221b Baker Street: The Seventeen Steps

Ian Lamb, MA, BEd (Hons)

Foreword

I have been a fan of the Sherlock Holmes tales since I was given The Long Stories and The Short Stories in 1961. So when I retired twelve years ago I decided that I would compile a book on Sir Arthur Conan Doyle, Sherlock Holmes and Dr Watson. The majority of the content is taken from newspaper and magazine articles from 1998-2011 and some book forewords, the greater part containing information which I had never seen or read before. All content has been referenced correctly so that readers may access it if they so wish. All this is spread over 34 chapters, 890 foolscap pages and 326,400 words. I hope you enjoy reading this book as much as I did while compiling it.

Ian Lamb
Deal, Kent February 2011

Published by New Generation Publishing in 2013

Copyright © Ian Lamb 2013

First Edition

The author asserts the moral right under the Copyright, Designs and Patents Act 1988 to be identified as the author of this work.

All Rights reserved. No part of this publication may be reproduced, stored in a retrieval system or transmitted, in any form or by any means without the prior consent of the author, nor be otherwise circulated in any form of binding or cover other than that which it is published and without a similar condition being imposed on the subsequent purchaser.

www.newgeneration-publishing.com

 New Generation **Publishing**

Contents

Chapter 1 7
Sir Arthur Ignatius Conan Doyle: A Definitive Study

Chapter 2 40
Sir Arthur Conan Doyle: A Biography

Chapter 3 46
Dr Joseph Bell (1837 – 1911)

Chapter 4 55
The Hound of the Baskervilles

Chapter 5 83
The Lost World

Chapter 6 85
The Detective in Film – A Survey

Chapter 7 101
Sherlock Holmes in Films & on Television 1903 - 2002

Chapter 8 110
The Principal Characters – Actors & Actresses

Chapter 9 132
A Collection of Pastiches

Chapter 10 140
Introductions; Prefaces; Publisher's Notes, Forewords, and Afterwords

Chapter 11 182
Miscellany I: 1997 – 2003 182

Chapter 12 217
The Tragedy at Scarsdale Villas - -A Real-Life Sherlock Holmes Mystery

Chapter 13 250
Miscellany II: 2004 – 2005
Chapter 14 277
The Strange Case of Sherlock Holmes and Arthur Conan Doyle

Chapter 15 290
New Books: 2005 – 2006

Chapter 16 309
Arthur Conan Doyle For The Defence

Chapter 17 318
The Case of Doctor Watson's Watch

Chapter 18 323
The Strange Case Of Mr James Phillimore

Chapter 19 335
Further Introductions & Prefaces

Chapter 20 357
Miscellany III: 2006-2010

Chapter 21 396
A Further Collection of Forewords, Introductions & Prefaces

Chapter 22 418
The Told & Untold Tales

Chapter 23 447
Sherlock Holmes & Jack the Ripper: 1888-2011

Chapter 24 496
Sir Arthur Conan Doyle's Sherlock Holmes Novels & Stories: A Complete Bibliography

Chapter 25 523
Final Collection of Forewords, Afterwords, Introductions, Prefaces & Prologues

Chapter 26 573
Miscellany IIII: 2008-2011

Chapter 27 583
The New Annotated Sherlock Holmes – Volumes I, II & III. Edited by Leslie S. Klinger

Chapter 28 591
The Case of Marion Gilchrist

Chapter 29 636
The Latest Sherlock Holmes Films – Boxing Day 2009 & Christmas 2011

Chapter 30 674
An Update On Undershaw

Chapter 31 685
The New TV Sherlock Holmes

Chapter 32 723
Sunday Times Magazine 14 March 2004

Chapter 33 731
Sir Arthur Conan Doyle: An Obituary

Chapter 34 736
New Books: October/November 2010/2011

Chapter 35: Addendum 744

Bibliography I 759

Chapter 1

Sir Arthur Ignatius Conan Doyle: A Definitive Study

Sir Arthur Conan Doyle, the creator of Sherlock Holmes, was born at No. 11 Picardy Place, Edinburgh[1] (demolished 1969) on Sunday May 22, 1859 and died at Windlesham Manor in Sheep Plain, Crowborough, East Sussex [2] on Monday July 7, 1930. (The house is now a residential nursing home). He was buried in the garden along with his wife, Jean Conan Doyle but their bodies were moved in 1955 to a grave at Minstead Churchyard in Hampshire where Conan Doyle had bought the half-timbered Bignell House, Bignell Wood in the New Forest at Wittensford Bridge near to the village. (Bignell House is now being used as a private psychiatric clinic). Undershaw, which was Conan Doyle's first house which he had built, was at Hindhead, Surrey and was turned into a hotel in 1976. The Conan Doyles and their two young children moved into the house in October, 1897. [**For further details on this house see Chapter 30**]. He knew the area well; it was while staying at a cottage on Emery Down in 1891 that he wrote *The White Company*, which was set there. His simple grave is on the south side of the village churchyard near open fields, and is inscribed *"Steel True, Blade Straight"* and describing him as a *"Knight, Patriot, Physician & Man of Letters"*.

Both his parents, who married in 1855 were Irish, devout Catholics and emigrated to Scotland. His father, Charles Altamont Doyle, was a clerk of works to the Scottish Office of Works. [Doyle used his father's middle name in his story "The Last Bow", giving it to the American agent {Sherlock Holmes} who thwarts von Bork]. His mother, Mary Foley had three daughters and one son besides Arthur. His mother's tales of the exploits of illustrious Irish forebears developed Doyle's adventurous and romantic nature. His father was melancholy, with a morbid disposition, suffered epileptic fits and was an alcoholic. He was firstly cared for at Fordoun House, a nursing home specialising in the treatment of alcoholism. Later, he was committed to Crighton Royal Institution, a Mental Hospital near Dumfries. He died in October, 1893 from, allegedly, swallowing his tongue during an epileptic seizure.

---

[1] Picardy Place EH1 3JT is still there today It runs off Broughton Street and into Leith Walk. A statue of Sherlock Holmes is erected outside and opposite is The Conan Doyle public house.

[2] The following is a reprint of an article published in *The News Of The World*, July 5, 1998, entitled **'Wat's On In Sussex Holmes?'** 'What's happening at Crowborough in Sussex this weekend? Elementary my dear Watson, it's celebrating its Sherlock Holmes Festival. Townspeople get togged up in Victorian dress, sport deerstalkers and capes and smoke Holmes-style pipes in honour of Sir Arthur Conan Doyle who lived there for the last 23 years of his life. And today there's a Hound of the Baskervilles Dog Show for family pets…plus a walk along the footpaths that gave Sir Arthur ideas for his many plots'.

At the age of nine Conan Doyle was sent to Hodder, at Whalley, near Blackburn, Lancashire, the preparatory school for Stonyhurst, the famous Jesuit college. At eleven-and-a-half he graduated to Stonyhurst proper, near Preston, Lancashire, which he attended until 1876. During his time at Stonyhurst he relished the books of Oliver Wendell Holmes.{Oliver Wendell Holmes (1809-94), was an American writer born at Cambridge, Mass. He became professor of anatomy at Dartmouth (1838-40) and at Harvard (1847-82). In 1857 he founded with Lowell the *Atlantic Monthly*, in which were published the essays and verse collected in 1858 as *The Autocrat of the Breakfast-Table*, a record of the imaginary conversation of boarding-house guests. This was followed by the *The Professor at the Breakfast-Table* and the novel *Elsie Venner* (1861).} It is reputed that Conan Doyle based the surname of his famous detective on this writer.

Conan Doyle then studied medicine at the University of Edinburgh (1876-81) where he qualified as a physician (MB, CM). Lack of finance meant Conan Doyle could only study for six months each year. During the remaining time he took various minor assistantships, and served as a ship's doctor on a Greenland whaling boat. At the port of Peterhead, on the afternoon of February 28, 1880, Arthur went aboard the *Hope* as the ship's surgeon. The *Hope* was a 400-ton whaling vessel with a crew of twenty-five Scots and twenty-five Shetlanders, which sailed to the fisheries between Greenland and Spitsbergen. He returned to Peterhead in September 1880. Following his graduation, he set forth on another and very different voyage, as surgeon aboard a 4.000-ton *Mayumba*, sailing with cargo and twenty passengers to the Gold Coast, in Africa on October 22, 1881. He returned to Liverpool docks on January 14, 1882.

In the summer of 1882, twenty-three-year-old Dr Conan Doyle set up a brass plate (which he had to polish himself after dark) at 1 Bush Villas, Elm Grove, (now demolished), a suburb of Southsea, the genteel end of Portsmouth, where he remained until 1890 (when he gave up medical practice after the publication of his first Sherlock Holmes book). He had to sweep the floors, sleep on a mattress of the straw packing from his medicine bottles, his pillow being Bristow's *Principles of Medicine* wrapped in his other suit. Worse still, he had to open his own front door. He could not afford a servant, so patients (such as they were) were ushered in by nine-year-old Innes (his brother). Only caller of the week was a top-hatted man who suffered from bronchitis, but had come to collect on the gas-meter. Luckily, Dr Doyle's grocer was an epileptic. They struck a bartering arrangement. When the patient had fits the doctor had butter. Then the wretched fellow died, reducing him to dry bread and saveloys. 'The throb of the charwoman's heart and the rustle of the greengrocer's lungs' never made Doyle more than £300 a year. In August 1890 he decided to become an ophthalmologist. He went to Vienna so that he could study the human eye at the Krankenhaus. The lectures were unfortunately incomprehensible through ignorance of German medical terminology. Back in London after his futile six months in Austria, he insisted on becoming an eye specialist even without the supporting diplomas. He found rooms at 23, Montague Place, directly facing an entrance to the British Museum and opened a small office and consulting room at 2, Devonshire Place. He was unable to attract a single patient. He then rented rooms in Harley Street – 'A waiting-room and a consulting room, where I waited in the consulting-room and no one waited in the waiting-room'. So he wrote about Sherlock Holmes from ten to four instead.

He married on August 6, 1885 (the year that he was awarded a doctorate from Edinburgh for his dissertation on syphilis [3]) his first wife, Louise Hawkins (he was to marry twice and have five children). Conan Doyle had treated her brother, Jack, who unfortunately had died the same year of cerebral meningitis. His first child, Mary Louise was born in February, 1889. (His second child and first son, Alleyne Kingsley was born in November, 1892). His first wife died at three o'clock on the morning of July 4, 1906. She was 49 years old. On September 18, 1907, Conan Doyle married Jean Leckie. In the last years of the decade, she became the mother of two sons, Denis and Malcolm, followed by a daughter, Jean. Jean Conan Doyle nee Leckie died in 1940.

Sherlock Holmes became one of the most vivid characters in English fiction and the prototype for the modern mastermind detective. The character generated the most enduring tradition in detective fiction. Holmes' friend, the good-hearted but comparatively obtuse Dr Watson, and the detective's principal enemy, the archcriminal Professor Moriarty, also have taken on an uncanny life beyond the page. An obvious example of a foil in literature (i.e. a character who is presented as a contrast to a second character so as to point to or show to advantage some aspect of the second character) is Dr Watson. In New York, the Baker Street Irregulars and in London The Sherlock Holmes Society peruses Holmesiana with cultist fervour, and similar groups exist on the Continent. The brilliantly eccentric hero, in deerstalker or dressing gown, has been portrayed in a variety of media and has put the author's other works – chiefly historical romances – somewhat in the shade.

While at Southsea, he began to send short stories to magazine editors, and his first published story, "The Mystery of Sasassa Valley" (1879), was accepted by *Chamber's Journal*, for which he was paid three guineas. In December 1887 his first long novel *A Study in Scarlet* appeared in *Beeton's Christmas Annual* and introduced readers to Sherlock Holmes, a fictional private detective who, with his ingenious skill of deductive reasoning, was based on Dr Joseph Bell, one of Doyle's university professors. *A Study in Scarlet*, narrated by Holmes's companion, Dr John H. Watson, was followed in 1890 by a sequel, *The Sign of Four*.

The Strand Magazine

Two short stories arrived on the desk of Greenhough Smith, literary editor of **The Strand Magazine**. *'A Scandal in Bohemia' and 'The Red-Headed League' by Dr A.C.Doyle, 2 Devonshire Place, W. (Conan Doyle had given up medical practice then and had gone to live at 12 Tennyson Road, South Norwood). These two stories were the first in a series of six published under the collective title of* **The Adventures of Sherlock Holmes**. *Conan Doyle was paid thirty guineas each for the first set of Holmes stories in* **The Strand**, *and fifty guineas for the second series.*

The Strand Magazine, launched in January 1891, was one of the most successful and influential magazines of its time. It ran until 1950, selling in its heyday half a million

---

[3] See, **The Edinburgh Stories**…AN ESSAY

copies a month. Making its mark immediately with publication of the first volumes of Sherlock Holmes stories, the magazine continued to publish high-quality detective fiction. What people remember about *The Strand Magazine* a hundred years after its birth, is that in the seventh issue appeared the very first Sherlock Holmes short story, 'A Scandal in Bohemia'.

The following year, Doyle began the first of several collections of Holmes tales in *The Strand Magazine* up to 1927, the first time that any writer had used a pair of recurring characters to link a series of stories. These included *The Adventures of Sherlock Holmes* (1892), *The Memoirs of Sherlock Holmes* (1893) – the last story of this series, *The Final Problem* appearing in *The Strand* in December, 1893, *The Hound of the Baskervilles* – the first instalment appearing in the January, 1902 issue. *The Return of Sherlock Holmes* (1905) and *The Casebook of Sherlock Holmes* (1927) together with a rare and highly entertaining pastiche of Conan Doyle's style, 'The Adventure of the First Class Carriage' (1947) by Ronald Knox. Writing bad imitation Holmes is not difficult, and many authors have done it, but Knox's story can almost stand beside the master. (*See Chapter 8 to read the story*).

Despite the success of the Sherlock Holmes adventures, Doyle was never comfortable with the popularity of his hero. While he wanted to devote his time to writing historical romances such as *Micah Clarke* (1889), *The White Company* (1891), a boxing story *Rodney Stone* (1896) and his play, *The Story of Waterloo* (1894), the public clamoured for more detective fiction, resulting in *The Mystery Of Cloomber* (1889) and *The Doings of Raffles Haw* (1892). In 1893 he attempted to resolve this problem by sending Holmes plunging to his death at the Reichenbach Falls, locked in the arms of his arch-enemy, Professor James Moriarty.

Accepting the inevitable, Greenhough Smith persuaded Conan Doyle to choose what he considered the best twelve Holmes stories, sealing the list in an envelope and confiding it to a locked drawer in the editor's room. Readers were then invited to send in their lists, a prize of £100 being offered for the one that most nearly coincided with the author's.

Lists came in from far and near. The winner was R.T.Norman of Spring Hill, Wellingborough, Northants., who correctly named in order ten out of Conan Doyle's twelve, which gave first place to *The Speckled Band* and the last place to *The Reigate Squires*. Scores of readers placed eight correctly. All included *The Speckled Band*, *The Red-Headed League*, *The Final Problem*, *A Scandal in Bohemia* and *The Five Orange Pips*.

The last of the fifty-six Sherlock Holmes published in *The Strand* through thirty-six years appeared in the issue for April 1927. It was entitled *The Adventure of Shoscombe Old Place*. The illustrator was F.Wiles, whose line was less gaunt than Sidney Paget's, his Holmes being slightly more refined in features.

In 1901 Doyle was forced by public demand to revive Holmes for a novel, *The Hound of the Baskervilles* (1902), and then, in a further series of short stories, revealed that the encounter at Reichenbach had been fatal only for Moriarty.

The following two excerpts are taken from the TELEGRAPH TRAVEL section. The first one was published on Sunday, February 4, 2001 entitled **How Sherlock found the alps**.*

Sir Arthur Conan Doyle helped introduce the world to winter sports, says **Tim Ring**, *when he took his famous character to Switzerland and then learned to ski himself'.*

'It was on a trip to Switzerland in spring 1893 that Sir Arthur Conan Doyle chose the Reichenbach Falls in the Bernese Oberland as the setting for Sherlock Holmes's demise. That autumn, the author's wife Louisa fell ill with tuberculosis – just as the high valleys of Switzerland's easternmost canton, the Grisons, were gaining a reputation as an environment for the treatment of the disease. The couple retreated to Davos, spending the next two winters in what was little more than an "unheard of and roadless collection of crude wooden chalets". Doyle set out to amuse himself. "In the early months of 1893," he wrote, "I developed ski-running in Switzerland."

He sent off to Norway, the home of skiing, for what proved to be "two strips of elm wood, 8ft long, 4in broad, with a square heel, turned up toes and straps in the centre to secure your feet". Helping him master the contraptions were two local tradesmen, the Branger brothers.

For some weeks, the trio afforded "innocent amusement to a large number of people who watched our awkward movements and complete tumbles".

Then they set off on a series of journeys around Davos on cross-country skis, following Scandinavian tradition. They climbed uphill with the skis on their backs, pushed themselves along on the flat and ran gently downhill.

At the end of the season, they accomplished the hazardous seven-hour crossing of the 7,976ft Furka pass between Davos and Arosa. Doyle's world-wide reputation brought this exploit to the public's attention. As he wrote at the time in the *Strand Magazine*, "Skiing opens up a field of sport which is, I think, unique. This is not appreciated yet, but I am convinced the time will come when hundreds of Englishmen will come for the skiing season between March and April."

Daily Mail, Saturday, September 4, 2004

Holmes and away!

Haven't a clue where to go in Switzerland? Try the dramatic waterfall where the great detective met his end, says **Robert Gore-Langton**

SWITZERLAND was where Sir Arthur Conan Doyle plotted the death of Sherlock Holmes.

Sick of writing stories about the sleuth, the author, who was a keen hiker, travelled around Switzerland and decided to make the spectacular Reichenbach Falls, near the village of Meiringen, the place to bump off his great detective.

And, so, on May 4, 1891, Holmes and his arch-enemy Professor Moriarty ('the Napoleon of crime') did battle on a tiny ledge on top of the falls. They supposedly vanished into the raging torrent whose noise was like a 'half-human shout which came booming up with the spray out of the abyss.'

The Reichenbach Falls are these days a shrine for fans of literature's famous character. A star marks the chilling spot from where Holmes fell. But fans of the stories wouldn't accept his death at the time. Conan Doyle was persuaded by a deafening public outcry to bring him back to life. In The Adventure of the Empty House, Holmes duly makes his return (Watson faints on seeing him) and explains how he escaped up the perilous cliff beside the waterfall having totally unbalanced his foe with a Japanese wrestling technique.

Today it is a giddy-making experience to watch great sheets of water crashing down the sheer rock face and imagine Holmes wrestling with his old adversary above the great cataract.

Indeed, nothing much has changed sine Conan Doyle's day. Except, that is, in winter when the water is 'switched off' and diverted for power generation.

The funicular railway up to the falls is still running a century after it was built for those who don't fancy the two-hour climb.

Although the village of Meiringen is now a modern town with plate-glass shopfronts, it was very popular with British tourists in the 19th century.

The 1880 hotel where Conan Doyle stayed still stands. He installed Holmes and Watson there and called it the Englischer Hof. Today it has 70 rooms with all mod cons, but the old belle-epoque décor has a period charm.

Next to the hotel is a square called Conan Doyle Place (the sign is in the London borough style) featuring a life-size-statue of the sleuth complete with deer-stalker, pipe and magnifying glass.

The bronze is inscribed with more than 60 fiendishly hard clues, each one referring to a Sherlock Holmes mystery.

Thanks to the Swiss National Tourist in Meiringen who supplied me with a copy of both the mysteries and the solutions as follows:

Solutions to the representation of each of the Sherlock Holmes stories on the bronze statue of Sherlock Holmes at Meiringen.

01 The Abbey Grange…Three wine glasses, with dregs in one
02 The Beryl Coronet….Broken coronet
03 Black Peter…………Harpoon
04 The Blanched Soldier…Elephant bullet
05 The Blue Carbuncle…..Carbuncle
06 The Boscombe Valley Mystery…The letters 'ARAT'
07 The Bruce-Partington Plans…Submarine (in the form of periscope)
08 The Cardboard Box……………...Severed human ear
09 A Case of Identity………………Typewriter
10 Charles Augustus Milverton…Visual representation of a plum followed by Rs LL (i.e. plumbers tools)
11 The Copper Beeches…………A severed plait of hair
12 The Creeping Man……………Creeping man, bent double
13 The Crooked Man……………Mongoose
14 The Dancing Men…Representation of an eye followed by 'count bright hours only'
15 The Devil's Foot….Cloven hoof slot
16 The Dying Detective…Oysters and half-crowns
17 The Empty House…….Oscar Meunier signature
18 The Engineer's Thumb…Hand with severed thumb

19 The Final Problem………Alpenstock
20 The Five Orange Pips…...Five orange pips
21 The Gloria Scott………...Ship (a barque)
22 The Golden Pince-Nez…..Pince-Nez spectacles
23 The Greek Interpreter……Slate
24 His Last Bow…………….Book
25 The Hound of the Baskervilles…Ship Barque=Bark=Hound
26 The Illustrious Client…………..Phial of vitriol
27 The Lion's Mane………………Jellyfish
28 Lady Frances Carfax…………..Coffin with two corpses inside

29 The Man with the Twisted Lip…Opium pipe
30 The Mazarin Stone……………..Diamond
31 The Missing Three-Quarter…….Rugger ball
32 The Musgrave Ritual…………..Oak tree and trigonometry symbols
33 The Naval Treaty   Visual representation of an umbilicus with a tree in the shape of a small 't' (i.e. naval treaty)
34 The Noble Batchelor…Wedding bouquet
35 The Norwood Builder…Metal trouser buttons
36 The Priory School……..Bicycle
37 The Red Circle………...Circle
38 The Red-Headed League…Pawnbroker's three balls
39 The Reigate Squires…Book, two candlesticks, ivory letter-weight and ball of twine
40 The Resident Patient…Hangman's noose
41 The Retired Colourman…A well
42 A Scandal in Bohemia…..Rocket (for plumbers rocket)
43 The Second Stain………..Sealed envelope
44 Shoscombe Old Place……The 'upper condyle of a human femur'
45 The Sign of Four…The hieroglyph '++++' (four crosses in line arms touching)
46 Silver Blaze………Horseshoe
47 The Six Napoleons…Bust of Napoleon
48 The Solitary Cyclist...Dark glasses and a false black beard
49 The Speckled Band…Snake
50 The Stockbroker's Clerk…Pair of braces
51 A Study in Scarlet………..Wedding ring
52 The Sussex Vampire……..Vampire bat
53 Thor Bridge…Revolver tied to string with stone at one end

54 The Three Gables…A 'huge knotted lump of a fist under (Holmes's) nose'
55 The Three Garridebs…Printing press plate for bank notes
56 The Three Students…..Three mortarboards
57 The Valley of Fear……The hieroglyph '_____'
58 The Veiled Lodger……Lion leaping out of cage
59 Wisteria Lodge………..A white cock (represented by the schematic

representation phallus
60 The Yellow Face..........Black child's face with mask

But eccentric though this might seem, it's nothing compared to the little 19th century English church in the town. The museum features an immaculate full-scale recreation of the doctor and detective's rooms at 221b Baker Street. It's designed to look as if the pair had rushed out on a case, leaving newspapers strewn about.

Amid the High Victorian décor are all the Holmesian touches: the slipper full of tobacco, the chemistry apparatus and, for eagle-eyed fans, the 'gasogene' (soda siphon) on the sideboard.

For fans of funiculars, cable cars and trains, Meiringen is heaven. The Eagle Express cable car to Planplatten with its circular Alpen Tower restaurant is not for the faint-hearted.

In winter, you ski down the mountain. In summer the descent on foot takes about three hours among the edelweiss, gentians, orchids and furry marmots which pop out of their burrows with a squeak. Ten minutes away by rail is the town of Brienz, perched on the edge of the stunning turquoise Lake Brienz, with the white-capped mountains rising all around the shore.

The cog-and-ratchet railway built up the side of the mountain in 1892 is the oldest steam line in Switzerland. The engine pushes two open-sided carriages up a series of gut-churning hairpin bends, 2,350m to the very top of the Brienz Rothorn Bahn.

It takes about an hour to reach the summit, where the air is like champagne and the views jaw-dropping.

Back down at the station, you can either take the boat to explore Interlaaken or go back to the hotel by rail.

The Park Hotel Du Sauvage holds murder mystery weekends through the year. In June 2005, the Sherlock Holmes Society will link with other fan clubs over the world for a Holmesian celebration in Meiringen. If you are planning to go, wear 19th century costume – deer-stalker and pipe obligatory for the chaps.

Sherlock Holmes has rather overshadowed Meiringen's other claim to fame. In the 17th century, a baker called Gasparini invented a delicacy made of egg whites and sugar, one which Napoleon found irresistible.

It is the meringue. Try one while saying 'My Dear Watson' with your mouthful. It's far from elementary.

(Compiler's note: The following two articles concern Sir Arthur Conan Doyle and skiing).
TELEGRAPH WEEKEND Saturday, February, 27, 2010

Quiteinteresting

A quietly intriguing column from the brains behind QI, of the BBC quiz show. This week: **QI goes skiing**

Conan Doyle

Lovers of Swiss ski holidays have the creator of Sherlock Holmes, Sir Arthur Conan Doyle to thank. He had fallen in love with the sport in Norway and thought Switzerland offered the perfect terrain. He imported some skis and encouraged two Swiss brothers to join him. The practised at night to avoid being teased by the locals. Conan Doyle later wrote: "I am convinced that the time will come when hundreds of English men will come to Switzerland for the skiing season."

Saturday, March 6, 2010 TELEGRAPH TRAVEL

Skiing

Conan Doyle and the height of cool

Value for money and an aversion to overdevelopment are turning Davos and Klosters into the most fashionable resorts in the Alps. **Peter Hardy** reports. (Excerpt)

" Elementary" was not the word that immediately springs to mind as I descended an icy *couloir* above Davos in the tracks of Sir Arthur Conan Doyle. There are occasional moments in life you wish you were somewhere – anywhere – but there you are. This was one. Even if the Hound of the Baskervilles had been hot on my heels, I could not have inched my way down any faster.

"The snow fell away here at an angle of from 50 to 60 degrees," wrote the creator of Sherlock Holmes in the *Strand* magazine," and as this steep incline, along the face of which we were shuffling, sloped away down until it ended in an absolute precipice, a slip might have been serious." More than a century later, I can report that the start of the off-piste epic from Davos to Arosa across the Maienfeld Furka pass has lost none of its initial bite. Sir Arthur was comforted by the security of having his local guides, the Branger brothers, standing beneath him to arrest any fall. "Skis," Sir Arthur told the readers of the *Strand*, "are the most capricious things on Earth. One day you cannot go wrong with them. On another, with the same weather and the same snow, you cannot go right. I am convinced that there will come a time when hundreds of Englishmen will come to Switzerland for the "skiing" season."

While the actual hardware has mercifully evolved from his eight-feet-long course elm planks, and the 19 miles of virgin white snowfields, which are the reward for the initial challenge of *couloir*, remain remarkably untouched by the passage of time.

Of course, the same can't be said for the town of Davos, where Sir Arthur was then living with his sick wife…

…Back on the Maienfeld Furka pass, just as Sir Arthur wrote: "We shot along over gently dipping curves, skimming down into the valley without a motion of our feet. In that great untrodden waste, with snowfields bounding our vision on every side and no marks of life save the tracks of chamois and of foxes, it was glorious to whiz along in this easy fashion. "A short zigzag at the bottom of the slope brought us, at half-past nine, into the mouth of the pass; and we could see the tiny toy hotels of Arosa, away down among the fir woods, thousands of feet beneath. My tailor tells me that Harris tweed cannot wear out. This is a mere theory and will not stand a thorough scientific test. He will find samples of his wares on view from the Furka Pass to Arosa."

Unlike Sir Arthur, I managed not to get down by the seat of my pants, but a new generation of skiers heading for Klosters and Davos, comfortably clad in Gore-Tex, will find that Switzerland's oldest ski area has lost none of its original appeal.

The second excerpt is from an article published in the TELEGRAPH TRAVEL, Saturday, March 24, 2001. Entitled **The case of the 'tec who wouldn't die.**' *Following Sir Arthur Conan Doyle to Meiringen,* **Gavin Bell** *finds evidence of Holmes' presence there'.*

"It is a fearful place. The torrent, swollen by the melting snow, plunges into a tremendous abyss, from which the spray rolls up like smoke from a burning house." Thus wrote John H. Watson, M.D, late of the army medical department, of the dreadful spot where he last saw the lonely figure of his friend Sherlock Holmes. It was on the afternoon of May, 4, 1891, that the pair reached the Reichenbach Falls, above the Swiss village of Meiringen, on an expedition to the hamlet of Rosenlaui.

And it was there, after Watson had been drawn away by a ruse, that Holmes had his fateful encounter with the Napoleon of Crime, the dastardly Professor Moriarty. Watson deduced that the two adversaries, locked in a desperate struggle, had plunged to their deaths in the maelstrom far below.

He was only half-right. The world may have seen the end of Moriarty, but Arthur Conan Doyle was compelled by public outrage to revive his great detective for a few more adventures.

If Holmes returned to Meiringen today, he would be bemused to find people whizzing and whooping down the mountains at seemingly reckless speeds in winter, and ascending them more slowly on bicycles in summer. The village on Bernese Oberland has grown since his day, but not much, to accommodate a new breed of visitors intent on skiing, hiking and trail-biking through some of the most splendid scenery in Switzerland.

He would also find some familiar sights, including a handsome bronze statue of himself, sitting on a boulder in a reflective mood, in the main square of the community which has been renamed Conan Doyle Place. Fashioned by the English sculptor John Doubleday, it is inscribed with 60 cryptic clues, each one referring to a Sherlock Holmes mystery.

There is an international competition to match them up, with a 1:10 model of the sculpture as a prize, but so far the closest anyone has got is 58. The case of the missing clues remains unsolved.

Doubtless Holmes would not take long to discover that his rooms at 221b Baker Street have been moved – to the basement of a 19th century English church a few steps from his statue. They are the centrepiece of a museum dedicated to the peerless private eye, and his creator, inaugurated on the centenary of his "death" in 1991.

Here we discover the true origins of Holmes and Moriarty – as fellow pupils of Conan Doyle at Stonyhurst College in the 1870s.

(Compiler's note: However, two recent newspaper articles suggest the linkage between Conan Doyle and Moriarty is through the game of golf). Both are reproduced as follows:

Daily Express Saturday April 19 2003. **Solved!** Mystery of Holmes Villain by **Richard Palmer.**

An old golf club register may hold the clue to one of the last Sherlock Holmes mysteries.

The identity of the man who inspired the great detective's arch-villain, Professor James Moriarty, has long puzzled literary detectives.

But new light was shed on the riddle yesterday after it was discovered that Holmes's creator, Sir Arthur Conan Doyle, was once a member of Sheringham Golf Club in Norfolk at the same time as a Mr C. Moriarty.

Club historian Douglas Blunden found the name Mr Moriarty in a visitors' book entry for 1901. He later became a full member. Sir Arthur, who often visited Sheringham, became a member in 1903. Now club officials are wondering if the two men met on holiday in Sheringham a decade earlier, when Conan Doyle first began writing about Holmes's battles with Moriarty.

Grace Riley, curator of the Sherlock Holmes Museum in London, said: "It is entirely possible that there could be a link with the Moriarty who played golf at Sheringham."

DAILY TELEGRAPH, Saturday, April 19, 2003. **Conan Doyle had golf links with Moriarty** by **David Sapsted**

Devotees of Sherlock Holmes are delighted by the disclosure that Sir Arthur Conan Doyle belonged to the same golf club as a man named Moriarty.

Until now, the only contender as the inspiration for Holmes's arch-enemy was a boy called Moriarty who attended school with the author. Yesterday, though, it emerged that a C Moriarty from Harrow was a member of Sheringham Golf Club on the Norfolk coast, where Conan Doyle played.

The discovery was made by Douglas Blunden, the club's historian. Although Mr Moriarty's name does not crop up until 1901, a decade after Professor James Moriarty first tangled with Holmes, there is speculation that Conan Doyle might have met the real Moriarty during his frequent visits to the Sheringham area,

Here also is evidence that Holmes lives on, in the hearts and minds of admirers who still write to him at his London address.

"It's a joke, right?" I suggest to Jurg Musfeld, curator of the museum, of the collection of letters that have been delivered to Baker Street. "Not at all," he says, "some are from stamp collectors, some people are just curious, but there are others who write to Holmes as a last resort to help them find missing cats and so on."

The point is made in a conversation between two elderly Englishmen, examining a display case: "That deerstalker, it's not old enough to have been Holmes's."

"Holmes was fiction, Charles."

"Oh yes, right."

Jurg Musfeld is the ideal guide to the Holmes trail depicted in "The Final Problem". He is not only largely responsible for creating the museum, he manages the belle époque hotel where Conan Doyle lodged in 1893, and he is the founder of the Reichenbach Irregulars, the Swiss branch of the Sherlock Holmes Society. "I suppose it's nostalgia," he says. "I personally wish I could have lived in the time of Holmes. There was a lot of class and elegance then, which doesn't exist now in my opinion. Men no longer stand up when a lady approaches their table." Watson, ever the gentleman, would doubtless have concurred.

Should Holmes return to the scene of Moriarty's last crime, he would find it chillingly familiar. There are waterfalls, and there are awesome, gut-churning, head-spinning cataracts that appear to have been gouged from the earth by a deranged god. The Reichenbach Falls are of the latter variety.

Imagine a torrent of water roaring off the edge of a 200ft. precipice, tumbling down a chasm of glistening black rock with the force of a tidal wave, and you get the picture. For perspective, add a few pine trees, clinging for dear life to inches of soil on the edge of the abyss.

From a viewing platform, which gives an uneasy sensation of being in mid-air, the place where Holmes and Moriarty engaged in mortal combat can be seen marked with a large, white star. It is on a hair-raisingly narrow path that ends abruptly at a cliff face, and is presumably visited by only the most determined and fearless followers of Holmes. It is not a place for a picnic.

The first resurrectionist Holmes short story, *The Empty House*, was published in the summer of 1903. Between 1908 and 1927 he continued to produce occasional Holmes adventures, and another novel, *The Valley of Fear* (1915). The final collection of stories was prefaced by his remark: "I fear that Mr Sherlock Holmes may become like one of those popular tenors, who, having outlived their time, are still tempted to make repeat farewell bows to their indulgent audiences." Doyle was proud that Holmes's methods had influenced contemporary police practice and, in 1907, turned detective himself to clear the name of George Edaljee, who in 1903 had been wrongly convicted of cattle-maiming.

Doyle's prolific output of magazine fiction produced some other memorable characters. A cycle of stories involving a young Napoleonic adventurer, Brigadier Gerard, and recounted with humorous irony, appeared in the *Strand* from 1895. *The Lost World* (1912) introduced the irascible and belligerent Professor Edward Challenger, and told of his encounter with dinosaurs and primitive humans on a South American plateau, and who reappeared in *The Poison Belt (1913)*.

Conan Doyle died in 1930, for *The Strand Magazine* the end of a long and exemplary relationship between author and editor. He was commemorated by a full-page photograph in which he looked like a universal uncle, and by the reprinting of *A Scandal in Bohemia*, the first Sherlock Holmes story that appeared in *The Strand*. It was illustrated by the original Paget drawings. *The Strand* even revived Sherlock Holmes, using the expedient of an apocryphal story *The Adventure of the First Class Carriage*, written by Ronald Knox, and illustrated by Tom Purvis, 'in loving memory of Sidney Paget'. Some said that Purvis's realisation of Holmes surpassed Paget's.

In 1921 *The Strand* published the author's valedictory:

'Sherlock Holmes began his adventures in the very heart of the late Victorian era, and has managed to hold his own little niche in these feverish days. Thus it would be true to say that those who first read of him as a young man have lived to see their grown-up children following the same adventures in the same magazine. It is a sterling example of the patience and loyalty of the British public'. The main feature of the Christmas number for 1921 was: "Fairies Photographed: An Epoch-Making Event".

A similar tribute could have been paid to Doyle. Despite many inducements, he had remained faithful to *The Strand* from the beginning of his association with it back in 1891.

Listeners to the 6p.m., 9p.m., and 10p.m. Home News bulletins of the BBC on December 13, 1949, heard the following item: *'The Strand Magazine, pioneer of British illustrated magazines, and for many years the most popular of its kind, is to cease publication with the March issue next year'*.

The Boer War & Spiritualism

Doyle served in the Second South African War (or Boer War) 1899 1902 as a senior physician of a field hospital, the Langman, in Bloemfontein. He commenced duties on April, 2 and completed them, returning to the England on July, 11. On his return, he wrote *The Great Boer War* (1900). This was followed by revised and much improved editions in 1901 and 1902. He also wrote *War in South Africa: Its Causes and Conduct* (1902), a vindication and justification of England's participation. For these works he was knighted on August, 9, 1902 at Buckingham Palace. Doyle was a great crusader – in 1890, he warned against an ill-tested cure for tuberculosis. In 1902, he defended the British Government against charges of misconduct in the Boer War. In 1906, he championed the cause of divorce law reform and was defeated as the parliamentary candidate for the Scottish seat of Hawick Burghs District, standing as an Unionist (Conservative). In 1909, he spoke out against the atrocities in the Congo. In 1910, he took up the case of Oscar Slater, a man falsely accused of murder. In 1914, he warned against the potentially devastating effects of a submarine blockade of Britain and the U-Boat war.

He was the first publicly to advocate the change in the Coronation Oath, deleting the insult to Catholics; he was responsible for the steel helmet and inflatable life jacket being introduced into the Army and Navy; he was a founder of the Pilgrims to promote Anglo-American relations; his work on the *Edalji* case led the Home Office to introduce the Court of Criminal Appeal and he first suggested the building of the Channel Tunnel between Britain and France. During World War I he wrote the *History of the British Campaign in France and Flanders* (6 volumes, 1916-1920) as a tribute to British bravery.

THE COTTINGLEY FAIRIES

Doyle had long been an advocate of spiritualism, but the death of his eldest son, Kingsley, from wounds incurred in World War I, intensified his interest in such matter. He lectured and published extensively on the subject (thirty books), becoming a leading member of the Psychical Research Society, and in *The Land of Mist* (1926), converted Professor Challenger to its doctrines. He was the victim of a famous hoax involving photographs of fairies, produced in 1917 by two young girls, Elsie Wright, aged 15, and her 10- year- old cousin Frances Griffiths from Cottingley, England.

The Strange Case of The Cottingley Fairies

The Daily Telegraph, Wednesday, March 14, 2001
News Bulletin

Fairies hoax fetches £6,000

Photographs of the celebrated Cottingley Fairies hoax sold for £6,000 at auction yesterday. The collection was bought at Bonhams & Brooks in London by an anonymous bidder. It was compiled by Edward Gardner who brought the case to the notice of Sir Arthur Conan Doyle, creator of Sherlock Holmes. Both men fell for the hoax perpetrated by Elsie Wright, aged 15, and her 10 year-old-cousin, Frances Griffiths, in 1937.

DAILY MAIL, Wednesday, October 15, 2008

SHERLOCK HOLMES AND THE CURIOUS CASE OF THE GARDEN FAIRIES

He was the creator of the most rational and intelligent detective of all time. So, why, asks a new book, was Arthur Conan Doyle fooled by this picture into believing in fairies? **By Russell Miller**
  The Adventures Of Arthur Conan Doyle by Russell Miller (Harvill Secker)

THE DAILY TELEGRAPH MONDAY, NOVEMBER 8, 2010

Obituaries (Excerpt)

Geoffrey Crawley

Scientific journalist who debunked the myth of the Cottingley Fairies and uncovered a well-intentioned hoax.

Geoffrey Crawley, who has died aged 83, was a scientific journalist specialising in photography and in 1982 exposed the world's longest-running photographic hoax – the myth of the so-called Cottingley Fairies. Between 1917 and 1920 a series of celebrated photographs purporting to show fairies and gnomes cavorting in woodland scenes were created by two young schoolgirls, Frances Griffiths, 10, and her 13-year-old cousin Elsie Wright, who as a prank had cut illustrations from books, propped them up and posed with them in front of a camera.

When the plates were developed, one appeared to show Frances surrounded by white blurs, possibly pieces of paper, while a second – underexposed and unclear – apparently depicted Elsie encountering a gnome. The images, taken in a garden of Cottingley, near Bingley, west Yorkshire, might have remained private curiosities, but for the intervention of Edward Gardner, a prominent figure in the Theosophical Society who chanced to hear about the photographs.

Realising that if he could show they were genuine, he could reinforce the theosophites' belief in a spirit world, so Gardner instructed a technician to produce better quality negatives. When these were developed, the new prints clearly showed images of fairy creatures.

In 1920 Gardner provided more cameras and 20 photographic plates and before long the girls had returned with three more "fairy" photographs. When they appeared in the *Strand* magazine the following year, they caused a sensation.

Although the results were never likely to convince modern eyes (a hatpin can clearly be seen holding up a flimsy gnome), many prominent people were fooled, including the creator of Sherlock Holmes, Arthur Conan Doyle. In 1922 Doyle, a fervent spiritualist who had lost a son in the First World War trenches, wrote *The Coming of the Fairies*, in which he defended the authenticity of the pictures.

The two girls could not have guessed that their whimsical hoax would keep the world guessing for more than 60 years. But in 1982 Crawley, the editor of the magazine *British Journal of Photography*, decided to apply his technical expertise to the pictures, and to settle the matter once and for all.

Crawley never believed the photographs could be genuine, but thought he should try to establish exactly how the images might have been created. He tested the original camera to see if they could have produced images as sharp and recognisable as the ones endorsed by Gardner and Conan Doyle.

He was convinced that they could not have done so, and that Gardner enhanced negatives had, by some trickery, transformed the original blurs into fairy images.

It was not until 1983 – after Crawley had demonstrated beyond doubt in a series of articles for his magazine that the photographs were faked – that the girls, then elderly women, admitted the deception.

At the same time as Crawley was testing the authenticity of the Cottingley pictures, the journalist Joe Cooper was conducting an independent investigation of his own. When he interviewed the two perpetrators of the hoax, they were contrite. "I don't see how people could believe they're real fairies," Frances Griffiths told him. She explained how, using a pair of sharp scissors borrowed from her mother, she and Elsie Wright had cut fairy illustrations from a children's book and secured them on a bank of earth using hatpins. A flying fairy was attached to a tree branch using the same method.

But the pair continued to insist that as young girls they had encountered real fairies in the area where the photographs were taken.

When he concluded his investigations into the Cottingley photographs, Crawley wrote to Elsie Wright with his findings. Gently sympathetic, he told her he understood why she had felt obliged to keep silent once Gardner, Doyle and various other experts had proclaimed to have proved the existence of fairies.

"Of course there are fairies – just as there is Father Christmas," he wrote. "The trouble comes when you try to make them corporeal. They are fine poetic concepts, taking us out of this at times too ugly real world. Conan Doyle, after the horrors of the First World War in which his son died, wanted to suggest a realm where spirit forms just might exist."

Elsie Wright told Crawley the whole affair had been a practical joke that had fallen flat on its face. "The laugh," she added, "was on us." Frances Griffiths died in 1986, and Elsie Wright in 1988. in 1997 the Cottingley episode inspired two films, *Fairy Tale: A True Story*, starring Peter O'Toole as Conan Doyle, and *Photographing Fairies*.

Fairy Tale – A True Story (2003)

The movie

Fairy Tale: A True Story is the story of two British girls who claim to see fairies in the woods at the back of their home. In itself, that's easy enough for the adults to dismiss as childish fancy, but when the girls produce actual photographs of these fairies, a storm of attention brews up, drawing in such famous men as Sir Arthur Conan Doyle and Harry Houdini, both profoundly interested in the supernatural and the paranormal. *Fairy Tale* is a cute movie, a reasonably entertaining piece that fits squarely into the "family entertainment" box. It's also a movie that feels like it wanted to be something more substantial.

When a modern eye looks at the "fairy photographs," they're so obviously faked that it's amazing that anyone believed in them for a moment. But they did: not just uneducated people, either, but and presumably intelligent people as well. Some of the answer lies in the novelty of the photographic process (we're much more familiar with it and aware of how photographs can be faked), but that's not the whole story. What made these photographs so compelling?

The film shows us part of the answer in the social context of the story: in the midst of World War I, popular culture in England and the United States became fascinated with "spiritualism" and "theosophy"; various names for ideas about how people could communicate with the dead, or see angels and guardian spirits, and so on. It's no surprise, then, that the claim of actual photographic proof of fairies (and thus some sort of spiritual life beyond ordinary human experience) was taken up with such enthusiasm by devotees of spiritualism.

Another key part of the story is in the personalities of the key people involved, particularly Sir Arthur Conan Doyle (Peter O'Toole), who is the prime mover in bringing the fairy photographs to the public eye. Conan Doyle is quite accurately portrayed in the film, as a kindly but gullible man, and one who was stuck in antiquated ideas about class; one telling line of dialogue has him comment that there was no way that two young and "working class" girls could have faked the photos.

Again, as in real life, Houdini (Harvey Keitel) is portrayed as the sceptic: as a master of illusion himself, Houdini was well aware of how seemingly "magic" occurrences could be faked, and devoted endless energy to exposing false mediums. However, the historical Houdini's exposes were motivated by his longing to communicate with his dead mother: he wanted to discover a medium who was not a fake, one who would truly let him speak with the dead and not just fool him into believing that he had. This aspect of Houdini's motivation is left unexplored in the film, although it would have formed a nice counterpart to Conan Doyle's willingness to rationalize just about anything if it bolstered his faith.

In a nice touch, the photographs that we see in the film are, in fact, the "real" photographs taken by the original two girls, including the most famous one.

In a sense, though, *Fairy Tale* chooses not to have the power that it could have, if it had really explored the ideas of the power of belief and how the desire to believe in something can blind people to the truth. It's the tension between truth and lies, the desire to believe and the desire to know the truth, that makes *Fairy Tale* an fascinating story.

Unfortunately, as the film moves on into its last third it moves away from exploring those interesting areas of the human heart, and sticks to a more conventional wish-fulfillment fantasy. The motivations and reactions of the girls aren't really developed, which isn't such a surprise considering that the film, at this point, is moving away from its basis in establishing fact and character, and toward a fantasy ending (in real life, the girls eventually admitted that they'd faked the images and explained how they'd done it). The plot thread of the investigative reporter is turned into a comic piece, which doesn't fit the tone of the film as a whole, and any potential loose ends are tied up neatly, leaving viewers nothing to wonder about. It's a light-weight and reasonably entertaining film, but I can't help wishing that the story of the 'Cottingley Fairies' had been given more depth.

Photographing Fairies (1997)

The movie

'Death is merely a change of state. The soul is a fresh expression of the self. The dead are not dust. They really are only a footfall away.'

It is the ensuing years after World War I, and Charles Castle (Toby Stephens) is eking out a living as a photographer in London after having spent time in the trenches of Europe photographing dead soldiers for posterity. Before the war, in 1912, he was married in Switzerland, but due to a mountain climbing tragedy, he became a widower before the honeymoon was over. He has become a mere shell of a man, going through the motions of everyday life, and unceasing in his wait for the day that he himself will cease to exist. His function in this life has been to debunk the world of the supernatural and all who claim to make contact with the spirit world.

At one such function, sponsored by the Theosophical Society, he lays waste to a set of photographs purporting to show to young girls with fairies dancing around them. A woman who attended the same function comes to his studio, showing photos of a different calibre – a little girl with a fairy obscured, standing on the end of her hand. Castle readily pooh poohs this display, and the woman leaves, satisfied and yet unfulfilled in her quest. Before long, Castle comes to realize, through a series of experiments, that there is a great deal of truth being portrayed in that photograph, and hence, he makes it his goal to travel to Birkenwell to confront his own demons and solve the mystery of life and death as we know it.

Photographing Fairies is a variation on a theme of a famous incident that happened in England in 1917 involving two young girls, Frances Griffiths and Elsie Wright of Cottingley, who claimed to have taken photographs of fairies in their garden. These photos were seized upon by no other than Sir Arthur Conan Doyle of Sherlock Holmes fame in 1921, and bandied about as absolute proof of theosophist theories that he was attracted to. Final proof of the girls and their duplicity was revealed in 1983, when Elsie wrote her famous confession and Frances followed suit. The article was posted in The Times.

Photographing Fairies is definitely not a film for children. It was released the same year as another film about fairies, Fairy Tale: A True Story, but is miles apart in telling a tale of fantasy and awe. While the latter asks us to believe that all we see happened as it was filmed, there is obviously a great deal of artistic license that is projected. Photographing Fairies differs for it asks us as viewers to take it or leave it as we see fit. It is a much darker story and obviously not a fairy tale with a happy ending, except in the mind of Charles Castle as he races on a course with death. It is truly a shame that this film was lost in the shuffle of Fairy Tale, for while both have their good points, Photographing Fairies has an absolute stranglehold on a story with teeth in it.

Toby Stephens plays Charles Castle as an enigma, and in doing so, has provided us with an entirely convincing performance. Emily Woof as Linda, governess to the little girls, Clara and Ana Templeton (Hannah Bould and Miriam Grant) is effective in her pursuit to keep Charles in this world and not the next. The girls are etched in innocence and peace of mind and never did one get the feeling that they were witnessing 'acting' by precocious children. Ben Kingsley as Reverend Templeton provides a strange and calculated portrayal, moving from frame to frame, changing his spots like a leopard, until the final denouement between Castle and himself in the forest. Edward Hardwicke as Sir Arthur Conan Doyle is simply doing what he does best; lending credence to a marvelous block of acting as has been his wont over a long and illustrious career. It's too bad that his role was so short in this film.

Nick Willing and Chris Harrald have taken the novel of the same name by Steve Szilagyl and worked miracles with it. The novel was simply an armature for an interpretation that is a vast improvement on a slight undertaking by Mr. Szilagyl. The better story is provided with the film, for complexities of human nature are betrayed that never quite see the light of day in the book. Both Willing and Harrald are relative newcomers to the world of film, but if Photographing Fairies is any indication of what stuff they are made of, then a productive, creative and applause filled road is theirs to travel.

When it first opened, critics made a great deal out of the fact that the visuals of the fairies had none of the requisite necessities that were needed to make the viewer think that they were actually seeing the agreed upon subject. What nitpicking! They failed to understand that only a visual was pertinent to the crux of the situation, and not a high tech, state of the art blow out. The merest hint of 'it's there' was all that was needed and it was achieved in spades.

Music by Simon Boswell was evocative of time and place and it shared mood duties with the death dirge of Beethoven's Seventh Symphony, which is played to full effect and in compliance with Castle's life and eventual fate. If there is a dry eye to be had at the conclusion of this film, then the person they belong to, has no heart or soul.

This reviewer was intrigued and swept away, into the world of make believe and what if's. The logical and yet as we know and are taught it, irrationality of the subject, melded together to present for our considerations, a well thought out and richly veined tale that stays with us long after the credits have rolled, the music has stopped and we have left the theatre. We are left with the possibilities of probabilities as we would like to think them to be. We are entreated entrance into a world of simple things and knowing souls who will guide us to another world where things will be complacent and serene, if we just believe.

Photographing Fairies is that rare commodity that comes along and stays with us like a cool breeze on a summer's day, and is just as quickly gone to adjust its policies. A seed has been planted and the questions we are left with take us back to a time of innocence, longing and understanding. Is there a place, a clearing, a glen that houses such things? We can only wish…

(**Compiler's note**: The above information on the two versions of the story came from the website IMDB.com).

His autobiography, *Memories and Adventures* (1924), relates his military exploits, his psychic beliefs, and his meetings with literary figures of the period, including Oscar Wilde and George Meredith.

The following is a reprint of an article by David Pirie published in the Daily Telegraph, Wednesday, December 29, 1999. The article was entitled **The man who was Holmes.** *Conan Doyle acknowledged that his old tutor was the model for Sherlock Holmes. But, asks David Pirie, writer of a new BBC drama, was the link closer than he admitted?*

'What is it about Sherlock Holmes? Other popular fictional characters of the 19th century, from David Copperfield to Dracula, may still be in print, may be internationally renowned and on TV.

But so far as I know, nobody actually writes to them. Their fictional homes have not become museums, surrounded by shops selling memorabilia; they are not the subjects of endless discussion groups that dwell on their habits and tastes. Nobody thinks of them as real.

Some argue that Sherlock Holmes has appeared real because he was the first detective. But that is simply not true. Other skilled literary detectives preceded him, even from famous writers such as Poe, who inspired Doyle. Many more came after. But not one ever achieved anything like this kind of Elvis effect. Reading the stories undoubtedly brings us closer to an understanding: for the truth is they have an odd and unexpected intensity. There is a genuine emotion in Doyle's portrayal of Holmes and Watson, which explains some of its impact, yet makes the creative origins of this emotion even more mysterious.

Doyle's own account of the origin of Holmes is of little help. It is thin and uninformative as Mary Shelley's account of the origins of Frankenstein. But facts are now emerging that shed a remarkable light on the making of the detective, and Doyle's early creative life. Many secrets were kept to the end and most of them were obviously extremely painful. It was on the basis of these secrets that I developed the idea of the TV serial *Murder Rooms*, which will be shown on January 4 and 5 on BBC2.

Though based on fact with many real characters, this is partly fiction. But as a result of my research I have incidentally, begun to wonder if the answer to the Holmes puzzle has not been staring us in the face the whole time. It may at first seem startling. But could it be that Holmes seems real because, in certain respects we are only just starting to appreciate, he *was* real. Of course it had long been known that the figure of Holmes was based on the charismatic teacher and physician Joseph Bell, who taught Doyle at Edinburgh University from 1878. One of the few letters of Doyle's in the public domain was written to Bell and acknowledges the debt openly: "It is certainly to you that I owe Sherlock Holmes."

Here is about the only serious autobiographical clue to the detective's origins we have. For, even now, the life of Doyle remains shrouded in a fog as thick as the ones that swirl through his stories. There have been many recent biographies but not one has had access to Doyle's own papers and letters. For most of this century, these have been locked away, unseen by anyone at all because of a mysterious court case concerning the estate, which shows no sign of progressing. As a result, the evidence is coming with painful slowness. But in the Eighties a remarkable discovery was made by Doyle's biographer Owen Dudley Edwards.

It was always known that the Doyle family existed in great poverty and must have struggled to send Arthur through medical school. More recently it was discovered that his father's decline into alcoholism and madness was reaching a peak when Arthur returned from boarding school to live at home in Edinburgh in 1876. This was bad enough for him but what may have been even harder was that Bryan Waller, a supercilious doctor and a vain, egotistical and arrogant man, appears at the same time to have moved both into the family home and the affections of Doyle's mother.

From about the same year Doyle returned, it was Waller, then aged only 25, who was paying the rent and enabling the family to survive. Given everything we know of the man, it seems unlikely that he would not have expected power in return. Waller would continue to live alongside Mrs Doyle, who was nearly 40 when he moved in, until her eightieth year.

The relationship may or may not have been sexual, but the pressure it must have placed on Arthur is surely extraordinary. When Doyle started his early years at Edinburgh medical school, he had not only a father who was deranged and whose condition had to be kept secret, but also, in the same house, an arrogant older rival for his mother's affection.

But at this critical time, someone appeared: a teacher opposite in every way to these other troublesome fathers. And his name was Joseph Bell.

There is no question that this charismatic, skilled, caring and glamorous scientific pioneer dazzled Doyle. Just like Holmes, Bell was the kind of teacher who could wow his audience with tricks of observation and memory. He would startle his students by pronouncing the profession and origins of some patient even down to the colour of the two horses he drove. But he was also a remarkable scientist, a skilled doctor, a social reformer and a detective. The relationship was cemented when, to Doyle's astonishment, Bell picked him out as the clerk who would assist him in all practical duties.

But does the "reality" of Holmes go further? In 1878, the year Doyle met Bell; a murderer called Eugene Chantrelle was hanged in Edinburgh for the slaying of his wife. Bell's crucial part in this case is recorded in several memoirs by his own pupils. And indeed, as he stepped onto the gallows, Chantrelle singled out Bell for solving the crime. Given these facts, and the letters Doyle wrote to Bell asking for material for the Holmes stories, it is extraordinary that Doyle refrained from making any such connection in public, even while acknowledging Bell as his model for Holmes. The silence is suggestive, and I can see only two possible reasons for it.

One is that Doyle wished to diminish the connection. But if this was the case, why so easily and publicly acknowledge it? The other is that he knew of Bell's criminal work but did not discuss it at all because, like so much in these Victorian lives, he regarded it as confidential. Bell certainly appears to have wanted this to be the case.

If this is true then Bell may have supplied Doyle with details of his criminal investigation which Doyle later put to such good use. There are even rumours, though I do not believe them, that a manuscript exists in which the young Doyle wrote accounts of some of Bell's work in criminal and forensic investigation. If such a book ever saw the light of day it would indeed be the true stories of Holmes.

We will probably never know. But I am certain that Holmes represented a telling truth for Doyle at a certain point in his life and the debt he acknowledged to Bell was not just technical but real and emotional. Little wonder that he looked back on the creation of Holmes with a certain pained memory, and sometimes wished to be rid of him'.

Murder Rooms: The Dark Beginnings of Sherlock Holmes

The following reviews are of the above television programme which was shown on BBC 2, Tuesday January 4 and Wednesday January 5, 2000.

Introduction: When medical student Arthur Conan Doyle became an apprentice to the maverick and pioneering master forensic pathologist Dr Joseph Bell in 1878 his fictional detective Sherlock Holmes was born – inspired by Bell's involvement in secret police investigations. In the authentically gloomy atmosphere of Victorian Edinburgh, David Pirie's two-part dramatisation introduces us to Doyle and the dour Bell, a murder inquiry proving the perfect model for Doyle's fertile imagination.

The first of these reviews was published in The Daily Telegraph, Wednesday, January 5, 2000 entitled **The origins of Sherlock Holmes** written by **James Walton** as follows:

'Nobody who watched last night's *Murder Rooms* is likely to have felt short-changed. Let's face it, few other recent television dramas have managed to blend literary history, biography, women's studies, a love story and two whodunnits in 60 minutes flat.

The programme started with a familiar deerstalker floating at the bottom of a familiar waterfall. Sure enough, newsvendors were soon shouting "Sherlock Holmes Dead – read all about it" through their mufflers, as crowds besieged the offices of *Strand* magazine, demanding to know why Arthur Conan Doyle (Robin Laing) had killed off the great man. The *Strand's* editor, not surprisingly, wanted to know the same thing – but Doyle's only response was to say "Because it was time" and to gaze distractedly into the distance. Cue a flashback to his days as an Edinburgh medical student and to the man who inspired it all…

That man, of course, was Dr Joseph Bell (Ian Richardson) whom we first saw whipping a corpse, then shooting it, and making careful notes of what happened as a result. (Not much it turned out). Before long, however, he was duly using the word "elementary" a lot; telling his students, "You see but you do not observe"; and generally deducing his socks off. He was also moonlighting as a forensic adviser to the local police – a job that largely consisted of solving implausibly intricate crimes while they stood around open-mouthed. Yet, for reasons unexplained, Bell couldn't be satisfied with life until he had convinced Doyle of the validity of his methods. He therefore conscripted the young sceptic as a clerk whose frankly Watsonian tasks were a) to be amazed; and b) to write up the cases. That Bell and Doyle are now engaged in finding the man behind a series of attacks on prostitutes indicates accurately, how *Murder Rooms* often fails to rise above the clichés of screen Victoriana. (The programme has already given us more dingy back-streets than you could shake a stick at – and as a general rule, the more misogynist a posh male character's utterances, the more liable he is to visit brothels). Nonetheless, with so much else going on, and especially with Ian Richardson in such magnificent form, this somehow doesn't matter as much as it should. Certainly, I can't wait for tonight's concluding episode, which promises to be even more incident-packed.'

(Compiler's note: The second of these reviews cannot be referenced, as the source of the original newspaper article was not noted).

'A lot more dramatic than *Longitude* and much more to my taste was **Murder Rooms: The Dark Beginnings of Sherlock Holmes** (Tuesday and Wednesday, BBC 2). The central idea had a real touch of brilliance: the true,
 or at least truish, story of how Sherlock Holmes came into being. Thus the young Arthur Conan Doyle became in effect Dr Watson, a sceptical and bumbling acolyte, studying at the feet of the Edinburgh surgeon, Dr Joseph Bell, and being invited to write up his case studies.

As well as having an authentically Holmesian atmosphere, David Pirie's script skilfully weaved episodes from Doyle's own past – his shame at his father's insanity – into a richly textured, constantly wrong-footed plot. A killer is on the loose in 1890s Edinburgh, slaughtering women too common to warrant the attentions of the Edinburgh police. The suspects are a suitably diverse lot, from the university chancellor to the mad Jesuit trying to exclude women from the university.

The denouement, in which Doyle's fiancée was herself murdered, launched him on the path to writing Holmes: creating an imaginary detective to dispel the insoluble crimes which haunted him. It was as clear as anything that had gone before. Robert Laing made an effective Doyle – dour and hot-headed but by no means unsympathetic – while Dr Bell allowed Ian Richardson plenty of scope to display that patrician vigour at which he excels. And the relationship between them, while taking its flavour from their fictional guises, had some very subtle emotional cross-currents of its own.'

Following the success of the first series, a second one of four stories ran for four Tuesdays during September 2001.
 An introduction was published on Monday, September 3, 2001 in the *Daily Express*. It was entitled **The sleuth truth** by **David Robson** who put BBC1's intriguing new Victorian Murder series, Murder Rooms, under the magnifying glass.

'Those reading this television preview are persons of discernment, more interested in their brains than their stomachs or their pockets. They place the problems of homo sapiens above dogs," said Holmes, "And of those who look at this before the article next to it, the majority are over 50."

"What leads you to reach those conclusions?" asked Watson, his expression something between disbelief and idolatry. "Because they will watch Murder rooms, tomorrow night on BBC1, rather than Food And Drink and Ainsley's Gourmet Express on BBC2; Who Wants To Be A Millionaire? On ITV or even The Dog Listener – a canine psychology programme on Channel 5," replied Holmes.

"Oh yes, I can see that," said Watson, "but how can you tell their age?" "Because," said Holmes with a self-satisfied flourish, "older people are known to be devoted fans of murder mysteries and a headline like the one above will prove to be an irresistible attraction."

"Remarkable, quite remarkable," said Watson with a shake of his head.

For the next four Tuesday evenings viewers will be drawn back into a dark and gripping world of Victorian murder, evil and insanity and the mind-boggling deductive leaps that were Sherlock Holmes's speciality although, as viewers of last year's first Murder Rooms series on BBC2 already know, the leading characters in these well-told and well-mounted detective stories are not Holmes and Watson but their creator, Arthur Conan Doyle, and his own mentor, the pathologist Dr Joseph Bell, who taught him when he was a medical student at Edinburgh.

Bell, played by Ian Richardson with the sinister knowingness of which he is master, was Conan Doyle's model for Holmes. He was an extraordinary character, often secretly used by the Edinburgh police force to solve mysteries that foxed them. But if the roots of Holmes's deductive methods can be traced to him, the genesis of the whole Holmes character and the terrible world in which he moved, lies much deeper. The full title of the series is **Murder Rooms: The Dark Beginnings of Sherlock Holmes**.

According to David Pirie, creator of the series and writer of tomorrow's story, Holmes was a product of Conan Doyle's profoundly miserable youth. He had been unhappy at school and bored by mediocre teachers at University until he fell under Bell's spell. As for his home life, his father had gone mad and his mother had taken in a supercilious arrogant doctor as a "lodger". He paid the bills (which was necessary), but made the house a most unpleasant place. Whether he and Conan Doyle's mother were having a sexual relationship is not known but, as Pirie says, it hardly matters. "It all added up to a sort of Hamlet situation," he says. "Looked at it another way, he had two bad fathers at home and one good father, Bell."

Although the Sherlock Holmes stories made Conan Doyle rich and famous, and although they were classed "entertainments", for Conan Doyle they were associated with pain. "The writer of Dracula and Frankenstein tried to explain their characters away, probably because of the dark emotions that spawned them. Doyle's attitude to Sherlock Holmes was the same."

Tomorrow's story, entitled "The Patient's Eyes" finds a penniless Conan Doyle (played by Charles Edwards) sharing a practice with an exploitative quack called Tumavine – this, too, is based on fact. He has a young patient, an attractive woman who believes she is seeing things, being pursued by a cloaked and ghoulish cyclist. Conan Doyle tries to get to the bottom of it, but cannot and enlists the help of Bell. It is a tortuous tale, but to find out what happens you will have to wave goodbye to Ainsley's Gourmet Express'.

A review by **John Preston** was published in the *Sunday Telegraph* Arts Section on September 9, 2001.

"I very much enjoyed the pilot of **Murder Rooms** (Tuesday, BBC1) when it appeared last year, and it has returned as a series of four feature-length episodes.

The premise is an ingenious one – the young Conan Doyle and his real-life mentor, Dr Joseph Bell, set out to investigate various crimes with Doyle effectively acting as Dr Watson to Bell's Holmes. But it needs to be done with a great deal of panache if it's not to suffer by comparison with the original Doyle stories. While the plot was fine and there were some excellent flourishes, it all felt simultaneously overdrawn and underpowered.

Doyle never properly took flight as a character, and the relationship between him and Bell lacked tone and depth. I sat through it happily enough, yet was left feeling undernourished afterwards.

The following are reviews of the first story in the series **"The Patient's Eyes"**. Firstly, by **Daniela Soave** in the *Daily Mail*, Tuesday, September 4, 2001.

'The excellent Ian Richardson reprises his role as Dr Joseph Bell – the real-life University lecturer upon whom Arthur Conan Doyle based his hero Sherlock Holmes – in a new series of four glossy feature-length films that resonate with Victorian melodrama. The first, entitled The Patient's Eyes, is set in the early days of Doyle's career as a doctor. Newly arrived in Portsmouth, Doyle (Charles Edwards) discovers that his employer, Dr Turnavine, is a charlatan and a madman and before long he is on his own. Worst still, he becomes embroiled in the dark goings-on of a patient, a troubled heiress named Heather. When Doyle writes to his mentor, Bell travels from Edinburgh to cast a practised eye over the evidence.'

Secondly, by **Simon Edge**, *Daily Express*, Wednesday September 5, 2001.

'Sir Arthur Conan Doyle has a lot to answer for. Ever since he gave the world Sherlock Holmes and Dr Watson, detective writers have been churning out weaker and weaker variations on the "all-knowing supersleuth plus know-nothing sidekick" theme. The lazier the author, the more miraculously the Holmes figure magics the truth out of the ether. The Watson figure may splutter in admiration, but we know better. This isn't detective genius so much as defective writing.

So there is a certain poetic justice that one of the sloppiest examples of this formula should feature an imagined version of Sir Arthur himself in the Watson role – or Dr Doyle as he is called in **Murder Rooms** (BBC1). The title makes it sound like a cross between Murder, She Wrote and Changing Rooms in which Angela Lansbury tries to work out which aggrieved couple garrotted Laurence Llewelyn-Bowen for the cold-blooded murder of their living room. If only it were half that good.

"There's something about this place, is there not? Is it because highwaymen were hanged on a gibbet back there?" observed Ian Richardson in last night's mystery. (The real mystery, of course, is what on earth possessed him. Even the best actors need to pay the bills? You may think that – I couldn't possibly comment.)

Richardson plays the Holmesian Dr Bell. "*The* Dr Bell? Head of operative surgery, who wrote the monograph on the adaptation of the eye to distance?" gasped one of the shiftier-looking of last night's suspects.

There was indeed something about the place, and it had nothing to do with gibbets. It was full of munitions tunnels, allowing a deranged former lover of orphaned Miss Grace (Katie Blake) to dress up like Darth Vader on a push-bike and sneak up on her when she wasn't looking. The idea was to frighten her into taking him back, but Miss Grace was made of sterner stuff, having arranged her own orphanhood some years earlier by bludgeoning her parents to death. She co-opted Darth Vader into stabbing a nuisance suitor through the heart and burying a nice young doctor's assistant up to his topknot.

The poor cast stumbled around as if all the scenes had been shot in the wrong order and nobody had seen the full script – including the director. At one point the wicked Dr Turnavine (a bewhiskered Alexander Armstrong from the awful Armstrong and Miller and the excellent Beast) confessed to "a little drama" involving Miss Grace. This was very confusing because he wasn't Darth Vader at all. What, precisely, was he owning up to? It brought to mind the famous story about the Usual Suspects, where Gabriel Byrne wrongly thought he was the killer right up to the cast screening.

There was also a marvellous moment when Doyle a charisma-bypassed (Charles Edwards) ran into a derelict house on a fine moonlit night and emerged through the window 10 seconds later into a torrential rainstorm. Explain that one, Sherlock'.

Thirdly, from the *Daily Mail*, Wednesday, September 5, 2001. Entitled **Less than ideal Holmes** by **Peter Paterson**.

'Good Lord, Holmes,' said Dr Watson, I thought I saw you on the television last night, but it turned out to be a certain Joseph Bell, who claims that you were modelled on him.'

'Bell is a complete imposter, I assure you, my dear Watson,' replied Sherlock Holmes, lighting another opium pipe.

'Only by getting that fellow Ian Richardson to play him did they have the slightest chance of convincing gullible viewers such as yourself that they were seeing the real thing.'

'They claim,' said Watson, warily eyeing Holmes's violin case and worrying that he might start at any moment to play, 'that Bell actually taught medicine to Sir Arthur Conan Doyle at the University of Edinburgh.

'And as you are well aware, Holmes, it was Conan Doyle who immortalised us both in his stories based on our career in detection.'

My career in detection, Watson,' Holmes corrected him, 'I fear you were no more than what is known nowadays as my sidekick.

'But I can assure you that no trained observer could possibly mistake this Bell for myself.'

Watson fidgeted for a moment with the poker at the fireside, feeling the comforting weight of the revolver in his inside pocket and wondering whether Holmes was in one of his more tiresome moods.

'Ian Richardson certainly looks quite as distinguished as yourself,' he said provocatively, 'and I must say, Holmes, that the way he goes about things is certainly reminiscent of that time we were on Dartmoor together – the Baskerville case, wasn't it, something to do with a dog that barked at the moment his master was murdered?'

'You're confusing Conan Doyle's effusions with those of G.K.Chesterton,' Holmes snapped irritably. 'Besides, I would never be seen dead in that top hat Richardson is wearing. Don't they know that one is required to wear a deerstalker and an Ulster coat when one is investigating a crime?

'It is my belief, Watson, that those tricky BBC people have noticed that the copyright on the Sherlock Holmes stories might be extended indefinitely by the EU.

(***Compiler's note***: *see the two newspaper articles on copyright and trademark at the conclusion of these reviews).*

'Inventing this Bell fellow for programmes like the one you saw last night – Murder Rooms: The Dark Beginnings of Sherlock Holmes, I believe it was called – is a way of negating that possibility.'

'These are deep waters,' said Watson.' I said that first,' admonished Holmes, preparing to retire to bed.

Fourthly, by **Edna Pottersman**, Tuesday, September 4, 2001 THE DAILY TELEGRAPH **Today's Choices**.

If you go down to the woods today, you'll find yourself again in the company of master pathologist and crime investigator Dr Joseph Bell (Ian Richardson). David Pirie's *The Patient's Eyes* marks the start of a series of indulgent but enjoyable costume who-dunits following last year's one-off drama. Charles Edwards plays Arthur Conan Doyle, no longer Bell's apprentice, but now a fully qualified and dedicated doctor in practice with a mad partner, living in Southsea and still haunted by the murder of his love. That explains his empathy with Miss Heather Grace (Katie Blake), a young lady of means and experience who consults him over her fears – mostly, of being followed on her bike by a hooded man. Bodies mount, so do the suspects; Doyle fancies the case – and Heather, of course…

Fifthly, from THE DAILY TELEGRAPH Wednesday, September 5, 2001. **Last night on television. Elementary inspiration** by **James Walton**.

If you saw last year's "one-off" (ie pilot) drama, **Murder Rooms: the Dark Beginnings of Sherlock Holmes**, you'll have known what to expect when the programme returned yesterday on BBC1 – almost anything. And so it proved. The show's premise is the fact that literature's most famous detective was based on Dr Joseph Bell, Arthur Conan Doyle's mentor when he was a medical student in Edinburgh. Yet, once again, *Murder Rooms* wasn't content merely to play fast and loose with Bell and Doyle's biographies so as to give them a mystery to solve, in a frankly Holmes and Watson style – and then to suggest that this is where Doyle found the inspiration for one of his stories. (Last night's episode contained several echoes of *The Adventures of the Solitary Cyclist*. Instead, it also threw in elements from Hammer Horror, *film noir*, the *Doctor* movies and possibly even *Scooby-Doo*).

Thus, the programme started with the young Doyle (Charles Edwards) joining his first practice in Southsea where his new boss took a robustly James Robertson Justice line towards all staff and patients. Next, the toothsome Heather (Katie Blake), a Victorian *femme fatale* with a particularly impressive bustle, arrived in Doyle's surgery. Every day, she told him, as she cycled through the woods, she was pursued by a spectral figure in a hooded cloak who had the apparent ability to disappear into thin air. (Curiously, this didn't cause her to change her route).

Doyle's initial investigations were predictably inept – but then Dr Bell (Ian Richardson) showed up. After a brief demonstration of his powers of perception ("You have lost nine and a half pounds since I saw you last Doyle" – which seemed a bit mean on Robin Laing, who played Doyle in the pilot), he got to work. Unfortunately, the plot immediately became so complicated that it was an hour before he could shout "Yes of course" and explain everything.

It was so complicated, too that the script didn't have time to let us in on the clues – which is why viewers familiar with punishments for traitors in the First Boer War of 1880-81 stood any chance of guessing even part of the solution.

And yet, *Murder Rooms* isn't the pile of old nonsense it theoretically should be. For one thing, its very eccentricity proves distinctly refreshing. For another, like all genuine eccentrics, it goes about its peculiar business without any self-consciousness whatsoever – behaving throughout as if it were the most unobjectionably normal TV series in the world. Its pace is unhurried, and rather than trying to be all ironic and camp, its central performances are delivered with the utmost seriousness. The result is an oddly yet undeniably enjoyable piece of television.

Finally, on this episode, from **THE MIRROR**, Wednesday September 5, 2001, entitled **Confused by Holmes truths** by **Tony Purnell**.

You did not have to be the world's greatest detective to work out who provided the model for Sherlock Holmes.

He didn't have a deerstalker and he didn't smoke a pipe but it was Dr Joseph Bell and no mistake.

The clues were there for all to see in **Murder Rooms (BBC1)** despite the fact that it was shot mainly in the dark.

Dr Bell was Sir Arthur Conan Doyle's tutor at university and came over as a right clever dick.

He was played with great relish by Ian Richardson who was Holmes in all but name. And who was the inspiration for sidekick Watson?

Elementary, dear reader, it was Doyle himself who hung on to his mentor's every word and was rather slow on the uptake. The drama was based on the real-life relationship between the two friends.

We joined the young Doyle, played by Charles Edwards, as he set up in practice on the south coast. An attractive girl patient complained that a hooded man kept following her as she cycled home through the woods.

She feared her eyes were playing tricks on her or she was slowly going mad. Doyle was immediately smitten. It was love at first eyesight examination.

He made it his business to follow her to catch the culprit but her hooded pursuer vanished into thin air. Doyle wrote to Dr Bell in Edinburgh and you just knew the snooty sleuth would soon book a train to Sherlock-On-Sea.

Melodrama has never been more Victorian. The girl's parents had been butchered by a serial killer and she had been jilted by a naval officer. She lived with a wicked uncle, a dodgy looking schoolteacher had asked for her hand in marriage and she was about to inherit a fortune.

Small wonder dopey Doyle was out of his depth.

Dr Bell who strode around the countryside in a black topper and carried a silver-topped cane got to the bottom of the caped cyclist mystery but not in time to prevent a number of grisly murders.

Whodunit? It was so complicated in the end I was past caring.

The second story was entitled *The Photographer's Chair* and was reviewed by **Edna Pottersman** in THE DAILY TELEGRAPH, Tuesday September 11, 2001.

"Memory can be a torment": Arthur Conan Doyle (Charles Edwards) has never recovered from his fiancée's death, her killer hasn't been found, and now he's challenged by a series of bodies washed up on the beach – all very different characters, though there are marked similarities in the method of murder. The problem lies in the investigating pathologist, with a reputation as an incompetent surgeon, a man from whom Dr Joseph Bell (Ian Richardson) has never had respect, and who consistently misses crucial evidence. With a fine mix of humour, tragedy, suspense and an excellent cast, Paul Billing's *The Photographer's Chair* keeps you hanging on, unbelievable though it is (but hey, somebody, turn the light up). As séance follows séance, it's soon clear that the medium has the message.

This episode was also reviewed by **Gerard O'Donovan**, Wednesday, September 19, 2001 THE DAILY TELEGRAPH.

Later, **Murder Rooms: the Dark Beginnings of Sherlock Holmes (BBC1)** caught up with an episode knocked out of the schedules last week by coverage of the tragedy in America. *The Photographer's Chair* was an agreeably daft murder mystery if you could overlook the re-casting of Arthur Conan Doyle's great fictional hero in the guise of his real life mentor, Dr Joseph Bell.

In this instance, Drs Doyle and Bell were transplanted to Portsmouth, where a serial killer was dumping bodies in the docks, strange marks on his victims' necks the only clue to his identity. Bell's proto-forensic methods duly unearthed chemical traces on one victim, indicating a photographer's involvement and – after a wild goose chase down avenues packed to overflowing with the set designer's impressive collection of Victoriana, and a storyline playing excessively on Conan Doyle's lifelong fascination with the supernatural – the victim was eventually unmasked. What the committed Conan Doyle enthusiast made of it I can't say but as television entertainment, I must admit I rather enjoyed it.

A third review came from the **Daily Mail**, Tuesday, September 11, 2001 and was written by **Sadie Austin**.

Continuing the atmospheric dramas, set in Portsmouth, about the early life of Arthur Conan Doyle, creator of Sherlock Holmes. Tonight sees our man concerned with the increasing number of corpses washing up on Portsmouth's shores. Through flashbacks we realise Doyle's girlfriend was murdered some years ago and he continues to be tortured by her death. Can his probe into these murders and a tumble into the world of spiritualism put him straight? Charles Edwards is wonderfully Victorian as our staunch hero, while Richardson, as usual, is compelling as his mentor, Dr Joseph Bell, who cuts to the heart of the mystery. Look out, too, for Scots actor David Hayman as a syphilitic photographer who has a fascination with death.

The fourth and final review was written by **Danny Scott** and published in the DAILY EXPRESS Tuesday September 11 2001.
Still shocked by the fatal poisoning of his beloved wife Elspeth, the young Arthur Conan Doyle, played by Charles Edwards, was probably hoping for a break from all this

death, murder, mystery and suspense malarkey. No such luck. This week's spooky story surrounds a dastardly fiend who seems to have a thing for beating up women and dumping them into Southsea harbour. A quick dip in the briny reveals a watery graveyard of bodies, and once again Ian Richardson's character Dr Joseph Bell and his student are called upon for their forensic expertise.

The third episode, entitled *The Kingdom of Bones* was reviewed, firstly by **Edna Pottersman**, THE DAILY TELEGRAPH, Tuesday 25, September 2001.

There's a tangible sense of affection growing between whimsical forensic pathologist Dr Joseph Bell (Ian Richardson) and his young protégé, Dr Arthur Conan Doyle (Charles Edwards), when a little of Doyle's troubled home background emerges tonight in *The Kingdom of Bones* – "a sort of Victorian *Raiders of the Lost Ark*," as the episode's author Stephen Gallagher describes it. It's an apt description of a tale that's even more barking and convoluted than last week's: a local museum curator, desperate to build his reputation believes he's in possession of a valuable mummified Egyptian princess. That it's murder with a hidden political agenda is elementary. As horse-drawn chase scenes go, it rattles along at a decent pace with a star cast including John Sessions and Crispin Bonham Carter. Originally scheduled for last Tuesday.

The second review is from The Daily Telegraph Television and Radio, September 22-28. Pick of the day: **Murder Rooms: The Kingdom of Bones**.

Ian Richardson stars as the pioneering forensic pathologist Dr Joseph Bell, with Charles Edwards as the tenacious Arthur Conan Doyle, in the third film of this intriguing series. *The Kingdom of Bones* begins in Southsea, where the curator of a local museum Reuben Proctor (Crispin Bonham-Carter) shows his friend Doyle a strange mummified body covered in hieroglyphs. Doyle persuades Bell to bring the eminent Edinburgh scientist, William Rutherford (John Sessions) to the south coast for a public unwrapping of the corpse.
   However, the doctor and the detective duo are shocked to discover that the body is not that of an Egyptian at all, but of a recently murdered Victorian. The shame of it all leads Proctor to kill himself. Meanwhile, Bell and Doyle become suspicious of Canadian art collector Heywood Donovan (Ian McNiece) and his beautiful daughter Gladys (Caroline Carver). As Bell stumbles across Donovan's secret, he puts both his and Doyle's life in danger.
   Written by Stephen Gallagher, this title pays homage not so much to Sherlock Holmes, but another of Arthur Conan Doyle's much loved books, *The Lost World*.

The third and final review was published in the **Daily Mail**, Wednesday, September 26, 2001 and was written by **Peter Paterson**.

MURDER Rooms, the Sherlock Holmes stories by proxy, caught up in last night's tale with our current preoccupation with terrorism. But The Kingdom of Bones was about Irish terrorism, which curiously doesn't seem to count in the new anti-terrorist war, and was, besides, mainly set in the Victorian period.

Its only Arab reference – firmly pre-Islamic – was the discovery of a modern corpse within the linen wrappings of what should have been an Egyptian mummy.

Instead of the great fictional detective in person, David Pirie's series gives us his creator, Arthur Conan Doyle, as a junior version of Dr Watson, and Dr Joseph Bell, Doyle's Edinburgh University medicine tutor and supposedly the inspiration for Holmes, as-well-Holmes by another name.

Doyle was already writing his detective stories while struggling as a General Practitioner in Southsea, near Portsmouth, where Murder Rooms is set. I doubt whether the town today (if it ever did) can boast the natural history and antiquarian museum it was given in Kingdom of Bones.

The museum curator was Doyle's friend Reuben Proctor (Crispin Bonham-Carter), who bought the supposed mummy for seven guineas and proudly arranged for a famous surgeon, Professor Rutherford (John Sessions), ceremoniously to reveal an Egyptian princess interred 3,000 years ago.

Rutherford, Dr Bell – played with feline smoothness by Ian Richardson – and Doyle (Charles Edwards) were astonished to find instead that the remains were of a stonemason called Hudson, and the hieroglyphics around the mummy mere gibberish. Proctor was so mortified that he hanged himself.

It would be tedious to explain the connection of this event with Irish terrorism, though the always watchable Ian McNeice played the Fenian villain of the piece with an occasional Irish lilt.

For dyed-in-the-wool Holmes fans there were teasing references to Conan Doyle's works scattered through Stephen Gallagher's script. The mummy may have been a nod to The Lost World – not a Sherlock Holmes story, but featuring another of Doyle's creations, Professor Challenger. And a fairground boxing booth sequence brought to mind his novel of the noble art, *Rodney Stone*.

For most viewers, I would guess, Ian Richardson, regardless of tiresomely being called Dr Bell, makes a fine Sherlock Holmes, even if we miss the occasional sartorial trappings. And, thankfully, he does not play the violin.

The final episode in the series **Murder Rooms: The Dark Beginnings of Sherlock Holmes** was *The White Knight Stratagem*. The following review is by **Edna Pottersman**, Tuesday, October 2, 2001 THE DAILY TELEGRAPH.

First one death, then another – and another: it doesn't take much to set tongues wagging up in Edinburgh. Dr Arthur Conan Doyle (Charles Edwards) returns to the stamping ground of his student days, where he first dabbled in the world of forensic pathology under his then tutor Dr Joseph Bell (Ian Richardson) – whose now as much a paternal figure in Doyle's personally troubled life as a friend and occasional work colleague.

Mill-owner Alicia Craine has killed herself; money-lender Henry Starr is murdered. Surely some connection? But the copper on the case Lt Daniel Blaney (Rik Mayall) is hardly Bell's great ally, making the investigation contentious to say the least. With several individuals implicated, a perfect degree of levity and superb performances, Daniel Boyle's intriguing tale closes the current run. And elementary it ain't.

As referred to on page 21, Sherlock Holmes was probably alluding to the case of Andrea Plunket. Two newspaper articles have been published and they will be reproduced here.

Firstly, **Sherlock Holmes and the strange case of the socialite** written by **Catherine Milner**, Arts Correspondent, *The Sunday Telegraph*, September 12 1999.

Sherlock Holmes, Britain's cleverest detective, is facing his most taxing problem – how to escape the clutches of a Hungarian socialite.

Andrea Plunket, 60, claims that she controls the rights to the fictional characters of Holmes, Dr Watson and all the others created by Sir Arthur Conan Doyle in his Baker Street novels.

As a result, if anyone wants to publish anything to do so with him – even fictional pastiches of the original works by Conan Doyle, or to manufacture such things as Sherlock Holmes deer-stalkers or mugs bearing his eagle-like features and meerschaum pipe, they must, she insists, apply to her for a licence. "A lot of people have been scavenging," Mrs Plunket said.

The story goes back to 1976 when Mrs Plunket was married to Sheldon Reynolds, a television producer who wanted to make a film about Holmes. To help him, her mother bought the copyrights and last year Mrs Plunket became the manager and administrator of these rights. The copyright on Conan Doyle's novels expired in 1980 but the European Community added a new twist last year. A Brussels directive extended the period of copyright from 50 to 70 years after the author's death – giving Mrs Plunket a fresh opportunity to cash in on the books, and to attempt to establish herself as the exclusive licenser of Sherlock Holmes material indefinitely.

Although the copyright runs out next year Mrs Plunket is trying to extend her hold over the Conan Doyle industry by licensing his characters and apparently trying to register Sherlock Holmes as a trademark.

Mrs Plunket controls not only the literary copyright, but according to her legal advisers she also has rights to images of Holmes. The characters as entities are separate from the copyright.

Her lawyers, Field Fisher Waterhouse, said last week: "Andrea Plunket is responsible for administering the rights in the Conan Doyle literary works. These rights include the right to exploit the fictional characters created by Conan Doyle in the literary works."

Mrs Plunket, who has had 15 plastic surgery operations, is the former mistress of Claus von Bulow, the languid aristocrat who in the Eighties was acquitted of attempting to murder his wife Sunny by injecting her with an overdose of insulin.

She stood by von Bulow during his legal battle, but he dropped her shortly after it was over. In 1991, she married her fourth husband – The Hon Shaun Plunket.

So far the BBC and Constable Books have acquiesced to Mrs Plunket's requests. The BBC, which recently produced a series of audio cassettes entitled *The Sherlock Holmes Pastiches*, is believed to have agreed to pay Mrs Plunket a two per cent royalty on the sale of any tapes in addition to £350 up front.

Constable Books have printed an acknowledgement that "the characters of Sherlock Holmes and Dr Watson and all other characters created by Sir Arthur Conan Doyle are the copyright of Andrea Plunket" in the front of some recent pastiches of Sherlock Holmes that they published.

But a number of smaller businesses are furious that the BBC and Constable Books gave in so easily.

"Those people who have agreed to Mrs Plunket's demands are unwise," said Martin Breese, one of Britain's leading publishers of the Sherlock Holmes novels.

"In British law you can't copyright a fictional character – and as a result you can't license them."

Mr Breese said that he had been "pestered" with several letters over the past year from Mrs Plunket's lawers and agents.

He added: "No one has given me a coherent explanation of what right these people have to interfere with my publishing business. They claim to have the right to license the use of the characters even after the copyright expires. You might just as well demand a toll for using a public highway – Baker Street for example."

Marcel Schulman, who owns the Sherlock Holmes Memorabilia Shop in Baker Street, said she has received two "threatening" letters from Mrs Plunket's lawyers.

The BBC refused to comment on why it had decided to pay Mrs Plunket and a spokesman for Constable Books said that acknowledging her as the Sherlock Holmes licence controller seemed to offer the course of "least resistance". But if she succeeds Mrs Plunket could set a precedent encouraging others who might be tempted to buy up rights to such national icons as Long John Silver or Toad of Toad Hall.

It might also mean that Sherlock Holmes pubs and even the bronze statue being erected in honour of Britain's greatest detective at number 221B Baker Street next week, might have to be licensed by Mrs Plunket.[4]

The second article was written by **John McEntee** and published in *The Express* Wednesday, April 12, 2000, entitled **Sherlock trademark mystery deepens**.

A bid by a New-York based socialite and former mistress of Claus von Bulow to wrest control of the name of Arthur Conan Doyle's legendary creation, Sherlock Holmes, has infuriated aficionados of the fictional detective.

Historian Count Nikolai Tolstoy last night denounced the attempt by New Yorker Andrea Plunket to register Sherlock's name as a trademark. If the application to the EU is successful, Plunket will control the rights to all Doyle's works featuring Holmes. Plunket, who has no other links with Holmes, may then be able to veto all books, magazines, films and even Christmas tree decorations.

Her application includes a request to register the classic silhouette image, showing Holmes wearing a deerstalker hat and smoking his Meerschaum pipe. Tolstoy fumes: "This seems like a ludicrous way to get around the copyright laws. It's another case of Euro-madness. Copyright law recently changed to extend the period to 70 years after an author's death.

---

[4] **The Daily Telegraph Monday, September 20, 1999.** News – Spotlight on the week. "SHERLOCK HOLMES: The great detective will be honoured on Thursday, when a 9ft statue will be unveiled outside Baker Street Underground Station. The sculptor, John Doubleday, has created one Holmes statue in Meiringen, Switzerland, near the Reichenbach Falls, and there are others in Edinburgh and Karuizawa, Japan. His creator, Sir Arthur Conan Doyle, however, appears to have no public statue anywhere. "

"If you can trademark a literary creation, you could effectively bypass this legislation, possibly within the life of an author. As Dr Watson would have said: 'These are still, deep waters and anything can happen'. Authors, more

than most people, create something unique. If I own a Rembrandt, it's a tangible artifact, but once copyright expires, anyone can use the author's work."

Since the copyright expires at the end of the year 2000 – 70 years after Conan Doyle's death in 1930 – any publisher could then freely republish his work but Plunket's application may jeopardise this. Marcel Schulman, owner of Baker Street's Sherlock Holmes Memorabilia Shop said: "Basically, it's an Americanism. It's a strange situation and no one really knows what she will own."

Meanwhile, Plunket declines my entreaties to comment.

*(**Compiler's note:** *Since the footnote newspaper article on the preceding page, the part about a statue to Sir Arthur Conan Doyle is no longer correct. A bronze statue has been erected in Crowborough, East Sussex at the junction of the four main streets. I have visited it and had a photograph taken in 2003*).

Chapter 2

Sir Arthur Conan Doyle: A Biography

Teller of Tales: The Life of Sir Arthur Conan Doyle by Daniel Stashower. This book was published in March 1999 and was the Winner of the 2000 Edgar Allen Poe Award for Best Critical/Biographical Work.

This biography examines the extraordinary life and strange contrasts of Sir Arthur Conan Doyle, the struggling provincial doctor who became the most popular storyteller of his age. From his youthful exploits aboard a whaling ship to his often stormy friendships with such figures as Harry Houdini and George Bernard Shaw, Arthur Conan Doyle lived a life as gripping as one of his own adventures. Exhaustively researched and elegantly written, *Teller of Tales* sets aside many myths and misconceptions to present a vivid portrait of the man behind the legend of Baker Street, with a particular emphasis on the Psychic Crusade that dominated his final years – the work that Conan Doyle himself felt to be "the most important thing in the world."

Best known for creating Sherlock Holmes, Sir Arthur Conan Doyle also wrote many historical novels, non-Holmensian mysteries, and even some works of science fiction. The Sherlock Holmes stories were easily the most profitable, but Conan Doyle quickly grew tired of his character's popularity. In addition to writing stories, he led a turbulent life as a doctor, playwright, avid sportsman and crusader for hopeless or unpopular causes. Stashower portrays Conan Doyle's very public belief in spiritualism as a lifelong interest rather than something brought on by senility or depression. This solid if somewhat dry account is liberally sprinkled with anecdotes, particularly of Conan Doyle's encounters with famous contemporaries. Stashower's analysis of his subject, however, could be stronger. Like Conan Doyle, he is best when he sticks to telling stories.

Three reviews will be presented here. Firstly, under Books Reviews in *The Sunday Telegraph*, February 27, 2000 under the title **An open and shut case**. Our most celebrated crime writer led a life of robust and scandal-free rectitude, finds **Kathryn Hughes** (who is the author of 'George Eliot, The Last Victorian').

'This is the age of "secret history" in which everyone is assumed to have led a double-life about which they would hate Posterity to know. The biographer's job is to hunt for truffles – a mad sister, an embarrassing disease, a financial scandal – anything to avoid the suggestion that the subject has somehow got away with it. But no matter how hard you look and whatever way you tell it, Arthur Conan Doyle's life reads like an open book. Even when he was at his weirdest – trying to convince the nation that there were fairies at the bottom of his garden – he did it with shining sincerity. Writing Conan Doyle's biography, Daniel Stashower is faced with that old literary dilemma: how to make goodness interesting.

Always seeming more like Watson than Holmes, Conan Doyle was a model of late Victorian (he was born in 1859) masculinity. He loved golf and cricket and was a pioneer of Alpine skiing which he did in Harris tweed knicker-bockers. He worked out with weights so effectively that, during one emergency, he was able to bear the weight of his Wolseley on his back. It was in this car that he managed to collect one of the first ever speeding tickets.

This physical robustness was combined with moral delicacy. Saddled with a consumptive wife who was routinely warned off sex by doctors, Conan Doyle refused the solution of paying for a prostitute or suing for divorce, even though he had left his family's Catholicism far behind him. Instead, he endured an excruciating 13 years of celibacy, concerning himself to arm-in-arm walks with the woman who was to become the second Lady Conan Doyle.

Even in the 1890s this kind of chivalry seemed quaint. A fan of Sir Walter Scott's novels and Macaulay's history, Conan Doyle would love to have done something similar. He worked hard on a series of historical plays and novels, but mostly they came out flat. What the British public really wanted, of course, was more of Sherlock Holmes. But the sage of Baker Street had been sent hurtling over the Reichenbach falls in 1893, a mere six years after his first appearance in *A Study in Scarlet*.

Desolate readers wore black armbands and *The Times* ran an obituary, a fancy which offended Conan Doyle, since his own father's recent death had failed to raise a single notice in a national newspaper. Holmes was left suspended over the Falls for eight years, before being recalled by popular request to tackle *The Hound of the Baskervilles*.

Eventually Conan Doyle made peace with the fact that he was always going to be known as the creator of Sherlock Holmes, rather than as a great literary novelist or military historian. He used his phenomenal fame to campaign for the release of wrongly-convicted prisoners and to push through various army reforms. He never managed his ambition of replacing the mounted cavalry with regiments on bicycles, but he did persuade the government to set up a kind of home guard during the First War.

Most famously, Conan Doyle threw his considerable bulk behind the cause of spiritualism. As a young man he had made that classic journey of so many scientifically-minded Victorians from devout faith to reverent doubt, always hoping that some crucial piece of evidence would appear to take him back into the fold. When that didn't happen, he dedicated himself to proving that life did indeed continue after death, and that it was possible to make contact with the spirits of the departed.

Conan Doyle's hunger to make this true, combined with his total lack of psychic ability, meant that he often ended up endorsing the most unlikely scams and frauds. He genuinely believed that Jerome K. Jerome and Joseph Conrad had made contact with him, and that Charles Dickens had begged him to finish *Edwin Drood*. Any remaining shreds of authority disappeared when Conan Doyle championed two little girls from Yorkshire who said that they had seen fairies in their garden and had the photographs to prove it. The pictures were obviously fake, but Conan Doyle so desperately wanted to believe in the little people that he was often to be seen tip-toeing bulkily through the woods on his Surrey estate in the hope of a sighting.[5]

---

[5] The following is a reprint of an article published in *The Daily Telegraph*, Wednesday, March 14, 2001, under News Bulletin and entitled **'Fairies hoax fetches £6,000'** '*Photographs of the celebrated Cottingley Fairies hoax sold for £6,000 at auction yesterday. The collection was bought at Bonhams and Brooks in London by an anonymous bidder. It was compiled by Edward Gardner who brought the case to the notice of Sir Arthur Conan Doyle, creator of Sherlock Holmes. Both men fell for the hoax perpetrated by Elsie Wright, aged 15, and her 10 year old cousin, Frances Griffiths, in 1917*'.

Daniel Stashower has written a scrupulously fair biography of Conan Doyle, never once making fun of his mockable beliefs. But in his determination not to judge or trivialise, Stashower fails to address quite legitimate issues in his subject's life. In particular, why did Conan Doyle's second wife, Jean Leckie develop a convenient capacity for automatic writing (in which she claimed her pen was seized and controlled by spirits) after her marriage to the convinced spiritualist? Was this, perhaps, her way of keeping Conan Doyle dependent on her, rather than on a whole array of other psychics or mediums (Yeat's young wife, after all, did much the same thing)?

Nor, more crucially, does Stashower make us see how the clumsy and credulous Conan Doyle was able to create the subtle sceptic of Baker Street. Still, in showing us that exemplary lives can still make riveting biography, he has done the genre a great service'.

The second review was published in *The Daily Telegraph* Saturday February 19, 2000 in the **arts and books** section. It was entitled *Champion of underdogs* and was written by **Allan Massie** who praises an even-handed biography.

'Graham Green began a review of Hesketh Pearson's Life of Arthur Conan Doyle (1943) by remarking that "one has seen that face over a hundred bar counters" – although Conan Doyle, ever mindful of his alcoholic father, was not much of a man for bar counters. Green's point was well made nevertheless: "could Sherlock Holmes have deduced from this magnificently open appearance anything at all resembling the bizarre truth?"

He praised Pearson's strengths as a biographer: "a plainness, an honesty, a sense of ordinary life going on all the time" – strengths that Daniel Stashower, Conan Doyle's latest biographer, abundantly shows. But then Green goes on to chide him, as one may also chide Stashower, for giving insufficient attention to the "poetic quality in Doyle, the quality which gives life to his work far more surely than does his wit". Greene continues: "(Conan Doyle) made Plumstead Marshes and the Barking Level as vivid and unfamiliar as a lesser writer would have made the mangrove swamps of the West Coast which he had also known and of which he did not bother to write".

One might add only that he may well have known those mangrove swamps better than he knew suburban London; for Stashower shows that, for the first Holmes stories, when Conan Doyle knew London only as an occasional visitor, he worked from Post Office maps of the city.

I should like, though, to put in a word – a stronger word than Stashower grants them – for Conan Doyle's historical novels. The first, *Micah Clarke*, the history of Monmouth's rebellion, owing much to his reading of Macaulay, is at least as good as *They Were Defeated*, the Civil War novel of Rose Macaulay (no relation of the historian). Doyle, although neither Calvinist or Republican, thought himself into the Roundhead spirit as displayed in that last flicker of the "Good Old Cause", just as later his imaginative vitality enabled him to inhabit 14th-century soldiers of fortune in *The White Company* and the raffish world of Regency prize-fighting in the entertaining *Rodney Stone*.

Conan Doyle was open-hearted and generous, an unusually good man, although Stashower shows him as more short-tempered and sometimes unreasonable than earlier biographers have allowed. But in almost all the public controversies in which Conan

Doyle involved himself he engages readers on his side, even when he was wrong, one feels that he deserved to be right.

He fought to redress miscarriages of justice – the case of Oscar Slater, found guilty of a murder in Glasgow of which he was innocent, is the best-known case. He remained friendly with, and sympathetic to, Wilde, after his trials and imprisonment; he did not abandon his friend Roger Casement, even though he himself was unquestioningly patriotic, and Casement unquestionably guilty of treason, but fought hard to have him reprieved. Of the notorious Casement diaries, he said merely that "as no possible sexual offence could be as suborning soldiers from their duty, I was not diverted from my purpose". Some readers, however, will be dismayed to learn that Conan Doyle thought Casement's homosexuality, and Wilde's, "pathological", and that in Wilde's case, "a hospital rather than a police court was the place for its consideration".

The last year of Conan Doyle's life (he died in 1930) was devoted to his crusade on behalf of spiritualism. This may seem stranger now than it did then. Sceptics of course vastly outnumbered believers, but spiritualism may have been a natural refuge sought by those whose orthodox Christian faith had been undermined by the science of the 19th century. That was certainly the case with the Jesuit-educated Conan Doyle. Interested in psychical research since his days as a young medical practitioner, he became the "St Paul of the Spiritualist Movement", which attracted thousands who had lost fathers, brothers, husbands or lovers in the mud of the Somme and Passchendaele.

If spiritualism, which between the wars attracted the attention of young writers such as Anthony Powell and Graham Greene, now seems a minority fad rather than, as Doyle thought, the revelation towards which all religions had been tending, that is because we live in a society dominated by a complacent materialism.

Conan Doyle's last years may seem sad, his quest futile. Stashower, not unaware of comic elements, nevertheless treats this part of his story with melancholy respect. He cannot accept the man's views, but presents them fairly. And, indeed, fairness is the quality that shines through this very readable and continuously interesting book'.

The third review is a reprint of an article entitled **It's elementary my dear Watson, I've been misunderstood** by Peter Lewis. This was published in the Books Section of the *Daily Mail*, Friday, March 24, 2000, and was the Critics' Choice.

'Everyone who knows the standard portrait of the creator of Sherlock Holmes: he was the bluff Scottish doctor with no patients who based his immortal detective on his one-time teacher, Dr Joseph Bell of Edinburgh.

He killed off Holmes because he was tired of him, reluctantly brought him back to make a fortune and spent the rest of his life writing unread historical novels and going barmy about spirits and fairies'.

So a book about the other side of Sir Arthur Conan Doyle is overdue. This well-told tale by an American crime writer is constantly surprising and shrewdly entertaining. It left me viewing Conan Doyle with enhanced respect as an honourable and quixotic man.

Like Holmes, the author has an eye for the arresting detail. What was Conan Doyle's next work after A Study in Scarlet? Holmesians would answer The Sign of Four – sorry, no.

It was a paper called Testing Gas Pipes for Leakage, which he translated amateurishly from the German. He was still needing to pawn his watch from time to time (A Study in Scarlet brought in only £25) and was glad of the commission.

Did Conan Doyle, like Holmes, take cocaine? Holmes's addiction was not particularly shocking in 1889 – cocaine was legally obtainable as a nerve tonic. As a medical student Conan Doyle had deliberately overdosed on a drug called Gelseminum and reported the (unpleasant) effects in the British Medical Journal.

Everyone seems to have liked him. This huge, burly man with hands like hams and a Scots burr loved sport (he scored a century at Lord's and pioneered skiing in Switzerland).

And he was always game for an adventure. As a young doctor he joined an Arctic whaler and a steamer which took him to Liberia. He served in a field hospital in dreadful conditions in the Boer War.

He was always campaigning – for divorce reform, about the atrocities in the Belgian Congo, for life-belts to be provided for the navy or armour for the army and on behalf of several victims of miscarriages of justice.

His ideals were those of the 'gallant, pious knights' of the chivalrous medieval romances which he loved to write and which he called 'my higher work'.

Like Don Quixote, he revered women and was ready to break a lance on behalf of anyone he saw as a victim.

To him, women were sacred, beginning with his mother to whom he took all his decisions for approval for as long as she lived. When his wife Louisa fell ill with terminal tuberculosis and sex was medically prohibited, he fell desperately in love with Jean Leckie, an accomplished, good-looking Scotswoman.

For six harrowing years he cared for his wife, while keeping company with Jean whenever he could. Everyone knew of their attachment – except Louisa. In effect they were waiting for her to die. But, says this biographer, 'there is every reason to suppose that he remained celibate for the rest of Louisa's life'.

Again, like Don Quixote, there was no shaking Conan Doyle once he believed something. When he first joined The Society for Psychic Research he was in respectable company. Arthur Balfour, a future Prime Minister, Sir Oliver Lodge and many scientists were members and standards of proof were stringent.

Then, in 1917, 'after 30 years of research' he declared himself a convinced spiritualist. It was a religious conversion. Having long rejected his Catholic upbringing, he badly needed a faith.

While on a lecture tour, he heard that his son, having survived the war, had died in the 1919 influenza epidemic. He calmly told the meeting that he knew his son had survived the grave. Soon afterwards, at a séance where the medium was tied to a chair groaning and muttering, he felt a hand and a kiss on his forehead and heard a voice whispering, 'Father! Forgive me!'.

That was enough. From that point no exposure of trickery in the séance room could shake his crusading zeal. The need to believe was too strong.

Not even the unconvincing photograph of 'The Cottingley Fairies' (snapped by two teenaged girls in their garden at Cottingley Glen) were a windmill too far for this Don Quixote. Why did he believe in them and write a book that made him the object of ridicule?

It appears fairies had a special significance for Conan Doyle. His father was an alcoholic who spent most of his time in the loony bin. He was always drawing fairies, goblins and elves and seemed to believe in them. Suppose he was right after all and not mad?

This is the author's interesting slant on an episode that seems to brand Conan Doyle as a fool. How could the creator of Sherlock Holmes have been so gullible?

He died in 1930, discredited as a serious author by his spiritualist crusading. He faced death serene in the knowledge that his 'most glorious adventure' awaited him.

Soon afterwards people packed the Albert Hall hoping to witness his return in the spirit. A chair on the platform bore a placard with his name.

His favourite medium tried for some time to make contact. Unbelievers were walking out when she suddenly shouted: 'He is here!' Six thousand people strained forward for a better view – of an empty chair. [6]

His real immortality is full of paradox. Almost no one takes his spiritualism seriously, like he did, while nearly everyone wants to believe that Sherlock Holmes, of whom Conan Doyle made light, was-or is-real.

---

[6] For a full description of this occurrence, refer to Stashower's book, Chapter 1 entitled *The Empty Chair*.

Chapter 3

Dr Joseph Bell (1837 – 1911)

'Spot diagnosis' was the clinical craze at the time. A girl working on the lucifers - making matches - was gleefully identified by phosphorous burns on her fingers. A sweatshop sempstress' left index finger was recognisably roughened from needle-pricks, a coachman's finger and thumb by the reins. Wee, sharp-faced, forty-three-year-old Dr Joseph Bell of Edinburgh could tell a copyist by the corn on his middle finger from a violinist with them on the tips of all four.

The following is a reprint of an article by Julian Champkin published in the Daily Mail, Thursday, May 20, 1999 *(with minor additions by the compiler)*. The article was entitled **As The Identity Of Our Greatest Fictional Detective Is Finally Revealed.** *Elementary! This is the <u>real</u> Sherlock Holmes.* The year is 1878. It is a Friday, the free clinic for the poor at Edinburgh's great Royal Infirmary in the Out-Patients Department. A doctor deals with cases quickly. A fascinated medical student, acting as his clerk (in this instance, surgical dresser Conan Doyle), writes down the eminent man's words and opinions as fast as he can.

A patient with a grotesquely swollen leg enters the room; he is poor, overawed – and unknown to either of them. The doctor holds forth:

'Well, my man, you've served in the army?' Dr Bell addressed the patient.

'Aye, sir' replied the civilian, mystified.

Dr Bell instantly declared him a recently discharged non-commissioned officer of a Highland regiment stationed in Barbados.

'You see, gentlemen,' he explained to the students with insufferable cleverness, 'the man was a respectful man but did not remove his hat. They do not in the army, but he would have learned civilian ways had he been long discharged. He had an air of authority and he is obviously Scottish. As to Barbados, his complaint is elephantiasis, which is West Indian and not British.'

(**Compiler's Note: Elephantiasis** [Gk., *elephas*, elephant, *osis*, condition], the end-stage lesion of filariasis, characterised by extensive swelling, usually of the external genitalia and the legs. The overlying skin becomes dark, thick, and coarse.

Elephantiasis results from filariasis of many years' duration.

Filariasis [L, *filum*, thread, Gk., *osis*, condition]. A disease caused by the presence of filariae or microfilariae in body tissues. Filarial worms are round, long and thread-like and are common in most tropic and sub-tropic regions. They tend to infect the lymph glands and channels after entering the body as microscopic larvae through the bite of a mosquito or other insect. The infection is characterised by occlusion of the lymphatic vessels, with swelling and pain of the limb distal to the blockage. After many years the limb becomes greatly swollen and the skin coarse and tough. The most effective means of preventing infestation is mosquito control.

And if that sound like Sherlock Holmes, it is because Conan Doyle, inspired by Dr Bell, created the great fictional detective. But new research seems to show that Bell was rather more than just an Edinburgh doctor – he may have been a real-life detective.

Many years after Bell's analysis of the soldier, Sir Arthur Conan Doyle put an almost identical deduction into the mouth of Sherlock Holmes in A Study In Scarlet. He made the soldier an artilleryman not long back from South Africa, but otherwise the dialogue and the deductions were the same.

Dr Joseph Bell was born in 1837. By the time young Conan Doyle arrived at Edinburgh to study medicine in 1876, Bell was established as a great surgeon and a great eccentric. Bell did his Holmes-like tricks not simply to show off: the correct medical treatment in those days depended on observation as much as on scientific analysis.

The Barbados case is the most well-known example of Bell's extraordinary real-life deductions, but by no means the only one. How, for example, could he tell that a woman patient with a small child lived in Fife, had travelled to Edinburgh by a particular road, had dropped off an older child before coming to the surgery – and worked in a linoleum factory? The accent gave him Fife, the clay on her shoes the road, the child's coat she was carrying was too big for the toddler and she had dermatitis on her right hand, caused by the caustic chemicals in the factory.

Conan Doyle acknowledged his debt. When, later, asked how he thought of the character, he said: 'I thought I would try my hand at writing a story where the hero would treat crime just as Dr Bell treated disease, and where science would take the place of chance'. 'A very remarkable man, in body and mind,' he wrote of his mentor. 'He was a very skilful surgeon, but his strong point was diagnosis, not only of disease, but of occupation and character.' And his portrayal was so accurate that fellow Edinburgh student Robert Louis Stevenson, reading a Sherlock Holmes story for the first time far away in Samoa, wrote to Conan Doyle: 'Only one thing troubles me: can this be my old friend Joe Bell?'

There was certainly a special relationship between the doctor and Conan Doyle. They may have met on Arran in the summer before Doyle began his studies. (**Compiler's note:** Whilst a medical student at Edinburgh University, Arthur Conan Doyle [*A Life In Letters*], before his second year began, took several weeks' holidays on the island of Arran. In a letter to Mary Doyle dated September 18, 1877 he said "I met no less a person than Dr Joseph Bell in Brodick yesterday. I wonder what he is doing here.") And of all his students Bell chose the young, penniless Conan Doyle to clerk for him. It was not only Holmes's mental powers that were modelled on Bell. Think of Holmes's appearance: 'Sparse and lean, with the long and sensitive fingers of a musician, sharp grey eyes, twinkling with shrewdness, an angular nose with chin to match.'

That is the Sherlock Holmes we all know and love; but in fact it is a description of Bell by Conan Doyle's biographer Martin Booth.

Conan Doyle criticised Bell for treating his patients as specimens, not people; and that, too comes across in the character of Holmes.

'I thought of my old teacher Joe Bell, of his eagle face, of his curious ways, of his eerie trick of spotting details. If he were a detective, he would surely reduce this fascinating but unorganised business to something nearer an exact science,' wrote Conan Doyle.

Doyle dedicated The Adventures of Sherlock Holmes to his old teacher. Bell was amused and flattered. And in his old age Dr Bell began to take an interest in the scientific detection of crimes.

He appeared as medical witness for the prosecution in several cases in the Scottish courts.

Thanks to Sherlock Holmes, his life began to imitate the fictional creation that was based upon it. This, at least, is what has always been believed. But now the British Broadcasting Corporation (BBC) would have us believe otherwise. David Pirie, script editor for a BBC series on Bell to be shown in the autumn of 1999 (see later notes), claims to have evidence that Bell was not only a doctor when Conan Doyle met him – he was a consulting detective as well.

Pirie claims that in 1878 Bell was responsible for sending a murderer to the gallows.

It was the year of the celebrated Chantrelle murder. Eugene Chantrelle was a Frenchman teaching in Edinburgh. He seduced a young pupil; married her; and, in 1878 gassed her to death. By that time domestic gas lighting had been in use in Edinburgh for some 30 years. The gas then contained deadly carbon monoxide. To murder with it, one had to do no more than wait until your victim was asleep, make sure the windows and doors were shut and turn on the gas tap.

As a method of murder in an age before forensic medicine it must have seemed close to perfect. Probably the only sign on the body would have been lips a little redder than usual, a side-effect of the gas.

A few years earlier, Chantrelle might have got away with it. But he was caught and hanged. His last note, says Pirie, reads: 'My compliments to Joseph Bell. He did a good job in bringing me to the scaffold.'

If this is true, it neatly reverses the version of events we have been told up to now. **(see: The Chantrelle Case overleaf)**

Holmes never investigated Jack the Ripper. Dr Bell did. With a friend he sifted through the evidence – though, as far as we know, he got nowhere. We do know that he appeared as medical witness for the prosecution in one of the most complex Scottish murder mysteries.

It involved a large sporting estate in the hands of a young boy; the boy's guardian in desperate straits for money; large loans raised with the estate as illicit security; insurance policies on the boy's life; and the death of the young laird as he and his guardian scrambled through scrambled through a ditch while out rabbit hunting.

No one knows if Alfred Monson shot Cecil Hambrough. Monson was tried and, despite Bell's evidence against him based on medical analysis of the body and pellets, the verdict was the peculiarly Scottish one of 'not proven' – neither guilty nor innocent.

If Bell was no more than a surgeon, he deserves to be remembered as inspiring the greatest fictional detective ever. Was he also the first true scientific detective?

As Holmes said, it is a capital mistake to theorise before one has data, but then, as he also said, when you have eliminated the impossible, whatever remains, however improbable, must be the truth.

Conan Doyle was so impressed that he depicted Sherlock Holmes as Dr Bell, 'with a great hawk's-bill of a nose, and two small eyes, set together on either side of it'. Everyman's Sherlock Holmes, lantern-jawed, beetle-browed, with insanitary pipe and lethally conspicuous headgear, is the younger brother of artist Sydney Paget, model for his illustrations in the *Strand Magazine* of 1891. 'The precise and intelligent recognition and appreciation of minor differences is the real essential factor in all successful medical diagnosis' – Dr Joseph Bell's words are enduring. 'Eyes and ears can see and hear, memory to record at once and to recall at pleasure the impressions of the senses, and an imagination capable of weaving a theory or piecing together a broken chain or unravelling a tangled clue, such are the implements of his trade to a successful diagnostician.'

The Case of Eugene Marie Chantrelle (1834 – 1878)

On page 41, David Pirie claimed that Dr Joseph Bell was instrumental in sending a convicted killer (Chantrelle) to the gallows. This statement is not under suspicion, but the method used in the killing presents an apparent discrepancy according to another source of evidence presented here by the compiler. This evidence has been obtained from the internet website of Edinburgh library through the kind co-operation of Andrew Bethune, Librarian, to whom my thanks are extended.

Eugene Marie Chantrelle was a Frenchman who came to live and work in Edinburgh in 1866. He taught at Newington Academy (3 Newington Road) where one of his pupils was Elizabeth Dyer (age 15). She became pregnant by him and they were married in 1868. The marriage was an unhappy one characterised by unkindness, infidelity, violence and financial difficulties. In 1877, Chantrelle insured his wife's life for £1000. She died on the 2nd January 1878 after a short illness. At the trial it was established that he had murdered her by the *administration of opium in orange juice and lemonade.*

Because this method is different to that put forward by David Pirie, I corresponded further with Andrew Bethune. The library holds a transcript of the trial, from which the following transcripts are quoted, along with comments from the librarian:
"I have had another look at the principal information source available to me – *Trial of Eugene Marie Chantrelle*; edited by A. Duncan Smith, Advocate (Notable Scottish Trials series, 1906). This includes the complete transcript of the trial. The indictment appears on page 20 and includes these words:

'you did wickedly and feloniously administer to, or cause to be taken by, Elizabeth Cullen Dyer or Chantrelle, your wife now deceased...in an orange, or parts or parts

thereof, and in lemonade, or in one or other of these articles, or in some other article of food or drink to the prosecutor unknown, a quantity or quantities of opium or other poison to the prosecutor unknown, and the said Elizabeth Cullen Dyer or Chantrelle, having taken the said opium or other poison by you administered or caused to be taken as aforesaid, did, in consequence thereof, die on the said 2nd day of January, 1878, and was thus murdered by you, the said Eugene Marie Chantrelle'.

Then follows some subsidiary clauses of the indictment concerned with Chantrelle's ill will and accusations against his wife.

On page 195 the jury is reported as having found the panel guilty of murder as libelled.

However, it does seem clear that there was a prolonged discussion about whether Mrs Chantrelle died from gas poisoning, and whether this was accidental or deliberate. There was also a discussion about whether or not Mr Chantrelle had administered the poison (opium) and whether the deceased's symptoms favoured gas or opium.

On page 89, Dr Henry Littlejohn states that Mrs Chantrelle's symptoms *were not* consistent with gas poisoning.

On pages 94-100 and 225-226 are statements from Professor Douglas Maclagan that Mrs Chantrelle's symptoms *were not* consistent with gas poisoning, but that they *were* consistent with opium poisoning.

I, (Andrew Bethune) don't think that the evidence was anything like conclusive, but the jury seems to have accepted Chantrelle's guilt.

On page 196 appears Chantrelle's speech to the court in response to the verdict. He seems to accept the verdict, but questions some of the evidence by which the verdict was reached. He said that he was satisfied that opium had been present on his wife's night gown, but that he had not put it there. He said that it had not proceeded from Mrs Chantrelle's stomach; that it was rubbed in *'by some person for a purpose which I do not know'*. He then states that *'opium was administered or taken in a solid form – that is perfectly evident'*. A few sentences later Chantrelle's speech was cut short by the judge, before he could say what had really happened".

Therefore, it cannot be accepted that David Pirie was correct in saying that the murder was carried out using carbon monoxide poisoning. Chantrelle's speech to the court in response to the verdict, appears to favour the method as administration of opium. After all, he had no axe to grind, he was going to hang anyway, whatever the method. As there was conflicting evidence between two forensic pathologists as witnesses, it appears to me, that a definite answer to the method used cannot be ascertained. I have tried on occasions to contact David Pirie for his comments, but to no avail.

Ely M. Liebow (2007) *Dr. Joe Bell. Model for Sherlock Holmes*. Popular Press.

The Case of the Chantrelle Murder

The Boston *Medical & Surgical Journal* implied that many people knew of his (Bell's) forensic activities, but stated positively that "Bell served as assistant to Dr. Littlewood [*sic*] as medical advisor to the British Crown in cases of medical jurisprudence." [7] He worked with one of the truly remarkable forensic experts of all time in Dr. Henry Littlejohn, equally well known as one of the first Commissioners of Sanitation in the western world.

So it would seem that Dr. Bell was one of the country's first consulting medical detectives, along with Dr. Littlejohn. One of his first well-known triumphs was the celebrated murder trial of Dr. Eugene Chantrelle, a suave, mutton-chopped Frenchman and one-time medical student.

Dr.Chantrelle, as he was called, was by all accounts a muscular handsome devil, who came to Edinburgh in 1866 as a teacher of languages. Before the end of 1867 he had seduced a fifteen-year-old pupil, one Elizabeth (Lizzie) Dyer and had to marry her, but for nearly ten years theirs was the stormiest relationship imaginable. They exchanged passionate letters in the beginning of their relationship; she swore she gave herself only to him; he cursed her, abused her, and finally told her he was seducing the servants. Their letters ran from…

"My dear Eugene,
I accept you, as my lawful husband," and
"My dear Lizzie,
I take you this day, as my lawful wife" to
"My dear Mama,
I might have been sleeping for an hour or more, when I was awakened by several blows. I got one [from him] on the side of the head which knocked me stupid…My jaw is out of place, my mouth inside skinned and festering and my face all swollen," etc.

He threatened her with a revolver, knives, and a final threat of poisoning her "so that not even the Edinburgh University faculty [*sic*] could detect his work." Almost ten years to the day, in October, 1877, the good doctor providentially insured his wife for over £1,000. Early one morning in December, less than three months later, the housemaid heard peculiar choking and moaning noises coming from her mistresses' bedroom.

Rushing into the room, she found Mme. Chantrelle unconscious. On the small French bedside table were a half-empty glass of lemonade, some orange segments, and some grapes. Keeping her wits, the maid called out for her master and then ran to fetch a doctor. Upon returning, she noticed the glass was now empty and the fruit gone, and her master making a hasty retreat from the window. The doctor immediately sent for Sir Henry Littlejohn, telling him he had a classic case of coal-gas poisoning. The great forensic man arrived with Dr. Joseph Bell. They both studied the bedroom, and had the wife taken immediately to the Royal Infirmary. She died within a few hours. On being told that his wife probably died of narcotic poisoning, Chantrelle told one and all that everyone knew they were having trouble with the gas in his wife's bedroom, but he was arraigned for murder.

Bell and Littlejohn found evidence of poison everywhere. There were many brownish spots on Mme. Chantrelle's pillow, a few on her nightgown, and analysis revealed that these spots contained opium in a solid form, along with minute traces of grape-seed fragments. The same combination was found in her alimentary canal. Dr. Bell learned from nearby chemists that Chantrelle had recently purchased at least thirty doses of opium.

---

[7] "Joseph Bell." *Boston Medical & Surgical Journal*. 165 (December, 1911), 584.

M. Chantrelle loudly protested his innocence, always harking back to the smell of gas in the room. The maid insisted she smelled gas only upon her return from the doctors. The gas company investigated and did indeed find a broken gaspipe behind a shutter outside the deceased woman's bedroom.

The maid, who had heard and seen the arguments and blows over the years, felt that Chantrelle himself had ripped the pipe loose. Chantrelle objected that he didn't know the pipe existed. Suspicious, and doing what a good detective would do at that point, Dr. Bell located a gasfitter who remembered repairing the pipe for Dr. Chantrelle about a year earlier. He also remembered that Chantrelle was more than a little interested in the entire repair operation. With this development and Chantrelle's many letters revealing his sad financial condition, he was brought to trial. The four-day trial was the talk of Edinburgh. After deliberating only seventy minutes, the jury brought in a verdict of "Guilty as libelled."

On May 31, 1878, the dapper Frenchman was led to the scaffold. Z.M. Hamilton who had heard such great things of Dr. Bell's classes that, even though not enrolled, he attended them regularly, gives an account of the condemned man's last mile: "The morning of the execution Chantrelle appeared on the scaffold beautifully dressed and smoking an expensive cigar. Dr. Littlejohn was there in accordance with his duty. Just before being pinioned, Chantrelle took off his hat, took a last puff on his cigar, and waving his hand to the police physician, called out, 'Bye-bye, Littlejohn. Don't forget to give my compliments to Joe Bell. You both did a good job in bringing me to the scaffold'. Joe Bell said no more about this trial than he would say about at least three others in which it is known he was working for the Crown, and perhaps many others.

Indeed, years later in a controversy, Adrian Conan Doyle, son of the author, rightfully said he could find Dr. Bell's name nowhere in the official accounts of the murder, but Sir Sydney Smith and two-on-the-spot witnesses, Drs. Z.M. Hamilton and Douglas Guthrie, attest to Dr. Bell's involvement.

THE SUNDAY POST, **May 6, 2007**

Edinburgh surgeon was the inspiration for Sherlock Holmes By Mike Duffy.

Amid the formaldehyde-drenched slices of gunshot-riddled kidneys and skeletons of long-dead babies within Surgeons' Hall Pathology Museum in Edinburgh is a corner devoted to a man who inspired the greatest detective the world has ever known.

There, prominently displayed, is a letter, addressed to the Victorian Scottish surgeon Joseph Bell, from one of his former students. In precise handwriting it includes the line, "It is most certainly to you that I owe Sherlock Holmes."

The letter is signed by Sir Arthur Conan Doyle.

It is one of several discovered in a widow's house in Edinburgh's Ann Street, in a detective mystery to rival the investigations of Holmes and Watson a century ago.

Speaking in the library of the Royal College of Surgeons of Edinburgh, Dr Alan Mackaill, a retired biochemist from Edinburgh University, described how he made the discovery.

"I have been working in the museum as a volunteer guide since my retirement and was approached by a Probus club to do a talk about 19th Century surgery. "As part of that I thought it would be interesting to include references to Dr Joseph Bell, because he was a former president of the Royal College and because of his connection to literature through Sherlock Holmes."

During his research, Alan read a biography about Bell, who was the first surgeon at the Edinburgh Sick Children's Hospital when it was founded in 1860.

Penned by an American doctor, Eli Liebow, in the forward written by the surgeon's great grandson Brigadier Nigel Stisted, who mentioned he had a portrait of Dr Bell in his house in Edinburgh.

Discovered

That was something to go on and, searching for an unusual name like Stisted, Alan discovered just one in the Edinburgh phone book. But when he tried to contact the retired brigadier he was informed by his wife Judith that her husband had passed away three months previously.

I thought I'd come to an abrupt end in my enquiries until she said there was an old box with some "bits and pieces" I might be interested in." when Alan went round to Judith's house in Ann Street which had been in the family for generations, he was shown a few letters taken from the box. The very first one she showed him was that auspicious revelation from May 4, 1892 in which Conan Doyle admitted his former mentor was the inspiration for his super-sleuth.

"Judith asked me, 'Do you find this interesting?' I was so excited I could hardly speak!" admits Alan.

"I don't think she realised quite how important this was as a historical document."

Given permission to root through the old cardboard box, Alan went on to discover several letters from Conan Doyle to Bell, photographs of the surgeon with his wife Edith and their three children, two copies of Bell's own books and his private journal. There was even a letter from Florence Nightingale.

Judith kindly gave the historical artefacts to Surgeons' Hall Pathology Museum where some of them are now on display in a new exhibition, *Conan Doyle and Joseph Bell: The Real Sherlock Holmes*, which runs until May 31.

Reputation

Dr Bell had a reputation within the medical world of Victorian Edinburgh for his shrewd diagnoses of patients, often gleaned by simply observing them.

It is said that Bell could tell of their habits, occupations, nationality and even names just from studying them.

But Alan is keen to point out that the keen eye for detail Bell shared with Holmes was as far as the similarities went.

"Sherlock Holmes is sometimes harsh and unreasonable and has a superiority complex and I don't think Bell was like that,

"Joseph Bell was a man of great compassion who cared deeply for his patients and their difficulties. He was deeply religious and hated missing church – and that is very un-Holmesian."

Whether Bell enjoyed his connection with Holmes is debatable. While there is no proof he disapproved, following his death in 1911 a colleague wrote that the surgeon had been unhappy with the association. Dr Bell's wife died of peritonitis and his son Benjamin died 20 years later. He never remarried and, perhaps due to his increasing reputation, when he died in 1911 his assets excluding his houses, came to more than £62,000 – about £4 million in today's money.

Interest in the great detective, meanwhile, seems undiminished.

Chapter 4

The Hound of the Baskervilles

From the Internet September 11 2000, Source: Agence France Presse, the following entitled **Murder charge for Sherlock Holmes' creator far from elementary**.

LONDON, Sept 11 (AFP) – A British writer has accused Sir Arthur Conan Doyle, creator of one of the world's most famous fictional detectives, Sherlock Holmes, of plagiarism and murder, causing outrage among the author's fans. Roger Garrick Steele, a former psychologist, claimed Monday that Conan Doyle stole the story of "The Hound of the Baskervilles" from one of his friends, Bertram Fletcher Robinson.

He explained that Conan Doyle had not only borrowed the name "Baskerville" from Robinson's coachman, but also stole a manuscript from him in 1900 which bore remarkable similarities to "The Hound of the Baskervilles."

In the true spirit of a Sherlock Holmes story, Garrick Steele claimed Conan Doyle then got rid of Robinson by persuading his wife, with whom he was having an affair, to poison her husband.

The success of the book, he suggested, made the presence of Robinson untenable. Garrick Steele, who said he spent eleven years sifting through letters, documents, death certificates and other documents, set down his theory in a 446-page manuscript which he called "The House of the Baskervilles."

He has written to present-day London detectives at what is now New Scotland Yard, calling on them to exhume Robinson's remains in order to prove that his theory is correct.

The letter "will be handed over to detectives who will contact Mr Garrick Steele. We have to investigate the allegations made," a police spokesman said. Bertram Robinson officially died of typhoid on January 21, 1907 at the age of 36. Garrick Steele's accusations were greeted with shock among associations and societies set up to celebrate Conan Doyle's work. Heather Owen, editor of the Sherlock Holmes Journal and members of the Sherlock Holmes Society of London described the allegations as "complete nonsense."

"He was a man of honour. He would have seen himself perhaps as being the knight in the stories that he wrote about the Middle Ages (…) and therefore he would have behaved in his own life in that sort of way".

Owen said Conan Doyle's admirable lifestyle was the opposite of that of a murderer.

"During the Boer War, he went out and worked as a field surgeon in the trenches, although he was in his fifties by then. He was serving his country…It was for that, for his services to his country, that he received his knighthood," she said.

The following article appeared in THE SUNDAY POST **September 17, 2000** entitled: **Curse of the Baskervilles strikes again!** Subtitled: *In the doghouse over Conan Doyle claims.*
By Farrah Baskerville

I've been dogged by dastardly deeds and cruel jibes about my surname all my life.

Now, following fresh claims over the authorship of Sir Arthur Conan Doyle's classic tale *The Hound of the Baskervilles*, my name has once again been struck by the Baskerville curse leaving me well and truly in the doghouse!

Edinburgh-born Conan Doyle has, of course, become a literary legend throughout the world thanks to his immortal stories of Sherlock Holmes. However *The Hound of the Baskervilles*, first published in 1902, ensured my name would also be immortalised.

I hated it when I was younger. My schoolmates used to go around the playground howling like mad dogs and if I ever again hear "Elementary, my dear Watson", I'll scream.

Super-sleuth

But the mystery, intrigue and drama surrounding these latest claims turned me, the roving reporter, into super-sleuth.

This case of alleged concealment begins with 58-year-old writer Rodger Garrick-Steele, from Dawlish in Devon – not all that far from dark, foreboding Dartmoor where the hound that roamed the lonely uplands killed off some of my Baskerville ancestors.

Rodger's controversial claim is that Conan Doyle betrayed his friend, Bertram Fletcher Robinson, by taking full credit for the book – when, says Rodger, Robinson was the largely unsung co-author of *The Hound of the Baskervilles*.

He goes on to say the name came from Robinson's coachman, Harry Baskerville.

After 11 years researching the relationship between Conan Doyle and Robinson, he has discovered a tangled web of information which even Sherlock Holmes and his confidant Dr Watson would have found hard to unravel.

He began in 1989 when he moved to Park Hill House, the very house on the edge of Dartmoor where Robinson had once lived.

Rodger recalls, "While I was unpacking my large pump-action screwdriver it disappeared and later turned up in a place I had already thoroughly checked.

"That was just the beginning. Three days later I heard snooker balls striking one another at three in the morning, even though I didn't have a snooker table."

He was later told there had been a games room in the house – and also learned that Conan Doyle had written *The Hound of the Baskervilles* there.

A month later, a picture of Conan Doyle and his father mysteriously appeared on Rodger's doorstep and he hung it on a wall. "The picture keeps jumping off the wall and I wondered if Conan Doyle or his father had done something to upset the Robinsons, so I began to dig even deeper."

As Holmes once said, "There is nothing like first-hand evidence."

So Rodger delved deep through tenancy documents, letters, maps, and marriage and death certificates and has amassed sheaves of photos, and newspaper cuttings concerning Conan Doyle and Robinson.

Now he has put his findings in a book aptly titled *The House of the Baskervilles* and is hoping to find an agent to publish it.

In the book, Rodger claims that Fletcher Robinson's original manuscript, *Adventures on Dartmoor*, was re-written by Conan Doyle, and that it was agreed that Robinson's name would appear on the front cover too. But, he says, as the newly-titled book became a worldwide success, Conan Doyle quickly forgot his friend's part.

"All Robinson received was an acknowledgement that "This story owes its inception to my friend Mr Fletcher Robinson, who has helped me both in the general plot and in the local details".

"I feel Robinson has been cheated and I want to put that right."

Another great Holmes saying is, "There is nothing more stimulating than a case where everything goes against you."

So the trail took me from Dartmoor to Edinburgh, where I spoke to the honorary president of The Arthur Conan Doyle Society, Owen Dudley Edwards, a reader in history at the university.

"The claims are a complete nonsense," Owen says, "Arthur Conan Doyle knew Fletcher Robinson, who gave him ideas about ghost stories in Devon.

"But Conan Doyle knew the country quite well – he was a doctor in Plymouth in 1882 and had written about Dartmoor in an earlier Sherlock Holmes tale (**Compiler's note**: *i.e. A Study in Scarlet [1887]*). So he didn't actually have to be told about Dartmoor or the Baskerville name.

"He'd heard of it before because when Robert Louis Stevenson had died, his family asked Conan Doyle if he'd finish a story Stevenson had written. Conan Doyle looked at fragments of Stevenson's work and came across a story called *Mr Baskerville And His Ward*.

"Secondly, Fletcher Robinson got an idea of collaboration and Conan Doyle seemed to pay him quite a bit of money. Although Robinson had written between two or four chapters of a book, none of this was ever used.

"I think Robinson wanted it to be a joint project but Conan Doyle had realised he wasn't up to it, so he wrote the entire book himself.

"Scholars say that it is the work of Conan Doyle. Why, if you had invented a detective called Holmes, would you want someone else to write Sherlock Holmes stories?

"Mr Garrick-Steele is very confused and erroneous in many of his statements."

Not much dubiety there, my dear Watson.

No evidence

Next, I spoke to Martin Booth, author of a biography of Conan Doyle. He says, "Any claims that this book was not written by Conan Doyle are laughable."

Finally, like a bloodhound I followed the scent back to the Sherlock Holmes Museum in London – in Baker Street, where else?

Museum Director Mrs Grace Riley said, "I am very sceptical about these claims. There is no real evidence being put forward. The story of *The Hound of the Baskervilles* was very much the work of Arthur Conan Doyle."

So just like Holmes in the book, this roving reporter turned super-sleuth finds herself at a dead end.

We may never know the truth, but I'm sticking with Conan Doyle. So let's stop hounding the famous man.

The following is a reprint of an article from the **Features** page of the **Daily Express** Saturday March 24, 2001 written by **Paul Callan**. The article is introduced by the heading "Was the creator of literature's greatest detective a real-life killer? If you look at the clues the answer, it seems, is far from elementary."

The title of the article is **"Sherlock Holmes and the mysterious hounding of Sir Arthur Conan Doyle. Ghostly dogs, fairies and the father of crime fiction.** It is 100 years since Sir Arthur Conan Doyle wrote his greatest Sherlock Holmes story. The Hound of the Baskervilles has fascinated – and terrified – generations and is now at the centre of a new and chilling mystery: Was Doyle himself in fact a murderer?"

A long, low moan, indescribably sad, swept over the moor. It filled the whole air; yet it was impossible to say whence it came. From a dull murmur it swelled into a deep roar, and then sank back into a melancholy throbbing once again.

So wrote the good Dr Watson, one not given to scaring easily. After all, he had been a military man, a soldier-doctor who had seen active service on the barbarous Afghan frontier and had witnessed mutilations and violent death in its many forms.

But the sound that echoed over Dartmoor that damp day had set a chill of fear into the very marrow of his bones. It was the howl of death, a spectral wail that tore at the soul. It was the deadly call of the Hound of the Baskervilles.

The blood-spattered tale of the ghostly dog that preyed on those who strayed on to the quagmires of Dartmoor – and members of the ill-fated Baskerville family in particular – has fascinated and thrilled millions since the mild-mannered former Edinburgh GP, Sir Arthur Conan Doyle, started writing it 100 years ago this month.

The book has always inspired controversy – even to the extent that, last year, Rodger Garrick-Steele, a former psychologist, suggested that Conan Doyle stole the idea from another writer. Sensationally, this latter-day sleuth has even theorised that Conan Doyle committed murder to keep his literary crime a secret. If so, the killing would be one of the crimes of the century.

It is fitting that this, of all Holmes's cases, should be at the centre of more intrigue. The Hound of the Baskervilles is Conan Doyle's most popular and enduring work – more than 20 films have been made of it. When it was first published The Strand Magazine, which released the story in cliff-hanging instalments, had to rush out thousands of extra copies. It was the habit to serialise stories in the late 19th and early 20th century and readers became addicted to their favourite writers and characters in much the same way as television soap opera audiences today.

The story brought back to an adoring public the razor-edged intellect and forensic skills of Conan Doyle's greatest creations – Sherlock Holmes and Dr Watson. He had first written of the detective's exploits in a rather lacklustre tale called A Study in Scarlet in 1887 and later completed 24 short stories under the titles The Adventures of Sherlock Holmes and The Memoirs of Sherlock Holmes. As a medical student in Edinburgh, Conan Doyle had been inspired by other future authors including Robert Louis Stevenson and James Barrie. But it was his tutor Dr Joseph Bell – a master of observation, logic and deduction – who was to be his main template for Holmes.

Despite the tepid initial response, the stories gained in popularity – so much so that Conan Doyle gave up medicine and devoted all his efforts to the adventures of Holmes and his faithful aide. But by 1893, Conan Doyle, now quite wealthy, had become bored by Holmes and promptly wrote The Final Problem in which the detective seemingly falls to his death after a fight with professor Moriarty ("The Napoleon of Crime") at the Reichenbach Falls in Switzerland.

But the public's clamour was such that by 1901 Conan Doyle decided to return Holmes to the scene (he had never made it clear if the character had really died) – and this he did with The Hound of the Baskervilles. In the story, Holmes is asked to investigate the Baskerville family curse, which started in the 18th century when the dastardly Sir Hugo Baskerville pursued on to Dartmoor a girl who had escaped his clutches. Both were found dead – she from fright and he from having his throat torn out by the hound.

Subsequent generations of the family were cursed and the latest, Sir Charles, is also found dead on the moor – frightened to death. The story involves a murderer who has escaped from the Dartmoor Prison, forays on to the treacherous moor and murderous attempts to wrest the title from the new baronet. Above it all looms the brilliant figure of Holmes (who does not enter the story until quite late) and Dr Watson, who emerges as a talented sleuth in his own right. Then there is the hound – howling and murderous, certainly, but in reality a large dog (probably a Great Dane) that has been turned mad with hunger and daubed with luminous paint to give it a ghostly appearance.

So is it possible that Conan Doyle stole the story from another author? Beyond dispute is the fact that the idea was first discussed with his long-term friend Bertram Fletcher Robinson, on their return voyage from the Boer War in South Africa where Conan Doyle had served as a doctor. And Fletcher Robinson can properly be credited with re-igniting Doyle's imagination with his tales of the dark legends of Dartmoor.

Conan Doyle even acknowledges his debt to Fletcher Robinson. Writing to his mother on April 2, 1902 he said: "[The Story] is a highly dramatic idea which I owe to Robinson." And to his friend Greenhough Smith he also wrote: "I must do it with my friend Fletcher Robinson and his name must appear with my own." A footnote to the first edition of The Hound of the Baskervilles reads: "This story owes its inception to my friend Fletcher Robinson who has helped me both with the general plot and the local details." He also saw to it that his friend was paid £25 per 1,000 words for help in the first instalment.

This active co-operation and the evidence of the footnote surely disproves Rodger Garrick-Steele's claims that Conan Doyle had not only stolen the idea for the book but also conspired with Robinson's wife, whom he claims Conan Doyle was having an affair, to poison him.

The murder theory has infuriated the Sherlock Holmes Society of London. "It is complete nonsense," says its secretary, Heather Owen. "Fletcher Robinson was rightly credited by Conan Doyle for his help."

Mr Garrick-Steele, who could not be contacted for comment this week, has tried in vain to have a book on the subject published. An American company has taken an option on it as a possible film – so far unmade.

Yet even without the evidence of the credit, the theory would surely take Holmes only moments to demolish. Although greatly helped by Fletcher Robinson, for instance, it is likely Conan Doyle was himself well aware of the goulish legends of Dartmoor. Owen Dudley Edwards, Conan Doyle's biographer and a distinguished historian at the University of Edinburgh, says the writer was "easily persuaded" to develop the idea.

"He probably listened very politely to young Fletcher Robinson as they voyaged home together from South Africa," explains Mr Dudley Edwards. "He would have known about such ghostly stories and since he had earlier been a doctor based at

Portsmouth, he would have known about the mysteries of Dartmoor. Conan Doyle was a great walker and amateur photographer and would have doubtless visited the area many times."

Dartmoor, because of its isolation, has become saturated with local myths and folklore but it is unlikely that this supposed murder will join them. Fletcher Robinson won't be remembered as the true author of one of the greatest detective stories. Posterity will have to make do with the knowledge that he was one of the first editors of the Daily Express. Ironically, today the moor is impassable due to foot-and-mouth disease, though the Baskerville Hounds, a Conan Doyle study group, still hopes to be able to hold a special centenary celebration there in August. Many of the myths that the group will once more explore centre on Dewer, a phantom huntsman who terrorises the countryside. He always appears with a pack of hounds known as "Whist Hounds" or "Heath Dogs". The legend is that anyone who meets these dogs will die hideously within a year. Another story has it that the pack will chase the wanderer over the Dewerstone, the cliffs on Dartmoor's southern tip. It is likely that Conan Doyle shaped his story by taking the traits of the "Whist Hounds" and combining them with another legend, "The Lone Black Dogs of Dartmoor". These were black hounds with flaming red eyes who struck fear into those travelling across the moors. What emerged, for simplicity of plot, was one blood-crazed black hound. Conan Doyle knew the geography of the area with some precision, changing only the names. Dartmoor's treacherous Fox Tor Mire was the model for the book's Great Grimpen Mire. These treacherous bogs can suck in careless walkers.

Baskerville Hall, however, is a total transplant – from the Welsh border village of Clyro. The great, gloomy house was the family home of the real-life Baskerville family until 1946 and Conan Doyle stayed there regularly when he walked the nearby hills and also joined shooting parties.

The house is today the Baskerville Hall Hotel and its owner, David Hodby, points out the great staircase and high gallery, both of which appear in the book. "He also includes the avenue of old trees which are still here today," says Mr Hodby. "Conan Doyle literally moves the house to Dartmoor for effect." The Hound of the Baskervilles was an outstanding success and led to a knighthood. Gossip had it that Edward VII was such an avid Holmes fan that he had Conan Doyle's name put on the honours list just to encourage him to write more stories. Conan Doyle was torn between writing and medicine and even dabbled with politics. He was highly intelligent but prone to outbursts of temper and periods of depression. But he retained his sense of humour and liked to sign "Dr John Watson" when asked for his autograph. A devout Catholic who attended a strict Jesuit public school, Doyle subsequently graduated as a doctor from Edinburgh University, and turned later to spiritualism. He married again after the death of his first wife and it would seem that his grief at the death of a son in the First World War spurred him towards the supernatural. Conan Doyle also later professed a belief in the existence of fairies – it was his support that led to the acceptance of the Cottingley Fairies, the 1917 hoax pictures by two young girls, the negatives of which sold for £6000 this month. It was an odd acceptance for a man who had created Holmes, a master of logic.

The Hound of the Baskervilles put Conan Doyle on a secure literary pinnacle. Many of his tales were dark and Gothic but it was his storytelling skills that really enticed his readers.

Conan Doyle's work was to influence almost every subsequent writer of detective fiction. There are shades of Holmes in Agatha Christie's Poirot, Dorothy L. Sayer's Lord Peter Wimsey, even Raymond Chandler's dissolute Philip Marlowe. And Colin Dexter's Morse is pure Holmes in intellectual mentality.

Conan Doyle died from a heart attack at his Sussex home on July 7, 1930. Some say a mournful howl was heard at Dartmoor at exactly that time – the Hound of the Baskervilles lamenting the passing of his creator. Doubtless another myth but Conan Doyle would have chuckled.

'Conan Doyle would have known all about Dartmoor's mysteries'.

The following is a reprint of an article published in the **Daily Express** MONDAY JULY 9 2001 **Comment** by **Andrew Taylor** entitled AS THE HOUND OF THE BASKERVILLES FINALLY GETS THE CREDIT IT DESERVES. This is one dog who will always have his day.

On Wednesday, Penguin Books will throw a party at Murder One, The crime fiction bookshop in London's Charing Cross Road, to mark the inclusion of The Hound Of The Baskervilles in its Penguin Classic series. Sir Arthur Conan Doyle's novel was first published almost exactly 100 years ago as a serial in the Strand Magazine, beginning in August 1901. It deserves a celebration – it's the best-known crime story in the world – but do we really know what we are celebrating?

We've watched the films (more than 20 of them), listened to the songs, played the computer games and licked the postage stamps. Hitler's personal film library at the Berchtesgaden included a print of one of the films.

Like Conan Doyle's hero, Sherlock Holmes, the hound is familiar to people who have never read a book. Its slavering jaws haunt the dreams of the unwary from Moscow to Valparaiso. Yet Doyle had never expected to write the book that inspired this international industry. Unlike his readers, the author had had enough of Sherlock Holmes. He arranged for him to die heroically while ridding the world of Professor Moriarty at the Reichenbach Falls. Some people have since claimed that Conan Doyle was not the only, or even main author of The Hound of the Baskervilles.

In 1899, Conan Doyle had sailed to South Africa to serve during the Boer War as an unpaid Army doctor (taking his butler with him). After his return, suffering from the after effects of fever, he went to Norfolk for a golfing holiday with a friend the journalist Fletcher Robinson. Here, one rainy day as Doyle sat before the fire, the Hound was born.

Conan Doyle was the first to admit that Robinson played an important part in its genesis. Robinson told Doyle some of the horrifying folk tales he had heard as a child near Dartmoor. There were similar stories in Norfolk and other parts of the country, many populated with phantom hounds. Among them is a ghostly boar hound on the Welsh borders, said to appear when there is a death in the Baskerville-Vaughan family.

Doyle had a taste for the supernatural and was inspired to use the material in a gothic thriller. At first, he did not intend it to be a Holmes novel. He and Robinson travelled to Dartmoor, explored the terrain and planned the story. As Holmes himself found with his penchant for cocaine, old habits die hard. Holmes and Watson sidled into the storyline.

Doyle's publishers were desperate for more Holmes stories and willing to pay well too but there were literary reasons for including Holmes, as well as financial ones. The rational processes of detection would both balance and accentuate the melodramatic horrors of the black hound and Dartmoor.

Conan Doyle sensed he was on to something. He wrote to his mother: "Robinson and I are exploring the moor over our Sherlock Holmes book. I think it will work out splendidly – Indeed I have done nearly half of it. Holmes is at his very best and it is a highly dramatic idea – which I owe to Robinson."

Originally, the friends planned to write it together but Robinson dropped out. Conan Doyle worked fast. The golfing holiday was at the end of April 1901 and in a little more than three months the first instalment appeared in *The Strand*.

Success breeds its own myths. When the Hound of the Baskervilles became so successful, stories began to circulate that Doyle was not the author. (One rumour even claimed that Conan Doyle had committed a murder for the sake of the book). One of the attacks on Conan Doyle's reputation was mounted by a real-life Baskerville – in, as it happens, the Daily Express.

Harry Baskerville had been the Fletcher Robinson family coachman and probably drove Robinson and Conan Doyle on at least one occasion. There's no doubt that he lent his surname to the novel. In the Express of March 16, 1959, Peter Evans reported a conversation with Baskerville (then 88), in which the old man claimed: "Doyle didn't write the story himself. A lot of the story was written by Fletcher but he never got the credit he deserved."

Adrian Conan Doyle sprang to his father's defence, minimising Robinson's contribution But Conan Doyle acknowledged a collaboration. The evidence suggests that Robinson was involved in the original idea and in planning the storyline but then they decided amicably that Conan Doyle should write it.

Robinson's contribution to the book may be debatable but the quality of The Hound Of The Baskervilles is unquestionable. Sir Charles Baskerville has died, apparently terrified to death by a black dog on Dartmoor. According to a family legend, this satanic animal preys on the family because of the misdeeds of an ancestor. The dead man's GP, Dr Mortimer, says there may be more to this than ghastly twaddle, leading to one of the immortal chapter endings of Western literature: "Mr Holmes they were the footprints of a gigantic hound!"

The story moves between the bright, crowded streets of London and Conan Doyle's phantasmagoric Dartmoor; the one setting contrasting with the other but both full of hidden dangers. First one boot and then another are stoles from outside a bedroom door in a London hotel. An anonymous letter arrives. A convict escapes from prison. A pony drowns in an insatiable bog on the moor. The butler and his wife behave oddly. Sir Henry, nephew and heir of Sir Charles, falls in love with the beautiful, mysteriously damaged sister of a moth collector. These disparate strands are woven together with enormous skill.

There's even time for sly humour. Dr Mortimer takes a scientific interest in Holmes's skull. "A cast of your skull, sir, until the original is available, would be an ornament to any anthropological museum. I confess that I covet your skull."

In the best Holmes short stories, Conan Doyle showed himself a master of narrative, combining the intellectual thrill of the investigation with a sensational storyline – often with added qualities of wit and humanity. The Hound Of The Baskervilles is quite simply one of the finest crime novels ever written.

Read it on the beach. In fact read it anywhere. Whether or not you have read it before, you will enjoy it. Entertaining reading doesn't get much better than this.

Still on the subject of Conan Doyle and The Hound of the Baskervilles – according to an article from the Property Section of the *Telegraph, Saturday, September 22, 2001*, written by **Suzanne Savill**, The Lion's Den, a hotel in Ashburton on the southern edge of Dartmoor, has historical links with The Hound of the Baskervilles.

That was when Sir Arthur Conan Doyle reputedly stayed at the then Golden Lion Hotel (in room 6), and was inspired by local legend to write his most famous story. His coachman (Conan Doyle was touring Dartmoor) called Baskerville told him tales about Lord Cabell who had lived nearby at Buckfastleigh and was supposedly so evil, that when he died, packs of hounds with flames belching from their nostrils were seen tearing up the driveway on their way to retrieve his soul.

Saturday, March 9, 2002 TELEGRAPH TRAVEL. **In the footprints of a gigantic hound**. Conan Doyle's canine monstrosity is 100 years old. A nervous **Christopher Somerville** plays literary sleuth on Dartmoor.

Whenever fans of Sherlock Holmes hear the name of Dartmoor, it is impressions of *The Hound of the Baskervilles* that come rushing to mind: a barren, mist-wreathed moor, a mysterious figure silhouetted against the rising moon, the face of an escaped convict "all seamed and scored with vile passions", and the blood-freezing howl of the fiery, fiendish Hound from the heart of the great Grimpen Mire.

Something about the moor fascinated Arthur Conan Doyle from the moment his friend Bertram Fletcher Robinson spun him a yarn about a spectral hound that haunted Dartmoor. Researching his tale in 1901, Conan Doyle drew inspiration from the gloomy baronial halls, sucking bogs, abandoned tin mines and lonely houses all around – not to mention the great grim prison.

Doyle had killed off his famous detective eight years before. But Holmes simply could not be left out of such a ripping yarn. It was a wise capitulation on Conan Doyle's part: *The Hound of the Baskervilles* has never been out of print, and rarely off the film and TV screens, since his first serialised publication in 1901-2 in *The Strand Magazine*. We love this Gothic horror tale, all of us, all over the world, whether we are dedicated Holmesians or mere casual browsers under the midnight lamp.

The Hound is 100 years old, but has never lost its fascination. When Philip Weller's admirable new book *The Hound of the Baskervilles: Hunting the Dartmoor Legend*, fell through my letterbox I knew that I was in the capable hands of a Holmesian *par excellence*. The author is chairman of The Baskerville Hounds, a group of enthusiasts dedicated to playing to the utmost what they term "The Great Holmesian Game" –

pretending that Holmes and Watson were real and fitting their adventures to actual dates, locations and historical circumstances.

Imagination is always the best set designer. But this book promised to introduce some fascinating actuality. The prospect of expert guidance around Dartmoor, to points from which I could gaze on the originals of doom-wrapped Baskerville Hall. Sinister Merripit House and the wastes of the great Grimpen Mire, was too good to pass up. I threw my Weller into a Gladstone, Looked out my stoutest boots and a trusty "Penang lawyer", (**Compiler's note:** *Penang lawyer- a type of heavy walking stick_ with a big nob, formerly sold in Penang and Singapore generally. It is popularly said to be so called either because the power and wisdom of lawyers lies in their nobs (heads) or because there was formerly no law in Penang and people were obliged to use a heavy stick in order literally to 'take the law into their own hands'. The name may actually be a corruption of Malay* pinang liyar, '*wild areca, or* pinang layor, '*fire-dried areca, referring to the species of palm from which it was made)* sent down to Stanfords for the Ordnance map and to Spar for a pound of their strongest shag, and took the M5 into Devonshire on a blustery autumn day of the year 20—.

Baskerville Hall, seat of the Hound-haunted Baskerville family, has always been one of the prime Gothic literary settings – a dark old house in a tree-blanketed hollow under the moor with a sombre tunnel of a drive, twin towers, ivy-smothered walls and that scary Yew Alley where Sir Charles Baskerville died of sheer fright after running for his life from the Hound. There are three main candidates for Baskerville Hall on the eastern edge of Dartmoor, the only feasible location given the relative positions of neighbouring places in the story.

Fowelscombe, not far from the village of Ugborough, was a strong contender, in spite of its lack of a view of the moor. When Doyle was researching on Dartmoor in 1901 this grand Elizabethan mansion – then newly abandoned to decay – possessed twin towers, mullioned windows, crenellations and long wings, just as in the novelist's description of Baskerville Hall. I found Fowelscombe sunk in its hollow in a sad state of dereliction; a poignant, ivy-choked ruin.

The next candidate, Hayford Hall, was perfectly positioned deep in a tree-filled cleft under Dartmoor's rim west of Buckfastleigh, and had an old yew alley leading out on to the moor. The drive was lined with beeches whose leaves were streaming away on the autumn gale. I could only catch a glimpse of tall, tower-like chimneys through the trees, but Weller's book assured me that the house itself answered none of Doyle's description of Baskerville Hall.

The third possible source of inspiration, Brook Manor, lay in a suitably deep valley a couple of miles east of Hayford Hall. What best recommended this ancient house, though, was the character of the man who owned it in the mid-17th century, Richard "Dirty Dick" Cabell. Dirty Dick married Elizabeth Fowell of Fowelscombe, but proved an absolute bounder – so wicked in fact, that legend says he was hunted to death on Dartmoor by ghostly black dogs.

In the churchyard of Holy Trinity Church at Buckfastleigh I found the mausoleum where Dirty Dick lies sealed into his tomb by a massive stone slab – he has a tendency to walk abroad, apparently. He might well have been Conan Doyle's inspiration for the character of wicked Hugo Baskerville, who became the first of his family to be hounded to death when he hunted an innocent maiden over the moor by night.

Identification of the prehistoric stone hut in which Sherlock Holmes camped out on the moor, unbeknown to faithful Watson could be a nightmare, since Dartmoor possesses the remains of well over a thousand such primitive dwellings. But Weller persuaded me that there were really only two candidates.

It's a fact that Arthur Conan Doyle and Bertram Fletcher Robinson visited Grimspound Dartmoor's best known enclosure of hut circles, in 1901. A suitably moody rainstorm welcomed me to the site, where I soon identified the hut in which Doyle and Robinson probably sat to smoke their pipes – Hut No 3, the most thoroughly restored and most central in the big walled compound.

Grimspound lies too far from the central moor to be the correct choice geographically; but Ryder's Rings, an oblong walled settlement a couple of miles South-west of Hayford Hall, is perfectly placed at the top of a steep brackeny slope above the River Avon. Its forgotten hut circles, collapsed in the bracken chimed exactly with the melancholy mood of the moor.

So to the scenes of the tale's denouement around Merripit House, the remote moorland dwelling of the ominous naturalist Stapleton and his exotically beautiful "sister", Beryl on the shores of the fearsome quagmire called the great Grimpen Mire. Stapleton is unmasked – to a typically acute piece of Holmesian observation – as a murderous Baskerville bastard intent on extinguishing the young rightful heir to the estate, Sir Henry Baskerville, and claiming title, house and fortune for himself.

Although other candidates exist, only one area properly fits the bill – the moor south of Princetown. Here Fox Tor Mires makes the perfect Great Grimpen Mire, while Nun's Cross Farm is surely the original Merripit House. In late afternoon rain I passed the gaunt Napoleonic barrack blocks of Dartmoor prison and walked the puddle track towards Nun's Cross Farm.

The shuttered building lay hidden in a walled quarter-acre of rough garden, it's grey walls battered by the weather. Nothing lonelier or more eerie could be imagined – save for the vast flat brown waste of Fox Tor Mires that filled the adjacent valley.

Along the track through a moor fog Sir Henry Baskerville had run screaming from the hellish, fire-breathing hound that Stapleton set on his trail. Here, Holmes gunned the Hound down in the nick of time. And over there, where the ruined walls of the old Whiteworks tin mines lay on the moor slopes, the desperate Stapleton, in flight from the collapse of his schemes, had leapt over the tussocks of the Great Grimpen Mire until a false step sent the murderer into the ooze to be sucked down to his awful end.

Weller in hand, I gazed on this scene so often conjured in the imagination's eye, now brought starkly and stunningly to life.

Three further entries for this chapter are from THE DAILY TELEGRAPH.

Firstly, Monday, July 30, 2001 entitled **Hero Holmes**. Fans of Sherlock Holmes will mark the 100th anniversary of the publication of *The Hound of the Baskervilles* at a convention this week in Ashburton, Devon.

Secondly, Friday, December 21, 2001 entitled **Chinese are right to be dead scared on the 4**[th] by **Nicole Martin**. People are dying of fright, researchers have found.

A study shows that Chinese and Japanese people are more likely to die from heart disease on the fourth day of the month, a date so foreboding that many choose not to travel on it for fear of tempting fate.

The researchers term dying of fright the "Baskerville effect" after Sir Arthur Conan Doyle's *The Hound of the Baskervilles* in which Charles Baskerville dies of a heart attack brought on by extreme psychological stress.

Writing in the *British Medical Journal*, Prof David Phillips, who led the team at the University of California, said that the higher death rates from heart disease on the fourth did not coincide with changes in diet, alcohol, exercise or drug treatment.

"Our findings of excess cardiac mortality on unlucky days are consistent with the hypothesis that cardiac mortality increases on psychologically stressful occasions," said Prof Phillips.

The team published its findings after comparing death certificates for Chinese and Japanese Americans with white Americans, who do not regard four as unlucky, between 1973 and 1998.

Lastly, Monday, April 1, 2002 entitled **BBC puts youthful slant on Hound of the Baskervilles** by **Tom Leonard** Media Editor.

Sherlock Holmes and Dr Watson will be portrayed as athletic young men in their mid-thirties in a glossy new BBC version of *The Hound of the Baskervilles*.

Richard Roxburgh, 40, and Ian Hart, 38 – who played Professor Quirrell in the Harry Potter film – will be the youngest Holmes and Watson since the pair first appeared on screen more than 60 years ago.

Although critics weaned on the likes of the portly Nigel Bruce – the first screen Watson – or Jeremy Brett – ITV's long running Holmes, may see the latest pair as one more example of television's increasing obsession with youth and good looks, the BBC insists not.

According to Christopher Hall, the film's producer, having a younger Holmes and Watson was a more accurate reflection of the original story.

It also fitted in with the energetic dashes the pair made across Dartmoor in pursuit of the fearsome hound, he added.

The film is being made by the same team that produced the BBC's Christmas adaptation of Arthur Conan Doyle's *The Lost World* and will use the special effects computer technology that was used in *Walking With Beasts* to create the great hound.

While the BBC's version of *The Lost World* introduced two new characters and played fast and loose with the story – notably creating the now obligatory love interest – the corporation insisted that it had not tampered with Conan Doyle's most famous Sherlock Holmes story.

Jane Tranter, the BBC's controller of drama commissioning, described the adaptation as a "chilling thriller for the 21st century" which was intended for an adult audience.

The cast also includes Richard E Grant as the archaeologist Stapleton and John Nettles as the local doctor.

The BBC's last adaptation of *The Hound of the Baskervilles* was a four-part serialisation in 1982 starring Tom Baker as Holmes and Terence Rigby as Watson.

In 1968, Peter Cushing and Nigel Stock played the pair in a two-part story for the BBC, as did Jeremy Brett and Edward Hardwicke 20 years later in the ITV adaptations.

In the cinema, Basil Rathbone made his first appearance as Holmes alongside Nigel Bruce in a 1939 version of *The Hound of the Baskervilles*. A Hammer version of the story in 1959 produced one of the more unlikely pairings, with Peter Cushing as Holmes and Christopher Lee as Watson.

What follows now are four introductions and one review of the latest BBC TV version of *The Hound of the Baskervilles*, referred to earlier, and shown on Thursday, December 26, 2002.

Firstly, *The Hound of the Baskervilles* by **John Preston**.

Sherlock Holmes made his British TV debut in a live broadcast in 1951, in the shape of Alan Wheatley – he went on to play the Sheriff of Nottingham in *The Adventures of Robin Hood*. Since then Holmeses have come thick and fast, reaching their high-water mark so far with Jeremy Brett's masterly portrayal in the 1980s ITV series. Perhaps the most unlikely Holmes of all remains the late Peter Cook who starred – along with Dudley Moore as Watson and a very friendly-looking Irish wolfhound – in a little-seen and critically excoriated adaptation of *The Hound of the Baskervilles* back in 1977.

The BBC's latest version of **The Hound of the Baskervilles** looks set to be the ideal antidote to post-Christmas gloom. Boasting a computer-generated hound with dripping fangs and rolling red eyes, it is produced by Christopher Hall (who made last Christmas's BBC hit, *The Lost World*). Richard Roxburgh stars as Holmes, while Ian Hart is Watson. They head for darkest Dartmoor where the luckless Sir Charles Baskerville has recently croaked, apparently from heart failure. But heart failure induced by whom, prey? Or what?

Secondly, **Say g'day to the darker side of sleuth Holmes** (writer unknown). Picking an antipodean to play Sherlock Holmes in The Hound of the Baskervilles might seem like an unusual choice. However, Australian Richard Roxburgh (Moulin Rouge, Mission Impossible II, Oscar and Lucinda) admits that he did not think twice about accepting the role.

This adaptation of Sir Arthur Conan Doyle's classic thriller begins with the death of Sir Charles Baskerville on Dartmoor. For some time, the Baskervilles have been convinced they are being hunted by a ghostly hound. So, while the circumstances of Charles's death seem above suspicion, the discovery of a giant canine footprint next to his body sends the family into panic, prompting a visit to Holmes at 221b Baker Street to help put their minds at rest.

The part of Sherlock Holmes is a coup for any actor. Unfortunately for Roxburgh, accepting this role meant that, not only was there a cultural divide for him to deal with, but there was also an age gap to overcome – he is much younger than previous actors who have taken on the role. So all credit to the 39-year old then who has just treated both as a challenge and has used the opportunity to present the little-seen darker side of the well-known detective.

"I find it interesting that Holmes was addicted to cocaine and took a seven per cent solution twice a day," he says. "He believed it helped his powers of reasoning and then he had to take morphine to relax."

Richard believes that this regular drug-taking shows that there is an emptiness to Holmes. "To me this indicates that there's something missing in his life. He's almost entirely cerebral – probably to the detriment of other areas of his life. Nobody is as untainted by life as Holmes is."

The actor believes that personality gap is largely filled through his partnership with Watson – and that together, this odd couple make a complete whole.

A strange unit they may be, but a good tale like this gothic treat needs more than just complex characters. Roxburgh believes that it is the combination of a number of mystical elements that made this story the top-notch detective thriller it is.

"It gets right to the heart of some of our deepest fears," he says. "The idea of a big, black dog, something outside the cave, something that could eat you. On top of that, it's set on the wasteland of the moors, which is perilous because if you get lost out there, you'd just die. Then there's someone out there who is committing murders.

"And it's all happening at night!"

Thirdly, from the Radio Times by **Alison Graham**.

Turn off the lights, turn up the central heating, find a big box of chocolates and prepare to be spooked by this new television dramatisation of arguably the greatest detective story of all time.

Richard Roxburgh is Sherlock Holmes and Ian Hart is his faithful chronicler and companion Dr Watson, in Conan Doyle's ripping yarn about the cursed Baskerville family and the legend of the hound that stalks Dartmoor, savaging its prey at will.

Holmes and Watson are drawn into this curious tale after the death of Sir Charles Baskerville, apparently from heart failure. His heir, Sir Henry Baskerville, arrives from the USA, but he's in the sights of an unknown stalker and soon receives an ominous and threatening letter. "As you value your life or your reason, keep away from the moor."

Naturally, Holmes's curiosity is tweaked and he dispatches Dr Watson to Baskerville Hall, where he's to keep a close watch on Sir Henry, a man whose obviously in great danger. Soon Watson makes the acquaintance of Sir Henry's neighbours, the charming Stapleton (Richard E. Grant) and his lovely wife. But soon the mists roll in and howls echo across the starkly beautiful moors as death visits Dartmoor once more.

One of the big problems with adapting such classics is that everyone who has ever read the book has their own mental picture of Holmes and Watson. Roxburgh is suitably austere, and Hart, in his commendable efforts to throw off the quite erroneous perception that Watson was a bit of a buffoon, ends up being colourless. And the computer-generated hound isn't actually as scary as you might expect. For some reason the eeriest feature is missing – the hound doesn't glow in the dark (in the book the beast was daubed with phosphorous to give it an unearthly look).

But any television of such a wonderful story is welcome, though if you are tempted to sit down as a family to watch, be aware that there are some bloody moments that might frighten very young children.

Fourthly, from THE DAILY TELEGRAPH Thursday, December, 26, 2002 **Today's Choices** by **Edna Pottersman**.

Out goes the deerstalker, in comes the syringe, in this splendid new version – more Conan Doyle than Basil Rathbone – of the classic mystery. Australian actor Richard Roxburgh plays the great deducer. Ian hart is Watson, and in Alan Cubitt's deliciously tangy adaptation both bring fresh nuances to their characters. The latter is particularly good, his Watson the beating heart and, intriguingly, moral compass of the story. There are some grisly moments which might upset younger viewers. And the computer-generated effects aren't very good. Otherwise, perfect seasonal viewing.

The review comes from THE DAILY TELEGRAPH Friday, December 27, 2002 by **James Walton**.

Boxing Day 2002 saw a troubling clash for all forms of television's answer to comfort food. Both **Hound of the Baskervilles** (BBC1) and **Goodbye Mr Chips** (ITV1) did exactly what they were supposed to do – which was to contain few surprises. Both duly turned out to be perfectly enjoyable, if not strictly necessary retellings of much-loved tales.

Hound of the Baskervilles was certainly the pacier of the two. The opening shots featured Sir Charles's twisted corpse looking like an extra from *Silent Witness*. Seconds later, Sedden the convict was haring across the moors – and seconds after that, the pursuing policeman had sunk into a swamp, leaving only his hat behind. Sir Charles's doctor (John Nettles) then consulted Sherlock Holmes (Richard Roxburgh) who, after a brief pause to shoot up some morphine, agreed to take on the case. And so we were off: heading to an apocalyptic Dartmoor for an appointment with a large dog. Like most people who've played Dr Watson since Nigel Bruce, Ian Hart tries hard to give the man some gravitas. Despite this, the programme – like the book – did flag when he was leading the investigation. Fortunately, once his clever friend reappeared, things soon livened up again.

Roxburgh's Holmes, in fact, was a bit of an action hero. The scene in which he beat information out of a cabbie unexpectedly recalled Inspector Regan from *The Sweeney*. A more sustained influence, though, seemed to be James Bond. Near the end, we even had a moment when the baddie explained precisely how he would kill him, before uttering the words, "Goodbye, Mr Holmes". And after escaping, Holmes celebrated with a wisecrack.

Conan Doyle purists may well have taken a dim view of these and other additions – but personally I thought the synthesis was pretty neatly done. Mind you, two other factors did rather mar the climactic chase. First, Richard E. Grant played the baddie – and, as viewers of *The Scarlet Pimpernel* will remember, he's rubbish at running (To use a technical term, he runs like "a great big girl".) Second, the dog itself looked on the initial appearance like a member of the Muppets, and on all subsequent ones like a refugee from *Walking with Beasts*. Apparently BBC's head of drama sent back *Hound of the Baskervilles* at the last minute so that the dog could be improved. From this we can make a simple deduction: the original one must have been absolutely hilarious.

To conclude this chapter, the following question was asked in the **Daily Mail**, Monday, July 7, 2003: **Which book (apart from the Bible) has had the most movie adaptations made from it?**

The answer: Sir Arthur Conan Doyle's story The Hound of the Baskervilles can claim this record. The first of many adaptations was a silent German version in 1914. This was followed by a version starring Eille Norwood made by Stoll Films in England in 1920. Another German version, in 1929, was the last silent Holmes feature. In England, Arthur Wontner starred as Holmes in the first sound version in 1932.

Possibly the most famous version is the 1939 production which featured Basil Rathbone's first appearance as Holmes. In 1959 another version hit cinema screens, from Hammer Films in England, starring Peter Cushing. The following decade Cushing reprised his role in a BBC TV series which, in 1968, included his second go at the story of Baskerville Hall. In the same year RAI (Italian Television) also produced a version.

In 1988 Granada presented its version of the story as part of the series with Jeremy Brett and Edward Hardwicke as Holmes and Watson.

Most recently, during the 2000 Christmas season, the BBC presented a new adaptation, an interesting production with many 'amendments' to the original story.

Daily Mail, Friday, October 31, 2003

Return to Baker Street by **Simon Brett**

The next classic tale to add to your children's Golden Library hardback book collection is The Hound of the Baskervilles by Sir Arthur Conan Doyle.

I hadn't touched a copy of The Hound of the Baskervilles since my schooldays. I had enjoyed it then – which was surprising since it was an O- level set text – but to re-read the book recently was unalloyed pleasure.

I was once again immediately immersed in the ghoulish, misty shadows of Dartmoor, and in Sherlock Holmes's race against time to save the new heir to Baskerville Hall from the ghostly fate which had destroyed his predecessors.

But while I was reading, I was also deeply struck by how much Conan Doyle had got right by the time this Sherlock Holmes adventure was published in 1902, and by how much his creation had influenced subsequent crime fiction.

Rarely can an iconic literary figure have burst so fully-formed from the creative imagination as did the sleuth of Baker Street. All the qualities for which a deerstalker hat is now internationally recognised shorthand were there in his 1887 debut, A Study in Scarlet. His very first exchange on being introduced to Watson is archetypal Sherlock Holmes.

'How are you?' he said cordially, gripping my hand with a strength for which I should hardly have given him credit. *'You have been in Afghanistan, I perceive'.*

'How on earth did you know that/' I asked in astonishment.

At once, the relationship was established – and what an influential relationship it proved to be. How many lesser pairings of masterminds and plodding chronicles have been perpetuated in crime fiction?

When millions of TV viewers watch Sergeant Lewis limping behind the dashing thought processes of Inspector Morse, they are following a path laid down by Conan Doyle. It is the stolid ness of Dr Watson's chronicling that makes the genius of his companion credible.

By the time he was writing The Hound of the Baskervilles, Conan Doyle had made Watson slightly less of a buffoon. The doctor is a fitter man for a start, less handicapped by the wounds he sustained in Afghanistan, and he can make a genuine contribution as detective's assistant.

But there is still no question where the real power in the relationship lies, and the book contains a wonderful moment when Holmes turns the tables on Watson, to show just how far he is on the investigative trail.

The supersleuth is also still capable of breathtakingly arrogant put-downs to his sidekick. 'I am afraid, my dear Watson, that most of your conclusions were erroneous. When I say that you stimulated me I meant, to be frank, that in noting your fallacies I was occasionally guided towards the truth.'

As in all Sherlock Holmes stories, this vital thread of humour sparkles through the narrative, without defusing the tension, or limiting the horror. And, although I don't like crime literature which involves the occult (for me, the introduction of spiritual forces moves the goalposts too far, with a resulting diminution of tension and interest), I find The Hound of the Baskervilles totally satisfying.

The horror is maintained, it seems that the only possible explanation for events can lie in the supernatural, and then Sherlock Holmes produces a perfect solution which involves only human agencies and human psychology.

Conan Doyle's detective stories are a bridge from the Victorian era into the 20th century. The scientific analysis at the root of Sherlock Holmes's investigation in The Hound of the Baskervilles looks forward to 20th century technologies, while the background of the story is pure Victorian melodrama.

Very good Victorian melodrama, to be sure, but it does have all the classic ingredients – a dark, old menacing house set in the middle of the moors, a family curse, an escaped convict, swirling mists, a treacherous marsh, and a genuinely terrifying monster – 'a foul thing, a great, black beast, shaped like a hound, yet larger than any hound that ever mortal eye had rested upon.'

Though this kind of scenario is from the world of Wilkie Collins, the resolution of The Hound of the Baskervilles, arrived at by Sherlock Holmes's deductive skills and analysis of the human mind, anticipates the world of Sigmund Freud.

Yet another enduring legacy of Conan Doyle is his hero's relationship with the police. At the beginning of his investigative career, the denizens of Scotland Yard may have been sceptical.

Not any more, by the time he's investigating the hound, 'I saw at once from the reverential way in which Lestrade gazed at my companion that he had learned a great deal since the days when they had first worked together.'

In the real world there never has been a successful amateur detective, certainly not one whose brilliance leaves professional policemen in a state of perpetual bafflement. Conan Doyle invented the species. Sherlock Holmes defined the character.

A Study in Scarlet defined the genre, and it was then superbly developed in The Hound of the Baskervilles – an exciting, witty, rattling good year.

THE DAILY TELEGRAPH Tuesday, June 1, 2004

The dubious pedigree of the Baskerville Hound By Richard Savill

SOLVING the mystery of the Hound of the Baskervilles may have been the easy part for Sherlock Holmes. For even the detective created by Sir Arthur Conan Doyle might find it hard to reach a conclusion about the origins of the ghostly beast.

Tradition has always had it that Holmes's most famous case was set on foggy Dartmoor and the inspiration for the story came from the area's people, places and folklore.

However, the thriller writer Phil Rickman believes that Herefordshire may also have played a part. And his claims, which are due to be published this week in the magazine *Sherlock*, have provoked a furore in Devon [see later entry].

Speculation that some of the story originated in Herefordshire began 50 years ago. Rickman claims to have "linked everything together" – and to have been convinced by a coincidence of related names.

The medieval Baskervilles had a castle at Eardisley, near Kington, Herefordshire, he wrote, "Consider also Dr Mortimer, who first enlists the aid of Sherlock Holmes in the affair of the hound. The Mortimers were the powerful Norman barons who controlled the Welsh Marches around Kington. Mortimer's Cross lies just a few miles away.

"Then there is Stapleton [the naturalist]. A few miles from Kington, complete with a ruined castle on a hill, is the hamlet of Stapleton." Rickman believes that Conan Doyle may have drawn some of his inspiration for the character of the wicked Hugo Baskerville from the legend of Black Vaughan of Kington and his dog.

Black Vaughan, a lord living about five centuries ago, was supposed to have appeared in Kington market place after his death in the Wars of the Roses as a black bull and to have devastated the church.

Many local people still refuse to walk near his home of Hergest Croft at night for fear of seeing his ghost and that of his black dog. Rickman made his claims after researching his latest book *The Prayer of the Night Shepherd*. He said: "The ghostly hound legend is well established around Kington and stories about Conan Doyle being related to the descendents of the Baskerville family and visiting on a regular basis are firmly rooted in the area.

"I believe the story is based on the Hergest hound but Conan Doyle blurred the sources by adding elements from Devon. The hound may have been a bit of a mongrel."

Guidebooks to Devon point to the ghostly hound connected with the death of Dartmoor's Sir Richard Cabell as the model for Hugo Baskerville. "The story is firmly set on Dartmoor and the fact that Conan Doyle may have found inspiration from stories in other parts of the country does not alter that fact," a spokesman for Dartmoor National Park said.

The Sherlock Holmes Society said: "This theory is not new. It's been batted about for years and, while we agree that there are Baskervilles in Herefordshire, Conan Doyle placed the story on Dartmoor and that's where it should remain.

"Mr Rickman is very brave and daring to go into print declaring that the origins of this most famous of Holmes's stories is Herefordshire – which of course it isn't."

Tracing the Footprints

Phil Rickman on the scent of *The Hound of the Baskervilles*

'Mr Holmes, they were the footprints of a gigantic hound.'

It's a resonant line, isn't it? Weighted in all the right places. Guaranteed, no matter how many times you've read it, to patter up your spine.

But if we follow those footprints back to the creature's lair, where do we end up? Fifty years after Maurice Campbell, a chairman of the Sherlock Holmes Society, published his controversial pamphlet *The Hound of the Baskervilles: Dartmoor or Herefordshire*? The issue remains unresolved.

Guidebooks to Devon point authoritatively to the ghostly hound connected with the death of Sir Richard Cabell, allegedly the most hated man on Dartmoor and an obvious model for the devilish Hugo Baskerville who enlisted the Powers of Darkness in his pursuit of a runaway maiden across Dartmoor and ended up having his throat torn out by the aforementioned gigantic hound.

But residents of Kington, on the Welsh border, maintain that the origins of Conan Doyle's Hound can be traced back to Hergest Court, a bleak stone and timbered farmhouse in a country lane on the edge of the town. And for them, this is still very much a live issue.

'I can tell you for a fact,' one local said to me last year, 'that there are people in this town now who will not go along that road after dark, either on foot or even in a car.'

It's not the kind of thing you say to a writer if you want him to go away. I live some miles down the Border from Kington. I'd already made a radio programme about the ghastly Hound of Hergest and had been threatening for years to write a novel exploring the legend and the possible link with Arthur Conan Doyle. Now, with my new novel, *The Prayer of the Night Shepherd*, I was finally seizing the Hound by the collar.

'I have the idea for a real creeper for the *Strand*', Conan Doyle wrote to Greenough Smith, editor of the London magazine, in 1901, adding ,'There is one stipulation, I must do it with my friend Fletcher Robinson.' Robinson, a 28 year old journalist, had been with Doyle on a golfing holiday in Norfolk when he lit the tapir of inspiration with his retelling of the tale of a ghostly hound. Robinson was a Devon man, and it was to Dartmoor that he and Doyle went to research the book, ferried around by a coachman by the name of Harry Baskerville.

Case closed, surely.

Apparently not. As Daniel Stashower ponts out in his Conan Doyle biography, *Teller of Tales* (1999) Greenough Smith later recalled that Robinson had admitted finding the hound legend in a 'Welsh guidebook'. And the proposed title *The Hound of the Baskervilles* had been divulged by Conan Doyle to his mother before he and Robinson had ever been to Dartmoor or, presumably, heard of Harry Baskerville.

Because the Vaughan family, to which the Hound of Hergest is connected, had very strong Welsh origins – all the back to the Princes of Brecknock – the legend is recounted in Welsh guidebooks to this day, invariably followed by the assertion that that this was where Sir Arthur found the inspiration for his most famous novel.

The Herefordshire town of Kington is on the very border of England and Wales. In fact there are those who say it shouldn't be in England at all as it lies on the Welsh side of Offa's Dyke. On the old border itself is windy Hergest Ridge, made famous by the musician Mike Oldfield, who lived there for a while and whose music became the soundtrack for the film *The Exorcist*.

And it's an exorcism that lies at the core of the legend of Hergest Court. The central figure here is Thomas Vaughan – Black Vaughan, who lived at the court when it was far grander and more fortified than the present farmhouse.

During the Wars of the Roses (it's interesting that the events in Doyle's Baskerville manuscript take place in the time of another great national division, the Civil War) Vaughan, in true Welsh border tradition, changed sides from Lancaster to York and is said to have been killed at a battle near Banbury. His headless body was brought back, to be buried by his widow Ellen Gethyn (the Terrible) who now lies by his side in a spectacular double tomb in the rather eerie Vaughan Chapel in Kington Church. Ellen has her own legend. After her favourite brother was killed in a fight with his cousin, she attended an archery contest disguised as a man and put an arrow through the cousin.

Vaughan himself has often been described as a notorious tyrant, but there's nothing in history to support this – the name Black Vaughan apparently referred to his hair and was used to distinguish him from a red-headed relative – and it was only after his death that he began to measure up to Hugo Baskerville's level of infamy. According to the local legend, his furious phantom would rampage through Kington and its environs, overturning farmer's carts, terrifying their wives and disrupting services at the church, where his body lies, by manifesting as a raging bull. A spectral hound was also seen. Soon, nobody wanted to come to Kington market and the economy of the town was in trouble. This was when it was decided that Vaughan should be exorcised.

It was a big job. It took twelve priests. Ella Mary Leather's *The Folklore of Herefordshire* (1912) contains a transcript of the lurid oral account of a ceremony in the course of which Vaughan makes a personal appearance, insisting he has now become a devil. Eventually subdued , after much shouting and extinguishing of candles, his spirit is shrunk down, confined to a snuff box and buried under a stone at the bottom of a pool close to Hergest Court.

Only the hound remained, to become allegedly, a harbinger of death in the Vaughan family and a general source of fear in Kington even after the immediate family died out in the nineteenth century.

During World War Two, it was seen by a man cycling home to Kington late at night, according to Bob Jenkins, a local journalist and Kington oracle. 'He'd been working at the munitions factory. Near Hergest Court, he saw this enormous hound which he'd never seen before and never saw again. The hound had huge eyes – that's what impressed him. He had a feeling that there was something that wasn't real about it.' The man, it seems, did not die afterwards. But then he wasn't a Vaughan.

To this day there are reports of psychic disturbance at the Court itself, where no Vaughan has resided since the death of The Rev. Silvanus Vaughan in 1706.

John Williams, a farmer, lived there in the 1980s. He described sound as a patter of huge paws in an upstairs room and hound-like shadow padding in front of him and into the inner hall. 'A prickly feeling,' he said, 'went up my back.'

Originally, *The Hound* was not going to be a Sherlock Holmes story. This was post-Reichenbach; Holmes was supposed to be dead. And at the time, Arthur Conan Doyle's obsession with spiritualism, fairies and anything otherworldly was developing fast. He would go on to write evangelical stories of the supernatural. Why he turned the Hound over to Holmes and a rational explanation has never been fully explained, but I've always liked to imagine it was in some way linked to his decision to switch the location from the Welsh border to Dartmoor. From such imaginings are crime novels born.

So, all right, what evidence is there that the story originated in Herefordshire? Actually, not at all, but I'm still inclined to believe that the Hound was, at the very least, a Vaughan/Cabell mongrel. The Holmes anoraks who refute this outright know nothing about novelists. This is what we do: gather as many different sources as we can find and then smudge the originals.

Around Kington, the story persists locally that Doyle was distantly related to what became the Baskerville-Mynors family and also had friends locally. It was said that he stayed at the Victorian Dunfield House, now a Christian study centre, but there is no documentary proof.

In the end, what impresses most is the coincidence of names. The medieval Baskervilles had a castle at Eardisley, about five miles from Kington. Their descendents owned the mansion at Clyro Court (it became a hotel and was recently renamed, for obvious reasons, Baskerville Hall) and the pub in the village of Clyro, a few miles over the Welsh border, has always been the Baskerville Arms.

Consider also Dr Mortimer, who first enlists the aid of Sherlock Holmes in the affair of the Hound. The Mortimers were the powerful Norman barons who controlled the Welsh Marches around Kington. Mortimer's Cross lies just a few miles away. And, more impressively, a few miles in another direction, with a ruined castle on a hill, famously haunted by one Lady Bluefoot, is the hamlet of…Stapleton.

OK, I realise that there are at least three other English villages called Stapleton, but this cluster of Hound-associated names still seems like more than coincidence.

As for the Hound itself, there are no recent sightings as far as I'm aware. But in 1987, a woman visiting the area from the Midlands reported that a spectral bull had manifested in front of her in Kington Church. I found her convincing.

'The inside of his nostrils – this was one of the most vivid things – were very, very, red, like a racehorse when it's just stopped running. And it was wet, it was dripping moisture or something on to the ground. It was as though it was hanging in strings…I'm a hard-headed business person, but I can't deny it. I've seen it.'

Her name, by the way, was Jenny Vaughan.

Researching *The Prayer of the Night Shepherd* last year, I talked to Alan Lloyd, historian and chronicler of the Vaughan family, who occasionally guides visitors around Hergest Court, where, if you recall, the spirit of Black Vaughan is supposed to lie in a snuffbox under a big stone at the bottom of the pool.

In *Herefordshire Folklore* (2002), Ray Palmer, who records that 'both Doyle and the Vaughans were connected by marriage to the Baskerville family', writes that when there were attempts to fill in the pool a few years ago, the project was abandoned after the water began to 'bubble ominously.'

A couple of years ago, when the water level dropped, it was decided to clean out the pool. A large stone was found in the middle. Keen to know if it might possibly be concealing a one-time receptacle for nasal stimulants. Alan Lloyd says he tried to persuade local farmers who owned mechanical diggers to help remove the rock.

None of them, he says, was prepared to touch it.

Following this article, four **Letters to the Editor** on the subject were published in THE DAILY TELEGRAPH as follows:

Wednesday, June 2, 2004

Hounded from Hereford

SIR – There is no doubt in my mind that *The Hound of the Baskervilles* owes its origins to Hertfordshire (report June 1). My grandmother was brought up at Clyro Court, the 19th century home of the Baskervilles, and was living there when Conan Doyle came across the story of Black Vaughan's dog on a visit to the Kington area.

I understand that it is important to Dartmoor that the story belongs there. However, when Conan Doyle asked the Baskerville family if he could use their name, as it had a more romantic ring, the family took a rather different view to the people of Dartmoor. Only if he promised to spirit the story away from the Welsh Borders would permission be granted. Conan Doyle stayed true to his word and, I believe, rented a house from the Duchy of Cornwall while writing the story. Furthermore, as far as I know, he never let on about the story's Herefordshire origins.

Geoffrey Hopton
Hay-on-Wye, Powys

SIR – Phil Rickman forgets the many connections that Conan Doyle had with Devon. It was the journalist Bertram Fletcher Robinson who suggested the idea of the hound. Bertram's father retired to Ipplepen in Devon and his coachman's name was Baskerville.

A.J. Robinson
Prestatyn, Denbighshire

Thursday, June 3, 2004

Hunting the hound

SIR – My grandfather, the mathematician WD Evans, met Conan Doyle several times in the 1920s and 1930s and was particularly keen on *The Hound of the Baskervilles* (Letters, June 2). He asked the author about its origins and Conan Doyle told him that both the ghostly hound and Sir Hugo Baskerville were based on legends he had heard in Herefordshire and Devon.

Jacqueline Worthington
Stansted, Essex

Friday, June 4, 2004

Scucca sucker

SIR – Further to the discussion on the origins of Sir Arthur Conan Doyle's Baskerville hound (Letters, June 3), arguably the most likely source is the legendary demon dog of East Anglia, the "Black Shuck". In March 1901, Conan Doyle took a golfing holiday on the Norfolk coast in the company of Fletcher Robinson (Letters, June 2). During their stay, it is believed they heard local stories of a sinister black dog the size of a calf with a black shaggy coat and eyes like glowing saucers. In local lore, the Black Shuck serves as a warning of death and disaster to all who encounter him. It has also been suggested that Cromer Hall provided the model for Baskerville Hall.

The name "shuck" is believed to come from an Anglo-Saxon word, "scucca", meaning demon or goblin, and there are reports of his appearance well into the 20th century, suggesting that he may be more than just a shaggy dog story.

Alan Murdie
Chairman, the Ghost Club
Bury St. Edmunds, Suffolk
THE DAILY TELEGRAPH TUESDAY, JULY 26, 2005

Did Conan Doyle poison his friend to cheat him out of The Hound of the Baskervilles? By Richard Savill

A TEAM investigating claims that Sir Arthur Conan Doyle murdered the true author of *The Hound of the Baskervilles,* is to apply to exhume a body from a churchyard in Devon.

The six-strong team, led by an author and a scientist, is to ask the Diocese of Exeter and the Home Office for permission to dig up the corpse of Conan Doyle's friend Bertram Fletcher Robinson, believed by some to have written the original.

The author Rodger Garrick-Steele and a scientist Paul Spiring, have formed the team, which included a pathologist and a toxicologist, to investigate whether Fletcher Robinson was given the poison laudanum shortly before his death in 1907.

There have been claims that Conan Doyle poisoned his former friend rather than let his plagiarism be discovered.

Fletcher Robinson, a journalist and barrister, and a former editor of the Daily Express, is buried at St Andrew's Church, Ipplepen, Devon.

The investigators are to meet the parochial church committee next week to discuss their proposal, before submitting a formal application to exhume the body. The official cause of death was typhoid.

"We believe there is evidence that what was put on the death certificate was not true and that the cause of death was much more likely to have been laudanum poisoning," said Mr Spiring, who began his investigations after moving to Ipplepen.

"That raises the question about why he should have been poisoned. We have got what we believe is refutable evidence that Fletcher Robinson was cheated out of a considerable sum of royalties because he was much more actively engaged in The Hound of the Baskervilles than was acknowledged by Conan Doyle."

Mr Spiring, a physicist and biologist, and a former policeman, said there was also evidence that Conan Doyle, to avoid being exposed as a fraud, persuaded Fletcher Robinson's wife, with whom he had had an affair, to poison him, possibly without her direct knowledge.

He added that if the exhumation failed to find any evidence of poisoning then the suggestion could be dismissed. However, if poison was found close to the root of Fletcher Robinson's hair then it would mean he had ingested it within a week before his death. "That would collaborate three or four strands of evidence," he said.

Sherlock Holmes enthusiasts and other literary scholars have dismissed the poison theory but have acknowledged that Fletcher Robinson's full role in creating the novel has been underplayed.

Fletcher Robinson showed Conan Doyle around Dartmoor, from where inspiration for the tale of the ghostly beast came. Baskerville was the surname of Robinson's coachman.

A footnote to the first edition of The Hound of the Baskervilles acknowledges Fletcher Robinson's contribution: "This story owes its inception to my friend Fletcher Robinson who helped me."

Fletcher Robinson is said to have enthralled Conan Doyle with the story of the evil squire Sir Richard Cabell, who sold his soul to Satan and was dragged to hell by a pack of hounds.

Heather Owen, of the Sherlock Holmes Society, said the poison theory seemed "highly unlikely and far-fetched".

"It would be entirely out of character," she said. He [Conan Doyle] wasn't a poisoning kind of person.

"His love life was already fairly complicated. He was faithful and true to his dying wife. But also he had an intense but platonic affair with Jean Leckie, who became his second wife. They were happily married for the rest of their lives.

"Conan Doyle wanted the book to be published in joint names but the publishers didn't like that idea because Conan Doyle was the selling point."

(**Compiler's note**: A very similar article was published in THE SUNDAY POST/**September 17, 2006** as follows):

Conan Doyle accuser wants body dug up By BOB SMYTH

A writer who claims Sir Arthur Conan Doyle was a murderer has handed church bosses a dossier he hopes will lead to the alleged victim's body being dug up.

It is a tale of intrigue that would delight Conan Doyle's famous creation Sherlock Holmes, author Rodger Garrick-Steele claims the author stole the idea for his most successful book *The Hound of the Baskervilles*, from a friend, Bertram Fletcher Robinson.

He says Edinburgh-born Conan Doyle then covered up his plagiarism by arranging for journalist Fletcher Robinson to be poisoned.

Theory

Rodger, who published a book, *The House of the Baskervilles*, outlining his theory, hopes to have Fletcher Robinson's body exhumed next year – the 100th anniversary of his death.

The Devon author says, "I believe he was poisoned by laudanum. If we can test the remains we can find out if that's true. Finding poison won't prove Conan Doyle was responsible, but it will back up my claims."

Last week he provided files of evidence to the Church of England's Diocese of Exeter, whose Consistory Court must now decide if the grave in a churchyard in Ipplepen in Devon can be disturbed. Fletcher Robinson is said to have entertained Conan Doyle with ghostly folk stories from his home in Dartmoor.

Conan Doyle was particularly taken with the tale of the mythical black hound that stalked the desolate moors at night, and the gruesome story of the evil squire Sir Richard Cabell, who sold his soul to the devil and was dragged to the underworld by a pack of hellhounds.

This was said to be the genesis of the Baskerville hound.

Rodger said, "After Conan Doyle was given his knighthood on the back of his success of the book, Fletcher Robinson began dropping hints that it was really his story.

"I believe Conan Doyle was having an affair with Fletcher Robinson's wife Gladys and blackmailed her into poisoning him by threatening to expose their adultery.

"Fletcher Robinson died unexpectedly in 1907. The official cause was typhoid. Gladys initially stated that he died from food poisoning but I believe the symptoms and circumstances of his death are more consistent with an overdose of laudanum."

The Sherlock Holmes Society has dismissed the claims as "complete bunkum and absolute nonsense."

Rodger said, "I had to provide a lot of detailed information in my exhumation application and I've shown there are no surviving relatives. A public notice has gone out and I had a meeting with local people last month. There were no major objections.

"The diocese will hopefully come up with a decision by the end of the year."

The tale has also caught the imagination of Hollywood movie company, ThunderBall Films, who want to turn it into a big-screen production, and a TV documentary, featuring the exhumation.

The Diocese of Exeter confirmed the exhumation bid was being considered.

The Sunday Telegraph SEVEN Magazine 25.01.09 Paperback/Books

TITLE DEED HOW THE BOOK GOT IT'S NAME

The Hound of the Baskervilles by Arthur Conan Doyle

The Hound of the Baskervilles (1901) was the story that reintroduced Holmes after his tumble into the Reichenbach Falls in 1893. Doyle redeployed his hero partly for the money – *The Strand* magazine coughed up double the usual fee – but also because he'd happened on an irresistible story. The spectral hound and the location in Dartmoor were suggested by his journalist friend, Fletcher Robinson; and it is at least possible that the Robinson family coachman, Harry Baskerville, whom Doyle met on his fact-finding tour of Dartmoor in May 1901, supplied the surname (although another strong candidate is the Baskerville family of Clyro Court, Hay-on-Wye). Support for the coachman theory comes also from the fact that Robinson, in his role as 'co-author', inscribed a copy of the novel to Harry Baskerville with apologies for using the name'. Harry went on to become a piece of walking Holmesiana, and died aged 91 in April 1962.

Daily Mail, Friday, November 13, 2009

Release the hound!

Question

A previous answer referred the squire Cabell, the ghostly hunter of Dartmoor, as the inspiration for Sir Arthur Conan Doyle's The Hound of the Baskervilles. Is this correct? What about Lord and Lady Baskerville of Crowsley Park, Henley-on-Thames?

Baskerville was the name of the coachman employed by a family called Fletcher Robinson, who lived in the village of Ipplepen in Devon. The Baskerville family farmed in our village of Landscove and their original farmland abuts ours, which at one time, belonged to the vicarage.

Conan Doyle met journalist Bertram Fletcher Robinson during the Boer War and, both being interested in spiritualism, struck up a friendship.

There has long been debate over the role played by Fletcher Robinson in the creation of The Hound of the Baskervilles. It was he who first entertained Conan Doyle with his ghostly folk stories from his home in Dartmoor.

Conan Doyle was impressed by the story of Squire Cabell, a huntsman who sold his soul to the Devil and was dragged to the underworld by a pack of hellhounds. When he died in 1677, black hounds appeared around his burial chamber. This was the genesis of the Baskerville Hound.

Fletcher Robinson invited Conan Doyle to Ipplepen and the book may have been a joint venture. Fletcher Robinson's coachman, Harry Baskerville drove the pair around the moors, the arrangement being that his name would be incorporated into the book.

The book was a success and, as the royalties began to flow in, Conan Doyle paid £2,500, a quarter of the advance, to Fletcher Robinson. Unfortunately, Fletcher Robinson died in 1907, age 36, of enteric fever, prompting Doyle to write in the preface *(see below)* to The Complete Sherlock Holmes Long Stories (1929), that the story 'arose from a remark by that fine fellow whose premature death was a loss to the world.'

There is a Baskerville family grave at St. Matthew's Church, Landscove, and one day, when walking through the graveyard. I thought I'd entered a time warp.

Several men were walking about in tweeds, wearing deerstalker hats and smoking Meerschaums. They were members of a Conan Doyle society and were visiting scenes associated with The Hound of the Baskervilles, including the Baskerville grave adjacent to our nursery.

Raymond Hubbard,
Landscombe, Devon.

PREFACE

The following stories paint Mr Sherlock Holmes and his activities upon a somewhat broader canvas where there is room for expansion. This expansion must express itself in action, for there is no room for character development in the conception of a detective. Whatever you add to the one central quality of astuteness must in my opinion detract from the general effect. Other writers may however succeed where I failed.

The *Study in Scarlet* was the first completed long story which I ever wrote, though I had served an apprenticeship of nearly ten years of short stories, most of which were anonymous. It represented a reaction against the too facile way in which the detective of the old school, so far as he was depicted in literature, gained his results. Having endured a severe course of training in medical diagnosis, I felt that if the same austere methods of observation and reasoning were applied to the problems of crime some more scientific system could be constructed. On the whole, taking the series of books, my view has been justified, as I understand that in several countries some changes have been made in police procedure on account of these stories. It is all very well to sneer at the paper detective, but a principle is a principle, whether in fiction or in fact. Many of the great lessons in life are to be learned in the pages of the novelist.

There was no American copyright in 1887 when the *Study in Scarlet* was written, so that the book had a circulation in the United States, and attracted some attention. As a consequence Mr Lippincott sent an ambassador over to treat for a successor. He had commissions for several British authors, and invited Oscar Wilde and myself to dinner to discuss the matter. The result was *The Picture of Dorian Gray* and *The Sign of Four*.

Then came *The Hound of the Baskervilles*. It arose from a remark by that fine fellow, whose premature death was a loss to the world, Fletcher Robinson, that there was a spectral dog near his home on Dartmoor. That remark was the inception of the book, but I should add that the plot and every word of the actual narrative was my own.

Finally, there is *The Valley of Fear*, which had its origin through my reading a graphic account of the Molly McQuire outrages in the coalfields of Pennsylvania, when a young detective drawn from Pinkerton's Agency acted exactly as the hero is representative as doing. Holmes plays a subsidiary part in this story.

I trust that the younger public may find these romances of interest, and that here and there one of the older generation may recapture an ancient thrill.

ARTHUR CONAN DOYLE

June 1929

Daily Mail, Thursday, December 3, 2009

ANSWERS TO CORRESPONDENTS Compiled by **Charles Legge**

QUESTION

A previous answer referred to Squire Cabell, the ghostly hunter of Dartmoor as the inspiration for Sir Arthur Conan Doyle's Hound of the Baskervilles. Is this correct? What about Lord and Lady Baskerville of Crowsley Park, Henley-on-Thames?

FURTHER to the earlier answer, Fletcher Robinson's coachman was interviewed in the Western Times and clearly believed the story came largely from Robinson's imagination.

The Hound of the Baskervilles has long been the subject of an inconclusive debate. Mr Baskerville said: 'Several generations ago, his family owned Heatree House and

Spitchwick, near Ashburton, too, but the time came when the spendthrift inherited the property'.

Heatree House, near Manaton, became Baskerville Hall in Conan Doyle's hands. "Harry, instead of being the master of Heatree House, found himself touching the forelock to the master of Parkhill, Ipplepen, the home to the Robinsons and to their guests, such as Conan Doyle.

During the same interview, Baskerville says, they [Conan Doyle and Robinson] definitely wrote it together' and to support this view he has his copy of the first edition autographed by Robinson, with apologies for using your name.'

On the other hand, Conan Doyle wrote in a foreword to this edition: 'My dear Robinson, it was to your account of the West Country legend that this tale owes its inception. For this and all your help in the details, all thanks.'

David Baskerville, Guilford, Surrey.

THE DAILY TELEGRAPH FRIDAY, JANUARY 7, 2011

In Brief

A partner in crime

Arthur Conan Doyle paid the equivalent of £45,000 to a friend who helped come up with the idea for **The Hound of the Baskervilles**.

The author Paul Spiring found an entry in Conan Doyle's bank book showing he paid Bertram Fletcher Robinson more than £500 in 1901.

Chapter 5

The Lost World

Two short entries from newspaper articles present up to date information on one of Conan Doyle's stories.

Firstly, from THE EXPRESS, Thursday, February 8, 2000 entitled **Professor Hoskins goes in search of the Lost World as the BBC dips into its drama millions** by **Ruth Hilton**.

Actor Bob Hoskins is returning to our TV screens in a classic tale of adventure.

He will star in the BBC drama The Lost World, based on the story by Sherlock Holmes creator Sir Arthur Conan Doyle.

The drama is to be filmed in New Zealand, which was chosen for the diversity of its landscape and wildlife.

Although the BBC will not confirm when the cast are to fly out, a dash to get a New Zealand visa for Hoskins earlier in the week suggests filming is imminent. "It all seemed very urgent and last-minute – they must only just have decided to sign him up," said a source.

"His assistant totally jumped the queue for visas."

The Lost World is a science fiction novel which centres on Professor George Edward Challenger, who faces various adventures high above the Amazon rainforest.

Hoskins is being lined up to take the role of the fascinating but not always likeable scientist.

The Lost World will be the actor's first small screen role for several years, but he is said to be looking forward to the challenge. A BBC spokeswoman said yesterday: The adaptation of Sir Arthur Conan Doyle's classic novel is part of the BBC's increased drive for drama and Bob Hoskins is set to be one of the leads.

"The final line-up and the exact number of episodes hasn't been decided but we expect the show to be ready for the winter schedule." *Columbo* star Peter Falk, Matthew Rhys, Elaine Cassidy and Tom Ward also have parts in the big-budget production.

Funding is being helped through £120 million allocated by the BBC for drama over the next two years.

The second article is taken from *The Sunday Telegraph*, November 12, 2000 by **Oliver Poole** entitled **BBC will strip Conan Doyle of racial overtones**.

The BBC is to adapt *The Lost World*, Sir Arthur Conan Doyle's tale of dinosaurs and empire builders, for television in a way that eliminates its "tone of racial superiority". The £10 million drama will be one of the highlights of next year's schedule.

Conan Doyle packed his adventure story with references to "sub-human natives noted for their savage behaviour and low intellects". The two-part adaptation will, however, portray the strange tribes encountered by British explorers as equal to the white men who invade their hidden territory.

Names that the corporation consider offensive to modern sensibilities, such as Zambo the giant "Negro" described as being as "faithful as a dog", will be expunged. To bring the story further up to date, a love interest, in the shape of the beautiful niece of a missionary, is to be introduced.

Christopher Hall, the programme's producer, said that although the drama would remain as close as possible to the original work there were elements that would not be acceptable to contemporary audiences.

"Some of the Victorian obsessions and concerns are now viewed slightly differently," he said. "There are things about Conan Doyle which are old-fashioned, particularly his view of natives. We feel differently now."

Conan Doyle's story of a scientific expedition by four high-spirited Englishmen who travel deep into Amazon jungle in South America was written in 1912, when views of Britain's imperial destiny and the superiority of the white man were common.

The BBC hopes that its adaptation will prove a ratings winner by combining the strengths of its costume drama department, responsible for successes such as *Pride and Prejudice*, with the special effects developed for its award-winning series *Walking with Dinosaurs*.

Nicknamed "frocks with teeth" by the makers, the two 75-minute episodes have gone into pre-production; filming will begin in New Zealand in February. It will then take five months for the computer-generated dinosaurs to be added. The drama will be directed by Stuart Orme, who made *The Sculptress*, the script was written by Tony Mulholland, who has worked on previous Conan Doyle programmes.

Philip Webber, the president of the Arthur Conan Doyle Study Group, said that the book was a classic and should not be altered.

"It is true that the treatment of the natives is very strange," he said. "it may not be politically correct but to judge Conan Doyle for this is to be anachronistic – you are applying standards that did not apply then."

Chapter 6

The Detective in Film – A Survey

The Master: Sir Arthur Conan Doyle

Perhaps it is only appropriate that this survey should begin with Sherlock Holmes, not only because Sir Arthur Conan Doyle's creation is virtually the prototype of the investigator involved in the art of detection for it's own sake, but also because Holmes was the *first* detective to be transferred to the screen (as early as 1903). Furthermore, the usage of Holmes on the screen has tended to reflect the movies' fluctuating interest in detective films generally. In the silent period, where the screen detective labored under the difficulty of not being able to conduct prolonged interrogations or oral deductions, he usually found himself shunted into the two-reeler or used in vehicles where the stress was on mystery or physical action rather than on literary-derived sleuthings. Certainly, Holmes fell into this pattern and, since dialogue and the enjoyable mixture of brilliance and the arrogant awareness of that brilliance are key factors in appreciating Holmes at work, it is not surprising that more of his forays into the silent film were markedly successful. In the sound period, Holmes twice reappeared as a kind of bird of good omen – once in 1929, and again in 1939 – hovering in the celluloid heavens in the forefront of prolific cycles of detective films, re-establishing the genre as a popular entertainment, and then withdrawing gracefully and allowing his disciples – from Charlie Chan and Philo Vance to Sam Spade and Nick Charles – to take over and carry on.

Sir Arthur Conan Doyle created Holmes in 1887, giving him a Baker Street address which in itself was a kind of tipoff to the kind of man he wanted Holmes to be. Baker Street was doubtless more fashionable in the eighteen-hundreds than it is today, at the same time it never represented the *height* of fashion. It was and is a kind of outskirt, boasting a railway station leading to the suburbs and close proximity to the London Zoo and Madame Tussaud's Wax Museum. It is close enough to the theatrical and business centres of London – and to the museums, universities and hospitals – to be quite convenient, and yet just sufficiently far removed for an inhabitant, if he so wished to consider himself "in" London without being "of" London. In other words, the perfect location from which a dilettante like Holmes, withdrawn from the bustle of central London, could devote himself to the art of deductive reasoning. Ostensibly, Doyle built the character of Holmes around that of one of his former teachers, and it is the character – rather than the plots – that has made Homes both a legend and a "problem" to cast. Holmesian students – and such international groups as the Baker Street Irregulars – "know" Holmes as a very real person with specifically designated physical characteristics and mental attitudes which to date have never been totally fulfilled by any one actor, though certainly Arthur Wontner and Basil Rathbone have come close.

None of the earliest attempts to transfer Holmes to the screen appear to have survived, but it is interesting that America and Scandinavia realized his commercial possibilities before Britain did. The first known Holmes film was *Sherlock Holmes Baffled*, made by the American Biograph Company, and since it was copyrighted in

February of 1903, the chances are that it was made at the end of 1902. While story films did exist before 1930's *The Great Train Robbery*, Biograph in its pre- D.W.Griffith days, showed little evidence of interest in dramatic structure. It is likely that this early Holmes effort was little more than a series of tableaux of a melodramatic nature without any real continuity; or like many other Biograph half-reelers of that period, it may have been little more than an excuse to show exterior views of the city – although, in view of the enormous popularity of the then fifteen-year-old Holmes, a New York or New Jersey location might just have been too incongruous for even such an infant industry. Since Biograph did not begin to use recognizable actors until much later, it is probable that Holmes was played by a studio employee or relative who happened to look like the traditional image of the detective. In late 1905, Vitagraph made a second Holmes film, which, since it carried two titles (*The Adventures of Sherlock Holmes* and *Held for a Ransom*) clearly had a specific story line and must have been a considerable advance on the previous film, even though it was still too early a film to warrant our entertaining any thoughts about it as a valuable contribution to Holmesian lore of the screen.

Three years later, another Holmes film – by the Crescent Company, one of a number of rapidly proliferating but generally short-lived independent companies – made its bow. Its title was *Sherlock Holmes and the Great Murder Mystery*, and the one traceable review was good, although it should be stressed that critical standards of such an early date cannot be regarded as too reliable. Its plot, involving murder by a gorilla, seems to incline more towards Edgar Allen Poe than towards Doyle!

Also, in 1908, the Nordisk Company of Denmark embarked on a whole series of Sherlock Holmes films directed by F. Holger-Madsen, who also played the role of Holmes. Unfortunately, a recent sojourn at both the Swedish and Danish film archives failed to turn up any surviving copies of the dozen or so films (all approximately a reel and a half in length) made in this series and presumably, they have been lost for some time since they are not even represented in the compilation films that the Scandinavian film industries have put together to record their early film history. This is a particularly sad loss, since the Scandinavian cinema of pre-World War I years was extremely advanced, turning out films comparable to (and, in the case of early feature-length productions, superior to) American films of the same period. Records indicate that the films had well-staged physical action, and a good deal of exterior shooting, and certainly no little showmanship. Apart from the utilisation of Professor Moriarty as Holmes' enemy in some of the films, others brought him face to face with Raffles, the debonair cracksman created by E.W.Hornung in 1899. Presumably Raffles was depicted more in a criminal than in an heroic light. Film makers in those days were none too scrupulous about recognising the still vague copyright laws or about using a characters name but changing his image entirely. (Thus, in America, O. Henry's Cisco Kid made his first bow in an early western as a thoroughly despicable villain and not as the good-badman cavalier). The Danish Holmes films were made over a three-year period. Alwin Neuss was cast as Dr. Watson.

Thereafter, Holmes began to appear with rather more regularity. In 1910 Germany made two Holmes films – with Arsene Lupin replacing Moriarty as Sherlock's sparring partner. Allegedly, Conan Doyle was personally involved in a 1912 series of Anglo-French two-reelers. The French also made a series of one-reelers in the same period which, from their titles (*The Speckled Band*, *The Copper Beeches*, *Silver Blaze*, did seem to be relying to a degree on the Doyle originals. One very battered print of *The

Copper Beeches surfaced quite recently, too shrunken to risk projection, and viewable only via the ultra-small image on a hand-cranked 35-mm viewer. Apart from having the distinction of being the earliest known extant Holmes film, it was a tedious and dull production, though it was difficult to assess its photographic and other production qualities under such circumstances. The French also made *A Study in Scarlet* and *The Hound of the Baskervilles* in 1914-1915 before abandoning the character and turning instead to their own native mystery specialists *Fantomas* and *Judex*.

Oddly enough, it was a British equivalent of Fantomas and Judex – Ultus – who dominated the mystery field in Britain at the same time. The several Ultus films directed by George Pearson took the limelight away from Britain's first two six-reel Holmes features: *A Study in Scarlet* (1914, with Fred Paul) and *Valley of Fear* (1916). Since they were both produced by G.B.Samuelson a noted British pioneer whose work was well above the admittedly not very high standards of the day (production expansion was very much curtailed by the war), one must assume that they were respectable little films, yet their success must have been modest since there were no follow-ups until 1922's *The Hound of the Baskervilles*.

Frankly, it was hardly an auspicious return for the master detective. This time Holmes was played by Eille Norwood, and his effectiveness was minimized by the fact that his Dr.Watson was of the same build and general appearance. Indeed, in the rather grey and washed-out print that has survived, it is often difficult to tell them apart! The plot stuck fairly closely to Doyle's original and would seem to have been foolproof – yet it is amazing how often this much-filmed Holmes adventure has come a cropper because of uninspired direction. The director in this case was Maurice Elvey, a reliable workhorse who turned out films with astonishing regularity between 1913 and 1957, tackling everything from historical pageantry and slapstick comedy to Dickens, war films, and science fiction. With a good plot, capable actors, and impressive sets, he could make thoroughly impressive films – as, for example, the 1935 *Transatlantic Tunnel* – but he wasn't an imaginative enough director to evoke mood or to create atmosphere from a script that didn't tell him how to. *The Hound of the Baskervilles*, of all films, needs *mood* far more than it needs logic or action, and mood is the one thing that this version consistently lacks.

Baskerville Hall, never seen in relation to its supposedly bleak surroundings, looks exactly like what it probably was – a London suburb townhouse belonging to someone of above-average but by no means spectacular wealth. The few forays on to Grimpen Mire suggest cheerful parkland, or possibly Hamstead Heath, but one never has the sense of desolation, of sweeping moorlands and treacherous quicksands. Not even miniatures or fog effects are pressed into service to heighten the feeling of natural menace and, undoubtedly aware of the shortcomings of his exteriors, Elvey keeps most of his action indoors. The one solitary touch of showmanship: the hound was tinted or hand-painted with a luminous glow, so that its infrequent appearances did carry a token shock value.

Quite coincidentally, *The Hound of the Baskervilles* had also been made in Germany (in 1917) by a director, Richard Oswald, who was an exact equivalent of Maurice Elvey. His work was literal, stodgy, unimaginative – and tremendously popular in his own country. It is perhaps unfair to criticize a film that is not available for reappraisal, but many of Oswald's German films (silent and sound) *are* still extant and apart from occasional pleasing camera compositions, none live up to their potential or generate much excitement. Oswald, who has a penchant for remaking his big commercial hits, redid *The Hound of the Baskervilles* in 1929, still as a silent, with Carlyle Blackwell singularly miscast as Holmes.

Although the 1922 British *Hound* had not been a marked success, Eille Norwood had been. With Maurice Elvey continuing as producer-director (and scenarist) and Hubert Willis cast as Dr. Watson throughout, Norwood played in close to fifty Holmes films. Some were two-reelers, others longer features, and they must have literally saturated the market since all were made over a three-year period. If the quality of *The Hound of the Baskervilles* is typical, then it is not surprising that the British promptly retired Holmes until the coming of sound!

Back in America, the first feature-length Holmes was made in 1916. Titled just *Sherlock Holmes*, it was based on the play written as a vehicle for himself by William Gillette. He had been playing the role on stage for some seventeen years and was the logical choice to star in the film version as well. (At this time, many stage personalities were being brought to Hollywood to re-create their famous theatrical roles and, incidentally, to bring a little prestige and respectability to what was still considered a bastard art. Many were too old to photograph well or convincingly; others could not adapt to movie technique. Only Douglas Fairbanks and John Barrymore were totally successful.) Although Essanay had a certain crudity, they were usually well photographed and generous with their close-ups. Their films, though well below the standards set by Vitagraph and Fine Arts, did provide useful showcases for actors. *Sherlock Holmes*, directed by Arthur Berthelet, was probably a valuable, if frustratingly mute, record of a famous actor in his finest role. It is tragic that this theatrically important record is apparently lost, while destiny has seen fit to preserve *The Count of Monte Cristo* as a record of James O'Neill's most famous stage role, but a film so primitive that no one ever gets a single close-up of the actor, and all we have to judge him by is a series of long-shot charades!

The same Gillette play formed the basis for the first really elaborate Holmes film: 1922's *Sherlock Holmes* produced by Sam Goldwyn and starring John Barrymore. Although Goldwyn was already very much concerned with prestige and production gloss, he was also a showman. His films of that period – and they included some of the very best Lon Chaney vehicles – were full of rich melodrama, giving the paying audiences what they wanted, but with added bonuses of directional flair and production values that they possibly didn't expect. Though *Sherlock Holmes* was criticized for its hokum, for being more of a Barrymore than a Holmes vehicle, it was immensely popular. (Barrymore's film career had started slowly in light comedy in 1915, established itself more firmly with *Dr. Jekyll and Mr. Hyde* in 1920, but was now solidly entrenched with the presold role of Holmes and a romantic flavoring to boot.) Exquisitely lit photography made the most of the classic Barrymore profile *and* of his love of the bizarre, as in the scenes where he masquerades – convincingly – as Moriarty, and in one sequence meets him face to face. Moriarty was played by the satanic-featured Gustav von Seyffertitz, perhaps too wholly evil and physically grotesque to be perfectly cast as Doyle's criminal genius. But he made an ideal facial foil and counterpart to Barrymore, who used him in a similar way (likewise involving a masquerade) in the later *Don Juan*. One of the most enjoyable aspects was its extensive location shooting in London: not just in the obvious "scenic" spots such as the Embankment by the Thames, but also in the quiet back streets of Kensington, or amid the bustle of a Piccadilly Circus that still had a goodly percentage of horse-drawn vehicles among the proud new automobiles and double-decker buses. Tragically, this enchanting film is also (at least partially) a lost work, and attempts to reconstruct it have taken on all of the characteristics of a Holmesian puzzle. Would that the Master himself were on hand to assist in the work! Rochester's George Eastman House, America's foremost film archive, some years ago was able to salvage several cans of negative of the film, each can consisting of short unconnected rolls. They were printed up, spliced together for viewing purposes, and found to be most intriguing but virtually incomprehensible. There was a little of everything – but not very much of anything. Some scenes ran for a few seconds; others would reappear with variations at regular intervals. One method of assuring longer film preservation is the removal of all the subtitles (which tend to decompose first) and except for a singular reference frame for each title, which sped by far too quickly to be read, there were no titles in the film.

Further adding to the puzzle, both Roland Young and Reginald Denny appeared with mustaches in some scenes, without them in others! (Later it became apparent that the hairless scenes belonged in a prologue or flashback to their younger days, while the mustaches represented a passage of time.) William Powell sneaked menacingly in and out of the proceedings, stealing all of the non-Barrymore scenes with ease even when one wasn't quite sure what he was doing. Anders Randolf, Carol Dempster, David Torrence, and Louis Wolheim made but token appearances, and Roland Young's Watson seemed to make few real contributions. All told, there were about 50 minutes of surviving footage, seemingly representing most of the sequences, but only about half of the total. The first move was to put it all in some semblance of order, so that it could be screened without becoming a surrealist nightmare. The second move was to screen it in London for the film's director, veteran Albert Parker (then an agent and married to actress Margaret Johnston), in the hopes that he could shed light on the missing scenes and help to restore the continuity.

Also present at that screening in late 1970 were Clive Brook and British historian and film maker Kevin Brownlow, Brook who later played Holmes three times himself, had mellowed gracefully and serenely into the kind of person that one would hope and expect that Brook – and Holmes – would become at age eighty (though Brook's handsome face and spry wit belied those years.) not a great deal was learned about the film at that initial screening, but unexpectedly – and most amusingly – Brook and Parker slid unwittingly and quite naturally into the Holmes and Watson roles (Brook sardonically pointing out the superiority of his version. Parker, forgetful and a little confused, assuming the Nigel Bruce interpretation of Dr. Watson). It was a delightful evening and one wishes it could be recorded on film but, apart from a few clues, it brought us no nearer to solving the puzzle of this jigsaw of a film. In the subsequent years, however, Kevin Brownlow, pouring over the fragments of film, matching up minute scene numbers printed on to the celluloid. Shooting and inserting stills to bridge gaps, restoring titles – has completed the major part of the reassembly process. If *Sherlock Holmes* has gone in its totality, at least a coherent and representative cross-section of it will shortly be available for archival study. One hopes that at its initial rescreening Brownlow will have the wit to deprecate all much-deserved congratulations with an underplayed "Elementary!"

Quite incidentally, although there may have been legal reasons for it, it seems more likely that the mediocrity of so many earlier Holmes films was the deciding factor in releasing the films in Britain under the title *Moriarty!* Barrymore's Holmes had been a youthful one, and the next major Holmes was to maintain the tradition. Clive Brook was introduced to the role in 1920's *The Return of Sherlock Holmes* and thus became the first Holmes to talk on the screen. The film was limited in its action, most of it taking place aboard an ocean liner, but the concentration on talk was what audiences wanted then – or at least what the executive offices *thought* they wanted. Brook's excellent diction made him vocally a fine choice, though his rather humorless acting style in that period tended to make Holmes unnecessarily priggish. The film was directed by Basil Dean, a commercially successful but never very enterprising British director, who was then not only a newcomer to films generally but a total novice to sound films. The film, with a contemporary setting, adapted from two Doyle stories ("The Dying Detective" and "His Last Bow"), offered Harry J. Morey as an effective Moriarty (using such colorful gimmicks as a cigarette case with a poisoned needle that was brought into play when the opening spring was pressed) and H. Reeves-Smith as Dr. Watson. It's odd that a property of such comparative importance, with an established star such as Clive Brook, should have been entrusted to a minor British director but, presumably, the thinking was that a man with British stage experience would be the best choice for such a British-oriented dialogue film. Although it was a Paramount release officially shot in Paramount's large Long Island studios, Brook recalls the film as having been shot very quickly and cheaply with few facilities. Some of the shipboard footage was shot on a trip from England to New York, while Brook describes the studio work as done at a small, cramped studio in midtown Manhattan.

That same year Clive Brook made a second appearance as Holmes in the studio's contribution in the all-star musical review cycle, *Paramount on Parade*. The Holmes skit introduced three of Paramount's leading stars and characters – Brook as Holmes, William Powell as Philo Vance, Warner Oland as Fu Manchu – and after some informal off-screen banter, let them loose in a wild-and-woolly satire of their own specialities, with all three killed off one by one by a mysterious assailant. (This is a minor historic footnote, since it represents the only time that Holmes died on screen!) It was all rather arch and not as funny as its writers and players thought it was, but it did have pace and a feeling of spontaneity and the atmospheric set was quite impressive. Coming very early in the film, it remained a highlight in a musical revue that was rather better and more spirited than the competitive entries from Warner's, Fox and MGM.

Brook's final appearance as Holmes in 1932's *Sherlock Holmes* for Fox, one of the most enjoyable and stylish of all Holmes films, though possibly a big disappointment for true Doyle devotees. Officially, it was based on the Gillette play once again but, apart from its similar emphasis on a deliberate confrontation between Holmes and Moriarty, there was little relationship. Oddly enough, even the official studio synopsis bears little similarity to the finished film, written by Bertram Millhauser (who would appear later as one of the perennial writers on Universal's Holmes series), updated to a contemporary thirties setting and drawing its basic inspiration from Doyle's "The Red Headed League." A hangover from the Gillette play was Holmes' romantic involvement with Alice Faulkner (played by Miriam Jordan) and his retirement to wedded bliss at the film's end. The contemporary setting was given added stress by having Moriarty import saloon bombings and other gangster methods from the States. Holmes was given virtually no opportunity for verbal reasoning and deductions, and the famous "Elementary, my dear Watson!" was used more as a joke following moments of quite ordinary observations. Watson himself, played by Reginald Owen, made but fleeting appearances, in fact, in the cast list Owen was billed *below* Herbert Mundin, who had a small and not very important character-comedy role.

But if the film was disappointing Doyle, it was still a first-class melodrama, William K. Howard who directed, was a master of slick polished thrillers, his highlight sequences always well composed and angled, edited with pace and precision, and prone to Germanic lighting and design. The first reel of the film is a model of how to combine theatrical bravura with real cinematic sense. In a series of strikingly lit silhouette and gauze shots, Moriarty (beautifully played by Ernest Torrence, who delivered every line with relish and an effective mock humility) is brought into court and in an address to the jury promises that the rope that can hang him has not yet been made – and that Holmes, the judge, and all others responsible for his sentence will precede him in death.

After a stately return to his cell – again in silhouette – and backed by the sombre chimes of Big Ben – we cut away to Holmes laboratory. Mainly as an excuse to realise some of the impressive Frankensteinian lab machinery that Fox had concocted for a number of science-fiction films of the period. Holmes is shown dabbling with some elaborate electrical gadgetry and demonstrating his new ray with which police can knock out the automobile motors of escaping crooks. It is his parting gift to Scotland Yard, and is accompanied by a neat little speech about the deadly weapon that the automobile has become. Alice Faulkner, Little Billy (rather obnoxiously affected and unconvincingly British, as portrayed by Howard Leeds) and Watson are introduced to some pleasantries, and then we are back to the prison, chaos; turmoil; guards running; whistles; hooters. George Pearson's smoothly flowing camera follows the prison guards as they race through the grim corridors and Howard cuts vividly from the muscular figures of prisoners, straining close to the bars to see what is going on, to a detail shot of a whistle hanging from the still fingers of a murdered guard. Finally, the camera tracks along the walls of a cell block, coming to rest on an open door and a message scrawled on the wall: "Tell Holmes I'm OUT – Moriarty!"

It would be difficult for any thriller to match the visual flair and excitement of these opening scenes and *Sherlock Holmes* doesn't quite make it. But it's a surprisingly short film and thus is able to keep its pace fairly taut. While its plot (involving Moriarty's revenge and his plan to force Holmes into a murder and thence to the gallows) is a good one. The bank robbery climax returns to the powerful visual style of the opening scenes, and the only really weak moment in the film is Holmes' totally unconvincing masquerade as a prissy maiden aunt. It's an amusing sequence, but that the disguise should fool the cunning Moriarty is a little hard to accept.

Despite his physical "rightness" for the role, and an undeniable screen "presence", Clive Brook fell somewhat short of being the ideal movie Holmes. His diction was fine, the detached imperturbability just right, and yet there was an air of condescension to his interpretation, as though the role wasn't quite worth taking seriously. Some directors (especially Josef von Sternberg with *Shanghai Express*) were able to take this acting trait and turn it to the advantage of the role, while Brook himself dispensed with it for roles he really believed in (as, for example, with Noel Coward's *Cavalcade*. Nevertheless, his 1932 *Sherlock Holmes* stands as one of the most interesting of a sudden plethora of Holmes films in 1930-33, most of them from Britain. Hollywood's only immediate follow-up was the independently made *A Study in Scarlet* (1933) with Reginald Owen graduating from the Watson role to the least-effective-ever Holmes interpretation. The story took nothing from the book and apart from an exceptionally strong cast for a small company like World-Wide (Anna May Wong, Alan Dinehart, and Warburton Gamble as Watson), the talkative and tedious film had little to recommend it.

Back in Britain in 1930, the Twickenham Studios introduced the best movie Holmes to date – and, in fact, still one of the best – in Arthur Wontner. Although his movie career was a long one and he was a fine and sensitive actor (witness the poignancy he brought to his brief scene as the elderly admirer of the antique automobile in *Genevieve*) who had been in films since 1915 – and on the stage before that – he was best known for his interpretation of Holmes in five films of the early thirties. Preceded by their reputation, based largely on the excellence of Wontner's performance. These films tend to disappoint audiences seeing them for the first time today. They are all "modern" versions of the Doyle stories, although since they stick largely to telling the stories by dialogue, with a maximum of interiors, the contemporary settings are not stressed and as the years go by they take on more and more the patina of a "period" background. Twickenham was an ambitious independent company but it was still an independent, and the lack of really elaborate production values (especially in the early thirties, when there was a big gap between the polish of lavish films and those of Hollywood) was readily apparent. Moreover, all of the Wontner films were directed by competent, journeyman directors, none of whom were able to do much in the way of creating mood and atmosphere from rather talkative scripts. The films did lack pace.

Nevertheless, in their concentration of the characterizations of Holmes and Watson and in the general fullness of their strong adaptations, they had an integrity that most of the other Holmes films lacked. Wontner was not only physically right as Holmes, but he also managed to achieve the right mixture of dedication and aloofness without sacrificing warmth and wry humour. Likewise, Ian Fleming (a familiar British character actor, not to be confused with the author of the James Bond stories) made a fine Watson – an intelligent, good-looking man whose intellect was admittedly not called upon too often, and who was at least no mere foil that so many Watsons (especially Nigel Bruce) seemed destined to play.

The first of the Wontner films was 1930's *The Sleeping Cardinal*, released in the United States under the title *Sherlock Holmes' Fatal Hour*, and based on two Doyle stories, "The Empty House" and "The Final Problem". It was the longest of the Wontner films, the slowest paced and by current standards the most dated, yet it was in many ways the best. Its leisurely pacing allowed for ample examples of Holmes' deductive reasoning, all arising naturally out of the plot and the clues and not dragged out merely for their own sake. Although the bulk of the plot line was developed on an intimate level, with Holmes trying to ferret out the identity of the elusive Moriarty from a small group of society friends, it was played against the larger background of Moriarty's world-wide crime organisation, with an opening bank robbery sequence suspiciously akin to those employed in Fritz Lang's *The Testament of Dr. Mabuse* two years earlier. The only disappointing aspect of the film was that since Moriarty was acting in the open as one of a group of above-suspicion citizens, he could not be portrayed by a bravura villain. Norman McKinn playing the role, thus had only two real opportunities to display his perfidy during the film: once when, heavily disguised, he confronts Holmes (and inadvertently reveals his identity when Holmes notices a peculiarity of his upper left molar!) and in the final showdown when his plans to murder Holmes are thwarted.

Despite the film's slow pace, it did have some enjoyable moments and highlight sequences reminiscent (in terms of content and photographic style) of the silent German cinema, still a fashionable model for British directors of that period. Moreover, its plot was well constructed; audiences were neither *ahead* of the game nor did they have their intelligence underestimated by sudden and illogical marshalling of facts and deductions that the film had not substantiated.

Wontner's second Holmes film (with Ian Hunter temporarily taking over as Watson) was *The Sign of the Four* (1932). Again it was a faithful adaptation. Curiously, any U.S. reviews criticized the film for substandard photography. Since the film had the most professional technical crew of any of the Wontner films – Hollywood's Rowland V. Lee producing; a good British veteran, Graham Cutts, directing; and *two* cameramen, including Hollywood's Robert de Grasse – this seems hard to accept. Possibly, since the American release was handled by an independent, second-rate laboratory work or an inadequate dupe negative may have been to blame.

Ian Fleming returned as Watson in *The Missing Rembrandt*, a good mystery with a good cast (Miles Mander, Francis L. Sullivan) and in 1935 Wontner and Fleming teamed again for *The Triumph of Sherlock Holmes* based on "The Valley of Fear," is set a good deal of its action – energetically, if not too convincingly – in America's West. Its main attribute was one of Britain's best villains: Lyn Harding as Moriarty. Harding, a big, bluff, hearty man, somewhat resembling a bearded Gibson Rowland, was a much underrated actor who, despite his bulk, could deliver dialogue with intelligence and subtlety at play for full-blooded melodrama when the occasion demanded. There has been a higher percentage of successful Moriartys than there has been of successful Holmeses – and Harding was one of the best. The last Wontner-Fleming film was *Silver Blaze*, the mildest and the weakest of their series, though still distinguished by their teamwork and the skill of Lyn Harding.

However, the plot to keep a horse out of the big race seemed unworthy of the talents of Moriarty, whose time would have been better spent in crime of a much broader scope, and equally unworthy of the attention of England's greatest detective. Frankie Darrow and Kane Richmond could have handled the case just as well. Too, the film showed its less imposing budget (Twickenham was then in its last throes as a producer-distributor, although the studio itself was still in use) and rarely got away from cramped interior sets. Even the horse spent most of its time in studio "ex-actors." While others of the Wontner films were released in America soon after their British showings, *Silver Blaze* was considered unworthy of importing. It did show up finally in the early forties, under the title *Murder at the Baskervilles*. Fortunately, much of the action had taken place at Baskerville Hall. And the new title none too subtly suggested a relationship to *The Hound of the Baskervilles*, which had just successfully launched Basil Rathbone's association with the Holmes saga.

Two other negligible Holmes films had come out of Britain in the early thirties, worthy of note only because of the actors playing the lead. *The Speckled Band* (1931) had Raymond Massey enacting Holmes as though he knew that he would one day play Lincoln. Athole Stewart was an adequate Watson. The year 1932 saw yet another remake of *The Hound of the Baskervilles*, with Robert Rendell as Holmes, Fred Lloyd as Watson, and Heather Angel as the heroine. Edgar Wallace worked on the scenario. Like other versions of the tale, it had quite elaborate reconstruction of the Baskerville legend, done this time as a prologue. Oddly enough, only the picture negative of this film seems to have survived, and in recent years it has been impossible to see the film with sound. Thus one cannot be on reliably firm ground in commenting on Robert Rendell's performance but, excellent actor though he was, he would seem to be quite inappropriate as the master detective. Short and alert, he suggests intellect certainly, but not a man of contemplative deduction. One would expect calm reasoning from such a man – but also quick decisions and swift action. Rendell was well cast in wartime films as the naval official in situations where he has the responsibility of making immediate decisions that also have to be the right ones. But as Holmes, while his performance was thoughtful and free of frivolity, he seemed badly miscast.

Hollywood gave Sherlock Holmes a spectacular comeback in 1939 with *The Hound of the Baskervilles*. This was a year in which many formerly popular genres were dusted off and given elaborate revivals, but in new formats which sought to combine the old values in slicker and glossier packages. Thus the gangster cycle was brought back, bigger and noisier than ever via *The Roaring Twenties*; *Stagecoach* revitalised a western format that had grown somewhat stale, while Son of Frankenstein, the longest and most expensive horror film to date, launched a new cycle of chillers. The detective film, which had fallen into a rut of formularised "B" pictures, could hardly have had a more stylish and impressive showcase than *The Hound of the Baskervilles*, with which Twentieth –Century Fox initiated the inspired casting of Basil Rathbone as Holmes and the equally shrewd (though less effectively written) utilization of Nigel Bruce as Watson. The best of the many versions of *The Hound of the Baskervilles*, it remains an impressive, handsomely mounted and certainly "respectful" treatment of Doyle, even if a little too measured in its pacing and never quite makes the most of its excitement potential.

Certainly, one of its shortcomings was the lack of an inspired director, for Sidney Lanfield (a specialist in light modern comedy) was no more suited to the subject than Britain's Maurice Elvey or Germany's Richard Oswald had been. With that cast and such a literate script, an imaginative director could have made of this the definitive Holmes essay. James Whale, for example, would have been a superb choice, or even such a lesser stylist as John Brahm. In fact, one of Brahm's minor horror films for Twentieth-Century Fox – *The Undying Monsters*, with its similar period, location, and even an overlapping plot line – provides a concrete example of just what cinematic wonders Brahms could work with such material, while his more elaborate *The Lodger*, a Jack the Ripper story, confirmed that increasing Brahm's budget increased the thrills proportionately.

The Hound of the Baskervilles also suffered from a surprising lack of background music. Since the thriller depends for its effect on the manipulation of audience fears, and since the use of music (and, at the same time, the dramatic use of silence) is a key factor in involving that audience, the lack of music (even in the alleged interests of realism) can reduce the thriller's impact considerably.

The London scenes, calling as they do on Fox's then remarkable array of standing sets, are totally convincing, but the bulk of the film, set at Baskerville Hall and its environs, does have a rather studio-bound quality. Studio "exteriors" had become a fine art in the thirties, particularly in the well-lit black-and-white cinematography of the day. (To see how much has been lost of this art, especially with the widespread usage of colour film, one has only to compare the exteriors in this film with those in the later Hammer films *The Mummy* and *Curse of the Mummy's Tomb*, where color only emphasises all the blank space and lack of real design.) When well done, studio exteriors can enhance rather than minimize the power of a scene, and certainly James Whale's studio exteriors in his horror films had a stylistic power that shooting in natural locations couldn't have duplicated.

But if you're going to build Dartmoor or Grimpen Mire in the studio, no matter how artfully you design it, you're not going to succeed unless you create an atmosphere of awesome desolation. *Son of Frankenstein*, which didn't really rely on outdoor sets, created that atmosphere via a few dead trees. Cunning and handsome as the moor sets are in *The Hound of the Baskervilles* – and they are enhanced by some barely perceptive use of gauzes over the lens – one never once has the feeling of boundless space, of being cut off from all help. One is all too aware that victim, pursuer, and rescuers are all carefully running around one basic set, with visibility minimized by the dry-ice created mists and rocks strategically placed to allow for a good variety of camera angles.

But to carp is perhaps unfair in the face of such an otherwise satisfying film. For one thing, it restored Holmes to his original period; it warrants respect and admiration not only for that, but for being about the most faithful to its source novel. The changes are minor: the butler, extremely well played by John Carradine and named Barrymore in the novel was rechristened Barryman for obvious reasons. The villain's *wife* in the novel became his sister in the movie without any notable change in her character although, presumably, the change made her more acceptable as a romantic partner for Sir Henry Baskerville. A séance *not* in the novel was written in probably out of deference to Doyle's well-publicized interest in spiritualism, and the villain (seldom has there been less doubt about the identity of a "mystery" villain!) quite definitely meets his end in Grimpen Mire in the novel while the film leaves it open to conjecture. Despite its slowness and the artificiality of its sets, the film's mounting and hand-picked cast make it solidly enjoyable throughout, though one rather resents the studio's newest romantic lead, Richard Greene, getting billing over Rathbone.

Lionel Atwill, bearded once more and wearing thick eyeglasses so sinister in appearance that he obviously *cannot* be the guilty party, plays another marvellous red-herring role, is favored with some fine low-key close-ups and launches into his lines with special enthusiasm when he has something particularly unpleasant to report. His final tribute to Holmes, however, is a sincere, underplayed scene, that reminds us what a good actor Atwill could be when given the material. Basil Rathbone, who often tended to overact (and did so outrageously in later Holmes films) here keeps his interpretation well in check – colorful yet sober, making his detailed deductions with pride and self-assurance, yet without smugness, and attacking his "disguise" scenes with relish. Nigel Bruce, a physically suitable choice as Watson, is presented as a loyal but not-too-bright aide. Unfortunately, Bruce's role was to be played more and more for comic pomposity in later films. One of the best sequences in *The Hound of the Baskervilles* was its recapitulation of the old legend, this time not done as a prologue but as a flashback, the story being shown over the turning pages of an old manuscript in the course of its being related to Holmes by Lionel Atwill. A further pleasant surprise was that, while the film was a product of the conservative Production Code -dominated years, we were still permitted to hear Holmes ask Watson for the needle as his graceful curtain line!

The film's success prompted an immediate sequel *The Adventures of Sherlock Holmes*, this time with Rathbone and Bruce getting the top billing they deserved. Although officially based-again-on the Gillette play, it bore no resemblance to it, or to the earlier Barrymore and Brook "adaptations" of the play. Again, its only similarity was to the dominance of the personal Holmes-Moriarty content. Holmes' romantic interest was removed too. The plot was a wild and woolly affair dealing with Moriarty's attempts to steal the Crown Jewels from the Tower of London. It's a pity that the story line was less impressive than that of *The Hound of the Baskervilles*, for in all other respects it was a superior product. Alfred Werker was a much better director than Sidney Lanfield and got much more out of his material; the pace and action were much faster; the concentration on a London locale ensured the continuing use of Fox's substantial standing sets and avoided the claustrophobic artifice of moorland and other exterior sets.

And, in George Zucco, we had one of the best Moriartys. Zucco's face not only had the ability to suggest intellectual superiority, but it also had the happy facility of being able to light itself up with satanic glee at his own perfidy. Obviously, his Moriarty enjoyed villainy for its own sake as well as for the rewards it brought. Moreover, being British himself and possessed of clear diction that had the same kind of built-in smugness and suavity that also characterized Rathbone's speech, he made a perfect mental as well as physical foil for Rathbone. Although, occasionally, Zucco was to play Scotland Yard detectives himself (as in such films as *Moss Rose*), clearly, he was temperamentally much better equipped to exist on the wrong side of the law. He was to cross swords with Rathbone on other occasions: in a later Holmes adventure, and especially effectively in *International Lady*, a wartime spy thriller in which Zucco's espionage agent was defeated by Rathbone's Scotland Yard detective with a penchant for Holmesian disguises.

The quality of Fox's two Holmes films was such that under ordinary circumstances a series would have been a forgone conclusion. But by the end of 1939 World War II was upon us; spies and saboteurs were much more logical than purloiners of the Crown Jewels and films like Hitchcock's *Foreign Correspondent* took the master criminal from his own environments and dropped him into the area of political intrigue. And, a year later, the unexpected success of the John Huston-Humphrey Bogart *The Maltese Falcon* suddenly gave new and greater impetus to the "private eye" detective thriller. With such opposition, Holmes and Watson must have seemed out of touch with the times indeed. Probably, Fox saw them as a serious commercial proposition for continuance on the same budgetary level, and too important (and too costly) to relegate to their "B" mystery series. Although Fox abandoned Mr. Moto in 1939, they still had Charlie Chan on their "B" payroll and Michael Shayne, private detective, in the person of Lloyd Nolan, would go to work for them too by the end of 1940.

Sherlock Holmes' position as an anachronism was somewhat confirmed when, in 1942, Universal put Rathbone and Bruce into a new series of twelve Holmes adventures – all updated, and the initial ones with a contemporary wartime setting that pitted Holmes against the Axis, and occasionally had Professor Moriarty lending his ingenious talents to the Nazi cause. There was some outcry at first from the purist Holmes devotees – especially as the films, though slick and streamlined, had none of the careful production values of the two Fox predecessors. Rathbone's fondness for overacting was a failing he indulged in more and more as the series progressed and, presumably, he was trying to find some outlet for his personal boredom. Rathbone's bravura acting was often a definite asset in his costumers and swashbucklers, and some directors (notably, Rowland V. Lee in *Love from a Stranger* and *Son of Frankenstein*) were able to harness his excess energy to the benefit of roles calling for neurosis and hysteria. But, in time, the increasingly frank "ham" of Rathbone's Holmes and the equally increasing stereotype fashioned for Watson began to work against the series.

The first films made at least a token attempt to retain recognizable plot elements from Doyle's stories and the second, and one of the best of the series, *Sherlock Holmes and the Secret Weapon*, benefited not only by its causal inspiration from *The Dancing Men* but, most spectacularly, from the inspired casting of Lionel Atwill as Moriarty. (Rathbone and Atwill, another Englishman, worked together as felicitously as Rathbone and Zucco, and had opposed each other in the past in *Son of Frankenstein* and *The Sun Never Sets*.) The macabre climax found Holmes playing for time by submitting to an operation whereby Moriarty systematically drains all the blood from his body. As the operation reaches its climax and Holmes is looking understandably pale and wan, Moriarty chortles that one more drop of blood will do the trick. But there is the inevitable timely interruption and, with astonishing energy for a man in his condition, Holmes gives vigorous chase to the disgruntled Moriarty, who falls to his death through a trapdoor.

Sherlock Holmes in Washington, which followed, was rather tamer and brought back Bertram Millhauser (scenarist for the '32 Fox film) who was to become a regular fixture on the series. Increasingly, his stories were "originals," with fleeting references, if any, to Doyle themes. After two years, Holmes' name was dropped from the titles of the films, which (via such titles as *The Scarlet Claw* and *The Spider Woman*) tried to lure the horror devotees as well as the Holmes aficionados. In fact, Gale Sondergaard's Spider Woman and Rondo Hatton's Creeper (from *The Pearl of Death*) spun off into negligible "B" horror careers on their own.

Among the best of the Holmes series were two from the midway point: *The Scarlet Claw* (1944) a genuinely eerie thriller with some echoes of *The Hound of the Baskervilles*, and 1945's *The House of Fear*. As always, however, with any "B" series of this type, eventually, the inspiration, the interest (and the money allocated), were drastically reduced.

The last three (*Pursuit to Algiers*, *Terror by Night*, and *Dressed to Kill*) made in 1945-46, were tedious and unexciting, with no recognizable link to any Doyle stories. The later entries were all much below the already none-too-exacting standards of the earlier ones, although they did eschew the sometimes patronizing and embarrassing hands-across-the-seas propaganda with which Holmes bombarded us in the wartime productions, mainly via stirring quotations from Churchill's speeches. The single highlight of the later films was the unexpected appearance of Professor Moriarty, in the capable hands of Henry Daniell in picture number nine, *The Woman in Green*. Toward the start of the series, Rathbone and Nigel Bruce had also parodied themselves via a brief and heavy-handed guest bit in the Olsen and Johnson musical *Crazy House*. Dennis Hoey appeared as Inspector Lestrade in six of the films though, like Watson, he was less bright than Doyle had intended.

When considerably more than a decade had passed and it seemed time to trot Sherlock Holmes out again, the always reliable *The Hound of the Baskervilles* was chosen as the Trial balloon. This time production was in England; Hammer Films produced, Terence Fisher directed, the film was back to its correct period and in colour. Hammer having by this time (1959) carved themselves a profitable niche as producers of horror films, the grislier aspects of Doyle's stories were emphasised. Peter Cushing was hardly an ideal Holmes; his earlier work as Van Helsing in the Dracula tales had set him up as a man of learning and meditation, with an appropriate professional stance. But as a man of action as well, on whom the fates of so many in the Grimpen Mire area depended, he inspired little confidence. Andre Morell, however, a fine British character actor, was a perfect realization of Doyle's conception of Dr. Watson. He was also taller and sturdier than Cushing and tended to seem the dominating half of the two.

Curiously, Cushing's cohort at Hammer, Christopher Lee, also essayed the Holmes role at this time (none too successfully) in a lurid German thriller, more reminiscent of Sax Rohmer than Conan Doyle, titled *Sherlock Holmes and the Deadly Necklace*. A final British entry, *A Study in Terror*, made virtually no impression.

For the time being, Holmes seemed to have been given the *coup de grace* by Billy Wilder's quite charming and unappreciated *The Private Life of Sherlock Holmes* in 1970. Wilder was in a difficult position at that time: his reputation for black comedy and the risqué had been all but stifled by the increasing permissiveness of the screen, in which far more outrageous things than had ever been in his once-notorious films were now not only the order of the day, but were themselves being constantly eclipsed. With the Sherlock Holmes theme by no means assured boxoffice – an earlier Broadway musical had not been a success – Wilder felt he had to pad out his extremely handsome and literate film with a number of "with it" ingredients. These turned out to include undue stress on Holmesian fondness for drugs and homosexuality. Not only did these subthemes introduce a note of vulgarity into what was otherwise a tasteful and affectionate film, but they also proved insufficiently strong to have the desired effect. The film was drastically shortened in an effort to streamline its episodic story, but all to no avail. It was a boxoffice flop and disappeared all too quickly – hopefully, to share the fate of another misunderstood satire, John Huston's *Beat the Devil*, and to reappear to a more receptive audience in a few years. Robert Stephens was a generally uninteresting Holmes but an unexpected bonus was Peter Cushing's extremely funny performance as the detective's brother – a most pleasant surprise after his disappointing showing as the Master some ten years earlier.

Since, in the seventies, the detective film was more and more emphasizing speed, action, violence, sex, and the kind of ultramodern and flashily directorial techniques that would inevitably be alien to a faithful and effective filming of Doyle, it is not surprising that Mr. Holmes bade the movies farewell. The other media, however, more prone to the traditional, continued to find Sherlock Holmes useful. On radio, there had been a long string of Holmes impersonators, Rathbone and Tom Conway among them. British television in the mid-fifties had made a long-running series of placid, comfortable, but quite enjoyable Holmes mysteries. Ronald Howard, son of Leslie, and unfortunately one of those perennial youthful actors who seems out of place in anything but light romantic comedy (where he has been a convincing juvenile for the past twenty-five years), had neither the looks nor the presence to play Holmes. Howard Marion Crawford was typecast as Watson, so that the team generated few sparks.

Holmes' first television spectacular was, however, held back until 1972 when, with stunning originality, Universal selected as a "prestige" thriller – *The Hound of the Baskervilles*! Probable *initial* intentions to use it as the launching pad for a new series of Holmes TV films were scotched by extremely lukewarm reviews. The principal shortcoming was its incredible cheapness: not only was it entirely studio-made, but standing sets were not even given a cursory reworking to adopt them to Holmes'

England. Florid Spanish architecture stood out like a sore thumb in a street exterior. The script was confusing and unexciting though, reportedly, the initial script had had some considerable novelty values which had vanished either prior to the shooting or during the editing. The only favourable comment one could make of this television enterprise is that at least its makers *did* take it seriously and didn't see the need to "camp" it up, and that Stewart Granger (as Holmes) and Bernard Fox (as Watson) were both quite good, although Granger's whitening hair seemed inappropriate. Curiously, Holmes was off-screen a good deal of the time, and by actual footage count Watson probably had more to do. It was a thorough disappointment, leaving Rathbone's version still out in the lead, though still not quite good enough in itself to rule out the possibility that this hardy old chestnut will one day provide the definitive Sherlock Holmes film.

In view of the dearth of really good Holmes films and the total absence of even one that could be termed a classic or a definitive filmic treatment, the amount of space herein devoted to Mr. Holmes might seem inappropriately generous. But, apart from the fact that it has attracted the attention of some outstanding actors and interesting directors from at least five countries and has been the only movie detective to span virtually the entire history of film, Holmes' influence (literary and filmic) on other detectives has been considerable. Britain's Sexton Blake is clearly a juvenile-level carbon copy, missing only Watson admittedly, but with Tinker substituting for the Little Billy of the Gillette play, and a protective landlady/housekeeper to fill the role of Doyle's Mrs. Hudson.

The basic Holmesian costume props – deerstalker cap, pipe, and magnifying glass – were adopted very quickly, perhaps *because* of their incongruity, by most movies spoofing the detective genre. Mack Sennett's very early *A Desperate Lover* starred Sennett himself, accoutered in such a manner, scouring the Hollywood hills for clues. One of the silent Mutt and Jeff animated cartoons, *Slick Sleuths*, fell back on those costuming devices, as did actors as divers as Michael Redgrave and Huntz Hall, and such comedy teams as Laurel and Hardy and Abbott and Costello. Even the name "Sherlock" rapidly became absorbed into filmic language as one of the words most used in the titles of detective satires: *Sherlock Junior, Miss Sherlock Holmes, Sherlock Brown, Shivering Sherlocks*.

And while in recent years there has been a general tendency to filmic lampoon of more modern detective *types* such as Sam Spade and James Bond, it is still Sherlock Holmes that has inspired the *specified* satires. One of the most enjoyable was the German spoof of the mid-thirties entitled *The Man Who Was Sherlock Holmes* in which Hans Albers and Heinz Ruhmann, in order to boost their unsuccessful private detective business, assume the identities of Holmes and Watson, one of the films best running jokes being their frequent encounters with an excessively British type who refuses to take them seriously, and is ultimately revealed as Conan Doyle. Much heavier-handed but similar in intent was an American comedy of the seventies, *They Might Be Giants*, in which George C. Scott believes himself to be Holmes against the incongruous background of contemporary New York.

However, it is difficult to satirize the Holmes films successfully. There is little to parody in them apart from the man himself – or men, if we extend the parody to include Watson and Moriarty. Comedy, to be effective, needs a certain amount of speed, and to manipulate the Holmes stories so as to provide faster pacing and physical action is to distort those basic contemplative elements which made them so unique and so popular.

Parodies of Holmes usually turn out to be parodies of a *genre* with Holmes as an interchangeable key figure. Satires of more conventional mystery forms – the Bulldog Drummond adventures, or the "old house-sliding panel" thrillers – have tended to be far more successful because they retain the ingredients to be good examples of the genre they are kidding even while they are simultaneously satires. The British *Bulldog Jack*, referred to later, is a prime example of this.

There has never been a deliberate parody of the Bible – although deMille and Sam Katzman have unwittingly come quite close at times – and with the modern trend to shock, outrage, and extreme antiestablishmentarianism, perhaps the biblical parody is inevitable. (*Jesus Christ, Superstar* suggests that it may well be.) But thus far, taste, decorum – and creative stumbling blocks – have prevented it. Since Sherlock Holmes is in a sense the Bible of all detective fiction and since Billy Wilder has already had his little joke at Sherlock's expense, perhaps the Master will remain immune, aloof – and a constant challenge.

Chapter 7

Sherlock Holmes in Films & on Television

1903 - 2002

Conan Doyle's classic fictional detective, around whom a detailed legend has been created by ardent followers, has a long screen history. 79 actors have played Sherlock Holmes, whose 215 big-screen cases make him the most filmed fictional character of all time.

There were American one-reel films featuring him in 1903, 1905 (*The Adventures of Sherlock Holmes*, an adaptation of The Sign of Four, starring Maurice Costello and directed by J. Stuart Blackton), and 1908. Also between 1908 and 1909 there began a series of twelve Danish one reelers. These were titled *The Adventures of Sherlock Holmes* (aka *Sherlock Holmes i livsfare*), numbered I – XII, and starring Forrest Holger-Madsen. In 1910 there were two German films and in 1912 six French. A second French series began in 1913, also in this year an American two-reel version of *The Sign of Four* featured Harry Benham. British six-reelers were made of *A Study in Scarlet* (1914), and *Valley of Fear* (1916); also in 1916 the famous stage actor William Gillette put his impersonation of Holmes on film for Essanay, entitled *Sherlock Holmes* and directed by Arthur Berthelet. (William Gillette performed 1400 times on stage as Sherlock Holmes. It was he who coined the phrase "Elementary, my dear Watson", though this never was used in any of Conan Doyle's stories of the great detective).

In 1917 came a German version of *The Hound of the Baskervilles*. Beginning in 1921, the British Stoll Film Company made a series of 15 two-reeler Sherlock Holmes and forty-seven *Adventures of Sherlock Holmes* films starring Eille Norwood who really resembled Professor Bell, capped off by a full-length version of *The Hound of the Baskervilles*, all directed by Maurice Elvey. In 1922 John Barrymore played Holmes and Roland Young was Watson in Goldwyn's *Sherlock Holmes* (aka *Moriarty*) (USA), based on Gillette's stage play with Moriarty played by Gustav von Seyffertitz, and directed by Albert Parker. In 1929 Carlyle Blackwell played Holmes in another German remake of *The Hound of the Baskervilles*. Also in 1929 Clive Brook played in a talkie, *The Return of Sherlock Holmes* (USA), with H. Reeves-Smith as Watson and Harry T. Morey as Professor Moriarty and directed by Basil Dean. Brook also appeared in a 1932 film entitled *Sherlock Holmes* with Reginald Owen as Watson and Ernest Torrence as Moriarty and directed by William K. Howard. Moriarty is sentenced to death, and Sherlock Holmes prepares to retire to the country and marry his girl [*sic*]. But Moriarty has sworn that Holmes, Lt-Col Gore-King of Scotland Yard, and his trial judge shall all be hanged too. When Moriarty escapes and proceeds to put his threat into operation, Holmes has to postpone his retirement.

Arthur Wontner, a perfect Holmes first played the role in *Sherlock Holmes' Final Hour* (**Fatal** in some books) (aka: The Sleeping Cardinal) (GB) 1931. Doctor Watson was played by Ian Fleming, and the director was Leslie S. Hiscott. Arthur Wontner later appeared in *The Sign of Four* (1932), *The Missing Rembrandt* (aka: *The Strange Case of the Missing Rembrandt, The Adventure of the Missing Rembrandt, Sherlock Holmes and the Missing Rembrandt* (1933), *The Triumph of Sherlock Holmes* (aka: *Valley of Fear* – Plot Summary: The detective uncovers an American secret society behind an apparent revenge murder. Holmes, retired to Sussex, is drawn into a last case when arch-enemy Moriarty arranges with an American gang to kill one John Douglas, a country gentleman with a mysterious past. Holmes' methods baffle Watson and Lestrade, but his results astonish them. In a long flashback, the victim's wife tells the story of the sinister Vermissa Valley (1935), and *The Silver Blaze* (1936). Raymond Massey was Holmes in *The Speckled Band* (GB) 1931, with Athole Stewart as Watson; in 1932 Robert Rendel was in *The Hound of the Baskervilles* (GB). Reginald Owen then played Holmes in *A Study in Scarlet* (US) 1933. The Germans made three more Holmes films in the mid-thirties, including yet another remake of *The Hound of the Baskervilles*. The other two films were *Sherlock Holmes* (aka: *Graue Dame, Die*, and *Sherlock Holmes und die graue Dame*), and *Der Mann, Der Sherlock Holmes War* (aka: *Zwei lustige Abenteurer*), both released in 1937. Starring Hans Albers as Sherlock Holmes, Heinz Ruhmann as Dr Watson and Paul Bildt as Sir Arthur Conan Doyle.

In 1939, by some genius of casting, Basil Rathbone and Nigel Bruce were signed to play Sherlock Holmes and Dr Watson in an adaptation of *The Hound of the Baskervilles* by Fox in Hollywood. Its immediate success prompted a follow-up that same year - *The Adventures of Sherlock Holmes*, (aka: *Sherlock Holmes*), in which Moriarty attempts to steal the Crown jewels from the Tower of London while sidetracking Holmes' attention by the mysterious murder of a girl being pursued by a clubfoot gaucho. George Zucco played Moriarty and it was directed by Alfred L.Werker, and was based on the play by William Gillette. These were beautiful, atmospheric productions, faithful to Doyle's stories. Two years later the series resumed with twelve "modern" films that never captured the flavour of the initial two (*The Scarlet Claw* came closest), but they were always worth seeing for the performances of the two stars: Rathbone – smooth, cunning, seldom caught by surprise; and Bruce – talkative, bumbling, never close to understanding the situation at hand. Every episode ended with a stirring ode by Holmes to the glory of England, America, Canada, or some comparable topic, in keeping with the wartime flag-waving nature of Hollywood films. Seldom faithful to Doyle, later episodes like *Dressed to Kill*, wearing thin, dialogue often awkward (*Sherlock Holmes in Washington*, for example), the Sherlock Holmes series relied on Rathbone and Bruce for enjoyment, and they never failed. The twelve films were as follows, and were directed by Roy William Neill, unless noted otherwise.

Sherlock Holmes and the Voice of Terror (1942) (aka: Sherlock Holmes Saves London (USA) & The Voice of Terror). Director: John Rawlins. Based on the story *His Last Bow*). England, and the start of WWII. Mysterious wireless broadcasts, apparently from Nazi Germany are heard over the BBC. They warn of acts of terror in England, just before they take place. Baffled, the Defence Committee call in Holmes.

Sherlock Holmes & The Secret Weapon (1942) (aka: Secret Weapon). Based on the story *The Dancing Men*. Starting in Switzerland, Sherlock Holmes rescues the inventor of a bomb-sight which the allies want to keep from the Nazis. Back in London, it seems that the inventor is not all that he seemed. Lionel Atwill is believingly malevolent as Holmes' arch enemy, the baleful Moriarty.

Sherlock Holmes in Washington (1942). In WWII, a British secret agent carrying a vitally important document is kidnapped en route to Washington. The British government calls on Sherlock Holmes to recover it. A contrived wartime flag-waver, probably the least convincing of the series.

Sherlock Holmes Faces Death (1943). During WWII several murders occur at a convalescent home where Dr. Watson has volunteered his services. He summons Holmes for help and the master detective proceeds to solve the crime from a long list of suspects including the owners of the home, the staff and the patients recovering there. With distinctive echoes from its Conan Doyle source story, *The Musgrave Ritual*, it's one of the most old fashioned of the series, which explains the craftsman-like grip it exerts.

Spider Woman (1944) (aka: Sherlock Holmes and the Spider woman). Based on the story *The Sign of Four*. In wartime Britain, Sherlock Holmes feigns death in order to investigate a spate of "pyjama suicides". His suspicions soon fall on the attractive but possibly deadly Andrea Spedding played by Gail Sondergaard. Poisonous gas is emitted from the fireplace of 221B Baker Street after she visits (see *The Devil's Foot*).

The Scarlet Claw (1944) (aka: Sherlock Holmes and the Scarlet Claw). Based on the "Sherlock Holmes" stories by Arthur Conan Doyle. Holmes and Watson investigate mysterious deaths by a murderous apparition that has reappeared after 100 years to terrorise a small village, La Mort Rouge, on the Canadian marshes. A tribute to Canada in wartime concludes the film.

Pearl of Death (1944) (aka: Sherlock Holmes and the Pearl of Death). Sherlock Holmes tracks down a famous pearl which is continually stolen, and the thieves responsible. Based on the story *The Six Napoleons*.

The House of Fear (1945) (aka: Sherlock Holmes and the House of Fear). Based on the story "The Five Orange Pips". Sherlock Holmes solves the series of murders of the Good Companions, all heavily insured in favour of the last surviving member.

The Woman in Green (1945) (aka: Invitation to Death. Sherlock Holmes and the Woman in Green). Holmes and Watson investigate a series of bizarre and apparently unconnected murders of young women who have their right forefinger removed. Holmes is called in after a man is blackmailed after spending the evening with a blond, and who is subsequently murdered. The trail leads to a society of hypnotists and the mysterious, glamorous, blond woman. She with Moriarty (played by Henry Daniell, who was reportedly hanged in Montevideo), are unmasked as leaders of the blackmail gang.

Pursuit to Algiers (1945) Holmes and Watson off to Scotland for some sun and fishing. Holmes notes that the late Moriarty "was a virtuoso on the bassoon"! Doctor Watson sings "Loch Lomond" and tells the story of Sherlock Holmes and the Giant Rat of Sumatra! A film that was hardly worth watching.

Terror by Night (1946) – About the transportation of the Star of Rhodesia diamond from London to Edinburgh.

Dressed to Kill (1946) (aka: Sherlock Holmes and the Secret Code. Sherlock Holmes in Dressed to Kill). A convicted thief in Dartmoor prison hides the location of the stolen Bank of England plates inside three music boxes. When the innocent purchasers of the boxes start to be murdered, Holmes and Watson investigate. The director was Roy William Neill and was the final appearance of Basil Rathbone as the famous sleuth and Nigel Bruce as Dr Watson (though Bruce happily continued playing Watson on radio for several years).

In 1954 a Franco-American TV series *"Sherlock Holmes"* starring Ronald Howard as Sherlock Holmes, Howard Marion-Crawford as Dr. John H. Watson and Archie Duncan as Inspector Lestrade.

In 1956 France produced *A la Maniere de Sherlock Holmes* (In the Manner/Style of Sherlock Holmes). It was directed by Henri Lepage and concerned a murder story set in Rouen. A British remake of *The Hound of the Baskervilles* with Peter Cushing and Andre Morell playing the leads was produced in 1959. It was shown on British television in August 2002 and the following are two reviews of the film.

Firstly by **Simon Horsford**, The Week in Films. **The Daily Telegraph**, Television and Radio Guide, August 24-30, 2002.

One of the best adaptations of the Sherlock Holmes story with all the necessary horrors of the Baskerville legend – and the dog from Hell. It's all deliciously Gothic as Holmes (Peter Cushing in terrific form) and Dr Watson (played with just the right touch by Andre Morell) stalk the house and foggy moors under the watchful eye of Sir Henry Baskerville (Christopher Lee). Under Terence Fisher's inventive direction, it couldn't really get much better. This was also the first version filmed in colour.

Secondly by **Yvette Huddleston**, Television mail. **Daily Mail**, Thursday, August 29, 2002.

Peter Cushing gives one of his best ever performances as Sherlock Holmes in the elegant Hammer Studios adaptation of the Conan Doyle novel. He is ably supported by Andre Morell as Dr Watson in a portrayal that is nicely underplayed; less bumbling and buffoonish than other well-known interpretations of the role. The eerie atmosphere is instantly established with Holmes and Watson being called out to Dartmoor following the mysterious slaying of Sir Charles Baskerville by what appears to be an enormous hound. Christopher Lee, as the heir to the Baskerville inheritance, is concerned that he may meet a similar fate and so it's up to the Baker Street duo to get to the bottom of the killing. Arguably the best Sherlock Holmes film made, this was a triumph for Hammer studios and that is due in no small part to Cushing's perfect casting in the lead.

In 1962 Christopher Lee and Thorley Walters played Holmes and Watson in a West German/Italian/French film *Sherlock Holmes und das Halsband des Todes* (aka: Sherlock Holmes and the Deadly Necklace. Sherlock Holmes et le colliere de la morte. Sherlock Holmes la valle del terrore. Valley of Fear). The directors were Terence Fisher and Frank Winterstein. Sherlock Holmes and Dr Watson try to solve the case of the stealing of Cleopatra's necklace, found by archaeologists in Egypt. They soon discover that the evil Professor Moriarty (played by Hans Sohnker) is behind it all. In 1965 John Neville and Donald Houston appeared in an original story involving the famous pair with Jack The Ripper: *A Study in Terror*. Also in 1965/66 a BBC TV series entitled "Sherlock Holmes" featuring Douglas Wilmer and Nigel Stock, with Peter Cushing later taking over as Holmes (1968). The 1965 series saw *The Disappearance of Lady Frances Carfax* (from 'His Last Bow'). 1966 saw *The Man with the Twisted* Lip (from 'The Adventures of Sherlock Holmes'). And 1968 saw *Shoscombe Old Place* (from 'The Case-Book of Sherlock Holmes'). The period atmosphere was carefully sought but the stories suffered from being padded out to the standard TV length.

In 1970 Billy Wilder produced and directed *The Private Life of Sherlock Holmes* with Robert Stephens as Sherlock Holmes, Colin Blakely as Watson and Christopher Lee as Mycroft Holmes. As the title suggests, Billy Wilder's neglected masterpiece concentrated more on the super-sleuth's emotions than his phenomenal powers of deduction (perhaps why it was such a box-office flop). But Robert Stephen's melancholy Holmes was surely the missing link between Basil Rathbone and Jeremy Brett, as for once the great man is distracted by affairs of the heart. This was apparently intended as a send-up but produced only a further pleasant variation. The complicated case involved a vanishing husband, six missing dwarves, dead canaries and the Loch Ness monster! In the same year, George C. Scott thought he was Sherlock Holmes in *They Might Be Giants* (as did Larry Hagman in the 1976 TV movie *The Return of the World's Greatest Detective*. Hagman gave Arthur Conan Doyle's infallible sleuth a comedy update. Unfortunately, as the LA cop who is convinced he is Sherlock Holmes, he shows little comic timing. The director was Dean Hargrove). 1971 saw a Czechoslovakian film entitled *Touha Sherlocka Holmese* (trans: Longing of Sherlock Holmes). Directed by Stepan Stalsky and starring Radovan Lukavsky as Holmes. A four episode film in which Sherlock Holmes was depicted as a violinist and detective who is never sure whether his real mission in life is to join the world of art or the sphere of criminology. In the same year, a TV series. *The Rivals of Sherlock Holmes* was produced.

1972 saw a TV version of *The Hound of the Baskervilles* starring Stewart Granger as Holmes and Bernard Fox as Watson. It was directed by Barry Crane. A poorly scripted TV pilot for a proposed Sherlock Holmes TV series was appallingly directed with no sense of atmosphere whatsoever. In 1975 Gene Wilder directed a spoof *The Adventure of Sherlock Holmes' Smarter Brother* (aka: Sherlock Holmes' Smarter Brother). Gene Wilder plays Sherlock Holmes' younger brother Sigerson, who is annoyed that he has to live in Sherlock's shadow for so long. When Sherlock (played by Douglas Wilmer) goes to the continent, he sends a case to his brother who constantly tries with varying success, to imitate Sherlock's deductive and observational tricks. Thorley Walters plays Dr Watson and Leo McKern is Moriarty. Nicol Williamson as Holmes was treated by Sigmund Freud in 1976's *The Seven Percent Solution*. Robert Duvall played Watson, Laurence Olivier was Moriarty and the film was directed by Herbert Ross. In the same year Roger Moore dons the deerstalker and pipe to play master sleuth Sherlock Holmes in *Sherlock Holmes in New York* (TV). Holmes is lured to New York by some theatre tickets supposedly sent by an actress with whom he's in love (Irene Adler). There he discovers Moriarty (John Huston) at the bottom of a kidnapping of her son and a plot to steal the world's gold supply. Dr Watson was played by Patrick Macnee and the director was Boris Sagal. An eyebrow was raised when old ham Roger Moore was cast as the great Victorian detective in this amiable spoof. Grizzled John Huston was also an odd bit of casting as Holmes' arch enemy Professor Moriarty. It was the half-serious, half-jokey atmosphere that was most interesting.

In 1978 there was a perfectly ghastly, supposedly comic *The Hound of the Baskervilles* with Peter Cook and Dudley Moore. Andy Warhol's one time collaborator, Paul Morrissey, directed this woeful lampoon of Arthur Conan Doyle's celebrated story. Peter Cook played the Baker Street sleuth while Dudley Moore's trio of roles included the doggedly dim Watson and Holmes' mother. Never did the comedy double act look so bereft of inspiration, however, as gag after gag falls flat, despite the supportive ministrations of such comic geniuses as Spike Milligan, Kenneth Williams, Terry-Thomas, Irene Handl, Max Wall and Roy Kinnear. These made an irresistible cast, but spoofing ends up further over the top than the fog. Morrissey is a notoriously unpredictable director, but in this case it's the shoddy screenplay, co-written by Morrissey, Cook and Moore, that is to blame.

In the same year Christopher Plummer as Holmes and James Mason as Watson starred in *Murder by Decree* (aka: Sherlock Holmes and Saucy Jack, Sherlock Holmes: Murder by Decree) directed by Bob Clark. Sherlock Holmes investigates London's most infamous case, Jack the Ripper. As he investigates, he finds that the Ripper has friends in high places. Christopher Plummer also starred as Holmes in a 1979 TV version of *Silver Blaze*.

1979 brought another TV series with Geoffrey Whitehead and Donald Pickering; but *Sherlock Holmes and Doctor Watson* was barely seen outside Poland where it was shot. Russia then produced three films directed by Igor Maslennikov and featuring Vasili Livanov as Sherlock Holmes and Vitali Solomin as Doctor Watson. These were entitled *Sherlok Holms i doktor Vatson* (aka: Sherlock Holmes and Dr. Watson) (1979) TV; *Priklyuucheniya Sherloka Holmsa i doktora Vatsona* (aka: Adventures of Sherlock Holmes and Dr. Watson) (1980) TV; and *Sherlock Holmes v dvadtsatom veki* (aka: 20th Century Begins, Sherlock Holmes in the 20th Century).

In 1983 Sy Weintraub made TV movies of *The Sign of Four* and *The Hound of the Baskervilles*. Director Desmond Davis' adaptation of Conan Doyle's novel saw Ian Richardson tackling the sometimes troublesome role of Sherlock Holmes. To his credit, Richardson turned in an impressive performance, and, along with his trusty sidekick Dr Watson (David Healy), set out to track down the stolen 'Great Mogul' – the second largest diamond in the world. Major Sholto (Thorley Walters) excelled as the villain at the centre of a plot bursting with murder and deception – the staple diet of any crime film fanatic. An ingenious solution coupled with some great scenes (the midnight chase along the Thames for instance) made this film well worth a watch. Unlike many attempts to bring Britain's most famous detective to the screen, Davis' came very close to the mark. Tom Baker starred in a BBC serial of *The Hound of the Baskervilles* in the same year. 1984 saw the release of the TV movie *The Murder of Sherlock Holmes* directed by Corey Allen. This was a pilot film for a detective series (USA) starring Angela Lansbury as Jessica Fletcher who played a best-selling detective story novelist who solved mysteries for real. (The series entitled "Murder, She Wrote" is still being repeated on BBC as late as 2010).

In the same year *Sherlock Holmes and the Masks of Death* (TV) was released starring Peter Cushing as Holmes and John Mills as Watson. Here Sherlock Holmes has retired, but when MacDonald asks him to take on another case, he says yes. There have been some mysterious murders, and there are no visible causes for the deaths. At the same time Graf Udo Von Felseck (played by Anton Diffring) gives him another case: find a young and missing prince to prevent war between Germany and England. But Von Felseck is not as honest as he seems.

1985 saw the film *Young Sherlock Holmes* (aka: Young Sherlock Holmes and the Pyramid of Fear). Directed by Barry Levinson and starring Nicholas Rowe as Sherlock Holmes and Alan Cox as John Watson with Roger Ashton-Griffiths as Lestrade. Here Sherlock Holmes and Dr Watson meet as boys in an English boarding school. Holmes is known for his deductive ability even as a youth, amazing his classmates with his abilities. When they discover a plot to murder a series of British women by an Egyptian cult, they move to stop it.

In 1984 Granada TV had a 13-hour series starring Jeremy Brett and David Burke. This highly detailed series recreated the adventures of Conan Doyle's Victorian detective in painstaking detail, sometimes to the extent of recreating the illustrations which accompanied the original story publication in the "Strand" magazine during the late 19th century. These 13 short stories were followed by three sequels – " The Adventures of Sherlock Holmes" (1985), " The Return of Sherlock Holmes" (1986/7/8) and "The Casebook of Sherlock Holmes" (1990). *The Return of Sherlock Holmes* (1986) saw Edward Hardwicke replace David Burke. Dr Watson finds a mystery in 'The Empty House', while Holmes and he solve the mysteries of 'The Abbey Grange', 'The Musgrave Ritual', 'The Second Stain', 'The Man with the Twisted Lip', 'The Priory School' and 'The Six Napoleons'.

1987 saw the TV production of *Sign of Four*. After the disappearance of her father, Miss Mary Morstan (Jenny Seagrove) receives a beautiful pearl every year and a mysterious, anonymous message. On the day of her summons by her benefactor, she arrives at 221B baker Street to consult Sherlock Holmes. He and Dr Watson piece together a series of clues and embark on a chase along London's streets and waterways in pursuit of a priceless hoard of Indian treasure – and the murderer whose ominous trademark is 'The Sign of Four'. 1987/88 saw two versions of *The Return of Sherlock Holmes*, the 1987 TV version with Michael Pennington as Holmes. The 1988 version starred Brett and Hardwicke as Holmes and Watson. Here, the great detective and his companion solved the mysteries of The Devil's Foot, Silver Blaze, Wisteria Lodge and The Bruce-

Partington Plans. Also in the same year, the two returned in the TV version of *The Hound of the Baskervilles*. Then came *Hands of a Murderer* (1990 TV) (aka: Sherlock Holmes and the Prince of Crime). Starring Edward Woodward as Holmes and John Hillerman as Watson. *The Casebook of Sherlock Holmes* (1990) saw Brett and Hardwicke solving the mysteries Disappearance of Lady Frances Carfax, Thor Bridge, Shoscombe Old Place, The Boscombe Valley Mystery, The Illustrious Client and The Creeping Man.

The same year saw a TV production entitled *Sherlock Holmes and the Leading Lady*. Here Christopher Lee played Sherlock Holmes and Patrick Macnee Dr Watson. Irene Adler turned up (played by Morgan Fairchild), as well as Sigmund Freud (again!) and Elliott Ness (The Untouchables! TV and film).

They both reappeared in 1991 in *Incident at Victoria Falls* (aka: Sherlock Holmes and the Incident at Victoria Falls; Sherlock Holmes: Incident at Victoria Falls; Sherlock Holmes: The Star of Africa; and The Star of Africa. Lily Langtree, King Edward and Teddy Roosevelt were all involved! 1991 also saw the TV production of *Sherlock Holmes: The Master Blackmailer*. A special two- hour film in the Sherlock Holmes series. Here Sherlock Holmes finds some of his cases become entwined and have at their root the ruthless blackmailer Charles Augustus Milverton (played by Robert Hardy) who has brought downfall and misery to numerous members of high society. Holmes finds employment in Milverton's house and tries to get hold of the incriminating letters held by Milverton.

The same year saw *Sherlock Holmes in San Francisco* and *Sherlock Holmes in Caracas* (Venezuela). Sherlock Holmes was played by Jean Manuel Montesinos and Dr Watson by Gilbert Dacouran. A satirical/comedy film with Holmes and Watson finding themselves in ludicrous situations and a fantastical case including a pagan-loving governess and an ex-Miss Venezuela who turns out to be a vampire!

1991 saw a new Sherlock Holmes and Dr Watson in *The Crucifer of Blood* (based on The Sign of Four). Holmes being played by Charlton Heston, Watson by Richard Johnson and Inspector Lestrade by Simon Callow. In 1993 *Sherlock Holmes Returns* was produced. Here, Anthony Higgins as Holmes, is awakened in modern times with a tale that he had invented a method of suspended animation that he had utilised on himself. Awakened he is joined by a new group of Baker Street Irregulars led by Zapper. His battles lead him to the evil Moriarty clan led by James Moriarty Booth who lives at 1994 Baker Street in San Francisco. (Dr Watson appears to have been missing in this film). Patrick Macnee returned the same year (but this time playing Sherlock Holmes rather than Dr Watson), in *Hound of London* (aka: Sherlock Holmes in The Hound of London).

1994 saw Brett and Hardwicke reprise their roles for the last time in *Memoirs of Sherlock Holmes*. Holmes, his friend Watson (or his brother Mycroft, played by Charles Gray) work to solve the mysteries of Three Gables, The Dying Detective, The Golden Pince-Nez, The Red Circle, The Mazarin Stone and The Cardboard Box.

There was a gap until 1997 when two films were made in the USA based upon **The Cottingley Fairies** (as noted in Chapter 1, page 10). One was titled *Fairy Tale: a True Story* and was directed by Charles Sturridge. It was a family tale based on the true story of two young girls who, in 1917 produced photographs of a group of winged, fairy-like creatures they had taken at the bottom of their garden. The story follows the subsequent controversy, as luminaries such as Sir Arthur Conan Doyle (Peter O'Toole) and Harry

Houdini (Harvey Keitel) debated the authenticity of the pictures. It was beautifully filmed, and infused with a sense of wonder. The second film was titled *Photographing Fairies*, where Sir Arthur Conan Doyle was portrayed by Edward Hardwicke.[8]

The final Sherlock Holmes film was *Without a Clue* produced in 1988 and directed by Thom Eberhardt. A farcical tale on the Sherlock Holmes stories. The premise that Sherlock Holmes was really a drunken actor, Reginald Kincaid (played by Michael Caine) hired by Dr Watson (Ben Kingsley) to impersonate his creation is the one-joke idea behind this lamentably elementary spoof. Professor Moriarty was played by Paul Freeman, Inspector Lestrade by Jeffrey Jones and Mrs Hudson by Pat Keen.

---

[8] The photographs taken by Elsie Wright and Frances Griffiths certainly existed. They were sold at auction in 1998, along with other items from Griffith's collection, for a total of £21,620.

Chapter 8

The Principal Characters – Actors & Actresses

Research for this chapter identified 98 Sherlock Holmes, 73 Dr Watson, 38 Inspector Lestrade, 17 Mrs Hudson and 35 Professor Moriarty

Sherlock Holmes

Maurice Costello
1905 *Sherlock Holmes Held for a Ransom* (USA)

F. Holger-Madsen
1908 *The Adventures of Sherlock Holmes* (12 Danish)

Viggo Larsen
1909 *Den Graa dame* (aka The Grey Dame/Lady)

Georges Treville
1912 *Mystere de Val Boscombe* (3 French)

Harry Benham
1913 *Sherlock Holmes Solves The Sign of The Four* (USA)

Frederick Paul
1914 *A Study in Scarlet*
1916 *Valley of Fear*

James Bragington
1914 *A Study in Scarlet*

Francis Ford
1914/II *A Study in Scarlet*

Alwin Neub
1914 I & II *The Hound of the Baskervilles*
1915 I & II *The Hound of the Baskervilles*

Eugen Burg
1915 *Dunkle Schlob* (aka The Hound of the Baskervilles)

William Gillette
1916 *Sherlock Holmes*

1939 *The Adventures of Sherlock Holmes*

Hugo Flink
1917 (3 German)

Ferdinand Bonn
1918 (1 German)

Willy Kaiser-Heyl
1920 *Der Hund Von Baskerville*

John Barrymore
1922 *Sherlock Holmes* (aka Moriarty, UK)

Eille Norwood
1920-1923 Starred as Sherlock Holmes in a total of 47 films

Clive Brook
1929 *The Return of Sherlock Holmes*
1930 *Paramount on Parade: Himself and Sherlock Holmes*
1932 *Sherlock Holmes*

Martin Fric
1932 (1 Czechoslovakia)

Reginald Owen
1932 *Sherlock Holmes*
1933 *A Study in Scarlet*

Arthur Wontner
1931 *Sherlock Holmes's Fatal Hour* (aka The Sleeping Cardinal)
1932 *The Missing Rembrandt* (aka Sherlock Holmes and the Missing Rembrandt USA)
1932 *The Triumph of Sherlock Holmes* (aka The Valley of Fear)
1937 *Silver Blaze* (aka Murder at the Baskervilles 1941, USA)

Raymond Massey
1931 *The Speckled Band*

Robert Rendell
1932 *The Hound of the Baskervilles*

Archie Hunter
1933 *The Blue Carbuncle*

Hans Albers
1937 *Der Man, der Sherlock Holmes war* (The Man Who Was Sherlock Holmes)

Louis Hector
1937 *The Three Garridebs* (TV)

Bruno Guttner/Siegfried Schurenberg
1937 *Hund von Baskerville, Der*

Basil Rathbone
1939 *The Adventures of Sherlock Holmes*
    The Hound of the Baskervilles
1942 *Sherlock Holmes and the Voice of Terror*
1943 *Sherlock Holmes and the Secret Weapon*
    Sherlock Holmes in Washington
    Sherlock Holmes Faces Death
1944 *The Spider Woman*
    The Scarlet Claw
    The Pearl of Death
1945 *The House of Fear*
    The Woman in Green
    Pursuit to Algiers
1946 *Terror by Night*
    Dressed to Kill (aka Sherlock Holmes and the Secret Code UK)

Jose Baviera
1947 *Arsenio Lupin*

Alan Napier
1949 *The Adventure of the Speckled Band*

John Longden
1951 *Sherlock Holmes: The Man Who Disappeared* (aka The Man with the Twisted Lip)

Alan Wheatley
1951 *The Second Stain*
    The Red-Headed League
    The Reigate Squires
    The Dying Detective
    A Scandal in Bohemia

Basil Rathbone
1953 *The Adventure of the Black Baronet* (TV)

Ronald Howard
1955 *Sherlock Holmes* (TV Series) (aka The Adventures of Sherlock Holmes)
    The Case of the Tyrant's Daughter
    The Case of the Diamond Tooth
    The Case of the Unlucky Gambler

The Case of the Neurotic Detective
The Case of the Haunted Gainsborough

Ernst Fritz Furbringer
1954 (1 German)

Wolf Ackva
1955 *Hund von Baskerville, Der* (TV)

Christopher Lee
1962 *The Speckled Band*
    Sherlock Holmes and the Deadly Necklace

Peter Cushing
1959 *The Hound of the Baskervilles* (TV)
1964 *A Study in Scarlet* (TV Series)
    The Boscombe Valley Mystery
    The Sign of Four
    The Blue Carbuncle
1968 *Wisteria Lodge* (TV)
    Shoscombe Old Place (TV)
    The Solitary Cyclist (TV)
    The Sign of Four (TV)
    The Blue Carbuncle (TV)
    The Hound of the Baskervilles (TV)
1984 *Sherlock Holmes and the Masks of Death* (TV) + 23 More

Jerome Raphael
1965 *The Doubled-Barrelled Detective Story*

John Neville
1965 *A Study in Terror*

Nando Gazzolo
1968 *The Hound of the Baskervilles* (TV)
    The Valley of Fear (TV)
    Sherlock Holmes (TV)

Erich Schellow
1968 (6 German)

Peter Jeffrey
1969 *The Best House in London*

Robert Stephens
1970 *The Private Life of Sherlock Holmes*

George C. Scott
1970 *They Might Be Giants*

Radovan Lukavsky
1971 *The Longing of Sherlock Holmes* (Czechoslovakia)

Stewart Granger
1972 *The Hound of the Baskervilles*

Douglas Wilmer
1964 *Sherlock Holmes* (TV Series)
1975 *The Adventure of Sherlock Holmes' Smarter Brother*

Rolf Becker
1974 *The Sign of Four* (TV)
      Le signe des quatre TV)

Raymond Gerome
1974 *Le Chien des Baskerville* (TV)

Roger Moore
1976 *Sherlock Holmes in New York* (TV)

Nicol Williamson
1976 *The Seven-Per-Cent Solution*

Larry Hagman
1976 *The Return of the World's Greatest Detective* (US TVM)

John Cleese
1973 *Elementary My Dear Watson* (TV)
1977 (as Arthur Sherlock Holmes) *The Strange Case of the End of Civilisation as We Know It*

Peter Cook
1978 *The Hound of the Baskervilles*

Christopher Plummer
1977 *Silver Blaze*
1979 *Murder by Decree*

Algimantas Masiulis
1979 *The Blue Carbuncle* (Soviet Union)

Geoffrey Whitehead
1979 *Sherlock Holmes and Dr. Watson* (TV Series 23 Episodes Poland)

Keith McConnell
1980 *The Treasure of Alpheus T. Winterburn*

Frank Langella
1981 *The Strange Case of Alice Faulkner* (TV)

Peter O'Toole
1983 *Sherlock Holmes and the Baskerville Curse*
    Sherlock Holmes and the Sign of Four
    Sherlock Holmes and A Study in Scarlet
    Sherlock Holmes and The Valley of Fear

Taichiro Hirokawa
1984 *The Evil Genius, Professor Moriarty* (TV)
    He's the Famous Detective (TV)

Fat Chung
1984 *The Return of Pom Pom* (HK)

Guy Rolfe
1984 *The Case of Marcel Duchamp*

Peter Evans
1984 *Elementary Steele* (from "Remington Steele" TV)

Nicholas Rowe
1985 *Young Sherlock Holmes*

Jeremy Brett (1) [Starred in a total of 41 Granada TV dramatisations]
1984/85 *The Adventures of Sherlock Holmes* (Australia TV)
    The Greek Interpreter
    The Norwood Builder
    The Resident Patient
    The Red-Headed League
    The Final Problem

Vasili Livanov
1986 *The Adventures of Sherlock Holmes and Dr. Watson*

James Downey
1986 *The Replacements* (TV)

Michael Pennington
1987 *The Return of Sherlock Holmes* (TV)

Jeremy Brett (2)
The Return of Sherlock Holmes

1986 *The Six Napoleons* (TV)
1987 *The Sign of Four* (TV)
1988 *The Return of Sherlock Holmes*
    The Devil's Foot (TV)
    Silver Blaze (TV)
    Wisteria Lodge (TV)
    The Bruce-Partington Plans (TV)
    The Hound of the Baskervilles (TV)

Rodney Litchfield
1988 *Testimony* (West Germany)

Michael Caine
1988 *Without a Clue*

Brian Bedford
1989 *My Dear Watson*

Edward Woodward
1990 *Hands of a Murderer*

Charlton Heston
1991 *The Crucifer of Blood*

Juan Manuel Montesinos
1991 *Sherlock Holmes in Caracas*

Rupert Frazer
1991 *The Consulting Detective Mystery* (from 'The Father Dowling Mysteries' TV Series)

Anthony Higgins
1993 *Sherlock Holmes Returns* (TV)

Patrick Macnee
1993 *The Hound of London* (TV)

Jeremy Brett (3)
The Case-Book of Sherlock Holmes
1991 *The Illustrious Client*
1991 *The Creeping Man*
1992 *The Master Blackmailer*
1993 *The Last Vampyre*
1993 *The Eligible Bachelor*

Radoslav Brzobomaty
1993 (Czechoslovakia)

Fan Al Li
1994 *Sherlock Holmes and the Chinese Heroine* (China)

Jeremy Brett (4)
The Memoirs of Sherlock Holmes
1994 *The Dying Detective* (TV)
    The Golden Pince-Nez (TV)
    The Red Circle (TV)
    The Mazarin Stone (TV)
    The Cardboard Box (TV)

Francisco Moran
1996 *Oscar y Sherlock* (TV)

Rheal Guevremont
1997 *J'en Suis!* (TV)

Jason Grey-Stanford
1999 *Sherlock Holmes in the 22nd Century* (TV)

Joaquim de Almeida
2001 *The Xango from Baker Street*

Herve Ganem
2001 *Sherlock Holmes a Trouville*

Matt Frewer
2000 *The Hound of the Baskervilles*
2001 *The Royal Scandal (in Bohemia)*
2001 *The Sign of Four*
2002 *The Case of the Whitechapel Vampire*
(TVM Canada)

Richard Roxburgh
2002 *The Hound of the Baskervilles* (TV)

James D'Arcy
2002 *A Case of Evil* (TV)
2002 *Sherlock* (TVM)

Rupert Everett
2004 *The Case of the Silk Stocking* (TV)

Ted Rooney
2005 *Who Shot Sherlock*

Eugenio Monclova
2005 (TV)

Johnathan Pryce
2007 *Sherlock Holmes And The Baker Street Irregulars* (TV)

Humphrey Ker
2007 *I Am Bob*

Benedict Cumberbatch
2009 *Sherlock*

Robert Downey Jr
2009 *Sherlock Holmes*

Dr. John H. Watson

H. Kyrle Bellew
1905 *Held for a Ransom* (USA)

Alwin Neuss
1908 The 12 Danish Holmes films

Charles Gunn
1913 *Sherlock Holmes Solves The Sign of the Four*

John Ford
1914 *A Study in Scarlet*

Edward Fielding
1916 *Sherlock Holmes*

Hubert Willis
1920-1923 Appeared in 45 Sherlock Holmes films

Roland Young
1922 *Sherlock Holmes*

Arthur M. Cullin
1923 *The Valley of Fear*

H. Reeves-Smith
1929 *The Return of Sherlock Holmes* (USA)

George Seroff
1929 *The Hound of the Baskervilles*

Ian Fleming
1931 *The Sleeping Cardinal* (aka Sherlock Holmes' Fatal Hour) (USA)
1932 *The Missing Rembrandt* (aka Sherlock Holmes and the Missing Rembrandt) (USA)
1935 *The Triumph of Sherlock Holmes*
1937 *Silver Blaze* (aka Murder at the Baskervilles) (USA)

Athole Stewart
1931 *The Speckled Band*

Reginald Owen
1932 *Sherlock Holmes*

Frederick Lloyd
1932 *The Hound of the Baskervilles*

Ian Hunter
1932 *The Sign of Four*

Warburton Gamble
1933 *A Study in Scarlet*

Fritz Odemar
1937 *Hund von Baskerville, Der*

William Podmore
1937 *The Three Garridebs* (TV)

Heinz Ruhmann
1937 *The Man Who Was Sherlock Holmes*

Nigel Bruce
1939-1946 Appeared in 14 Sherlock Holmes films

Campbell Singer
1951 *The Man with the Twisted Lip*

Raymond Francis
1951 Appeared in 6 Sherlock Holmes stories

Martyn Green
1953 *The Adventure of the Black Baronet* (TV)

Harald Manni
1954 (German TV)

Amulf Schroder
1955 *The Hound of the Baskervilles*

Andre Morell
1959 *The Hound of the Baskervilles*

Thorley Walters
1962 *Sherlock Holmes and the Deadly Necklace*
1969 *The Best House in London*
1975 *The Adventure of Sherlock Holmes' Smarter Brother*
1977 *Silver Blaze* (TV)

Nigel Stock
1964-1968 TV Series – 30 Episodes

Donald Houston

1965 *A Study in Terror*

Gianni Bonagura
1968 *The Hound of theBaskervilles* & *The Valley of Fear* Italian TV

Paul Edwin Roth
1968 German TV 6 Episodes

Colin Blakely
1970 *The Private Life of Sherlock Holmes*

Vaclav Vosca
1971 *Sherlock Holmes*

Bernard Fox
1972 *The Hound of the Baskervilles*

William Rushton
1973 *Elementary My Dear Watson*

Roger Lumont
1974 *The Sign of Four* (German TV)

Andre Haber
1974 *The Hound of the Baskervilles* (French TV)

Patrick Macnee
1976 *Sherlock Holmes in New York* (TV)
1992 *Incident at Victoria Falls* (TV)
  Sherlock Holmes and the Leading Lady (TV)

Robert Duvall
1976 *The Seven-Per-Cent solution*

Dudley Moore
1978 *The Hound of the Baskervilles*

Vitali Solomin
1979-1986 TV 9 Episodes (Soviet Union)

James Mason
1979 *Murder by Decree*

Donald Pickering
1979 *Sherlock Holmes and Dr. Watson* (TV) 23 Episodes

Laurie Main
1980 *The Treasure of Alpheus T. Winterborn* (TV)

David Healey
1981 *The Sign of Four*

Richard Woods
1981 *Sherlock Holmes* (TV)

Donald O'Connor
1982 *Save Sherlock Holmes* (TV)

Terence Rigby
1982 *The Hound of the Baskervilles* (TV Series)

Donald Churchill
1983 *The Hound of the Baskervilles*

Hubert Rees
1983 *The Baker Street Boys*

Kousei Tomita
1984 TV Episodes (2)

John Mills
1984 *Sherlock Holmes and the Masks of Death*

Lewis Arquette
1984 *Sherlock Holmes, the Detective*

David Burke
1985 *The Adventures of Sherlock Holmes* TV Episodes (13) Australia
1995 *Sherlock Holmes: The Great Detective* (TV Episode)

Alan Cox
1985 *Young Sherlock Holmes* (aka Pyramid of Fear)

Laurie Main
1986 *The Great Mouse Detective*

Edward Hardwicke
1987-1994 TV Episodes (28)

Ben Kingsley
1988 *Without a Clue*

Derek Waring

1989 *Sherlock Holmes* (TV Series)

Patrick Monkton
1989 *My Dear Watson*

John Hillerman
1990 *Hands of a Murderer*

Richard Johnson
1991 *The Crucible of Blood*

Gilbert Dacourman
1991 *Sherlock Holmes in Caracas*

John Scott-Paget
1993 *The Hound of London* (TV)

John Payne
1999 *Sherlock Holmes in the 22nd Century*

Kenneth Welsh
2000 *The Hound of the Baskervilles*
2001 *The Sign of Four*
    The Royal Scandal
2002 *The Case of the Whitechapel Vampire* – All TVM Canada

Ian Hart
2002 *The Hound of the Baskervilles* (TV)
2004 *Sherlock Holmes and the Case of the Silk Stocking* (TV)

Roger Morlidge
2002 *Sherlock* (TVM)

Phil Vischer
2006 *Sherlock Holmes and the Golden Ruler*

Bill Paterson
2007 *Sherlock Holmes and the Baker Street Irregulars* (TV)

Jim Piddock
2008 *Batman: The Brave and the Bold*

Martin Freeman
2009 *Sherlock*

Jude Law
2009 *Sherlock Holmes*

Inspector Lestrade

Arthur Bell
1921 *The Tiger of San Pedro*
    The Resident Patient
    The Empty House
    The Noble Bachelor

Tom Beaumont
1923 *The Cardboard Box*

Philip Hewland
1931 *Sherlock Holmes' Fatal Hour* (aka The Sleeping Cardinal)
1932 *The Missing Rembrandt* (aka Sherlock Holmes and the Missing Rembrant USA)

Alan Mowbray
1933 *A Study in Scarlet*

Charles Mortimer
1935 *The Triumph of Sherlock Holmes*

John Turnbull
1937 *Silver Blaze* (aka Murder at the Baskervilles USA)

Dennis Hoey
1942 *Sherlock Holmes and the Secret Weapon*
1943 *Sherlock Holmes Faces Death*
1944 *Sherlock Holmes and the Spider Woman*
    Sherlock Holmes and the Pearl of Death
1945 *Sherlock Holmes and the House of Fear*
1946 *Terror by Night*

Archie Duncan
1955 *Sherlock Holmes* TV Series 28 Episodes

Peter Madden
1965 *Sherlock Holmes* TV Series 4 Episodes

Frank Finlay
1965 *A Study in Terror*
1979 *Murder by Decree*

Hans Schellbach
1968 German TV 3 Episodes

William Lucas
1968 *A Study in Scarlet* (TV)

Alan Caillou
1972 *The Hound of the Baskervilles* (TV)

Dieter Kirchtechner
1974 *The Sign of Four* (German)

Bronislav Brondukov
1979-1986 Soviet Union TV 8 Episodes

Patrick Newell
1980 *Sherlock Holmes and Dr. Watson* (TV)

Hubert Rees
1982 *The Hound of the Baskervilles* (TV)

Ian Abercrombie
1982 *Save Sherlock Holmes* (TV)

Ronald Lacey
1983 *The Hound of the Baskervilles*

Stanley Lebor
1983 *The Baker Street Boys* (TV)

Gerry Gibson
1983 *Voyagers! Jack's Back*

Roger Ashton-Griffiths
1985 *Young Sherlock Holmes*

Colin Jeavons
1984/5 *The Adventures of Sherlock Holmes* (TV Series)
1986 *The Return of Sherlock Holmes* (TV 3 Episodes)
1990 *The Case-Book of Sherlock Holmes* (TV 2 Episodes)
1992 *Sherlock Holmes and the Master Blackmailer* (TV)

Jeffrey Jones
1988 *Without a Clue*

Alan Shearman
1988 *Elementary, Dear Data* (TV)

John Colicos
1989 *My Dear Watson* (TV)

Terence Lodge
1990 *Hands of a Murderer* (TV)

Simon Callow
1991 *The Crucifer of Blood*

Kenway Baker
1992 *Incident at Victoria Falls* (TV)

Colin Skinner
1993 *The Hound of London* (TV)

Akiko Morison
1999 *Sherlock Holmes in the 22nd Century*

Julian Casey
2001 *The Royal Scandal* (TV)
2002 *The Case of the Whitechapel Vampire* (TV)

Danny Webb
2002 *The Hound of the Baskervilles*

Nicholas Gecks
2002 *Sherlock* (TV)

Neil Dudgeon
2004 *Sherlock Holmes and the Case of the Silk Stocking* (TV)

Rupert Graves
2009 *Sherlock*

Eddie Marsan
2009 *Sherlock Holmes*

Mrs Hudson

Madame E'Sterre
Early 1920s with Eille Norwood

Minnie Rayner
1931 *Sherlock Holmes' Fatal Hour* (aka The Sleeping Cardinal)
1932 *The Missing Rembrandt*
1935 *The Triumph of Sherlock Holmes*
1937 *Silver Blaze*

Mary Gordon
1939 *The Adventures of Sherlock Holmes*
1942 *Sherlock Holmes and the Voice of Terror*
1943 *Sherlock Holmes Faces Death*
1944 *Sherlock Holmes and the Spider Woman*
1944 *Sherlock Holmes and the Pearl of Death*
1945 *The Woman in Green*
1946 *Dressed to Kill*

Edith Schultz-Westrum
1962 *Sherlock Holmes and the Deadly Necklace*

Irene Handl
1970 *The Private Life of Sherlock Holmes*

Marjorie Bennett
1976 *Sherlock Holmes in New York*

Betty Woolfe
1979 *Murder by Decree*

Rina Zelyonava
1979-1986 (Soviet Union)

Rosalie Williams
1984/85 *The Adventures of Sherlock Holmes* (TV Series)
1986/88 *The Return of Sherlock Holmes* (TV Series)
1987 *The Sign of Four* (TV)
1990 *The Case-Book of Sherlock Holmes* (TV Series)
1992 *Sherlock Holmes and the Master Blackmailer* (TV)
1994 *The Memoirs of Sherlock Holmes* (TV Series)

Jenny Laird
1984 *Sherlock Holmes and the Masks of Death* (TV)

Pat Keen
1988 *Without a Clue*

Faith Kent
1990 *Hands of a Murderer* (TV)

Sophie Thornley
1993 *The Hound of London*

Kathleen McAuliffe
2001 *The Sign of Four* (TVM Canada)

Anne Carroll
2004 *Sherlock Holmes and the Case of the Silk Stocking*

Geraldine James
2009 *Sherlock Holmes*

Una Stubbs
2009 *Sherlock*

Professor James Moriarty

Ernest Maupain (aka Maupin)
1916 *Sherlock Holmes*

Booth Conway
1916 *The Valley of Fear*

Gustav von Seyffertitz
1922 *Sherlock Holmes* (aka Moriarty) UK

Percy Standing
1923 *The Final Problem*

Harry T. Morey
1929 *The Return of Sherlock Holmes* (USA)

Norman (aka Robert) McKinnell
1931 *The Sleeping Cardinal* (aka Sherlock Holmes' Final (or Fatal) Hour (USA)

Ernest Torrence
1932 *Sherlock Holmes*

Jack Macreath
1933 *The Hound of London*

Lyn Harding
1931 *The Speckled Band*
1935 *The Triumph of Sherlock Holmes*
1937 *Silver Blaze* (aka Murder at the Baskervilles 1941 USA)

George Zucco
1939 *The Adventures of Sherlock Holmes* (aka Sherlock Holmes UK)

Lionel Atwill
1942 *Sherlock Holmes and the Secret Weapon* (aka Secret Weapon) USA

Henry Daniell
1945 *The Woman in Green* (aka Sherlock Holmes and the Woman in Green) USA
Hans Sohnker
1962 *Sherlock Holmes and the Deadly Necklace* (USA)

Spike Milligan
1963 *The Telegoons* (TV)
1968 *The Goon Show* (TV)

Bill Maynard

1973 *Elementary My Dear Watson* (TV)

Leo McKern
1975 *The Adventure of Sherlock Holmes' Smarter Brother*

John Huston
1976 *Sherlock Holmes in New York* (TV)

Laurence Olivier
1976 *The Seven-Per-Cent Solution*

Victor Yevgrafov
1980 *The Adventures of Sherlock Holmes and Dr. Watson*

George Morfogen
1981 *Sherlock Holmes* (TV)

Mel Ferrer
1982 *Save Sherlock Holmes* – Episode of Fantasy Island (TV Series)

Francois Maistre
1982 *Sherlock Holmes* (TV)

Colin Jeavons
1983 *The Adventure of the Winged Scarab* from *The Baker Street Boys* (Children's TV Series)

Eric Porter
1984/85 *The Adventures of Sherlock Holmes* (TV Series 2 Episodes) Australia
1986 *The Return of Sherlock Holmes* (TV)

Hamilton Camp
1985 *Sherlock Holmes, the Detective* (TV 27 Episodes)
Anthony Higgins
1985 *Young Sherlock Holmes* (aka Pyramid of Fear)

Paul Freeman
1988 *Without a Clue*

Daniel Davis
1988 *Elementary, Dear Data* TV Star Trek: The Next Generation
1993 *Ship in a Bottle*

John Colicos
1989 *My Dear Watson* (TV)

Anthony Andrews

1990 *Hands of a Murderer* (TV)

Jack Macreath
1993 *The Hound of London* (TV)

Richard Newman
1999 *Sherlock Holmes in the 22nd Century*

Vincent D'Onofrio
2002 *Sherlock* (TVM)

David Herman
2003 *Futurama* (TV Episode)

Richard Roxburgh
2003 *The League of Extraordinary Gentleman*

Chapter 9

A Collection of Pastiches

This chapter comprises pastiches collected and read by the compiler. Some of these can be deemed to follow closely the style of Conan Doyle's writing, whilst others from a literary and literal point of view leave the reader with a sense of unfulfilled expectation.

As noted on pages 5 and 10 of this book, Ronald Knox's story, *The Adventure of the First Class Carriage* can "...almost stand beside the master." Therefore, it seems appropriate to begin this chapter by reproducing this story.

The Adventure of the First Class Carriage by **Ronald Knox**.

The general encouragement extended to my efforts by the public is my excuse, if excuse were needed, for continuing to act as chronicler of my friend Sherlock Holmes. But even if I confine myself to those cases in which I have had the honour of being personally associated with him, I find it difficult to make a selection among the large amount of matter at my disposal.

As I turn over my records, I find that some of them deal with events of national or even international importance; but the time has not yet come when it would be safe to disclose (for instance) the true facts about the recent change of government in Paraguay. Others (like the case of the Missing Omnibus) would do more to gratify the modern craving for sensation; but I am well aware that my friend himself is the first to deplore it when I indulge what is, in his own view, a weakness.

My preference is for recording incidents whose bizarre features give special opportunity for the exercise of that analytical talent which he possessed in such a marked degree. Of these, the case of the Tattooed Nurseryman and that of the Luminous Cigar-Box naturally suggest themselves to the mind. But perhaps my friend's gifts were more signally displayed when he had occasion to investigate the disappearance of Mr Nathaniel Swithinbank, which provoked so much speculation in the early days of September, five years back.

Mr Sherlock Holmes was, of all men, the least influenced by what are called class distinctions. To him the rank was but the guinea stamp; a client was a client. And it did not surprise me, one evening when I was sitting over the familiar fire in Baker Street – the days were sunny but the evenings were already falling chill – to be told that he was expecting a visit from a domestic servant, a woman who 'did' for a well-to-do, childless couple in the southern Midlands. 'My last visit,' he explained, 'was from a countess. Her mind was uninteresting, and she had no great regard for the truth; the problem she brought was quite elementary. I fancy Mrs John Hennessy will have something more important to communicate.'

'You have met her already, then?'

'No, I have not had the privilege. But anyone who is in the habit of receiving letters from strangers will tell you the same – handwriting is often a better form of introduction than hand-shaking. You will find Mrs Hennessy's letter on the mantelpiece, and if you care to look at her j's and her w's in particular, I think you will agree that it is no ordinary woman we have to deal with. Dear me, there is the bell ringing already; in a moment or two, if I mistake not, we shall know what Mrs Hennessy, of the Cottage, Guiseborough St Martin, wants of Sherlock Holmes.'

There was nothing in the appearance of the old dame who was shown up, a few minutes later, by the faithful Mrs Hudson, to justify Holmes's estimate. To the outward view she was a typical representative of her class; from the bugles on her bonnet to her elastic-sided boots everything suggested the old-fashioned caretaker such as you may see polishing the front doorsteps of a hundred office buildings any spring morning in the city of London. Her voice, when she spoke, was articulated with unnecessary care, as that of the respectable working-class woman is apt to be. But there was something precise and business-like about the statement of her case which made you feel that this was a mind which could easily have profited by greater educational advantages.

'I have read of you, Mr Holmes,' she began, 'and when things began to go wrong up at the Hall it wasn't long before I thought to myself, if there's one man in England who will be able to see light here, it's Mr Sherlock Holmes. My husband was in good employment, till lately, on the railway at Chester; but the time came when the rheumatism got hold of him, and after that nothing seemed to go well with us until he had thrown up his job, and we went to live in a country village not far from Banbury, looking out for any odd work that might come our way.

'We had only been living there a week when a Mr Swithinbank and his wife took the old Hall, that had long been standing empty. They were newcomers to the district, and their needs were not great, having neither chick nor child to fend for; so they engaged me and Mr Hennessy to come and live in the lodge, close by the house, and do all the work of it for them. The pay was good and the duties light, so we were glad enough to get the billet.'

'One moment!' said Holmes. 'Did they advertise, or were you indebted to some private recommendation for the appointment?'

'They came at short notice, Mr Holmes, and were directed to us for temporary help. But they soon saw that our ways suited them, and they kept us on. They were people who kept very much to themselves, and perhaps they did not want a set of maids who would have followers, and spread gossip in the village.'

'That is suggestive. You state your case with admirable clearness. Pray proceed.'

'All this was no longer ago than last July. Since then they have once been away in London, but for the most part they have lived at Guiseborough, seeing very little of the folk round about. Parson called, but he is not a man to put his nose in where he is not wanted, and I think they must have made it clear they would sooner have his room than his company. So there was more guessing than gossiping about them in the countryside. But, sir, you can't be in domestic employment without finding out a good deal about how the land lies; and it wasn't long before my husband and I were certain of two things. One was that Mr and Mrs Swithinbank were deep in debt. And the other was that they got on badly together.'

'Debts have a way of reflecting themselves in a man's correspondence,' said Holmes, 'and whoever has the cleaning of his wastepaper basket will necessarily be conscious of them. But the relations between man and wife? Surely they must have gone very wrong indeed before there is quarrelling in public.'

'That's as may be, Mr Holmes, but quarrel in public they did. Why, it was only last week I came in with the blancmange, and he was saying, *The fact is, no one would be better pleased than you to see me in my coffin.* To be sure, he held his tongue after that, and looked a bit confused, and she tried to put a brave face on it. But I've lived long enough Mr Holmes, to know when a woman's been crying. Then last Monday, when I'd been in drawing the curtains, he burst out just before I'd closed the door behind me, *The world isn't big enough for both of us.* That was all I heard, and right glad I'd have been to hear less. But I've not come round here just to repeat servants'-hall gossip.

'*Today, when I was cleaning out the waste-paper basket, I came across a scrap of a letter that tells the same story, in his own handwriting. Cast your eye over that, Mr Holmes, and tell me whether a Christian woman has the right to sit by and do nothing about it.*'

She had dived her hand into a capacious reticule and brought out, with a triumphant flourish, her documentary evidence. Holmes knitted his brow over it, and passed it on to me. It ran: 'Being of sound mind, whatever the numskulls on the jury may say of it.'

'Can you identify the writing?' my friend said.

'It was my master's,' replied Mrs Hennessy. 'I know it well enough; the bank, I am sure, will tell you the same.'

'Mrs Hennessy, let us make no bones about it. Curiosity is a well-marked instinct of the human species. Your eye having lighted on this document, no doubt inadvertently, I will wager you took a look round the basket for any other fragments it might contain.'

'That I did, sir; my husband and I went through it carefully together, for who knew but the life of a fellow-creature might depend on it? But only one other piece could we find written by the same hand, and on the same notepaper. Here it is.' And she smoothed out on her knee a second fragment, to all appearances part of the same sheet, yet strangely different in its tenor. It seemed to have been torn away from the middle of a sentence, nothing survived but the words 'in the reeds by the lake, taking a bearing at the point where the old tower hides both the middle first-floor windows'.

'Come,' I said, 'this at least gives us something to go upon. Mrs Hennessy will surely be able to tell us whether there are any landmarks in Guiseborough answering to this description.'

'Indeed there are, sir; the directions are plain as a pikestaff. There is an old ruined building which juts out upon the little lake at the bottom of the garden, and it would be easy enough to hit on the place mentioned. I daresay you gentlemen are wondering why we haven't been down to the lakeside ourselves to see what we could find there. Well, the plain fact is, we were scared. My master is a quiet-spoken man enough at ordinary times, but there's a wild look in his eye when he's roused, and I for one should be sorry to cross him. So I thought I'd come to you, Mr Holmes, and put the whole thing in your hands.'

'I shall be interested to look into your little difficulty. To speak frankly, Mrs Hennessy, the story you have told me runs on such familiar lines that I should have been tempted to dismiss the whole case from my mind. Dr Watson here will tell you that I am a busy man, and the affairs of the Bank of Mauritius urgently require my presence in London. But this last detail about the reeds by the lakeside is piquant, decidedly piquant, and the whole matter shall be gone into. The only difficulty is a practical one. How are we to explain my presence at Guiseborough without betraying to your employers the fact that you and your husband have been intruding on their family affairs?'

'I have thought of that, sir.' Replied the old dame, 'and I think we can find a way out. I slipped away today easily enough because my mistress is going abroad to visit her aunt, near Dieppe, and Mr Swithinbank has come up to Town with her to see her off. I must go back by the evening train, and had half thought of asking you to accompany me. But no, he would get to hear of it if a stranger visited the place in his absence. It would be better if you came down by the quarter-past ten train tomorrow, and passed yourself off for a stranger who was coming to look at the house. They have taken it on a short lease, and plenty of folks come to see it without troubling to obtain an order-to-view.'

'Will your employer be back so early?'

'That is the very train he means to take; and to speak truth, sir, I should be the better for knowing that he was being watched. This wicked talk of making away with himself is enough to make anyone anxious about him. You cannot mistake him, Mr Holmes,' she went on; 'what chiefly marks him out is a scar on the left-hand side of his chin, where a dog bit him when he was a youngster.'

'Excellent, Mrs Hennessy; you have thought of everything. Tomorrow, then, on the quarter-past ten for Banbury without fail. You will oblige me by ordering the station fly to be in readiness. Country walks may be good for health, but time is more precious. I will drive straight to your cottage, and you or your husband shall escort me on my visit to this desirable country residence and its mysterious tenant.' With a wave of his hand, he cut short her protestations of gratitude.

'Well, Watson, what did you make of her? asked my companion when the door had closed on our visitor.

'She seemed typical of that noble army of women whose hard scrubbing makes life easy for the leisured classes. I could not see her well because she sat between us and the window, and her veil was lowered over her eyes. But her manner was enough to convince me that she was telling us the truth, and that she is sincere in her anxiety to avert what may be an appalling tragedy. As to its nature, I confess I am in the dark. Like yourself, I was particularly struck by the reference to the reeds by the lakeside. What can it mean? An assignation?'

'Hardly, my dear Watson. At this time of the year a man runs enough risk of cold without standing about in a reed-bed. A hiding-place, more probably, but for what? And why should a man take the trouble to hide something, and then obligingly litter his waste-paper basket with clues to its whereabouts? No, these are deep waters, Watson, and we must have more data before we begin to theorize. You will come with me?'

'Certainly, if I may. Shall I bring my revolver?'

'I do not apprehend any danger, but perhaps it is as well to be on the safe side. Mr Swithinbank seems to strike his neighbours as a formidable person. And now, if you will be good enough to hand me the more peaceful instrument which hangs beside you, I will try out that air of Scarlatti's, and leave the affairs of Guiseborough St Martin to look after themselves.'

I often had occasion to deprecate Sherlock Holmes's habit of catching trains with just half a minute to spare. But on the morning after our interview with Mrs Hennessy we arrived at Paddington station no later than ten o'clock – to find a stranger, with a pronounced scar on the left hand side of his chin, gazing out at us languidly from the window of a first-class carriage.

'Do you mean to travel with him?' I asked when we were out of earshot.

'Scarcely feasible, I think. If he is the man I take him for, he has secured solitude all the way to Banbury by the simple process of slipping half a crown into the guard's hand.' And, sure enough, a few minutes later we saw that functionary shepherd a fussy-looking gentleman, who had been vigorously assaulting the locked door, to a compartment further on. For ourselves, we took up our post in the carriage next but one behind Mr Swithinbank. This, like the other first-class compartments, was duly locked when we had entered it; behind us the less fortunate passengers accommodated themselves in seconds.

*'The case is not without its interest,' observed Holmes, laying down his paper as we steamed through Burnham Beeches. 'It presents features which recall the affairs of James Phillimore, whose disappearance (though your loyalty may tempt you to forget it) we investigated without success. (**Compiler's note:** see Chapter 17 for four pastiches on The Strange Case of Mr. James Phillimore). But this Swithinbank mystery, if I mistake not, cuts even deeper.*

Why, for example, is the man so anxious to parade his intention of suicide, or fictitious suicide, in the presence of his domestic staff? It can hardly fail to strike you that he chose the moment when the good Mrs Hennessy was just entering the room, or just leaving it, to make those remarkable confidences to his wife. Not content with that, he must leave evidence of his intentions lying around in the waste-paper basket. And yet this involved the risk of having his plans foiled by good-natured interference. Time enough for his disappearance to become public when it became effective! And why, in the name of fortune, does he hide something only to tell us where he has hidden it?'

Amid a maze of railway tracks, we came to a standstill at Reading, Holmes craned his neck out of the window, but reported that all the doors had been left locked. We were not destined to learn anything about our elusive travelling-companion until, just as we were passing the pretty hamlet of Tilehurst, a little shower of paper fragments fluttered past the window on the right-hand side of the compartment, and two of them actually sailed in through the space we had dedicated to ventilation on that bright morning of autumn. It may easily be guessed with what avidity we pounced on them.

The messages were in the same handwriting with which Mrs Hennessy's find had made us familiar; they ran, respectively, 'Mean to make an end of it all' and 'This is the only way out.' Holmes sat over them with knitted brows, till I fairly danced with impatience.

'Should we not pull the communication-cord?' I asked.

'Hardly,' answered my companion, 'unless five-pound notes are more plentiful with you than they used to be. I will even anticipate your next suggestion, which is that we should look out of the windows on either side of the carriage. Either we have a lunatic two doors off, in which case there is no use in trying to foresee his next move, or he intends suicide, in which case he will not be deterred by the presence of spectators, or he is a man with a scheming brain who is sending us these messages in order to make us behave in a particular way. Quite possibly, he wants to make us lean out of the window, which seems to me an excellent reason for not leaning out of the window. At Oxford we shall be able to read the guard a lesson on the danger of locking passengers in.'

So indeed it proved; for when the train stopped at Oxford there was no passenger to be found in Mr Swithinbank's carriage. His overcoat remained, and his wide-awake hat; his portmanteau was duly identified in the guard's van. The door on the right-hand side of the compartment, away from the platform, had swung open; nor did Holmes's lens bring to light any details about the way in which the elusive passenger had made his exit.

It was an impatient horse and an injured cabman that awaited us at Banbury, when we drove through golden woodlands to the little village of Guiseborough St Martin, nestling under the shadow of Edge Hill. Mrs Hennessy met us at the door of her cottage, dropping an old-fashioned curtsey; and it may easily be imagined what wringing of hands, what wiping of eyes with her apron, greeted the announcement of her master's disappearance. Mr Hennessy, it seemed had gone off to a neighbouring farm upon some errand, and it was the old dame herself who escorted us up to the Hall.

'There's a gentleman there already, Mr Holmes,' she informed us. 'Arrived early this morning and would take no denial; and not a word to say what business he came on.'

'That is unfortunate,' said Holmes. 'I particularly wanted a free field to make some investigations. Let us hope that he will be good enough to clear off when he is told that there is no chance of an interview with Mr Swithinbank.'

Guiseborough Hall stands in its own grounds a little way outside the village, the residence of a squire unmistakably, but with no airs of baronial grandeur. The old, rough walls have been refaced with pointed stone, the mullioned windows exchanged for a generous expanse of plate-glass, to suit a more recent taste, and a portico has been thrown out from the front door to welcome the traveller with its shelter. The garden descends at a precipitous slope from the main terrace, and a little lake fringes it at the bottom, dominated by a ruined eminence that serves the modern owner for a gazebo.

Within the house, furniture was of the scantiest, the Swithinbanks having evidently rented it with what fittings it had, and introduced little of their own. As Mrs Hennessy ushered us into the drawing-room, we were not a little surprised to be greeted by the wiry figure and melancholy features of our old rival, Inspector Lestrade.

'I knew you were quick off the mark, Mr Holmes,' he said, but it beats me how you heard of Mr Swithinbank's little goings-on; let alone that I didn't think you took much stock in cases of common fraud like this.'

'Common fraud?' repeated my companion. 'Why, what has he been up to?'

'Drawing cheques, and big ones, Mr Holmes, when he knew that his bank wouldn't honour them; only little things of that sort. But if you're on his track I don't suppose he's far off, and I'll be grateful for any help you can give me to lay my hands on him.'

'My dear Lestrade, if you follow out your usual systematic methods, you will have to patrol the Great Western line all the way from Reading to Oxford. I trust you have brought a drag-net with you, for the line crossed the river no less than four times in the course of the journey.' And he regaled the astonished inspector with a brief summary of our investigations.

Our information worked like a charm on the little detective. He was off in a moment to find the nearest telegraph office and put himself in touch with Scotland Yard, with the Great Western Railway authorities, with the Thames Conservancy. He promised, however, a speedy return, and I fancy Holmes cursed himself for not having dismissed the jarvey who had brought us from the station, an undeserved windfall for our rival.

'Now, Watson!' he cried, as the sound of the wheels faded away into the distance.

'Our way lies to the lakeside, I presume.'

'How often am I to remind you that the place where the criminal tells you to look is the place not to look? No, the clue to the mystery lies, somehow, in the house, and we must hurry up if we are to find it.'

Quick as a thought, he began turning out shelves, cupboards, escritoires, while I, at his direction, went through the various rooms of the house to ascertain whether all was in order, and whether anything suggested the anticipation of a hasty flight. By the time I returned to him, having found nothing amiss, he was seated in the most comfortable of the drawing-room armchairs, reading a book he had picked out of the shelves – it dealt, if I remember right, with the aborigines of Borneo.

'The mystery, Holmes!' I cried.

'I have solved it. If you will look on the bureau yonder, you will find the household books which Mrs Swithinbank has obligingly left behind. Extraordinary how these people always make some elementary mistake. You are a man of the world, Watson; take a look at them and tell me what strikes you as curious.'

It was not long before the salient feature occurred to me. 'Why, Holmes,' I exclaimed, 'there is no record of the Hennessy's being paid any wages at all!'

'Bravo, Watson! And if you will go into the figures a little more closely, you will find that the Hennessy's lived on air. So now the whole facts of the story are plain to you.'

'I confess,' I replied, somewhat crestfallen, 'that the whole case is as dark to me as ever.'

'Why, then, take a look at that newspaper I have left on the occasional table; I have marked the important paragraph in blue pencil.'

It was a copy of an Australian paper, issued some weeks previously. The paragraph to which Holmes had drawn my attention ran thus:

ROMANCE OF RICH MAN'S WILL

The recent lamented death of Mr John Macready, the well-known sheepfarming magnate, has had an unexpected sequel in the circumstance that the dead man, apparently, left no will. His son, Mr Alexander Macready, left for England some years back, owing to a misunderstanding with his father – it was said – because he announced his intention of marrying a lady from the stage. The young man has completely disappeared, and energetic steps are being taken by the lawyers to trace his whereabouts. It is estimated that the fortunate heirs, whoever they be, will be the richer by not far short of a hundred thousand pounds sterling.

Horse-hoofs echoed under the archway, and in another minute Lestrade was again of our party. Seldom have I seen the little detective looking so baffled and ill at ease. 'They'll have the laugh of me at the Yard over this,' he said. 'We had word that Swithinbank was in London, but I made sure it was only a feint, and I came racing up here by the early train, instead of catching the quarter-past ten and my man in it. He's a slippery devil, and he may be half-way to the Continent by this time.'

'Don't be down-hearted about it Lestrade. Come and interview Mr and Mrs Hennessy, at the lodge, we may get news of your man down there.'

A coarse-looking fellow in a bushy red beard sat sharing his tea with our friend of the evening before. His greasy waistcoat and corduroy trousers proclaimed him a manual worker. He rose to meet us with something of a defiant air; his wife was all affability.

'Have you heard any news of the poor gentleman?' she asked.

'We may have some before long,' answered Holmes. 'Lestrade, you might arrest John Hennessy for stealing that porter's cap you see on the dresser, the property of the Great Western Railway Company. Or, if you prefer an alternative charge, you might arrest him as Alexander Macready, alias Nathaniel Swithinbank.' And while we stood there literally thunderstruck, he tore off the red beard from a chin marked with a scar on the left-hand side.

'The case was difficult,' he said to me afterwards, 'only because we had no clue to the motive. Swithinbank's debts would almost have swallowed up Macready's legacy; it was necessary for the couple to disappear, and take up the claim under a fresh alias. This meant a duplication of personalities, but it was not really difficult. She had been an actress; he had really been a railway porter in his hard-up days. When he got out at Reading, and passed along the six-foot way to take his place in a third-class carriage, nobody marked the circumstance, because on the way from London he had changed into a porter's clothes; he had the cap, no doubt, in his pocket. On the sill of the door he left open, he had made a little pile of suicide-messages, hoping that when it swung open these would be shaken out and flutter into the carriages behind.'

'But why the visit to London? And, above all, why the visit to Baker Street?'

'That is the most amusing part of the story; we should have seen through it at once. He wanted Nathaniel Swithinbank to disappear finally, beyond all hope of tracing him. And who would hope to trace him, when Mr Sherlock Holmes, who was travelling two carriages behind, had given up the attempt? Their only fear was that I should find the case uninteresting, hence the random reference to a hiding-place among the reeds, which so intrigued you. Come to think of it, they nearly had Inspector Lestrade in the same train as well. I hear he has won golden opinions with his superiors by cornering his man so neatly. *Sic vos non vobis*, as Virgil said of the bees; only they tell us nowadays the lines are not by Virgil.'

Chapter 10

Introductions; Prefaces; Publisher's Notes, Forewords, and Afterwords

This chapter consists of the above taken from the compiler's collection of various editions of Sir Arthur Conan Doyle's Sherlock Holmes stories. Also from a variety of books and pastiches which are referenced within the book and noted in the bibliography at the conclusion.

Firstly, an introduction to *Detective Stories* from *The Strand* by **Jack Adrian**.

The immediate, enormous, and for the time unparalleled success of the *Strand Magazine* – the lavishly illustrated monthly launched in 1891 and which ran for nearly sixty years – was due to a great extent to the abundant energy and shrewd and promotional abilities of its founder and proprietor, George Newnes. Newnes was the very epitome, almost to the point of caricature, of the late nineteenth-century entrepreneur and a man of action, who had a sudden idea, saw immense moral possibilities or financial benefits in it, and then pursued it relentlessly, even ruthlessly, until it was 'made flesh'. In the case of George Newnes this was true in a very real sense.

Ten years earlier, in the late summer of 1881, Newnes spotted in his evening paper a paragraph about a runaway train. There were no fatalities, though at the climax of their headlong journey the carriages smashed through buffers, then a brick wall, and into a printing shop, partly demolishing it. The story mentioned the remarkable escape of some children on the train who were shaken but otherwise unharmed, and was buried in a page of similarly brief news items. In his unpublished memoirs he recalled thinking, 'Why shouldn't there be a paper filled with tit-bits like that?'

At the time Newnes was in haberdashery, with no experience of printing or anything remotely connected with the publishing industry. He had no capital and could not get credit. Yet two days short of two months later – on 22 October 1881 (the news item he'd read about had appeared in the Manchester *Evening News* for 24 August) – the first issue of *Tit-Bits from All the Most Interesting Books, Periodicals and Newspapers in the World* was published. In the end the problem of his lack of capital had proved easily surmountable: he had simply opened a vegetarian restaurant which, within a few weeks, he sold at the useful net profit of £400.

Tit-Bits was successful. It was clearly what a vast public had been waiting for and was eager to read. Newnes filled it with all kinds of trivia – news items, sensational murders, strange coincidences, curious facts – a good deal of which (copyright laws being virtually non-existent) he simply lifted, often unacknowledged, from other sources. It was a scissors-and-paste enterprise on a grand scale. If he did make any acknowledgement – for an interesting chapter from a travel book, perhaps, or a précis of conclusions from a volume of popular science – and the injured author demanded a fee, Newnes testily pointed out that he was giving the book free publicity and that as the extract would be seen by tens of thousands of readers, really the author ought to be paying him.

This cavalier treatment soon ceased when circulation, and thus profits out of which such payments could be made, took off in a spectacular fashion. Half-way through its first year, selling only in the Manchester area, *Tit-Bits* reached a figure of 40,000 copies a week, and one of the businessmen from whom Newnes had originally tried to beg a mere £500 for a half-share in the paper, prior to launch, now offered £16,000. Newnes refused. When, still before the end of its maiden year, the paper's circulation soared to over 100,000 an offer of £30,000 was made. Newnes refused that too. As he remarked to his brother-in-law, in mildly awe-struck tones, 'I believe I'm going to be rich.'

He was. His bright idea launched a publishing empire, soon enabled him to turn philanthropist, and was in the long run responsible for the baronetcy bestowed on him in less than two decades. It was also responsible for the *Strand*.

In 1884 Newnes removed himself and his burgeoning publishing business to rooms and an accommodation address in London, a year later setting up shop in Burleigh Street, just off the Strand. In that same year, 1885, he became MP for Newmarket on the Liberal ticket. He enjoyed the fame of being proprietor of the biggest-selling weekly paper in the land, indeed in publishing history – and even enjoyed the later success of younger entrepreneurs whom he had groomed and nurtured and who had struck out on their own. Alfred Harmsworth (later Lord Northcliffe, founder of the *Daily Mail*) was employed by Newnes for a time, left, and in 1888 launched *Answers to Correspondents*, quickly shortened to *Answers*, in direct competition to *Tit-Bits*; then *Harmsworth's Magazine*, later retitled to *London*, as a rival to the *Strand*. Arthur Pearson, another bright young journalist, strode out along much the same road, starting *Pearson's Weekly* in 1890 and *Pearson's Magazine* in 1896. It had been the same in the first few years after *Tit-Bits* itself was launched: a multitude of imitations, some quite shameless – *Sketchy Bits, Rarebits, Bits and Pieces, Quick Bits*. None of this worried Newnes, whose confidence in himself and his publications was boundless. Whatever was thrown together by others, as far as he was concerned his product was, quite simply, better. In any case, as he pointed out, 'The world is wide.' Even so, although he was gratified by the popularity of *Tit-Bits* – which alone, was soon giving him a personal income of £30,000 a year, net –the paper in no way bestowed on him the *gravitas*, certainly as an MP, he now sought. He had long since thrust into the very deepest recesses of his mind the genuine horror he had experienced on discovering, in the early months of the paper, that his clever title had indecent connotations. A naïve man, it had never occurred to him that the reason some retailers were anxious to take the paper while others resolutely refused to have anything to do with it because in certain quarters a 'tit-bit' was a dirty joke. By the time this had been explained to him it was far too late to alter the title, or do anything other than ignore the sniggers and hope for the best.

Happily, the jokes were soon forgotten as *Tit-Bits* rapidly became a household name. Even so the outstanding success of the paper brought only a measure of dignity: it was too popular, too (as it would be termed today) downmarket. The obvious answer was to move 'upmarket', but instead of aping the schilling 'literary' monthlies such as the *Cornhill, Temple Bar,* or *Belgravia,* full as these were of columns of dreary type and little else, the magazine would have to be quite different, if possible unique.

Opinion is divided as to who actually devised the *Strand Magazine*. Newnes' name was on the masthead and whenever an anniversary occurred (the hundredth issue, say, or the tenth year) Newnes himself invariably provided a signed – though by no means swaggering – editorial; it was surely he who wanted something with 'pictures on every page' in it (the columns of *Tit-Bits* were full of cartoons and sketches), and no one but the canny Newnes would have decided on a price of sixpence instead of a shilling at which all the stodgy monthlies were priced. Nevertheless, it is more than likely that the man who came up with the overall package – a budget of fiction, illustrated articles, popular politics ('From Behind the Speaker's Chair' ran for years), art features, and interviews with the great and the good – was the journalist (ex *Temple Bar*) H. Greenhough Smith, who was initially awarded the post of 'literary editor' but whose steadying hand directed the entire enterprise. From the outset the *Strand* gave Newnes the respectability he craved. No snob, he was yet attracted to the highborn, and was certainly in awe of the monarchy. One of the reasons for the magazine's eventual success was that it was seen to have received the royal imprimatur at an early stage. In one number it published an etching of Queen Victoria's first child, and executed half a century before Her Majesty herself, and now printed with her blessing. This was a distinct coup. Others followed. Not too long afterwards there appeared an extended article on Victoria's dolls, the proofs of which she read and to which she appended notes. She also revised an article dealing with her studies in Hindustani and 'graciously accorded permission' to a Strand journalist to write a nineteen-page piece on Buckingham Palace, interiors and all.

Though the magazine's premier number was dated January 1891, Newnes had it on sale well before Christmas 1890, advertising it energetically in *Tit-Bits* and the trade, and bill boarding it all over the country, especially in mainline railway stations. Astonishingly – even allowing for the extensive promotion and the magazine's innovative aspect and approach – it not only sold out but had to be reprinted three times. In all, nearly 300,000 copies of that first issue were moved.

Still, while 300,000 copies of the magazine's first number is a colossal figure, in periodical publishing it is axiomatic (then as now) that a triumphant launch is no indication of future success; indeed, however, excellent the product, however muscular the promotion, sales will inevitably fall after 'the shock of the new' has been absorbed, more often than not after the first half-dozen issues. With the *Strand* the reverse was the case. Sales actually rose after the first half-dozen issues, and kept on rising, finally reaching a quite extraordinary peak of nearly half a million copies a month, a figure which held well into the 1930s (with a probable readership of between two and three million).

All this was due to a remarkable stroke of good fortune which neither Newnes or Smith could have foreseen, and which had nothing to do with the look of the magazine, its revolutionary nature, or even its price. In the late spring of 1891 Smith received two short stories from a contributor who had already appeared in the magazine with a neat and ingenious twist-ending tale. The contributor was a Dr A.C. Doyle; the two stories which featured a detective called Sherlock Holmes, were entitled 'A Scandal in Bohemia' and 'The Red-Headed League'.

(**Compiler's note** – The following extract is taken from an article in the *Sherlock Holmes Gazette,* Spring 1995):
'A Case of Identity', first published in 'The Strand' in September 1891, was actually the second story in the series which became 'The Adventures of Sherlock Holmes', but

Greenhough Smith, editor of the magazine, believed that 'The Red-Headed League' was the stronger piece and so published it first. This was in spite of the fact that in 'The Red-Headed League' there is reference to 'A Case of Identity'.

Another element within the latter story which exposes the incorrect chronology is Holmes' reference to his newly acquired snuff box: 'It is a little souvenir from the King of Bohemia'. This backward glance to 'A Scandal in Bohemia' was obviously a ploy by Conan Doyle to enhance the idea of continuity. While each adventure was complete in itself, Doyle intended to create a sense of unity by such references. He had not reckoned on editorial decisions.

When Doyle, now Sir Arthur Conan Doyle, died in 1930 Smith wrote a tribute. 'I at once realized that here was the greatest short story writer since Edgar Allan Poe. I remember rushing into Mr Newnes' office and thrusting the stories before his eyes.'

This sounds like hyperbole, if not being wise after the event. Yet whatever Smith's real reactions on that spring day in 1891 they were surely something akin to those he recalled to mind, for the two stories were quite different from anything that had been published in the *Strand* thus far; indeed, quite different from any story published in any of the monthly magazines of the day.

The good fortune was that Doyle sent them to Smith in the first place, since at that time he could easily have tried them out on any one of half a dozen, perhaps more, periodicals to which he had successfully sold over the past two or three years – such as *London Society, Belgravia* , the *Cornhill,* or *Cassell's Saturday Journal*. He could have sent them to Tillotson's Fiction Bureau, which specialised in buying material from not quite front-line authors and syndicating it in provincial newspapers across the north of England. Fees were by no means regal (Doyle had sold the story to the chain in 1889, receiving four guineas for two placings in that year), but Tillotson was hungry for copy: he had a giant maw to feed and the more an author produced the more he was paid. He could certainly have offered them to *Lippincott's Magazine*, the prestigious American whose editor had already commissioned *The Sign of Four* from him, had wined and dined them at the Langham Hotel (with Oscar Wilde as table-mate), and paid him the not inconsiderable sum of £100 for the rights to the 45,000-word novella.

That Doyle did none of these things, sending the two detective stories instead straight to the *Strand*, is almost certainly due to the enthusiastic reception Smith had given to the first (non-Holmes) story he had tried out on the new magazine, 'The Voice of Science', which had appeared anonymously in the *Strand's* first issue (although Doyle was credited on the contents page). About that earlier story Smith was to write much later: 'Here, to an editor jaded with wading through reams of impossible stuff, [came]...a godsend in the shape of a story that brought a gleam of happiness into the despairing life of this weary editor – there was no mistaking the ingenuity of the plot, the limpid clearness of the style, the perfect art of telling a story.'

This is a penetrating judgement. Doyle is indeed an outstanding story-teller who effortlessly engages the reader's attention. His style is simple and straightforward, with none of the late-Victorian *fustian* to be found in the work of so many of his peers, indeed so many of his own followers, and even when he is mildly pedantic – 'I find it recorded in my notebook that it was a bleak and windy day...' 'In glancing over the somewhat incoherent series of memoirs...' – he charms. In any case, he was also capable of writing a sentence such as 'I clapped a pistol to his head', and could handle action sequences with rare mastery.

Doyle admired the *romans-poiliciers* of the French writer Gaboriau ('he had rather attracted me by the neat dove-tailing of his plots') and the ingenuity displayed by Poe in his Chevalier Dupin tales. Combining the sensational with the clever, the exciting with the cerebral, and serving it up in short-story form with a continuing character, he had struck a new and rich vein that was to revolutionize popular fiction.

Ironically, he cared little for Holmes, tiring of him even while working the first half-dozen stories. Indeed six, at £30 a time, were all he ever intended to write, and once he had finished them he refused to write more. This would have been perfectly acceptable to Greenhough Smith were it not for the undeniable fact that with the publication of the first three stories his readers had gone, so it seemed, Sherlock Holmes mad. Letters praising the series in intemperate terms were arriving by every post; retailers were reporting unprecedented enthusiasm and were re-ordering copies in massive quantities. He urged Doyle to reconsider his decision. Doyle thought he might, for another £20 a story, certain that George Newnes would never sanction such a high-handed demand. Smith wrote back by return of post, agreeing and urging him to send copy as soon as possible (Doyle could have no idea then that the final Holmes story – 'Shoscombe Old Place', to be written thirty-six years in the future – would bring him, from both US and UK first sales, a sum approaching £2,400).

Doyle had created what every popular fiction writer dreams of creating and so seldom does: a cult hero. When in the December 1893 issue of the *Strand*, he finally rid himself of the succubus that was draining (so he thought) his talent away from the great historical dramas he wanted to write, there were any number of his fellow-authors, both male and female, who were eager to fill the yawning breech left by Holmes' 'death'. In fact no one came anywhere near to emulating Doyle's immense popularity or success.

Arthur Morrison, who had previously been penning larky articles on zoos for the *Strand*, created Martin Hewitt, plump and genial where Holmes had been lean and hungry. The stories were attractive, but no more than that. After a single series Morrison took his hero off to the *Windsor Magazine*, one of Newnes' newer rivals. Of rather more interest were the various stories by Mrs L.T.Meade (usually in tandem with a collaborator who supplied the technical data), whose stories were an engaging blend of late-Victorian sensationalism and strange science, often with more than a hint of the weird. Something of a Stakhanovite (her canon ran to upwards of 250 books written over a forty-year period), Mrs Meade was responsible for two series of 'Stories from the Diary of a Doctor' as well as 'The Sorceress of the Strand','Stories from the Sanctuary Club', and 'The Brotherhood of the Seven Keys', amongst others. Grant Allen, the 'new woman' novelist and science populizer, tried the oblique approach by writing a series around a confidence trickster, 'An African Millionaire', about a spirited blue-stocking who turns sleuth; his final series, 'Hilda Wade', was completed after his death by Conan Doyle himself.

It has to be said that in many ways Doyle's success had a deleterious effect on the genre, his influence lying like a dead hand over the efforts of his fellow-authors, far too many of whom tried far too hard to write precisely in his style, and always failing (not a few – Sapper, for instance – simply plagiarised his plots). Despite those who complained that after Holmes returned from the dead in 1903 he was never quite the same, Doyle's Holmesian appearances – spasmodic after 1905 – are distinctly refreshing when compared to those of the detectives of most of his rivals in the *Strand*.

The truth is, Doyle's real rivals – those who were indebted to Doyle's original breakthrough but whose approach to the genre now deviated from source – were not writing in the *Strand* at all. R. Austin Freeman, whose Dr Thorndyke was undeniably Holmes – inspired (even down to his faithful but slightly obtuse henchman/chronicler), was inventing an entirely fresh sub-genre: the 'inverted' crime story, in which the reader is told who commits the crime and how it is done, and then follows Thorndyke on the criminal's trial. Thorndyke's exploits appeared mainly in *Pearson's Magazine*. Baroness Orczy's unusul 'Old Man in the Corner', the first 'armchair' detective who solves all his criminous problems in a Lyon's corner shop, appeared in the *Royal Magazine*, whilst G.K. Chesterson's Father Brown stories were mostly published in *Cassell's Magazine* and *The Storyteller*. The inevitable conclusion is that while Conan Doyle was still alive there was simply no room in the *Strand* for experimentation.

During the 1920s, though pure detective fiction still surfaces, the mystery genre that featured most prominently in the *Strand* was the thriller, its principal exponent being Edgar Wallace, who in 1921, contributed a profoundly influential series of murder stories set around his characters the Four Just Men. Wallace's work was clever and always absorbing but was not lit by any brilliant deductive shafts; his restless temperament was ill suited to the painstaking planting of clues within the body of a story. E.

Phillips Oppenheim, who had cornered the market in Riviera make-believe, and like Wallace, was disinclined to grapple with the puzzle story, was the author who appeared most often on the *Strand's* content pages from 1920 to 1930. A hugely successful writer, whose thrillers sold in their hundreds of thousands, his stories have a surface glamour only; too much Oppenheim palls.

Conan Doyle in 1930; Greenhough Smith, his most loyal champion (save in the matter of Spiritualism and fairy photographs), retired from active duties in the same year. Almost at once the Bright Young Hopes began crowding in. The 1930s, under the *Strand's* second editor Reeves Shaw (erstwhile editor of *The Humorist*, who welcomed writers with the lighter touch), is the decade of Agatha Christie, Marjory Allingham, Dorothy Sayers, E.C. Bentley (hardly young, to be sure, but suddenly reinvigorated after an absence from detective fiction of over twenty years), Richard Keverne, Frank King, and John Dickson Carr (who wrote under his own name and 'Carter Dickson' and whose speciality was that most appealing of 'sub-genres, the 'impossible' crime). This final decade before the Second World War, far more than the 1920s, may be considered a genuine 'Golden Age', rich in ingenious nuggets, psychological twists, fast cars, literary allusions, brain-wracking complexities, corpses in conservatories.

The 1940s, a starker decade altogether – the *Strand* was dying slowly, its half a million circulation now shrivelled to 95,000 – is notable for the virtual absence of detective stories in the classic, or indeed any, tradition. Those that do appear gleam like beacons. Nicholas Blake's 'The Snow Line' is a puzzle story in which the reader is asked to join in the investigation, spot the clues, name the guilty party – solution at the end of the issue. It is cleverly and entertainingly done. But perhaps the most striking story of all (in a way most melancholy) is one that takes the reader back over half a century to a different world, another time, and the fountainhead and inspiration itself, Sherlock Holmes, in a dazzling pastiche by Mgr. Ronald Knox of which, surely Arthur Conan Doyle himself would have approved.

In a sense, the *Strand Magazine* created the detective story, one of two genres at which it excelled. The other, the weird tale, bay be experienced in this anthology's companion volume, *Strange Tales from* The Strand. Here, however, are collected all manner of mysteries, devised by some of the best and most cunning writers of the past hundred years. Some are known; some, today, wholly unknown. All knew how to entertain.

Secondly, publishers' notes to *The Exploits of Sherlock Holmes* and *More Exploits of Sherlock Holmes* by Adrian Conan Doyle and John Dickson Carr.

No reader of the *Strand Magazine* in 1887 could have guessed that Sherlock Holmes and Dr Watson, then making their debut, would soon become the world's most famous characters of fiction. Certainly their creator, Sir Arthur Conan Doyle, had no thought of it at the time, nor many years later when, having done away with Holmes by contriving his death at the Reichenbach Falls, he was compelled by public clamour to bring him back to life and to the familiar surroundings of his lodgings at 221B Baker Street.

In view of Holmes's immense popularity it is not perhaps so surprising that among the hundreds of millions to whom his name is familiar, there are some who believe that he was a living person. In fact, Holmes is much less of an invention than some people think. The chivalry of Holmes, his penetrating mind, his erudition, his physical feats, and his character are those of the genius who created him. Sir Arthur in real life, as Holmes in fiction, came to the rescue of people convicted for crimes they had not committed and he used the very logic and deductive reasoning that enabled Holmes to solve the problems of his clients. Sir Arthur, like Holmes, was a man of unusual physical strength who might have become a great boxer had he not chosen to become first a doctor and then a writer. And in their background both were descended from a line of country squires and both had a grandmother of French extraction. On the Doyle side Holmes comes of a creative family of which five members within three generations provide records of achievement in the *Dictionary of National Biography* and include John Doyle the famous political cartoonist in the early nineteenth century, Richard ('Dicky') Doyle the designer of the *Punch* cover and James Doyle the compiler of *The Chronicle of England*.

Despite all his many claims to fame, and despite the success of his historical novels, to which he devoted so much of his heart, Conan Doyle is now best known to the world for having created Sherlock Holmes. Since 1887, the Sherlock Holmes stories have been translated into almost every known language and have never been out of print. Holmes has been the hero of fifteen legitimate stage plays, one hundred and ten films, over a thousand radio dramatizations, and has made his debut on television. Many of the investigation methods created for Holmes by Sir Arthur were adopted by Scotland Yard, the French Surete, and police forces of many other nations. Holmes has even become the cult of many societies and the object of many imitations, all of which have failed to catch the spirit of the man about whom Somerset Maugham says, in his recent book *The Vagrant Mood*: 'No detective stories have had the popularity of Conan Doyle's and, because of the invention of Sherlock Holmes, I think it may be admitted that none has so well deserved it.'

The Exploits of Sherlock Holmes are based on the unsolved cases to which Dr Watson refers in the original fifty-six short stories and four novels. The plots are new, but the stories are faithful reproductions of the originals, in construction as well as in texture. They were written for the millions of Holmes admirers by Sir Arthur's younger son, Adrian Conan Doyle, who was brought up in the tradition of the Victorian era and in close contact with his father. The son, who is the author of two books about his deep-sea fishing expeditions – *Heaven Has Claws* and *Lone Dhow* – has a lust for adventure, cherishes relics of the past and values the same sense of chivalry that so completely characterized his father…or should we say Holmes. Using the desk on which his father wrote, and surrounded by the same objects that his father handled, he has in every way endeavoured to re-create each particle of atmosphere that formed Sir Arthur's environment.

The stories in *More Exploits of Sherlock Holmes* were written by Adrian Conan Doyle in collaboration with John Dickson Carr, the author of that remarkable *Life of Sir Arthur Conan Doyle* and some of the best contemporary detective novels.

The *Exploits* and *More Exploits* were concerned with the single desire of producing stories of the 'old vintage'; of re-creating those moments of delicious anticipation when the approaching steps of a new client indicates that 'the game is afoot' and our two friends are ready to exchange remarks such as those celebrated four lines from *Silver Blaze* when Watson asks Holmes:

'Is there any point to which you wish to draw attention?'
'To the curious incident of the dog in the night-time.'
'The dog did nothing in the night-time.'
'That was the curious incident,' remarked Holmes.

Third, Introduction to *The Edinburgh Stories* by Own Dudley Edwards, *Department of History, University of Edinburgh.*

ARTHUR CONAN DOYLE is a paradoxical figure among Edinburgh writers. Although almost all of the last fifty years of his life were spent in England, he took trouble to retain his Scottish accent, his wit and humour had a distinctively Scottish dry, analytical quality, he thronged his papers with memorable characters deriving in part from the Edinburgh intelligentsia and his vivid depiction of urban scenes owed far more initially to his birthplace than to the cities – notably London – in which they were normally located. Yet posterity has hitherto granted little of this. His most recent biographer, the brilliant historian of the detective story Julian Symons, tells us "he took away little from Edinburgh except his degree" and Trevor Royle's charming and erudite literary history of Edinburgh, *Precipitous City*, largely concurs.

But formative years were particularly critical in the case of so impressionable and creative writer distinguished for a phenomenally retentive memory, and the legacy of his Edinburgh experiences from birth to 1859 to departure in 1881 was a powerful one, although the two most substantial works with an Edinburgh location, the short story "John Barrington Cowles" and the short novel *The Parasite*, have been lost to sight for many years. The former survived for some time in the successive reprints of the author's early anthology *The Captain of the 'Polestar'* but was not brought into his later collections of his works; the latter, published as a single work, had several printings between 1894 and 1897 and then went out of print, and what stood most strongly against the reprinting of both stories was their length. The Sherlock Holmes short stories moved Conan Doyle from his often somewhat sprawling narratives of the 1889s to splendidly economic use of space in the 1890s and thereafter. He had, in fact, made himself the model for the multitude of professional short story writers who sprang into activity after his success in the *Strand* and poured out their offerings in its pages and those of its rivals to the time of his death.

The two stories fully merit survival. "Cowles" is certainly the work of a young author still in pursuit of a style, and while executed with remarkable power, occasionally shows a looseness in sentence-structure contrasting with the music and precision of his short-story writing from 1891 onward; but the admirers of Sherlock Holmes will find it in something of the same blend of scientifically presented evidence highlighting the judicious anticipation and ultimate horrific climax of a plot all too worthy of Scottish literary traditions of fear and darkness. The Edinburgh setting, largely muted in *The Parasite* by reason of its special narrative form, plays a major part in the retrospection of "Cowles". A minor detail – having John Barrington Cowles win an actual and still existing prize in the Edinburgh medical school – reminds us at once both of those touches of personal humour with which Conan Doyle would surreptitiously introduce phenomena of his own experience into his fiction, and of the underlying tone of realism which has wooed so many enthusiasts into obsessions with Holmes, Watson and their adventures as creatures of fact.

The Parasite by contrast is a work of a mature writer of great technical skill. The narrator of "Cowles", benevolent but not particularly distinctive, has given way to a self-portrait of the protagonist worked out with the power for first-person narration which Doyle had by now shown in the creation of Watson. The use of the professor's day-to-day notes on the events at once conveys the mind of a scientific enquirer becoming gradually overwhelmed with his investigations, with dual effects both for character-depiction and for structural development. It is evident that Doyle had "Cowles" in mind in writing *The Parasite* and thus exemplifies what a remarkable craftsman could do in reworking ideas of which he had earlier made insufficient use. Above all else, Conan Doyle was a supreme master of literary economics. Another example of such reconsideration is the transformation of the conventional concept of a supremely attractive if diabolical beauty in "Cowles" to an essentially repulsive but even more dangerously destructive woman in *The Parasite*. Conan Doyle rejected the crude acceptance of Roman Catholic doctrine, with all of its certainties, which his school training had sought to inculcate, but also remained doubtful about the equal self-assurance of scientific scepticism as transmitted by the Edinburgh University medical school. His life, both literary and spiritual, constantly reflected a mental conflict between science and the supernatural. Ultimately, Doyle was to find resolution of his long internal conflict in the spiritualistic faith, and to express the victory of spirit over science in the conquest of Professor Challenger, but a finer artistic expression of that resolution is to be found in the passages where the scientific Holmes acknowledges his belief in the spirit. This resolution lay far in the future during the writing of *The Parasite*, and part of the novel's strength is its revelation of the terrible vulnerability of seemingly all-conquering science. It is worth stressing that Doyle, conscious of his own Celtic antecedents, is also playing skilfully with the question of whether what is at stake is science or magic; as modern historians of science have testified, the two were decidedly allied, sometimes in the single persons of their medieval practitioners. Location plays an interesting contrasting role in another aspect. The care of usage of local references in "Cowles" is in part intended to offset the plot, which could be located anywhere. Cowles might have met his fate whatever his city and profession, and the final scenes on the island are intended to imply just such a removal from normal social life. (They also offer a fascinating anticipation of the last great scene in "The Final Problem", where Watson calls into the deep from the cliff for the presumably dead Holmes, to hear a strange half-human response much as Armitage does for Cowles: again, the evidence of the growth of professional literary skill in the interval between composition of the two stories is highly suggestive.) In *The Parasite* the greater tension of the story is achieved by the disruption of Edinburgh social and academic life by the enchantment. The fate of Professor Gilroy affects this reader much more than that of Cowles, because the surroundings and circumstances come so much closer to the lives of reader and writer. Hesketh Pearson's *Conan Doyle* saw something of the strength of *The Parasite* but weakened itself by its own facetiousness, the English Pearson finding it ludicrous that Gilroy could be suspended from his chair for talking nonsense in lectures. But Doyle was thinking of his Edinburgh, when lectures were strictly linked to students' fees and were absolutely pre-eminent in the University system, having nothing of the comforts of the Oxbridge tutorials about them.

The sexual implications of both stories are notable, but they require rather more conservative analysis than Mr Charles Higham has offered in the biography where he so rightly seeks to rescue them from their obscurity. Conan Doyle's medical research for his doctorate was concerned with the effects of syphilis, and indeed some of his medical fiction, such as "The Third Generation" and "A Medical Document", introduces the theme in highly dramatic form. Given the readiness to label him a typical Victorian it is important to stress here, as elsewhere, he was in fact seeking to open up far more realistic dimensions to fiction. Moreover, as a medical student, he knew far more about sexual impulses and their possible consequences than most writers, and believed their discussion to be natural and necessary. "Cowles", composed at the time when he was finishing his doctoral thesis, is in part a metaphor for syphilis: human destruction by love for an instrument of murderous contagion. The metaphor is also present in *The Parasite*, but by making the destruction mental rather than physical, it is strengthened, while retaining the medical basis that syphilis and its effects also destroy the mind. Lord Randolph Churchill was presenting a tragic proof of the fact in the House of Commons during these very years.

The diabolical women themselves, however, reflect a different aspect of Doyle. He was a believer in "the new woman" in many respects: the great creative period which produced *The Parasite* also included two very powerful statements for the rights of women in professional life, "The Doctors of Hoyland" and *Beyond the City*. In our two stories the women are evil, and women in Doyle's fiction are normally forces for good, if at times ambiguous and frustrated in that work. Doyle believed in the superiority of women, very largely because of his overwhelming admiration for his own mother, who kept a struggling family together despite his father's alcoholism and inability to take responsibility. These two stories show a female superiority turned to evil consequences, but the testament to that superiority is still there. Elsewhere in this work the point is as vigorously made in happier contexts. It will be remembered that the first of the Holmes short stories, which were to put him on the road to immortality, was a firm, almost brutal, assertion of his defeat at the hands of a woman.

The alcoholism of Charles Doyle and, it may be, a few wild nights with fellow students on the part of Conan Doyle, gave rise to another aspect of the stories: the terror of losing control of normal social impulses and destruction of self-respect. Only a minor character in "Cowles" is actually presented in a state of alcoholism, but Cowles's own obsession is easily translated to – and from – that of a likeable person who cannot see his own doom in his love of alcohol. In the case of Gilroy, alcoholism and its effects form an even more obvious basis for what in the story is the Professor's irrationality under enchantment. Conan Doyle's writing reached a very sympathetic and involved audience during its frequent references to the proximity of struggling professionals to socio-economic destruction; his own family background had perpetually teetered on the verge of that brink; and Professor Gilroy's case turns on the terrible vulnerability of professional responsibility, alcoholism being one of the most frequent threats to survival in that world. Experience of alcoholics and their treatment, even their attempts at self-treatment, certainly gave a grim quality to Gilroy's attempts to fight off the seductive power of his own enemy.

The three other items in this volume possess a different interest. The full M.D. dissertation which Conan Doyle wrote at Southsea was presented with success to Edinburgh University in 1885, is too large, too technical and, in part, too obsolete to justify inclusion in a popular work. But it merits brief quotation to exhibit a point hitherto ignored. If Doyle's medical knowledge lent a scientific basis and a tone of realism to his writing, whether in Holmes's consulting-room, medical demonstration or surgeon-lecture techniques, or in the almost clinical presentation of certain characters, his own developing prowess as a writer of fiction made curious inroads on his medical research. One singular passage in his dissertation, presented here, shows a recital of symptoms gradually evolving into a biography of the patient, and a world of minor characters and background detail gradually coming alive in the doctoral candidate's mind. The scholar informed the writer; but the writer was struggling to break out of the scholar. A more predictable way in which the thesis would go on to influence future fictional work, particularly detective-work, is the later passage on a personal case-study based on an actual patient, and the charm of the irony with which Doyle concludes that portion of the narrative is both characteristic and highly suggestive. It also foreshadows those intriguing stories in which Conan Doyle presented his readers with a truncated conclusion, circumstances preventing the final clearing-up of the case – "Case of Identity", "The Five Orange Pips", "The Engineer's Thumb", "The Resident Patient" and "The Greek Interpreter" being but a few, obvious, examples.

Among the many points in our extracts from the dissertation which throw new light on Conan Doyle's later writing is the coldly scientific citation of his research into remedial drugs by making experiments on himself to see how large a dose might safely be prescribed. It is a remarkable indication of the courage and dedication which he brought to his investigation and shows how deeply his scholarly enthusiasm and desire for the betterment of humanity dominated him. Here, certainly, is a clear revelation of Conan Doyle himself among the other human originals for Sherlock Holmes. Holmes's readiness to conduct experiments on himself was one of the first points made about him, and indeed is mentioned to Watson before he meets Holmes at all. But it is evident that Doyle's literary imagination as well as his retrospective reconsideration led him to reflect on the dangerous possible side-effects of experimentation with an overdose of drugs, and from this it was a short step to making Holmes a cocaine addict. A final use both of self-experimentation, and of subsequent remorse for the failure to consider other consequences of it in the fever of the chase, is made in the most horrific possible form in "The Devil's Foot", where Holmes and Watson nearly blast their own minds while attempting to discover the nature of the drug which killed Brenda and Mortimer Tregennis and drove into insanity their brothers George and Owen.

But it would be misleading to see Conan Doyle's writings for or about Edinburgh University and its staff and students as exclusively concerned with darker themes. His rich vein of comedy and irony found expression in far more of his work than has been generally recognised: much of the charm of the Holmes stories, for instance, derives from concealed as well as open humour, and the same is true of the bulk of his long and short stories. Of these latter a remarkable volume, *Round the Red Lamp*, published in 1894, was entirely concerned with medical life. It was natural that at least one of his stories should have been directly set in the atmosphere of his own student days. The date of its composition is uncertain: a few of its companion stories had been written some years previously, but most were previously unpublished and the confidence of style suggested that the theme recommended itself when he was writing the bulk of the stories for book publication. If, then, it comes from 1893-94, it is clear that his recollection of his world of some fifteen years earlier was excellent, and he evidently derived a nostalgic satisfaction in the mention of Rutherford's pub in Drummond street, opposite Old College. It is probable that some of the reactions of the younger student in the story were indeed Conan Doyle's own at first operation; but it seems likely that the actual incident, if it had no foundation in fact, befell a more nervous and suggestible student – of the relative weakness of will depicted in several protagonists elsewhere in this present collection. The little story is of considerable interest to the social historian, being clearly very close indeed to what normally transpired in Edinburgh operations before a student audience, and the casual conversation of the surgeon indicates a source for Holmes's small-talk to Watson in the intervals of discussing his cases – very notably during the chase led by the mongrel Toby in *The Sign of Four*.

And Sherlock Holmes himself was in fact brought directly into confrontation with Conan Doyle's Edinburgh in a story unknown to almost all readers of what they mistakenly took to be the complete Sherlock Holmes. The dissertation was not Conan Doyle's last offering to his old university. On November 20, 1896, the Edinburgh University *Student* appeared with a number of contributions from distinguished alumni and friends in furtherance of a charitable appeal (whose nature will present itself in the text). Sherlock Holmes had been formally buried in the Reichenbach in the *Strand* for December 1893, but in a response to a call from the students, Conan Doyle resurrected him for a brief frivolous moment: it would be five more years before *The Hound of the Baskervilles*, and two more yet before Holmes's divorce from Reichenbach was made absolute in *The Return of Sherlock Holmes*. Conan Doyle even wickedly headed his self-parody "The Field Bazaar" with the same title as the book publication of what he had intended to be the last Holmes stories: *The Memoirs of Sherlock Holmes*. It merits serious critical attention as a reminder of the intense amusement he derived from his own literary composition, part of the joke turning on self-identification with Watson in this little story (although there was much more of himself in Holmes than he troubled to assert). The apparent Englishness of Holmes (an Englishness less apparent to those who, like Doyle's family, heard his adventures read in the author's high Scottish intonation) led many interested commentators to puzzle *ad nauseam* as to whether Holmes had been to Oxford or Cambridge. In fact, Holmes's university career is clearly based on the university Doyle knew: but he only gives Edinburgh warrant for claiming Watson, albeit Holmes's awareness of university cash priorities suggests personal knowledge of the same institution. Anyhow, any university could congratulate itself on a pupil with the humanity, decency and literal genius of Watson. It was eminently characteristic of Conan Doyle to respond with such generosity (and at some cost to his own wish for emancipation from Holmes) to the *Student*'s appeal. Ten years ago *Student* became the basis for the creation of the Edinburgh University Publications Board, now directors of Polygon Books. It is, therefore, with the greatest pride and pleasure that we reprint the work given us by our most celebrated author. We express our thanks in the way he would most have wished, that of dedicating his gift to us, together with its accompanying Edinburgh works, to his surviving daughter, Dame Jean Conan Doyle, to whom, indeed, our own thanks are due for her very kind interest in the present book, and for several most helpful pieces of information which have been of great benefit to this introduction. We would also like to express our appreciation to Air Vice-Marshall Sir Geoffrey Bromet, to Professor W.W. Robson, to Mr Colin Affleck, to the National Library of Scotland, to the Edinburgh University Library (and especially its Keeper of Special Collections, Dr J.T.D. Hall), to Professor George Shepperson, to Mr Bill Campbell, and to the permanent staff of the Board, notably Mrs Margaret Roxton, Mr Neville Moir and Mr Adam Griffin. Mr Timothy Willis, Chairman of the Board, and research associate of the introducer, encouraged us throughout. Miss Louise Simson joined our operation most effectively at the proof-reading stage. Mr James Hutcheson took particular pains to give us a striking and imaginative cover design. Dr Graham Sutton, editor of the Board's medical journal, *Synapse*, very kindly undertook the work of reading the manuscript of the doctoral dissertation and of editing the material selected from it: the notes are his. The publication of the book was directed by Mr Graham Richardson, despite his onerous duties as Honorary Treasurer of the Edinburgh Students' Association. It has been a privilege to have worked under him in the enterprise, and I think Conan Doyle would be proud of him.

From the dust-jacket:

Deceived perhaps by the location of Sherlock Holmes' Baker Street rooms, many avid readers of Sir Arthur Conan Doyle have imagined the author to be a southerner born and bred. Yet his dry, analytical sense of humour and wry intonation must always serve to remind us of his Scottish birth, upbringing and university education, and its influence throughout his life.

His years at Edinburgh were critically formative ones, and the five pieces printed here both illustrate and illuminate its effects on his writing career.

Previously unpublished extracts for his M.D. thesis for Edinburgh University demonstrate an exciting fictional style of writing intruding on what might have been dry documentation. Both the Edinburgh short story *John Barrington Cowles*, published in the mid-1880s, and the short novel *The Parasite* of 1894 deal with women with extraordinary effects on men, in part supernatural and in part scientific. (*The Parasite* is clearly set in Edinburgh University circles, despite vague references to being in "England", here apparently used as a synonym for Britain.) The conflict of science and the supernatural, indeed, dominated much of Conan Doyle's life and writing.

The unsettling power and strength of *The Parasite* is brilliantly offset by the wit and precision of *The Field Bazaar*, a story about Holmes and Watson which Conan Doyle wrote for the Edinburgh University *Student*. Three years after officially sending

Sherlock Holmes into the Reichenbach Falls, Conan Doyle briefly resurrects his hero in honour of the city to which he owed so much. Finally, the half-reminiscence, half-fiction *His First Operation* presents in miniature to us Edinburgh's medical students and Royal Infirmary as they were a century ago in Conan Doyle's day.

"The Field Bazaar" – An Unknown Sherlock Holmes Case [9]

"I should certainly do it," said Sherlock Holmes. I started at the interruption, for my companion had been eating his breakfast with his attention entirely centred upon the paper which was propped up by the coffee pot. Now I looked across at him to find his eyes fastened upon me with the half-amused, half-questioning expression which he usually assumed when he felt that he had made an intellectual point.

"Do what?" I asked.

He smiled as he took his slipper from the mantelpiece and drew from it enough shag tobacco to fill the old clay pipe with which he invariably rounded off his breakfast.

"A most characteristic question of yours Watson," said he. You will not, I am sure, be offended if I say that any reputation for sharpness which I may possess has been entirely gained by the admirable foil which you have made for me. Have I not heard of debutants who have insisted upon plainness in their chaperones? There is a certain analogy."

Our long companionship in the Baker Street rooms had left us on those easy terms of intimacy when much may be said without offence. And yet I acknowledge that I was nettled at his remark.

"I may be very obtuse," said I, "but I confess that I am unable to see how you have managed to know that I was…I was"

"Asked to help in the Edinburgh University Bazaar."

"Precisely. The letter has only just come to hand and I have not spoken to you since."

"In spite of that," said Holmes, leaning back in his chair and putting his fingertips together. I would even venture to suggest that the object of the bazaar is to enlarge the University cricket field."

I looked at him in such bewilderment that he vibrated with silent laughter.

"The fact is, my dear Watson, that you are an excellent subject," said he.

You are never *blasé*. You respond instantly to any external stimulus. Your mental processes may be slow but they are never obscure, and I found during breakfast that you were easier reading than the leader in the *Times* in front of me."

"I should be glad to know how you arrived at your conclusions," I said.

"I fear that my good nature in giving explanations has seriously compromised my reputation," said Holmes. "But in this case the train of reasoning is based upon such obvious facts that no credit can be claimed for it. You entered the room with a thoughtful expression, the expression of a man who is debating some point in his mind.

---

[9] The Field Bazaar was written in 1896 as a fund-raiser for Edinburgh University, which was Sir Arthur Conan Doyle's Alma Mater. It was published in THE STUDENT, the Edinburgh University Undergraduate Magazine and reprinted by Atheneum Press in 1934. The story was republished by the Baker Street Irregulars in pamphlet form.

The Atheneum Press version is listed as Number Thirty-nine in Otto Penzier's 100 Indespensibles in Sherlock Holmes.

In your hand you held a solitary letter. Now last night you retired in the best of spirits, so it was clear that it was this letter in your hand which had caused the change in you."

"This is obvious."

"It is all obvious when it is explained to you. I naturally asked myself what the letter could contain which might have this effect upon you. As you walked you held the flap side of the envelope towards me, and I saw upon it the same shield-shaped device which I have observed upon your old college cricketing cap. It was clear, then, that the request came from Edinburgh University – or from some club connected with the University. When you reached the table you laid down the letter beside your plate with the address uppermost, and you walked over to look at the framed photograph upon the mantelpiece."

It amazed me to see the accuracy with which he had observed my movements. "What next?" I asked.

"I began by glancing at the address, and I could tell, even at the distance of six feet, that it was an official communication. This I gathered from the use of the word 'Doctor' upon the address, to which, as a Bachelor of Medicine, you have no legal claim. I know that University officials are pedantic in their correct use of titles, and I was thus enabled to say with certainty that your letter was unofficial. When on your return to the table you turned over your letter and allowed me to perceive that the enclosure was a printed one, the idea of a bazaar first occurred to me. I had already weighed the possibility of its being a political communication, but this seemed improbable in the present stagnant conditions of politics.

"When you returned to the table your face still retained its expression, and it was evident that your examination of the photograph had not changed the current of your thoughts. In that case it must itself bear upon the subject in question. I turned my attention to the photograph, and saw at once that it consisted of yourself as a member of the Edinburgh University Eleven, with the pavilion and cricket-field in the background. My small experience of cricket clubs has taught me that next to churches and cavalry ensigns they are the most debt-laden things upon earth. When upon your return to the table I saw you take out your pencil and draw lines upon the envelope. I was convinced you were endeavouring to realise some projected improvement which was to be brought about by a bazaar. Your face still showed some indecision, so that I was able to break in upon you with my advice that you should assist in so good an object."

I could not help smiling at the extreme simplicity of his explanation.

"Of course, it was as easy as possible," said I.

My remark appeared to nettle him.

"I may add," said he, "that the particular help which you have been asked to give was that you should write in their album, and that you have already made up your mind that the present incident will be the subject of your article."

"But how - !" I cried.

"It is as easy as possible," said he, "and I leave its solution to your own ingenuity. In the meantime, "he added raising his paper, "you will excuse me if I return to this very interesting article upon the trees of Cremona, and the exact reasons for their pre-eminence in the manufacture of violins. It is one of those small outlying problems to which I am sometimes tempted to direct my attention."

Fourth, an Introduction to *The Complete Sherlock Holmes and Other Detective Stories* by **Owen Dudley Edwards**, a leading critical authority on Conan Doyle's detective stories and author of *The Quest for Sherlock Holmes*.

Sherlock Holmes (said the late, great W.W. Robson, Masson Professor of English Literature at Edinburgh University, a century after Arthur Conan Doyle studied medicine there) is 'arguably the most famous [fictional character] in literature'. Conan Doyle himself insisted that Holmes merely walked in the footsteps of C. Auguste Dupin, the detective with whom Edgar Allan Poe, the great pathfinder of so many literary genres, had launched modern detective fiction in the late 1840s. In his invaluable celebration of his favourites in English Literature, *Through the Magic Door*, Conan Doyle called Poe 'to my mind, the supreme original short story writer of all time.' All detective stories, insisted the Edinburgh-born Irishman, went back to the work of the American; each writer's 'main art must trace back to those admirable stories of Monsieur Dupin, so wonderful in their masterful force, their reticence, their quick dramatic point. After all, mental acuteness is the one quality which can be described to the ideal detective, and when that has once been admirably done, succeeding writers must necessarily be content for all time to follow in the main track.' Holmes might be rude about Dupin in *A Study in Scarlet*, or parody his thought-reading in 'The Cardboard Box', but Conan Doyle meant that as an indication of Holmes's weakness, vanity, not of his strength.

Posterity does not agree. Sherlock Holmes is synonymous with infallibility, incorrectly no doubt (see 'The Greek Interpreter' or 'Wisteria Lodge'). Sherlock Holmes inspires endless movies, TV and radio versions, pastiches, full-length spurious imitations: he has been portrayed as an artificial clone for the future, as Jack the Ripper, as an early Freud patient, as a pornographically insatiably gay, as a World War II geriatric. Minor figures in the stories, such as Professor Moriarty or Inspector Lestrade have been made modern fictionists' central characters to buoy up whole series of somewhat indifferent quality. Poe is a more famous name, perhaps, than Conan Doyle: but his box-office winners are The House of Usher, or the Black Cat, or the Red Death, or even the Raven – Dupin opens no cheque books. Ironically, Conan Doyle has been served with the reverse injustice: if Holmes is immortal, the world has pursued him with the relative indifference to such excellent stars as the Brazilian Cat, the Lost Special, the Man with the Watches, the Terror of Blue John Gap, or the Horror of the Heights. If Dupin had been submerged by his master's galaxy of rival creations. Holmes in reality merits his star status because *his* maker was also capable of other great things. And while Conan Doyle wrote on kind of straight detective fiction, his versatility in the detectiveless detective story demands the homage it has not yet fully won.

So what are we giving you here for the first time in one volume is the chance to encounter Sherlock Holmes among his author's other detective creations. This requires a wide net. If you have invented the most famous detective the world has ever known, you hardly wish to write other stories which field an inadequate substitute. Conan Doyle's problem went the other way: he worried that the pressure on him to produce series of Holmes stories would mean that Holmes was dragged into perfectly good plots which really did not need a great detective. Holmes's appeal goes far beyond the detective story, owing so much of its strength to the wit, the humour, the atmospherics, the brilliant use of Watson to bring the exotic and adventurous into our own ordinary family-doctor-overshadowed lives. It had been one thing to write a story mixing a whole series of Edinburgh medical types into the two figures of Holmes and Watson and structures with the science of a medical case-study and the art of Plato's dialogues, Cervantes's Don-Quixote-and-Sancho-Panza comedy in reverse. Boswell setting up Johnson to knock everyone down, Poe's plucking forth mystery from the accumulation of trifles, Emile Gaboriau's human fox-hounds on the Scent, Wilkie Collin's complexities of cross-purposes among striking protagonists to deepen the quest – indeed with his own enjoyment of knight-errantry later celebrated in his romances of Fourteen-century England and France *The White Company* and *Sir Nigel*, Conan Doyle endowed Holmes and Watson with the roles of knight and squire on quests. These things in *A Study in Scarlet*, begun in 1886, published (after several rejections) in 1887 by Ward, Lock in their *Beeton's Christmas Annual*; if not fully developed, as they would be, all the ingredients seem present in embryo. The, possibly on a suggestion from Oscar Wilde (Conan Doyle and he met at a dinner where work was commissioned from them both by *Lippincott's* magazine, Wilde's contribution turning out to be *The Picture of Dorian Gray*), Conan Doyle produced a sequel, *The Sign of the Four*. Then the newly-founded family magazine the *Strand* found itself with a winner when Arthur Conan Doyle offered a series of short stories with the same principal two characters encountering separate adventures each month, so you could miss an episode without losing track of the plot, as you would if you missed an instalment in a serial. We think of the procedure as automatic today, and TV would be lost without it: but Conan Doyle pioneered it. And in the short story he had found his true art-framework: as he says in *Through the Magic Door* 'It takes more exquisite skill to carve the cameo than the Statue. But the strangest thing is that the two excellences seem to be separate and even antagonistic. Skill in the one by no means ensures skill in the other.' He constructed most of his own longer stories episodically, and the long Holmes stories are in three of the four cases made up of two self-standing parts. *The Hound of the Baskervilles* is a single entity, and works well as such, partly by varying Watson's retrospective account with his own reports and diaries: but it is short. And Arthur Conan Doyle thought of works like his fellow-Scot Stevenson's *Treasure Island* as short stories. He would have thought of one of the greatest of all modern derivatives From Holmes and Watson, F. Scott Fitzgerald's *The Great Gatsby*, as a short story.

So now, at 32, the young doctor was famous, had removed from Portsmouth to London (having left his native Edinburgh for good at 22), and his six Holmes short stories had become twelve, at the *Strand*'s urgent request, and the twelve became twenty-four. But the twenty-four ended with Holmes's supposed death, in a noble act of literary integrity which rained curses on Conan Doyle's head from an enraged and astronomically expanding band of followers. He had even thought of killing off Holmes at the end of the first twelve stories, and when he respected his mother's advice not to, the resultant story, 'The Copper Beeches', rejoiced in brilliant dialogue (Holmes's suspicions of rural turpitude, one of the finest anti-pastorals in literature), infectious fear (Arthur Conan Doyle's sisters were governesses whose dangers clearly worried him), and high literary antecedents (his mother was now living in the rural location of Charlotte Bronte's *Jane Eyre* with effects on the scenario she prompted) – but gave Holmes little impact on the main drama. Much of his detective-work is peripheral to the principal action in several of the *Memoirs* – e.g. 'The Gloria Scott' or 'The Crooked Man' – and in a few he is either avowedly ('The Yellow Face') or less openly wrong

('The Stockbroker's Clerk, in which enquiry at Mawson and Williams in London instead of travelling to Birmingham would have averted the crime). The need to supply so many Holmes stories so quickly meant that a plot might take the author into unfamiliar territory. 'Silver Blaze' is one of the finest short stories ever written, and its exchange on the dog in the night-time one of the most memorable, as well as one of the most instructive, epigrams ever coined, but Conan Doyle would later sardonically recall that persons who knew racing better than a struggling doctor-author could afford to do, said it contained enough violation of racing legalities to ensure all persons connected with the running of 'Silver Blaze' would be warned off the turf for life with some of them (including Holmes) in danger of imprisonment as well. So Holmes was sent by his maker to meet Moriarty: ironically the miniature epic in which they supposedly hurtled to destruction violated all the rules of rationality so dear to Holmes's heart and wielded the weapons of the eternal struggle of Good and Evil so engagingly that it completed Holmes's conquest of the reading public for 1893 and the ensuing century.

Freed of Holmes (forever, as he may have thought, but why was that airgun in 'The Final Problem' left unexplained?), Conan Doyle first created a new and magnificent hero, but not, very much not, a master mind: Brigadier Etienne Gerard was to be the protagonist. Arthur Conan Doyle came back to detective fiction as a new kind of literary vehicle: a Holmesless carriage. The 'Round the Fire' stories of the late 1890s twice introduced a Holmes-sound 'amateur reasoner' (in 'The Lost Special' and 'The Man with the Watches') but as the late D. Martin Dakin, Prince of Sherlockologists, put it, while the phrases were Holmesian 'the theories advanced in the letters are not merely wrong, but rather silly; in other words, Arthur Conan Doyle, tongue in cheek, used them as a means for anti-Holmesian detective fiction. The deluge of detectives who followed Holmes made (wholly unconvincing) attempts to show their distance from Holmes by insisting on their difference of method: Conan Doyle in these two stories shows that if anyone can put it across the Great Detective, it is his own creator. And those pseudo-Holmes Lampoons are mere details, like Scotland Yard theories: the real solutions leave no reader adrenalin unsatisfied, all the more because the confessions are so credible in human terms, from judicially opposed types of evil and good. But more generally the 'Round the Fire' tales are centred around victims, and it seems highly deliberate that the most sympathetic is a self-confessed crook ('B.24). That story is also indicative of Conan Doyle's craftsman's eye, seeing how it might be reworked to a much more favourable view of a protagonist, in this instance resulting in the 'Abbey Grange' (when Holmes has Returned).

The 'Round the Fire' Series is the work of an accomplished writer who has brought his literary economics to a fine art, knows how to build his location and atmosphere, establish his characters, work up his pace, and retire leaving his audience emotionally breathless and intellectually replete. Holmes in *The Sign of the Four* opens with an entertaining critique of *A Study in Scarlet* which suggests Arthur Conan Doyle's Jesuit teachers at his boarding school Stonyhurst College had well taught him to be your own devil's advocate: and here Holmes demands that reports of his cases should be like Euclidian geometry. Oddly enough, Conan Doyle's detective fictions do not leave readers with a sense of neat conclusions analogous to a Euclidian proof, but this is not primarily because of the scientific perfection of the solution (many Holmes solutions are not perfect, and the story's magic does not demand that they are perfect, merely that the story's discourse can make them seem so for the time being). These are adventures, quests, great narratives in miniature, not puzzles for the most part: we read them because of the story, not because of the problem. Our jaded palates, suerfeited with every known contrivance in detective fiction, do now turn to Holmes for the same wine in old bottles: we go to Holmes because he gives us literature, however unpretentious. The geometrical satisfaction has much more to do with moral and emotional pleasure at the conclusion. This is not to say the stories have happy endings: very often they do not, and the Holmesian or Holmesless unveiling of the mystery leaves tragic background conditions irredeemably present, or with their memory hauntingly inescapable. But some form of justice has been done, as a rule. It may be that the justice comes in the courage of one protagonist to face a horrifying and unjust condition, as in one of the very last stories, 'The Veiled Lodger' (a little gem, beginning with high farce, turning into retrospective mystery, ending with towering nobility in the midst of every incentive to despair). When a story concludes with flagrant injustice, it is the reader's compassion that supplies the justice: and Conan Doyle can stimulate reader emotions with all the skill of a practiced physician. But in speaking of the emotions we come closer to Watson's province than to Holmes's. Holmes may be a priest like figure (as in his absolutions to criminals) or a Christ like one (as in 'The Final Problem' or 'The Dying Detective', respectively recalling the Crucifixion and the Temptation in the Desert). So impressively could his severely scientific personality become identified with Good that a modern Christian apologist and major literary critic C.S. Lewis readily mixes 'The Final Problem' with Milton's *Paradise Lost* when having Good battle with Evil for the future of a planet in its Garden of Eden phase (*Perelandra*). But Watson works from within us; Watson's reactions are our reactions; Watson testifies to our inability to keep emotions out of our would-be scientific analysis of life. And to develop a Watson required consistent practice, reflection, trial and error. The very earliest story Conan Doyle was ready to reprint 'That Little Square Box' written when he was barely 22, is a satirical detective story, in which the narrator from the first must alienate our sympathies (where Watson would invade and conquer them). It is curious how a lifetime in some art-form may begin with satire upon it. Eric Ambler, for instance, began his career as a great thriller-writer with *The Dark Frontier*, whose hero, having gone mad, imagines himself to be the hero of a cheap thriller.

 Our first stories here show Arthur Conan Doyle making his way as future Holmes-maker, with the note of satire and pastiche very prominent. Future skits on Holmes involving his self-detection as criminal prove to have been lacking in originality even as skits: 'The Silver Hatchet' said it first. Some of Arthur Conan Doyle's work gives us clues to how his data were obtained, 'The Cabman's Story', for instance, not only having its individual merits but also showing how its material would be startlingly deployed for *A Study in Scarlet*. For all of the comic genius which makes Conan Doyle one of the most amusing writers of detective fiction as well as perhaps the greatest, his young life was cruelly overshadowed by the descent of his gentle, artistic father into alcoholism and epilepsy, with consequences visible in early mysteries such as 'The Surgeon of Gaster Fell', 'A Pastoral Horror', or 'Our Midnight Visitor'. Arthur Conan Doyle's voyage to the West African coast as a ship's doctor on the *Mayumba* would result in a fateful meeting with the dying American black antislavery leader, Henry Highland Garnet, from whom the boy doctor learned of the tragedies of racial oppression in the United States from a black standpoint, with results unique for his time in the authenticity of 'J. Habakuk Jephson's Statement', 'The Five Orange Pips', and 'The Yellow Face'.

Conan Doyle's early work, even some that he would discard, often reaches great heights – 'Habakuk Jephson', for instance, whose power led to its indignant denial by a consular official ready to assume it would be taken for truth, while its more grammatical version of the actual abandoned ship (*Marie Celeste* for *Mary Celeste*) has prevailed over the real name in virtually all allusions. But he is learning his trade: 'Uncle Jeremy's Household' is included here as a definite early mystery, but in later work Conan Doyle would not discard potential sources of entertainment as casually as he here throws aside Jeremy, the Yorkshire Bard. He became a master-artist of the absurd, as figures such as Thadeus Sholto, Athelney Jones, Dr Grimsby Roylott, Reginald Musgrave, Mycroft Holmes, Professor Sergius Coram, Lord Mount James, Frankland of Lafter Hall, and many others bear witness. Roylott in particular deserves study, proving impressively in 'The Speckled Band' how a figure of fun can simultaneously flourish as a figure of terror. Thadeus continues fascinated with his own hypochondria in the midst of death; Athelney Jones acknowledges 'there's a flaw here when Holmes points out his theory of the crime requires that 'a dead man very considerately got up and locked the door on the inside'; Reginald Musgrave fears he 'hardly' follows Holmes's deduction that the butler had more brains than Musgrave and his preceding nine generations of ancestors; Frankland is reputed to sue an archaeologist for opening a Neolithic grave without the consent of the next of kin (while disinheriting his own unfortunate daughter.

With or without Holmes, Conan Doyle could produce some startling criminals. The present collection not only includes a python, a giant blind underground bear, and a collection of undiscovered stratospheric airfish, but a gentleman of a considerable turn of speech notwithstanding his venerable age of several thousand years. If it be argued that to place the responsibility for the crime on a non-human agency is to cheat, the defence calls as its first witness Poe's orang-utan in 'The Murders in the Rue Morgue. The detective story was in fact founded on the widest construction of criminality. The late non-Holmesian problem, 'Danger!' offers a more usual plot than any: instead of guessing who done it, we know who is the criminal (or more correctly, agent of destruction) and that his victim is Britain: what we seek to discover is why Britain surrendered to her minor opponent. It is a fascinating instance of the application of detection-methods to international politics, in this instance Arthur Conan Doyle's crusade for a Channel Tunnel which has so belatedly been vindicated. In the event, the story would be quoted favourably during World War I not by the British but by the Germans, to its author's horror, thus he needed the aid of Sherlock Holmes in 'The Last Bow' to martial the arts of propaganda in fiction to reassert his devout patriotism.

In the latter part of Conan Doyle's life his devotion to the cause of spiritualism diverted him most of the time from his usual directions in fiction, save for Holmes. And critics, partly in irritation at the survival of familiar names, were ready enough to dismiss the last stories as weak. The charge is in some respects unjust. Perhaps Holmes was weakened by the want of competition from non-Holmes stories, and the exigencies of meeting cost of spiritualistic crusades meant that Holmes had to be revived when a story might have been better without him. 'The Blanched Soldier', for instance, is outstanding, as W.W. Robson established, when Holmes (for the first time a narrative voice for an entire story) is not speaking but listening to his client or to the victim who clears up the mystery at the close. 'The Lion's Mane' was originally intended to be

Holmes recounting his own defeat as a naturalist, and the story was weakened when the idea (and the naturalist) were discarded, but some fairly torrid cameos supplying positive motive remained to give the story strength. The use of Holmes and of a third-person narrator shows us that the aged Conan Doyle wanted to go on experimenting with new departures in story-telling. Conan Doyle was not afraid of the 'twenties': he took on the dollar decade with great vehemence in Holmes cutting the Gold King down to moral size in 'Thor Bridge', he used the new freedom of sexual allusion to striking effect, even making homosexual incest a motive for sibling murder in 'The Sussex Vampire', and showing a daughter's terror of paternal rape in 'The Creeping Man'. The vitriol-throwing in 'The Illustrious Client' is a particularly powerful description. And Holmes's tears in fear that Watson has been killed in 'The Three Garridebs' are the culmination of a Platonic relationship economically developed over 40 years and 60 stories.

Of course it is not only the mutual respect and affection of Holmes and Watson that develops over the years, but also their own stature as characters. Holmes begins as the humanised automaton who ruthlessly excludes literature and philosophy from his consideration for reasons of relevance, but he rapidly becomes a commentator on both. And in the same way, the work of Conan Doyle shows that the detective story can be both literature and philosophy. The question of 'who done it?' has more profound implications than the case – or the corpse – in hand. Conan Doyle showed how a doctor in mind and training can have much to teach the creative writer and the historical investigator. And, in a wholly unpriggish way, the stories have much to teach us about ourselves and our quandaries. They are the work of a good, as well as a great, man; and it will require no Sherlock Holmes to work that out.

ACKNOWLEDGEMENTS

This edition would not have been possible without the support and goodwill of Michael Cox, of Oxford University Press; I would not have undertaken the present commission without it, given my personal gratitude for his aid in the making of *The Oxford Sherlock Holmes*. I have not troubled my former colleagues in that enterprise, Christopher Roden and Richard Lancelyn Green **(Compiler's note**:*Deceased April, 2004. See Chapter 11 for further details*), but the benefit of their wisdom and insight then has been invaluable to the present work. So, too, was that of beloved co-editor, W.W. Robson, whose death is irreparable but whose influence is eternal. I am also deeply obliged to Bonnie, Leila, Sara and Michael Dudley Edwards. I remain perpetually indebted to Dame Jean Conan Doyle for her advice and encouragement in my days as a biographer: there could have been no justification for troubling her now, but her wisdom and nobility are a perpetual source of inspiration.

My deepest thanks are due to Edwin Moore, my commissioning editor at *HarperCollins*, who has been a joy to work with on the *Strand* magazine. Sherlock Holmes would have been out of the Reichenbach five years earlier than he was, so irresistible is his good nature. And as always I must present my heartfelt gratitude to the staff of the National Library of Scotland, and to that of Edinburgh University Library. Fortunate indeed is Arthur Conan Doyle in the biographical guardians of his native city.

Next, an Introduction and an Afterword from two publisher's editions of the Conan Doyle collection *The Adventures of Sherlock Holmes*.

Firstly, the Introduction by **Eric Ambler** to the edition published by Book Club Associates.

I first read the early Sherlock Holmes stories over fifty years ago. They still give me pleasure. I can say that of few other books read at the time. The kind of pleasure they gave me now is, of course, different; but my first experience of them remains in the memory as an episode of importance, like learning the truth about Santa Clause or going to the grammar school. For the boy of twelve these stories were more than an entertainment; they opened doors to rooms about which he might not otherwise have known so soon.

Conan Doyle was one of those writers who, having taken the trouble to acquire special knowledge, feel obliged to pass it all on, every last scrap, to their readers. In what he thought of as his serious work, the historical novels, this propensity was responsible for their major defects. In the Sherlock Holmes stories it had happier consequences.

Thus, Holmes is not only a great detective but also a aphorism-dropper. Moved, as he often is, to reflect sardonically upon the human condition, he turns usually for the apt comment, the summing up, to French or German writers. 'Goethe is always pithy,' he may remark, or, 'The French have a neat way of putting these things.' Driven by compassion he may go further afield – to such recondite sources as the poet Hafiz, for example – but the French and Germans are his preferred authorities. Moreover, few concessions are made to Watson's, or the reader's possible ignorance of the languages used. True, Hafiz is rendered in English – presumably not even *The Strand Magazine* was prepared to set in Farsi – but the French and German tags are invariably given in the original with no other clues to their meaning than those provided by context. When he uses French quotations Holmes makes things even more difficult. In 'The Red-Headed League', admittedly, *L'homme c'est rien – l'oeuvre c'est tout* is attributed to Flaubert, but that is unusual; most of the French sources are left unidentified. Since Watson never asked, 'Who said that?' I could only assume that he always knew, an assumption strengthened when I found him passing an idle hour with Murger's *Vie de Boheme*. This troubled me. Obviously, Watson, though often silly, was an educated man, and that was what I wanted to be. If being educated meant knowing instantly what Holmes was saying when he quoted Goeth's German, and who he was quoting when he lapsed into French, clearly I had extra-curricular work to do.

I did it in the public library and it was valuable exercise. For instance, tracking down Holmes's sneer at the Scotland Yard worthies, *Un sot trouve toujours un plus sot qui l'admire*, taught me a lot about using books of reference; and if at the same time I acquired a certain amount of pretty useless information – the author of that particular quip was Nicolas Boileau (1636-1711) – you never knew when it might come in handy. Naturally, I had my failures. In *The Sign of Four* another Scotland Yard man is dismissed with a shrug and *Il n'y a pas de soits si incommodes que ceux qui ont de l'esprit*. I couldn't find this one anywhere and finally concluded that Holmes had simply paraphrased Moliere's line about an erudite fool being more foolish than an ignorant one; though why the oafish Athelney Jones should have been credited with having *de l'esprit* was beyond me.

But Holmes influenced my reading in other, more exciting ways. When he urged Watson to read Winwood Reade's *The Martyrdom of Man*, Watson was cool. I was more receptive. I took Holmes's advice eagerly, though certain hazards had to be overcome before I could do so. By then I knew my way about the public library and could find most things unaided; but not Winwood Reade's book; for that I had to ask. I always tried to avoid the librarian himself – there had been a humiliating encounter with him over my request for Holmes's monograph on tobacco ashes – and so approached his woman assistant. She gave me an odd look and went away. After a bit, and with an elaborate pretence of browsing among the shelves, I followed to see where she had gone. To my dismay I saw her with the librarian in the latter's glass-partitioned office. He had a book in his hands and was flipping through the pages. Clearly, they were trying to decide, neither of them having read it, whether or not *The Martyrdom* was suitable for a boy of my age. Finally, the librarian stopped flipping, shrugged and gave it back to her. No smut apparently, therefore harmless. I got the book. It took me a long time to read and I relished every moment.

The church, the Bible and religious instruction at school had always bored me. After years of regular church-going I still had to watch the rest of the congregation in order to know when to stand, sit or kneel. The words of the service were still to me meaningless. I loathed hymns, found the clerical voice grotesque and the uttering of responses absurd. Of course, I had kept these thoughts to myself. Religion wasn't something one was permitted to like or dislike. You accepted it in the form provided, as you accepted tap water, or you were damned. Young clergymen sometimes had doubts, it appeared, but as these always turned out to arise from some theological quibble or a dispute over ritual, they were small consolation to a doubter who was against clergymen of all ages and denominations. Now though, here at last, was a book by an articulate, and patently educated, writer which proclaimed, with a wealth of historical evidence and reasoned argument to support its case, that the whole thing was, and always has been, an elaborate hoax. That, at least, was how I interpreted Reade's findings, and I was sure that Holmes had done the same. It was an enormous relief. My own doubts could now be explained in terms other than those of innate wickedness or incipient madness.

The emphasis, however, was brief. Priggish youngsters seeking theoretical justification for their likes and dislikes are, though often successful, not always as fortunate as I was. After the first excitement of recognizing in Winwood Reade a kindred spirit had worn off, and I had grown used to what Watson called 'the daring speculation of the writer', I became more interested in the paths by which he had arrived at them than in the speculations themselves. Before long I had begun an explanation of social history which still continues.

I remain grateful to Holmes.

Today the things which most impress me about these stories are the natural skills with which they are told and the quite subtle ways in which even the most fanciful plots are made believable. In *The Adventures* Conan Doyle was still putting flesh on the characters of Holmes and Watson, giving them the kind of substance which would make the reader's suspension of belief instant and automatic. If among the establishments he used were those closest at hand, the cultural titbits which had taken his own fancy, he chose them shrewdly. With Watson epitomizing the virtues and prejudices of the

Victorian middle-class Englishman, the agnostic polymath Holmes had to be made as cosmopolitan in his tastes as possible. Although Conan Doyle himself greatly admired Dr. Johnson and Macaulay, he never made the mistake of wishing them on Holmes. It is Goethe to whom Holmes turns for pithiness and obscure satirists like Boileau who are called upon to provide the 'neat way of putting things' which so appeals to him. Of course, the supply of *mots justes* must sometimes have run low. Conan Doyle's biographers have been silent on the subject, but it is unworthy to suspect that somewhere on his travels he picked up a dictionary of French quotations, and that it was among the entries in it under *sot* that he found the sticks needed to beat Lestrade, Gregson and Athelney Jones? Perhaps, though I think the suggestion might have amused him. He was almost always a man who could laugh a little at himself.

In 1891 he could well have been amazed at himself too. In that one year he abandoned medicine to become a full-time professional writer and suffered a bout of influenza that nearly killed him; he left his consulting room in Devonshire Place and moved to a house in South Norwood; he started a long historical novel called *The Refugees* and he became famous by writing for *The Strand Magazine* all the stories in this book.

I wish that I were about to read *The Adventures of Sherlock Holmes* for the first time, and envy those who will be doing so. Still, it is comforting to know that in rereading them yet again I shall not be disappointed.

Secondly, an Afterword to the Reader's Digest Association edition.

This afterword has been excerpted from "The Greatest Detective Who Ever Lived" by Fred Strebeigh, originally published in Smithsonian. *Strebeigh, a member of the English faculty at Yale University, spent three months traveling across America to meet some of the thousands of Sherlock Holmes admirers who celebrated the great detective's centennial in 1987.*

In the winter of 1887 a declining London magazine called *Beeton's Christmas Annual* published a tale of murder titled "A Study in Scarlet." Written by a struggling doctor, the story had suffered multiple rejections before arriving at *Beeton's*, which considered it "cheap fiction" and paid the poor doctor wretchedly. *Beeton's* soon failed. But by then it had launched probably the most successful literary character of the past century and, some would argue, of all time – the great detective Sherlock Holmes.

Anyone who reads that first tale finds the protagonists in full stride. He mocks his most eminent predecessor, C. Auguste Dupin, the detective created by Edgar Allan Poe. He dismisses the London police as a bad lot and treats his loyal friend and chronicler, Dr. John H. Watson, as a dummy. He boasts that his deductive powers allow him to judge a man's profession from such details as his expression and his trouser knees. He grouches that crime and criminals have deteriorated so far that none can test him. And finally, of course, he gets his man and then watches Scotland Yard steal the credit.

Arrogant, brilliant, unappreciated, Holmes soon bestrode the world. His cases can be read in 57 languages, including Azerbaijani, Frisian, and Urdu. The works of his creator, Sir Arthur Conan Doyle, have earned royalties in at least 72 currencies. Though Holmes himself rarely left London, his image has circled the globe on stage, screen, radio and television, personified by such actors as William Gillette and Basil Rathbone.

Lean and angular, dressed in deerstalker hat and Inverness cape, smoking a pipe and wielding a magnifying glass, Holmes remains – one century after his debut – the world's detective. But no land on earth – not Japan or England or Denmark (all of which have Holmes fan clubs), not Iceland or India or Armenia (all of which has published his tales) – gives him the reverence that he receives in the United States. Strange as it seems, the British sleuth has become one of the great American heroes.

Followers of Sherlock Holmes may not be confined to any one country, but they do have their own language. Fans are *Sherlockian*s. The 60 original Holmes stories are the *Sacred Writings* or, more simply, the *Canon*. Arthur Conan Doyle is merely the *Literary Agent*. As such, he represented Dr. Watson, who became not Holmes's fictional chronicler but the true *Author*. When a Sherlockian achieves the pinnacle of Canonical knowledge, he becomes a Baker Street *Irregular*, if he is a man. Women, as a rule become *Adventuresses* of Sherlock Holmes. Each Irregular or Adventuress receives a name from a Holmes case, which becomes his or her *Investiture*.

Most American Sherlockians, whether or not they reach the pinnacle, join the offshoot of the Irregulars called a *Scion*. Some scions take names directly from Canonical adventures. "The Speckled Band" of Boston or "The Six Napoleons" of Baltimore. Others make adjustments: "The Hounds of the Baskerville" of Chicago or "The Solitary Cyclists" of South Bend. Still others play loose: "Boss McGinty's Bird Watchers" of Wilkes-Barre, "The Confederates of Wisteria Lodge" of Atlanta, or "The Great Alkali Plainsmen" of Kansas City. From Alaska ("The Bering Strait Irregulars") to Florida ("The Tropical Deerstalkers"), more than 80 scions hold meetings in at least 39 states, and what unites them all is Sherlock Holmes, the best and wisest man who ever lived, "The Master." Meeting across the land? Speaking a language others cannot understand? Calling themselves strange names? Honoring as real a man whom most of the world believes is a splendid fiction? Sherlockians may be this country's most benign cult – but a cult they are, indisputably, and one of enormous proportions.

Other nations, to be sure, honor Sherlock Holmes. In England, for example, the corporation whose headquarters encompass 221B Baker Street employs a secretary to answer every letter sent there for Holmes. But four of every five letters, some 800 of 1,000 a year come from America. In England, also, guides lead tours in Holmes's supposed footsteps – from Charing Cross Station to Scotland Yard to the Sherlock Holmes pub. But nine of every ten Holmes-walkers are American. Even the membership of England's most important Holmesian club, the Sherlock Holmes Society of London, is one-quarter American. According to the society's chairman, Anthony Howlett, a retired lawyer, British Holmesians are interested in serious scholarship. "Americans go more for the fun of the situation," he says. "You like dressing up much more than we do." He pointed to the deerstalker emblem woven across the wings of his butterfly bow tie. "That," he said for a Holmesian, "is about the height of eccentricity."

What an English Holmesian calls eccentricity, an American Sherlockian calls dedication to the cause. In New Mexico, on every Thursday after Halloween for the past 15 years, "The Brothers Three of Moriarty" have gathered at the Frontier Saloon, which sits just west of the Chaparral Truck Stop on a strip of old route 66 that runs through the town of Moriarty. They come from across the state to curse the memory of Holmes's archenemy, the villainous Professor Moriarty. They offer toasts to Holmes. They present scholarly papers. They take quizzes on stories from the Canon.

Although English scholars in the early 20th Century produced the first Higher Criticism on Holmes, in the 1920's an American doctor from St. Louis, Gray Chandler Briggs made a breakthrough: he chose to study Holmes as a real person. Briggs travelled to England to track down Holmes's house, which he decided must have stood at 111 Baker Street (221 did not yet exist). In 1930 Christopher Morley, columnist for the *Saturday Review of Literature*, wrote an introduction to the first American collection of all the Holmes stories, popularising the great detective as a subject for careful study. The flames of Sherlockian interest spread quickly, with Morley acting as bellows. By 1934, through his column in the *Saturday Review*, he had created the Baker Street Irregulars, taking their name from the street urchins whom Holmes used to ferret out information. Its creation inspired the rapid organisation of its first overseas counterpart, the English Sherlock Holmes Society, and the first American scion, the Five Orange Pips of Westchester County, New York. The Irregulars soon included America's greatest Sherlockian biographer, Vincent Starrett, and the greatest Sherlockian politician, President Franklin D. Roosevelt, who never attended a meeting but who contributed to the Higher Criticism with a series of letters arguing that Sherlock Holmes was an American.

In 1973, before Roosevelt joined the Irregulars, John Bennett Shaw started his Sherlockian Library, today consisting of 12,000 volumes, 4,000 periodicals, and 20,000 press clippings. Eventually it will move to the University of Minnesota, where it will merge with the university's own collection to create the world's leading Holmes center. But for now, the 74-year-old Shaw continues to serve as unpaid librarian to all Sherlockians. Requests flow in – from an Argentinian studying a Scotland Yard detective, an Englishman preparing a Holmes biography, a Nebraskan analyzing Holmes's use of the telephone, a Japanese seeking first editions. He responds with detailed letters and some 400 photocopies per month, bearing almost all the expenses himself. "Bread cast upon the waters," says Shaw.

Religious zeal typifies more than one Sherlockian. Richard Warner of Tulsa, Oklahoma, a retired forklift dealer, wrote on Holmes's behalf to Pope John Paul II, seeking to correct an error of omission. Warner lamented that the moon had a geographical feature that commemorated the great detective – Sherlock Crater, named by Sherlockian astronaut Harrison Schmitt – but the earth had none. So he set his sights on an Oklahoma hillock and decided to name it for the great detective. The hill's owner, however, had died leaving it equally to two universities and the Catholic Diocese of Tulsa. The universities agreed to Warner's request, but the Bishop of Tulsa objected. Undaunted, Warner went to the top, reminding His Holiness that Holmes had twice served the Vatican, albeit "fictional service to a prior pope." Warner was informed that since the diocese no longer owned a share of the hill, he was free to christen it "Holmes Peak."

Not all Sherlockians go to the Vatican to show their dedication. Some go to the racetrack. In Baltimore, 77 Sherlockians have sponsored a horse race at Pimlico for 16 years. It is called the Silver Blaze, and it commemorates the case in which Holmes restored England's greatest thoroughbred, Silver Blaze, to its rightful place in the winner's circle. Other Sherlockians sponsor Silver Blaze races in New York, Chicago, St. Louis, and Los Angeles. The Sherlockian better, however, doesn't look for a horse with fast times or impressive victories. He looks for links to the Canon – a jockey named Watson, an owner named Sherlock, or a horse racing in the colours of the original Silver Blaze.

Sherlockian devotees need not create memorials or wager money. Most often, they pursue knowledge. On the lower West Side of Manhattan, the Priory Scholars hold bimonthly meetings at a restaurant called Bogie's. They also take bimonthly quizzes. The quizzes challenge members to recall "Mycroft's yearly salary" or "the length of Oberstein's prison sentence" or "the number of plans taken from the Woolwich arsenal" – all parts of the same Holmes story. Such quizzes may seem intended to flunk out nonscholars. In practice, however, most scions exclude no one, and the most accessible one is the Sherlock Holmes Wireless Society, which meets within hearing range of any ham radio operator.

But not all of the groups are so unrestricted. The Red-Headed League grants membership only to Sherlockians who have red hair. The Bruce-Partington Planners claim to admit only Sherlockians who work "inside the military-industrial complex" and who can pass an entry exam that demands "access to classified data." The Planners are coordinated by an official from the Pentagon.

The only closed societies that engender resentment are those few who exclude women, the most conspicuous being the Baker Street Irregulars. Its mostly-male history began rather oddly. In 1934, when Christopher Morley announced his plans to form the group, he wrote to "all those" who sent him correct solutions to a difficult Sherlockian crossword puzzle would "automatically become members of the Baker Street Irregulars." Of the 21 solutions which Morley judged correct, at least 7 came from women. Morley then invited the men who passed the test, along with a few who made no attempt, to the first formal meeting of the Irregulars. "This first meeting," said the invitation's final sentence, "Will be stag." Stag they have remained for 53 years – despite the Investiture of two female Irregulars.

What pulls Americans so strongly, 100 years after his literary birth, towards Sherlock Holmes? Isaac Asimov, the well-known science-fiction writer (invested by the Irregulars as "The Remarkable Worm Unknown to Science"), suggests that Holmes may be "the most successful fictional character of all time" because he represents the triumph of the "gifted amateur who could see clearly through the fog." Dr. David Musto ("Dr. Anstruther"), of the Yale Medical School and the Yale Sherlock Holmes Society, says that Holmes appeals to modern readers because he represents a life unencumbered by the petty details of human existence. When you read a Holmes story, says Musto, "you enter a world in which people have breakfast but never use the toilet." Holmes's world is an "exciting place, but it's also peaceful – a world of modified danger." Other Sherlockians give different answers. At a meeting of an inner circle of the Irregulars, often called the "Sacred Six" members offered a range of explanations for Holmes's appeal: the human scale of the 19th. Century London, said "The Cardboard Box." The influence of the age of radio that began in the 1930's, said "Wiggins," when the voices of Gillette and Rathbone brought Holmes to the homes of millions. The mythic vitality of the characters, said "Sahara King."

The Canon totals only 60 stories, said the "Commissionaire Emeritus," Dr. Julian Wolff, a retired physician. "The real scholars," continued Dr. Wolff, who presided over the Irregulars from 1960 until his retirement this year, "are studying Shakespeare and the Bible. But we have a very limited amount of knowledge, so we can be professors, and be very, very wise. Because it's easy to know it all."

These and other answers ring true enough, but something more basic may lie beneath them. Sherlockian America links travel agent and tax accountant, funeral director and forklift dealer, commercial artist and army officer, legal secretary and state supreme court justice, stockbroker and music store owner. In a country that seems large and fragmented at times, Sherlockian have forged a nation of neighbors. That nation depends on one great game. The game depends on a few basic rules; that Watson *wrote* the stories; that Holmes *lived*. These rules stand no more open to challenge than the rule that a baseball hit left of third base will be called a foul. Sherlockians grew numerous because in America, as Holmes would say, the game is afoot. And any of them, traveling in almost any part of the country, know they can find a kindred spirit ready to play their game.

Next, an Introduction to **The Return of Sherlock Holmes** (Book Club Associates) by **Angus Wilson** (1974).

The return of Sherlock Holmes is more successful than his disappearance. A criminal master-mind bent upon desperate revenge among the lofty peaks and awful chasms of the Swiss Alps – calls for a combination of Doctor Mabuse and Frankenstein which is a contradiction of all that Holmes, the Man of Reason, stands for. Conan Doyle could splendidly invent the Gothic, out-Poe Poe when he liked, but to no other end than a rational refutation by Holmes of the superstitious fears and occult alarms that his creator had raised in the reader. Yet Holmes could hardly rationalize his own death (or, at any rate, not in the story in which it takes place). And so the Reichenbach Falls, which cry out for some phenomenon apparently supernatural to set off against nature at her wildest, remain obstinately a tourist background to a contrived tourist mishap. One feels sure that the notice of Holmes's fall to his death, which appeared in the *Journal de Geneve* on May 6th, 1891 was at best a second-page feature; alas, Watson's account of the terrible death of his friend is also among the most pedestrian of his narratives – especially as, by the nature of the story, he could not be an eye-witness to the dreadful event he is reporting in later tranquillity. In fact, I am afraid, a touch of Conan Doyle's boredom with the great detective seeps through into the story of his passing.

It is also true, I think, that the foreign scene is not the best of settings for Holmes. So far as I remember, Conan Doyle wisely only uses such a setting in one other story – 'The Disappearance of Lady Frances Carfax'

in *His Last Bow*; and even there the denouement is set in London – for the rest, the foreign adventures that won Holmes the Legion of Honour are wisely mentioned rather than recorded in full.

Perhaps the most remarkable achievement of the Sherlock Holmes stories – particularly when viewed from our distance in time – is their wonderful evocation of late Victorian England; not only the famous gas-lit fog-murky, four-wheeler London, but Surrey, the Home Counties, indeed all England south of Yorkshire. To these magnificently designed stage, 'abroad' can only be noises off, and these not the thunderous waters of the Reichenbach Falls, but the ominous grumbles of the machinations of the Great Powers in lost treaties or murdered spies, or, more congenially still, the lawless, brash voices of those returned newly rich from the goldfields or diamond mines of Australia or South Africa or even California (for Holmes, like his creator, expressly hoped that the follies of George III could be undone and the English-speaking peoples once more united). Imperial England, in fact, is Holmes's England. And in such a world the second most dangerous man in London, Colonel Moran, is far more effective than the first most dangerous man, Professor Moriarty. A mathematical genius, however criminal the streak within him, is but a general figure, whereas the 'best heavy game shot that our Eastern Empire ever produced', now turned crooked gambler in the West End clubs, is exactly the perfect eighteen-nineties London adversary for Sherlock Holmes. Nothing short of the colonel's tiger-shooting coolness, his jungle ruthlessness and his perfect marksmanship could really satisfactorily explain Holmes's need to lie low for three years after his supposed disappearance in Switzerland – for we must see his visit to the Lama in Tibet, his pilgrimage to Mecca, his 'interesting visit to the Khalifa at Khartoum', not to say his investigations into coal-tar derivatives at Montpelier, as no more than diversions of enforced idleness. With Colonel Moran, the old Shikari tiger-hunter, stalking Holmes in the darkness of midnight Baker Street, himself snarling tigerishly when the great detective brings him to bay, we are at the very heart of Conan Doyle's wonderful world in that Darwinian jungle, not only of London's bricks and mortar, but of the English countryside tamed by man, where the wild beasts are the criminals in every class and Holmes is the ever-vigilant warden.

Watson's narrative in the stories contained in *The Return of Sherlock Holmes* comes back often in its imagery to this jungle theme. 'I know not what wild beast we were about to hunt down in the dark jungle of

Criminal London,' Watson says as he sets forth with Holmes upon the first adventure of their new life together; and when that 'beast' is at last captured, he tells us of Colonel Moran that 'with his savage eyes and bristling moustache, he was wonderfully like a tiger himself'. Then, as Holmes and Watson keep their midnight vigil with the young detective Stanley Hopkins, to surprise the mysterious intruder into the murdered Black Peter's cabin, Watson tells us:

it brought with it something of the thrill which the hunter feels when he lies beside the water-pool and waits for the coming of the thirsty beast of prey. What savage creature was it which might steal upon us out of the darkness? Was it a fierce tiger of crime, which could only be taken fighting hard with flashing fang and claw, or would it prove to be some skulking jackal, dangerous only to the weak and unguarded?

> (Of course, in keeping with Holmes-Doyle's puncturing of all sinister, irrational fears, it turns out to be neither, but a pathetic, frightened, innocent young man.) Speaking of the blackmailer' Charles Augustus Milverton, Holmes says, "Do you feel a creeping, shrinking sensation, Watson, when you stand before the serpents in the Zoo and see the slithering, gliding, venomous creatures, with their deadly eyes and wicked, flattened faces?"

Beppo in 'The Six Napoleons' snaps at Watson's hand 'like a hungry wolf'. The clue to the distasteful character of the Norwood builder lies in the 'shocking story of how he had turned a cat loose in an aviary'.

And, in a peculiarly happy imaginative flash, Watson, at the start of 'The Dancing Men', tells us that Holmes himself 'looked from my point of view like a strange, lank bird, with dull grey plumage and a black top-knot'. In short, in the stories of *The Return of Sherlock Holmes* the world of beasts is never far away as a shadow world behind the strange or dreadful events which Holmes reduces to questions of orderly reason.

I do not think it fanciful to suggest that this gives to the book a special power, because it links so closely to the general metaphysic which governs Holmes's universe. Doyle had, we know, after leaving Stonyhurst, lapsed not only from Catholicism but from all religious belief into the current *fin de siecle* Darwinian pessimism. We also know that by the early years of the new century he was searching for some theistic creed – not least through exploration of occult phenomena – and that, from the time of the First World War until his death, he became a zealous, untiring preacher of the truth of spiritualism as the revelation of a Christian after-life. But whatever may have been emerging religious beliefs of his creator, Holmes, when he returned to life with the publication of 'The Empty House' in the *Strand Magazine* for October 1903, is still strictly rational. Indeed, he remained so always, long after his creator had given most of his life to affirming the truth of spiritualism, right into the last stories collected in *The Case-Book of Sherlock Holmes*, which was published as late as 1927. In fact a vital clue to Sherlock Holmes's extraordinary force as a fictional character comes from his personification of the *zeitgeist* of the turn of the century. His is a Hardyesque, blind world in which only incessant mental activity, incessant close reasoning, preserves him from despair and cocaine. In the opening of 'The Missing Three-quarter' in the present volume, Watson tells us,

> For years I had gradually weaned him from that drug mania which had threatened once to check his remarkable career. Now I know that under ordinary conditions he no longer craved for this artificial stimulus; but I was well aware that the fiend was not dead, but sleeping, and I have known that the sleep was a light one and the waking near when in periods of idleness…

Anyone who doubts that Conan Doyle was a subtle artist as well as a great entertainer should note how this underlining of Holmes's ever-looming despair introduces by contrast the only story which concerns athletes, those young rugger-players whose simple physical mode of life precludes all nervous pessimism. Justice (not always the justice of the British law, but the justice of the jungle law, something which Holmes himself decides as we see in 'The Abbey Grange' – "I had rather play tricks with the laws of England than with my own conscience"), reason, decency, these are Holmes's religion, practised to preserve the balance which alone in a Darwinian world keeps the beasts under control.

But Holmes's world (for all his aloofness and arrogance) is essentially a human one; this, I believe, is the clue to the extraordinary fascination which we feel in each of the stories as a new client enters the Baker Street room, a new man or woman who immediately (for all the brevity of description) interests us in his or her own right. As for the solar system, if it is not concerned with human life, then it is no concern of Sherlock Holmes, and he shrugs it away as an unnecessary irrelevance for a man who has misleading footprints to measure or subtle poisons to detect. Only once, so far as I remember, in the great outburst at the end of 'The Cardboard Box' in *His Last Bow*, does Holmes voice his dissatisfaction (always working in his creator) at the mechanical universe he inhabits –

> What is the meaning of it Watson? What object is served by this circle of misery and violence? It must tend to some end, or else our universe is ruled by chance, which is unthinkable. But what end? There is a great perennial problem to which human reason is as far from an answer as ever.

One outburst, and, for the rest, Holmes's great reasoning powers are given to establishing justice as far as may be in an unjust world. Yet how little satisfied either he or his creator were with a godless universe we may tell from the unpleasant nature of Professor Coran in 'The Golden Pince-nez', whose life is given to writing 'a work which will cut deep at the very foundations of revealed religion.'

Justice is here in the thirteen (away with superstition!) stories in this volume. The background to Holmes's return from supposed death is well known. Conan Doyle had come to see the enormous popular success of Holmes as a barrier to his own (and the public's) concentration upon his serious historical novels like *The White Company* or *Rodney Stone*. In 1892 he killed off Holmes in 'The Final Problem' (a death took place in 1891 and was made public to the world in 1893). Editors, however, reflecting public opinion, continued to press for more of the great detective. Chance events on a holiday in 1901 set Conan Doyle to thinking of a story essentially made for Holmes, and in 1902 he produced *The Hound of the Baskervilles*. He finally laid this novel in the days before Holmes had supposedly fallen to his death, locked in the arms of Professor Moriarty; nevertheless, by bringing his hero into print again, he soon found himself committed to resurrecting him from the Reichenbach abyss. Beginning in 1903 with Holmes's unexpected return into Watson's life disguised as an eccentric second-hand book dealer in 'The Empty House', he produced the stories in the present volume in rapid succession for magazine publication. In 1905 they were published in book form as *The Return of Sherlock Holmes*. In my opinion, this writing to the purpose of making up a book, far from lessening the qualities of *The Return of Sherlock Holmes* compared with its more chancely compiled predecessors, makes it a superior compilation, for Conan Doyle, though a considerable artist, was first of all a superb, professional writer of entertainment; yet the collection has not the tiredness which goes with a much later collection like *The Case-Book*. Conan Doyle is at his height, and what is perhaps more delightful to the reader, Sherlock Holmes himself, as Watson tells us, is also at the height of his reputation. These stories are set in the years between 1894 ('The Empty House') and 1898, the year of 'The Dancing Men', which is specifically said to have taken place in the year after the Jubilee.

Holmes had not lost his knowledge of the London under-world, as we learn in the first story "he is a harmless enough fellow, Parker by name, a garrotter by trade, and a remarkable performer upon the Jew's harp", but his advice is now sought by the highest in the land. As Watson says in 'Black Peter', 'I have never known my friend to be in better form, both mental and physical, than in the year '95. His increasing fame had brought with it an immense practice, and I should be guilty of an indiscretion if I were even to hint at the identity of some of the illustrious clients who crossed over our humble threshold in Baker Street.' He then goes on in 'The Priory School' and 'The Second Stain' to describe in detail these identities at which he must not hint. As Holmes remarks on reading the career of the Duke of Holderness, in 'The Priory School', "Well, well this man is certainly one of the greatest subjects of the Crown." And in the last story of the book, 'The Second Stain', Watson feels that, with Holmes retired to bee-keeping in Sussex, the time is at last right for the release to the public of a drama in which for some days the peace of Europe was at stake, a drama in which Holmes's clients are no less than the Prime Minister and the Secretary for European Affairs. Here we are indeed behind the scenes of the greatest world stage. 'His [the Secretary's] handsome face was distorted with a spasm of despair, and his hands tore at his hair. For a moment we caught a glimpse of the natural man – impulsive, ardent, keenly sensitive. The next the aristocratic mask was replaced.' Holmes's reaction to this grand world in which he is now called to move is mixed, and, I think, sympathetic. For all that, as he tells Watson elsewhere, he comes of country gentry stock, he is impressed by social distinction: "We are moving in high life, Watson – crackling paper, 'E.B.' monogram, coat-of-arms, picturesque address," he says in 'The Abbey Grange'; and the touch of irony does no, I think, prevent us from detecting the genuine snobbery. Yet when the greatest in the land offend Holmes's moral sense, as with the miserly old Lord Mount-James in 'The Missing Three-quarter' or even more with the great Duke of Holderness himself in 'The Priory School', Holmes does not spare them. He is truly at the height of his power.

This is well reflected, too, in his relations with Scotland Yard. True, Inspector Lestrade is still suspicious, jealous, and even, on occasion, offensive. But even Lestrade is at last forced into genuine, whole-hearted tribute to Holmes's skill in 'The Six Napoleons' – "We're not jealous of you at Scotland Yard. No, sir, we are very proud of you, if you came down tomorrow there's not a man, from the oldest inspector to the youngest constable, who wouldn't be glad to shake you by the hand." And there is a new generation at Scotland Yard in these mid- and late 'nineties to whom Holmes is a hero and a father figure. One of the most likeable men in the whole Holmes saga first appears in 'Black Peter' – 'Stanley Hopkins, a young police inspector for whose future Holmes had high hopes'. Who else in Holmes's world, dominated by a general desire to outcap the great man's omniscience, would have the natural modesty to say as Hopkins does in 'The Golden Pince-nez', "It means that I can make neither head nor tale of it"? As a result of this new friendly relation of Holmes with the conventional lawkeeper, based on his now accepted supremacy, Watson can pay a (some-what absurd it must be admitted) high tribute to British law in 'The Dancing Men' – I guess the very best case I can make for myself is the absolute naked truth," [says the American gangster]. "It is my duty to warn you that it will be used against you," cried the inspector, with the magnificent fair-play of the British criminal law,' It is not alone a familiarity with the highest in the land and a natural ascendancy over the conventional authority of Scotland Yard that mark the outward form of Holmes's gigantic intellectual superiority in these years of his triumph, it is clear that he also prospers at will in the ordinary base financial sense. For the most part he dispenses rather capriciously with fees, but when he does accept one, as in 'The Priory School', the size of the payment - £6,000 (in the mid-'nineties) – is enough to make us believe that Holmes was well able to afford to but Watson out of his practice, through an intermediary, for a handsome some. But there, of course, lies the real glory of this decade in Holmes's life, between his return from supposed death and his retirement to bee-keeping: the complete and happy union with Watson-Holmes, with cocaine (and, indeed, scraping on the violin) almost behind him; Watson bereaved of a superfluous wife. Each is assured of the other's steadfast affection after that moment in 'The Empty House' when Holmes's removal of his disguise causes Watson to faint and the great man himself to be openly moved – "I had no idea that you would be so affected!" This is demonstrative indeed in that late Victorian man's world of stiff upper lips, chaff and unspoken emotion, where women exists only on a throne far above mundane right and wrong.

Not all women, it is true. Holmes maintains his Olympian curtness with housekeepers – "Mrs Marker, you may go"; even Mrs Hudson, the lynchpin of the Baker Street establishment, is hardly fulsomely thanked for risking her life by moving the dummy in line with the bullets of the "best heavy game shot that our Eastern Empire ever produced" – she must be content to cherish he lodger-master's simple "All right Mrs Hudson, I am much obliged for your assistance." But *ladies* – from those like Miss Violet Smith, the solitary cyclist of the story of that name (perhaps the best in the book), who have fallen into genteel penury, up to the great Lady Hilda Trelawney Hope herself – may err but they never leave their thrones; they may even, as in 'The Golden Pince-nez' be Nihilists and be forgiven. The physical type of the ideal lady does not vary – 'tall, graceful and queenly', 'she stood proudly defiant, a queenly figure' – yet, despite this reverential attitude (or, no doubt because of it) there is also patronage, as when Holmes speaks protectively of miss Violet Smith, for all her queenly height as "that little woman". There is a certain nullity about the regal refinement of these ladies (a refinement, be it noted, which extends to those from far-flung Australia or America) that perhaps puts Holmes off his stroke, for the only two surely less than purely rational deductions he makes in these stories concern women. "I nearly fell into the error of supposing that you were typewriting. Of course it is obvious that it is music. You observe the spatulate finger end, Watson, which is common to both professions? There is spirituality about the face however" – he gently turned it towards the light – "which a typewriter does not generate. This lady is a musician.'" And again: "it is inconceivable that anyone who wore such glasses could be slatternly in other respects." There are other forces at work than pure reason when Holmes makes deductions about ladies. But for the rest, for the crowd of men of all kinds and conditions that jostle their way into Holmes's consulting-room, with a wide range and what an exact brevity in portraying it Conan Doyle had – from the Headmaster of the Priory School announcing himself with *Huxstable's Sidelights on Horace* to the captain of the Cambridge Rugby Football Fifteen's amazement at not being known to Holmes (' "Great Scott! Why, I was first reserve for England against Wales and I've skippered the 'Varsity all this year" '). It is a magnificent pageant of late Victorian England seen in late Victorian terms; and, of course, a pageant reaching far beyond England to the Empire, to the men tougher, more direct both in villainy and in decency than the Little Englanders, the men returned from the prairies, the Veldt and the outback. And it is not an empire of the past only, as Holmes makes clear to the erring undergraduate in 'The Three Students': "As to you, sir, I trust that a bright future awaits you in Rhodesia." Such is the splendidly realised world to which Sherlock Holmes, to our happiness as well as Watson's, returns, in this book, from a terrible death.

Secondly an Afterwod to **The Return of Sherlock Holmes** (Reader's Digest Association) by **John L. Cobbs**, Ursinus College, December 1991.

Orson Wells once called Sherlock Holmes "the man who never lives – and will never die"; and with each new generation of Holmes fans, it becomes more evident that this supersleuth is among the most durable of literary characters. Sherlock Holmes lives in our imagination in the pantheon of immortal literary heroes, right alongside King Arthur, Robin Hood, and the Count of Monte Cristo.

Unless we are Holmes scholars, like the members of the Baker Street Irregulars, who devote themselves to the study of Holmesiana, we don't pay much attention to the order of the adventures. We may well read *The Hound of the Baskervilles* or "The Bruce-Partington Plans" after *The Sign of the Four* or *A Study in Scarlet*. But for the detective's first fans, British and American readers at the turn of the century, Holmes arrived as Sir Arthur Conan Doyle wrote him – in a distinct sequence, and with each story tantalizingly delayed. Through the early 1890s the stories followed each other regularly in *The Strand Magazine*, usually every month. Today we can hardly imagine how shattered Holmes admirers must have been when they opened the December 1893 of *The Strand* to read a new adventure, 'The Final Problem,' only to discover that Doyle had killed off their beloved hero! In that story, Holmes died in the arms of his arch-enemy, Professor Moriarty. Christopher Morley, the critic and Holmes devotee, writes of "the wave of dismay that went round the English-reading world" when it appeared that the man whose mind had seemed equal to *any* problem had finally met his match.

A decade would pass before Doyle could be persuaded to raise Holmes from his watery grave – or rather, to indicate that he never entered it. Published in 1903 and 1904, the stories that appeared in *The Return of Sherlock Holmes* represent the triumph of the great detective over his creator's determination to dispose of him. Happily, this baker's dozen of stories was cut from the same cloth as the others. A few Holmes purists contended that they are inferior to Doyle's earlier "classics," but a careful reading of *The Return of Sherlock Holmes* reveals that these tales stand with the best.

"The Dancing Men," "The Solitary Cyclist," "The Priory School," "The Six Napoleons," "The Abbey Grange" – all display that melding of ingenious plot and rich atmosphere that mark the finest tales in the Holmes canon. Not a single story in the collection is weak. Even "The Adventure of Charles Augustus Milverton," which contains almost no detecting per se, has a dramatic immediacy that makes the narrative come to life. In reading *The Return of Sherlock Holmes*, we should remember that Holmes represents only half of Arthur Conan Doyle's divided literary personality, and the less dominant half at that. The cerebral Holmes – exacting, unemotional, and scientific – is the epitome of 19th- century reasoning, and he takes arms against a sea of troubles. Holmes does battle again and again with dragons and demons, and always he rips off their masks in a demonstration of the power of the rational mind over the forces of disorder.

But Arthur Conan Doyle was a man of many worlds, and only one of them involved orderly logic. Reason and precision were the products of Dr. Arthur Conan Doyle the ophthalmologist, and it was this precision that became the source of Holmes's mentality. But Arthur Conan Doyle the writer was a man of romance and passion. This was the man who wrote *The White Company* and a dozen more novels of chivalry and derring-do; who conceived *The Lost World* and other stories that resemble the science fiction of Jules Verne; and who devoted the last decade of his life to the pursuit of spiritualism.

Doyle's romantic nature shines through most of the stories in *The Return of Sherlock Holmes*. Often it reveals itself in the tale's rich gothic flavour and tense melodrama, as in "Black Peter":

It was a long and melancholy vigil, and yet it brought with it something of the thrill which the hunter feels when he lies besides the water pool and waits for the coming of the thirsty beast of prey. What savage creature was it which might steal upon us out of the darkness?

In other stories, Doyle's flair for the romantic leads to dramatic exaggeration of character. Thus, we are introduced to "the second most dangerous man in London" (after Moriarty), Colonel Sebastian Moran, Holmes's would-be assassin "The Empty House":

It was a tremendously virile and yet sinister face which was turned towards us. With the brow of a philosopher above and the jaw of a sensualist below, the man must have started with great capacities for good or for evil.

Reality versus romance – in story after story, Doyle establishes this tension. On the one hand, Holmes is the supremely objective thinking machine; on the other, he lives amidst the exciting excesses of Victorian London. Holmes's Olympian mind always triumphs, but not before the reader is titillated by sordid suggestiveness (what theatre critics of the time called "blue fire" theatrics). This blend of ingenious rationalism and lush romanticism accounts, no doubt, for the phenomenal success of Doyle's books.

These 13 stories lie at the very core of the Holmes canon, and in some ways they are the most representative. In "The Solitary Cyclist" Watson tells us "that from the years 1894 to 1901 inclusive, Mr. Sherlock Holmes was a very busy man. It is safe to say that there was no public case of any difficulty in which he was not consulted during those eight years." Doyle wrote these stories in 1903 and 1904, but the action takes place from 1894 to 1901. the Holmes who returns to us in "The Empty House" is not the young Holmes of the early tales. The young Holmes, although brilliant and eccentric, was an unformed eminence, notably more for his clever oddity than for his commanding intellect. We feel with Watson an occasional rankling at his arrogance, and an astonishment at his tours de force. By the time of *The Return of Sherlock Holmes*, however, Holmes is at the height of his powers, and we, who know him so well, are admiring, but beyond astonishment. Watson's sketch of him at the beginning of "Black Peter" is appropriate: "I have never known my friend to be in better form, both mental and physical, than in the year '95. His increasing fame had brought with it an immense practice, and I should be guilty of an indiscretion if I were even to hint at the identity of some of the illustrious clients who crossed our humble threshold in Baker Street. Holmes, however, like all great artists, lived for his art's sake…"

Humble threshold? Perhaps, but the great detective himself is hardly humble. Holmes moves in elevated circles in these middle years of his career. Watson tells us that during this period Holmes won the Order of the Legion of Honour and a letter of thanks from the president of France, and was of service to "the most illustrious persons in the land." In "The Adventure of the Second Stain" ("the most important international case which he has ever been called upon to handle") Holmes's clients are "the illustrious Lord

Bellinger, twice premier of Britain" and "the right Honourable Trelawney Hope, Secretary for European Affairs, and the most rising statesman in the country." In "The Adventure of the Priory School" he is employed by the duke of Holderness, "one of the greatest subjects of the crown."

In this last story, Holmes displays the supreme self-confidence that characterises this stage of his career. He humbles the haughty duke, ferreting out his lordship's indirect complicity in the kidnapping of his own son, then berates the nobleman for moral laxity: "The proud lord of Holderness was not accustomed to be so rated in his own ducal hall. The blood flushed into his high forehead, but his conscience held him dumb" – his conscience, and the impressive talents and demeanour of Holmes. "You seem to have powers that are hardly human," says the duke. Indeed, by the time of *The Return of Sherlock Holmes*, the detective has passed into the realm of the mythical. He has become, in the words of one critic, something of "a Victorian prototype for Superman." We feel that there is nothing he cannot do, no worlds he cannot conquer.

Many would present themselves to Holmes. Great Britain's global reach is something of a theme for all the Holmes stories, and for *The Return of Sherlock Holmes* in particular. Doyle forged the boilerplate for all his plots in his first two novels. *A Study in Scarlet* and *The Sign of the Four*. In both books Holmes investigates a murder committed in civilized London and discovers the roots of the crime in the primitive passions and vices of foreign lands – in the first case, in once-colonial America; in the second, in British India. The imperial pattern, if we may call it that, persists in some form through most Holmes tales, but it's particularly strong in this collection, in which all but two stories have foreign elements. Abe Slaney of "The Dancing Men," for example, pursues his lost love from America to England, bringing murder in his violent wake. Similarly, "The Abbey Grange," "The Golden Pince-nez," "The Solitary Cyclist," and "Black Peter" bring murderers or murders from beyond the sea home to England for Holmes to solve. Even in tales in which the foreign motif is less critical, is still instrumental: James Wilder, the kidnapper of "The Priory School," flees to Australia; the exam cheater in "The Three Students" does penance by joining the Rhodesian police; "The Six Napoleons" involves the expatriate Italian community; and "The Second Stain" is overshadowed by the international ramifications of a diplomatic theft. Only "The Norwood Builder" and "The Missing Three-quarter" seem wholly English in setting and plot.

As is so often the case in Holmes stories, the great world beyond England and her happy breed of men is a festering spawning ground of violence and vice. Exotic evils boil up out of the colonies, or stout Englishmen like Colonel Sebastian Moran and Black Peter Carey are corrupted by the uncivilized laws of jungles of palm and pine. Frequently, as is appropriate for mysteries, the foreign evils assume a sinister caste, sometimes with gothic overtones of the supernatural. Outside the solid walls of 221B Baker Street, man is a wolf unto man. As the critic Andrew Wilson has noted, "Watson's narratives in the stories contained in *The Return of Sherlock Holmes* comes back often in its imagery to this jungle theme." Indeed, many of the tales involve setting a trap in which the criminal hunter becomes the prey.

As always Holmes is the imposer of order and the voice of absolute reason. He may not prove that the evils of the world are cardboard wolves with painted teeth, but he demonstrates that they are flesh and blood, subject to the laws of biology, chemistry, and physics. Furthermore, their evil will yield to the cool application of a superior mind.

The crafty vengeful Norwood builder is flushed from his lair; the brutal Abe Slaney hoist by his own petard when Holmes uses his own code to lure him; and Colonel Moran is snared like the tigers he has bagged. "You cunning, cunning fiend!" Moran hisses as Inspector Lestrade drags him off to jail; but we know it is he who is the fiend. Holmes's reason not only tames the monster but analyses his deviant psychology: "There are some trees, Watson, which grow to a certain height, and then suddenly develop some unsightly eccentricity. You will see it often in humans. I have a theory that the individual represents in his development the whole procession of his ancestors, and that such a sudden turn to good or evil stands for some strong influence which comes into the line of his pedigree." The voice might be that of Charles Darwin.

It was also the voice of imperial England at the turn of the century. It is no coincidence that *The Return of Sherlock Holmes* overlaps with the period of Great Britain's glory. The 1890s was a halcyon decade before the Boer War, the death of Queen Victoria, the Coal Strike and, of course, World War I. It was a golden moment in British history, when literate Englishmen could believe that civilization, order, and reason would prevail over the forces of violence, superstition, and emotion. The sun never set on the British flag, and London was the great heart of the world, imposing discipline on every corner of Great Britain's far-flung empire. The "lesser breeds without the law" might bridle at the imposition of the British rein. They might produce, momentarily, chaos and mystery, but both could be resolved by the cool British mind. Nowhere in English literature is that mind more forceful and dramatic than in *The Return of Sherlock Holmes*. After all, once Holmes had proven that he could come back from the dead – entirely rationally of course – we would willingly accept his unravelling of life's lesser, but not less exciting, mysteries.

A Study in Scarlet

In a long story whose title was changed by its author from *A Tangled Skein* to *A Study in Scarlet*, Sherlock Holmes was born. It appeared first in Beeton's Christmas Annual of 1887 and received little attention from either critics or the public. Yet it laid the foundation of the greatest literary cult of the 19th.century, is now a world classic and in the first edition is extremely valuable.

Introduction by **Hugh Green** (1974)

If Conan Doyle had had the bad luck to fall under a hansom cab in 1887, after the publication of *A Study in Scarlet*, or even in 1890, after the publication of *The Sign of Four*, the name of Sherlock Holmes and Dr Watson would probably be known today only to a few specialists and the subsequent history of the detective story would have been different. It was the publication in the *Strand Magazine*, and afterwards in book form, of the great short stories beginning with *The Adventures of Sherlock Holmes* in 1891 and continuing with *The Memoirs* and *The Return* which gave Conan Doyle and his characters their immortality. In fact Conan Doyle sold the copyright of *A Study in Scarlet* to Ward, Lock & Co. for £25 and never, apparently, at the same time made another penny out of it. (He thus shared the experience of Fergus Hume who, at almost exactly the same time, sold the copyright of *The Mystery of a Hansom Cab*, the greatest detective-story bestseller of all time, to a group of speculators for $50).

A Study in Scarlet first appeared in November 1887 in the 28th. issue of *Beeton's Christmas Annual*, which cost one shilling: a first edition in the original pictorial picture wrappers might well fetch £1000 or more today. An important element in the creation of the Sherlock Holmes legend proved to be the illustrations contributed by Sidney Paget to the *Strand Magazine* from *The Adventures* onwards. Who today remembers D.H. Friston, James Greig, George Hutchinson, Charles Kerr and F.H. Townsend, who illustrated various early editions of *A Study in Scarlet* and *The Sign of Four*? It was Paget who first drew the Holmes and Watson we know today, even though he did not see the characters exactly as Conan Doyle saw them.

The third edition of *A Study in Scarlet*, which appeared in 1891 with George Hutchinson's illustrations, including a publisher's note identifying Conan Doyle's old master Dr Joseph Bell as the original of Sherlock Holmes. Dr Bell's 'intuitive powers', says Conan Doyle, were 'simply marvellous'. The patient would step up, "I see," said Dr Bell, "you're suffering from drink. You carry a flask in the inside breast pocket of your coat." Another case would come forward. "Cobbler, I see." Then he would turn to the students, and point out to them that the inside of the knee of the man's trousers were worn. That was where the man had rested the lapstone – a peculiarity only found on cobblers. All this impressed me very much.

Conan Doyle goes on to describe Dr Bell's 'sharp, piercing eyes, eagle nose, and striking features'. It was, he admits the impression made on him by Dr Bell that eventually led him to give up medicine for story-writing, although some of Sherlock Holmes's habits, such as drug-taking, were presumably not drawn from Bell, the two men clearly had much in common.

Dr Bell himself, in a further note reprinted in the same edition from *The Bookman*, describes his own methods such as Holmes might have done: 'The precise and intelligent recognition and appreciation of minor differences is the real essential factor in all successful medical diagnosis…Eyes and ears which can see and hear, memory to record at once and to recall at leisure the impression of the senses, and an imagination capable of weaving a theory or piercing together a broken chain or unravelling a tangled clue, such are implements of his trade to a successful diagnostician.'

One also does not have to look very far to find the original of Dr Watson. Conan Doyle, who was a very modest man, clearly saw himself as Watson, and he drops many clues to this in the stories. Holmes's critical attitude to the style in which Watson records his adventures may be taken to apply to his creator, as when Holmes remarks: 'Your fatal habit of looking at everything from the point of view of a story instead of as a scientific exercise has ruined what might have been an instructive and even classical series of demonstrations.' Even physically Conan Doyle resembles Watson, and when I occasionally caught a glimpse of him in Crowborough in the last years of his life one might have been looking at Dr Watson.

In spite of his experience and skill as a historical novelist, Conan Doyle only once, in *The Hound of the Baskervilles*, successfully overcame the problem of constructing a full-length detective story. What defeated him, as it defeated many of his contemporaries, was a final, convincing explanation of the crimes and the detection he had so vividly described. *A Study in Scarlet* is a case in point.

It begins excellently, with Dr Watson at a loose end in London after being badly wounded in the second Afghan war. The characters of Holmes – evidently a younger Holmes than the one we get to know later in the short stories – and of Watson are established with admirable economy. In a few pages they have set up house in the rooms at 221B Baker Street: 'a couple of comfortable bedrooms and a single large airy sitting-room, cheerfully furnished, and illuminated by two broad windows'. Holmes astonishes Watson with his deductions as he was to continue to do throughout their long life together. Holmes plays the violin. Holmes carries out chemical experiments and is the author of a monograph on cigar ashes. Watson would have suspected Holmes of being addicted to narcotics, 'had not the temperament and cleanliness of his own life forbidden such a notion'. This is a subtle touch. Watson got to know Holmes better later on. In a few more pages the hunt is up. 'A minute later we are both in a hansom, driving furiously for the Brixton Road.' Sentences like that can still, after any number of re-readings, make the heart beat a little faster. But when the book is barely half finished the hunt is over and the murderer is struggling in the arms of Holmes and his despised Scotland Yard colleagues, Lestrade and Gregson, who 'sprang upon him like so many staghounds'.

The explanation of all the murderous goings-on which takes up the last half of the story, a rather conventional account of adventures among the Mormons, fails in my view to come up to the standard of the detection in the first half. Conan Doyle seems to have been attracted by the theme of revenge arising from the activities of American sects and secret societies: he returned to the same line of country 28 years later in *The Valley of Fear*. And yet how readable Conan Doyle is, even at his weakest, compared with his predecessors in the field of the detective story, if one leaves aside Edgar Allan Poe and Wilkie Collins. Before the coming of Sherlock Holmes the Victorians had to pass the time on their railway journeys with a stodgy, and now pretty unreadable, succession of bogus police memoirs, mostly published a 'yellow-backs', such as *Experiences of a Real Detective, Recollections of a Detective Police-Officer, Recollections of a Sheriff's Officer, Diary of an Ex-Detective,* and *Revelations of a Private Detective.*

Conan Doyle was a true original and it is fair to say that even his most gifted contemporaries would not, could not, have written as they did if the Sherlock Holmes short stories had never appeared in the *Strand*. Some of those contemporaries occasionally wrote stories, and created characters, which approach the standard set in the first three books of Sherlock Holmes short stories, and which, in my opinion, are often better than Holmes in decline. I am thinking particularly of Austin Freeman, with the astute and completely realistic (not an adjective one would use about Holmes) Dr Thorndyke and Arthur Morrison, with his kindly and patient Martin Hewitt and his unscrupulous and brutal Dorrington. But they could not, as Conan Doyle did, create a still-living world. They do not make the heart beat faster: they lack the touch of imaginative genius.

A Study in Scarlet & The Hound of the Baskervilles (One volume).

Afterword by G.K. Chesterton entitled **Larger Than Literature: The World's Most Famous Detective**.

This afterword has been adapted from two essays by G.K. Chesterton (1874-1936), the British author and Critic known for the detective stories featuring his own Sleuth, Father Brown.

The return of Sherlock Holmes to the Strand Magazine some years after his death put a finishing touch to the almost heroic popularity of a figure whose reality was like the universally admitted reality of some hero of medieval fable. Just as Arthur and Barbarossa were to return again, men felt that this preposterous detective must return again. He had emerged out of the unreality of literature into the growing reality of legend, and in proof of this he has inherited the most widespread and pathetic of the characteristics of legendary heroes: that characteristic which makes men incredulous of their death. A slight and fantastic figure in a fugitive and ironical type of romance, he may seem too insignificant a subject for such a description. Nevertheless, the fact remains that Mr. Conan Doyle's hero is probably the only literary creation since the creation of Dickens which has really passed into the life and language of the people and become a being like John Bull or Father Christmas. It is remarkable to notice that although we possess many writers whose popularity is attested by enormous sales and general discussion, there is hardly one of them except Conan Doyle in this instance whose characters are familiar to everyone as types and symbols. Rudyard Kipling, for example, is undoubtedly a popular writer. But if we were to go up to any man in the street and say that a particular problem would have puzzled Strickland he would receive it with a very different expression of countenance to that which he would wear if we said that it would puzzle Sherlock Holmes. Mr. Kipling's stories give inexhaustible intellectual delight, but the personality which we remember is the personality of the story, not the personality of the character. We remember the action but forget the actors. In no other current creation except Sherlock Holmes does the character succeed, so to speak, in breaking out of the book as a chicken breaks out of the egg.

The fact that Sherlock Holmes alone has succeeded in familiarising himself at once with the cultured and the uncultured, and turned his name into almost as descriptive a word as Dr. Guillotine or Captain Boycott, involves certain conclusions, which are for the most part worthy and reassuring. The phenomenon corrects finally, for example, much of the foolish and foppish talk about the public preferring books because they are bad. The stories of Sherlock Holmes are very good stories; they are perfectly graceful and conscientious works of art. The thread of irony which runs through all the solemn impossibilities of the narrative gives it the position of a really brilliant addition to the great literature of nonsense. The notion of the greatness of an intellect, proved by its occupation with small things instead of with great, is an original departure; it constitutes a kind of wild poetry of the commonplace. The intellectual clues upon which the development of each story turns are perhaps incredible as fact; they are such problems as a great lawyer might extract from two bottles of champagne; they are full of the very revelry of reason. The figure of Conan Doyle's detective is, in its own wild and trifling way, good literature.

Now, there are in London more than nine hundred and ninety-nine detective stories and fictitious detectives, nearly all of which are bad literature, or rather not literature at all. If, as the saying goes, the public like books because they are bad, it would not be the fact that the one fictitious detective who is familiar to the whole public is the one fictitious detective who is a work of art.

All English people have read the stories about Sherlock Holmes. Work like this is so good of its kind that it is difficult to endure patiently the talk of people who are occupied only in pointing out that it is not work of some other kind. The specific quality of a story of this sort is strictly what may be called wit; it is obliged to have some definite invention, construction and point, like a joke in the comic papers. Such work is inexpressibly superior to most mediocre serious work. There has to be something in it; it cannot be an entire imposture. A man can pretend to be wise; a man cannot pretend to be witty. His jokes may be much worse in your opinion than they are in his opinion; but after all they must be jokes; they cannot be entirely shapeless mysteries, like many modern works of philosophy. Many men can make an epic who could not make an epigram. I would rather have the man who devotes a short story to saying that he can solve the problem of a murder in Margate than a man who devotes a whole book to saying that he cannot solve the problem of things in general. Sir Arthur Conan Doyle certainly weakened his excellent series of stories by being occasionally serious, but the greatest error of the Sherlock Holmes conception remains to be remarked: I mean the error which represented the detective as indifferent to philosophy and poetry would not be good for a detective. Sherlock Holmes would have been a better detective if he had been a philosopher, if he had been a poet, nay, if he had been a lover. It is remarkable to notice (I assume you are as intimate with Dr. Watson's narratives as you should be) – it is remarkable to notice that the very same story in which the biographer describes Holmes's inaccessibility to love and such emotions, and how necessary it was to the clear balance of his logic, is the very same story in which Holmes is beaten by a woman because he does not know whether a certain man is her fiancé or her lawyer. If he had been in love, he might have known well enough. The only real danger is that Conan Doyle, by spreading the notion that practical logic must be unpoetical, may have encouraged the notion, too common already, that imagination must be absent-minded. It is a false and dangerous doctrine that a poet must be absent-minded. The purely imaginative man could never be absent-minded. He would perceive the significance of things near to him as clearly as he perceived the significance of things far off. In the highest imaginative sense man has no right whatever to forget his teacup because he is thinking about Plato. If he does not understand his teacup which he has seen, how shall he understand Plato whom he has not seen? The best and last word of mysticism is an almost agonising sense of the preciousness of the whole universe, which is like an exquisite and fragile vase, and among other things the preciousness of other people's teacups. The last and best word of mysticism is not lavishness, but rather a sublime and sacred economy.

The perfect mystic would always be socially alert. The perfect mystic would be always correctly dressed. To such heights of transcendentalism some of us may find it difficult to soar; and such honest and unselfconsciousness failure, though it is certainly a weakness, is not an unpardonable or inhuman one. Some of the best men in the world have been specially remarkable for being conventional in theory and unconventional in practice. But if once a man is unconventional in theory, then the situation is atrocious. It almost certainly means either that a man has no morals or that he has no brains. The type of man does exist who says clearly and deliberately that he does not want to observe the little laws that surround him, that he is proud of being absent-minded, that he is proud of his disdain of detail. Whenever this occurs, it certainly arises in another and most literal sense from absence – of Mind.

The real moral of the popularity of the adventures of Sherlock Holmes lies in the existence of a great artistic neglect. There are a number of perfectly legitimate forms of art which are almost entirely neglected by good artists – the detective story, the farce, the book of boyish adventures, the melodrama, the music-hall song. The real curse of these things is not that they are too much regarded, but that they are not regarded enough; that they are despised even by those who write them. Conan Doyle triumphed and triumphed deservedly, because he took his art seriously, because he lavished a hundred little touches of real knowledge and genuine picturesqueness on the police novelette. He substituted for the customary keen eyes and turned-up collar of the conventional detective a number of traits – external and pictorial, indeed, but honestly appropriate to the logical genius – traits such as an immeasurable love of music and an egotism which was abstract and therefore almost unselfish. Above all, he surrounded his detective with a genuine atmosphere of the poetry of London. He called up before the imagination a new and visionary city in which every cellar and alley hid as many weapons as the rocks and heather-bushes of Sir Walter Scott's Roderick Dhu. By this artistic seriousness he raised one at least of the popular forms of art to the level which it ought to occupy.

He wrote the best work in a popular form, and he found that because it was the best it was also the most popular. Men needed stories, and he had been content to take bad ones; and they were right, for a story in itself is a marvellous and excellent thing, and a bad story is better than no story, just as half a loaf is better than no bread. But when a detective story was written by a man who refused to despise his art, who carried all their dreams to fulfilment, they preferred him to the bungling and irresponsible authors who catered to them before. It is no discredit to them that psychologies and philosophies had not sated their need for the rush of a climax and the fascination of a riddle. It would be as reasonable to blame men for not accepting cats as watchdogs, or using pocketknives as fireirons. Men must have detective stories; they must have forces and melodramas and comic songs. For anyone who is honest enough to take trouble and invoke inspiration over these other forms, the road lies open to rich and many-coloured fields of undiscovered art.

Chapter 11

Miscellany I: 1997 – 2003

This chapter consists of newspaper articles that contain up-to-date information associated with Sir Arthur Conan Doyle and Sherlock Holmes.

THE SUNDAY POST/**MAY 4, 1997**

Meet the man who answers the great detective's fan mail

The legend of Sherlock Holmes lives on

CLEARLY the little girl was upset. "Dear Sherlock Holmes," she wrote, "I have lost my little dog.
"We went for a walk in Central Park and he ran away. I am sure he has been stolen. Would you please help us find him. My daddy says you are the best detective in the world."
Like hundreds of other letters which arrive each month at Abbey House, London – head office of the Abbey National Bank – it was a touching request, written in the firm belief the ace detective is still alive.

Deer-stalker

This year – 67 years after the death of Holmes' creator Sir Arthur Conan Doyle – 250,000 letters will have been received, mostly from abroad.
And every one will have been answered by a succession of secretaries to Sherlock Holmes.
Gug Kyriacou (30), whose parents were born in Cyprus, is the latest to wear the famous deer-stalker hat.
He's a press officer with the bank which has an office in the massive white stone building occupying numbers 215 to 229 Baker Street in Central London.
Gug has become something of an expert in the Holmes phenomenon. He constantly re-reads the 60 stories the author wrote.
"I've been fascinated by the character, so I'm happy to keep the legend alive," he enthuses.
Gug is in good company. There are scores of Sherlock Holmes Societies all over the world. They include the Baker Street Irregulars, the Speckled Band, and the Scandalous Bohemians of Boston.
In the 1880s, when Conan Doyle began writing detective stories, Baker Street was much shorter than it is today. Number 221b did not exist except in the imagination of the author.
But today the Post Office accepts the fictional gas-lit residence of Holmes and Watson does exist. Even letters marked "Sherlock Holmes, London, England" are faithfully delivered.

Genuine

First job for Gug is to sort out the jokers from the serious enquirers. Most replies maintain Sherlock is "away at the moment" or "busy with his bees in Sussex".

"From reading every letter, I estimate the majority are genuine," says Gug. "Like the student at West Point military academy who wrote asking Sherlock what mystery novels he enjoyed reading. For a prompt reply he even included five dollars for postage.

"So many people really believe Sherlock exists so we never disappoint them."

Signed photo

One letter from Acapulco wanted to meet the great man any time he was in Mexico. A fan in Sapporo, Japan, addressed his letter to "Sharrock Homes" and a mother in Indianapolis asked for a signed photograph.

A woman in Alabama wrote – "There is a guy who lives a few blocks down the street who reckons he knows who killed Sharon Tate. He says it wasn't Manson at all. Can you come over and sort this out?"

Many who write are youngsters between 12 and 16 who are reading about Sherlock Holmes for the first time. They get special consideration.

"The last thing we want to do is destroy the myth. So when I reply I enclose a picture of the great man, a badge, a bookmark and a booklet about him," says Gug.

There are more than 80 Sherlock Holmes Societies around the world – thanks to the outcry which greeted the fictional death of Holmes in May, 1891.

Conan Doyle became so fed up with his fictional character that he "arranged" his death early in Holmes' career.

But the public refused to accept their hero had been done to death at the Reichenbach Falls by the evil Moriarty.

They clamoured for more. Black armbands were worn in the City and letters of protest flooded in to the newspapers.

In 1901 Conan Doyle was persuaded to resurrect the great detective, and *The Hound of the Baskervilles* was published.

Daily Mail, Saturday, June 21, 1977 **BOOKS**

Unmasked: The real Moriarty, master criminal
THE NAPOLEON OF CRIME; THE LIFE AND TIMES OF THE REAL MORIARTY by **Ben Macintyre** (*Harper Collins, £18*) by **Christopher Hudson**

Sir Arthur Conan Doyle created the first great master-criminal of fiction – Professor Moriarty. Tall, thin and pale, with a domed forehead and sunken eyes, Moriarty hid his malevolent genius behind a veneer of respectability and vast learning.

'He is the Napoleon of crime, Watson,' Sherlock Holmes tells his faithful friend in The Final Problem, before he and Moriarty clash and tumble to their deaths over the Reichenbach Falls.

Just as Doyle was persuaded to resurrect Holmes, so Ben Macintyre has now resurrected Moriarty – though as a figure of fascinating fact, not fiction.

Conan Doyle's chief inspiration for his master criminal was Adam Worth, or Wirth. Born in 1844, the son of German-Jewish immigrants to America, he grew up in New York when it was one of the most concentratedly criminal cities on earth.

His education in crime he picked up from people with names such as Boiled Oysters Malloy, Ludwig the Bloodsucker, Hell-Cat Maggie, who filed her teeth to points, and the saloon-keeper Gallus Mag, who bit the ears off rowdy customers and kept them in a pickling jug.

'Little Adam' became a purse-snatcher; then graduated to robbing banks. In 1869, in partnership with 'Piano' Charley Bullard whose deft fingers could charm open any safe, he stole about £1 million from a Boston Bank, and fled to Britain with his share, just ahead of the pursuing Pinkerton detectives.

Overnight he became a prosperous Yankee merchant banker, no longer Adam Wirth but Henry J. Raymond – the name filched from the irreproachable founder-editor of the New York Times.

After robbing a Liverpool pawnbroker, Raymond and Bullard made their way to Paris, where they set up a large-scale gambling operation disguised as an American social club.

In Liverpool, both men had met and fallen in love with an exuberantly beautiful, flirtatiously Irish barmaid, Kitty Flynn. Although she married Bullard, she had two children by Raymond and was to be one of the two enduring passions of the master criminal's life.

Pinkerton's agents eventually got the French police to shut down the Paris operation but, by then, Raymond had refined his *modus operandi*. Using trusted associates, Raymond would farm out robberies, which he had planned in impeccable detail, to petty criminals who never knew his name.

Returning to London, he bought Western Lodge on Clapham Common and a lavish flat in Piccadilly. He hosted dinner parties, bought a yacht and a string of racehorses, and became accepted as a man about town.

Steadfastly loyal to his friends and generous to those in need, he made it a rule that violence should be no part of any crime he planned.

His close associates all ended up in jail, but the Metropolitan Police couldn't lay a finger on Raymond, despite staking out his homes. He was to claim that throughout the 1880s he made about £63,000 a year, equivalent to £2.5 million today.

At about the time that Kitty, his first great passion, walked out of his life into the arms of a Cuban-American millionaire, Henry Raymond acquired the second, who made him internationally famous.

In 1876, Thomas Gainsborough's wonderfully seductive portrait of Georgiana, Duchess of Devonshire, was sold at auction for 10,000 guineas, the highest price ever paid for a work of art.

While she was still on exhibition, Henry Raymond was hoisted up to the first-floor window of Agnew's in Old Bond Street, wrenched it open, cut Georgiana out of her frame and walked off with her inside his frock coat.

Raymond entered into negotiations with Agnew's, then abruptly broke them off. Ben Macintyre suggests that he fell in love with the portrait, in which he saw not only echoes of Kitty, but a symbol of his relationship with a gilded society he both despised and wanted to be part of.

He held on to the Duchess for 20 years, keeping her under the mattress of his bed and travelling with her stashed in a false-bottomed trunk.

His criminal enterprises flourished – banks robbed in Paris, London and Sacramento, mail-trains plundered in France and Belgium, large quantities of diamonds abstracted from post offices in South Africa – but always Raymond, like Macavity, wasn't there.

Detective skills were in their infancy. There was no Interpol. Police communications, even between regions, barely existed. Not until the 1890s did telephones and photographs start to make a difference.

Raymond could have retired – he now had a wife and two young children – but he loved his work too much.

In the end, bored or perhaps thinking himself invulnerable, he courted arrest, attempting to rob a mail-van in the streets of Liege.

Captured, Adam Wirth (Raymond the gentleman no longer) spent the next five years in a Belgian prison. Old associates ratted on him. His business partner seduced Wirth's wife and sold the family possessions before fleeing with the cash.

By 1897, when Wirth was released, his spirit broken, suffering from TB, Professor Moriarty was a household name, his own had been forgotten.

He attempted to return to his life of crime, but his heart wasn't in it. The only man he respected was the great detective, William Pinkerton. Through him, he arranged with Agnew's to return Gainsborough's Duchess of Devonshire, and passed the proceeds on to his children before turning his face to the wall.

Wirth's son joined Pinkerton's; his grandson created Pan-American Airways. Georgiana eventually found her way back to Chatsworth where she belonged.

(**Compiler's note**: see also article on the same subject, page 246)

THE EXPRESS: THURSDAY JUNE 26 1997

TURNING POINT: A weekly look at how history could have been different.
Eliminated, my dear Watson

Why it would be a crime to lose arch-detective Sherlock Holmes. That dear old deerstalker of deduction has spawned many films and souvenirs, plus millions of letters and visitors to 221B Baker Street and it is an essential part of our lives and literature, proves writer and broadcaster BRIAN SIBLEY

THE FACT that millions of people every year write to 221B Baker Street, London, seeking the advice of Mr Sherlock Holmes, private consulting detective, is testimony to the creative powers of Arthur Conan Doyle, the man who (with a little help from Dr John H. Watson) chronicled Holmes's career.

Conan Doyle, a doctor with literary aspirations, was initially grateful that the popular success of the Sherlock Holmes stories enabled him to devote time to his serious writings. Later, he dismissed Holmes as belonging to a lower stratum of literary achievement and did his best to be rid of the ace detective – going so far as to hurl him over the Reichenbach Falls.

Responding to public demand, Conan Doyle reluctantly resurrected Holmes but, even if he had not, we should still have remembered the man who once observed that when you have eliminated the impossible, whatever remains, however improbable, must be the truth.

But what if Sherlock Holmes had never been brought into existence?

That, as the detective would say, is quite a three-pipe problem. However, we know his methods, we need only apply them.

Detective fiction would obviously have been saved half a century of emulating Holmes's style and another 50 years of trying to throw off the cape, cast aside the deerstalker and jettison the rest of Holmesian paraphernalia. And detectives would have been spared the anxiety of having to look out for facts with Zen-like significance, such as a dog that does not bark in the night.

Scotland Yard would undoubtedly have had a higher rate of unsolved crime, the Reichenbach Falls would be a minor Swiss beauty spot and London would be robbed of Sherlock Holmes pubs and Mrs Hudson dining rooms. The famous Baker Street would be just another thoroughfare without any shops selling souvenir plates, mugs and toby-jugs; everything in fact, from nesting Russian dolls to detective teddy-bears.

Since, as Holmes remarked, little things are infinitely the most important; we should not forget that we would have been denied hundreds of stage, film, TV and radio versions of the adventures. We would never have seen those beak-nosed portrayals by Basil Rathbone, those coldly cadaverous performances by Peter Cushing, or the wild-eyed fanaticism of Jeremy Brett.

Unwrite the 56 short stories and four novels about Holmes and so much mystery, intrigue and exoticism would have been lost to us: no sinister Man with the Twisted Lip, no Veiled Lodger or Solitary Cyclist; and definitely no gigantic hound stalking the mist-shrouded moors.

Above all, society would have been boringly free of all those arch villains; no Professor Moriarty to be dubbed "The Napoleon of Crime" and no Irene Adler to be known by the sobriquet, "The Woman".

To deduce that the world would have been poorer for the absence of Mr Sherlock Holmes is, as the great man himself would have said, "Elementary!"

DAILY MAIL, Tuesday, May 5, 1998

The best of Brickish. Japanese flock to admire our building blocks of history.

Daily Mail Reporter

Squat and solid, they are regarded with hushed awe by the visitors who file past every day.

Treasured for their shape and texture and marvelled at for their lasting quality, these are the precious prize exhibits in a Japanese museum.

British bricks, it seems, are building up a reputation for themselves.

Back home, they can be found cluttering up back gardens, littering building sites or even propping open doors.

But the Japanese believe our bricks deserve more respect.

At the World Brick Museum in Maizuru, north-west of Kyoto, specimens are kept lovingly in glass cases and treated as works of art. More then 10,000 visitors a month go to look at them. The Japanese fascination with British bricks probably has something to do with the rarity of brick buildings in Japan.

The high risk of earthquakes has made building with bricks a risky business.

So when the museum hosted an exhibition of just 16 bricks, titled 'Sherlock Holmes and English Bricks', Record number of visitors flocked through the doors.

They feasted their eyes on a collection of clay from Covent Garden, Scotland Yard, the Royal Albert Hall, St. Pancras Station and 221B Baker Street – the detective's home address.

The museum curators enlisted the help of the city of Portsmouth to compile the exhibition after discovering that Sir Arthur Conan Doyle created the character of Sherlock Holmes while living there in 1887. Council officials, quickly realising the tourism potential, frantically began tracking every spare brick they could find from the most famous sites in the Sherlock Holmes books.

But the Japanese brick appreciation is broadening rapidly. Soon Sherlock Holmes themes won't be enough. So council staff have resorted to plucking ordinary bricks from the city's Guildhall Square and fortifications to be sent to the museum. They will be displayed alongside photographs and documents about Portsmouth and its architecture.

An 18in specimen from the Anglican Cathedral, along with a lump of cathedral stone, is ready for shipment to Japan. Next in line is a brick from Charles Dickens's birthplace, in Old Commercial Road, Portsmouth. But this is proving a little more delicate.

'We simply can't go down and chip one out, we have to wait until one becomes available,' said council spokesman Mark Ludmon, explaining that many of the bricks have been recovered during renovation work in the city.

'The Japanese are genuinely very interested in our bricks, they are very enthusiastic about them indeed,' he added.

'Sometimes the bricks are mailed or sometimes they are carried by visiting delegations.'

Museum director Yukio Kohigashi said the Sherlock Holmes exhibition had been a great success. 'Many visitors seemed to be deeply impressed with the beautiful and magnificent buildings which are made of red bricks,' he said.

'They are impressed with buildings such as St Pancras station and Scotland Yard and they must have imagined Sherlock Holmes pursuing criminals in them'.

Brick fans don't always have to go to the museum to appreciate the best in bricks. Maizuru also hosts a Red Brick Festival and Red Brick Summer Jazz Concert each year.

The Daily Telegraph Monday, June 28, 1999

Sparing Sherlock's Blushes by **Charles Holland**

The mystery of why a Sherlock Holmes story, *The Adventure of the Cardboard Box*, was suppressed from publication by its creator, seems to have been solved.

A postcard from Sir Arthur Conan Doyle to an unknown recipient has revealed that he considered the story too risqué for publication and, instead, lifted sections of the tale for use in another work.

In the postcard dated May 10 1927, and headed "From Sir Arthur Conan Doyle, Bignell Wood, Minstead, Lyndhurst, Hants", the author wrote: "There was a certain sex element in the Cardboard Box story and for this reason I discarded it when I published it in book form.

"As there was a bit of good deductive reasoning in it I took it out and inserted it in another story *The Adventure of the Resident Patient*.

"Years later I was publishing another Sherlock Holmes collection and, as I was rather short, I put in the Cardboard Box after all. But I forgot that a bit of it had already been used…"

Conan Doyle's explanation has surfaced from a private source at the auctioneers Southeby's in London, where it is expected to fetch up to £1,500 at the sale on July 15.

A Southeby's specialist, Dr Peter Beal, said yesterday: "This postcard would appear to confirm the provisional conclusions reached by Doyle's bibliographers as to why Doyle dropped *The Adventure of the Cardboard Box* from English editions of the second collection of Sherlock Holmes stories, *The Memoirs*, published in 1894.

"The story only appeared in the American edition, not appearing in Britain until the collection *His Last Bow* was published in 1917.

"However, he was reluctant to drop the superb line of deductive reasoning used by Holmes on Watson at the beginning and so transferred it to *The Adventure of the Resident Patient*.

"In English editions the resulting duplication went unnoticed until the John Murray omnibus volume was published in 1928."

The Sunday Telegraph OCTOBER 3, 1999

COMMENT 'An insult to my ancient university' by **Isla McKelvie**, Edinburgh.

I am a fourth-year undergraduate at Edinburgh University, which, you suggest, Prince William may choose to attend and state dismissively the university is redbrick (News, September 26). Seeing that it was founded in 1583 in its current form, it is an older establishment than quite a few Oxford and Cambridge colleges including the really redbrick Keble College and the plate-glass-and-concrete St. Catherine's College. Or did you, even more insultingly mean to write provincial?

The university was the *alma mater* of such famous alumni as Oliver Goldsmith, Sir Walter Scott, Sir Arthur Conan Doyle, Robert Louis Stevenson, David Hume and William Playfair (not to mention James Boswell) so surely an apology is forthcoming.

Daily Mail, Saturday, January 8, 2000

As a £3 million Cezanne disappears, the story of the master criminal who might have inspired the painting's audacious thief…The priceless portrait, a racy duchess and the most daring theft of all time by **Trevor Grove**.

Certainly, it is tempting to think there was something romantic about the New Year's Eve theft of a Cezanne from Oxford's Ashmolean Museum. The stolen painting, Auvers-Sur-Oise, would have made a memorable gift to a lover on millennium morning.

To greet 2000 with a post-Impressionist landscape worth £3 million would have put in his place the chap who swims torrents and scales cliffs to deliver a box of chocolates.

Though the thief may have used the celebrations as a cover, it was not simply a case of festive opportunism by some undergraduate. And as it would be impossible to unload such a well-known painting on the market, the thief was probably stealing to order.

He planned the heist meticulously, breaking into the gallery via the roof. To avoid being identified on the closed-circuit TV cameras, he detonated a smoke grenade and used a fan to fill the room with fumes. The police found a hold-all containing gloves, sticky tape and a scalpel.

Reading these details, filmgoers must have felt a frisson of *déjà vu*. Surely, this was the nailbiting climax of movies such as The Thomas Crown Affair or Mission Impossible? So is Auvers-Sur-Oise being gloated over by a master criminal straight out of the pages of James Bond or **Sherlock Holmes**?

This may seem a frivolous notion until you consider the precedents – works of art have been snatched from public view to become the love object of a single pair of eyes.

One of the best-known cases concerned the master criminal of his age, who hid his prize for a quarter of a century, and whose notoriety was such that he became the model for **Sherlock Holmes's** most villainous opponent, **Professor Moriarty**.

The disappearance in 1876 of one of Thomas Gainsborough's finest portraits was the most sensational art theft in history, involving the then most expensive painting in the world.

It baffled the police of two continents for 25 years, despite underworld rumours and tip-offs. But the main reason for the public interest was the portrait's subject: the beautiful loose-living, witty, hard-drinking Georgiana, Duchess of Devonshire.

In her lifetime (1757-1806), she was the unchallenged queen of fashionable society, famous for her charm, extravagance and sense of style.

Born Georgiana Spencer, she married the duke in 1774 when she was 17 and immediately, by her own account, 'launched into the vortex of dissipation'.

For much of their life together, the Devonshires lived with the duke's mistress in an uneasy *ménage a trios*, while the duchess had a passionate love affair (and a child) with Charles Grey, a future prime minister.

Georgiana cut much the same sort of public figure in her day as her great-great-grand-niece Princess Diana was to do two centuries later.

After Georgiana's death, the Gainsborough portrait inexplicably vanished, until it was discovered 35 years later hanging over the hearth of a retired school-mistress. She had hacked off the duchess's legs so the picture would fit above the fireplace.

After the death of its owner, the portrait was put on display by Christie's in 1876, prior to being auctioned, and it caused a sensation. The picture of the loveliest, louchest Georgian society belle titillated Victorian London.

'Anyone passing the neighbourhood of St James's Square might well have supposed that some great lady was holding a reception and this, in fact, was pretty much what was going on,' reported The Times on May 6, 1876, the day of the sale.

'All the world had come to see the beautiful duchess and were conquered by her fascinating beauty'.

The other conquest of that day belonged to West End art dealer William Agnew. His winning bid of 10,100 guineas – worth more than £450,000 today – made it the costliest picture bought at auction, and was met with foot-stamping and cries of 'bravo'.

Among the crowds who flocked to view the duchess at Agnew's gallery during the next three weeks was a small, dapper man with dark, penetrating eyes and heavy whiskers. This inconspicuous figure was the 33-year-old American Adam Worth (or Wirth, or Werth), also known as Henry or Harry J. Raymond.

His closest friends, which included some of the worst hoodlums in the U.S. and Europe, called him Little Adam. But when Scotland Yard detective Robert Anderson called him 'the Napoleon of the criminal world' he was referring not merely to Worth's 5ft 4in height. It was also a salute to the little man's international stature as the 19th century's boldest, most resourceful and successful crook.

Conan Doyle used the same words to describe his fictionalised version of Worth, the arch-villain **Moriarty**, in The Final Problem: 'He is the Napoleon of crime, Watson – he is a genius, a philosopher, an abstract thinker.'

Unlike the evil professor, Worth did have some redeeming features. According to Ben Macintyre, author of a gripping biography called (of course) The Napoleon of Crime, he avoided violence, was widely generous when in the money – which thanks to the shrewdness of his operations, was most of the time – and staunchly loyal to his criminal companions.

It was a filial impulse that drew Worth to the portrait of Georgiana. His brother John, an incompetent crook who joined his elder sibling's London gang, was on remand in Newgate jail at the time, after a bungled forgery operation.

Adam Worth was unable to put up the £3,000 bail without revealing his connection with the forgers. So he conceived the idea of stealing the portrait to use as a hostage to force the respectable William Agnew to pay the bail.

Worth was sure that Agnew would be desperate to play along, the picture's value having increased sharply since the auction. The identity of the duchess's 'kidnapper' need never be known. And the freed John could then jump bail and do a bunk back to the U.S.

The robbery took place on a May night in 1876. Worth took two of his gang: the rat-like Joe Elliott to act as lookout and the slow-thinking, bull-like Jack 'Junka' Phillips.

Outside Agnew's Old Bond Street gallery, Worth climbed on to Junka's massive shoulders, prised open a window and let himself into the upstairs room where the portrait of the duchess was on display.

It was the work of moments for him to cut the portrait from its frame, roll it up carefully to avoid cracking the paint, and slip down to the street again. As always, he left no clues, except the mark of a hobnail boot on the lead outside the window. By the next morning, the theft was on its way to becoming the most celebrated crime on earth. According to one report, 'the hue and cry raised in Bond Street spread to every civilised corner of the globe, and all nations, peoples and languages were talking of it'.

The Daily Telegraph said: 'Nothing but the poisoning of a favourite racehorse or the disappearance of a famous dog could have aroused equal concern in the average British mind.'

Thanks to Worth – bank robber, forger, mail raider, diamond thief – the fame of the duchess and her portraitist was suddenly universal. Millions who had never before heard of Gainsborough knew all about the painting. As one newspaper commented wryly, whoever had stolen the painting was, in a sense, 'an apostle of culture'.

Ironically, Worth's brother John was soon released from Newgate on a legal technicality, so the duchess was no longer needed as a hostage. But, by then her new protector had started to fall in love with her. So much so that he hid her under his four-poster bed.

Later, Worth would describe himself as having 'eloped' with the duchess.

Certainly there was much to explain his swift and obsessive attachment to the painting. For the owner of two fine London houses, a string of racehorses and a 110ft yacht with a crew of 25, the possession of the most famous painting in the world, even in secret, must have seemed like the crowning glory of a brilliant criminal career.

But the value and fame of the painting do not explain in full his growing obsession. At the time of the theft he was a heartbroken man. His mistress, Kitty Flynn – the Irish barmaid whom he had shared with his former partner 'Piano' Charley Bullard and mother of his two daughters – had deserted him to return to the U.S.

Now here was the seductive Georgiana, bearing enough of a resemblance to Kitty to provide some consolation.

So as the hullabaloo erupted around Worth's gangster base in Piccadilly, just a few yards from Agnew's gallery, the master criminal decided it would be discrete to go abroad for a while – accompanied by his new paramour.

Worth had a large trunk fitted with a hidden panel in the bottom in which the stolen portrait could be safely and securely accommodated. Together, the pair boarded a ship bound for New York.

For several months, Worth conducted desultory transatlantic negotiations with Agnew for the return of the painting, sending shreds of canvas to prove he had it. But eventually he decided he did not want to be parted from 'The Noble Lady', as he called her.

The sands of time apparently closed over the extraordinary affair, but not as far as the Napoleon of Crime was concerned. Georgiana seems to have become his Josephine. Wherever his criminal activities took him, he took her, too, in the false-bottomed trunk.

At home, she had her special place under his bed. Aboard Shamrock, Worth's lavish yacht, she lived in the chartroom, secreted among the logbooks.

Throughout the 1880s Worth continued to steal and racketeer with seeming immunity. But as the last decade of the century began, his luck began to waver.

Both Scotland Yard and the Pinkerton detective agency in the U.S. had suspected for years that Worth was behind the Gainsborough mystery. Now Joe Elliott, who had been the lookout on the night of the theft, was arrested – and began to squeal.

Then in 1892 Worth was arrested while trying to rob a Belgian mail train. This time the man whom the Daily Telegraph referred to as the 'prince of cracksmen' failed either to bribe or break his way out of trouble, as he had done so many times before all over the world. He was sentenced to seven years' solitary confinement with hard labour.

Astonishingly, Worth was given more than one chance to avoid his sentence and even earn a generous reward if he would reveal the whereabouts of the missing Gainsborough. But he flatly refused.

Perhaps he suspected that the offers were merely tricks to relieve him of his secret. All the same, Worth's obstinacy about even discussing the matter was striking.

'The painting was safely stashed in a Boston warehouse, but during the 17 years that Worth had travelled the world with his duchess in his trunk, yacht and bed, an extraordinary bond had grown up between them which meant far more to him than money, more even than his freedom,' writes his biographer Ben Macintyre.

'The law and the world may know him as a rogue, imposter, villain and liar, but as long as he controlled the duchess he was still, at least in his perception, a worthy gentleman and mighty thief.'

In 1898, Worth was released from prison, ill and broken-spirited. The following year, he sought a meeting with his oldest and shrewdest adversary, William Pinkerton. The two men became fast friends during a series of remarkable meetings in which Worth treated the famous detective like a father confessor.

Even so, it took two years of negotiations with Pinkerton acting as go-between for Worth to finally bring himself to part with his duchess.

William Agnew's son Morland agreed to come secretly to the U.S. to collect the painting. The handover took place in a Chicago hotel in cloak-and-dagger fashion, with a messenger coming to the door of Agnew's room carrying a brown paper roll under his arm.

The messenger was probably Worth in disguise, playing the role of the great con man to the end.

On January 4, 1902, Agnew delivered the Duchess of Devonshire to her new owner, the American magnate J. Pierpont Morgan, who had paid £30,000 for the portrait.

Four days later, the criminal who had stolen her and kept her from the world for 25 years died.

The death notices in Britain and the U.S. were, on the whole, admiring. They praised Worth's resourcefulness, his daring and his avoidance of violence. The New York Sun concluded that the Gainsborough theft was the most remarkable crime of the 19th century.

The thief who stole the Cezanne from the Ashmolean on New Year's Eve may know Worth's story and may be feeling a little cocky about being counted in such company.

If so, maybe he should think again. Auvers-Sur-Oise is a very fine landscape, but it is not in the same league as Gainsborough's portrait of the famous and fascinating Duchess of Devonshire.

The New York Journal said of Adam Worth's death: 'His demise marks the closing of a singular modern romance.'

The romance would have been less singular had it not been the captivating Georgiana who had shared it with Adam Worth for a quarter of a century.

THE DAILY TELEGRAPH Thursday, August 24, 2000

NEWS £5m for house that enchanted Conan Doyle by Caroline Davies

A SEVENTEENTH century moated manor house, once described by English Heritage as "one of those houses which more than very many others defines what makes us English", is up for sale.

The owner, Andrew de Candole, a property developer, is asking for offers above £5 million for Groombridge Place, near Tunbridge Wells, Kent, which inspired literary works by Sir Arthur Conan Doyle and Vita Sackville-West. The house, set in 200 acres and surrounded by a moat dating back to 1230, is most famous for its gardens which were landscaped by Ivan Hicks, the surrealist garden designer. The property attracts up to 100,000 visitors a year.

Mr de Candole, 47, who bought the house eight years ago, said he was selling "reluctantly". Speaking from America, he said: "I have become increasingly involved in the IT sector and I am spending much of my time overseas.

"I feel I can no longer give Groombridge Place the attention it needs."

Grade 1 listed, the 10-bedroom house and its grounds featured in the 1983 film *The Draughtsman's Contract*.

Once described by Kent Historic Buildings Committee as "one of the finest 17th-century classical houses", it was a favourite haunt of Conan Doyle, who created Sherlock Holmes. The writer took part in séances there.

He used the house for his plot in *The Valley of Fear*, published in 1902, in which it was renamed Birlstone Manor. A shrine to Conan Doyle stands in the garden.

Sackville-West, another visitor, used Groombridge as the setting for *The Heir*.

Mr de Candole has long had a passion for gardens. The son of a former governor of Libya, he was brought up in Rudyard Kipling's house, Batemans in East Sussex.

He hired Hicks to restore the grounds of Groombridge and create a 50-acre enchanted forest, a landscape of pools, fern valleys, mazes and grottoes.

A glittering ballroom sphere dangles above pools and mirrors are set into tree trunks.

The garden will remain open to the public until the end of October.

DAILY EXPRESS SATURDAY NOVEMBER 18 2000

It's elementary, my dear reader by **Anna Hunt**
The Mandala of Sherlock Holmes Edited by Jamyang Norbu.

One of the most cherished detectives is given a new lease of life in a novel that takes the great Sherlock Holmes on a perilous journey to India…

It was not without a degree of reservation that I embarked on this book which purports to record the renowned detective's exploits during his two-year disappearance following his supposed death at the hands of Professor Moriaty. Sequels and prequels of classics – and everything in between when written by the hand of a stranger – are an invariable disaster. Or so I thought.

This delightful novel in which Jamyang Norbu presents Holmes's exploits as recorded by the wonderfully amusing Hurree Chudner Mookerjee, is a total success. The narrative is fast-paced and action-packed. Mookerjee, an overweight double agent with an interest in ethnology, is a fascinating character in his own right and a perfect companion to the intrepid Holmes on his journeys to India and Tibet.

Following his struggle with Moriaty, Holmes anticipates attempts on his life from the criminal's associates and decides to go underground. The Mandala of Sherlock Holmes sees Holmes arrive in Bombay, survive an attempt on his life, travel to the hillside town of Simla and from there, journey into deepest Tibet.

It is here that Holmes is employed to protect the Dalai Lama-in-waiting, who, in a fitting parallel to Modern Tibet, is under threat from the Chinese government. Given his circumstances, it is not surprising that Holmes is going through a more introspective period at the time of the novel.

The scholarly Mookerjee provides wonderful and hitherto unprecedented insights into Holmes's situation and state of mind: "Holmes was not a happy man. It seemed that the great powers he possessed were sometimes more of a curse than a blessing to him."

We see a softer side to the impregnable detective, whose very physiognomy summarises his cool dispassion and focused determination in all things. Holmes is a rounder, fuller figure than descriptions of his detective employment have hitherto allowed.

Monkerjee's observations have prepared the reader for the Buddhists' premonition that the famed detective whom they describe as "one of us", is the key to ensuring the safety of the Dalai Lama. In a brilliant twist, Holmes' past catches up with him in the form of Professor Moriarty, whose own involvement in Buddhism turns the battle into a fight of epic dimension.

The book is brilliant. Our view of Holmes is transformed, but it is certainly for the better. He is a more credible human being, a more believable character, with his own frustrations and worries – and it is testimony to Norbu's skill that, far from diminishing him, these insights into Holmes' make-up serve only to increase his standing in our estimation. If you are a fan of the detective, you must read this book.

The Sunday Telegraph FEBRUARY 4 2001

REVIEW **One of the best imitators of Conan Doyle is Barrie Roberts, whose latest addition to Dr Watson's chronicles, Sherlock Holmes and the Crosby Murder,** presents, for the most part, the authentic Watsonian style.

The famous detective's hunt for a mysterious killer who has presented Scotland Yard with his victim's shrunken head leads to an exciting chase in a deserted Thames-side warehouse. Doyle's own work was most successful in short-story format and, although entertaining, this is fairly slim material to sustain a full-length novel.

THE DAILY TELEGRAPH THURSDAY, FEBRUARY 15, 2001
NEWS Public Records Office

Vengeful butler is prime suspect in Holmes' last case By Neil Tweedie

IT was a whodunit worthy of fiction's greatest detective. The crime library of Sir Arthur Conan Doyle, creator of Sherlock Holmes, vanishes with a treasure map shortly before his death only to resurface on the far side of the Atlantic in the hands of an American collector.

Was it the work of the author himself, or could it have been the final revenge of the butler he dismissed?

The mystery of the 79 books came to occupy the finest minds in Scotland Yard and the FBI when the British enlisted the help of J. Edgar Hoover to establish who had stolen the raw material for the adventures of literature's most famous sleuth.

The story, contained in Scotland Yard files released at the Public Record Office yesterday, began in June 1946, when Insp Symes of the Metropolitan Police CID was visited by Sir Arthur's sons, Denis and Adrian.

The brothers were concerned about the fate of the crime library, which they believed had been taken from their father's house at Crowborough, Sussex, and put into storage after his death at the age of 71 in 1930.

An examination of the stored contents of the house in 1940 revealed that virtually all of the collection was missing, along with a map relating to sunken treasure. But matters rested until 1946 when the Conan Doyle family were alerted by an article in an American magazine advertising an exhibition of "Sherlockiana" owned by one of the world's leading dealers in rare books and manuscripts.

The owner turned out to be Dr A.S. Rosenbach of Fifth Avenue, New York, who explained that he had purchased the books at auction at Southeby's in London in 1931 for £95.

In a magazine article, Rosenbach wrote that he had "every volume he [Conan Doyle] used for reference when he created Sherlock Holmes and his countless adventures".

Scotland Yard turned to Hoover, who responded by ordering his G-men to check out Rosenbach's story. Inquiries were also started about the map following an article about a treasure hunt in the waters off western Mexico using a suspiciously similar chart.

The volumes had indeed been sold at Southeby's and the auction house produced records showing that the sale of the property had been made by order of Sir Arthur.

The Scotland Yard investigation was ended, and the FBI also ceased inquiries, but not before Hoover had ordered a thorough examination of those involved in the treasure hunt off Mexico.

The chart that was being used turned out to be a different one from the one that was missing from Sir Arthur's house.

However, the author's family were not convinced. Insp Symes wrote: "The sons are positive that their father would not have disposed of the books before his death, and they have not since authorised any such disposal."

In October 1946, Adrian Conan Doyle sent a letter to Scotland Yard from the Grand Hotel in Venice asking why no progress had been made.

Seemingly unaware that inquiries had ended, he wrote: "You will recall that we asked that the Scotland Yard authorities should request the New York police to demand from Doctor Rosenbach the details of the manner in which he acquired my father's library in view of the fact that there is no record of my father having sold these books that he prized so highly."

Despite the family's objections, the books stayed in America.

But there was one other possibility. During his inquiries, Insp Symes came across a suspect with an intimate knowledge of Sir Arthur's home, and a possible motive.

He wrote: "For future reference, it may be mentioned that in 1928, Charles Roy Harris, alias Henry Thornton, was circulated as wanted for the theft of property belonging to Sir Arthur Conan Doyle, by whom he had been employed as a butler.

"Harris was not traced and in 1935 the circulation respecting him was cancelled."
Maybe it was the butler who done it.

THE DAILY TELEGRAPH THURSDAY, FEBRUARY 22, 2001

NEWS Mystery of the doctor's role in Holmes tale By **Will Bennett** Art Sales Correspondent

SIR Arthur Conan Doyle, creator of Sherlock Holmes, had a mysterious collaborator who helped with early works, a letter to be auctioned shows.

The 1889 letter discloses what is thought to be a previously unknown working title for *The Sign of Four*, a Holmes story, although the auctioneers are not yet disclosing it.

Conan Doyle's letter, found in a house in the Lake District, is addressed to "My dear doctor" and refers to a "little story which we invented together".

Catherine Cook, curator of the Sherlock Holmes Collection in Marylebone Library, said it was likely to be Dr Reginald Ratcliffe Hoare, a friend. It is expected to fetch £1,000 to £1,500 at Dominic Winter Book Auctions in Swindon on March 8.

The Mirror, Monday April 2, 2001

IDEAL HOLMES

Robson & Jerome targets for £6m Sherlock Series

Robson Green and Jerome Flynn are being lined up to star as Sherlock Holmes and Dr Watson in a £6million revival of the famed detective series. TV bosses hope the duo, who shot to fame in the drama Soldier, Soldier, will play younger versions of the sleuth and his aide.

Although the new drama will be set in the dingy backstreets of 19th century London, there are some controversial changes in store for Sir Arthur Conan Doyle's legendary crimebusters which will outrage fans.

Sherlock's trademark pipe, deerstalker and tweed cap will be binned. And rather than being a confirmed bachelor, the detective will have a girlfriend. ITV bosses are to offer Sherlock's lover to Cracker actress Geraldine Somerville.

And they hope Sharp star Sean Bean will play the investigator's arch enemy Moriarty.

An insider said: "We'll re-do the series from a 21st century point of view. It will be set in backdrop of pimps, prostitutes and opium dens. But it'll be a gritty, sexy look at the 1800s. Sherlock and Watson will be younger and hipper to appeal to today's viewer. Sherlock wouldn't have worn his deerstalker at that age. He'll be trendier, more with it. Even the woman in his life has a dark side to her."

Drama boss Andy Harries is in talks with writers and cast to make twelve hour-long episodes. The series will be shot at Granada's Manchester studios, where the Baker Street set still stands.

ITV's original Sherlock Holmes series which ran for 10 years from 1964, drew audiences of 14million.*

Sherlock Holmes was then played by Jeremy Brett, loved for his brooding portrayal of Holmes. He died of a heart attack in 1995.

Many other actors have tackled the role including Hollywood legend Basil Rathbone. *(**Compiler's correction:** The series were broadcast between 1984 and 1994. This above drama had no basis in fact – see Chapter 12, page 333 for an explanation).

The Daily Telegraph Sunday, April 15, 2001

News in Brief

Sir Arthur's Statue

A life size bronze statue of Sir Arthur Conan Doyle, who created the fictional detective, Sherlock Holmes, was erected in Crowborough, East Sussex, where he lived for 23 years. Fans attended from America and Japan.

Daily Mail, Wednesday, July 25, 2001

QUESTION **Did Hercule Poirot ever make reference to that other great detective, Sherlock Holmes?**

ANSWER 1 In Hickory Dickory Dock, first published in 1955 we find: 'He did not admit to himself that he had been rather bored of late and that the very triviality of the business attracted him.

'The parsley sinking into the butter on a hot day,' he muttered to himself.

'Parsley? Butter?' Miss Lemon looked startled.

'A quotation from one of your classics,' he said. 'You are acquainted, no doubt, with the adventures, to say nothing of the exploits of Sherlock Holmes.'

There is also a reference to Holmes in The Mysterious Affair at Styles – the novel that introduced Hercule Poirot – when Captain Hastings and Mary Cavendish are discussing the art of sleuthing.

'Well, I've always had a secret hankering to be a detective!'

'The real thing – Scotland Yard? Or Sherlock Holmes?'

'Oh, Sherlock Holmes by all means.'

ANSWER 2 In the 1963 novel The Clocks, Hercule Poirot makes reference to Sherlock Holmes in conversation with Detective Inspector Hardcastle:

'One comes almost to regard actual cases in the light of fiction. That is to say, if I observe that a dog has not barked when he should bark, I say to myself: "Ha! A Sherlock Holmes crime!"

ANSWER 3 Daily Mail, Friday, August 3, 2001

Further to the earlier answers, in chapter five of The Dumb Witness (1937) Captain Hastings makes an observation over a letter Poirot has received in the morning post: 'Poirot, I – the humble Watson – am going to hazard a deduction.' Poirot replies: 'You are indeed the Sherlock Holmes!'

ANSWER 4 In chapter 14 of The Clocks (1963), Hercule Poirot picks up a book: 'The Adventures of Sherlock Holmes,' he murmured lovingly, and uttered reverently the one word 'Maitre!'…'Ah, non, non, not Sherlock Holmes! It is the author Sir Arthur Conan Doyle, that I salute. These tales of Sherlock Holmes are in reality far-fetched, full of fallacies and most artificially contrived. But the art of writing – ah, that is entirely different!'

THE DAILY TELEGRAPH Monday, July 30, 2001

In Brief

Hero Holmes

Fans of Sherlock Holmes will mark the 100th anniversary of the publication of *The Hound of the Baskervilles* at a convention this week in Ashburton, Devon.

Reader's Digest AUGUST 2001

Elementary, My Dear Doyle

Fancy yourself a sleuth? Try this quiz about Sherlock Holmes's creator

By IAN CUNNINGHAM

A HUNDRED years ago this month Sir Arthur Conan Doyle's novel **The Hound of the Baskervilles** was unleashed on the public when the first instalment was published in **The Strand Magazine**.

It was the third novel and, in the opinion of many, the best of the tales featuring Sherlock Holmes and his admiring friend Dr Watson.

Although he wrote them on and off for 40 years (the last was published in 1927), Conan Doyle could never understand how the Holmes stories, which he could polish off in a matter of days, enthralled the public, while his more serious literary offerings were greeted with comparative indifference.

But it is for Sherlock Holmes and Dr Watson, and their gas lit sanctum at 221b Baker Street, that the author will always be remembered.

Here's your chance to turn sleuth and find out how much you know about Conan Doyle and his most famous creation.

1 As well as writing, Conan Doyle was renowned for his proficiency at what sport?
A. Table tennis
   A.   Badminton
   B.   Cricket

2 Sherlock Holmes's gift for deductive reasoning was based on a legendary figure Conan Doyle met in his youth.
What was the man's profession?

A. Night watchman
B. Surgeon
C. Portrait painter

3 In his autobiography, Conan Doyle described his early manhood as a time "I divided among my _____ and literature. It is hard to say which suffered most." What's missing?

A. Patients
B. Long-suffering wife
C. Sporting activities

4 What was the name of Holmes's landlady?

A. Mrs Hudson
B. Mrs Bridges
C. Mrs Collins

5 "How often have I said to you", Holmes asks Watson in the novel *The Sign of Four*, "that when you have eliminated the impossible, whatever remains, *however improbable*, must be the truth?" The remark originally appeared, almost word for word, in a story Conan Doyle particularly admired. Who was the author?

A. Charles Dickens
B. Bram Stoker
C. Edgar Allan Poe

6 The phrase, "Elementary, my dear Watson", appears how many times in the Holmes stories?

A. 74
B. 11
C. Never

7 "You won't! You can't! You mustn't!" Conan Doyle's mother wrote to him in 1891. What had he threatened to do?

A. Divorce his wife
B. Kill off Holmes
C. Become a monk

8 After a ten-year hiatus, Conan Doyle wrote what is probably the most famous Holmes story *The Hound of the Baskervilles*. Where is it set?

A. The Highlands

    B. The Fens
    C. Dartmoor

9
In 1905, the author was convicted of what offence?

    A.   Breach of copyright
    B. Bigamy
    C. Speeding

10
Conan Doyle devoted his last ten years to which cause?

    A. Spiritualism
    B. Republicanism
    C. Antidisestablishmentarianism

Answers

1c) Arthur Ignatius Conan Doyle was born in Edinburgh on 22 May, 1859, the third of 11 children. Partly to protect him from his alcoholic father, a government clerk and architect, Arthur was sent to a boarding school in Lancashire, where he excelled at **cricket**. He also discovered his gift as a storyteller, inventing tales to entertain the other boys.

2b) At 17, Conan Doyle enrolled at medical school in Edinburgh, where he studied under the **surgeon** Dr Joseph Bell. Bell's gift for gleaning detailed information on the patients was summed up in a celebrated encounter with a new patient.
  "Well, my man," Bell said," you have served in the army."
  "Aye, sir."
  "Not long discharged?"
  "No, sir."
  "A Highland regiment?"
  "Aye, sir."
  "A non-commissioned officer?"
  "Aye, sir."
  "Stationed at Barbados?"
  "Aye, sir."
  Bell turned to his students. "you see, the patient was a respectful man, but he did not remove his hat. They do not in the army, but he would have learnt civilian ways if he had been long discharged. He has an air of authority and is obviously Scottish. As to Barbados, his complaint is elephantiasis, which is West Indian, and the Scottish regiments are at present in that particular island."
  Years later, Conan Doyle wrote to Bell: "It is most certainly to you that I owe Sherlock Holmes."

3a) After graduating as a Bachelor of Medicine and Master of Surgery, Conan Doyle worked as a medical officer on a steamer and at the medical practice of one of his fellow students, before setting up on his own at Southsea. Short of money, he wrote fiction to help pay the bills. Louisa Hawkins, his first wife, was the sister of one of his **patients**.

4a) Sherlock Holmes first appears in *A Study in Scarlet*, written when Conan Doyle was 26. It was the first of 60 tales featuring the detective, all but four narrated by Holmes's companion and on-off flatmate Dr John Watson. Three publishers turned down the novel before a fourth reluctantly accepted it for a one-off fee of £25.

In the novel Holmes and Watson move into 221b Baker Street. Though not introduced until the second Holmes tale, *The Sign of the Four*, their heroically patient landlady, **Mrs Hudson**, appears in 14 of the adventures. As Watson observes in "The Dying Detective", (1913), Holmes's habits – late-night violin playing, indoor revolver practice and malodorous scientific experiments – "made him the very worst tenant in London".

5c) The American **Edgar Allan Poe** had pioneered the detective genre more than 40 years earlier with his tales of the Parisian sleuth Monsieur Dupin. Holmes, however, was the first detailed portrait of what Conan Doyle termed "a scientific detective who solved cases on his own merits and not through the folly of the criminal".

Although *A Study in Scarlet* was only a modest success, Conan Doyle was commissioned to write a second adventure followed by a series of short stories. Serialized in *The Strand Magazine*, they were a phenomenal success, eventually earning him the then handsome fee of around £800 per story.

6c) Holmes's popularity was due partly to a series of plays based on the stories. The phrase "Elementary, my dear Watson" was probably used first by the star, William Gillette, but **never** by Conan Doyle. Holmes's cocaine habit, on the other hand, had to be toned down for the stage.

7b) Conan Doyle became increasingly weary of his hero. He planned to **kill off Holmes**. In a letter to his mother he explained "He takes my mind from better things" – meaning more serious novels, such as *The White Company*, his tale of fourteenth century knight errantry. He carried out his threat in "The Final Problem" (1893), in which the detective plunges to his death from the Reichenbach Falls after a battle with his arch-enemy Professor Moriarty. The public were horrified. One woman attacked Conan Doyle with a handbag; others wore black armbands. An unrepentant Conan Doyle told the Authors' Club it was "self-defence, since if I had not killed him, he would certainly have killed me".

8c) In 1901, Conan Doyle wrote a new Holmes story *The Hound of the Baskervilles*, though he was at pains to point out this was a tale from the past and Holmes was irredeemably dead. Such was the popularity of the tale, about a **Dartmoor** baronet and his family haunted by "a gigantic hound", that the author finally agreed to write another Holmes series, starting with "The Adventure of the Empty House", in which we learn precisely how Holmes escaped death.

9c) In 1900 Conan Doyle sailed to South Africa to run a battlefield hospital during the Boer War. Knighted two years later and now a wealthy man, he used his income from the Holmes tales to indulge his numerous interests. Fascinated by technology, he built a monorail in his garden and in 1905 became one of the first people to be fined for **speeding** in his car.

10a) Conan Doyle's wife died of TB in 1906 and the following year he married Jean Leckie. But it was the death of his brother and son Kingsley over a decade later that reawakened an interest in **spiritualism** and the afterlife. Conan Doyle wrote towards the end of his life that, "All other work which I have ever done, or could ever do, was as nothing compared to this." He died in 1930.

Daily Mail, Tuesday, November 6, 2001

QUESTION **Is there a quantifiable limit as to how much information the human brain can store?**

Further to the earlier answer, there is a limit if you believe the great detective Sherlock Holmes.
　Justifying his poor knowledge of the solar system, he replies to Watson in Arthur Conan Doyle's A Study in Scarlet: 'I consider that a man's brain is a little like an empty attic, and you have to stock it with such furniture as you choose.
　'A fool takes in all the lumber of every sort that he comes across, so that the knowledge that might be useful to him gets crowded out.
　'Now the skilled workman is very careful, indeed, as to what he takes into his brain attic. He will have nothing but the tools that may help him in doing his work, and all in the most perfect order.
　'It is a mistake to think that the little room has elastic walls and can be distended to any extent. Depend upon it, there comes a time when for every addition of knowledge you forget something that you knew before.
　'It is of highest importance, therefore, not to have useless facts elbowing out the useful ones.'

Daily Mail, Thursday, November 8, 2001

QUESTION **In Conan Doyle's A Study in Scarlet, a violinist called Norman Neruda is mentioned. Who was he?**

ANSWER 1 The Norman-Neruda referred to was, in fact, Wilhelmina (Wilma) Neruda, second wife of German-born pianist and conductor Charles Halle (1839-1911), founder of the Halle Orchestra. Her first husband's name was Norman.
　Born in Moravia, she was taught by her father, Joseph Neruda, a respected organist, and by the famous violinist Leopold Jansa. She made her debut in Vienna aged seven.
　After many years of touring Germany, France, Russia, Britain and Holland, she settled in Stockholm, where she married Ludwig Norman, the musical director of the Swedish court, and changed her surname to Norman-Neruda.
　They divorced in 1869 (he died in 1885) and Wilma went to London, where she continued her career with great success, finally marrying Herr Halle in 1888. She is one of the most famous women in the history of violin playing.

Answer 2 While investigating A Study in Scarlet, keen violinist Holmes would have been happy spending an afternoon at the Halle, where the renowned violinist Wilhelmina Norman-Neruda was performing.

Holmes said: 'And now for lunch and then Norman-Neruda. Her attack and bowing are splendid. What's that little thing of Chopin's she plays so magnificently? Tra-La-La-Lira-Lira-Lay.'

Like Holmes, she owned a Stradivarius violin, presented to her in 1876 by the Duke of Saxe-Coburg-Gotha and Earls of Dudley and Hardwicke as a token of their appreciation. She died in 1911.

SUNDAY MIRROR, November 18, 2001

TREASURE HUNTERS TV's James Breese on the world of collectibles.

Q. I have a pair of old-style handcuffs made by Hiatt with the key and an old police truncheon, wooden and red/orange in colour. Any info?
A. There are a number of books on the subject of collecting police memorabilia. Sherlock Holmes used very similar Hiatt cuffs in his fictional adventures. Your pair, because of the presence of the key, might be worth £75, while the truncheon could make £45.

The Joke

Excerpt from THE DAILY TELEGRAPH, Thursday, December 20, 2001

Entitled: **Best joke is elementary, my dear Watson**.

By: Roger Highfield, Science Editor.

The world's funniest joke was named yesterday by scientists investigating the psychology of laughter.
 "The response has been enormous with over 10,000 jokes submitted and over 100,000 people from over 70 countries rating them," said Dr
 Richard Wiseman, from the University of Hertfordshire, who devised "Laughalab".
 A joke about Sherlock Holmes and Dr Watson submitted by Geoff Anandappa, from Blackpool emerged the overall winner, with a top rating from 47 per cent of those taking part.

The Joke

Sherlock Holmes and Dr Watson go camping, and pitch their tent under the stars. During the night, Holmes wakes his companion and says: "Watson, look up at the stars, and tell me what you deduce." Watson says: "I see millions of stars, and even if a few of those have planets, it's quite likely there are some planets like Earth, and if there are few planets like Earth out there, there might also be life." Holmes replies, "Watson, you idiot. Somebody stole our tent…"

DAILY TELEGRAPH Friday, December 21, 2001

Chinese are right to be scared on the 4th By Nicole Martin

People are dying of fright, researchers have found.

A study shows that Chinese and Japanese people are more likely to die from heart disease on the fourth day of the month, a date so foreboding that many choose not to travel on it for fear of tempting fate.

The researchers term dying of fright the "Baskerville effect" after Sir Arthur Conan Doyle's *The Hound of the Baskervilles* in which Charles Baskerville dies of a heart attack brought on by severe psychological stress.

Writing in the *British Medical Journal*, Prof David Phillips who led the team at the University of California, said that the higher death rates from heart disease on the fourth did not coincide with changes in diet, alcohol intake, exercise or drug treatment.

"Our findings of excess cardiac mortality on unlucky days are consistent with the hypothesis that cardiac mortality increases on psychologically stressful occasions," said Prof Phillips.

The team published its findings after comparing death certificates for Chinese and Japanese Americans with white Americans, who do not regard four as unlucky, between 1973 and 1998.

THE TELEGRAPH Saturday, September 7, 2002

Top five portrayals of Sherlock Holmes chosen by Tim Robey

Jeremy Brett A new dramatisation of Sir Arthur Conan Doyle's *The Hound of the Baskervilles* opened at the Belgrade Theatre in Coventry this week with Julian Forsyth the latest in a long line of gaunt thespians to don the deerstalker on stage and screen. Of all Holmes portrayals, the one closest to British hearts is probably that of the neurotic, saturnine Jeremy Brett in Granada's exhaustive, 41-episode 1980s TV series. Brett also treated the West End to a psychological re-evaluation of his performance in 1988, for Jeremy Paul's play *The Secret of Sherlock Holmes*, in which Professor Moriarty turned out to be some sort of schizophrenic alter ego. The actor's anxiety about the presentation of Holmes's opium addiction meanwhile, was such that he insisted on a symbolic syringe-burying scene being added to one of the most disturbing stories, *The Devil's Foot*.

Basil Rathbone Eille Norwood's record of 47 big-screen appearances as Holmes (in a series of silent films) has never been topped. But most of these have been lost to us, unlike the 14 evergreen features in which the businesslike Rathbone opposite Nigel Bruce's notoriously bumbling Watson, made the role his own, starting with *The Hound of the Baskervilles* in 1939. Rathbone was quoted at the time as saying that he'd rather play Holmes than Hamlet but, by 1953, and the sad coda of a final, failed attempt to recreate the role on stage, he seemed thoroughly bored with the routine. "When you become the character you portray, it's the end of your career as an actor," he said.

Peter Cushing Hammer's 1959 version of *The Hound of the Baskervilles*, the first colour adaptation, is considered something of a high-water mark among Holmes films. But the story's illusionary terrors were a disappointment to fans craving the real monster action of Hammer's early Dracula and Frankenstein's movies, and the film was not successful enough to spawn the hoped-for sequels. The mercurial Cushing got the chance to revisit the role for TV in the late 1960s instead. His co-star Christopher Lee (as Sir Henry) went on to play Holmes himself for the very same director, Terence Fisher, in 1962's *The Speckled Band*, and then played the detective's brother Mycroft, opposite Robert Stevens, in Billy Wilder's 1970 comic romance *The Private Life of Sherlock Holmes*.

Ian Richardson Among the less well-known incarnations of Holmes is Ian Richardson's, in two stylish films (*Baskervilles* again, directed by Desmond Hickox, and *The Sign of Four*, directed by Desmond Davis for American TV). Richardson's amused and lugubrious reading of the part is offset by some impressively atmospherics: Hickox's uses of Dartmoor locations pays off particularly well. More recently, Richardson performed a variation on the same theme, playing a possible real-life Holmes, the Edinburgh surgeon Dr Joseph Bell, in the speculative BBC series *Murder Rooms*.

Michael Caine Of all the "revisionist" Holmes interpretations (*Young Sherlock Holmes*, *The Seven Per Cent Solution*, *The Adventure of Sherlock Holmes' Smarter Brother*), none is as radical as the one propounded in the watchable silly 1988 comedy *Without a Clue*: that Watson (Ben Kingsley) was the real brains behind the operation, and Holmes was merely a ham actor hired to play the part. Caine, needless to say, is all wrong for the job, but that's part of the joke. Sort of.

THE DAILY TELEGRAPH Thursday, October 17, 2002

Strange case of Holmes, FRSC By David Derbyshire Science Correspondent

A MEDAL was placed around a statue of Sherlock Holmes outside Baker Street Underground station in London yesterday to mark the award of an honorary fellowship to the great detective by the Royal Society of Chemistry.

The award, usually reserved for Nobel Laureates and distinguished academics, is the first by the society to a fictional character and was made in recognition of Holmes's pioneering use of forensic science.

The presentation by Dr John Watson a fellow of the RSC, who shares the name of Holmes's fictional biographer, marked the centenary of his best known case, *The Hound of the Baskervilles*.

Although the award was welcomed by the leading Sherlock Holmes society, some aficionados expressed surprise that it was not awarded to the detective's creator, Sir Arthur Conan Doyle.

Alexander Chancellor Footnote.

MY FIRST reaction on learning that the Royal Society of Chemistry had awarded an honorary fellowship to Sherlock Holmes was that it must be something to do with his well-known addictions to opium and cocaine. But this would have been like honouring Soho House for failing to Hoover up ecstasy tablets from the floor. So, of course, that wasn't it. Holmes was honoured "for his love of chemistry and the way he wielded such knowledge for the public good." The society noted that he "published papers on using tobacco ashes, shapes of ears, cryptography, dating of documents, tattoos and footsteps as clues".

(**Compiler's note** – should not this be **footprints**?)

He had anticipated 120 years ago the use of chemistry in the battle against crime, it said.

That would doubtless be a good reason for awarding somebody an honorary fellowship of the Royal Society of Chemistry, but Holmes wasn't somebody – or indeed anybody. He didn't exist, except in the imagination of Sir Arthur Conan Doyle. And the society itself boasts that he is the first "fictional character" to be so honoured. The aim presumably was to attract publicity to this not tremendously well known organisation, but it was carrying whimsy too far. You can hardly take seriously an institution that hands out honours to fictional characters. What would we think if the Nobel committee decided to give its prize for economics to Mr Micawber? He might have deserved it if he had existed. So why didn't the Royal Society of Chemistry bestow its honour on Holmes's creator, Conan Doyle, who did actually graduate as a doctor from Edinburgh University?

Not famous enough, I suppose.

Boxing Day Thursday, December 26, 2002

Four previews of BBC 1's *Hound of the Baskervilles*

Sherlock Holmes made his British TV debut in a live broadcast in 1951, in the shape of Alan Wheatley – he went on to play the Sheriff of Nottingham in *The Adventures of Robin Hood*. Since then Holmeses have come thick and fast, reaching their high-water mark so far with Jeremy Brett's masterly portrayal in the 1980s ITV series. Perhaps the most unlikely Holmes of all remains the late Peter Cook, who starred – along with Dudley Moore as Watson and a very friendly-looking Irish wolfhound – in a little-seen and critically excoriated adaptation of *The Hound of the Baskervilles* back in 1977.

The BBC's latest version of **The Hound of the Baskervilles** looks set to be the ideal antidote to post-Christmas gloom. Boasting a computer-generated hound with dripping fangs and rolling red eyes. It is produced by Christopher Hall (who made last Christmas's BBC hit *The Lost World*). Richard Roxburgh stars as Holmes, while Ian Hart is Watson. They head for darkest Dartmoor where the luckless Sir Charles Baskerville has recently croaked, apparently from heart failure. But heart failure induced by whom, pray? Or what?

(From the Radio Times) By **Alison Graham**

Turn off the lights, turn up the central heating, find a big box of chocolates and prepare to be spooked by this new television dramatisation of arguably the greatest detective story of all time. Richard Roxburgh as Sherlock Holmes and Ian Hart is his faithful chronicler and companion Doctor Watson, in Conan Doyle's ripping yarn of the legend of the hound that stalks Dartmoor, savaging its prey at will.

Holmes and Watson are drawn into this curious tale after the death of Sir Charles Baskerville, apparently from heart failure. His heir, Sir Henry Baskerville, arrives from the USA, but he's in the sight of an unknown stalker and soon receives an ominous and threatening letter: "As you value your life, or your reason, keep away from the moor."

Naturally, Holmes's curiosity is tweaked and he dispatches Dr Watson to Baskerville Hall, where he's to keep a close watch on Sir Henry, a man who is in obvious great danger. Soon Watson makes the acquaintance of Sir Henry's neighbours, the charming Stapleton (Richard E. Grant) and his lovely wife. But soon the mists roll in and howls echo across the darkly beautiful moor as death visits Dartmoor once more.

One of the big problems with adapting such classics is that everyone who has ever read the book has their own mental picture of Holmes and Watson. Roxburgh is suitably austere, and Hart, in his commendable efforts to throw off the quite erroneous perception that Watson was a bit of a buffoon, ends up being colourless. And the computer-generated hound isn't actually as scary as you might expect. For some reason its eeriest feature is missing – the hound doesn't glow in the dark (in the book the beast was daubed with phosphorus to give it an unearthly look).

But any television version of such a wonderful story is welcome, though if you are tempted to sit down as a family to watch, be aware that there are some bloody moments that might frighten very young children.

Say g'day to the darker side of sleuth Holmes (*newspaper article, date not noted*)

Picking an antipodean to play Sherlock Holmes in the Hound of the Baskervilles might seem like an unusual choice. However, Australian Richard Roxburgh (Moulin Rouge, Mission Impossible II and Lucinda) admits that he did not think twice about accepting the role.

The adaptation of Sir Arthur Conan Doyle's classic thriller begins with the death of Sir Charles Baskerville on Dartmoor. For some time, the Baskervilles have been convinced that they are being hunted by a ghostly hound. So, while the circumstances of Charles's death seem above suspicion, the discovery of a giant canine footprint next to his body sends the family into panic, prompting a visit to Holmes at 221b Baker Street to help put their minds at rest.

The part of Sherlock Holmes is a coup for any actor. Unfortunately for Roxburgh, accepting this role meant that, not only was there a cultural divide for him to deal with, but there was also an age gap to overcome – he is much younger than previous actors who have taken on the role. So all credit to the 39-year-old who has just treated both as a challenge and has used the opportunity to present the little-seen darker side of the well-known detective.

"I find it interesting that Holmes was addicted to cocaine and took a seven per cent solution twice a day," he says. "He believed it helped his powers of reasoning and then he had to take morphine to relax."

Richard believes that the regular drug-taking shows that there is an emptiness to Holmes. "To me this indicates that there's something missing in his life. He's almost entirely cerebral – probably to the detriment of other areas of his life. Nobody is as untainted by life as Holmes is."

The actor believes that personality gap is largely filled through his partnership with Watson – and that together, this odd couple make a complete whole.

A strange unit they may be, but a good tale like this gothic treat needs more than just complex characters. Roxburgh believes that it is the combination of a number of mystical elements that made this story the top-notch detective thriller it is.

"It gets right to the heart of some of our deepest fears," he says. "The idea of a big, black dog, something outside the cave, something that could eat you. On top of that, it's set on the wasteland of the moors, which is perilous because if you got lost out there you'd just die. Then there's someone out there who is committing murders.

"And it's all happening at night!"

Thursday, December 26, 2002 THE DAILY TELEGRAPH

Today's **Choices** By **Edna Pottersman**

Out goes the deerstalker, in comes the syringe, in this splendid new version – more Conan Doyle than Basil Rathbone – of the classic mystery. Australian actor Richard Roxburgh plays the great deducer, Ian Hart is Watson, and in Allan Cubitt's deliciously tangy adaptation both bring fresh nuances to their characters. The latter is particularly good, his Watson the beating heart and, intriguingly, moral compass of the story. There are some grisly moments which might upset younger viewers. And the computer-generated effects aren't very good. Otherwise, perfectly seasonal viewing.

Finally, a review by **James Walton** THE DAILY TELEGRAPH Friday, December 27, 2002 entitled **Traditional comforts**.

Boxing Day 2002 saw a troubling clash for all fans of television's answer to comfort food. Both **Hound of the Baskervilles** (BBC1) and **Goodbye Mr Chips** (ITV1) did what exactly what they were supposed to do – which was to contain few surprises. Both duly turned out to be perfectly enjoyable, if not strictly necessary retellings of much-loved tales.

Hound of theBaskervilles was certainly the pacier of the two. The opening shots featured Sir Charles's twisted corpse looking like an extra from *Silent Witness*. Seconds later, Selden the convict was haring across the moors – and seconds after that, the pursuing policeman had sunk into a swamp, leaving only his hat behind. Sir Charles's doctor (John Nettles) then consulted Sherlock Holmes (Richard Roxburgh) who, after a brief pause to shoot up some morphine, agreed to take on the case. And so we were off: leading to an apocalyptic Dartmoor for an appointment with a large dog.

Like most people who've played Dr Watson since Nigel Bruce, Ian Hart tried hard to give the man some gravitas. Despite this, the programme – like the book – did flag when he was leading the investigation. Fortunately, once his clever friend had reappeared, things soon livened up again.

Roxburgh's Holmes, in fact, was a bit of an action hero. The scene in which he beat information out of a cabbie unexpectedly recalled Inspector Regan from *The Sweeney*. A more sustained influence, though, seemed to be James Bond. Near the end, we even had a moment when the baddie explained precisely how he would kill him, before uttering the words, "Goodbye, Mr Holmes". And after escaping, Holmes celebrated with a wisecrack.

Conan Doyle purists may well have taken a dim view of these and other additions – but personally I thought the synthesis was pretty neatly done. Mind you, two other factors did rather mar the climactic chase. First, Richard E. Grant played the baddie – and, as viewers of *The Scarlet Pimpernel* will remember, he's rubbish at running. (To use a technical term, he runs "like a great big girl".) Second, the dog itself looked on its initial appearance like a member of the Muppets, and on all subsequent ones like a refugee from *Walking with Beasts*. Apparently BBC's head of drama sent back *Hound of the Baskervilles* at the last minute so that the dog could be improved. From this we can make a simple deduction: the original one must have been absolutely hilarious.

DAILY TELEGRAPH Saturday, April 19, 2003

Conan Doyle had golf links with Moriarty By David Sapsted

Devotees of Sherlock Holmes are delighted by the disclosure that Sir Arthur Conan Doyle belonged to the same golf club as a man named Moriarty.

Until now, the only contender as the inspiration for Holmes's arch-enemy was a boy called Moriarty who attended school with the author. Yesterday, though, it emerged that a C Moriarty from Harrow was a member of Sheringham Golf Club on the Norfolk coast, where Conan Doyle played.

The discovery was made by Douglas Blunden, the club's historian. Although Mr Moriarty's name does not crop up until 1901, a decade after Professor James Moriarty first tangled with Holmes, there is speculation that Conan Doyle might have met the real Moriarty during his frequent visits to the Sheringham area.

Daily Express Saturday April 19 2003

Solved! Mystery of Holmes villain By Richard Palmer

An old golf club register may hold the clue to one of the last Sherlock Holmes mysteries.

The identity of the man who inspired the great detective's arch-villain, Professor James Moriarty, has long puzzled literary detectives.

But new light was shed on the riddle yesterday after it was discovered that Holmes's creator, Sir Arthur Conan Doyle, was once a member of Sheringham Golf Club in Norfolk at the same time as a Mr C Moriarty.

Club historian Douglas Blunden found the name of Mr Moriarty in a visitors' book entry for 1901. He later became a full member. Sir Arthur, who often visited Sheringham, became a member in 1903. Now club officials are wondering if the two men met on holiday in Sheringham a decade earlier, when Conan Doyle first began writing about Holmes's battles with Moriarty.

Grace Riley, curator of the Sherlock Holmes Museum in London, said: "It is entirely possible that there could be a link with the Moriarty who played golf at Sheringham."

Daily Mail, Monday, July 7, 2003

Holmes is top dog

QUESTION **Which book (apart from the Bible) has had the most movie adaptations made from it?**

ANSWER Sir Arthur Conan Doyle's Sherlock Holmes story The Hound of The Baskervilles can claim this record. The first of many adaptations was a silent German version in 1914.

This was followed by a version starring Eille Norwood made by Stoll Films in England in 1920. Another German version, in 1929, was the last silent Holmes feature. In England, Arthur Wontner starred as Holmes in the first sound version in 1932.

Possibly, the most famous version is the 1939 production from Fox, which featured Basil Rathbone's first appearance as Holmes.

In 1959 another version hit cinema screens, from Hammer Films in England, starring Peter Cushing. The following decade, Cushing reprised his role in a BBC TV series which, in 1968, included his second go at the story of Baskerville Hall. In the same year, RAI (Italian television) also produced a version.

In 1979, Peter Cook took the role of Holmes with Dudley Moore as Dr Watson in a comedy version.

In 1988 Granada presented its version of the story as part of the series with Jeremy Brett and Edward Hardwicke as Holmes and Watson.

Most recently, during the 2002 Christmas season, the BBC presented a new adaptation, an interesting production with many 'amendments' to the original story.

DAILY MAIL, Saturday, August 30, 2003

The curious case of the literary goalie

QUESTION **Was Sir Arthur Conan Doyle once goalkeeper for Portsmouth FC?**

ANSWER 1 ON OCTOBER 14, 1884 a group of enthusiasts, led by prominent local architect Arthur Cogswell, met at the Blue Anchor public house in Portsmouth and decided to form a club to play football under Association rules.

Portsmouth Football Club proceeded to play in local amateur leagues. Their first goalkeeper, listed as 'A.C. Smith' was, in fact, Conan Doyle under an assumed name, to protect his status as a doctor in the genteel district of Southsea.

He played for Portsmouth Cricket Club under his proper name, but that was regarded as more of a gentleman's sport.

Over the next couple of seasons, played at 'keeper and also at full back for the club, alternating the two positions in successive games'.

The club adopted a uniform which was a foretaste of today's strip – dark blue jersey with the Borough arms in white, white knickerbockers and dark blue stockings – but with a peaked velvet quarter cap.

The full story of Conan Doyle's involvement with both clubs can be found in Geoffrey Stavert's 1987 book, *A Study In Southsea*.

ANSWER 2 **Daily Mail**, Tuesday, October 7, 2003

Further to the earlier answer, Conan Doyle (aka A.C. Smith) was an enthusiastic member of Portsmouth FC and played for the club for six seasons, making at least 91 appearances as either goalkeeper or full-back, and scoring once.

He was present for the club's first ever match, in which they beat Hayling Island 5-1. In 1885 and 1886, Portsmouth were successful, playing and winning four matches over Christmas and New Year, scoring 21 goals to four against. In 1887, they played 33 games, winning 25 and scoring 87 goals to 30 against.

They later won the Portsmouth And District Challenge Cup, beating Woolston 1-0. The trophy was presented by General Howard, who accidentally let the cat out of the bag that Smith was really A.C.Doyle.

Doyle was also a fine batsman, opening for Portsmouth Cricket Club, of which he was captain for five years until 1890.

The Daily Telegraph Tuesday, September 2, 2003

Proof that you can judge a book by its cover. By Will Bennett Art Sales Correspondent.

'Throwing away the dust jacket of a novel or children's book could be the most expensive mistake the owner has made according to a survey.

Top ten UK adult fiction first editions 1900 to present:

1. Arthur Conan Doyle – *The Hound of the Baskervilles* (1902) £80,000 with dust jacket; £5,000 without.

Anthony Howlett, born Peterborough, December 30, 1924. Died London, August 21, 2003, aged 78.

Two obituaries: firstly from the DAILY TELEGRAPH (exact date unknown), and secondly, from the **Daily Express** Tuesday September 9 2003 By **Dominic Egan**.

Anthony Howlett Barrister who restarted the Sherlock Holmes Society and re-enacted the encounter at Reichenbach Falls.

ANTHONY HOWLETT, who died on August 21 aged 78, was a barrister at the Board of Trade and Remembrancer of the City of London; but he was more widely known as founder and presiding inspiration of the Sherlock Holmes Society of London.

The original Sherlock Holmes Society, founded by A G Macdonnel in 1934, had been a casualty of the war (and of the founder's indiscretion with the wife of the president). The origins of the new society were laid in 1951 at the time of the Sherlock Holmes Exhibition, which was mounted by Marylebone Public Library as its contribution to the Festival of Britain.

Tony Howlett, then a newly-fledged barrister with too much spare time on his hands, had haunted the Marylebone library to lend what help he could; the frequency of his visits was not uninfluenced by the presence of Miss Freda Pearce, the assistant librarian who, a year later, became his wife.

Howlett raised the idea of reviving the pre-war society, with the purpose of bringing together like-minded enthusiasts to study the life and work of Sherlock Holmes, to hold meetings and to publish a journal. A notice about the society appeared in *The Times* on April 19 1951, and it held its first meeting at the Victoria and Albert Museum on July 17.

Howlett was the first honorary secretary, twice chairman, and the president from 1992, by which time the society had 1,000 members and a long waiting list. For more than 30 years he would organise annual film evenings, an annual dinner (with a star guest) and visits to sites mentioned by Conan Doyle.

His finest hour came in 1968, when, with Albert Kunz of the Swiss National Tourist Office, he organised the first pilgrimage to Switzerland to re-enact the encounter between Holmes and his arch-enemy Moriarty at the Reichenbach Falls. Members of the society wore Victorian costume and played characters from the stories, while the Swiss, who reaped excellent publicity, laid on brass bands, horse-drawn carriages and steam trains. Sir Paul Gore-Booth (then Permanent Under-Secretary at the Foreign Office) was to have played Sherlock Holmes, but as he could only leave London for a few days, Howlett assumed the role in his absence, with great aplomb. He worked closely with Kunz on subsequent visits in 1978, 1987, 1988 and 1991, and was largely responsible for the reconstruction of the Sherlock Holmes sitting-room which is the centrepiece of the Sherlock Holmes Museum at Meiringen.

On the later trips he took on the role of Moriarty, "the Napoleon of crime", on each occasion re-enacting the famous tussle during which two clothed dummies are seen to fall over the cliff into the Falls. "I've spent most of my life being pompous and serious," said Howlett. "This is the perfect relaxation."

Anthony Douglas Howlett was born in Peterborough on December 30 1924 and grew up at Grantham, Lincolnshire. After leaving King's School he joined the Royal Naval Volunteer Reserve. He served in landing-craft during the Second World War and crossed the Channel on D-Day plus one.

On demobilisation Howlett went up to Trinity, Cambridge, to read Law, and was called to the Bar by Gray's Inn in 1950. The next year he joined the legal department of the Board of Trade, where he was in charge of export credit guarantees (1972-75) and of merchant shipping (1975-81). He was the British delegate at the London diplomatic conference on the limitation of liability for maritime claims in 1976, and at several other international maritime conferences.

Howlett left the Board of Trade in 1981 to become Remembrancer of the City of London, a post dating back to the reign of Queen Elizabeth I which involved him, for the next five years, in arranging state banquets and acting as liaison between the City and the Palace. It brought him many honours, including the Order of King Abdul Aziz II of Saudi Arabia, the Order of Oman, and of Qatar. He was also appointed a Commander of the Order of Orange Nassau, an Officer of the Legion d'honneur, and a Commander of the Order of the Lion of Malawi.

Howlett's recreations included book-browsing, sailing, opera, photography, maritime history, as well as service in the RNVSR (1951-60) and RNR (1960-75). But none of these took up so much of his spare time as Sherlock Holmes.

His favourite Holmes story was *The Hound of the Baskervilles* and its film history was the subject of his earliest contribution to the *Sherlock Holmes Journal* (in the first issue in May 1952). He later provided readers with reviews and background for new films as they appeared. He helped Michael Pointer, a friend from school with what became a definitive history, *The Public Life of Sherlock Holmes* (1975), which is dedicated to Howlett.

Howlett was a master of tact when dealing with Conan Doyle's sons, Denis and Adrian, and became a close personal friend of the author's daughter, Dame Jean Conan Doyle. He was closely involved in planning the statue of Sherlock Holmes outside Baker Street underground station and that of Conan Doyle at Crowborough, in Sussex, and he did much else to further appreciation of Holmes and his creator.

His wisdom and enthusiasm, his sense of fun, and his innate understanding of what was appropriate ensured that the society prospered.

He is survived by his wife.

EXPRESS OBITUARIES Anthony Howlett, City grandee.

Sherlock fan who menaced as Moriarty.

A barrister and and former civil servant, Anthony Howlett spent several years as a senior functionary of the City of London organising banquets for presidents and kings. He was rewarded with top laurels from around the world, including the coveted Legion d'Honneur from France's President Mitterrand, but nothing gave him greater pleasure than trips he organised to the Reichenbach Falls in Switzerland to re-enact the famous battle between Sherlock Holmes and his arch-enemy Professor Moriarty.

The founder of the Sherlock Holmes Society of London, Howlett assumed the role of his great hero at the first re-enactment in 1968 but came into his own in later years, when he played Moriarty, producing memorable performances that seethed with menace. Playing the villain, he declared, was much more fun.

A big man with a personality to match, he was the heart and soul of a society that now has more than 1,000 members. As its first honorary secretary and later as chairman and president, his enthusiasm, administrative skills and wit proved essential to its success. "I've spent most of my life being pompous and serious," he said. "This is the perfect relaxation."

Anthony Howlett was born in 1924 in Peterborough but grew up in Grantham, Lincolnshire. He joined the Royal Navy Volunteer Reserve in 1939, served in landing craft and put down on a Normandy beach just 24 hours after D-Day.

After the war he read law at Trinity College, Cambridge, and was called to the Bar by Gray's Inn in 1950. He joined the legal department of the Board of Trade in 1951 and became head of the export credit guarantees and merchant shipping sections. He served as the British delegate at a number of international maritime conferences.

In the early Fifties he began making regular trips to the Marylebone public library, where one of the assistants, Freda Pearce, had caught his eye. They married in 1952 and remained devoted to each other for more than 50 years.

Through the library, home to one of the world's best Sherlock Holmes collections, he revived the Sherlock Holmes Society. Founded in 1934, the original had boasted famous members including Dorothy L Sayers, creator of another famous fictional detective, Lord Peter Wimsey. It has stopped meeting during the Second World War and had also been rocked by a scandal involving its founder, AG Macdonnell and the wife of its president.

The new society held its first meeting at the Victoria and Albert Museum on July 17, 1951. It later published its own journal and organised film evenings, an annual dinner and visits to sites mentioned in the Sherlock Holmes stories. The high points of its activities were the trips to the Reichenbach Falls, arranged in conjunction with the Swiss National Tourist Office. Members of the society wore Victorian costume, while the Swiss hosts provided steam trains, horse-draw carriages and brass bands. The most recent trip was in 1991.

Working once more with the Swiss National Tourist Office, he played a key role in recreating the sitting room that forms the centrepiece of the Sherlock Holmes Museum in Meiringen. He was also closely involved in planning the statue of Holmes that stands outside Baker Street Underground station in London and that of Sir Arthur Conan Doyle at his adopted home town of Crowborough in Sussex.

In 1981 he left the Board of Trade to become Remembrancer of the City of London. The office dates back to the reign of Queen Elizabeth I and requires the encumbent to wear a long court coat, breeches and full-bottom wig. In addition to organising banquets he acted as liaison between the City and Buckingham Palace.

His success in the post was such that he was showered with honours, including the Order of King Abdul Aziz II of Saudi Arabia, the Order of Oman and the Order of Qatar. He was also appointed a Commander of the Order of Orange Nassau, a coveted Dutch honour, and of the Order of the Lion of Malawi.

He retired in 1986 and is survived by his wife.

Daily Mail, Friday, October 31, 2003

Return to Baker Street by **Simon Brett**

The next classic tale to add to your Children's Golden Library hardback book collection is The Hound of the Baskervilles by Sir Arthur Conan Doyle.

I hadn't touched a copy of The Hound of the Baskervilles since my schooldays. I had enjoyed it then – which was surprising, since it was an O-level set text – but to re-read the book recently was unalloyed pleasure.

I was once again immediately immersed in the ghoulish, misty shadows of Dartmoor, and in Sherlock Holmes's race against time to save the new heir to Baskerville Hall from the ghastly fate which had destroyed his predecessors.

But while I was reading, I was also deeply struck by how much Conan Doyle had got right by the time this Sherlock Holmes adventure was published in 1902, and by how much his creation has influenced subsequent crime fiction.

Rarely can an iconic literary figure have burst so fully-formed from the creative imagination as did the sleuth of Baker Street. All the qualities for which a deerstalker hat is now internationally recognised shorthand were there in his 1887 debut, A Study in Scarlet. His very first exchange on being introduced to Dr Watson is archetypal Sherlock Holmes.

'How are you?' he said cordially, gripping my hand with a strength for which I should hardly have given him credit. *'You have been in Afghanistan, I perceive'*

'How on earth did you know that?' I asked in astonishment.

At once, the relationship was established – and what an influential relationship it proved to be. How many lesser pairings of masterminds and plodding chronicles have been perpetuated in crime fiction?

When millions of TV viewers watch Sergeant Lewis limping behind the dashing thought processes of Inspector Morse, they are following a path laid down by Conan Doyle. It is the stolidness of Dr Watson's chronicling that makes the genius of his companion credible.

By the time he was writing The Hound of the Baskervilles, Conan Doyle had made Watson slightly less of a buffoon. The doctor is a fitter man for a start, less handicapped by the wounds he sustained in Afghanistan, and he can make a genuine contribution as detective's assistant.

But there is still no question where the real power in the relationship lies, and the book contains a wonderful moment when Holmes turns the tables on Watson, to show just how far he is on the investigative trail.

The supersleuth is also still capable of breathtakingly arrogant put-downs to his sidekick. 'I am afraid, my dear Watson, that most of your conclusions were erroneous. When I say that you stimulated me I meant, to be frank, that in noting your fallacies I was occasionally guided towards the truth.'

As in all the Sherlock Holmes stories, this vital thread of humour sparkles through the narrative, without defusing the tension, or limiting the horror.

And, although I don't like crime literature which involves the occult (for me, the introduction of spiritual forces moves the goalposts too far, with a resulting diminution of tension and interest), I find The Hound of the Baskervilles totally satisfying.

The horror is maintained, it seems that the only possible explanation for events can lie in the supernatural, and then Sherlock Holmes produces a perfect solution which involves only human agencies and human psychology.

Conan Doyle's detective stories are a bridge from the Victorian era into the 20th century. The scientific analysis at the root of Sherlock Holmes's investigation in The Hound of the Baskervilles looks forward to 20th century technologies, while the background of the story is pure Victorian melodrama.

Very good Victorian melodrama, to be sure, but it does have all the classic ingredients – a dark, old menacing house set in the middle of the moors, a family curse, an escaped convict, swirling mists, a treacherous marsh, and a genuinely terrifying monster – 'a foul thing, a great, black beast, shaped like a hound, yet larger than any hound that ever mortal eye had rested upon.'

Though this kind of scenario is from the world of Wilkie Collins, the resolution of The Hound of the Baskervilles, arrived at by Sherlock Holmes's deductive skills and analysis of the human mind, anticipates the world of Sigmund Freud.

Yet another enduring legacy of Conan Doyle is his hero's relationship with the police. At the beginning of his investigative career, the denizens of Scotland Yard may have been sceptical.

Not any more, by the time he's investigating the Hound. 'I saw at once from the reverential way in which Lestrade gazed at my companion that he had learned a great deal since the days when they had first worked together.'

In the real world there never has been a successful amateur detective, certainly not one whose brilliance leaves professional policemen in a state of perpetual bafflement. Conan Doyle invented the species. Sherlock Holmes defined the character.

A Study in Scarlet defined the genre, and it was then superbly developed in The Hound of the Baskervilles – an exciting, witty, rattling good read.

Chapter 12

The Tragedy at Scarsdale Villas

A Real-Life Sherlock Holmes Mystery

The Daily Telegraph Saturday, April 24, 2004

Mysterious death of Holmes expert By Catriona Davies

A LEADING expert on Sherlock Holmes grew paranoid that people were plotting against him before being found garrotted in his bed, an inquest was told yesterday.

Richard Lancelyn Green, 50, who co-edited a book about Sir Arthur Conan Doyle, creator of the fictional detective Holmes, was found dead at his home in Kensington, west London, with a shoelace tightened around his neck using a wooden spoon.

Dr Paul Knapman, the Westminster coroner, recorded an open verdict and said it was a "very unusual death".

Prof Sir Colin Berry, a pathologist who gave the cause of death as asphyxia due to garrotting, said the form of death was so unusual that he had only come across it once before in 30 years.

Mr Lancelyn Green's friend Nicholas Rathbone Utechin, a relative of the Sherlock Holmes actor Basil Rathbone, said his death had revived rumours of "the curse of Conan Doyle", that several people associated with the late author have suffered breakdowns or untimely deaths.

However, Dr Knapman said: "I would not wish to stress the importance of any conspiracy theories."

The inquest was told that Mr Lancelyn Green, a former chairman of the Sherlock Holmes Society of London, whose body was found on March 27, developed an intense paranoia that he was being followed.

The Sunday Telegraph Magazine 30 May 2004

Was it murder? Or was it suicide? And what did Conan Doyle's lost archive have to do with it? William Langley investigates the mysterious death of a Sherlock Holmes enthusiast.

What lay behind the hideous death earlier this year of the world's leading Sherlock Holmes expert? William Langley investigates a story worthy of Conan Doyle himself, and finds the answer far from elementary.

IN the strange, lost hours before his death, Richard Lancelyn Green, the world's foremost authority on Sherlock Holmes, shut himself away among the spoils of a lifetime's obsession. From the outside 39 Scarsdale Villas, London W8, looked like a typically elegant Kensington townhouse, but its basement was a shrine to the great detective and his creator, Sir Arthur Conan Doyle. Almost everything in the world that mattered to Lancelyn Green was there, and, as fear and suspicion took over his mind, it was the place he retreated to.

Lancelyn green, 50, had so much in common with his hero. He was highly intelligent, diligent and not by nature given to flights of fancy. So when, in spring last year, he began to suggest that people were plotting against him and that his movements were being monitored, those close to him were bewildered. Had Richard, they asked been spending too long in the realms of fiction?

It was a fair question. Lancelyn Green was immersed in the world of Holmes to a degree that went far beyond the normal boundaries of enthusiasm or even scholarship. As a schoolboy he had turned the attic of his family's home into a replica of the fictional detective's study at 221b Baker Street, complete with violin, tobacco case and coal scuttle. From an early age he had been able to recite entire chapters of the Conan Doyle oeuvre. Most boys eventually grow out of their crazes, but Lancelyn Green never did. Nor did he ever marry. It was assumed that his passion for Holmes left no room for other loves, but the truth, it would emerge, was somewhat different.

On the night of February 26 March Lancelyn Green made a number of telephone calls. One was to Nick Rathbone Utechin, editor of the *Sherlock Holmes Journal* and a friend for 25 years. 'I found it extremely disturbing,' recalls Utechin, a distant relative of Basil Rathbone, the actor who played Holmes in the classic 1940s films. 'He sounded frightened and confused, and completely unlike his usual self. He got agitated and started making accusations against me and other people; then there were long pauses in his conversation. I said to him, "Richard, why are you doing this?" There was a long silence. Then he said, "Perhaps it's because I'm strange."

The next day, alerted by Lancelyn Green's anxious sister, Priscilla West, who had also received a disturbing telephone call, the police went to the Kensington house. Receiving no answer at the door, they broke in. Richard was dead in his bed, surrounded by an assortment of cuddly toys – the googly-eyed Muppet from *Sesame Street* called Elmo, his childhood teddy bear and a Snoopy. He had been garrotted with a shoelace tightened by a wooden spoon.

Professor Sir Colin Berry, one of Britain's most eminent pathologists, told the inquest into Lancelyn Green's death that in 30 years he had encountered only one comparable case. Even in the rare instances where self-garrotting is chosen as a means of suicide, the victim almost always uses a scarf or blanket to protect the neck from being painfully cut as the cord tightens. There were other puzzling aspects to the case. Lancelyn Green, a highly proficient writer, had left no note. Nor, as is common in suicide cases, had he talked to anyone about taking his life. There were, though, no signs of forced entry to the house, or of a struggle, and convincing evidence was given of the dead man's apparently disturbed state of mind. Describing the death as 'very unusual', the Westminster coroner, Dr Paul Knapman, recorded an open verdict, observing – pointedly – that he was 'a little surprised' that the CID had not been called in to look more closely at the circumstances.

Why was Lancelyn Green's mind in turmoil? What accounted for the anxiety that pursued him through the last weeks of his life? Who was the mysterious American he claimed was threatening him? Let us consider a mystery we'll call *The Case of the Missing Papers*.

When Sir Arthur Conan Doyle died in 1930 he left a large store of personal documents. The papers were carefully stored by his widow, Jean, and upon her death in 1940 the bulk of them passed into the hands of Conan Doyles' eldest surviving son, Adrian.

Adrian, a man of expensive tastes, kept the papers in the vaults of his Swiss home, the Chateau de Lucens, near Lake Geneva. To finance those tastes he periodically sold manuscripts, mostly to American collectors, but he guarded the core of the archive jealously, to the extent of occasionally denying its existence. As far as is known, only two outsiders were ever allowed to see the papers. One was John Dickson Carr, an American mystery writer, who was commissioned to write an authorised Conan Doyle biography. The other was Pierre Nordon, a French student who struck lucky while working on his thesis.

Although dull and deficient in scholarship, Carr's book caused a sensation among Conan Doyle devotees. At the back of the volume was an index of the archive. It listed the contents by subject but gave no further details. Ever since, Conan Doyle scholars have been tormented by the thought of what the papers might actually reveal.

Conan Doyle has the power to enthral – even to possess the minds of his admirers like no other writer, and Doyleans, as his disciples are known, hail from all over the world. While eminently capable of falling out with each other, they have, in recent years broadly agreed on two things. One was a need for a modern biography. The other was that Richard Lancelyn Green was by far the best qualified to write it. No one else had the same depth of knowledge or the same degree of literary pizzazz. Yet Lancelyn Green had a problem. He didn't have the precious archive. He wasn't even sure what had happened to it.

After Adrian Conan Doyle's death in 1970 the papers disappeared. The chateau and its contents were surrendered to the Vaud canton in lieu of death duties, but a search of the premises revealed no sign of the archive. Had it been secretly sold? Had it – as was rumoured – been destroyed?

In fact the papers – 15 boxes of them – were quietly brought back to Britain. For the next 25 years, while Doyle's descendants argued about who owned them, their whereabouts remained unknown to the world at large. Only with the deaths of Adrian's wife, Anna in 1991, and Arthur Conan Doyle's daughter Jean, in 1997, was the question of ownership resolved. Earlier this year Christie's announced that the papers had been found in the offices of a London solicitor, and were being put under the hammer.

When he first heard the news Lancelyn Green was understandably ecstatic. 'He came in to see us and we went over the material,' says Tom Lamb, head of books and manuscripts at Christie's. He was absolutely thrilled. For anyone with an interest in Conan Doyle the archive is the holy grail. Richard had dreamt of the day all this would be available. I wanted him to be involved, and he was very keen to help.

The cache was indeed spectacular. Among its treasures was a fragment of the first story Conan Doyle had written, aged six, about a Bengal tiger; an unpublished and untitled first novel; a gripping account of a whaling trip to the Arctic in 1880; various outlines for Sherlock Holmes plots; and an angry letter from Lord Alfred Douglas,

Oscar Wilde's lover, suggesting that 'The proper way to deal with a man such as you [Conan Doyle] would be to give you a thrashing with a horse whip.'

As the preparations for the auction began, however, Lancelyn Green's enthusiasm lessened noticeably. The archive was being sold in 137 separate lots. There was every chance a substantial part of it would be sold on as sublots. Lancelyn Green began to express the view that it would be better if it all went to the British Library, where it would be available for study. This, he argued, was what Conan Doyle's family would have wanted. Above all, it was clear that Lancelyn Green feared his biography would never be written if the papers – having been missing for so long – were scattered into private hands. In the event there were, according to Christie's, 'two or three main buyers' (at least one private American buyer) at the sale earlier this month which made a total of £950,000. At the time of going to press their identities had not been revealed. [see later notes on the auction – *Sherlock* magazine Issue 60].

Friends who talked to Lancelyn Green began to detect an uncharacteristic note of anger and resentment; those who didn't share his objections to the sale were 'against' him. He talked of plots to keep him quiet and claimed powerful interests – particularly in the shape of a sinister, unidentified American – were trying to destroy his reputation. So began Lancelyn Green's descent into what his sister, Priscilla, describes as 'a Kafkaesque world' in which he would lose first his reason, then his life.

Richard Lancelyn Green was born in 1953, the youngest of three children of the successful children's author Roger Lancelyn Green. Roger himself was a lifelong Holmes devotee. When he introduced his 11-year-old son to the stories, he caught the bug instantly. 'When Richard was four,' says Priscilla, 'he was blinded in one eye. He was never going to be a rugger player, so it was natural for him to gravitate towards books. And in Sherlock Holmes, he found a ready-made world.'

Richard read English at Oxford, and upon leaving – sustained by a modest allowance from a family trust – embarked on the only career he would ever have: the quest for Doylean knowledge. 'Obsession is by no means too strong a word to describe what Richard had,' says Nick Utechin. 'He took literally Dorothy L. Sayers remark that "The game of Sherlock Holmes must be played as seriously as a county cricket match at Lord's." But he wasn't a crank. There are some people to whom Holmes is, to all intents and purposes, a real person. Richard wasn't like that. He knew his business. He was, I suppose, a gentleman scholar of the kind that doesn't exist now.'

For 30 years the gentleman scholar devoted his life to collection and study. His most treasured piece was a rare 1887 edition of *Beeton's Christmas Annual* in which Holmes makes his first appearance in 'A Study in Scarlet'. When, after years of searching, he finally obtained a copy, he sent Utechin a card with a two-word message: "At last!" And all the time he was preparing for the task ahead: the definitive biography of Conan Doyle. All he needed, he would say, was the last archive.

As a person, many people found Lancelyn Green, unnervingly reserved. 'You could go further,' says Philip Porter, the chairman of the Sherlock Holmes Society of London, 'and say that he seemed a little superior, or even supercilious. And he had this funny eye. But when you got to know him better, and shared a bottle of wine with him, you could break through and find he was warm and modest and very amusing. But he wasn't the kind of man who told you a lot about himself.'

Indeed Richard's private life – and his sexuality – remained a mystery until his death. Hardly anyone, including those who were closest to him, realised he was homosexual. 'I assumed that he wasn't,' says his sister Priscilla. 'Not that it was the kind of thing we talked about. It seemed more likely that he just hadn't found the right woman.' The fringes of the Holmesian world would buzz with theories that the sleuth and Dr Watson, two unmarried men sharing rooms, were gay. If so, they could not have done a better job of hiding it than Richard. 'I had absolutely no idea,' says Utechin. 'I didn't have a clue,' says Porter. As for Priscilla: 'It is a comfort to know there was love and friendship in his life.'

Indeed, on the evening before his death, Lancelyn Green went to a restaurant in Kensington High Street with an old boyfriend, Lawrence Keen, a care-worker from south London. The pair had known each other for eight years but had, says Keen, been lovers only for the first two. At dinner, Lancelyn Green was agitated. He drank heavily throughout, Keen told the inquest, and when they had finished eating they returned to Scarsdale Villas. Lancelyn Green wanted to talk more, but not indoors where, he said, he suspected their conversation would be bugged. So they went into the garden, despite the chilliness of the night, and drank coffee in the darkness. Richard talked of his fear of the mysterious American, his dismay at the impending sale of the archive, and his belief that someone was out to destroy him. When Keen left, Lancelyn Green went inside. He was not seen alive again.

Three possibilities present themselves. Lancelyn Green killed himself, or was murdered, or was engaged in a fetishistic sexual act that accidentally led to his death. The police made an assumption of suicide on the spot, which the coroner, and those who knew the dead man's state of mind, have since accepted as the most probable explanation.

Yet questions remain. Why did Lancelyn Green choose such a grotesque and uncertain form of suicide? Why did so meticulous a man not leave a note? Who were the people he claimed were threatening him? And why, if the auction was the source of his anxiety, did he not want to see its outcome before taking such a drastic step?

'Personally I don't believe that the sale could have pushed him over the edge,' says Tom Lamb. 'I saw him not long before his death, and he seemed quite all right. He was a lovely man and somehow things went wrong for him. What happened happened.

Priscilla takes a different line. 'I'm glad the verdict was left open,' she says. 'Although I'm 99 per cent certain it was suicide, his world had become Kafkaesque, and we cannot be sure what was happening in it. Richard wasn't equipped to deal with life's difficulties. People didn't behave towards him as he expected. He felt threatened. I believe there was some deliberate psychological bullying which may have contributed to his state of mind.'

Perhaps Conan Doyle himself sums the matter up best: 'This tragedy has been so uncommon, so complete and of such personal importance to so many people, that we are suffering from a plethora of surmise, conjecture, and hypothesis,' he has Sherlock Holmes say in 'Silver Blaze'. The words could hardly be more fitting to the strange death at Scarsdale Villas. The missing papers were the key not only to Conan Doyle's life but to Richard Lancelyn Green's. And one way or another they almost certainly killed him.

Sherlock Magazine Issue 60 June 2004

Newsdesk – Richard Lancelyn Green 1953-2004

With the tragic, untimely death of Richard Lancelyn Green, reported in many of the national newspapers, the world has lost one of the great Doylean and Holmesian scholars.

He was an avid collector, owning one of the most important collections of Holmesiana and Doyleana in private hands. His collection contained many rare items, including a copy of *Beeton's Christmas Annual* for 1887, in which Holmes first appeared, and private films of Arthur Conan Doyle and his family.

Richard was also a writer of great skill and with John Michael Gibson compiled the authoritative *Bibliography of A. Conan Doyle* (1983). As an editor he produced some wonderful collections, including an anthology of pastiches, *The Further Adventures of Sherlock Holmes* (1985); [see an Introduction to this book by Richard Lancelyn Green later in this chapter]. And an anthology of associated Doyle writings, *The Uncollected Sherlock Holmes* (1993). His latest publication was an introduction and notes to the Raffles stories last year. He also wrote many articles for Sherlockian publications and, indeed, contributed to this magazine in the past.

Richard joined the Sherlock Holmes Society of London in 1966, becoming thirty years later, an active, talented and inspired chairman.

Beneath his apparently shy and diffident exterior, Richard was a man of great wit, charm, modesty and, above all, kindness. He was respected and liked on both sides of the Atlantic, receiving his investiture from the Baker Street Irregulars in 1985.

A Personal Note from David Stuart Davies (Editor)

To lose a great Sherlockian is one thing; to lose a friend is another. Richard was a friend. We met through the Sherlock Holmes Society in the late 1980s and our friendship grew over the years. I knew I could always rely on Richard for help, especially when I was in need of a picture for the front cover of the magazine. I never quite realised how vast his collection of media material was until I came to write *Starring Sherlock Holmes*, my book on the film career of the Great Detective. Richard agreed to let me plunder his collection to provide some of the illustrations for the book. I spent the day at his house selecting the stills. He brought out drawer upon drawer of pictures for me to examine. For a film-loving Sherlockian it was like entering Aladdin's cave. I left at the end of the day with a suitcase bulging with stills. Approximately seventy percent of the images in *Starring Sherlock Holmes* were from Richard's collection and I will be forever grateful for his help. He would always respond to a request to share his knowledge and his collection with others, like last year when I was in London working on a DVD 'featurette' – an interview with Edward Hardwicke for one of the Granada TV Holmes DVD releases. We needed a picture of Adrian Conan Doyle. I didn't have one, but I knew a man who did. A quick phone call and Richard jumped into a taxi and arrived at the recording studio bearing the requisite still.

But it wasn't all Sherlock business: we also shared many happy social times and in company he was urbane, funny and a splendid raconteur. The Sherlockian world has lost a giant; but those who knew him have lost a very special, kind friend. Our thoughts are with his family.

Newsdesk – The Doyle Auction

By the time you read this the collection of 137 items from a Conan Doyle Archive will have gone under the hammer at Christie's in London. It is claimed that the material had been owned by Doyle's son Adrian and then by his widow, Anna, and then by Anna's heirs, Richard Doyle, Catherine Doyle and Charles Foley and it is they who have sent it to auction. While there were hardly any items directly relating to Sherlock Holmes in the auction, there was a wealth of interesting pieces providing a fascinating glimpse into this author's life from the pages of his first unpublished (non-Holmes) novel to letters concerned with Spiritualism written towards the end of his life.

There was also a wonderful array of letters from famous individuals who corresponded with the author including Winston Churchill, George Bernard Shaw, WG Grace, PG Wodehouse, Bram Stoker, HG Wells and Oscar Wilde.

Also included was a brass name plate stating 'Dr CONAN DOYLE Physician & Surgeon' from his Southsea days. In his autobiography **Memoirs & Adventures** *Doyle described how he arrived at Portsmouth in July 1882 to set up in practice as a general physician after a false start in Plymouth. His worldly possessions were contained in a small trunk and he had less than £10 to meet expenses and to furnish a house. He managed to rent Bush Villa in Southsea (the residential part of Portsmouth) for £40 a year and there he put up the plate which he had made earlier during a brief partnership in Plymouth. He wrote, 'Servants, of course, were out of the question, so I polished my own plate every morning, brushed down my front steps, and kept the house reasonably clean.'*

Of the scant Sherlockian items there were some documents which went under the auction heading of 'Sherlock Holmes – Plots & Ideas'. This referred to a collection of letters and other documents relating to real-life mysteries investigated by Conan Doyle, or potential plots for Sherlock Holmes stories. Five of the letters relate to a mystery dubbed 'The Case of the Missing Fiancé, 1909, the result of an appeal by a nurse, whose Danish fiancé had vanished without trace, there are three letters from the nurse, and two from an employee of the Danish East Asian Company, enabling the identification of the missing man as a fraudster.

The other two letters, 1901 and 1907, also relate to real-life missing persons. The typescript is a suggested plot for a Sherlock Holmes story, a murder case involving a pistol, a ladder, and the framing of an innocent man. The manuscript map is apparently a spoof: 'Rough plan of a field where a battle with Germans took place', 'Holmes' aeroplane', 'Moran's aeroplane', 'Gravel pit whence Holmes flung Egg into river', 'Bridge blown up by Holmes', and 'Knoll where Stanley Hopkins stood'. A printed book in Chinese was equally irreverent, being Xiao Qing's **An Account Between Two Cunning Rivals,** *(possibly extracted from a literary journal), a version of the rivalry between Sherlock Holmes and Arsene Lupin.*

There was also William Gillett's Sherlockian Greetings card for Christmas 1901, with autograph inscription by Gillette to Sir Arthur Conan Doyle, 'Did you ever imagine that Sherlock Holmes would be sending his compliments to his maker?' with printed greeting 'Mr. Sherlock Holmes at the Lyceum Theatre, London, presents his compliments and the best wishes of the season', bound with four illustrations, original ribbon tie.

We hope they all find a good home, but how much more pleasing would it have been for the collection to have gone to a public institution where we could all *see these historical gems.*

DAILY MAIL, Friday, August 6, 2004

A new home for Sherlock Holmes

A collection of Sir Arthur Conan Doyle memorabilia, including a hint of how Sherlock Holmes got his name, is moving.

Writer Richard Lancelyn Green, who died in March, has left the 20,000 items, worth more than £2million, to Portsmouth library.

Conan Doyle had a medical practice in the city and wrote his first two Holmes books there. The collection includes first editions, manuscripts, film scripts, photographs, jigsaws, videos, posters, Toby jugs – and a small medical book by a Doctor Sherlock, possibly inspiring the detective's name.

DAILY TELEGRAPH Friday, August 6, 2004

Conan Doyle fan leaves £2m hoard to library By David Sapsted

An avid collector of Sir Arthur Conan Doyle memorabilia, who died in circumstances bizarre enough to have attracted the attention of Sherlock Holmes, has bequeathed his £2million collection to a city library.

Richard Lancelyn Green, 50, a writer and ex-chairman of the Sherlock Holmes Society, was found dead in bed, surrounded by cuddly toys, in his London home in March. He had been strangled with a shoelace, but a coroner recorded an open verdict, saying he was unsure whether it was suicide, murder or a sexual act gone wrong.

Mr Lancelyn Green had collected 20,000 items, including a recreation of 221b Baker Street. His will, published today, leaves them to the library service in Portsmouth, where Conan Doyle lived and worked between 1882-1890 and where he helped to found Portsmouth Football Club, becoming its first goalkeeper.

The collection will be catalogued before going on display in 2006.

The Sunday Telegraph DECEMBER 12 2004

Case of the Sherlock Holmes fanatic 'who killed himself but made it look like murder'
By **Elizabeth Day**

A LEADING authority on Sherlock Holmes took his own life in a way meant to suggest that a rival had murdered him, it is claimed.

Richard Lancelyn Green, 50, a prolific author and collector of memorabilia relating to the fictional detective, was found garrotted on his bed by police in March after trying to stop a £2million auction of Sir Arthur Conan Doyle's papers.

Although the coroner returned an open verdict, friends and relatives of Mr Lancelyn Green now claim that the evidence suggests he took his own life in a manner that would implicate an American rival.

In an interview with The New Yorker *magazine, James Gibson, who co-edited the first comprehensive Conan Doyle biography with Mr Lancelyn Green in 1983, concludes that his colleague had "wanted [his death] to look like murder", and that he had set up a trail of "false clues". Mr Lancelyn Green's body was found in his flat in Kensington, west London, on March 27 with a shoelace tied round his neck and a wooden spoon, which had been used to tighten the noose, still entangled in the cord.*

In the weeks leading up to his death, Mr Lancelyn Green had expressed concern that a forthcoming auction of Conan Doyle papers at Christie's, consisted mostly of items that the author's daughter, Dame Jean Conan Doyle, had left as a bequest to the British Library. Mr Lancelyn Green, a former chairman of the Sherlock Holmes Society, wanted access to the papers to research a biography of Conan Doyle.

Mr Gibson said that the more curious elements of the evidence – which had revived talk of a Conan Doyle "curse" – could be explained by Mr Lancelyn Green's suicide. He told The New Yorker. *He had to have used [the wooden spoon] to tighten the cord. If someone else had garrotted him, why would he need the spoon? The killer could simply use his hands.*

"I think things in his life had not turned out the way he wanted. This sale brought everything to a head."

Before he died Mr Lancelyn Green had made several telephone calls to friends and journalists claiming that an American whom he did not identify was pursuing him. He feared that his opposition to the forthcoming auction could result in his death and his behaviour is said to have become increasingly erratic.

Although "the American" is not named in The New Yorker, *there has been speculation among Holmes enthusiasts that Mr Lancelyn Green was becoming increasingly paranoid about Jon Lellenberg, a policy strategy analyst in the office of Donald Rumsfeld, the US defence secretary, and a respected author of books about Holmes. He was in London to see the Sherlock Holmes Society in the week Mr Lancelyn Green was most erratic.*

The men had collaborated on a number of Holmesian articles but fell out in the mid-1990s over the Mr Lancelyn Green's close relationship with Dame Jean.

One friend said "the American" played on Dame Jean's sensitivities about her father's reputation and "twisted" some of Mr Lancelyn Green's more candid published works to drive a wedge between them.

Shortly before Mr Lancelyn Green died he gave his sister a piece of paper containing the names of three people and their telephone numbers and told her to keep them safe. When she called his flat on the night his body was discovered, Mr Lancelyn Green's answering machine had been replaced by an American voice, which caused her to raise the alarm.

Mr Gibson said: "I think he wanted it to look like murder. That's why he didn't leave a note. That's why he took his voice off the answering machine. That's why he sent that message to his sister with the three phone numbers on it. That's why he spoke of the American who was after him.

"He must have been planning it for days, giving us false clues. He created the perfect mystery."

The puzzle of the answering machine message was solved by Mr Lancelyn Green's sister, who said that the machine had been made in America and had a built-in automated message. When her brother took off his message, a pre-recorded American voice answered his calls. The three telephone numbers proved to be unimportant. Two of them were reporters Mr Lancelyn Green spoke to and the other was someone at Christie's. If the theory is proved correct, Mr Lancelyn Green's death would echo the plot of one of the last Sherlock Holmes mysteries, The Problem of Thor Bridge *(1922)*, in which a wife is found lying dead on a bridge, shot in the head at point-blank range. All the evidence points to the governess with whom the husband had been flirting but Holmes shows that she had killed herself to frame her rival.

David Grann, the journalist who wrote the article in The New Yorker, concluded that Mr Lancelyn Green could have been so enraged with the loss of the archive "that he might have done something similar, and even tried to frame the American, whom he blamed for ruining his relationship with Dame Jean".

The suicide theory was dismissed, however, by Owen Dudley Edwards, a Conan Doyle scholar who worked closely with Mr Lancelyn Green to stop the auction.

He claimed that Mr Lancelyn Green was murdered because he had transferred various of Dame Jean's papers to her solicitor's office at her request and could testify that she wished to bequeath them to the library. When the archive came up for sale, Mr Lancelyn Green suspected foul play.

"Murder: I fear that is what the preponderance of the evidence points to," said Prof Dudley Edwards. "Richard told me that he had moved [the archive papers]. So his knowledge was really quite dangerous."

After the auction on May 19, however, it was revealed that Dame Jean had made a last-minute deed of appointment while dying of cancer, splitting the archive between herself and the three heirs of her ex-sister-in-law, Anna Conan Doyle. The auction papers went to the heirs and Dame Jean left the most important papers to the library. In the event, the 3,000 letters, notes and manuscripts fetched just under £1million.

"The tragedy is that Richard could still have written his biography," said Mr Gibson. "He would have had everything he needed."

The Sunday Telegraph December 19 2004

Correction

Last Sunday we published a picture, stating that it was Richard Lancelyn Green, who died in March this year. It was, in fact, a picture of his brother Scirard Lancelyn Green, who is very much alive. We apologise for this error.

The Further Adventures of Sherlock Holmes By Richard Lancelyn Green.

INTRODUCTION

The Strand Magazine *for December 1893 revealed that Sherlock Holmes and Professor Moriarty had perished at the Reichenbach Falls. That at least was the belief of Dr Watson and of his creator. 'Holmes died in the Xmas number,' said Conan Doyle, 'so there's an end to his adventures.' He had failed to see how potent was the spirit he had conjured up and how indestructible was the myth to which he had given birth. The public would not accept the demise of such a popular character and many people were anxious to see the vacuum filled.*

'Suppose someone imagining himself to be "on the same intellectual plane" as Mr Conan Doyle should drag Sherlock Holmes to life again. What would be Mr Doyle's remedy?' asked the St James Gazette, *pointing to stories which used characters created by Dickens, to Walter Besant's sequel to Ibsen,* The Doll's House and After, *and to the sham* Don Quixote *by Avellaneda. The truth was that there was no remedy, for Holmes had already assumed an independent existence.*

Few authors could resist the temptation of writing a Sherlock Holmes parody, or of interviewing him, or of composing memorial verses in his honour. They haunted the Reichenbach Falls in their attempt to resuscitate the great detective or they summoned up his ghost. They welcomed him into their books and they called him by other names. Sherlock Holmes was popular wherever he went. New stories were already appearing in Germany, Spain and Russia which bore his name; he was soon pitting his wits against France's foremost gentleman-cambrioleur; and, as his brother Mycroft said, he was to be heard of everywhere.

Scholars began to unravel the confused chronology and to search for answers to some of the biographical problems. It seemed that readers would never be content, for they could not know enough about Sherlock Holmes. Doyle's hand was forced and forced again, and he would go down in the vaults of Cox & Co., at Charing Cross, to retrieve further stories, but still the public wished for more. And so it was that experts of the highest calibre one of whom according to Doyle knew more about the subject than he did himself, took up the pen for Dr Watson and helped him to chronicle a number of previously unrecorded cases.

THE ADVENTURE OF
THE FIRST-CLASS CARRIAGE

Ronald Knox is one of the most learned authorities on Sherlock Holmes and the person who first showed how the methods of 'Higher Criticism' and classical scholarship might be applied to the stories. He was born in 1888, the youngest son of an Anglican bishop, and he died in 1957 having been for forty years a convert to the Catholic faith. Like his brother, E.V. Knox, he became an early and ardent admirer of Sherlock Holmes through reading the stories in the Strand Magazine. It was one of the few secular periodicals allowed in the Knox household and the first to which children had access. 'Quotations from the epistles of Dr Watson,' his brother said later, 'were considered proper by myself and my brothers on all suitable and unsuitable occasions.'

A family magazine provided them with the opportunity to write an essay on the inconsistencies found in the stories and this in turn served as the basis for the famous paper, 'Studies in the Literature of Sherlock Holmes', which Ronald read to the Gryphon Club in Oxford in 1911. Both essays were sent to Conan Doyle, who, if he failed to give his opinion of the first, at least found much to amuse him in the second. He read it in the Oxford Blue Book where it was first published in July 1912. It then became one of Ronald Knox's most popular talks and gained widespread acclaim in 1928 when it was included in his Essays in Satire.

Knox's other Sherlockian writings include his first book Juxta Salices of 1910, in which Holmes forms a member of the symposium, and Memories of the Future of 1923, where Lady Opal describes the great statue of the detective in Baker Street; there were also reviews, leading articles, letters to the Press, and an essay on 'Mycroft and Moriarty' in H.W. Bell's 1934 anthology, Baker Street Studies.

Knox was a close friend of G.K. Chesterton and a member of the Detection Club. He edited The Best Detective Stories of the Year 1928, giving in the introduction his famous decalogue or list of rules to be adhered to by mystery writers, and he was the author of six detective novels, most of which it must be said feature the rather characterless and unmemorable amateur sleuth, Miles Bredon.

For a time Knox became disenchanted with the Sherlockian world. 'I can't bear books about Sherlock Holmes,' he told an editor who had asked him to review one. 'It is so depressing that my one permanent achievement is to have started a bad joke. If I did start it.' But his old enthusiasm was revived after the war and it was then that he agreed to write 'The Adventure of the First-Class Carriage' for the Strand Magazine.

Many people felt that Sherlock Holmes was the only person who could restore the magazine's flagging fortunes. The editors were finding it more and more difficult to compete with the newer and brasher pocket magazines which their own by then resembled. Richard Osborne, in a review of The Annotated Sherlock Holmes in 1967, explained what the problems were. He said that he was sorry that the compiler had not included any of the articles which E.V. Knox had written for Punch:

I'd also like to have seen again that complete Holmes story that we got Ronald Knox to write for the dying (dear old) Strand in 1947. 'The Adventure of the First-Class Carriage'. I say 'we', I was assistant to Macdonald Hastings, who edited the Strand in its last three years. We were ourselves as hag-ridden by the Holmes legend in those days as the magazine's readers (not very many) appeared to be. The Strand had meant Holmes to us as boys, and the Holmes/Paget face scowled in at the window as we wondered how to make the pocket-size (paper shortage) Strand profitable again. Half the time we wanted to kill its crippling name and start on a new formula, with nudes and shorties to rival the money-making Lilliput and Men Only. The other half of the time we wanted to recall Doyle, Kipling, Jacobs, and Wodehouse and to go back complete to gaslight, assegais, and hansom cabs. When the Strand *finally folded in 1950, my old sixth-form master wrote to me regretfully: 'I loved the dear old* Strand. *To tell you the truth, I have not opened a copy of it in this century.' Perhaps he was the typical reader we were up against.*

Knox's story appeared in the February 1947 issue and an attempt was made to re-create the original atmosphere. 'Do you remember this?' asked the editorial over a photograph of the opening page of 'The Adventure of Shoscombe Old Place': 'It was the last of the Sherlock Holmes stories, published in the Strand Magazine *in 1927. In this issue, Monsignor Ronald Knox, faithfully imitating the style of the great master, recalls Holmes and Watson to the pages of the* Strand *again. To the immortal memory of Sir Arthur Conan Doyle, we offer the first Apocryphal Adventure of Sherlock Holmes.' A* Strand Magazine *heading by Gareth Jones (the artist who designed the covers for* The Hound of the Baskervilles), *dating from before the First World War, and illustrations by Tom Purvis, 'In loving memory of Sidney Paget', completed the effect. It bore as a main title, 'The Apocryphal Sherlock Holmes', and was intended to be the first of a series, but in the event it was the only one published.*

The story is original and is not one of those mentioned by Dr. Watson, but it is firmly in the tradition and has many touches which are highly evocative and convincing. Even if it is not based on actual fact the case of the disappearance of Mr Nathaniel Swithinbank would easily pass as the work of the deutero-Watson who, according to Knox's earlier thesis, had himself written pastiches after the demise of his friend.

Spurious Dr Watson has been the curse of scholars ever since the real first one put pen to paper. Two in particular have had undue attention paid to their work as it was discovered among Conan Doyle's own papers. One is the plot outline for a story involving the use of stilts, and the other is a complete story.

THE ADVENTURE OF
THE SHEFFIELD BANKER

The 'Star Man's Diary' of 13 June 1942 announced a 'Sherlock Holmes "Find"'. It was nothing less than the 'manuscript of an unpublished adventure of the greatest of all fiction detectives', and news of its discovery had been given by 'the author's son', Adrian Conan Doyle, who had come across it when going through his father's papers in search of material for a biography being written by Hesketh Pearson. 'Unfortunately,' the Diary continued, 'our inevitable curiosity is not to be satisfied; there is no likelihood of the story being published.' No reason was given, but the writer of the piece was left in no doubt that it was indeed in Doyle's own handwriting. 'Every line of my father's stories, from the earliest days, was in his own neat writing,' Adrian told him, and then, quoting a remark first made in 1914 by a proof-reader of the Strand Magazine, *he added: 'It was so meticulously clear that the publishers always referred to him as the "Printer's Friend".'*

Word of the discovery soon reached America and William King, the London representative of the Associated Press, was asked to find out more about it. In his dispatch, dated 12 September 1942, he reported that the story had been in a chest with other family documents and that the envelope containing it had a note by Doyle's widow which explained that her husband had refrained from publishing it because he felt that it was not up to his usual standard. Both Adrian Conan Doyle and Hesketh Pearson agreed that the standard was lower than usual, but neither appeared to doubt its authenticity; indeed, rather the reverse, for King ended up by saying: 'The story was written several years before Sir Arthur died, but the state of the paper would indicate, his son said, that it was not among the last of his Sherlock Holmes stories. It is in the same neat handwriting which characterised all his manuscripts.'

No one was more eager for the work to be published than Edgar W. Smith of the Baker Street Irregulars. He said in a letter to the Saturday Review of Literature on 10 October 1942 that its discovery was of 'cosmic importance', and no matter how inferior the story was, no argument designed to justify its suppression would have any validity. 'The world is too eager, too insistent, for more – no matter what – of Sherlock Holmes!'

The first opportunity for the public to judge for themselves came in August 1943 when the Strand Magazine published the chapter from Pearson's biography containing extracts from it. But the full story was still withheld. An offer of $20,000 from an American magazine was declined, and Adrian Conan Doyle also refused to cable the story to the president of the Baker Street Irregulars so that it might be read out at the annual dinner after the guests had been sworn to secrecy.

Nothing more was heard of it until 1947 when a further batch of Conan Doyle manuscripts came to light in a bank vault at Crowborough, including the essay called 'Some personalia about Mr Sherlock Holmes' which was written in 1917. This came to the attention of the editor of Hearst's Cosmopolitan and he asked if he might publish it, but as it had already been published in the Strand Magazine and in Doyle's autobiography, he was offered instead 'The Man who was Wanted' and gladly accepted it. He was under the impression that it had also been found in the bank vault and that it was in manuscript form. 'Found!' said the cover of the August 1948, 'The Last Adventure of Sherlock Holmes. A hitherto unpublished story by Sir Arthur Conan Doyle.' It was, as those who had seen it been warned, somewhat below the usual standard. 'We are aware,' the editor admitted, 'that there are several inconsistencies in this story. We have not tried to correct them. The story is published as it was found except for minor changes in spelling and punctuation.'

In England, the story was offered to the Strand Magazine but the editors turned it down as they could not afford the fee, and it was still available when the editor of the Sunday Dispatch contacted Denis Conan Doyle on 12 August 1948. Negotiations dragged on until December when a price of £250 was agreed, and the literary agents, Pearn, Pollinger, and Higham, who had replaced A.P. Watt and Son, then arranged very advantageous terms for the sale of foreign rights. The first part of the story appeared in the paper on 2 January and the rest followed on 9 and 16 January. Once again there was a warning about the inconsistencies and, to forestall further criticism, the editor added a statement by Denis Conan Doyle which said: 'My father apparently withheld publication of "The Case of the Man who was Wanted" because he did not consider it to be up to his usual standard. His family took the same view and for that reason have withheld publication until now, but public interest in this story has been so great that we have finally yielded to pressure and decided to allow it to be published in the Sunday Dispatch.'

When news of the story was first given, many people urged that it should be published and, in the words of Edgar Smith, called for 'the immediate subsumption of this new Revelation into the full canon of the Sacred Writings'; but when this was done *they were less kind. 'Some notable Sherlockians are pretty severe,' Vincent Starrett admitted in his 'Books Alive' column in the* Chicago Tribune *on 19 September 1948:*

Joseph Henry Jackson thinks the story 'falls flat on its face'. Russell McLauchlin inclines to the belief that it was written, a few years ago, by Adrian Conan Doyle, son of that Sir Arthur who was, as we all know, Dr Watson's literary agent. H.B. Williams thinks the two Doyle boys, Adrian and Denis, may have found the tale in fragmentary form among their father's papers and have completed it as best they could. Jeremiah Buckley declares the work to be a forgery and its perpetrator an American. Prof. Finlay Christ also hints at forgery, and so the game goes on.

In fact, as Starrett was soon to learn, it was not by Conan Doyle and nor was it a forgery. The true author was Arthur Whitaker. He was born in 1882 and married in 1909, and was an architect by profession. Shortly after his marriage, he found that he had time on his hands and, having always been a great admirer of Sherlock Holmes, he worked out some half-dozen plots. One of these, the story in question, he wrote out in full and sent it to Conan Doyle suggesting they might collaborate. Doyle replied on 7 March 1911, saying:
Dear Sir,

I read your story. It is not bad and I don't see why you should not change the names, and try to get it published yourself. Of course you could not use the names of my characters.

It is impossible for me to join with another in any case for the results would be that my price would at once be pushed down 75 per cent by Editors.

Sometimes I am open to purchase ideas which I lay aside and use at my own time and in my own way. I did this once before and gave 10 guineas for the idea, working it on my own lines. If you wished I would do this for you, but I could not guarantee to use it, and you could get no personal credit for it. On the whole you would be wiser to use it yourself.

Yours faithfully,

Arthur Conan Doyle.

Whitaker decided he would accept the offer and a cheque for ten guineas was sent to him on 14 March 1911. Then, inspired by new literary enthusiasm, he wrote four or five of the other stories, one of which, 'The Missing Bales', featured a private detective called Harold Quest, was published in Novel Magazine *in April 1913. But the remainder were set to one side. Throughout his life his abiding interest was natural history. Before writing the Holmes story he had had an article on bats published in the* Naturalist, *and others were to follow, while his collection grew to be one of the finest in the country (the bird notes and diaries are now divided between the Edward Grey Institute in Oxford and the British Trust for Ornithology in Tring, while the birds' eggs, butterflies, and moths went to the Sheffield City Museum). His interest in ornithology tended to take precedence over his work as an architect, but he did design at least one cinema and a number of town houses in his home town of Sheffield. His name was also* occasionally seen in the correspondence columns of the local papers where he would often write in verse – as he did on his hand-drawn Christmas cards and in letters to his friends.

Whitaker retained a carbon copy of the story, and this was read by his brother and sister (to whom he gave the Doyle letter), and by other friends (including one to whom he gave the inscribed visiting-card from Doyle which had accompanied the cheque), but he had almost forgotten about it when in September 1945 he chanced to read Hesketh Pearson's biography and came across the incorrect attribution. He wrote to Pearson pointing out that he was the author. 'My pride,' he said, 'is not unduly hurt by your remark that "The Man who was Wanted" is certainly not up to scratch for the sting is much mitigated by your going on to remark that it carries the authentic trade-mark! This, I feel, is a great compliment to my one and only effort at plagiarism.'

Pearson acknowledged the letter on 26 September, saying that the opening of the story was certainly good enough for him to have claimed it as authentic and suggesting that he would add a note to all future editions, to read as follows:

Two years after the publication of this book I heard from Mr Arthur Whitaker of Sheffield that he had written the unpublished story entitled "The Man who was Wanted" about 35-years before. He had sent it to Doyle suggesting a collaboration. Doyle replied that the story should be rewritten, but added that he was prepared to give £10.10 for it, as he was open to purchase ideas for plots to be used how, when and if he liked. Mr Whitaker accepted the offer, and Doyle filed the story among his papers. Owing to its characteristic opening, I believed it to be his own, and there was nothing in writing to suggest that it was not.

Although a new edition did appear in 1946, under the Guild Books imprint, it did not contain the note as the proofs were not sent to the author in time.

On 31 October 1948, Pearson again wrote to Whitaker, having just received press cuttings from America which made it clear that the story had been published under Doyle's name. He was thinking of writing an article about it, but by December, after he had contacted Vincent Starrett and received a copy of the **Cosmopolitan**, he decided that he would do nothing further, mainly because of the animosity previously shown towards him by Doyle's sons. 'Whatever I do or say in the matter of this story,' he explained, 'they will probably regard it as malicious, which is the reason I have decided to keep out of the business as far as possible, let Starrett have the main facts, and leave the matter entirely in his hands.' He and Whitaker each wrote to Starrett but, with the publication of the story in the **Sunday Dispatch**, Whitaker felt that he should in all fairness disclose the truth to Denis Conan Doyle without further delay. This he did on 12 January 1949. The letter was then forwarded to Adrian Conan Doyle in Tangier. He replied on 21 January and angrily demanded evidence of Whitaker's authorship. 'Unless such proof is forthcoming to satisfy our lawyers, we give you fair warning that we will at once bring action for damages in the event that any person casts any aspersion, without solid proof, against our MS.'

Whitaker was astonished at the tone of the letter and pointed out that he had the original carbon copy and could produce a score of witnesses who had seen and read the story long before Doyle's death. But the matter was already in the hands of Vertue, Son & Churcher, the solicitors for the Conan Doyle estate. Whitaker therefore turned to his own solicitors, Lapage Norris Sons and Saleby. On 3 February 1949 he was able to produce the original letter from Conan Doyle, and on 15 February the affair was brought to a satisfactory conclusion. The Doyles acknowledged that the story was indeed by Arthur Whitaker and, though he expected no remuneration, they agreed to pay him part of the proceeds (£150 in all, of which £21 went on legal expenses). The press had meanwhile been kept at a distance, but once the matter was resolved, the Sunday Dispatch carried an article by John Bingham setting the record straight and explaining how the confusion had arisen. Whitaker had little time to savour his new-found fame, as he died suddenly on 10 July 1949.

The curious history entitles the story to a place in this collection and, though it was criticized at the time when thought to be Conan Doyle's own because of the disconcerting double time-scale, erratic dating, and impossible references to Mary Morstan (who was dead by 1895), it is nevertheless of a high standard, and, as it deceived Doyle's widow, his sons, and two biographers, both Hesketh Pearson and John Dickson Carr, it will always have a special place in the Sherlock Holmes apocrypha.

THE ADVENTURE OF
THE UNIQUE HAMLET

Vincent Starrett, who, as has been seen, was one of the first to learn the truth about Arthur Whitaker, and who had also been one of the first in America to mention the story of 'The Man who was Wanted', as he had done so in the Chicago Tribune on 12 September 1942, was born in Toronto in 1886 and began his 'career of Conan Doyle idolatry' when he was ten years old. In 1918 he wrote his first article, 'In Praise of Sherlock Holmes', for Reedy's Mirror; it was a 'paean of gratitude' following the publication of His Last Bow, and a copy was sent to Conan Doyle. It was to be the inspiration for a series of articles which were collected in 1933 as The Private Life of Sherlock Holmes. But before then he had made his second contribution to the 'literature of the legend'. This was 'The Adventure of the Unique Hamlet', which was written in 1920 and privately printed by Walter Hill for distribution at Christmas among their friends (one of whom was Conan Doyle). It is described as a 'hitherto unchronicled adventure of Mr Sherlock Holmes', but the author also hoped that it would be read as a 'genial satire on book collecting and Shakespearean commentators'.

Starrett was a man of many parts, a noted critic, essayist, journalist, anthologist, poet, biographer, and book collector, but he will be best remembered as a 'Sherlockophile'. In 1934 he was a founding member of the Baker Street Irregulars; in 1940 he edited an anthology of Sherlockiana (which included this pastiche); and thereafter he produced a stream of poems, articles and introductions. 'The fact is,' he admitted later, 'I can scarcely write a paragraph on any subject now, without bringing Holmes into the argument.' Under Conan Doyle's influence he wrote a fictional account of the Oscar Slater case, Too Many Sleuths, and his detective novels were indebted to Sherlock Holmes. One of them The Casebook of Jimmie Lavender, was actually dedicated to 'Dr John H. Watson, formerly of Baker Street, London, who wrote the original prescription'. Although not a great crime writer, Starrett had by the time of his death in 1974 established himself as one of America's greatest book-men and the doyen of the Sherlockians.

As well as appearing in his own anthology, 221B, 'The Adventure of the

Unique Hamlet' *was also included in Ellery Queen's* Misadventures of Sherlock Holmes *of 1944, and in the revised edition of* The Private Life of Sherlock Holmes *published in 1960. It was Starrett's only pastiche, though he once said that he might do something similar by creating a 'synthetic' story. He explained his reason for wanting to do so in a letter to Ellery Queen:*

I've always wanted to do a synthetic Holmes – the beginning of one story, the middle of another, and the conclusion of a third; or perhaps six or eight of the adventures merged into a perfect Holmes tale. I may yet do it. The reason would be to produce a Holmes adventure that I could completely admire, and which would contain everything I like – the opening at the breakfast table, with a page or two of deduction; the appearance of Mrs Hudson, followed instantly by the troubled client, who would fall over the threshold in a faint; the hansom in the fog, and so on. I think it could be done. I find when I think of the Holmes stories that almost instinctively I think of just such a yarn, wonder which one it is, then realise it's a cento existing only in my mind.

Two other writers of Sherlockian pastiche may be mentioned in connection with Starrett; they are Harry Bedford-Jones and August Derleth.

Shortly after the publication of The Private Life of Sherlock Holmes, *Starrett learned from Dr Logan Clendenning that a series of unpublished Sherlock Holmes stories had come to light; they had been sent to Alexander Woolcott by Mr H.E. Twinells, of Palm Springs, with an ingenious explanation of how they came to be in his custody. Starrett was greatly intrigued and soon Clendenning obtained copies for him. 'Although obviously pastiches,' Starrett said later, 'the tales were extremely clever. I knew at once, however, that they were not by Conan Doyle and shortly, by a series of deductions, worthy of the master himself, I was certain that they* were *by my old friend Bedford-Jones. As with Hosmer Angel, Mr Twinells was betrayed by his typewriter and paper for they were identical to those used by Bedford-Jones.*

There were at least three of these stories, each based on a title given by Dr Watson. One concerned the Atkinson brothers of Trinconmalee; another dealt with the fate of the barque, Matilda Briggs; *and a third contained an account of the case of the Aluminium Crutch. This last was published as a Sherlock Holmes pastiche in the* Palm Springs News *in January and February 1936 (and later in the* Baker Street Journal*), but the other two had the names changed and were made into ordinary detective stories.*

The pastiches by August Derleth were on a more ambitious scale and eventually developed into a parallel saga complete with its own Higher Criticism and a Society. Derleth was born in Sauk City, Wisconsin, in 1909 and became one of America's most prolific writers, as well as being an editor and publisher of note. He died in 1971 with over a hundred and thirty books to his name.

He became fond of Sherlock Holmes when he was a boy, and his first pastiche was written in the autumn of 1928 when he was in his junior year at the University of Wisconsin. His intention was to produce a new series of Sherlock Holmes stories. Their form, he said later, was not to be the 'ridiculing imitation designed for laughter', but the 'fond and admiring one less widely known as pastiche'. Doyle, however, refused to allow him to use the names of Sherlock Holmes and Dr Watson, so he settled instead on 'Solar Pons', which was syllabically similar and implied a 'bridge of light'; the companion became Dr Lyndon Parker and they had lodgings in Praed Street. The first story, 'The Adventure of the Black Narcissus', was published in Dragnet *in February*

1929. Ten more stories followed in rapid succession, with three being written during a single day, and Pons was then consigned to limbo. There he would have stayed but for the interest of Ellery Queen, who included 'The Adventure of the Norcross Riddle' in The Misadventures of Sherlock Holmes *and thereby made the name of Solar Pons known to a wider audience. Derleth was then persuaded to revise the earlier stories and to publish them in book form. This had the title* In Re: Sherlock Holmes, *which was the entry which Derleth had placed in his diary before writing the first story; there was an introduction by Vincent Starrett; and a specially created imprint, Mycroft and Moran. Many more adventures followed in the years ahead, including long stories and a novel.*

Solar Pons evolved out of Sherlock Holmes but became a distinct character, a distinction which was highlighted when the author of the Baker Street Journal *published 'The Adventure of the Circular Room' using the names of Holmes and Watson. As a Pons story, it is a success; but as a Sherlock Holmes pastiche, it has serious shortcomings. As Starrett said, 'Pons was an ectoplasmic emanation of his great prototype', a clever impersonator, and a brilliant pupil, but he was definitely not Sherlock Holmes. He was more in the tradition of the Picklock Holes stories of R.C. Lehmann which first appeared in* Punch *in 1893, as a precursor of the Schlock Homes stories by Robert L. Fish.*

THE ADVENTURE OF
THE MARKED MAN

The original Schlock Homes story was published in the 'Department of "First Stories"' in Ellery Queen's Mystery Magazine *in 1960, and it proved so popular that the author, a consulting engineer, was persuaded to write more. He continued to do so from time to time until his death in 1981.*

Fred Dannay and Manfred B. Lee, who were the two halves of 'Ellery Queen', played a very significant role in the fostering of detective literature. Their memories were long, their tastes catholic, and their patronage widespread, and they were directly responsible for many stories and sequels which might otherwise never have been written. They had a virtual monopoly of the Schlock Homes stories; they also encouraged Barry Perowne to continue his sequels to Raffles which he had begun in the 1930s, and from Michael Harrison (whose theories on the origin of Sherlock Holmes they published) they got a series of new Dupin tales. All the great mystery writers, living and dead, have been represented in the pages of their magazine and there has been a steady flow of Sherlockian parody and pastiche. One of the earliest of these was 'The Adventure of the Marked Man', which appeared in the July 1944 issue. It was one of two Sherlock Holmes stories written specially for them by Stuart Palmer, the other being 'The Adventure of the Remarkable Worm', which was published in The Misadventures of Sherlock Holmes.

Palmer was born in 1905 and died in 1968. He came across the name of Sherlock Holmes for the first time at the age of twelve when he read The Pursuit of the House-Boat *by John Kendrick Bangs. Within a few years he knew all the original stories by heart and had even taken the trouble to write a letter of appreciation to Sherlock Holmes at his Baker Street address. He made his debut as a detective story writer in 1931, but it was his second book,* The Penguin Pool Murders, *which established his reputation and that of his heroine, the schoolteacher turned sleuth, Miss Hildegarde*

Withers. *'She could never have existed at all,'* he said later, *'if it had not been for her illustrious predecessor.'* Her love of the abstruse, her curiosity, and her habit of withholding information until the last denouement owed their origin to Sherlock Holmes.

The two pastiches, one serious and one comic, were written while Palmer was marooned at an army post in Oklahoma, where he was serving as an instructor, and both, he said, were *'patterned in the great tradition and yet conceived in all humbleness and respect'*. They were the only two he wrote, though his interest in Sherlock Holmes and in the unrecorded cases mentioned by Dr Watson never diminished. The fate of the Dutch steamship Friesland, *the singular adventures of the Grice-Patersons in the island of Uffa and the other 'lost delightful stories'* would, he insisted, always be more precious to him than the missing songs of Sappho.

THE ADVENTURE OF
THE MEGATHERIUM THEFTS

For S.C. Roberts, later to become one of the leading authorities on the life of Dr Johnson, it was the first six volumes of the Strand Magazine *which served as his introduction to Sherlock Holmes. He was born in 1887 and was a scholar, then fellow, and finally master of Pembroke College, Cambridge. He was Secretary to the University Press between 1922 and 1948, and Vice-Chancellor of the university from 1949 to 1951.*

Although he met Conan Doyle in 1911, his first contribution to the literature of Sherlock Holmes (which was privately printed) was 'A Note on the Watson Problem' in the Cambridge Review *of 25 January 1929, this being a commentary on the studies by Ronald Knox which had appeared in* Essays in Satire. *It was followed by an essay on the early career of Dr Watson, a 'prolegomena to the study of a biographical problem', which was published in* Life and Letters *in February 1930, and in an* Essays of the Year *anthology, and was then made into one of Faber and Faber's Criterion Miscellanies, where it was extended to include details of Watson's later years. This became, as* The Times *said, the 'standard of life' of Dr Watson and it placed Roberts in the forefront of the new scholarship, scholarship which reached its climax in 1932 with the publication of a 'really authoritative biography' of Sherlock Holmes by T.S. Blakeney, and of a 'textbook for advanced students' by H.W. Bell, giving the chronology of the stories. Both books were reviewed by Roberts in the* Observer. *He also became a member of the first Sherlock Holmes Society of London and was a contributor to Bell's* Baker Street Studies.

Of his four Sherlockian pastiches, the first was a short play called Christmas Eve, *which was privately printed in 1936 for distribution at Christmas. Then in 1945, following the theft of some books from the Athenaeum library, he published 'The Strange Case of the Megatherium Thefts'. Later, in July 1951, to coincide with the Sherlock Holmes Exhibition in Baker Street and under the auspices of the National Book League, he gave a public lecture at the Victoria and Albert Museum on 'The Personality of Sherlock Holmes' which included a few tantalizing extracts from Dr Watson's account of 'The Death of Cardinal Tosca'. At the same time, he was made Life President of the new Sherlock Holmes Society, and it was in that capacity (and as a Trustee of Shakespeare's birthplace) that in 1963 he revealed his discovery of the unpublished manuscript by Dr Watson of 'The Case of the Missing Quarto', a counterpart to the earlier story by Vincent Starrett. All his early articles, essays, and pastiches, including the introduction to the World's Classics edition of Sherlock Holmes stories, were collected in 1953 as* Holmes and Watson: A Miscellany, *and he remained an active Sherlockian until his death in 1966.*

THE ADVENTURE OF
THE TRAINED CORMORANT

W.R. Duncan Macmillan's story, originally called 'Holmes in Scotland', provides an account of perhaps the most intriguing of the unrecorded cases, the one referred to in 'The Veiled Lodger' concerning the trained cormorant, the politician and the lighthouse keeper.

The origin of the title would appear to date back to Conan Doyle's days in Edinburgh when he visited the Isle of May in the Firth of Forth. The island had little to recommend it but it did have a lighthouse, cormorants, and solan geese, and Doyle used it twice in the early 1880s, first in a semi-autobiographical sketch, 'After Cormorants with a Camera', which was published in the British Journal of Photography *in 1881, and again in 'John Barrington Cowles', which appeared in* Cassell's Saturday Journal *in 1884. It is appropriate therefore that the story should have been written by a Scotsman, that it should have a Scottish setting, and that it should have first appeared in an Edinburgh magazine. And it is also appropriate that it should have been* Blackwood's Magazine *and this was a periodical in which during his early years Doyle was most anxious to have a story published. Unlike* Chambers's Journal, *which accepted his first story in 1879,* Blackwood's, *rejected many manuscripts which he offered them, including two which have been claimed as prototypes of the Sherlock Holmes stories, 'The Haunted Grange of Goresthorpe' and 'Uncle Jeremy's Household'. The first was sent to them in about 1880 and never returned, while the second reached them in 1884 and was eventually published in the* Boy's Own Paper.

Duncan Macmillan's story was published in Blackwood's *in September 1953 and was originally prefaced by a short account of its origin. The author said that he seemed to be walking with Dr Watson in the Shades. He asked if Sherlock Holmes had ever been guilty of egotism or boastfulness, but Watson denied it. He then asked if the claims which Holmes had made about his earlier cases were justified, and, on being pressed to give an example, mentioned the case involving the trained cormorant. Watson immediately felt at ease and when they had seated themselves in a convenient bower he gave an account of the case. When it was over, his listener asked him if it was indeed the true story of the statesman, the lighthouse keeper, and the trained cormorant. 'Yes, my dear sir,' said the doctor in a voice both placid and content, 'it is indeed.'*

THE ADVENTURE OF
ARNSWORTH CASTLE

The stories which make up The Exploits of Sherlock Holmes *were almost contemporary with 'Holmes in Scotland'. They were based on the titles mentioned by Dr Watson and were written by Adrian Conan Doyle and John Dickson Carr.*

Adrian was the youngest son of Sir Arthur Conan Doyle and was born in 1910. His whole life was to be dedicated to the memory of his father. As a boy, he accompanied him on lecture tours to Australia, America, South Africa, and Scandinavia, where he witnessed both the fulsome praise given to the creator of Sherlock Holmes and the sometimes harsh criticism directed against the 'apostle of spiritualism'. His formal education was limited to a few years at a crammer and thereafter he devoted most of his time to his hobbies of motor racing, painting, and zoology. He was married in 1938 and soon afterwards visited the Cameroons on a reptile-hunting expedition. Too headstrong to submit to the discipline of the Armed Forces, he spent the war years in virtual retirement at Bignell Wood, in the New Forest, where he was surrounded by a collection of armour, old keys, and family papers.

The running of the literary estate was initially left to his brother, Denis, but in 1943 Adrian entered the fray by accusing Hesketh Pearson of having written a fraudulent biography which did not do justice to his father, and in 1945 produced his own panegyric in pamphlet form called **The True Conan Doyle**. A year or two later, John Dickson Carr was chosen as the official biographer and the two men became friends. Both shared the belief that England was in decline and that, under the new Labour government, it was no longer a fit place in which to live. Carr, having completed his biography, returned to America, while Adrian went into a self-imposed exile, settling first in Tangier, later in Portugal, and finally in Switzerland. The two men met in New York in 1952 when Adrian was there to supervise the opening of his Sherlock Holmes Exhibition, which included the reconstruction of the sitting-room at 221B which he had purchased from the Marylebone Council. They had on earlier occasions discussed the possibility of reviving Sherlock Holmes, but now a firm decision to do so was taken.

Carr already had some experience in this field as he had written two humorous sketches for the Mystery Writers of America. The first 'The Adventure of the Conk-Singleton Papers', was performed in April 1948, and the other, 'The Adventure of the Paradol Chamber', a year later. In one Queen Victoria was accused of having attempted to poison Gladstone, while the other had the French ambassador removing his trousers in her presence. Despite being in poor taste, Carr insisted that he meant no disrespect to Sherlock Holmes.

The first of the **Exploits**, 'The Adventure of the Seven Clocks', was a full-scale collaboration based on an idea provided by Carr. 'Some of it is written line by line alternately,' said Adrian at the time of its publication. 'We cannot tell, nor can anyone else, who wrote which phrase. When we write, our brains are each a half, forming a whole.' Another two were written in the same way but the collaboration was not easy. Carr found it hard to write in a style other than his own and did not always feel that the stories were improved by the emendations made by Adrian. He wrote three more on his own and then 'fell ill', leaving Adrian to complete the series. In America, the first story was taken by **Life** and the rest by **Collier's**, while in England they appeared in the London **Evening Standard** and other regional newspapers.

The reaction from the readers was mixed and Sherlockians were divided among themselves. Some allowed their judgement to be clouded by the resentment which they felt for Adrian, while others welcomed his change of attitude as he was now giving his blessing to a literary form which he and his brother had previously tried to suppress. He said, for example, in a letter to the **Irish Times**:

By trying to carry on with the unwritten cases of Sherlock Holmes referred to by Dr Watson in the original tales, and by painstakingly preserving the original style and setting of the stories, I am doing exactly what my father would have wished, i.e. to give a little more of the Baker Street secrets from a Conan Doyle pen for the pleasure and amusement of the old friends of Mr Sherlock Holmes and Dr Watson.

It was not only what his father might have wished, it was also in many ways what his father had done, for the later stories were pastiches of his own earlier style. But they were authentic in a way which Adrian's could never be. The fact that he was Conan Doyle's son or that he was able to handle his father's magnifying glass or write on his father's desk was no guarantee of his ability as a writer and such things could not by themselves create plots or provide examples of logical reasoning. This did however come with practice and while some of the earlier stories in the series are derivative, and even cumbersome, with clumsy manipulation of plot, the later ones have a certain elegance of their own. The last story, which is included here, is undoubtedly the most memorable.

After the publication of The Exploits of Sherlock Holmes in 1954 and the death of his brother a year later, Adrian became more closely involved with his father's estate. There were various court cases and controversies: one was the attempt to get unpaid loyalties from Russia, another was the argument with Irving Wallace over whether Dr Joseph Bell or Doyle himself was the 'original' of Sherlock Holmes. In 1959 Adrian edited and paid for a large scrapbook to commemorate his father's centenary, and in 1963 he helped to found Sir Nigel Films which, in association with another film company, produced the Sherlock Holmes film, Fog or A

Study in Terror, *and which later was responsible for a disastrous film based on the Brigadier Gerard stories.*

His other major concern was with his share of the family archives. In 1955 he had promised them to Dublin; in 1962 he gave them to the city of Geneva, and in 1965, with the help of the Swiss government, he purchased the Chateau de Lucens and opened it to the public the following year as the Sir Arthur Conan Doyle Foundation. It was intended as a permanent memorial to his father, but under financial pressure he tried to sell part of the collection to an American university and suffered the indignity of being 'exposed' by the Sunday Times *in April 1969. He died on 2 June 1970. the chateau was sold and the papers which remained were transferred to a local library.*

Adrian Conan Doyle made a significant contribution to the literature of Sherlock Holmes and one which will outlive any damage which he may unwittingly have done to his father's reputation by his somewhat excessive zeal.

THE ADVENTURE OF
THE TIRED CAPTAIN

The Sherlock Holmes Journal *is the source of the next story. The* Sherlock Holmes Society's *magazine was first issued in 1952 and from 1956 was edited by Lord Donegall. Unlike its older rival, the* Baker Street Journal, *which has published a flood of parodies and pastiches of varying merit, the* Journal *has included only a few. Pastiches, the editor explained later, were anathema to him unless they were exceptionally brilliant, and only three ever came into this category, one by A. Lloyd Taylor and two by Alan Wilson. Taylor's concerned Vamberry, the wine merchant (which was appropriate as he had been responsible for the decorations in the Sherlock Holmes Public House),* and Alan Wilson's were 'The Adventure of the Tired Captain' and 'The Adventure of the Paradol Chamber'.

Wilson was born in 1923 and was introduced to the Sherlock Holmes stories by his father. By the age of twelve he had read them all many times with the exception of 'The Solitary Cyclist', which for some reason escaped his notice. It was this story which helped to revive his earlier enthusiasm when he came back across it after the war.

Lord Donegall felt that 'The Adventure of the Tired Captain' had 'achieved perfection' and was 'a hundred per cent Watson', and it was with this that Alan Wilson first made his mark in 1958. 'The Adventure of the Paradol Chamber', which described Senor Paradol's connection with Vigor, the Hammersmith Wonder, followed in 1961. There were also articles on the date of **The Valley of Fear** *(he opted for 1891); on Watson's integrity as an author; on the location of the opium den mentioned in 'The Man with the Twisted Lip'; and on 'Holmes the Histrionic'. The last of these put forward the thesis that Holmes had trained for the stage and had only left the profession when passed over in favour of Henry Irving. It was a subject on which Wilson spoke with authority as he had been to drama school and was himself an actor.*

Wilson was also a member of the Milvertonians of Hampstead, a branch society founded by Humphrey Morton and Peter Richard which became active in 1958 with the publication of its own Christmas card. It's aim was to further the study of Milvertonians and to this end the society published a series of well-researched papers. It was most active between 1958 and 1963, though it continued in existence until Morton's death in 1969. 'Son of Escott', an article which dealt with Holmes's flirtation with the maid of Charles Augustus Milverton and its unexpected sequel, was Wilson's major 'Milverton story'. It was like 'The Giant Rat of Sumatra' a story for which the world was not prepared – indeed for which the world would never be prepared – and it appeared in the Baker Street Journal.

In addition, Alan Wilson adapted 'Black Peter' for the radio and was the winner of the Sherlock Holmes Society Photographic Competition of 1963. He also compiled an encyclopedia, listing all the characters and places mentioned in the stories. **Give Me Data** *was ready for publication in the early 1960s but was set to one side when another book appeared covering much of the same ground. His Sherlockian activity ceased in 1963 when he left England to become a staff director for the New Zealand Drama Council.*

THE ADVENTURE OF
THE GREEN EMPRESS

It is appropriate that 'The Adventure of the Second Stain' ('The Adventure of the Green Empress') should follow 'The Adventure of the Tired Captain', as both took place at the same period. At the start of 'The Adventure of the Naval Treaty', Watson says:

The July which immediately succeeded my marriage was made memorable by three cases of interest in which I had the privilege of being associated with Sherlock Holmes and of studying his methods. I find them recorded in my notes under the headings of 'The Adventure of the Second Stain', 'The Adventure of the Naval Treaty', and 'The Adventure of the Tired Captain'.

He was not then at liberty to describe the first because it implicated so many of the first families in the kingdom and he feared that the new century would have come before the facts could be made public. It had, however, provided an excellent example of Holmes's methods and the detective's handling of the case had impressed all those associated with it. 'I still retain,' Watson added, 'an almost verbatim report of the interview in which he demonstrated the true facts of the case to Monsieur Dubuque of the Paris police, and Fritz von Waldbaum, the well-known specialist of Danzig, both of whom had wasted their energies upon what proved to be side-issues.'

In 1903, when the public first heard of Holmes's return, many people were curious to learn about the 'second stain', and the editors of the New York Bookman were particularly anxious to see it published as it had always intrigued them. 'The mere title of the story shows genius of a high order,' they said, 'and rouses the most intense expectation.' Indeed, it was so important to their peace of mind that the junior editor was dispatched to Paris to discuss the matter with Monsieur Dubuque and on the same tour met Conan Doyle and asked him to do everything in his power to ensure that the story was written. Doyle immediately obliged, but the 'Adventure of the Second Stain' as published did not contain any references to Monsieur Dubuque or to Fritz von Waldbaum. Sherlockian scholars realized that there must have been three cases bearing the same name, the one mentioned in 'The Adventure of the Naval Treaty', another referred to in 'The Adventure of the Yellow Face', and the one which Doyle had written. It was left to the Sunday Times *of Johannesburg to discover details of the first.*

On 18 June 1967, the paper announced an 'Intriguing Contest for Our Readers', saying that as part of its duty to encourage good writing, it would be offering a prize of 200 rand for a Sherlock Holmes story based on the description of 'The Adventure of the Second Stain' given in 'The Adventure of the Naval Treaty'. The closing date was 30 September 1967 and the length was to be between 5,000 and 7,000 words. The paper later said that the other reference to the case and the one bearing its name were to be ignored.

Ninety-five separate versions were received by the closing date and on 27 November, after two months of deliberation, the joint winners were announced. They were F.P. Cillie and Miles Masters. The first had chosen a suitably aristocratic setting and the other had used the Jack the Ripper mystery. The runners-up had chosen a wide range of subjects, including national and international politics, espionage, domestic scandals, the Boer War, and the gold mines.

Francois Paulus Cillie, whose entry was published in the Johannesburg Sunday Times *on 3 December 1967, was educated in Port Elizabeth and took an honours degree in economics at Stellenbosch University. An addict of the Sherlock Holmes stories since his boyhood, he was only twenty-four at the time of the competition. His story was written in the evenings and at night while his fiancée was doing night duty at a hospital; and by day he was working as an economist on the staff of a commercial bank.*

THE ADVENTURE OF
THE PURPLE HAND

Many people of all ages have turned their hand to Sherlockian pastiche and examples of their work are to be found in many small publications such as a booklet issued in 1976 called The Non-Canonical Sherlock Holmes. *But few can compare with those written by D.O. Smith, whose stories have been appearing annually since 1982 under the imprint of Diogenes Publications. 'The Adventure of the Purple Hand' was the first and has been followed by 'The Unseen Traveller' and 'The Zodiac Plate'; it is the author's intention to produce a full volume in the course of time.*

Denis Smith was born in 1948 and, as with so many other authors represented here, became interested in Sherlock Holmes at the age of twelve. He tried his hand at a variety of jobs before going to York University where he read philosophy. That and his other interests, which include logic, literature, the railways of Britain, and maps (which he sometimes 'reads' for hours on end), added to his detailed knowledge of the Sherlock Holmes stories which he has analysed from every conceivable angle, will help to explain why he is so proficient in this field. He is a regular contributor to the **Sherlock Holmes Journal** *and hopes one day to produce the definitive chronology of the stories.*

THE ADVENTURE OF
HILLERMAN HALL

All the stories in this volume, with the exception of the last, date from the years when Holmes was at the height of his activities, but 'The Adventure of Hillerman Hall' by Julian Symons is set in the 1920s during his retirement.

Julian Symons was born in 1912 and first made his mark in the 1930s as the editor of **Twentieth-Century Verse,** *then as a biographer, social historian, and critic. He turned to crime writing in a light-hearted way before the war and soon afterwards established himself as a leading exponent of it, though his use of irony to show the violence behind the respectable masks of society place many of his books on the level of the orthodox novel. He is an authority on detective fiction and has written a standard history on it, as well as books about Edgar Allan Poe and Conan Doyle.*

'The Adventure of Hillerman Hall' comes from **The Great Detectives.** *The book was originally to have been a series of 'biographies', but the author decided that as too much was known about some and too little about others, he would vary the technique in each case. 'The story should suggest the master,' he reflected, 'without ever attempting to enter into competition with him.' Parody would be avoided and, although the book was to have excellent colour illustrations by Tom Adams, the text was to be independent of them. Of the first story, originally called 'How a Hermit was Disturbed in His Retirement', he said: 'The Sherlock Holmes story relies very little upon biographical detail, chiefly because there is no shortage of biographies and biographical essays in the form of full-length books, which may easily be consulted. What is offered here is Sherlock in retirement, and a narrative which has a tease, if not exactly a twist, in the tail.'*

It is one of a number of works which demonstrate the fascination which Symons has always felt for the myth of Sherlock Holmes. In 1974 he wrote **A Three Pipe Problem,** *concerning a television actor, Sheridan Haynes, who wears the mask of Sherlock Holmes and assumes his character. The book neatly reversed the usual theme of the criminal behind the mask by having a rather commonplace man wearing the mask of the great detective.*

Julian Symons was the guest of honour at the annual dinner of the Sherlock Holmes Society in 1975 but, despite being in some ways the literary heir of Dorothy L. Sayers, he has never indulged as she did in Sherlockian scholarship, preferring instead to concentrate on the character of Conan Doyle and on those writers who influenced him or were influenced by him.

THE UNTOLD TALES
OF DR JOHN H. WATSON

Dr Watson provides the names of some forty cases other than those which he described. His yearbooks covering the period when Holmes was in active practice filled a shelf and there were a number of dispatch-cases crammed with notes. It is therefore not surprising that further details should from time to time be made public, but it is remarkable that the new adventures and misadventures should now exceed the number of the originals. For the curious or insatiable reader there is a wide choice. He may opt for further stories from the pen of Dr Watson, such as 'The Adventure of the Purple Maculas' by James C. Iraldi concerning Henry Staunton, whom Holmes had helped to hang. Or there is 'The Darkwater Hall Mystery' by Kingsley Amis, in which Watson describes his own attempt at deduction and at seduction. Or there are reminiscences by those who knew the great detective, such as J.C. Masterman's 'The Case of the Gifted Amateur', which is told by Inspector Lestrade. Or there are the novels which have cross-fertilized fact and fiction so that Edwin Drood, Raffles, Dracula, Tarzan and their ilk seek the detective's advice in the company of such distinguished personages as Sigmund Freud, Oscar Wilde, Queen Victoria, the Tsar, and Theodore Roosevelt. Or there are those in which Holmes or his children, or his children's children, investigate a more recent mystery, or in which Moriarty or his brother try in vain to clear their family name. The list it seems is endless and continues to grow with each succeeding year.

Apocryphal Sherlock Holmes stories are not designed to compete with the originals, as that may be left to the many rivals who have followed in his wake, their intention is rather to reflect and enhance the achievements of Mr Holmes. If the stories in this book can kindle afresh the fire in the rooms in Baker Street, or echo the noise of the hansom cabs, or catch the sound of a foot upon the stairs, then they will have achieved their end.

Finally in this chapter from the Baker Street Bulletin, A True Sherlockian Murder Mystery:

The Unsolved Death Of Richard Lancelyn-Green

By Richard Milner

He was king of the Sherlockians, but he wore his crown lightly.

In the world of Baker Street irregulars, Richard Lancelyn-Green, who died last year under mysterious and still hotly-debated circumstances, was thought by many to be the world's top Sherlock Holmes and Sir Arthur Conan Doyle scholar. Everyone who wrote a serious biography, book or essay or put together a television programme on the subject sought him out, and he was unfailingly generous with his time and expertise – often supplying illustrations and photographs from his unparalleled archive.

He was a quiet, courtly, unassuming gentleman, a man of inherited wealth whose father, Roger Lancelyn-Green, was a scholar of heroic myths and children's literature. From Roger, who wrote about Greek and Roman myths, Robin Hood and Arthurian legends, he inherited not only a family history documented to before the Norman invasion, but also a love of collecting books and immersing himself in the tales of legendary heroes, especially of Sherlock Holmes. As a boy, Richard was inspired by the Holmes adventures to construct a replica of 221B Baker Street in the family attic, complete with the bullet holes in the wall and the famous Persian slipper filled with shag tobacco.

When once asked if he came from the industrial north, Richard replied, "No, the preindustrial north. My family has lived on the same estate in the Wirral, near Liverpool, for 900 years." The Greens came over with the Norman Invasion, and then settled in the north as spoils-of-war landlords. (His ancestors fought in the battle of Hastings, and were allied to the invaders who killed King Harold.) Richard's brother, Scarred [10], told a journalist that the family had lived quietly there for almost a millennium, "so as not to attract the attention of any subsequent royals."

Some who came to know the subtle twists and turns of Richard's sceptical mind, expressed dismay at his less than idolatrous attitude towards the Doylean canon and its creator. For despite his love of Conan Doyle and the Sherlockian adventures, he had a shyly perverse penchant for picking holes in both – using his bemused, not always gentle humour. Even his detractors and jealous rivals agreed, however, that Richard's collection of Doylean literary rarities and memorabilia – valued after his death at over 2 million pounds – was a world-class treasure, without peer or precedent.

I was privileged to have been his friend for eight years, during which he always happily made time to see me when I visited London. I first approached him when I was investigating the possibility that Sir Arthur was the mastermind behind the Piltdown man hoax, one of the greatest fossil frauds in the history of science. Someone had planted a modern orang-utan jaw with parts of an old human skull and planted them near the Piltdown golf course in Sussex, where Conan Doyle came frequently to play. Some have speculated that he had created his own real-life mystery by tossing the bones into a gravel pit during golfing practice – thus giving a new meaning to the term "missing links."

Richard listened with interest to my circumstantial evidence, which included clues an American anthropologist thought he saw in Conan Doyle's prehistoric fantasy adventure "The Lost World." Was it a case of taking revenge on the scientists who had thrown cold water on his obsession with spiritualism? Richard thought "it would not be out of character," given Conan Doyle's history of pranks and jokes, such as the time he donned long beard and makeup as his own fictional character, Professor George Challenger. In addition, Richard thought, the author's preoccupation with ghosts was in serious and ludicrous contradiction to his insistence on evidence and deduction in the Sherlock Holmes tales.

Richard found it plausible that the ape-man hoax may have been Conan Doyle's attempt to turn the tables on the scientists. It would show that they, who had accused him of accepting flimsy evidence for Spiritualism, would be eager to embrace any shred of bone that would bolster their own beliefs about evolution. After he attended my Piltdown lecture at the Linnean Society of London, Richard checked his files to see where the author might have been during the days when the Piltdown incident had

---

[10] According to **The Sunday Telegraph** December 19 2004 Richard Lancelyn Green's brother was named as Scirard.

occurred. "My father always said that a good biographer can tell you where his subject was and what he was doing on any given day of his life," he said. (According to Richard's files, Conan Doyle had done a good bit of travelling around Europe but returned to Crowborough in the fall of 1911 to finish "The Lost World," and stayed around during the time that the bones were "discovered" in 1912 at Piltdown.)

A few months before Richard's death, he finally invited me into his sanctum sanctorum to see the heart of his collection. I had been to his house in South Kensington many times before, but had never gone into the sacred basement. I was well aware that it was a rare honour that had been granted to only a handful of Sherlockians.

I could scarcely believe what I saw. Dozens of sketches and illustrations by Sidney Paget for the original Strand stories, mock-ups of the statues of Conan Doyle (Richard had helped design the full-size bronze that stands today in Crowborough) and Sherlock Holmes, (which stands in Marylebone Road, near Baker Street). Even some of Conan Doyle's pipes (they still smelt of tobacco) and spectacles (I looked through them) and one of his waistcoats, neatly pressed on a hanger. And these gems in addition to the thousand of first edition books, articles, and ephemera in mint condition – including that holy grail of Sherlockians, the rare and valuable Beeton's Christmas Annual of 1887, in which the first Sherlock Holmes story appeared.

The very day I returned to London several months later, I rang Richard, wanting him to look over the typed pages of interviews from tapes we had made. But there was a new, unfamiliar voice on his answering-machine. He didn't return my calls and I soon found out why. Mutual friends told me that his body had been discovered the day before.

Who killed the king of the Sherlockians – and why?

Within a few days of his demise at the age of 50 on March 27, 2004, newspapers from the Guardian to the New York Times were buzzing with theories and speculations.

Richard's death came only days before a long-sequestered treasure trove of Conan Doyle's personal papers, letters, and manuscripts was to be auctioned at Christie's in London. The author's family had been a contentious lot, fighting tooth and claw over the scraps of their patriarch's literary legacy. According to Richard, who had once been friends with his daughter, Dame Jean Conan Doyle, the lion's share of the papers were meant to be donated to the British Library, where scholars would have access to them. He had looked forward for many years to getting his hands on them – the missing material he needed to finish the massive Conan Doyle biography that had been his life's work.

After Dame Jean's death in 1977, however, it transpired that she only had control of a portion of the papers, which she had indeed promised to the British Library. Other boxes of valuable papers had been earmarked for various heirs, who had decided to auction them off. Richard felt personally betrayed, and feared that most of this national treasure would fall into the hands of private collectors and become scattered all over the world. He wrote letters to newspapers decrying the sale, condemning its legitimacy, and raising hell over what he saw as an impending disaster that was looming over his life like a monstrous tsunami. (Yet, when asked, he dutifully cooperated with Christie's, even lending photographs for use in the auction catalogue.)

During his last days, he told friends that he believed his home was bugged with listening devices, that someone was out to get him, and that he feared for his life. He even rang a national newspaper and said, "Something might happen to me." Yet he did not identify his shadowy enemies except to mention a mysterious American. According to those who spoke with him, he appeared paranoid and consumed by irrational fears of imminent doom. In light of his subsequent death, other acquaintances believed that his fears may have been based on reality, not delusion.

As matters now stand, no one really knows what happened. Richard was found strangled by a shoelace that had been twisted round his neck with the help of a large wooden spoon. The bed was surrounded by soft toys and an open bottle of gin was nearby. When his worried sister, who could not reach him by phone, rushed over to check on him – she discovered the gruesome scene.

The coroner refused to rule the death a suicide, a murder, or an accident. He announced that there was no conclusive evidence as to what had happened, adding that he thought the police had made a botch of the scene and had not gathered any forensic evidence. After the inquest, he ruled an "open verdict," and will re-open the case if anyone can produce new evidence.

Those who knew Richard cannot believe that he committed suicide as, although he was fearful for his life, he did not seem depressed during his final days. A notable American Sherlockian who was often at odds with him and represented the Conan Doyle estate, was pursued by the press and politely asked if he was the mysterious Yank who had murdered Lancelyn-Green. He just as politely replied that he had certainly not. Indeed, according to the police, there was no indication that another person had ever been in the house on the night that Richard died.

Sadly, there is another possibility – a distasteful spectre lurking in the shadows like a hideous Baskerville hound from hell. That is the scenario that he died from erotic auto-asphyxiation, a practice of unintentional self-strangulation which claims the lives of thousands of men each year – but I don't want to dwell on it.

Richard Lancelyn-Green was an extremely dignified and private man, and the necessary contemplation of this grotesque manner of death has no doubt brought additional pain and sorrow to his family. Best, then, to remember him as he was in life – the extraordinary learned, humorous, talented and generous soul that he was. Blessed with a quiet charisma, a wicked wit, a loveable gentility and a touch of pixie dust.

I can't help but recall something he once said to me when we were speaking about great bibliophiles dying and their libraries being dispersed. "It's just not the collections that are lost," he said, "but when someone like that dies, a tremendous wealth of knowledge dies with him." I never thought that statement would apply to him so soon. There was no time for his last bow.

An ironic postscript: Sidestepping the most obvious choice of the British Library, which had initially ignored his entreaties to buy the entire archive, Richard Lancelyn-Green bequeathed his magnificent collection to the modest library at Portsmouth. (It was in Portsmouth that Conan Doyle once conducted his medical practice and wrote his first Sherlock Holmes story.)

Soon after Richard's death, perhaps belatedly responding to his entreaties, the British Library purchased most of the important Doyle papers at the Christie's auction, and will make them available to scholars. Had Richard lived, he would have had access to all the materials he needed to complete his long-deferred Conan Doyle biography.

That he never lived to finish it makes this a double tragedy.

Keeping the memory Green. First glimpse of Richard Lancelyn Green's Conan Doyle collection. By **Dr Neil McCaw**.

The world's largest collection of Conan Doyle and Sherlock Holmes material has gone on display for the first time at Portsmouth's City Museum and Records Office. The collection is the product of one man's lifetime dedication over four decades of auction-room spending.

Following the death of Richard Lancelyn Green in March 2004, one of the world's leading experts on Holmes and Conan Doyle, Portsmouth City Council was given the opportunity to become the custodian of his unique collection. Portsmouth was Lancelyn Green's first choice to house his life's work. The Libraries and Museums and Record Services of the local authority gladly took up the opportunity, and the huge range of books, objects, and archival material was transferred to its care.

Portsmouth had been the first choice because it was the 'birthplace' of Sherlock Holmes, Arthur Conan Doyle, having lived in Bush Villas, Elm Grove, Southsea from 1882-1890, during which time he not only set up in practice as a doctor, and became a well-known local figure, but he also began his career as a writer of fiction, most notably creating the world's greatest detective, Sherlock Holmes. The first two Holmes novels were written and published while Conan Doyle was living in the city.

During the eight years in which he was a Portsmouth resident, Conan Doyle played an active part in all areas of local life, giving regular talks at the Literary and Scientific Society, establishing himself as a doctor of some repute, and also showing great skills as a sportsman. Not only was he the first goalkeeper of what was to became Portsmouth Football Club, but he was also captain of the local cricket and bowls teams, as well as a skilled tennis and billiards player. He was also active in political life as vice-president of the local Liberal Unionists, and he became secretary of the Literary and Scientific Society as well.

Richard Lancelyn Green's collection, now formerly known as The Arthur Conan Doyle Collection, Richard Lancelyn Green Bequest, eventually arrived in Portsmouth over two days in July 2005. It was transported from London via two lorries carrying over 400 large boxes containing more than 16,000 items; this was the largest bequest to a UK library or museum this century. The many and various items in the collection had filled Richard's flat in Kensington, as well as taking up sizeable space in the family home – Poulton Hall in Cheshire – where his passion for Sherlock Holmes began when he was a small boy.

The mammoth task of sifting, sorting and cataloguing the collection began over the summer of 2005. This is a mammoth task, and it is estimated that it will take another year or so before all of the material is recorded properly. The idea is then to publish a full catalogue of the collection, and to make this available to scholars, afficionados (sic), and the general public from 2007 onwards.

As part of the process of developing the collection, Portsmouth Museum and Record Service decided to stage an introductory exhibition of materials from the collection in 2006, before the cataloguing was completed. The exhibition serves as a taster for the collection as a whole, and is intended to whet the appetite for a more wide-ranging display planned for 2007.

Visitors to the introductory exhibition are greeted by a short film put together especially for the occasion. This includes footage of Sir Arthur Conan Doyle himself talking about his life, his creation of Sherlock Holmes, and his lifelong interest in spiritualism. Conan Doyle wonders at the popular fascination with his great detective, and the fact that he was receiving letters from all over the world addressed to Sherlock Holmes and Dr Watson, asking for advice or else expressing a desire to act as housekeeper for Holmes. The film also includes an introduction to the collection by Stephen Fry, the patron of the collection, who is also a lifelong devotee of Conan Doyle's work.

Fry talks of the importance of Conan Doyle's writing, noting how he personally would 'walk a mile in tight boots just to read his letters to the milkman.' He also talks about Richard Lancelyn Green, his background and how he came to amass the most wide-ranging collection of Conan Doyle and Sherlock Holmes material in the world.

For those interested in the man behind the writing, there is a specially assembled Conan Doyle family album that shares intimate glances of the great man and the rich life he led. Flicking through the album, visitors can see images from his childhood, through his time as an undergraduate to his years in Portsmouth and ultimately the decades of success as a writer and thinker. The album tells his life in pictures, the story of an adventurer, traveller, sportsman, celebrity, and family man.

A selection of the huge number of posters in the collection are also on display, including original Holmes film posters in an array of languages, examples of how Holmes has been used in advertising and merchandising, and playbills for the numerous adaptations of the Holmes stories across the twentieth century.

One of the highlights of the exhibition has to be the extremely rare first edition of Beeton's Christmas Annual *containing the first Holmes story that Conan Doyle penned,* A Study in Scarlet. *First published in 1887, this book is one of the very few copies left in the world; a similar copy fetched more than $90,000 only a handful of years ago.*

Other items on display include furniture collected by Richard Lancelyn Green and used to recreate Holmes's 221B Baker Street study in the attic of his family home in the Wirral, personal items belonging to Conan Doyle himself, such as a cigar box, spectacles, and boxing gloves, along with more novel items such as a Holmes Toby jug and a Snoopy lamp in which the famous beagle is dressed as the great detective.

One of the most remarkable inclusions in the exhibition is a letter from the then President of the United States of America, Franklin D. Roosevelt, accepting honorary membership of the Baker Street Irregulars, one of the main Sherlock Holmes societies in the US. In the latter (sic), *President Roosevelt notes that 'Baker Street' is also the name given to one of the hideouts used by the secret servicemen whose job it is to guard him.*

The exhibition also includes a special Sherlock Holmes mystery trail based on some of Conan Doyle's stories. This has been created especially for the occasion, with the aim of making the exhibition more accessible to families and young people. Visitors can explore objects and toy-based clues to unravel the mysteries, such as who stole the Blue Carbuncle, the subject of one of the most famous Holmes stories of all.

The fuller exhibition of material from the Arthur Conan Doyle Collection will take place in Portsmouth over the summer of 2007, when the intention is to display a much greater proportion of the collection as a whole. By this time the City Council will also have established a charitable trust to oversee and manage the collection on its behalf; trust status is vital for the collection to attract sponsorship and donations from the UK and especially overseas, which will have a significant impact on the ways in which the collection can be developed for the benefit of everyone.

It is true to say Portsmouth is proud and honoured to have been trusted with the care of the Arthur Conan Doyle Collection, the most remarkable collection of its kind in the world.

'The Case of the Portsmouth Doctor': The introductory Exhibition to the Arthur Conan Doyle Collection is currently at Portsmouth City Museum and Records office, Museum Road, open 10am to 5pm daily. Admission is free to all.
For more information, visit the collection website –

©www.conandoylecollection.co.uk

or email –

©lancelyngreencollection@portsmouthcc.gov.uk

Chapter 13

Miscellany II: 2004 – 2005

The Sunday Telegraph, FEBRUARY 8 2004 (Extract)

Q. When, according to the BBC, is a repeat not a repeat?
A. When it happens on ITV first.

By Chris Hastings & David Bamber.

What does the BBC do when it runs out of old programmes to repeat? Elementary, my dear Watson, it buys some older ones from ITV.

In a new twist on the policy of padding out its daytime schedules with 20-year-old BBC dramas, the corporation is now filling such slots with old ITV hits including *Sherlock Holmes*.

The BBC insists that the shows, which were first broadcast during the 1980s and early 1990s and have since been screened on digital channels, cannot be classed as repeats because they have never appeared on the BBC.

Viewers' organisations have criticised the move and have accused the corporation of failing to spend enough money on new programmes. However, the BBC's policy does appear to be successful. An episode of *Sherlock Holmes*, which was first screened in 1984 and stars the late Jeremy Brett, gained 2.9 million viewers when it was broadcast on BBC2 eight days ago in an afternoon slot which would typically attract a much lower audience figure.

The reappearance of Sherlock Holmes on a different channel has surprised some of the detective's biggest fans, who were unable to persuade ITV to re-run the series.

David Stuart-Davies, a member of the Sherlock Holmes Society, who has written extensively about Granada's original television series, said that he welcomed the BBC's decision to screen the programme.

"I was a little surprised to discover the BBC were repeating the show.

"There was a feeling at Granada that the series, although brilliant for its first few years, ran on a little too long and went past its sell-by date," he said.

"I think the BBC must have thought, 'Isn't it time we did a Sherlock Holmes programme' and then realised just how expensive a proposition that would have been. Buying one already done by Granada must have seemed an ideal solution."

A BBC spokesman said that the corporation had decided to buy *Sherlock Holmes* for its *Watching the Detectives* slot, which was proving enormously popular with viewers.

SHERLOCK Magazine Issue 60 June 2004

Newsdesk – Sherlock Fry and Dr Laurie

On 30 March the **Daily Mirror** published the following news item.

'Comedy duo Hugh Laurie and Stephen Fry are to reunite as Sherlock Holmes and Dr Watson in a major new ITV drama.

The pair were last on the screen together as Jeeves and Wooster more than a decade ago.

Now Fry, 46, a devoted Holmes fan, will play the Baker Street detective, with 44 year old Laurie as his loyal friend Watson.

ITV 1 Drama Chief Nick Elliott said: 'Stephen is absolutely passionate about Sherlock Holmes and Hugh will make a superb Watson.

…The £2 million adaptation of a so far unnamed Conan Doyle book will be screened next year – and a series could follow. It will be written by Ashley Pharoah, creator of BBC's Down to Earth.'

Strangely, the **Mirror** was the only paper to run this story, so the NewsDesk sleuth hounds went into action to investigate further. It became clear after talking to Fry's agent and the production company that this project is very much in the embryo stage and Pharoah's agent knew nothing of the matter. Fry's representative told us: 'At present this is just an idea, nothing more, and it is far too early to comment further.' In other words the **Mirror** story was premature. Rather like the declaration a few years ago that Robson Green was to appear as Holmes in a new Granada series, it has no real foundation.

We at SHERLOCK would not be all that unhappy if this 'major new ITV drama' is all pie in the sky after all. While at first glance the casting of Fry and Laurie as Holmes and Watson may seem to have a certain attraction, in reality these talented performers are not ideal casting. Especially Stephen Fry who is far too chubby for the lean detective and whose acting range seems somewhat limited to give full range to the diverse characteristics of Sherlock Holmes. Think Jeremy Brett and you'll see what we mean.

What happens next is anyone's guess – but keep watching this space.

(**Compiler's note**: Though the Daily Mirror was the only paper to publish an article on the above topic on 30 March, this was followed by The Sun and The Daily Express as follows:

THE SUN, Wednesday, June 16, 2004 TV Biz edited by **Emily Smith**

'Stephen Fry and Rupert Everett are going head to head – with BOTH playing detective Sherlock Holmes.

The BBC will screen 45-year-old movie actor Rupert's drama at Christmas, his first British TV role since The Far Pavilions in 1984. Stephen, 46, will portray the famous sleuth on ITV 1 in January, with former comedy partner Hugh Laurie as sidekick Dr Watson.

Daily Express Friday June 25 2004

As one of the nation's leading experts on Sherlock Holmes, Stephen Fry, will not have to do much research when he plays the part in a new TV drama. Such is his knowledge of the famous detective that, when he chose Holmes as his specialised subject on the celebrity edition of Mastermind, he won hands down.

(**Compiler's note**: A transcript of the programme appears on page 341 of this chapter).

But the 46-year-old heavyweight actor has admitted that he has to undergo some training for the role. Fry admits that at the moment he is not physically quite right to step into the Victorian sleuth's shoes. "I'm having to go on a diet and, horrors of horrors, attend the gymnasium. I have scoured the books from beginning to end but, sadly, no where does Conan Doyle suggest that Holmes was a lardy wobble-bottom," he said.

Fry is teaming up with his old comedy partner Hugh Laurie for the series and confesses they will both need to alter their appearance before filming begins. He continues: "If we are going to be faithful to the original, then Holmes should be the lithe one, while Dr Watson should be the more cuddly one. At the moment we are the wrong way round."

THE DAILY TELEGRAPH Tuesday, June 1, 2004

The dubious pedigree of the Baskerville Hound By Richard Savill

SOLVING the mystery of the Hound of the Baskervilles may have been the easy part for Sherlock Holmes. For even the detective created by Sir Arthur Conan Doyle might find it hard to reach a conclusion about the origins of the ghostly beast.

Tradition has always had it that Holmes's most famous case was set on foggy Dartmoor and the inspiration for the story came from the area's people, places and folklore.

However, the thriller writer Phil Rickman believes that Herefordshire may also have played a part. And his claims, which are due to be published this week in the magazine *Sherlock*,[11] have provoked a furore in Devon.

Speculation that some of the story originated in Herefordshire began 50 years ago. Rickman claims to have "linked everything together" – and to have been convinced by a coincidence of related names.

The medieval Baskervilles had a castle at Eardisley, near Kington, Herefordshire, he wrote, "Consider also Dr Mortimer, who first enlists the aid of Sherlock Holmes in the affair of the hound. The Mortimers were the powerful Norman barons who controlled the Welsh Marshes around Kington. Mortimer's Cross lies just a few miles away.

"Then there is Stapleton [the naturalist]. A few miles from Kington, complete with a ruined castle on a hill, is the hamlet of Stapleton."

Rickman believes that Conan Doyle may have drawn some of his inspiration for the character of the wicked Hugo Baskerville from the legend of Black Vaughan of Kington and his dog.

Black Vaughan, a lord living about five centuries ago, was supposed to have appeared in Kington market place after his death in the Wars of the Roses as a black bull and to have devastated the church.

Many local people still refuse to walk near his home of Hergest Croft at night for fear of seeing his ghost and that of his black dog. Rickman made his claims after researching his latest book *The Prayer of the Night Shepherd*. He said: "The ghostly hound legend is

---

[11] This article is reproduced on page 337

well established around Kington and stories about Conan Doyle being related to the descendents of the Baskerville family and visiting on a regular basis are firmly rooted in the area.

"I believe the story is based on the Hergest hound but Conan Doyle blurred the sources by adding elements from Devon. The hound may have been a bit of a mongrel."

Guidebooks to Devon point to the ghostly hound connected with the death of Dartmoor's Sir Richard Cabell as the model for Hugo Baskerville. "The story is firmly set on Dartmoor and the fact that Conan Doyle may have found inspiration from stories in other parts of the country does not alter that fact," a spokesman for Dartmoor National Park said.

The Sherlock Holmes Society said: "This theory is not new. It's been batted about for years and, while we agree that there are Baskervilles in Herefordshire, Conan Doyle placed the story on Dartmoor and that's where it should remain.

"Mr Rickman is very brave and daring to go into print declaring that the origins of this most famous of Holmes's stories is Herefordshire – which of course it isn't."

Following this article, four **Letters to the Editor** on the subject were published in THE DAILY TELEGRAPH as follows:

Wednesday, June 2, 2004

Hounded from Hereford

SIR – There is no doubt in my mind that *The Hound of the Baskervilles* owes its origins to Herefordshire (report, June 1). My grandmother was brought up at Clyro Court, the 19th-century home of the Baskervilles, and was living there when Conan Doyle came across the story of Black Vaughan's dog on a visit to the Kington area.

I understand that it is important to Dartmoor that the story belongs there. However, when Conan Doyle asked the Baskerville family if he could use their name, as it had a more romantic ring, the family took a rather different view to the people of Dartmoor. Only if he promised to spirit the story away from the Welsh Borders would permission be granted.

Conan Doyle stayed true to his word and, I believe, rented a house from the Duchy of Cornwall while writing the story. Furthermore, as far as I know, he never let on about the story's Herefordshire origins.

Geoffrey Hopton

Hay-on-Wye, Powys

SIR – Phil Rickman forgets the many connections that Conan Doyle had with Devon. It was the journalist Bertram Fletcher Robinson who suggested the idea of the hound. Bertram's father retired to Ipplepen in Devon and his coachman's name was Baskerville.

A.J. Robinson

Prestatyn, Denbighshire

Thursday, June 3, 2004

Hunting the hound

SIR – My grandfather, the mathematician WD Evans, met Conan Doyle several times in the 1920s and 1930s and was particularly keen on *The Hound of the Baskervilles* (Letters, June 2). He asked the author about its origins and Conan Doyle told him that both the ghostly hound and Sir Hugo Baskerville were based on legends he had heard in Herefordshire and Devon.

Jacqueline Worthington

Stansted, Essex

Friday, June 4, 2004

Scucca sucker

SIR – Further to the discussion on the origins of Sir Arthur Conan Doyle's Baskerville hound (Letters, June 3), arguably the most likely source is the legendary demon dog of East Anglia, the "Black Shuck".

In March 1901, Conan Doyle took a golfing holiday at Cromer on the Norfolk coast, in the company of Fletcher Robinson (Letters, June 2). During their stay, it is believed they heard local stories of a sinister black dog the size of a calf, with a black shaggy coat and eyes like glowing saucers. In local lore, the Black Shuck serves as a warning of death and disaster to all who encounter him. It has also been suggested that Cromer Hall provided the model for Baskerville Hall.

The name "shuck" is believed to come from an Anglo-Saxon word, "scucca", meaning demon or goblin, and there are reports of his appearance well into the 20th-century, suggesting that he may be more than just a shaggy dog story.

Alan Murdie

Chairman, the Ghost Club
Bury St. Edmunds, Suffolk

Tracing the Footprints

Phil Rickman on the scent of *The Hound of the Baskervilles*

'Mr Holmes, they were the footprints of a gigantic hound.'

It's a resonant line, isn't it? Weighted in all the right places. Guaranteed, no matter how many times you've read it, to patter up your spine.

But if we follow those footprints back to the creature's lair, where do we end up? Fifty years after Maurice Campbell, a chairman of the Sherlock Holmes Society, published his controversial pamphlet *The Hound of the Baskervilles: Dartmoor or Herefordshire?* The issue remains unresolved.

Guidebooks to Devon point authoritatively to the ghostly hound connected with the death of Sir Richard Cabell, allegedly the most hated man on Dartmoor and an obvious model for the devilish Hugo Baskerville who enlisted the Powers of Darkness in his pursuit of a runaway maiden across Dartmoor and ended up having his throat torn out by the aforementioned gigantic hound.

But residents of Kington, on the Welsh border, maintain that the origins of Conan Doyle's Hound can be traced back to Hergest Court, a bleak stone and timbered farmhouse in a country lane on the edge of the town. And for them, this is still very much a live issue.

'I can tell you for a fact,' one local said to me last year, 'that there are people in this town now who will not go along that road after dark, either on foot or even in a car.'

It's not the kind of thing you say to a writer if you want him to go away. I live some miles down the Border from Kington. I'd already made a radio programme about the ghastly Hound of Hergest and had been threatening for years to write a novel exploring the legend and the possible link with Arthur Conan Doyle. Now, with my new novel, *The Prayer of the Night Shepherd*, I was finally seizing the Hound by the collar.

'I have the idea for a real creeper for the *Strand*,' Conan Doyle wrote to Greenhough Smith, editor of the London magazine, in 1901, adding, 'There is one stipulation, I must do it with my friend Fletcher Robinson.'

Robinson, a 28 year-old journalist, had been with Doyle on a golfing holiday in Norfolk when he lit the taper of inspiration with his retelling of the tale of a ghostly hound. Robinson was a Devon man, and it was to Dartmoor that he and Doyle went to research the book, ferried around by a coachman by the name of Harry Baskerville.

Case closed, surely.

Apparently not. As Daniel Stashower points out in his Conan Doyle biography, *Teller of Tales* (1999) Greenhough Smith later recalled that Robinson had admitted finding the hound legend in a 'Welsh guidebook'. And the proposed title *The Hound of the Baskervilles* had been divulged by Conan Doyle to his mother before he and Robinson had even been to Dartmoor or, presumably, heard of Harry Baskerville.

Because the Vaughan family, to which the Hound of Hergest is connected, had very strong Welsh origins – all the way back to the Princes of Brecknock – the legend is recounted in Welsh guidebooks to this day, invariably followed by the assertion that this was where Sir Arthur found the inspiration for his most famous novel.

The Herefordshire town of Kington is on the very border of England and Wales. In fact, there are those who say it shouldn't be in England at all as it lies on the Welsh side of Offa's Dyke. On the old border itself is windy Hergest Ridge, made famous by the musician Mike Oldfield, who lived there for a while and whose music became the soundtrack for the film *The Exorcist*.

And it's an exorcism that lies at the core of the legend of Hergest Court.

The central figure here is Thomas Vaughan – Black Vaughan, who lived at the court when it was far grander and more fortified than the present farmhouse. During the Wars of the Roses (it's interesting that the events in Doyle's Baskerville manuscript take place in the time of another great national division, the Civil War) Vaughan, in true Welsh border tradition, changed sides from Lancaster to York and is said to have been killed at a battle near Banbury. His headless body was brought back, to be buried by his widow Ellen Gethyn (the Terrible) who now lies by his side in a spectacular double tomb in the rather eerie Vaughan Chapel in Kington Church. Ellen has her own legend. After her favourite brother was killed in a fight with his cousin, she attended an archery contest disguised as a man and put an arrow through the cousin.

Vaughan himself has often been described as a notorious tyrant, but there's nothing in history to support this – the name Black Vaughan apparently referred to his hair and was used to distinguish him from a red-headed relative – and it was only after his death that he began to measure up to Hugo Baskerville's level of infamy. According to the local legend, his furious phantom would rampage throughout Kington and its environs, overturning farmers' carts, terrifying their wives and disrupting services at the church, where his body lies, by manifesting as a raging bull. A spectral hound was also seen. Soon, nobody wanted to come to Kington market and the economy of the town was in trouble. This was when it was decided that Vaughan should be exorcised.

It was a big job. It took twelve priests. Ella Mary Leather's *The Folklore of Herefordshire* (1912) contains a transcript of the lurid oral account of a ceremony in the course of which Vaughan makes a personal appearance, insisting he has now become a devil. Eventually subdued, after much shouting and extinguishing of candles, his spirit is shrunk down, confined to a snuff box and buried under a stone at the bottom of the pool close to Hergest Court.

Only the hound remained, to become allegedly, a harbinger of death in the Vaughan family and a general source of fear in Kington even after the immediate family died out in the nineteenth century.

During World War Two, it was seen by a man cycling home to Kington late at night, according to Bob Jenkins, a local journalist and Kington oracle. 'He'd been working at the munitions factory. Near Hergest Court, he saw this enormous hound which he'd never seen before and never saw again. The hound had huge eyes – that's what impressed him. He had a feeling that there was something that just wasn't real about it.'

The man, it seems, did not die soon afterwards. But then he wasn't a Vaughan.

To this day there are reports of psychic disturbance at the Court itself, where no Vaughan has resided since the death of The Rev. Silvanus Vaughan in 1706.

John Williams, a farmer, lived there in the 1980s. He described sound as a patter of huge paws in an upstairs room and hound-like shadow padding in front of him and into the inner hall. 'A prickly feeling,' he said, 'went up my back.'

Originally, *The Hound* was not going to be a Sherlock Holmes story. This was post-Reichenbach; Holmes was supposed to be dead. And at the time, Arthur Conan Doyle's obsession with spiritualism, fairies and anything otherworldly was developing fast. He would go on to write evangelical stories of the supernatural. Why he turned the Hound over to Holmes and a rational explanation has never been fully explained, but I've always liked to imagine it was in some way linked to his decision to switch the location from the Welsh Border to Dartmoor. Of such imaginings are crime novels born.

So, all right, what evidence is there that the story originated in Herefordshire? Actually, not at all, but I'm still inclined to believe that the Hound was, at the very least, a Vaughan/Cabell mongrel. The Holmes anoraks who refute this outright know nothing about novelists. This is what we do: gather as many different sources as we can find and then smudge the origins.

Around Kington, the story persists locally that Doyle was distantly related to what became the Baskerville-Mynors family and also had friends locally. It was said that he stayed at the Victorian Dunfield House, now a Christian study centre, but there is no documentary proof.

In the end, what impresses most is the coincidence of names. The medieval Baskervilles had a castle at Eardisley, about five miles from Kington. Their descendents owned the mansion Clyro Court (it became a hotel and was recently renamed, for obvious reasons, Baskerville Hall) and the pub in the village of Clyro, a few miles over the Welsh border, has always been the Baskerville Arms.

Consider also Dr Mortimer, who first enlists the aid of Sherlock Holmes in the affair of the Hound. The Mortimers were the powerful Norman barons who controlled the Welsh Marches around Kington. Mortimer's Cross lies just a few miles away. And, more impressively, a few miles in another direction, with a ruined castle on a hill, famously haunted by one Lady Bluefoot, is the hamlet of…Stapleton.

OK, I realise that there are at least three other English villages called Stapleton, but this cluster of Hound-associated names still seems like more than coincidence.

As for the Hound itself, there are no recent sightings as far as I'm aware. But in 1987, a woman visiting the area from the Midlands reported that a spectral bull had manifested in front of her in Kington Church. I found her convincing.

'The inside of his nostrils – this was one of the most vivid things – were very, very, red, like a racehorse when it's just stopped running. And it was wet, it was dripping moisture or something on to the ground. It was as though it was hanging in strings…I'm a hard-headed business person, but I can't deny it. I've seen it.'

Her name, by the way, was Jenny Vaughan.

Researching *The Prayer of the Night Shepherd* last year, I talked to Alan Lloyd, historian and chronicler of the Vaughan family, who occasionally guides visitors around Hergest Court, where, if you recall, the spirit of Black Vaughan is supposed to lie in a snuff box under a big stone at the bottom of the pool.

In *Herefordshire Folklore* (2002), Ray Palmer, who records that 'both Doyle and the Vaughans were connected by marriage to the Baskerville family', writes that when there were attempts to fill in the pool a few years ago, the project was abandoned after the water began to 'bubble ominously.'

A couple of years ago, when the water level dropped, it was decided to clean out the pool. A large stone was found in the middle. Keen to know if it might possibly be concealing a one-time receptacle for nasal stimulants, Alan Lloyd says he tried to persuade local farmers who owned mechanical diggers to help remove the rock.

None of them, he says, was prepared to touch it.

Daily Express Friday June 25 2004

Mastermind BBC2

Stephen Fry – TV Presenter & Author

Specialist Subject: The Sherlock Holmes stories of Sir Arthur Conan Doyle

Q. Where did Sherlock Holmes deduce Dr Watson had been at their first meeting in A Study in Scarlet?
A. Afghanistan.

Q. What sort of creature was The Lion's Mane who killed Fitzroy Macpherson in the story of the same name?
A. Jellyfish.

Q. In the Hound of the Baskervilles which disease killed Roger Baskerville?
A. Yellow fever.

Q. In A Scandal in Bohemia what was the name of the lawyer Irene Adler marries?
A. Godfrey Norton.

Q. In A Case of Identity on what was Holmes going to write a monograph on and it's relation to crime?
A. The typewriter.

Q. In The Adventure of the Six Napoleons whose shop in Kennington is where the first bust is broken?
A. Morse Hudson's.

Q. What name did Ferguson's spaniel in The Sussex Vampire share with Jethro Ruscastle's mastiff in The Copper Beeches?
A. Carlo.

Q. In The Adventure of the Three Students, a chapter of which ancient Greek historian's work must be translated in the examination for the Fortesque scholarship?
A. Thucydides.

Q. Which of the Crown Jewels is Holmes asked to recover by the Prime Minister, though Lord Cantlemere opposes his involvement?
A. The Mazarine Stone.

Q. In The Valley of Fear which work by Moriarty was so intellectually refined that there was no man in the scientific press capable of criticising it?
A. The Dynamics of an Asteroid.

Q. In The Adventure of the Second Stain which international agent blackmails Lady Hilda Trelawney Hope into stealing a confidential document from her husband's dispatch box?
A. Eduardo Lucas.

Q. What was the title of the last Sherlock Holmes case to be published in Liberty magazine in 1927?
A. The Adventure of Shoscombe Old Place.

Q. In The Sign of Four what is Dr Watson expecting to find when he opens the Benares metalwork box?
A. The Agra treasure.

Q. In The adventure Silver Blaze what is the name of Colonel Ross's other horse that he scratches from the Wessex Cup?
A. Bazard.

Sherlock Magazine Issue 63 December 2004
SHERLOCK STATESIDE By **Pat Ward**

Andrea Plunkett, the former wife of producer Sheldon Reynolds, has made a career of claiming copyright control over the characters of the Holmes stories based on her husband's ownership of the rights to the characters for his television productions of the 1950s and 1980s. Ms. Plunkett has lost every legal challenge she has filed against individuals and companies who have ignored her claims. A judge recently summarily dismissed her suit against the USA cable network regarding the 2002 television film *A Case Of Evil*. The courts ruled in favor of the network, awarding attorneys' fees to USA Cable, and found that it was 'objectively unreasonable' for the lawsuit to have been filed.Excerpt from Sam Leith's **Notebook**

Another discovery I made this week concerns Sherlock Holmes's hat.
　Everyone of course knows that nowhere in the canon does he actually say: "Elementary, my dear Watson." But new on me was that the famous deerstalker was an invention of the illustrator Sidney Paget.
　Only once, in the kidnapped-racehorse yarn *Silver Blaze*, does Conan Doyle mention something like it: an "earflapped travelling cap". Nor, while we're at it, does the textual Holmes – furious smoker that he is – confine himself to a pipe.

THE DAILY TELEGRAPH Thursday, December 2, 2004

NEWS BULLETIN

Conan Doyle debut on display

The manuscript of Sherlock Holmes creator Sir Arthur Conan Doyle's unpublished debut novel will go on display for the first time today at the British Library. Conan Doyle apparently thought **The Narrative of John Smith** had been lost in the post, and wrote in 1897: "I must in all honesty confess that my shock at its disappearance would be as nothing to my horror if it were suddenly to appear again – in print.

DECEMBER 5 2004 The Sunday Telegraph

The New Annotated Sherlock Holmes ed. By Leslie S. Klinger. W.W. NORTON £35.

Sherlock Holmes originally appeared in 24 short-stories before he disappeared – presumed dead – after his grapple with Professor Moriarty at the Reichenbach Falls. Thanks to public demand Arthur Conan Doyle brought him back to life in a further 32 adventures which appeared sporadically in *The Strand* magazine up to 1927. This handsome two-volume boxed set brings together all five collections of Holmes short stories complete with annotations elucidating the text (by 1880 the Metropolitan police force numbered 16, 943, one officer for every 430 citizens), numerous reproductions of the evocative early illustrations and, for serious addicts, the latest theories coming out of the weird and wonderful world of Holmes scholars (according to one expert, by the time he returned in October 1903 the detective had apparently handled some 1,700 cases). This large-scale production has an attention to detail that the great man himself would surely have appreciated.

[Review by Michael Prodger]

THE DAILY TELEGRAPH Monday, December 27, 2004

Holmes was right, women will rescue the photos first

By DAVID DERBYSHIRE Consumer Affairs Editor

A PIECE of folklore that helped Sherlock Holmes solve one of his earliest and most famous cases still holds true after a century: women will choose to save the photograph of a loved one above anything else from a burning house.

A survey has shown that, given the choice of saving just one precious thing from their home, most women will rescue a family picture.

The findings confirm the plot twist of Sir Arthur Conan Doyle's *A Scandal in Bohemia*, the first of the Sherlock Holmes short stories which was published in *The Strand* magazine in 1891.

In the story Holmes is hired by the king of Bohemia to retrieve a compromising photograph from the clutches of the protagonist Irene Adler. She unwittingly reveals the location of the hidden photograph when the detective tricks her into believing her home is burning down.

Holmes later tells Dr Watson: "When a woman thinks that her house is on fire, her instinct is at once to rush to the thing which she values most. It is a perfectly overpowering impulse, and I have more than once taken advantage of it."

Now Holmes' assertion has been put to the test in a snap-shot survey on 84 people carried out by eDV, a firm which archives family photographs.

It found that about a third of women would choose to save a family photograph above any other possession in a burning building.

Older women in particular value photographs above other memorabilia. Every woman over 55 named them as the most important items. Essential documents such as a passport, driving licence or marriage certificate were next most popular, followed by letters and mobile phones. Jewels came next followed by money and books.

Other personal and more expensive items barely got a look in, although three women mentioned an iPod music player as the item they would save above all.

Richard Williamson, the president of eDV, a London-based company, said: "People sometimes give us 40 years worth of boxes of photographs and old cine to put on film and they frequently comment on how it's the most important thing that they have.

"I was in my 30s before I had my children and they are not going to know their grandparents as well. That means family photographs are increasingly important."

THE SUNDAY POST/**August 28, 2005**

Elementary, my dear spiritualists By **James Millar**

HE MAY have created one of literature's most logical characters, but Sir Arthur Conan Doyle left hundreds of pounds in his will to the cause of spiritualism.

The contents of his will have just been released by the National Archives. It shows the Edinburgh-born creator of Sherlock Holmes left around £700 to various spiritualist causes.

Conan Doyle became fascinated by spiritualism following the death of his son during World War 1.

When the writer died in 1930 he left £200 to the Psychic College and £100 each to the Spiritualist Alliance of London, the National Spiritual Union and the Spiritual Community. *The Psychic Gazette* and various independent spiritualists were also left smaller gifts.

In total, the will was worth £80,346 – around £3.5 million today.

Archives Awareness Campaign Officer Lucy Fulton got first look at the will. She said, "I knew he had an interest in spiritualism and it's nice when you open a file and find the facts fit with the knowledge you already have.

"It's interesting Sherlock Holmes is so logical yet Conan Doyle had this strong belief in the power of the supernatural and was willing to defend clairvoyants publicly."

Another file held by the National Archives at Kew reveals Conan Doyle got involved in the case of a clairvoyant called Madam Estelle.

The gypsy foretold a young male customer would meet a rich lady. When he didn't he complained and the local police sent along two female police officers to investigate by having their fortunes told.

Conan Doyle leapt to the defence of Madam Estelle, writing to the Press and the Home Office to complain she had been set up by the police.

Lucy added, "This file is just the tip of the iceberg. It takes a bit of work to uncover a gem like this, but there's a wealth of fascinating information in archives which you can discover for yourself."

AUGUST 29 2004 The Sunday Telegraph

Revealed: the cruelty of Conan Doyle to his eldest daughter. A new biography by a member of the Doyle family exposes the callous nature of the creator of Sherlock Holmes, reports **Chris Logan**

Sir Arthur Conan Doyle, the creator of the world's celebrated fictional detective, Sherlock Holmes, behaved cruelly towards his first-born daughter, a new biography has revealed.

It details how the Scottish-born Victorian author rejected his daughter, Mary, from his first marriage to appease the jealousy of his much younger second wife.

Conan Doyle once denied the teenager permission to return home for Christmas, even though she begged to be allowed to travel back from music school in Germany.

When he died in 1930, he left Mary £2,000 (the equivalent of about £80,000 today). Crucially, however, she was not included in his copyright bequest: all the royalties from his hugely successful books, which would run into millions of pounds over the following decades, went to his second wife and their three children.

The revelations about his hard-hearted behaviour towards his first-born child will shock many fans of his stories and could lead to a re-evaluation of his personality.

Until now, biographies have portrayed Conan Doyle as a man dedicated to duty and selfless family devotion. His three children from his second marriage kept a close watch on what was written about their father and censored material to make certain he was shown in the best light.

A different picture of the author, however, emerges in *Out of the Shadows – The Untold Story of Arthur Conan Doyle's First Family*, written by Georgina Doyle, the widow of one of the writer's nephews, John. It is published by Calabash Press in Canada and is available through the Broadway Bookshop in Crowborough on 01892 652409 (£25).

Mrs Doyle, 68, drew on previously unpublished letters and diaries and spent 16 years researching and writing the book. "I wanted to set the record straight," she said last week at her home in Iwerne Minster, Dorset.

"I didn't set out to denigrate Arthur. I just wanted to set out the facts as I knew them from my husband John and others in the family who knew Arthur's second wife and what she was like.

"It was mean of Arthur not to include Mary in the copyright and I believe it was because of Jean. She wanted everything for herself and her children."

Conan Doyle was already one of Britain's wealthiest and most famous writers when his first wife, Louise, died of tuberculosis in 1906 after a long illness. He had met the woman who was to be his second wife, Jean Leckie, some years earlier but always insisted that the relationship had remained platonic at least until Louise's death. He married Jean a year later, he was 47 and she was 31.

The couple moved from the home in Hindhead, Surrey, where Conan Doyle had lived with Louise, to Crowborough, East Sussex. At this point, however, says Mrs Doyle, the doctor-turned-author became so desperate to keep his new wife happy that he bowed to her possessive jealousy and treated Mary and her brother Kingsley, coldly.

At 17 Mary was sent against her will to Dresden to study music, while Kingsley boarded at Eton. Mary wrote to her brother: "My dear, I'm feeling awfully low and depressed just now. In answer to my letter to Daddy about Xmas, he not only flatly refused to hear of my coming home till next August but blamed me sharply for great weakness of character for even asking such a thing…I can't think why my father is so hard – I have not had one gentle word, or sign of love from him during the whole two years since Mother died".

In later letters, Mary made it clear that she felt that Jean was influencing the way her father was behaving towards her and Kingsley, who was to die aged 26 from influenza in 1918 while he was training to be a doctor.

At one stage Mary, a talented pianist and singer, was told by her father that he might have to cut her funds and withdraw her from music school. He told her that her voice had "a sweet quality but can never stand out from others".

Mary, devastated by the criticism, was convinced that her stepmother, a trained mezzo soprano, was behind the threat.

Conan Doyle's treatment changed Mary from being an extrovert to being "shy and retiring and lacking in confidence", according to Mrs Doyle. When she returned to England she became involved in her father's spiritualist campaigns and ran his psychic bookshop in London. Yet when Conan Doyle died, aged 71, Mary was dealt a further blow in his will.

The bulk of the estate, including the copyright to all of Conan Doyle's works, was left to Jean and the three children from their marriage, Adrian, Denis and Jean.

Mrs Doyle's book tells how, while Mary lived frugally and lunched for 2s 6p in cafes, Adrian and Denis lived the life of playboys thanks to their father's royalties.

Mary, a spinster, died in 1976, aged 87, with only a small terrace house in Twickenham and little money to her name.

"I feel very sorry for Mary," said Mrs Doyle. "She led a rather difficult, unfulfilled life. Arthur was very mean to her because he was so besotted with Jean.

The revelations in Mrs Doyle's book have shocked fans of the man who created one of literature's most enduring characters.

Catherine Cooke, the curator of the Sherlock Holmes Collection at Marylebone Library in London, said: "This is a side to Conan Doyle that we've never seen before. I'm saddened by the picture that emerges and I feel deeply sorry for Mary. She had a raw deal from her father."

Brian Pugh, the curator of the Conan Doyle Establishment in Crowborough, said: "My opinion of Conan Doyle the writer hasn't changed, but my opinion of Conan Doyle the man has gone down a bit. He seems to have virtually disowned Mary and Kingsley."

Daily Mail, Saturday, September 4, 2004

Holmes and away!

Haven't a clue where to go in Switzerland? Try the dramatic waterfall where the great detective met his end, says **Robert Gore-Langton**.

SWITZERLAND was where Sir Arthur Conan Doyle plotted the death of Sherlock Holmes.

Sick of writing stories about the sleuth, the author, who was a keen hiker, travelled around Switzerland and decided to make the spectacular Reichenbach Falls, near the village of Meiringen, the place to bump off his great detective.

And, so, on May 4, 1891, Holmes and his arch-enemy Professor Moriarty ('the Napoleon of crime') did battle on a tiny ledge at the top of the falls.

They supposedly vanished into the raging torrent whose noise was like a 'half-human shout which came booming up with the spray out of the abyss.'

The Reichenbach Falls are these days a shrine for fans of literature's famous character. A star marks the chilling spot from where Holmes fell. But fans of the stories wouldn't accept his death at the time. Conan Doyle was persuaded by a deafening public outcry to bring him back to life. In The Adventure of the Empty House, Holmes duly makes his return (Watson faints on seeing him) and explains how he escaped up the perilous cliff beside the waterfall having totally unbalanced his foe with a Japanese wrestling technique.

Today it is a giddy-making experience to watch great sheets of water crashing down the sheer rock face and imagine Holmes wrestling with his old adversary above the great cataract.

Indeed, nothing much has changed since Conan Doyle's day. Except, that is, in winter when the water is 'switched off' and diverted for power generation.

The funicular railway up to the falls is still running a century after it was built for those who don't fancy the two-hour climb.

Although the village of Meiringen is now a modern town with plate-glass shopfronts, it was very popular with British tourists in the 19th. century.

The 1880 hotel where Conan Doyle stayed still stands. He installed Holmes and Watson there and called it the Englischer Hof. Today it has 70 rooms with all mod cons, but the old lifts belle-epoque décor has a period charm.

Next to the hotel is a square called Conan Doyle Place (the sign is in the London borough style) featuring a life-size statue of the sleuth complete with deer-stalker, pipe and magnifying glass.

The bronze is inscribed with more than 50 fiendishly hard clues, each one referring to a Sherlock Holmes mystery.

But eccentric though this might seem, it's nothing compared to the little 19th-century English church in the town. The museum features an immaculate full-scale recreation of the doctor and detective's rooms at 221b Baker Street. It's designed to look as if the pair had rushed out on a case, leaving newspapers strewn about.

Amid the High Victorian décor are all the Holmesian touches: the slipper full of tobacco, the chemistry apparatus and, for eagle-eyed fans, the 'gasogene' (soda siphon) on the sideboard.

For fans of funiculars, cable cars and trains, Meiringen is heaven. The Eagle Express cable car to Planplatten with its circular Alpen Tower restaurant is not for the faint-hearted.

In winter, you ski down the mountain. In summer the descent on foot takes about three hours among the edelweiss, gentians, orchids and furry marmots which pop out of their burrows with a squeak. Ten minutes away by rail is the town of Brienz, perched on the edge of the stunning turquoise Lake Brienz, with the white-capped mountains rising all around the shore.

The cog-and-ratchet railway built up the side of the mountain in 1892 is the oldest steam line in Switzerland. The engine pushes two open-sided carriages up a series of gut-churning hairpin bends, 2,350m to the very top of the Brienz Rothorn Bahn.

It takes about an hour to reach the summit, where the air is like champagne and the views jaw-dropping.

Back down at the station, you can either take the boat to explore Interlaaken or go back to the hotel by rail.

The Park Hotel Du Sauvage holds murder mystery weekends through the year. In June 2005, the Sherlock Holmes Society will link with other fan clubs over the world for a Holmesian celebration in Meiringen. If you are planning to go, wear 19th-century costume – deer-stalker and pipe obligatory for the chaps.

Sherlock Holmes has rather overshadowed Meiringen's other claim to fame. In the 17th century, a baker called Gasparini invented a delicacy made of egg whites and sugar, one which Napoleon found irresistible.

It is the meringue. Try one while saying 'My dear Watson' with your mouthful. It's far from elementary.

Daily Mail, Monday, November 29, 2004

QUESTION **What is the Christian name of Dr Watson in the Sherlock Holmes stories?**

ANSWER Sir Arthur Conan Doyle's first Sherlock Holmes story, A Study in Scarlet, written in 1886, starts with a thumbnail sketch of Dr Watson.

A chance meeting with a friend in London is described, which in turn leads to an introduction to an unusual research chemist who is looking for someone with whom to share rooms in Baker Street. That was how Dr John H. Watson MD came to meet Sherlock Holmes.

Daily Mail, Wednesday, December 1, 2004

ANSWER Further to earlier answers, there is an alternative Christian name for Dr Watson.

Although he's called John in the first story, A Study in Scarlet, his wife doesn't seem to have realised this because in a later story, The Man With The Twisted Lip, she addresses him as James.

Some have suggested that James was a nickname, based on a possible interpretation of his middle name. For this, the initial 'H', given in A Study in Scarlet, is said to stand for 'Hamish' – the Scots equivalent of James.

The reason probably lies in Conan Doyle's inability to remember the details he put in his earlier stories. Holmes's landlady, Mrs Hudson, turns into Mrs Turner in one story, (see below) and Professor James Moriarty (named in full in The Empty House) also has a brother called James, named in The Final Problem.

Daily Mail, Friday, December 10, 2004

ANSWER Further to earlier answers, where the character of Mrs Turner was proposed as a memory fault by Conan Doyle (instead of Mrs Hudson), this character appeared in the story A Scandal in Bohemia, bringing in a tray with 'the simple fare that our landlady has provided'.

Mrs Turner was, in fact, either the cook or a servant.

(**Compiler's note**: In David L. Hammer's 1995 book *The Before Breakfast Pipe of Mr Sherlock Holmes* Gasogene Press Ltd., it was noted that '…Mrs Hudson had been summoned to attend a death-bed in the North, together with her sister, Mrs Turner, who normally attended to our needs in the absence of Mrs Hudson…'

The Sunday Telegraph July 4 2004

My Darling Watson Mandrake By **Tim Walker**

EVER the rebel, Rupert Everett tells Mandrake that he will not be sporting the traditional deerstalker when he plays the title role in the BBC's Christmas drama *The Return of Sherlock Holmes*. Scholars of the work of the late, great Sir Arthur Conan Doyle will, however, be far more concerned that the gay Ampleforth-educated actor also says – predictably, perhaps – that he sees the fictional detective's relationship with his sidekick, Dr Watson, as "a love affair, albeit one that is not really expressible".

It is just as well that Dame Jean Conan Doyle is no longer with us. Shortly before her death seven years ago, Sir Arthur's daughter told Mandrake that her father would have been aghast at such a suggestion. "I think that my father immersed himself in the story of these two men precisely because he wanted to take his mind off sex," she told me. Her father had fallen in love with her mother, Jean Leckie, as his beloved first wife, Louise, died a long lingering death from tuberculosis. Sir Arthur behaved impeccably, and it was only a year after his bereavement that he permitted himself to marry Miss Leckie. And think about sex again.

Sherlock Holmes and The Case of the Silk Stocking
BOXING DAY, 2004, BBC1

Daily Mail WEEKEND Magazine, Saturday 11th December 2004

Holmes is where the heart is

More than 100 years after his creation, Sherlock Holmes remains one of fiction's most intriguing characters. Writer **Allan Cubitt** (talking to Julian Champkin) tells how he came up with a new Christmas TV adventure for the detective.

Although I read and hugely enjoyed The Hound of the Baskervilles, and many other Sherlock Holmes stories as a child, Holmes is actually a very adult character. Sir Arthur Conan Doyle created the great detective as a manic-depressive with a brooding darkness within him. And that complexity is one of the reasons Holmes has become a classic role on stage and screen.

The late Jeremy Brett was Sherlock Holmes on TV for a decade, and described the role as tougher than Hamlet or Macbeth. Brett became so obsessed with playing Holmes that he was once discovered outside Doyle's former London house, begging to be released from the spirit of the master detective. In the 1940s Basil Rathbone made the role his own in radio broadcasts and Hollywood films. For Christmas 2002, I adapted The Hound of the Baskervilles for BBC television with Richard Roxburgh playing Holmes. This Christmas, my offering is Sherlock Holmes And The Case Of The Silk Stocking, with Rupert Everett in the lead role. He is a fascinating choice.

First of all there's the look – Conan Doyle describes Holmes as over six foot tall, with black hair, dark brows, a hawk-like nose and piercing eyes. Everett has all these.

But Holmes is a strange, complex man. A genius; but flawed, volatile, solitary. Holmes is more familiar than other fictional detectives. His faults are greater, too – the arrogance and rudeness, the disparaging of his companion Watson; the lethargies, the drug addiction. Can Everett cope with all that. I think so.

However, there will be no deerstalker hat and no pipe – these were introduced by William Gillette, the American actor who first played Holmes on stage in 1899. Everett will, though, as his own tongue-in-cheek tribute, utter the immortal line, 'Elementary, my dear Watson' – never actually said by Holmes. Is his detective a little too glamorous? Perhaps, though Holmes is charismatic, with an almost hypnotic power over both men and women. Is he too sexy? In fact, Everett attempts to be asexual, which is how Conan Doyle wrote Holmes. Women usually enter Holmes' life only as clients, although he is outwitted by one woman, Irene Adler, whom he admires for her brains and ruthlessness.

Ascetic, monkish? Up to a point. Off-duty Holmes enjoys good food, wine and music, and the drugs of his choice – tobacco and cocaine. Watson knows his friends weaknesses, and in the first Sherlock Holmes novel, A Study In Scarlet, he lists them – among other failings Holmes claims either to know nor to care whether the earth goes round the sun or is still.

Too often, Watson has been presented as the amiable old duffer, the comic sidekick. This ignores his role as Holmes' biographer, the man who writes the stories. Nigel Bruce, who played opposite Basil Rathbone, based his Watson on Doyle himself – a tweedy, big, bluff, hearty chap, sporting a gentleman's moustache. Watson does not have Holmes' genius, but that does not make him stupid. Luckily, Ian Hart, who was in The Hound, is reprising his role – an actor of tremendous integrity and power who has really got under Watson's skin.

Adaptors face other problems with Sherlock Holmes and Dr John Watson – or is it James? Conan Doyle himself could not remember, and in different stories gave the doctor different Christian names. Nor could he even remember whether Watson's old Afghan war wound was in an arm or a leg. In A Study In Scarlet, he makes Watson limp around the room from it. Four pages later it has moved to his left arm. And was Watson married once or twice? Doyle gives him another wife in a story set after his first wife has supposedly died – though we are never told the second lady's name, or anything else about her. I therefore felt justified in inventing a fiancée for Watson – an American widow, Mrs Vandeleur, played with customary brilliance by Helen McCrory.

Conan Doyle killed off Sherlock Holmes in 1891, in a struggle with his archenemy, Moriarty. Eleven years later, he reluctantly resurrected him due to public demand – and for the money – and sent him travelling, before pitting him against the dastardly Colonel Sebastian Moran in foggy London in The Adventure Of The Empty House.

The Hound Of The Baskervilles came about in much the same way. Doyle had a story about a dog and realised that he would get more money for it if he made it a Sherlock Holmes story. The Hound is by far Doyle's best story for tension and dramatic effect.

After that, there was really nowhere left for the television adaptor to go. The short stories have all been done and do not easily extend to 90 minutes anyway. There is an honourable tradition among Sherlockians of writing new stories for their hero – and that is what I did.

I set it in 1902, the Edwardian era. It gives us ringing telephones, instead of the telegrams and telegraph boys of the earlier Victorian stories. It lets us use fingerprinting, which was new and exciting back then. Doyle – and Holmes – were fascinated by new technology.

We have to start with a murder. In 1889 a man called Stoddart, the editor of Lippincott's magazine, brought Conan Doyle and Oscar Wilde together for dinner. Stoddart commissioned each man to write a story. Doyle produced his second Holmes story, The Sign Of Four; while Wilde wrote The Picture Of Dorian Gray. My first idea was to combine them – to have Holmes investigate the murder of Basil Hallward and the strange case of the man who never seemed to grow old – but whose picture hidden in the attic aged instead. The trouble was that Holmes is a strictly logical man. He debunks the supernatural, and I could not think of a rational explanation for Wilde's supernatural tale. I had to start again.

I turned to a real-life Victorian murder case; the most famous of all, and unresolved at that. There are no serial killers in Doyle's stories. In one story, a severed ear is sent through the post, but the criminal is a repentant jealous husband, not a psychopath. There are brutes who tie up their wives and beat them, but nothing that comes close to the real horror of the Whitechapel murders. When Jack the Ripper spread his terror, some understood perfectly the psychological profile of the killer. And what is Holmes if not a profiler of criminals, a man who can deduce their description, their habits, their passions, from the clues they leave at the scene? It is easy to see that the Ripper was a frenzied maniac, a psychopath who must have been hardly able to function in normal society.

At the height of the Ripper murders, George Bernard Shaw wrote to the newspapers asking how great would be the outrage if the Ripper was killing not prostitutes but duchesses? Panic in the East End was so great that, when rumour got around that the Ripper was a doctor, innocent men were attacked in the street for carrying black bags. What would a West End Ripper produce? And that got me thinking. Elegant daughters of the wealthy disappearing. One by one. In thick, turn-of-the-century fog…A case for Holmes, I think.

Ideal Holmes By Jeff Dawson. **Radio Times Exclusive** 18-31 December 2004

Rupert Everett wants to make Sherlock Holmes his own – but what's the distinctive ingredients he just couldn't leave out? Elementary…

London. 1902. A pea-souper , another debutante has been murdered and Scotland Yard is damned if it can fathom it all. Thank goodness for Sherlock Holmes, a man who'll puff on his pipe, browbeat Dr Watson and finger a culprit before Mrs Hudson can wheel in the crumpets. But hello, what's this? Britain's finest detective lies stoned out of his gourd in an opium den, having jacked in the sleuthing altogether.

Welcome to Sherlock Holmes and the Case of the Silk Stocking, starring Rupert Everett as a grittier version of our most famous literary crime-stopper. "To play Sherlock Holmes without touching on his drug addiction would be like playing Winston Churchill without a cigar," says Everett. "Holmes offers us an interesting viewpoint on the late Victorian/Edwardian age: this amazing juxtaposition between high moral tone and total debauchery."

But assured, Holmes does snap out of his stupor. But Everett is correct. Devotees of Arthur Conan Doyle will attest that Holmes's copious drug indulgences (strictly legal in those days) are in the original stories. It's just that, for so long, we've settled for a more wholesome image: the deerstalker, tweeds and magnifying glass, which are the inventions of Victorian illustrator Sidney Paget – an illusion compounded by the Basil Rathbone films of the 1940s. "Holmes is such an establishment subject, but he'd pretty much been hijacked," says Everett. "There's something exciting about playing characters that are so deeply ingrained in the culture."

Everett's in esteemed company. Over 80 years, John Barrymore, Roger Moore, Raymond Massey, Stewart Granger, Christopher Lee, Christopher Plummer, Ian Richardson, Charlton Heston, Edward Woodward, Peter Cushing and Tom Baker have all had a pop at Holmes. The most faithful reconstructions are considered to be Granada's series, starring Jeremy Brett, between 1984 and 1994 (recently revived on BBC2).

This time, the adventure is an original one, by Allan Cubitt, who dramatised *The Hound of the Baskervilles* for BBC1 two Christmases ago (with Richard Roxburgh as Holmes and Ian Hart, as he is this year, as Watson). "It struck me that I'd need to make one up, because I'd started with the biggest and strongest," Cubitt explains. "A lot of the stories are extremely short, and many hinge on dramatic turns that aren't the stuff of a 90-minute Boxing Day extravaganza, but I think everything I've done has a precedent in the books."

Would Conan Doyle have been fussed? Though Holmes appeared in 56 short stories and four novels and could turn his hand to anything (the violin, fencing, boxing, Buddhism), it seems that even his creator got bored with him. Feeling that Holmes was thwarting his higher literary ambitions, Conan Doyle killed him off in 1893, in a scrap with arch-villain Moriarty at the Reichenbach Falls in Switzerland. Ten years later, thanks to popular demand, he was resurrected, Dirty-Den style, plodding on to his final case in 1926.

Arguably as compelling as Holmes was Conan Doyle himself. A Scottish doctor who relocated to England's south coast, he was a true Renaissance man: an expert on the supernatural, social reformer and proponent of the new sport of association football (he's surely the most scholarly man ever to have played in goal for Portsmouth FC). Moreover, his legacy is enormous. From Miss Marple to CSI, the debt is obvious. "Holmes is a psychological profiler, but he's the first person in literature to say, "Secure the crime scene," so he's a forensic detective, too," says Cubitt. "He established the mould for the detective and the sidekick. He's Holmes, arrogant, opinionated, vain, brilliant and depressive. It's a gift to have him and Watson to write for."

If the American tourists who disgorge themselves daily from Baker Street Tube station are anything to go by, then the popular conviction – that Holmes was actually real – is surely the ultimate tribute. And are there any other detective lines as famous as "Elementary, my dear Watson"? Though not originally scripted for this particular drama – and indeed, not appearing anywhere in Conan Doyle's stories – the phrase was included at Everett's behest. "I did get a kick out of it," the actor gushes "I insisted on putting it in, because that's part of the fun."

BOXING DAY TODAY'S CHOICES *Radio Times*

Sherlock Holmes and the Case of the Silk Stocking by **Alison Graham**

Tonight a new Sherlock Holmes and a new Sherlock Holmes story go head to head with that other great fictional detective, Miss Marple, over on ITV1.

Rupert Everett makes a good job of Holmes – he's naturally ascetic with a slightly unnerving sexuality. Pity he's let down by the plot. Things start intriguingly enough – a serial killer is stalking and killing the young debutantes of Belgravia.

It builds into a gripping tale, complete with echoes of *The Silence of the Lambs* and a touch of criminal profiling (thanks to Dr Watson's psychologist fiancée played by Helen McCrory. But did they have criminal profiling in those days, I wonder?

A good cast – Ian Hart as Watson, Neil Dudgeon as bumbling Inspector Lestrade – do their best, but they can't help it when things slowly get ridiculous and weird, with a very unlikely resolution that will probably leave you thinking: "What???" Pity.

[Mrs Hudson was played by Anne Carroll].

Daily Mail WEEKEND Magazine Boxing Day – **Nigel Andrew's** VIEW.

A couple of Christmases ago, BBC1 showed a generally unsatisfactory dramatisation of *The Hound of the Baskervilles*. Now the same writer, Allan Cubitt, has been let loose on Sherlock Holmes again – but this time there's a new Holmes, in the elegant shape of Rupert Everett, and Cubitt has invented his own Storyline. The result is ***Sherlock Holmes And The Case Of The Silk Stocking.***

Everett's languid, aphoristic, almost Wildean Holmes works brilliantly – with Ian Hart a suitably doughty Watson – and it's a handsome, atmospheric production. The problem is the story, which is simply a modern 'psychological' serial-killer thriller in Edwardian dress – with an ending as ridiculous as *The Hound of the Baskervilles*.

Pick of the day By **Sophie Heath**

Rupert Everett as Sherlock Holmes? No, I wasn't convinced either, but prepare to be amazed. Despite believing that Jeremy Brett was the only person capable of filling Basil Rathbone's shoes in the role of the great detective, I must report that, in this dark but compelling production, Everett is actually quite spiffing, as he brings a tantalisingly laconic arrogance to his portrayal of the enigmatic sleuth. The year is 1902, and Holmes is lured out of his opium-addicted retirement when a serial killer starts targeting young debutants. A splendid Christmas surprise.

Pick of the Day by GERARD O'DONOVAN

There's no doubt that Rupert Everett makes a superb Holmes, Ian Hart's not half bad as Watson and the exquisite camerawork, sets and costumes do wonders to conjure up turn-of-the-century London from a permanent pall of fog. But what a stinker of an anachronistic storyline to lumber us with, as the world's greatest detective tries to save the daughters of the aristocracy from the predators of…a homicidal foot-fetishist? From the outset there's much to provoke the purist but, surely, Helen McCrory's role as Mrs "I'm a trained psychoanalyst" [in 1902!] Vandeleur must go down as one of the worst Holmes travesties, ever.

Daily Mail, Monday, December 27, 2004

Something a bit special by **Christopher Matthew** (excerpt)

Sherlock Holmes, as re-invented by Rupert Everett, should have been a lot more special than it was. It had everything going for it – a languid and unusually drug-fuelled sleuth, a terrier-like Watson in Ian Hart, Neil Dudgeon's dim Inspector Lestrade, plenty of over-the-top acting by the likes of Jonathan Hyde (George Pentney) and Eleanor David (Mary Pentney), lashings of production values, oodles of fog.

All that was missing was a decent plot. Ah well, at Christmas you can't win 'em all.

THE DAILY TELEGRAPH Monday, December 27, 2004

The weekend on television by James Walton (extract)

Now, Christmas TV wouldn't be the same without some top-hatted figures making their way through a London fog. The gap was filled last night with **Sherlock Holmes and the Case of the Silk Stocking** starring Rupert Everett. Everett proved an interesting (and as far as my wife was concerned, inspired) choice. Despite looking more like James Bond than Sherlock Holmes, he did a fine job of bringing out the man's less comfy aspects, including drug addiction and an all-round weirdness.

The other elements of the drama were well done too – except for a surprisingly ropey plot. Alan Cubitt's script basically took a bog-standard serial-killer yarn from our own times and plonked it down in 1902. This led to plenty of unEdwardian – sounding psychobabble. It also meant that our understanding was also ahead of Holmes's – which surely can't be right.

Finally, JANUARY 2, 2005 *The Sunday Telegraph* by **John Preston**

The biggest mystery about *Sherlock Holmes and the Case of the Silk Stocking* was why anyone had seen fit to make up a feeble new Holmes story instead of sticking to one of the originals. Without looking as if he was going to make 221B Baker Street his own, Rupert Everett wasn't all that bad – a more Edwardian figure than usual, and a good deal less misogynistic.

However, Alan Cubitt's script allowed him oddly little opportunity to do much actual sleuthing. Instead he sat about doing suitably Holmesian things like playing the violin – far too well for my taste – while the story unfolded creakily around him. As he proved two year's ago, in an excellent *Hound of the Baskervilles*, Ian Hart is a first-class Watson, but there was little opportunity here for him and Holmes to establish much rapport.

Amid fog so thick I thought my television had short-circuited, the plot lumbered to a much flogged climax. Strangely enough, it was only in the last shot of all that the essence of Holmes shone through. Watson goes off to get married, leaving Holmes alone and with nothing to do. As the camera closed in on Everett's face, desolation crept into his eyes. Not for him the pleasures of the hearth, or the heart. Nothing for him except isolation and ennui.

The Sunday Telegraph May 22 2005

REVIEW BOOKS

How did celebrated books get their names? Continuing our series, we look at the story behind Arthur Conan Doyle's **A Study in Scarlet** by Gary Dexter

BEHIND Sherlock Holmes stand two older fictional detectives: Edgar Allen Poe's Dupin and Emile Gaboriau's Lecoq. Both were exponents of the deductive method, both were ardent examiners of footprints and cigar ash, and both had devoted sidekicks whose main function was to be testily interrupted. Arthur Conan Doyle was quite open about his debt to both Poe and Gaboriau, *A Study in Scarlet*, the story in which Holmes first meets Watson contains a concealed homage to Gaboriau: the title is in fact a pun on Gaboriau's *L'Affaire Lerouge*. Despite his acknowledgement of these influences, some contemporary commentators were less than indulgent when they discovered the extent of Conan Doyle's debt. As Arthur Guiterman's poem *The Case of the Inferior Sleuth* put it: "Holmes is your hero of drama and serial; All of us know where you dug the material."

TELEGRAPH TRAVEL Saturday, June 25, 2005

Not quite the city of scribblers

The Scottish capital can be justly proud of its literary heritage, says **Max Davidson**, but it should polish up its plaques.
 An extract of the above article:

The Scottish capital, which last October was named a City of Literature by the UN – the first city to be so honoured. In principle I am all in favour. We do not do nearly enough to celebrate our literary heritage.
 Or I thought I was all for it. I started to waiver when I visited the statue of Sherlock Holmes in Picardy Place, near the site where Sir Arthur Conan Doyle was born. The deerstalker hat was almost white. It did not need the Baker Street sleuth to work out that the culprits were 1,000-plus pigeons – and that nobody had bothered to scrub off their handiwork.
 Conan Doyle studied medicine in Edinburgh, where it was one of his teachers, Dr Joseph Bell, who provided the model for Holmes. Opposite Picardy Place, there is a pleasant pub called the Conan Doyle, with some interesting memorabilia on the walls: violins; tobacco pouches; covers from *Strand* magazine; even a cricket bat. Conan Doyle was a keen amateur cricketer and once took the wicket of the great WG Grace.
 But the biographical details on the back of the menu were so comically off-beam ("the creator of the infamous detective Sherlock Holmes") that I could imagine Dr Watson spluttering into his leek and potato soup.
 "Holmes, this is a scandal. Why INFAMOUS? These people must be half-wits. It was Professor Moriarty who was infamous. You…"

"Elementary, my dear Watson. Where you see gross illiteracy, I see the conservative social attitudes for which Edinburgh is renowned. I take cocaine, therefore I am infamous. It is as simple as that."

THE DAILY TELEGRAPH TUESDAY, July 26, 2005

Did Conan Doyle poison his friend to cheat him out of the Hound of the Baskervilles? By Richard Savill

A TEAM investigating claims that Sir Arthur Conan Doyle murdered the true author of *The Hound of the Baskervilles* is to apply to exhume a body from a churchyard in Devon.

The six-strong team, led by an author and a scientist, is to ask the Diocese of Exeter and the Home Office for permission to dig up the corpse of Conan Doyle's friend Bertram Fletcher Robinson, believed by some to have written the original.

The author Rodger Garrick-Steele and a scientist Paul Spiring, have formed the team, which included a pathologist and a toxicologist, to investigate whether Fletcher Robinson was given the poison laudanum shortly before his death in 1907.

There have been claims that Conan Doyle poisoned his former friend rather than let his plagiarism be discovered.

Fletcher Robinson, a journalist and a barrister, and a former editor of the Daily Express, is buried at St Andrew's Church, Ipplepen, Devon.

The investigators are to meet the parochial church committee next week to discuss their proposal, before submitting a formal application to exhume the body. The official cause of death was typhoid.

"We believe there is evidence that what was put on the death certificate was not true and that the cause of death was much more likely to have been laudanum poisoning," said Mr Spiring, who began his investigations after moving to Ipplepen.

"That raises the question about why he should have been poisoned. We have got what we believe is refutable evidence that Fletcher Robinson was cheated out of a considerable sum of royalties because he was much more actively engaged in The Hound of the Baskervilles than was acknowledged by Conan Doyle."

Mr Spiring, a physicist and biologist, and a former policeman, said there was also evidence that Conan Doyle, to avoid being exposed as a fraud, persuaded Fletcher Robinson's wife, with whom he had had an affair, to poison him, possibly without her direct knowledge.

He added that if the exhumation failed to find any evidence of poisoning then the suggestions could be dismissed. However, if poison was found close to the root of Fletcher Robinson's hair then it would mean he had ingested it within a week before his death. "That would collaborate three or four further strands of evidence," he said.

Sherlock Holmes enthusiasts and other literary scholars have dismissed the poison theory but they have acknowledged that Fletcher Robinson's full role in creating the novel has been underplayed.

Fletcher Robinson showed Conan Doyle around Dartmoor, from where inspiration for the tale of the ghostly beast came. Baskerville was the surname of Robinson's coachman.

A footnote to the first edition of The Hound of the Baskervilles acknowledges Fletcher Robinson's contribution: "This story owes its inception to my friend Fletcher Robinson who helped me."

Fletcher Robinson is said to have enthralled Conan Doyle with the story of the evil squire Sir Richard Cabell, who sold his soul to Satan and was dragged to hell by a pack of hounds.

Heather Owen, of the Sherlock Holmes Society, said the poison theory seemed "highly unlikely and far-fetched".

"It would be entirely out of character," she said. He [Conan Doyle] wasn't a poisoning kind of person.

"His love life was already fairly complicated. He was faithful and true to his dying wife. He also had an intense but platonic affair with Jean Leckie, who became his second wife. They were happily married for the rest of their lives.

"Conan Doyle wanted the book to be published in joint names but the publishers didn't like that idea because Conan Doyle was the selling point."

(**Compiler's note:** A very similar article was published in THE SUNDAY POST/**September 12, 2006** – see Miscellany III).

Chapter 14

The Strange Case of Sherlock Holmes and Arthur Conan Doyle

BBC2 Wednesday 27 July 2005

THE DAILY TELEGRAPH Thursday, March 19, 2005

New dramas in BBC2's forthcoming schedule include *The Strange Case of Sherlock Holmes and Arthur Conan Doyle*, starring Douglas Henshall, about the author's tortured relationship with his most famous creation.

Radio Times 23-29 July 2005

BROKEN HOLMES

Why did Arthur Conan Doyle want to kill his finest creation? **David Pirie**, writer of a new biographical drama on Doyle, explains that truth was stranger than fiction.

Arthur Conan Doyle conquered the world with his literary creation, Sherlock Holmes, yet the author was always ambivalent towards his detective. Of course, writers grow tired of their creations, but this was an exceptional case. It was a mere two years after Holmes's success that Doyle took it upon himself – despite the pleading of everyone around him – to kill him.

Why? It's a subject that's perplexed many. TS Eliot called the relationship between Doyle and Holmes "the greatest of mysteries". He concluded his reflections with a question: "Sir Arthur Conan Doyle…what has he to do with Holmes?"

What indeed? Doyle always evaded the issue, talking of more serious work and a vague sense of impatience. But authors are often the worst people to discuss their own artistic motivation, and there are grounds for supposing Holmes was a more loaded subject than Doyle ever acknowledged – that he was born out of a desperate desire for sanity, order and authority in the difficult early years of Doyle's life.

In order to understand this, we need to understand more about that life but that's not as easy as it sounds. Doyle was scrupulous in tailoring the image that reached the public: so much so that even today, 75 years after his death, no biographer has had unrestricted access to his papers.

For a long time the estate was tightly controlled and, though a few writers were allowed to see the papers, Arthur's son Adrian oversaw anything that was published as a result. When Adrian died in 1970, matters might have changed, but it was then that a complex legal dispute began within the family, which has only just been resolved. Some papers are at last emerging, but the bulk of his letters are yet to be revealed, if they still exist at all.

Most of what we have dates from his later life, when the image of the sportsman, amateur scientist and crusader for various causes was presented to the public. About his first 50 years, less is known, but heroic detective work by researchers has uncovered why Doyle would not have wished some aspects of it to be explored too closely. *The Strange Case of Sherlock Holmes and Arthur Conan Doyle* uses this evidence to unravel the mysteries of his life, and link them to his greatest creation.

Doyle revered Edgar Allan Poe, and his own upbringing could be a Poe tale of terror. His father Charles – a struggling artist who made wild drawings of supernatural phenomena – was diagnosed as a lunatic and incarcerated. He would probably now be considered as merely an alcoholic with manic tendencies, but it's hard to overestimate the effect his condition might have had on an impoverished yet respectable Edinburgh family of the 1870s. The strain of keeping it secret must have been immense.

There are other equally suggestive mysteries, including the shadowy figure of a doctor called Waller, only six years older than Doyle, who effectively took over the household, and whom Doyle came to hate with a passion. Many questions surround his relationship with Doyle's mother. Yet if the situation at home had aspects of *Hamlet*, into his world at this darkest hour stepped Doyle's university professor, the charismatic, handsome Joseph Bell, one of the foremost medical academics of his generation. Bell was to be his guide and inspiration at that difficult time, and the model for Sherlock Holmes.

But the intrigue in Doyle's life is not to be found merely in his younger days. In 1893, Doyle killed Holmes, only to see him mourned by the whole world, while at almost the same time his father died in abject circumstances and his wife Louise was diagnosed with terminal consumption. Doyle, a doctor by training, felt culpable and fought to save her, but also fell in love with another woman, the dark, captivating Jean Leckie.

Doyle's fiction deals obsessively with bizarre subjects: family secrets, brutal murders, monsters in locked rooms. Now we're beginning to see why they were there. The details of his own life are as dramatic as anything he ever wrote.

Daily Mail WEEKEND Magazine Saturday 9th July 2005
WHO KILLED SHERLOCK HOLMES?

When Sir Arthur Conan Doyle wrote about the demise of his most famous creation, his motives were far from elementary. As a new TV drama recreates the troubled world of the author, ALICE FOWLER investigates.

Walking down a London street, Conan Doyle's eye is caught by a stranger, his face in shadow. When the man turns, Conan Doyle sees he is grotesquely mutilated: one ear ripped clean away, his face wet with blood. An instant later, the man – if he existed at all – is gone. At the height of his literary success, the creator of Sherlock Holmes is left doubting his own sanity.

For Conan Doyle, as depicted in a new BBC drama, such moments of Gothic horror were all too common. In The Strange Case Of Sherlock Holmes and Arthur Conan Doyle, the best-selling author – played by Douglas Henshall – is a troubled man, at war with the fictional detective who made his name. Set in the 1890s, it describes a time in Conan Doyle's life when the pressures of success, coupled with deep personal trauma, threatened to destroy him.

The source of much of Conan Doyle's anguish was his relationship with his father, Charles Doyle, an alcoholic and epileptic. While Arthur was a boy, his father was kept shut away in the attic of the family home in Edinburgh. Later, Conan Doyle's mother, Mary, unable to cope with her husband's behaviour, arranged for him to be locked up in an asylum.

'In those days, there was no sensitive treatment for alcoholism,' Henshall explains. 'You were stuck in a sanatorium: an asylum, essentially. Arthur and his mother found themselves in a terrible position. This man was ruining their lives, but should they have him released from the asylum or not? In the end, they were both complicit in him being kept there.'

When Charles finally died in 1893, Arthur – 34 and already a successful writer – was racked with grief and guilt. Soon afterwards he endured another bitter blow: his wife, Louise, was diagnosed with tuberculosis. Conan Doyle, a qualified doctor, would nurse his consumptive wife for the next 13 years.

Later, Conan Doyle took an extraordinary step. With his father dead and his wife dying, he decided to kill off the detective with whom he was indelibly, but annoyingly associated. As he wrote to his mother: 'I am weary of his name.' He dispatched Sherlock Holmes to his death at the end of that year, in a short story called The Final Problem, in which Holmes plunges down a Swiss waterfall locked in lethal combat with his old enemy Moriarty, 'the Napoleon of crime'.

Holmes fans were devastated. Mourners wore black armbands, while Conan Doyle himself was threatened and insulted. Unperturbed, he maintained that Holmes's demise was justifiable homicide.

But why did Conan Doyle kill off the detective who brought him fame and fortune? 'The history behind it was difficult to bear,' says Henshall. 'He associated Holmes with his father, and the guilt he felt about him became wrapped up with his writing. Also, Holmes was a cocaine addict. When his father died, he wanted to get away from that.'

For Henshall, playing Arthur Conan Doyle brought back memories of his own family; not struggles with an ailing father; he says, but Conan Doyle's closeness to his mother, the formidable Mary (played in the drama by Sinead Cusack). 'Conan Doyle's relationship with his mother was very important,' Henshall insists. 'I was brought up in a female household, with two sisters and a strong-willed mother, so, from that point of view, I can relate to him.'

Henshall, 39, was very close to his mother, who died eight years ago. Talking about her death publicly for the first time, the notoriously private actor softens. 'She had a massive coronary while watching a documentary about Terry-Thomas [the gap-toothed comedy actor]. You could say she died laughing. It took the ambulance man 15 minutes to get her heart started again. I was on stage in London at the time, and got home from a party to find she was in hospital. I knew that it was serious.'

Rushing to Glasgow, Henshall joined his family at her bedside. 'She was on life-support for 36 hours, but she didn't regain consciousness,' he says quietly. 'Too much damage had been done in that 15 minutes. Then the doctors took out the tubes and turned off the machine that was keeping her heart going. It was quite nice, actually – as much as something like that can be. It brought us together.'

The gap left by his mother is evident. 'She knew me back to front,' he says wryly. 'Mothers do, don't they? Someone said to me, "Of course your mother knows how to push your buttons. She's the one who sewed them on." And that's right.' Had he been her favourite child? 'I was the youngest, blond-haired and blue-eyed. I was cursed from day one,' he jokes. 'I was certainly her favourite son.'

Playing Conan Doyle brought back memories of watching old Sherlock Holmes films as a child. 'My mother was a huge Basil Rathbone fan,' he remembers. 'I loved him and Jeremy Brett [who played Holmes for television in the 1980s and 1990s]. But I'd never read the books until I did this. The stories were fantastic and I read them just for pleasure. I didn't know much about Conan Doyle, to my shame, as I ought to have done. He was an extraordinary man.'

We meet at Ardgowan, an impressive stately home outside Glasgow. With its opulent rooms and air of genteel decay, it provides a perfect location for filming. Henshall, attired as a Victorian gentleman, also looks the part, complete with a prominent ginger moustache.

Growing up in Barrhead, near Glasgow, he first became involved with acting through the Scottish Youth Theatre. 'It looked like great fun, but I never quite had the courage to audition. Then, a girl I had a massive crush on told me I'd look good on stage. I was easily flattered. I thought "My God, maybe." I auditioned, and realised she'd been very clever: they badly needed more guys. However, it got me in.' And did it get him the girl? 'It didn't get me the girl – but it got me a career.'

At 18, abandoning his dreams of becoming a sports journalist, Henshall headed south to train at the Mountview drama school in north London. Still, success seemed a distant prospect. 'I never went into this business because I wanted to be famous. The idea of success didn't seem possible, really.'

In fact, Henshell's star has soared rapidly. His first big break was working with Dennis Potter in the acclaimed Lipstick On Your Collar, and since then he has starred in the Channel 4 drama Psychos. Currently on stage in Death Of A Salesman in London, playing Willie Loman's troubled son Biff, Henshall seems tailor-made for moody, misunderstood heroes who set female hearts aflutter.

Briefly married in his 20s, Henshall had a short but high-profile relationship with the model Sophie Dahl, whom he met during a radio production of Romeo and Juliet. His private life today remains – as he likes it – private. 'When he was suggested for Arthur Conan Doyle, I thought he was perfect,' confirms the drama's writer David Pirie. 'He conveys a sense of physical and mental turmoil – Conan Doyle's inner world, the stuff he doesn't want to show.'

But how much of The Strange Case Of Sherlock Holmes & Arthur Conan Doyle is true? The BBC calls it a 'fictional exploration' – and, as the drama unfolds and a mysterious biographer arrives to solve the riddles of Conan Doyle's life, it is clear that art is taking over from fact.

Nonetheless, its themes are rooted in reality. As he grew older, Conan Doyle became increasingly drawn to spiritualism. He attended séances, trying in vain to make contact with his dead father. Ironically, the man who, through his creation of Sherlock Holmes, displayed such breathtaking logic, preferred a far more ethereal approach in his own life. His spiritualist involvement was widely mocked when he endorsed pictures of fairies cavorting in an English garden – the photographs were soon exposed as fakes.

Conan Doyle's relationship with Jean Leckie, a young Scotswoman 14 years his junior, whom he met in 1897, is based on fact. He fell in love with a passion exceeding anything he had felt for his wife. But he still cared for the invalid Louise, pledging to nurse, cherish and be faithful to her until death. His relationship with Jean remained platonic. Little wonder if, as David Pirie suggests, the author's mind became unhinged. Pirie believes that Conan Doyle suffered a sort of nervous breakdown. 'I find 1899 a very interesting year in his life,' he says. 'He had been living in Louise's sick room for years, while obviously madly in love with Jean. His books weren't very successful at this point, and his reading public desperately wanted him to bring back Sherlock Holmes. The whole thing became untethered. There was no public breakdown; life continued solidly in the proper Victorian manner. But something was going on'.

By the following year, however, the crisis in Conan Doyle's life was resolved. Aged 40, he determined to fight in the Boer War. Rejected as a soldier, he served as a doctor instead, tending injured British soldiers at Bloemfontein. Conan Doyle was shocked by the chaos and suffering of war, yet his own mental turmoil seems to have been relieved. By the time he returned, in 1900, his mind was calmer. The old haunting images, of bloodied faces and severed ears, was gone.

And, to the joy of fans, he resurrected Holmes in The Return of Sherlock Holmes and The Hound of the Baskervilles, published the following year. The tale of the ghostly Dartmoor dog became a worldwide sensation and the most popular of all the Holmes books.

Louise died in 1906, and it was said Conan Doyle wept like a baby. A year later, he married Jean, the great love of his life. As he wrote in his memoirs, ' the sunshine of my Indian summer now deepens into a golden autumn'. As he neared his 50th birthday, the creator of Sherlock Holmes had faced down his own demons.

THE DAILY TELEGRAPH Saturday, July 23, 2005

Why Holmes was murdered

Was Arthur Conan Doyle's decision to kill off his famous sleuth connected with his mad father and terminally ill wife? TV writer **David Pirie** offers a solution to a mystery.

In May 4, 1891, Sir Arthur Conan Doyle committed a murder. With a few strokes of his pen, the author sent Sherlock Holmes plummeting down into the "dreadful cauldron" of the Reichenbach Falls, destroying his own star character, and creating one of the most enduring mysteries in literary history. The deerstalker-wearing detective was the sole source of Doyle's fame and a character that could bring in a million pounds in today's money for a single set of stories. Why, after two years of popular success, did Doyle send Holmes to his death?

My quest to solve this mystery began one winter morning at Paddington station, with a phone call from a TV producer inviting me to write a drama on Doyle. I am no obsessive Sherlockian, just a screenwriter who had read and loved the Holmes stories from childhood, but when the producer suggested it was time to approach Doyle's stories from a new angle by taking a look at the author's own life, I was too intrigued to refuse the challenge.

But Doyle had no intention of making biographical investigations easy. Almost everything I knew about him – the public man of letters, the amateur scientist, the believer in spiritualism, the crusader for good causes – dated from the last two decades of his life. About the first 50 years, which included the creation and dispatch of Holmes, nearly all his greatest books and most formative moments, far less was known.

There are no published letters (from a man whose correspondence was legendary). Nor has a single biographer ever had unfettered access to Doyle's papers. It almost felt like the author had covered his tracks; but how? The answer was part skill, part chance. After his death, Doyle's own reluctance to reveal the more personal side of his life was honoured by his sons. When the last surviving heir, Adrian Conan Doyle, died in 1970, the embargo might have been lifted. But, instead, a protracted legal dispute about the ownership of Doyle's papers began, and continued for decades.

Examining the clues that have emerged in the work of recent biographers such as Michael Baker, the image of Doyle as the safe, dull, solid Victorian vanishes. Early sections of his life in Edinburgh were harrowing, reflecting violent hues and patterns of his beloved Edgar Allan Poe. Doyle's father Charles was a talented (yet failing) artist, who specialised in the most macabre and supernatural subjects, and who gradually lost his senses through alcoholism and manic depression. Such a thing would be bad enough for any family today: in the respectable Edinburgh of the 1870s, the stigma must have been unbearable for the young Doyle.

Eventually, Charles Doyle became an inmate of (at least) three asylums, from one of which he attempted to escape. By the end, it seems, there was little contact with his family, and four years before his death he declared they had forgotten him. He wrote of himself bitterly as "a madman" and claimed that he kept sending them paintings that were never acknowledged.

Then there is the shadowy figure of a good-looking aristocratic doctor, only six years Doyle's senior, called Bryan Waller. Waller assumed control over the household. Doyle came to hate him with a passion. The exact nature of Waller's relations with Doyle's mother remains unclear but about the character of the man there is no confusion whatsoever. No one seems in any doubt that he was an arrogant, snobbish, cruel and imperious aristocrat – every inch the villain.

The cast of amazing characters in the young Doyle's life didn't end there. If he found torture at home he encountered a true hero at university. Charismatic, dark and handsome with the long fingers of a pianist and the aquiline features of an actor, Dr Joseph Bell was one of the foremost medical academics of his generation. The doctor employed Doyle as his medical clerk, becoming the young writer's guide and ultimately inspiring, as Doyle himself acknowledged, the birth of Sherlock Holmes.

I used some of this as the basis for the screenplay of my detective drama *Murder Rooms*. The high ratings for this when it screened in 2000 suggested that there was still a huge audience for Doyle. So when I was invited to write a drama about his life, I jumped at the chance to return to the subject and consider the decade in which Doyle actually did the deed and killed off his detective.

The last decade of the 19th.century was almost more extraordinary for Doyle than anything that had preceded it. Doyle was by now perhaps the most famous writer in the world but his wife, Louise, had been diagnosed with terminal consumption. The author was under enormous pressure, and friends remarked that his posture became rigid. He wrote in confidence to his mother of suffering nerves "more than most people know".

On October 10, 1883, Doyle's father died at the Crichton Royal Asylum in Dumfries, and, though details are sketchy, there is evidence that the end was expected for some time. Two months later, in spite of desperate pleading from everyone around him, including his mother, Doyle finally went to print with his detective's own death at the Reichenbach Falls. Almost immediately, there was a great public backlash. And then, as if all this were not dramatic enough, Doyle, who already felt guilty about his failure to diagnose his wife's consumption in time to save her, fell deeply in love with another woman, the darkly captivating Jean Leckie.

Throughout his life, Doyle did what he could to conceal these startling events, and the emotional turmoil they inspired. But in the process of writing the screenplay for *The Strange Case of Sherlock Holmes and Arthur Conan Doyle*, I became convinced that these were the experiences that inspired not only the creation of Holmes, but also the pain that led Doyle to send his great detective over the cliff into the foaming waters of the Reichenbach.

THE SUNDAY POST/**July 24, 2005**

Television highlights by Kevin Bridges

Arthur Conan Doyle received hate mail

Outrage after the death of Sherlock

Ask most folk how they imagine legendary writer Arthur Conan Doyle and they'll probably conjure up a picture of a rather straight-laced gent.

They probably don't expect the Scot who created the immortal Sherlock Holmes to have ever been a young man with a turbulent private life.

Your perception of the author should change if you tune in to the new period drama from BBC Scotland, *The Strange Case Of Sherlock Holmes And Arthur Conan Doyle*.

Based on real events, the drama deals with the period when Doyle decided to kill off his beloved detective creation.

The decision caused outrage among his countless fans and Doyle received hate mail.

Asylum

Well, imagine what would happen if JK Rowling decided to make Harry Potter a villain!

What made matters worse for Doyle was that his wife Louise contracted TB, his father died in an asylum and Doyle found himself falling for another woman. Enough meaty drama for anyone!

Scottish actor Douglas Henshall was more than happy to get his teeth into the role of Doyle.

"I really like the way we play everyone as real human beings with feelings and emotions, rather than buttoned-up archetypes of Victorian times."

Douglas, like most people, had read a few Sherlock Holmes mysteries when he was younger, but decided to immerse himself in the stories once he got this part.

"I found I enjoyed them so much I actually read them all just for pleasure. They're a great read and I also love all the films. Basil Rathbone and Jeremy Brett were great as Holmes."

The role was a first for Douglas as he found himself playing a real person and, what's more, he had the chance to actually listen to a rare recording of Doyle talking.

"Few people really know what Doyle sounded like and anyway the performance isn't about giving an impersonation – as an actor you just go with your feeling for the character."

He was also pleased that it allowed him to work in Scotland, as the entire drama was shot entirely on location north of the border.

They used real country homes such as Ardgowan House in Inverclyde and Hunterstone House in Ayrshire.

There was an aspect of the character he didn't care for – the fact he needed to have a moustache.

"I didn't like having glue on my face and I didn't want to have to spend hours in make-up, so I grew my own moustache. But as soon as it was feasible it came off."

This new one-off drama helps reveal a little of the mystery of the man who has brought so much pleasure to millions and still does by dealing with the basic facts of the story.

Almost elementary in fact!

What follows are a selection of previews and reviews of the drama.

Radio Times 23-29 JULY 2005

TODAY'S CHOICES By **Alison Graham**
The title says it all really – this truly is a very strange tale, an odd, dark drama about the birth and death of Arthur Conan Doyle's creation, Sherlock Holmes.

Douglas Henshall does a good job as the troubled Doyle, tormented by his father's death in a lunatic asylum, and Tim McInnerny is riveting as his funereal, mysterious biographer Selden. The scenes between the two of them are the highlights of what is an otherwise slow-moving, vaguely supernatural essay from writer David Pirie (who wrote *Murder Rooms: the Dark Beginnings of Sherlock Holmes*). It purports to look at the demons that drove Doyle to create Holmes, then to kill him off, albeit temporarily, during that last tussle with Moriarty at the Reichenbach Falls.

Brian Cox, too, makes a few brief appearances as Doyle's mentor and the supposed model for Holmes, the brilliant forensic investigator Joseph Bell.

It's a curious piece that doesn't end particularly satisfactorily, though there's a nice sense of place and period. And connoisseurs of such things will be delighted to note that it features a very fine example of Costume Drama Cough from Doyle's ailing wife.

The Daily Telegraph Television & Radio 23-29 July 2005

Pick of the Day by CHRIS RILEY

An impressive Douglas Henshall plays Sherlock Holmes's creator Arthur Conan Doyle in David Pirie's drama. Pirie wrote the BBC's *Murder Rooms* stories spun around the relationship between the student Doyle and his Edinburgh University mentor, pioneering criminologist Dr. Joseph Bell. In some respects, this picks up a version of that Doyle character in his mid-30s, when married and internationally feted for his Holmes stories. It's an intriguing and thoughtful examination of a darkly troubled writer and his complex relationship with his creator. "Sherlock Holmes takes my mind from better things," cries Doyle, haunted by his past and a character he feels compelled to kill. "If I don't finish him, he could finish me." And it's a psychological mystery, too, as biographer Selden (Tim McInnerny) starts to chronicle Doyle's life and tiny but revealing shards of information – about Bell (Brian Cox), the Holmes persona and a Doyle family secret – begin to emerge. Intelligent and absorbing.

The Sunday Telegraph TV & Radio 24-30 July 2005

Programme of the day by Claire Murphy

David Pirie, the writer of the *Murder Rooms*, revisits the same milieu for another elegant Victorian Gothic, this time a dramatisation of the life of Arthur Conan Doyle (played with handsome intensity by Douglas Henshall) between the years he created then 'killed off' his most famous character, Sherlock Holmes.

After his father tragically dies in an asylum, Conan Doyle's life enters ever more turbulent waters as he cares for his dying wife, is tortured by his unconsummated passion for a new love, and attempts to put an end to his accursed creation (Holmes). References to Sherlock Holmes stories abound as Conan Doyle receives disturbing drawings and severed ears through the post, and takes a trip to Reichenbach Falls (scene of Holmes's supposed demise).

But the intrigue only gets really underway when Conan Doyle allows the shadowy Selden (Tim McInnerney, lipsmackingly sinister) to become his biographer. Gradually, Selden turns the tables on Doyle and initiates a psychological battle worthy of the great detective himself.

Daily Mail WEEKEND Wednesday 27 July 2005

Nigel Andrew's VIEW

The Strange Case Of Sherlock Holmes And Arthur Conan Doyle is a clever and impressive piece of work, taking an ingenious route through the life of the great detective's troubled creator. However, I cannot honestly say that it gripped me. The structure seemed rather contrived, even ponderous, and Douglas Henshall as Doyle somehow lacked depth. Still, I'm sure many will get more out of David Pirie's drama than I did.

PICK of the day by DANIELA SOAVE

In his time, Arthur Conan Doyle was the most famous writer in the world. His creation, Sherlock Holmes, had made him exceedingly wealthy, and he was the toast of the literary world. So why did Doyle kill off his detective, to the distress of his public and publishers? This feature-length drama, by David Pirie (who also wrote *Murder Rooms* and scripted *The Woman in White*), delves into Doyle's little-known past to reveal a dark and tortured family history that was much more closely linked to his fictional creation than his readers could imagine. Douglas Henshall stars as Doyle, Brian Cox as his mentor Joseph Bell, Sinead Cusack as Doyle's mother, and Tim McInnerny as the mysterious biographer, Selden.

THE DAILY TELEGRAPH THURSDAY, JULY 28, 2005

Last night on television

Literary deductions by **James Walton**

BBC2's **The Strange Case of Sherlock Holmes and Arthur Conan Doyle** took a while to build up any momentum. For at least 30 minutes, it consisted of short, discrete scenes from Doyle's life. He visited his alcoholic father in a mental asylum. His wife coughed up some blood. He decided to kill off Sherlock Holmes. He learned that his father had died. His wife was diagnosed with consumption. He was suddenly in the middle of an intense platonic relationship with Jean Leckie.

Each of these scenes was beautifully staged and performed. Taken as a whole, though, they were rather too short and discrete to be very gripping.

Fortunately, things then perked up with the arrival of a biographer (Tim McInnerny). Speaking in the widely hushed tones of an undertaker on Valium, Selden proved a pretty good observational detective himself. By interviewing Doyle and the people who knew him, he gradually came up with a theory of Holmes's genesis – and so brought the programme some much-needed coherence.

Summarised somewhat starkly, Selden's theory was that all those dark family secrets in Doyle's stories were linked to the shame of having a mad and drunken dad. His mother's financial and possibly sexual reliance on a young doctor whom Doyle hated was another indignity that found its way into the fiction. Later, Dr Joseph Bell became a surrogate father – and so, in a way, did Sherlock Holmes, whose deductive methods Bell famously inspired. This is why Doyle's relationship with Holmes was so weirdly troubled, going far beyond the usual resentment of authors towards the characters that upstage them.

David Pirie's script made many suggestive connections between Doyle's life and work, all backed up with apt quotations. It did a fine job too of keeping Selden genuinely mysterious. At first, he seemed to be a biographer sent by Doyle's publisher – but then we discovered that the publisher had never heard of him. So, did he actually exist? Was he a flesh-and-blood con man, a creation of Doyle's guilty conscience, or the ghost of Sherlock Holmes? The answer remained pleasingly uncertain.

But, to try a little theory of my own, whatever else he might have been, Selden surely represented as well a fantasy version of David Pirie. Pirie is clearly fascinated by Doyle. (His other work for television includes *Murder Rooms: the Dark Beginnings of Sherlock Holmes*.) As a result, he must have thoroughly enjoyed creating a character who not only cracks the central mysteries of Doyle's life using Pirie's own ideas, but also has the opportunity to have them confirmed by a squirming Doyle himself. The behaviour of a biographer towards his subject can be a ruthless, even slightly cruel business. Last night Pirie explored – and perhaps embodied – that too.

All of which might make the programme sound more like a thesis (albeit an interesting one) than a drama, and at times it probably was. Yet, the central relationship between Selden and Doyle was certainly and authentically dramatic. Essentially, it was concerned with that old chestnut about what's lurking behind a respectable Victorian façade. Nonetheless, by keeping the particulars of the case so assiduously particular, Pirie avoided laziness or cliché.

The quality of the acting also helped. Douglas Henshall powerfully conveyed just how much Doyle had at stake in seeking to guard his secrets. Tim McInnerney made Selden's endless politeness seem increasingly menacing. Meanwhile, characters that in other hands might have felt a bit thin were solidly fleshed out by a strong supporting cast – including Sinead Cusack as Doyle's mother, and, best of all, Brian Cox as Joseph Bell.

The result was undeniably an odd programme, which about halfway through still looked as if it might be too carefully constructed for its own good. That late rally, however, ensured that it ended up as an intelligent and satisfying piece of entertainment.

Daily Mail, Thursday, July 28, 2005

television **mail Conan the barbarian** by PETER PATERSON

TO MAKE a story from the life of a real historical character, it is usually best to ignore the obvious and attribute his actions and behaviour to the most complicated explanation.

Especially if you are contracted to fill 90 minutes of prime-time TV.

Filling the allotted span seemed to be a burden for last night's psycho-drama, The Strange Case Of Sherlock Holmes And Arthur Conan Doyle.

This was a tale that – for all its stylishness – required of the viewer a great deal of concentration and patience.

In essence, it was an attempt to explain why Conan Doyle, as a young novelist, abruptly killed off his most successful and lucrative character, the great detective Sherlock Holmes.

And why, a few years later, he triumphantly brought Holmes back to life, despite the entire world believing that he had died in a struggle with his greatest enemy, the evil Moriarty, when they both plunged into the seething Reichenbach Falls in Switzerland.

Nowadays, of course it is quite common for TV cynically to revive a dead character if there's thought to be sufficient commercial mileage (and audience gullability) in dusting him down for a further series: you just have to recall the second coming of Bobby Ewing in Dallas, and those of Dirty Den and Grant Mitchell in Eastenders.

But Conan Doyle's approach was far less crude than TV's. He made clear that Holmes's reappearance in the 1901 publication of The Hound of the Baskervilles, was not an act of reincarnation.

Instead, it was the recollection by the detective's companion, Doctor Watson, of an adventure which took place *before* his friend's fatal encounter with Moriarty in The Adventure of the Final Problem.

But a public disappointed by the demise of Holmes naturally preferred to believe that he was not dead after all.

David Pirie, the author of last night's biographical speculations, is a paid-up Sherlock Holmes fanatic (from which the word fan, of course, derives).

For he wrote the entertaining series, Murder Rooms, which charted the connection between Conan Doyle's creation and the pioneering criminologist Joseph Bell – a template for Holmes's method of solving crimes by observation and deduction – who was Conan Doyle's tutor at Edinburgh University.

Pirie took events in Conan Doyle's life – his wife Louise's struggle with TB and his own failure, as a doctor, to diagnose her, his guilt over his intense but platonic affair with Jean Leckie (who became his second wife), the death of his father in an asylum – and turned them into a crisis that caused him to focus his discontent on Sherlock Holmes.

His most brilliant stroke was to introduce his own fictional phantom figure into Conan Doyle's life, in the form of Tim McInnerny's Selden, a lugubrious writer researching the novelist's life for a book on the extent to which Sherlock Holmes had emerged from the experiences of his creator's troubled younger days.

Obviously, Pirie wanted to give Joseph Bell, played here by Brian Cox, his due share of credit as the original model for Sherlock Holmes, and the university scenes, with Conan Doyle listening entranced to Bell's lectures, were well done.

Darker themes also emerged. The affair with Jean Leckie (Emily Blunt), starting with a flirtation at a spiritualist séance, must have troubled Conan Doyle's conscience.

But it's hard to connect that with the extinction of Holmes, since a married man with an existing family needs money to maintain an extra relationship, even one that is unconsummated, and Sherlock Holmes was a money-making machine.

A T THE end of the 19th century, when the author was in his mid-30s, mental illness was a matter of shame, so his father's incarceration and death in a Scottish asylum was not something to be advertised.

Taking a leaf from Conan Doyle's near contemporary, Sigmund Freud, Pirie constructed another guilt trip for his subject, hinting that the author's mother abandoned her husband for a wealthy doctor.

Charles Doyle, the story implied, was not the mad monster and violent drunkard of the official family version, but a once kindly, playful and loved figure, an artist, who became ill and was betrayed by his wife and son.

Coupled with the extraordinary claim this week that Conan Doyle stole the outline of The Hound Of The Baskervilles and had the man who brought him the story poisoned by his wife (with whom Conan Doyle allegedly had an affair) to hide the fact, this is not a particularly good time for Sherlock Holmes fans.

To hear now that he let down his father and his wife, used séances to flirt with another woman and deprived millions of readers of the pleasure of his Sherlock Holmes tales in a fit of pique is all rather lowering.

Douglas Henshall, who played Conan Doyle last night, always conveyed too much brimming confidence as the successful author for us to be taken in by much of the psychology with which David Pirie surrounded him.

And I was pleased by Conan Doyle's defence of the historical novels (which I happen to prefer to the detective stories) he wrote during Holmes's absence.

Nevertheless, Pirie's final twist, that Selden was a figment of Conan Doyle's imagination, would have worked as well in a detective story as it did here.

Finally, **arts telegraph** Saturday, July 30, 2005

Television by **Martha Dunstan**

With anachronistic political correctness, Douglas Henshall was allowed only a few furtive puffs of his pipe as the creator of **The Strange Case of Sherlock Holmes and Arthur Conan Doyle**, but then literal authenticity wasn't what David Pirie's drama was striving for. The costumes were sumptuously "period" but Pirie had used his own investigation into the author's mysterious early life to make a satisfying piece that was part psychoanalysis, part historical research.

Why did the incredibly successful Doyle kill off Holmes? Was it connected to the death of his mad, alcoholic father in an asylum or the discovery, at Reichenbach Falls, of his wife's fatal TB? Could Holmes's resuscitation have had anything to do with his acceptance of his mother's affair and his own renewal and remarriage?

To investigate, Pirie furnished Doyle with a mysterious biographer, Mr Selden, whose mission was to discover the origins of Doyle's creativity. He scratched away at real family secrets and, in increasingly familiar bravura displays of logic, extrapolated Doyle's formative experiences from the author's novels. Selden naturally turned out to be Holmes himself, a character pleading with his miserable, repressed author for his literary life.

Contrived? Certainly, but infinitely more absorbing than the umpteenth remake of *The Hound of the Baskervilles*, particularly when it is as well realised as this. No one matched the accumulated power of Tim McInnerny's Selden, but it was a surprise to find that what Douglas Henshall did best on screen was fall in love – which he did quite beautifully in an Edinburgh tea room. His face was full of fluttery delight as he piled scone upon cake upon cream bun in front of his new love. Of course Emily Blunt's Jean couldn't resist him.

Chapter 15

New Books: 2005 – 2006

CHABON, M. (2005) The Final Solution. Fourth Estate (h/b)

THE DAILY TELEGRAPH Saturday, February 12, 2005

This is an edited version of an article by Michael Chabon in the Feb 12 edition of 'The New York Review of Books'.

THE MAKING OF HOLMES

No one can quite explain the lasting appeal of the Sherlock Holmes stories. Michael Chabon, whose new novella is inspired by the great detective, looks for clues in their creator's strange life.

More than 100 years after Sherlock Holmes's first appearance in print, in the pages of *Beeton's Christmas Annual* for 1887, fans and non-believers alike seem to feel compelled to try to explain the lasting appeal of Sherlock Holmes, as if the stories of the adventures with Dr Watson were a system, like semaphore or the pneumatic post, that ought long since to have been superseded. Inherent in these explanations, buried or explicit, is a feeling that the 56 stories and four short novels that make up the so-called canon are not worthy of such enduring admiration.

There has always been doubt about the literary merit of the Holmes stories and the fault lies squarely with the author. It is well known Arthur Conan Doyle regretted his Holmes work, and disparaged it: "I have had such an overdose of [Holmes]," he wrote, "that I feel towards him as I do toward pate de foie gras, of which I once ate too much, so that the name of it gives me a sickly feeling to this day." In 1893, in "The Final Problem", he made a sincere attempt to have Holmes murdered (by Prof Moriarty at Reichenbach Falls). Even the first Holmes story, *A Study in Scarlet*, suffers from the author's lack of faith in his creation, since for most of its second part it wanders forlornly, *sans* Holmes or Watson, amid the Mormon wastes of Utah.

The next Holmes adventure, *The Sign of Four*, opens with a chapter that features the first of many metacritcisms the detective would offer about the literary efforts of Dr Watson and, by extension, of the cash-strapped young doctor who held their strings. "I glanced over it," Holmes remarks to Watson, referring to *A Study in Scarlet*, and continues:

> Honestly, I cannot congratulate you upon it. Detection is, or ought to be, an exact science, and should be treated in the same cold and unemotional manner. You have attempted to tinge it with romanticism, which produces much the same effect as if you worked a love-story or an elopement into the fifth proposition of Euclid.

Some of us feel, of course, that the fifth proposition of Euclid would only be improved by a nice juicy elopement. This is a typical bit of good-humoured self-mockery, with Conan Doyle displaying the sly wit for which he is too rarely given credit. Whilst he was busy scorning the Holmes stories and planning Holmes's death (and nursing the suppurating pride of a would-be Walter Scott condemned, first by necessity and then by success, to write popular fiction), Conan Doyle was also tangibly having fun. It seems to have been characteristic of the man that he was unusually having it at his own expense.

Like most writer, Conan Doyle wrote for money. His misfortune as an artist was to make piles of it, and become famous around the World, by writing stories he did not consider worthy of his talent; and to be so freehanded in his philanthropy, wild schemes and spending habits, and so well-endowed with children, that the piles of money were never quite tall enough. Few writers wrote more determinedly for cash than Conan Doyle. That the results of this arrant and effective hack work have endured so long testifies not only to Conan Doyle's art and storytelling gift, and to the magic of the central heroic duo, but also to the quickening force – neglected, derided and denied – of money and the getting of it on a ready imagination.

Secret-sharers, deception and disguise, imposture, buried shame and repressed evil, madwoman in the attic, the court life of London, the concealment of depravity and wonder beneath the brick façade of the world – these are familiar motifs of Victorian popular literature. In 1889, JM Stoddart, the American editor of *Lippincott's Magazine*, took Oscar Wilde and another writer to lunch, over which he proposed that each man write a long story for his publication. One of his lunch guests that day went off and dreamed up a tale of an uncanny, bohemian, manic-depressive genius who stalks the yellow fog of London, takes cocaine and morphine to ease the torment of living in this "dreary, dismal, unprofitable world", and abates his drug habit by compulsively scheming to peel back the surface of other people's lives, betraying secret histories of violence and vice. Stoddart published Conan Doyle's second Holmes story as *The Sign of Four*. Wilde, for his part, turned in *The Picture of Dorian Gray*.

The Victorian habit of seeing double, of reading hidden shame into ordinary human lives, reached its peak with the detective stories of Sigmund Freud, and persists to our time. It is tempting to read Conan Doyle's biography as a classic Victorian narrative of this kind, of success haunted by shameful failure, marital fidelity that conceals adulterous love, robust scientific positivism that masks deep credulity.

Conan Doyle's life was founded on a series of braided pairs: Irishman and Scotsman, Celt and Englishman, doctor and novelist, athlete and aesthete, loving family man and callous wanderer, champion of truth and inveterate concealer.

The series was perfected by Holmes and Watson, an archetypal pair who have only Quixote and Sancho as rivals in the hearts of readers and in the annals of imaginary friendship, that record of widely limited men who find in each other, and only in each other, the stuff, sense and passion of one whole man.

Arthur Conan Doyle was the grandson of a caricaturist, the nephew of the designer of the original cover of *Punch*, and the son of Charles Doyle, an architect and painter who died, in a sanatorium, of drink and of a bitter, self-aware madness that sees itself as damnation through an excess of sanity. His was the kind of madness that reads the random text of the natural world and finds messages and secret connections, the agency of elves and demons and other liminal beings. Charles Doyle burdened his son with an eccentric way of looking at the world, of making it, against all reason, cohere. The father's fecklessness, epilepsy, alcoholism and eventual committal to an institution were for the son the black axioms of existence, never acknowledged, sometimes denied.

Conan Doyle's mother, Mary, whom he always called "the Ma'am", seems to have been a model of Victorian motherhood, beribboned, cased in whalebone. She was also an Irishwoman who thrilled and terrified her children by the fireside, on long winter evenings, with ghost stories and legends of heroes and *sidhe*, or fairy people. A mother of 10 (seven of whom survived childhood), a model of propriety, modesty and self-sacrifice, she none the less maintained a long relationship with a lodger 15 years her junior. Evidence of a sexual liaison between her and the lodger, a pathologist named Bryan Waller, is scanty but suggestive. Waller's residence in the Doyle house predated the institutionalism of Conan Doyle's father, as did the birth of Mary's last child, a girl who was given the name Bryan Julia Doyle. Julia being the name of Waller's mother. It does not require "the most perfect reasoning and observing mind the world has ever known" to draw the readiest conclusion. When Waller bought a house in Yorkshire, he took Mary and Bryan Doyle to live with him. He supported young Arthur financially, and Conan Doyle's decision to attend medical school was almost certainly determined by the wishes of his mother's mysteriously powerful lodger. And yet, in all his autobiographical writings and letters, he never mentioned Bryan Waller, neither to thank him nor to settle a score. There is an enigmatic reference in his memoirs: "My mother has adopted the device of sharing a large house, which may have eased her in some ways, but was disastrous in others."

A number of Holmes stories centre on the activities of sinister lodgers in boarding houses, machinating step-parents, or people who keep their loved ones locked away. Reproachful ghosts of the immured father, imprisoned for his own supposed good can be glimpsed in the eponymous figure of "The Adventure of the Blanched Soldier" – the Boer War veteran hidden in a "detached building of some size" on the family estate in the belief that he had contracted leprosy in Africa. Freud might conclude that Conan Doyle never entirely recovered from the pain and humiliation of watching his mother cuckold his demented father in his own house, and then being obliged to stand by as the old man was packed off to the Montrose Royal Lunatic Asylum, never to return.

(**Compiler's note**: In fact, Doyle's father died on October 10 at the Crighton Royal Institution, a mental hospital near Dumfries, according to Stashower's biography).

Conan Doyle's home life was played out in a city that mirrored its duality and duplicity. Edinburgh in the 19th century embodied the Jekyll-and-Hyde impulses of the Victorian mind. It consisted of two distinct cities, the Old Town and the New. The old medieval centre, "this accursed, stinking, reeky mass of stones and lime and dung", as Thomas Carlyle called it, was notorious throughout Europe for its foulness. At the end of the 18th century, it had, like Charles Doyle, been supplanted, though not fully replaced, by a stately city of grey stone, erected on a ridge to the north of the old burgh.

This partly successful act of deliberate moral self-improvement reflected the predicament, and the achievement, of Conan Doyle himself, who lived his dreary and anxious childhood amid failure, genteel poverty, and the unimaginable oblivion of his father, on the one hand, and the relative fame and splendour of his successful, artistic Doyle grandfather and uncles in far-off London; between the weird, Irish-Catholic world of his mother's hearth tales and the overtly empirical, Protestant narrative of urban Victorian Scotland.

In medical school at Edinburgh University, Conan Doyle got a decisive demonstration that his father's way of reading the world for messages could be combined with his mother's gift for making a story. In 1876, he began attending lectures and working as a clerk in the Royal Infirmary, presided over by Dr Joseph Bell, FRCS, an ingenious practitioner of what might be called narrative diagnostics. We might also call it prose fiction, or the science of detection.

Joe Bell was a legend of the medical school. His favourite trick – he relished, like the character he would one day inspire, the *coup de theatre* – was to diagnose patients in the waiting room without speaking to or directly examining them. As Dr Harold Emery Jones recorded it in a memoir:

> Gentlemen, a fisherman! You will notice that, though this is a very hot summer's day, the patient is wearing top-boots. When he sat on the chair they were plainly visible. No one but a sailor would wear top-boots at this season of the year. He is concealing a quid of tobacco in the furthest corner of his mouth and manages it very adroitly indeed gentlemen...Further, to prove the correctness of these deductions, I noticed several fish-scales adhering to his clothes and hands, while the odour of fish announced his arrival in a most marked and striking manner.

The principle behind these feats of inspired guessing, of taking the sum of a set of physical facts, many of them not apparent to the untrained eye, and checking them against an internal reservoir of knowledge based on prior observation, was to awaken the young Conan Doyle to the wealth of signs, symptoms and shortcuts a patient provided. The patient came in spouting and strewing great fiery gouts of information; he or she was a Petri dish of facts that it required only patience and a highly trained eye to read and diagnose.

But such observational and interpersonal skills were not the whole of the doctoring game, any more than they are for writers and detectives. To succeed as a narrative diagnostician, or a novelist, or a detective, you also needed the art that, if you were Conan Doyle, you learned from your mother: you needed the feeling for story, both for the "history" to be inferred from the signs and symptoms and for the way that story could be reconstructed, in therapeutic terms, for the benefit of the patient. Bell treated his patients, in part, by telling them their own stories, as if threading a coherent narrative were itself a therapy.

Conan Doyle had little luck, and took as little pleasure, in his chosen career. (At least one writer has suggested that he might have managed to kill a patient, through ineptitude or otherwise; he subsequently married the dead man's sister, and took control of the income that she inherited from her brother.) Like so many Scotsmen of his time, those engineers, overseers, managers, merchant princes, foot soldiers, and rationalisers of the Empire, Conan Doyle had a powerful taste for adventure. In seeking to elude the fate that Waller, his personal Moriarty, had determined for him, Conan Doyle made two inconclusive or ill-fated attempts at becoming a ship's doctor, and a rash and doomed decision to abandon general practice for the study, in Germany, of ophthalmology, in spite of the fact that he barely understood German.

In his late twenties, Conan Doyle found himself stuck in a series of difficult, tedious or failing medical practices, with a young wife whose health was poor and the first of his eventual five children to support, indebted, too proud in his agnosticism to go to his devout Doyle relations for help, yearning for the kind of adventure that his mother's stories had kindled in him. His horizons were lowering, his promise going unredeemed. He had witnessed Joseph Bell work a kind of salvation, through storytelling, in the infirmary in Edinburgh. It may have been inevitable that his thoughts would turn to Bell now as, trapped in his desolate consulting rooms, like Holmes taking up the cocaine needle, he took up his pen.

I know I run the risk of hokum in dwelling very long on the connection, at least as old as Rabelais, between doctors and literature, storytelling and healing. So I'll just mention that when the first dozen Holmes stories were collected and published in *The Adventures of Sherlock Holmes*, a book that made Conan Doyle famous and rich, and saved him forever from the life he had never resigned himself to living out, they came dedicated to Dr Joseph Bell.

THE DAILY TELEGRAPH Saturday, February 19, 2005

NOVEL OF THE WEEK **The Final Solution** by **Michael Chabon**

There's a healthy dollop of Conan Doyle in this charming war-time detective story, argues **Benjamin Markovits**

The parrot holds the key

Michael Chabon is, in his way, a writer's writer. He is still moved by the child's ambition to write, the romance of the novelist: someone who suffers from what he calls "the midnight disease". Chabon has the air of a good schoolteacher, who uses strange words precisely – "aspergillum" or "echolalia" – and shows a highbrow relish for low slang: suitcases, for example, are always "grips". His characters, naturally enough, talk like people in books, but that's partly because they are the kind of people who aspire to talk that way. Pupillages play a part in his stories. His heroes are usually either teaching or being taught how to write, or how the world works, or both. What connects the two kinds of knowledge is the budding writer's necessary faith that the world is simple enough to be imagined. From scratch. *The Final Solution*, Chabon's new book, more novella than novel, bears the imprint of his taste in reading. It's a kind of war-time detective story. A Jewish evacuee, a mute boy with a parrot, arrives in the English countryside in the summer of 1944. The parrot sings and talks for the silent child, erupting from time to time into strings of German numbers. Various parties have an interest in deciphering these lists: are they part of a secret military code, or perhaps the account numbers to a Swiss stash? Mr Shane, who lodges with the boy's hosts (posing as a milking equipment salesman), is killed trying to steal the bird, which disappears. A retired detective, an old man on his last legs, and his last case, tries to find the parrot for the boy's sake, and stumbles on the murderer.

It's a light story in both senses of that phrase: short and sweet. And it's hard to know what to make of the mostly shirked heaviness the plot shoulders on Chabon: Holocaust, murder, London in the Blitz. One of Chabon's gifts as a writer is the fatal facility to make anything pleasant in the telling, and *The Final Solution* is further evidence of that talent. Chabon always writes like he's having fun, like he's writing a book he wouldn't mind picking up himself: "he has heard the tales, the legends, the wild, famous leaps of induction pulled off by the old man in his heyday, assassins inferred from cigar ash, horse thieves from the absence of a watchdog's bark". There's a healthy dollop of Conan Doyle here, and the novella contains other ingredients from the larder of good reads, including bumbling constables, drunk vicars, teasing puzzles and talking animals. And the sum, more or less, lives up to its parts.

Still, there's something unsettling about the deployment of so many literary tricks. Writing, of course, isn't easy: and Chabon's *Wonder Boys* (1995) is an amusing commentary on the many ways a novelist has of getting lost. Brevity, in it's narrator's view, is the holy grail, always sought, sometimes found, usually lost again; writers go wrong when they try to match the world in complex length. According to that standard, *The Final Problem* is an absolute triumph.

Its charm is really the charm of the imagination itself: how easy revelation seems, in book at least. And Chabon likes to tease his characters with it. One of the boy's hosts suddenly sees that he is a "faithless middle-aged minister, drunk and in flight from the ruin of his life". He relishes the illusion, as he accompanies the old detective in his search for the lost parrot, "that they were penetrating to the heart of some authentic mystery of London, or perhaps of life itself", that "he might discover some elucidation of the heartbreaking clockwork of the world". It's a nice idea and Chabon knowingly indulges the character, though the novelist is smart enough, at other times, to insist on "the world's beautiful refusal to yield up its mysteries without a fight".

In this context, the old man's detection is really a stand-in for Chabon's other writerly obsessions. The character has begun to suffer from periodic blackouts, moments when the world appears to him unlit by the vanity of understanding: "a page of alien text". He begins to fear that it is "the insoluble problems – the false leads and cold cases – that reflected the true nature of things". The parrot's list of numbers turn out to be neither meaningless nor significant.

Such dilemmas make for wonderful reading, but I'm not sure how closely they capture the human problems of his characters. Chabon, in cooking them up, has gone heavier on epiphany than circumstance. This, too, belongs to the romance of the novelist: that everything can be beautifully explained: that it's the explanations that matter. *The Final Solution* is perched, not quite comfortably, between fable and whodunit: genres with a very different interest in the facts of the case. It is to the novel's credit that it doesn't belong to either?

THE DAILY TELEGRAPH Saturday, March 5, 2005

BOOK CLUB *The Final Solution* had readers on tenterhooks finds **James Francken**

'A deliciously easy read'

Jocelyn, the woman who runs the reading group in Karen Joy Fowler's rollicking novel *The Jane Austen Book Club*, likes to dig her heels in. She has no time for trash and wants to handpick every member of her "all-Jane-Austen-all-the-time" club. At first, it appears as though men will not be allowed to take part – they pontificate rather than communicate, one character says, and they talk more than their fair share. Besides, "men don't do book clubs. They see reading as a solitary pleasure. When they read at all."

Men were in the minority when the book group attached to the West End Bookshop in West Hamstead, London, met to discuss the second selection of *The Daily Telegraph* Book Club, Michael Chabon's slim, Sherlock Holmes-inspired novel, *The Final Solution*. And for most of the evening they managed to play by the rules. The club has grappled with some big books: members are expected to read at a clip and they steamed through *Don Quixote* and *Moby Dick* in their first two months. The last book they took on was Saul Bellow's *Henderson the Rain King*. Chabon's 127-page wartime detective story was going to be a quick read. Helen was not the only person in the group to look at the novel for a second time. The first time through she put herself in the place of the detective, trying to pick up clues and puzzle out the central, knotty problem. Only on a second reading could she make sense of the book as a whole, and tidy up its loose ends. The novel poses a mystery that is never satisfactorily explained: Linus, a young boy who has escaped the Nazis and lives on the South Downs, has an African grey parrot that jabbers a sequence of numbers in German. Are they a secret naval code or the key to a Swiss bank account?

The sleuths in the book group homed in on the question. For Jerry, the string of numbers brought to mind the tattoos of concentration camp victims. Marie thought they had something to do with the numbers on the sides of the train carriages that were bound for the camps. Susan agreed, and pointed to the final line of the novel – which draws attention to "the clamour of the passing train" – as evidence.

But Mimi, who enjoyed getting caught up in the novel's arcana, scuppered this interpretation. She described her husband as a "serious train enthusiast" whose photographs of freight wagons of the period showed that the parrot's sequence of numbers didn't match the numbers on the cars. Could Chabon have got his facts wrong? The detective in the novel is a beekeeper; Mimi had "done her research" and asked a beekeeping friend how accurate the details were. He thought that they were spot on. But at one point in the story we are told that the detective "fastened all the zips of his bee suit". The novel is set in 1944 – and in 1944 would the suits have had zips?

The identity of Chabon's unnamed detective is fudged. Mimi thought that the character was an older version of Sherlock Holmes – Marie was unconvinced – and their discussion led on to the question of the novelist's prose style. Val found the book convoluted and overly descriptive at times; Janet, who brought her copy of *The Collected Sherlock Holmes* to the meeting, thought that the original Holmes stories were pacier and more conversational than Chabon's novel. Jim agreed: "Could you imagine Conan Doyle having written this book?"

Elspeth enjoyed the novel's old fashioned feel and its use of arcane language – looking up words such as "echolalia" in the dictionary gave her the sense of having learned something from the book. But Andy argued that the novel had its shortcomings and took aim at passages that he considered to be overwrought. He singled out three eye-glazing sentences: Chabon, in his mind, was guilty of "pretending to be Henry

James". Jerry tried to talk about Chabon's outdated use of punctuation, but the conversation was brought to a standstill by Marie: "I want to read the book, I don't want to take a PhD in it. I didn't notice the punctuation marks – and more importantly, it was a delicious easy read."

This, finally, was the consensus: the group agreed that *The Final Solution* had its faults, but felt that Chabon should be let off lightly. His novel had kept their attention, and they had to read to the end with escalating pleasure.

Arthur & George by Julian Barnes 2005 Jonathan Cape

The Sunday Telegraph Magazine 3 July 2005

The inconsistent novelist

Julian Barnes sets out to reinvent himself as a writer each time he brings out a new book – one reason why his many readers adore him. Is the novelist as unpredictable in person as he is on the page? **Nigel Farndale** finds out.

Though known as 'Barnesy' to his friends, Julian Barnes doesn't seem like a Barnesy when you meet him. Nor does he strike you as being much of a 'Jules', which is what Martin Amis used to call him before they had their falling out a few years ago. (It was over…Well, we'll come to that, or at least I will, because he prefers not to discuss it.) Both nicknames seem too frivolous for a serious novelist, or rather for a novelist who can be wry, but who takes himself, and his craft, seriously.

Julian Barnes seems like what he is, a Julian Barnes: tall, self-contained 59-year-old with a slightly fussy, Victorian air about him. Perhaps it is something to do with his appearance: the side-parted mousy hair, the pale-blue, unblinking eyes, the long, thin nose, and the one-sided smile – a 19th –century parson with a furtive passion for fly-fishing and antiquarian books. Today he has a cold, but he doesn't allow that to interfere with his routine: whenever he has lunch at the Lord Palmerston, a bare, wooden-floored pub around the corner from his house in Tufnell Park, north London, he asks for a single glass of red wine and a bowl of pasta. His life is ordered. He does not seek variety, except in his writing. His new book, *Arthur & George*, is typical of his novels – in that it is unlike the rest. The Arthur is Arthur Conan Doyle. The George is George Edalji, a solicitor whose father is Indian and mother Scottish. In the novel, based on a true case, George is falsely accused of slashing horses. He is arrested, tried and sentenced to seven years' hard labour. Incensed at this racially motivated miscarriage of justice, Doyle seeks to clear Edalji's name. The form of the book is unusual, alternating every few pages between the seemingly separate stories of Arthur and George. When I ask Barnes about his apparent aversion to literary convention, he delivers a forkful of pasta to his mouth, chews on it thoughtfully for a moment and swallows. 'It is a combination of literary principle and paranoia about repeating myself,' he says. 'It is also out of boredom. There has to be some sort of technical challenge. In this case I found it an interesting exercise to see how long I could keep the two central characters and their stories apart.'

Barnes does not hold with the view that the author's biography or psychological landscape is relevant to a novel. 'The answers are in the work,' he typically explains.

I'm sure that he is sincere in his belief that a literary principle is at stake, but it may also be a convenient camouflage. After all, literary gossip, like literary convention clearly bores him – and there was quite a bit of it a few years ago when his wife, the literary agent Pat Kavanagh, whom he married in 1979, had a brief fling with the novelist Jeanette Winterson. There was also much gossip when Martin Amis left Kavanagh's agency after 23 years and went with the American agent Andrew 'the Jackal' Wylie instead. In response to this Barnes wrote a letter to Amis in which, among other things, he told his former friend to 'f...off'. Amis called it a 'blunderingly ugly' and 'self-defeating' letter. These uncomfortable episodes, then, are presumably part of the reason why Barnes argues that curiosity about a writer's life is redundant. And yet it does seem to have a bearing on his latest novel. I remember hearing him on *Desert Island Discs* a few years ago when he revealed that he is obsessed by the subject of death, that he thinks about it every day. And towards the end of *Arthur & George* there is a passage in which George looks across Hyde Park towards the Albert Memorial and realises with horror that he and everyone else there is mortal: 'He returned the binoculars to their case, and moved his attention from the monochrome, frozen figures to the colourful, moving ones around him, from the sculpted frieze to the living one. And in that moment, George was struck by the realisation that everyone was going to be dead…the woman with the parasol would be dead, and her mother next to her dead sooner, and those small children dead later…'

Surely he, the author, is speaking through his 'fictional' George in this instance? 'No, because George comes to this realisation late in life whereas I was about 13 when it hit me. There are moments for me, when life seems at its most celebratory and flamboyant, that I notice that it is all going to come to an end. There are times I can be relied upon to think about death, one of them being whenever I watch a Six Nations rugby match. Right at the beginning of the match I will think about being dead. It's now in the wiring of my brain. It must be because I find I can almost lose myself in the pleasure of watching rugby. Almost. It's as if I have to remind myself about death at all times, even though I don't get anywhere thinking about it in this way. I don't become wiser about it or more accepting of it.'

Barnes's parents – both French teachers – died within a few years of each other in the 1990s. I ask if their deaths heightened his sense of moral panic. 'Not really. When I was young I had a sense of their being two barriers between me and death, my grandparents and my parents. What I didn't appreciate then, and do now, is that death is on a parallel track to you all the time. There is no rule about when you die; it doesn't have to be after your parents. War, after all, is when parents bury their children.' Does he like to keep his affairs in order in case he dies unexpectedly? 'I used to have a severe fear of flying and though I am better about it now I always clear my desk before a flight. I also find my self writing unnecessary cards or thank-you notes to people, ones I don't really need to send. At the back of my head is the thought, "Well, at least another person will think I'm a good guy if I die." Then I get back from holiday and start writing vile letters to everybody again."

After graduating from Oxford in 1968 with a degree in modern languages, Barnes became a lexicographer. He the trained as a lawyer but, shortly after passing his Bar finals, he became a journalist instead, joining the *New Statesman* in the late 1970s. The editor of the magazine then was Anthony Howard and so Barnes became one of what was known in Fleet Street as 'Howard's boys' – Christopher Hitchens, Martin Amis,

James Fenton, Blake Morrison, Russell Davies and Clive James – a prodigiously talented group of young *New Statesman* writers who became firm friends. Was it all chain-smoking, wisecracking and debating the finer points of *Das Kapital* into the small hours? 'Not really. There was a lot of ping-pong though.'

Was he quite useful with a ping-pong ball? 'Pathetically, I can still remember I was both tennis and table-tennis champion of the *New Statesman*. Given that there were only about 15 people working there and some of them were drunk it wasn't much of an achievement.' A sip of red wine. A lopsided smile. 'For me there was no point in playing tennis unless you wanted to win. I didn't see it as an aesthetic exercise. If I lost I'd feel terrible. I'd be very grumpy for a few hours afterwards.' He shakes his head at the memory. 'I've given up tennis now. The only thing I still play competitively is snooker. Now I care more about making a good break than winning badly. I'm getting there. By the time I'm too old to play I'll have the right attitude to sport.'

Is he competitive about his writing too? 'No, because it doesn't work like that. I have some of the things which all writers share, such as a moment of schadenfreude when a contemporary gets a bad review. I'm not immune to that. But it seems to me silly to line up the writers of my generation and see who is doing best. It's all pointless newspaper gossip.

There is no proper way of measuring literary success in your own lifetime.'

But does he care about his reputation? 'Of course, I care what readers think and what my fellow novelists think. But I've never read a word that has been written about me that has made me write any differently.' He's not lacking in self-confidence then? 'No, I have doubts. Put it this way, the first two novels I wrote I prepared for their critical reception by writing the worst review I could of them myself, pointing out all the faults I could – and no one picked out these faults. So I thought, "I'm not going to do that again. I'll keep quiet."'

His first novel, *Metroland*, took nearly ten years to write and was published in 1980 when Barnes was 34. 'Sometimes when I was signing that book,' he recalls, 'I would flick through it and see people's notes and there would be the word "Irony!" in the margin.'

I confess that before the interview I went through my old copies of his books and found that in his second novel, *Before She Met Me*, I had written 'Not convinced' in the margin. It was next to a passage in which one character, Jack, contrives a meeting with a friend in a sports shop, just so as he can fart in the cricket-bat section and deliver the seemingly off-the-cuff line, 'Wind in the willows'. 'I know,' says Barnes. 'It was probably a joke-led scene. It depends how much you believe in Jack.' Is he thick skinned about such petty carping? 'At this distance I don't feel remotely sensitive about it and, in fact, I think you are probably right about that example. I feel more sensitive about new stuff. I get reviews heavily filtered. At first what you get out of a review is "masterpiece" and "deep insight". After a while all you want is a truthful and exact description. You want the review to reflect the density, tone and colour of the novel. It becomes irrelevant whether a reviewer is nice or nasty. You just want the book to be rendered accurately.'

His third novel was *Flaubert's Parrot*, which has now been in print for 20 years, was shortlisted for the Booker and gained him a strong French following (he is the only writer to have won both France's *prix medicis* and it's *prix femina*). The next big novel of Barnes's career was *A History of the World in 10 ½ Chapters*, which took a distorted, postmodern lens to the subject of truth. Next came the most accessible of his novels, *Talking It Over*. It is a story of a love triangle and functions without an authorial voice, with each character directly addressing the reader in turn and arguing for his or her version of the truth, then leaving the reader to decide what the facts are of this three-way relationship. His tenth novel, *Love, Etc*, was a sequel to this. There were others in between – as well as the odd non-fiction book – and there has been a collection of short stories since, but *Arthur & George* marks a return to novel-writing for Barnes after a five-year lacuna.

He thinks that he probably comes across in person as aloof and ideas-ridden, but he describes himself to me as 'generally cheerful with a melancholy undertone'. When I ask him if he feels fulfilled, he says, 'I don't ask myself that. No, I don't think so. But I'm not sure being fulfilled is what I want. I feel surprised that I am a novelist who has written all those novels. I never set out to occupy a particular literary territory. I've always jumped around and so I never feel that I have to run my race.'

He thinks he may have been driven in the early part of his career by the need to impress his rather hard-to-impress parents. 'I don't think you ever really get the approval of your parents when you are a writer,' he says. 'Perhaps that is why you keep writing. I think they were proud of me. I don't think they undermined me in any way but they thought showing pride in your children was vulgar. I would occasionally hear back from other people that my mother had been boasting about something I or my brother had done. [His older brother Jonathan is a professor of ancient philosophy in Geneva.] I think she thought there was too much sex in my books. That never inhibited me from including sex in them, though I never worried what they would think. When you're at your typewriter it is as if everyone you know who might take offence is dead.' He smiles his calm, crocodile smile again. 'I sent my parents my first book and there was a long silence and when I next went home – I had a distant relationship with them – my father said, "I read your novel. Quite a good first effort. Mind you, the language was a bit lower-deck." My mother didn't comment at all.'

He has not gone down the parenthood road himself, and he dismisses the suggestion that his books might in some way be child substitutes. I ask him if he thinks successful writers have to be quite selfish and single-minded, though, in the way they organise their lives and pursue their careers. 'Not necessarily. Self-disciplined, which isn't the same. If you are working at home, as I do, you deal with the window-cleaner and the milkman. It's not as if you disappear into the clouds.' He drains his glass. 'I don't like distractions, though. I don't have music in the background, for example. I'm amazed people can write fiction to music. I think it would f--- up the rhythm of your prose. My typewriter faces the wall. I don't look out of the window. When it is flowing I will work intensely, weekends and Christmas day.' Does that make him difficult to live with? 'You'd have to ask my wife. I'm remote while I'm in my study but when I come out I'm a reasonably normal human being.'

It is telling that in his memoirs Martin Amis describes Barnes as 'uxorious' – that is, excessively dependent on his wife. Perhaps that comment was sourness on Amis's part, but it is curious that Barnes always dedicates his novels to his wife. I ask him why he does this. 'Actually I don't write the dedication until I finish the book,' he says. And then it always seems appropriate to dedicate it to Pat. I changed it this time for *Arthur & George*. It's a period dedication: PK. I thought that was more ACD.

It seems an apposite dedication for this most Victorian of figures to make. And it occurs to me that a better nickname for Julian Barnes, better at least than Jules or Barnsey, would be 'JB'.

THE DAILY TELEGRAPH Saturday, August 20, 2005

The Italian Secretary: a Further Adventure of Sherlock Holmes by **Caleb Carr**. Little Brown.

But would Sir Arthur approve?...Review by **Mark Richards**

In his story "The Final Problem", Arthur Conan Doyle rid himself of his most celebrated creation by having him plunge to his death over the Reichenbach Falls, along with his nemesis, Moriarty. Sherlock Holmes's end was shortlived, however; following an outcry from devoted readers, he was resurrected, in "The Adventure of the Empty House". Spiritual descendents of those devoted readers have been equally unwilling to let dead detectives lie, and Caleb Carr's *The Italian Secretary* is the latest in a long procession of resuscitations of the Baker Street regular.

The plot is set in motion by a cryptic telegram from Holmes's brother Mycroft, who is in Scotland to safeguard Queen Victoria, and Sherlock and Watson are soon aboard a train for Edinburgh. Reports of two strangely mutilated bodies found in the grounds of the Palace of Holyroodhouse remind Holmes of the case of David Rizzio, "private secretary, music instructor, and confident to Mary, Queen of Scots", murdered in a similarly grotesque fashion three centuries before, and said to haunt the rooms he was killed in.

The principal pleasure of any detective story, it goes almost without saying, lies in the rational explanation of the initially mysterious. While not the first detective in literary history to pursue the deductive method – Edgar Allan Poe's Auguste Dupin preceded him – Sherlock Holmes is certainly its most celebrated adherent and most eloquent expositor. Which is what makes it doubly odd that, while *The Italian Secretary* is an enjoyable if slightly stretched piece of literary ventriloquism, at its heart lies – spoiler alert – a presence that remains unexplained: the ghost of the Italian secretary himself, David Rizzio.

Admittedly, we are given many warnings that the story may take a supernatural turn, but the hope throughout is that Holmes is engaged in another of his bluffs. That Carr had doubts about the advisability of his resolution, or lack of one, is implied by the final chapter, which is little more than a chance for Holmes to expound upon his theory of the supernatural: Within the study of crime, Watson...phenomena occur that we are powerless to explain...the unexplained nature of these phenomena gives them extraordinary force...This is power, indeed; and what possesses power, we must admit, possesses actuality." Really?

The suspicion is confirmed by an extraordinary Afterword, written by the American representative of the estate of Conan Doyle, Jon Lellenberg. It is part encomium to Carr, part request for him to write a book featuring Sherlock Holmes and Carr's own detective Dr Laszlo Kreizler, and part justification for the supernatural elements of the novel. But even Lellenberg, the instigator of the project, has his doubts: "I am not sure that Sir Arthur Conan Doyle would approve," he admits. Lellenberg *also* reveals the reason for the novel's thinness; it was originally commissioned as a short story. At least that's one mystery solved.

Review

Fiction Mycroft = Moriarty

Alfred Hinkling finds that the fruits of the Sherlockian labours are fun to read

The New Annotated Sherlock Holmes Volume 3: The Novels edited by Leslie S Klinger. Norton.

Sherlock Holmes: The Unauthorised Biography by Nick Rennison. Atlantic Books.

Sherlock Holmes has been ranked as one of the three most recognisable icons of the western world, alongside Father Christmas and Mickey Mouse. Yet there is no shortage of Sherlockian scholars prepared to dispute this on the grounds that, among the three, only the great detective was real.

The state of Sherlock studies is now so advanced that, far from it seeming incredible that anyone should believe that Holmes actually existed, it is a wonder that there is anyone still prepared to suggest that he didn't. Ever since William S Baring-Gould published the first biography of the detective in 1962, there has been an increasing number of scholars determined to disprove the fiction that Holmes was in any way fictional, while Baring-Gould's *Annotated Sherlock Holmes* remained the bible for this school of thought for almost 40 years.

Not any longer. Its pre-eminence has been seriously challenged by Leslie S Klinger's monumental *New Annotated Sherlock Holmes*, which now comes to completion. The first two volumes, published last year, contained the 56 short stories as they appeared in the Strand magazine between 1887-1927. The concluding part presents the four novel-length adventures.

(**Compiler's note**: See Chapter 25 for further details).

Far more significant, however, is the state-of-the-art Sherlockian arcane it contains, produced by a tribe of obsessives who believe that Conan Doyle simply acted as Watson's agent; that 221B Baker Street was an actual address; and that the real brains behind al-Quida is Professor Moriarty. Klinger has overseen a handsome project – elegantly produced, lavishly illustrated and scrupulously well organised. The only slight perversity is that the volume containing the first meeting of Holmes and Watson (in *A Study in Scarlet*) should be published last; though this might be a simple reflection of the fact that Sherlockian scholars do not like anything to be simple. Indeed non-specialists may find themselves slightly disoriented by the fact that one barely reaches the second paragraph before the text breaks off to engage in a prolonged discussion of Dr Watson's war wound.

Yet the issue of Watson's wound is a prime example of the kind of controversy this edition attempts to resolve. The doctor's initial report of an injured shoulder sustained in Afghanistan contradicts, as many scholars are eager to point out, plentiful testimony elsewhere in the Canon that he was shot in the leg. Attention is drawn to WB Hepburn's paper, the Jezail Bullet, which rather logically concludes that the good doctor may have been shot twice. Yet this is too rational a solution for most Sherlockians: and Klinger also considers various theories accounting for how the bullet may have penetrated both places at the same time. My favourite among these is Peter Brain's proposal that Watson was shot from below while squatting over a cliff to relieve himself (though how Watson managed to avoid toppling backwards in shock Mr Brain declines to say).

The degree of industry evidenced in these volumes is astonishing. When Holmes casually mentions that he once authored a monograph classifying different types of cigar ash, it comes as no surprise to learn that a real-life chemist, Raymond J McGowan, has verified these findings in the laboratory. And the musicologist William Smith has minutely analysed the complete piano works of Chopin in order to identify "the little thing" that Holmes sings as: "Tra-la-la-lira-lira-lay" (it's potentially the Fourth Polonnaise (*sic*) in C Minor, if you're interested). One continually marvels at the extent of these experts' ingenuity, while rather wondering if they do have anything better to do with their time.

Yet such speculation inevitably arises given the tantalising lack of reliable sources. Watson is often characterised as the Boswell of detective fiction, a diligent and dependable chronicler of his friend's career. Yet as Nick Rennison points out in his new biography, of a calculable 1,800 cases in the detective's career, Watson and Conan Doyle provide accounts of only 60 – in other words, more than 96% of Holmes's investigations are unrecorded.

For an inventive biographer, this leaves the field wide open for fantasy and supposition, though Rennison's account feels rather stolid and dependable. According to Rennison, Holmes was brought up in windy isolation on the North Yorkshire Moors, received his early education at home, and had an abortive stint as an actor with Sir Henry Irving's company before settling down to become the world's first consulting detective.

As with all Sherlockians, Rennison has to be at his most resourceful while attempting to explain what happened during "the Great Hiatus", the period between 1891-94 when Holmes was assumed to have tumbled to his death at the Reichenbach Falls. Rennison rejects some of the more outré theories (that he travelled to Russia, disguised as a tobacco merchant, at the invitation of Anton Chekov, for example) and constructs a plausible argument that throughout this time Holmes followed a semi-official roaming brief on behalf of his elder brother Mycroft, the inscrutable Whitehall mandarin.

Am I quite mad, but has nobody yet tried to advance the theory that Mycroft and Moriarty are possibly one and the same? If not, perhaps it is worth drawing attention to the fact that both are furtive, elusive, super-brains whose names begin with M. And get this – if you subject "Mycroft" to a spell-check, the automatic correction becomes "Microsoft". I confidentially look forward to these findings being incorporated in the new, *New Annotated Edition* in due course.

THE DAILY TELEGRAPH Saturday, December 24, 2005

Christopher Silvester applauds an ingenious biography that invests Sherlock Holmes's life with credibility

Maintaining the illusion to the last

Can fictional characters have a life beyond the confines of their original author's imagination? In this delightful *jeu d'esprit* – elaborate, richly textures and impressively sustained – Nick Rennison establishes beyond peradventure that there was a vast hinterland to Sherlock Holmes's public identity. This is no act of frivolous disrespect. While in Rennison's version of events Conan Doyle is reduced to little more than a ghost-writer and literary agent, it is, of course the brilliance of Conan Doyle's creation that permits Rennison to invest Holmes's parallel life with such credibility. And it is Rennison's achievement that the result is so much fun.

Unlike the *Annotated Sherlock Holmes* (now in its third volume), which simply provides commentary on Conan Doyle's stories as if Holmes was a real person, Rennison goes further and seeks to show that Holmes was secretly involved in many of the incidents of British and European public life from the 1870s to the 1920s. The Fenian outrages of the 1880s (in which, according to Rennison, Professor Moriarty, an Irish native, was a key participant), the Whitechapel murders of Jack the Ripper, the Cleveland Street conspiracy (a homosexual prostitution scandal involving members of the establishment), the Tranby Croft "cheating at cards" affair, numerous celebrated murder cases, even the Siege of Sydney Street – are all grist the Rennison's mill.

Indeed, Rennison uses a brief paragraph in one of Watson's accounts referring to his friend's two-year visit to Tibet, which was followed by sojourns in Persia, Mecca and Khartoum, to construct a detailed account of the Great Hiatus in Holmes's life. It should come as no surprise to learn that at the instigation of his brother Mycroft, the grey eminence of Whitehall, and indulging in his well-attested craving for adventure and exotic stimulation, Sherlock Holmes should have embarked on secret service work for the British Empire as part of that geopolitical struggle known as the Great Game. Rennison also has his working on trailblazing chemical experiments in France with Pierre and Marie Curie, shortly before their discovery of radioactivity.

Although Rennison must perforce lean heavily on the testimony of Dr Watson and his writing partner Conan Doyle he is quick to admit that Watson is an unreliable narrator: "Mixing together real cases and real people with individuals whom he disguised under pseudonyms and locations that he altered for his own purposes, he created a narrative in which it is often difficult to disentangle the actuality from the inventions." Rennison interweaves the Holmes we already know with the Holmes he believes we ought to know, and where seams are occasionally apparent he deals with them clearly.

It is fashionable for modern biographers to uncover some secret sexual transgression on the part of their subject, but Rennison resists the temptation. Dismissing suggestions that Holmes was homosexual, merely because he "knew and liked the work of so-called 'decadent' writers and artists of the 1880s and 1890s" he concludes that by his late twenties Holmes had become a "sexual outsider" or celibate.

He does turn up one hitherto unknown aspect of Holmes's youth, namely his brief career as a professional actor in Henry Irving's company at the Lyceum theatre in 1874. In his own words, Holmes was someone who "can never resist a dramatic situation" and Rennison persuades with his assertion that there was always a theatrical element in Holmes's investigations.

He also portrays Holmes as a wry observer of his own celebrity, even taking an interest in the earliest film productions based on his life. Again, contrary to Watson's oft-repeated assertion that Holmes was scornful of publicity and the vulgarities of fame,

Rennison argues that "in truth, Holmes was one of those men who enjoyed backing into the limelight." Holmes died peacefully in his bed in 1929, having just been administered a shot of his beloved morphine, apparently whispering: "My friend Watson would not approve."

The overall result of Rennison's efforts is that Holmes is presented as a more human and, at the same time, a more accomplished figure: "As we have seen, he made some serious errors of judgement in his career, most notably in his dealings with Moriarty and the Irish question, but his influence on British history between the 1880s and the First World War was more significant than his Boswell allowed."

Rennison is no slouch. Maintaining the illusion to the very last, there is even a cod author's note about imaginary manuscript sources which he was able to consult but from which he was not allowed to quote directly. One need not be a Sherlock Holmes obsessive to appreciate this peculiar enterprise. Described as erudite though pointless by one critic, Rennison's book is a marvel of ingenuity. Its point lies in the sheer enjoyment it affords.

Seven Magazine JANUARY 1 2006 THE SUNDAY TELEGRAPH

The New Annotated Sherlock Holmes: Volume 3: The Novels Edited by Leslie S. Klinger.

Sherlock Holmes: The Biography By Nick Rennison.

Christopher Tayler DETECTS PLOT HOLES, RED HERRINGS AND THIN JOKES

'Sherlokian scholarship' as its practitioners call it, got off the ground in 1911, when Ronald Knox – a crime-writing Oxford chaplain who later became a famous Catholic apologist – gave a lecture called 'Studies in the Literature of Sherlock Holmes'. Knox wasn't the first to point out continuity errors in Holmes's adventures, but his mock-scholarly analysis amused Conan Doyle, who admitted that 'you know a great deal more about it than I do, for the stories have been written in a disconnected (and careless) way without referring back to what had gone before.'

Conan Doyle wasn't bothered because he didn't take Holmes very seriously: he planned to be remembered for his long-forgotten historical romances. Knox, in turn, had examined such questions as Dr Watson's first name – John, so why does his wife call him 'James'? – in order to make fun of contemporary Biblical scholarship, which, as he saw it, was too preoccupied with inconsistencies and anachronisms. Nevertheless, the idea of treating the stories as historical documents written by Watson turned out to be irresistible to fans of donnish whimsy, and the joke staggers on to this day.

The latest full-dress Sherlockian productions both toil in the shadow of W.S. Baring-Gould, who perpetrated an early 'biography' of the great detective as well as an *Annotated Sherlock Holmes* (1976) bristling with archly conjectural footnotes. Leslie S. Klinger, the editor of *The New Annotated Sherlock Holmes*, argues that the field has moved on since Baring-Gould's day, and process it by drawing on an enormous range of self-consciously pointless writings. A chemist has tried to reproduce Holmes's 'special study' of tobacco ash. There's a monograph on Baker Street drug use called *Subcutaneously, My Dear Watson*.

Klinger's addition of the longer stories is a beautiful thing to look at, reproducing as it does many of the earlier illustrations – including the famous ones by Sydney Paget – along with maps and pictures of Victorian London. Some of the annotations raise a smile or two: Sherlockians have produced an amazing range of explanations for the fact that Watson's war wound seems to migrate from his shoulder to his leg. In general, though, there's only so much comic mileage in such aggressively trivial footnotes as "This is the only reference in the Canon to Holmes's eyebrows."

Reading the stories with Klinger's annotations also makes Conan Doyle look more slapdash than you'd otherwise notice, since the authorities cited are largely interested in his mistakes. Sherlockians like nothing better than filling in plot-holes with extravagant hypotheses, the hastily-written yarns give them numerous opportunities to do so. On the other hand, they're equally obsessed by a game started by Conan Doyle himself when he threw in teasing references to such unrecorded cases as the giant rat of Sumatra, 'a story for which the world is not yet prepared' – evidence that Watson left quite a few things out.

Nick Rennison's 'biography' uses both approaches to fill in Holmes's shadowy life story. Rennison has him grow up in Yorkshire, the offspring of minor gentry, before sending him to Sidney Sussex, Cambridge. (Mercifully he leaves out the chortling Oxford-v-Cambridge debate relished by Holmes's plumier admirers.) After a brief stint as an actor, Holmes sets up as a consulting detective and gets mixed up with real-life late Victorian crime and espionage. Professor Moriarty turns out to be a Fenian, and Holmes soldiers on until 1929, dealing with Dr Crippen as well as Jack the Ripper.

Rennison's style is so impressively dry that his parodies of routine biography-speak are often as numbing as the genuine article. For a while, his mixture of real and fake scholarship makes it seem as though he intends to use Holmes to lighten up a serious study of Victorian and Edwardian society. This turns out not to be the case, however, and the result is a peculiar hybrid work – a fictional biography written at such a distance from the original stories that it's hard to detect the ingenious interpretations that Rennison is presumably foisting on them.

Despite the rigorously-worked conceit, he's affectionate towards Conan Doyle, Watson's 'literary agent' in the Sherlockian universe. Although he was in some ways a conventional jingo (*The Sign of Four*'s depiction of Andaman Islanders as blowpipe-wielding cannibal pygmies draws a lot of flack from Klinger's ace fact-checkers). Holmes creator was a thoughtful, decent man, and Rennison admiringly records his interventions in the cases of George Edalji and Oscar Slater, which helped to clear up two miscarriages of justice, as well as his efforts on behalf of Roger Casement and Oscar Wilde.

But unless you're a fully paid-up member of the Baker Street Irregulars, both of these books reveal more about the spending power of the subculture they're aimed at than they do about Watson, Holmes and their creator. Klinger's high-end three-volume edition will set you back at least 70 quid, which, judiciously spent, could pay for the authoritative, non-Sherlockian Oxford paperbacks as well as a second-hand copy of Stevenson's *Suicide Club* – which has an even better Mormon interlude than *A Study in Scarlet* – and maybe a copy of *Raffles, The Amateur Cracksman*.

Daily Mail, Friday, January 20, 2006

Books on Friday by **Hephzibah Anderson**

CHABON, M. (2006) *The Final Solution.* **Harper Perennial (p/b)**

BILLED as a 'story of detection', this perfectly formed novella is much more besides. Taking the classic 19th-century detective story as its template, it introduces an 89-year-old bee-keeper, rumoured to have been a celebrated sleuth in his prime.

One day, his solitary existence is disturbed by the arrival of Linus Steinman, a knobbly-kneed nine year old who appears from nowhere with an African grey parrot perched on his shoulder. While Linus seems to be mute, the parrot has plenty to say for himself, squawking a string of German numerals over and over again – odd, yes, but in England in 1944 downright suspicious.

When a man turns up murdered and the parrot vanishes, our cantankerous hero hauls himself out of retirement, determined to solve the mystery. It's a suspenseful, witty tale, but the book's real brilliance lies in the subtle revelation of Linus' tragic past, a story hinted at through a trail of clues that begins with the title.

THE DAILY TELEGRAPH Saturday, January 28, 2006

PICK OF THE **PAPERBACKS** by **Jeremy Sheldon**

While Linus Steinman, a nine-year-old Jewish refugee, arrives at a South Down village in 1944 the rekindles the "old appetite and energies" of an unnamed but celebrated octogenarian detective living out a hermitic retirement. Linus is mute and carries on his shoulder an African grey parrot that spouts a stream of mysterious German numbers.

When another mysterious newcomer to the village is killed and the parrot disappears, our frail and elderly hero sets out about solving the case.

At times a poignant study of loneliness, at others a playful homage to the golden age of British detective fiction, this lyrical and soulful novella sees Chabon revisit the subject of wartime refugees that formed the fulcrum for his Pulitzer Prize-winning book, *The Amazing Adventures of Kavalier & Clay*. This is imbued with the same absorbing psychological and linguistic details that have made all his precious writing so enjoyable.
(**Compiler's note:** See Addendum for a new 2011 book by Anthony Horowitz).

Chapter 16

Arthur Conan Doyle For The Defence

BBC 4, 9.05pm Christmas Day 2005

The Daily Mail WEEKEND Magazine Christmas & New Year Edition

Sherlock Holmes guaranteed literary immortality for ARTHUR CONAN DOYLE. But, as a Christmas TV series shows, the author himself turned detective to clear the names of two men wrongly accused of appalling crimes. By NIGEL JONES.

Elementary my dear Doyle

The great detective prowled the green fields, poking the mud with his stick, examining a suspicious footprint with a magnifying glass, gazing around the shed with the old bloodstains where the crime had been committed. He recalled his own words: 'It is my belief, Watson…that the lowest and vilest alleys in London do not present a more dreadful record of sin than does the smiling and beautiful countryside.'

Yet the man with the magnifying glass was not the immortal yet fictional Sherlock Holmes, but his creator, doctor turned author Arthur Conan Doyle, and the case he was investigating in the rural Midlands 100 years ago was not some fanciful product of his fertile imagination, but a savage real-life crime – and one that had landed an innocent man behind bars. It was an injustice that Doyle was determined to correct.

Arthur Conan Doyle For The Defence is one of a season of BBC programmes devoted to the author of the Sherlock Holmes stories on this Christmas, and it shows a neglected side of Doyle – as a crusader for justice. 'Doyle was a highly moral man,' says Andrew Lycett, who is writing Conan Doyle's biography. 'He hated injustice, and once he was convinced that an innocent man was being unjustly punished, he spared no effort to save them from the clutches of a corrupt legal system – and, in the end, his patience and persistence paid off.'

The first of these high-profile cases in which Doyle donned Sherlock Holmes' cape and deerstalker hat for real, was that of George Edalji, a young lawyer who lived in the Staffordshire village of Great Wyrley with his sisters, and his English mother and Indian father. George's father, Shapurji Edalji, was an Indian Parsee who had converted to Christianity and, after being ordained in the Church of England, found himself posted to Great Wyrley as the parish's vicar. 'An Indian family in rural Edwardian England was a rarity,' says Lycett. 'And although they lived blamelessly in the village for 30 years, the Edaljis were the object of widespread suspicion and open racism.

In the 1890s, an anonymous hate campaign began against them. They were persecuted by poison-pen letters full of abuse and threats; adverts insulting local worthies and falsely purporting to be from the Edaljis were placed in local newspapers, and they became highly unpopular as a result. The Chief Constable of Staffordshire, a

Captain Anson, openly accused George of stealing a school key that had been mysteriously found on the vicarage doorstep – and vowed to have the young man jailed.

So when, in 1903, a particularly nasty spate of animal mutilations began in the Great Wyrley area, police suspicion soon fell on young George. More anonymous letters arrived accusing him of the crimes – letters which, amazingly, the police accused George of writing to himself – and he was arrested after a pit pony was disembowelled. He was tried, convicted – despite a petition calling for a retrial that attracted 10,000 signatures – and jailed for seven years. George spent three years in prison, but indignation about the thinness of the case against him mounted, and he was suddenly freed with no explanation or compensation.

George wrote a pamphlet in his own defence, which was read to Doyle. 'I realised I was in the presence of an appalling tragedy,' the author later wrote, 'and that I was called upon to do what I could to set it right.'

Doyle, then at the height of the fame generated by the Holmes stories, agreed to put his Holmesian deductions to work to help clear George's name. Arriving late for their first meeting, Doyle noticed that George was reading a newspaper – and peering with his face only inches from the print. With his medical training, Doyle realised that George was so short-sighted as to be almost blind. Yet police alleged that he had left the bedroom he shared with his father, and made his way, on a pitch-black night, through a police cordon – thrown around the village after the earlier outrages – in order to carry out the mutilation of the pony. Doyle proved that horse hair found on George's jacket had been planted by police – and that, anyway, he had worn a different jacket at the time of the crime. He proved that mud on George's shoes did not come from the place where the mutilations had happened; and he showed that the deep wounds on the pony could not possibly have been inflicted by George's cut-throat razor, as the police had claimed.

But not only did Doyle's detective work clear George; his painstaking enquiries and his analysis of the anonymous letters identified the likely culprit – a butcher ironically named Sharp – with access to the necessary knives and enough knowledge of animal anatomy to perform the mutilations. Doyle's suspicions were confirmed when he, too, began to receive anonymous hate mail and death threats, similar in style to those that had plagued George.

Doyle's forensic skills and dedicated detective work finally forced the authorities to grant George a grudging pardon – though he never received a penny for his years in jail and his ruined reputation.

A website – **The Chronicles of Sir Arthur Conan Doyle** – contains further information on this case as follows:

It was a moment straight out of a Sherlock Holmes novel. In January of 1907 Conan Doyle walked into the lobby of a hotel. He was late for an appointment. He was to meet with a man who was trying to clear his name. As Conan Doyle entered the lobby he spotted the man he was looking for, George Edalji. In a flash Conan Doyle knew that Edalji was innocent of the crime for which he'd served three years in prison. George Edalji grew up in Great Wyrley, northwest of Birmingham. His father was a Parsee Indian who had converted to the Church of England and became a vicar. Reverend

Edalji married an English woman and together they had three children, including George.

The Edalji family endured much racial intolerance. There was name-calling and practical jokes. In 1888 there were also anonymous, disturbing letters. A disgruntled servant of the Edalji family confessed to sending the letters.

However in 1892 another series of letters began. This time sixteen-year-old George was accused of being the culprit by local law enforcement. At the time George was a student at the Walsall Grammar School. He was considered an excellent student. No reason or evidence was given for the accusations against him. The letters ceased soon after George was accused of writing them and the matter was dropped.

In 1903 something much more troubling happened in the Great Wyrley area. Sheep, cows and horses were being killed. The animals were mutilated in the middle of the night. Long shallow cuts to the stomach caused the animals to bleed to death.

The anonymous letters began again. The letters taunted the police and named the perpetrator of the crimes. George Edalji was named as the person behind the hideous crimes.

By this time Edalji was a successful solicitor. While it was true that he didn't seem to have many friends that seemed to be the worst that could be said of him. Nevertheless evidence was gathered and a trial was held. George Edalji, vicar's son and former solicitor was found guilty and sentenced to seven years' hard labour.

Not everyone who was aware of the case was convinced that justice had been done. A petition was organised to protest Edalji's conviction and to press for his release. Ten thousand people signed the petition. Because of the publicity Edalji was released after three years. No reason was given for his release, his name was not cleared and no compensation was given for the three years of imprisonment.

While Edalji was happy for his freedom he couldn't practice *(sic)* as a solicitor because of the conviction. He also thought he should receive some sort of compensation for all the time he'd lost and everything he had to endure. Since he hadn't had much luck with the legal system, Edalji took his case to the press. He published an account of the entire matter.

Conan Doyle read about the Edalji case and felt compelled to act. In December of 1906 he began to investigate the matter and everything he found confirmed his initial feelings that an innocent man had been convicted.

As he reviewed the facts it seemed to Conan Doyle that the evidence was overwhelming. Edalji was innocent. The bloody razors found in the Edalji home were later discovered to be merely rusty razors. The handwriting expert who testified that Edalji's handwriting matched the writing on the taunting letters was discovered to have made a serious mistake on another case causing an innocent man to be convicted. The mud on George's boots was of a different soil type than that of the field where the last mutilation took place. The killings and letters continued after Edalji was prosecuted.

And then there was the final piece of evidence that Conan Doyle gathered. The evidence that he saw in an instance the first time he set eyes on George Edalji, Conan Doyle stated, "He had come to my hotel by appointment, but I had been delayed, and he was passing the time by reading the paper. I recognised my man by his dark face, so I stood and observed him. He held the paper close to his eyes and rather sideways, proving not only a high degree of myopia, but marked astigmatism. The idea of such a man scouring field at night and assaulting cattle while avoiding the watching police was ludicrous...There, in a single physical defect, lay the moral certainty of his innocence..."

Conan Doyle wrote a series of articles for the *Daily Telegraph* about the Edalji case. He outlined everything in great detail. These articles caught the public's attention and that caught the attention of the British government. At that time there was no procedure for a retrial so there was a private committee meeting to consider the matter. In the spring of 1907 the committee decided that Edalji was innocent of the mutilations, but still found him guilty of writing the anonymous letters.

Conan Doyle found anything less than a finding of innocent on all charges a miscarriage of justice, however the decision made a huge difference for Edalji. The Law Society readmitted him. Edalji was once again able to practice *(sic)* as a solicitor. It is important to note that partially as a result of the case the Court of Criminal Appeal was established in 1907. So not only did Conan Doyle help George Edalji, his work helped to establish a way to correct other miscarriages of justice.

In 1910, Doyle heard about a second suspect case: that of a convict, Oscar Slater, serving a life sentence for killing a wealthy Scottish spinster, Marion Gilchrist. 'Having expended so much time and energy on the Edalji case, he was extremely reluctant to get involved again,' says Lycett, 'but once more a blatant injustice fired his indignation.' Doyle felt the Slater case was an even worse miscarriage of justice than that of George Edalji. After studying the case, in which the victim had been brutally battered in her own flat, he concluded that, 'This unhappy man had...no more to do with the murder for which he had been condemned than I had.'

Slater's case reminded him of George's: the convicted man was again an unpopular foreigner (Slater was a German Jew who made his living as a gambler, con man and pimp); police again got the weapon used in the crime wrong (they said that Slater had battered the victim with a hammer, whereas the murder weapon had been a chair); and the authorities had stubbornly ignored mounting evidence, not only of Slater's innocence – but that, as a convenient and unpopular fall guy, he had been framed by the police and legal establishment to protect a well-connected Scottish family from whose ranks the real killer had come.

Once more, Doyle set to work as a gumshoe: he visited the scene of the crime, which he knew well, as Scotland had been the place where he first picked up his deductive skills. As a young medical student, his teacher, Joseph Bell's methods of diagnosing illness had made him the real-life model for Holmes. Doyle found witnesses to prove that Slater had been elsewhere when the brutal killing had been committed – and he shot holes in the flimsy prosecution evidence in a book he wrote on the case.

At first, his efforts to secure justice for Slater, who continued to languish in Peterhead prison, came to nothing. An inquiry in 1914 backed the original verdict, and then the case was forgotten amid the greater tragedy of World War I. It was only in the mid-1920s, when prosecution witnesses began to admit that their original statements had been concocted or forced from them by the police, that Slater was finally freed. 'Again, the authorities had refused to admit that an innocent man was rotting in jail,' says Lycett. 'And again, Doyle's hard work – and money, since he had paid Slater's legal bills – forced them to free him, albeit only after he had already spent 18 years inside, and only after the Prime Minister, Ramsay MacDonald, had intervened.'

Lycett believes that Doyle's passion for justice was first kindled when, he had himself come under suspicion following the death of a young man lodging in his own home in Southsea, Hampshire. 'It was only after the dead man's sister became Doyle's first wife that the cloud of suspicion lifted,' says Lycett. 'But he never forgot how easily the innocent can be accused if there is gossip and malicious rumour at work.'

Sadly, Doyle subsequently fell out with Oscar Slater, an ungrateful character who refused to repay those who had spent money on his behalf, despite receiving a large compensation cheque. Slater survived until 1948 and again saw the inside of a prison when he was interned as an enemy alien during World War II. George Edalji, by contrast, was guest of honour when Doyle married his second wife, Jean Leckie. 'Although Doyle was a respected Establishment man,' says Lycett, 'fighting these two injustices shook him to the core. He realised there were people at the heart of the legal system prepared to see innocents suffer. He would not rest until he had righted that wrong.'

Daily Mail, Friday, January 6, 2006

Television **mail – By George, Holmes!**

Conan Doyle For The Defence by **Christopher Matthew**

JULIAN BARNES must be feeling pretty cheesed off. As one of our most successful novelists, he can hardly be desperate for publicity. His latest book, *Arthur & George*, is a huge critical and commercial success.

Even so, he must have been more than a little miffed that BBC2 broadcast a programme about Sir Arthur Conan Doyle's enthusiasm for solving real-life crimes every bit as chilling and baffling as those tackled by his fictional hero Sherlock Holmes, and never once mentioned Barnes.

The reason being that one of Doyle's more successful cases, featured in the programme, was the subject of *Arthur & George*.

The George in the title was a young lawyer called George Edalji. The eldest son of a Bombay-born vicar of Great Wyrely in Staffordshire, he was put on trial for injuring a horse some time during the night of August 17, 1903.

It was not the first time such a thing had happened. All through that summer a maniac had been on the loose in the neighbourhood slashing horses and cattle and leaving them in agony to bleed to death.

A series of anonymous letters, suggesting that a little girl would be the next victim, prompted the police to raid the vicarage, where they took away a coat smeared with blood and horsehairs, and a pair of shoes which matched footprints in the muddy field where the horse had been kept. George, with his odd looks and staring eyes, was not surprised when he was arrested.

'I've been expecting it for some time,' he said.

When cross-examined in court, he explained that he had come home from work at 6.30pm and gone for a long walk, during which he had met various locals.

His father, with whom he shared a bedroom, testified that he had gone to bed at 10.30 and hadn't left the house again that night. But the forensic evidence was enough to ensure the poor fellow got seven years hard labour.

Following a 10,000-signature petition, Edalji was released after three years – at which point Conan Doyle took up his case.

Using the same techniques of observation and deduction that he had learned as a young medical student in Edinburgh from his tutor, Joseph Bell (himself something of a sleuth), and which he had bestowed on Holmes, Doyle showed that it could have been quite impossible for anyone as seriously short-sighted as George to have found his way in the dark to the field.

A HOME Office Committee concluded that Edalji had been wrongly convicted, and that he had written the letters and brought trouble on himself.

Doyle was convinced that the real culprit was a disturbed ex-pupil of Walsall Grammar School, but it was never proved – nor did he get anywhere with his accusations of institutional racism within the Staffordshire police force.

As one who had himself, as a young doctor in Southsea, very nearly been unjustly accused of murder, Doyle felt a strong bond of sympathy with Edalji, and invited him to his second wedding.

Doyle was also responsible for the release after 18 years of the German Jewish gambler and pimp, Oscar Slater, who had been wrongly convicted of the brutal murder of the elderly Miss Gilchrist in Glasgow in December 1908.

It wasn't until many years later that the real murderer was shown to be a relative of the victim, and that because the Procurator Fiscal and the Lord Advocate were friends of his family, they framed an innocent man.

Owing to his obsession with spiritualism and fairies, Doyle later became discredited as a sleuth. Even so, this fascinating documentary showed why so many believed that the great man really was Sherlock Holmes all along.

Further information on this case comes from the same website as previously noted.

In 1925 William Gordon was released from Peterhead Prison in Scotland. Unbeknownst to the authorities Gordon smuggled out a message from fellow prisoner, Oscar Slater. The message, written on waterproof paper and hidden under Gordon's tongue, was a plea for help. It was to be delivered to none other than Sir Arthur Conan Doyle.

Conan Doyle first heard the name of Oscar Slater years earlier. He became aware of the case when Slater was sentenced to death for the murder of Marion Gilchrist.

The crime occurred on December 21, 1908 in Glasgow. Helen Lambie, the sole servant of the elderly Marion Gilchrist, left her employer for a few minutes to get a newspaper. Shortly thereafter, Arthur Adams, who lived in the apartment directly below Miss Gilchrist said he and his sisters heard three knocks on the ceiling.

Thinking that Miss Gilchrist wanted his assistance, Adams went to investigate. When he arrived at Miss Gilchrist's door he rang the bell. Although no one came to the door he heard noises inside the apartment. He returned downstairs, but his sisters urged him to check on Miss Gilchrist one more time. He returned upstairs and was in front of the door when Helen Lambie returned from her errand. At about this time they glimpsed a man in the building's hallway. However it didn't strike either of them as unusual. Perhaps it was another tenant or visitor. At any rate, Adams told Helen what had been going on and together they entered the apartment.

To their horror they discovered that Miss Gilchrist had been bludgeoned to death. Her personal papers had been rifled and a diamond brooch was stolen.

There was a public outcry against the brutal murder. The police and the public wanted the crime to be solved quickly and the murderer put behind bars. Within five days the police announced that they were looking for a suspect. His name was Oscar Slater.

At first glance it did seem that the police had found their man. Slater lived near Miss Gilchrist. He was known to the police for running an illegal gambling operation. He had recently pawned a diamond brooch. Even more damning was the fact that soon after the murder Slater left the country under an assumed name.

Slater was discovered in America. Once he was made aware of the accusations against him Slater willingly returned. He was positive he could prove his innocence.

The brooch that he pawned did not match the description of Miss Gilchrist's brooch.

He also had witnesses who could testify as to his location at the time in question.

The police were not swayed by Slater's evidence. They were sure that he was the culprit. In addition to Slater's criminal history was the fact that the police had witnesses. After some coaching by the authorities, these people including Helen Lambie, were sure that they'd seen Slater leaving the scene of the murder. Also the police believed they found the murder weapon after a small hammer was found in Slater's possession.

The trial was held in 1909. Despite the conflicting evidence Oscar Slater was found guilty of the murder of Marion Gilchrist and sentenced to death. Slater's lawyers started a petition that urged mercy. Two days before he was scheduled to die, Slater's sentence was changed to imprisonment with hard labour for life.

Slater's lawyers also contacted Sir Arthur Conan Doyle. While Conan Doyle didn't approve of Slater or his lifestyle it was clear that he was not the murderer of Marion Gilchrist. In 1912 Conan Doyle published *The Case of Oscar Slater*. It examined evidence brought forward at the trial and point by point proved that Slater was not the killer.

For example, Conan Doyle explained that Slater traveled *(sic)* under an assumed name because he was traveling *(sic)* with his mistress. He was trying to avoid detection by his wife, not the police. And while it was true that Slater did possess a small hammer it wasn't large enough to inflict the type of wounds that Miss Gilchrist had sustained. Conan Doyle stated that a medical examiner at the crime scene declared that a large chair, dripping with blood, seemed to be the murder weapon. Conan Doyle also concluded that Miss Gilchrist had opened her door to the murderer herself. He surmised that she knew the murderer. Despite the fact that Miss Gilchrist and Oscar Slater lived near one another, they had never met.

The case of Oscar Slater caused some demand for a new trial. However the authorities said the evidence didn't justify that the case be reopened. In 1914 there were more calls for a retrial. New evidence had come to light. Another witness was found that could verify Slater's whereabouts during the time of the crime. Also, it was learned that before Helen Lambie named Slater as the man she'd seen in the hallway the day of the murder she had given the police another name. Unbelievably, the officials decided to let the matter rest.

Conan Doyle was outraged. "How the verdict could be that there was no fresh cause for reversing the conviction is incomprehensible. The whole case will, in my opinion, remain immortal in the classics of crime as the supreme example of official incompetence and obstinacy."

Throughout the years Conan Doyle raised the issue of the injustice against Oscar Slater. However he was not successful in his efforts. Then in 1925 he received the message smuggled out of Peterhead Prison. Oscar Slater didn't offer any new revelations. There was no new evidence. It was just a note from a desperate man who wanted justice. He begged Conan Doyle not to forget him and try one more time to free him.

Conan Doyle could not ignore Slater's heartfelt request. He fired off a fresh barrage of letters. He wrote to his influential friends, the press and to the secretary of state of Scotland. He made public appearances and began to gather other likeminded people to the cause. The movement slowly began to gather steam. The turning point was in 1927 when a book by Glasgow journalist, William Park, was published.

The Truth About Oscar Slater re-examined the case. Park came to the same conclusion that Conan Doyle did years ago, Miss Gilchrist had likely known the murderer and had invited him into her home. Park speculated that Miss Gilchrist had argued with this person about a document that she possessed. During the argument she was pushed and hit her head. Her assailant was then forced to make a decision.

What would be worse? To have Marion Gilchrist recover from her wounds and charge him with assault or to kill her and be done with the matter? He chose to kill her. Libel laws prevented Park naming this person in the book, however he believed the murderer to be the victim's nephew.

The book caused a huge uproar. Newspapers were full of information about the case. Witnesses came forth to talk about the police coaching them into naming Slater as the man they'd seen around the building that fateful day.

On November 8, 1927 the secretary of state for Scotland issued the following statement "Oscar Slater has now completed more than eighteen and a half years of his life sentence, and I have felt justified in deciding to authorize his release on license as soon as suitable arrangements can be made." Within a few days Oscar Slater was a free man.

However the case was not totally a happy ending as far as Conan Doyle was concerned. Slater was released, not pardoned. As a result the case had to be reopened and retried. At that point Slater could apply for compensation from the government for the years of wrongful imprisonment. Conan Doyle and others gave money to Slater for his legal fees.

In the end Slater was cleared of all charges and awarded £6,000 in compensation. Conan Doyle assumed that Slater would reimburse his supporters for his legal fees. After all, it was what Conan Doyle would have done. However Slater saw the matter in a different way. He thought it was ridiculous that he had to pay court costs at all and so he shouldn't have to pay them back.

Conan Doyle didn't need the £1,000 that he had given for Slater's legal fees. What bothered him was that Slater seemed ungrateful for the support he was given. Honor *(sic)* was very important to Conan Doyle and he believed that Slater had behaved in a dishonourable manner. Conan Doyle wrote to Slater saying, "You seem to have taken leave of your senses. If you are indeed responsible for your actions, then you are the most ungrateful as well as the most foolish person whom I have ever known."

Had Conan Doyle been alive in 1948 he probably would have disagreed with the newspaper notice about Oscar Slater's death: "Oscar Slater Dead at 78, Reprieved Murderer, Friend of A. Conan Doyle."

For further details of these two cases see Costello's book *The Real World of Sherlock Holmes*.

Chapter 17

The Case of Doctor Watson's Watch

In *The Sign of Four*, Chapter 1. The Science of Deduction, Dr Watson says to Sherlock Holmes:

"I have heard you say that it is difficult for a man to have any object in daily use without leaving the impress of his individuality upon it in such a way that a trained observer might read it. Now, I have here a watch which has recently come into my possession. Would you have the kindness to let me have your opinion upon the character or habits of the late owner?"

I handed him over the watch with some slight feeling of amusement in my heart, for the test was, as I thought, an impossible one, and I intended it as a lesson against the somewhat dogmatic tone which he occasionally assumed. He balanced the watch in his hand, gazed hard at the dial, opened the back, and examined the works, first with his naked eyes and then with a powerful convex lens. I could hardly keep from smiling at his crestfallen face when he finally snapped the case to and handed it back.

"There are hardly any data," he remarked. "The watch has been recently cleaned, which robs me of my most suggestive facts."

"You are right," I answered. "It was cleaned before being sent to me."

In my heart I accused my companion of putting forward a most lame and impotent excuse to cover his failure. What data could he expect from an uncleaned watch?

"Though unsatisfactory, my research has not been entirely barren," he observed, staring up at the ceiling with dreamy lack-lustre eyes. "Subject to your correction, I should judge that the watch belonged to your elder brother, who inherited from your father."

"That you gather no doubt, from the H.W. upon the back?"

"Quite so. The W suggests your own name. The date of the watch is nearly fifty years back and the initials are as old as the watch; so it was made for the last generation. Jewellery usually descends to the eldest son, and he is most likely to have the same name as the father. Your father has, if I remember right, been dead many years. It has, therefore, been in the hands of your eldest brother."

"Right, so far," said I. "Anything else?"

"He was a man of untidy habits – very untidy and careless. He was left with good prospects, but he threw away his chances, lived for some time in poverty with occasional short intervals of prosperity, and, finally, taking to drink, he died. That is all I can gather."

I sprang from my chair and limped impatiently about the room with considerable bitterness in my heart.

"This is unworthy of you, Holmes," I said. "I could not have believed that you would have descended to this. You have made inquiries into the history of my unhappy brother, and you now pretend to deduce this knowledge in some fanciful way. You cannot expect me to believe that you have read all this from his old watch! It is unkind, and, to speak plainly, has a touch of charlatanism in it."

"My dear doctor," said he, kindly, "pray accept my apologies. Viewing the matter as an abstract problem, I had forgotten how personal and painful a thing it might be to you. I assure you, however, that I never even knew that you had a brother until you handed me the watch."

"Then how in the name of all that is wonderful did you get these facts? They are absolutely correct in every particular."

"Ah, that is good luck. I could only say what was the balance of probability. I did not at all expect to be accurate."

"But it was not mere guesswork?"

"No, no: I never guess. It is a shocking habit – destructive to the logical faculty. What seems strange to you is only so because you do not follow my train of thought or observe the small facts upon which large inferences may depend. For example, I began by stating that your brother was careless. When you observe the lower part of that watch-case you notice that it is not only dinted in two places, but it is cut and marked all over from the habit of keeping other hard objects, such as coins or keys, in the same pocket. Surely it is no great feat to assume that a man who treats a fifty-guinea watch so cavalierly must be a careless man. Neither is it a very far-fetched inference that a man who inherits one article of such value is pretty well provided for in other respects."

I nodded, to show that I followed his reasoning.

"It is very customary for pawnbrokers in England, when they take a watch, to scratch the number of the ticket with a pin-point upon the inside of the case. It is more handy than a label, as there is no risk of the number being lost or transposed. There are no less than four such numbers visible to my lens on the inside of the case. Inference – that your brother was often at low water. Secondary inference – that he had occasional bursts of prosperity, or he could not have redeemed the pledge. Finally, I ask you to look at the inner plate, which contains the keyhole. Look at the thousands of scratches all round the hole – marks where the key has slipped. What sober man's key could have scored those grooves? But you will never see a drunkard's watch without them. He winds it at night, and he leaves these traces of his unsteady hand. Where is the mystery in all this?"

"It is as clear as daylight," I answered. "I regret the injustice which I did you. I should have had more faith in your marvellous faculty."

The reason I, the compiler, have included the above is in order to draw the attention of the reader to the work of the author David Pirie. Between 2001 and 2004 he had had published a trilogy of fictional novels with the overall title *Murder Rooms: The Dark Beginnings Of Sherlock Holmes*. In the first of these, *The Patient's Eyes*, and the second, *The Night Calls*, there are sections concerning 'the watch'. The difference here is that Dr Watson has been replaced by a young Conan Doyle and Sherlock Holmes by Dr Joseph Bell, otherwise, the similarity with the original Conan Doyle story becomes apparent. I have included both extracts as follows:

The Patient's Eyes

… 'Yes,' he (Bell) admitted with much less resistance than I had anticipated, 'just so. Anyone can follow the reasoning afterwards and talk of what would later be discovered. I only wish there were a way I could illustrate it better for you.'

'Perhaps there is,' I (Doyle) said. He stared at me gloomily, an eyebrow raised. 'You have written in one of your essays that it is difficult for a man to keep any object in daily use without leaving his personality about it. That is an example of your method in its purest form, is it not?'

'Certainly,' he agreed.

'Well, then.' I took out my father's watch as I spoke.

'If you make something useful of this watch, you may convince me.'

The watch, with its chain and gold facia, gleamed in the light of the fire. 'Months can go by without a single case. I would rejoice in a challenge...' he said and the watch was duly handed over.

I still remember Bell's expression as he studied it. His face was a perfect picture of disappointment. In fact, I could hardly keep from laughing. But there are hardly any data,' he said miserably. 'This has recently been cleaned.'

'Yes, I know,' I said. 'I oversaw its cleaning myself. So you see, Doctor, I rather feel this illustrates the limitations of your so-called method.'

The Doctor could certainly be arrogant, but he was never a bad loser and I expected him to return the watch to me with a shrug of defeat. But he did no such thing. He held on to it, and turned it round and round under the light, opening its back and studying the works. Then he took out a powerful concave lens to examine it and at last, still a little crestfallen, he handed it back to me.

He sat in his chair, eyes half closed. 'Yes,' he mused.' Perhaps you are right. But my investigation was not entirely barren. The watch is about fifty years old. Its owner is a man of untidy habits – very untidy and careless. He was left with good prospects but threw away his chances. He has lived some time in relative poverty with a few short intervals of prosperity. After that he took to drink and his mind went. That is all I can honestly tell you.'

I jumped to my feet in anguish. I felt in that moment as if he had casually ripped my soul apart. Here was the awful downward spiral of my father's life, a downward spiral that we lived through day after day, a secret torture to me and all my family, being recounted like some casual smoking-room anecdote.

'This is unworthy of you, Dr Bell,' I said. 'I could not believe you would descend to it.'

He looked at me in amazement. 'I do not follow.'

'This is the watch of my father. You have somehow got wind of our family history and now you pretend to deduce this knowledge in some fanciful way! To parade a painful family secret in such a fashion is not merely unkind, it...is pure malice.'

The Doctor looked quite concerned. 'My dear Doyle,' he said with some feeling, 'viewing the matter purely as an abstract problem, I had not considered your personal reaction. But I can assure you I am quite unaware of your family situation. You could have been an orphan for all I know.'

His tone was so genuine that slowly some of my rage ebbed away. 'Then in heaven's name,' I asked, 'how?'

He came to me, then, took the watch and looked at me with a directness I had rarely seen before. 'The same as always,' he said quietly. 'Observe the small facts on which larger inferences depend. Careless? Well, the lower part of the watch is dented and cut and marked from the habit of keeping other hard objects such as coins and keys in the same pocket. To treat a fifty-guinea watch like that marks a careless man.'

Now he opened the watch and continued in the same soft, mesmerising tone, determined to let me see the process he had followed: 'Through the lens I can see many pawnbroker's remarks – hence the hard times. But clearly sometimes he had money to redeem his pledge. Finally, look at the scratches round the keyhole – mark where the key has slipped! What sober man's keys could have scored those grooves? And then you will observe here how they become seriously disturbed and destructive, well beyond mere drunkenness.'

We looked at each other. So he had indeed stumbled through his deductions upon our darkest family secret, a secret my mother, my sisters and I were at such pains to conceal. I was impressed, but in that moment my humiliation was so intense I could only nod.

'So have I shown you something at last?' His voice was still very gentle, as was his expression.

'Yes, you have,' I told him. But my heart felt it would break. And shortly afterwards I left him.

The Night Calls

...I (Conan Doyle) had never from the beginning quite been able to accept the vast claims Bell made for his system of deduction. And so it was that one afternoon in February, shortly after he took me into his confidence. I had been bold enough to try and test the man's deductive powers.

Among the many claims Bell made for his precious method, one of the most outlandish was that a close study of any object could lay bare the character of its owner. I was highly dubious of this and had therefore offered him my father's watch as a trial. It had been recently cleaned so I felt absolutely confident that he could get nowhere with it. However, Dr Bell proceeded to use every mark and feature of that watch – certain indentations, some pawnbroker's marks, the tiny scratches around the key – to expose in unbearable detail its owner's mental condition. It was utterly horrifying to me to hear the secret my family had struggled to conceal being analysed and reviewed in so casual a fashion. To his credit, the Doctor saw my anguish and tried his best to make me aware he had been indulging in pure deduction. But even so, for some time after that day, I did my best to avoid him and pleaded my studies as an excuse.

Readers can now appreciate that David Pirie has closely copied the story of 'the watch', noted especially, almost word for word in *The Patient's Eyes*. I ask, did David Pirie obtain permission from the estate of Sir Arthur Conan Doyle, or is this a case of plagiarism?

Finally in this chapter, notes on 'the watch' from *The New Annotated Sherlock Holmes: Volume 3*.

Jewellery usually descends to the eldest son, and he is most likely to have the same name as the father.

This remark suggests that Holmes knew Watson's father's Christian name, which we do not.

Surely it is no great feat to assume that a man who treats a fifty-guinea watch so cavalierly must be a careless man.

The reader will recall that Watson's daily pension was 11s.6d. The watch represents almost a full two years' pension.

Finally, I ask you to look at the inner plate, which contains the keyhole. Look at the thousands of scratches all round the hole – marks where the key has slipped.

Watches that could be wound without a key were a relatively recent invention (the patents for a crown winder were filed between 1845 and 1860), and Watson's father's watch may well have predated the introduction of practical keyless watches. An earlier invention was the so-called Breguet key, also referred as the tipsy key, which could only be turned in one direction.

He winds it at night, and he leaves these traces of his unsteady hand.

Holmes may be right that this feature always shows up on the watch of a drunkard, but it is faulty reasoning to say that the scratches prove that the owner is a drunkard. For example, the owner could suffer palsy or simply be careless, with little regard for possessions.

Chapter 18

The Strange Case Of Mr James Phillimore

Sir Arthur Conan Doyle's novel *The Hound of the Baskervilles* has been credited with more film and television adaptations than any other of his Sherlock Holmes novels or short stories.

Similarly, the name of James Phillimore has resulted in four pastiches found during my research for this book.

The first mention occurred in the story *Thor Bridge* (1922) from *The Case-Book of Sherlock Holmes*. Here Dr Watson is discussing the contents of his dispatch-box which contains papers which are records of cases which Mr Sherlock Holmes had at various times to examine. Among these unfinished tales is that of Mr. James Phillimore, who, stepping back into his own house to get his umbrella, was never more seen in this world.

The second mention was in the apocryphal story *The Adventure of the First Class Carriage* by Ronald Knox (1947), *viz,* 'This case (the disappearance of Mr. Nathaniel Swithinbank) is not without its interest,' observed Holmes, laying down his paper as we steamed through Burnham Beeches 'It presents features which recall the affairs of James Phillimore, whose disappearance (though your loyalty may tempt you to forget it) we investigated without success.'

Adrian Conan Doyle and John Dickson Carr wrote the first pastiche entitled *The Adventure of THE HIGHGATE MIRACLE* from the volume *More Exploits of Sherlock Holmes* (1964).

The second was written by June Thomson from *The Secret Files of Sherlock Holmes* (1990) entitled *The Case of the Vanishing Head-Waiter*.

The third by Alan Stockwell from his volume of stories *The Singular Adventures of Mr Sherlock Holmes* (2003) entitled *The Singular Adventure of The Eccentric Gentleman*.

The final pastiche, *The Adventure of the Forgotten Umbrella* by Mel Gilden from Michael Kurland's (Ed) My Sherlock Holmes (2003) – Untold Stories of the Great Detective.

A synopsis of these four tales follows.

THE ADVENTURE OF THE HIGHGATE MIRACLE

It was late December of the year 1893 – I was not living in Baker Street but I had come for a few days to visit old haunts. Under the heading for this year, my notebook records few cases. Of these only one, the affair of Mrs. Ronder, the veiled lodger, have I seen fit so far to set down: and Mrs. Ronder's problem afforded little scope for my friend's great powers.

Thus Holmes entered a brief period of stagnation and desperation. Until, that is, he received a telegram which ran thus:

'Can you imagine man worshipping umbrella? Husbands are irrational. Suspect chicanery with diamonds. Will call upon you tea-time. – Mrs. Gloria Cabpleasure.'

When Mrs. Cabpleasure arrived at 221B Baker Street, the consultation got off to a bad start as Mrs. Cabpleasure insisted most vehemently that Holmes state his exact fee for his services as she did not want to take the risk of being overcharged by a professional spy!

After this outburst Holmes asked Watson to escort Mrs. Cabpleasure out. However, she aroused his interest as to why her husband cherished, worshipped, idolized a pestilent shabby umbrella, never letting it out of his sight.

Holmes wondered if the umbrella had great financial or sentimental value. Seemingly not so, it cost seven and sixpence two and a half years ago. An idiosyncrasy? Not according to Mrs. Cabpleasure who described her husband as selfish, inhuman, soulless, cruel, abnormally strong and inordinately proud of a very heavy, very glossy brown moustache, worn for many years. He did not drink, interest himself in other women, keep his wife short of money or gamble and never did anything without very good reason.

Mr. James Cabpleasure was the senior partner of the firm of Cabpleasure and Brown, well-known diamond-brokers of Hatton Garden. He had just returned from a protracted six months' business journey to Amsterdam. This period of time was apparently the longest he and his wife had been apart during the fifteen years of their marriage. It became clear at this point that although the umbrella was purchased two and a half years ago, it was only over the past year that Mr. Cabpleasure had worshipped it.

Watson at this point in the narrative proposed that the handle of the umbrella was probably hollow and that diamonds could be secreted in it. Mrs. Cabpleasure soon shot this idea down in flames having had an artisan dissemble the umbrella and show that there was nothing inside of it. If the umbrella is left behind in the house or office even for a few seconds, her husband utters a cry of dread and rushes back for it. Holmes does not see how he can help, as no crime seems to have been committed. However, it seems that Mr. James Cabpleasure stole a large number of diamonds from the safe belonging to himself and his partner. This was followed by a telegram from Mr. Mortimer Brown asking him whether he had removed the diamonds belonging to the Cowles-Derningham. Her husband crept downstairs that night and had a whispered conversation in which Mrs. Cabpleasure overheard only two sentences spoken by her husband: "Be outside the gate before eight-thirty on Thursday morning. Don't fail me!"

Mrs. Cabpleasure assured Holmes that this meeting was to take place outside their house tomorrow morning. Holmes agreed to be there at the appointed time.

The next morning Holmes and Watson were outside the house in Highgate. Holmes noted the semi-circular carriage drive to the front door with a narrow branch to the tradesmen's entrance. Suddenly, Holmes saw Inspector Lestrade and two police constables (both of whom were bulky and wore heavy moustaches) by one of the gates in the wall. It turned out that Inspector Lestrade had been visited by Mrs. Cabpleasure. While they were discussing the matter of Mr. Cabpleasure they were interrupted by Lestrade dashing off to apprehend a portly and florid-faced gentleman, rather nervous-looking in a grey top-hat and a handsome grey overcoat. He turned out to be Mr. Harold Mortimer Brown, the partner of Mr. James Cabpleasure. Holmes was about to ask Mr. Brown a question when he was interrupted by Lestrade who noted a horse-drawn milk-wagon arrive and stop by the front door. The milkman jumped down, went into the entry to fill a small milk-jug waiting for him outside the front door.

Then the slam of the front door and the appearance of Mr. James Cabpleasure, deduced correctly by Watson – minus his umbrella. This resulted in a wordless cry from him and he rushed back into the house. This occurrence astonished the milkman who glanced back, said something inaudible, and then climbed back on to the seat of his wagon.

Lestrade saw it all now – Mr. Cabpleasure and the milkman were close to each other in that entry, and Mr. Cabpleasure could have passed the diamonds to the milkman! Lestrade bullied the milkman (who was, in fact, one Alf Peters) off his wagon, where he was searched by the two constables. No diamonds were found on his person, so Lestrade wanted the milk churns emptied out and even suggested that the milkman had swallowed the diamonds!

Holmes suggested to Lestrade that if Mr. Cabpleasure wanted to hand over the diamonds to an accomplice, why did he not do so on the Tuesday night when he had the secret conversation described by his wife?

Suddenly, Holmes exclaimed that Mr. Cabpleasure was taking a long time to leave the house with his umbrella and had probably vanished! Lestrade said that this was impossible as he had constables watching every door and window. Nevertheless, Lestrade blew his police whistle and plunged towards the house. This gave time for the milkman and Mr. Mortimer Brown to rapidly take their leave.

At this point Holmes explained to Watson that the matter was extremely simple once the significance of the umbrella was explained. At the end of an hour Lestrade rushed out of the house to confirm Holmes's suspicion that Mr. Cabpleasure had in fact disappeared from the house leaving only his hat, greatcoat and umbrella by the front door. Only his wife was left in the house, and Mr. Cabpleasure having driven the servants out of the house last night and appears to have drugged his wife as she had not been aroused by what had been going on since Holmes and Watson had arrived at the house this morning. This proved to be correct as Lestrade had found traces of powdered opium in her cup of hot meat-juice which she took every night before bed.

Lestrade still could not fathom out how Mr. Cabpleasure had managed to leave the house without being seen. Holmes suggested that Lestrade think about the use of a disguise. His conclusion on thinking this over was – as Mr. and Mrs. Cabpleasure had never been seen together, and as he had found a false moustache in the house, and as Mrs. Cabpleasure was presently in the house, he (Mr. Cabpleasure) had gone back into the house this morning and had become Mrs. Cabpleasure! Lestrade rushed into the house and a scream from Mrs. Cabpleasure illustrated the fact that Lestrade had imparted his idea on disguise being the answer to the problem!

At this point Holmes said he had certain lines of enquiry to pursue and asked Watson to return to 221B Baker Street to await a telegram from Mr. Mortimer Brown. This telegram when it arrived, basically said that Mr. James Cabpleasure had every right to take the diamonds as the company belonged to him, Mr. Mortimer Brown being only a nominal partner. His first telegram was only to ensure that the diamonds had arrived safely. He was no thief!

That evening when Holmes returned, Watson put forward an explanation of the whole business – he, Mr. Cabpleasure, did not vanish, he was there all the time – disguised as a police constable, allowing him to leave unobserved. However Holmes reminded Watson that Mrs. Cabpleasure described her husband as being of medium height and was thin or lanky, so could not have impersonated a policeman, who tended to being tall and beefy.

At this point the downstairs doorbell rang followed by footsteps upon the stairs, the door opened…and a man clad in evening clothes, cape and top hat entered…none other than Mr. Alf Peters alias Mr. James Cabpleasure!

Holmes then proceeded to explain all to an astonished Watson.

Mr. Cabpleasure had removed his heavy moustache, rather than assuming one, for his disguise. Holmes in fact had recognised that a hoax or imposture was being carried out in order to deceive Mrs. Cabpleasure. Holmes had traced him through the milk company, had showed them a photograph of Mr. Cabpleasure without a moustache and had confirmation that the photograph was of Alfred Peters who had worked for the company for six months and had requested leave of absence for Tuesday and Wednesday – to 'return' as James Cabpleasure with a false moustache. You then started acting suspiciously, had a conversation with a non-existent 'co-conspirator', dismissed the servants, drugged your wife and left the house. You returned next morning as 'Alf Peters', went into the entrance and 'changed' into Mr. Cabpleasure. Leaving the house you 'forgot' your umbrella, went back for it and became Alf Peters, giving the illusion that the two men had passed each other in the entrance.

Lestrade swore he had seen you before on the milk-wagon, but could not remember where! You must have shared the secret with Mr. Mortimer Brown who appeared this morning to draw attention away from the milkman, which he failed at. Your plans could not have succeeded without the worship of the umbrella. Now Holmes asked Mr. Cabpleasure why he could not have left her without all this imposture? It turned out that Mrs. Cabpleasure was already married when she married Mr. Cabpleasure! And now she wanted to return to her first husband.

It turned out that Cabpleasure was not his real name, it was forced upon him by his uncle, who founded the business. He wanted a new life under his real name of James Phillimore, by leaving all his possessions to his wife, except for twenty-six costly diamonds.

Holmes commented that when a milk-wagon is driven to the front door instead of the tradesman's entrance this helped to identify the social standing of the driver.

Holmes concluded the story as follows:

"From diplomatic necessity, until the day you die, Watson shall call the problem of your disappearance unsolved. Assume what other name you choose. But Mr James Phillimore must never more be seen in this world!"

THE CASE OF THE VANISHING HEAD-WAITER

The adventure began one Friday morning in late May (last 1880s or early 1890s) when I called on Sherlock Holmes, who gave me a letter to read. The writer was one Charles Nelson who wished to visit Holmes concerning the disappearance of his friend, Mr James Phillimore a head-waiter who vanished on Tuesday morning.

I felt that the case was too commonplace for Holmes to investigate, and should be left to the police. Holmes was unconvinced until after he had spoken to the writer of the letter. (While awaiting Mr Nelson, Holmes noted from the daily paper that there had been another burglary in Knightsbridge, this time at the home of Lady Whittaker whose emeralds had been stolen. Holmes wondered if Inspector Lestrade would be visiting with regards to the case).

Mr Nelson arrived on time with a companion, Miss Cora Page, the fiancée of James Phillimore, who promptly took charge of the interview. It turned out that she was feeling humiliated by the fact that her fiancé had disappeared when they were due to marry next month and all arrangements had already been made. She became more distressed as the interview progressed. At this point, Holmes asked me to take Miss Page downstairs to Mrs Hudson for tea and biscuits.

Having done that I returned upstairs to find Mr Nelson talking to Holmes and seemingly more at ease. Mr Nelson seemingly accompanied Mr Phillimore every morning to Clapham Junction station in order for them both to catch the eight-five train into town for their work, Mr Nelson as a solicitor and Mr Phillimore as a head-waiter. Prior to their walk to the station on the Tuesday morning in question, Mr Phillimore was standing by his gate as usual when Mr Nelson arrived from his lodgings. Deciding that it might rain, Mr Phillimore went back indoors for his umbrella, leaving the front door ajar, and that was the last Mr Nelson saw of him! He waited for five minutes, went into the house and with Mr Phillimore's housekeeper searched the house and the garden to no avail. Mr Phillimore could not have climbed over the garden fence as it was too high. Neither could he have left by the tradesmen's entrance as neither his housekeeper saw him pass by the kitchen window nor Mr Nelson standing by the front gate.

Holmes then questioned Mr Nelson about the character of Mr Phillimore. He was described as very quiet, unassuming, regular in his habits, reliable, thought highly of by his employers with no financial problems. He lived modestly on his wages and his tips (which seemed to surprise Holmes, as if he had never heard of the word), and didn't smoke, drink or gamble. The house in Laburnum Grove, from where he disappeared was his, following the death of his parents, and it was there that he planned to set up home with Miss Page.

However, when Mrs Phillimore was alive, she did not see eye to eye with Cora Page, neither of them willing to share the same house with the other. She was a bit of a tartar and led her son a terrible dance. So as soon as she died, Miss Page insisted on naming a wedding day, which was highly unlikely now to take place. Watching Mr Nelson and Cora Page's body language as they walked away down Baker Street, Holmes said to me that unless Mr Nelson is very careful he will find himself married off sooner or later to his friend's fiancée and she won't take no for an answer!

Holmes thought he detected a whiff of conspiracy. They both left then to examine the house from where Mr Phillimore had disappeared. Here they met Mrs Bennet, the housekeeper, Holmes questioned her about the morning of the disappearance. She confirmed that Mr Phillimore's behaviour was the same as every morning. Dr Watson thought it significant that the paper Mr Phillimore glanced at over breakfast was *The Times*. She then went on to confirm what Mr Nelson had already told Holmes and Watson about the search that took place of the house and garden. Holmes noticed that Mr Phillimore's umbrella was still in the hall-stand. Mrs Bennet said that her employer had left everything behind except what he stood up in. He had not even so much as gone on holiday except for the week in Margate after his mother died. This occurrence interested Holmes who wondered where he had stayed. Mrs Bennet said only that it was a boarding –house with a funny, foreign-sounding name. Holmes inquired whether Mr Phillimore had recently changed his routine in any way. Seemingly he had taken to locking his wardrobe over the past few days, but that it was now unlocked, a fact that Holmes had expected without viewing the wardrobe. Before Mrs Bennet left she confirmed that no one had passed by the kitchen window overlooking the passage of the tradesman's entrance.

Holmes was obviously interested in the matter of the locked wardrobe, and I in *The Times*, during our discussion in the sitting-room. Holmes then examined two drawers of a sideboard and handed me a small bundle of printed sheets. These turned out to be music-hall programmes – Mr Nelson having mentioned in his meeting with Holmes that Mr Phillimore treated himself to a seat in the upper circle at a music-hall. Holmes and I then examined the house and garden – in the house Holmes noted that the wardrobe in Phillimore's bedroom was roomy – and in the garden found nothing to explain the disappearance of Mr James Phillimore.

We left the house then, walked to the bottom of the hill, where Holmes hailed a cab. Holmes asked me what he thought the lifetime's ambition of Phillimore was. I felt it would be to retire, but Holmes thought it would be to own the establishment where he worked, and I agreed with him. Then Holmes said the most extraordinary element of the case was the timing of Mr Phillimore's disappearance – why Tuesday, why not Monday or Friday? I suggested that maybe something had happened to detain him on Monday. Holmes exclaimed that I may have put my finger on the key to the whole mystery! Holmes also suggested that Miss Cora Page might be the reason for his disappearance and if we unearthed Phillimore I must not mention the possibility of Miss Page transferring her affection to Charlie Nelson, lest Mr Phillimore came out of hiding to save his friend from the clutches of Cora Page! I had noted earlier Phillimore's regularity of habits and Holmes felt that this aspect of his personality would provide the answer to his secret.

He decided to return to Laburnum Grove at the same hour of the morning in which Phillimore disappeared in order to see what Charles Nelson and Mrs Bennet had missed. The following morning we were outside 17 Laburnum Grove in a hansom on the opposite side of the road and a little distance from the house. We observed Charlie Nelson at precisely seven thirty hesitate outside number 17, and then carry on in the direction of Lavender Hill to get his train to work.

Then Holmes became very interested in the arrival of a baker's van drawn by a pony. It stopped outside number 17 and the delivery man, a tall youth of about 18 or so, dressed in a cap and a long white apron, climbed off his seat and, taking a basket of bread, went off down the tradesman's passage, reappearing a few moments later. Holmes then leapt out of the cab and left me to return to my surgery, for I had a patient to see.

We met up again for lunch the next day at 221B Baker Street. During lunch Holmes told me that he was now fairly confident that he could find Mr Phillimore because of his regular routine and habits. Though he had disappeared, he would certainly reappear in some environment where he will feel almost as much at home. [At this time Holmes reminded me of Harry Beecham, the notorious forger who escaped the clutches of police but was caught by Holmes because he always went to the same barber, a habit he could not shake off].

This environment had to be the Margate boarding-house then, I suggested, to which Holmes agreed, but how to find it? The foreign-sounding name mentioned by Mrs Bennet, probably was "Mon Repose", a favourite with seaside landladies, according to Holmes, and one with a neat garden and freshly-whitened front doorstep.

We arrived at Margate and instructed the cabby from the rank outside the station to take us to boarding houses with the name 'Mon Repose'. The fourth one we came to was not unlike Phillimore's house in Clapham and had a neat front garden. Holmes leapt out, knocked on the front door, telling the lady who answered the door that he was enquiring after a Mr James Phillimore. At that, a man emerged from a door leading off the hall, and approaching us made it clear that he knew who we were, and from his initial remark about Charlie Nelson, we knew him to be none other than the missing Mr James Phillimore!

Holmes told Phillimore that he knew the method by which he contrived his disappearance, but not his reasons. How he 'disappeared' was, when he returned for his umbrella, he went upstairs to his bedroom and dressed as a bread-man using the clothes he had in his locked wardrobe. He then left the house by means of the tradesman's passage, passing Sammy Webb the real bread-man, who of course, was in on the conspiracy. Neither Mrs Bennet nor Charlie Nelson paid any attention to the 'bread-man'. When Mr Nelson went into the house to look for his friend, Webb then left by the side gate and returned to his closed van, Phillimore having in the meantime climbed into the back of the van.

Phillimore explained that the reason for his disappearance was the landlady, Ellen, whom he had fallen in love with when he stayed at the boarding-house before. He was making arrangements to have his house made over to Charlie Nelson and for an annuity to be paid to Mrs Bennet. As for Cora Page, he was going to give her his savings of a hundred pounds or so. Holmes also knew that Phillimore had investments from the "tips" he received at the restaurant by being able to lip-read (for the benefit of his deaf mother) business clients' discussions about stocks and shares. The reason he had disappeared on a Tuesday was because on the Monday the market was particularly buoyant, as he gleaned from *The Times*. He made £5,000 and was going to use the money to buy a nice, comfortable hotel on the sea-front which had recently come on the market, and to marry Ellen.

Holmes and I wished him well. However Holmes wondered why he had 'disappeared in such a spectacular fashion', instead of just leaving a letter and walking out of the house? It was due, said James Phillimore to Marvello the Great Magician from the music-hall, whose assistant vanished from behind an umbrella! This gave him the idea to vanish in style as Marvello did in a cloud of coloured smoke!

Holmes and I then bade goodbye to Mr James Phillimore and returned to London. But not before Holmes reminded me that I may write up the story, but on no account was I to publish it. Otherwise Miss Cora Page, on reading it, would turn Margate inside out in order to sue Mr James Phillimore for breach of promise. It must, therefore, remain one of those cases which Sherlock Holmes was unable to solve.

THE SINGULAR ADVENTURE OF THE ECCENTRIC GENTLEMAN

In one of my previous writings I made mention of the strange case of the city gentleman who, stepping back into his house for his umbrella, was never seen again. It occurs to me that now the time is right for me to give a full explanation of this bizarre event. An event that was to become the first of several such odd happenings throughout London in that winter of 1887.

A London cab driver called at 221B Baker Street carrying a typical leather suitcase, about which the cabby proceeded to tell Holmes the following tale. Yesterday he had been called to a fare off Park Lane. A Mr James Phillimore wanted picking up at twenty-three minutes past two. Holmes thought the accuracy of the time strange and the cabby agreed.

He arrived at about quarter-past and waited for twenty-three minutes past. But a couple of minutes later the gent appears and hands him this heavy suitcase which he hands into the cab followed by Mr Phillimore, who jumps out and returns to the house to get his umbrella which he's forgotten. After about ten minutes and no Mr Phillimore, the cabby goes up to the house and knocks on the door. The servant girl who answers looks at him as if he's mad when he asks for Mr Phillimore and the butler who appears says that no one of that name lives in this house! The cabby asks on either side, but no Phillimore lives there either. He returns to the cabbie's shelter after half-an-hour and following a discussion with his mates, he turns up at 221B Baker Street with his tale.

Holmes asked the cabby if he was sure that he had not carried Mr Phillimore before. The cabby said no, but that he would have remembered him if he had been dressed as he was yesterday – perfectly normal – except for a bright yellow top hat!

Holmes then opened the suitcase which contained nothing but seven common house bricks wrapped in a great quantity of old newspapers. Holmes gave the cabby a half-sovereign and off he went. Holmes left the matter at this point saying that James Phillimore was at great pains to establish the time of this affair and that this was the key to the whole matter.

Some days later, two odd incidents took place, the second of which appeared to involve Mr James Phillimore. Firstly was a newspaper report about a diner at Simpson's in the Strand who stood on his chair and harangued the diners. He left quietly when the manager threatened to call the police. The second occurred a few days later when I was passing through Trafalgar Square. A man was feeding the pigeons, conspicuously encouraging them in a loud voice. He then loudly declared that it was now past five o'clock, he had been there over an hour, and it was now time to go! With that he donned a yellow top hat and disappeared into the crowd and was lost to view. On reporting the incident to Holmes, he suggested we make a note of the dates and times of the incidents and look for any further examples of bizarre but harmless behaviour. A number of sightings of eccentric behaviour were reported in the newspapers, but none seemed to involve Mr Phillimore. The trail was going cold and Holmes was involved in the affair of The Copper Beeches.

Then one day a Samuel Gossage called at 221B for Holmes's advice. He told the following long story to Holmes and myself.

He commenced with a family history, the most interesting fact being that his late mother was murdered by a servant girl, Eliza Lawson! This servant girl was a criminal, stealing from her employer and consorting with unsavoury types from the garrison at Chatham. It appeared that his mother went down to the cellar to give the girl a week's notice because of her behaviour. An argument must have ensued, whereupon the girl, who had been chopping firewood, struck his mother on the head with the axe, killing her instantly. She then removed his mother's dress, stuffed it down the privy, then dragged the body upstairs, and laid it on the bed. She then washed his mother's face as the bleeding had stopped and changed her dress as it was spotted with blood.

Suddenly, there came a knock at the door, Lawson panicked, and grabbing a knife, she slit her own throat! It wasn't the police at the door only two lads who wanted to know if the household wanted their snow shovelled. When they saw the state of Lawson, they came and got me as they knew I only lived a couple of streets away. She told me that two dustbin men had attacked them, tried to rape her and murdered my mother! Also, they washed my mother's face and bolted the door behind them when they left! In spite of the damming evidence, said Mr Gossage, Lawson was found *Not Guilty*. He wanted Sherlock Holmes to have the verdict overturned. Holmes explained to him that as the law stood this would not be possible. At this point, Holmes excused himself to consult a book which might help with Mr Gossage's case. Strangely, I thought, that all his books were on shelves in the room with us or in his bedroom, but that he did not head in that direction. Holmes then returned, having been unable to find the book in question. [What Holmes had actually been up to, I found out later, while out of the room, was to arrange for a Baker Street Irregular to follow Gossard to find out where he really lived]. He advised Mr Gossard to see one of the top criminal lawyers. Our visitor thanked us, gave Holmes his address, and left, noting that he had arrived at 8.00pm and that it was now 8.30pm.

Holmes then threw himself into his armchair and laughed and laughed. The reason for his mirth was because, he told me, we had been in the presence of none other than Mr James Phillimore! He had come to 221B in order to provide himself with a timed alibi. When he asked Holmes for help following the murder of his mother, he did not realise Holmes's prodigious memory for past criminal cases. Gossage's 'murder case' took place fifty years ago! It was all a charade to provide him with a water-tight alibi. But for what reason?

A week later Holmes asked me to tail Phillimore/Gossage from his house near Regent's Park, where the Baker Street Irregular had followed him to. Holmes expected him to draw attention to himself and the time of this occurrence. Whatever he did, I had to ensure that he was arrested and detained at least overnight in jail. Holmes in the meantime would follow his partner (Holmes was sure that he had one), and hope to catch him red-handed.

At 6.30 that evening the two of us were concealed opposite a house near Regent's Park. Soon Phillimore emerged and I followed him, leaving Holmes still watching the house. Phillimore made his way by cab to the Lyceum Theatre, followed not too closely by me-to prevent him recognising me. I obtained a seat in the pit to watch the show.

During the interval I heard comments about a person in the dress circle (where Phillimore had a seat), who was behaving excessively noisy, causing discomfort to the rest of the audience around him. This must be Phillimore I thought. I then had a brainwave – I unfastened my fobwatch and tucked it into my side pocket. At the final interval I made my way to the salon of the dress circle where I engaged 'Mr Gossage' in pointless conversation until the bell for the final act was rung. I then went to the manager (Bram Stoker) and complained that I had been robbed of my pocket watch. I asked that the police be summoned as I suspected that the thief was the man from the dress circle who had been causing trouble to the patrons of the Lyceum.

At the conclusion of the play Stoker took the subject into his office where my watch was found in the suspects pocket (where I had placed it during our meeting in the salon). He was arrested and taken to Bow Street police station, where I was told to attend the following morning to give evidence. There I found Holmes (who had not returned the previous evening to 221B), and Inspector Lestrade – who wanted to know what the connection was between the burglar he had arrested last night and the person that I had had arrested.

We looked at this prisoner and Lestrade was astounded to see that it was the same man who was at Scotland Yard! Holmes explained that he was one half of a pair of zygotic twins who formed a team for nefarious purposes. While one drew attention to himself the other committed crimes, each giving the other an alibi. Holmes worked this out by keeping a record of the dates and times of various burglaries and their relationship to the singular and curious happenings.

Hence, concluded the Phillimore/Gossage events of an eccentric nature.

THE ADVENTURE OF THE FORGOTTEN UMBRELLA

This story is written in the first person singular as follows:

I, Mr. James Phillimore, still being very much in this world, take the liberty of explaining myself what happened on that chilly April morning – believing that the true and correct details of the case should be preserved. The facts are both less mysterious and more dramatic than some of the fantastic suppositions that have been put forward in the more sensational stories of the daily press – having to do with neither black magic nor abduction by Mr. Well's Martians, but only with human greed.

Five years ago I met Alice Madison and we fell in love with each other and married. Alice would stop at my office, where I was vice-president of Morehouse & Co., an investment company, so that we could lunch together. In the corner of my office was a large safe containing money and stocks, bonds, contracts and other important papers. Only Mr. Morehouse and I knew the combination.

My life continued without any problems until the evening I came home to find my wife in serious conversation with a man who I could only describe as a scruffy individual with an unpleasant manner towards both of us. When I tackled him about his attitude towards my wife, he left with a sneer as to whether she was indeed my wife.

Once she had settled down, Alice astonished me by saying that her visitor could ruin our lives and the police would be unable to help. It turned out that Alice was married before we met and that she was *still* married! The man she had married was the unpleasant man who had just left, Mr. Harvey Maynard. He turned out to be a violent drunk who beat Alice. She wanted to divorce him, but could not because of the shame it would entail.

One morning he did not return and Alice found out that he had been arrested for a brutal robbery and sent to Dartmoor prison. Some years later she was notified that he had died crossing the moor during an escape attempt. However, this turned out to be untrue as it was he who James Phillimore had found accosting his wife. It appeared that he had met and killed a man on the moor after forcing him to exchange clothes. Maynard had only come to gloat over his escape and to tell her that he was going to South America where the police would never find him.

Even though Alice was a bigamist I could not stop loving her, and now that Maynard had left, it was the end of the incident. Or so I thought. But it turned out that he had not gone to South Africa after all and in the meantime had forced my wife to commit a crime.

A few days later Alice came to the office as usual, albeit earlier. I carried on with my business, leaving the room for a few minutes to obtain a signature from Mr. Morehouse. When I returned I locked the safe and Alice and I went for our customary lunch. Alice's mind was not on the meal but she said there was nothing amiss. That evening I found Alice in tears again and inquiring what was the matter, she told me that she had a terrible admission to make.

The reason for Maynard's visit was to force her to give him £1,000 or he would report her bigamy to the papers. She had tried to pawn her jewelry but could not raise the amount specified. So she stole the money out of the safe while I was out of the office as I had left the door ajar.

Knowing that I would be the main suspect for the robbery once it came to light tomorrow morning, I sent Alice off to her sister's in Kent, so that I could put an idea I had into play.

The next morning I gave the cook and maid the day off. I donned a painter's cap and smock over my clothes, applied a false moustache and climbed a ladder at the side of the house and began painting the wall. Soon a hansom drew up outside my house, a man jumped out followed by a group of police who quickly surrounded the building. Just as the plainclothes officer was about to knock on the front door, he was hailed by a man who I recognised as Sherlock Holmes, he having been pointed out to me by one of my clients. The policeman and Mr. Holmes spoke together, then he knocked on the door.

I quickly climbed in the window, removed my painting clothes and moustache and went to answer the door. The policeman introduced himself as Inspector Lestrade and told me I had to accompany him to Scotland Yard as I was suspected of having been involved in a robbery at my office. As we left I said that it looked like rain and could I go back for my umbrella and Inspector Lestrade agreed. As soon as the front door was closed I dashed upstairs, put on my painting garb and moustache, climbed out of the window and continued painting the wall. One of the policemen shouted up to me as to whether or not I had seen Mr. Phillimore. I answered that if he was the bloke who lived in this house, the answer was no. Shortly afterwards all the police left to search for me and I was congratulating myself on my escape, when a voice from below hailed me. It was Mr. Sherlock Holmes who asked me to come down. I continued to try and bluff along as a painter, but Mr. Holmes saw through my disguise because there were no splatters of paint on my shoes. Holmes said that things would go better for me if I returned the money. When I said I could not as I didn't know where it was, Holmes escorted me to 221B where we could continue to talk without any interference from the police.

I asked Mr. Holmes how he happened to be at my house this morning. Simple really, Morehouse & Co. had employed him to retrieve the money they believed I had stolen. I then told him the story behind the theft of the money. After listening intently Mr. Holmes convinced me that not only would he recover the money but also would bring Mr. Harvey Maynard to justice. Holmes now brought out his handkerchief, unfolded it, and revealed a piece of sawdust which he had picked up from the entryway to my house. Mr. Holmes informed me that, from the odour of the sawdust, that it had come from the floor of a public house, and had been left by Maynard.

I had noted to Mr. Holmes earlier that Maynard had ignored two cabs when he left my house. This suggested to Mr. Holmes that the pub was within walking distance of my house. A study of an ordnance map on London convinced Mr. Holmes that the commercial hotel and pub was The Twin Lambs and was situated in an alley in a low part of St. Marylebone. Before visiting the pub we shared a breakfast prepared by Mrs. Hudson, Mr. Holmes' landlady.

We finished our breakfast, armed ourselves (I had Dr. Watson's revolver), and set off for the pub. We entered the dingy, dirty premises, found an empty table and sat down. We ordered two mugs of beer and while drinking these I told Mr. Holmes that Maynard was not there. Suddenly, a man exploded through a door at the back of the room, followed swiftly by a second man who set about beating the first man, who, I told Mr. Holmes was the man we sought. Before we knew it, the entire room had joined in the fight. Suddenly a shot rang out, Maynard fell to the floor mortally wounded, and all the men rushed from the pub.

Mr. Holmes went across to Maynard's body, searched his pockets and removed a packet containing a sheaf of ten-pound notes – the money he had stolen from me. Mr. Holmes put the packet into his own coat pocket, and we hurriedly left. Back in his rooms Mr. Holmes arranged for me to travel to Kent and from there Alice and I would leave for the United States of America, never to return to England. Mr. Holmes would return the money and that would be the end of the story.

Chapter 19

Further Introductions & Prefaces

The Sherlock Holmes Illustrated Omnibus

Dust jacket

Here for the first time are all the Sherlock Holmes stories which Sidney Paget illustrated, in facsimile, as they originally appeared in *The Strand Magazine* in the 1890s and 1900s. Although two long stories had previously been published elsewhere, it was in the pages of *The Strand* that Sherlock Holmes really attracted the enormous following which has been his ever since. As Leslie Fiedler says in his Introduction, 'the face we are likely to recall when we think of Sherlock Holmes is not the invention of Conan Doyle' but that of his most important illustrator, Sidney Paget. Paget became in effect Holmes' 'co-creator, his author's collaborator. It seems therefore, only fitting in this edition the true text – icon and words – are reproduced as it first appeared in *The Strand*.

The story goes that Paget was commissioned by mistake, in place of his brother Walter, the illustrator of Rider Haggard and Robert Louis Stevenson. By a nice twist Sidney did in fact use Walter's features as his model for Holmes. The only regret is that Sidney Paget died in 1908 and so did not illustrate the later stories.

In the past only those lucky enough to own a set of *The Strand Magazine* have been able to appreciate how the flavour of these marvellous stories is brought out when accompanied by the Paget illustrations, but this double pleasure is now available to everyone.

INTRODUCTION

Art in the Blood: Some Notes on Sherlock Holmes

By Leslie Fiedler (1976)

During the last two decades of the nineteenth century, there occurred in England an extraordinary event still unnoticed in the respectable literary histories of the period: the emergence of a new mythology which has possessed the imagination of the world ever since. It is a mythology especially appealing to those otherwise culturally underprivileged, to children, and to the minimally literate and those who can read only images on the screen. But it also moves the educated classes, who, though they are familiar with the books that preserve classical and Judaeo-Christian mythology, are no longer moved by them to wonder and assent; and who, therefore, turn to the mass media – quite like their less-educated brothers and sisters, or sons and daughters – in quest of satisfaction once provided by High Literature and Scripture.

For the contemporary mass audience, then, at both its poles, highbrow and lowbrow, traditional gods and demons have been effectively replaced by those larger-than-life figures who first appeared in certain popular illustrated Victorian journals, in the form either of short stories or of serialized novels; then passed rapidly into the public domain – reworked not merely by parodists and imitators in the same medium, but by painters, playwrights, and eventually makers of movies. Most of us in the last decades of the twentieth century, in fact, tend to remember such characters first of all as they were re-embodied in certain films of the 1930s, though the first of them, Frankenstein's Monster, pre-dated Queen Victoria. Most of them surfaced, however, in late-Victorian times, as part of a strange breakthrough – the resurgence of all that had been repressed in the name of rationality and gentility, which also included a renaissance of pornography and pop occultism, the peaking of an especially violent wave of feminism, and a renewed interest in the fairy tale and the freakshow.

But the longest-lived aspect of that breakthrough was the new popular fiction, a series of books most of which have never been out of print since, though a good many of them have been ignored or even condemned by literary critics, even as they have continued to be read behind their backs. Just to recite the names of their mythological protagonists is enough to stir a response at once too deep and too shamefaced to be classified as merely esthetic: Sherlock Holmes, Dracula, Long John Silver, Dr. Jekyll and Mr. Hyde, Ayesha or "She," Mowgli the Jungle Boy, Gunga Din and Kim, the Time Traveller, Dorian Grey, and (extending over geographical boundaries a little) Tom Sawyer, Injun Joe, and Huckleberry Finn. How different our response to a corresponding set of names picked at random out of, say, the Victorian books prized by an elitist critic like F.R. Leavis: Dorothea Brook, Gwendolyn Harleth, Hyacinth Robinson, Heyst, Razumov. For an equally equivocal but authentic tremor we would have to compile a list out of certain immensely popular works created over the succeeding forty years during which Conan Doyle continued to re-imagine Holmes: Dorothy and the Wizard of Oz, for instance, and Tarzan – or shifting medium and going beyond Conan Doyle's death, King Kong, Superman, Donald Duck, and Mickey Mouse.

Kipling's Kim, Wells' Time Traveller, Twain's Tom and Huck, along with Wilde's Dorian Grey represent borderline cases, perhaps, since – after long debate – the critics have either granted them full status as o.k. literature, or at least have admitted them into the demimonde of "children's books," rather than dismissing them as the sort of junk appropriate only to a mass audience too hurried and harried to read sensitively. But the mass audience has been as indifferent to the critics' approval as to their disapproval – loving with equal and undiscriminating fervour Holmes and Huck, Dracula and Dorian Grey, and rewarding them with an accolade out of the control of the critics: success in the marketplace.

The mass audience had, indeed, begun to control the marketplace for a century and a half before Conan Doyle began to publish; from the moment at which Samuel Richardson first created Pamela and Clarissa: fictional characters who seemed to a new group of readers – devotees of the first pop form of literature, the bourgeois novel – as real or even more real than life itself, precisely because they embodied not their shared waking experience but their common dreams.

By 1880, however, that audience had increased immensely in size, as the Common Schools spread literacy to more and more members of a more and more overwhelmingly urban population, and new advances in Gutenburg technology made possible mass-produced, illustrated magazines in which their hunger for appropriate archetypal tales could be widely distributed. *The Strand*, in which – beginning in the year 1891 – the adventures of Sherlock Holmes were published, was just such a magazine. And, typically, it was snatched from the railway station bookstalls by travellers on the run, commuters from city to city who longed for a literature that could be consumed in transit and tossed aside when their journeys were done: a disposable literature, unpretentious and certainly unaware that it was creating new myths of city life and of exotic places outside the city such as could be dreamed only by city dwellers.

Paris had been the first modern city mythologized by popular fiction, chiefly in the works of Eugene Sue. And when Edgar Allan Poe created the detective story, the first specifically urban pop genre, he kept that city as his setting. But Conan Doyle, though he modelled his amateur sleuth on Poe's Auguste Dupin, moved him to his own gaslit late-nineteenth-century London, a city to which he returned again and again as he grew older and it grew evermore distant from him in time. No electric lights ever illuminated the streets of his imagination, nor did motor cars speed through them, nor airplanes overfly them – though at the moment he wrote the last adventure of Holmes, Lindbergh's "Spirit of St. Louis" may well have been passing above his head. It was not a matter of choice for Conan Doyle, whose readers – as well as whatever deep in his psyche responded to their mythological and therefore unchangeable needs before they were able to express them – kept him bound to one time and place. He may have preferred to live outside of London, towards which he was in fact deeply ambivalent, describing it in the first adventure of Holmes as "that great cess-pool into which all the loungers and idlers of the Empire are irresistibly drained"; yet it is to purge that cesspool that Holmes exists, boasting just before his (presumed) death at the hands of Moriarty, "The air of London is the sweeter for my presence." But Holmes could not, of course, die; rather, he had to die and be reborn over and over, so that the fog-shrouded scene of violence and deceit could be purged over and over – yet remain always the same.

Holmes is, in short, like the city in which he dwells, and myth and therefore immortal, unkillable even by his creator. Like Frankenstein's Monster and Dracula, Tarzan and Rider Haggard's Ayesha, he began to detach himself at the very start from those printed texts in which we first learn of his existence, persisting as a name of immense mythic resonance and a series of visual images, or icons, that continue to haunt us long after we have forgotten the plots which were their occasion and the words in which they were first formulated.

In fact, the face we are likely to recall when we think of Sherlock Holmes is not the invention of Conan Doyle, who imagined him more gaunt, ill-favored and grotesque than we can any longer quite believe. Nor is it even the face of one of the famous actors who recreated him on stage and screen, like William Gillette or Basil Rathbone; they were already accommodating their makeup to the image created – in spite of Conan Doyle's own descriptions – by Holmes' most important illustrator, Sidney Paget. Paget attributed to Holmes the features of his own beloved, balding, and saturnine but finally handsome brother, thus becoming, in effect, his co-creator, his author's collaborator. It seems, therefore, only fitting that in this edition the true text – icon and words – be reproduced as it first appeared in *The Strand*.

But in order that a fuller context be established, it is necessary that the reader hear ringing in his inner ear as he reads Doyle's own words certain lines of dialogue ("Elementary, my dear Watson" and "Quick, Watson, the needle!"), which he will find neither here in this omnibus nor in any of the other sixty canonical tales. Where these lines came from is hard to say – out of some forgotten dramatic version perhaps, or some snide travesty, or most probably, out of the imaginary ur-text continually revised by the popular imagination, to which they seemed more and more its own creation, as Doyle's protagonists came to be known even to some who had not read a single one of his stories.

Eventually the popular audience became a full collaborator with Doyle in his lifelong task, not just in retrospect but in prospect as well – suggesting to him (like his own mother, an ardent fan who provided him with at least one story idea) plots for future tales, and, of course, refusing to let him abandon his series right up to the moment of his death. But the name "Sherlock Holmes," so richly resonant that it seemed a myth in itself, or at least something from which the whole myth can be inferred, was his own invention. It came to him as if from someplace else, in a kind of vision, at first a little blurred, then slowly sharpening into focus.

"Sherrinford Holmes," Doyle jotted down as his private investigator's name in the notes written to himself before he had yet contrived an action for him to perform. And "Sherrington Hope" was his second try, his second miss. But then, for reasons hard to fathom, there apparently emerged in his undermind the image of another mythological figure, equally hawkbeaked, lean and lonely, the Jew Shylock, and the name Sherlock was born of the grafting. Doyle, however, could not even begin to imagine such an antimask of his own stolid self – so Hyde-like a dope addict, housebreaker, a compounder of felonies (though always, to be sure, in the name of a "higher justice"), so resolute an enemy of women and rebel against the bourgeois family – until he had first imagined a Jekyll-like mask for himself as author: a kind of living pseudonym as it were, through whom he could spin a series of yarns that he might otherwise have been reluctant to acknowledge, in part because they celebrate one whose lifestyle was profoundly different not just from his own, but from that of "the average male Briton" who was Doyle's ideal reader.

That self and that ideal reader are represented, of course, by Dr. Watson, with his "average male Briton's" name. Doyle began by calling him "Ormond Sacker," a palpably absurd appellation for that hefty and moustached medico, who not only resembled him physically, but, like him at the moment he began his series, was just back from the Imperial wars, in quest of a wife and ready to turn author. It is hard to understand in light of all this how some commentators have persuaded themselves that the good doctor was modelled on someone else, and that Holmes is a barely camouflaged self-portrait of the author.

Never mind that Holmes was thin, Doyle fat. Or that Holmes lay indolently on his couch between cases, poisoning himself with the fumes of cigars, cigarettes, and pipes, or shooting up cocaine and morphine, while Doyle subscribed to Sandow's body building courses and worked out with barbells. And forget, too, that Holmes was prey to bouts of melancholia and ennui, while Doyle roved restlessly through the world, running for Parliament, espousing lost causes, and singing the glories of Empire. But what are we to make of the fact that Holmes despised team sports even more than he did politics, while Doyle was a frantic footballer and cricketer until age and multiple broken bones benched him; that Holmes played the violin and admired the baroque musician Lassus, while Doyle performed only on the tuba and the banjo. And especially, how to explain the portrayal of Holmes as a sceptic, a total rationalist, who refused ever to deal with the "supernatural" except by exposing its manifestations as delusions and hoaxes, while

Doyle was a lifelong seeker after the occult, who flirted with theosophy and ended as a convert to spiritualism.

But what most completely differentiates the two are their attitudes towards women. Doyle, for all his occasional outbursts against the more violent feminists of his time, lived always in the shadow of the other sex: his mother first of all, whom he never ceased to consult and adore; two wives, the second of whom he loved passionately, though platonically, during the years his first wife was dying a lingering death; and finally a daughter. But Holmes inhabited a bachelor apartment, presided over only by a housekeeper who never seems to have tidied up its masculine clutter, and he was – as far as the text tells us – apparently not even born of woman. Certainly, there is no mention in the sixty tales of a mother, much less a sister or former mistress – though there are female clients in great plenty, and even a couple of adventuresses praised for having proved better in a battle of wits than Holmes himself.

If his consulting detective represented any aspect of Doyle, it was precisely that aspect which his whole public life and stance denied: his shadow self, which is to say, not merely the thin man that popular wisdom tells us persists inside of every fat man, but the diabolical antimask ordinarily released only in nightmares or madness. It is true that Doyle would, perhaps could, never quite confess how diabolical Holmes really was – splitting his psychic underside of himself down the middle once more by creating Holmes' enemy twin, Professor Moriarty – so that when, in the last story in this collection, they die offstage in each others' arms, Dr. Watson can describe his friend – in terms that suggest Socrates or even Jesus Christ – as "the best and the wisest man whom I have ever known."

But when in his autobiography Doyle poses the question of which of his two "puppets" is most like himself, asking "whether I myself had the qualities which I depicted [in Holmes], or whether I was merely the Watson that I look," the words which occur to him in reference to these characters spun out of his "inner consciousness" are "villains," "grim as doom," "dim ill-boding shadow,"

> Darkling figures, stern or quaint,
> Now a savage, now a saint,
> Showing fitfully and faint

In the gloom

Clearly, Watson is not a creature of that interior gloom, like Moriarty or Colonel Moran, the declared villains of the tales, or even like Holmes who more resembles such villains that he does his ingenuous comrade-in-arms. The point is that Watson functions within the fiction as Holmes' author, whereas Holmes plays the part of his *daemon*, the Heathcliffe to his Catherine.

To be sure, they are both projections of Doyle; but the dependable and obtuse doctor represents everything that Doyle suspected he had – choosing the road of respectability – become; while the "bohemian" detective stands for what he might have become had he chosen otherwise, or rather, had he been able to so choose. The relationship of such masturbatory complementary fantasies is typically rendered in novels (as the comparison with *Wuthering Heights* suggests) erratically. And there has always been a few readers who have suspected that Holmes and Watson, after those dinner and theatre dates, nights out together at the Turkish Baths, or the long smoking bouts which followed the completion of some breathless adventure, may well have ended up in bed together. But if Doyle, in the darkest recesses of his "inner consciousness," imagined them in so supremely antibourgeois an embrace, he does not confess it. We are not given, as a matter of fact, very precise information about the sleeping arrangements at 221b Baker Street – and so in a sense are left free to fantasize as we will.

But we do know from Conan Doyle's autobiography how thoroughly he disapproved of homosexual relationships, boasting that not even in prep school was he exposed to their temptations – thanks to the vigilance of the Jesuits who presided over his own schooling. "We were never allowed for an instant to be alone with each other," he tells us, " and I think that the immorality which is rife in public schools was at a minimum in consequence." And a little later remembering Oscar Wilde, he speaks disapprovingly though compassionately ("a hospital rather than a police court was the place for its consideration") of "the monstrous development which ruined him." There seems little doubt in my own mind, however, that Wilde "already famous, as the champion of estheticism" when Doyle met him was one of the models for the dandiacal and decadent side of Holmes – who was like him a practitioner of "art for art's sake," seeking refuge from the tedium of late-Victorian respectability in drugs.

Doyle speaks often of Holmes as a "scientist," and indeed, we first meet him bending over a test tube; but he proves finally to be an odd sort of a scientist. Not only is he utterly contemptuous of physics and astronomy – boasting of his indifference to whether earth revolves about the sun or vice versa, but he is not even a very scientific detective – eschewing for instance the use of fingerprints in detecting crime (the only fingerprint which appears in the whole canon is a forgery) though by 1894 Mark Twain had already used the techniques of Bertillon to resolve the plot of *Pudd'nhead Wilson*. But even more often Doyle refers to Holmes as an "artist," remarking at one point the effect on him of his painter forbears in a phrase that continues to resonate in my mind, "Art in the blood is liable to take the strangest forms."

It seems to me, in fact, that it is precisely as the detective that the *poete maudit*, the alienated artist, enters the domain of pop literature; first of all, of course, in the form of Auguste Dupin, the alter ego of Edgar Allan Poe, who was himself both a dandy and a hack writer for popular magazines. About the debt of Doyle to Poe in this regard there is no doubt, the name of Dupin appearing just after those of "Ormond Sacker" and "Sherrinford Holmes" in the notes for *A Study in Scarlet*. And though Holmes alludes to his predecessor rather smugly, it is clearly out of defensive vanity; since speaking in his own voice, Doyle bestows unstinting praise on Dupin. Between *A Study in Scarlet* and *The Sign of Four*, however, Doyle met Wilde, which is to say, a Dupin-Poe in the flesh, and it is in the latter work that the decadent Holmes is first clearly sketched. "Sherlock Holmes," the opening sentence runs, "took his bottle from the corner of the mantelpiece, and his hypodermic syringe from its morocco case...."

Moreover, though the revelation of Wilde's scandalous secret lay still far in the future, Doyle seems somehow to have sensed the centrality to his lifestyle of that courtly contempt for women which also plays so important a role in Poe and the genre he invented. Poe's misogyny had been noticed long before Holmes began to write; Baudelaire, for instance, remarked that "Another peculiar feature of his writings is that they are entirely antifeminine...." But Doyle was the first to exploit that peculiarly intimate relationship between master and disciple, investigator and narrator, which fills the vacuum created in a story like *Murders in the Rue Morgue* by the absence of heterosexual love – identifying it with the relationship of a condescending professor to an adoring student in the all-male college classroom, or more specifically, his own relationship to his old anatomy teacher, Dr. Joseph Bell, whom, he liked to suggest to inquiring reporters, *was* the model for Sherlock Holmes.

That the kind of detective story Doyle thus created is a literature of masculine protest – at once superficially compatible with and radically subversive of Victorian codes of chivalry – seems to me undeniable. And the immediate acceptability – on the level of dream-wish and fear – of Holmes' antimask to the general reading public is based largely on that fact. An underground hostility to the tyranny of domesticity and the image of Women as the spotless Angel of the House must have been widely shared by Doyle's audience, both male and female, though they were not (except for a handful of feminists) ready to express that hostility in open revolt.

It is true, to be sure, that Holmes expresses admiration for certain women he encounters; but they are invariably killers and deceivers of men: Dark Ladies (their named suspiciously Jewish) who prove his repeated contention that their sex is dangerous – though splendidly enough to compel a certain fearful respect. The clinging and subservient females, on the other hand, whom Watson admires (and at least one of whom he marries) remain shadowy and interchangeable figures, usually called Violet. The women, therefore, who constituted a smaller but by no means unimportant part of Holmes' readership must have identified with his equivocal villainesses, that is, when they were not dreaming of intruding into his bachelor retreat in the guise of housekeepers and luring him away from what they must have understood as his priestly commitment, his life-long chastity.

To the men in his audience, however, for whom the reading of Doyle's tales was in itself an escape from domestic obligations, the ambiguous suggestion of a homoerotic bond strong enough to protect Holmes forever from household routine must have constituted an appeal, all the more alluring for being, even by their own conscious standards, taboo. And they must, therefore, have despaired when at the end of *The Sign of Four*, Watson threatened to leave Holmes forever for the sake of holy matrimony. Even Watson himself seems to hesitate at the prospect, observing ruefully, "The division seems unfair. You have done all the work in the business. I got a wife out of it…pray, what remains for you?" And Holmes answers, reaching a pale hand up towards the shelf where he keeps his drugs, "For me, there still remains the cocaine bottle…."

It must have been as evident to Doyle as it is to us now, that such a conclusion meant an end not just to their equivocal relationship but to the saga of Sherlock Holmes as a whole; since after Watson has been eliminated, there remains no one capable of stirring Holmes out of his indolence, or indeed of recording what befalls him. If, however, Doyle believed that marrying Watson off had really delivered him from the demands of his audience, he was rapidly disabused of the notion; neither they, nor his publishers – who responded to their pressure by raising the price offered for new stories – would let Watson remain faithful to his marital vows. With no apparent pangs of conscience, he runs off from his new bride (and a job necessary to sustain his household) whenever Holmes beckons; and in a little while, Doyle seems to have forgotten that she ever existed.

Some later commentators, looking for consistency to life rather than myth, have even argued that the first Mrs. Watson must have died or been divorced – and that when in later stories Doyle begins again to refer to a wife, she must be a second one. But the second succeeds no better than the first in keeping Watson at home – or in releasing Doyle from his increasingly resented obligation. When, therefore, in the final story of the *Memoirs*, he tried once more to be done, he chose to kill Holmes rather than marry off his narrator. But with a deviousness of which even he himself seems to have been at first unaware, Doyle killed Holmes offstage and without witnesses or a *corpus delicti*; so that when his audience – less confused than he about the exigencies of the myth – refused to accept that death as irreversible, he could resurrect him without straining the credulity of even the most realistically minded among them.

The reborn Holmes is, however, in some ways rather different, having, for instance, kicked his cocaine habit, though he continues to smoke with almost suicidal assiduity. Moreover, though he pursues criminals still, he seems less the human foxhound, hungry for prey, and more the artist, i.e., the virtuoso dispellar of illusion. Indeed, what appears to compel him now is not so much a desire to expose the criminal as a need to frustrate the smug and misguided police. And though occasionally he delivers someone up to the courts and the due process of law, more often he reveals that there has been no crime at all, no victim or no culprit, or that the violence or deceit that had motivated his investigation was itself an act of justice. He functions, in short, less and less as the instrument through which society avenges itself against the hybristic individual who has taken its powers into his own hands, and more and more as precisely such a hybristic lover, achieving single-handedly what the organised community has failed to accomplish.

From the very beginning, indeed, *organisations* represented to Holmes the supreme evil, whether they functioned outside the law like the Ku Klux Klan, the Molly Maguires, or the Elders of the Mormon Church, or whether they purported to represent the law itself, like the police. Despite his habit of contemptuously giving them the public credit for his private triumphs, Holmes always refers scornfully to the official guardians of the city – like Inspector Lestrade and his obtuse successors – who would, if left to their own devices, not prevent or punish crime, but compound it by convicting the innocent. If the popular audience of Doyle's time refused to let his private investigator die, it was because – like the avant-garde of the same period – they had come to believe that innocence is best protected and order most effectively restored not by the bumbling efforts of a self-defeating bureaucracy, but by the art of the self-exiled eccentric.

Why then did Doyle deprecate those stories in which he had made of his own antimask an archetypal figure able simultaneously to express and allay the wish of a mass society to subvert a growingly repressive order, which at the same time it yearned desperately to maintain? In part, surely, because he was as much the victim of that same ambivalence and understood it as little as the least educated of his readers. But also, it is clear, because he distrusted the genre to which these stories belonged, as most of his readers did not, holding the tale of detection in as low esteem as his elitist contemporary, Henry James, who in his earliest fiction Conan Doyle had tried unsuccessfully to emulate. Doyle invariably spoke of the adventures of Holmes with scant respect, claiming to have written them only for money and assuring a correspondent that "I have never taken them seriously myself." Just before beginning *His Last Bow*, in fact, he wrote to his mother, "I think of winding him up for good and all. He takes my mind from better things."

Ironically, however, he meant by "better things" a genre that James would have found quite as vulgar as any detective story: a kind of historical novel modelled on

Charles Reade's *The Cloister and the Hearth* and Stanley Weyman's *Under the Red Robe*, both of which have since been remanded by the critics to children's libraries, where they remain largely unread. Indeed, his own *Micah Clarke* and *The White Company*, upon which he believed his claim to literary fame rested, have suffered a similar fate, because – like his models – they are not only insufferably genteel and pretentious, but hopelessly lacking in mythic resonance.

Doyle was finally, in his wrong headed effort to create "better things," the victim of a division of fiction into "serious" and "popular," for which James was largely responsible, and which, for some readers, still makes it possible to enjoy the saga of Sherlock Holmes only by pretending they are "slumming," much as Doyle did when he composed it. Certainly he never realised the kinship of his detective to Dracula, Ayesha, or even Dr. Jekyll and Mr. Hyde – or his own role in creating a new urban mythology, whose rise was coincident with (and in some sense dependent upon) that division. Thanks, however, to the taste of the mass audience, which cared nothing for the opinion of critics like James, and the marketplace through which they enforced their taste, Doyle continued to write his "humbler" tales until the year he died, even as we have continued to read them ever since.

In the final story of the collection called *The Return of Sherlock Holmes* (1904), which begins with his resurrection, Doyle tried once more to cast him off forever; confiding to us, in the voice of Dr. Watson, that *this* tale constitutes the often-promised but this time absolutely guaranteed "last of those exploits of my friend," who has not died again (by now Doyle had learned that Holmes could never die), but has withdrawn into absolute exile, giving up detection for "bee farming on the Sussex Downs." Moreover, since at long last "notoriety has become hateful to him," he has exacted from Watson the vow to write of him no more.

But twice more Doyle reneged on his promise, living long enough to publish two more collections, *His Last Bow* appearing in 1917, and then in 1927 *The Casebook of Sherlock Holmes*, in the preface to which he indicates for the first and only time a real sense of what he had all along so grudgingly achieved. His tone is still a little condescending, but there is a recognition at least that his "humbler" fictions, which he confesses finally have not really kept him from higher pursuits, are grounded in the sort of primordial myth and magic capable of producing in readers what has traditionally been called *ekstasis*: an alteration of consciousness, a momentary yet somehow timeless release from the tyranny of reason and the ennui of the commonplace, from which Holmes sought to escape by the cocaine bottle, and we by precisely such books as these.

And so, reader, farewell to Sherlock Holmes! I thank you for your past constancy, and can but hope that some return has been made in the shape of that distraction from the worries of life and stimulating change of thought which can only be found in the fairy kingdom of romance.

The Sherlock Holmes 2nd Illustrated Omnibus

Dust jacket

Here is the sequel to the popular first illustrated Omnibus published in 1978. Sidney Paget who illustrated the *Adventures, Memoirs, Return,* and *The Hound of the*

Baskervilles, died in January 1908. So when Conan Doyle began yet again to write Sherlock Holmes stories later that year after a gap of nearly four years, *The Strand Magazine* had to look around for another source of pictorial images to accompany the vivid verbal ones which its star writer provided. The solution adopted was not to plump for one particular artist. Instead the seven stories published between 1908 and 1917 and then collected in *His Last Bow* had seven different artists. *The Valley of Fear*, appearing in the early months of the War, was a long story and needed a single artist – Frank Wiles. The *Case Book* stories of 1921 to 1927 were shared with two exceptions between Wiles and Howard K. Elcock.

There was no question of a departure from the image of Holmes that Paget had created from the features of his brother Walter (who incidentally did the drawings for 'The Dying Detective'). But within the convention of the masterly brow, inquisitorial nose and commanding jaw, there are some intriguing variations of gauntness. While Watson continues to wear stick-up collars and Holmes a turned-down collar with bow tie tucked under, the deer-stalker only reappears at the last minute in 'Shoscombe Old Place'.

It is often regretted that Sidney Paget did not live to illustrate these nineteen short stories and *The Valley of Fear*, but it must also be acknowledged that his successors rose to the challenge both of his example and of the stories themselves.

The Penguin Complete Sherlock Holmes

Preface by Christopher Morley

IN MEMORIAM SHERLOCK HOLMES

IT WAS UNFAIR of Conan Doyle to say (as he did in his delightful autobiography, *Memories and Adventures*) that Dr. Watson had never shown a gleam of humor nor made a single joke. Let me refute this at once. In the first chapter of *The Valley of Fear* the good doctor, after some rather sharp taunting by his friend, caught Holmes fairly off guard.

They were speaking of Professor Moriarty.
"The famous scientific criminal," says Watson, "as famous among crooks as ---."
"My blushes, Watson!" Holmes murmurs in a deprecating voice.
"I was about to say, as he is unknown to the public."
Even Holmes admitted that this was "a distinct touch."

But other evidence of Dr. Watson's mischief was his frequent sly allusions to the unrecorded adventures. All Holmes-and-Watson lovers must have brooded sadly on the titles of these untold tales. "The shocking affair of the Dutch steamship *Friesland*, which so nearly cost us both our lives," the case of Wilson the notorious canary-trainer, the repulsive story of the red leech, the story of the giant rat of Sumatra "for which the world is not yet prepared," the singular affair of the aluminium crutch, the Curious Experience of the Patterson Family on the Island of Uffa – these are some of the yarns we have had to do without; having only the melancholy assurance that the documents were safely on file in that famous dispatch box in the vaults of Cox's Bank at Charing Cross. Perhaps most of all I deplore that we were never told "the story of the politician, the lighthouse, and the trained cormorant." In this allusion we surely find Watson in a deliberately pawky vain. --- We hoped against hope for some of these stories; we can never have them now.

But there is one omission in the long Holmes-Watson history that some generous survivor could supply. It must not be forgotten that it was a certain "young Stamford" also a medico, who first introduced Watson to Sherlock Holmes; and the chance that brought this about was that Stamford and Watson met at the Criterion Bar in London. Young Stamford was so specifically outlined in those first pages of *A Study in Scarlet* that I had always thought he might reappear some day in one of the adventures. I don't believe he ever did. But at least his immortal service in bringing the pair together should be remembered. A small tablet in that famous bar-room would be a grateful memento; I think it should be erected by the London publisher who bought the complete copyright of *A Study in Scarlet* for £25. And in any healths drunk in the matter by visiting pilgrims I suggest also a grateful side-look to the gallant Murray, the orderly who saved Dr. Watson's life in Afghanistan.

The whole Sherlock Holmes saga is a triumphant illustration of art's supremacy over life. Perhaps no fiction character ever created has become so charmingly real to his readers. It is not that we take our blessed Sherlock too seriously, if we really want the painful oddities of criminology let us go to Bataille or Roughead. But Holmes is pure anesthesia. We read the stories again and again; perhaps most of all for the little introductory interiors which gave us a glimpse of 221B Baker Street. The fact that Holmes had earlier lodgings in Montague Street (alongside the British Museum) is forgotten. That was before Watson, and we must have Watson too. Rashly, in the later years, Holmes twice undertook to write stories for himself. They have not quite the same magic. No, we are epicures. We must begin in Baker Street; and best of all, if possible, let it be a stormy winter morning when Holmes routs Watson out of bed in haste. The doctor wakes to see the tall ascetic figure by the bedside with a candle. "Come, Watson, come! The game is afoot!" If that is not possible, then I prefer to find Holmes stretched on the sofa in a fit of the dumps, perhaps he is scraping on the violin, or bemoaning the dearth of imaginative crime and reaching for the cocaine (a habit he evidently outgrew, for we hear little of it in the later adventures). We have a glimpse of the sitting-room, that room we know so well. There are the great volumes of scrapbook records; the bullet marks on the walls; the mysterious "gasogene" which appears occasionally in English fiction and which I can only suppose to be some sort of siphon-bottle. (There is also a sort of decanter-holder called a "tantalus" now and then set out on the sideboard; another mystery for American readers, and now more than ever true to its name.) The Persian slipper for tobacco and the coal-scuttle for cigars don't appeal to me so much. They are more conscious eccentricities. In comes Mrs. Hudson with a message or a "commissionaire" with a letter, and we are off. Gregson and Lestrade will get the credit, but we have the fun. Already we are in a hansom rattling through the streets of Waterloo or Charing Cross or Paddington. (Holmes rarely takes trains at Euston or King's Cross or Liverpool Street.)

It is a kind of piety for even the least and humblest of Holmes-lovers to pay what tribute he may to this great encyclopaedia of romance that has given the world so much innocent pleasure. Already the grandchildren of Holmes's earliest followers are beginning upon him with equal delight. I was too young to know the wave of dismay that went round the English-reading world when Sherlock and Professor Moriarty supposedly perished together in the Reichenbach Falls, but I can well remember the sombre effect on my own ten-year-old spirits when I first read the closing paragraphs of the *Memoirs*. The intolerable pathos of the cigarette-case on the rocky ledge; the firm clear handwriting of that last stoic message! I then put in two or three years in reading everything else of Dr. Doyle's. One walked downtown to the old Enoch Pratt Free Library on Mulberry Street in Baltimore and got out a book – *The Firm of Girdlestone*, or *The Captain of the Pole Star* or *Beyond the City*, or *A Duet*, or *Round the Red Lamp*, or *The Stark Munro Letters* or *The Doings of Raffles Haw*. For I specialized chiefly in the lesser known tales, and regret Sir Arthur's tendency (in his autobiography) to make light of some of these yarns. As for *The White Company* and *The Refugees* and *Micah Clarke* and *Uncle Bernac*, these were household words. When one found at the library a Conan Doyle he had not read, he began it at once on the walk home. It was quite a long trudge from Mulberry Street to the 2000 block on Park Avenue, and the tragedy often was that, loitering like a snail, almost like the locomotion of a slowed moving picture, the book was actually finished by the time one got home. There was all the journey to do over again the next day.

But all that time I knew, deep in some instinct, that Holmes was not really dead. In the first place I had noted that the date of his Reichenbach crisis lacked only one day of being my own birthday; and I felt positive that the eve of my festival would not have been marred by the death of my hero. So you may imagine the thrilling excitement – in 1903, wasn't it? – when the *Return* began printing in *Collier's*. Then we saw how Dr. Doyle had got himself out of his predicament. He had revived Holmes, but (to be fair all round) he had killed off Mrs. Watson. We had been tolerant of Mrs. Watson because she was nee Mary Morstan in *The Sign of Four*, but obviously she was a little in the way. Her patience was certainly exemplary in allowing the doctor to rush off on various expeditions; but it could not last. One of the unsolved questions, by the way, is the second Mrs. Watson. Evidently the good doctor, who was always persevering had tried again; for Holmes in January 1903 (see *The Adventure of the Blanched Soldier*) refers to an existing Mrs. Watson. But who or why this second lady we have no data.

One of the blissful ways of passing an evening, when you encounter another dyed-in-the-blood addict, is to embark upon the happy discussion of minor details of Holmesiana. "Whose gold watch was it that had been so mishandled?" one may ask; and the other counters with "What was the book that Joseph Stangerson carried in his pocket?" Endless delicious minutiae to consider! There was Dr. Verner, "a distant relative of Sherlock Holmes," who bought out Watson's practice. Undoubtably this was an Anglicization of the name of Holmes's grandmother, Vernet. She was French, a sister of the French military artist of that name. (A real and very distinguished family of painters, incidentally; undoubtedly suggested to Doyle by his own artistic family inheritance. I wonder if the Vernet family in France realize that the world-famous detective has thus been grafted onto their genealogy?) Or there are the glimpses of Moriarty to be talked over: his youthful treatise on the binomial theorem "which had a European vogue." Or Mycroft Holmes, seven years older than Sherlock: we would gladly have heard more of him and the Diogenes Club. How was it that Dr. Watson happened to cherish a portrait of Henry Ward Beecher, but had never had it framed? Or we might air a minor grievance that the devoted Mrs. Hudson had never been implicated in a mystery of her own. There was a mystery about a landlady, but a certain Mrs. Warren was brought in for the purpose. And why did Gregson and Lestrade gradually fade out of the picture? Why does Billy the page-boy remain only a phantom? Holmes speaks once of having been at college: what college was it? And Dr. Watson's wound from the "Jezail bullet": was it in his shoulder or in his leg: apparently Sir Arthur was not quite sure.

Such are the questions that the Holmesians argue with innocent satisfaction. Even in the less successful stories we remain untroubled by any naivety of plot; it is the character of the immortal pair that we relish. It is not mere chance that they are well-loved. Doyle himself must have been a singularly lovable man. There is an anecdote in his *Memories and Adventures* that reveals very clearly the fine instinct of delicacy in his massive personality. He was visiting George Meredith in the latter's old age, and they were walking up a steep path to the little summer-house Meredith used for writing. In Doyle's own words:

> The nervous complaint from which he suffered caused him to fall down occasionally. As we walked up the narrow path I heard him fall behind me, but judged from the sound that it was a mere slither and could not have hurt him. Therefore I walked on as if I had heard nothing. He was a fiercely proud old man, and my instincts told me that his humiliation in being helped up would be far greater than any relief I could give him.

I can think of no truer revelation of a gentleman than that.

The character of Holmes, Doyle has told us, was at any rate partly suggested by his student memories of Dr. Joseph Bell of the Edinburgh Infirmary, whose diagnostic intuitions used to startle his patients and pupils. But there was abundant evidence that the invention of the scientific detective conformed to a fundamental logic in Doyle's own temper. The famous case of Oscar Slater was one example; another was his ingenuity in transmitting news of the war in cipher to British prisoners in Germany. This he did by sending books in which he had put needle-pricks under various printed letters so as to spell out the desired messages; but beginning with the third chapter, believing that the German censor would examine the earlier chapters more carefully. Of his humor there is a pleasant income-tax story. In his first year of independent medical practice his earnings were £154, and when the income-tax paper arrived he filled it up to show that he was not liable. The authorities returned the form with the words *Most Unsatisfactory* scrawled across it. He returned it again with the subscription *I entirely agree*. As many readers must have guessed, *Round the Red Lamp* and *The Stark Munro Letters* were very literally drawn from his own experiences in medicine.

"Art in the blood is liable to take the strangest forms," Sherlock Holmes once remarked. Understandably Doyle was thinking also of his own inheritance (both artistic and Irish) and certainly he himself, though he looked so solidly Watsonian, gave his friends many surprises in the mutations of his vigorous career. One of the quaintest of these must have been his collaboration with Barrie in an operetta. Of the finest spiritualist phase only those who have made careful study of those problems can profitably speak. But there was no stage of the life, from the poor student doing without lunch to buy books to the famous author enduring painful hostility for his psychic faith, which did not reflect the courage, the chivalry, the sagacity we would have expected from the creator of Holmes. Certainly it was characteristic of that student of mysteries to attack the greatest one we know.

Those of us in earliest boyhood gave our hearts to Conan Doyle, and have had from him so many hours of good refreshment, find our affection unshakable. What other man led a fuller and heartier and more masculine life? Doctor, whaler, athlete, writer, speculator, dramatist, historian, war correspondent, spiritualist, he was always also the infracaninophile – the helper of the underdog. Big in every way, his virtues had always something of the fresh vigor of the amateur, keen, open-minded, flexible, imaginative. If, as Doyle utterly believed, the spirits of the dead persist and can communicate, there is none that could have more wholesome news to impart to us than that brave and energetic lover of life.

A blessing, then, on those ophthalmic citizens who did not go to that office at 2 Devonshire Place, near Harley Street, where in 1891 Dr. A. Conan Doyle set up consulting rooms as an eye specialist. It was there, waiting for the patients who never came, that he began to see the possibilities in Sherlock Holmes. No wonder that Dr. Watson too sometimes rather neglected his practice.

The Celebrated Cases Of Sherlock Holmes

INTRODUCTION

SIR ARTHUR CONAN DOYLE HAS been the recipient of tributes from readers and criminologists throughout the world. One of his greatest admirers was Sir Winston Churchill, who remained a lifelong devotee both of the historical novels and the detective stories. The French Surete honoured Conan Doyle by naming their renowned criminal laboratory in Lyons after him. J. Edgar Hoover remarked that his investigative methods had been substantially incorporated into the FBI network and, when Doyle himself was travelling in Egypt in 1896, he discovered that his stories had been translated into Arabic and were being issued to the local police as an instruction manual.

Born into an Irish Catholic family in Edinburgh in 1859, Conan Doyle was educated at Stoneyhurst and Edinburgh University. Qualifying as a doctor, he then practised from 1882 to 1890 at Southsea. It was during this period that he began writing stories showing the influence of both Poe and Wilkie Collins. *A Study in Scarlet* appeared in 1887 in *Beeton's Christmas Annual* and marks the inception of the great Sherlock Holmes saga; it attracted little attention at the time but has since emerged as immensely popular. The editor of *Lippincott's Magazine* thought highly enough of it to invite Conan Doyle to try his hand at another story. The result was *The Sign of Four* (1890), a story published by *Lippincott's* both in America and England that also took time to achieve widespread popularity.

Early in 1891 Conan Doyle set himself up in London as an eye specialist, but sitting in his Harley Street office from ten to four every day without any patients, he started writing more stories to keep the wolf from the door. Thus began the famous series of Sherlock Holmes short stories for which Conan Doyle is chiefly remembered today. They were published in the then recently founded and very popular *Strand Magazine*. It was not long before the public's enthusiasm had been whipped into a positive frenzy, especially over such stories as *The Red-Headed League* and *A Scandal in Bohemia*. After the series of twelve which make up *The Adventures of Sherlock Holmes* (1891-2), he was prevailed upon to write another series, *The Memoirs* (1892-3), at the rate of £50 a story. Seven years before he had been reduced to selling *A Study in Scarlet* outright for £25, but now he was in a position to dictate his own terms. His popularity in America led to an invitation in 1894 to make a lecture tour, which proved immensely successful.

By this time, however, Conan Doyle was already tiring of Holmes. While his success was providing him with the good things of life, he also found it a millstone around his neck and grew weary of the endless magazine deadlines. Moreover, it was not for the Holmes stories that he wished to be remembered; he had a strong sense of the pageantry of history and wanted to do for England what Scott had done for Scotland, in recreating an exciting past that would come alive for his readers. It was to this end that he wrote *The White Company* (1891), set in 14th century England and France, and *Micah Clarke* (1894), a story of the Monmouth Rebellion in 1685 and its aftermath in the Bloody Assize. The credit due to Conan Doyle as a skilful and exciting historical novelist has been overshadowed by the cult-like popularity of Sherlock Holmes, in spite of the fact that Conan Doyle himself considered these, and other novels like *Rodney Stone* (1896) and *The Exploits of Brigadier Gerard* (1896), by far his most worthwhile. As a result of all these factors he decided to kill off Holmes at the end of the *Memoirs* in the famous fall with Moriarty over the Reichenbach Falls. The public reaction to this came as a surprise to Conan Doyle: one lady wrote to him a letter, beginning 'You Brute…' and some people went so far as to wear black ties in mourning.

Despite a great deal of pressure, Conan Doyle could not be persuaded to take up his pen again for some time on behalf of Sherlock Holmes. In 1901, however, faced with money worries and his imagination sparked off by a story of a gruesome death and a ghastly dog on Dartmoor, he started writing *The Hound of the Baskervilles,* stressing that this was an early adventure of Holmes. Finally in 1903 he succumbed to everyone's persuasion and to the lure of *Lippincott's* offer of $5,000 a story and the *Strand's* of £100 per thousand words. The result was *The Empty Room* (*sic*) *House* in which Holmes's escape from death is ingeniously explained, and from then until the end of his life in 1930 he continued to write Sherlock Holmes stories.

Conan Doyle stated that the original model for Sherlock Holmes was Dr. Joseph Bell, a brilliant surgeon under whom Doyle studied in Edinburgh. He was dark and thin, with an aquiline nose and delighted in the sort of deductive reasoning that Doyle developed to such a pitch of perfection. One example of this was when a new case was brought in, Bell remarked, 'this man is a left-handed cobbler' and then explained. 'You'll observe, gentlemen, the worn places on the corduroy breeches where a cobbler rests his lapstone? The right-hand side, you'll note, is far more worn than the left. He uses his left hand for hammering the leather'. But Bell was not the only influence. The extremely successful formula of a brilliant detective with a less intelligent assistant and interpreter as a foil had already been used by Poe and the French novelist, Emile Gaboriau. Holmes united glamour and excitement, mingled with the familiarity of an old friend. Ascetic and unique, bowing only to society's morals by rational decision rather than deeply implanted habit, he appealed to the escapist dreams of ordinary people. Watson was the perfect 'straight man' for Holmes's clever explanations and also represented the average conventional reader in outlook and abilities, being somewhat blinkered and without a far-reaching imagination.

In Conan Doyle himself there can be seen an intriguing mixture of Dr. Watson and Sherlock Holmes. In outward appearance he was very Watson-like; a big man, an above-average athlete in his youth, he was very much the solid late Victorian citizen imbued with ideals about the value of the family and the Empire. He was almost always on the side of the establishment except if he believed there had been a serious miscarriage of justice, in which case he could prove a very tough opponent. In 1906 he took up the case of George Edalji, a half-Indian solicitor who had been wrongfully imprisoned and subsequently released, but without having his name cleared. He had been accused of writing illiterate, anonymous letters of a threatening nature (to his own family) and of stealing around the countryside at night damaging stock. Using Holmesian observation and deductive techniques, Conan Doyle clearly proved Edalji's innocence beyond all doubt and also uncovered the true criminal.

The First World War brought him both fulfilment and loss. He was 55 years old when it started and therefore could not take part physically but he was passionately involved, full of practical suggestions and a dedicated propagandist. But he also lost several people close to him, and it is at this time that he developed an interest in spiritualism. While being very practical and capable of grasping the latest scientific advances (he owned a motor car as early as 1903), he also had a very highly developed imagination inherited from both his mother and father which allowed him to believe in spiritualism, as well as have a deep appreciation of art and nature.

But despite his vast literary output of more than fifty books published on a wide range of subjects, it is for the immortal Sherlock Holmes that Conan Doyle will be remembered. In addition, it is the evocation of late Victorian England which so fascinates modern readers: foggy, gas-lit London, the sound of horses' hooves and rattling hansom cab wheels, the contrast between the monied ease of a small confident section of the population and the poor, working man – a world in which Englishmen felt that England and her moral values were unquestionably the best.

TELLER OF TALES - Biography by Daniel Stashower

PREFACE

Not long ago, in the London showroom of a dealer in rare books, I asked to have a look at a first edition of *The Hound of the Baskervilles*. No price was posted, but I knew that a "bright and unrubbed" copy could go for £600, so my interest was largely theoretical. The assistant manager – an indulgent, friendly sort of person – opened the glass display case and waited patiently as I fingered the brittle volume. After a moment, when I handed it back, she mentioned that there might be some other Conan Doyle material in the back room. If I could wait a moment while she helped another customer, she would check with the manager. After five minutes or so, when my scan of the floor-to-ceiling bookshelves brought me as far as Thackeray, I happened to find myself outside the manager's open door. "There's a customer out front," I heard the assistant say. "He's interested in Conan Doyle."

"Oh, God," came the answer. "It must be an American."

I freely confess to being an American. But I'm not entirely sure why an interest in Conan Doyle should reveal this to a rare book dealer. Was it because only an American could afford the prices he was asking? Or was it, as his tone suggested, that only an American, with an American's suspect taste in literature, would be interested in a second-rater like Conan Doyle?

It was not the first time I'd had this reaction. Many times over the past five years I've presented myself at British bookshops and auction houses as a collector of Conan Doyle material – always taking care to look under D for Doyle, but also C for Conan Doyle, the compound surname he preferred. The response is invariably polite, but it generally carries a quiet note of sympathy, as though I'd just confessed some exotic intestinal complaint. "Conan Doyle? Well, Sherlock Holmes was brilliant, but Doyle went a bit potty at the end, didn't he? Fairies, ghosts, and that."

"Fairies, ghosts, and that" have been the millstone of Conan Doyle's reputation for the better part of a century. Toward the end of his life, Conan Doyle came to believe that communication with dead souls was possible. His efforts to spread this message, which he considered the most important work of his life, proved to be his undoing. The British public watched with growing incredulity as he made one foray after another into the spirit realm. On any given day he might pronounce upon a ghostly photograph of fallen World War I soldiers, or speculate on a possible literary collaboration with the late Charles Dickens. In America, where such reports were less frequent, it was possible to remain sympathetic, if bemused. In Britain, the general public's tolerance began to fray. "Poor Sherlock Holmes," ran one headline, "Hopelessly Crazy?"

The result was inevitable. Though Sherlock Holmes remains a colossus among cultural icons, Conan Doyle, once the most popular author of his generation, has been sharply downgraded. In Edinburgh, where Walter Scott is commemorated with a towering Gothic monument, Conan Doyle's birthplace is marked by a statue of his fictional detective. *The White Company* and *Sir Nigel*, the books Conan Doyle regarded as his finest work, are seldom read. Conan Doyle's portrait is not currently displayed at London's National Portrait Gallery. Though such decisions owe something to the quality of the portraits involved, it seems curious that Agatha Christie, Dorothy Sayers, and Daphne du Maurier are all on view while Conan Doyle remains in storage.

Conan Doyle once declared that he would gladly sacrifice whatever literary reputation he enjoyed if it would bring about a greater acceptance of his spiritualist message. To a large extent, he made the sacrifice without achieving the objective. The critic Sherman Yellen, writing of Conan Doyle's spiritualist novel *The Land of Mist* in 1965, offered a view shared by many: "*The Land of Mist* demonstrates that Conan Doyle had made his greatest sacrifice to his spiritualist beliefs; he had relinquished his literary power to it."

Any writer who would address this delicate topic must first declare a position on the paranormal. I should admit, then, that I never had any traffic with the spirit realm, that I am a supporter of the Committee for Scientific Investigation of Claims of the Paranormal, and that it has been some years since I believed in fairies. At the same time, I also belong to the Society for Psychical Research. I once shook hands with Uri Geller, and some of my closest friends claim to be psychic. I consider myself, then, a cordial disbeliever.

None of which diminishes my regard for Conan Doyle in any way. Like most of his admirers, my introduction came through Sherlock Holmes. In fact, at the age of eleven I sported a deerstalker hat, carried a magnifying glass in my pocket, and was much given to declarations of "Brilliant deduction!" and "Elementary!" – which greatly endeared me to teachers, friends, and family. Some time later, as I was rereading *The Valley of Fear* for perhaps the ninth time, I noticed on the title page that the author had some twenty or thirty other books to his credit. I found a copy of *The Lost World* at my local library and never looked back.

Sooner or later, though, every Conan Doyle fan bumps up against *The Vital Message* or *The Edge of the Unknown* or one of the author's many other spiritualist works. Most readers simply shrug and look elsewhere, and only a very singular taste would prefer

Conan Doyle's two-volume *History of Spiritualism* to *The Adventures of Sherlock Holmes*. In my own case, after dutifully slogging through *The Wanderings of a Spiritualist*, I found myself wondering about the author's state of mind. As John Dickson Carr wrote in 1949, echoing the popular attitude of Conan Doyle's contemporaries, "For a quarter of a century he had loomed thick-shouldered as the sturdy Briton, with no damned nonsense about him. What was wrong? What ailed the man?"

The answer, like the man himself, was far more complicated than it first appeared. Yes, Conan Doyle lost a son in the First World War and, like so many others, sought consolation in the séance room. This was not, however, where his involvement began. Conan Doyle's interest in the spirit realm took root some thirty years earlier, well before his son's birth. This interest was by no means unique; the Society of Psychical Research was already a going concern when Conan Doyle joined in 1893, and its members included prominent scientists, philosophers, members of Parliament, and a future prime minister. For many years Conan Doyle was a mere dabbler in psychic research. He experimented with table-tipping and automatic writing as possible methods of contacting the spirits, and had a short-lived interest in mesmerism and thought transference. Only later, when the testimony of those closest to him erased his lingering doubts, did he become a zealous crusader. For many, he became the living embodiment of the spiritualist craze, rather than its most vocal proponent. His outspokenness, weighed against the cool logic of Sherlock Holmes, seemed to invite public scorn.

"We who believe in the psychic revelation," he wrote near the end of his life, "and who appreciate that a perception of these things is of the utmost importance, certainly have hurled ourselves against the obstinacy of our time. Possibly we have allowed some of our lives to be gnawed away in what for the moment seemed a vain and thankless quest. Only the future can show whether the sacrifice was worth it."

"Personally," he added, "I think it was."

If Conan Doyle's generation was quick to dismiss his queer ideas, our own generation – with its power crystals, White House astrologers, and Area 51 – must admit to harbouring some queer ideas of its own. It is too much to say that Conan Doyle's version of a spiritualist utopia has come to pass, nor is it likely that it ever will. The question is not whether we must accept Conan Doyle's beliefs to understand the man. The question is whether it is now possible, nearly seventy years after his death, to examine this aspect of his life with sympathy rather than derision.

Personally, I think it is.

INTRODUCTION

One morning in 1930, not long before his death, Sir Arthur Conan Doyle struggled to his writing desk and reached for pen and paper. He had done a great deal of writing in the previous months – mostly correspondence and letters to the press – but that morning he decided instead to try his hand at a sketch. He worked at it for some time, squinting intently over a troublesome detail or a tricky bit of lettering, gazing from the window when inspiration flagged. At length he set down his pen and pushed the drawing aside.

Today, a copy of the sketch hangs in London's Sherlock Holmes pub. It shows a flea-bitten workhorse pulling a heavy baggage cart. A tall pile of packing cases weighs the cart down, and each case bears the label of a different aspect of Conan Doyle's life and work. "Medical Practice" is piled alongside "Historical Novels." "Elections" rests on top of "Psychic Research," "Tales" and "Drama" prop up "Poems" and "The Great War." Perhaps the heaviest case in the pile is the one sandwiched in between "500 Lectures" and "Australia 1921." It reads "Sherlock Holmes."

Self-pity played no part in Conan Doyle's character. Moreover, his heartfelt belief in spiritualism left him with no fear of death. But though his drawing strikes a light-hearted, self-deprecating tone, there is an unmistakable note of melancholy at its core. Conan Doyle came from a long line of artists – his grandfather was a pioneer of political caricature – and he knew the value of a well-chosen image. This was how he viewed himself as death approached: a draft animal hauling a cart. And Sherlock Holmes, his legendary fictional detective, was just another piece of heavy cargo.

Conan Doyle had lived long enough to realize that Sherlock Holmes would, in Watson's phrase, "eclipse and predominate" the rest of his work. Already the historical novels by which he hoped to be remembered had fallen out of fashion, and his poetry, plays, and wartime chronicles had largely disappeared from view. His dedication to spiritualism, and his vigorous campaign to spread his beliefs to others, had taken a heavy toll on his reputation as a serious man of letters. Many found it difficult to reconcile that the creator of Sherlock Holmes, the "perfect reasoning and observing machine," could have given himself so wholly to a cause that appeared to defy logic. A man who espoused such ideas, it seemed, could not be taken seriously as a writer.

In person, however, Conan Doyle seemed the very model of reason and sincerity. Interviewers were struck by his easy manner and lack of pretension. As he grew older, and thicker around the middle, Conan Doyle's heavy eyelids and drooping mustache made him look more and more like a genial walrus. "He was a great, burly, clumsy man," wrote one friend, "with an unwieldy-looking body that was meant for a farm bailiff, with hands like Westphalian hams, and a nervous halting voice whose burrs recalled the banks and braes of Scotland."

His looks were deceiving. Behind the placid, sleepy-eyed demeanour was a man of strong convictions, some of them absurd, all of them deeply felt. Conan Doyle's life had been a series of hard-fought crusades, of which spiritualism was only the latest. In 1890, he warned against an ill-tested cure for tuberculosis. In 1902, he defended the British government against charges of misconduct in the Boer War. In 1906, he championed the cause of divorce law reform. In 1910, he took up the case of Oscar Slater, a man falsely accused of murder. In 1914, he warned against the potentially devastating effects of a submarine blockade. In each case Conan Doyle fought his corner with skill and resourcefulness, marshalling whatever advantages could be wrought from his fame and natural eloquence. Many of his causes were unpopular, but Conan Doyle's private sense of honor mattered more to him than public opinion. "He seemed to us," his daughter Jean once wrote, "to be the very personification of the chivalry of the stories of King Arthur's Round Table."

It was probably not how he would have described himself. *The Strand* magazine where the bulk of Conan Doyle's work first saw print, took a poll of its leading writers in 1927. Of all the characters of literature, the editors asked, which one would you most like to have created?

H.G. Wells put forward the name of Shakespeare's Falstaff, as did John Buchan. Compton Mackenzie expressed his preference for Don Quixote. The names of

D'Artagnan, Don Juan, and Robinson Crusoe were raised by other prominent writers. Conan Doyle's answer, as the editors of *The Strand* were quick to point out, was "characteristic of him as a writer and a man." Conan Doyle gave the name of Colonel Newcome, a character from a Thackeray novel published shortly before his birth. The reason was simple. This character, Conan Doyle said, was "an ideal English gentleman."

Conan Doyle was not English – his family was Irish, and he himself had been born in Scotland – but he was very much a gentleman. In a sense his own character had been molded with greater care and ambition than that of Sherlock Holmes, Brigadier Gerard, Professor Challenger, or any of his other fictional heroes. It projected his natural decency, and expressed a wistful strain of nostalgia for the orderly values of a previous age. Of all his novels, he most prized the historical romances that celebrated the Regency period or the Napoleonic era. In later life, this insistence on old-fashioned values and propriety caused some to regard him as a quaint, if charming, old party, somewhat out of step with the times. Conan Doyle lived until 1930, but he remains fixed in the popular imagination as a figure of gaslight and hansom cabs. The final decade of his life saw the publication of *Lady Chatterley's Lover*, *A Farewell to Arms*, *The Great Gatsby*, *Ulysses*, and *To the Lighthouse*. Conan Doyle, by contrast, published a book in which undersea explorers travel to Atlantis.

And through it all, Sherlock Holmes, whose adventures he considered to be "on a different and humbler plane" from the rest of his books, continued to thrive. "I've written a good deal more about him than I ever intended to do," Conan Doyle said in 1927, forty years after Holmes first saw print, "but my hand has been rather forced by kind friends who continually wanted to know more. And so it is that this monstrous growth has come out, out of what was really a comparatively small seed."

Indeed, this "monstrous growth" had long since taken on a life of its own. "Sherlock Holmes and Dr. Watson are household words; both names have passed into the language," remarked H. Greenhough Smith, Conan Doyle's editor at *The Strand*. "This was a feat any author might feel proud of. Sherlock Holmes, without question, is the most familiar and most widely known character in English fiction." Even the *Times* of London, celebrating the great detective's longevity in 1930, felt compelled to offer a word of consolation to Conan Doyle's other creations: "Those who follow the fortunes of Rodney Stone, of the White Company, of the Brigadier Gerard, of Micah Clarke, and a crowd of others, share momentous events by the side of intimate friends, and this double gift of providing at once good company and stirring deeds is displayed by Conan Doyle in his short stories as well as his books. Seeing what perils they ran, and how nobly, it is easy to understand the resentment of the rest of the Conan Doyle characters that pride of place must always be yielded to a lean and somewhat inhuman scientific student of crime, living not in the brave and brutal fourteenth century or at the heart of the Napoleonic epic, but amid the hansom cabs and street urchins of the later eighties."

Today, Sherlock Holmes has become a cultural archetype – like Robin Hood, Romeo and Juliet, or the Three Musketeers. Children in Zaire and Tibet recognise his image as easily as that of Santa Claus or Mickey Mouse. He has been featured in countless books, movies, television programs, musicals, stage plays – even a ballet. The familiar hawk-nosed profile appears on teapots, chess pieces, dinner plates, board games, computer programs, and chewing gum packages. He has acquired a cult of followers whose devotion borders on the mystical. Sherlockians, as they call themselves, can be found in every corner of the globe – and, increasingly, on the Internet – discussing such matters as the depth to which a sprig of parsley might sink in butter on a hot day or the true location of Dr. Watson's strangely transient war wound. Ask a Holmes buff for news of the giant rat of Sumatra and he or she will answer, gently, that it is a tale for which the world is not yet prepared.

"Every detective story writer makes mistakes," wrote Raymond Chandler, "and none will ever know as much as he should. Conan Doyle made mistakes which completely invalidated some of his stories, But he was a pioneer, and Sherlock Holmes is mostly an attitude and a few dozen lines of unforgettable dialogue."

Chandler's assessment, however cavalier, strikes at an essential truth. Sherlock Holmes can be read over and over again for the sheer joy of Conan Doyle's writing. It is not that we have forgotten who killed Sir Charles Baskerville or who stole the Bruce-Partington Plans. We return to Baker Street to watch a genius at work. Once heard, the call is never forgotten: The singular worm unknown to science. Wilson the notorious canary trainer. The curious incident of the dog in the nighttime. "Come, Watson, come. The game's afoot."

But in the rush to lionize Sherlock Holmes, Conan Doyle has been nudged aside. Too often Conan Doyle is dismissed as a figure who happened to be present when Holmes sprang into being – or, as some Sherlockians would have it, the "literary agent" who helped Dr. Watson's writings find their way into print. This would have been a great sadness to Conan Doyle. Though he played down his own achievement with Holmes, he understood that he had taken a little-known genre and pulled it into the light.

Conan Doyle is often portrayed as "the man who hated Sherlock Holmes," but this is only partially true. At times he sickened of his famous creation – as evidenced by the early attempts to kill him off – but in his final years he was able to strike a conciliatory note: "I have not in actual practice found that these lighter sketches have prevented me from exploring and finding my limitations in such varied branches of literature as history, poetry, historical novels, psychic research, and the drama. Had Holmes never existed I could not have done more, though he may perhaps have stood a little in the way of the recognition of my more serious literary work."

Perhaps. Though some would argue that these "lighter sketches" were the work of an innovative genius, breaking new ground and lighting the way for future generations of writers, while the more "serious" work remains hopelessly tethered to the past. Even so, Sherlock Holmes constitutes only a small part of Conan Doyle's total body of work, and if his admirers could be lured away from the bright lights of Baker Street for a few moments, they would find an interesting and rewarding writer waiting in the shadows. Conan Doyle gave the world a great deal of pleasure. He deserves, at least for a moment, to be taken on his own terms.

"I have led a life which, for variety and romance, could, I think, hardly be exceeded," he once wrote. "I have known what it was to be a poor man and I have known what it was to be fairly affluent. I have sampled every kind of human experience. I have known many of the most remarkable men of my time. I have had a long literary career after a medical training which gave me the M.D. of Edinburgh. I have tried my hand at very many sports, including boxing, cricket, billiards, motoring, aeronautics and skiing, having been the first to introduce the latter for long journeys into Switzerland. I have travelled as Doctor to a whaler for seven months in the Arctic and afterward in the West Coast of Africa. I have seen something of three wars, the Sudanese, the South African and the German. My life has been dotted with adventures of all kinds. Finally I have been constrained to devote my latter years to telling the world the final result of thirty-six years' study of the occult, and in endeavouring to make it realize the overwhelming importance of the question. In this mission I have already travelled more than 50,000 miles and addressed 300,000 people, besides writing seven books on the subject. Such is the life I have led."

And such is the story that follows.

Chapter 20

Miscellany III: 2006-2010

THE DAILY TELEGRAPH THURSDAY, JANUARY 19, 2006

By **Nigel Reynolds** Arts Correspondent

The second most valuable book according to *Book & Magazine Collector* are first editions of Arthur Conan Doyle's *The Hound of the Baskervilles* (1902), complete with rare dust jacket, at £80,000.
[The most valuable book was James Joyce's *Ulysses* at £100,000].
[See also page 484].

SUNDAY TELEGRAPH **February 5 2006**

Letters to the Editor

On the road to Kandahar

Can you substantiate your claim that Kipling made the battle of Maiwand famous (International News, January 29)?
 Although nobody has dealt more with Afghan affairs and mindset, he did not write up Maiwand. Some have seen a faint echo in *The Drums of the Fore and Aft*; and if so, it is very faint. The poem "That Day" is thought to draw on it, but never by name. Probably the only work which can, with confidence, be assigned even to the Second Afghan War, as opposed to some later North West Frontier campaign, is "Ford o' Kabul River".
 Conan Doyle might have given Maiwand more publicity, as it was where Dr Watson probably acquired his gammy leg.
 In Afghan eyes, Maiwand is pretty much their Trafalgar and Waterloo in one, inspiring monument, square and boulevard in the capital.

PG URBEN
Kenilworth, Warwickshire

SUNDAY TELEGRAPH **February 12 2006**

Letters to the Editor

Where Dr Watson caught the bullet

It is highly improbable that Conan Doyle's Dr Watson acquired his lame leg at the Battle of Maiwand (Letters, February 5). There was one British infantry battalion in the battle and, after the Indian troops fled, the British were surrounded and annihilated by the Afghan forces.

If Dr Watson sustained his wound in the Afghan campaign as suggested by your correspondent, it was probably at the Battle of Kandahar fought 36 days after Maiwand, on September 1, 1880. The Afghan army was routed and all its guns and equipage were captured.

PJ SMITH
Bridlington, East Yorkshire

SUNDAY TELEGRAPH **February 19 2006**

Letters to the Editor

Dr Watson was not alone

The fictional Dr Watson – and the question of his gammy leg – aside (Letters, February 12), there were indeed British survivors of the Battle of Maiwand who fell back under fire to the city of Kandahar.

Charles Baffin of the 66th Foot was one of those men and I am privileged to be the custodian of the campaign medal awarded to him for services in Afghanistan.

Peter Weedon
Upper Bucklebury, Berkshire

SUNDAY TELEGRAPH **February 26 2006**

Maiwand survivor

My grandfather, Sgt Thomas Benjamin Stephenson of the 66th Foot, survived the defeat at Maiwand in July 1880 (Letters, February 19) and left the Army six years later. He promptly married and sired nine healthy children before his death in 1901.

Robert Stephenson
Henley-on-Thames, Oxfordshire

MONDAY, MAY 8, 2006 **THE DAILY TELEGRAPH**

WORLD NEWS

Japanese to honour Briton who saved them from cholera (Extract) **By Colin Joyce in Tokyo**

IF WILLIAM Kinninmond Burton is remembered at all in Britain, it is as a childhood friend of Sir Arthur Conan Doyle.

But in Japan he is revered as the foreign engineer who saved the country from cholera in the 19th century and built the country's first skyscraper.

Burton's father, John Hill, was a historian and sponsor of struggling writers including the young Conan Doyle. In his youth, the creator of Sherlock Holmes, lived for a while with the Burton family and his book *The Firm of Girdlestone* is dedicated to "my old friend" William K Burton.

THE SUNDAY TELEGRAPH Seven Magazine 03.09.06

BOOKS/FICTION Paperbacks Review by **Katie Owen**

ARTHUR & GEORGE By Julian Barnes. VINTAGE

Meticulous, impressive, and arguably heavy-going, this is Barnes's recreation of the background to a famous real-life 19th-century court case. Sir Arthur Conan Doyle took on a mission: to clear the name of an obscure half-Indian solicitor. George Edalji was accused of killing animals in his home village, but Conan Doyle believed in his innocence. The story is a vehicle for Barnes to pose questions about different versions of truth and reality as well as issues of social prejudice.

TELEGRAPH REVIEW Saturday, September 9, 2006

PICK OF THE PAPERBACKS
Arthur & George by Julian Barnes. Jonathan Cape

Based on the notorious Great Wyrley Outrages of 1906, this riveting mix of fact and fiction was pipped for last year's Man Booker by John Banville's *The Sea*. Arthur is Sir Arthur Conan Doyle, hide-bound and morally conscientious, wrestling with literary fame and love for another woman while his wife lies dying. George is a solicitor from rural Staffordshire, the son of an Indian priest. When his family starts to get hate mail they assume it is racial prejudice, and report it. The police, however, think George is the author of the notes and then, when someone starts mutilating horses in the nearby fields, they accuse him of the crime and charge him on the flimsiest of evidence. He is given seven years in prison. Conan Doyle takes up cudgels on George's behalf without either man, both beautifully delineated in Barnes's precise prose, understanding one another's motivations at all. What really sticks in the mind, though, is the hate mail, reprinted as it was written, and the product of a shockingly deranged mind.

Toby Clements

THE DAILY TELEGRAPH WEDNESDAY, DECEMBER 27, 2006

Letters to the Editor

Jeeves's crease

SIR – The tailors Gieves and Hawkes might have enjoyed the patronage of such well-dressed men as Bertie Wooster, but would be shocked at the allegation that they inspired the name of his manservant (Travel, December 23).

They would surely know that Jeeves was named after the Warwickshire cricketer Percy Jeeves (1888-1916), whom PG Wodehouse saw play at Cheltenham in 1912. Wodehouse confirmed this and added that he was following the example of Arthur Conan Doyle, who liked naming his characters after professional cricketers.

N.T.P. Murphy
London N11

Telegraph Review, Saturday, December 30, 2006

Books Feature

The detective's dark side

Ian Thomson delights in Conan Doyle's masterpiece, 'The Hound of the Baskervilles.'

In 1893, Sir Arthur Conan Doyle murdered Sherlock Holmes. After writing two dozen stories, Doyle was sick of his creation and felt he was distracted from more serious literature. So, in *The Adventure of the Final Problem*, he drowned his detective in the foaming abyss of the Reichenbach Falls, Switzerland. "Couldn't you bring him back?" Doyle was repeatedly asked. "He is at the foot of the Reichenbach Falls," he retorted crossly, "And there he stays."

It was not to be. Nine years later, in 1901, Doyle was forced to "revive" his subtle, hawk-eyed detective in what was to become his masterpiece, *The Hound of the Baskervilles*. The sleuth's disappearance had caused such a public outcry that Doyle relented. Sherlockians had marched in protest down Fleet Street and sent letters of complaint to the Prince of Wales. Readers of *The Strand* magazine, which serialised Holmes, threatened to cancel their subscriptions. Now the greatest investigator of all had risen again, complete with pipe, Stradivarius and magnifying glass (though not deerstalker: the hat was added by the illustrator Sidney Paget).

The result was a Victorian whodunnit of extraordinary brooding power. Doyle took a literary risk with his new monster. The use of a canine rather than Professor Moriarty, say, as the villain of *The Hound of the Baskervilles* was a brilliant device. Given the British fondness for dogs, the hell-hound must have given readers of *The Strand* a peculiar frisson. Dogs are common in the Sherlock Holmes tales, but not murderous ones: Conan Doyle's own dog – half spaniel, half lurcher – was the model for the virtuous Toby, who brings the criminals to book in the second of the Holmes novels, *The Sign of Four* (1890). A precursor of the Baskerville hound (never named, but certainly not Rover) is found in Doyle's short story "The King of the Foxes", where a monstrous fox turns out to be a wolf escaped from a menagerie. Yet the Baskerville hound remains unique in British literature and has become a legend.

Fans of the Baker Street detective can rejoice that all nine of the Sherlock Holmes mysteries are republished this month. The reprints, with suitably atmospheric covers (baying phantom dogs; swirling London fog) are aimed at younger readers who will have heard of Doyle but not necessarily have read him.

Sherlock Holmes is name-checked by Arctic Monkeys, for example, in their song *A Certain Romance*. Stephen Fry is a die-hard Sherlockian, as is Alexander McCall Smith.

The best Holmes stories were written before 1917, when Conan Doyle converted to Spiritualism. A hybrid of mysticism and Low Church gloom, the pseudo-religion flourished amid the bereavement of the First World War; Doyle had lost a son in the conflict. He had dabbled in mediums and moonshine before *Baskervilles* was published in 1902, the fire-breathing beast might really have come from the Beyond, as we are first led to believe.

Instead, *The Hound of the Baskervilles* is leavened by a marvellous corny humour. ("I have ample evidence," Holmes tells Sir Henry Baskerville, "that you are being dogged in London.") And, memorably, it's the only Sherlock Holmes tale, short or long, where the story overshadows the detective, Holmes being "absent" for almost half of the narrative (though really on the moors in disguise).

The detective's darker side, made explicit in the drug-taking of *The Sign of Four*, contradicts the familiar deerstalker image. Sherlock Holmes was addicted to cocaine and injected himself with morphine to stave off the bouts of boredom. Did his creator also have a weakness for narcotics? Conan Doyle was familiar with stimulants from his medical studies at Edinburgh University in the early 1880s, and later witnessed varieties of addiction (notably to rum) as a trainee surgeon aboard a whaling ship. It is possible that hallucinogens helped Doyle appreciate the shimmering, greenish light emanated by certain spiritualist mediums.

In 1891, two years before he precipitated the Reichenbach Crisis, Conan Doyle moved with his family to the nondescript London Suburb of South Norwood, where he would later write his two-volume *History of Spiritualism* and call for a new science of the paranormal: Plasmology. A number of the Sherlock Holmes stories unfold in Norbury and other parts of London south of the river; Brixton is the scene of the gruesome ritual murder in *A Study in Scarlet* (1888); Woolwich and Croydon crop up in *His Last Bow* (1917). The Holmes adventures are, among other things, metropolitan fantasies, atmospherically fixed in the outskirts of Victorian London.

The Baker Street mysteries, however, make up only a small part of Doyle's literary output. As well as whodunits, he wrote a variety of non-fiction works including *The Coming of the Fairies* (1922), in which he tried to authenticate photographs of wood nymphs. Hopelessly in thrawl to table-rapping and other fog-bound marvels, Doyle was convinced that the deceased could return to life through luminous voice trumpets. Even if many in post-Somme Britain were communing with the war dead, only the creator of *The Hound of the Baskervilles*, one feels, could have travelled to the Welsh mining village of Penylan (not a noted pocket of the paranormal) in search of clairvoyants. Unfortunately, there is no doubting Doyle's sincerity. Spiritualism, the first of the modern heresies, eclipsed all other concerns in his adult years; Doyle had found an alternative in crystal-balling to the hard Catholicism of his upbringing (at Stonyhurst College he was routinely birched by Jesuits). In spite of his spook-dabbling, Doyle was a steely moralist, who campaigned on behalf of battered wives and against the persecution of Jews and the iniquities of the Belgian Congo. His best-selling pamphlet *The War in South Africa*, issued in 1902, condemned British cruelty towards the Boers. But the real drama in Doyle's life remained Sherlock Holmes, even though in 1912 he tried once more to elude his morphine-hungry sleuth with *The Lost World*, a science fantasy about pterodactyls and stegosauri. The 60th and final Holmes adventure, "Shoscombe Old Place" (from *The Casebook of Sherlock Holmes*), was published three years before Doyle died in 1930. By then the tall, ascetic scientist-sleuth had given pleasure to millions.

Doyle's troubled relationship with his creation was fraught with dark, father-son undercurrents, and was far from elementary. What other fictional detective has become so charmingly real to his readers as the occupant of 221b Baker Street? The revival of Sherlock Holmes is a treat. Meanwhile, a spectral bogey hound continues to prowl the Baskerville moors, reappearing to each new generation of Holmes readers as the Fido from hell.

Daily Mail WEEKEND Saturday 17th March 2007

Sherlock Holmes and the case of the vanishing pipe

No deerstalker, no pipe. The new Sherlock Holmes is the most PC yet, but will there be fire without smoke? By **Jill Parkin**

An evil genius is on the loose, a child is missing and something gory has just been discovered lying among the dripping fronds in the orangery. So the world's greatest detective is called in to solve the mystery with his legendary powers of deduction. We're on the set of Sherlock Holmes and The Baker Street Irregulars, the latest Holmes drama to visit our television screens, and with his cadaverous looks and gaunt appearance, Jonathan Pryce is perfect for the part of the famous sleuth. Bill Paterson plays Watson, his loyal but plodding sidekick.

Together, the actors look so convincing you could almost believe they *are* Holmes and Watson and, indeed, as many people still believe, that their fictional characters were once real investigators. Pryce and Paterson talk about the popular 'mythology' that has grown around Arthur Conan Doyle's creation. 'I do say "elementary", though not in the same context as the mythology has it,' says Pryce. 'Holmes never actually said, "Elementary, my dear Watson." As for the deerstalker hat he is usually depicted as wearing, I shouldn't think there'd have been much call for one of those in London.'

Pryce is wearing a homburg hat for the orangery scene, but he won't confirm rumours that a deerstalker makes an appearance in the BBC drama. There's a pipe on the set, but, as yet, no actual wreathes of smoke drifting up to the ceiling as Holmes ponders his latest case. In fact, it has been reported that his tobacco habit has been the victim of historical airbrushing as he enters a more health-conscious age. We're chatting in between filming in a glasshouse at Dublin's National Botanic Gardens. It is misty, pouring with rain and just right for dark deeds among the giant palms.

The Irregulars of the title are the street urchins who appear in the original Conan Doyle stories, such as The Sign of Four, helping Holmes with their knowledge of low life in London and their ability to move around the capital virtually unnoticed.

'This Holmes is more contemporary to attract a younger TV audience,' says Pryce, 59. 'What I liked about this version is the sense of fun and enjoyment. There are murders, but you don't see any blood. Most TV has gone much too far the other way. You just can't talk about a dead body any more, you have to go into graphic detail.'

'Every other Sherlock has been for an adult audience,' explains Michael Maloney, 49, who plays Inspector Stirling, the policeman who's at least one step behind Holmes. 'But there's a lot here that children will like. There's an extremely powerful brain for once; instead of an extremely powerful body or magical abilities. Part of Holmes's appeal is his absolute rationality. He has a tremendous enjoyment of the problematic, of logic and reasoning. Of course, children's fantasy is very big at the moment, but there are lots of children out there who find reasoning and logic very appealing.'

Of course, there are also a lot of children who might find it slightly odd that Holmes and Watson live together; this generation wasn't brought up with Morecambe and Wise and their cosy chats in bed together. But this Holmes has a romantic past to explain all that, and a new arch rival. Move over, Moriarty, Holmes's traditional adversary – Irene Adler's here.

'We have Irene's story being revealed for the very first time, which is fun,' says Pryce. Irene was introduced in A Scandal in Bohemia. Holmes was in love with her, though he resists those feelings. She deceived him and he avoided further relationships after that.' Without me giving away too much of the plot, it turns out that Irene is a heartless mistress of disguise. Holmes seems irked as much by his former love's brilliant mind as by her wickedness. He's not an emotional man, which makes him hard on himself as well as others.

'He's also quite severe with the Irregulars, even when one of them might be dead. He's quite ruthless with the missing boy's sister, saying that life goes on and she may as well get used to it,' explains Pryce. 'But he does give them help and advice.'

Paterson, who played Ally Fraser in Auf Wiedersehen, Pet, and Pryce have been friends for 25 years and have long thought about playing the detective and his partner. When the chance came Pryce's way, he immediately suggested Paterson as the other half of the duo. 'We've known each other for a long time,' says Paterson. 'We've grown up together; we have daughters the same age; we've lived near each other and we meet often. It always goes like this: after three glasses of wine, I'll say, "We should do Holmes and Watson some day, you know." He'll reply, "Yes, yes, we should. We really should, yes." And we've gone on like this for 15 years, and got through lots of wine. Then we actually got the chance to do it. What luck.'

During the next filming break, some disreputable-looking kids appear, dodging the drips of water that come through the glasshouse roof. Looking distinctly underfed and sharp, as if they're on their way back to Fagin's den, they are the Baker Street Irregulars: Finch, Jack, Sadie, Tealeaf and Jasmine. 'The story has that Oliver Twist thing that children love; rather like the Lost Boys in Peter Pan,' concludes Pryce.

Megan Jones, 14, from London, who plays Jasmine, a sort of drama queen of the gutter, explains, 'It's something that could happen now and be nasty, but it's done in an old-fashioned way. I wouldn't like it if my mum and dad really weren't around, but it's fun if they're not there to tell you what to do. That's what it's like for the Irregulars.'

MONDAY, MARCH 26, 2007/**THE DAILY TELEGRAPH**

Last Night on Television By **James Walton**

Sherlock Holmes and the Baker Street Irregulars (BBC1) is a plucky attempt to revive the Sunday-teatime serial for children. Happily too, yesterday's episode didn't make us wait long for our first foggy London alleyway – which came in the opening scene.

The programme is clearly intended as a cheering fantasy for younger viewers. The irregulars of the title are a group of street children, mentioned in Doyle's *A Study in Scarlet*, who assist the great detective when required. Here, though, they're required all the time. By the end yesterday, they were even charged with saving Holmes's bacon – after he'd been somewhat implausibly arrested for the murder of two policemen.

Grumpier adult viewers might wonder if these 19th-century characters would be quite so fluent in modern slang. And yet, of course, that's the point. The idea is to let modern children imagine themselves as the irregulars: getting into scrapes, impressing Holmes with their sleuthing, and basically outwitting the grown-ups at every turn. (Think *Hustle* remade in the style of a Victorian *Bugsy Malone*.)

In fact, they're so good that, despite being played by Jonathan Pryce, Holmes himself is content to let them dominate proceedings. Yesterday, he even paid their leader the ultimate compliment, by praising his choice of magnifying glass: "Ah, the Zeiss optimiser 600."

THE SUNDAY POST, **May 6, 2007**

Edinburgh surgeon was the inspiration for Sherlock Holmes By Mike Duffy.

Amid the formaldehyde-drenched slices of gunshot-riddled kidneys and skeletons of long dead babies within Surgeons' Hall Pathology Museum in Edinburgh is a corner devoted to a man who inspired the greatest detective the world has ever known.

There, prominently displayed, is a letter, addressed to the Victorian Scottish surgeon Joseph Bell, from one of his former students.

In precise handwriting it includes the line, "It is most certainly to you that I owe Sherlock Holmes."

The letter is signed by Sir Arthur Conan Doyle.

It is one of several discovered in a widow's house in Edinburgh's Ann Street, in a detective mystery to rival the investigations of Holmes and Watson a century ago.

Speaking in the library of the Royal College of Surgeons of Edinburgh, Dr Alan Mackaill, a retired biochemist from Edinburgh University, described how he made the discovery.

"I have been working in the museum as a volunteer guide since my retirement and was approached by a Probus club to do a talk about 19th Century surgery. "As part of that I thought it would be interesting to include references to Dr Joseph Bell, because he was a former president of the Royal College and because of his connection to literature through Sherlock Holmes."

During his research Alan read a biography about Bell, who was the first surgeon at the Edinburgh Sick Children's Hospital when it was founded in 1860.

Penned by an American doctor, Eli Liebow, in the foreword written by the surgeon's great grandson Brigadier Nigel Stisted, who mentioned he had a portrait of Dr Bell in his house in Edinburgh.

Discovered

That was something to go on and, searching for an unusual name like Stisted, Alan discovered just one in the Edinburgh phone book. But when he tried to contact the retired brigadier he was informed by his wife Judith that her husband had just passed away three months previously.

"I thought I'd come to an abrupt end in my enquiries until she said there was an old box with some 'bits and pieces' I might be interested in."

When Alan went round to Judith's home in Ann Street, which had been in the family for generations, he was shown a few letters taken from the box.

The very first one she showed him was that auspicious revelation from May 4, 1892, in which Conan Doyle admitted his former mentor was the inspiration for his super-sleuth.

"Judith asked me, 'Do you find this interesting?' I was so excited I could hardly speak!" admits Alan.

"I don't think she realised quite how important this was as a historical document."

Given permission to root through the old cardboard box, Alan went on to discover several other letters from Conan Doyle to Bell, photographs of the surgeon with his wife Edith and their three children, two copies of Bell's own books and his private journal. There was even a letter to him from Florence Nightingale.

Judith kindly gave the historical artefacts to Surgeons' Hall Pathology Museum where some of them are now on display in a new exhibition, *Conan Doyle and Joseph Bell: The Real Sherlock Holmes*, which runs until May 31.

Reputation

Dr Bell had a reputation within the medical world of Victorian Edinburgh for his shrewd diagnoses of patients, often gleaned by simply observing them.

It is said that Bell could tell of their habits, occupations, nationality and even names just from studying them.

But Alan is keen to point out that the keen eye for detail Bell shared with Holmes was as far as the similarities went.

"Sherlock Holmes is sometimes harsh and unreasonable and has a superiority complex and I don't think Bell was like that.

"Joseph Bell was a man of great compassion who cared deeply for his patients and their difficulties. He was deeply religious and hated missing church – and that is very un-Holmesian."

Whether Bell enjoyed his connection with Holmes is debatable.

While there is no proof he disapproved, following his death in 1911 a colleague wrote that the surgeon had been unhappy with the association.

Dr Bell's wife died of peritonitis and his son Benjamin died 20 years later. He never remarried and, perhaps due to his increasing reputation, when he died in 1911 his assets excluding his houses, came to more than £62,000 – about £4 million in today's money.

Interest in the great detective, meanwhile, seems undiminished.

An original manuscript of one of Conan Doyle's last stories, *The Adventure of The Three Gables*, is to be auctioned in New York in June when it's expected to fetch more than £250,000.

And today and tomorrow at Surgeons' Hall Pathology Museum on Nicolson Street in Edinburgh, they are holding a special detective weekend from 10am-4pm.

Visitors will have the opportunity to try on deerstalker hats and capes, there are hands-on microscope sessions and quizzes and readings about the great detective by historian and writer Owen Dudley Edwards.

Sunday Telegraph **Seven** Magazine, 16 September 2007.

Books/Non-Fiction Biography – The first of two reviews.
Conan Doyle: The Man Who Created Sherlock Holmes by Andrew Lycett. Weidenfeld & Nicholson.

Philip Hoare on the Paradoxical, Indefatigable Conan Doyle.

For the sedentary occupation of a writer, Arthur Conan Doyle's life was one of extraordinary action. The man never stood still. A doctor by training, an athlete by aspiration, and an author by ambition, he prospered in an age when a man need not be restricted by one particular career. In Andrew Lycett's hugely enjoyable new biography, the sheer breathtaking dynamism of the man shines through.

Born of Irish parents, with a Roman Catholic upbringing and education – at Stonyhurst (where his school report described him as 'sulky', 'slovenly' and 'snappish') – Doyle's father was an artist and an alcoholic who ended up in an asylum.

As Lycett points out, the shame haunted his son, who feared he might go the same way. That in itself might explain the non-stop nature of Conan Doyle's adult life – and his thirst to earn money. As a result of Charles Doyle's illness, his wife Mary – whose intellect their son did inherit – experienced severe bouts of poverty. Conan Doyle would later become one of the richest authors in Britain.

He did so by dint of application. Having trained in Edinburgh as a doctor, he spent six months on a whaling ship in the Arctic as a ship's surgeon. The SS Hope caught just two whales; but the experience produced one of Conan Doyle's spookiest early stories, 'The Captain of the Polestar'. The tale is evidence of the influence of Edgar Allan Poe, a favourite writer of Conan Doyle's and inventor of the detective story.

Conan Doyle was already publishing his short stories when he set up shop as GP in Southsea – where a young H.G. Wells, his future rival, was working as a draper's assistant. There Conan Doyle discovered spiritualism, through the wonderfully eccentric character of Alfred Drayson; a professional soldier whose interests ranged from astronomy to mesmerism and who, in one séance, witnessed fresh eggs, fruit and flowers descend from the ceiling of his Woolwich quarters, a phenomenon which must have surprised his fellow officers.

Lycett's impeccably researched book correctly emphases how important spiritualism was to Conan Doyle. Having discarded his Catholicism, he placed implicit faith in his new religion – to an extent that would blind him to its frauds. He was certainly a man of enormous paradox. On one hand, he financed to proto-Fascist British Brothers League which, in the paranoid years before the First World War, lobbied to keep German Jews out of the East End.

Yet he also fought fiercely on behalf of George Edalji, a Parsee Indian living in Staffordshire who had been wrongly imprisoned for the horrific maiming of animals in the countryside. Conan Doyle's alliance with Roger Casement in exposing the atrocities committed in King Leopold's Congo similarly does justice to the more benevolent aspects of the British Empire. But he also managed to find time to box with friends in his garage, play cricket with W.G. Grace, and get some of the first speeding tickets issued in Surrey.

It is a measure of the man's energy that his most famous creation sometimes seems almost incidental to Lycett's book – despite its subtitle. As the biographer shows, Conan Doyle felt cursed by the success of Sherlock Holmes, announcing even as early as after the first six stories, that he would never write another. Of course he did – tantalised, if not tormented by public acclaim, and by munificent cheques from publishers.

'Becoming a spiritualist so soon after creating the quintessentially rational Sherlock Holmes: that is the central paradox of Arthur's life,' writes Lycett. Holmes – named after Conan Doyle's favourite American writer, Oliver Wendell Holmes, himself a doctor, and friend of Emerson and Melville, was hyper-rational and diagnostic. (Conan Doyle openly acknowledged that his Edinburgh tutor, Joseph Bell, was the inspiration for this aspect of his detective).

But Holmes was also a Bohemian drug addict and melancholic who sometimes resembles an invention of Oscar Wilde. Indeed, in another of his telling anecdotes, Lycett describes how it was shortly after meeting Wilde that Conan Doyle wrote *The Sign of Four* – his second Holmes adventure, with its own specifically Wildean character – whilst Wilde went off and wrote *The Picture of Dorian Grey*.

Conan Doyle's success could only have been in his age. With the advent of Armageddon, that gloriously certain world which waited with baited breath for the next Sherlock Holmes fell apart. From his Surrey home Conan Doyle could hear the guns of Flanders. He visited the Front, wrote a history of the war even as it was in progress; and became more convinced than ever of the verities of spiritualism.

'I seemed suddenly to see that this subject with which I had so long dallied was…really something tremendous…a call of hope and guidance to the human race at the time of its deepest affliction.' Conan Doyle, like Kipling, lost his son in the war; his brother, too: but it was his implacable belief that they had merely moved on to a 'summerland' – where, indeed he contacted them beyond the grave.

To the end of his own life, he continued to champion the faith, believed in the Cottingley Fairies, and even appeared at his own funeral – if the attendant clairvoyant is to be believed – 'I saw him distinctly. He was wearing evening dress.' One would expect nothing less.

Telegraph Review Literary Biography Books **Saturday, October 20, 2007**

A life that was far from elementary- By **Jane Stevenson**

It is interesting reading Andrew Lycett's biography of Arthur Conan Doyle alongside Jon Lellenberg, Daniel Stashower and Charles Foley's edition of letters, mostly from Conan Doyle to his mother – **Arthur Conan Doyle: a Life in Letters**. Harper Press.

The letters reveal a man perpetually boyish in his capacity for wild enthusiasms, and supportive of his younger siblings. But no man will ever tell the whole truth to his mother, especially not one who is forced to assume his father's place as provider. From his schooldays on, the letters imply: "See what a good boy I'm being." Cheery and breezy, they make light of difficulties: they tell "the Mam" what she wants to hear. Never, they imply, did he experience resentment or anger at the burdens his family put upon him.

Certain subjects were not discussed on paper, or if they were, have been censored by subsequent family members. They include, for example, Charles Doyle's alcoholism and lamentable failure as a husband and father. Mary Doyle's relationship with a doctor called Bryan Waller, who made himself to some extent financially responsible for the family, and Conan Doyle's attitude to his supplanter (except in a single mystifying letter that suggests he actually beat up the older man on one occasion).

Even apart from this, all was far from sweetness and light in Conan Doyle's life, especially after his wife Louise, developed TB. He fell in love with a younger and prettier woman, but his wife survived as a chronic invalid for nine years, keeping him apart from the girl he loved.

It is unsurprising to find him protesting his righteousness to "the Mam", and assuring her that his wife did not suffer in the least from the fact that he was in love with another woman. Like Dickens, whom he resembles, Conan Doyle had a tremendous capacity for convincing himself.

His editors take his version at face value but Lycett, more subtly, observes that one of the later Holmes stories, "The Problem of Thor Bridge", deals with a woman in Louise's position, driven by jealousy that attempts to implicate her supplanter as her murderer. The story suggests Conan Doyle's recognition that his wife might have seen things differently.

This is the most stark of the instances in which the editors fail to engage seriously with the central question of how far Conan Doyle's self-presentation can be trusted. The brief linking passages of *A Life in Letters* fill in all manner of factual minutiae, but fail to weigh the value of the author's words. By contrast, Lycett's sophisticated account reveals a character with far more light and shade, capable, on the one hand, of generosity and courage and, on the other, of self-deception, emotional blackmail, mental cruelty (especially towards his first wife and her children) and sheer silliness (especially towards the second family). The letters reveal that he canonised his eldest son, Kingsley, after his early death, while Lycett suggests that he treated Kingsley quite badly during his life, so guilt had something to do with this.

If there is too little of the Letters loving, honourable son in Lycett, this is partly because the letters in question were not available to him. Unpublished letters are legally the property of the writer's natural heirs: literary biography is therefore often hampered by "professional descendants". This is abundantly the case with the Conan Doyle estate. The family letters that fell to the share of his daughter by his second wife went to the British Library on her death, but Foley, by virtue of being both Conan Doyle's sister Ida's grandson, and named as heir by the widow of Conan Doyle's youngest son, was in a position under the daughter's will to remove "documents merely of family interest" from public access. It is these documents that are published as *A Life in Letters*.

But while Lycett's narrative is competent if a little colourless, the afterword in which he reveals these machinations is the most entertaining part of the book, written with a degree of sustained fury that makes the words crackle off the page. And for all the impediments in his way, Lycett's is by far the better book.

Daily Telegraph Saturday, October 20, 2007

Property Section

Ipplepen, in Devon, forms the rugged, rural backdrop to Sherlock Holmes's greatest detective. **Clive Aslet** revisits it.

My sons have been reading *The Hound of the Baskervilles*, not only the greatest of detective stories but a novel with a vivid sense of place. Arthur Conan Doyle heard about the Dartmoor hound legend, or a medley of hound legends, while recuperating from a fever caught in South Africa during the Boer War. He was staying at a hotel with Fletcher Robinson (known as Bobbles to some friends, although not to Conan Doyle) whom he had met on the ship home. It was 1901 and Robinson had recently inherited a house at Ipplepen, Devon, nine miles from the moor. His father's coachman went by the suggestive name of Harry Baskerville.

I am indebted for these facts to Philip Weller's *The Hound of the Baskervilles: Hunting the Dartmoor Legend*. Weller tracks down likely inspirations for the places described in the book with the persistence of Holmes himself. Conan Doyle did his homework, staying variously at Robinson's house at Ipplepen, at a hotel in Princetown and spending a night, like Holmes, in a stone hut on the moor (although with Robinson for company).

Baskerville Hall and the great Grimpen Mire are composites, but there are compelling precedents for other places. Nun's Cross Farm, shown as a primitive and cheerless building in contemporary photographs, was the model for Merripit House, home of Stapleton and his beautiful "sister". There would be a couple of 4x4s standing outside it now. The house that Conan Doyle built for his family in Surrey – Undershaw, at Hindhead – seems to have contributed something; according to Weller, it was exceptionally gloomy. (Alas, it must be even gloomier now. Waverley Borough Council served the owner with an urgent works notice in January.)

Robinson's Park Hill House at Ipplepen was an unremarkable villa, and Conan Doyle made nothing of it. If only he had known that the village lay in the hundred of Black Torrington; that sounds sufficiently stern to have been woven in somewhere. Perhaps he came to the same verdict as the great landscape historian WG Hoskins in his 1972 volume on Devon: "A grey and rather dismal village, with much bad modern building," he wrote, admitting only that the perpendicular windows in the church are "notably good". It cannot be said, looking at some of the property for sale at the moment, that Hoskins was altogether wide of the mark.

Clive Aslet is Editor-at-Large of 'Country Life'.

Compiler's note: The rest of the article concerns houses for sale in Devon.
DAILY MAIL WEEKEND Magazine, November 2007

The case of the **crooked nose**

Richard E. Grant is a huge fan of Sherlock Holmes, but just one thing stops him playing the great detective on screen. By DAVID THOMAS

This weekend, Richard E. Grant presents an ITV documentary investigating the truth about Sherlock Holmes direct from 221B Baker Street – the home of the world's most famous detective. In the course of the programme, *Elementary, My Dear Viewer*, he dons a cape and deerstalker hat, while sucking on a pipe, just as Sherlock Holmes liked to do. All in all, it looks awfully like a job application for the next time a producer needs someone to play the great detective. In many ways Grant, 50, seems perfect for the role. He's loved Sir Arthur Conan Doyle's novels since he was a teenager. 'Holmes is an outsider-insider,' he says. 'He's not in the police force. He's not officially on the radar. And yet he solves these crimes. That appeals to the amateur detective in all of us.'

An 'outsider-insider' is an excellent description of Grant himself. He is a successful actor, yet he has the instinctive detachment of a born writer: he has published two volumes of diaries and a novel, all critically acclaimed. His languid, confident voice is pure English public school, but his real name is Richard Grant Esterhuysen, and he was born and raised in Swaziland, in Southern Africa, where his father was Minister for Education. Grant grew up in the dying days of colonial rule, a child of the white governing class, in a world he describes as 'an equatorial Ealing'. As a boy, he witnessed his mother having sex with one of his father's closest friends. She then ran off with her lover, leaving Richard and his brother, Stuart, behind with their grief-stricken father, who became a violent alcoholic. This gave Grant something in common with Conan Doyle, another son of a drunken father.

The experience inspired Grant's autobiographical film Wah-Wah, which he wrote and directed. At last, he found himself able to forgive his mother for her desertion. 'It was enormously helpful. The writing was the cathartic bit. Having to write forces you to act your way into what it would have felt like for the other characters, who in this case were my parents and their friends.'

Grant has been married for 21 years to Joan Washington, one of the film world's top dialect coaches, with whom he has had two children. Contentedly domesticated, he has spent his entire career away from tabloid gossip. Still, the long-term consequences of his childhood experiences have not been entirely overcome.

Grant is capable of being witty at his own and other people's expense. He can also deliver performances that are tours-de-force of arrogance and extroversion. But off-screen he is riven with insecurity. He hasn't seen his Holmes documentary because he never watches any of his screen appearances. As he explains, 'You only see your own failure. I'd rather just have the experience of working and leave it at that. The actor Steve Martin said to me that it's usually five years before a person realises that their career is over. They're still trundling along thinking it's going well, but in fact it's stalled years before. The point is, you never know.'

That's pessimism made amusing. But Grant has suffered from genuine depression, too, culminating in a minor nervous breakdown in 1999. In fact, he seems somewhat depressed when we meet. A teetotaller, Grant is obsessed by fitness. 'I run four miles every morning. It seems better than lying in bed.' All his interviewers comment on his manic energy. Yet when our conversation begins, he is about as energetic as a Valium-addicted sloth. I'm not the only one to have noticed. When he appeared on This Morning, his performance was so laid-back, Fern Britton asked him if he was tired. 'No,' he replied, 'just 50.'

All his contradictory traits seem perfectly suited to Holmes, that most neurotic of detectives. Grant even looks the part: tall, slender, with penetrating, pale-blue eyes. But he insists that he could never be Sherlock himself. His first problem, he explains, is his nose.' Rupert Everett was the last person who did Holmes, for the BBC, and his profile makes him almost perfect. According to the original drawings of Holmes, you've got to have a hooked nose and Rupert has a very distinct nose, which I don't. So, in the nose department, I fall short.'

Even if he got the part Grant doubts whether he'd enjoy the experience. 'Essentially, Holmes is a loner,' he says. 'He has the very male thing of being able to deal with everything, but have no emotional involvement in it. His only emotion is clinical and obsessive, but disconnected from real feelings. To play that would be interesting the first time you did it. But in the same way that Conan Doyle got sick of writing that character, to be unemotional, and not having real contact with other people, would not be very satisfying to play for long as an actor.'

He played the title role in that greatest of all cult comedies, Withnail & I, giving a performance so brilliant he may never equal it again. And he has had lots of jobs, everything from turkeys such as Hudson Hawk, with Bruce Willis, to three films – The Player, Pret-a-Porter and Gosford Park – made by director Robert Altman. Grant says that his mood at home depends on his relationship with the director and co-stars with whom he's working. And the happiest film sets were Altman's. He may have paid his actors less money than any other director – but they all got as little as each other. 'When I was working on Pret-a-Porter, it was the only time I knew I was going to get the same money as Julia Roberts,' says Grant. 'There was no opportunity for one ego to dominate. That made an enormous difference. So, inevitably, someone like Julia is a completely different person, compared to when she's in a massive Julia Roberts vehicle.

But the worst of all, says Grant, are writers. 'I was at a writer's festival in Australia. Meeting other writers, I was amazed at how competitive and ungenerous a lot of them were.'

Sadly, he is completely right. He has instinctively uncovered the dirty little secret we scribes would rather keep hidden. But then, I told you he was a natural Sherlock.

Daily Mail, Thursday, November 8, 2007

Newly published letters from Sherlock Holmes's creator Arthur Conan Doyle reveal how he betrayed his dying wife by embarking on an affair with a younger lover.

Adultery, my dear Watson by Glenys Roberts

ARTHUR CONAN DOYLE, creator of the world's most famous fictional detective Sherlock Holmes, is a British institution, his prolific body of work as popular today as when he died 77 years ago.

Physician, sportsman, crusader for social justice, war correspondent, military historian – he was also a convinced spiritualist who believed the most unlikely tales from beyond the grave – his life was as gripping as any of his books.

But there is a less well-known side to this larger-than-life figure. Though a respected pillar of Edwardian society, Conan Doyle scandalously fell in love with the much younger woman who would become his second wife, while his first was mortally ill.

Ever since his first biographer John Dickson Carr revealed that the couple's close friendship predated their 1907 wedding by a whole ten years, scholars have yearned to know the extent of their passion. Did Arthur, as he maintained publicly, keep their relationship platonic out of respect for his family? Or did he succumb to a physical relationship long before he was free.

A fascinating new book *(A Life In Letters)*of his hitherto unpublished letters strongly suggests he did. Throughout the love affair, Conan Doyle related his most intimate thoughts to his mother Mary, finally becoming so bold that the reader does not need the forensic gifts of Holmes to deduce the truth: his mother was not just his confidante, she was his accomplice.

Arthur always found time to write to Mary from wherever he was in the world. More than 1,000 of his letters to her survive from the time he was sent away to boarding school aged eight till her death in 1920. He confided in her about everything: the highs and lows of writing, his finances, his famous friends and his passionate political views. The letters paint a fascinating picture of the vulnerable, restless and determined man behind the huge reputation.

From the beginning, Arthur was a mercurial spirit who was destined to accomplish more in life than his alcoholic artist father, who would drink the furniture varnish if there was nothing stronger to hand. Cricket, fell-walking, rock climbing, classical theatre, foreign languages, new countries, skiing, riding, he plunged himself into each successive pursuit, recording his enthusiasm in millions of words.

But he was also unusually disciplined. 'I am studying very hard – harder than I have ever studied before, and like it very much,' he wrote in 1874, when he was 15.

Yet Conan Doyle also loved physical pursuits. As a young man, he took part in a whaling expedition in sub-zero temperatures, and recorded that he had never felt better. His wanderlust lasted till his death, consuming a great deal of money and his careful mother was trying to act as a brake on his spending habits.

But, then if it hadn't been for his money troubles we would never have had Sherlock Holmes or his doctor friend who occasioned the famous catch-phrase 'Elementary, my dear Watson'. Conan Doyle invented them only because crime fiction sold so well. He was always trying to kill them off so he could write about philosophy instead while his practical mother was always begging him not to.

The first seeds of Sherlock were sown when Conan Doyle studied medicine at Edinburgh University in 1876. He hated his studies, especially the mathematics course, and later made his villain Moriarty a mathematician. At Edinburgh he also met the prototype for Holmes, a professor of medicine called Joseph Bell, whose powers of observation were so acute he boasted he could diagnose patients even before they came into the room.

BELL made a profound impression on his young pupil, but it would be some time before Conan Doyle drew on the memory. After his whaling trip, he went to work as a ship's doctor on a boat to Nigeria.

He finally took a post as a doctor in Portsmouth, and as he struggled to make ends meet started to write short stories. At first they were usually rejected, but in 1882 his spirits were lifted by the sale, for a whole ten guineas, of a ghost story, The Captain of the Pole Star. It so boosted his confidence, he immediately planned a lucrative future in letters. 'I want some three-figure cheques, and I shall have them, too,' he wrote home.

When in Portsmouth, he also started to go to spiritualist séances, but to begin with he kept them secret from his staunchly Roman Catholic mother. But soon there was something more pressing on his mind: his marriage to Louisa [sic]'Touie' Hawkins, the sister of one of his patients.

The marriage went ahead in 1885, and with a wife to support, Conan Doyle decided to concentrate on lucrative crime fiction. Enter Sherlock Holmes, making his first appearance in 1887 in A Study in Scarlet. The birth of the author's daughter Marie [sic] Louise in 1889 – he delivered her himself – prompted him to work even harder, and two years later he was doing so well he gave up medicine and moved to the quiet of the London suburbs to concentrate on writing.

He chronicled the birth of his son Kingsley, in 1892, his passion to write an opera, and a book on medical stories and a Napoleonic saga.

In the meantime, his worries about his wife – who had succumbed to tuberculosis – saw him take her to Switzerland for her health and there in 1894, he became the first Englishman to cross an alpine pass in snow shoes. But, bored with Sherlock, Conan Doyle killed him off at the country's Reichenbach Falls, as every Holmes aficionado will know.

The great detective made a comeback, not least because Conan Doyle needed the money to fund his restless lifestyle. In all he would publish 60 Holmes stories, but it would be eight years before the next appeared.

Meanwhile Conan Doyle embarked on a worldwide search to find a climate in which his wife would flourish, visiting Egypt, Italy and Colorado, before settling in Surrey, where his famous house, Undershaw, became a place of pilgrimage for admirers. There, in the good air of Hindhead, the highest point in the county, he hoped Touie would thrive.

But Conan Doyle was rapidly acquiring some expensive tastes. Having taken up hunting, he needed horses and stabling. He was also trying to stand for Parliament and was soon feeling the financial pinch only Sherlock Holmes could relieve.

In 1897, at the age of 38, he fell in love at first sight with Jean Leckie, a beauty 14 years his junior, and, as his letters home show, he would much rather indulge in romantic pursuits such as writing poetry, playing music and throwing parties to impress his new love, than attend to Holmes.

Conan Doyle did not tell his mother the reason for his new interests immediately, but in the way lovers do, he used any excuse to include his beloved's name on the page. In 1899 he told how he had had lunch with her parents, who gave him an exquisite Christmas present of a diamond and pearl stud. He also embarked on a book about a man, a mistress and a wife called The Duet. It is easy to see the source of his inspiration.

By June he could no longer keep his relationship with Jean secret and was rapturising to his mother about it, assuring her that he would never cause his wife any pain. Yet it is tempting to read the next lines as a confession that he and Jean were already physically involved. 'She is as dear to me as ever,' he wrote about Touie, 'but there is a large side of my life which was unoccupied, but is no longer so.' Are these words proof that, having given up marital relations with his wife because of her illness, he had turned to Jean instead?

Mary Doyle was more concerned with stopping her son from going to report on the Boer War. All her entreaties failed, and by April 1900 he was in South Africa writing long letters from the front. 'There are only two things for which I wish to return to England,' he wrote. 'One of them is to kiss my dear mother once more.'

THE other, presumably, was to see Jean. By August he was back in London and seeing a good deal of his girlfriend. He took her to Lord's for the cricket, causing a terrible family row when they bumped into his sister Connie and her husband. Arthur explained that the relationship was strictly platonic and they all agreed to meet the next day.

Then, as he revealed petulantly to his mother, Connie pleaded a toothache and refused to meet. Conan Doyle, though in the wrong according to any social mores, was outraged. 'I refused to speak further on such a sacred matter,' he declared to Mary Doyle, flattering he that though she was sensitive enough to understand the real situation, others – like his sister – were intolerably petty-minded. Mary sided with her daughter. But soon Arthur had given up all discretion and was telling his mother about golfing breaks when Jean would turn up. 'Jean came down,' he wrote breathlessly. 'We had such a healthy, innocent time.'

He even invited Mary to chaperone Jean on these breaks. And surprisingly, she agreed. It looks as if Touie, too, was becoming aware of his infidelities. Suddenly Arthur was complaining to his mother that his wife had dropped plans to go to France for her health as usual, and was insisting on going to Torquay, where he'd have to join her. He suggested that his mother, now in league with him, should invite Jean to Scotland, where he would visit them both.

Since he had an avid social life in London – his regular contacts included Winston Churchill – the now famous author took a room near Charing Cross, and it is tempting to think that he saw even more of Jean

He also started taking his mistress on sentimental journeys alone back to his first postings in his new car.

It was Jean, not poor Touie, languishing with worsening TB, who had taken to fussing about his own failing health. 'It is a fateful, heaven-sent thing and inspirational,' he wrote his mother about their love.

Mary clearly agreed, for she started sending the woman in her son's life gifts of family jewellery. Indeed, his mother seems to have accepted their relationship so completely that Arthur even sent her Jean's love letters to read.

While Touie's health declined, Arthur spent more time away from home with his 'darling J', without a single reproach from Mary.

Her priority was that he should accept the knighthood he had been offered, even though he maintained he did not want it, declaring that even if the three people he loved best in the world – Jean, his sister Lottie, and his mother – were all down on bended knee, he wouldn't accept it. His wife is noticeably not mentioned.

OF COURSE, Conan Doyle did accept a knighthood in October 1902, and managed to remain extraordinarily prolific as a writer despite juggling mistress, family and public life, for this was the year Holmes finally made a comeback in

The Hound of the Baskervilles.

Meanwhile, his wife was coming to terms with his affair, because before she finally died, delirious and paralysed in 1906, she instructed her daughter to give her father her blessing if he married again.

Condemned to a year of mourning, Conan Doyle fell into a depression until he married Jean the following September. As he wrote to his mother from honeymoon in Constantinople and the Greek Islands, he was more and more in love with his beautiful, intelligent bride. He soon had three more children with her.

Then came World War I and the tragic deaths [sic] of his son Kingsley. Conan Doyle's later letters shows that his lifelong confidence was dealt a fatal blow by this, and he turned more and more to spiritualism in the hope that he could commune with his lost son. His beliefs brought him plenty of criticism from his mother, yet he carried on writing to her till she died.

With his lifelong confidante gone, Conan Doyle survived only ten more years. He died of a heart attack in his Surrey garden in 1930, aged 71, and his last words were for his beloved wife. 'You are wonderful,' he told her.

Arthur Conan Doyle: A Life In Letters, edited by Daniel Stashower, Jon Lellenberg and Charles Foley (Harper Press, £25).

The Sunday Telegraph DECEMBER 23 2007

Mandrake By **Tim Walker** with Richard Eden

Elementary help

STEPHEN FRY'S hopes of playing Sherlock Holmes in a television series may so far have come to nothing, but he clearly retains a close interest in the fictional detective. Conan Doyle's biographer Andrew Lycett tells Mandrake that he relied on Fry when writing his book.

"Stephen is a great Sherlock Holmes enthusiast," he says. "When he appeared in *Celebrity Mastermind*, Conan Doyle's detective was his special subject."

Fry, helped Lycett gain access to the extensive collection of Sherlockiana assembled by the late scholar Richard Lancelyn Green, who died three years ago in circumstances that were sufficiently strange to have been "a three-pipe problem" for the great sleuth. Green's collection was bequeathed to Portsmouth's museums and libraries, where the ubiquitous Fry became its patron.

Cataloguing and assembling the material took much longer than expected, though, and Lycett was not able to view it until Fry helped cut through the red tape. "With Stephen's help I was able to pin down a lot of interesting detail about the Conan Doyle family, and the selection of photographs there is superb," he adds. "I am looking forward to him playing Sherlock Holmes. He would undoubtedly be superb.

"There was some talk of it three years ago – a series with him and Hugh Laurie in the role of Dr Watson – but I understand the contractual details have still to be finalised."

THE DAILY TELEGRAPH WEDNESDAY, JUNE 25, 2008

INBRIEF

£180,000 Austen

An inscribed presentation copy of a first edition of *Emma* by Jane Austen fetched £180,000 in Bonhams in London yesterday – a world record price for an Austen novel.

SATURDAY, JULY 5, 2008 **THE DAILY TELEGRAPH**

MANDRAKE Tim Walker

Cohen to cut it as Holmes

News that **Sacha Baron Cohen** has signed up to play Sherlock Holmes in a Hollywood comedy has excited his barber, **Carmelo Guastella**.
 "Because Holmes always wears his deer-stalker on duty, I reckon the sideburns are the most important thing," says the Sicilian-born Guastella, whom Baron Cohen holds in such high regard that he recruited him as an adviser when he starred in *Sweeny Todd: The Demon Barber Of Fleet Street*.
 "Holmes is an eccentric character and I reckon he doesn't get much time to go to the barbers, so his hair should not look too perfect.
 "It should be shiny, as back then gel was unknown and greasy products such as Brillantine were used."
 Heaven knows what the late **Dame Jean Conan-Doyle** would have made of it.
 The redoubtable Dame Jean, who died 11 years ago, had enough trouble with **Sir Robert Stephen's** mildly comic portrayal of the detective in *The Private life of Sherlock Holmes*.
 "My father never intended the character to be played for laughs," she told me.

DAILY MAIL, Wednesday, October 15, 2008

SHERLOCK HOLMES AND THE CURIOUS CASE OF THE GARDEN FAIRIES

He was the creator of the most rational and intelligent detective of all time. So why, asks a new book, was Arthur Conan Doyle fooled by this picture into believing in fairies **by Russell Miller**

COTTINGLEY, a village outside Bradford in Yorkshire, would have remained in much deserved obscurity had not 16-year-old Elsie Wright taken a remarkable photograph of her ten-year-old cousin, Frances Griffiths, playing with fairies on the banks of a stream which ran behind the garden of Elsie's house.
 A few days earlier, in the summer of 1917, Frances had slipped and fallen into the stream. When she got home, her mother demanded to know why her dress was soaked and the tearful girl offered the excuse that she had fallen into the water while she was 'playing with the fairies'.

Her mother, unamused, sent her up to the attic bedroom she shared with Elsie where, later that afternoon, the two girls hatched a childish prank that would make headlines around the world, severely damage the reputations of eminent public figures and generate a controversy that endured for generations.

The saga of the Cottingley fairies began with a mischievous idea from Elsie. She suggested they should take a photograph of the 'fairies' to prove to Frances' mother that she had been telling the truth.

By happy circumstance, the family owned a copy of Princess Mary's Gift Book, published in 1914 to raise funds for charity. The girls flicked through its pages looking for suitable fairy pictures and found them in the illustrations for a poem by Alfred Noyes called A Spell For A Fairy.

They cut them out and pasted them on to cardboard. With a few long hatpins on which to mount their 'fairies' and a roll of zinc oxide bandage tape, they were ready.

Arthur Wright willingly agreed to lend his daughter his camera when she said she wanted to take a photograph of Frances by the stream.

The girls set off, blissfully unaware that they were about to create one of the most reproduced photographs in history.

They arranged the four fairies – three with wings and one playing a piped instrument – in front of Frances, who put flowers in her hair and, curiously stared intently at the camera rather than at the fairies when Elsie took the picture.

Wright developed the exposed plate in the darkroom he had built for himself under the stairs at his home on Main Street, Cottingly. The image was a sweet picture of Frances, with what Wright at first thought were 'bits of paper' in front of her.

When he asked Elsie what they were, she told him they were the fairies that she and Frances played with by the stream. Wright dismissed it as girlish nonsense, filed away the plate and forgot about it.

A month later, the girls produced another 'fairy' photograph. This time it was taken by Frances and showed Elsie sitting on the grass with her skirt spread around her, reaching out to a gnome-like figure about a foot high, who appeared to be prancing on the hem of her skirt.

Wright was irritated that the girls refused to admit it was a joke and, as a punishment, said they could no longer borrow his camera.

Polly Wright, Elsie's mother, and her sister, Annie Griffiths, Frances' mother, faced with the 'evidence' of the photographs, were less inclined to dismiss the girls' story.

Both women were interested in theosophy – a religious philosophy popular after World War I which believed all religions were attempts by 'spiritual hierarchy' to help humanity evolve, and that each religion therefore had a portion of the truth.

They took the photographs to a meeting of the Theosophical Society in Harrogate. Many of those present believed that the pictures offered the first evidence that countless accounts of fairy sightings were true.

This was the heyday of 'spirit photography', when the Spiritualist movement fed the insatiable hunger of the war bereaved, and the unscrupulous photographers made a handsome living producing portraits with ghostly images of a loved one lost in the war hovering in the background.

KNOWLEDGE of photography was not widespread at this time and few understood that the 'spirit' could be introduced by a double exposure on the same photographic plate.

As a result, many Spiritualists were encouraged to believe that the camera could 'see' what the naked eye could not, a belief which helped legitimise the Cottingley fairy photographs.

That Elsie and Frances were young and pretty also undoubtedly helped within the spiritualist movement it was widely believed that prepubescent and adolescent girls often possessed psychic powers.

Word of the Cottingley fairies soon spread. Sir Arthur Conan Doyle, famous as the creator of Sherlock Holmes, heard about the pictures from a friend at a time when he was preparing an article about fairy sightings for The Strand magazine.

By then he had virtually given up writing fiction to devote himself to promoting the Spiritualist cause around the world.

On June 30, 1920, Conan Doyle wrote separate registered letters to Elsie and her father. His letter to Arthur Wright was entirely businesslike: 'Dear Mr Wright, I have seen the very interesting photos which your little girl took. They are certainly amazing. I was writing a little article for The Strand upon the evidence for the existence of fairies, so I was very much interested.'

He asked permission to use the photographs to accompany his article, offering a fee of £5 (about £150, today) or a five-year subscription to the magazine, and guaranteeing the family anonymity so that they would not 'be annoyed in any way'.

Conan Doyle's offer was hardly generous, since he would be receiving £500 (£15,000 today) from The Strand for the article.

His letter to Elsie was friendly, flattering and clearly designed to recruit her co-operation at some later date. 'Dear Miss Elsie Wright, I have seen the wonderful pictures of the fairies which you and your cousin Frances have taken and I have not been so interested for a long time. I will send you tomorrow one of my little books for I am sure you are not too old to enjoy adventures. With best wishes. Yours sincerely.'

Arthur Wright was suitably awed to receive a communication from the great author and, perhaps on this account, forbore to mention his doubts about the pictures' authenticity.

The Christmas 1920 edition of The Strand had blazoned across its cover the headline: 'Fairies Photographed – An Epoch Making Event Described by A. Conan Doyle.' Inside, the picture of 'Iris and the Dancing Gnome' was captioned as 'one of the most astounding photographs ever published'.

ALTHOUGH Conan Doyle opened his article in non-committed fashion, calling for the scenes portrayed to be repeated before a 'disinterested witness' in order to 'remove the last faint shadow of doubt', the reader was left in little doubt where he stood: 'It seems to me that with fuller knowledge and with fresh means of vision, these people are destined to become just as solid and real as the Eskimos.'

He explained that he had examined the photographs 'long and earnestly' with a high-powered lens. Obviously intent on using the Cottingley fairies to advance the Spiritualist cause, Conan Doyle concluded there was a strong case for the pictures' authenticity.

Seemingly carried away by the implications of the discovery, he fondly speculated about how the world would change.

'These little folk who appear to be our neighbours, with only some small difference of vibration to separate us, will become familiar. The thought of them, even when unseen, will add charm to every brook and valley and give romantic interest to every country walk.'

The Fairies edition of The Strand sold out across the country in three days. Conan Doyle had hoped that his article would cause a sensation, and it certainly provoked a heated debate as to whether the photographs were genuine or crude fakes.

But there was also a genuine astonishment that a man such as Conan Doyle, a trained doctor, a man who embodied common sense, would write such a piece. How could someone who had created Sherlock Holmes, the epitome of a cool, calculating thinking machine, believe in fairies? It was inexplicable.

In truth, it could fairly be said that Conan Doyle was almost genetically programmed to believe in fairies. His family originated in Ireland and his Celtic heritage was populated by many stories about the 'little people'.

His unhappy father, Charles Altamont Doyle, an alcoholic committed to a lunatic asylum in Scotland, filled page after page of a sketchbook with fantastical drawings of fairies, elves, goblins and sprites.

His uncle, the artist Richard Doyle, made his reputation with fairy paintings. 'Dicky' Doyle designed the famous cover of the Punch magazine, which featured swarms of 'little people' in various poses.

Conan Doyle's spiritualism was inspired in part by the death of his son, Kingsley, in 1918 from pneumonia while recovering from his injuries in the Battle of the Somme.

By the time The Strand had revealed the existence of the Cottingley fairies, Elsie and Frances had produced three more pictures – one showing a fairy offering a posy of flowers to Elsie, a second slightly out of focus, captured a fairy in flight, and a third portrayed a fairy bower in a tree. Having examined them, Conan Doyle concluded they were 'beyond the possibility of fake'.

All five Cottingley fairy pictures were featured in an exhibition mounted later that year at the Theosophist Hall in Brompton Road, London.

It was not an unqualified success. While Theosophists and Spiritualists inevitably hailed the pictures as a historic breakthrough, cynics sneered.

Why, they asked did the fairies conform so precisely to traditional illustrations in fairy tales? Why were they so fashionably attired and coiffed?

Why did the 'gnome' appear to have a hatpin stuck in his midriff? Why, in the first picture, was Frances looking directly at the camera and not at the fairies allegedly prancing in front of her?

But Conan Doyle refused to budge, and in another article for The Strand attempted to elaborate on the fairy world as revealed by the photographs.

It revealed more about his extreme credulity and his willingness to use his imagination to fill in the details: 'Elves are a compound of the human and the butterfly, while the gnome has more of the moth. This may be merely the result of under-exposure of the negative and dullness of the weather.

'Perhaps the little gnome is really of the same tribe, but represents an elderly male, while the elves are romping young women. Most observers of fairy life have reported, however, that there are separate species, varying very much in size, appearance and locality – the wood fairy, the water fairy, the fairy of the plains, etc.'

THEN in 1922, Conan Doyle, as always utterly unmoved by the potential for embarrassment or the prospect of public ridicule, wrote the Coming of the Fairies, a book which was undoubtedly the nadir of his non-fiction work and in which the story of the Cottingley fairies was knitted into his fanciful, not to say fatuous, theories about fairy life, supported by numerous fairy sightings from around the world.

The Cottingley photographs, he wrote, represented 'either the most elaborate and ingenious hoax ever played upon the public, or else they constitute an event in human history which may in the future appear to have been epoch-making in its character'. He made it clear which he favoured: 'I have convinced myself that there is overwhelming evidence for the fairies.'

And that is what he believed until he died, at the age of 71, in 1930. In his final years, he filled the garden of his country home in the New Forest with plaster gnomes in the hope they would encourage fairies to emerge from the forest.

The gardener's eight-year-old daughter was occasionally persuaded to sit on the stump of an old tree, on the forest side of the garden gate, while Conan Doyle played ethereal music on a portable gramophone with a camera to capture images of the elusive sprites the moment they appeared.

Controversy over the Cottingley fairies continued for decades, long after Conan Doyle's death.

Arthur Wright died in 1926, puzzled that 'our Elsie, and her at the bottom of the class' could have stirred up such a controversy.

Elsie and Frances stuck doggedly to their story for years. Not until March 1893, when she was 76 years old, did Frances finally confess that the fairies on four of the five pictures had been cutouts traced from Princess Mary's Gift Book and secured by hatpins.

'I'm fed up with all these stories,' she complained. I hated those photographs and cringe every time I see them. I thought it was a joke, but everyone else kept it going. It should have died a natural death 60 years ago.'

Elsie at first refused to comment, but later confirmed her cousin's story: 'I do not want to die and leave my grandchildren with a loony grandmother to remember.'

Frances continued to claim, contrarily, that she had seen fairies and that the fifth photograph – the fairy bower – was authentic. She died in 1986; Elsie died two years later.

'The joke was only meant to last two hours,' said Elsie towards the end of her life. 'It lasted 70 years.'

Russell Miller (2008) The Adventures of Arthur Conan Doyle. Harvill Secker.

A review of this book was published on Saturday, November 8, 2008 in the Telegraph Review by David Flusfeder

The man for supreme moments

"All our lives have been but a preparation for this supreme moment," wrote Arthur Conan Doyle in 1914. He happened to be writing this sentence in a propaganda pamphlet to muster public opinion against Germany in the Great War, but it could have been written at almost any moment in his life, with any number of objects in mind. Conan Doyle was a man for the supreme moment. His enthusiasms – detective fiction, the Channel Tunnel, submarines or motor cars – and some of his animosities – miscarriage of justice, inequitable divorce laws – were, for the first part of his life, broadcasts to a sleepy population from someone alert to the rhythms of the future. His later enthusiasms, for spiritualism and fairies, were not so in step.

Russell Miller is serviceable on the story of his subject's life and works. We get the facts: the family background, his father's alcoholism and madness, his Catholic education and subsequent scepticism, his medical studies and career, his married lives. The "Adventures" of the title is, however, putting it strongly: Miller shows none of his subject's narrative swagger.

After Conan Doyle made his doomed attempt to kill off Sherlock Holmes at the Reichenbach Falls, the *Strand* magazine lost 20,000 subscribers, and workers in the City of London wore mourning crepe tied around their top hats. Conan Doyle was assaulted in the street. "It was as if a God had been destroyed by treachery," one critic wrote.

But Conan Doyle had had enough of his greatest and most profitable creation. He wanted respect as a writer of historical romances. And he had his causes to fight. He was a sportsman (he kept the bat with which he had hit a century at Lord's) a moralist, a doctor, novelist and campaigner. Despite his Scottishness, he represented an exemplary Englishness to the world. Like Holmes, he worked from data. By the time of the Boer War, however, his patriotism was getting ahead of his empiricism. He could not believe that the British were conducting the war with anything less than gentlemanly dignity, and refused to countenance reports of atrocities. During the First World War, some of his reports were horribly wrong-headed. Visiting the front line just before the Battle of the Somme, he wrote in a kind of rapture that this was "surely the most wonderful spot in the world".

It's hard to disagree with the opinion of Edgar Wallace, one of Conan Doyle's successors on the bestsellers lists, that his last and most long-winded enthusiasm, for spiritualism, was "dreary nonsense". (Especially so as Miller devotes so much space to it.) Conan Doyle kept his passion, courage and imagination to the end, but in his interests and preoccupations, he became silly. The creator of the logician Holmes turned into a flag-waver for spiritualism and the "Cottingley Fairies", a photographic mock-up made by two whimsical girls.

Miller is a mostly reliable guide to the whats and whens of Conan Doyle's life. But as the book goes on, his carelessness increases: it's generally agreed that the solicitor and amateur palaeontologist Charles Dawson was the perpetrator of the Piltdown Man fraud, contrary to Miller's remark that "the perpetrator of the hoax remains as elusive to this day as the missing link'''. And the as yet unborn Aldous Huxley was not, as Miller claims, an early opponent of spiritualism, unless there's more to the pseudo-science than meets the eye.

He is far less sure-footed on the whys and hows. Miller is not the man to turn to for psychological perception. He writes that, because of his Irish ancestry, "it could fairly be said that Conan Doyle was genetically programmed to believe in "fairies" before going on, a little more persuasively, to remind the reader that Conan Doyle's father Charles "had filled page after page of a sketchbook with fantastical drawings of fairies, elves, goblins and sprites while he was an inmate of the Montrose Royal Lunatic Asylum".

Given the paternity and also the deaths of both his brother and his son in the aftermath of the "supreme moment" of the Great War, perhaps the question might not be how Conan Doyle's shrewd mind could become seduced by such delusions as spiritualism and belief in fairies, but rather to marvel at how strongly and for how so long it had clutched on to empiricism and logic.

THE DAILY TELEGRAPH WEDNESDAY, JANUARY 21, 2009

British diplomat as Bollywood Holmes?...it's elementary

By Dean Nelson in New Delhi

A PIPE-SMOKING British diplomat is to star as Sherlock Holmes in a Bollywood production.

Simon Wilson, 50, Deputy High Commissioner in Calcutta, is using "Bollywood Diplomacy" to improve Angle-Indian relations by appearing in a remake of *The Sign of Four* by acclaimed Indian director Ashoke Viswanathan.

Mr Wilson, a keen amateur thespian, initially agreed to help research Sir Arthur Conan Doyle's links to India and the role India played in the novel.

But after impressing the director, Mr Wilson was persuaded to follow in the footsteps of Peter O'Toole and Peter Cushing and star as Holmes. In Mr Viswanathan's Indian version, a detective called Prashant Saigal is investigating a series of murders but hits a dead end. He seeks inspiration from the iconic British detective and – in true Bollywood fashion – Holmes emerges from a misty river, complete with cape and pipe.

The film, which also stars Victor Banerjee, the Indian actor who played Dr Aziz in *A Passage to India*, was shot on location in Shillong, the former Raj capital, which is known in India as the "Scotland of the East" for the green hills and colonial architecture.

Mr Viswanathan said "I wanted to do a Sherlock Holmes classic and we agreed on *The Sign of the Four*, in which Watson falls in love. My film is entirely set in India but we have a surreal version of the original Sherlock Holmes who helps Saigal solve the case.

"We have Simon Wilson playing Sherlock, who I found to be a fine actor who could handle a pipe and speak at the same time. Most Indian actors can't do that."

Mr Wilson said his job as a diplomat meant he had little time for acting. Appearing in a cameo, however, gave him a rare chance to act as well as an opportunity to promote English literature and its ties to India.

"Many Indians are very well versed in English literature, there's a love for P.G. Wodehouse and Arthur Conan Doyle. They're very familiar with Sherlock Holmes. So I decided to do my bit," he said. "It would have been difficult for a non-pipe smoker."

Daily Mail, Monday, May 25, 2009

A wooden actor

QUESTION Was Actor Basil Rathbone awarded the Military Cross in World War I for conspicuous bravery in the field while disguised as a tree?

ANSWER Second Lieutenant Basil St John Rathbone, of the 2/10th Liverpool Scottish Battalion, The King's Liverpool Regiment, reported for duty on May 23, 1917, at Erquinghem, a short distance west of Armentieres, where he was posted to B Company.

It was a sector of the front line known as Streaky Bacon and La Rolanderie Farms, where the men rested when not on the front line. My uncle William Frederick Bate, a member of the same regiment, was killed in action three days after Rathbone arrived at the front.

At the time that he won the Military Cross, Rathbone was Scouting Officer whose job it was to crawl out into No Man's Land, taking with him a sniper and one other, and to hide close to the enemy forward posts in an effort to collect useful information.

He persuaded his military superiors to use his gift to scout enemy positions during daylight, which was usually considered too dangerous. On one such expedition he shot dead a German, after coming face to face with him, crawling towards the British lines.

Rathbone had a considerable gift for disguise and camouflage – a gift he was later to attribute to his screen character Sherlock Holmes. It is the frequency with which Rathbone conducted these dangerous patrols that won him his Military Cross; both men who went with him on these raids were awarded the Military Medal.

In an interview in 1957 with Edward R. Murrow, the U.S. broadcast journalist. Rathbone related the story of how he disguised himself as a tree to get near the enemy camp to obtain information, though it might have been tongue in cheek.

'I went to my commanding officer, and I said that I thought we'd get a great deal more information from the enemy if we didn't fool around in the dark so much…and I asked him whether I could go out in daylight,' he said.

'I think he thought we were crazy. I said we'd go out camouflaged – made up as trees – with branches sticking out of our heads and arms. We brought back an awful lot of information and a few prisoners.'

Rathbone was only one of many brave young men who served with 'the Liverpool Scottish'. One other was their medical officer, Captain Noel Chavasse, V.C. and Bar, M.C., (R.A.M.C.). He was the only soldier serving in World War I to be awarded the Victoria Cross twice.

Stan Bate, St Helens, Merseyside

Daily Mail WEEKEND Magazine 30 May 2009

HOUSE AND HOLMES

House is back on Sky 1 this week. But did you realise the know-all doctor was inspired by the great Sherlock Holmes? Here are the tell-tale clues…

*Holmes and House both exhibit remarkable powers of observation and a tendency to come to rapid conclusions after the briefest examination of the circumstances.

*They both only have one close friend – Holmes had Dr Watson, House has Dr Wilson.

*House's name is obviously inspired by Holmes's. Gregory Shed wouldn't have worked nearly so well.

*Both the detective and the doctor share a fondness for recreational drugs. To relieve his boredom while not on a case, Sir Arthur Conan Doyle's fictional character indulged in cocaine and morphine. Some episodes suggest House also used hard drugs before he developed his current dependency on Vicodin, a prescription pain-reliever. In the episode *Distractions*, House used LSD to treat a migraine. And this man is a doctor?

*In the pilot episode of House, there is a patient called Rebecca Adler, while in the first Holmes short story, A Scandal in Bohemia, he is outwitted by Irene Adler.

*Neither man has the faintest idea what the word 'humility' means.

*In the episode *No Reason*, the man who shoots House has the surname Moriarty, echoing Holmes's nemesis, Professor Moriarty.

*In the episode *Failure to Communicate*, the physician asks his staff to solve a riddle about a room with an all-southern view and a polar bear. This is the same riddle given by the Victorian sleuth to Dr Watson in the 1985 film Young Sherlock Holmes.

*Both live in a residence numbered 221B. It must save on the rent and the bills, though there'd probably be terrible arguments over who had the last of the morphine.

*Conan Doyle based Sherlock Holmes on Joseph Bell, a doctor noted for deductive reasoning and skill in the new science of forensic medicine. The character of House has finally fulfilled the writer's original vision.

Daily Mail, Wednesday, July 29, 2009

EPHRAIM HARDCASTLE

AN early Afghanistan casualty was Dr. John Watson, an assistant surgeon of the Army Medical Department invalided home after being shot 'at the Battle of Maiwand'. Watson, of course, was created by Arthur Conan Doyle as the companion of his fictional detective Sherlock Holmes. But there was a real Battle of Maiwand, in 1880, in which many British soldiers died.

BBC 2 Friday 28.08.09 **Mastermind**

Roy Watson Davis – Teacher

Specialist Subject: **The Sherlock Holmes Films of Basil Rathbone**

Q Based on Sir Arthur Conan Doyle's *The Dancing Men* which of Roy William Neal's films opened with the word Switzerland emblazoned on the screen?

A *The Secret Weapon*

Q Which actress appeared in *The Spider Woman* as Andrea Spedding?

A Gale Sondergaard

Q "I won't forget that morning not if I live to be a hundred. I counted the men as they marched out of the yard, they'd hardly slept for weeks". Are the opening lines to which film?

A *Woman in Green*

Q Although the majority of the films were directed by Roy William Neal, who made the second film *The Adventures of Sherlock Holmes*?

A Alfred Werker

Q In which house on the west coast of Scotland did the seven men of the Good Companions live in *The House of Fear*?

A Drearcliffe

Q In *The Woman in Green* Dr Watson says that Professor Moriarty was hanged in which city only minutes before Professor Moriarty pays Holmes a visit?

A Montevideo

Q How is the body of Guy Davis identified even though it had been burnt beyond recognition?

A By his cuff-links

Q Which film starts with a bell tolling in a gloomy graveyard?

A *The Scarlet Claw*

Q In *The Secret Weapon* Dr Watson says that Sir Reginald Bailey played for which rugby club?

A Blackheath

Q What single word does the bird called Charlie utter several times in the Rat & Raven public house?

A Blood

Q Which art gallery auctioned the three musical boxes that are central to the plot of *Dressed To Kill*?

A Gaylord

Q What's the price of the grilled salmon in the Soho oyster house. It's clued in the number of the house that Holmes and Watson have to visit?

A 2/6

Q Which actor featured in *The Pearl of Death* as the Hoxton Creeper?

A Rondo Hatton

Q In *Sherlock Holmes in Washington* Holmes said that he would write a monograph some day on the noxious habit of accumulating useless… What?

A Trivia

Q Better known for a later TV role, who plays Sir Henry Baskerville in the first of the Rathbone/Bruce films, *The Hound of the Baskervilles*?

A Richard Green

Q In *Pursuit to Algiers* Holmes comments to Watson that the late Professor Moriarty was a virtuoso on which instrument?

A The bassoon

Q What's the name of the firm of ornamental plasterers on whose premises Giles Conover finds the bust of Napoleon containing the Borgia Pearl?

A Gelder

Q In *Terror by Night* Inspector Lestrade pretends to be going on holiday to Scotland. Who does Sherlock Holmes say that he is giving an excellent imitation of?

A Izaak Walton

Daily Mail, Friday, April 2, 2010

It's Friday! Theatre

Elementary error, I fear, Sir Arthur

Arthur & George (Repertory Theatre, Birmingham)
Verdict: Sherlock-lite. Three Stars (out of five)
Review by Patrick Marmion

NOVELIST Julian Barnes and playwright David Edgar have gone to great lengths to create a cunningly un-Sherlock-like Conan Doyle drama. It's based on real-life events, when Sherlock Holmes's creator Sir Arthur Conan Doyle investigated a miscarriage of justice involving an Asian West Midlander called George Edalji – a small-town Indian solicitor framed in a nasty case of horse slashing.

Like his fictional alter ego, Conan Doyle prides himself on being a man of sharp instinct, re-deploying Holmes's shrewd forensic intellect to his own personal ends.

It's a journey that leads him and his Watsonian assistant through a landscape of benighted country folk who, in time-honoured tradition, advise the upstart Londoner to 'leave it well alone'.

The ingredients of Barnes's 2005 novel about the episode and Edgar's staging bear all the hallmarks of a Conan Doyle classic.

Sadly, though, Sir Arthur is not allowed to get one over on Holmes with a real-life, last-minute rabbit-out-of-the-hat trick in which the dastardly villain is brilliantly exposed. Conan Doyle is instead more or less told off for the sin of pride in seeking to outwit his fictional creation.

Personally, I'd rather have had the brilliant hat trick, but there are elementary pleasures in Rachel Kavanaugh's production, which scales up a modest studio play for the Rep's chasm-like arena.

Chris Nayak as George, the hapless victim who becomes the cause celebre which gave us the Court of Criminal Appeal in 1097, is a loveable nerd whose innocence might have benefited from being more in doubt.

Kirsty Holles, Arthur's rather matronly love interest, exists, I fear, merely to satisfy political correctness, and tut-tut the menfolk for their clubbish misogyny.

Thankfully, Adrian Lukis saves the day as Conan Doyle. Although his Scottish accent only just makes it to Jedburgh, he gives the audience what they came for: an unmistakable Sherlock.

He is like a barrister addressing some invisible jury, halting mid-stride and stroking his chin at moments of insight. All that's missing is the cape and deerstalker.

Patrick Marmion

MONDAY, MAY 10, 2010 **THE DAILY TELEGRAPH**

News Bulletin

Holmes clue leads to burglar

A burglary victim unmasked a thief using a clue described in a Sherlock Holmes story, a court heard. Scott Baldwin suspected he knew the burglar as his dog had not barked. He confronted his nephew Carl Nesbitt, 21, who confessed to stealing £700 and an Xbox console in January.

At Newcastle Crown Court, Judge Guy Whitburn said that, like the story *Silver Blaze*, it was a case of "the dog that didn't bark in the night". Nesbitt, of Chopwell, Gateshead was given a 51-week suspended jail term and ordered to carry out 100 hours community service.

FRIDAY, MAY 22, 2009 **THE DAILY TELEGRAPH**

We still believe in Holmes, even in the age of DNA

150 years after his birth, Conan Doyle lives on in his greatest creation, says **Melanie McDonagh**

Sir Arthur Conan Doyle was born 150 years ago today, but it doesn't feel like that, does it? There are some authors you don't feel separated from by the mere passage of time; that's true of Conan Doyle, but still more of his most famous creation, Sherlock Holmes. He's the premier brand name in detective fiction, the archetype of the sleuth. Of course, Conan Doyle didn't invent the concept of the analytical detective. This distinction belongs to Edgar Allan Poe and his C. Auguste Dupin, who came complete with the soon-to-be traditional detective brilliance and dim sidekick. But Conan Doyle achieved a feat that belongs as much to popular fiction as to great novels: he invented a character who was utterly memorable. Holmes's appeal shows no sign of diminishing, but in an odd way, he has become less relevant than ever. In my edition of the stories, the publisher assures readers that Scotland Yard had incorporated Holmes's scientific methods into its own investigations. But the science outran the deduction: practically every contemporary crime (and practically every contemporary crime drama) seems to revolve around the use of DNA or forensic evidence, which renders the Holmes method pretty well redundant. I can't, alas, think of a single modern murder that could have been cleared up by a man with a magnifying glass and a remarkable capacity for reasoning. It's the size of the DNA database that delivers modern criminals to justice.

The Sherlock Holmes novels, then, bring us back to a more human and edifying kind of crime, whose perpetrators aren't identified by scraps of genetic material at the crime scene, mobile phone logs or the simple assumption that it was the boyfriend/husband who dunnit. Today, the brilliant amateur could never edge out the professionals, because it's the police who have the technology. With Holmes, we're back in happier times, when ratiocination ruled.

Of course, an immortal character has some elements of caricature. Conan Doyle insisted that Holmes was, as a man, modelled on his old teacher, Dr Joseph Bell, with "his eagle face…his curious ways…the eerie trick of spotting details". It was that combination of instantly recognisable characteristics as much as the plots that the public fell for – though we don't now dwell on Holmes's cocaine habit. Poor Conan Doyle thought it was his historical novel, *The White Company*, that "would live and illumine our national traditions". Nope: it was the creation he "regarded as a lower stratum of literary achievement" who lived instead.

Conan Doyle stands out for other things than his writing. He was, for instance, a great champion of spiritualism, a creed he embraced after a series of bereavements. It's a reminder that even men of high intelligence can fall for hokum – as is his belief in the Cottingley Fairies, a hoax perpetrated by two girls who became famous for the photos they concocted of creatures at the bottom of their garden.

These days, we don't read his historical novels much, but the Brigadier Gerard stories, about the adventures of a Napoleonic officer, are funny and touching; *The White Company* certainly doesn't deserve oblivion; and his autobiography is very funny. I'm also a sucker for the Professor Challenger novels, or at least the first one, *The Lost World*, in which he gives Jules Verne a run for his money with a valley full of dinosaurs.

Ultimately, though, it is his famous sleuth for whom Conan Doyle will always be remembered – however far the fashions of detection drift from his flamboyant techniques.

TUESDAY, MAY 25, 2010 **THE DAILY TELEGRAPH**
News digest

Stately Holmes Sleuth's debut to fetch £400,000.

A rare inscribed copy of the book in which Sherlock Holmes made his first appearance is expected to fetch up to £400,000 when it goes under the hammer.

A copy of *A Study in Scarlet*, the debut novel by Sir Arthur Conan Doyle, is one of only two inscribed examples known to exist. Sotheby's will auction the work, which it described as "one of the rarest books of modern times", in London on July 15.

The work, published in *Beeton's Christmas Annual* in November 1887, had been rejected by a succession of publishers.

It sold out in 14 days and was republished, but Conan Doyle had given up all the rights for £25 and never received another penny for the work.

His inscription reads: "This is the first independent book of mine which was ever published, Arthur Conan Doyle."

Peter Selley, a senior specialist in Sotheby's books and manuscript department, said of the novel – the first inscribed copy to ever come up for auction: "It is highly unlikely that such a copy will ever become available again.

"The sale represents an opportunity to acquire the finest copy of the most important cornerstone of any collection of detective literature in the world."

THE DAILY TELEGRAPH TUESDAY, JUNE 29, 2010

Bloomsbury Auctions London 8 July 2010
Strand Magazine VOL. 1 – VOL 84, 1891-1897
A complete run that includes all the Arthur Conan Doyle issues
Est. £7,000-10,000.

Saturday, July 3, 2010 TELEGRAPH WEEKEND

Book Club

Mystery of Sherlock's childhood revealed

A new series uncovers the ace detective's youth. By **Christopher Middleton**

Y ou don't have to be a detective to work out there's a murder mystery at the heart of our Family Book Club choice for July. However, the hero of *Young Sherlock Holmes: Death Cloud* is not quite the character we have all come to expect.

"I decided to make him a younger version of his adult self," says Andrew Lane, the author commissioned by the Sir Arthur Conan Doyle estate to write a whole series of Young Sherlock Books. "The thing is, Holmes is insufferable enough as an adult. Give him the same characteristics when he was a 14-year-old boy, and you'd just want to slap him around the face.

"Far more interesting, I thought, to develop him from scratch, to see him as an adolescent starting out in life and gradually acquiring the different aspects of his personality."

Not that it looks like he's going to reach adulthood, given the dangers he faces during the course of this first book in the series. Apart from the obvious hazard mentioned in the title, young Sherlock finds himself trapped inside a burning barn, attacked by savage dogs, surrounded by club-wielding thugs and at the wrong end of a riding whip wielded by sadistic megalomaniac Baron Maupertuis.

As with no Dr Watson to watch his back, the junior Holmes has to rely on the help of Matty, a wily young Victorian street urchin, and Virginia, the resourceful (and somewhat unnervingly attractive) daughter of his tutor, Amyus Crowe.

What, cry the purists? The famous misogynistic Holmes having anything to with a woman who isn't either a client or Mrs Hudson, his landlady?

"He hasn't yet developed the massive distrust of women that he will have in later life," explains Lane. "But even at this early stage, we see the seeds being sown."

We certainly do. Apart from the sparky Virginia, most of the other females in young Sherlock's life are a poor advertisement for their sex: his mentally fragile (and absent mother), the loopy aunt with whom he is sent to live and the malevolent housekeeper Mrs Eglantine, whose first words to him are, "Child, be aware you are not welcome here."

As well as not having acquired immunity to emotion, the teenage Holmes has also not perfected the powers of observation and analysis that will mark him out in later life. We only get one glimpse of his fledgling perspicacity when, by looking at the crumples in elder brother Mycroft's trousers, he can deduce by what mode of transport he has travelled (their father's carriage which has a clumsily repaired rip in the upholstery).

"A small bit of me regrets putting that even one scene into the book," admits Lane, a prolific crime and science-fiction writer in his own right (*Dr Who, Torchwood*). "I really wanted to preserve the distinction between the young and old Sherlock."

An obsessive Holmes fan since childhood, Lane has gone to great lengths to capture the period detail, providing vivid descriptions of rail journeys, fair grounds and unhygienic public highways (the manure-rich streets of Farnham). And he has refused to allow anything into his books that might conflict with the original Conan Doyle stories.

The Sunday Telegraph MAGAZINE 15.08.10

Theatre Extraordinary, Holmes

Jeremy Paul's homage to the great detective is thoroughly on the case. By TIM WALKER

Sir Arthur Conan Doyle sat down to write his Sherlock Holmes stories as some men would venture into cold showers. His wife, Louise, was dying a long, lingering death from tuberculosis and he had found the love of another woman in Jean Leckie. Sir Arthur remained faithful to his first wife until the end, and, out of loyalty to her, only permitted himself to marry Jean a year after Louise's death.

Dame Jean Conan Doyle, Sir Arthur's daughter by his second marriage, was the jolly-hockey-sticks type of woman in The Joyce Grenfell mould, and she told me towards the end of her life that her father had made two men the central characters of his detective stories precisely because he wanted to put sex as far out of his mind as possible.

Predictably, she did not approve of Robert Stephen's dashingly romantic performance in the title role of *The Private Life of Sherlock Holmes*, and she was nothing less than aghast at the prospect of a pornographic film whose name she could not bring herself to utter. Mercifully, *Sherlock Homo and Dr Wet Thong* did not, in the event, come out, in any sense of the phrase.

Had Dame Jean lived to see *Sherlock* – the BBC's attempt to set Sir Arthur's stories in a modern setting, starring Benedict Cumberbatch and Martin Freeman – she would not, I fear, have been a whole-hearted admirer. Still, adaptations that are true to the spirit of the original stories are still to be had.

The Secret of Sherlock Holmes would, I am certain, have pleased Dame Jean greatly. What Jeremy Paul has written amounts to *un hommage* to the books. There is a lot more of Peter Cushing's cold obsessiveness to Peter Egan's Holmes than Cumberbatch's lusty grandstander, and it is all the more faithful and welcome for that. Robert Daws is no bumbling slow-witted Nigel Bruce or Andre Morell as Watson, but a sensitive and intelligent man with whom one could readily imagine Holmes wishing to consort.

There is a splendidly atmospheric recreation of 221b Baker Street by the designer Simon Higlett, some bracing sound design and music by Matthew Bugg, and as for the director Robin Herford, he extracts every last ounce of atmosphere out of his limited budget in the tradition of all the great Hammer horror films. It all puts the grand into Holmes's guignol.

THE DAILY TELEGRAPH WEDNESDAY, NOVEMBER 17, 2010

Obituaries (Excerpt)

Bernard Davies

Sherlock Holmes scholar who identified Baskerville Hall and the real 221B Baker Street

BERNARD DAVIES, who has died aged 86, devoted much of his life to the study of "the more neglected regions of Sherlock Holmes topography" and was also founder-president of the Dracula Society.

Davies joined the Sherlock Holmes Society of London in 1958 and made his mark the following year in the society's journal with a paper entitled *Was Holmes a Londoner?* quickly followed by *The Back Yards of Baker Street*. In both papers he drew on an unrivalled familiarity with the entire Conan Doyle canon and the results of years spent in the British Museum Reading Room pouring over old maps, directions and, of course, back numbers of *Bradshaw's Monthly Railway* and *Steam Navigation Guide*. In his first article, an exhaustive and comprehensively footnoted analysis of the most ephemeral of clues in the Sherlock Holmes stories led him to conclude that Holmes had in all probability been born and brought up "in the districts known loosely as Kennington and Stockwell, where his useful associations seem most concentrated".

In his second article he addressed the "abiding mystery" of the true location of No 221B Baker Street (which does not exist) and, by analysing fleeting references to the topography of the house and surrounding streets, made what Holmes aficionados regard as a "virtually unassailable" case for its being No 31 Baker Street.

In other papers (published by the Sherlock Holmes Society in 2008 in a two-volume collection entitled *Holmes and Watson: Travels in Search of a Solution*) Davies addressed such knotty problems as did *The Sign of Four* take place in September or July and was it 1887 or 1888?"

A series of "radical rethinks on Baskervillean problems" yielded the conclusion that the most likely original for the village of Grimpen was the Devon village of Postbridge, and identified the nearby manor of Cator Court as the probable location of Baskerville Hall.

Davies admitted to playing the Holmesian game "with all the seriousness of a cricket match at Lords", and seemed to have picked up some of the Great Detective's methods and even his voice. Describing his apprenticeship he wrote: "My own ideas developed slowly during the years in which I was engaged in formulating principles for the topographical detection which, while they did not exclude the logical use of inference, placed it firmly on the basis of detailed map-work and research in the field."

A mere layman might have obtained the impression that Davies sometimes lacked a sense of proportion – as when he suggested that, "in terms of world influence," *A Study in Scarlet* "stands at least on a par with *Das Kapital*".

He was proud of the fact that one of his grandfathers had been a Metropolitan Police inspector who was drafted into Whitechapel at the time of the Jack the Ripper murders.

In his years as a professional actor, Davies took part in only one Sherlock Holmes production, playing two roles in a 1970 audio dramatisation of *Shoscombe Old Place*.

The same year (1958) he joined the Sherlock Holmes Society of London. By this time Davies had already devoted around a decade of his life to Holmes research. He went on to write some 30 meticulously researched papers which, in addition to topographical studies, included essays on the ancient Cornish language and a spirited defence of Dr Watson's war record. In addition he contributed to all but nine of the society's 25 expedition handbooks and gave numerous lectures and tours.

In 1984 he was made a member of the Baker Street Irregulars, the American Holmes society. He served as Chairman of the Sherlock Holmes Society of London from 1983 to 1986.

Daily Mail, Friday, November 26, 2010

Curious case of 221a

QUESTION Do we know who occupied 221a Baker Street, next door to Sherlock Holmes?

THERE was no actual Number 221a Baker Street. The 'b' in Sherlock Holmes's famous address represented the French designation *bis* (meaning twice), denoting the address is a subsidiary one, this case on an upper floor, Holmes's landlady Mrs Hudson being in residence on the ground floor.

In Sherlock Holmes's day, Baker Street was quite short, running north to south with numbered addresses from 1 to 85. There was no 221.

In 1930, some of the surrounding streets were renamed, buildings were renumbered and Baker Street became much longer. So 221 Baker Street became a real address.

In 1932, the original 221B Baker Street was demolished and the block of odd numbers from 215 to 229 was assigned to an Art Deco-style building known as Abbey House, home of the Abbey Road Building Society, which the society and its successor Abbey National occupied until 2002.

Subsequently, the inside of the building was demolished, though the distinctive façade and tower were retained, to be integrated into a new, mixed-use office, retail and residential development.

Abbey National sponsored the creation of the bronze statue of Sherlock Holmes that has stood at the entrance to Baker Street Tube station since 1999.

The firm received so much mail from Sherlock Holmes fans that it appointed a 'secretary to Sherlock Holmes' to deal with it.

Colin Jackson, London W6.

I have found further information on the above in June Thomson's book *Holmes and Watson. A Study in Friendship* (2000), which I include here as follows:

APPENDIX TWO THE SITE OF 221B BAKER STREET

Various theories, too numerous to describe in detail, have been suggested for the site of 221B Baker Street. These include, among others, 21, 27, 49, 59, 61, 63 and 66. Mr James Holroyd's claim for number 109, based on evidence in *The Adventure of the Resident Patient*, was apparently supported by Dr Chandler Brigg's discovery that the house opposite, number 118, was actually called Camden House and must therefore must have been the same house from which Holmes and Watson kept watch on 221B Baker Street in *The Adventure of the Empty House* (1894). Unfortunately, it has since been shown that Camden House was then in use as a private school and would therefore not have been empty.

Mr Bernard Davies's claim for number 31 seems more likely. Basing his theory on a large-scale map of Baker Street, he demonstrated that number 34, fitted the description of the Empty House, having rear access through a mews and a yard, its front door to the right when faced from the road, and no street lamp nearby. Number 31 has since been demolished to make way for a block of flats.

However, according to the street directory for the period, in 1894 number 34 was occupied by Arthur Canton, a dentist and surgeon, and therefore would also be ineligible as the Empty House.

Wherever 221B was situated, it was almost certainly on the east side of Baker Street, facing west, for in *The Adventure of the Cardboard Box*, Watson refers to the morning sun shining on the facades of the houses opposite. It must also have been far enough away from the station in Marylebone Road for Alexander Holder (*The Adventure of the Beryl Coronet*) to consider taking a cab there.

Watson's references to a 'bow' window are confusing. When the houses were built in the eighteenth century, all of them had tall, narrow sash windows. There is no record of any of them being bow-shaped. Nor is there any evidence either in nineteenth-century photographs or other documentation that a bow window was installed in any of the houses prior to Holmes' and Watson's time. As the properties were leasehold, it is doubtful if the ground landlord, the Portland estate, would have allowed such an alteration to the fabric of the building.

It is also significant that in Watson's initial description of the sitting-room in *A Study in Scarlet*, recording his first visit to the lodgings, he refers only to 'two broad windows'. There is no reference to a bow window until much later in *The Adventure of the Beryl Coronet*, published in May 1892, and *The Adventure of the Mazarin Stone*, published in October 1921, by which time not only was Holmes' fame as a consulting detective already established but also Watson's as his chronicler.

It is possible Watson introduced the bow window as a deliberate ploy to throw curious readers off the scent in case they came looking for 221B Baker Street. It would have been embarrassing for many Holmes' clients, many of whom were important and influential people, to find sightseers gathered around the house.

Alternatively, Watson may be referring to the arched brick soffit, or inner curve, to the semi-circular head of the window opening.

Daily Mail, Wednesday, March 31, 2010

ANSWERS TO CORRESPONDENTS Compiled by Charles Legge

An elementary error

QUESTION Did Sir Arthur Conan Doyle really play for Portsmouth FC?

AS A lifelong Portsmouth FC supporter, I wish that was the case, but alas it is not. It is a common misconception that Conan Doyle played for Pompey and an excellent book, popular in the city, Sherlock Holmes Was A Pompey Goalkeeper, perpetuates the myth.

After his writing became successful, Conan Doyle left a struggling doctor's practice in Southsea for pastures new in 1891. The professional football club Portsmouth FC wasn't founded until 1898.

My research for a forthcoming book about the city shows that while he was in Southsea, Conan Doyle played for an amateur club called Portsmouth Association Football Club.

This was not the forerunner of the professional club – that sprang from Portsmouth Royal Artillery, whose team played on the Services sports ground within the sound of the town hall chimes. Hence the famous Pompey Chimes – 'Play Up Pompey, Pompey Play Up' – sung by the supporters when the bells rang.

Conan Doyle was an ardent sporting man whose interests included bowls, boxing, ski-ing and baseball, which he tried to introduce to Britain after a visit to the U.S.

As a footballer he played in goal and 'at back', but he was no Gordon Banks or Bobby Moore. What skills he lacked he made up for by using his tall, 15-stone frame and restless energy.

The story goes that, tired of kicking his heels in defence, he would often run the length of the pitch to support an attack – without ever receiving the ball – before running back.

However, he excelled at cricket. He was captain of Portsmouth Cricket Club and later played for Marylebone Cricket Club, once taking seven wickets for 51 runs against Cambridgeshire, making him one of the early Lord's legends.

Chris Horrocks, Southsea, Hants.

(**Compiler's note:** I sent an email to Portsmouth Football Club on the above subject, which elicited the following reply on 1.04.2010: 'He (ACD) was a member of Portsmouth Football Association Club in the mid 1880s. More than ten years before Portsmouth Football Club as we know it today was formed).

Chapter 21

A Further Collection of Forewords, Introductions & Prefaces

The Sherlock Holmes Companion by Michael & Mollie Hardwick

FOREWORD

One thing which has struck us most forcibly while compiling *The Sherlock Holmes Companion* has been the illusion that we were dealing with a figure of real life rather than of fiction. How vital Holmes appears, compared with many people of one's own acquaintance! From how many eminent lives could one distil so balanced a philosophy, so vivid a self-portrait, so penetrating a view of human nature and contemporary society? Compare Holmes's sayings with those of any public figure, Victorian or otherwise. Perhaps the same wisdom will be found, or the pungency of wit, or the perception – but seldom all together. It is as though the sensitive mind of Sir Arthur Conan Doyle, which was later to be so sincerely of 'a world elsewhere', had unwittingly summoned from that world a spirit of such rare quality that it refused to return to the shadows, or to leave its sometimes unwilling master. Perhaps that other figure of vast reality, Falstaff, was such another spirit, and tormented Shakespeare as Holmes tormented Conan Doyle. Both were killed off in desperation by the man who had called them into being; and both were restored to life by the prayers of their worshippers.

This volume should, perhaps, more properly bear the title 'The Sherlock Holmes Reader's Companion'; for that is what it is intended to be. Our chief aim has been to tempt the uninitiated reader into the inevitable delight of reading all of Sherlock Holmes for himself, while at the same time to provide for the well versed a quick reference guide to more than two hundred significant characters, all sixty plots, and a good deal else, using only the information to be found in the text. We have resisted, as far as we could, the temptation to speculate upon chronology, geography, and those anomalies and inconsistencies which provide such rich material for the application of certain of Holmes's own methods. Anyone wishing to refresh his memory as to which story deals with the strange affair of young Cadogan West, who abruptly left his fiancée standing in a fog-bound street, never to be seen by her again, will find his answer here. If, troubled by a nagging half-recollection, someone should find himself in straits over the occupation of a certain Mr. Mordecai Smith, or the name of the partner in bigamy of Miss Hatty Doran, he can quickly find the answers here. Admittedly, in writing the biographies of Holmes and Watson we have permitted ourselves a certain latitude of inference and assumption. In summarizing the stories we have endeavoured to set the scenes and pose the problems without giving away too many details of the plots; a reservation which applies particularly to the *Who's Who* section, for, as Holmes himself found, "It is always awkward doing business with an alias."

Our warm thanks are due to Mr. Adrian Conan Doyle for his enthusiastic co-operation and good wishes; to Mr. Alan Robertson, our erudite fellow member of the

Sherlock Holmes Society of London, for scrutinizing the manuscript; and to Messrs. George Newnes for permission to use the Sidney Paget illustrations, and Mr. Michael Holder, manager of their Press Services Department, for his good offices in this direction.

The date given after each entry in the section of story summaries refers to first publication in any form, whether in England or the United States.

Lest it be charged that our preoccupation with Holmes and Watson has seduced our thoughts away from their 'onlie begetter,' we hasten to say that nothing could be less true. We yield to none in admiration of Sir Arthur Conan Doyle as writer and as man. It would also be an omission not to pay tribute to Sidney Paget. We believe that this volume contains the widest selection of his definitive illustrations ever assembled outside the original *Strand Magazine* – and, of course, many more have had to be excluded. Paget died in 1908 and subsequent stories were ably illustrated by others. But, for us, Sidney Paget is always *the* illustrator.

It only remains for us, like Watson, to ask: "Has anything escaped us" We trust there is nothing of consequence which we have overlooked?"

Alan Stockwell- **The Singular Adventures of Mr Sherlock Holmes**

Dust jacket:

Alan has been a professional puppeteer for forty years and was awarded the MBE in 2000. Like many devotees he re-reads the original Sherlock Holmes canon regularly and wishes there were more stories; hence the present volume.

"I suppose, Watson, we must look upon you as a man of letters," said Mr Sherlock Holmes. "How do you define the word singular?"

"Curious – extraordinary," I suggested.

He shook his head at my definition. "There is surely something more than that," said he; "some underlying suggestion of the weird, the strange, the odd."

Dr Watson delves into his battered dispatch-box in the vaults of Cox & Co. and draws out fifteen more cases from the career of his friend the eminent consulting detective. Why does a man wear a yellow top hat to feed the pigeons in Trafalgar Square? Why should a dead tree affect a son's inheritance? How can a cyclist disappear in the snow without leaving any traces?

The answer to these and many other enigmas are revealed in this collection of new stories written in the authentic manner.

Mr Sherlock Holmes
1854 – 1928

VERY little is known about the early life of Mr Sherlock Holmes who has recently died. It is thought he was descended from a long line of country squires. His grandmother was a sister of Vernet, the French artist. His only relative was a brother Mycroft, seven years his senior, who pre-deceased him. Sherlock Holmes cultivated his natural talent for observation and logical deduction by undertaking an erratic course of study at Oxford University and St. Bartholomew's Hospital. His researches embraced chemistry, anatomy and botany with special references to poisons. Early on he gained a reputation for eccentricity when in the anatomy class he belaboured the specimens with a stick to study the bruising. All his studies had the object of making himself an expert in criminal detection and in this aim he triumphantly succeeded. Setting up in business in 1878, he soon became the leading consulting detective of his generation and a pioneer of methods that have since become standard practice throughout the police forces of the world.

Sherlock Holmes was an expert single stick player and swordsman and one of the finest amateur boxers of his weight. However, he preferred not to expend his energies wastefully and considered unnecessary physical activity deprived him of food for the brain and would recline for hours on the sofa, and even retire to bed for several days, to husband his thought processes. Yet, when enthused by the chase of combating crime, he would spring into action and show the vast reserves of strength that resided somewhat improbably in his tall, spare frame.

Sherlock Holmes had a large store of *outré* knowledge gained from extensive reading and, although he had an interest in all the muses, his chief love was music, perhaps the most mathematical of all the arts, and owned a Stradivarius violin which he played excellently but often preferred to scrape tunelessly across his knees when in deep thought. His *bete noire* was ennui and he rebelled at an inactive brain, at times choosing to keep stagnation at bay by means of injecting himself with a seven per cent solution of cocaine. His career spanned some twenty-three years and in hundreds of cases he defeated the enemies of law and order in several countries. In June 1902 he refused a knighthood and retired in 1903 to keep bees on the Sussex Downs where he died peacefully in his villa on Sunday last. This is the second time that Sherlock Holmes' death had been announced. In 1891 it was thought that he had perished in the Reichenbach Falls in mortal combat with the criminal Professor Moriarty but this proved to be a false alarm and Holmes returned from obscurity in 1894 to resume his career. He was a man of ascetic character and had one friend only – myself, John H. Watson, MD, Late Indian Army.

Reproduced from the Daily Telegraph by kind permission of the editor.

PREFACE

OVER many years I placed before an indulgent public a series of adventures depicting the life and work of my friend Mr Sherlock Holmes. When I laid down my pen after relating the case I called *The Adventure of Shoscombe Old Place* I determined that should be the end of my effusions lest I should weary my public. I did not want to place myself in the position of the aged actor-manager who is forever dragging his weary bones around the provinces on an endless farewell tour.

Recently, however, the announcement of the death of Sherlock Holmes has caused new interest in that remarkable man and the public press has beaten a path to my door in their search for memoirs and anecdotes. Several publishers have pressed me to write a personal biography of Sherlock Holmes but I have declined to do so. The fact is that Holmes' life was nothing more than his career. He eschewed all the comforts, emotions and yearnings of mortal man to turn himself into a calculating machine. His sole *raison d'etre* was to fight crime, anything that caused him to deviate from this quest was ruthlessly eliminated from his life.

In the vaults of the bank of Cox & Co, at Charing Cross, there is my battered dispatch-box crammed with papers appertaining to the dozens of cases of my friend which I intend to preserve for the interest of posterity. The flurry of recent attention, however, has encouraged me to re-examine this extraordinary file of notes as there are many cases of great interest which I was unable to reveal to the public at the time. Sherlock Holmes served many of the crowned heads of Europe and, of course, these cases must remain secret as national securities are at stake. Others with possible libellous consequences and some concerning the honour of private persons will be destroyed. However, many years have now passed and the bulk of my notes concern a period when the present King's grandmother was on the throne of our great country and in most cases the necessity for discretion has been removed.

I have purposed, therefore, to lay before the public one last collection of a dozen cases. (**Compiler's note:** there are in fact 15 cases in the book).

Selected from throughout the long and extraordinary career of my friend Mr Sherlock Holmes. I have endeavoured to give some idea of the many and varied talents of this prodigious man and that has been the sole basis of my selection. The compilation of this volume has been of the utmost pleasure to me but has been onerous on my fragile state of health and I fear I shall write no more.

John H. Watson, MD, Late Indian Army
London & Hastings 1929

A Sherlock Holmes Handbook by Christopher Redmond

Dust jacket

Here, in one convenient book by a noted Sherlockian scholar, is everything needed for the study and enjoyment of the Holmes canon: information on the stories and their publishing history; an assessment of a century of illustrators; a biography of Arthur Conan Doyle and a bibliography of his other writings; commentary on the films and plays about Sherlock Holmes; and synopses of the stories and information about their characters; a survey of Victorian life and on the geography and social scene of 1895 London; and information on current Sherlockian organisations. A final section comments on the lasting appeal of Sherlock Holmes and what he means to generations of readers.

INTRODUCTION

Hardly a village library anywhere is without some volume of Sherlock Holmes. Hardly a cartoon or show business figure has never dressed up in "deerstalker" hat and magnifying glass to communicate instantly to a universal audience that here is the great detective, known to North American toddlers as "Sherlock Hemlock" and to late-night watchers as the hyperactive, overcoated Basil Rathbone. If the creator of Holmes, Arthur Conan Doyle, was once identified as "the best-known living Englishman", Sherlock Holmes has a claim to be the best-known Englishman who never-quite-lived.

Everyone who is literate knows Sherlock Holmes vaguely, and may some day wish to know more. A few enthusiasts already know far, far more, to the point that they exchange trivia at the regular meetings of Sherlock Holmes societies from Tokyo to Toronto. This book is intended for both kinds of people. For the enthusiasts, the Sherlockians, it may serve as a key to larger libraries, including their own shelves as well as to the largest imaginable library of Sherlockiana. It has been designed, too, as a ready reference for information currently scattered in often inaccessible places in the great Sherlockian literature. I hope it will stand beside the chief existing reference work for Sherlockians – Tracy's *Encyclopedia Sherlockiana*, the DeWall bibliographies, the Gibson & Green *Bibliography of Arthur Conan Doyle*, William D. Goodrich's *Good Old Index*, and the valuable though flawed *Annotated Sherlock Holmes*. For general readers, it may be of use as a companion to *The Complete Sherlock Holmes*, or to whichever smaller volume of Holmes stories may be at hand. By no means could I imagine including all knowledge about Sherlock Holmes in a single volume, but the essential facts are here, along with generalizations that provide a context for them, and a good many indications about what else has been said or written for those who want to know more. I welcome corrections, comments and suggestions.

I hope the style of these pages makes it clear that I take the stories of Sherlock Holmes seriously, but enjoy them at the same time. It would be a pity not to take them seriously, for they demonstrate such insight, and can teach us so much. It would be a disaster not to enjoy them as four generations have already done. As entertainment they generally speak for themselves, but perhaps this book will be a little help for those who hope to understand a little better the language in which Sherlock Holmes, and Arthur Conan Doyle, make themselves known.

In writing this book I have of course drawn on many sources. At my elbow I have kept the Canon itself, as well as the Goodrich *Index* and the Gibson and Green *Bibliography*. But rarely have I managed to write a paragraph without jumping up to consult some other volume: one of these standard reference works, or perhaps Steinbrunner and Michaels's *The Films of Sherlock Holmes*, Hugh Harrington's privately printed *Canonical Index*, *Bigelow on Holmes*, the indexes to the *Baker Street Journal*, and Bill Rabe's 1962 *Sherlockian Who's Who and What's What*. Practically every other volume on my shelves, I think, was needed at least once during the several months in which I drafted the pages that follow.

In the same way, many individuals have been of great help. Some were asked for information on specific points (and while I cannot provide an exhaustive list, I must certainly acknowledge Cameron Hollyer and Victoria Gill of the Metropolitan Toronto Reference Library). My good friend Barbara Rusch has encouraged me throughout the writing, and was of particular help as I planned, wrote and revised my chapter on the Victorian background. I take pleasure in acknowledging the help of Kate Karlson – once or twice she provided specific suggestions, but more generally she has, during my long friendship with her, contributed enormously to forming my view of the Sherlockian literature and the Sherlockian world, on which this book is based, and developing my knowledge of both. In the same way I am greatly indebted to my father, Donald A. Redmond, whose guidance and companionship have made my Sherlockian work possible. Further, he has read most of this book during its preparation and provided valuable suggestions.

My dear wife, Susan, resolutely resists becoming a Sherlockian (a policy that helps keep me in modest touch with the real world outside my study) but has provided affectionate moral support throughout the writing of these chapters. As I finish them, our Christopher is just reaching the stage of real literacy, with a special enthusiasm for *Nate the Great*. I look forward to the day when he may find this book a tool in truly discovering Sherlock Holmes.

CAR
May 1993

Michael Kurland **My Sherlock Holmes. Untold Stories of the Great Detective**

Dust jacket

FOR MORE THAN A CENTURY, readers have thrilled to the exploits of Sherlock Holmes through the tales narrated by his sidekick and official chronicler, Dr. John Watson. But do Dr. Watson's tales really tell the true story of the great detective? In this collection of thirteen original tales, each told by a side character in the original canon, ranging from the famous (IRENE ADLER, PROFESSOR JAMES MORIARTY, and MYCROFT HOLMES) to the decidedly minor (BILLY THE PAGE BOY, WIGGINS OF THE BAKER STREET IRREGULARS, and both MRS. WATSONS), readers finally get to hear another side of the legend.

From what INSPECTOR LESTRADE really thought of Holmes to the untold tale of his encounter with DR. FU MANCHU, from the bitter reminiscences of him by C. AUGUSTE DUPIN to the thoughts of his longtime landlady, MRS. HUDSON, the totality of the veil of mystery over the legend that is Sherlock Holmes is at last removed. With stories from Barbara Hambly, Cara Black, Peter Tremayne, and Michael Kurland, among others, *My Sherlock Holmes* is a unique and compelling entry into the literature of the world's most famous detective.

INTRODUCTION

O for a muse of fire, that would ascend the brightest heaven of invention; a kingdom for a stage, princes to act and monarchs to behold the swelling scene! Then – well, then you'd be reading Shakespeare instead of Sherlock Holmes. *Henry V*, or Hank Cinque, as we like to call him, to be exact. What do William Shakespeare and Arthur Conan Doyle have in common? They both, without really trying, created fictional characters that have attained the literary equivalent of immortality.

Without really trying? Yes, I think it's true of both Shakespeare and Conan Doyle. Not that they weren't doing their best to create wonderful stories for their public, but neither assumed that his creations would outlive him by centuries. Look at what Shakespeare named some of his plays: *The Comedy of Errors* – hey, it's a comedy; the characters keep making these errors, that's what makes it funny. *As You Like It* – as good as saying, "I think this plot is dumb, but the groundlings like this sort of thing, so here it is." *Much Ado About Nothing* – how self-effacing can you get? *Love's Labours Lost* – sounds like a bad sitcom. (Shakespeare apparently also wrote a play entitled *Love's Labours' Won*, which has been, er, misplaced. If you can find a copy, say on the back shelf of some old library, you might get a favourable mention in a couple of textbooks yourself.)

And Conan Doyle, as we all know, thought so little of his popular consulting detective that he did his best to kill off, to leave himself more time to write his serious historical works, like *Micah Clarke* and *The White Company*.

What can one possibly say about Sherlock Holmes that hasn't been said before? His exploits have been written up by Sir Arthur Conan Doyle (we'll drop for the moment the pretence that Conan Doyle was merely the "agent" for Dr. John Watson); expanded on by Adrian Conan Doyle, John Dickson Carr, and others; pastiched by August Derleth, Robert L. Fish, Anthony Boucher, John Lennon, and scores of others; parodied by Mark Twain, Stephen Leacock, P.G. Wodehouse, and untold legions of others.

Every aspect of Holmes's fictional existence has been discussed, dissected, and the conclusions disponed and disputed by such literary luminaries as Vincent Starrett, William Baring-Gould, Ronald Knox, Rex Stout, and Dorothy Sayers, to name just the ones who come to mind most easily. (If you are a Holmes aficionado you probably have your own list of favourite Irregulars, and you're slightly miffed at me for not mentioning Paul Anderson, Isaac Asimov, John Kendrick Bangs, Martin Gardner, Michael Harrison, John Bennett Shaw, Nicholas Meyer, John Gardner, or possibly Colin Wilson. Well, sorry; they just didn't come to mind.)

It has been said, by the sort of people who say these things, that there are only five universally recognised fictional characters: Santa Claus, Romeo, Superman, Mickey Mouse and Sherlock Holmes. Some would expand the list to add Don Quixote, Don Juan, King Kong, Dorothy (the Wizard's Dorothy, you know), Bugs Bunny, Wonder Woman, Charlie Chan, James Bond, and perhaps Peter Pan to that list, and, as my grandmother used to say, they're right too.

Then there are the ones that have fallen by the wayside. Fifty years ago almost any literate adult whose native language was English could recognize Raffles, Nick Carter, Stella Dallas, Ephram Tutt, Bertie Wooster, and Bulldog Drummond, for example. But membership in this club for the fictional elite is transient for most; characters age and fade away from the public consciousness to be replaced by more youthful, contemporary creations.

But Sherlock Holmes lives on.

It has been estimated, by the sort of people who estimate these things, that there are over a billion people living today who could tell you, at least in some vague fashion, who Sherlock Holmes was. Many of them don't realize that he is a fictional character, or that if he were real he'd be well over a hundred years old now, as is shown by the volume of mail the London post office continues to get addressed to 221B Baker Street.

What is there about this creation of Dr. Conan Doyle's that enabled him to so quickly enter the pantheon of fictional immortals, rise to be numbered among the top five, and remain there for over a century? I'll give you my theory, but you'll have to put up with a little digression. Here goes.

The detective story took some time to come into being. Edgar Allen Poe is usually credited with being its first practitioner, with his stories involving the Chevalier C. Auguste Dupin. (Did Holmes ever meet Dupin? See "The Adventure of the Impecunious Chevalier," from the quill pen of Richard Lupoff, in this very volume.) There have been detectives in stories before Dupin; there have been stories of detection before Dupin. What, then, made Poe's *The Murders in the Rue Morgue* the first true detective story?

Simply it was the first story where:

∗ The detective is the main character of the story.

* The matter to be detected is the principal problem of the story.

* And the detective *detects* ; that is, he solves the problem by the application of observation guided by intelligence.

The last Dupin story was published in 1845. Over the four decades, until Arthur Conan Doyle decided to call the main characters in his first detective novel Sherlock Holmes and John Watson instead of Sherringford Holmes and Ormond Sacker (as indicated by a rough page of preliminary notes, still preserved, plotting out *A Study in Scarlet*), few detectives worthy of the name were introduced to the world of fiction. Charles Dickens's Inspector Bucket (*Bleak House*, 1853) and Wilkie Collins's Sergeant Cuff (*The Moonstone*, 1868) are credible police officers, and their actions advance the plots of their respective books, but they are minor characters (no less than four other characters do their share of detecting during the course of the Moonstone), and in each book the solving of the crime takes second place to the novelists' examination of how the situation affects the other characters.

With *L'Affair Lerouge* (English title: *The Lerouge Case*: U.S. title *The Widow Lerouge*), first published in 1866, Emil Gaboriau introduced Lecoq, a detective who uses observation, reflection, and raciocination (Poe's word for what Dupin did; it means thinking logically) to solve his cases. Lecoq is an amalgam of Dupin and Francois Eugene Vidocq, a real detective who rose from being a professional thief to head the Paris Police Department in 1811. Vidocq wrote four volumes of memoirs after his forced retirement in 1827, which gave highly fictionalised accounts of his prowess as a detective.

It seems fitting that the first English-language detective novel was written by a woman: Anna Katherine Green. It was called *The Leavenworth Case*, it was first published in 1848, and it was a bestseller. In his book *Bloody Murder*, Julian Symons recounts *The Leavenworth Case* was the favourite reading of British prime minister Stanley Baldwin. Since Baldwin didn't serve as prime minister until 1923, it's clear that the book, as we professionals put it, had legs.

There were also any number of inferior imitators of Poe and Gaboriau and Green. From 1870, with the publication of "The Bowery Detective" by Kenward Philp, until the 1920s the so-called dime novels published hundreds, perhaps thousands of detective stories; strong on action, suspense, disguises, racy dialogue, good men turned bad, bad men who want to be good. They were weak on characterization, plot, and anything approaching detection; but they moved fast and, with a combination of non-stop action and exotic locales, they provided a welcome anodyne from the dullness and drudgery of everyday life.

And then, in 1887, came *A Study in Scarlet*, and all lesser attempts were washed away as though they had never been. Sherlock Holmes was instantly recognised as a master of detection, by a public who had been waiting for just such a hero without knowing what it was they were waiting for until it appeared.

To the readers of the latter years of the nineteenth century Sherlock Holmes was the perfect Victorian; not as we today imagine Victorians: uptight, prudish, repressed, overly mannered, and ridiculously dressed prigs, but as the Victorians thought of themselves: logical, clearheaded, scientific, thoroughly modern leaders of the civilized world. Perhaps Holmes was a little too logical, a bit too cold and emotionless; but this merely permitted his readers to admire him without wishing to be him. And, like Darwin, Pasteur, Maxwell, Bell, Edison, and the other scientific geniuses of the period, he solved mysteries that baffled other men. And you could watch him do it! You could see the results as that mighty brain attacked the problem of *Thor Bridge*, or *The Second Stain*, or *The Dancing Men*.

"It is my business to know things," Holmes explains in *A Case of Identity*. "Perhaps I have trained myself to see what others overlook."

And today? We have all of that, with the added delight of visiting what is, for us, the alien wonderland, of tantalus and gasogene, of hansom cabs and four-wheelers – "Never take the first cab in the rank" – of spending an hour or a day in a London where, as Vincent Starrett put it, "it is always 1895."

It was perhaps inevitable that, when Conan Doyle gave up writing the continuing saga of Sherlock Holmes, others would take up the pen. Even before Holmes retired to take up beekeeping, the parodies and pastiches had begun. Vincent Starrett, Mark Twain, John Kendrick Bangs, all couldn't resist the impulse to pastiche or parody the creation of Dr. Doyle. In a 1973 German magazine article, Pierre Lachat notes that over 300 Holmes rip-offs appeared between 1907 and 1930. And that's only in English, and doesn't count the Spanish, or Portuguese, or the extensive German series, *Aus den Geheimakten des Weldtetektvis* (*From the Mystery Files of the World Detective*), which features Sherlock Holmes, but does away with Watson, replacing him with a youth called Harry Taxon.

But they were, at best, weak evocations of the Master. And most of them were not at anything approaching best. Perhaps the most successful of those authors who drew from the canon not merely their inspiration, but their mise-en-scene, were those who chose not to find another ancient notebook of Watson's in the lockbox at Cox, but who tell their stories in another voice than that of the long-suffering doctor, although the tales are set in the world of Sherlock Holmes. In some of them Holmes is still a major character, as in my own Professor Moriarty novels, and in others Holmes appears briefly, if at all.

The continued existence of a fictional character, not only in the steadily reprinted works of the author, but in new works created by other authors, is one of the signs of literary immortality. If this is so, then Holmes and Watson are more immortal (yeah, I know, being "more immortal" is like being "less dead", but it's only an expression fer crissakes) than most and we're adding to his longevity here in a big way, with some great writers.

Sherlock Holmes appears in all the stories in this collection. His "Watson" in each story is not the good doctor himself, but one of the legion of memorable secondary characters that Conan Doyle created with such ease. What reader can forget – to cite a few examples not appearing in this volume – Dr. Thorneycroft Huxtable, M.A., principal of the Priory School and author of *Huxtable's Sidelights on Horace*? Or Jabez Wilson, pawnbroker of Coburg Square, with his blazing red hair? Or Hosmer Angel. The fiancé of the myopic Mary Sutherland, who found it easy to vanish on his wedding day because he never really existed?

And so onward, for one more look at Sherlock Holmes through the eyes of some of those who knew him best, but who haven't, until now, had the chance to tell their stories.

This book is a compilation of new stories about Sherlock Holmes, told from the point of view of various people mentioned in the original stories *except* Dr. Watson or Sherlock Holmes. The authors of these stories, freed from the limitation of having to speak in Watson's voice, have taken their tales in several interesting directions. How did

Mrs. Hudson, Holmes's long-suffering landlady, acquire such an illustrious tenant? And just who was Mr. Hudson and what became of him? Find out in Linda Robertson's "Mrs. Hudson Reminisces." "A Study in Orange," By Peter Tremayne, will give some idea of what Colonel Sebastian Moran thought of his adversary and nemesis. In George Alec Effinger's "The Adventure of the Celestial Snows." Reginald Musgrave witnesses Sherlock Holmes's encounter with the infamous Dr. Fu Manchu.

Cara Black shows us Irene Adler's later relationship with Sherlock Holmes, a tale that, even if Watson had known about it, would have remained locked up in his battered tin dispatch box in the vaults of Cox & Co. We will learn of the early relationship between Sherlock Holmes and his maths instructor, James Moriarty. Richard Lupoff describes an unsuspecting relationship between a young Sherlock Holmes and the Chevalier C. Auguste Dupin.

I should mention that, as we know, the passage of time creates lapses of memory, and, as Ryunosuke Akutagawa pointed out in his story "Rashomom," different people will see the same event from vastly different perspectives, and may relate versions of the event that seem to have no relation to each other. So it is with some of these stories. Ask not which ones are true: they all are, and they are all lies.

Murder in Baker Street, Robinson London

INTRODUCTION

"THIS I AM sure of," Arthur Conan Doyle once remarked, "that there are far fewer supremely good short stories than there are supremely good long books. It takes more exquisite skill to carve the cameo than the statue."

The author was speaking from long experience. Some years earlier, in April 1891, Conan Doyle's career as a medical practitioner had reached its lowest point. He had recently abandoned a modestly successful practice in Southsea, near Portsmouth, to study diseases of the eye. Now, having moved his family to London, the 31-year-old physician declared himself ready to "put up my plate as an oculist."

Eager to establish himself, Conan Doyle set up a consulting room at 2 Upper Wimpole Street, a short distance from Harley Street, where the more established medical men plied their trade. "I was aware that many of the big men did not find time to work out refractions," he wrote. "I was capable in this work and liked it, so I hoped that some of it might drift my way."

None did. The young doctor's lease entitled him to a consulting room and a share of a waiting room, but as Conan Doyle ruefully admitted, "I was soon to find that they were both waiting rooms."

Undeterred, Conan Doyle set out each morning from his flat in Montague Place and walked the fifteen minutes or so to Upper Wimpole Street. There, he sat at his desk until late afternoon – "with never a ring to disturb my serenity."

As he had already enjoyed some success as an author by this stage, Conan Doyle's thoughts naturally turned to literature. Sitting alone in his consulting room, he hit on an idea which may well have been the single greatest inspiration of his career.

For some time, Conan Doyle had poured most of his literary energies into novels, because the disjointed collection of short stories from his early days had done nothing to advance his career. Now, with his financial reserves dwindling, he decided on a new direction. It struck him that there might be some benefit in writing a series of stories featuring a single, continuing character. This offered an advantage over the more conventional serialized novel, because the reader would not lose interest if one instalment or another was missed. Conan Doyle realized, of course, that the serialization of novels had done no harm to Charles Dickens, but there were now far more magazines on the stands, and a far greater number of literate people to read them, not all of whom would have the patience or the means to follow a continuing saga.

"Looking round for my central character," he wrote, "I felt that Sherlock Holmes, whom I had already handled in two little books, would easily lend himself to a succession of short stories."

The importance of this decision cannot be overstated. Not only had Conan Doyle made a very canny marketing decision, but he had also found an especially good showcase for the talents of Sherlock Holmes. In the two previously published Holmes novellas – "A Study in Scarlet" and "The Sign of the Four" – the detective had been obliged to trundle offstage for long patches of exposition. The short story format offered a compact execution and brisk pace, and highlighted Conan Doyle's singular talent for puzzle plots. Of the sixty tales comprising the complete Sherlock Holmes adventures, fifty-six are short stories. Sherlock Holmes was a sprinter, not a distance runner.

Having charted this new course, Conan Doyle needed only to find a magazine receptive to the idea. For ten years, a journal called *Tit-bits* had been a fixture at every corner newsstand. Made up of nuggets, or "tit-bits," of informative material, humor and stories, the magazine made a fortune for its founder, George Newnes, who parlayed the success into an entire stable of periodicals. The latest of these, as Conan Doyle set to work on his Sherlock Holmes short stories, was *The Strand* magazine, which began publication in January of that year under the editorship of H. Greenhough Smith.

Within weeks, Conan Doyle began sending the first of his Sherlock Holmes short stories to *The Strand*. In later years, Greenhough Smith would often speak of the day when those stories crossed his desk: "What a God-send to an editor jaded with wading through reams of impossible stuff! The ingenuity of plot, the limpid clearness of style, the perfect art of telling a story! The very handwriting, full of character, and clear as print."

And the rest – in a cliché that the good Dr. Watson would have abhorred – is history.

The editors of the present volume, though not overly concerned with handwriting, share Mr. Smith's concern for plot, style and the art of storytelling. It is a particular pleasure, therefore, to present this collection of new stories in the grand tradition of Sherlock Holmes by eleven of today's best crime writers. In addition, we have the honor to present three pieces of nonfiction on the subject of the Great Detective and his world, including a series of entertaining reminiscences from Conan Doyle himself.

Once again, the game's afoot.

David Stashower

New Sherlock Holmes Adventures (Ed) Mike Ashley

FOREWORD

One of the most famous opening paragraphs in a Sherlock Holmes story is that found in "Thor Bridge" (which was first published in the 1920s). Dr Watson says: "Somewhere in the vaults of the bank of Cox & Co., at Charing Cross, there is a travel-worn and battered tin dispatch box with my name John H. Watson, M.D., Late Indian Army, painted upon the lid. It is crammed with papers, nearly all of which are records of cases to illustrate the curious problems which Mr Sherlock Holmes had at various times to examine." Readers had already been offered tantalizing details of many unrecorded cases in preceding stories, but this confirmed that he had a "long row of year-books which fill a shelf, and there are the dispatch cases filled with documents". He rightly called it "a perfect quarry for the student, not only of crime, but of the social and official scandals of the late Victorian era". It is into these that the authors represented in the present volume have dipped.

The influence of Sherlock Holmes made itself felt within months of the publication of the first short stories in the *Strand Magazine*. There was plagiarism which achieved its apogee with Sexton Blake who had rooms in Baker Street, and there were rivals who knew they could succeed only by being different. The "Golden Age" of detective fiction was littered with a strange array of private inquiry agents who were fat, blind, Belgian or of the opposite sex. Yet for all their attempts at being different, they never entirely escaped the shadow of Sherlock Holmes. As Scotland Yard had discovered, his longest shots invariably hit their mark, and even when he was outwitted, as he was by Irene Adler, his reputation was enhanced.

It is the art of a great writer to leave the reader anxious for more, and Dr Watson was such a writer. He often erred on the side of discretion, and he intrigued the reader because of his less than perfect grasp of detail. Where his knowledge failed he resorted to imagination and was not unduly concerned when this led to contradictions and inconsistencies within the text. He introduced colour and variety and irrelevance, which added to the myth and gave the reader a picture which was sharp in its essentials, but blurred at the edges.

No reader has ever put down the stories believing that Watson had said the last word on the subject. For some their was an irresistible urge to parody the style and to play with the name of Sherlock Holmes (which lends itself well to imitations such as Shylock Bones, Sherluck Gromes, Picklock Holes, or Sheerlecoq Omes). The parodies made fun of the contrasting characteristics of Holmes and Watson, between the infallible brain which could distinguish 144 types of cigarette ash or recognise clay or earth from the counties of England (something still denied to the most sophisticated computers of the late twentieth century), and the obtuseness of the all-admiring friend.

The greatest scope for other writers lay in the unrecorded, unfathomed and unfinished cases. When Watson made it known that Holmes survived the struggle at the Reichenbach Falls, there were demands that he should furnish the public with details of the cases which he had already mentioned, and he proceeded to do so with "The Second Stain" (to which he had referred on two occasions). Even then there was an alternative literature provided by others, including major writers such as Bret Harte, and Mark Twain (who introduced Holmes into his late novel, *A Double-Barrelled Detective Story*).

The early apocryphal works did not profess to be part of the original 'canon', for the concept only developed after Ronald Knox had elevated the study of Sherlock Holmes to new and rarefied heights in 1911 with his famous satirical essay, "Studies in the Literature of Sherlock Holmes". This gave impetus to the serious study of the stories and raised the possibility that there was not one but two authors (as has been suggested in the writing of the *Odyssey*) or that Watson had described the early cases as they happened, but had invented the later ones to satisfy public demand. The new scholarship opened the way for others to take up their pens to continue the saga, while remaining faithful to their subject as had the story-tellers of old who created heroic deeds for Alexander the Great of which historians were previously unaware. The apocryphal Sherlock Holmes story need not be a great detective story, but it has to be a convincing story of the great detective. The character is more important than the case. It is his method which appeals to the reader. It is the special relationship with Dr Watson, who holds up a mirror to nature and occasionally distorts the image to add glamour to the reflection. The additional stories should conform to the formula and yet should add variety. The purist might prefer the seemingly insignificant trifle that turns out to be important, and the humble and eccentric client often makes a better entrance at Baker Street than the representations of the reigning houses of Europe or the emissaries of the Pope. The introduction of historical figures such as Oscar Wilde or Jack the Ripper is not always advisable as it could be said they add an element of fiction to the self-contained world of Sherlock Holmes, and characters whose exploits have been documented by others have difficulty crossing the threshold at Baker Street. Watson could describe a case in which Sherlock Holmes outwitted Raffles, but it would not be the Raffles who is known to us through the writings of his friend, Bunny Manders. There again, there is no reason why Holmes's grandson should not ape his grandfather and form a working partnership with Dr Watson's granddaughter, but it is Dr Watson, and his work, who will always be most in demand. Whatever other cases remain in the battered dispatch box, readers are most anxious to have details of the cases which are known to them by name and which were solved by Sherlock Holmes.

This volume is exactly what is required. It contains an impressive array of cases which Watson mentioned and it has a scholarly status as it is arranged in chronological order with a connecting narrative which provides a biographical background. It is entertaining and informative, it is remarkable for the many distinguished writers who are among the contributors. It is a book which can be recommended and is in every sense a *magnum opus*.

Richard Lancelyn Green

INTRODUCTION

The Life & Adventures of Sherlock Holmes

For more years than I care to remember I have been researching the life of the first and best known of all private consulting detectives, Mr Sherlock Holmes. It has not been easy. Devotees of the Sherlock Holmes cases will know that his friend and colleague Dr John Watson kept an assiduous record of many of the cases after they first met in January, but he was not involved in them all.

When Holmes was reflecting over his cases in the hours before his cataclysmic struggle with Professor Moriarty in "The Final Problem", he remarked to Watson that he had investigated over a thousand cases. That was in April 1891. In "The Adventure of the Solitary Cyclist" Watson comments that between 1894 and 1901 Holmes had been involved in every public case of any difficulty plus many hundreds of private cases. Watson goes on to say that "I have preserved very full notes of all these cases." Yet when you look at the standard omnibus volume of Sherlock Holmes you will find only fifty-six short stories and four novels, sixty cases in all. In writing up these cases Watson makes tantalizing passing references to others, such as the repulsive story of the red leech, or the singular adventures of the Grice Patersons on the island of Uffa, but though he kept notes of these stories he did not complete all of them as finished cases. Even then he refers to just short of a hundred cases, which is likely to be less than a tenth of all the cases Holmes investigated. How wonderful it would be to know about the others. This has been my life's work.

The obvious starting point was Watson's papers. He told us in "The Problem of Thor Bridge" that they were filed away in a despatch box stored in the vaults of Cox & Co., at Charing Cross. Imagine my horror when, many years ago, in attempting to gain access to these records I discovered two things. Firstly that Watson was clever and had stored only some of his records in that bank vault, and that others were hidden elsewhere. But more frustrating was that I had been pipped at the post. The Cox Bank papers had already been collected by someone else and though he provided a name and identity for the purposes of the bank, I have never been able to trace him, and suspect the identity was false. Watson was fearful that his papers might be stolen. When he published the case of "The Veiled Lodger" in January 1927 he alerted the public to the fact that attempts had already been made to gain access to his papers and he gave a warning to one individual, whom he doesn't name, that facts would be revealed about him if he didn't desist. Occasionally stories purporting to be from these files have surfaced in books and magazines. Some may well be genuine, or at least give that appearance, but most are almost certainly false, written by those seeking to gain some reflected glory from the fame of Sherlock Holmes.

Over the years I have tracked down some of the original cases from papers at Scotland Yard, old newspaper files, and documents held in private archives. On rare moments I have stumbled across papers which almost certainly came from Watson's despatch box, but I fear that most of those records are hidden in one or more private collections, possibly not even in England, purchased, I dare say, for a phenomenal price.

The trail is complicated by many false avenues and windings. Not even Watson was helpful. Frequently in his published cases he disguised the names of individuals, for obvious reasons, and falsified dates and locations, so that when he recorded that Holmes was investigating such-and-such a case it was likely that Holmes was somewhere else at that time involved in a very private affair. Watson did his job well in masking the trail, and it will probably never be fully uncovered.

However, the time has come for me to share the product of some of my research. It is far from complete, but for fear that something may happen to me or to my own papers, I thought it was right to place some of it in print. Perhaps the existence of this book may bring me into contact with others who have access to further papers. Who knows?

In this volume I have pieced together something of the investigations of Sherlock Holmes and have presented twenty-six new cases completed by fellow researchers who have helped me in my quest. I have endeavoured to show where these cases fit into Holmes's career and how they relate to the known cases. In an appendix at the end of this book I also provide a complete chronology of Holmes's life and known cases, including some of the other write-ups of his investigations where I believe there has been a genuine effort to get at the truth.

Let us begin our quest, therefore, and return to the early days of Sherlock Holmes.

Mike Ashley
May 1997

PART I: THE EARLY YEARS

There is precious little record of Holmes's early life. It is unusual that someone so famous could keep the details of his life so secret that it becomes necessary to think that it was deliberate. Holmes had little interest in the trivia of personal biography, so it is unlikely that he would have bothered to have disguised the trail. But others may certainly have done so in order to protect him, and thoughts turn immediately to his elder brother Mycroft Holmes who had considerable influence in government circles and could have easily pressed the right buttons in order to close whatever shutters were necessary.

We must therefore rely on what Watson himself tells us. In "His Last Bow", which takes place in August 1914, Watson refers to Holmes as "a tall, gaunt man of sixty". It is the only occasion when he mentions his age. We must be careful as he was describing Holmes in disguise as the Irish-American spy Altamont. Had Holmes aged himself or made himself look younger? We don't know. And did Watson mean precisely sixty, or was he in his sixtieth year – in other words fifty-nine? If we accept it at face value, and since no other clue is given as to Holmes's birthday, then we must conclude that Holmes was born in either 1853 or 1854, or at latest in 1855. I prefer the earlier date because in "The Boscombe Valley Mystery" Holmes refers to himself as middle-aged which suggests forty-something. That story took place in 1889 or 1890 which would make Holmes's year of birth earlier than 1850, but middle-aged is an indeterminate phrase and we can assume that a birth year somewhere in the early 1850s is as close as we'll get. We may take some clue from the year in which Holmes retired, which was at the end of 1903. Did he do this on his fiftieth birthday? It would be an appropriate landmark.

Holmes came from a line of country squires but somewhere in his veins was the blood of the French artist Claude Vernet, from whose family Holmes also claimed descent. We do not know where Holmes was born, but his general dislike of the countryside suggests that he was raised somewhere remote, and as we shall see he certainly spent some of his youth in Ireland. This coupled with his reticence to discuss his childhood suggests that it might not have been happy, and we can imagine an almost reclusive child already intent upon his studies in logical deduction. Holmes was almost certainly educated at a private school before progressing to university.

It is at university that his abilities as a solver of puzzles came to the fore. Two of the recorded cases throw some light on Holmes's University days. "The Gloria Scott", Holmes tells us, was the first case in which he was engaged. He refers to the case again in "The Musgrave Ritual" saying that the Gloria Scott case "first turned my attention in the direction of the profession which has become my life's work." It is thus of some importance to date this investigation, but it is here that we first encounter Watson's masking of facts. We could put a rough dating on it on the assumption that Holmes went to university when he was about eighteen or nineteen, which would place it in the period 1868 to 1872, and he talks about it occurring after two years at university, or between 1870 and 1874. In "The Veiled Lodger" Watson tells us Holmes was in active practice for twenty-three years. Since he retired in 1903, counting back would bring us to 1880, but we must also deduct the years of the Great Hiatus between "The Final Problem" in

April 1891 and Holmes's return in "The Empty House" in early 1894, a gap of three years. So he established himself as a consulting detective in 1887. We know from "the Musgrave Ritual" that Holmes set up his practice soon after university, so we can imagine he finished his university years around 1876. A span of university education from 1872 to 1876 therefore sounds realistic in the chronology and would place the Gloria Scott case in about 1874.

However, in the case of "The Gloria Scott" Holmes refers to events aboard the ship having taken place thirty years earlier in 1855, which would place the story in 1885. This has to be wrong, because Holmes and Watson met in 1881 by which time Holmes had been in practice for four years. Clearly there is some deliberate shifting of dates in this story, perhaps through Holmes's faulty record keeping (always possible, as he was not a great record-keeper of things he regarded as unimportant), or Watson's erroneous transcription of the case or, we should not forget, through Watson trying to hide the time of Holmes's university years.

In fact my own research has revealed two episodes that happened to Holmes while at university that have previously gone unrecorded. They reveal that Holmes's years at university were not without incident and it is not surprising that it has been difficult to tie him down, since he spent time at two universities. I am grateful to Peter Tremayne and Derek Wilson for their help in bringing the record of the episodes into their final form from scraps of evidence left by Watson. I have deliberately set the stories in reverse order of internal events because of the relative discovery of the episodes by Watson. The first happened during the period of Holmes's apparent death, whilst Watson learned of the second after Holmes's return. Here then for the first time ever, are the earliest records of Sherlock Holmes.

Nick Rennison - Sherlock Holmes *The Unauthorised Biography*

The year is 1895. London is swathed in dense yellow fog. As the greasy clouds swirl up the streets and condense in oily drops on windowpanes, two men peer out from rented rooms at 221B Baker Street. One is tall and gaunt with a narrow face, hawk-like nose and high, intellectual brow. The other, shorter and stockier, is square-jawed and moustachioed. Outside, the smog envelops a vast city that holds a thousand sinister secrets but inside is a haven of comfort and bachelor domesticity. Suddenly, out of the surrounding gloom, a hansom cab emerges. A young woman descends from it, and looks up briefly at the two men at the window before ringing the doorbell of 221B. Another client, with a tale of mystery and potential danger, has come to consult Sherlock Holmes. The game is once again afoot, and Holmes and Dr Watson will soon be in pursuit of the truth about another dark story from the hidden metropolis.

Few individuals in English history are as well known as Sherlock Holmes. From the moment in 1887 when, in a narrative published in *Beeton's Christmas Annual* for that year, his colleague and friend Dr John Watson revealed the detective's extraordinary powers of analysis and deduction, he captured the imagination of the public. As Watson continued to act as Holmes's Boswell, recording more of his exploits and adventures in magazine articles and books, his fame spread. Watson's accounts have been translated into dozens of languages from Afrikaans to Yiddish, from Armenian to Vietnamese. Students of Swahili can read *Mbwa wa Familia ya Baskerville*. Those fluent in Slovak can turn the pages of *Pes Baskervillsky*. There are versions of the stories in Esperanto, in

Pitman's shorthand and, of course, in Braille. There is even a translation of 'The Dancing Men' into the code that plays a central role in that story.

Dramatized versions of Holmes's life began to appear in the 1890s and have continued to be performed to the present day. On any given day in 2005 an amateur dramatic society somewhere in England or America will be staging a play in which Sherlock Holmes makes an appearance. He has been the subject of hundreds of films from the early silent era to the present day. *Sherlock Holmes – The Musical* by Leslie Bricusse, screenwriter of the Dr Doolittle movie, opened in London in 1989. (Admittedly, it closed almost immediately and has rarely been seen on the stage since.) There has been a ballet called *The Great Detective*, produced at Sadler's Wells in 1953, and at least one opera has required a tenor Holmes and a bass Watson to sing feelingly of their mutually rewarding partnership and the joys of detective work.

Although Holmes has been dead for more than seventy years, people still write from around the world to ask for his help. Until recently Abbey House, the headquarters of the Abbey National Building Society, which stands on the site of his one-time lodgings in Baker Street, employed a secretary to answer the letters that were delivered to the address. Since his death in 1929, a growing army of Holmes scholars has produced a library of theses and dissertations on his life and work. In half the countries of the world there are Sherlock Holmes societies, their members dedicated to the minute examination of his life and work: the Singular Society of the Baker Street Dozen in Calgary, Canada; the Copenhagen Speckled Gang; Le Cercle Litteraire de l'Escarboucle Bleue in Toulouse; the Tokyo Nonpareil Club; the Ural Holmesian Society in Ekaterinburg; the Illustrious Clients of Indianapolis; the Friends of Irene Adler in Cambridge, Massachusetts; the Six Napoleons of Baltimore. All these and many more are devoted exclusively to the study of Sherlock Holmes. Even writers of fiction have taken the basic facts of his life and expanded them into novels and short stories of varying degrees of credibility.

Like other emblematic figures from the nation's past – Henry VIII, Robin Hood, Winston Churchill – he has been seized upon by the heritage industry. Pubs and hotels are named after him. Tours of Sherlock Holmes's London wind daily through the streets of the capital. Holmes memorabilia crowd the shelves of gift shops and tourist boutiques. Should you feel so inclined, it is possible to buy silver statuettes of Holmes and Watson, Sherlock Holmes fridge magnets, Hound of the Baskervilles coffee mugs, a 221B Baker Street board game and a Sherlock Holmes plastic pipe designed to provide the authentic Holmes aura without actually encouraging smoking. There is even a Sherlock Holmes teddy bear dressed in an Inverness cape and deerstalker hat.

Yet Holmes himself remains a curiously elusive figure. Apart from a few monographs on arcane subjects (types of tobacco ash; the polyphonic motets of the Renaissance composer Orlande de Lassus; ciphers and secret writings) as well as a manual on beekeeping, he published nothing under his own name. In one narrative ('The Adventure of the Cardboard Box') Holmes claims to have published two short monographs on ears in the *Journal of the Anthropological Institute* but a trawl through nineteenth-century back numbers of that periodical suggests that he was referring to works that he had merely planned rather than completed. Two narratives of his work, which he wrote in the first person, were published in *The Strand Magazine* in 1926, three years before his death. Otherwise the record is blank. His preferred means of communication was the telegram, more impermanent in his time than the e-mail is today, and no irrefutably authentic letters written by him survive.

For any student of Holmes's life and work, the alpha and the omega of their research remains the texts written by his colleague and friend Dr John H. Watson. There are fifty-six short narratives and four longer ones, which all scholars and Holmesians agree are the work of Watson or (in two instances) Holmes. There are a few texts ('The Case of the Man Who Was Wanted', 'The Story of the Lost Special') that some commentators wish to claim for the canon but their status remains disputed. There are also those unidentified papers, which once, almost certainly, existed but which seem to have disappeared.

'Somewhere in the vaults of the bank of Cox & Company at Charing Cross,' Watson wrote in 'The Problem of Thor Bridge', 'There is a travel-worn and battered tin dispatch-box with my name upon the lid. It is crammed with papers, nearly all of which are records of cases to illustrate the curious problems which Mr Sherlock Holmes had at various times to examine.' Cox & Company's building in Charing Cross was destroyed in the London Blitz and, if there were still papers in the vault, a decade after Watson's death, they were lost in the conflagration.

It is always worth remembering just what a small proportion of Holmes's cases is recorded in Watson's surviving narratives. In *The Hound of the Baskervilles* Holmes refers in passing to the 'five hundred cases of capital importance which I have handled.' The events in the Baskerville case took place more than a decade before Holmes's supposed retirement and, as we shall see, more than thirty years before his actual and final retirement from all involvement in criminal cases. From a total of approximately 1,800, Watson gave us accounts of sixty. In other words, only between 3 and 4 per cent of the extant cases are recorded by the doctor.

Yet the primary source for Holmes's life remains the work of Watson and, as Holmes scholars have long known, Watson's narratives, for a variety of reasons, have to be interpreted with care. Often Holmes himself muddied the waters by misleading Watson, providing him with false information and spurious facts that merely sent the doctor off in pursuit of red herrings. Often Watson deliberately obscures the truth, hiding real characters under pseudonyms or disguising towns and cities beneath invented names. Sometimes he is quite simply wrong. It is easy to forget the circumstances in which Watson wrote his narratives. Although, as he points out in 'The Adventure of the Solitary Cyclist', 'I have preserved very full notes of these cases,' and clearly he must have had his notes beside him as he wrote, the full stories that he handed over to Arthur Conan Doyle for publication were not produced until years, sometimes decades, after the events they describe. 'The Adventure of the Devil's Foot', for instance, shows Holmes investigating the macabre deaths in the Tregennis family whilst he was holidaying in Cornwall with Watson in the spring of 1897 but it was not written up in full until 1910. In the case of the investigation known as 'The Adventure of the Creeping Man', Watson is recalling events from 1903 but the story was not published for another twenty years, appearing in *The Strand Magazine* for March 1923. In these circumstances it is not surprising that Watson occasionally slipped up. Even the most egregious errors – setting one of the stories at a time when Holmes was assumed to be dead – became understandable to a degree.

Despite the difficulties imposed by the shortage of authentic records, few Victorian lives deserve study as much as does that of Sherlock Holmes. And a Victorian he undoubtedly was. Although he was only in his late forties when Victoria died, he remained rooted in the world into which he was born and in which he grew up. We think we know the Victorians. In contrast to our contradictory selves, grappling with the complexities of modernity and post-modernity, they seem the products of a simpler era. Frozen in the clichéd poses we have imagined for them, the Victorians appear immune to the fears and anxieties that trouble us. Staring at us from sepia-tinted photographs, they look certain of the world and their own place in it in a way we cannot hope to match. Nothing, however, could be further from the truth. Anyone born, like Holmes, in the 1850s and growing up in the late Victorian era, lived through a period of intellectual and social upheaval just as dramatic and threatening as any the twentieth century was to offer. Religious beliefs were crumbling under the assault of new theories of man and his place in the world. The British Empire, on which the sun was supposed never to set may have appeared to be everlasting but the seeds of its ultimate collapse had already been sown. Germany and America had emerged as its competitors on the world stage. New ideologies – socialism, communism, feminism – began to shake the foundations of state and family on which Victorian confidence and security were built. Scratching the surface of Victorian complacency soon reveals the underlying angst about a world that was changing rapidly and unpredictably.

The ambiguity of Holmes's character mirror those of the age in which he came to maturity. Highly rational and committed to the idea of progress, he was haunted by darker dreams and more troubling emotions. Drawn into the service of an empire that he knew, intellectually at least, had already passed its zenith, he remained steadfast in his commitment to it. Yet, even as he fought to preserve stability and the solid values of the age, he himself was driven by a lifelong search for change, stimulation and excitement. His own innermost beliefs – social, aesthetic, scientific – often clashed with those that he outwardly professed. To follow Holmes through the twists and turns of his career in the 1880s and 1890s is to watch the Victorian era battling with its own demons.

Richard Lancelyn Green & John Michael Gibson (1983) **A Bibliography of A. Conan Doyle.** Hudson House.

FOREWORD

Don Quixote and Sancho Panza, Pickwick and Sam Weller, Huckleberry and Tom Sawyer, Stephen Daedalus and Mr Bloom: these are the great pairs of fiction, and it would be churlish to refuse Sherlock Holmes and Dr Watson a claim to a place among them. The contrast between two characters has given them life. Don Quixote would have only been half a character without Sancho; Daedalus, as we know from *A Portrait of the Artist*, needed Mr Bloom to come to full life. Dr Watson created Holmes.

Doyle may not have been a great writer (his style except at moments of intensity was pedestrian, and sometimes in historical novels, it must be admitted, fustian), but he was certainly a great story-teller. There are many moments in life when, like children, we demand to be told a story, periods of pain or anxiety from which we cannot be distracted by the finest writing. Mrs Dalloway fails to take us away from our cares into her poetic Regent Street, and we cannot lose ourselves in *Howards End*.

Doyle's first published was *A Study in Scarlet* (I am happy to own a copy of the first issue in Beeton's Christmas Annual of 1887) in which, rereading it now, I am surprised to find a Holmes who is a young man. How quickly he grew up in *The Sign of Four* (my own favourite among the Holmes novels even though it derives a little too closely from *The Moonstone*) and in the short stories that followed. Who cares about the carelessness of Doyle's memory? – that Holmes in *A Study* had never heard of Carlyle and yet proves extremely literate in the later stories: that in *The Sign of Four* a letter received 'the next day' and dated July 7 is brought hot-foot to Holmes in September: that in *The Adventures* a police agent turns suddenly from an Athelney to a Peter Jones: even the name of his famous housekeeper Mrs Hudson is a second thought. Some of the charm of the story-teller lies in the errors, as though we're listening to someone improvising a story for our amusement by our bedside. Doyle, I feel, was right in never bothering to correct his mistakes in future editions.

I am not one of those who regard Doyle only as a detective writer. In some moods I prefer Brigadier Gerard to Holmes, and that dynamic figure Professor Challenger of *The Lost World* and *The Poison Belt*. His historic novels did not please me as a boy, but I appreciate them better: *Micah Clarke* with the memorable portrait of the Duke of Monmouth and its anticipation in one scene of *The Hound of the Baskervilles*: *The White Company* and *Sir Nigel* and even *The Refugees*. (Surely his learned and excellent bibliographers have missed the chief source of that narrative – The Memoirs of Saint-Simon.)

I have found the bibliography fascinating, especially for the notes on each book. How I would love in some obscure junk shop to stumble on the 1893 Continental Edition of *My Friend the Murderer and Other Mysteries and Adventures* (one story was removed from copies sold in Russia with a sharp knife by the Czar's censors), or the manuscript of his first novel, *The Narrative of John Smith*, which was lost in the post. (Does it lie still in some neglected corner of the dead-letter office?) And who would not give half his fortune to have been a guest at that dinner in the Langham Hotel in 1889, with Oscar Wilde present, when Lippincott's agent agreed to publish *The Sign of Four* and *The Picture of Dorian Gray*?

GRAHAM GREEN

PREFACE

We have tried to include all the published works of A. Conan Doyle in English. We have not attempted a list of translations, except for those which contain new prefaces and those which were issued in England as propaganda.

A number of minor contributions and letters which are known to us, but which we have been unable to trace, have had to be omitted. We have also failed to find copies of three small pamphlets, one on George Edalji (a non-copyright publication) and two on Divorce Law Reform, but they are described in such detail as is possible. There are also a few leaflets which we have thought best to omit; these include reprints of the author's articles on the funerals of Queen Victoria and Edward VII, and a leaflet on 'The Beauteous Beyond' (Seed-Corn Leaflets. – No. 3), which contains extracts from a speech made at Yarmouth. Reports and proceedings of the various societies and institutions with which the author was connected, especially the Psychic Bookshop, often carry his name and may on occasion have been written partly by him.

The publishing history derives for the most part from the publisher's records, but access to these has not always been possible. In such cases the figures are based on the A. P. Watt records and on the royalty returns, though these are no longer complete.

'First edition' is used to denote the first printing of the first edition; 'Colonial issue' to denote the first printing of the Colonial issue. 'Second issue' denotes either a second impression which is undesignated, or a reprint to which an alteration has been made. 'Second edition' is only used where the book has been entirely reset. 'Reissue' denotes the use of sheets printed for the first edition and bound later with new preliminaries or merely a cheaper binding.

We are deeply indebted to the many people who have helped us with their advice and loaned books or other material: Sir Arthur Conan Doyle's daughter, Dame Jean Bromet, without whose assistance, encouragement, and friendship over many years, this book would not have been attempted; M. Etienne Hofmann and the staff of Bibliotheque Cantonale et Universitaire at Lausanne for access to the papers deposited by the Arthur Conan Doyle Foundation; the following people associated with the Cataloguing and Development project for the Mary Kahler and Ohilip S. Hench Conan Doyle Collection in the Special Collections and Rare Books Division of the University of Minnesota Library – the Principal Investigator, Professor E.W. McDiarmid; the Arthur Conan Doyle Bibliographer, Andrew Malec, who has checked parts of the book in manuscript and offered advice and information which has been invaluable; the Curator and Assistant Curator, Austin McLean and John Jenson. Cameron Hollyer and the Metropolitan Toronto Library Board were kind enough to let us use the Sir Arthur Conan Doyle Collection. We also wish to acknowledge the assistance of the librarians and staff of the British Library (particularly the newspaper division at Colindale), the Bodleian Library, the National Library of Scotland, and many other libraries among them the Edinburgh Public Library, the Manchester Central Library, Cambridge University Library, the Portsmouth Central Library, and the libraries at the London School of Economics and at the University of London.

We are also indebted to A. P. Watt & Son for permission to examine their files; the Berg Collection in the New York Public Library for the use of the royalty statements; John Murray and his staff for their unfailing courtesy and help with books bearing their own imprint and that of Smith, Elder and Company; Longmans and the Librarian and staff at Reading University Library for permission to examine the Longman archives; Hodder and Stoughton and the Guildhall Library for the use of their archives; Methuen, Samuel French and the other publishers who have supplied information. Our thanks are also due to the editor and staff of *Psychic News*.

We also wish to thank Mr William Cagle and staff of the Lilly Library, Bloomington, Indiana, for the use of the McClure papers and the Appleton archives; the Librarian and staff of the Humanities Research Centre at the University of Texas at Austin for the use of the Arthur Conan Doyle Spiritualist Library; and the following for permission to quote from unpublished manuscripts and for other services: The Library of Congress; The New York Public Library; The Houghton Library, Harvard; The Beinecke Library, Yale; The Huntington Library, Santa Monica; and the library of the university of South Carolina. Use has also been made of microfilms in the public libraries at Boston, Philadelphia, Cincinnati, San Francisco, Oklahoma, Richmond, and the Carnegie Library at Pittsburg, and the university libraries at Minnesota and Indiana.

For information on the continental editions and translations, we are indebted to the National Library of Sweden and to the Royal Library of Denmark.

So many people have helped with their time and advice that it is not possible to list each one individually, but our special thanks go to James Edward Holroyd, Stanley Mackenzie, Marvin Epstein, Redmond A. Burke, Rollin van N. Hadley, and Dr R.J. Hetherington.

It only remains to thank our families and friends who have helped in many ways to make the task of preparing this book for publication as pleasant and enjoyable as it has been.

Any errors and omissions are wholly our responsibility and for these we apologise.

London, J.M. GIBSON
December 1981 R.G.L. GREEN

Chapter 22

The Told & Untold Tales

INTRODUCTION

During the twelve years I have been compiling the content for this book, my research has identified stories mentioned by Sherlock Holmes or Dr Watson, but not written up by Sir Arthur Conan Doyle. The natural progression from these findings is to ascertain whether authors have taken up these untold stories either as apocryphal tales or pastiches.

A STUDY IN SCARLET (November 1887)

Chapter I: Mr. Sherlock Holmes

Whilst working in the pathological laboratory at St. Bartholomew's Hospital, London, Sherlock Holmes developed a superior test for detecting bloodstains to the one which was currently available.[12]

---

[12] If Holmes's discovery were valid, argues Remsen Ten Eyck Schenck, in "Baker Street Fables," it would be universally used today. The fact that it is not leads Schenck to label "unfounded" the notion that only haemoglobin caused the agent to react. "Presumably," Schenck continues, "[Holmes] discovered on further study that a similar result was obtained with other common substances, or else that it was not due to haemoglobin at all, or rather to some other ingredient in the blood, but not peculiar to it." Holmes was even wrong about the concentration of his blood solution: Schenck estimates that the ratio of a "drop" of blood to a litre of water would have actually been one part blood to 30,000 parts water, rather than the "one in a million" proportion Holmes cites shortly (although a "drop" is an imprecise unit, the smallest unit used in medicine is a "minim," .06 of a millilitre, which would produce a ratio of 1 in 60,000). The detective no doubt soon bitterly regretted that he had even mentioned his test, even to Watson," Schenck concludes, "and this could well explain why it was never again referred to."

But Leon S. Holstein, in "7. Knowledge of Chemistry – Profound" disagrees, suggesting that the test was an early version of the present-day haematochromogen test, which is used to identify bloodstains. When blood is present, haematochromogen crystals turn pinkish, which is perhaps, as Holmes surmises, a shade not that far removed from the "dull mahogany colour" that Holmes observes.

Christine L. Huber, in "The Sherlock Holmes Blood Test: the Solution to a Century-Old Mystery," identifies the test as one "rediscovered" in the 1930s, when it was "discovered" that haemoglobin A is denatured by sodium hydroxide ("white crystals") and then precipitated with saturated ammonium sulfate (a "transparent fluid"). [T]he Holmes Test...has been in almost daily use in hospitals and research laboratories as a part of the electrophoretic process, since its rediscovery," she claims. "How it was lost in the first place and why Holmes never received acknowledgement for it remains a mystery."

In another test for haemoglobin (and consequently for the presence of blood), the greenish-brown resin of the guaiacum tree, or lignum vitae, was mixed with alcohol; this substance was

He mentioned five cases – Von Bischoff at Frankfort, Mason of Bradford, the notorious Muller, [13] Lefevre of Montpellier, and Samson of New Orleans [14] - where the outcome of their crimes would have been different had his test been available then. Having not found any further references to these cases, it appears that Holmes did not investigate them. Instead, he used them as illustrations of cases where his test would have been useful.

Chapter III: The Lauriston Garden Mystery

"Then, of course, this blood belongs to a second individual – presumably the murderer, if murder has been committed," said Sherlock Holmes. It reminds me of the circumstances attendant on the death of Van Jansen, in Utrecht, in the year '34. Do you remember the case, Gregson?" [15]

---

added to the liquid being tested and then shaken with a few drops of hydrogen peroxide in ether. The presence of haemoglobin would turn the mixture bright blue. The test was first reported in 1861 in a modified form by J. Van Deen.

R. Austin Freeman describes this test in *The Shadow of the Wolf* (1925), an account of the great medico-legal detective Dr. John Evelyn Thorndyke – whose cases, like those of Holmes, were written up in several other books, from *The Red Thumb* (1907) to *The Jacob Street Mystery* (1942). After pouring some tincture of guaicum on a questionable stain, Thorndyke watches as the liquid spreads outward, then adds the ether and allows the two liquids to mix. "Gradually the ether spreads towards the stain, "Freeman writes, "and, first at one point and then at another, approached and finally crossed the wavy grey line; and at each point the same change occurred: first the faint grey line turned into a strong blue line, and then the colour extended to the enclosed space until the entire area of the stain stood out in a conspicuous blue patch. 'You understand the meaning of this,' said Thorndyke, 'This is a bloodstain.'"

P.M. Stone asserts in "The Other Friendship: A Speculation," that Holmes and Thorndyke actually met and exchanged views at some point. "[I]t is not unlikely," comments Edgar Smith in his introduction to the essay, "that Sherlock Holmes…was inclined to seek variety – and shall we say relief? – in intellectual converse on the higher plane with someone whose capacities and inclinations were just a little closer to his own."

There were in fact eleven original tests for haemoglobin between 1800 and 1881, and numerous variations were proposed. The tests, several of which remain in modern use, are summarised in Raymond J. McGowan's "Sherlock Holmes and Forensic Chemistry."

Michael Harrison surmises that Holmes offered his test to the British police, who snubbed him. It is no wonder, then, Harrison suggests that Holmes, "nursing an unconquerable prejudice against the British police system, preferred to go his own highly individual way."

[13] "D. Martin Dakin notes that "Muller" cannot have been the Franz Muller who was the first railway murderer (1864) since he was convicted and that not by bloodstains, but by him absentmindedly going off with his victim's hat!"

[14] Owen Dudley Edwards observes "Holmes is evidently shooting off these names at great speed with the obsessiveness of a devotee determined to bombard his audience with proofs of their own ignorance in a field he intends to evangelise."

[15] Utrecht, in the Netherlands, was the site of a series of peace treaties signed from 1713 to 1714. Under the Peace of Utrecht, France and Spain came to terms with a number of European powers to conclude the war of Spanish Succession. Holmes's interest in Utrecht would have likely been

Chapter VI: Tobias Gregson Shows What He Can Do

Watson noted from the *Daily Telegraph*...and the Ratcliff Highway murders. [16]

Chapter XIV: The Conclusion

Holmes noted – "The forcible administration of poison is by no means a new thing in criminal annals. The cases of Dolsky in Odessa, and of Leturier in Montpellier, will occur at once to any toxicologist."

I have not found either of these two cases as published stories.

THE SIGN OF FOUR (February 1890)

Chapter II: The Statement of the Case

"I have come to you, Mr. Holmes," said Miss Morstan, "because you once enabled my employer, Mrs. Cecil Forrester, [17] to unravel a little domestic complication. [18] She was much impressed by your kindness and skill."

---

more natural than political, as the province was a center for bee-keeping, with a bee-market held nearby in Veenendaal.

Curiously, for over two hundred years, Utrecht was the headquarters of Jansenism, a Roman Catholic movement founded by the theologian Cornelis Jansen (1585-1638). Jansenists claimed to be disciples of St. Augustine and opposed the Jesuits in many theological respects. Yet there is no known connection between the sect and the "Van Jansen" that Holmes mentions. "Jansen" (the Dutch equivalent of Johnson) is, in fact, a common name in Holland.

[16] Ratcliff Highway, located in the East End near the docks, became notorious early in the nineteenth century when it was the scene of a series of murders committed at the end of 1811. Thomas De Quincey, who wrote about the crimes in his *Murder Considered as One of the Fine Arts*, called the area one of "manifold ruffianism." Among the murders were those of the draper Mr Marr, his wife, their infant child, and a boy who worked in the Marrs' shop. *The Complete Newgate Calendar*, Volume V (1926), recounts that when a servant girl and a watchman rang the Marrs' bell and received no answer, a number of neighbours scaled the wall and entered the house; "and there was presented the most woeful scene that, perhaps, ever disgraced human nature: the bodies of Mr Marr and his shop-boy, the latter of whom appeared from evident marks to have struggled for life with the assassins, near each other. That of Mrs Marr in the passage, and the infant in its cradle – all dead, but yet warm and weltering in their blood." At final count, seven people were killed over a course of eight days. Although the murders were no doubt the work of more than one perpetrator, the only person arrested was a man named John Williams, who escaped trial by committing suicide in his cell at Coldbath Fields Prison.

As a result of the murders, the street acquired such sinister repute that its name was changed to St. George's Street. By 1895, when depicted in *The Queen's London*, it was reported that the streets once regarded as unsavoury and dangerous was "now...chiefly remarkable for the shops of dealers in wild beasts, birds, *etc.*"

[17] Donald A. Redmond, in *Sherlock Holmes: A Study in Sources,* identifies her as Mary Anne Forester, widow of David Ochterloney Dyce Sombre and daughter of Edward Jervis, 2nd. Viscount St. Vincent, who married George Cecil Weld, 3rd. Baron Forester of Willey Park, on November 8, 1862. Mrs. For[r]ester died in 1895.

"Mrs. Cecil Forrester," he repeated thoughtfully. "I believe that I was of some slight service to her." [19]

Chapter VI: Sherlock Holmes Gives a Demonstration

Athelney Jones – "It's Mr. Sherlock Holmes, the theorist. Remember you! I'll never forget how you lectured us on all causes and inferences and effects in the Bishopgate jewel case. [20]

Devotees of Sherlock Holmes will remember that Dr Watson met his future wife, Mary Morstan, when she sought Holmes's help in the case of "The Sign of Four". In introducing herself she reminded Holmes that he had once helped her employer, Mrs Cecil Forrester, to "unravel a little domestic complication." Holmes had to think for a while to remember and then recalled that the case "was a very simple one".

A few years ago that excellent scholar of ghost and mystery fiction **Barbara Roden**, *was undertaking research in a firm of insurers on another matter entirely, when she*

---

[18] Robert Keith Leavitt suggests (in "Who Was Cecil Forrester?") that Mr. Cecil Forrester, Farintosh of "The Speckled Band," Woodhouse of "The Bruce Partington Plans," and Colonel Upwood of *The Hound of the Baskervilles*, were all one and the same man – "former friend of Captain Morstan and probably of the none-too-scrupulous Major Sholto, sometime husband of Mary Morstan's employer, party hanger-on, card-sharp and all-too-dubious hero of the strange adventure of the politician, the lighthouse and the trained cormorant" (the latter referred to in "The Veiled Lodger").

And Ruth Douglass, in "The Camberwell Poisoner," advances the speculation that the "little domestic complication" in Mrs. Forrester's household was the Camberwell Poisoning mentioned in "The Five Orange Pips"; that the poisoner was Mrs. Forrester; that she escaped justice and used Mary first as bait (for Watson) and then as a tool (in order to obtain poison, through Mary, from Watson's medical cabinet). She finally killed Mary.

[19] Rosemary Michaud, in "Another Case of Identity," proposes that the woman here was not Mary Morstan but rather the daughter of Mrs. Cecil Forrester. Holmes knew perfectly well who she was but, presented with a pearl, went along to find out what the case was about. Miss Morstan had died earlier. Michaud suggests, and the Forresters – swindlers by trade – decided to pursue the *Times* advertisement themselves. Holmes had no knowledge of how serious relations had become between "Miss Morstan" and Watson until too late and probably assumed that recovery of the treasure would put and end to "Miss Morstan's" interest in Watson. This thesis also explains the reference in "The Five Orange Pips" to Mary visiting her "mother".

An alternative but equally startling suggestion is made by Charles A. Meyer, in "The Remarkable Forrester Case." Meyer suggests that Mrs. Forrester and Holmes had an affair and that only after the passions had cooled for ten years was Mrs. Forrester comfortable in recommending Holmes. This explains, in Meyer's view, the otherwise "dull" behaviour of Miss Morstan in accepting for so many years the twin mysteries of her father's disappearance and the annual pearls.

[20] Bishopsgate Street, called "Bishopgate" Street in many older publications, is in Bethnal Green, and Bishopsgate Station is a station of the London Underground. In Holmes's time, it was actually bifurcated in common reference into "Bishopsgate Street Within" (the City) and "Bishopsgate Street Without" and was the main northern thoroughfare out of the City.

*chanced upon some information about a certain Mr Forrester, and piece by piece she was able to rebuild **"The Adventure of the Suspect Servant"**. (see Mike Ashley's book).*

THE ADVENTURES OF SHERLOCK HOLMES (July 1891- June 1892)

A Scandal in Bohemia

'From time to time I heard some vague account of his doings: of his summons to Odessa [21] in the case of the Trepoff murder, [22] of his clearing up of the singular tragedy of the Atkinson brothers [23] at Trincomalee, [24] and finally of the mission which he had accomplished so delicately and successfully for the reigning family of Holland.' [25]

The story of the Trepoff murder has been written by Adrian Conan Doyle & John Dickson Carr in their book "More Exploits of Sherlock Holmes" under the title 'The Adventure of the Seven Clocks'.

'In the case of the Darlington Substitution Scandal it (fire) was of use to me, and also in the Arnsworth Castle business.'

"The Darlington Substitution Scandal" has been written by David Stuart Davies – see Mike Ashley's book. The Arnsworth Castle business has been written by Adrian Conan Doyle in his book "The Exploits of Sherlock Holmes" under the title 'The Adventure of the Red Widow'. It is also included in "The Further Adventures of Sherlock Holmes" collected by Richard Lancelyn Green.

---

[21] Odessa, at the time the third largest city in Russia (now part of Ukraine), was one of the chief centres of the 1905 uprising against the tsar. A mutiny took place that year on board the warship *Potemkin*, docked in Odessa, and Sergey Eisenstein's classic film *Potemkin*, filmed in the city and on the docks, memorialised the suffering of the rebels.

[22] One Fyodor Fyodorovich Trepoff (1803-1889) was military policemaster of St. Petersburg. Might he be connected with Holmes's "summons to Odessa in the case of the Trepoff murder"? Such an identification would mean that Trepoff was not the victim but perhaps the murderer. Another possibility, suggested by Richard Lancelyn Green, is *General* Trepoff, who was shot by a nihilist on January 24, 1878.

[23] The Vanishing of the Atkinsons by Eric Brown (see Mike Ashley's book).

[24] Trincomalee is in the eastern province of Ceylon. This is not the only reference to Ceylon, then a British territory and now Sri Lanka; in *The Sign of Four*, Holmes displays a mastery of the subject of Buddhism in Ceylon, suggesting that he actually visited there.

[25] The "reigning family of Holland" was that of William III (1817-1890), who married Princess Emma of Waldeck-Pyrmont; they produced only one child, Wilhelmina, born 1880. When William died in 1890, Wilhelmina became queen.

The Red-Headed League

'You will remember that I remarked the other day, just before we went into the very simple problem presented by Miss Mary Sutherland,…' [26]

'It is not too much to say that once or twice, as in that business of the Sholto murder and the Agra treasure…'
  See June Thomas's book The secret Archives of Sherlock Holmes *The Msn with the Twisted Lip.*

No other tales mentioned.

A Case of Identity

"This is the Dundas separation case, and, as it happens, I was engaged in clearing up some small points in connection with it. The husband was a teetotaller, there was no other woman, and the conduct complained of was that he had drifted into the habit of winding up every meal by taking out his false teeth and hurling them at his wife…" [27]

"In these cases, save for one intricate matter which has been referred to me from Marseilles…" [28]

(**Compiler's note:** Mr. James Windibank has a second mention in Adrian Conan Doyle & John Dickson Carr's book *More Exploits of Sherlock Holmes* in the story 'The Highgate Miracle' when Holmes says: "I recall a similar case in Riga in 1876 and is faintly reminiscent of an impersonation by a Mr. James Windibank in '88."

'I (Miss Mary Sutherland) came to you, sir, because I heard of you from Mrs. Etherege, whose husband you found so easy when the police and everyone had given him up for dead.'

'You will find parallel cases, if you consult my index, in Andover in '77, and there was something of the sort at The Hague last year.'

---

[26] "A Case of Identity," the case of Miss Mary Sutherland was not published in the *Strand Magazine* until September 1891, the month *after* publication of "The Red-Headed League."

[27] "This interesting case…involved a bit of leg-pulling, I'm afraid, for…even today, with all the skill of modern dental science, we cannot construct a set of artificial teeth that would withstand such violent and frequent abuse," Dr. Charles Goodman writes in "The Dental Holmes." Michael Ramos, D.D.S., a prominent collector of dentures, opines, however, that the "vulcanised" rubber dentures of the last century might well have stood up to such abuse where modern porcelain or even plastic dentures would not. "The rubber dentures often had a horrible smell, but they were hard as stone," states Ramos in a letter to this editor.

[28] France's main seaport and oldest city, Marseilles prospered greatly in the nineteenth century with the conquest of Algeria by France and the opening of the Suez Canal. Could this "intricate matter…from Marseilles have involved the "great claret importers Westhouse & Marbank" and their employee Mr. James Windibank?

No further reference to these three cases have been found.

The Boscombe Valley Mystery

No other tale is referred to in this story.

The Five Orange Pips

'When I glance over my notes and records of the Sherlock Holmes cases between the years '82 and '90, I am faced by so many which present strange and interesting features, that it is no easy matter to know which to choose and which to leave...The year '87 furnished us with a long series of cases of greater or less interest, of which I retain the records. Among my headings under this one twelve months, I find an account of the Paradol Chamber, [29] of the Amateur Mendicant Society, [30] of the facts connected with the loss of the British barque *Sophy Anderson*, [31] of the singular adventures of the Grice Patersons in the island of Uffa, [32] and finally of the Camberwell poisoning case.' [33] In the latter, as may be remembered, Sherlock Holmes was able, by winding up the dead man's watch, to prove that it had been wound up two hours ago and that therefore the deceased had gone to bed within that time – a deduction which was of the greatest importance in clearing up the case. [34]

From *The Annotated Sherlock Holmes Volume I* 'it was noted...' As early as July 1901, the editor of *The Bookman* complained that the *Adventures* and the *Memoirs* were replete with "allusions to affairs of which the reader knows nothing" and demanded that the author "clear away the mystery of all the titles." There are over 110 "unrecorded cases" mentioned in the Canon, according to Christopher Redmond, but John Hall, in

---

[29] Numerous pastiches have explored this strange reference, but Klas Lithner, in "A Key to the Paradol Chamber," identifies the chamber as the residence of Lucien-Anatole Paradol, a French journalist and political figure.

[30] The Amateur Mendicant Society published as 'The Case of the Amateur Mendicants' by June Thomson from *The Secret Files of Sherlock Holmes'*. Also, '*The Adventure of the Amateur Mendicant Society*' by John Gregory Betancourt. (see Mike Ashley's book).

[31] The Case of the Vanishing Barque. The Sophy Anderson. By June Thomson from *The Secret Notebooks of Sherlock Holmes*.

[32] Produced in Mike Ashley's book as *The Adventure of the Silver Buckle* by Denis O. Smith.

[33] Published as *The Adventure of the Gold Hunter* by Adrian Conan Doyle & John Dickson Carr in More Exploits of Sherlock Holmes.

[34] The word "ago" becomes "before" in American editions. Lord Donegall, in "The Horological Holmes," observes, "Dr. Watson's statement as it stands is palpable nonsense. Holmes would have had to wind the watch *and let it run down completely* before being able to tell how many turns of the key or pendant represented 2 hours – even approximately...Watson must have omitted some essential link in the chain of reasoning."

The Abominable Wife, points out that there is meaningful information about only thirty-nine of these cases.

'I have heard of you, Mr Holmes. I heard from Major Prendergast how you saved him in the Tankerville Club Scandal.' [35]

'The Case of the Paradol Chamber' by June Thomson in *The Secret Chronicles of Sherlock Holmes*. A pastiche similar to 'The Adventure of the Blanched Soldier.'

The Blue Carbuncle

"So much so," I remarked, "that of the last six cases which I have added to my notes, three have been entirely free of any legal crime." [36]

No other tale was noted in this story.

The Speckled Band

"I have heard of you Mr Holmes from Mrs Farintosh, whom you helped in the hour of her sore need." (The case concerned an opal tiara. "I think it was before your time, Watson.")

Hence, no record has been found of this case.

The Engineer's Thumb

"…there were only two (cases) which I was the means of introducing to his notice, that of Mr. Hatherley's thumb and that of Colonel Warburton's madness." [37]

See 'The Adventure of the Sealed Room' by Adrian Conan Doyle and John Dickson Carr.

---

[35] I have been unable to find any published details of this story.

[36] Fletcher Pratt computes that by 1914, when the record of Holmes's detective activities ceases, no crimes had taken place in one quarter of the total published cases. In nine of these cases, there was no legal crime. In six no crime took place because Holmes intervened in time to prevent its occurrence.

[37] Arthur Conan Doyle received his M.D. in 1885 at the University of Edinburgh together with one Colonel William Pleace Warburton. Although there is no record of William Pleace Warburton suffering any mental disturbance, it is possible that he is the subject of the matter brought to Holmes's attention and was introduced through Conan Doyle's relationship with Watson.

The Noble Bachelor

"Your morning's letters, if I remember right, were from a fishmonger and a tide-waiter." [38]

"Oh, you mean the little problem of the Grosvenor Square furniture van. That is quite cleared up now – though, indeed, it was obvious from the first." [39]

"Without, however, the knowledge of pre-existing cases which serves me so well. There was a parallel instance in Aberdeen some years back, and something on very much the same lines at Munich the year after the Franco-Prussian War. It is one of those cases – but hullo, here is Lestrade…"

No tale referring to Aberdeen has been located, and Lestrade interrupted the identification of the second tale.

The Beryl Coronet & The Copper Beeches

No mention of other tales related during these stories.

THE MEMOIRS OF SHERLOCK HOLMES (December 1892 – December 1893)

Silver Blaze

No other case mentioned.

The Cardboard Box

"The Cardboard Box" appeared in the *Strand Magazine* in January 1893 and in *Harper's Weekly* (New York) on January 14, 1893. The first edition of *Memoirs of Sherlock Holmes* published in London in 1894 by George Newnes, Limited, contained only eleven "memoirs," excluding "The Cardboard Box" from the series of twelve that had appeared in the *Strand Magazine*. The first American edition of *Memoirs of Sherlock Holmes*, published by Harper that same year, contained all twelve stories; almost immediately afterward, however, a "new and revised" Harper edition appeared that, like the British edition, omitted "The Cardboard Box."

Theories about the odd handling of this story are sketchy at best. Arthur Bartlett Maurice, in an article entitled "Sherlock Holmes & His Creator" (*Collier's*, August 15, 1908), surmises that the story's recounting of an "illicit love affair" led a cautious Doyle to put the piece aside when preparing the collection for publication. Eminent bookseller David Randall, in his *Catalogue of Original Manuscripts, etc.,* subsequently concludes that the American publisher Harper, having seen the story in the *Strand*, was unaware that Doyle had any objections to including all twelve stories in book form; upon

---

[38] A customs officer who awaited the arrival of ships (formerly coming in with the tide) and boarded them to prevent the avoidance of custom-house regulations.

[39] Grosvenor Square, close to the Baker Street Station of the Metropolitan Line, comprised many aristocratic residences. It is now the site of the American Embassy.

publication, Doyle must have issued a protest, hence the quick issuance of a new *Memoirs* edition. The first American edition is now considered quite rare. Curiously, not one of the numerous biographers of Arthur Conan Doyle has a word of explanation of the self-censorship, nor did Doyle himself comment upon it in his *Memories and Adventures*.

(See p. 500 for mention of a tale).

The Yellow Face, The Stockbroker's Clerk & The 'Gloria Scott'.

Again, no other cases mentioned.

The Musgrave Ritual

"Here's a record of the Tarleton murders (no mention), and the case of Vamberry, the wine merchant, [40] and the adventure of the old Russian woman, [41] and the singular affair of the aluminium crutch, [42] as well as a full account of Ricoletti of the club foot and his abominable wife. [43]

No mention of this tale appears to have been recorded.

The Reigate Squires

---

[40] Vamberry is identified by several scholars with Arminius, or Armin, Vambery (Hermann Vamberger, 1832-1913), a Hungarian professor of Oriental languages at the University of Buda-Pesth and a renowned wine collector. In his twenties he travelled throughout Armenia and Persia for several months, disguised in native dress, writing about his experiences in such books as *Sketches of Central Asia* (1868), *The Life and Adventures of Arminius Vambery* (1884), and *The Story of My Struggles* (1904). According to David Pelger, Vambery travelled to London in 1885, where he spent three weeks lecturing to the public on the Russian threat in Central Asia. He and Holmes may have met then. The character of Professor Van Helsing in the work *Dracula* is said by some to be drawn from Vambery, whom Bram Stoker may have consulted for his expertise on Romania and vampirism.

[41] Written up as "*The Case of The Old Russian Woman*" by June Thomson in 'The Secret Chronicles of Sherlock Holmes'.

[42] Written up as "*The Case of the Aluminium Crutch*" by June Thomson in 'The Secret Notebooks of Sherlock Holmes'.
Aluminium crutches were certainly not commonly available as medical devices at the time of "The Musgrave Ritual." In 1886, only 15 tonnes of aluminium were produced worldwide, and the modern technique for producing aluminium was not invented until 1886. Before the "Bayer Process" for commercial smelting was developed in 1888, aluminium was far more precious than gold or silver. By 1900, production had risen to 8,000 tonnes, and aluminium became a common industrial metal.

[43] D. Martin Dakin points out that the native name for the Abominable Snowman is "yeti" and suggests that what Holmes really said was "the wrinkled yeti of the clubfoot and his abominable life."

'The whole question of the Netherland-Sumatra Company and of the colossal schemes of Baron Maupertuis…'

See June Thomson's story "The Case of the Maupertuis Scandal" in *The Secret Journals of Sherlock Holmes*.

Nothing identified on the Netherland-Sumatra Company.

The Crooked Man & The Resident Patient

No other tales mentioned during these two stories.

The Greek Interpreter

Mycroft Holmes: "…I expected to see you round last week to consult me over the Manor House case."

Nothing noted in the *New Annotated Sherlock Holmes* about this case.

The Naval Treaty

"I find them recorded in my notes under the headings of 'The Adventure of the Second Stain', 'The Adventure of the Naval Treaty,' and 'The Adventure of the Tired Captain.'"

The Adventure of the Green Empress published as 'The Adventure of the Second Stain" by F.P. Cillie in 'The Further Adventures of Sherlock Holmes' collected by Richard Lancelyn Green.

See *The Adventure of the Tired Captain* by Alan Wilson in 'The Further Adventures of Sherlock Holmes' collected by Richard Lancelyn Green.

The Final Problem

"During the winter of that year and the early spring of 1891, I saw in the papers that he had been engaged by the French Government upon a matter of supreme importance…"

No record found of this case.

"Between ourselves, the recent cases in which I have been of assistance to the Royal Family of Scandinavia, and to the French Republic…"

Neither of these tales have been published to the best of my knowledge.

THE HOUND OF THE BASKERVILLES (August 1901 – April 1902)

Chapter V: Three Broken Threads

"At the present instant one of the most revered persons in England is being besmirched by a blackmailer [44] and only I can stop the disasterous scandal."
See, 'The Adventure of the Two Women' by Adrian Conan Doyle in *Exploits of Sherlock Holmes*.

Chapter XIII: Fixing the Nets

"Students of criminology will remember the analogous incident in Grodno, in Little Russia, in the year '66, [45] and of course there are the Anderson murders in North Carolina..." [46]

Chapter XV: A Retrospection

"Since the tragic upshot of our visit to Devonshire he had been engaged in two affairs of the utmost importance, in the first of which he had exposed the atrocious conduct of Colonel Upwood [47] in connection with the famous card scandal of the Nonpareil Club, [48]

---

[44] Michael P. Malloy, who dates "Charles Augustus Milverton" after *The Hound of the Baskervilles*, identifies the Blackmail victim as Milverton's murderess. Philip Cornell, in a fine piece entitled "Blackmail's Dark Waters," demonstrated that Holmes seems to react particularly strongly to cases of blackmail and to exhibit more sympathy for the victims of blackmail than he does for the victims (see, for example, "The 'Gloria Scott,'" "The Boscombe Valley Mystery," "The Second Stain," and most notably "Charles Augustus Milverton"). Cornell suggests that Holmes may have had an experience, either personally or in his family, that led to this intense aversion. Of course, we learn later that there *was* no blackmail case at hand, but Cornell finds it noteworthy that when Holmes needs a pretext, it is a case of blackmail that springs to his lips.

[45] Grodno was a Lithuanian district of Western Russia, near St. Petersburg, heavily Jewish, in the area now known as Belorussia; "Little Russia" was the Czarist name for the area now called Ukraine. That is, Grodno was not in Little Russia. In some American editions, the town os given as "Godno," a non-existent location.

[46] Possibly Holmes meant *South* Carolina. In 1866, Lt. Charles Snyder, commander of the military post of Anderson, S.C., reported the fatal shooting by Reuben Golding, a "desperate and ruffianly" white man, of A. Payton, a black man. The murder shocked the community, and other crimes of Golding's may have been brought to light. What possible reliance the case had to the one at hand is unknown. *Fort* Anderson was an important Civil War emplacement in North Carolina, but Anderson County and the town of Anderson were located in South Carolina.

[47] Dr. Julian Wolff, in his *Practical Handbook of Sherlockian Heraldry*, identifies Colonel Upwood with Sir William Gordon-Cumming, a lieutenant-colonel in the Scots Guards during the Zulu War (1879). In 1891 Sir William brought an action for slander against a family who had accused him of cheating at the illegal card game baccarat. A long-term friend of Gordon-Cumming's , the Prince of Wales – the future King Edward VII – himself was subpoenaed as a witness; hw was the first in the Royal Family ever to give evidence in a civil court action, and had been compelled to appear (by Gordon-Cumming's lawyer, Sir Edward Clarke) on the basis of Article 42 of the Queen's Regulations for the army, which directed that anyone who saw an illegal action being performed by a soldier or officer report it to the appropriate commanding officer, largely because of the Prince's evidence under vicious cross-examination by Gordon-Cumming's counsel, who delved into the Prince's personal life. Sir William lost the Baccarat

while in the second he had defended the unfortunate Mme. Montpensier from the charge of murder..."

See '*The Adventure of the Abbas Ruby*' by Adrian Conan Doyle in 'The Exploits of Sherlock Holmes'. (The Nonpareil Club).

See '*The Adventure of the Black Baronet*' by Adrian Conan Doyle & John Dickson Carr in 'More Exploits of Sherlock Holmes'. (Madame Montpensier).

THE RETURN OF SHERLOCK HOLMES (October 1903 – December 1904)

The Adventure of the Empty House

"But you handled the Molesey Mystery with less than your usual..."

"...and here is Morgan the poisoner, and Merridew of the abominable memory, and Mathews who knocked out my left canine..."
"You may have some recollection of the death of Mrs. Stewart, of Lauder, in 1887."

No mention has been found of any publication of these five cases.

The Adventure of the Norwood Builder

"...for I find, on looking over my notes, that this period includes the case of the papers of ex-President Murillo, [49] and also the shocking affair of the Dutch steamship *Friesland*, [50]..."

Case, as it became known. The case aroused great interest, with many people convinced of Sir William's innocence; some believed it was perhaps Edward who had committed some unknown illegal action not revealed in the course of the trial, and that Gordon-Cumming was merely covering for his friend. As a result of the scandal, public opinion turned for a time against the Prince, but ultimately his reputation was undamaged. The effect on Gordon-Cummings life, on the other hand, was complete and devastating. He was ostracised from society.

[48] In "Who Was Cecil Forrester?" Robert Keith Leavitt writes that the Nonpareil must have been "a discrete, footnote kind of club composed of journalists." He hazards this guess on the basis of the fact that Nonpareil was a type-face. Originally, the name signified the type's unsurpassable beauty; in 1886, at the urging of type-founder inventor Nelson C. Marks, who was working to regularise printer's nomenclature, the word "nonpareil" was adopted by the U.S. Typefounders' Association and other groups as a size designation (6-point).

[49] Most scholars accept this as a reference to "Wisteria Lodge," in which "ex-President Murillo" of the fictitious country of "San Pedro" figures, although the reference to "papers" is puzzling, for "papers" are not directly involved in the case.

[50] Although Friesland is located in the Netherlands, the S.S. *Friesland* was actually of Belgian registry. The transatlantic passenger liner was owned and operated by the Red Star line, carrying scores of emigrants from Antwerp to New York throughout the 1890s. In 1903, supplanted by faster, larger steamships, she was transferred to charter service between Liverpool and Philadelphia and was finally scrapped in 1812. Christopher Morley, who sailed on the *Friesland*

The Affair of Don Murillo, the Tiger of San Pedro, the Central American dictator – mentioned in *The Singular Adventure of the Flat-Top Desk* by Alan Stockwell.

"You remember that terrible murderer, Bert Stevens, who wanted us to get him off in '87?"

No mention of this tale has been unearthed.

See June Thomson's book The Secret Archives of Sherlock Holmes *The Adventure of the Norwood Builder*.

The Adventure of the Dancing Men

No other case mentioned during this story.

The Adventure of the Solitary Cyclist

"... for he was immersed at the moment in a very abstruse and complicated problem concerning the peculiar persecution to which John Vincent Harden, the well-known tobacco millionaire..."

See 'The Case of the Millionaire's Persecution' by June Thomson in *The Secret Journals of Sherlock Holmes*.

"You remember, Watson, that it was near there that we took Archie Stamford, the forger." [51]

The Adventure of the Priory School

"I am retained in this case of the Ferrers Documents, and the Abergavenny murder..."

The Adventure of the Dark Angel by Adrian Conan Doyle in 'Exploits of Sherlock Holmes.' (The Case of the Ferrers Documents).

The Case of the Suicidal Lawyer by Martin Edwards in Mike Ashley's book. (The Abergavenny murder).

---

from Philadelphia to Liverpool in September 1910, described her as "a beauty, a smart little Red Star liner." Several scholars point out that in Arthur Conan Doyle's *The Lost World*, it was the S.S. *Friesland*, a Dutch-American liner, that sighted Professor George Edward Challenger's pterodactyl when it escaped from the Queen's Hall.

[51] In "The Sad Case of Young Stamford," Jerry Neal Williamson speculates that he was the "Archie" of "The Red-Headed League" and also the young Stamford who introduced Holmes to Watson. The manuscript of "The Solitary Cyclist" continues here: "Hughes, the poisoner, also came from there." Apparently Watson was not then ready to reveal the facts of the Hughes case.

The Adventure of Black Peter

"In this memorable year '95…ranging from his famous investigation of the sudden death of Cardinal Tosca [52]…down to his arrest of Wilson, the notorious Canary trainer [53] …"

See June Thomson's book The secret archives of Sherlock Holmes *The Adventure of Black Peter*.

See *The Case of the Cardinal's Corpse* by June Thomson and *The Case of the Notorious Canary Trainer* in The Secret Files of Sherlock Holmes.

Also, "The Adventure of the Deptford Horror" by Adrian Conan Doyle from 'The Exploits of Sherlock Holmes'.

Charles Augustus Milverton

No other tales noted during this story

---

[52] Cardinal "Tosca" is identified by Francis Albert Young as Cardinal Luigi Ruffo-Scilla, whose collapse and death at the age of fifty-five in Rome on May 29, 1895, came as a great surprise to many. A different churchman is suggested by Mark. E. Levitt, namely, the Monsignor Isodoro Carini, who was a significant part of the effort to bring the church and the Italian government to a *rapprochement* in the 1890s and who died in a "sudden and mysterious" way (according the the *London Times* of February 1, 1895).

[53] The meaning of Watson's allusion here is murky. According to E. Cobham Brewer's *Dictionary of Phrase and Fable,* a canary can be slang for a guinea or sovereign – gold coins are yellow in colour. So, too, does the dictionary list "canary bird" as a convict: Certain "desperate" prisoners once wore yellow uniforms, and the jail was considered their cage. Donald A. Redmond adds that "The Old Canaries" was the nickname given to the Third Dragoon Guards, after their yellow facings (although there were no Third Dragoon officers named Wilson). Redmond continues that "canary" could be taken to mean any soldier sporting a yellow armband, or "an instructor at a gas school, or one of the Sanitary Corps of the R.A.M.C. ; batallion Sanitary Orderlies.'"
Some dismiss the idea that the "canary" of Wilson's infamy is anything but a bird. "There is absolutely nothing whatsoever in any way, shape, or form notorious about canaries," declares "Red" Smith in "The Nefarious Holmes." "However, a bird trainer can branch out, as Hirsch Jacobs has demonstrated in our day; Mr. Jacobs began with pigeons and went on to become America's leading horse trainer in eleven of twelve consecutive years. It stands to reason that Holmes's man, Wilson, followed a similar course…"
Numerous contradictory theories abound, *New York Times* music critic Harold C. Schonberg, in "Sherlock and Malocchio!," argues that the case may have been connected with threats against the life of the famous soprano Adelina Patti. David Roberts proposes that Wilson was in the business of training informants, or "stool-pigeons." Carol Paul Woods suggests that Wilson was a trainer of prize-fighters, and that he and his fighter protégé hailed from the Canary Islands.

The Six Napoleons

"You will remember, Watson, how the dreadful business of the Abernetty family…" [54]

The dreadful business of the Abernetty family came to Holmes attention because of the depth that the parsley had sunk into the butter, an example of how not to overlook what may appear trifling detail. This case has baffled Sherlockians for decades but at least we can repeat it in full as "The Case of the Incumbent Invalid" by Claire Griffen. (See Mike Ashley's book).

"…and get out the papers of the Conk-Singleton forgery case."

See June Thomson's book The Secret Archives of Sherlock Holmes *The Adventure of the Six Napoleons*.

The Adventure of the Three Students

No reference to any other tale(s) found in this story.

The Adventure of the Golden Pince-Nez

"As I turn over the pages, I see my notes upon the repulsive story of the red leech [55] and the terrible death of Crosby the banker. Here also I find an account of the Addleton tragedy and the singular contents of the ancient British barrow. The famous Smith-Mortimer succession case comes also within this period, and so does the tracking of Huret, the Boulevard assassin…" [56]

---

[54] Numerous pastiches and analyses of the "Abernetty business have been written and are surveyed in detail in William Hyder's "Parsley and Butter: The Abernetty Business." Hyder concludes, without foundation, that no less than murder was involved. It is not equally likely that a business – perhaps an inn or tavern – run by the Abernetty family was "dreadful" (that is, kept in poor sanitation), and that condition was first brought to Holmes's notice having been left out on a hot day? The connection between this observation and the ensuing investigation remains undetermined. A number of scholars consider whether and how fast parsley will sink into butter. Not surprisingly, they do not agree.

[55] It is the rare leech that is red in colour. Most such parasites, as Lord Gore-Booth comments in "The Journeys of Sherlock Holmes: A Topographical Monograph," are olive-green or brown. A. Carson Simpson gathers that Watson might have been using the word's more archaic meaning and making a derogatory reference to a physician, perhaps one who had red hair (taking a name such as "Eric the Red"), wore predominately red clothing (Count Amadeo VII of Savoy was known as "il Conte Rosso"), favoured blood-letting as a treatment, or had communist sympathies.

[56] "The Golden Pince-Nez" is generally thought to have occurred in the late autumn of 1894 (see *Chronological Table*). M. Jean-Paul-Pierre Casimir-Perier (1847-1907) was the President of France from June 24, 1894 to January 15, 1895, succeeding Marie-Francois Sadi-Carnot, who was assassinated by the Italian anarchist Sante or Santos Caserio.

No tale of the ancient British barrow has been found.

"The Adventure of Foulkes Rath" – Here also I find an account of the Addleton tragedy." By Adrian Conan Doyle in *The Exploits of Sherlock Holmes*.

"The Case of the Addleton Tragedy" and "The Case of the Smith-Mortimer Succession" by June Thomson in *The Secret Journals of Sherlock Holmes*.

From Mike Ashley's book see "The Mystery of the Addleton Curse" by **Barrie Roberts**; "The Case of Huret the Boulevard Assassin" by **Robert Weinberg** and **Lois Gresh**; and "The Adventure of the Touch of God" by **Peter Crowther** (The Case of Crosby the Banker); "The Repulsive Story of the Red Leech" by **David Langford**.

The Adventure of the Missing Three-Quarter

"There is Arthur H. Staunton, the rising young forger," [57] said he, "and there was Henry Staunton, whom I helped to hang..." [58]

The Adventure of the Abbey Grange

No other tale mentioned during this story.

The Adventure of the Second Stain

William E. Fleischauer considers which president of France would have been the target of the "Boulevard assassin" and which wrote a letter of thanks (to Holmes). He concludes that Sadi-Carnot was the target but rejects the identification of Huret with Caserio, for although the assassination took place in a *boulevard* (old fortification) in Paris, there was no "tracking" involved – Caserio was arrested on the spot. Sadi-Carnot. Fleischauer suggests was the intended victim of another, earlier assassin supplied by the Moriarty organisation. Holmes was able to stop that assassin (and thus won the gratitude of Sadi-Carnot) but failed to prevent the subsequent successful attempt. Watson, anxious to mention Holmes's medal but embarrassed to lay out the facts in light of the eventual assassination of Sadi-Carnot, obfuscated.

Michael Harrison, in *The World of Sherlock Holmes*, reaches a contrary conclusion. He asserts that Holmes tracked Huret, and that in December, using then-President Casimir-Perier as the "bait," Holmes lured the would-be assassin to Montpellier. Montpellier was of course well-known to Holmes, for he had just finished his researches into coal-tar derivatives there before returning to London in April 1894 ("The Empty House"). Huret hid himself in the old fortifications in Montpellier, but Holmes quickly flushed and captured him, leading Casimir-Perier to express his gratitude.

[57] The Reverend Arthur Henry Stanton, according to Donald Redmond's *Sherlock Holmes: A Study in Sources*, was wrongly accused of authorship of a book of Catholic prayers.

[58] Michael Harrison, in *In the Footsteps of Sherlock Holmes*, points out that the omission of Louis A. Staunton, who with others of his family was convicted of murdering his wife in 1877 and surely would have been in Holmes's index.

"And yet the motives of women are so inscrutable. You remember the woman at Margate whom I suspected for the same reason. No powder on her nose – that proved to be the correct solution."

No further mention of this tale has been found.

THE VALLEY OF FEAR (1914 – 1915)

No mention of another tale during this long story.

HIS LAST BOW (September 1908 – September 1917)

The Adventure of Wisteria Lodge

1. The Singular Adventure of Mr John Scott Eccles

"My dear Watson, you know how bored I have been since we locked up Colonel Carruthers." [59]

2. The Tiger of San Pedro

"Henderson," the inspector answered," is Don [60] Murillo, once called the Tiger of San Pedro…His name was a terror through all Central America…[61] From that moment he

---

[59] This is not Bob Carruthers of "The Solitary Cyclist," who had no apparent military connections. Carruthers is another in the long line of colonels of questionable integrity – see, for example, Colonel Lysander Stark, no doubt an alias ("The Engineer's Thumb"); Colonel Dorking, whose conduct may have been cause for blackmail ("Charles Augustus Milverton"); Colonel James Barclay, "David" to his wife's "Bathsheba" ("The Crooked Man"); Colonel Warburton, the madman ("The Engineer's Thumb"); Colonel Openshaw of the Confederate Army ("The Five Orange Pips"); Colonel Upwood, guilty of scandalous conduct ("The Hound of the Baskervilles); Colonel Emsworth, guilty of overreaction ("The Blanched Soldier"); Colonel Valentine Walter, guilty of treason ("The Bruce-Partington Plans"); Colonel James Moriarty, guilty of brotherhood ("The Empty House"); and Colonel Sebastian Moran, guilty of almost everything ("The Empty House"). Only Colonel Ross of "Silver Blaze," Colonel Spence Munro of "The Copper Beeches," Colonel Hayter of "The Reigate Squires," and Colonel James Damery of "The Illustrious Client" seem free of taint.

[60] A Spanish title applied in courtesy to all of the "better" classes. It preceded the bearer's Christian name (as in "Don Juan"). Thus the inspector's reference to "Don Murillo" is improper.

[61] Any attempt to guess the true location of "San Pedro" by looking for clues in the fateful note ("Our own colours, green and white") is fruitless, for green and white, as Julian Wolff points out in *Practical Handbook of Sherlockian Heraldry* are not the colours of any Central American flag. Wolff does notice that green and *yellow* are the colours of Brazil's flag, a close enough match to support a possible correlation there. Cindy Stevens makes an excellent case for Hispaniola as "San Pedro". Other suggestions include Nicaragua, El Salvador, and Guatemala.

had vanished from the world, and his identity had been a frequent subject for comment in the European Press…" [62]

The Adventure of the Cardboard Box

"…who helped us in the bogus laundry affair…"

No reference to this tale has been found.

The Adventure of the Red Circle

"You arranged an affair for a lodger of mine last year," she said – "Mr Fairdale Hobbs."

No reference to this found.

"The hero of the Long Island Cave mystery?" said Holmes. [63]

---

[62] Operating on the assumption that the green and white colours of Garcia's note were actually meant to be the green and yellow colours of the Brazilian flag. Julian Wolff identifies the "Tiger" as Dom Pedro de Alcantara, or Pedro II, the last emperor of Brazil. Pedro II reigned from 1831 until 1889, when a military coup forced him into exile in Europe. Far from being a "lewd and bloodthirsty tyrant," Pedro II was widely popular; under his reign the slaves were emancipated, export revenues increased, and the railway system expanded. It was the monarchy's ties to a traditionally elite feudal system, more than dissatisfaction with Pedro II himself, that caused pro-capitalist groups – among them the urban middle class, coffee farmers, and the military – to push for a new system of government. Wolff explains the contradiction between Pedro's actual nature and the violent description accorded him here by pointing out that Holmes and Watson were getting information from the point of view of the opposition. Although Watson seems to recall reading about Dom Pedro in the press, his recollection of these press reports may well have been coloured by the passions of Garcia and his confederates. As Wolff puts it, "Anyone who has read the opposition's opinion of our best and wisest men will easily understand."

Evan Wilson concludes instead that the country in question is El Salvador, the dictator Rafael Zaldivar, who ruled from 1876 to 1885 and oversaw numerous Indian uprisings. Charles Higham, in *Adventures of Conan Doyle*, suggests Jose Santos Zelaya (1893-1909), president of Nicaragua. Zelaya, a true dictator who annexed the Mosquito Coast, incited revolutions in neighbouring countries, and attempted to assume control of the Central American Federation, made plenty of enemies – including the U.S. government, which, frustrated by his refusal to allow a canal to be built through Nicaragua, encouraged his Conservative opposition to revolt. Zelaya was forced to resign and go into exile, but not until one year after "Wisteria Lodge" was first published. In a detailed examination of the problem, Henry Dietz also fingers Zelaya as the Tiger, arguing that Watson "anticipated the end of the adventure before it took place in the hopes of hurrying Zelaya's downfall."

Klas Lithner is persuasive in arguing for Justo Rufino Barrios, a dictator of Guatemala from 1873 to 1885. Most fancifully, Rick Lai proposes that Murillo was the man named Mayes, known as the "Tiger of Haiti," whose evil deeds were recorded by Arthur Morrison in *The Red Triangle* (1903), a record of the adventures of Holmes's rival Martin Hewitt.

[63] "The mystery, on true Sherlockian principles, is that there are no caves on Long Island," writes Christopher Morley, the quintessential New Yorker, in "Was Sherlock Holmes an American?" W.E. Edwards suggests that the word was "cove," noting that Glen Cove is a landmark for the golfer and the starch-manufacturer. David H. Galerstein, in "A Solution to the Long Island Cave Mystery," proposes a *man-made* cave on the north shore of Long Island.

The Adventure of the Bruce-Partington Plans

"Suppose that I were Brooks or Woodhouse, or any of the fifty men who have good reason for taking my life…"

No further mention of these two characters.

The Adventure of the Dying Detective

"Place it here among the papers. Good! You can now go and fetch Mr Culverton Smith, of 13, Lower Burke Street…a well-known resident of Sumatra." [64]
  See June Thomson's book The Secret Archives of Sherlock Holmes *The Adventure of the Dying Detective.*

The Disappearance of Lady Frances Carfax

"You know I cannot possibly leave London while old Abrahams is in such mortal terror of his life."
  No further mention in a tale has been found.

See June Thomson's book The Secret Archives of Sherlock Holmes *The Disappearance of Lady Frances Carfax.*

The Adventure of the Devil's Foot

"In March of that year (1897) Dr. Moore Agar, [65] of Harley Street, whose dramatic introduction to Holmes I may some day recount…" [66]

  Other scholars challenge the assumption that Long Island, N.Y., was meant: Long Island, Tennessee, and Long Island, Alabama, are suggested. D. Martin Dakin proposes that Cave (spelled with a capital) was the name of the criminal or victim involved. William Ulrich makes the interesting suggestion that the "Cove" referred to was a term used to describe a cell of the Bohemian Brethren, a secret society, located on Long Island.

[64] Stephen Hayes suggests that the "giant rat of Sumatra" – the mystifying case that Holmes mentions in passing in "The Sussex Vampire" – may have been an experimental animal used by Culverton Smith in his study of bacteria. It was, Hayes continues, Holmes's investigation of the plague-stricken ship *Matilda Briggs* (also mentioned in "The Sussex Vampire") that carried the rat from Sumatra to London and led Holmes to uncover Smith's misdeeds. Mary Ann Kluge identifies Smith himself as the giant rat of Sumatra.
[65] Charles Thomas, writing as "Percy Trevelyan," in *Mr. Holmes in Cornwall* identifies Agar as the cousin of the Agar-Robertes family, chief landowners of the parish of Mullion. He suggests that Dr. Agar specifically directed Holmes to travel to Poldhu, thinking that his cousin might be of assistance and that the ozone-laden air of Cornwall would have "therapeutic values."

[66] Watson never published this case.

Dr Moore Agar – See 'The Tragedy of Saxon's Gate' in David Stuart Davies book "The Game's Afoot" & 'The case of the Faithful Retainer' by Amy Myers in Mike Ashley's book.

THE CASE-BOOK OF SHERLOCK HOLMES (Oct.1921-Apr.1927)

The Adventure of the Illustrious Client

"You may remember his negotiations with Sir George Lewis [67] over the Hammerford Will case."

This case was not published.

"De Merville of Khyber fame?" [68]
"A complex mind," said Holmes. "All great criminals have that. My old friend Charlie Peace [69] was a violin virtuoso. Wainwright [70] was no mean artist."

---

[67] Sir George Lewis (1833-1911), of the firm of Lewis & Lewis, was the most famous solicitor in England, the confidant of the Prince of Wales and countless others.

[68] The battle of the Khyber Pass occurred in the second Afghan war (1878-1879), one of three wars in which Britain – threatened by Russia's interest in Afghanistan – attempted to seize control of the territory for itself. Under terms of the 1879 Treaty of Gandamak, Yakub Khan, the emir of Afghanistan, ceded the Khyber Pass to the British; and by the end of the year, following the murder of a British envoy, British forces had occupied Kabul. Watson carried out his military service in this second Afghan campaign.

[69] Irving Fenton describes Charles Peace (1832-1879) as a "burglar, murderer, liar, wife-beater, braggart, actor, inventor [and] violin virtuoso." A native of Sheffield, Peace started his criminal career as a teenager, spending several stints in jail for burglarising people's homes. Between prison terms, he taught himself to play a violin with one string billing himself as "the modern Paganini" at fairs and other venues. Fenton credits Peace with inventing the burglar's kit, improving the machinery at Dartmoor's prison, and fashioning a "smoke helmet" for firemen, among other innovations. His downfall was the 1876 murder of Arthur Dyson, the husband of Peace's purported mistress. Eluding capture by living as "Mr. Thompson" in London for two years, he was finally caught committing burglary in Blackheath. Pearce was recognised and quickly sentenced to death – the jury was out for only ten minutes – and, writes Fenton, "on February 25, 1879, the law ended his terrestrial friendship, at least with Sherlock Holmes." His collection of violins and banjos, one of the best in England, was auctioned off after his death. One wonders whether Holmes purchased one of Peace's violins as a souvenir.

Like Holmes, Peace was a master of disguise, capable of altering his appearance merely by jutting out his lower jaw or wearing a pair of goggles. For a time he posed as a one-armed man, hiding his real limb underneath his clothes. An 1894 *Strand* article entitled "Burglars and Burglary" notes that Peace used this effect to conceal the tell-tale fact that he was missing the forefinger of his right hand. "After he left Sheffield on 29th. November, 1876," the article recounts, "his description was posted at every police station in the country. So he made himself [a false arm] which he placed in his sleeve, hanging his violin on the hook when engaged in walking about and taking stock of 'crackable' residences, and screwing in a fork in the place of the hook for use at meals. For something like two years, the impressible Peace walked this earth short of a hand, while the police were looking for a man short of a *finger*.

No other tale mentioned during this adventure.

The Adventure of the Blanched Soldier

"I had also a commission from the Sultan of Turkey which called for immediate action…" [71]

Holmes mentioned in this story that he was once able to do Sir James Saunders a professional service, but no tale appears to have developed.

The Adventure of the Mazarin Stone & The Adventure of the Three Gables

No other tales mentioned during these adventures.

The Adventure of the Sussex Vampire *

* See *The Case of the Vampire's Mark* by Bill Crider in 'Murder in Baker Street.'

The letter to Holmes from Morrison, Morrison, and Dodd [72] – "We have not forgotten your successful action in the case of Matilda Briggs." [73]

---

[70] This might have been Thomas Griffiths Wainwright (1794-1852), a painter, art critic for *London Magazine* (writing essays under the pen names Egomet Bonmot and James Weathercock) and suspected murderer. Attempting to evade suspicion for the deaths of his uncle, his mother-in-law, and his sister-in-law, he lived in France for six years but, upon returning to England, was convicted on an old forgery charge and exiled to Tasmania for the remainder of his life. Or Holmes might be referring to Henry Wainwright (?-1875), a brush manufacturer who killed his mistress and was caught attempting to dispose of her dismembered body parts. The artistic abilities of Wainwright who maintained his innocence but confessed just before being hanged, are unknown.

[71] Abdul-Hamid II (1842-1918) assumed the throne in 1876 after his brother, Murad V suffered a mental breakdown. A cruel despot who relied upon his secret police and censorship to keep the populace in line. Abdul-Hamid dismissed Parliament and suspended the constitution, ruling in seclusion from his palace and adopting a Pan-Islamic stance for Turkey. He was deposed in 1909 by the revolutionary Young Turks movement, which was agitating for a constitutional government. In 1901 and 1902, Turkish encroachments on Aden had created dangerously high tensions between England and Turkey, and perhaps Mycroft and his cronies asked Sherlock to assist the sultan in smoothing the diplomatic waters by looking into the early stirrings of the revolution.

[72] The combination of vampires, tea brokerage, and a law firm specialising in machinery produces a rather strange marriage indeed, and later in the tale, Ferguson recounts that he met his Peruvian wife during a business transaction involving the importation of nitrates – which would not seem to have anything remotely to do with tea. Gordon B. Speck expresses scepticism of the entire situation in "The Adventure of the Sussex Vampire, Hoax, Jokes and Hubris." The combination of vampires, South America and nitrates suggests to him that Ferguson may well have been involved with the importation of bat guano. Was Ferguson too embarrassed to admit how he made his living?

"Matilda Briggs was not the name of a young woman," Watson, said Holmes in a reminiscent voice. "It was a ship which is associated with the giant rat of Sumatra, a story for which the world is not yet prepared." [74]

See *The Case of the Sumatran Rat* by June Thomson in 'The Secret Chronicles of Sherlock Holmes.'

"...Vittoria, the circus belle...Vanderbilt and the Yeggman [75]... and Vigor the Hammersmith wonder. [76]

See: *The Adventure of Vittoria the Circus Belle* by Edward D. Hoch in Mike Ashley's book.

Also: *The Case of the Itinerant Yeggman* By June Thomson in 'The Secret Files of Sherlock Holmes.'

---

[73] Richard W. Clarke discovers that the *Matilda Briggs* was owned by the Oriental Trading Company, based in Shanghai. Another, more intriguing angle is pursued by Edgar W. Smith, who calls attention to the ill-fated *Marie Celeste*. Found mysteriously abandoned between the Azores and Portugal in 1872, she had sailed from New York under the leadership of Captain Benjamin Spooner Briggs. The captain had been accompanied by his wife, Sarah Elizabeth Briggs, and their daughter, Sophie Matilda Briggs.

[74] This was probably the species *Sundamys infraluteus,* discovered by Guy G. Musser and Cameron Newcomb and reported in 1893 in their 270-page article in the *Bulletin of the American Museum of Natural History*. They describe the adult male, indigenous to the tropical forests of Sumatra, as weighing in excess of 22 pounds and measuring 24 inches long, including the tail. Having obtained six specimens for study, Musser and Newcomb note that the rat "is difficult to catch and its habits are unknown."

[75] A yegg, or yeggman, is a burglar or a safe-cracker. Although the exact origins of the term are murky. William Pinkerton, of the Pinkerton National Detective Agency, believed both "yegg" and "hobo" to be related to gypsies. Excerpts from speeches given by Pinkerton between 1900 and 1907 reveal the following logic: "When a particularly clever thief is found among a gypsy tribe, he is selected as the 'Yegg' or chief thief. This expression is now adopted by the better class of thieves among tramps and hobos of this country. As late as twenty years ago, one tramp meeting another and wishing to be sure of his identity as a professional tramp would address him as 'Ho-Beau.' This expression subsequently developed into the word 'hobo.' If a tribe or band of tramps found a particularly persistent beggar or daring thief, they, using the expression of the gypsies, calling him a 'Yegg.' Then came the name of 'John Yegg' and finally the word 'Yeggman.'"

[76] One is tempted to connect this "wonder" with the famous ornate *fin-de-siecle* gilt and velvet auditorium of the Lyric Theatre, Hammersmith, which opened in 1895 and was undoubtedly well known to the musical Holmes. Howard Lachtman identified the "wonder" as a mechanical horse produced by the Vigor company. Its virtues are described in the Victorian advertisement on p. 1558, Volume II, *The New Annotated Sherlock Holmes*.

The Case of the Hammersmith Wonder by June Thomson in 'The Secret Chronicles of Sherlock Holmes.'

The Adventure of the Three Garridebs

"I remember the date very well, for it was in the same month that Holmes refused a knighthood for services which may perhaps some day be described." [77]

No other tale was mentioned during this short story.

The Problem of Thor Bridge

"Among those unfinished tales is that of Mr. James Phillimore, who, stepping back into his own house to get his umbrella, was never more seen in this world." [78]

I have identified five pastiches on the disappearance of Mr. James Phillimore as follows:

Adrian Conan Doyle & John Dickson Carr wrote the first entitled *The Adventure of the Highgate Miracle* from the volume 'More Exploits of Sherlock Holmes' (1964).

June Thomson *The Case of the Vanishing Head-Waiter* from 'The Secret Files of Sherlock Holmes' (1990).

Alan Stockwell *The Singular Adventure of the Eccentric Gentleman* in 'The Singular Adventures of Mr Sherlock Holmes' (2003).

Mel Gilden *The Adventure of the Forgotten Umbrella* from Michael Kurland's 'My Sherlock Holmes – Untold Stories of the Great Detective' (2003).

F. Gwynplaine MacIntyre *The Enigma of the Warwickshire Vortex* in Mike Ashley's 'New Sherlock Holmes Adventures' (2004).

"No less remarkable is that of the cutter *Alicia* which sailed one spring morning into a small patch of mist from where she never again remerged, nor was anything further ever heard of herself and her crew." [79]

---

[77] In "The Golden Pince-Nez," Watson reports that Holmes accepted a Legion of Honour from the French president for assisting in "the tracking and arrest of Huret, the Boulevard assassin." This makes Holmes's refusal of a knighthood all the more curious. Trevor H. Hall explains the discrepancy by guessing that Holmes accepted the Legion of Honour in tribute to his grandmother, the sister of the French artist Vernet. The spurned offer of a knighthood may have been part of Edward VII's coronation honours, which coincidentally (or perhaps not) included the knighthood of Arthur Conan Doyle.

[78] Phillimore's mysterious disappearance has inspired the "James Phillimore Society," a group of Sherlockians who are devoted to magic and science fiction.

"A third case worthy of note is that of Isadora Persano, the well-known journalist and duellist, who was found stark staring mad with a match box in front of him which contained a remarkable worm said to be unknown to science." [80]

Startingly, in the manuscript of "Thor Bridge," Watson originally records the "worm" as a caterpillar.

See: *The Remarkable Worm* by Carolyn Wheat in 'Murder in Baker Street.'

Also: *The Case of the Remarkable Worm* by June Thomson in 'The Secret Files of Sherlock Holmes.'

The Adventure of the Creeping Man

See June Thomson's book The Secret Archives of Sherlock Holmes *The Adventure of the Creeping Man.*

The Adventure of the Lion's Mane

As above.

The Adventure of the Veiled Lodger

"The source of these outrages is known, and if they are repeated I have Mr. Holmes's authority for saying that the whole story concerning the politician, the lighthouse, and the trained cormorant will be given to the public." [81]

---

[79] Philip Weller notes, "*Lloyd's Sailing Vessels* for 1891-92 includes a wooden see bark *(sic)* called the 'Alicia', which was built in 1887, and which was wrecked in 1891."

[80] Speculations abound regarding the remarkable worm. Edgar W. Smith embraces the amusing suggestion of Rolfe Boswell, who thought the worm not as a biological specimen but as an optical illusion used in the Gestalt school of psychology. One could hypnotise oneself, or possibly go mad, by staring at a whirling spiral an inch in diameter. Boswell likened the effect to that of staring fixedly at a coiled watch spring, and noted that the *Shorter Oxford Dictionary* gave one definition of "worm" as "A spring or strip of metal of spiral shape 1724." "Presumably," Boswell wrote, "if you gaze at such a worm long enough, you'll be *Persano non grata*, if not 'stark staring mad.'"

A more serious effort is put forward by R.P. Graham, who unearths an 1891 article that was written by Sir John Ross (uncle of famed Antarctic explorer Sir James Clark Ross, both of whom sailed in search of the Northwest Passage in 1818) and entitled "A Voyage of Discovery, made under the Orders of the Admiralty, in His Majesty's Ships *Isabella* and *Alexander*, for the Purpose of Exploring Baffin's Bay and Enquiring into the Probability of a North-West Passage." Ross's work contains the intriguing text, "we sounded with the deepsea clamms, which brought up a quantity of mud, in which were *five worms of a species that had not been seen before.*" Graham asks, "Who of Ross's crew…preserved these Baffin Bay worms, and who put one of their descendents into a match-box to help drive poor Isadora Persano 'stark staring mad'?"

See: *The Case of the Abandoned Lighthouse* by June Thomas in 'The Secret files of Sherlock Holmes.'

Also: *The Adventure of the Trained Cormorant* published as 'Holmes in Scotland' (*Blackwood's Magazine*, September 1953); copyright 1953 by W.R. Duncan Macmillan.

No other tale mentioned during this story.

The Adventure of Shoscombe Old Place

"It is a very fine demonstration," he answered. "In the St. Pancras case you may remember that a cap was found beside the dead policeman." [82]

No tale mentioned during this story.

The Adventure of the Retired Colourman

"You know that I am preoccupied with this case of the two Coptic Patriarchs, which shall come to a head today." [83]

No other tale mentioned during this final short story.

---

[81] Donald A. Redmond, * in "Still Sits the Cormorant," identifies the politician as Joseph Chamberlain, who was associated with a scandal in the 1890s related to a mutual assurance company lampooned by *Punch* as the "Cormorant Friendly Society." Derek Hinrich suggests that the "politician" was "Dollman," the pseudonym of the English traitor described in Erskine Childer's *Riddle of the Sands* (1903), whose plans for a British invasion involved a German troop ship called the *Kormoran* (cormorant).

* According to the Selected Sources in *The New Annotated Sherlock Holmes*, Volume II, the article cited was by Christopher Redmond, *not* Donald Redmond.

[82]."The former borough of St. Pancras is home to St. Pancras Old Church, built in the fourteenth century and thought to be the first Christian church in England. That a policeman was murdered in the isolated and somewhat mysterious place – 'Walk not there too late,' counselled one Elizabethan topographer." area evinces little surprise, for as Peter Ackroyd notes, the area around the church "has always been an isolated and somewhat mysterious place – 'Walk there not too late' counsellec one Elizabethan topographer."

[83] Professor Coram of "The Golden Pince-Nez" was engaged in a study of documents found in Coptic monasteries. Strangely, only in the year 1899 were there two Coptic patriarchs in office, Cyril Maqar, head of the Catholic Patriarchate (which was founded in 1895 but named no patriarch until 1899), and Cyril V, known as Hanna al-Nasikh, who served as patriarch of the Coptic Orthodox Church from 1874 to 1927 (with a short respite in 1912). Wladimir V. Bogomoletz suggests that Dr. Watson may have confused the date of "The Retired Colourman" when he stated that it occurred in the "summer of 1898." Of course, the "two Coptic patriarchs" for whom Holmes acted may not both have actually been holding that office – Holmes may have acted for both men in 1898, and Watson, writing up the story many years later, simply *called* both patriarchs, as honorifics due them.

Conclusion

From the four novels and fifty-six short stories I have re-read for this chapter, the following pastiches, parodies and apocryphal tales have been noted as follows:

Stories mentioned in the canon and published – 59

Stories mentioned in the canon and not published – 57

Making a total of 116 stories in all.

Footnotes for this chapter and reference came from *The New Annotated Sherlock Holmes*, Volumes I, II & III.

References

A Study in Scarlet

SCHENCK, R.T.A. "Baker Street Fables." *Baker Street Journal* 2, No.2 (April. 1952): 85-92.

HOLSTEIN, L.S. "7, Knowledge of Chemistry – Profound," *Baker Street Journal* 4, No.1 (Jan. 1954): 44-49.

HUBER, C.L. "The Sherlock Holmes Blood Test: The Solution to a Century-Old Mystery." *Baker Street Journal* 37, No. 4 (Dec. 1987): 215-220.

STONE, P.M. "The Other Friendship: A Speculation." In PROFILE BY GASLIGHT: AN IRREGULAR READER ABOUT THE PRIVATE LIFE OF SHERLOCK HOLMES, edited by Edgar W. Smith, 97-103, New York: Simon & Schuster, 1944.

McGOWAN, R.J. "A Chemist's Evaluation of Sherlock Holmes's Monograph on Tobacco." *Sherlock Holmes Journal* 19, No.3 (Winter 1989): 86-88.

The Sign of Four

REDMOND, D.A. SHERLOCK HOLMES: A STUDY IN SOURCES. Kingston & Montreal: McGill-Queen's University Press, 1982.

LEAVITT, R.K. "Who Was Cecil Forrester?" *Baker Street Journal* [O.S.] 1, No.2 (Apr. 1946): 201-204.

DOUGLASS, R. "The Camberwell Poisoner." *Ellery Queen's Mystery Magazine* 9. No. 39 (Feb. 1947): 57-63.

MEYER, C.A. "The Remarkable Forrester Case." *Canadian Holmes* 13, No. 4, (Summer 1990): 26-27.

The Adventures of Sherlock Holmes

GOODMAN, C. D. D.D.S. "The Dental Holmes." *Baker Street Journal* [O.S.] 2, No. 4. (Oct. 1947): 381-393.

The Return of Sherlock Holmes

WOLFF, C. "I Have My Eye on a Suite in Baker Street." *Baker Street Journal* [O.S.] 1, No. 3 (July 1946); 296-299.

STEVENS, C. "The Location of San Pedro." In ANNUAL REPORT 1992: THE WISTERIA LODGE CONTRACT, edited by Philip Weller, 47-49. Hampshire, England: Franco-Midland Hardware Company, 1992.

WILSON, E. M. "Sherlock Holmes and Latin America: An Identification and Some Lovely Ladies." *Baker Street Journal* 22, No. 3 (Sept. 1972): 148-152.

DIETZ, H. A. "Murillo and San Pedro: An Excursion in Identification." *Baker Street Journal* 39, No. 3 (Sept. 1989): 153-168.

LITHNER, K. "San Pedro Revisited." *Baker Street Miscellanea* 50 (Summer 1987): 27-30.

LAI, R. "The Savage Reversion." *Golden Perils* 6, No. 4 (May 1986): 22-25.

---------- "The Tiger of Haiti." *Wheelwritings* 8. No. 3 (Jan. 1986): 18-24.

MORLEY, C. "Was Sherlock Holmes an American?" In 221B: STUDIES IN SHERLOCK HOLMES, edited by Vincent Starrett, 5-15 New York, Macmillan Co., 1940.

GALERSTEIN, D.H. "A Solution to the Long Island Cave Mystery." *Baker Street Journal* 33, No. 4 (Dec. 1983): 233-234.

ULRICH, W. "Notes After an Evening in the Cave." *Prescott's Press* [N.S.] 15 (Sept. 1992): 7-8.

KLUGE, M. A. "Looking Back at the 'Dying Detective.'" *Camden House Journal* 7, No. 7 (July 1985): 2.

The Case-Book of Sherlock Holmes

FENTON, I. "On Friendship." *Baker Street Journal* 9, No.1 (Jan. 1959): 23-25.

SPECK, G.R. "Holmes, Heroics, Hiatus: A Man to Match Swiss Mountains." In COMMANDING VIEWS FROM THE EMPTY HOUSE, edited by William R. Cochran & Gordon R. Speck, 111-113, Indianapolis: Gasogene Books, 1997.

CLARKE, R.W. "On the Nomenclature of Watson's Ships." *Baker Street Journal* [O.S.] 1, No. 2 (1946): 119-121.

SMITH, E.W. "From the Editor's Commonplace Book." *Baker Street Journal* [O.S.] 1, No. 2 (1946): 187-194.

LACHTMAN, H. "Vigor: A Case for Identity." *Baker Street Journal* 27, No. 1 (March 1977): 37-40.

GRAHAM, R. P. "The Unknown Worm." *Baker Street Journal* [O.S.] 2, No. 2 (Apr. 1947): 212.

REDMOND, C. "Still Sits the Cormorant." *Sherlock Holmes Journal* 11, No. 2 (Summer 1973): 58-63.

HINRICH, D. "The Politician, the Lighthouse and the Trained Cormorant: An Hypothesis." *Sherlock Holmes Journal* 21, No. 1 (Winter 1992): 22-23.

Chapter 23

Sherlock Holmes & Jack the Ripper: 1888-2011

Introduction

Much conjecture has taken place over the years amongst Sherlockians and other interested parties. This revolves around the vexing question – **"Why was Sherlock Holmes not involved in the Jack the Ripper murders?"** The Whitechapel murders took place between the summer and autumn of 1888. Mike Ashley notes in his book that – "Throughout the months of August – November 1888 Holmes was probably consulted on the Jack the Ripper case but this was one series of murders that Watson did not write up and probably explains some of the confusion in dates during this period."

In this chapter I have attempted to draw together as much information as possible on the Ripper murders, but whether this comes anywhere near answering this question, readers will have to wait and see and form their own opinions.

Holmes & Crime

The Victorian public was fascinated by sensational crime, and the press eagerly satisfied that fascination. Watson describes Holmes himself as having an immense knowledge of sensational literature. There do seem to have been fashions in crime, probably as a result of imitations of some of the more lurid crimes given coverage by the newspapers. There was a great popularity in late-Victorian London for dismembering murder victims and distributing the parts around the city. One particularly audacious murderer travelled by omnibus, carrying the head of his victim wrapped in a napkin on his knees. It is probably apocryphal, however, he almost gave himself away after asking the fare and being told that it was "sixpence a head"!

Much of the crime at the time was, however, less grotesque, although of a nature which was particularly abhorrent to the middle and upper classes of Victorian society, being crimes against property. As with many other aspects of Victorian morals, there was ambivalence between the supposed public attitudes to crime and actual private, individual attitudes. At the end of the century Doyle's brother-in-law, E.W. Hornung, began to produce a series about an upper-class gentleman-criminal called Raffles, a character who quickly caught the admiration of a wide audience. Holmes himself was not averse to committing such crimes as burglary in the pursuit of those he suspected, and he occasionally acted as his own court of law in deciding whether those he discovered to be criminally guilty should be brought before the official courts.

The question must, almost inevitably, be asked as to why Holmes does not appear to have been called in to assist the police with the most notorious crime of the age, the "Jack the Ripper" murders that occurred in 1888. It does seem unlikely that Holmes would not have been involved himself in the investigation, even if he had not been consulted officially, and it would seem equally unlikely that – being who he was – he would not have found the criminal, or criminals, involved. Thus it is possible that he did just this, and that there was no subsequent public recognition of the fact because of some political, high-society or simple police embarrassment involved in the solving of a notorious crime. It certainly seems strange that the hundreds of extra policemen drafted into the Whitechapel district were all suddenly withdrawn shortly after the last murder, when no culprit had been found. It is a fact that the Metropolitan Police Commissioner of that time deliberately interfered with some of the evidence, and that he was later forced to resign in the face of public allegations of incompetence. It is also true that the Scotland Yard documents were closed to public inspection for many decades, and that some of these documents are now missing. Perhaps these missing documents revealed not only the criminal but also that a certain consulting detective had been foremost in discovering his identity.

The Real World of Sherlock Holmes: The true crimes investigated by Arthur Conan Doyle by Peter Costello (1991) Carrol & Graf Publishers Inc. New York.

The Trail of Jack the Ripper

ON WEDNESDAY, 19 APRIL 1905, Conan Doyle was one of a small group from the Crimes Club who met in the East End of London to follow up the trail of Jack the Ripper.

Conan Doyle had long been familiar with the story of the mysterious scourge of Whitechapel who had murdered a series of at least five women in the autumn of 1888 – the year that *A Study in Scarlet* was published as a book. These seemingly motiveless crimes had thrilled and shocked the whole country, indeed the whole world, and ripples of the wave of horror had even reached Conan Doyle in Southsea, so placid in its respectability. During September 1889 the Hampshire Psychical Society was formed, with Dr Conan Doyle and Prof. William Barrett among the Vice-Presidents. A little later, in November, a local paper suggested that Conan Doyle in his twin roles as crime novelist and spiritualist, should attempt to trace Jack the Ripper by calling up the spirit of what some thought was the latest victim of his dissecting knife.

The mutilated trunk of a female had been found under a railway bridge in Pinchin Street on 10 September 1889. The head and legs were never found, and the woman was never identified. Even at the time the police did not connect this crime with Jack the Ripper, and though it received sensational coverage in the papers, it is not now accepted as one of the series.

This piece of local facetiousness suggests that even at that date Conan Doyle was known locally for his interest in real-life crime. What role spiritualism was to play in solving the mystery of Jack the Ripper we shall see in due course, and although nothing as sordid as the Whitechapel murders now appears in his fiction, Conan Doyle, like every other criminologist, remained fascinated by Jack the Ripper and the enigma of his identity.

On 2 December 1892 Conan Doyle visited the notorious Black Museum at New Scotland Yard, along with Dr Gilbert, the medical officer at Newgate, his brother-in-law E.W. Hornung who was later to achieve fame with his tales about ace "cracksman" *Raffles*; and Jerome K. Jerome at the time editor of the *Idler*, but better known for his widely acclaimed *Three Men in a Boat* of three years before. This gruesome show, housed in a cold, ill-lit room in the basement of the building on the Thames Embankment contained relics of crime and murder going back several decades.

Of all the grim exhibits, Conan Doyle's attention was caught by a fading photograph of the disembowelled corpse of the Ripper's last victim, Mary Kelly, and by a letter and postcard written in red ink signed by him. Sir Robert Anderson claimed that these communications, later removed from the Black Museum, [84] were the work of a journalist, but he refused to name him. However, from internal evidence it is clear that they were really written by the murderer.

The letter is dated 25 September. By that date the Whitechapel murderer had killed two women: Mary Ann Nichols on Friday, 31 August in Buck's Row, and Annie Chapman called "Dark Annie", on 8 September in Hanbury Street. (Two earlier murders, those of Emma Elizabeth Smith on April 3 and Martha Tabram on 6 August, had been bracketed with the Ripper murders but subsequently eliminated.) The killings had caused a sensation and the writer was exploiting this. The envelope was postmarked "London East Central, 28 September 1888". It was addressed to the Central News Agency office who passed it on to the police, but the text was not released until after the double murder of Elizabeth Stride and Catherine Eddowes on 30 September. For Conan Doyle these letters brought the criminal vividly alive.

Dear Boss,
I keep hearing the police have caught me but they won't fix me just yet. I have laughed when they look so clever and talk about being on the right track. That joke about Leather Apron gave me real fits. I am down on whores and I shan't quit ripping them till I do get buckled. Grand work the last job was. I gave the lady no time to squeal. How can they catch me now? I love my work and want to start again. You will soon hear of me with my funny little games. I saved some of the proper red stuff in a ginger beer bottle over the last job to write with, but it went thick like glue, and I can't use it. Red ink is fit enough I hope ha ha. The next job I do I shall clip the lady's ears off and send to the police officers just for jolly – Wouldn't you keep this letter back till I do a bit more work, then give it out straight. My knife is nice and sharp I want to get to work right away if I get a chance. Good luck.
  Yours truly,
  Jack the ripper
Don't mind me giving the trade name. Wasn't good enough to post this before I got all the red ink off my hands curse it. They say I'm a doctor now ha ha.

The postcard, postmarked "London East, October 1", not only referred to the previous letter which was still unpublished, but also to details of the next two which were not as yet public knowledge by the time the card arrived at the Central News Office.

---

[84] They were returned anonymously in the autumn of 1988

I was not codding dear old Boss when I gave you the tip. You'll hear about Saucy Jack's work tomorrow. Double event this time. Number one squealed a bit. Couldn't finish straight off. Had no time to get ears for police. Thanks for keeping last letter back till I got to work again.
    Jack the Ripper.

These communications had been sent to the editor of the news agency. An understanding of how news agencies work and their role in modern publicity implies a high level of education, which the demented style of the letters scarcely hides. As the denizens of the East End had already realised ("They say I'm a doctor"): Jack the Ripper was a "Toff".

The murders on 30 September – the Ripper's double event – of Elizabeth Stride in Berner Street just before 1am and of Catherine Eddowes in Mitre Square about half an hour later, were followed by a pause. All doubts about there being a maniac at large were gone, and the population of London was thrown into a fever of fear and excitement.

Then on Friday 9 November Mary Jean Kelly, an Irish girl of about twenty-five, was butchered in her room in Miller's Court off Dorset Street. This was the last Ripper murder in a series of five. Then the killer, whoever he was, vanished as mysteriously as he had arrived.

What did Conan Doyle think at that time of the case? In the summer of 1894 he outlined to an American journalist just how Sherlock Holmes would have set about tracing the culprit.

I am not in the least degree either a sharp or an observant man myself. I try to get inside the skin of a sharp man and see how things strike him. I remember going to Scotland Yard Museum and looking at the letter which was received from the Ripper. Of course it may have been a hoax, but there were reasons to think it genuine, and in any case it was well to find out who wrote it.

It was written in red ink in a clerkly hand. I tried to think how Holmes might have deduced the writer of that letter. The most obvious point was that it had been written by someone who had been in America. It began "Dear Boss", and contained the phrase "fix it up" and several others which are not usual with Britishers. Then we have the quality of the paper, and a round, easy, clerkly hand. He was, therefore, a man accustomed to the use of a pen.

Having determined that much, we can not avoid the inference that there must be somewhere letters which this man has written over his own name, or documents or accounts that could readily be traced to him. Oddly enough, the police did not, as far as I know, think of that, and so they failed to accomplish anything. Holmes's plan would have been to reproduce the letters in facsimile and on each plate briefly indicate the peculiarities of the handwriting. Then publish these facsimiles in the leading newspapers of Great Britain and America and in connection with them offer a reward to anyone who could show them a letter or any other specimen of the same handwriting. Such a course would have enlisted millions of people as detectives on the case.

In fact the Metropolitan Police issues facsimiles of both the letter and the postcard on a poster on 3 October 1888, asking anyone who recognised the writing to communicate with them or the nearest police station. Such answers as they received led nowhere. But they did not issue an analysis of the handwriting which well might have made tracing the writer easier. Even in 1894 this might have been done and the Ripper caught, but there is good reason to believe that by then the police knew the culprit was either dead or well out of the way in a lunatic asylum.

Among the members of the Crimes Club there was so great an interest in the case that Ingleby Oddie, then a lawyer, arranged with Dr Frederick Gordon Brown, the City of London Police Surgeon, to visit the scenes of the murders with Churton Collins, H.B. Irving, Dr Crosse, and of course Sir Arthur Conan Doyle.

They were to be guided by Dr Brown himself and by City of London Police detectives familiar with the details of the crimes. In this they were lucky Brown was one of the doctors who had been called to Mitre Square to examine the body of Catherine Eddowes, on which he later performed the post-mortem. He told the Coroner that some anatomical knowledge was displayed by the killer's work, but whether this was from medical training or skill in cutting up animals was not clear. The entrails had been removed and deliberately placed on the right shoulder – which has since led some writers to see this as an example of Masonic ritual murder. Brown's notes on his post-mortem as well as a set of mortuary photographs survive, from which the horror of the crimes can clearly be seen. From him Conan Doyle would have gained a direct and grim idea of the real nature of the murders.

The party met at the Police Hospital in Bishopsgate on a wet and dreary afternoon. At that date, long before the bombs of the Second World War, Whitechapel had changed little since the heyday of the Ripper. Here Conan Doyle, who had seen many aspects of life now, was exposed to a new experience.

It was the Eve of the Passover, and the Jewish community of the East End was crowding into the narrow streets, especially Petticoat Lane. The party could not use their umbrellas, or even keep together so great was the crush. It all seemed immensely curious and foreign, especially "the strange articles of food." As Oddie later recalled:

Most of the married women wore black wigs, the idea being that they should conceal their charms from the eyes of all save their lawful husbands. Many of the women carried hens under their arms, on there way to having their throats cut by a priest according to ritual with a clean knife without a notch on the blade which was carefully shown to and inspected by all his patrons.

There were other booths where chickens could be plucked; and others where cows could be milked into the women's clean jugs. Moses as Oddie observed, was acting as an unqualified assistant to the local Medical Officers of Health.

One theory about the identity of Jack the Ripper was that he might have been one of those Jewish ritual slaughtermen, and that the local Jewish community was hiding him. After the Mitre Square murder an inscription was found in a hallway: "The Jowes are not the people who will be blamed for nothing." Nearby was a bloodstained fragment of the victim's apron cut off by the murderer on which he wiped his hands. This writing was removed for fear of inciting anti-Jewish feelings, very much alive in Whitechapel after the trial of Israel Lipski the year before.

But the Juwes are not the Jews, but the celebrated murderers of Masonic tradition:[85] yet another clue which has been taken up as pointing to some Masonic connection with the crimes.

The Crimes Club party also saw inside a dosshouse and other cheap lodgings typical of the area, the sort of places that the victims of the Ripper lodged in, and for which they raised the rent by walking the streets. According to John Churton Collins in his diary record of the walk:

Conan Doyle seemed very much interested, particularly in the Petticoat Lane part of the expedition, and laughed as I said "Caliban would have turned his nose up at this."

But they had not come for local colour, but for local crimes. As they toured them, the sites of the Ripper murders all presented one common characteristic: they were dark, obscure and secret. Yet all were chosen to be easy to escape from. Buck's Row, Hanbury Street, Mitre Square and Miller's Court, all were provided with exits and with cover. Churton Collins records what he and Conan Doyle saw in Miller's Court where Mary Kelly died:

This latter place was a dismal hole seen on a dark, wet, gloomy afternoon. It consisted of one very small room, with a small window, a fire, a chair and a bed. It was sombre and sinister, unwholesome and depressing, and it was approached by a single doorstep from a grimy covered passage leading from Dorset Street into a courtyard.

Here, behind the safety of a locked door, Mary Kelly was murdered and butchered, her nose, breasts and intestines cut out and placed on the table beside the bed. The murder scene was also photographed by the police. Conan Doyle and his friends were shown the picture: "a mass of human flesh," recalled Oddie. "In my twenty-seven years as a London Coroner I have seen many gruesome sights, but for sheer horror this surpasses anything I ever set eyes on."

That had been the last Ripper murder, on 9 November 1888. Were the earlier murders mere gratuitous, or were they all part of a pattern which led up to the death of the unfortunate Mary Kelly? She had been born in Limerick, Ireland, and lived in Wales until her husband was killed in a mine explosion. She had been in "a fashionable house" in the West end of London, and claimed she had lived in France as the mistress of a mysterious protector who was never identified.

From there she had escaped into the East End, only to meet her death. Had someone been hunting her and her associates down, someone from her past? What is the significance of the fact that Catherine Eddowes, who had lived with a man named John Kelly, had called herself "Kate Kelly"? Had she been killed by someone who knew only that he sought a woman called Kelly? What was the secret that those unfortunate women, all of whom lived in the neighbourhood of Dorset Street, shared in life and in death?

---

[85] Jubelo, Jubela, and Jubelum, who, during the time of the building of Solomon's Temple, murdered Hiram Abiff, the Grand Master. In fact they are known as the "ruffians" more frequently than the "Juwes".

Dr Gordon Brown, the Crimes Club guide, had been the doctor who attended the corpse of Catherine Eddowes at Mitre Square. According to Churtun Collins in his diary the next day:

He was inclined to think that he [the murderer] was or had been a medical student, as he undoubtedly had a knowledge of human anatomy, but that he was also a butcher, as the mutilations slashing the nose, etc., were butcher's cuts.

The suggestion that the Ripper might be some kind of medical man was an early and persistent one.

Yet curiously (for remember we are in 1905) Dr Brown concluded that there was absolutely no foundation to the theory that the Ripper was a homicidal maniac doctor, whose body had been found in the Thames, though this was the theory of Scotland Yard. He was more of the opinion that the murderer suffered from a sort of homicidal satyriasis – that sexual perversion had led to the murders.

In fact there seem to have been two theories at Scotland Yard, and the homicidal maniac taken from the Thames was the one espoused by Sir Melville McNaughton and by Conan Doyle's friend Major Arthur Griffiths – both to be members of the Crimes Club. Sir Robert Anderson, writing five years later in 1910, said that Jack the Ripper was a low-class Polish Jew, later named as Aaron Kosminski.

What were Conan Doyle's own ideas, now that he had been given a chance to see the scenes of the crimes? By now he was as familiar as anyone with the details of the crime of the century. He is recorded as believing that "Jack the Ripper disguised himself as a woman in order to escape from the scenes of his crimes." This notion perhaps arose from the finding of burnt-up women's clothes in the fireplace of Miller's Court. One of the better informed writers on the Ripper murders, Tom Cullen, wrote to Adrian Conan Doyle in 1962 to ask about his father's theories. Adrian replied:

More than thirty years have passed, it is difficult to recall his views in detail on the Ripper Case. However, I do remember that he considered it likely that the man had a rough knowledge of surgery and probably clothed himself as a woman to approach his victims without arousing suspicion on their part.

Among Conan Doyle's fellow-members of the Crime Club, Jack the Ripper was an object of particular interest. Arthur Diosy, the Hungarian authority on things Japanese, for instance, was convinced that there was a Black Magic element in the murders, from the way new coins were set out near the bodies. Ingleby Oddie (who the murders knew him from the dinners of "Our Society") says that Diosy believed that the murders had been arranged in the form of a pentagram, a five-pointed star, and this meant that the murderer was seeking a magical "elixir of life", "one of the ingredients of which must come from a recently killed woman".

Whatever the truth about the elixir, the locations of the murders can be constructed only into the most lopsided of stars. The police in their dull practical way, were not convinced, although we do know that the murders ceased a week or two after Diosy took his ideas to Scotland Yard. Meanwhile, in Edinburgh, Dr Bell and a medical friend were working separately on detailed reports of the crimes. "There were two of us in the hunt," Bell later recalled. "and when two men set out to find a golf ball in the rough, they expect to find it where the straight lines marked in their mind's eye to it, from their original positions, crossed. In the same way, when two men set out to investigate a crime mystery, it is where their researches intersect that we have a result."

From the suspects investigated by the police, Dr Bell deduced the name of the murderer. He wrote the name on a piece of paper and put it in an envelope. His friend had done likewise. When they opened the envelopes the same name was in each. They contacted Scotland Yard at once, and a week later the murders ceased. Was this merely a coincidence as I suspect it was with Arthur Diosy, or had they stumbled on a clue which in some way led to the murderer? The murders ceased certainly – but Jack the Ripper was never brought to trial.

I don't think that Conan Doyle knew of this incident in the life of the original Sherlock Holmes till after Dr Bell's death in October 1911.

(**Compiler's note:** For further details of this aspect of the case see Ely M. Liebow's book *Dr. Joe Bell – Model for Sherlock Holmes* later in this chapter).

But to return to Conan Doyle's own original ideas about the Ripper. If the letters contained, as he suggested, American expressions, did that mean that the murderer was an American? In fact among the witnesses to the murder victims were some, including a policeman, who encountered a mysterious American accented seaman. As a result, sailors around the docks, and cowboys at the International Fair were questioned by the police without success. Was the Ripper really an American? It is an intriguing thought, but not a theory that has commended itself to any of the recent writers on the case.

Current theories about the identity of Jack the Ripper are that he was variously:

- a Russian named Alexey Pedachencko
- an English barrister named Montague John Druitt, who had medical connections and was found drowned in the Thames
- a mad surgeon named Dr Stanley revenging the death from venereal disease
- a Jewish slaughterman
- a Jill the Ripper, possibly an abortionist covering up her mistakes
- HRH Albert Victor, Duke of Clarence
- James Kenneth Stephen, the Duke's tutor and cousin of Virginia Woolf
- A literary Black Magician, Dr Roslyn D'Onston Stephenson
- And finally, the royal doctor, Sir William Gull, assisted by the painter William Sickert and his coachman John Netley.

The evidence for these various theories is never completely convincing. Of them all, I myself incline to believe the last theory, which has been developed by the late Stephen Knight in his book *Jack the Ripper: the Final Solution* (1976) though his evidence has not always stood up to re-investigation by recent writers.

These theories have nearly all been developed by writers since Conan Doyle's day – the first book wholly devoted to the mystery appeared only in 1929, Leonard Matters' *The Mystery of Jack the Ripper*. There is one aspect of the case which did interest Conan Doyle and his friend and biographer John Lamond, who shared his belief in spiritualism. For in his later life, with an increasing interest in the uses of clairvoyance, Doyle learnt more about the possible identity of Jack the Ripper.

In July 1889 Scotland Yard received yet another letter purporting to be from Jack the Ripper:

Dear Boss
You have not caught me yet you see, with all your cunning, with all your "Lees" with all your blue bottles.
   Jack the Ripper

Whoever wrote this letter, and it may well have been the person who wrote the letters of 1888 that so impressed Conan Doyle, it remained secret in the files of the Metropolitan Police. But the passing mention of Lees is striking.

The reference is to the leading Christian Spiritualist, Robert James Lees. He had found favour with Queen Victoria who was anxious to contact the departed Prince Albert, and had many other influential friends. At the time of the Ripper murders he had a troubling vision of one of them which he reported to Scotland Yard, but the police, pestered daily by cranks, ignored him. Another murder followed. Shocked by his visions Lees and his wife took a holiday abroad. On their return they were riding in a tram through Notting Hill when once again he became troubled. A man boarded the tram.

"That is Jack the Ripper," he told his wife.

She did not take him seriously. "I am not mistaken. I feel it."

Leaving the tram, Lees followed the man down Park Lane from Oxford Street. At Apsley House the man caught a cab and disappeared into the Piccadilly traffic.

After the awful orgy of violence in Miller's Court, Lees concentrated his powers on his vision of the murderer. Then he took his "information" to the police. Together with a police inspector he went to a house in the heart of fashionable Mayfair. There he challenged the wife of the resident, who confessed to worries about her husband's recent activities. The man was Dr William Gull. Years later his daughter told Mr William Stowell, the distinguished pathologist, that one evening Lady Gull had been annoyed by the appearance at her house of a man calling himself a medium who had a policeman with him. According to her Gull himself came downstairs and spoke of lapses of memory and of finding bloodstains on his shirt front.

Soon after, Gull made his will, and following a stroke, died in 1890. Or so it was said. Stephen Knight believed that he was in fact committed to an asylum under the name of Thomas Mason, dying only in 1892.

That Robert James Lees had tracked down the Ripper was, as the letter shows, a current rumour in 1889. The rumour made its way into print in 1895 in an American newspaper, though Gull was not actually named in this article. Although Lees' role was revealed in detail in the 1930s, it was not until the 1970s that the facts relating to Dr Gull began to filter out from several different sources. The story, however, was widely current in those spiritualist circles in which Conan Doyle and his friend the Rev. John Lamond moved.

Though Conan Doyle felt that the police should make more use of clairvoyance in detecting recent crime, he was even more enthusiastic about its use in historical cases such as Jack the Ripper.

After all, the occult knockings involving the Fox sisters at Hydesville, New York State, in 1848, led to the uncovering (it was then claimed) of the secretly buried body of a murdered pedlar. It was his tortured soul which was trying to communicate through the sisters with the living. And there were, as Conan Doyle was never tired of pointing out, many other very similar cases. But the manifestations of the occult forces properly belong to a later chapter of his life and this book.

The fictional use of Holmes and Watson to solve the Ripper murders – or indeed commit them – indulged in by modern writers as eminent in their field as Ellery Queen would undoubtedly have shocked and dismayed Conan Doyle.

Nevertheless, in those long conversations over their cigars and brandy the members of the Crimes Club found much food for thought and speculation in the topic of London's "Autumn of Terror". Several members were closely connected with the case: G.R. Sims, Sir Melville McNaughton, Lord Aberconway, Major Arthur Griffiths, Arthur Diosy, and even a relative of one of the putative Ripper suspects, the Duke of Kent.

Arthur Lambton, in his autobiography *The Salad Bowl*, recalls that in the early days of the club a certain member of the peerage wished to join. He offered to read a paper on the Whitechapel Murders. But the members knew a great deal about, or rather, against the noble lord, and did not wish to accept him. How could they put him off? J.B. Atlay drafted a letter for the Honorary Secretary to send him in his own name:

Dear ----,
I am desired by the committee to thank you very much for your kind offer to read a paper on the Whitechapel Murders, but you will appreciate the reason we cannot accept it when I tell you that the Whitechapel Murderer happens to be a very near and dear relative of one of our most popular members...

Sherlock Holmes & Jack the Ripper

Introduction

A Scholarly Case Study

The Problem of Sherlock Holmes & Jack the Ripper by **P.L. Anness** from *The Life & times of Sherlock Holmes* by **Philip Weller & Christopher Roden** (1993) Bracken Books.

Lastly, and most controversially, we come to the greatest mystery in Holmes's career – on the principle of the dog that didn't bark – which is his apparent lack of involvement in the case of Jack the Ripper: the brutal slaying of five (or six, depending on the theory espoused) prostitutes in the East End of London between August and November 1888. At this time Holmes was at his prime, and although he had not yet established his huge popular reputation, his work was well known and highly regarded in forensic circles, and he had already become the first point of call for the officials of Scotland Yard when they found themselves at a loss. It seems possible, on the face of it, that he would not have been consulted on a matter which had so obviously baffled the authorities and which became, for a time, an issue which looked likely to destroy the nation's trust and belief in its police force – almost to the point of public disorder and riot.

A number of theories have been put forward to cover this omission. The commonly accepted explanation was that Holmes was involved in the case, and indeed solved it, but that the perpetrator was so positioned in the community – perhaps even of royal blood – that the detective was begged and persuaded not to reveal his findings for the good of the country. A second view, along the same lines, is that Holmes caught the criminal, but decided, again perhaps for political reasons, to take the matter into his own hands, and executed the killer himself rather then depending on the official mechanism.

Unfortunately there is a further theory, which, though abhorrent to right-thinking people (including the authors of this volume), is included herein for the purposes of academic completeness. This is the hypothesis that Holmes himself was Jack the Ripper.

A profile of the Ripper was developed by the police at the time: necessarily primitive in those pre-Freudian days when neither the psychological nor the scientific field of criminal investigation had reached any degree of sophistication. Essentially they were looking for a man who was almost certainly not a doctor, but who had some medical training or knowledge; someone who could move at will through the lowest sections of the community without drawing attention to himself; someone who could come and go as he pleased, with no parents, wife or friend living at home with him to observe his movements, demeanour, and condition; perhaps someone who had a knowledge of police procedures, so that he could anticipate and make counter moves against them; and certainly a man who had an antipathy towards women, who had perhaps been slighted or damaged by one, or who imagined some threat against him from a female.

It is regrettable that Holmes fits the bill so precisely. Although not specifically trained in medicine, he took courses at the University of London Medical School, and his knowledge of anatomy is confessed by Watson to be "accurate, but unsystematic". Stamford, perhaps indicating something more sinister than was realized at the time, states that "he has amassed a lot of out-of-the-way knowledge which astonish his professors". At the University he would have mixed with medical students, and had access (as he was allowed into the building without supervision) to equipment, tools, and, potentially corpses. Remember, the evidence of Stamford in that he has seen Holmes experimenting on the "subjects" (donated bodies) in the dissecting room by beating them with a stick. He innocently accepts Holmes's explanation that he is investigating "how far bruises may be produced after death", but is this the truth? If it is, then is it not much more bizarre to suggest that the murders of the Whitechapel prostitutes may have been the grotesque scientific experiments of a diseased mind, unable any longer to differentiate between live and dead subjects.

Holmes's talent for disguise is well established. Due to the circumstances of the Ripper murders, no reliable descriptions were ever obtained. These that were received were contradictory, implying that the murderer took some pains to change his appearance from time to time. Nothing would have been simpler for Holmes – often seen as a groom, a loafer, a seaman, and even a priest – to take on the guise of a person whose presence would have raised no comment in Whitechapel. There were even fantastic rumours at the time that the Ripper was a woman – and Holmes, as we know, could easily assume a female role.

Regarding his ability to come and go as he pleased, Holmes was, at this time, living alone in Baker Street, as Watson, having met Mary Morstan, was almost certainly living with his new wife. This is one of the most confusing aspects of the history. Watson had clearly become engaged following the *Sign of Four* case, which occurred, we are told, "some years after" *A Study in Scarlet*, which we gather took place in March 1887. Yet *A Scandal in Bohemia*, which is dated March 1888 (five months before the first Ripper killing), Watson states that "my marriage had drifted us away from each other" and that he was living away from Baker Street. This brings us to Watson's role in the affair. It was often suggested that the Ripper had a helper, but given our knowledge of the doctor's character we can hardly suspect him of any active role. On the other hand somebody who lived so close to the man could not, realistically, have been totally absent of some suspicions, however mild or informed. The confusion of the dates by Watson is consequently interpreted as an unconscious suppression of facts that may have implicated his friend. Regardless, it is very highly probable that Holmes was living alone at this time, and could therefore act unobserved. He had, in any case, the contacts in the East End, and the intelligence, to set up a sanctuary for himself there if he thought it advisable. Indeed, it has been pointed out that Holmes had only to inform the police that he was investigating the crimes, and he could have set himself up a temporary headquarters in the area and come and go as he pleased – he was uniquely above suspicion.

His knowledge of police procedure, and contempt for it, are legendary – he could easily have double-crossed Abberline, or any of the other officers on the case. Again, it has been suggested that his scorn for the authorities, and his almost obsessive desire to make them look foolish and show himself superior, may have been a key motivating factor in the crimes. His other characteristics – the sociopathic desire for instant gratification and fear of boredom; manic mood swings from frenetic activity to overwhelming lassitude; an obsessive fascination with crime and its processes; and intensely secretive nature, intermingled with an uncontrollable desire for publicity; a tendency towards drug-taking; and a superiority complex which on innumerable occasions allowed Holmes to place himself above the law as a determiner of justice – complement the picture of a typical serial-killer.

The principal motivating factor, and the last item in the police profile, was obviously a hatred of, or contempt for, women. Unfortunately Holmes again falls under suspicion. Although Watson normally – perhaps once more, unconsciously protecting his friend – describes Holmes's misogyny as a simple lack of interest, it is not difficult, reading between the lines, to develop a more sinister interpretation. One wonders what was really said when Holmes is reported, on hearing of his friend's engagement: "I really cannot congratulate you…love is an emotional thing, and whatever is emotional is opposed to that true cold reason which I place above all things. I should never marry myself, lest I bias my judgement." More ominously, he is described by Watson in *A Scandal in Bohemia* in the following terms: "as a lover he would have placed himself in a false position. He never spoke of the softer passions, save with a gibe and a sneer."

The report by Watson entitled *A Scandal in Bohemia* is particularly important to the Holmes-as-Ripper theory. It has been noted that it dates from March 1888, shortly before the Ripper killings began, and that it opens with the barely veiled admission of Holmes's mental hatred of women at the time. There is every possibility that this hatred had been fostered by Watson's marriage and desertion. Without commenting on Holmes's sexuality, if we review the events of the previous two years in his life, we can see what a shock Watson's departure from Baker Street would have caused in an already sensitive mind. We know that Holmes was a lonely man (rationalising loneliness by constant protestations of misanthropy and concentration on his all-important work), brought up effectively as an only child as his brother Mycroft was seven years his senior and too old for sibling companionship. His isolation from his parents is confirmed by the fact that, in all the thousands of words of Watson's reports, no mention is ever made of them. That his isolation is caused by the difficulties of his personality is affirmed by the reluctance of Stamford to encourage Watson to share lodgings with Holmes: "You mustn't blame me if you don't get on with him…You proposed this arrangement, so you must not hold me responsible." That Watson is nervous is also an undisputed fact. "It seems to me, Stamford…that you have some reason for washing your hands of this matter."

Having overcome all the normally insurmountable hurdles he encounters when forming relationships, and settled down with Watson in what can only be described as a pseudo-marriage, it can readily be considered that this previously shunned and lonely person might well have placed too high an emotional value on what the formidably heterosexual Watson naturally treated as a domestic arrangement of convenience. All the signs are there – showing off; playing hard to get; alternative moods of self-aggrandizement and feigned stupidity – to suggest that Holmes went through a courtship ritual with Watson, which went unnoticed by the simple focus of his attention. Then comes the unexpected blow of the engagement. Watson, in Holmes's mind, is announcing that he is to divorce him, and marry, of all things, a woman.

The Adler case (*A Scandal in Bohemia*) could therefore not have come at a worse time from Holmes's psychological point of view. Perhaps on the way to recovery from being cut out of his friend's life and having his "marriage" destroyed by one woman, he is now bested and outwitted by another. This surely, if one is ever to espouse the Holmes-as-Ripper thesis, it is the critical point, as it is easy to see how between March and August 1888 Holmes's mind might further deteriorate so that a few months later he was ready to start killing symbolic representations of the women who had disrupted both his personal and business life. That prostitutes should have been chosen is no surprise: they represented the antithesis of the purity of Mary Morstan; the logical extension and embodiment of Irene Adler's career as courtesan, and the dark side of the femininity in his own murder.

It is well known that in most instances of serial killing that remain unsolved, the murders come to a halt because the killer, coming to a realisation of what he is doing, commits suicide. Indeed, this is the reason given in the Ripper case for strong suspicion against Montague Druitt. Holmes, as ever, must be considered too remarkable a man for such a simple resolution. The most likely theory is that he "caught himself", when investigating the case, and came to terms with what he had done. After a period of self-analysis, completed in 1891 by his faked disappearance from the world while he travelled, among other places to Tibet, his rehabilitation was complete, and he then made amends by devoting the rest of his life to good.

Others have, of course gone further. There is a theory that Holmes did not mend his ways, but stopped the serial killing because he feared capture. Then, having constructed the Reichenbach Falls mystery as an elaborate alibi, he slipped back into England to murder Mrs Watson, thereby regaining the affection of his lover, who rejoined him in Baker Street on his return. It is, indeed, strange that Holmes, freshly back from isolation in foreign parts, should appear to know so much about Mrs Watson's demise (see *The Empty House*). Others again have theorized that Professor Moriarty never existed, but was the black side of Holmes's own nature. The flight from Moriarty was Holmes's flight from his own black, murdering personality (the Ripper), and the struggle at the Falls was a Jungian symbol for Holmes's wrestling with all his darkest instincts in the wilderness. Having killed Moriarty (his desire to murder), he was free once more to re-enter society.

Whatever is believed about Holmes and the Ripper by others, the authors of this volume, though forced out of academic integrity to include these facts in order to present a well-rounded and comprehensive testament, nevertheless wish to distance themselves from such scurrilous speculation however well founded.

A Sherlock Holmes Handbook (1993) by Christopher Redmond. Simon & Pierre.

Jack the Ripper

Most dramatic of all Victorian crime stories is that of Jack the Ripper. Unlike other monsters of popular culture, the Ripper did exist, though no one was ever identified ("Saucy Jack", he called himself in one taunting letter to the police) or charged with the killings attributed to him in London in 1888. Five victims – all prostitutes in the east end of London – are definitely considered the Ripper's work:

*Mary Ann (Polly) Nichols – Buck's Row, August 31.

*Eliza Ann Chapman – Hanbury Street, September 8.

*Elizabeth Stride – Berner Street, September 30.

*Catherine Eddowes – Mitre Square, September 30.

*Mary Jeannette Kelly – Dorset Street.

Several other cases (notably the August 7 murder of Martha Tabram, or Turner, in George Yard buildings) are sometimes associated with the Ripper, but do not entirely fit the pattern, which included gruesome and increasingly elaborate disembowelling.

Several features of the Ripper cases are particularly interesting:

*The taunting letters to the police and the press, including one signed "Jack the Ripper" (origin of the enduring name), and one in which the author claimed to have eaten part of the kidney of one victim.

*A chalked message, "The Juwes are not the men who will be blamed for nothing," erased by police commissioner Sir Charles Warren because it might lead to violence against the large Jewish population in the East End. Some later analysts have seen a Masonic meaning in this message and in the details of the atrocities.

*Incompetent police work, under Warren's direction, and general hysteria from the population, leading to many false arrests.

*A plethora of suggestions about the killer's identity, from Prince Albert Victor, Duke of Clarence (who, however was in Scotland at the time of some of the killings) to barrister Montague John Druitt.

The most probable suggestions involve not celebrities but local residents, such as ""Kosminski, a Polish Jew, referred to in contemporary police files.

For the literal-minded Sherlockian, the important question is why Holmes did not solve the Ripper case. Several parodies and films have him doing so, notably, *A Study in Terror* (novel by Ellery Queen, published in England as *Sherlock Holmes Versus Jack the Ripper*, 1966; film the same year) and "Murder by Decree" (film 1979). The most recent effort of this kind is *The Whitechapel Horrors* (1992), a novel by C. Douglas Baker. *The Baker Street Journal* published a "Ninetieth Anniversary Jack the Ripper Memorial Issue" in 1978, with a number of articles dealing with aspects of the case from a Sherlockian viewpoint, and *Canadian Holmes* had a similar issue in 1988. Other such articles have appeared from time to time.

Useful books about the Ripper case include *The Ripper File* (1975) by Elwyn Jones and John Lloyd; *The Complete Jack the Ripper* (1975) by Donald Rumbelow; *Jack the Ripper, One Hundred Years of Mystery* (1987) by Peter Underwood. A summery of sources and data is *Jack the Ripper: A Bibliography and Review of the Literature*, by Alexander Kelly (1984)

Sherlock Magazine Issues 57, 58 (2003) & 59 (2004). Atlas Publishing Ltd.

Jack the Ripper & Popular Culture

Part One of Paul M. Chapman's new series on Jack the Ripper.

Shadow of the Knife

Despite the perennial British fascination with violent crime relatively few cases have actually burned their way into the national psyche with any lasting effect. Yesterday's sensations tend to remain precisely that. Few non-specialists are now familiar with the details of the Thurtell-Hunt murder case of 1823 or even the murder of Maria Marten by William Corder in 1827, now better remembered, if at all, as the subject of a famous melodrama. Yet both were familiar subjects for decades after the actual crimes were committed. In the contemporary world the names of the Moors Murderers, the Yorkshire Ripper, Fred and Rose West, and the James Bulger case are full of ready associates, but with time these too will lose some of their impact.

There is only one name from British criminal history which remains as potent to modern ears and sensibilities as it did when first heard in 1888, a name which perhaps more than ever comes replete with any amount of associated imagery and cultural baggage: Jack the Ripper.

As with many other cases from the nineteenth century (and even closer to the present day) few people could accurately list his crimes – which, of course remain unsolved – but most believe they are familiar with his short reign of terror (which lasted just over two months), and its accompanying film set in fog and squalor, because of his, or more accurately his shadowy image's prolific permeation into so many aspects of popular culture. It is a remarkable achievement for a totally anonymous historical figure who, with regard to his fame, actually made no deliberate positive contribution to society.

Although there have been arguments forwarded for the murder of Emma Smith, who was mortally injured in an attack of 4th April 1888, and Martha Tabram, stabbed to death on the night of 6th/7th August 1888, as Ripper victims, it seems unlikely, especially in Smith's case. It is more probable that his killing spree really began with the murder of Mary Ann Nichols, whose corpse was discovered in Buck's Row, to the east of Whitechapel parish, in the early hours of 31st August 1888. Her throat had been cut, but what made her death particularly notable was the fact that her body had been deliberately mutilated in the region of the abdomen and genitals. This would become the true mark of Jack the Ripper and grows progressively worse as the series continued.

Nichol's murder created a certain amount of trepidation, but, apart from the disturbing mutilations, was seen as nothing unusual in the district of London rather too used to violence. However, with the second murder, that of Annie Chapman in Hanbury Street on 8th September, genuine concern, if not actual panic began to surface. Chapman's mutilations were significantly worse than Nichol's, and this time the killer had removed his victim's uterus. Despite the singular nature of this crime and a number of promising initial leads the police were ultimately left at a loss. Such circumstances are the natural breeding ground for rumour and conjecture and soon the birth of the legend of Jack the Ripper (although he did not yet carry that name) was beginning.

For almost a month there was no further atrocities, but on the night of the 29th/30th September there occurred two murders: Elizabeth Stride and Catherine Eddowes, the former in Dutfield's Yard, Berner Street, the latter in Mitre Square in the territory of the City of London Police. Stride had simply had her throat cut, leading to the conclusion either that she was not a Ripper victim or that he had been disturbed before he had time to embark upon future mutilations. Eddowe's body, however, was horrifically attacked, leaving police in no doubt that the Ripper had returned.

Following this so-called 'double event' there was a further lull until the killer struck again on 9th November, the day of the Lord Mayor's parade. The victim was his youngest, Mary Kelly. She was also the only one to be killed indoors, in her room in Miller's Court, Dorset Street. This time the destruction of the body was complete. So, it came to be seen with time, was the cycle of killings. Following Kelly's death there were two worrying false alarms with the murders of Alice McKenzie on 17 July 1889 and Frances Coles on 14 February 1891. Neither, however, bore the true Ripper imprint.

In themselves this series of murders, although horrific, and gothic enough to exert a disturbing and ghoulish fascination, are not sufficiently significant in themselves to warrant the endurance of the legend of Jack the Ripper into the twenty first century. What has ensured this is the perpetual air of mystery and the fascinating blend of contemporaneous circumstances at the time of the killings, not least amongst which was the rise of the popular press, ideally poised to exploit (and, if necessary, embellish) a suitably sensational story. For some time before the Jack the Ripper killings, social conditions in the East End of London had been attracting a number of middle- and upper-class reformers and political radicals, including for example, Annie Besant, who was fighting for a seat on London County Council at the time of the Ripper scare. Together they saw a chance of turning the press attention focused upon the area by the murders to their advantage by advertising the case for social reform, claiming that the Ripper's activities were a direct consequence of the intolerable conditions daily endured by its working class population. George Bernard Shaw famously went further, employing the Shavian wit in the pages of the radical newspaper the *Star*.

'Whilst we conventional Social Democrats were wasting our time on education, agitation and organisation, some independent genius has taken the matter in hand, and by simply murdering and disembowelling four women, converted the proprietor press to an inept sort of communism.' Despite his comments being in questionable taste, and his assessment of the reaction of the established press rather overstated Shaw was essentially correct. Although the press agenda was driven by more radical and populist papers like the *Star* and W.T. Stead's *Pall Mall Gazette*, the press as a whole recognized that the Ripper story was selling newspapers and that it afforded far more scope than mere ghoulish reportage. There was political capital to be made, whether from the viewpoint of the social reformer or the enemy of the police, whose operations were hampered by unwelcome press attention, and their political masters.

There was also a story to be told. The bare details of the murder cases were simply waiting to be 'improved', sentimentalised and made even more horrific and mysterious. The Ripper scare was an inventive journalist's dream, and in the work of these Victorian hacks, writing for a wider and more literate public reaping the benefits of the 1871 Education Act, can be found the printed origins of the Jack the Ripper legend which persists to this day.

Indeed, it was probably a journalist who gave the murderer his famous soubriquet. Following the murder of Mary Ann Nichols an elusive figure known only as 'Leather Apron' was the subject of much gossip, which was further fuelled by the fact that a leather apron (totally unconnected to the case) was found near Annie Chapman's body. One unfortunate Jewish boot-finisher, John Pizer, suspected of being 'Leather Apron', even found himself temporarily in custody. But 'Leather Apron' was soon to be forgotten. On 27 September a letter was posted to the Central News Agency (a location in itself suggesting the hand of a journalist). This was followed by a postcard on 1 October. Both referred to the recipient as 'Boss' and were signed 'Jack the Ripper'. It was a stroke of genius. The name was perfect, and a gift for the press. It is testament to its power that it still endures and resonates.

If some of the press attention reaped positive benefits there was also a more sinister side to be found. In particular, certain articles were responsible to a degree for agitating racial and social tensions in the East End, an area which, because of its close association with the commerce of the Thames, had a considerable immigrant – particularly Jewish – and transient population. Anti-Semitic feeling had already been stirred in 1887 by Israel Lipski's murder of Miriam Angel in Batty Street ('Lipski' remained a popular insult at the time of the Ripper scare), and many wanted to believe that the Ripper was a Jew. Their view even seemed to be supported by the dubious evidence of the Goulston Street graffito, often attributed to the killer, which read either 'The Juwes are the men That Will not be Blames for nothing' or 'The Jews are not The men That Will be Blamed for nothing'. It is also notable that a number of witness statements of the time describe suspects as 'foreign looking' a common euphemism for 'of Jewish appearance'.

Jews were not the only group to be singled out for attention. Doctors, too, came under popular suspicion , especially following the pronouncement of Dr George Bagster Phillips, H Division's police surgeon, at Annie Chapman's inquest, that in his opinion the killer 'showed some anatomical knowledge'. To a population already wary of doctors this was not what they wanted to hear, and it is the figure of the doctor, with his black bag and formal dress that most helped to contribute to the popular perception of

Jack the Ripper's appearance, even more so than the idea of the bloodthirsty slumming toff, who on the whole, was a later addition to the legend.

Because of the nature of the mutilations inflicted by the Ripper it was also assumed in certain quarters that he was mentally disturbed or possibly escaped or discharged from an institution. This view was principally fostered by the alienist L. Forbes Winslow, but was effectively popularised by Marie Belloc Lowndes' highly successful novel *The Lodger* (1913) which was later filmed by Alfred Hitchcock in his first stint in the director's chair. *The Lodger* was the first significant Ripper fiction and Lowndes claimed it was inspired by overhearing a guest at a dinner party state that he knew a couple who were certain they had once let a room to Jack the Ripper.

Lowndes' work to a certain extent renewed interest in the Ripper who was, by that time, on his way to becoming little more than a shadowy figure from the East End's past, a London character on a par with the semi-legendary Spring-heeled Jack whose own reign of terror had lasted between 1837-38.

The next book to find a new wave of public interest was nominally a work of non-fiction, Leonard Matters' *The Mystery of Jack the Ripper* (1929), in which the author claimed that a certain Dr Stanley, whose son had died of syphilis contracted from Mary Kelly, who was finally tracked down and killed by the distraught father. Although his argument is largely unconvincing, and reads rather too much like fiction (it inspired the melodramatic 1959 film *Jack the Ripper*), Matters' book is a significant milestone, being the first notable serious study of the case, and for helping to inspire what would later be known – somewhat derisively – as 'Ripperology'. He also reviewed the doctor theory, which, in a very different form, would prove highly controversial in a future major phase of Ripper interest, during which the cultural and historical stakes would be further raised, and even lead to the involvement of no less a figure than Sherlock Holmes.

Part 2 of Paul M. Chapman's new series on Jack the Ripper

Shadows in the Fog

By the time Marie Belloc Lowndes wrote the first version of her classic Jack the Ripper story, *The Lodger*, in 1911, the original murders had already entered the realms of popular legend. The final serious, if unlikely, 'Ripper' scare, the murder of Frances Coles, had occurred twenty years previously and in the intervening time the killer's actual resonance, although not entirely dismissed, had come to be replaced by a phantom presence, a localised form of evil spirit. Indeed, as Ripper commentator Denis Meikle has remarked, *The Lodger* itself carries more than a hint of the mechanics and atmosphere of a ghost story.

However, the theory underpinning Lowndes' story, that the Whitechapel murderer may have been a discharged or escaped mental patient, was genuinely contemporaneous with the killings themselves, and most enthusiastically advocated by the noted alienist L. Forbes Winslow. But unlike Winslow (and Lowndes) popular and press opinion held that the obviously insane – who but a madman could have perpetrated these outrages? – murderer was of working class, possibly immigrant, probably Jewish, origin. The grotesque caricature quality of the line illustration 'sketches of supposed murderer' which appeared in such wide-circulation new-sheets as the *Illustrated Police News* pander to a popular prejudice which had, even before the murder of Annie Chapman – the probable second victim, on 8th September 1888, began to characterise the killer as a nebulous Jewish misogynist known only as 'Leather Apron'.

Following the inquest on Annie Chapman a further line of theory was firmly planted in the popular psyche when Dr George Bagster Phillips attested that in his opinion whoever killed Chapman had handled the knife which seemed to indicate great anatomical knowledge. Perhaps the murderer was a doctor. Although Phillips was not casting direct aspersions upon his own profession (slaughterman and butchers, after all, also possessed anatomical knowledge), the idea of a medical killer soon gained a level of popular credence – although one modern commentator's assertion that 'the suggestion that [the] Ripper might be a doctor…who had an obsession with destroying prostitutes, was by far the most popular, and accessible, explanation' seems rather overstated. The idea of a working class Jewish murderer never really lost its popular appeal, as was shown by Sir Charles Warren's insistence on the deletion of the Goulston Street graffito, with its provocative reference to 'Juwes', prompted by a genuine fear that it could have produced a pogrom.

Nevertheless, there did exist a certain degree of popular prejudice against doctors throughout the poorer districts of the metropolis. Despite the fact that the greater proportion of the profession were genuinely committed to serving their communities they were still largely representative of a different social class and, significantly, through their specialist knowledge, held sway over the bodies of their patients – a power similar to that wielded by the Ripper. A number of the century's more sensational crimes had already involved rogue doctors, a fact to which Sherlock Holmes alluded in *The Speckled Band* (1892), following on from an assertion that '[w]hen a doctor goes wrong he is the first of criminals. He has the nerve and he has knowledge.'

Although it is unlikely that many of the working class residents of Whitechapel and Spitalfields would have been particularly familiar with Robert Louis Stevenson's *Strange Case of Dr Jekyll & Mr Hyde* (1886), or with the theatrical adaptation starring the American actor Richard Mansfield which was playing at the Lyceum Theatre at the time of the Ripper's killing spree, the story did provide some (perhaps too) convenient indicators as to the type(s) of personality the killer may have been. The principal character is, of course, a doctor who deliberately releases the beast within himself. Stevenson was very circumspect in describing Hyde's crimes, and nowhere does he even hint that some of these may have been of a sexual nature. But with the advent of the Ripper case analysis naturally became coloured, and at least one contemporary theatregoing correspondent wrote to the City of London Police informing them that he 'felt at once that [Richard Mansfield] was the Man Wanted' for the killings. Such is the power of popular drama and ill-digested ideas. Mr Hyde, however, like Frankenstein's monster before him, represents much more than the product of a misguided individual medical experiment; he can – amongst other things – be interpreted as representing the dark side of the upper strata of society. This book, for example, can be read as a metaphorical description of Edinburgh, the city of Stevenson's formative years, with its ostensibly respectable and professional New Town and the more liberated Old Town. Hyde retains something of the surface veneer of a gentleman, but, without the requisite moral boundaries and self-discipline, he is a degenerate example.

The idea of Jack the Ripper as a slumming toff, acting out sadistic sexual fantasies of the bodies of vulnerable working class women, is relatively recent and actually speaks more for modern prejudices and concerns than about the reality of Victorian society. Although doctors were genuinely regarded with a jaundiced eye at the time of the killings, and supplied some of the imagery now associated – despite little hard evidence – with the Ripper, there was no real suggestion at the time that a bored or perverted representative of high society was guilty of the murders. Most eyewitness accounts of Ripper suspects depicted someone of relatively unobtrusive appearance. The only major exception was a description of a suspicious character seen with Mary Kelly shortly after her death, supplied by George Hutchinson, who knew the victim:

'Age about 34 or 35, height 5ft. 6, complexion pale, dark eyes and eyelashes, slight moustache curled up each end and hair dark, very surly looking; dress, long dark coat, collar cuffs trimmed astracan [sic] and a dark jacket under, light waistcoat, dark trousers, dark felt hat turned down in the middle, button boots and gaiters with white buttons, wore a very thick gold chain, white linen collar, dark tie with horseshoe pin, respectable appearance, walked very sharp, Jewish appearance.'

This remarkably detailed picture, however, does not suggest someone of actual social standing. Besides its vaudevillian quality, this is a flash rather than a dapper individual. And finally Hutchinson exposes his own prejudices by adding 'Jewish appearance'.

Even diehard socialists at the time of the murders did not seriously suspect or suggest that they could have been the work of a decadent aristocrat. To them the real crimes committed by the ruling elite were to allow widespread poverty and its attendant problems to prevail in the East End, and to compound this by virtually ignoring the situation; until, of course, Jack the Ripper highlighted it.

The murderous toff image really developed with the growth of the moving picture, whose practitioners took the basic template of an upper class music hall villain and embellished it. To the doctors black bag they appended the formal evening clothes of a fading generation, including the distinctive defining top hat and cloak, thereby serving the appeal of nostalgia whilst also providing a useful visual shorthand to indicate both the villain and his background.

Before the advent of a serious and systematic approach to the study of the Ripper murders in the 1970s, this figure was taken largely for what he was an entertaining caricature with little basis in reality. But in 1970 Dr Thomas Stowell published an article in *The Criminologist, Jack the Ripper – A Solution*, which grabbed the popular imagination, for Stowell's suspect, although he tried to disguise his identity behind the letter 'S', was none other than Prince Albert Victor Christian Edward, Duke of Clarence and Avondale and Heir Presumptive to the throne. Although Stowell was not the first to forward the theory publicly (Philippe Jullian alluded to it in his *Edouard VII* in 1962) it was his article which really began the process of cementing two staple ingredients of British popular culture; Jack the Ripper and the Royal Family. Stowell's article was merely a prelude, and his theories relatively straightforward, when compared to the release of two books in the mid-1970s; *The Ripper File* (1975) by Elwyn Jones and John Lloyd, which accompanied a BBC television drama documentary, *Jack the Ripper*. Which posited the involvement of Freemasons in the case, and then more sensationally, Stephen Knight's best-selling, if mis-named, *Jack the Ripper: The Final Solution* (1976).

Based on a story told by Joseph Sickert, who claimed to be the son of the artist Walter Sickert. Knight's book claims that far from being the work of an independent serial killer the Jack the Ripper murders were the result of a wide-ranging conspiracy which involved the highest in the land and supposedly originated with Prince Albert Victor's clandestine, unconstitutional, and consummated marriage to Annie Crook, a working class girl who, Knight wrongly asserts, was a Roman Catholic. Hearing of this union sinister establishment figures subsequently arranged for the happy couple to be apprehended by the Special Branch in order to silence Crook. However, she had already informed a number of her friends of her good fortune, but instead of keeping the news to themselves they foolishly threatened the establishment with blackmail.

Acting on the instruction of fellow Freemason Lord Salisbury, Sir William Withey Gull, physician-in-ordinary to Queen Victoria, recruited a driver and a third conspirator, Walter Sickert, in order to arrange the deaths of these women. Believing himself to be acting on highest orders Gull slaughtered his victims according to Masonic ritual. Thus the famous mutilations are merely indicative of a warped logic, rather than sexual or psychological in origin. Once the task was complete the myth of Jack the Ripper usefully disguised any suspicion of an organising hand. The whole plot is a farrago of nonsense, and totally unsupported by any reliable hard evidence, but Knight, a journalist, wrote so fluidly and convincingly, seldom allowing breathing – and more importantly, thinking-space that his arguments took firm hold and have yet to be entirely dispelled.

Part 3 of Paul M. Chapman's new series on Jack the Ripper

Chasing Shadows

Throughout much of the twentieth century Jack the Ripper remained little more than a resonant name attached to an anonymous yet legendary figure who was steadily becoming part of the folklore fabric of London's East End, a locale in itself constantly and evocatively mythologized by outsiders. The semi-fictionalised existence was, of course, only strengthened by subsequent popular literature and film – a process which the purveyors of yellow journalism had already fuelled during the Ripper's reign of terror itself, but which really coalesced with the initial appearance of Marie Belloc Lowndes' *The Lodger* in 1911 (in which the killer none too convincingly disguised behind the nom-de-plume 'The Avenger') and its numerous celluloid variants. It was even, possibly unwittingly, helped by the first significant full-length ostensibly factual study of the case, Leonard Matters' *The Mystery of Jack the Ripper* (1929), which later formed the basis of Robert S. Baker and Monty Berman's melodramatic film, *Jack the Ripper* (1959), which was scripted by Jimmy Sangster, one of Hammer Films' regular principal writers, and cheerfully utilised all the visual clichés now so readily associated with the Ripper story; swirling fogs, top hats, capes and black bags, and, naturally plenty of chirpy good time Cockney girls.

The reality was significantly more squalid and a number of early entries into the library of what would later, often mockingly, come to be termed 'Ripperology', attempting to evoke something of the urban mire in which the killer wallowed and his victims lived and died, most notably the pioneering work of the journalist Daniel Farson who, in a television documentary in 1959, revealed the initials of a genuine police suspect whose body had been retrieved from the Thames in December 1888. Farson's source was the so-called Macnaghten Memoranda, a series of notes collated by Sir Melville Macnaghten, who held a number of senior posts in Scotland Yard's CID between 1890 and 1908. Although not actively involved in the Ripper investigation itself Macnaghten obviously had access to the relevant files which allowed him to draw his own informed conclusions. These have been constantly challenged by later researchers, but nevertheless remain cogent.

Recognising the growing popular interest in the case Farson actually made the Macnaghten Memoranda public property in his book *Jack the Ripper* (1972), although the suspect whose body was recovered from the Thames had already been named in fellow journalist Tom Cullen's important volume *Autumn of Terror* which was published in 1965. Jack the Ripper was finally emerging from the shadows, although Macnaghten's assessment of his three principal suspects is undeniably couched in the terminology of categorisation:

'(1) A Mr M.J. Druitt, said to be a doctor and of good family, who disappeared at the time of the Miller's Court murder, whose body (which was said to have been upwards of a month in the water) was found in the Thames on 31st Dec…He was sexually insane and from private info I have little doubt but that his own family believed him to have been the murderer.

(2) Kosminski, a Polish Jew and resident in Whitechapel. This man became insane owing to many years indulging in solitary vices. He had a great hatred of women, especially of the prostitute class, and had strong homicidal tendencies, he was removed to a lunatic asylum about 1889. There were many circs connected with this man which made him a strong 'suspect'.

(3) Michael Ostrog, a Russian doctor, and a convict, who was subsequently detained in a lunatic asylum as a homicidal maniac. The man's antecedents were of the worse possible type, and his whereabouts at the time of the murders could never be ascertained.'

Although Macnaghten does lend human form to the Ripper through these suspects, all of whom were genuine personalities, it is interesting to note how they all conform to certain 'types' associated with the killer by the general public and the press, as well as the police, in 1888. Druitt and Ostrog are both described as doctors, which is untrue in Druitt's case, he was a teacher, and far from certain in Ostrog's as he was a professional con artist; lying was his trade. But as doctors they fit one popular profile of the Ripper. Similarly, and more obviously, Kosminski and Ostrog are both dismissed as 'homicidal' and it is made quite clear that neither Kosminski nor Druitt were considered to have had normal sex lives. All, of course, were insane.

Oversimplified as Macnaghten's assessment may appear to contemporary attitudes, at least his suspects remained in the realm of probability. At around the same time as Cullen and Farson were using his notes to present a relatively balanced and realistic overview of the events of 1888 – an approach which has been followed by most genuinely serious 'Ripperologists' since – Dr Thomas Stowell, an otherwise distinguished figure, presented his own conclusions on the case, which appeared (he referred to his subject only as 'S') to accuse Prince Albert Victor Christian Edward, Duke of Clarence and Avondale and Heir Presumptive to the British throne of being Jack the Ripper. Although Stowell made a half-hearted attempt at retraction when his theory was published in 1970 the damage was already done. Interesting as Macnaghten's conclusions were they could not hope to compete in the popular arena with the intriguing and beguiling idea of a member of the British Royal Family butchering prostitutes in Whitechapel.

Although it soon became obvious, for various reasons – including some cast iron alibis – that Prince Albert Victor could not have been the Ripper the idea of a royal connection could, or would not be readily dismissed and throughout the following years stimulated a miniature publishing industry. Few of these books were written by serious scholars of the crimes, much less by qualified historians, but, of course, they encouraged a wide readership and inspired a number of films, and their legacy of damage to sober scholarship persists, particularly with regard to Stephen Knight's *Jack the Ripper: The Final Solution* (1976), perhaps the single most important and influential – mostly for the wrong reasons – volume on the Ripper crimes ever published. Knight, a journalist acting on a story told by Joseph Gorman Sickert, posited a wild theory in which the Ripper was a myth invented to cover the bloody actions of a group of rogue Freemasons, headed by Sir William Withey Gull, physician-in-ordinary to Queen Victoria, whose aim was to silence the small group of working class women who had supposedly witnessed Prince Albert Victor's secret Catholic marriage to one of their number.

Knight's informant Sickert (whose story underwent periodic fluctuations), claimed to be the illegitimate son of the noted artist Walter Sickert and was apparently upset when Knight reached the conclusion that Sickert Senior was actively involved in the murders. Although, again, there is no real evidence that would stand up to legal or historical scrutiny. Knight had not been alone in accusing Walter Sickert. Jean Overton Fuller and, more recently and significantly, Patricia Cornwell, have both written book-length studies accusing him of being Jack the Ripper, on the flimsiest of 'evidence', mostly involving hearsay and the supposed proof of his complicity provided by hidden clues in his paintings for those with eyes to see. Cornwell's case is particularly interesting. She appears to have developed a deep antipathy towards Sickert and his work and, using her own fame and standing as a crime writer, has embarked upon a single-minded crusade to damage him both as an artist and a man. However, her much vaunted attempt to extract DNA evidence from his paintings is a fool's errand and totally unconvincing, yet her use of her reputation is a worrying development. She has the popular attention and writing skills necessary to manipulate uninformed public opinion, damaging both Sickert's artistic reputation and years of patient historical investigation into the events in Whitechapel in 1888. Although Walter Sickert was undeniably fascinated by the Ripper murders and occasionally enjoyed masquerading as a mysterious and sinister character he never confessed to being the infamous Whitechapel fiend. Apparently Liverpool cotton merchant James Maybrick did just that. In 1992 a Victorian journal, which appeared to be the handwritten confession of Jack the Ripper, entered the public arena. Internal evidence pointed to its author being James Maybrick, the apparent victim at the heart of one of Liverpool's great criminal trials in which his widow, Florence, was accused and found guilty – on dubious evidence, of his murder. At first the connection of these two great Victorian murder cases was difficult to resist, but soon caution asserted itself. The diary is of very uncertain provenance and ultimately unconvincing. Although it still has its supporters it has been widely dismissed as a fake. The Maybrick case may have been a Victorian *cause celebre*, but today it is very much the province of criminal and social historians. Maybrick's celebrity is not transcendent enough. And the memory of the Hitler diaries fiasco in the 1980s remains all too fresh in many minds. Reputations are not easily rebuilt.

The initial media circus surrounding the 'Maybrick diary' and the recurrence of the accusations made towards Walter Sickert and claims of Royal involvement in the Ripper murders remains indicative of the prevalent popular mindset. The Whitechapel killings of 1888 were, in themselves, of little consequence, other than to the victims and those who may have cared for them, and to the police who were unfairly pilloried for their inability to catch the killer. Yet simply because he was not caught, and because these murders were so public and irresistibly gothic, a legend quickly built which has gained rather than diminished with the years. At the time their repercussions were politically significant, helping to focus attention upon the appalling conditions within Whitechapel and Spitalfields. In the modern world their significance is more cultural. Those who feel that Jack the Ripper should be forgotten would appear to be in a minority of the Ripper industry, which encompasses books, films, walking tours and dubious merchandise, is any proof of a continuous widespread public interest.

In an age bedazzled by celebrities Jack the Ripper has become the ultimate anonymous criminal star. Yet in life it is probable that, despite the theories which insist that he was an eminent Victorian – Sir William Gull, Walter Sickert, Algernon Swinburne, Lewis Carroll – he was actually a nobody. The need for him to have been a somebody, especially a member of the establishment, demonstrates both an inherent distrust of authority and an unwillingness to accept that significant events can be driven by the actions of the lowly. But most serial killers, whose infamy (so easily mistaken for fame) is a direct result of their transgressions, are insignificant individuals. Murder, it would seem, can provide a route to public visibility, the possible implications of which for a celebrity-hungry society are rather worrying.

In Alan Moore's graphic novel *From Hell*, following Sir William Gull's killing of Mary Kelly his accomplice, John Netley, asks, 'Is it finished with?', to which gull replies, 'It is beginning, Netley. Only just beginning. For better or worse, the twentieth century. I have delivered.' This may be an understatement. Jack the Ripper's cultural legacy may ultimately prove to be immeasurable.

Christopher Redmond (1993) **A Sherlock Holmes Handbook**. Simon & Pierre.

William S. Baring-Gould's *Sherlock Holmes of Baker Street* (1962) introduces a number of ideas that are sometimes accepted by Sherlockians as authentic parts of Holmes, although they are best classified as folklore:

That he assisted in the solution of Jack the Ripper murders in 1888. Biographers have been fond of describing Doyle's intervention in two prominent criminal cases, those against George Edalji and Oscar Slater. But a remarkable book by Peter Costello, *The Real World of Sherlock Holmes* (1991), reports dozens of crimes in which Doyle took an interest, and sometimes an active role. Costello manages to include the affair of Jack the Ripper in this category, on the strength of an investigation carried out in 1905 – seventeen years after the murders took place – by the Crimes Club, a private group of connoisseurs of which Doyle was a member.

Social Classes

Donald Rumbelow, setting the social stage for the strange crimes of Jack the Ripper, describes how people lived in the poorer districts, as analysed by a contemporary, Charles Booth:

At the bottom were the occasional labourers, loafers and semi-criminals. Above them were the "very poor" and the "poor". The word "poor" he defined as those who had a meagre but regular income of between 18 shillings and 21 shillings a week, and the "very poor" were those whose income fell below this level. The former struggled to make ends meet and the latter lived in a state of chronic want. The condition of the lowest class of all, which doesn't get a rating, can be imagined. At a rough guess there were about 11,000 of them…This figure includes the "dossers" and the homeless outcasts who slept on staircases, in doorways and even in dustbins and lavatories for warmth. Their lives, Booth said, were the lives of savages, "with vicissitudes of extreme hardship and the occasional excess".

And about the slightly less desperate classes:

The commonest work was sweat shop tailoring. For trouser finishing (sewing) linings, making button holes and stitching on the buttons a woman might get twopence ha'penny a pair and have to buy their own thread…Fifty five per cent of East End children died before they were five…*The Lancet*…had estimated that in 1857 one house in every sixty was a brothel and one woman in every sixteen was a whore…[In lodging houses] a double bed was eight pence a night and a single bed fourpence.

Daily Life

The "social evil" was that lower-class prostitution continued, providing the context for Jack the Ripper's bloody work in 1888, but the newspapers spoke more about the need for social reform, and less about the stylish carriages of aristocratic men's mistresses.

For the literal-minded Sherlockian, the important question is why Holmes did not solve the Ripper case. Several parodies and films have him doing so, notably *A Study in Terror* (novel by Ellery Queen, published in England as *Sherlock Holmes Versus Jack the Ripper*, 1966; film the same year and "Murder by Degree" (film 1979). The most recent effort of this kind is *The Whitechapel Horrors* (1992), a novel by C. Douglas Baker. *The Baker Street Journal* published a "Ninetieth Anniversary Jack the Ripper Memorial Issue" in 1978, with a number of articles dealing with aspects of the case from a Sherlockian viewpoint, and *Canadian Holmes* had a similar issue in 1988. Other such articles have appeared from time to time. Useful books about the Ripper case include *The Ripper File* (1975) by Elwyn Jones and John Lloyd; *The Complete Jack the Ripper* (1975) by Donald Rumbelow; *Jack the Ripper: One Hundred Years of Mystery* (1978) by Peter Underwood. A summary of sources and data is *Jack the Ripper: A Bibliography & Review of the Literature* (1984) by Alexander Kelly.

Nick Rennison (2005) *Sherlock Holmes. The Unauthorised Biography*. Atlantic Books, London.

This was the man (Mycroft Holmes) that the Prime Minister now approached. Salisbury knew and respected Mycroft, although he had never met him, he knew of his younger brother's growing reputation of being able to throw light on the most impenetrably dark mysteries. Thus, through Mycroft, the suggestion was made that Holmes might consider tracking down Jack the Ripper. The only surprise is that it had taken so long for Holmes to become drawn into the investigation. The possible explanation for this is that, caught up in their continuing investigations into the Fenians and other Irish nationalists, Mycroft and Sherlock were unwilling to be distracted by what they may have seen as a series of murders that, however brutal, were of less significance than threats to national security. Instructions from the widow of Windsor, however, were not to be ignored.

There are more candidates for the true identity of Jack the Ripper than there were dark alleyways in Whitechapel in 1888. The most unlikely and bizarre theories have been put forward to explain the motives behind the murders. Perhaps the most notorious was the claim, entertainingly advanced by Stephen Knight in his 1978 book *Jack the Ripper: The Final Solution*, that the murders were part of a conspiracy to cover up the fact that Prince Albert Christian Victor Edward ('Eddy to his friends, son of the Prince of Wales and second in line to the throne, had fathered a love-child). The mother was not only an East End prostitute but, even worse, a Roman Catholic. Other prostitutes knew of the child's existence and who he was. To make sure they remained silent, they were all killed and the blame placed on a phantom serial killer. More recently the thriller writer Patricia Cornwell has argued that the painter Walter Sickert was the Ripper and his dark secret is hidden away in hints and details in his later work. It is no less unlikely than the earlier scenario. Even more preposterous notions have been advanced, presumably in all seriousness, to explain the killings.

One theory claims that the true culprit was Dr Thomas Neill Cream, a deranged abortionist and poisoner who was executed in 1892 for administering strychnine to two prostitutes in South London. Cream is alleged to have been attempting a last-minute confessions on the gallows when the executioner pulled the lever and he dropped through the trap. He got as far as, 'I am Jack...' before he fell. The difficulty with this story is that, at the time of the Whitechapel murders, records show that Cream was not only several thousand miles away but behind bars, serving a sentence in Joliet Penitentiary in Illinois. Some researchers, unwilling to relinquish a good story, have got round this apparently conclusive fact by arguing that it was possible that he paid a double to serve his sentence. The most generous assessment of this theory is that it seems implausible. An American researcher once 'proved' that elaborate analysis of the works of Lewis Carroll showed him to be the real Jack the Ripper. Even in the overheated world of Ripperology, this claim was not received with any great enthusiasm.

As for Holmes, his first task was to dispose of the idea that the letters had actually been sent by the murderer. Within days of joining the investigation, he had proved not only that they were fake but at least one of them was the work of gutter press journalist Tom Bulling. Although alert to the increasing importance, Holmes was contemptuous of most journalists. He would have to agree with Matthew Arnold's claim that the new journalism of the period was 'full of ability, novelty, sensation, sympathy, generous instinct: its one failure is that it is feather-brained. It throws out assertions at a venture, because it wishes them to be true...and to get at the state of things as they truly are, seems to have no concern whatever'. Pressure was placed on Bulling and he collapsed under it, admitting that Holmes was right and that he was the author of one of the most sensational letters. Why this information was not more widely publicized is difficult to fathom but many people today continue to believe that the Ripper letters were genuine.

(**Compiler's note:** However, see the final two pages of this chapter).

Holmes carried on with his investigation of the murders but his usual methods of working were soon causing difficulties. When first dragooned into accepting that the consulting detective should investigate the case *sub rosa*, the Assistant Commissioner of the CID, Robert Anderson, had naively believed that Holmes could be kept firmly under control. Anderson knew Holmes from the work they had both done to combat Irish terrorism earlier in the decade and, to some extent, he liked and trusted him. However, he did not want him 'interfering' (as he saw it) in the Ripper case if it could be avoided. He seemed to expect Holmes to work on the case solely under the narrow guidelines he issued. Holmes, who was not an easy man to work with, had other ideas. 'As sensitive to flattery on the score of his art as any girl could be of her beauty', as he is describes in *A Study in Scarlet*, Holmes needed the kind of tactful handling and freedom to manoeuvre that Anderson was not prepared to give. His habit of disappearing into the East End for days at a time, and returning to Scotland Yard dressed as a swaggeringly cocky costermonger to give enigmatic reports of his progress, did not endear him to Anderson and other senior policemen. Yet he did get results where so many had failed.

Trawl through the memoirs of the police officers involved in the Ripper case, from Sir Robert Anderson's to Walter Dew's, and you will find plenty of suggestions that someone, usually the officer whose recollections you are reading, knew who the Ripper was or, at the very least, had a strong suspicion of the killer's identity. Unfortunately, no two officers seem to agree. Often there is speculation that the Ripper committed suicide soon after the murder of Mary Kelly. All these stories can be traced back to Holmes who was the first to be convinced that the killer was himself and began to make converts to this theory among the higher echelons of the police. Other apparent murders, particularly those of Rose Mylett in December 1888 and Alice McKenzie, shook many in this belief but not Holmes. He pointed out that Mylett's death was almost certainly not a murder at all and that Alice McKenzie's killer had been left-handed, not, like the Whitechapel murderer, right-handed. To Holmes the evidence was clear and pointed in one direction only. By the spring of 1889, Holmes was convinced that he knew the identity of the Ripper. The killer who had terrorized the East End was a man called Montague Druitt. The body of Druitt, an Oxford-educated [86] barrister and schoolmaster with a family history of mental illness, was fished out of the Thames on 31 December 1888. Holmes, newly involved in the investigation, had immediately decided that the Ripper could have committed suicide. With his usual devotion to scouring the more sordid details of the press, he had come across a report in Druitt's demise in the pages of an obscure West London paper and had been intrigued. Further investigation into Druitt at first seemed to cast doubt on the possibility that he was indeed the murderer. The barrister was living at Blackheath at the time of the killings and train schedules suggested that it would have been impossible for him to travel freely from there to the East End at the times required. Holmes also discovered that Druitt, a keen sportsman,

---

[86] Druitt had been at Winchester before going up to Oxford. It is just possible that, although five years younger, he may have attended the school at the same time as Watson.

had played in a cricket match at Blackheath on 8 September a mere six hours after the murder of Annie Chapman. Druitt's legal chambers at 9 King's Bench Walk, however, were within walking distance of Whitechapel and, although unlikely, it was not inconceivable that a psychotic killer could have been practising his off spin soon after committing a murder.

Holmes was sufficiently impressed by coincidences of dates between the killings and Druitt's whereabouts, and by the similarity between the barrister's appearance and several of the witness descriptions of a man seen with the victims, to delve more deeply. In one of his forays into the East End in disguise, he seems to have picked up more conclusive proof that Druitt had a taste for the low-life and for slumming in the pubs and dives of Whitechapel. The clinching evidence appears to have come from an interview with Druitt's brother in which it became clear that the barrister's closest surviving relative had suspected, before the killing of Mary Kelly, that Montague was guilty of the murders. Holmes himself, in the wake of this interview, was equally convinced. His difficulty lay in winning over others.

Holmes's maverick approach to the investigation worked against him. By antagonizing Anderson and others in the police, he made it unnecessarily difficult to persuade them that he was right in his identification of Druitt. Eventually he grew weary when that was, to him, blindingly obvious remained, for others, one possibility among many, and he withdrew from the enquiry in disgust. The sole surviving evidence of Holmes's solution to the Jack the Ripper mystery lies in a memorandum written by one of the policemen involved in the case, Melville MacNaghten, 'From private information,' MacNaghten writes, referring to Holmes, 'I have little doubt that his own family suspected this man of being the Whitechapel murderer; it was alleged that he was sexually insane.'

Daily Mail, Saturday, December 2, 2006

THE SKELETON IN MY CUPBOARD

Many of us have dark family secrets. But when one writer saw a TV documentary about Jack the Ripper this week, he was forced to confront a chilling possibility…

By **Michael Thornton**

Last week, in an absorbing Channel Five television documentary, three criminologists attempted to apply modern forensic science to put a name and face to the most notorious serial killer in criminal history. For more than ten weeks in the terror-stricken autumn of 1888, an unknown solitary assailant stalked the noisome alleys of Whitechapel, in London, killing and mutilating five prostitutes, and possibly 13 other women.

He has entered folklore as Jack the Ripper. Yet after 118 years of concentrated investigation, millions of words, more than 200 suspects, and every sort of conspiracy theory and myth imaginable, we are still no nearer to discovering his identity.

Last week's ingenious attempt (by Laura Richards, a behavioural psychologist with the violent crime directorate at New Scotland Yard, John Grieve, former head of the

Yard's murder squad, and Dr Kim Rossmo, of the Department of Criminal Justice in Texas) to find out who he was, ended in failure.

A shawl allegedly taken from the butchered body of the Ripper's fourth undoubted victim, Catherine Eddowes, failed to render DNA – either her own or her killer's. The door appeared to have slammed shut on the last chance of solving the greatest unsolved crime of all time.

Despite this, I found myself watching the documentary transfixed, and with an overwhelming morbid fascination.

Some of the content in the documentary startled me and forced me to confront an alarming possibility that I had rejected and pushed to the back of my mind for almost 30 years. Could Jack the Ripper have been a member of my own family?

I was 37 and living in a flat opposite the Royal Mews in Buckingham Palace Road in 1978, when I first heard this astonishing story from my half-sister, Doreen Gillham, who was 25 years my senior, and the child of my father's first marriage.

She told me: 'Grandpa was a rather funny man – funny peculiar. Very peculiar in fact. Grandpa was a man who had secrets.

'When I was 16, I remember Granny telling me once: "Len has a dark side to his life." And for a long time she would never tell me what she meant.

"Then one day, not long before she died, it all came out. They had married for love, but the first years of their marriage were really difficult. There were differences between them – sexual differences, also religious differences. The, three years after they got married, Grandpa was investigated by the police, who thought he was Jack the Ripper.' He was never charged but Granny suspected it was true, and I am convinced of it. Doreen was sometimes given to bold statements, but this time I thought she had lost the plot.'

I asked incredulously: 'You think our grandfather was Jack the Ripper?' She looked back at me with a calm, unblinking stare. 'Yes' she said. Doreen was 63 at that time and I attributed this pronouncement to the aging process. My sister, Jean Wheeler, the last surviving member of the family who knew my grandparents, says: 'I don't believe this story, but no one knew them as well as she did.'

Before last week's documentary, I had not realised the police tracked down 13 eye-witnesses in 1888, all of whom saw the Ripper as he went about his murderous onslaughts.

To my astonishment, the physical details described – in terms of age, height, colouring and appearance – matched my grandfather with uncanny precision. This caused me to look more deeply into his life. Leonard Booker Thornton ('Len' to his family) was born on September 24, 1859 at 24 London Terrace, Bethnal Green, a short walk away from the dark Whitechapel streets where the Ripper went about his gruesome work.

Len's ancestors had been rectors of Birkin, Yorkshire. One branch of the family became extremely rich and influential, producing a banker, an MP, and the celebrated novelist E.M. Forster, of whom his cousin, my grandfather, disapproved deeply on account of his homosexuality.

The other branch, by comparison, was poor. My grandfather was the son of a well-to-do master linen draper, Tom Thornton. He owned several shops, but when he discovered his son did not intend to follow him into the business, planning to study medicine instead, he told him he must earn the money to pay for his tuition.

Accordingly, Len, at 18 went to work for a Bethnal Green blacksmith, transporting lame, sick and elderly horses to the slaughterhouse in Whitechapel where he learnt the grim task of dismembering the carcasses.

In time, he earned enough money to train at the London Hospital in Whitechapel Road, the merest stone's throw from the scene of the Ripper gruesome murders.

There he studied anatomy, performed amputations and other surgical procedures, and found himself deeply affected by the poverty and disease in the area.

In his diary, now in my possession, he wrote of 'the terrible bacilli of consumption. There, under the specialist's eye was the minute life more vicious than a hungry beast, more deadly than a sword'.

Late at night, invariably short of money he would walk home alone through the darkened streets, sometimes bloodstained from his work, ignoring the blandishments of the prostitutes, and carrying his surgical tools in a little Gladstone bag, an accessory that has become an indispensable part of Ripper folklore.

By the age of 25, he had qualified as a chemist and druggist, and on July 26, 1885, he married Hannah O'Sullivan, an Irish Catholic and a member of the famous O'Sullivan clan of County Cork.

Her family felt she was marrying beneath her, and they were aghast when she abandoned her Catholicism to marry in a Wesleyan Methodist chapel in Lambeth.

Their first child, Mabel, was born the following year, but was to be sickly all her life, dying unmarried at the age of 23.

It was during Hannah's second pregnancy, which began in December 1887, that the Ripper murders commenced. By that time, there was already trouble in the marriage on both religious and sexual grounds. Len, an atheist, wrote in his diary: 'Religion is the opium of the poor,' and added: 'I consider religion to be a mania when it interferes with the legitimate development of human nature.'

According to Hannah's later revelations to her granddaughter, Len, deprived by the pregnancy of sexual relations, he became moody and began coming home in the middle of the night.

'I could not help noticing that his clothes were often blood-stained,' she said, 'but he told me this was from his hospital work.'

Two Whitechapel prostitutes, Mary Ann Nichols – 'Polly', and 'Dark' Annie Chapman, had been killed and mutilated, the latter on September 8, 1888, only two days before the birth of Len and Hannah's son, my father, Reginald Leonard Thornton.

There was a respite of almost three weeks before two more prostitutes, Elizabeth ('Long Liz') Stride and Catherine Eddowes, were butchered on the same night.

The last and most terrible of the Ripper murders, that of Mary Jane Kelly, followed on November 9. She had been horribly mutilated, and her sexual organs and other parts distributed around her room.

Dennis Halstead, a doctor at the London Hospital, observed that these mutilations had been performed with 'great surgical skill'. It was shortly after the Kelly murder that the police descended on my grandfather. He owned two houses, with servants, and two chemist's shops in Lambeth, but his outward respectability did not prevent him from becoming a suspect.

The eye-witness accounts of the Ripper all described a man between 25 and 30. My grandfather was 29. The killer was said to stand between 5ft 5in and 5ft 7in. My grandfather was 5ft 7in. The murderer was said to have a brown moustache, 'carroty in colour'. My sister, Jean, who sat on his knee aged six, remembers my grandfather's moustache as 'gingery'.

Doreen was told by our grandmother that Len had not been arrested by the police – but they were clearly very suspicious of him, even though they had no evidence. He was asked some searching questions, and for a time he was followed by plain clothes officers. Len's diary entry of the time, scrawled in black ink, often seemed to reveal a man deeply troubled.

On one page he wrote: "The devil will lead you down into hell'. On another: "The mainspring of human actions is *human passions*. For good or evil, passions rule this poor humanity of ours.'

My grandfather's name does not appear in any surviving record of the Ripper investigation. Nor in the list of more than 200 suspects. Many of the names proposed, like that of Prince Albert Victor, Duke of Clarence, Queen Victoria's grandson, have long been discredited by serious Ripperologists on the grounds that they have alibis for the dates of the murders.

Other preposterous non-starters are the Queen's physician, Sir William Gull, author Lewis Carroll, painter Walter Sickert and poet Francis Thompson.

One ingenious theory presents the murders as part of an organised conspiracy by Freemasons, but there is no proof to support it. Virtually every other Ripper suspect has been discredited over the years.

Christabel, Lady Aberconway told me in 1972 that her father Sir Melville MacNaghten, formerly an assistant chief constable with the CID, was 'convinced' the Ripper was Montague John Druitt, a 31-year-old barrister who drowned himself in the Thames soon after the murder of Mary Jean Kelly.

'He was sexually insane,' wrote MacNaghten. But inspector Frederick Abberline, who led the Ripper investigation, disagreed, believing there was no real evidence against Druitt.

In the years following the Ripper killings, my grandfather became a respected analytical pharmacist who frequently gave evidence in murder cases, especially those involving poison.

In 1910, he assisted pathologist Sir Bernard Spilsbury to analyse human tissue found in the cellar of 39 Hilldrop Crescent, Holloway, which led to Dr Hawley Harvey Crippen being hanged for the murder of his wife. My father, who was 22 at the time, commented that Crippen had 'got what he deserved'. My grandfather replied: 'You should feel pity for him. Men can be driven by provocation into all manners of extremism.'

My grandfather became increasingly distant from my father, who, when the Irish 'troubles' began in 1916, took to calling himself 'Pat', and went around London with a gun in his belt, announcing himself as 'a founder member of the IRA'.

When my father's first wife, Mary, died in 1926 at the age of 41, leaving three young children, my grandfather was deeply sympathetic, but his Victorian sense of propriety was scandalised when my father married again, only 16 months later, his new wife my mother, Anne Roberts, a young Welsh nurse.

After the death of his wife on March 21, 1932, at the age of 72, my grandfather appeared a haunted and broken man. He was distressed by the activities of his convent-educated elder granddaughter, Irene, who went on the stage as the blond assistant of a magician.

She married a chorus boy from Ivor Novello's musicals, and outraged my grandfather by appearing on stage at the Windmill Theatre, wearing no clothes. Later, her glamorous looks won her a small role in the film The Mill on the Floss, but she was to die at only 32 from pulmonary tuberculosis.

In old age, Len became increasingly preoccupied by the plight of fallen women. 'Poverty of pain is a crime.' He wrote in his diary, 'particularly in the case of a girl, because it can make a girl desperate, and all the tea-shop girls suffer from poverty of pay'.

When Len developed cancer, and was nursed by my half-sister, he said to her: 'Thank you for looking after me, but if you know what I have done in my life, you would not even come near me.' He died on September 23, 1935, at the age of 75.

Just the other day, I stood by his grave, which I am planning to restore. The memorial stone has blackened with age, so that the name Thornton is almost indistinguishable. It looks as if time is trying to shroud our family mystery in secrecy.

Was my grandfather Jack the Ripper? The truthful answer is I don't know. But while I cannot prove my half-sister's belief that he was, I equally cannot prove that he wasn't. There are too many coincidences to dismiss.

And just how many of us are fully acquainted with all the skeletons in our family cupboards, or get to know the innermost secrets of the generations that went before us?

Behavioural psychologist Laura Richards believes the killer was 'socially skilled' and 'probably came across on a superficial level as charming'. She says: The police thought they were looking for an obvious lunatic, someone more animal than man. But I don't buy into that. The offender is someone who's been totally overlooked because he's so ordinary and so mundane.'

What last week's television documentary made clear is we shall never know the identity of the man who brought horror and carnage to the dark streets of London's East End during that long-ago autumn of terror.

Andrew Lycett (2007) **Conan Doyle. The Man Who Created Sherlock Holmes**. Weidenfeld & Nicolson.

…As the author of a recent study about a London-based detective, Arthur might have taken an interest in the spate of horrific murders of young women, almost all prostitutes, which had recently occurred in the city's East End. However if he enquired about what became known as the Jack the Ripper affair, he kept quiet about it, and had to suffer the ignominy of a satirical article in a Portsmouth paper calling on him, as a known spiritualist, to use his psychic powers to solve the murders that were front-page news.

…In December 1892 Conan Doyle visited Scotland Yard's crime museum where he was shown a letter supposedly written by Jack the Ripper and wondered why Scotland Yard, true to fictional form, had not taken more trouble to investigate its handwriting. Sherlock Holmes, he confidently said, would have made a facsimile of the signature and published in the leading newspapers of the world to see if anyone could come up with a match.

…Arthur accompanied members (of the Crimes Club) two months later on a tour of Jack the Ripper sites in Whitechapel. John Churton Collins, an English lecturer at Birmingham University, recalled that 'Conan Doyle seemed very much interested, particularly in the Petticoat Lane part of the Expedition, and laughed when I said "Caliban would have turned up his nose at this"'.

Between November 2007 and January 2008 an art exhibition entitled: "Walter Sickert: The Camden Town Nudes" took place at the Courtauld Institute/Gallery, London. What follows are extracts from two articles:

Seven The Sunday Telegraph Magazine 4 November 2007

MURDEROUS ENIGMA by Michael Prodger

Six years ago, the crime novelist Patricia Cornwell spent about £2 million of her royalties buying up 31 paintings by Walter Sickert, as well as some of his letters and his desk. It was not from love of his work: she cut one canvas into pieces and subjected the rest of her hoard to forensic examination. She was looking for evidence to support her theory that Sickert was in fact Jack the Ripper.

Unsurprisingly, none emerged. If Sickert wasn't to blame for the Whitechapel mutilations he was nevertheless partly responsible for Cornwell's act of mutilation. If he hadn't painted the four pictures known collectively as the Camden Town Murders series it is doubtful she would have marked him down as a serial killer. These paintings are now on show for the first time, as a centrepiece of a small exhibition of Sickert's nudes – paintings, pastels and drawings – at the Courtauld Gallery in Somerset House.

In 1907 a prostitute called Emily Dimmock was found with her throat cut in a dingy rented room in Camden Town. Sickert's paintings show just such a shabby bedroom with a naked woman lying on a cheap bed and a fully clothed man sitting or standing at her side. Their faces are shrouded in shadow and absolute stillness reigns. There is, however, no blood, no violence and no weapon…

THE DAILY TELEGRAPH TUESDAY, NOVEMBER 6, 2007

An underworld stripped bare

A richly rewarding show reveals the intelligence that Walter Sickert poured into his paintings of London low life, says **Richard Dorment**

…Although I don't for an instant agree with Patricia Cornwell's far-fetched theory that Sickert was Jack the Ripper, looking at the way Sickert draws the eyes to the vaginas of the prostitutes in so many of these pictures while at the same time "mutilating" their faces I can see why someone might entertain the idea.

For a prostitute, savagery of another sort was an occupational hazard. On September 12, 1907 a young prostitute named Emily Dimmock was found naked in a flat in Camden Town, her throat cut from ear to ear. Sickert followed with fascination the lurid cover of the murder and its aftermath – the arrest and acquittal of Robert Wood, the only suspect…

Ely M. Liebow (2007) **Dr. Joe Bell: Model for Sherlock Holmes**. Popular Press.

Late in 1888, according to the *Edinburgh Evening News*, Dr. Joseph Bell tried his hand in solving the biggest puzzle of them all: The identity of Jack the Ripper. It must be remembered, as Dr. Z.M. Hamilton reminded readers of the *Calgary Historical Bulletin*, Dr. Bell himself went on record, observing that "Dr. Littlejohn is the medical adviser, and he likes to have a second man with…and it so happens that for more than 20 yrs we have done a great deal together, and it has come to be the regular thing for him to take me into cases with him." At the height of the Ripper hysteria Joe Bell received a report detailing all aspects of the case [87] The identity of "the greatest fiend of modern times" was never established. All evidence pointed to a person (women were not ruled out) possessed of no little anatomical skill; one who had a "thing" about prostitutes; and one who was calculating and adroit, as evidenced by his uncanny stealth and elusiveness.

All of the murders took place in the Whitechapel Area of London's East End. From four to seven women were brutally slaughtered, dissected, and eviscerated by the murderer, probably starting in April of 1888 and ending at the very end of the year. Emma Elizabeth Smith, a widow, was the first of the official victims of the fiend. She was found in a Whitechapel gutter with her throat showing to jagged, parallel slashes that almost "carried" to the backbone. In early August Martha Turner, prostitute was found dead on a tenement stoop, her body horribly mutilated. Three weeks later Anne Nichols, prostitute, "her body slit apart," was found in yet another Whitechapel gutter. On September 8 the body of Annie Chapman, a 40-year-old prostitute, was found in the back yard of a tenement, her head nearly severed and her organs laid out symmetrically around her – some change and jewelry at her feet. On September 30 there was a double murder. First, a man riding a pony evidently came across the Ripper as he was dissecting the body of 42-year old Elizabeth Stride. She had been attending a party. The murderer fled and seemed to disappear magically into the labyrinthine alleys of

---

[87] The entire account may be found in one of Conan Doyle's favourite popular magazines: "The Real Sherlock Holmes," *Tit-Bits*. LI (October 21, 1911), 127.

Whitechapel; later that night, the blood-drenched body of 43-year old Katherine Eddowes was found in a public square. The last and most horrible murder took place on November 8. Mary Jeanette Kelly, an attractive 24-year old prostitute was found naked on her huge, old fashioned brass bed. Her throat had been cut through; her ears and nose sliced off, her organs had been removed and placed neatly around the body. On her pillow, above her twisted head – her bleeding heart. "The operator, according to Scotland Yard, must have been at least two hours over this hellish job. The madman [in a scene faithfully recreated by two recent movies] [88] made a bonfire of some old newspapers, and by this dim, irreligious light, a scene was enacted which nothing witnessed by Dante, in his visit to the infernal regions, could have surpassed."

Along with the police who nailed rubber strips to their shoes to promote silence as they walked in pairs around Whitechapel, Joe Bell was well aware that the killer used a long, razor-sharp knife; had a diabolic sense of the dramatic; and took unbelievable risks (everyone who owned a long-handled knife and knew anything about anatomy or woodcarving or slaughtering animals was suspect).

Some of the major suspects: a medical student with a pathological hatred of vice; a respectable English doctor (**Compiler's note:** Correction, he was in fact a barrister) whose body was found floating in the Thames; a Polish barber named Koslowski, seen running from the Ripper murders; an American sailor; an insane Russian doctor; and, ironically, a real life butcher.

Joe Bell was fascinated not only by the Ripper's letters to the London papers as well as the handwriting itself but also by the killer's maniacal delight in sending such things as human kidneys to the police. It is believed that, working out his own theory, he may have been instrumental in having the following story inserted on page 7 of the *Scotsman*:

Wed., Oct. 10, 1888

THE LONDON MURDERS

Detectives on a "New Scent"

The sudden disappearance of a man from a hotel in which he left a black bag, and is represented to have contained some articles of a compromising character. This man came to London from Scotland ten years ago. He is a duly qualified surgeon, but has lost his standing through dissipation. Since he began to slide the scale, his father has been in the habit of sending remittances. The sums have been squandered away among the class of women who have fallen victim to the murderer's knife, and on one occasion he was robbed of a case of surgical instruments by them. Since then, he has, it is said, harboured intense hatred against them.

According to the *Edinburgh Evening News*, Joe Bell spoke to a "journalist-friend" of Jack the Ripper murders, and related how he and another friend who liked solving deep problems, went about the unmasking of the fiendish murderer. "There were two of us in the hunt, and when two men set out to find a golf ball in the rough, they expect to come across it when the straight line marked in their mind's eye to it [sic], from their original

---

[88] "A Study in Terror" (1965) and "Murder by Decree" (1979).

positions, crossed. In the same way, when two men set out to investigate a crime mystery, it is where their researches intersect that we have a result." [89]

He and his anonymous friend, taking into account all the Scotland Yard suspects and at least two additional suspects from Scotland deduced the murderer; each wrote a name on a piece of paper; put the paper in an envelope; and then exchanged envelopes. Evidently both men had the same name (never revealed!). Dr. Bell immediately notified Scotland Yard. A week later, the murders came to an end. Was this coincidence? Did Dr. Bell and his unnamed friend have something to do with solving the case – or stopping the carnage? The answer will never be known, just as Jack the Ripper has never been positively identified. Sherlock Holmes, as a literary creation, was not yet a year old.

Conclusion

Patricia Cornwell (2002) **Portrait of a Killer. Jack the Ripper. Case Closed**. Berkley.

(*Including Compiler's note*)

This chapter presented information on Jack the Ripper by twenty-six authors/writers. Of these, seven can be discounted as their work was published after Cornwell's book. However, the books/articles by the remaining authors/writers came out between 1929 and 1993. Checking Cornwell's bibliography – primary and secondary sources – not one of these works were referenced.

These omissions make me ponder on Cornwell's research skills, as these works should, in my opinion (as a retired Senior Lecturer in Research) have been included in her background reading, especially Knight's book – "Perhaps the most important and influential volume on the Ripper crimes ever published" (Paul Chapman).

A new exhibition, 'Jack the Ripper and the East End' is being held at The Museum in Dockland until November 2. Two newspaper/Magazine articles have been published on the exhibition.

The first of these comes from The Daily Telegraph TELEGRAPH TRAVEL . **Saturday, May 17, 2008.**

Back to the London of Jack the Ripper.

A new exhibition debunks the myths surrounding a serial killer and paints a vivid portrait of the Victorian city. **Nigel Richardson** reports.

It is a repulsive and fascinating item and true obsessives will make a beeline for it. "This is the original 'Dear Boss' letter," confirmed Julia Hoffbrand, the co-curator of a new exhibition dedicated to Jack the Ripper. The letter marks the point in the Ripper story at which reality turned into myth.

It was sent to the head of a London news agency on September 25, 1888. following the murders of three women in a month in the East End. Written in red ink, it starts

---

[89] Irving Wallace, *The Sunday Gentleman*, New York. Bantam Books, 1976. p. 470. Originally published in 1965 by Simon & Schuster.

"Dear Boss", gives a warning that "I am down on whores and I shunt [sic] quit ripping them till I do get buckled, and is signed "Yours truly, Jack the Ripper".

This was the first time the name had been used and it was swiftly adopted and ascribed to the unidentified serial killer who committed savage murders of women (the exact number remains, like so much, a matter of speculation) in Whitechapel and Spitalfields, a decade or so before the turn of the 20th century. Since then the name and his deeds have developed into a bloated myth which this excellent exhibition at London's Museum in Docklands – just a hansom cab ride from the Ripper's killing fields – aims to expose and dissect.

It seems amazing, given the continuing and frenzied industry in books and films about Jack the Ripper, that this should be the first serious exhibition on the subject. But, discounting waxworks and other horror tableaux, it is indeed the first time that Ripper-related artefacts – more than 200, many original and not seen by the public before – have been brought together in a rigorous context.

Scrupulously avoiding any whiff of sensationalism (even if some of the marketing is in questionable taste), the exhibition steers a consistently thought-provoking line. "What's different here is that we are looking beyond the murders to the world in which they took place – what they tell us about London and life at the time," said Julia Hoffbrand. She and her team are also anxious to give the story back to its rightful owners – the murdered women.

"Usually they are bandied around as foils to Jack the Ripper himself," she said. "In the exhibition we always refer to the victims by their names." The bare facts are that, between April 1888 and February 1891, 11 murders were investigated that may or may not have been committed by one man, Jack the Ripper. Within those 11, five are regarded by "Ripperologists" – the fanatics who continue to speculate on the Ripper's identity – as "canonical".

By this they mean that these murders in particular bear unmistakable Ripper hallmarks, but Julia Hoffbrand finds the word canonical distasteful. "It is not historically appropriate," she said. Neither is she impressed by the undoubted "iconic" status of the red-ink letter in which the name Jack the Ripper was first used – and not just because it could well have been a hoax.

The 'Dear Boss' letter *is* iconic," she conceded, "whereas the police reports aren't as sought-after. But for me as a curator, when you read the documents it becomes real. It wasn't a game, something which Jack the Ripper has turned into: a game, a myth."

The exhibition debunks that myth, relating the story murder by murder and placing it in a series of contexts. By a coincidence that no doubt boosted the myth, the Ripper killings happened at a time of growing public interest in both the criminal mind and the possible means of understanding and thwarting it.

In 1887, a year before the killings started, the first Sherlock Holmes story had been published; and during 1888, when most of the murders took place, a stage adaptation of Robert Louis Stevenson's *Strange Case of Dr Jekyll and Mr Hyde* was playing in the West End. The exhibition features a double-exposure photograph of the actor Richard Mansfield, playing both the good doctor and his malevolent alter ego. At the same time social reformers and journalists were beginning to realise that the land to the east of the great City of London was an affront to the world's most powerful nation. The publicity surrounding the Ripper case was to expose once and for all the reality of one of Britain's darkest corners.

The few square miles of Whitechapel and Spitalfields in which the killings took place were a maze of alleys, courtyards and common lodging houses haunted by the desperately poor and vulnerable. The infant mortality rate was 20 per cent and alcoholism and prostitution – all the Ripper's victims were alcoholics and prostitutes – were a way of life. A highlight of the exhibition is the "poverty map" of London – compiled by the social scientist Charles Booth and published in 1889 – on which streets and neighbourhoods are coloured according to the wealth of the people who lived there. "It goes from yellow, which is very wealthy" – Julia pointed to the West End – to dark blue and black, the very poorest."

And now her finger hovered over the dark shaded areas to the north and south of Whitechapel Road, representing what she called "the abyss". Its denizens are captured in a series of photographs not seen before. Retrieved from the archives of the Museum of London – of which Museum in Docklands is an offshoot – they show streets and alleys peopled by defiant, proud, sometimes downtrodden-looking women in threadbare bonnets and shawls. "Somebody could have murdered any one of these women," Julia said.

The press cut its red-top teeth on the Ripper murders, revelling in details that today's tabloids would not be allowed to publish. The Birmingham *Daily Post*, reporting on the killing of Mary Ann Nichols, gloated that: "The throat was gashed in two cuts, penetrating from the front of the neck to the vertebrae."

The original police reports, written in black ink on yellowing official forms, are no less chilling for being dryly written. Detailing the death of Mary Ann, Inspector John Spratling noted that [the doctor] arrived quickly and pronounced life to be extinct…she had been disembowelled." The final part of the exhibition consists of an oval gallery with white walls into which are recessed a series of postcard-sized photographs. A notice gives warning that the images are of "a distressing nature". Here, finally, we see the women murdered by the man known as Jack the Ripper. Needless to say, no one took these women's photographs while they were alive. These are police pictures taken in death.

"When you see these images, you see what this is about," said Julia. "These are real women and their lives were cut short and this is what's important. There's nothing glamorous about Jack the Ripper, and there's nothing glamorous about what happened. I hope people will leave contemplating that."

My route took me through Whitechapel, so I decided to visit Mitre Square, where the body of Catherine Eddowes was found on September 30, 1888. The old buildings have been replaced by modern offices but the square is still cobbled, and towering over it is the glass skin of the office block known as The Gherkin.

I sat on a bench and studied a copy of the original map of the murder, trying to get my bearings. And a shudder ran through me as I worked out that I was sitting on the very spot where Catherine was found.

The second article is from The Sunday Telegraph **Seven** Magazine 18 MAY 2008-07-21.

Why Jack the Ripper still has us in his grip

Alex Werner was talking to Alastair Smart

Just mention London's Victorian East End and you will instantly conjure up a vision of the darker side of urban life – dimly lit alleys, foggy nights, prostitutes, poverty and the menacing footsteps of history's most notorious serial killer. Welcome to the world of Jack the Ripper.

I've been a senior curator at the Museum of London for more than 20 years, and whenever we have asked visitors who they would most like to see featured in an exhibition, it is the Ripper whose name keeps coming up. Our exhibition committee has always been uncertain about the idea: wasn't it sensationalist fare, better suited to the Chamber of Horrors at Madame Tussauds? In the end, though, we decided a serious treatment was long overdue.

We opted against finger-pointing and making bold new claims about who the Ripper was – though we do offer a 'Suspect's Wall', which portrays a few likely candidates from the 200-plus who have been suggested over the years. Dr Barnardo, Lewis Carroll and pretty much anyone slightly eccentric and well-known at the time have all been put in the frame. In the late 1960s and early 1970s, for example, when conspiracy theories were rife, the grandson of Queen Victoria, Albert Victor, became a suspect. He had always had a reputation as a dodgy character, based on his frequenting the infamous Cleveland Street rent-boy brothel and it was reckoned that there may have been a royal cover-up in the 1880s to hide his identity as Jack the Ripper.

New theories have these days become an industry in themselves, and Ripperology is big business. Most famously and most recently, the American crime writer Patricia Cornwell has pointed her finger at the English painter Walter Sickert, although evidence suggests he was in France in the late summer of 1888, when many of the murders took place. I don't suppose that Sickert popped back over the Channel each night to kill, but the attention Cornwell's theory has attracted goes to show that the Ripper case is far from closed. It's the ultimate whodunit that everyone's compelled to try to solve.

In the museum there are about 250,000 objects relating to London's social and working history, which are held in trust for future generations and housed in our warehouse stores in Hackney and Swindon. They range from ephemera, such as old tool boxes, to the serious – for example, we'll be displaying the skull of the late-19th- century syphilis sufferer (you can tell he had the disease from the pitted marks in the skull), with a view to highlighting the sexual disease and prostitution that was rife in those days.

My job is to document and research archival material and to pull different parts of it together for exhibitions of London history. It took more than two years to prepare for the Ripper exhibition, such was the wealth of material

One item I unearthed was a starkly titled map 'Modern Plague of London', which was published by the National Temperance Movement in the 1880s and marks, with red dots, the location of all the pubs in central London. There were 48 pubs in a one-mile section of the Whitechapel Road, which is interesting when you think that the women murdered by the Ripper were alcoholics. In a world of extreme deprivation, drink offered comfort and escape.

Our aim was to contextualise the Whitechapel murders and build a better picture of what life was like in the East End. In the mid-1880s, a trade depression had caused mass unemployment in London. Port and riverside workers struggled to feed and house their families. Tensions rose, culminating in demonstrations and riots. Some felt society was on the edge, with the establishment fearing the 1889 centenary of the French Revolution might be marked by a similar overthrow in Britain.

Into this troubled context came the Ripper. At the same time, the theatrical adaptation of *Dr Jekyll and Mr Hyde*, with its disturbing tale of an ordinary man becoming a violent and murderous beast, was smash-hit in the West End. Sherlock Holmes, too, was getting his first outings, as Arthur Conan Doyle's 'A Study in Scarlet' appeared in the pages of *Beeton's Christmas Annual*. Holmes's detective methods – including laboratory analysis , a practice as yet unused by the Met – foreshadowed later advances in forensic science, and during the Ripper murders, his intelligence and success, albeit fictional, highlighted the incompetence and failures of London's police. Conan Doyle's own Ripper theory was that the killer was a woman, probably a midwife, thus ensuring an easier escape from the murder scene. Midwives, after all, worked all hours and wore bloodstained clothing.

We are also presenting many documents that, are after more than a century in the National Archives, going on display for the first time. These include police reports that reveal how the murdered women's bodies were dismembered ('her throat cut from ear to ear' reads one), witness statements and detectives' case reports.

One highlight piece, though, is the 'Dear Boss' letter, dated 25 September, 1888. Received by the Central News Agency on 27 September and then forwarded to the Metropolitan Police, it is handwritten in blood-red ink, purportedly by the Ripper himself, and contains the foreboding message: 'My knife's so nice and sharp. I want to get to work right away.'

Its prediction of events to come was particularly chilling, in the context of the double murder of Catherine Eddowes and Elizabeth Stride just days later. The Met officers were pretty confident that it was a hoax carried out by a Central News Agency journalist interested in upping newspaper sales, yet the letter still caused a major public stir – facsimiles of it appeared in the press and on posters in the hope that someone would identify the handwriting. And just as interestingly for us, the sign-off 'Yours truly, Jack the Ripper' was the first time that moniker had been used.

(**Compiler's note**: Chief Inspector Walter Dew investigated both the Jack the Ripper murders and the case of Hawley Harvey Crippen).

NOVEMBER 9 2008 **The Sunday Telegraph**

Clues that could finally unmask the Ripper
File on leading suspect is among documents from high security hospital to be available to public for first time

Wendy Moore and **Ben Leach**

FOR MORE than a century, the identity of Jack the Ripper has eluded detectives and historians. Now, files released from Broadmoor High Security Hospital will provide tantalising new evidence that could finally help to crack Britain's most notorious unsolved murder case.

Among the patients whose files are to be disclosed, as the psychiatric hospital opens its archives to public view for the first time, is Thomas Hayne Cutbush, who was identified at the time as a leading suspect in the killing and mutilation of at least 11 women in the East End of London between 1888 and 1891.

Cutbush, who is described by one author writing a book about the Ripper murders as the "number one suspect", was sent to Lambeth Infirmary in 1891 suffering delusions thought to have been caused by syphilis. But he immediately escaped, stabbed a woman, and then attempted to stab a second.

He was pronounced insane and committed in 1891 to Broadmoor, where he remained until his death in 1903. From the day he was detained, the Ripper murders ceased.

The Broadmoor file on Cutbush is understood to contain about 20 documents. They include admittance details, medical notes on his behaviour, documents relating to his death and a letter from the hospital Medical Superintendent to Cutbush's mother.

They are also understood to include detailed descriptions of Cutbush that match eyewitness accounts of Jack the Ripper. In one document he is described as having "brilliant blue eyes" and a limp, fitting a description provided by someone who had seen the murderer. The file is also understood to include letters written by Broadmoor staff detailing Cutbush's rants while at the hospital. He was said to have repeatedly threatened to "rip" them open with a knife.

Cutbush first came under suspicion in 1894 when a newspaper claimed to know the identity of the Ripper. Although it did not name the suspect, the details clearly pointed to Cutbush, the nephew of a Scotland Yard superintendent who killed himself two years later. The newspaper article claimed that Cutbush's defence team had thought he was Jack the Ripper, and had evidence of this. But it was never shown to the court because Cutbush was sectioned.

David Bullock, who is writing a book about the Ripper killings called *The Man Who Would Be Jack*, said the files would shed "invaluable light" on Cutbush's role in the killings. "Cutbush really is the number one suspect. He was a known psychopath and his family actually suspected him of having to do with the killings because of his strange behaviour. "He was nocturnal, would spend the day studying medical books and would often spend the night walking the streets of London and come home covered in mud and blood," Mr Bullock said. "There is all sorts of evidence that point to him as the killer, but I have never seen any evidence that rules him out. There is even a conspiracy theory for why he was never put forward as a suspect by the police. Imagine the uproar if the public found out that he was a suspect, and that his uncle was a senior member of the Met."

Experts researching the Ripper case have previously approached the Broadmoor authorities seeking permission to view the Cutbush files, but have been turned away. Broadmoor's unique collection of historical records, which dates back to the hospital's opening in 1863, will provide a rich hunting ground for historians, family history enthusiasts and criminologists. Among many famous patients whose records became available from November 18 is the artist Richard Dadd, who painted many of his best-loved pictures during his time in Broadmoor. Another patient who used his time in Broadmoor creatively was William Chester Minor, an American army doctor committed to the hospital in 1872 after killing a man while in a delusional state. Granted two comfortable rooms complete with library, he contributed innumerable entries to the first *Oxford English Dictionary*, giving his address simply as Crowthorne (the village nearest to Broadmoor), Berkshire.

Edward Oxford was transferred to Broadmoor in 1864 after firing a pistol at Queen Victoria 24 years earlier. When he revealed the gun had contained blanks and doctors declared that he had been sane all along, he was released in 1867 on condition he left the country. The decision to open the archive to the public follows requests under Freedom of Information legislation. Only records more than 100 years old will be available to view by appointment at Berkshire Record Office, in Reading.

RIPPER SUSPECTS

Among the leading suspects in the Jack the Ripper case have been:

Walter Sickert

A German-born artist who painted the low-life of the East End. Sickert had a morbid fascination with the murders, and was thought to have a suspiciously detailed knowledge of the victims' injuries.

Sir William Gull

The Queen's physician, Gull features in the seemingly most far fetched theory. Queen Victoria's grandson Prince Albert Victor, according to urban legend, secretly married a Catholic girl named Annie Crook, who gave birth to his child. To avoid scandal, she was put in a lunatic asylum and Sir William was appointed to silence all who knew of the affair.

John Pizer

A Jewish shoemaker, Pizer resembled the description of Jack the Ripper that was circulated at the time: a short man with a dark beard and moustache, who spoke with a foreign accent. His name was cleared later by a solid alibi, leading to a libel payout.

Daily Mail, Monday, November 24, 2008

A leading suspect in the Jack the Ripper case – and a notorious murderer of women – Thomas Hayne Cutbush – was pronounced insane and died in Broadmoor in 1903. From the day of his arrest, the Ripper murders ceased.

The Sunday Telegraph NOVEMBER 16 2008

The article (report, November 9) pointing the finger at Thomas Hayne Cutbush as being the Ripper reinforces a theory I have long held that there is an industry which would die were the identity of the Ripper ever be proved. However, the identity was proved, beyond reasonable doubt, at the time. My great grandfather, Donald Sutherland Swanson, was the detective in total charge of the Ripper murders. His private papers contain his handwritten identification of Aaron Kosminski as the Ripper. Along with others of his papers, I have loaned them to the Metropolitan Police Museum at new Scotland Yard, where researchers may be able to study them.

Neville Swanson Worcester

The Sunday Telegraph NOVEMBER 23 2008

TO THE EDITOR

The Ripper's identity

Neville Swanson (Letters, November 16) wrote regarding the unsolved Whitechapel murders of 1888 and the unknown murderer known as Jack the Ripper. The identity of the killer was not "proved beyond all reasonable doubt at the time" and the then Chief Inspector Donald Sutherland Swanson, did not provide "handwritten identification of Aaron Kosminski as the Ripper." In fact, the police adduced no hard evidence against anybody in the case and there was no consensus of opinion in police circles as to the possible identity of the killer.

Stewart Evans Ely, Cambridgeshire

Daily Mail WEEKEND Magazine 20 June 2009

SEVEN DAYS **Nigel Andrew's** guide to the week's TV

Wednesday 24 June – Jack the Ripper: Tabloid Killer – Revealed

Kelvin MacKenzie applies his experience of newspapers and circulation-boosting stunts to the Jack the Ripper case, and nails the author of the notorious letter that gave the serial killer his grisly nickname. More than 120 years after he committed his crimes we are still fascinated by Jack the Ripper – no more so than former tabloid editor Kelvin MacKenzie. As the first serial killer in history to cause a media sensation, The Ripper has caught MacKenzie's imagination. – 'My intent lies in separating the facts from the newspaper fiction,' he explains in this first of a new series of Revealed, in which he names the man who wrote the notorious 'Jack the Ripper' letter – but is he right? He says that a jobbing journalist on 'The Star', Frederick Best wrote the 'Dear Boss' letter. The editor had to know that Best had written the letter. A sample of Best's handwriting from his estate was examined closely by a graphologist who definitely said that the two samples had been written by the same person but that was extremely unlikely to be the Ripper.

Kent on Sunday, January 30, 2011

News The Interview **By Nick Ames** (Excerpt)

When Sherlock Holmes chased Jack the Ripper

THE true life crimes of Jack the Ripper shocked Victorian London, with their brutality and exert a fascination for many mystery enthusiasts to this day.

The fact that no-one has ever been identified beyond doubt as the killer adds to the macabre interest in a shadowy figure stalking helpless women through the maze of slums which comprised 19th century Whitechapel. Likewise the character of Sherlock Holmes has continued to appeal, with last year seeing the very 21st century take on Sir Arthur Conan Doyle's 'consulting detective' who lived at 221b Baker Street in an era of hansom cabs, gaslights and pea-soup fogs.

Several Hollywood films – notably Murder by Decree starring Christopher Plummer – have brought together the factual killer and the fictional sleuth.

Books have also been written on the subject – in one case putting forward the theory that they were one and the same man.

Maniac

But now David Pybus has written a stage show asking how Holmes "would have investigated the killer whose identity has baffled experts for more than a century.

Mr Pybus said: "It is true that many people think Sherlock Holmes really existed.

"I have heard the question asked – 'why was the world's greatest detective, at the height of his ability as the supreme detective reasoned, not brought in on the Ripper murders?'

Well the answer is obvious – one is real and one isn't. But I thought I would have a go at bringing their worlds together."

Mr Pybus put together a format which includes clues as to his theories on the identity and motives of the homicidal maniac, so the audience can investigate alongside Holmes.

He said, "There were more than 100 suspects originally identified by the police as possibly being the killer and I have narrowed that down – via expert opinions from people who have studied the cases – to 20.

"These I outline in one of the talks and then Holmes comes along. I've made it part of the plot that he wasn't originally consulted because of internecine rivalry within the police – the Metropolitan and City of London forces both had crime on their patch attributed to the Ripper. "So what I've done is looked at a murder which had similar aspects to the killings but took place in 1905 – well after the Ripper's reign of terror. "I have suggested that Holmes is brought in to allay public fears that a fresh outbreak of killings are to take place as Jack is back."

Mr Pybus, has kept as much face as possible with Doyle's vision of Holmes and his world.

He said: "There are other characters involved – Dr Watson and a wife I have given him – an American expert in psychology.

"There is also a top US detective who helps to put the puzzle together. Meanwhile the audience can take part with riddles and ciphers to see what they come up with.

"Naturally I'm not giving it away – but the conclusions I have reached is an outstanding one."

THE SUNDAY TELEGRAPH May 15 2011

Battle for the Ripper secrets

Scotland Yard fights investigator over 123-year-old files because they contain the names of informants

DAVID BARRETT Home Affairs Correspondent

SCOTLAND YARD is fighting an extraordinary legal battle to withhold 123-year-old secret files which experts believe could finally provide the identity of Jack the Ripper.

Four thick ledgers compiled by Special Branch officers have been kept under lock and key since the Whitechapel murders in 1888.

Trevor Marriott, a Ripper investigator and former murder squad detective, has spent three years attempting to obtain uncensored versions of the documents.

But he has been repeatedly refused because the ledgers contain the identities of police informants – and the Metropolitan Police insist that revealing the information could compromise the gathering of information from "super grasses" and other modern-day informants.

Last week, Mr Marriott took Scotland Yard to a tribunal in a 1st-ditch attempt to see the journals – containing 36,000 entries – which he believes contains evidence which could finally unmask the world's famous serial killer.

The legal case has cost the taxpayer thousands of pounds and has even involved a senior Scotland Yard officer giving evidence anonymously from behind a screen. The ledgers provide details of the police's dealing with thousands of informants from 1888 to 1912, including some who provided information during the original Ripper investigations. Only two pages, deemed not to contain sensitive information have been given to Mr Marriott.

A sample of about 40 pages from the Scotland Yard ledgers was released to last week's tribunal, but with the names of informants and other key details blacked out.

Mr Marriott says the files contain the names of at least four new suspects, as well as other pieces of evidence.

He said: "I believe this to be the very last chance that we may have to solve the mystery of Jack the Ripper.

"To have any possibility of getting near the truth about those horrific crimes we must see what these ledgers contain.

"It may be that within them we find the final piece of the jigsaw that would unlock this mystery and lead to the identity of the killer, or killers, albeit 123 years too late."

Jack the Ripper slaughtered at least five women between August and November 1888 in the slums of Whitechapel, east London, but experts have claimed other murders may have been committed by the killer. The police made several mistakes in the inquiry and detection techniques were basic, with no fingerprinting and science unable even to distinguish between animal blood and human blood.

As a result, there is no conclusive evidence to point to the true identity of Jack the Ripper and the case remains one of the world's great unsolved mysteries.

Among the long list of possible suspects are Queen Victoria's grandson the Duke of Clarence, who died in an asylum in 1892, and the painter Walter Sickert.

Mr Marriott, who joined the Bedfordshire Police in 1970 and worked as a detective constable until the mid-1980s, began researching the Jack the Ripper case in 2003.

He has published a book on the subject which put forward the name of Carl Feigenbaum, a German merchant executed for the murder of a woman in New York, as a new suspect.

On uncovering references to the ledgers in 2008, Mr Marriott applied to see the documents under the Freedom of Information Act.

The Met refused and he appealed to the Information Commissioner who also decided the books should not be revealed.

Now Mr Marriott has appealed to the Information Tribunal, in which the case is heard by three judges.

The three-day hearing involved a detective inspector, identified only as 'D', speaking to the court from behind a screen because of his role running intelligence-gathering operation from informants.

Detective Inspector 'D' told the tribunal that unveiling the files could deter informants from coming forward in the future, and could even put off members of the public from phoning Crimestoppers or the anti-terrorist hotline.

"The interpretation on the street will be that the police have revealed the identity of informants," said 'D'. "Confidence in the system is maintaining their safety, regardless of age."

Det Insp 'D' said the passage of time did not make publication of informants' identities less sensitive because their descendants could be targeted by criminals with a grudge.

"Look at one of the world's best-known informants, Judas Iscariot.

"If someone could draw a bloodline from Judas Iscariot to the present day person then that person would face a risk, although I know that seems an extreme example," the officer said.

Another senior officer, Det Supt Julian McKinney, told the tribunal that releasing names would make the police less able to preventing terrorists attacks and organised crime, and make informants vulnerable to attack

Det Supt McKinney said: "Regardless of the time, regardless of whether they are dead, they should never be disclosed."

They come to us only when they have the confidence in our system that their identity will not be disclosed."

But Mr Marriott said that a number of historical files have been released which contained details of informants.

He argued there was no evidence to show descendants of informants who have been named had come to harm.

The tribunal decision is expected later this year.

Editorial Comment

A snitch in time

Hard-boiled policeman to quivering suspect: "Now look here, sonny, you tell me what I need to know, or it's the high jump for you." Quivering suspect: "I can't turn nark, copper, I can't. Otherwise my great-grandchildren, and my mate's great-great-grandchildren, might find out more than a century later. As dialogue goes, it is not especially convincing. Yet this, according to Scotland Yard, will be the result of its opening Special Branches' files on the Jack the Ripper murders, which contain evidence provided by informants: today's "super grasses", worried that the police's commitment to maintaining their anonymity will be less than absolute, will become less likely to co-operate.

We are not, we must admit, entirely convinced of the thesis. Also, we cannot help feeling that the Ripper missed a trip. If he really wanted to disguise his identity, surely he should have done what so many celebrities seem to these days: take out a super-injunction.

THE SUNDAY TELEGRAPH May 22 2011

Letters to the Editor

Ripper's true identity

SIR – Your piece today takes the view that Jack the Ripper was not identified by Scotland Yard. Actually, there is strong evidence from the writings of Sir Robert Anderson, assistant commissioner at the Metropolitan Police at the time, that senior officers at the Yard were aware who the Ripper was. The Yard's top detective in overall charge of the case was Chief Inspector Donald Sutherland Swanson, by great-grandfather.

Handwritten notes of his, which came to light around 100 years after the killings, named the suspect as Aaron Kosminski.

Nevill Swanson

Worcester

Daily Mail, Saturday, August 6, 2011

Detective leading hunt 'was Jack the Ripper'

SUSPECTS have ranged from a member of the Royal Family to a local butcher – but it is now claimed that Jack the Ripper was the very detective who led the hunt for the killer.

Chief Inspector Frederick Abberline of Scotland Yard was the man who murdered and mutilated at least five women in Victorian East London – at least according to Spanish writer Jose Abad, 84.

He makes the claim in his book Jack the Ripper: The Most Intelligent Murderer in History, published in Spain this week.

Mr Abad is a handwriting expert and has compared Abberline's writing with that in the Ripper diary – which surfaced in Liverpool in 1992. Mr Abad says: 'I have no doubt Abberline was the Ripper. Handwriting does not lie'.

The diary was attributed to a Liverpool cotton dealer called James Maybrick – whom others have identified as the Ripper. But many experts say the diary is a hoax. Mr Abad believes it is real, but that the author was Abberline, not Maybrick.

Other theories link the Ripper murders to Queen Victoria's grandson, Prince Albert Victor.

Chapter 24

Sir Arthur Conan Doyle's Sherlock Holmes Novels & Stories: A Complete Bibliography

Each entry will be preceded by publishing details and the introduction from the New Annotated Sherlock Holmes, edited by Leslie S. Klinger.

A Study in Scarlet (1887)

Beeton's Christmas Annual, 1887; Ward Lock, 1887; Philadelphia, Lippincott, 1890.

Scholars and casual Sherlockians alike have come to regard *A Study in Scarlet* (1887) as a fascinating book of Genesis, as it marked the very first public appearance of Sherlock Holmes. Here, after a brief glimpse of Watson's life before Baker Street, we are witness to a momentous occasion: the initial meeting between Sherlock Holmes and his "Boswell," Dr. John H. Watson, in a hospital laboratory. ("I've found it! I've found it," are Holmes's first words, appropriately enough.) The two men decide to share lodgings, and Watson discovers that his new roommate has an unorthodox occupation, as the world's sole consulting detective. Soon enough, the unsuspecting doctor finds himself involved in a dark tale of revenge and murder. Central to Watson's account of Holmes's brilliant detection is a "flashback"-type narrative, penned by an unknown author, of the Mormons in Utah under the leadership of Bringham Young. Arresting and lively, the account nevertheless reflects Victorian England's distorted views of the Mormons and their history in the American West.

When one compares this picture of the youthful Holmes (he was only twenty-seven when he met Watson) to the balance of the Canon, it is apparent that the Master's character changed little over the years of his remarkable career. His secretiveness, his bohemian habits, and his low opinions of the official police are all on display here; and while Holmes's drug use is only hinted at, his other vices and virtues are quickly revealed to the reader (although Watson's early assessment of Holmes's "limits" are soon disproved). The author of A Study in Scarlet may have earned little commercial reward from the book's early publication, but the stage was set for what would later become the most successful series of stories ever published.

The Sign of Four (1890)

The Sign of Four was published in *Lippincott's Monthly Magazine* in February 1890; under the title "The Sign of the Four"; or "The Problem of the Sholtos"; London, Spencer Blackett, in October 1890; Philadelphia, Lippincott, 1893.

The first British book edition was published as *The Sign of the Four* by Spencer Blackett...Numerous American and English editions, both authorised and pirated, contain countless textual variations. The original manuscript is in private hands and unavailable. Newt and Lillian Williams's *Annotated "Annotated"* provides a useful compilation of the variations, almost none of which makes any significant differences to the sense of the story.

No longer the newly minted consulting detective of A Study in Scarlet, Holmes is at his most confident in The Sign of Four (1890), irresistibly drawn to the plight of his client, Mary Morstan, a beautiful woman plagued by a mysterious past. Holmes occupies centre-stage for virtually the full length of this supremely satisfying tale of detection, while Watson, not to be outpaced, comes into full flower as a human being in a case that sadly shows Holmes steeped in his drugs and ends with a break-up of the shared lodgings of the two men in Baker Street. Only seven years have passed since the events of A Study in Scarlet, but Holmes seems in the interim to have accumulated a lifetime's experience, which he brings to bear on an adventure – rooted in the Indian Mutiny – that is packed with cinematic elements: occult figures of a pygmy and a wooden-legged man, a desperate hunt, a dependable dog, and a breathless chase down the Thames. The subject of English colonisation and its impact on the Victorian world is encapsulated during the final minutes of the novel in the back-story of murder, robbery, betrayal, and revenge related to Holmes's prey.

The Adventures of Sherlock Holmes

As published for the first time in the *Strand Magazine*, Vols. II & III, July 1891-June 1892. First published in book form by George Newnes Ltd. On October 14, 1892, in an edition of 10,000 copies, with 104 illustrations by Sidney Paget. The first American edition was published by Harper & Brothers, New York, on the following day (4,500 copies).

1 A Scandal in Bohemia

"A Scandal in Bohemia" is the first of the Sherlock Holmes stories to have appeared in the Strand Magazine; eventually, all of the works but the novel A Study in Scarlet and The Sign of Four appeared there. "A Scandal in Bohemia" is memorable for what it reveals about Holmes's attitude towards women, and it is the only story in which we see Holmes defeated – although he may well have decided that he was on the wrong side in the matter and had been glad of his "defeat." The opera singer "heroine," Irene Adler, has inspired generations of women Sherlockians, leading to the 1965 formation of the "Adventuresses of Sherlock Holmes" by women who were banned from joining the Baker Street Irregulars (a rule subsequently reversed). In "Scandal," we see for the first time the partnership of Holmes and Watson in action. Watson is no longer the reporter, as he is in A Study in Scarlet or The Sign of Four, and his participation is essential in carrying out Holmes's plans. There is little mystery in this first tale, but the reader's interest is seized by Watson's opening words: "To Sherlock Holmes she is always *the* woman.

II The Red-Headed League

Published in the *Strand Magazine* August 1891

"The Red-Headed League" has appeared in dozens of collections of short stories. Best remembered are the buffoonish Jabez Wilson, the bizarre spectacle of Fleet Street crowded with red-headed men, the first of the many night watches to appear in the Canon, and the intricate plan of John Clay, the "fourth smartest man in London." Almost in the manner of a conjurer, Holmes rattles off a series of quite startling deductions, perhaps matched only by Holmes's dissection of a hat in "The Blue Carbuncle." And then, to our delight, Watson records Holmes's deflation by Wilson: "I thought at first you had done something clever, but I see there was nothing in it at all." Watson kindly refrains from comment, but our understanding of the friendship of Holmes and Watson is enriched.

III A Case of Identity

"A Case of Identity" was published in the September 1891 issue of the *Strand Magazine*. It appeared simultaneously in the September-October copy of the New York edition of the *Strand Magazine* and was widely printed in newspapers in America that month.

As in "A Scandal in Bohemia," no crime is actually committed in "A Case of Identity," and scholars wonder why Watson chose to include it among the sixty published cases out of more than 1,000 that Holmes handled. Could the villain be more wicked that the events reveal? While the near-comic Mary Sutherland, the whispering Hosmer Angel, and the student James Windibank are only minor characters on Watson's stage, we are reminded that a single woman of Holmes's are can get along quite nicely on £60 per year. The "gasfitters' ball," a grand social event for the plumbing trade at which Mary meets her fate, has inspired many Sherlockian societies to hold similar galas. Her, too, we first see the masterful side of Holmes, as he hands out punishment and withholds information as he alone sees fit.

IV The Boscombe Valley Mystery

"The Boscombe Valley Mystery" was published in the *Strand Magazine* in October 1891.

Australia, particularly as the movement for independence grew, fascinated the Victorians in the later nineteenth century. Because of Australia's history as a penal colony for British convicts and political dissidents, it held a position not unlike the Wild West in America. The Victorian public readily believed that Australians in England were frequently involved in violent crime, and so they would have preconceptions about the characters of the McCarthys and the Turners, the key players in "The Boscombe Valley Mystery." It is the first in the short stories in the Canon to involve murder and the first short-story appearance of Inspector Lestrade of Scotland Yard. In Lestrade's earlier case with Holmes, recorded by Watson as A Study in Scarlet, Holmes called him and his partner Inspector Gregson "the pick of a bad lot." Lestrade is treated little better here. Holmes calls him an "imbecile." As in "A Case of Identity," Holmes has little use for the "regulars" and takes it upon himself to be both jury and judge.

V The Five Orange Pips

"The Five Orange Pips" was published in the *Strand Magazine* in November 1891 and in the American *Strand Magazine* in December 1891.

In "The Five Orange Pips", which takes place in 1887, Sherlock Holmes tells his client that he has been beaten only four times in his career. When Holmes fails to take immediate steps to protect his client, however, we must conclude that Holmes has been beaten again. Yet the case is a favourite among readers, not least for its tantalising mention of cases that Watson never records, including those of the Paradol Chamber, the Grice Patersons "in the island of Uffa," the Camberwell poisoning, the loss of the barque "Sophie Anderson," and the Amateur Mendicant Society. Repeating his formula from A Study in Scarlet, Watson shrewdly selects an adventure with an American setting featuring vengeance by a secret society. In the former case, Holmes tracks down a killer who took revenge on the avengers. Here, Holmes himself seeks revenge on the wrongdoers. We are left to wonder whether Holmes truly seeks justice or is merely trying to sooth his bruised ego

VI The Man with the Twisted Lip

"The Man with the Twisted Lip" was published in the *Strand Magazine* in December 1891. It appeared in the *Philadelphia Inquirer* a month before its appearance in the New York *Strand Magazine* (January 1892) as "The Strange Tale of a Beggar."

"The Man with the Twisted Lip" opens in an opium den in the crime-ridden East End of London, a milieu vivid in the Victorian popular imagination. Watson's tale is one of the earliest examples of a "play-fair" mystery, in which all of the clues are known to the reader at the same time as the detective. Holmes solves the puzzle in a manner available to the reader – by sheer intellect – and Watson draws the indelible image of Holmes, surrounded by pillows, sitting cross-legged in his dressing gown, smoking his pipe and contemplating the problem before him. There are tantalising hints of a romantic interlude between Holmes and the lovely Mrs. Neville St. Clair, but Watson's unexpected appearance on the scene leaves her longings apparently unfulfilled, and the reader is left to wonder whether Watson's cynical views of Holmes's feelings towards women (expressed in his opening remarks in "A Scandal in Bohemia") are accurate.

VII The Adventure of the Blue Carbuncle

"The Blue Carbuncle" was published in the *Strand Magazine* in January 1892 and in the New York *Strand Magazine* in February 1892. It also appeared in January 1892 in American newspapers, including the *Philadelphia Inquirer*, where it ran under the title "The Christmas Goose that Swallowed a Diamond."

Esteemed Holmes scholar and writer Christopher Morley referred to "The Blue Carbuncle" as "a Christmas story without slush," and some readers favour the story – the only tale in the Canon set in the holiday season – over such traditional fare as Dickens's "A Christmas Carol." Like Frank Capra's brilliant film "It's a Wonderful Life," the tale of the stolen gem commemorates the triumph of compassion over justice,

There are gems within the story, to be sure: Holmes's tour-de-force deductions from hapless Henry Baker's hat, Holmes's deception of Breckinridge, the sporting seller of geese, and the clever but ultimately foolish plan of the criminal to smuggle the countess's carbuncle to his fence in Kilburn. What draws us back each year, however, is the evident warmth of the friendship between Holmes and Watson, as Watson travels from his married household to visit his bachelor friend and wish him "compliments of the season." Sherlock Holmes, too, appears more human, less the "perfect reasoner," again taking the law into his own hands. After all, he concludes magnanimously "It is the season of forgiveness."

VIII The Adventure of the Speckled Band

"The Speckled Band" was published in the *Strand Magazine* in February 1892.

Scholars have delighted in the minutiae of "The Speckled Band," arguing over the identity of the "speckled band" (whose characteristics defy those known to science), whether Holmes again takes justice into his own hands or an accident occurs, and the geographical sources of cheetahs and baboons. Conan Doyle, knowing a good story when he heard it, turned Watson's tale into a highly successful stage play. Perhaps only second to "The Red-Headed League" in its popularity, "The Speckled Band" has Gothic elements to thrill every reader, and the confrontation between Dr. Grimsby Roylott and Sherlock Holmes is broadly melodramatic and highly satisfying.

IX The Adventure of the Engineer's Thumb

"The Engineer's Thumb" was published in the *Strand Magazine* in March 1892.
"The Engineer's Thumb" is the only case ever brought to Holmes by Dr. Watson himself. When a late-night call from a thumb-deprived patient rouses Watson, he displays good sense (if not good doctoring) in whisking his patient over to see Holmes. Here, a strange tale of German counterfeiters unfolds, in which we meet the first of the many corrupt colonels who populate the Canon. There is little actual detection in the tale, and Holmes appears to take scant interest in catching the crooks. The physical evidence of the titular amputation seems incongruous with the explanation offered by the young Victor Hatherley, and we may be left to wonder whether he is covering up for his own criminal activities.

X The Adventure of the Noble Bachelor

"The Noble Bachelor" was published in the *Strand Magazine* in April 1892.

In "The Noble Bachelor," Holmes meets society in the form of Lord Robert St. Simon. St. Simon is something of a fop, and middle-class British readers must have delighted in Holmes's "putdown" of the young lord. English women complained of an American "invasion" of young (rich) women in search of husbands from among the poorer members of England's upper crust. Here, Holmes is asked to trace a vanishing American bride. Correctly reading the signs, he finds her – and another man! Although some scholars insist that the beautiful heroine was a criminal. Holmes is forgiving; but his diplomacy fails when he tries to bring together the Old and New Worlds over breakfast. Holmes's cheery, democratic attitude and his expressions of faith in the future of the English-speaking peoples was copied in the utterly non-Canonical "Sherlock Holmes" films of Universal Pictures starring Basil Rathbone and Nigel Bruce.

XI **The Adventure of the Beryl Coronet**

"The Beryl Coronet" was published in the *Strand Magazine* in May 1892.

In a tale reminiscent of Wilkie Collin's highly successful mystery *The Moonstone*, which involves a priceless gem kept in an unlocked cupboard, Holmes must recover a valuable national treasure put at risk by an unnamed peer (likely understood by the readers to be the Prince of Wales, the highly popular but slightly disreputable Albert Edward, oldest son of Queen Victoria). Set in a suburb of London, "The Beryl Coronet" features another one-legged man from Watson's casebook (the first appeared in The Sign of Four); meanwhile, Holmes reveals both his knowledge of the criminal underworld of London and his bank account balance.

XII **The Adventure of the Copper Beeches**

"The Copper Beeches" was published in the *Strand Magazine* in June 1892 and was the last of the first series of "Adventures" published in that magazine.

Women in distress, especially governesses, constituted a large portion of Holmes's clientele. One of Conan Doyle's sisters was a governess, and it was a respectable employment for the emerging class of working women. Although Holmes scoffs that his practice is turning into "an agency for recovering lead pencils, and giving advice to young ladies from boarding-schools," he admits the case of Miss Violet Hunter (the first of four Violets to cross his path) is an exceptional one. In "The Copper Beeches," the last tale of the series collected as the *Adventures*, the freckled-faced Miss Hunter calls upon Holmes for "backup" as she accepts a job that pays too much. Watson feels Hunter is quite capable of taking care of herself, but Holmes uncharacteristically worries, muttering about "no sister of his" taking a situation such as Miss Hunters. Scholars have (with little success) tried to make these remarks into background material about Holmes's family. Others speculate that "Violet the Hunter" may have set her cap for Holmes, perhaps with encouragement from Dr. Watson. As the story concludes, Holmes dismisses Violet Hunter as merely one more "petty problem," and Watson duly records her marriage to another, although a note of sadness – perhaps over Holmes's indifference to the charms of Miss Hunter – is evident in the Doctor's voice.

The Memoirs of Sherlock Holmes

First published in book form (without "The Cardboard Box") by George Newnes, Limited, in an edition of 10,000 copies, as volume three of *The Strand Library* on December 13, 1893, containing 90 illustrations by Sidney Paget. The first American edition was published on February 2, 1894 by Harper and Brothers, New York, and included "The Cardboard Box."

As published for the first time in the *Strand Magazine*, Vols. IV, V and VI, December 1892-December 1893, in the *Strand Magazine* (New York) in January 1893.

XIII **The Adventure of Silver Blaze**

"Silver Blaze" the first case of the Memoirs (a series that commenced five months after conclusion of the Adventures), is one of the most famous sporting mysteries ever penned. Watson presents the case, set in racing circles, as another "fair-play" murder mystery, with the villain concealed in plain view. Holmes's well-known remark about "the curious incident of the dog in the night time" has been widely repeated in many contexts and has become a catch-phrase for a "negative inference." Although many question the accuracy of Watson's reporting of the sporting details of the adventure, few would dispute that Holmes's powers are here at their peak. His computation of the speed of the train has been amply demonstrated to be accurate, and his careful observation of sheep leads to the capture of an unlikely killer. The only blemish on the tale is the evidence that Holmes placed an unethical bet on the race.

XIV **The Cardboard Box**

"The Cardboard Box" appeared in the *Strand Magazine* in January 1893 and in *Harper's Weekly* (New York) on January 14, 1893. The first edition of *Memoirs of Sherlock Holmes*, published in London in 1894 by George Newnes, Limited, contained only eleven "memoirs," excluding "The Cardboard Box" from the series of twelve that had appeared in the *Strand Magazine*. The first American edition of *Memoirs of Sherlock Holmes*, published by Harper the same year, contained all twelve stories; almost immediately afterwards, however, a "new and revised" Harper edition that, like the British edition, omitted "The Cardboard Box." Theories about the odd handling of this story are sketchy at best. Arthur Bartlett Maurice, in an article entitled "Sherlock Holmes & His Creator" (*Colliers*, August 15, 1908), surmises that the story's recounting of an "illicit love affair" led to a cautious Doyle to put the piece aside when preparing the collection for publication. Eminent bookseller David Randall, in his *Catalogue of Original Manuscripts, etc.*, subsequently concludes that the American publisher Harper, having seen the story in the *Strand*, was unaware that Doyle had any objections to including all twelve stories in book form; upon publication, Doyle must have issued a protest, hence the quick issuance of a new *Memoirs* edition. The first American version is now considered quite rare. Curiously, not one of the numerous biographies of Arthur Conan Doyle has a word of explanation of this self-censorship, nor did Doyle himself comment upon it in his *Memories & Adventures*.

(**Compiler's note**: Another explanation for the non-inclusion of "The Cardboard Box," can be found in Andrew Lycett's biography).

"The Cardboard Box" is one of Watson's finest stories, combining brilliant detection and a powerful human drama. Easily the darkest tale in the entire Canon, Holmes and Watson here investigate a case that begins with the delivery of a gruesome packet and ends with a revelation of alcoholism, adultery and murder. Following up the slenderest of clues, wholly overlooked by Inspector Lestrade of Scotland Yard, Holmes discovers serious crime where the police see only grotesque humour. Even Holmes, the hardened criminal investigator, is deeply troubled by his discoveries: "What is the meaning of it, Watson?...What object is served by this circle of misery and violence and fear?" In fact, the case is so stark in its portrayal of human emotions that Arthur Conan Doyle suppressed publication of the story in the first edition of the *Memoirs*, deeming it unsuitable for younger readers. A poor editorial job on the story left its opening muddled; here it is restored to its original version from the pages of the *Strand Magazine*, as Watson intended it.

XV The Yellow Face

"The Yellow Face" was published in the *Strand Magazine* in February 1893 and in *Harper's Weekly* (New York) on February 11, 1893

Some students question why Watson included "The Yellow Face" among the *Memoirs*. Mr. Grant Munro's problem completely baffles Holmes, who can only propose outlandish theories with no evidence, and many suggest that Holmes was completely taken in by Munro's wife. Mindful of his failure, Holmes urges Watson to whisper "Norbury" in his ear whenever he becomes too arrogant, and perhaps it is to present this view of Holmes – the less-than-perfect reasoner – that Watson wrote up the case. Contemporary readers may deplore the apparent racial attitudes of the case, which suggests that interracial marriage was intolerable to English society, but a careful reading reveals that Watson applauds the tolerance of Mr. Munro. On a lighter note, it is gratifying to see Effie Munro call her husband Grant by the name "Jack," if only to bear out that John Watson's wife may well have called him James!

XVI The Stock-Broker's Clerk

"The Stock-Broker's Clerk" was published in the *Strand Magazine* in March 1893 and in *Harper's Weekly* (New York) on March 11, 1893.

The world of money has changed little in 100 years, and "The Stock-Broker's Clerk" tells the thrilling tale of "identity theft" that might be drawn from today's headlines. Here Holmes and Watson must tread unfamiliar turf, the "City," the realms of banks, brokerage firms, and high finance, to foil a daring robbery. Watson reveals an ear for Cockney slang in recording young Hall Pycroft's encounter with mystery. Strangely, the criminals of "The Stock-Broker's Clerk" appear to have been familiar with Holmes's cases, for the plot is certainly reminiscent of "The Red-Headed League." Scholars date it to 1888 or 1889, and therefore the plotters could not have read the published version of "The Red-Headed League." However, if Professor Moriarty had a hand in both, the similarities are no coincidence. The case also provides uncharacteristic revelations of Watson's personal life, providing details of his return to medical practice after his marriage.

XVII The "Gloria Scott"

The "Gloria Scott" was published in the *Strand Magazine* in February 1893 and in *Harper's Weekly* (New York) on April 15, 1893.

Virtually all that we know of Holmes before his fateful meeting with Watson in 1881 is contained in The "Gloria Scott" and the case that follows, "The Musgrave Ritual." The former is a recollection by Holmes, in which he tells Watson of his first case, brought to him by Victor Trevor (one of only three persons acknowledged by Holmes to be his friend) while attending college. Trevor's father, about whom Holmes makes some startling deductions, sets Holmes on the path to his career as a consulting detective. Holmes helps Victor to discover the truth about his father when the latter dies suddenly, but Holmes's skills are less than impressive. He solves a simple cipher and reads a confession. Watson has no active role in the account, so we must count the case as the first example of Holmes's own narrative voice. There are many gaps in Holmes's account of those early years – most intriguingly, what college he attended. The clues in this tale and several others have fuelled generations of speculation.

XVIII The Musgrave Ritual

"The Musgrave Ritual" was published in the *Strand Magazine* in May 1893 and in *Harper's Weekly* (New York) on May 13, 1893.

"The Musgrave Ritual" is one of the most famous "treasure-map" of cases of all time. T.S. Eliot, in his great play *Murder in the Cathedral*, borrows deliberately from it, and the recitation of the Ritual itself has become a rite of the Baker Street Irregulars annual dinner. Set, as is The "Gloria Scott," in the pre-Watson years, it tells of another case brought to Holmes by a college classmate. As in The "Gloria Scott," Holmes unconsciously reveals his useful naivety, for it appears unlikely that his verdict of "accidental death" may be sustained. The story's frame, recorded by Dr. Watson also teases us with several unpublished cases and reveals Holmes the decorator, as he draws a large "V.R." on the apartment wall with gunshots!

XIX The Reigate Squires

"The Reigate Squires" appeared in the *Strand Magazine* in June 1893 as *The Reigate Squire* (singular); in *Memoirs of Sherlock Holmes* it was changed to *The Reigate Squires*. In *Harper's Weekly* (June 17, 1893) it was altered to *The Reigate Puzzle*.

Holmes is suffering the effects of overwork, having brought to a successful conclusion the "Netherlands-Sumatra Company case, about which we know virtually nothing. Watson coerces him to vacation in Surrey, at the house of a military companion of Watson (Colonel Hayter, perhaps the only reputable colonel in the entire Canon). Suddenly, his rests ends, as he is thrust into "The Reigate Squires," an investigation of a robbery-murder. His father-and-son "clients" are strangely reluctant to have Holmes involved, and Holmes appears to be functioning at less than full capacity. Although Holmes's claim of twenty-three deductions from the handwritten note central to the case sounds preposterous, handwriting analysis was highly regarded in Victorian times, and there is much sound information which can be drawn from the note, even without Holmes's help. However, no scholar has solved the mystery of Annie Morrison.

XX The Crooked Man

"The Crooked Man" was published in the *Strand Magazine* in July 1893, in *Harper's Weekly* on July 8, 1893, and in the *Strand Magazine* (New York) in August 1893.

Knowledge of the Bible helps Holmes solve the locked-room puzzle Watson calls "The Crooked Man." The case is rooted in the evils of the Indian Mutiny, the uprising of native troops against the British rule of India. Although Watson's own military service and his circle of friends are the usual reasons for the frequent military connections to the Canon, this case is brought to Watson by Holmes himself. The tale commences late one evening, while Watson's wife lies upstairs sleeping. The tranquil domestic scene is quickly contrasted with Watson's picture of another household, the home of Colonel James Barclay with his wife, Nancy. The colonel lies dead on his hearth, with the door locked from the inside, with his wife insensible beside him. Holmes's careful observations reveal two other mysterious visitors to the room, and he uses the Baker Street Irregulars to track them down. Although the tale ends with a confession, some suggest that Holmes may be misled by the near-Biblical tale he hears.

XXI The Resident Patient

"The Resident Patient" was published in the *Strand Magazine* in August 1893 and in *Harper's Weekly* (New York) on August 12, 1893.

The text of "The Resident Patient" was badly mangled when the editors of the *Memoirs* deleted "The Cardboard Box" and moved its opening scene to Watson's account of this case. Here it is restored to its original version from the *Strand Magazine*. When Holmes is called in by young Dr. Percy Trevelyan to uncover the mystery of his "resident patient" (that is, a patient who shares living quarters with the doctor, a practice in which Conan Doyle himself once engaged), Holmes discovers waters far deeper than those imagined by Trevelyan. Holmes does little "deducing" in the case, relying instead on his immense knowledge of the sensational literature of the era and his docket-like recollection of unsolved crimes. Because the case also reflects the trials of a young doctor building a practice – a subject sure to elicit the sympathies of Drs. John Watson and Arthur Conan Doyle – we may understand why the case was included in the *Memoirs*.

XXII The Greek Interpreter

"The Greek Interpreter" was first published in the September 1893 edition of the *Strand Magazine* and in *Harper's Weekly* (New York) on September 16, 1893. Therefore Watson's "long and intimate acquaintance," mentioned in the first sentence, probably lasted less than twelve years.

"The Greek Interpreter" is not one of Holmes's most admirable performances, for he nearly loses his client and fails to prevent the murder of an innocent. However, as one of only two cases in which Holmes's brother Mycroft plays an active role (the other is "The Bruce-Partington Plans"), it is indispensable reading for a Sherlockian. Seven years Sherlock's senior, Mycroft is the smarter, less active brother, who cannot be bothered to leave his arm-chair to deal with a problem. Described as "larger and stouter" than Sherlock, "corpulent," with fat, flipper-like hands, Mycroft Holmes is said to be an auditor of some departments of the British government. In "The Bruce-Partington Plans," however, when Sherlock Holmes has become more certain of Watson's discretion, he reveals that Mycroft "occasionally…is the British government." Some like to see Mycroft as a Victorian secret agent, the head of a British "Central Intelligence Agency." Mycroft's actions in this case, however, are not all logical, and some scholars speculate that he may have had his own nefarious "agenda" in the matter.

XXIII The Naval Treaty

"The Naval Treaty" was published in two parts in the *Strand Magazine* in October and November 1893 and in *Harper's Weekly* (New York) on October 14 and 21, 1893.

The longest of all the "short stories" penned by Dr. Watson, "The Naval Treaty is a case brought to Watson by a classmate from prep school days. Percy "Tadpole" Phelps has risen high in the Foreign Office, and a treaty has been stolen from his office. Although suffering from the euphemistic "brain fever," Phelps begs Watson to bring in Holmes. When Holmes recovers the treaty, based primarily on his careful observations of the two key locations involved. Holmes cannot stop himself from revealing his success in a cruel but dramatic manner. But while the treaty is unquestionably recovered, scholars speculate that Holmes may have missed the real "brains" behind the crime. If Watson's physical description of the characters are accurate, there is reason to suspect that Holmes was deceived and that the real villain went unpunished.

XXIV The Final Problem

"The Final Problem" was published in the *Strand Magazine* in December 1893, in the *Strand Magazine* (New York) Christmas Number 1893, and in a number of American newspapers in late November and early December 1893.

To paraphrase Watson, it was with heavy hearts that *Strand Magazine* readers began the tale Watson recorded as "The Final Problem," which purported to include Watson's "last words" about Sherlock Holmes. The story stunned the British public, cost the *Strand Magazine* twenty thousand subscribers, and led to an outbreak of black armbands. Watson kept his silence until 1901, eight years after the publication of "The Final Problem," when he published *The Hound of the Baskervilles*, another reminiscence of Holmes. The modern reader knows that Holmes did not die, as Watson evidently believed at the close of this account, but instead returned to London in 1894. For obscure reasons, Holmes refused to allow Watson to disclose this information to his readers until 1903, when Watson was permitted to reveal the true conclusion of the events of "The Final Problem" in connection with his report of "The Adventure of the Empty House," the first story of the volume entitled The Return of Sherlock Holmes. But "The Final Problem" is a fine drama in its own right, with the tense and thrilling encounters between Holmes and Professor Moriarty (copied by William Gillette with great success in his play *Sherlock Holmes* and aped in countless films thereafter). Moriarty, who has achieved near-legendary status as the arch-nemesis of Holmes, appears only in "The Final Problem," "The Empty House," and *The Valley of Fear*, and so the information about him has been carefully mined by scholars.

The Hound of the Baskervilles (1902)

The Hound of the Baskervilles appeared in the *Strand Magazine*, in monthly parts, from August 1901 to April 1902 (vols. 22 and 23). The first book edition was published by George Newnes in 1902, before the first instalment appeared in the *Strand*. The first American edition, published by McClure, Phillips & Co., also appeared in 1902. See *Appendix 2*, The Source of *The Hound of the Baskervilles* in Klinger's book for a discussion of the various acknowledgements.

The immortal words "Mr. Holmes, they were the footprints of a gigantic hound!" conjure fear as few others in the twentieth-century canon. Based on local legends of black dogs and vengeful ghosts, and called the greatest mystery ever penned, *The Hound of the Baskervilles* (1902), a tale of Gothic horror set in the fantastic moors of England, enthralled readers of the *Strand Magazine* (in which it was serialised) with its strange warnings and clues and clever host of suspects. Watson shines here, both as the narrator and as the principal investigator until Holmes sweeps down on the scene to ratchet up the drama one more notch. Widely acknowledged to be one of the century's first bestsellers, the novel did little to quell the disappointment of readers who longed for a resolution of the question of whether Holmes – killed off in 1893's "The Final Problem" – had somehow cheated death at the hands of the villainous Professor Moriarty. The novel, the faithful realised unhappily, recounted events which predated Holmes's apparent death. The public had to wait until 1093, when "The Empty House" was published, for news that Holmes was firmly back in the land of the living.

The Return of Sherlock Holmes

First published in book form by George Newnes, Ltd., in an addition of 15,000 copies, on March 7, 1905, containing illustrations by Sidney Paget. Simultaneously a Colonial edition of 15,000 copies, bearing the imprint of Longman's Colonial Library was issued. The first American edition was published in February 1905 by McClure, Phillips and Co., with illustrations by Charles Raymond Macauley. Over 28,000 copies of the American edition were published.

The Adventure of the Empty House

"The Empty House" may be the most widely hailed story of the entire Canon. When it was published in the *Strand Magazine*'s October 1903 issue, ten years after the public was informed of Holmes's death (in "The Final Problem"), the magazine made no pretence of that issue's contents: bold letters at the top of the cover trumpeted "Sherlock Holmes," with the story title in smaller letters below, and the first page of the story declared "The Return of Sherlock Holmes" in large letters above the title. In September 1903, the *Strand* had announced: "Fortunately, the news of [Holmes's] death, though based on circumstantial evidence which at the time seemed conclusive, turns out to be erroneous." While many read the story for the highly emotional scene of Holmes and Watson's reunion, there are scholarly issues as well: The murder of Ronald Adair seems impossible as described, unless Moran was on the top of a passing bus. Another puzzle is why Moran escaped the Gallows for his crime. Finally, there are clues to the location of the "real" 221 Baker Street provided by the description of the "empty house" across the street.

II The Adventure of the Norwood Builder

"The Norwood Builder" was published in the *Strand Magazine* in November 1903 and in *Collier's Weekly* on October 31, 1903. The manuscript is in the Berg Collection of the New York Public Library.

With publication of "The Empty House" and Holmes in retirement (although the latter was unknown to the public), Watson was free at last to draw on his entire casebook of Holmes's career to select his tales. His first post-Return effort was "The Norwood Builder." The case is the first in the Canon to feature fingerprints as the key clue, and Holmes was clearly ahead of his law enforcement colleagues and the courts in recognising their significance. Scholars also raise questions about the strange will produced by Holmes's client and suggest his incompetence as a lawyer.

III The Adventure of the Dancing Men

"The Dancing Men" was published in the *Strand Magazine* in December 1903 and in *Collier's Weekly* on December 5, 1903.

When Hilton Cubitt hires Sherlock Holmes to discover his wife's secret past, Holmes must decipher the message of "The Dancing Men." Some would rank this case as one of Holmes's failures, for he is unable to prevent tragedy; yet he does bring the criminal to justice. Although Americans figure in numerous cases, only twice before had Watson written of an American criminal (in *A Study in Scarlet* and "The Five Orange Pips"). The case, with his mention of Holmes's friend Wilson Hargreave of the New York Police Bureau, hints that Holmes may have been to America himself. Conan Doyle had travelled there for lecture tours, and the play "Angels of Darkness" suggest that Watson, too, spent some time in America. Here we also learn a bit more about Watson: his friend Thurston, his fondness for billiards, and his apparent spendthrift nature. The cipher itself has been the subject of extensive study, by professional and amateur crypto analysis as well as Sherlockians, and its ingenuity and originality make Dr. Watson's tale a perennial favourite.

IV The Adventure of the Solitary Cyclist

"The Solitary Cyclist" was published in *Collier's Weekly* on December 26, 1903, and in the *Strand Magazine* in January 1904.

In "The Solitary Cyclist," we glimpse one of the British "frontiers," the mines of South Africa, which are the source of unexpected danger to yet another Violet (there are four damsels in distress with that name in the Canon). Bicycles, the great fad of the late Victorian era, play a central role in the case, which is set in 1895. Although Watson records in *A Study in Scarlet* that Holmes is an expert boxer, we have only two instances of his pugilistic skills, "The Naval Treaty" and here. While the case has very little mystery about it, scholars raise interesting questions about the marriage laws of England and the irrational behaviour of the villains.

V The Adventure of the Priory School

"The Priory School" appeared in *Collier's Weekly* on January 30, 1904, and in the *Strand Magazine* in February 1904.

"The Priory School" begins comically enough, with the preposterous figure of Thorneycroft Huxtable, M.A., Ph.D., etc., lying prostrate on the bearskin rug at 221 Baker Street. The case soon darkens, however, when Holmes learns that he must save a kidnapped boy from great danger. Even Holmes is surprised by the revelation of the kidnapper. Scholars argue over the true identity of the "Duke of Holderness," Watson's pseudonym for the boy's father, and Holmes's bold deduction from bicycle tracks (and his acceptance of an enormous fee) are questioned by many.

VI The Adventure of Black Peter

"Black Peter was published in *Collier's Weekly* on February 27, 1904 and in the *Strand Magazine* in March 1904.

It is hard to decide whether the criminal in "Black Peter" is worse than his victim. This tale of mistaken identity and murder begins with Holmes returning from the butcher's (*sic*) where he has been mysteriously harpooning pigs. We follow Holmes to one of the few undisguised locations in the Canon, the Brambletye Hotel in Forest Row, which now sports a Black Peter Bar. There Holmes saves his client by clearing up a twelve-year-old mystery. Dr. Watson's account also includes tantalising references to two more unpublished cases, the "death of Cardinal Tosca" (explained by J. Regis O'Connor in *The Sacred Seal*, 1998) and "the notorious canary-trainer," revealed in *The Canary Trainer* by Nicholas Meyer (author of the highly successful *Seven-Per-Cent Solution*, 1974) to be a story of Holmes and the *Phantom of the Opera*.

VII The Adventure of Charles Augustus Milverton

"Charles Augustus Milverton" was published in *Collier's Weekly* on March 26, 1904, and in the *Strand Magazine* in April 1904. Arthur Conan Doyle featured Charles Augustus Milverton in his play *The Speckled Band* in 1910; he was a blackmailer attempting to extort the Dutchess of Ferrers before her marriage.

After threats and subtleties fail, Holmes and Watson turn lawbreakers in the case of Charles Augustus Milverton as they seek to foil the blackmail plot of "the worst man in London." The two men find themselves unwilling witnesses to murder, and some question the ethics of their behaviour and wonder how the murderer got away. Whether the case occurred before or after Holmes's Great Hiatus from 1891 to 1894 is unclear, but Watson withheld publication until 1904. He may have done so solely out of concern for those victims whose reputations might still be damaged by Watson's revelations, or possibly out of concern that the police might still be chasing him!

VIII The Adventure of the Six Napoleons

"The Six Napoleons" was published in the *Strand Magazine* in May 1904 and in *Collier's Weekly* on April 30, 1904.

A favourite of readers, "The Six Napoleons" finds Holmes on the track of a jewel thief, just as in "The Blue Carbuncle." However, where Holmes sees the traces of a relentless burglar, Inspector Lestrade sees only a madman on the loose. Set in the closing years of Holmes's career, the case reveals that notwithstanding Holmes's constant criticism of Scotland Yard, he is revered there. In perhaps the first recorded instance of deliberate manipulation of the news, Holmes declares, "The Press, Watson, is a most valuable institution, if only you know how to use it."

IV The Adventure of the Three Students

"The Three Students" appeared in the *Strand Magazine* in June 1904 and in *Collier's Weekly* on September 24, 1904.

"The Three Students" provides a trove of background information for scholars regarding Holmes's university years. The crime presented here – regarding a student who cheats on an exam – pales in comparison to those of other stories, but the wealth of details regarding college life makes for a rewarding tale. What also makes the case memorable is that one of the first published pieces of Sherlockian scholarship, written by editor and critic Andrew Lang, examined its events in length. So implausible are the facts of "The Three Students" that some suggest the entire case was a diversion, a joke created by Watson and an old friend of Holmes to mystify the detective.

X The Adventure of the Golden Pince-Nez

"The Golden Pince-Nez" was published in the *Strand Magazine* in July 1904 and in *Collier's Weekly* on October 29, 1904.

The period following Holmes's return in the year 1894 was apparently a busy one for Holmes and Watson, because in "The Golden Pince-Nez," Watson notes no fewer than five unpublished cases, and at least three other published cases occur in that year. We learned that Holmes earned the French Order of the Legion of Honour for his capture of "the Boulevard assassin," leading to speculation about Holmes's French connections. The case is also noteworthy for its Russian background: Although Russia and its recent violent history was much on the public's mind in 1904 (the Russo-Japanese War broke out in February 1904, and in 1903, a general strike in Russia was widely reported), this is the only Canonical reference to nihilism and the terrors of the czarist police state.

XI The Adventure of the Missing Three-Quarter

"The Missing Three-Quarter" was published in the *Strand Magazine* in August 1904 and in *Collier's Weekly* on November 26, 1904. The manuscript is at the British Library.

"The Missing Three-Quarter" is the only case in the Canon to involve amateur sports directly. Conan Doyle and Watson both were active team sportsmen, the former an avid cricket player, the latter a rugby player (as we learn in "The Sussex Vampire"), Holmes himself excelled at individual sports, such as fencing, singlestick, and boxing. Here, he is called in to find a star rugby player in time for a crucial match. Two other players in the drama draw our attention: Lord Mount-James, perhaps the richest man in England (and the stingiest), and one Dr. Leslie Armstrong, who bids to be a most interesting villain only to turn out to be a friend. The Cambridge setting of the case provides scholars with more clues to Holmes's university years, adding to the hints in "The Three Students," published two months earlier. Her Holmes's efforts to use a dog as a tracker proved successful, reversing his failure with mongrel Toby in *The Sign of Four*.

XII The Adventure of the Abbey Grange

"The Abbey Grange" was published in the *Strand Magazine* in September 1904, three months before publication of "The Second Stain," and in *Collier's Weekly* on December 31, 1904.

In this, one of the four cases in which Holmes's protégé Inspector Stanley Hopkins appears (the others being "The Missing Three-Quarter," "Black Peter," and "The Golden Pince-Nez," all recorded in *The Return*), we witness Holmes's knowledge of wine, contrasted with a disdain for the upper class first viewed in "The Noble Bachelor." Most emblematic of the detective's complicated views is the wealthy Sir Eustace Brackenstall, the murder victim, who is unfavourably contrasted with the plucky heroine and her seaman friend. The self-reliant Lady Mary Brackenstall awakens Holmes usual sympathy for Australians (as seen by his treatment of them in "The Gloria Scott" and "The Boscombe Valley Mystery"), and as in those cases, Holmes takes the law into his own hands. Here, however, his sympathies may have overridden his judgement. Many scholars believe that Holmes lets himself be fooled by a villainess cleverer than he credited.

XIII The Adventure of the Second Stain

"The Second Stain" was published in the *Strand Magazine* in December 1904 and in the January 28, 1906 issue of *Collier's Weekly*. The manuscript is in the possession of Haverford College.

In "The Naval Treaty," Dr. Watson mentions "The Adventure of the Second Stain" as a case involving "interests of such importance and implicate[ing] so many of the first families in the kingdom that for many years it will be impossible to make it public." The case is definitely not this case. (For one thing, the former was published in 1892, over a decade before the definite setting of 1904 given by Dr. Watson here.) Yet this "Second Stain" is also a case of great international importance and one of the few reported matters to involve Holmes with political crimes, the others being "The Naval Treaty" and "The Bruce-Partington Plans," The events that take place are reminiscent of those in Edgar Allan Poe's "Purloined Letter," and it becomes clear that Holmes – who, in *A Study in Scarlet*, decries C. Auguste Dupin, the detective of the "Purloined Letter," as "a very inferior fellow" – is not copying the tactics of the era's other famous detective. "The Second Stain" is also noteworthy as the last case handled by Holmes before his retirement. The news of Holmes's retirement closed the series of stories known as *The Return of Sherlock Holmes*, and the public had to wait until 1908 for any further tales of the detective.

The Valley of Fear

The Valley of Fear was published in serial form in the *Strand Magazine* from Sept. 1914 to May 1915. Uniquely among the serialised long stories, each instalment was introduced by text prepared by the editors. The first British book edition was published in June 1915 By Smith, Elder and Co.; the first American edition appeared earlier, in Feb. 1915, published by George H. Duran Co. of New York. Many changes occurred between the *Strand Magazine* and the American texts. See Generally David A. Randall's "*The Valley of Fear* Biographically Considered."

The Valley of Fear, published at the onset of the Great War and comprising the last long account of Holmes and Watson, combines to near perfection a classic "locked-room" mystery – which comes to Holmes's attention via a tip from a disaffected lieutenant of Professor Moriarty's – a hard-boiled detective story, set twenty years earlier and featuring the victim in Holmes's case. Modern readers may quickly penetrate the mystery itself, as it features a clever device that has by now been so frequently copied as to become a cliché. For Edwardian readers, however, the story (serialised in the *Strand Magazine*) was enthralling. So, too, was the backstory, which recounted the violent history of the Molly Maguires, a secret organisation enmeshed in labour unrest in the Pennsylvania coal mines of the 1880s. Drawn from Allan Pinkerton's significantly fictionalised book *The Molly Maguires and the Detectives* (1877), this portion of *The Valley of Fear* takes a critical view, as did most people at the time, of the Irish miners and the violence in which they purportedly engaged. And while modern historians find the Mollies to be less villainous than oppressed, the role of the Pinkertons distorted, and the character of the "hero" less than spotless. Watson's version remains a gripping account of courage in the Valley of Fear.

His Last Bow

As published for the first time in the *Strand Magazine*, Vols. XXXV, XXXVI, XL, XLI, XLII, XLVI and LIV September 1908-September 1917.

The first English edition of the collection entitled *His Last Bow* was published by John Murray on October 22, 1917; 10,122 copies were printed. A Colonial edition of 10,122 copies was published simultaneously by G. Bell and Sons, Ltd. The first American edition was published by George H. Doran Company the same month.

1 **The Adventure of Wisteria Lodge**

"The Adventure of Wisteria Lodge" appeared as a title for this story only when book and omnibus editions were published. In *Collier's Weekly* (August 15, 1908), the story was entitled "The Singular Experience of Mr. J. Scott Eccles," and in England the *Strand Magazine* titled "A Reminiscence of Mr. Sherlock Holmes," calling the first instalment (September 1908) "The Singular Experience of Mr. Scott Eccles," and a second instalment (October 1908) "The Tiger of San Pedro." Indeed, until collected in book form, the entire series of stories, appearing from September 1908 to December 1913 (not including "The Cardboard Box" or "His Last Bow"), was entitled "Reminiscences of Sherlock Holmes."

As Watson reported in the preface to *His Last Bow*, a collection of eight stories published in 1917, Holmes may have been retired, but the accounts of plenty of his cases remained to delight his fans. The seven new stories that Watson added to "His Last Bow" as part of the collection (also included was "The Cardboard Box", properly part of *The Memoirs*) had appeared in the *Strand* sporadically from 1908 through 1917. "Wisteria Lodge," the first, is misdated by Watson (probably by accident), who places it in 1892, when Holmes was missing and thought dead. Here, as in "The Golden Pince-Nez," Holmes deals with a political fugitive, this time from South America. Although voodoo is a staple of twentieth-century thrillers, the earliest book in the British Library on the subject was published in 1893, and this story may be the earliest literary reference to voodoo. Unusually, Holmes is assisted by that rarity in Dr. Watson's accounts, a competent local policeman.

Notes

"A Reminiscence of Mr. Sherlock Holmes" is now known as "Wisteria Lodge."

"The Cardboard Box" is not included here, although it now forms part of *His Last Bow*. It was illustrated by Sidney Paget and therefore appeared in the first *Illustrated Omnibus*.

II **The Adventure of the Red Circle**

The original title in the manuscript is "The Adventure of the Bloomsbury Lodger." The manuscript is owned by the Lilly Library of Indiana University and is described by Spencer and Kennedy in "The Adventure of the Red Circle: An Examination of the Original Manuscript." "The Red Circle" was published in the *Strand Magazine* in March and April 1911.

Long before Mario Puzo and Francis Ford Coppola romanticised the Mafia for the American public "The Red Circle" involved Holmes with an Italian secret society so powerful that Watson was compelled to disguise its name. The "Italian colony" in London, although a distant feature of the landscape, by and large kept itself apart from the rest of the population, and only one other case, "The Six Napoleons," involves Italians. Here, Holmes accidentally joins forces with the Pinkertons, America's premier detective agency of the nineteenth century, to capture a cross-Atlantic killer. The Pinkertons appear again in *The Valley of Fear*, but this is the only record of Holmes working with them. Scholars consider Holmes may well have been duped by the beautiful heroine into letting the real murderer go.

III The Adventure of the Bruce-Partington Plans

"The Bruce-Partington Plans" was published in the *Strand Magazine* in December 1908 and in *Collier's Weekly* on December 12, 1908.

Regarded as one of the finest mystery stories in the annals of detection, both for its innovative clues and for its unexpected villain, "The Bruce-Partington Plans" is only the second one in which Sherlock's brother Mycroft plays an active role (the other is "The Greek Interpreter"). Here, Sherlock reveals to Watson that his brother is not just an auditor working for the British government, as he told him in "The Greek Interpreter"; occasionally his brother is the British Government. At the core of the story is an important government secret: the plans for the "Bruce-Partington" submarine, which Mycroft predicts will make naval warfare impossible. Submarines fascinated Conan Doyle, who wrote a story "Danger!" in 1914, warning of the perils of submarine warfare before they were widely appreciated. Scholars ponder why the British failed to develop the "Bruce-Partington," which could have played a significant role in the Great War. There is also much argument about Watson's description of the railways of London and puzzlement over the strange security procedures of the Admiralty.

IV The Adventure of the Dying Detective

A facsimile of Sir Arthur Conan Doyle's manuscript of "The Dying Detective was published 1991. There are minor textual differences between the manuscript dated July 27, 1913, and the version eventually published in the *Strand Magazine* in December 1913; significant differences are noted in *The New Annotated Sherlock Holmes*.

The only one of seven new cases reported in *His Last Bow* to occur before Holmes's disappearance in 1891, "The Dying Detective" (which scholars generally place between 1887 and 1890) has stirred up controversy over Holmes's cruel treatment of his closest friend, Dr. Watson. Here Holmes feigns illness (the practice known in Victorian times as "malingering") to deceive a murderer. In doing so, he not only allows Watson to believe that he is dying, he pretends to denigrate Watson's talents as a doctor. While Holmes's capture of the criminal is undeniably dramatic, it is the strain on the relationship between Holmes and Watson that holds our attention. Holmes's deception of Watson foreshadows his far greater (and crueller) deception in "The Final Problem" in 1891, when he allowed Watson to believe for three years that he, Holmes was dead. The late publication of this tale may indicate Watson's reluctance to reveal the cold side of his beloved friend's character.

VI The Adventure of the Devil's Foot

"The Devil's Foot" was published in the *Strand Magazine* in December 1910. The manuscript is in the Berg Collection of the New York Public Library.

The exploration of Africa captured the public imagination in the mid-nineteenth century, when the continent was no longer considered *terra inognita* by 1897, when the events of "The Devil's Foot" occurred (or 1910, when it was published). Hence the "great lion hunter and explorer" Dr. Leon Sterndale, the central figure of the case, is already something of an anomaly – even a bit of a caricature – when Holmes and Watson encounter him while on holiday in Cornwall. The case has been scrutinised in detail by scholars, who argue over the Cornwall locations and the nature of the "devilish drug" (reminiscent of LSD and PCP), but its real value lies in the revelation of the depth of the friendship between Holmes and Watson. Here, too, is the unforgettable repartee between Holmes and a suspect: "I followed you." "I saw no one." "That is what you may expect to see when I follow you."

VII His Last Bow

"His Last Bow" was published in the *Strand Magazine* in September 1917 and in *Collier's Weekly* on September 22, 1917. The manuscript is owned by a private collector. Dr. Watson may not have shared the manuscript with Arthur Conan Doyle before June 1916, for Sir Arthur reported (in *A Visit to Three Fronts*) that when he visited the Argonne French front at that time, its director, General Georges-Louis Humbert questioned him about Holmes: "'Sherlock Holmes, est ce qu'il est un soldat dans l'armee Anglaise?' The whole table waited in an awful hush. 'Mais, mon general,' I stammered, 'Il est trop vieux pour service.'"

In the tale entitled "His Last Bow," we learn of Holmes's undercover service in the Great War. Conan Doyle reported that while touring the front lines in 1916, he was asked what Holmes was doing for his country. Out of ignorance he answered, "He is too old to serve." Happily, that was not so. Like one other story in the Canon, "The Mazarin Stone,"

"His Last Bow" is written in the third person, not a Watsonian narrative, raising questions about its authorship. Scholars generally agree that it is Watson's work – otherwise, it seems unlikely that Watson would have included it in the collection under his preface. Because Watson was not present for much of the action of the episode, he may have felt more comfortable adopting an "omniscient" point of view. Here we learn details of Holmes's retirement and his celebrated beekeeping, and there are hints of Watson's retirement as well. The tale is a sentimental favourite of many readers, and the 1940s Holmes films starring Basil Rathbone and Nigel Bruce echoed its patriotic themes. Published in 1917, before the end of World War I, Holmes's vision of a beneficial "east wind coming" (that is, a wind that would blow over England from the Continent expressed the hopes of the millions of people around the world who wished for peace.

The Case-Book of Sherlock Holmes

I The Adventure of the Illustrious Client

"The Illustrious Client" was published in two parts in the *Strand Magazine* in February and March 1925, and its first American appearance was in *Collier's Weekly Magazine* on November 8, 1924. The first English edition, of 15,150 copies was published under the title *The CaseBook of Sherlock Holmes* on June 16, 1927 by John Murray. The Colonial edition of 5,000 copies, bearing the imprint "Murray's Imperial Library," appeared on the same date. The first American edition under the title *The Case-Book of Sherlock Holmes*, was issued by George H. Doran Company simultaneously.

The final collection of short stories, entitled *The Case-Book of Sherlock Holmes* consists of twelve stories published from 1921 through 1927 in the *Strand Magazine*. Curiously, it contains a preface by Arthur Conan Doyle, and doubt has been raised as to whether Dr. Watson wrote all of the stories credited to him in the volume. There are suggestions that some of the stories were penned by Watson's wife or cousin; some may even have been written by Sir Arthur Conan Doyle! "The Illustrious Client" is a tale of the mature Holmes, set in 1902. Holmes is physically attacked in the case, but as in "The Six Napoleons," he uses the power of the press to fool the villain. Although Holmes calls upon Watson to disguise himself as a connoisseur of Chinese pottery, scholars point out that Holmes's plan makes little sense. The case open with another example of Holmes's "reverse snobbery" in his dealings with the foppish Sir James Damery, and the contrast is startling when we later meet "Porky" Shinwell Johnson, an "underworld" operative of Holmes's.

II The Adventure of the Blanched Soldier

"The Blanched Soldier" is one of two cases written up by Holmes rather than Watson. The other, "The Lion's Mane," also appears in *The Case-Book*. Neither can be said to be a literary triumph: the contrast with Holmes's superb storytelling in stories such as "The Gloria Scott" and "The Musgrave Ritual" is pronounced. Both stories similarly show Holmes presented with a problem which he solves by knowledge known only to him – an early style of mystery fiction that Arthur Conan Doyle publicly disdained. Published in 1926, when the Boer War was but a dim memory to the British public, "The Blanched Soldier" demonstrates Holmes's knowledge of medicine rather than his detective skills. The case is also a harsh reminder of public attitudes towards mental illness and contagious diseases, even as late as 1903, when the events occur. The real doctor in the case, Sir James Saunders, made such an impression on Sherlockians that there now exists the "Sir James Saunders Society, a dermatological scion of the Baker Street Irregulars," which meets annually and administers a strict "re-certification" examination to its members.

III The Adventure of the Mazarin Stone

"The Mazarin Stone" appeared in the *Strand Magazine* in October 1921; its first American publication was in *Hearst's International Magazine* in November 1921. Only months before, on May 2, 1921, a play by Arthur Conan Doyle entitled *The Crown Diamond: or An Evening With Sherlock Holmes* opened at the Bristol Hippodrome, after which it toured for eighteen months. The play and the events of "The Mazarin Stone" have much in common, and it is difficult to understand why Dr. Watson would have given Sir Arthur access to his notes for purposes of producing a play. The play was published in 1958 by the Baker Street Irregulars.

"The Mazarin Stone" is written in the third person, like "His last Bow." Notwithstanding that the account opens with a passage of Watson's thoughts and emotions, most scholars doubt that he wrote it. The events all take place in one room of the Baker Street lodgings; and some suggest that the story is an adaptation (by Sir Arthur Conan Doyle) of his own script for *The Crown Diamond*, a moderately successful play that ran contemporaneously. Holmes seems to be uncharacteristically sarcastic. Parts of the story seem to be copied from Watson's "The Empty House," and the description of the layout of the sitting room at Baker Street contradicts Watson's account in other stories. When Granada Television produced "The Mazarin Stone" for television, Jeremy Brett (who had appeared in the previous thirty-nine episodes) was too ill to appear as Sherlock Holmes, and so the producers rewrote the story to make brother Mycroft the detective. In view of the likelihood that "The Mazarin Stone" is a work of fiction, they may be forgiven.

IV The Adventure of the Three Gables

"The Three Gables" was published in the *Strand Magazine* in October 1926; its first American publication was in *Liberty* on September 18, 1926.

Another case scholars doubt Dr. Watson wrote is "The Three Gables" (not to be confused with "The Three Garridebs," which also appeared in *The Case-Book*). Holmes sarcastic remarks to Steve Dixie, certainly racist by modern standards, displays an attitude markedly different from his evident racial tolerance on view in "The Yellow Face." There is little detection evident in the tale, and Holmes seems slow to grasp the clue of untouched luggage in the entry hall. Yet there are certain elements of the tale that seem accurate: Holmes's connection with Langdale Pike, a Victorian "gossip columnist," conforms to our idea of Holmes's "organisation." Holmes would have needed a source of information about "society" and the "upper classes," which neither the Baker Street Irregulars (the street urchins) or even "Porky" Shinwell Johnson could provide. Holmes's high-handed meeting with Isadora Klein also rings true to Holmes's character, for we have seen him repeatedly take the law into his own hands (for example, in "The Boscombe Valley Mystery," "The Blue Carbuncle," and "The Abbey Grange"). Without careful analysis of the manuscript, which is in the hands of a private collector, the authorship of "The Three Gables" must remain unsettled.

V The Adventure of the Sussex Vampire

"The Sussex Vampire" was published in the January 1924 issues of the *Strand Magazine* and *Hearst's International Magazine*.

That "The Sussex Vampire" is the genuine article – a Watsonian tale – is unassailable, which means that the suspicions that swirl around other stories in the Canon are blissfully nonexistent here. No scholar questions Watson's report of Holmes's great index, with references to Victor Lynch, the forger; the giant rat of Sumatra, "a story for which the world is not yet prepared"; Vanderbilt and the yeggman; Vittoria the circus belle; and Vigor, the Hammersmith wonder. Reference to Watson's youth, when he played rugby for Blackheath, also support the authenticity of the account. There is no record of the reaction to Watson's friend Sir Arthur Conan Doyle to such a mystical tale. Doyle, who by 1924 was known as "St. Paul of Spiritualism" and had committed his life to sharing his belief in the reality of the supernatural, might have harboured a particular fondness for "The Sussex Vampire." In striking contrast to Doyle, Holmes declares himself to be a confirmed sceptic: When a supernatural explanation is proffered for the mystery at hand, Holmes remarks, "This Agency stands flat-footed upon the ground, and there it must remain…No ghosts need apply." This is consistent with Holmes's pragmatic attitude in *The Hound of the Baskervilles*, when he rejects a diabolical explanation: "In a modest way I have combatted evil, but to take on the Father of Evil himself would, perhaps, be too ambitious a task."

VI The Adventure of the Three Garridebs

"The Three Garridebs" was first published in *Collier's Weekly Magazine* on October 25, 1924, and in the January 1925 issue of the *Strand Magazine*.

No scholar has yet found anyone with the genuine name of "Garrideb," and the uniqueness of the name plays a critical role in this tale. "The Three Garridebs" is undoubtedly a late case, probably occurring in 1902, and it may well be that the criminal was a reader of Dr. Watson's works, for the crime strongly resembles the deceptions employed in "The Red-Headed League" and "The Stockbroker's Clerk." The case is most noteworthy for what it reveals about the partners: As in "The Devil's Foot," another late case, Holmes expresses a moving concern for Watson's safety. Perhaps as a sign of Holmes's age (48) or his impending retirement in 1904, Holmes's and Watson's relationship has grown from that of mere flatmates in 1881 to the closest of friendship.

VII The Problem of Thor Bridge

"Thor Bridge" was published in the *Strand Magazine* in February/March 1922 and in *Hearst's International Magazine* in February/March 1922. The title page of the manuscript, which is owned by a private collector, shows that the tale had several alternate titles: "[The Little Tin?] Box," "The Adventure of the Second Chip," "The Problem of Rushmere Bridge" – and the *final* title was "The Problem of Thor's [*sic*] Bridge."

Although Watson is surely the writer of "Thor Bridge," here he mistakenly claims service in the "Indian Army." Perhaps his memory was beginning to dim as he celebrated his seventy-first birthday in 1922, when the case was published. In this tale, Watson records another confrontation of Holmes's with money and power, in the guise of Neil Gibson, the "Gold King." Although the true identity has been the subject of much speculation, this American millionaire seems to be almost a caricature of the British idea of "Gilded Age" Americans – fabulously rich, crude, stubborn, cold and violent. Here too are other staples of Holmes's world: the beautiful governess, the dark South American beauty. But all is not what it seems here, and Holmes much reach deep to solve the clue of the chipped stonework.

VII The Adventure of the Creeping Man

"The Creeping Man" was published in the *Strand Magazine* and in *Hearst's International Magazine* in March 1923.

"The Creeping Man" is more of a science-fiction story than a mystery, but the science of the tale is well grounded in medical trends of the day. In this story, Holmes is called in to discover the reasons that the respectable Professor Presbury has taken up courting a woman his daughter's age. Watson demonstrates here that Holmes's attitude towards dogs has changed markedly from his cold (but not cruel) dog poisoning in *A Study in Scarlet*. Now Holmes sees dogs as the mirror of their household, and he evens plans a monograph on the topic. While the case, with its outlandish plot of a drug-based "fountain of youth," has elements that seem laughable today, the obsessions of Professor Presbury and his fellow Victorians are not dissimilar from those reflected in current medical headlines.

IX The Adventure of the Lion's Mane

A facsimile of the original manuscript of "The Lion's Mane" was published by the Westminster Libraries and the Sherlock Holmes Society of London in 1992. There are numerous differences between the original text and the final published version, and significant additions to and deletions from the initial version are discussed in context, below…

The principal question for the student of "The Lion's Mane" must be why Holmes wrote it. While the case has the appearance of a crime, Holmes solves the mystery merely by recollecting that he has read the true explanation in a book. In fact, there is no crime at all. The tale is noteworthy, however, because it is the Canon's only depiction of Holmes's retirement. July 1907 sees Holmes resident in Sussex, and the story gives many clues as to the location of Holmes's last known home (where readers long to believe he still lives). Maud Bellamy, whose fiancée is the victim of the alleged crime, is a singularly attractive figure, and some suggest that Holmes had "feelings" for her. Appealing as the notion may be, we can only speculate, for there is no mention of her in "His Last Bow."

X The Adventure of the Veiled Lodger

"The Veiled Lodger" was published in the United States in *Liberty* on January 22, 1927, and in England in the *Strand Magazine* in February 1927.

"The Veiled Lodger" is the shortest of Dr. Watson's stories, and there is virtually no detection on exhibit. As in "The Red Circle," a troubled landlady asks Holmes to investigate her own lodger, a woman despondent over a murder plot gone horribly wrong. Holmes, who has never hesitated to ignore society's rules himself, nonetheless moves to prevent the woman from committing the ultimate rejection of society: suicide. While some question Watson's authorship of the tale, the attitudes expressed here by Holmes about higher justice coincide with those evidenced by him in "The Blue Carbuncle" and "The Boscombe Valley Mystery." Also, none can doubt the Watsonian tone to the narrator's deliberate suppression of "a story concerning the politician, the lighthouse and the trained cormorant."

XI The Adventure of Shoscombe Old Place

At the end of "The Retired Colourman," published in the January 1927 issue of the *Strand Magazine*, a forthcoming Holmes story was announced with the title "The Adventure of the Black Spaniel." It eventually took the title "The Adventure of Shoscombe Old Place" and became the last Holmes case to be published individually, appearing first in the United States in *Liberty* in March 1927 and then in the *Strand* in April 1927. When included in the first published edition of *The Case-Book of Sherlock Holmes*, it was moved to its present position as the penultimate tale. It turns out that the story could claim not two titles, but three: Arthur Conan Doyle, who wrote a preface to the John Murray edition of *Sherlock Holmes: The Complete Short Stories* in 1928, referred to the story as "The Adventure of Shoscombe Abbey" (although he misdated it as appearing in 1925) and the manuscript (published in facsimile in 2002 by the Bibliotheque Cantonale et Universitaire Lausanne) plainly bears that title.

Watson wrote no preface to *The Case-Book of Sherlock Holmes*, turning the task over to Arthur Conan Doyle. Thus for reasons forever unexplained, these were the last words that readers would hear from Holmes's devoted friend. "After this," in the words of June Thomas in *Holmes and Watson*, "the rest, as Hamlet says, is silence."

There is nothing about Watson's narrative of "Shoscombe Old Place" to suggest that Watson planned it to be the last tale he would write of Sherlock Holmes. Yet it was, appearing in 1927, when Watson was seventy-six years old. Perhaps Watson suffered some sudden illness or debility preventing him from further writing. Perhaps his wife urged him to lay down his pen, or perhaps she died. There is something fitting about a case of concealed death and investigation of crypts as a finale. In any event, as the tale opens, Holmes is still on the "cutting edge" of detective work, pioneering the use of the microscope as an investigative tool. Watson reveals that he was (at least in 1902, when the case likely took place) an habitué of the race track. As in "The Creeping Man," Holmes uses his newly found skills as an observer of dogs to uncover the mystery. Once again, he demonstrates his disdain for the "upper classes," as he confronts the amoral Sir Robert Norberton: "As to the morality or decency of your own conduct, it is not for me to express an opinion," he demurs coldly.

XII The Adventure of the Retired Colourman

"The Retired Colourman" was published in *Liberty* on December 18, 1926, and in the *Strand Magazine* in January 1927.

"The Retired Colourman" is the last story of the last volume of Holmes tales. Written in late 1926, when Watson celebrated his seventy-fifth birthday, it probably occurred several years before Holmes's retirement in 1904. Watson seems pleased to recollect his active partnership with Holmes, who, at age 72, may well have vanished from his life. Holmes first concludes that the case is merely "the old story": a fickle wife and a treacherous friend. He hands the investigation over to Watson, and (Holmes says) Watson characteristically misses everything of importance. However, when Holmes's "hatred rival on the Surrey shore" (of whom we have heard nothing before) turns up in the case, Holmes realises that a cold-blooded murder has occurred. There are a few untidy details in the tale, but no account of Watson's is free of flaws, and no true Sherlockian could accept one scholar's thesis that this – the story on which we must close the book on Sherlock Holmes and Dr. Watson – is a fabricated account. As to why it appears last in the book, we can only speculate, keeping in mind that Arthur Conan Doyle (as is evident from his preface in the *Case-Book*) and not John Watson put together this last volume.

Chapter 25

Final Collection of Forewords, Afterwords, Introductions, Prefaces & Prologues

NICHOLAS MEYER (Ed.) (1974 **The Seven Per Cent Solution. Being a reprint from the reminiscences of John H. Watson, M.D.** Coronet Books/Hodder and Stoughton.

Book cover

'Splendid stuff'. SUNDAY TELEGRAPH

'Here, in a newly discovered memoir, Dr Watson makes a startling confession: far from struggling with Professor Moriarty on the edge of the Reichenbach Falls in 1891, a cocaine-addicted Sherlock Holmes was hallucinating in Vienna under the care of Sigmund Freud…a brilliant piece of spoofery…The game is afoot again. Who can resist it?' THE GUARDIAN

'This intelligent and witty extension of the Sherlock Holmes myth…a marvellous new detective story…What happens as one mastermind pitches wits against the other and as Freud proceeds to psychoanalyse Holmes and get to the heart of his secrets makes a marvellously entertaining treat for the most jaded palate.' PUBLISHERS WEEKLY

Winner of the Crime Writer's Golden Dagger Award for 1976.

FOREWORD

The discovery of an unpublished manuscript by John H. Watson may well engender in the world of letters as much scepticism as surprise. It is easier to conceive of the unearthing of one more Dead Sea Scroll than yet another text from the hand of that indefatigable biographer.

Certainly there has been a surfeit of forgeries – some of them admittedly well done and others merely preposterous – so that the appearance of one more supposedly authentic chronicle may automatically arouse bored hostility in the breasts of serious students of the Canon. Where did *this* one come from and why not before now? Are the inevitable questions students are forced to pose time and time again, before going on to catalogue the myriad inconsistencies in style and content that brand the piece a hoax.

For the present manuscript, it does not matter whether or not I believe it to be genuine; for what it is worth, let me say that I do. As to how it came into my possession, that is a matter of nepotism as the letter from my uncle, quoted in full below, will serve to indicate.

London, March 7th, 1970

Dear Nick ---,

I know that both of us are busy so I'll come right to the point. (and you needn't worry, the enclosed bundle does not represent my attempt to make a stock-broker's life look glamorous and /or easy!)

Vinny and I bought a house in Hampshire three months ago from a widower named Swingline (if you can believe it!). The poor man's wife had just passed on – she was only in her middle fifties as I understand it – and he was quite broken up; couldn't wait to leave the house. They'd lived in it since the war, and the subject of the attic was simply too painful to bear. All the effects and mementos and papers (how much one accumulates during a lifetime!) that he wanted were in the house proper, and he said if we didn't mind clearing out the attic ourselves, anything we found up there we could keep!

Well, it isn't always you get to rummage around in someone else's junk and take what you like but, to be truthful, the more I thought of doing it, the less enthusiastic I became. The place was jammed with furniture, bric-a-brac, standing lamps, dusty what-nots and even old travelling steamer trunks (!), but there was something distasteful about going through poor Swingline's past – even with his permission.

Vinny, even though she felt the same way, is a homemaker. She wondered if there was anything we could use up there, furniture prices being what they are, and also she had items of her own she wanted to store out of the way. So up she went and down she came, choking with dust and smudged all over like a chimney sweep.

I won't bore you with all the details, but we found the enclosed, Xeroxed a copy, and are sending it on to you. Apparently the late Mrs. Swingline was a typist (her maiden name being Dobson), and in that capacity she worked at the Aylesworth House, an old folk's affair recently taken over by the National Health (hurrah, hurrah). In the course of her work – which included helping the patients write letters – she transcribed onto her typewriter (also in the attic, by the by, and in mint condition) the enclosed, which was dictated to her – he states so himself – by one 'John H. Watson, M.D.'!

It took me a while to read the thing and I was three pages or more into what he called his 'Introductory' before I realised what the hell it was. Of course it occurred to me the whole thing might be some sort of incredible hoax, a hoax that never came off and got buried in the attic, so I checked into it. In the first place, Swingline knew nothing about it. I asked him casually and he didn't recall it at all, much less express any interest. Then I went to Aylesworth House and asked them to check the files for me. There was some question about whether they were still accurate that far back – the war messed up everything – but my luck held good. In 1932 a Dr. John H. Watson was admitted (with severe arthritis) and it stated in his health record that he had been attached to the Fifth Northumberland Fusiliers! There could no longer be any doubt, at least in my mind, and I would fain have looked at the record in detail (wouldn't you have liked to know where Watson was *really* wounded?) but Matron wouldn't let me. She hadn't the time to stand around, she said, and the file was confidential. (Ah, bureaucracy, what would the National Health do without you?)

Anyway, it offers substantial confirmation as to the authenticity of the enclosed, which I am forwarding to you for whatever purpose you think best. You are the Sherlockian in the family and will know what to do with it. If it comes to anything we split the profits!!

Fondest regards to you,
HENRY

P.S. Vinnie says we have to cut her in, too – she found it.

P.P.S. We are retaining the original manuscript. We'll see if Southeby's is interested in auctioning it.

Authentic or not, the manuscript required editing, and preparing a definitive edition of Plutarch could not be more difficult than the problem posed by a newly unearthed text of Watson's. I corresponded extensively with Sherlockians too numerous to mention here; all of them proved invaluable, tireless in offering advice, comments and insights regarding the newly discovered material. The only proper acknowledgement of the debt this book owes them is the book itself. I have, with their help, preserved as much of Dr. Watson's narrative as makes for a consistent story.

For reasons which are not definitely known, Watson never (to our knowledge) got to edit the manuscript. His own death, possibly, or the vagaries of war prevented him. Therefore, readying the work for publication, I have tried to function as I believe he would have. I have struck out redundancies. Old people have a tendency to repeat themselves, and although Watson's memory of events apparently remained intact, he was prone to reiterate significant details. I have also eliminated digressions which he made from time to time when his mind appears to have strayed from the story and wandered unchecked into the intervening years. (These memories are themselves not without interest and in subsequent editions I shall no doubt include in the form of appendices). Knowing that footnotes are especially irksome in the course of a narrative, I have deliberately kept them to a minimum and made the necessary ones as informal as possible.

For the rest, I have left well enough alone. The doctor is an experienced hand at telling a tale and needs no help from me. Aside from succumbing to the irresistible temptation to telescope or streamline an awkward phrase here and there (which the good doctor no doubt would himself have corrected in his revisions), all is as the faithful Watson set it down.

NICHOLAS MEYER
Los Angeles
October 30th, 1973

INTRODUCTORY

FOR MANY YEARS IT was my good fortune to witness, chronicle, and in some instances to assist my friend, Mr. Sherlock Holmes, in a number of the cases which were submitted to him in his unique capacity as a consulting detective. Indeed, in 1881,[90]

---

[90] *A Study in Scarlet*, written by Watson after the case took place in 1881, was not published until December, 1887, when it appeared in Beeton's *Christmas Annual* under the pen name A. Conan Doyle. N.M.

when I committed to paper the substance of our first case together, Mr. Holmes was, as he said, the world's *only* consulting detective. The ensuing years have seen that situation remedied to the satisfactory degree that today, in 1939, consulting detectives (if not actually known by that name) flourish both within and without the police contingent of nearly every country in the so-called civilised world. Many of them, I am grateful to see, employ the methods and techniques first developed by my singular friend so long ago – though not all of them are gracious enough to give his genius the wealth of credit it deserves.

Holmes was, as I have always endeavoured to describe him, an intensely private individual, reclusive in certain areas to the point of eccentricity. He was fond of appearing impassive, austere and somewhat aloof, a thinking machine not in direct contact or communication with what he considered the sordid realities of physical existence. In truth, this reputation for coldness was deliberately and completely of his own manufacture. It was not, moreover, his friends – he admittedly had few – nor yet his biographer whom he sought to convince regarding this aspect of his character. It was himself.

The ten years since his death have provided me with ample time for reflection upon the question of Holmes's personality, and I have come to realise what I always really knew – but did not know that I knew – that Holmes was a deeply passionate human being. His susceptibility to emotion was an element in his nature which he tried almost physically to suppress. Holmes certainly regarded his emotions as a distraction, a liability, in fact. He was convinced the play of feelings would interfere with the precision demanded by his work and this was on no account to be tolerated. Sentience he eschewed; those moments during his career when circumstances forced open floodgates of his reserve were rare indeed, and always startling. The observer felt he had witnessed a brilliant flash of lightning on a darkling plain.

Rather than indulge in such explosions – whose unpredictability threw him off balance as much as it did any witnesses – Holmes possessed a veritable arsenal of resources whose specific purpose (whether he acknowledged it or no) was to relieve emotional stress when such relief became imperative. His iron will having cauterised the more conventional outlets of expression, he would resort to abstruse and frequently malodorous chemical experiments; he would improvise by the hour upon the violin (I have stated elsewhere my admiration for his musical talents); he would adorn the walls of our residence in Baker Street with bullet pocks usually spelling out the initials of our gracious sovereign – the Old Queen – or some other notable whose existence was then calling itself to the attention of his restless mind.

Also, he took cocaine.

It may seem strange to some that I am beginning yet another chronicle of my friend's brilliant achievements in this roundabout fashion. Indeed, the fact that I am proposing to relate another history of his at this late date may seem strange in itself. I can only hope, after commencing my narrative, to explain its origins and to account for my delay in setting it before the public.

The origins of this manuscript differ sharply from those of past cases recorded by me. In those accounts I made frequent mention of the notes I kept at the time. No such notes were kept during the period occupied by the present narrative. The reasons for this apparent dereliction of duty on my part are twofold. Firstly, the case commenced in so peculiar a manner that it was well under way before it was borne in upon me that it was actually a case at all. Secondly, once I realised what was happening I became convinced it was an adventure which, for many reasons, should never see the literary light of day.

That I was mistaken in this assumption, the present manuscript happily bears witness. Fortunately, though I was morally certain that the occasion would never arise when I would find myself recording this history, the case is one which I have good reason to recall in every particular. I may say, in fact, that the fixtures of it are engraved in my memory and will be until my death and possibly after, though such metaphysics are beyond my competent speculations.

The reasons for the delay involved in setting the narrative before the public are complex. I have said that Holmes was a private person, and this is a case that cannot be set down without some exploration of his character, an exploration that would certainly have been distasteful to him while he was alive. Let it not be thought, however, that his being alive was the only obstacle. If that were true, there was nothing that should have prevented my writing this history ten years ago when he breathed his last amongst his precious Sussex Downs. Nor should I have felt qualms about writing the case 'over his dead body', as I believe the phrase runs, for Holmes was notoriously sceptical about his reputation in the hereafter and entirely careless of the repercussions on his character on earth, once he himself had journeyed to that undiscovered country from whose bourne no traveller returns.

No, the reason for delay is that there was another party in the case, and it was esteem for this personage and a sense of delicacy on Holmes's part where this personage's reputation was concerned that caused him to enjoin me – under the strictest of oaths – to disclose nothing of the matter until such time as this second party had also ceased to breathe. If that event did not occur before my own demise, then so be it.

Fate, however has resolved the matter in favour of posterity.

The person in question has died within the last twenty-four hours, and while the world resounds with eulogies of praise (and from some quarters, with utterances of damnation), while biographies and retrospectives are hastily printed and published, I – while I still have the strength of hand and clarity of mind (for I am eighty-seven and that is old) – likewise hasten to set down what I know no one else knows.

Such a revelation is bound to stir up controversy in several quarters, the more so as it involves my declaration that two of the cases I penned concerning Holmes were total fabrications. Attentive students of my writings have pointed out my apparent inconsistencies, my patent falsification of a name or a date, and have proved to the satisfaction of all that the man who wrote these cases down was a blundering fool, or, at least an absentminded dotard. Some more astute – or more charitable – scholars have suggested that my seeming errors were in fact deliberate signs of commission and omission, designed to protect or disguise the facts for reasons that were either obvious or known only to myself. It is not my intention here to enter into the lengthy process of correction and restitution of data. Let an apology suffice, and the timid explanation be advanced that when the cases were often set down in extreme haste, it chanced that I frequently chose what seemed to me the simplest way out of a difficulty imposed by the need for tact or discretion. In retrospect, this practice has proved more cumbersome than the truth would have been, had I been so bold, or in some cases so unscrupulous, as to write it.

Yet these same astute scholars mentioned earlier have never with a certainty branded as spurious the two cases which I spun almost entirely of whole cloth and separated them from the others. I speak not here of forgeries by other hands than mine, which include such drivel as 'The Lion's Mane', 'The Mazarin Stone', 'The Creeping Man', and 'The Three Gables'.

I refer to 'The Final Problem', with its account of the death duel between Holmes and his arch-enemy, the fiendish Moriarty, and to 'The Adventure of the Empty House', the companion case, which relates the dramatic reappearance of Holmes and details briefly his three years of wandering through Central Europe, Africa, and India, in flight from the minions of his deceased opponent. I have just re-read the cases and marvel, I must confess, at my lack of subtlety. How could attentive readers have missed my overbearing emphasis on 'the truth' that I claimed to be telling?

As Sherlock Holmes remarked on more than one occasion, evidence which seems to point unerringly in one direction, may, in fact, if viewed from a slightly altered perspective, admit of precisely the opposite interpretation. So, I venture to suggest, it is in writing as well. My repeated emphasis in 'The Final Problem' on the undiluted truth which it contained should perhaps have aroused the suspicions of my readers and served to put them on their guard.

It is just as well, however, that nothing of the sort occurred, for secrecy, as it will shortly be seen, was essential at the time.

Now the real story may be told, the conditions stipulated by Holmes so long ago having at last been met.

I have remarked parenthetically that I am eighty-seven, and though I comprehend intellectually that I am in the general vicinity of death's door, yet emotionally I am as ill-equipped to grapple with oblivion as a man half or even a quarter of my age. Nevertheless, if the narrative which follows occasionally fails to bear the impress of my usual style, age must partly share the blame, along with the fact that years have elapsed since last I wrote. Similarly, a narrative which is not based on my usually copious notes is bound to differ considerably from previous works, however perfect my memory.

Another cause for variation is the fact that I am no longer actually writing – arthritis having made the attempt impossible – but rather dictating this memoir to a charming typist (a Miss Dobson), who is taking it down in some sort of coded abbreviation which she will subsequently transcribe to English – or so she promises.

Lastly, my style may appear dissimilar to that of my earlier writing because this adventure of Sherlock Holmes is totally unlike any that I have ever recorded. I shall not now repeat my earlier mistake and attempt to overbear the reader's scepticism by stating that what follows is the truth.

JOHN H. WATSON, M.D.
AYLESWORTH HOME
HAMPSHIRE, 1939

COSTELLO, P. (1991) **The Real World of Sherlock Holmes. The true crimes investigated by Arthur Conan Doyle**. Carroll & Graf Publishers, Inc.

Dust jacket

This fascinating book is based on a remarkable discovery: Sherlock Holmes methods of deduction and observation were actually those of his creator and used in order to solve real crimes.

Peter Costello draws on entirely new research to follow the tracks Conan Doyle left us as he entered the real world of Sherlock Holmes.

For Scotland Yard Sherlock Holmes really existed in the form of his creator; it was to him that they wrote when attempting to solve some of the most notorious elusive and brutal cases in criminal history.

Costello has, for the first time, pieced together the evidence and the background to the mysterious Oscar Slater case, uncovering a staggering police cover-up which protected a prominent Scottish doctor from being implicated in the case. He reveals that it is largely towards Conan Doyle that we must look to discover the mind behind the detection of George Smith, the ruthless Brides in the Bath murderer, and the discovery of the hidden grave at Moat House Farm. Again the marks of Conan Doyle's unparalleled powers of 'elementary' deduction are revealed in his correspondence concerning the identity of Jack the Ripper.

Like his fictional character, this arch sleuth was able to solve cases that had defied and mislead the greatest criminologists of the day, including the perplexing Langham Hotel Mystery. Among other extraordinary insights Costello reveals exactly how Conan Doyle established the innocence of George Edalji and identified the real culprit of a series of uncommonly vicious crimes.

These and many other detailed investigations illustrate how the Sherlock Holmes stories were the direct result of the author's hidden career as amateur detective and criminologist.

Sherlock Holmes's astonishing investigative powers, and the adventures that they lead to, are literally brought to life as one witness, for the first time, just how his creator turned the skills of his great detective to solving true crime cases from the gaslight era.

About the author: Peter Costello has written over eight books, including the highly acclaimed *Life of Joyce* and *Leopold Bloom*, *Jules Verne* and a biography of Flann O'Brien, as well as having contributed to a wide range of journals from the Dublin *Independent* and the *Irish Literary Supplement* to *Antiquity*. He has also been a consultant to various television programmes, including "Q.E.D" for BBC Television and documentaries for RTE.

THOMSON, J. (1995) **Holmes and Watson: a study in friendship.** Constable & Company. This edition (2000) Allison & Busby Limited.

The cover

This fictional biography celebrates the most famous friendship ever recorded. In the course of tracing its development, June Thomson, herself a highly respected writer of seventeen crime novels and three collections of Holmesian stories, gives fascinating insights into the personalities of these two very different individuals whose relationship was to last for over forty-six years.

Those interested in the many theories which surround the canon, such as the dating of The Hound of the Baskervilles or the location of 221B Baker Street, will find answers here. In addition, June Thomson supplies suggested chronologies to help with the vexed question of dating, as well as supplying two intriguing theories of her own concerning the identities of the King of Bohemia and the second Mrs Watson – both of which have been the subject of much debate among Sherlockian scholars.

Other controversial aspects of Holmes' and Watson's relationship are also explored. Was the relationship homosexual? What was the motive behind Holmes' decision to disappear for three years?

She has relied largely, not on conjecture but on the evidence supplied within the canon or from other sources of information, making it quite clear when, in the absence of precise data, she has been forced to speculate.

Those who have enjoyed the accounts of Holmes and Watson's adventures, whether in story form or in the many adaptations for film, television or radio, will find this book indispensable in providing a detailed and enthralling account of Sir Arthur Conan Doyle's two immortal characters whose names have become household words.

Prologue

Any attempt to write a biography of Holmes and Watson is fraught with problems. Not only is the canon itself immense, amounting approximately to 700,000 words, but Sherlockian commentators have, over the years, written many thousand more words about it and around it, their contributions ranging from suppositions regarding Holmes' astronomical sign – was he a Scorpio or a Virgo? – to a full-length novel by Cay Van Ash, *Ten Years Beyond Baker Street*, in which Holmes, having brought about the downfall of Professor Moriarty, takes on no less a protagonist than Dr Fu Manchu.

It is impossible to refer to all these writings in detail within the scope of this biography. I have therefore chosen only those which tend to affect the chronology of the subjects' lives. Rather than hold up the narrative by including these in the main part of the book, I have placed the references to them in two appendices, in which those readers interested in particular areas of Sherlockian research, such as the dating of some of Watson's accounts or the location of 221B Baker Street, will find the relevant theories set out in condensed form.

Wherever possible, I have kept to the facts given by Holmes and Watson in the canon and, where there are gaps, have used other sources of information to supply the missing data. When that has been impossible and I have been forced to speculate, I have made this quite clear.

Because readers might find it tedious, I have also limited the number of attributions to the places in the canon where direct quotations can be found and, with some of the less important data, have given no references at all. However, where any detail is stated as fact, readers may be assured that this is based on given information. Nor have I supplied, except in a few cases, potted accounts of the inquiries in which Holmes and Watson were involved. I have assumed that the readers are already acquainted with the narratives or would prefer to read them for themselves.

In the case of this biography, I have also put forward some theories of my own, for example, those regarding the identities of the King of Bohemia and the second Mrs Watson, both of which, as far as I know, are original. Some Sherlockian commentators may find this unacceptable, as they may find much else that is in the book.

But the biography is not intended for the experts. It was written with a very different reader in mind: the ordinary man or woman who, like me, has found much pleasure in Watson's chronicles of his adventures with Holmes and would like a more detailed account of their lives as well as background information about the period in which they lived.

My main concern, however, as the title suggests, is to celebrate the friendship between Holmes and Watson, arguably one of the most famous ever recorded, and to chronicle its progress, including the setbacks from which it inevitably suffered.

It was not, I believe, homosexual although some evidence in the canon might suggest, on first reading, a homoerotic relationship, such as the fact that Holmes and Watson share a double bedroom during The Man with the Twisted Lip inquiry or that Holmes bundles Watson out of sight in the Dying Detective case with the words 'Quick, man, if you love me!' Although on occasions he might have been naïf, Watson possessed a great deal of common sense and, knowing, as he must have done, the penalties of social ostracism should sexual deviation be suspected, or imprisonment should he be found engaging in homosexual activities, he would hardly have risked rousing suspicion by publishing these admissions unless he knew his own and Holmes' sexual behaviour was beyond reproach.

Watson also married twice, on both occasions for love. No one who has read his account of his courtship of Mary Morstan and his description of his feelings for her can doubt they are anything other than genuine. Nevertheless, Rohase Piercy in his book *My Dearest Holmes* has claimed that Watson, who was in love with Holmes, married Mary for convenience only, in order to appear respectable and to cloak his own homosexual practices.

I consider this a quite erroneous interpretation of his relationships both with Holmes and Mary Morstan. Watson, one of whose most endearing qualities was an inability to lie convincingly, was incapable of carrying through a sustained deception on his readers.

His relationship with Holmes was therefore exactly as he describes it: a close friendship and an example of male bonding which, though not unusual in itself, especially in an age of single-sex schools and gentlemen's clubs, is unique because of the detailed account of it which Watson has given us and also for its strength of endurance, despite the many strains to which it was subjected. It was a friendship which was to last for at least forty-six years.

CHARNOCK, I.A. (2000) **Watson's Last Case. A Sherlock Holmes Adventure**. Breese Books Ltd.

In the *Elementary Cases of Sherlock Holmes* by Ian Charnock, Stamford told of some of Sherlock Holmes's early cases. Now in *Watson's Last Case*, Stamford reveals what happened after Watson had joined up with his old service in 1914.

Stamford also tells us about his own youthful adventures and indiscretions and also gives details of those fascinating aspects of Holmes's life which so intrigue students of the world's first consulting detective.

Amongst the riveting tales in this exciting book are the following: *Mycroft Remembers*, *The Diogenes*, *The Report*, *The Solitary Student*, *The Attendant Three-Quarter* and *The Dresser*. Ian Charnock's Sherlockian pastiches are amongst the best ever written.

JANDA, A. (2001) **The Secret Diary of Dr Watson: Death at Reichenbach Falls**. Allison & Busby Limited.

The path of the biographer is fraught with peril, and insanity may not be the least of its dangers. I no longer think, if I ever did, that it is merely a matter of recording the truth as it happened.

These are the despairing words of Dr John Watson, as he attempts to set down the adventures of the famous master detective Sherlock Holmes. Not only does his editor at *The Strand* magazine require stories of no more than 9,000 words and Holmes himself complicate matters by exercising his right to censorship, but Watson's adoring wife Mary has her own opinions on the project in hand. At her instigation, Watson begins his secret journal.

Within these pages you will find the answers to many questions surrounding the most famous sleuthing pair in the history of fiction. What were the real circumstances behind the mystery of 'The Blue Carbuncle'? What actually happened on Dartmoor as they tracked 'The Hound of the Baskervilles'? How many adventures never made it into print? But most intriguing of all, how did Holmes die in his final duet with Moriarty – and then come back to life?

Charting the course of the two men's friendship, this ingenious pastiche draws on the entire canon and is a delight from beginning to end. Rich in scholarship, wit and period detail, this remarkable novel will delight fans of Sir Arthur Conan Doyle.

LYCETT, A. (2007) CONAN DOYLE. **The Man Who Created Sherlock Holmes**. Weidenfeld & Nicolson, London.

Dust jacket

It is one of the most intriguing dichotomies in literature. On the one hand you have fiction's most enduring character, Sherlock Holmes, the epitome of cold calculation and reason. On the other is his creator Sir Arthur Conan Doyle, a bundle of contradictions, who was a life-long follower of spiritualism (to the extent he was convinced that photographs of the Cottingley Fairies were real).

The complexities started early. Born in Scotland to an artistic Irish family, Conan Doyle became the archetypal Englishman and advocate of the British empire. With an alcoholic father and dominating mother, he rejected his family's Roman Catholicism. Seeking salvation in the scientific certainties of medicine, he became a doctor. But this proved inadequate: he needed scope for his imagination in writing, and for his repressed religious feelings in spiritualism.

The result was a fascinating personality and strong individualist, someone who, despite the trappings of convention, was prepared to take on the establishment in innumerable struggles for justice.

Never content with Sherlock Holmes, Conan Doyle was also a prolific writer of horror stories, histories and poetry. He was a sportsman, politician, clubman, polemicist, and much more besides.

While he sought to square his divergent philosophical attitudes, he was torn between dutiful devotion to his tubercular wife and passion for his beautiful young mistress.

With access to vast amounts of previously hidden archival material, Andrew Lycett shows the agonies, struggles and humanity of this great author as never before. Sir Arthur's literary career is played out in the middle of intense personal drama. With

Lycett's mastery of the historical background, Conan Doyle's life becomes a symbol of Victorianism battling to make its accommodation with the modern world. It makes for a scintillating biography of the highest quality.

ANDREW LYCETT read history at Oxford University. He worked for some years as a journalist, specialising in foreign reporting. He has been a full time biographer since 1992, with highly praised lives of *Ian Fleming, Rudyard Kipling* and *Dylan Thomas*. He lives in north London.

AFTERWORD

It was a game of golf that did it. A decade ago, while researching a biography of Kipling, I visited Brattleboro, Vermont, where the bard of empire had somewhat incongruously built himself a house called Naulakha. Just over a century earlier, in 1894, Arthur Conan Doyle had made the same trip when Kipling was living there. After comparing notes about literature and the state of the world, the two men went outside and played golf. Somewhere I read that Conan Doyle had introduced this sport to the United States which was stretching the truth (along with the claim that he brought skiing to Switzerland).

But the image of these two great authors teeing off on the rolling fields outside Naulakha had caught my imagination. I resolved that, after finishing Kipling, I would look into writing a life of Conan Doyle. A few months later, in November 1997, I read of the death of his daughter Dame Jean Conan Doyle and, with it, speculation that a vast family archive which had long been kept under lock and key, the subject of a protracted legal dispute, would finally be made available to the public.

Not long after my *Rudyard Kipling* was published in late 1999 I began doing what biographers do and enquired about the new heirs. I learnt that an American called Jon Lellenberg might be a useful intermediary. In telling him of my interest, I mentioned I had written a biography of Ian Fleming. This proved a good move since (something I did not know at the time) Lellenberg was a leading light in the Baker Street Irregulars, a US-based group of Sherlock Holmes enthusiasts.

He put me in touch with Charles Foley, Arthur's great nephew and the new representative of the Conan Doyle estate, who agreed to see me when he next visited London from his base in Sussex. We met in the Royal Automobile Club where Conan Doyle had been a member. From him and later from others I learnt some of the background to the estate.

Although Mary, a daughter from Conan Doyle's first marriage, survived into the mid-1970s, she was not an heir to his literary heritage. This position was reserved for the children of his beloved second wife, also Jean, on whose death in 1940, her three children, Denis, Adrian and Jean had shared the proceeds of the estate.

Denis and Adrian (and the latter in particular) were both spendthrift playboys. Denis married Nina Mdivani, who claimed to be a Georgian princess. (Her brothers made a habit of marrying and discarding a succession of Hollywood actresses and American heiresses.) Adrian took a more sober Danish woman, Anna Andersen, as his wife, but lived in a chateau in Switzerland, surrounded by Ferraris and mistresses.

These two sons used the Conan Doyle estate as a milch-cow. (Here I call upon other people's witness rather than Foley's.) Because neither man ever did anything useful in his life, they both took pleasure in making things difficult for anyone to write about their father. They even bridled at the Baker Street Irregulars' conceit of playing the game since this meant taking their father's name slightly in vain. (Inevitably if one regards Dr Watson as Sherlock Holmes's biographer, the role of Arthur Conan Doyle is rather devalued.)

But even the two sons realised that a good biography can be useful for a dead author's reputation. In this respect the relationship between an estate and a biographer is intriguing, as the former struggles to balance a natural retinence [*sic*] **Compiler's correction:** reticence about its subject's (often its close relation's) private life with a need to keep his or her name in the public eye as part of a modern media-savvy process of brand creation.

The race to write a life of Sir Arthur began as soon as he died. Even before 1930 was out, his widow Jean had rejected the advances of a jobbing author W.H. Hosking, plumping instead for the Reverend John Lamond, a committed spiritualist, who she knew would give due emphasis to Sir Arthur's passionate interest in the paranormal.

But this was not what the world wanted to read. Even her sons realised the resulting book was not satisfactory. So, after Jean's death in June 1940, they grudgingly allowed Hesketh Pearson, a prolific man of letters, to have another shot. Pearson had idolised Conan Doyle from an early age, even if when he met him at his relation Francis Galton's before the First World War, he was disappointed to find a thick-set broad-faced man with 'no more mystery about him than a pumpkin' fulminating against Sherlock Holmes for preventing him from writing the historical novels he wanted.

But the two brothers with Pearson's sprightly effort which they thought demeaned their father by suggesting that the secret of his success that he was the 'common man'. Adrian threatened criminal proceedings against Pearson's 'fakeography' when it appeared in paperback, he published his own riposte *The True Conan Doyle*, and he sought out Emil Ludwig, author of a life of Beethoven (such was the comparison to which he aspired), to write the definitive biography.

After Ludwig declined, Adrian allowed access to his father's unpublished letters and papers to John Dickson Carr, an American writer of detective stories, who had worked on a radio adaptation of *The Lost World* and was hoping to compile an anthology of Conan Doyle's works. Dickson Carr's biography, published in 1949, was a lively read – perhaps too lively, with its made-up dialogue, its lack of precision and its novelist's fanciful touches.

Usefully for future biographers, Dickson Carr included an appendix in which he listed eleven boxes, over thirty envelopes, more than fifty notebooks and commonplace books and sixty scrapbooks which he had used in his work and which he described as family papers. Around this time, Adrian, Denis and their sister Jean carried out what they called the Family Division, in which they shared out various papers and mementoes. For example, each heir chose seven of Sidney Paget's original Sherlock Holmes drawings for the Strand magazine. In addition, Jean wanted a Sherlock Holmes bust, Denis his father's writing desk and Adrian a table which the family had used to entertain such distinguished visitors as Dickens and Thackeray over the years.

In March 1955 Denis died at the age of forty-five. Before the end of the year Windlesham was put up for sale and the bodies of Sir Arthur and his wife were transferred from its garden to a new resting place at All Saints church, Minstead, in Hampshire, near the family's former house at Bignell Wood. (Even this caused controversy. Not only did the re-internment require Home Office approval, but the Church of England was wary about a spiritualist who had never hidden his hostility to established churches. So the Conan Doyles were buried at the outer extremity of the graveyard, though the rumour that they were laid to rest standing up is mere superstition).

Now the official manager of the estate, Adrian moved to Switzerland, where he was soon confronted by a formidable widow in Nina who, while protesting her love for her late husband, wasted little time (in the tradition of the 'marrying Mdivanis') in replacing him with Anthony Harwood, a former hairdresser who had been Denis's secretary.

Before long Adrian and his sister-in-law were feuding like wild cats. In September 1957 he alleged that Denis's estate owed him and his sister Jean $189,000. Nina retaliated with the claim that Adrian, as manager of the Conan Doyle royalties, had been holding back the third share she was owed as Denis's heir. Ken McCormick, editor in chief at Sir Arthur's American publisher, Doubleday, noted succinctly, 'I shiver at the thought of getting involved in this because everybody in that family is so unbelievably unpleasant.'

Adrian was determined to make something of the literary property at his disposal. In 1959 he oversaw a memorial volume put out by his friend, the London publisher John Murray, to celebrate the centenary of his father's birth. When he tried to interest Doubleday in this volume, he drew a blank, and was reduced to fulminating against their ingratitude to the man who he wrongly claimed had rescued the company from bankruptcy in 1894. (When the BBC commissioned an anniversary talk from Hesketh Pearson, Adrian announced that if it went ahead it would never broadcast another Sherlock Holmes story. The Corporation cravenly caved in.)

Adrian co-edited this book with Pierre Nordon, a student preparing a Ph.D. thesis on Conan Doyle at the Sorbonne. Impresses by Nordon's scholarly approach, he allowed the young Frenchman to develop his work into another biography, which appeared in France in 1964 before being translated into English by Frances Partridge, one of the last of the Bloomsbury group, and published by John Murray two years later.

Adrian now decided to put the family archive on show at the Chateau de Lucens, north of Lausanne. In June 1965 he made a deal with the Canton of Vaud. In return for financial help in buying the Chateau, and for additional tax breaks, he agreed to set up the Sir Arthur Conan Doyle Foundation whose aim was defined as the deposit, conservation and public exhibition of 'archives, manuscripts and books' left by the late creator of Sherlock Holmes.

An article in the Foundation's statutes gave Adrian and four other members of its council free rein financially, but declared the collections and the Chateau itself to be inalienable. The problem was that the collections were not defined. No inventory of the manuscripts and letters was attached, though a booklet subsequently put out by the Foundation referred to its ownership of the 'originals of literally thousands of documents forming the Conan Doyle biographical archives'.

Extraordinarily, this did not stop Adrian negotiating with the University of Texas through a New York book dealer to purchase the Chateau, complete with its contents. The University's Harry Ransom Centre had already accumulated a significant amount of Conan Doyle material, much of it through the same dealer, Lew Feldman, who, trading as the House of El Dieff (a pun on his initials), had over the years been acting for both Adrian and Denis.

In May 1966 Adrian was asking $2 million for the Chateau and its contents. He was not put off when the University offered only half this price. But when Texas's representative Dr Joe Neal visited Lucens a couple of years later to inspect the manuscripts supposedly included in the deal, he found little of interest and dropped out of the bidding. Adrian, however, persisted in trying to sell manuscript material on the American market. He claimed this amounted to 6,000 letters, including 1,500 from his father to his grandmother, Mary Doyle.

At this stage Adrian's sister Jean began voicing her concerns. The nature-loving former tomboy 'Billy' had forged a career in the Women's Royal Air Force, becoming its director (with the title of 'Dame') in 1963. Two years later, at the age of fifty-two, she had married Air Vice-Marshal Sir Geoffrey Bromet, a First World War flying ace, who was more than twenty years her senior.

In a letter from Geneva dated 23 April 1969 Adrian angrily brushed off her enquiries, stating high-handedly that her inquisitiveness had only started with her marriage to Bromet. He went over the details of the Family Division in the late 1940s, asserting that she and Denis had chosen manuscripts, while he had gone for family letters and papers. He added that, when their father was alive, Sir Arthur had given him an additional pile of letters which were stuck together after a glue pot had spilled over them. Adrian had spent long hours prising these letters apart with steam and razor blade, which explained, he said, why many in his collection still retained a patina of glue.

Feeling the need to defend himself against suggestions that he had been hoarding jointly owned material, he told Jean that he had been charged by their mother to burn two boxes of her love letters from their father. On the day of her death he had gone to Windlesham and, though aware of the sacrilege, had carried out her instructions.

He claimed that, ever since buying his first Conan Doyle letter in 1932, he had been the true guardian of their father's name. At one stage, he had run a regular advertisement in *The Times* offering, through a box number, to purchase any of Sir Arthur's correspondence. However to preserve this heritage – and, with it, the Foundation – he now needed to sell some of this accumulated material, 90 per cent of which had been bought by him over the previous thirty-five years, the remaining 10 per cent being from the Family Division. Under his stewardship, he claimed the estate's income had grown from £3,000 to £30,000 since 1956. But if his sister wanted, he offered to sell her the Foundation for Sw Fr 1.2 million. This would allow him to recoup over £100,000 he had previously lent the Foundation, but he warned she would also take over a £250,000 mortgage on the Chateau, plus its overheads.

Any fruitful conclusion to these negotiations were cut short by Adrian's own death in June 1970. But this only initiated an even more acrimonious battle between the widows of the two brothers and Dame Jean over the estate. As expected, the Canton of Vaud took over the Chateau and the small amount of artefacts kept there. (Any letters and photographs were transferred to the University of Lausanne.)

This time Nina Harwood chose to do battle not about the papers accumulated by Adrian but about the stewardship of the copyrights in Sir Arthur's published material, particularly the Sherlock Holmes stories. On the premise that the estate was not generating enough income, she hired Jonathan Clowes, a London literary agent, to look into improving matters. He suggested selling the property to Booker Brothers, a multinational company which had developed a tax efficient sideline in owning the copyrights of major authors including Ian Fleming and Agatha Christie. Unimpressed with this idea, she negotiated to buy the Sherlock Holmes literary rights through an Isle of Man company Baskerville Investments. By then the other two women, Dame Jean Bromet and Anna Conan Doyle, Adrian's widow, were relieved to be shot of this responsibility, though all three retained their interest in the estate's unpublished material which was brought back from Geneva to London in 1976 to languish in a solicitor's vault.

Matters again became complicated when Nina was unable to keep up the payments on the bank loan she had taken for this purchase. As a result in 1977 she was forced to sell to Sheldon Reynolds, an American film producer who had made a Sherlock Holmes television series in the 1950s starring Ronald Howard, son of the actor Leslie Howard.

The real owner (and the person who financed the deal) was Reynolds' Hungarian-born wife Andrea, whose mother had come into a fortune as the widow of Sir Oliver Duncan, an heir to Pfizer chemicals. Andrea Reynolds subsequently became well-known when, after leaving her husband, she fell for the Danish aristocrat Claus von Bulow. She stood beside him when, in a much publicised 1890s court case (later the subject of a feature film *Reversal of Fortune*), he was charged with and later acquitted of the attempted murder of his wealthy wife Sunny.

Subsequently re-married to Shaun Plunket, a former page to the Queen, she has continued to market her Sherlock Holmes rights, but found the Conan Doyle estate frequently opposing her in court.

Meanwhile Adrian's collection of letters and other material still gathered dust at the estate's London solicitor. Nina's death in March 1987 did not help matters as she bequeathed her interest in this to the US-based Mdivani relations who died intestate shortly afterwards.

The surviving heirs, Dame Jean and Anna, invoked provisions in US law which facilitate the retention of copyright interests by close family members. But then in December 1990 Anna died, leaving her share of the estate to three people – Charles Foley, grandson of Sir Arthur's sister Ida, who ran a sound equipment business in Brighton, and Richard Doyle and Catherine Beggs, grandchildren of Sir Arthur's brother Innes.

According to Foley, when he travelled to Anna's funeral in Switzerland, he was as surprised as anyone to learn that he had been designated one of Anna's heirs. At least he had some experience of the estate as he had spent time at the Chateau de Lucens in the 1960s when his father, also called Innes, worked as Adrian's assistant.

Towards the end of 1990 Dame Jean gave a rare interview to Christopher Roden, founder of the Arthur Conan Doyle Society, expressing the hope that all disputes over the family archive would soon be resolved and that it would become available to 'people studying my father's life'. She added her wish that it should remain in Britain.

She was, however, talking only about her own share of the family archive, which had to wait until shortly before her death in November 1997 to be formally divided. The now elderly Jean chose to keep her father's letters to his own mother, together with a few other items, while Anna Conan Doyle's heirs retained the rest. A deed of consignment was duly drawn up. The executors of Dame Jean's will were Charles Foley and Michael Pooley, her step-grandson.

When I met Charles Foley three years later I had no idea of this background. I did not know that the family papers were split between Jean's and Anna's heirs, and that Foley straddled both camps. When I broached the matter of the archive which I had read about after Dame Jean's death, he said he was still sorting through it at the solicitor's. However, although non-committal, he seemed happy to countenance the idea of a new biography. He said he would talk to other family members and, if there was any consensus, get back when there was movement and the papers could be consulted.

Over the next three years I called him a couple of times to ask how matters were proceeding. He replied that he was still looking through the documents and I understood him to say he would let me know when he was finished. But I heard nothing and got on with another project – a life of Dylan Thomas.

I was astonished therefore to read a lavishly illustrated article in the Sunday Times magazine of 14 March 2004 about the forthcoming auction of the Conan Doyle archive at Christie's. Little more than a puff for the sale, this emphasised the range of correspondence (from writers such as Winston Churchill, Oscar Wilde and Rudyard Kipling), artefacts and other treasures in the archive.

I was not the only person taken by surprise. The collector Richard Lancelyn Green, widely regarded as the most knowledgeable Conan Doyle scholar, was more than that: he was incensed. He was adamant that Dame Jean had wanted the collection to go to the British Library. But here were Anna Conan Doyle's heirs putting their share up for sale which would mean it being dispersed across the globe.

Lancelyn Green took his concerns to *The Times* which reported his attempts to halt the auction. But despite support from scholars and MPs, nothing could be done. Sadly Lancelyn Green had not understood the stark materialistic fact of life that the Conan Doyle archive had been owned (at its end) by one elderly woman and the executors of another and that the interests of the two did not necessarily coincide. Later Lancelyn Green took his own life. (It is true that the coroner recorded an open verdict but, having attended the inquest, I have little doubt that this is what happened.)

(**Compiler's note**: see Chapter 11 for further details of this tragedy).

At this stage I re-entered the scene. Having completed my book on Dylan Thomas, I was thinking again of Conan Doyle and, with the sale looming, I secured a commission from *The Independent* to write about this curious background. Using my previous contact, I prevailed on Charles Foley to give his side of the story for the first time.

Over tea at the Grosvenor Hotel he filled me in on the background to the sale. Shortly before her death, Dame Jean had indeed made her choice of items in the archive. These had been hers to dispose of as she wished (mostly to the British Library), while the rest were for Anna Conan Doyle's executors to do with as they pleased.

The sale duly went ahead and, though it failed to reach anything like the estimated £2 million and a quarter of the items remained unsold, it did realise £948,545 which after buyers' premium was divided between Anna Conan Doyle's three heirs.

Luckily some of the most important biographical material – letters between Conan Doyle and his brother and sisters – was bought by the British Library. When this was added to the letters and manuscripts which Dame Jean had bequeathed to the Library under her will, it made a significant corpus of work for a biographer to feast on.

I quickly moved to ensure that I would be the first biographer to work on these papers. I approached the British Library which promised to make its material available, even though it was uncatalogued. I also made contact with the Lancelyn Green family. Under the term of Richard's will he had bequeathed his substantial Sherlock Holmes and Conan Doyle collection (said to be worth £2 million, rather more than the estate had realised at Christie's) to Portsmouth, the city where, over a century earlier, the young

Conan Doyle had doubled as a doctor and writer before plumping for the latter profession after the success of his first Sherlock Holmes novel *A Study in Scarlet*.

I travelled to Poulton Hall in Cheshire, where the Lancelyn Green family has lived for over a thousand years. Richard's mother June and his brother and executor Scirard graciously offered to help me as much as they could with access to his collection which was now technically owned by Portsmouth City Council, while his sister Cilla in Oxfordshire allowed me to take print-offs from Richard's computer.

Encouraged that I could now call on material from not only the estate but also Richard Lancelyn Green, I secured contracts from my publishers in London and New York to write a new biography of Conan Doyle.

Imagine my astonishment when on one of my early visits to the British Library's manuscript room I found Charles Foley at a nearby table. I learnt that he was going through all the letters Dame Jean had left to the Library with the intention of withdrawing significant numbers. He was apparently allowed to do this under article 6 of Dame Jean's will which gave the British Library all her 'right title and interest' in the physical property of the unpublished material she had bequeathed, but not in any published version not in 'any document or documents which my Trustees in their absolute discretion may decide are documents merely of family interest and my Trustee's decision in this respect shall be final and binding on all parties'.

When I asked Foley about his criteria for selection, he declined to answer, saying this was a matter for him and his co-executor. However I acquired a list of seventy-five items which Foley intended removing from the Library. Ninety per cent were letters from Conan Doyle to his mother. It will be interesting to see if any of these documents 'merely of family interest' are included in the volume of Conan Doyle's letters which Foley is editing with Jon Lellenberg, now the estate's American agent, and Daniel Stashower.

After the co-operation I had gained from the British Library, and the speed with which it had made its material available, I now had a frustrating time gaining access to the Lancelyn Green collection in Portsmouth. Despite his family's support, I was repeatedly told that the items had not been properly sorted or catalogued and that, from a curatorial point of view, it was unlikely I would be able to view the material before the end of 2007.

Eventually in early 2007, with my book close to delivery, I enlisted the help of Stephen Fry, the collection's patron. With typical good humour he argued my corner. In April I was at last able to spend some productive hours with the collection and to make useful additions to my text. I am convinced that Richard Lancelyn Green chose well in making his bequest to Portsmouth. The team there is enthusiastic and deserves success in making its city a major port of call in Conan Doyle studies.

In the meantime I kept up sporadic dealings with the estate. I worked hard to keep these friendly because I knew at some stage I would need its permission to quote from copyright material. In this respect a biographer's job can be extraordinarily obsequious (and therefore stressful). I tried to promote the idea that our books were complementary, but it clearly looked on mine as competition.

Prior to this book, I have had to request permission from three main literary estates. I have usually been asked for a list of the quotations I want to make. In one case I simply had to say how many words I wanted to use and that was sufficient. But the Conan

Doyle estate was not satisfied with the actual words (which I had supplied together with sources). Foley asked for the contexts in which I wanted to use them.

Of course an estate is at liberty to make whatever demands it wants before granting its permission to quote. But as I am not aware of the Conan Doyle estate having made this request before, I took this to be an unfriendly act. Even if it was not the intention to hold me up at a crucial stage, this was certainly the effect, which was exacerbated when I was subsequently refused permission to quote 150 or roughly 40 per cent of the copyrighted items I wanted. (These were almost all from letters and other unpublished material written by Conan Doyle and his family. Generally Conan Doyle's published writings, and certainly all the Sherlock Holmes stories, are out of copyright in the United Kingdom, though the situation differs slightly in the United States.)

Oddly I was not allowed to use certain copyright material which had been published elsewhere, including in previous biographies. Foley said he was taking this line to protect the interests of the estate which had a substantial financial interest in the success of the edition of Conan Doyle's letters it was preparing.

As a result I had to spend further time deleting or paraphrasing quotations which I had painstakingly assembled in my text. This was exhausting and annoying, though I was also grateful that the estate had been fair enough to agree to the remainder of my copyright requests. Readers will have noted no lack of Conan Doyle's authentic voice in this biography.

I am left contemplating the relationship between a biographer and a literary estate. Some authors, particularly in America, are endeavouring to be more assertive of their rights to access and use copyright material for the purposes of scholarship. I can only speak of an interesting learning experience. I am constitutionally averse to regulations, particularly when not required. But when Kipling and Conan Doyle played their golf, there was a set of rules. At least, as a result of my research in the Conan Doyle archives, I have now seen the weathered card of their round of foursomes to prove it.

Review

"The man who created Sherlock Holmes" is a modest subtitle for a book that shows Arthur Conan Doyle as a doctor, spiritualist and goalkeeper for Portsmouth. Andrew Lycett's prose is quaint and academic: Conan Doyle's lover Jean Leckie was "a beautiful young creature…who struck an attractive compromise between the competing female role models of the age". And he overdoes the detail, Conan Doyle's surgery had "16 paintings on its walls, including nine by his father. As a result, it could not accommodate a new bookcase which had to be put in the dining room."

Anthony Cummins
Telegraph Books Saturday, October 4, 2008

NORMAN, A. Dr. (2007) **Arthur Conan Doyle. Beyond Sherlock Holmes**. Tempus Publishing Limited.

Dust jacket

In the year 1900, Sir Arthur Conan Doyle was at the height of his success as a qualified doctor, keen sportsman, writer of historical novels, champion of the oppressed and, most notably, the creator of that honourable, brave and eminently sensible master detective Sherlock Holmes.

Every new Holmes story was greeted with great anticipation and confidence in the knowledge that, however complex the crime, the supremely intelligent and logical detective would solve it. But in 1916 Conan Doyle surprised his readers by declaring that he believed in spiritualism. And when, in 1922 Doyle published a book in which he professed to believe in fairies, his devotees were nonplussed. How could the creator of the inexorably logical Sherlock Holmes claim to believe in something as vague and unproven as the paranormal?

In this fascinating study of the life of the creator of one of the greatest detectives of all times, Dr Andrew Norman traces the story of Sir Arthur Conan Doyle's strange beliefs from his early childhood. Can it be that Doyle's alcoholic father holds the key to the unanswered questions about his son? What was Doyle's involvement in the infamous Cottingley fairy affair? By delving into medical records and the writings of Doyle himself, Dr Norman unravels a mystery as exciting as any of the cases embarked upon by Sherlock Holmes.

(**Compiler's Note:** See Addendum for latest article, November 8, 2010).

About the author

Dr Andrew Norman graduated in animal physiology from St Edmund Hall, Oxford before qualifying in medicine from the Radcliffe Infirmary. He worked as a GP until 1983, and is now an established writer. He is the author of several biographies, including *Agatha Christie: The Finished Portrait*, and *Adolph Hitler: The Final Analysis*, also by Tempus. He lives with his wife Rachel in Poole, Dorset.

Preface

It is the year 1900 and Arthur Conan Doyle, now aged forty-one, is at the height of his powers. A qualified doctor who has travelled widely; a keen and able sportsman who once bowled out the legendary Dr W.G. Grace in a cricket match (a favour which the great cricketer was quick to return!), chronicler of the South African War (which he witnessed at first hand); a writer of historical novels and patriotic pamphlets, and a champion of the oppressed and the underdog. Most of all, however, he is known for being the creator of that honourable, brave, scientific, and eminently sensible master detective Sherlock Holmes.

Every new Holmes story is greeted with great anticipation and confidence in the knowledge that however complex the crime, the eminently intelligent and logical Holmes will solve it. It comes as a great surprise to his readers, when in the year 1916, the author, Now Sir Arthur (he was knighted in 1902), declares that he believes in spiritualism. How can the creator of the inexorably logical Sherlock Holmes behave like this? And when, in 1922, Doyle publishes a book in which he professes to believe in fairies, the vast majority of his devotees are, frankly, nonplussed. For many, this was too much. Suddenly the iconic figure of Doyle instead became a figure of fun; a subject of ridicule, mirth and derision.

Having an enquiring mind like Doyle, I was prompted to ask what he was seeking when he renounced his former Roman Catholic religion and became a spiritualist. Was there something lacking in his life which led him into an investigation of the paranormal? As for believing in fairies, this seemed altogether too bizarre. So how could one account for it?

As I commenced my research my first instinct was to empathise with Doyle, not for his strange beliefs, but for the reason that like him, I am a former medical practitioner who became a writer (in my case, following a spinal injury). What if he had walked into my former surgery in Poole, Dorset (his being in Southsea, Hampshire) one day as a patient, and told me his story? Perhaps, the first thing I should have asked him, discreetly of course, would have been if there were any other members of the Doyle family who had had similar experiences? Unfortunately, for obvious reasons, it is impossible for me to question Doyle himself.

Nonetheless, when I came to investigate Doyle's psyche using his own writings (both factual and fictional) as my predominant source. I found the journey just as exciting as any of the cases embarked upon by the great Sherlock Holmes, and all the more extraordinary because this was *real life!* Like Holmes, I was now looking for clues which I largely found subtly concealed in Doyle's own writings.

The trail led to Scotland, to the remote hamlet of Blairerno near the east coast; to Montrose; to Edinburgh; and to Dumfries. In all of these places Doyle's father Charles Altamont, had been forcibly incarcerated in various institutions for both his own safety and for that of others. Could it be that Charles held the key to the unanswered questions about his son?

My investigation led me to conclude that Doyle's father had suffered not only from alcoholism and epilepsy, as has previously been described, but more importantly from a serious mental illness. Not only that, but this illness was itself a heritable disease, in other words, one which Charles may have handed down to his son via the genes. Suddenly I realised that I now had an opportunity to solve what I consider to be the ultimate mystery, that of the bizarre and extraordinary nature of Sir Arthur Conan Doyle himself!

Epilogue

Sir Arthur Conan Doyle died on 7July 1930 aged seventy-one, at his home Windlesham, where his remains were interred in the garden. The following Sunday, a memorial service was held for him at London's Royal Albert Hall, organised by the Marylebone Spiritualist Association. His wife Jean died in 1940, and was buried beside him. In 1955 (Windlesham having previously been sold by the family), both bodies were exhumed and reburied at All Saints Church, Minstead, not far from Bignell Wood, the Doyle's family retreat in Hampshire's New Forest.

Inscribed on Doyle's tombstone, which incidentally takes the form of a Christian cross, are the words: 'Knight, Patriot, physician and man of letters Steel true, blade straight.' (The last line being a quotation from a poem by Robert Louis Stevenson entitled *My Wife*).

Looking back over Doyle's life, it is difficult to see how anyone could have fitted more into it, unless of course they were superhuman! Medicine, writing, sport, politics, and latterly the paranormal being subjects of consuming interest. In the typical British way he was strongly motivated to support the underdog. Above all, his quest was to discover the true meaning of human existence and more specifically, to overcome the seemingly insurmountable barrier between life and death. It is this which drove him onwards. It is as if he simply could not bear to accept the idea of death as meaning a final separation from loved ones.

His prodigious output of books has already been touched upon and his single-mindedness in producing them is illustrated by his son Adrian:

…before he wrote *The White Company*, he buried himself for a year in a tiny cottage in the New Forest, his sole companion being sixty-five works of reference on every aspect of the fourteenth century. Usually, he was at work in his study by 6.30 each morning, an hour's sleep in the afternoon, work until 11 at night, and then to bed with the Bible, a treatise on the recent evacuations in Egypt or, perhaps, all the newspaper reports on the Heavyweight (Boxing) Championship…

In *The Times*, at time of the South African War, he wrote, suggesting the formation of the Imperial Yeomanry…When Queen Victoria died, he wrote [again] to *The Times* advocating the change in the Coronation Oath which would delete the insult to Catholics. Before the Great War he saw exactly how Germany would use her submarines against our food carriers…, and had a story [published] in the *Strand* [Magazine] to illustrate it, after sending memoranda, in vain, to the Navy and War Office.

Adrian goes on to give an account of his father's sporting prowess, albeit a somewhat exaggerated one, which is nonetheless illustrative of the enormous and talent of a man who was burly, well built, over 6ft in height, and weighed in at about 15 stones:

I believe that I am correct in stating that Conan Doyle played for Hampshire in both football and cricket. He most certainly figured much in first-class cricket with the M.C.C.; reached the third round of the amateur billiards championship; was a hard rider to hounds, drove as one of the British team in the Prince Henry race against Germany [Prince Heinrich – 'Henry' – of Prussia, brother of Kaiser Wilhelm II, who loved to engage in motor sports]; introduced skiing into Switzerland [In fact, Doyle merely claimed that he had introduced skis into the Grisons division (canton) of Switzerland], and finally, was a dangerous man with the [boxing] gloves.

Doyle's generosity was touched upon by his mother Mary, in a letter that she wrote in December 1892:

My son is very good and generous to us. He pays half of his brother's [Innes's] expenses at Woolwich [Army Academy], besides paying for one sister abroad at school and keeping two sisters living with him. He had his own wife and children to maintain. I knew he would help me sooner than have his father out [i.e. released from the asylum].

Of Doyle's patriotism and sense of duty there is no doubt, and yet having witnessed two wars at first hand he is quite sanguine when it comes to the subject of international conflict. For example, in *The Adventure of the Cardboard Box*, he describes (vicariously through his character Sherlock Holmes), 'this method of settling international questions' – i.e. resorting to war – as 'ridiculous'. Although this was a reference to the American Civil War, Doyle no doubt intended the same sentiment to be applicable to all wars.

Neither is he at all jingoistic when it comes to the subject of war, and he was even respected by his former enemies the Boers, whom he had encountered at first-hand in the South African War, as this account by his son indicates:

His (Doyle's) history *The Great Boer War* is still accepted as the classical account and was so fair in its contents that the most full and flattering review of it was written from St Helena by one of the Boer leaders extolling its impartial and chivalrous spirit.

Despite Doyle being high achiever in many different fields, it seems highly likely that a man of his discernment and intuition would have lived his life with the thought always in the back of his mind that one day he might succumb to the same mental illness as his father Charles had done. He would doubtless have been relieved to reach middle age without such an untoward event occurring. However, when mental illness did finally overcome Doyle, he failed to recognise it, the illness itself having nullified his ability to have insight into his own condition.

With the death of Doyle, the trait of mental instability present in the family that had affected both him, his father Charles, and possibly his uncle Richard appears to have come to an end; although it has to be said that at least two of his children, his first wife Louise's daughter Mary and his second wife Jean's son Denis, shared his psychic interests. So what became of his surviving family?

Of his siblings, Annette became a governess in Portugal, where she died in 1890; Lottie married Captain Leslie Oldham of the Royal Engineers, who was killed in the First World War as already mentioned; Connie married journalist E.W. Hornung; Ida, following in Annett's footsteps, became a governess in Portugal and later married Nelson Foley, a distant relative and wealthy industrialist; Dodo married the Reverend Charles Cyril Angell.

Of Doyle's children by Louise, Mary managed his psychic bookshop in London, as already stated. Of his children by Jean, Denis married a Russian princess and assisted Doyle with his spiritualist 'propaganda' work; Adrian took a Danish wife and participated in motor racing and big game hunting, becoming a Fellow of the Zoological Society. He also added to his father's collection of Sherlock Holmes stories by writing several of his own. Jean became Air Commandant and Director of the Women's Royal Air Force.

Author Georgina Doyle states that neither Denis nor Adrian were '... trained to do any proper work. It seemed that his sons gradually dropped Arthur's spiritualist cause. Driving fast cars was a far more natural and enjoyable pursuit for young men.'

After his mother Jean's death in 1940, Adrian is said to have had 'some sort of nervous breakdown', and displayed 'subsequent erratic behaviour'. Adrian's doctor described him as having 'an overanxious nature', with 'grand, unrealistic ideas about his capabilities.' (This is reminiscent of the type of grandiose delusions suffered by Doyle himself).

In the final chapter of his autobiography entitled *The Psychic Quest*, Doyle anticipated the coming of a very different world, where:

...the sources of all force would be traced rather to spiritual than to material causes.

In religion one can perhaps see a little more clearly. Theology and dogma would disappear. People would realize that such questions as the number of persons in God, or the process of Christ's birth, have no bearing at all upon the development of man's spirit, which is the sole object of life.

All religions would be equal, for all alike produce gentle, unselfish souls who are God's elect. Christian, Jew, Buddhist, and Mohammedan would shed their distinctive doctrines, follow their own high teachers on a common path of morality, and forget all that antagonism which has made religion a curse rather than a blessing to the world.

We shall be in close touch with other-world forces, and knowledge will supersede that faith which has in the past planted a dozen different signposts to point in as many different directions.

Such will be the future, so far as I can dimly see it...

Perhaps it should be left to Doyle's son Adrian to have the final word, with this description of his father, who, even in his latter years, was still living and enjoying life to the full.

In the most cavalier manner possible, [he, Doyle] would lose far more money than he could afford in support of every wild project of treasure trove or sunken galleon; the adventurer who in the last year of his life would insist that he should experience the sensation of 120 m.p.h. in the mechanic's seat of a racing car; the companion who strode across the moonlit moor holding forth in the most fascinating manner on the Weald strata or the or the bloody history of the Ashdown smugglers and roaring out sea chanties [shanties] in a manner that leaves memory behind it as fresh and as happy as the salt wind in one's face.

ELY M. LIEBOW (2007) **Dr. Joe Bell. Model for Sherlock Holmes**. Popular Press.

FOREWORD

It is a great privilege to have been asked by Professor Ely Liebow to write a forward to his book on Dr. Joseph Bell. This task has been a true labour of love as my great grandfather has been a great favourite of mine since my earliest childhood. Although he died twenty years before I was born, I have felt always that I have known him. His almost life size portrait, used to hang between those of his parents above the sideboard in my grandparent's dining room. Now it hangs on the stairs in our house in Edinburgh. I like to think that I can remember him from the age of three during my first visit to see my grandmother, his daughter, when my parents brought me back with them on leave from India.

To the family Dr. Bell was referred to as 'Gigs', a name by which he was known by those grandchildren who were old enough to have met him. To me his portrait displays a very kindly and intelligent individual, who looks down upon those who pass as a friend and confidant. Without a doubt there is a touch of sadness in his eyes, which seem to follow you as you pass on the stairs.

I have been brought up always to believe that he is the person upon whom Sir Arthur Conan Doyle based the character of Sherlock Holmes. My grandmother told me that she was convinced that he was the teacher who gave his pupil the original idea of that great fictional figure. This is borne out by one of the letters written by Sir Arthur Conan Doyle to my great grandfather on 4th May 1892, which is in my possession. In it he says: 'It is most certainly to you that I owe Sherlock Holmes, and though in the stories I have the advantage of being able to place him in all sorts of dramatic positions, I do not think that his analytical work is in the least an exaggeration of some effects, which I have seen you produce in the outpatient ward. Round the centre of deduction and influence and observation which I have heard you inculcate, I have tried to build up a man who pushed the thing as far as it would go – further occasionally – and I am so glad that the result has satisfied you, who are the critic with the most right to be severe.'

It is no easy task to sum up Dr. Joseph Bell in a few words. On the professional side he was an eminent and dedicated surgeon, who was held in high esteem by all those who came in contact with him. He was, without a doubt, a man of very high principles with a deep religious conviction. He was a strong family man, whose life was saddened by the early deaths of his wife, only son and eldest grandson. Despite these great setbacks he bore no grudge to the world and continued to do all that he could to alleviate the sufferings of others. He took a great interest in life in general, kept himself very fit by shooting and walking and loved the countryside. In his private diary, which lies before me as I write, he recorded the major events of his life over a period of thirty years after leaving school.

It has been a great pleasure for me to have been in a position to help Professor Ely Liebow in some of his research. To you who read on, be you Sherlockians or not, I can do no better than to commend to you all the results of his detailed study and research. It is a fascinating and human tale of a remarkable man.

J.N. STISTED   January 1982   Edinburgh

J. LELLENBERG, D. STASHOWER & C. FOLEY (Eds.) (2007) **Arthur Conan Doyle. A Life in Letters**. Harper Press.

Dust jacket

More than 75 years after his death, Arthur Conan Doyle remains one of the world's best-loved authors. Famed as the creator of Sherlock Holmes, Conan Doyle was a fascinating man in his own right – physician, sportsman, crusader for social justice and war correspondent. From his early whale-hunting days to his later celebrity, Conan Doyle's life was as gripping as any of his own adventure tales.

Throughout, his mother Mary Foley was his principal confidante, the recipient of a stream of startlingly frank letters from her devoted son. Over a thousand letters between them survive from the time Arthur was sent away to boarding school in 1867 until her death in 1920. His letters to her, and to some other family members and friends, reveal a man whose early career was marked by a distinct lack of success as Conan Doyle struggled to establish a medical practice of his own, filling days by scribbling short stories that would result in the creation of Holmes.

In later years, Conan Doyle evolved into an impassioned figure. A deeply moral man of uncompromising political convictions, he nevertheless spent much of his married life passionately in love with another woman. His Catholic mother sympathised with her son and encouraged him. And yet neither she nor public ridicule could convince him to abandon the eccentric Spiritualist beliefs he embraced in later life.

This stunningly candid volume of never-before published letters sheds fascinating light on a man who has remained largely hidden behind his most famous character. Gracefully written and consistently revealing, these letters illuminate Conan Doyle's life, character and career as never before.

About the editors

Last year Jon Lellenberg concluded a long career at the Pentagon in Washington, D.C., where he was a strategist in the Office of the Secretary of Defense. He is the editor of the biographical study *The Quest for Sir Arthur Conan Doyle*, and the agent for the Conan Doyle Estate in America. A Baker Street Irregular, he is also a long-time member of the Sherlock Holmes Society of London, and a frequent contributor to its *Sherlock Holmes Journal*, as well as to other publications. He and his wife have three children, and live in Chicago.

Daniel Stashower is the author of the Edgar award-winning *Teller of Tales: The Life of Sir Arthur Conan Doyle*, and *Edgar Allan Poe & The Murder of Mary Rogers*, amongst many other works of fiction and non-fiction. A free lance journalist since 1986, Stashower's articles have appeared in *The New York Times*, *The Washington Post*, *Smithsonian Magazine*, *National Geographic Traveller* and *Connoisseur*. Like his co-editors, Stashower is a member of the Baker Street Irregulars. He lives with his wife and two sons in Washington, D.C.

Charles Foley is the great-nephew of Arthur Conan Doyle and great-grandson of Mary Foley Doyle. The present executor of the Conan Doyle Estate, he is also a member of the Sherlock Holmes Society of London, the Baker Street Irregulars, and the Arthur Conan Doyle Society founded in England in 1989. He lives in Hove.

INTRODUCTION

> *'Your ingenious habit of not dating your letters will make your biographer curse.'*
> -Conan Doyle's lifelong friend James Ryan

More than seventy-five years after his death Conan Doyle remains one of the most popular and best-loved authors of modern times, and his legendary creation, Sherlock Holmes, remains a towering phenomenon. For all his success, he aspired to be more than a mere writer, and his life was not spent simply cranking out book after book. He was also a physician, a sportsman, a crusader for criminal and social justice, a war correspondent, a military historian, and ultimately a spokesman and missionary for a new religion. Conan Doyle lived a life as gripping as any of his own adventure tales, and his activities frequently placed him on the leading edge of public controversies.

Each chapter of his life was rife with drama. As a schoolboy he confounded his masters' low expectations of him and became a prize-winning student. As a medical student he faced a torturous academic grind at Edinburgh University, and found some relief in spending six months as a ship's surgeon on an Arctic sealing and whaling expedition, risking his life upon the ice floes. As a penniless young doctor he overcame the treachery of a duplicitous colleague to establish a practice of his own, under constant threat of financial ruin. Upon finding fame as the author of the Sherlock Holmes stories, he travelled to America and became an apostle of what came to be known as 'the special relationship' between the two great English-speaking powers. He forged friendships with other writers such as Rudyard Kipling and James Barrie, and crossed swords with George Bernard Shaw. He helped introduce skiing to the Alps at a time when the sport was unknown there, and played cricket against some of the best professionals.

There was tragedy and controversy in his life as well. In the early days of his fame Conan Doyle learned that his wife had contracted tuberculosis, and he took her to the restorative climates of Switzerland and Egypt seeking a cure. His character and resolve were sorely tested when he met and fell in love with another woman during the years of his wife's decline. A staunch patriot, he went off to war in South Africa at the age of forty-one, wrote a history of it, then defended the British cause against slanderous attacks by its enemies. When his service to the Crown brought a knighthood, he initially intended to refuse it; he finally accepted only at his mother's insistence. At home and abroad he campaigned tirelessly for the victims of injustice and for military reform as well, as he watched war with Germany approach. Too old to serve in the army in World War I, his determination to contribute took him to both Downing Street and the front lines. The war took half a dozen of his family, including his only brother and his oldest son. And when he confronted anew the spiritualist uncertainties of his youth, he found comfort in a new religious belief, he was ridiculed for it.

Conan Doyle came from a distinguished family of artists who were Irish in origin, but by this time had lived in England for generations. His grandfather, John Doyle, was a celebrated political cartoonist known as 'H.B.', whose originals were sought by the

British Museum. His uncle Richard designed the famous cover of the *Punch* magazine, his uncle James compiled *The Official Baronage of England*, and his uncle Henry founded the National Gallery of Ireland. Three generations of Doyles, including Arthur himself, earned places in the *Dictionary of National Biography*.

His own father, Charles Doyle, was an artist as well. As a young man he went to Edinburgh to take a position with the City's Office of Works, and there he met and married Mary Foley, a young Irish girl of seventeen, and they began to build a large family. 'My father was in truth a great unrecognized genius.' Conan Doyle said: 'any sense I have for dramatic effect corresponds to the artistic nature of my father.' But Charles Doyle fell prey to alcohol in Edinburgh, and more and more the burden of supporting and raising the children came to rest upon their mother.

Mary Foley was remarkable in her own right. She was better educated than women usually were in Victorian Britain, spoke French and got much of her information about the world from the *Revue des Deux Mondes*, did heraldry for a hobby, and was greatly interested in genealogy and history – the origin of the historical fiction that her son loved to write more than anything else. 'My real love for letters, my instinct for storytelling, springs from my mother,' said Conan Doyle, 'who is of Anglo-Celtic stock, with the glamour and romance of the Celt very strongly marked. In my early childhood, as far back as I can remember, the vivid stories she would tell me stand out so clearly that they obscure the real facts of my life. It is not only that she was a wonderful storyteller, but she had an art of sinking her voice to a horror-stricken whisper when she came to a crisis in the narrative, which makes me goose-fleshy now when I think of it. It was in attempting to emulate these stories of my childhood that I began weaving dreams myself.' Though small in stature, she was a commanding personality who raised seven children largely on her own, and saw in Arthur the greatest hope of the family.

Born in Scotland, with parents of Irish descent, Conan Doyle nonetheless thought of himself as an Englishman, though the cultural strains of all three peoples would remain with him throughout his life. 'I am half Irish, you know,' he once told one of London's press lords, after losing his temper over a newspaper story, 'and my British half has the devil of a job to hold the hotheaded rascal in.' He was always conscious of his diverse makeup, living his adult life in England among its literary and social circles but standing for Parliament twice in Scotland, and taking a lifelong interest in the Irish Home Rule questions. Not all his colleagues managed to balance these disparate traits so successfully; two of his Irish-born collaborators in social and military reform movements would later be convicted of treason, and executed.

CONAN DOYLE'S LETTERS

Conan Doyle was a tireless correspondent, and few writers have left as full or vivid a record of their life and literary work. While he wrote hundreds of letters to the press and professional associates, the many he wrote to his mother were far more personal and introspective in nature, revealing a side of the man not previously known.

Conan Doyle admired his mother greatly, and she was his principal confidant his entire life. He went away to boarding school at the age of eight in 1867 (a year earlier than previously believed), starting the flow of letters that lasted until her death at the end of 1920, fifty-four years later. Roughly a thousand have survived, touching on nearly everything going on in his life, and letting us into his mind. They were among papers of his that were locked away for over fifty years because of family disagreements. They finally came to his youngest child, Dame Jean Conan Doyle, not long before her death in 1997, and were bequeathed by her to the British Library. Complementing them here are other letters to his father, his brother and sisters, and other figures in his life, which we have arranged and annotated to provide his life in letters. The correspondence constitutes a far more candid autobiography than the one that Conan Doyle published in the 1820s – called *Memories & Adventures* – which was long on adventures but deliberately short on the memories.

Virtually no aspect of Conan Doyle's life and work goes unmentioned in these letters, and they depict his personality and life far more completely and candidly than any previous treatment. They also contain many discoveries that greatly extend and often contradict the existing knowledge of his life. Other members of his family come into sharper focus as well, including his father. Charles Doyle has been accused on little if any evidence of being a volatile, even violent figure in the home, but there is no sign of that in the many references here, only regret over the infirmities that blighted his life and strained the family's resources. Other discoveries have led to previously unknown Conan Doyle work – including the only known example of his advertising copywriting, in verse, and a talk before four hundred physicians and the Prince of Wales that he called his most successful he'd ever given.

Gracefully written and consistently revealing, Arthur Conan Doyle's letters illuminate every phase of his life, tracing his development from a schoolboy through his years as a fledgling storywriter, then to the years of his immense success as a writer, becoming one of the most popular and influential voices of his time. He was a man of his era, occasionally prone to his prejudices, though perhaps less than one might expect in the private correspondence of a man born in 1859. And occasionally he had a temper as well. We have left intact examples of these, and of what some today would call his politically incorrect views on various subjects. When Sidney Paget, the artist who illustrated Sherlock Holmes for the *Strand* magazine, came to paint Conan Doyle's portrait in 1899, the author insisted upon being depicted 'warts and all'. This is likewise a warts and all portrait, as he would not have approved of being presented as other than he was.

MARY FOLEY DOYLE

His mother's influence is evident in every aspect of her son's character. 'The Mam', as he called her,[91] raised seven children in Victorian Edinburgh (two more died in infancy or childhood) in what was certainly straitened if not absolutely Dickensian circumstances. In later years Conan Doyle said his childhood had been spent in 'the hardy and bracing atmosphere of poverty', but that was a rather sunny way of looking at it, even though it appears to have been a genteel sort of poverty, usually with at least one servant in the household.

---

[91] His son Adrian, who exerted a considerable sway over his father's early biographers, insisting that his grandmother was, very grandly, 'The Ma'am'. In fact, Conan Doyle seldom addressed letters to his mother as 'Dearest Ma'am'; the term he used most frequently by far was 'Mam' – and after that 'Mammie'.

But Charles Doyle's alcoholism led to him being pensioned off when still in his forties, deepening the family's plight; and when he entered the first of a long series of sanatoria and asylums, it was his wife, Mary, who struggled successfully to hold the large family together. Throughout his life Conan Doyle felt a powerful debt to her, and a keen awareness of the many sacrifices she made to secure his education and his start in life. In his 1895 autobiographical novel, entitled *The Stark Munro Letters*, Conan Doyle gave an admiring portrait of his mother:

You must remember her sweet face, her sensitive mouth, her peering, short-sighted eyes, her general suggestion of a plump little hen, who is still on the alert about her chickens.

But you cannot realise all that she is to me in our domestic life. Those helpful fingers! That sympathetic brain! Ever since I can remember she has been the quaintest mixture of the housewife and the woman of letters, with the high-bred spirited lady as a basis for either character. Always a lady, whether bargaining with the butcher, or breaking in a skittish charwoman, or stirring the porridge, which I can see her doing with the porridge-stick in one hand, and the other holding her *Revue des Deux Mondes* within two inches of her dear nose. That was always her favourite reading, and I can never think of her without the association of its browny-yellow cover.

She is a very well-read woman is the mother; she keeps up to date in French literature as well as in English, and can talk by the hour about the Goncourts, and Flaubert, and Gautier. Yet she is always hard at work; and how she imbibes all her knowledge is a mystery. She reads when she knits, she reads when she scrubs, she even reads when she feeds her babies. We have a little joke against her, that at an interesting passage she deposited a spoonful of rusk and milk into my little sister's ear-hole, the child having turned her head at the critical instant. Her hands are worn with work, and yet where is the idle woman who has read as much?

Even at the peak of his fame, Conan Doyle solicited his mother's advice on nearly every aspect of his life and career – and even when he did not, she often provided it anyway – including, in one famous example, persuading him to refrain from killing off Sherlock Holmes. (She not only pleaded successfully for the detective's life, but also gave her son the plot device for a new story. 'He still lives,' Conan Doyle told her at the end of the first series of the stories, 'thanks to your entreaties.') But not all her advice was literary; she also counselled him on his tortuous love for the young woman who would become his second wife, while his first wife was still struggling against tuberculosis. While he did not preserve many of her letters to him, he did save the ones in which she strove vehemently to dissuade him from volunteering for the Boer War in 1899. In those letters her will and intellect shine every bit as forcefully as those of her famous son.

In addition, there were several more women in Conan Doyle's life whom he regarded as 'second mothers', addressing them, as he did his own, by the honorific 'Mam'. They did not exert the same developmental influence upon him as his own mother did, but he clearly regarded them with an esteem that went beyond simple family friendship. There was Mrs Charlotte Drummond, a close family friend in Edinburgh with whose two children Conan Doyle had grown up. His letters to her are in the Sherlock Holmes Collections of the University of Minnesota Library. Another was Mrs Amy Hoare, the wife of a Birmingham doctor, Reginald Ratcliff Hoare, under whom Conan Doyle worked a number of times as both a medical student and a fledgling doctor. Both Hoares became second parents to him, and his letters to them are in the Henry W. & Albert A.

Berg Collection of English and American Literature at the New York Public Library. Finally, there was Mrs Margaret Ryan, of Edinburgh, the mother of the one life long friend he made at school, James Ryan. Some of his letters to her are among his papers now at the British Library.

CONAN DOYLE'S TIMES (Excerpt)

His letters deal with a range of subjects that defined the age, including the literary and theatre worlds of both Britain and America, the British struggle for empire in Egypt and the Sudan; his country's bitterly controversial war in South Africa; bitterly contested politics at home (including his own two campaigns for a seat in The House of Commons); the sunnier world of sports (including the early days of the Olympic Games); the perennial and unsolvable question of Ireland; divorce law reform and women's suffrage (he was in favour of the first, and against the second); warnings about Germany's intentions in the days before World War I and reports from the front after the war broke out; the coming of automobiles, motorcycles, airplanes, submarines, radio, and motion pictures; and many insights into famous contemporaries.

The result is both an intimate memoir and a window opening onto a bygone age. In these letters, especially the ones to his mother, Conan Doyle held few things back, from the lofty ambitions of youth – 'We'll aim high, old lady, and consider the success of a lifetime, rather than the difference of a fifty pound note in an annual screw' – through the critical disappointments of his struggle to free himself from the public's demand for more and more Sherlock Holmes, and his restless search for 'some big purpose' that would define his life and career.

EDITING CONAN DOYLE'S LETTERS

Conan Doyle, like Dr Watson, had a tendency to be careless with dates. Of the many hundreds of letters written to his mother over more than fifty years, only a handful were dated. It was a daunting, at times maddening task to determine the chronology of the letters based on stationary, return addresses (when present), and internal evidence. 'The novel goes well,' he often wrote, but which novel? 'I have written a fine story', but which story? 'Many thanks for the birthday wishes', but which birthday? Sherlock Holmes himself might have found it a three-pipe problem, and we would not be surprised to find the occasional letter out of place.

Conan Doyle was also careless with spelling and punctuation, a boyhood habit that persisted to some degree his entire life. Except where important for purposes of clarity, we have let spelling and punctuation errors stand as they appear in his letters.

Whenever possible Conan Doyle has been allowed to speak for himself. Many important things in his life occurred outside the compass of these letters. For the most part, the interconnective narrative we have provided tries not to stray from the spirit and content of what Conan Doyle himself chose to convey in his letters, in order to reflect as far as possible the weight and emphasis he gave the matters he chose to report. But readers should keep in mind that his actual interests and activities and associations were even broader and more numerous than the many referred to here.

Conan Doyle lived at home with his family while attending Edinburgh University in the late 1870s and early 1880s, and therefore had no occasions to write letters describing, among many other striking features of a medical student's life, his remarkable instructor Dr Joseph Bell, who helped inspire the character of Sherlock Holmes. In this instance, and in others, the void has been filled with other accounts from Conan Doyle's own pen, so as to extend the fabric of personal narrative wherever possible.

Some liberties have been taken in editing the letters for publication. Shirley Nicholson points out in her book *A Victorian Household* (Stroud, UK: Sutton, 1994) that Victorians were constantly concerned for, indeed vocal about, their health. Conan Doyle, though living an active, robust, in fact athletic life was no exception. From boyhood he claimed to suffer from neuralgia, and his letters constantly report head colds and sore throats. We have left intact enough variations on 'I have a cold' and 'I have one of my throats' to give the idea, but have stricken many more for fear of exhausting the reader's patience. Similarly, Conan Doyle often conveyed tedious financial information to his mother in his letters, with scrupulous attention to the status and outlook of their investments. We have let many such references stand, but only the most single-minded reader would wish for all of them.

Finally, these letters do not solve all the mysteries about Conan Doyle's life. It seems evident that the eight-year-old boy was not sent away to school in order to protect him from a drunken father – but Charles Doyle still remains a misty figure about whom scholars would wish to know more. The letters provide more information about the turbulent influence of Dr Bryan Charles Waller, who became part of the household in Edinburgh for a time in the 1870s – but nowhere near as much as students of Conan Doyle's life would wish. And while Conan Doyle's investigation of psychic phenomena and spiritualism began while he was a struggling doctor in Southsea in the early 1880s, he told his apparently unsympathetic mother next to nothing about it until 1916, when he finally embraced Spiritualism to fill the religious vacuum in his life.

Whatever gaps remain, these letters will allow Conan Doyle's admirers to come to know him as never before – as a boy and a man, a physician and a writer, a public figure and a private person. For many readers past and present, Sherlock Holmes is a far more vivid presence on the literary landscape than the versatile and intriguing man who created him. Now, perhaps for the first time, Conan Doyle himself emerges whole from the shadows of Baker Street, as distinctive and memorable as any of his literary creations.

DAVID STUART DAVIES (Ed) (2008) **Sherlock Holmes: The Game's Afoot**. Wordsworth Editions.

Book cover

Once more, the game's afoot as Sherlock Holmes of Baker Street returns in twenty new adventures specially commissioned for Wordsworth's Mystery & Supernatural Series. The celebrated detective, along with his friend and biographer, Dr Watson, investigate a variety of baffling mysteries that will delight fans of the famous sleuth. Striding through the foggy gas-lit streets of London, Holmes tackles such cases as *The Puzzle of the Green Skull*, *The Secret of the Brown Box*, the conundrum of the *Dragon of Lea Lane*, as well as coming face to face once again with *The Sussex Vampire*. We also learn what really happened at the Reichenbach Falls when Holmes had his fateful encounter with Dr Moriarty.

David Stuart Davies, Denis O. Smith, Mark Valentine, Matthew Booth, M.J. Elliott and the other talented writers who have contributed to this collection have followed closely in the footsteps of Arthur Conan Doyle in creating a wonderful feast of Sherlockian entertainment.

INTRODUCTION

When the young doctor Arthur Conan Doyle sat down in his surgery in Southsea in 1886 and set about making notes for a novel involving a mystery which would be solved by a detective character called Sherrinford Holmes he could have had little idea of the phenomenon he was about to unleash on the world. (He changed the first name to Sherlock once he began writing the story). To be fair, it took some time before the public took much notice of the thin, hawk-nosed sleuth who shared rooms in Baker Street with a Dr Watson, who narrated his adventures. Holmes first appeared in *A Study in Scarlet*, a novella which was included in *Beeton's Christmas Annual* for 1887. The story and the character passed by virtually unnoticed. Even Holmes's second appearance in *The Sign of Four* (1890) failed to raise much interest amongst the reading public. But when the detective's adventures began appearing in the new publication *The Strand Magazine* in 1891, he became a rip-roaring success. Within a few months, the Sherlock Holmes short story was the main reason people purchased *The Strand* and the sales rocketed. Overnight it seemed that Sherlock Holmes and his creator Conan Doyle became household names.

It is difficult to imagine at this distance the effect Doyle's magical character had on the public at the time. There was no radio, television or movies and so reading was one of the main leisure activities, and the Holmes stories were lapped up by an eager populace. The detective achieved the status one today might equate with a pop star, a world-class footballer, a famous film star – or Harry Potter!

But Doyle soon tired of his character. He found the chore of being having to create a baffling mystery for Holmes to solve every month too demanding, and so he killed him off at the Reichenbach Falls in the story *The Final Problem* (1893). There was a public outcry. It is said that men wore black armbands in the City as a mark of mourning, and Doyle received many abusive letters from his readers. One woman wrote calling the author a 'brute' for killing Holmes.

It is well known that some years later Doyle brought Holmes back to solve the mystery of *The Hound of the Baskervilles* (1902), claiming at the time that Holmes had not returned to life but that this was an investigation from an earlier period in his career. However, pressure from publishers and financial inducements eventually led Doyle to relent and he brought the detective back permanently in the story *The Empty House* (1904), explaining that Holmes had escaped death at the Reichenbach Falls and had been travelling for some years before returning to London, to Baker Street, to Dr Watson and to solving crime once more. It was a less than credible explanation, but neither publishers nor the readers cared. The thing that mattered was the return of the Great Detective. Doyle's Holmes stories appeared sporadically and, it has to be said, with lessening effect and quality, until 1927, a few years before the author's death in 1930.

However, before the end of the nineteenth century, there were already parodies, plays and even music hall songs about the deer-stalkered one. And by the time Doyle died, there had been many films featuring Holmes's detective exploits. He had not only become a national institution but an international one as well. The silhouette of the sharp-featured fellow in a deerstalker cap smoking a curly pipe became recognised around the world. For the greater part of the twentieth century, the cinema, radio and later television carried the Sherlockian torch forward. Most of these productions were based on Doyle's original tales but in particular the radio series featuring Basil Rathbone (and Nigel Bruce as Dr Watson) in the 1940s included many new plots. When they ran out of Doyle's stories, other writers were employed to come up with fresh tales 'in the style of'. This approach was also reflected in Rathbone and Bruce's famous film series for Universal, which ran concurrently with the radio series. Gradually, the detective began to have a career independent of Arthur Conan Doyle's stories.

In the early 1950s, Doyle's son Adrian collaborated with the crime writer John Dickson Carr to create an enchanting set of new stories, *The Exploits of Sherlock Holmes*, which really captured the flavour, mood and piquancy of the originals. However, it has to be said that it was not until the mid-1970s that the Holmes pastiche bandwagon started rolling in a considerable way. This was down to one book: *The Seven-Per-Cent Solution* (1976) by Nicholas Meyer. This novel attempted to explain the real relationship between Holmes and Professor Moriarty and why Holmes disappeared from London for some time after his encounter with the Moriarty at the Reichenbach Falls. For some reason the book hit a nerve with the reading public at the time, became a worldwide bestseller, and was made into a Hollywood movie. Suddenly, Sherlock Holmes was in vogue once more.

In essence the novel *The Seven-Per-Cent Solution* opened the floodgates. There was an interest in Holmes again as a literary character and in 1980, when Doyle's work came out of copyright [sic], others – many others in fact – attempted to emulate Meyer's success. Since the publication of *The Seven-Percent Solution*, there has been a steady stream – no, let's be honest, there has been a deluge of pastiches featuring Sherlock Holmes, Dr Watson and indeed various of the satellites of his Baker Street world such as Mrs Hudson, Lestrade, Moriarty and even the Baker Street Irregulars, the little street arabs who occasionally helped the sleuth in his investigations. Even I am guilty of penning five Holmes novels and two one-man plays, *Sherlock Holmes-The Last Act* and *The Death and Life of Sherlock Holmes*. (Two of my novels: *The Tangled Skein* & *Sherlock Holmes & The Hentzau Affair* are currently available in Wordsworth's Mystery & The Supernatural Series). It would seem that the appetite for Holmes is insatiable. Arthur Conan Doyle wrote only 56 short stories and four novels featuring the character; but now there are thousands of his exploits penned by numerous hands from all continents of the world. Harry Potter eat your heart out.

It is impossible to explain fully why this character has such a mesmeric hold on the public. There are even statues erected to him in London, Edinburgh and Japan. There are many other brilliant detectives in fiction who, while having a certain popularity, come nowhere near to accruing the fanatical following that Sherlock Holmes generates. Why is this? Let us consider the elements which make up a Holmes story. There are the mysteries, of course: the conundrums which baffle not only Watson but the reader, and are clearly explained at the end when Holmes demonstrates his detective brilliance. Then there is the wonderful Victorian period with its pea-souper fogs, hansom cabs and gas-lit cobbled streets. This period is of course fascinating to the modern reader. Victorian London now seems another world with almost fairytale resonances, but it must be remembered that when these stories were first written this was the contemporary scene. The settings, the characters and the everyday details would be as familiar to Doyle's original readers as motorways, iPods and computers would be to us today. That is one reason why the period detail seems so natural and presents itself in an unobtrusive fashion in the original stories, unlike many modern writers who, when setting their mysteries in the past, tend to burden their writing with period detail they have unearthed in their research.

Another attraction of the Holmes stories is the wonderful set of bizarre and remarkable characters who people their pages, such as the blackmailer Charles Augustus Milverton, the worst man in London; the vengeful one-legged murderer, Jonathan Small, the avaricious red-headed pawnbroker, Jabez Wilson, and the strange creeping Professor Presbury, to name but a few. Then there is the friendship between Holmes and Watson. Here Doyle carries out a wonderful balancing act of presenting this as both reserved, in keeping with the Victorian modes of conduct, and yet emotional. We weep with Watson when he believes that he has lost his friend – 'the best and wisest man I have ever known' – at the Reichenbach Falls, and we are touched by Holmes's sudden and unexpected display of emotion in 'The Three Garridebs' : 'For God's sake, say you're not hurt, Watson. For God's sake say you are not hurt.' Holmes and Watson are not only one of the great partnerships in literature, but one of the great friendships also.

All these aspects combine to make these Holmes stories magical and somehow enable them to speak to readers of many nations. But there is something more, something else that, in truth, beggars description. Something, I suspect, that even Conan Doyle could not explain. When reading the stories, we feel it, we comprehend it, but we cannot describe it. It is the X factor, an intangible ingredient, which appeals to both the mind and the heart but defies recognition. I, for one, do not want to find out what it is. When the mysterious is explained, the magic dissolves. Holmes makes a similar observation to Watson when he explains one of his deductions in *A Study in Scarlet*:

You know a conjuror gets no credit when once he has explained his trick; and if I show you too much of my method of working, you will come to the conclusion that I am a very ordinary individual after all.

So let us just accept that these stories are unique, as are the characters of Sherlock Holmes and Dr John H. Watson, and be content that they still fascinate and entertain. And here in *The Game's Afoot* we have a new batch of twenty adventures to do just that: to fascinate and entertain you. These stories, collected together for the first time, have been penned by authors who not only are skilled storytellers but also have great knowledge and understanding of the Holmes canon and so can replicate in the best possible way the mood, tone and fidelity of the original tales.

Indeed, apart from a few exceptions, entertaining divertissements to add a little variety along the way, the majority of the stories in this collection aim to provide the reader with a traditional Sherlock Holmes story containing all the elements we have already referred to, including that mysterious X factor. That does not mean that they are slavish copies of Doyle with no spark of their own or that there will be no surprises for the reader along the way; it means that there is no attempt to introduce elements into the stories that are at odds with the original conceptions. There are no instances where Watson reveals himself to be Moriarty after all, or that Mycroft is a woman or that Holmes is in fact an alien. Neither is there a parade of other literary figures such as Dorian Gray, Raffles or Count Dracula calling on Holmes for assistance. In other words, there is little in these tales that Arthur Conan Doyle would not have penned himself.

I like to think of these stories as new vintage Holmes. I hope you agree.

So settle down, allow your mind to travel back to the London of very long ago, to those foggy, gas-lit streets with the sound of the lonely cab clip-clopping through the gloom, and get ready to join Sherlock Holmes and Dr Watson investigating another baffling mystery because, my friend, once more, the game's afoot.

DAVID STUART DAVIES

ALISTAIR DUNCAN (2008) **Eliminate the impossible**. An examination of the world of Sherlock Holmes on page and screen. Lightning Source UK Ltd.

Cover

Sherlock Holmes, arguably the most famous fictional private detective, is known to many purely through his appearances on film. However he had a life on the page long before he made it to the silver screen. This book looks at the origins of the character, examines the original stories and their inconsistencies before moving on to look at his film career and the many actors who have portrayed him. (**Compiler's note**: Readers will have already read detailed information about this in Chapter 7).

INTRODUCTION

Sherlock Holmes is one of the most recognisable and well known characters in literature. The image of him and Watson travelling along fog covered Victorian streets in search of clues is one that most people can easily conjure.

Like many people I gained my first glimpse into this world through television. I dimly remember, as a boy of less than ten years old, seeing the Basil Rathbone series for the first time. Rathbone *was* Sherlock Holmes for me for many years until I eventually started to see other adaptations. Despite this, for a long time afterwards, if I read one of the stories Rathbone was the Holmes of my imagination.

Although I have since discovered the inaccuracies of these films they were still responsible for getting me engrossed in arguably the best known series of detective stories to date. Since that first introduction I have watched many television adaptations and read all of the original stories along with a number of pastiches by other authors. My interest has naturally extended to other crime authors but none of them for me generates the same magical imagery as the work of Sir Arthur Conan Doyle.

So many books have been written on the subject of Holmes, Watson and Conan Doyle himself that you may wonder why I am adding yet another. I am well aware from my research that many of the anomalies in the stories and films that I will later refer to have been covered to some degree in other works. I have tried as much as possible to bring a fresh perspective to some of these puzzles. Where I have been unable to contribute anything new I have attempted to weigh the pros and cons of the opinions expressed in the hope of allowing the reader to come to their own informed conclusions.

This book was originally conceived as an introduction to the canon for those who had not given the world of Holmes more than a cursory glance. However as I wrote more and more and delved more deeply into some of the issues I became aware that I had created a work that to some extent would appeal to people who are long-standing fans as well as novice Sherlockians. However, I can state with absolute certainty that this book is not for you if you have not read at least some of the original stories.

My last word to the reader concerns the title of this book. As any author knows, choosing a title is one of the hardest aspects of writing a book. With a book about Sherlock Holmes it is even more so. With so many books out there, all the more obvious titles have been taken. I was lucky to find a title that most Holmes fans will recognise and yet had not been used.

However please note that it is purely a title and not a mission statement. I am not offering any definitive solutions to any of the puzzles that have been faced by generations of Sherlockian scholars. I am simply offering my own viewpoint.

ALISTAIR DUNCAN-London, 2008.

RUSSELL MILLER (2008) **The Adventures of Arthur Conan Doyle**. Harvill *Secker* London

Dust jacket

As the creator of Sherlock Holmes, 'the world's most famous man who never was', Arthur Conan Doyle remains one of our favourite writers; his work is read with affection – and sometimes obsession – the world over. Writer, doctor, cricketer, public figure and family man, his life was no less fascinating that his fiction.

Conan Doyle grew up in relative poverty in Edinburgh, with the mental illness of his artistically gifted but alcoholic father casting a shadow over his early life. He struggled both as a young doctor and his early attempts to sell short stories, having only limited success until Sherlock Holmes became a publishing phenomenon and propelled him to worldwide fame.

Whilst he enjoyed the celebrity Holmes brought him, he also felt that the stories damaged his literary reputation. Beyond his writing, Conan Doyle led a full life, participating in the Boer War, falling in love with another woman while his wife was dying of tuberculosis, campaigning against injustice, and converting to Spiritualism, a move that would bewilder his friends and fans.

During his lifetime Conan Doyle wrote more than 1,500 letters to members of his family, most notably his mother, revealing his most innermost thoughts, fears and hopes. Russell Miller is the first biographer to have been granted unlimited access to Conan Doyle's private correspondence. (**Compiler's note**: Lellenberg, Stashower and Foley's book *Arthur Conan Doyle. A Life in Letters* was published a year earlier in 2007). *The Adventures of Arthur Conan Doyle* also makes use of the writer's personal papers, unseen for many years, and is the first book to draw fully on the Richard Lancelyn Green archive, the world's most comprehensive collection of Conan Doyle material.

Told with panache, *The Adventures of Arthur Conan Doyle* is an unprecedentedly full portrait of an enduringly popular figure.

FOREWORD

THROUGHOUT HIS LONG AND remarkable life, Sir Arthur Conan Doyle was an amazing industrious correspondent, writing thousands of letters to friends, family, colleagues and acquaintances. He was a man more comfortable revealing his emotions on paper than by word or gesture. His adored mother received no fewer than 1,500 letters from her son, in one of which he confessed, for example, that he had fallen in love with another woman, while his wife was dying of tuberculosis. Thereafter he kept her up to date with every intimate development of the affair. Conan Doyle's candid letters provide a unique insight into the man and form the backbone of this book, the first biography to enjoy virtually unlimited and unfettered access to his private papers.

The background to the Conan Doyle archive is complicated. During his lifetime Conan Doyle sold at least seven manuscripts to raise money for the Red Cross during the First World War and a further six Sherlock Holmes manuscripts were put up for auction at the American Art Galleries in New York in 1922. At his death on 7 July 1930, all his remaining papers – original manuscripts, research notes, journals and voluminous letters, almost his entire life's work – were lodged at Windlesham, his house in East Sussex. He left everything to his wife, who, over the next decade, added her own notes and memories to the collection. When Lady Conan Doyle died in 1940, her three children – sons Adrian and Denis and daughter, Jean – shared the estate. While Jean would carve out a successful career, eventually becoming a Dame and Commandant of the Woman's Royal Air Force, her two brothers were feckless playboys who rarely worked and shamelessly used their father's estate to finance their extravagant lifestyles. Adrian Conan Doyle, who liked to describe himself as a motor racing driver and big game hunter, was appointed executor and became the unlikely custodian of his father's memory, establishing at his chateau in Lucens, Switzerland, a Sherlock Holmes Museum. It was Adrian's absurd thesis, against all the evidence, that his father was the role model for Sherlock Holmes.

In the late 1940s Adrian invited the American thriller writer, John Dickson Carr, to write an authorised biography of his father, offering him the use of the archive. Carr's book *The Life of Sir Arthur Conan Doyle*, first published in 1949, included an appendix briefly listing the contents of a number of boxes in the archive, although little use appeared to have been made of the material in the narrative, almost certainly because Adrian Conan Doyle was exercising strict editorial control. Ten years later, a French scholar, Pierre Nordon, was also granted access for his Sorbonne thesis, later published as a similarly anodyne biography.

Through the 1950s and 60s Adrian Conan Doyle sold manuscripts and certain of his father's papers, mainly in the United States, where there was a ready market for Conan Doyle memorabilia. In 1969 he had the complete archive shipped secretly to New York with the intention of selling it in its entirety to a wealthy collector in Texas for a huge sum, but no agreement had been reached by the time of his death, from a heart attack, the following year. Thereafter the archive, amounting to 15 boxes, now somewhat disorganised but still containing all of Sir Arthur's personal papers, would be lodged in the offices of a London solicitor for nearly 25 years while legal squabbles between the family dragged on.

No one was more frustrated by these events than Richard Lancelyn Green, one of the world's leading experts on Sherlock Holmes and Conan Doyle. A prominent and popular member of the Sherlock Holmes Society of London, Lancelyn Green had devoted his life to collecting Conan Doyle memorabilia and had a reputation as a brilliant and witty raconteur with an encyclopaedic knowledge of his subject. He travelled widely, delivering lectures with theatrical flair to other Sherlock Holmes societies around the world and established his scholarly reputation in 1983 as co-editor of *A Bibliography of A. Conan Doyle*, which was judged one of the most comprehensive and authoritative bibliographies ever produced, of any writer.

But the culmination of his life's work, a definitive biography, remained resolutely unachievable while the bulk of Conan Doyle's papers were the subject of continuing dispute within the family. The feuding finally ended in 1990, after the widows of both Adrian and Denis had died, when the estate was split between Dame Jean Conan Doyle and three cousins – the grandson of Conan Doyle's sister Ida and the grandchildren of his brother Innes. Dame Jean's share included her father's letters to his mother, which she bequeathed to the British Library.

Lancelyn Green believed that the entire archive rightly belonged in the British Library and was thus dismayed to learn, early in 2004, that the three cousins intended to sell their share of the estate through Christie's auction house. An article in the *Sunday Times Magazine* about the forthcoming sale revealed that it was indeed a treasure trove being offered. It included fascinating correspondence with public figures including Winston Churchill, P.G. Wodehouse, Theodore Roosevelt and Oscar Wilde; Conan Doyle's tan lizard-skin wallet, its contents intact; the illustrated logs he kept as a surgeon on a whaling ship in the Arctic; an armband with a red cross which he wore as a doctor in South Africa during the Boer War; and the manuscript of an unpublished novel, his first, written in the mid-1890s.

Lancelyn Green, alarmed at the prospect of this material being dispersed around the world, mounted a vigorous campaign to try and block the sale, contacting Members of Parliament and writing letters of protest to newspapers. But his efforts were to no avail and, seven weeks before the date of the auction, he was found dead, garrotted, at his Kensington home. A coroner recorded an open verdict, but many of Lancelyn Green's fellow 'Sherlockians' believe he killed himself in despair.

The sale at Christie's went ahead in May, as planned. Had Lancelyn Green lived he would have been relieved that many of the most interesting lots were purchased by the British Library. Not long afterwards, it was announced that Lancelyn Green had left his own huge collection of memorabilia, including rare first editions, letters and research notes, to the city of Portsmouth, where Conan Doyle first practised as a doctor and where he wrote the first two Sherlock Holmes stories.

The sudden and unexpected emergence of all this material into the public domain, combined with the generosity of Charles Foley, Conan Doyle's great-nephew and the current executor of his literary estate, make this book possible. While the British Library physically owns the most important letters, the copyright is still vested in the Conan Doyle Estate with Charles Foley's kind permission for me to make unlimited use of his great-uncle's papers, this book would be greatly diminished.

I was also the first biographer to have full access to the extraordinary Richard Lancelyn Green Collection at Portsmouth City Council and I particularly want to thank Sarah Speller, the project coordinator, for her help during the many hours my wife and I spent in the Guildhall going through box after box of papers. Grateful thanks, too, Owen Dudley Edwards, who was generous with his time in Edinburgh, despite planning his own book on Conan Doyle as a subject, just as, many years ago, he put forward the idea for my first book. I also want to thank Georgina Doyle, Christopher Roden, founder of the Arthur Conan Doyle Society, Caroline Hay of Christie's, Peggy Purdue at the Toronto Public Library, the helpful and friendly staff at the British Library, John Gibson, Jon Lellenberg, Roger Oldfield, my agent Michael Sissons and my superb editor, Stuart Williams. Renate, my wife, helped enormously with the research and read through many drafts of the manuscript with diligence, patience and good humour; as always she is my loving first-line editor.

Russell Miller,
Brighton, 2008.

EPILOGUE

IN THE DAYS FOLLOWING THE death of Sir Arthur Conan Doyle, 620 letters of condolence and 83 telegrams arrived at Windlesham.

'Sir Arthur Conan Doyle sets before us an example which must inspire all the best in us. It is by knowing great men and learning to love and admire them that we can shape our own characters. Conan Doyle stands out as an example to all men of activity, intelligence and noble thought.' General Sir Hubert Gough, GCB, GCMG, KCVO (Commander in Chief, Fifth Army, 1916-18).

'Conan Doyle was one of the best men I have ever known. There can never have been a more honourable.' Sir James Barrie.

'His passing from this earth leaves a very great gap. It is of him as a man, even above all his triumphs of the pen, that we feel his going most.' Lord Gorell, Chairman of the Society of Authors.

'Though Sir Arthur's fame as a writer is secure, he will be remembered no less as a defender of the defenceless.' R. Hodder Williams, publisher.

'Literature has lost a great figure. The Strand is proud that it was the means of bringing Sir Arthur's genius to an appreciative world.' Sir Frank Newnes, proprietor, *Strand* magazine.

'One of the most fearless and honest men that I ever knew. His friendship was a precious jewel.' H.E. Gwynne, editor of the *Morning Post*.

'The recollection I cherish is of the impression of courteous strength and the tremendous loyalty that made him the pattern of modern knight-errant. He was indeed a very gentle giant.' Francis Hiley, artist and illustrator.

'Only a big man, big of brain, big of heart, big of human understanding could have written such a letter to a lifer in present.' A convict serving a life sentence in Sing Sing prison.

'Big-bodied, big-brained, big hearted Conan Doyle.' Jerome K. Jerome.
'Just as a headland juts out dominatingly into the sea, dwarfing its immediate surroundings, so does Conan Doyle stand out in my memory, as a very headland of honesty and helpfulness to others, among some of us, his contemporaries, with our small insecurities, our small mean-ness and our small self-seekings.' Coulson Kernahan, novelist.

'How thankful we were to receive them [the swimming collars] on the destroyer I was serving in. I know only too well many a poor sailor thanks you, although I didn't know it was you he was blessing.' Able Seaman L. Mitcham, served on a destroyer in 1915.

'His methods are not mine, he regarded himself as a missionary, a trustee of a great truth which he felt bound to share with others, whether they would receive it and whether they would reject and ridicule it, but one cannot but admire the completeness and self-sacrificing character of his life and doctrines. Occasionally, I think, he lacked the wisdom of the serpent, but the goodness of his motives must be manifest to all.' Sir Oliver Lodge.

Three hundred people – family, friends and fellow spiritualists – attended the funeral, held on 11 July, in the rose garden at Windlesham, where the oak coffin rested on trestles on the lawn. The family had let it be known that there should be no mourning, rather a celebration. None of the blinds in the house was drawn and the ceremony was conducted on a gloriously sunny day in a cheerful garden-party atmosphere with most of those present wearing everyday clothes. Mary Conan Doyle accompanied hymns on the piano and the 121st Psalm was read ('I will lift up mine eyes unto the hills from whence cometh my help…'), with some of Conan Doyle's favourite biblical quotations. Then Lady Conan Doyle, in a grey chiffon summer dress with a crimson rose pinned to the shoulder, read the tribute she had written herself: 'God bless him for his beautiful and unselfish life, for his courage and fearlessness, for his never failing championship of those suffering injustice, and for the help he gave to those in sorrow. No man truly walked in his Master's footsteps…'

The gathering followed the coffin across the tennis court and down a garden path to the graveside, close to the rough-hewn garden hut where Conan Doyle often worked. Inside, his chair was drawn up to his desk and a notepad still bore the indentations of his last written words. Flowers sent in his memory covered the grass all around. As the coffin, decked in red roses, was lowered slowly into the ground, Lady Conan Doyle stepped forward and dropped a single red rose into the grave. The moment was almost too much and she looked close to fainting; Adrian stepped forward to support her. Later she assured friends that her husband would stay in touch with those he loved: 'We know that it is only the natural body that we are committing to the ground. The etheric body, or as Saint Paul said, the spiritual, is the exact duplicate and lives on and is able, when the psychic conditions are attuned to the spiritual, even to show itself to earthly eyes.'

Two days later, on the evening of Sunday, 13 July, a memorial service was held at the Albert Hall in London, organised by the Marylebone Spiritualist Association. Long before the service was due to begin at seven o'clock the hall was packed and throngs of people, many in evening dress, milled outside. Not all were friends or fellow spiritualists – a rumour had spread that Sir Arthur might make an appearance, in voice or perhaps even in body, and it was an event no one wanted to miss. Newspapers the following day would estimate that 10,000 people were present, almost twice the capacity of the hall.

A row of chairs was lined up on the flower-filled stage and propped on the seat of the centre chair was a large card bearing the name 'Sir Arthur Conan Doyle'. By the time the family appeared, Denis and Adrian in tail suits and carrying top hats, Lady Conan Doyle, Mary and daughter Jean in formal evening dresses, it was standing room only within the great concert hall and there were still many stranded outside. Lady Conan Doyle took the seat to the left of the chair reserved for her late husband, the place she had faithfully occupied at countless spiritualist rallies around the world for more than a decade.

George Craze, chairman of the Marylebone Spiritualist Association, opened proceedings, welcomed those present and read a statement from Lady Conan Doyle: 'At every meeting all over the world I have sat at my beloved husband's side, and at this great meeting to which people have come with respect and loving thoughts to do him honour, his chair is placed here, as I know that in psychic presence, he will be next to me, although our earthly eyes cannot perceive beyond the earth-obvious. Only those with the God-given extra sight, called clairvoyance, will be able to see his beloved form in our midst. I want in my children's name and my own and my husband's to thank you all from my heart for the love for him which brought you here tonight.'

After a hymn, an invocation by the Reverend C.D. Drayton Thomas, a two-minute silence and the recitation of the Lord's Prayer, friends and colleagues stepped up to offer their memories. They spoke of his great qualities as a spiritual leader, his devotion to the cause, the sacrifices he and Lady Conan Doyle had made in travelling to the ends of the earth to deliver their message, the labour expended writing letters to thousands of bereaved people. He had suffered for his beliefs, receiving venomous letters and attracting derision, but in assuming leadership of the movement he felt he was answering a call from heaven.

One speaker made the audience laugh with a jocular tale about Sir Arthur's love of cricket; another reduced many to tears when he suddenly looked upwards, raised his hands and cried: 'We thank you! God bless you, Doyle!' Fellow spiritualist Ernest Hunt referred to the rumours that Conan Doyle would be materialised during the course of the evening. Pointing at the vacant chair, he said: 'It would be a very trifling thing if any people here with hectic imagination were to persuade themselves imaginatively that they could see Sir Arthur's form there…But it would be a great thing for you to see in the vacant chair a symbol of God's call to you to qualify for being Doyle's successors.' Sir Oliver Lodge could not attend but sent a stirring message: 'Our great-hearted champion will still be continuing his campaign on the Other Side with added wisdom and knowledge. *Sursam Corda*! [Lift up your hearts!]'

The tributes ended with an organ voluntary and a collection for the spiritualist movement. Then Craze returned to the microphone and generated a ripple of excited murmurs through the audience with an announcement: 'This evening we are going to try and make a very daring experiment with the courage implanted in us by our late leader. We have with us a spirit sensitive who is going to try and give impressions from this platform. One reason why we hesitate to do it in such a colossal meeting as this is a terrific strain on the sensitive. In an assembly of ten thousand people a tremendous force is central upon the medium. Tonight, Mrs Roberts will try to describe some particular friends, but it will be the first time this has been attempted in such a tremendous gathering. You can help with your vibrations as you sing the next hymn, "Open My Eyes".'

As the final notes of the mystical hymn died away, Estelle Roberts stepped up to the microphone wearing a long black dress with a white collar and a bouquet of roses pinned to the shoulder. Then 41 years old, she was one of the best-known medium in London and a favourite of Conan Doyle. The audience waited expectantly as she stood for a moment or two with her arms outstretched, communing with the other world. 'There are vast numbers of spirits here with us,' she said eventually, 'they are pushing me like anything.' Later in the performance, she would stagger about the stage, as if being jostled by invisible forces. 'All right,' she snapped at thin air. '*All right*!'

Shielding her eyes from the light, she began pointing at members of the audience: 'There is a gentleman over there with hardly any hair. Yes, there! That's right. I see standing there in front of you a spirit form of a young soldier. He looks to be about 24, in khaki uniform. Upright. Well built. Broad. Mouth droops a little at the corners. He passed suddenly. He gives me 1916 as the year of his passing. He calls you Uncle, Uncle Fred. Is that correct?' Each time she rapped out 'Is that correct?', she received a nod or a wave of assent.

After half an hour of this, some members of the audience were restless; they had not come for a public demonstration of clairvoyance but to see the still conspicuously empty seat occupied. A few people got up to leave. 'I am afraid I cannot go on with people walking in and out,' Mrs Robert complained. When her words had no discernable effect on the increasing numbers heading for the exit, she suddenly stopped them in their tracks by shouting, 'He's here!' There could be no doubt who she meant: everyone switched their attention to the empty chair and Lady Conan Doyle jumped to her feet, eyes sparkling. The medium appeared to be following with her eyes an invisible figure moving towards her. 'He's wearing evening clothes,' she said, inclining her head as if to listen to something being said very quietly. Only those sitting nearby overheard the exchange that followed. 'Sir Arthur tells me that one of you went into the hut this morning. Is that correct? Lady Conan Doyle, beaming, agreed it was so. 'I have a message for you,' the medium said. At this point someone signalled for the organist to strike up. Estelle Roberts could be seen whispering urgently to Lady Conan Doyle, who was smiling and nodding, for several minutes. She was still smiling broadly as the service broke up with a closing hymn and benediction.

After the service, Mrs Roberts, still in a highly nervous state, spoke to reporters and claimed that she had first seen Sir Arthur 'in a flash' during the two-minute silence, that he had walked across the stage and taken a seat in the chair reserved for him, from where he later silently encouraged her clairvoyance. 'I received a message from Sir Arthur Conan Doyle and gave it to the family,' she said. 'It was a message to Lady Conan Doyle and her family, especially to one of them. I shall not divulge more. It was a perfectly happy message.'

'I am perfectly convinced,' Lady Conan Doyle confirmed, 'that the message is from my husband. I am as sure of the fact that he has been here with us as I am sure that I am speaking to you. It is a happy message, one that is cheering and encouraging. It is precious and sacred. You will understand that it was a secret to me.'

She never revealed its nature.

Recent Acquisition (2009)

JACK TRACY (1977) **The Encyclopedia Sherlockian** Or **A Universal Dictionary of the State of Knowledge** Of **SHERLOCK HOLMES AND HIS BIOGRAPHER JOHN. H. WATSON, M.D.** Doubleday & Company, Inc. Garden City, New York.

INTRODUCTION

Only twenty years ago a book like this would have been absurd. Anyone who grew up before World War II had any number of roots in the Victorian and Edwardian eras which serve as the settings for Sherlock Holmes; many of the people living in the 1930s and 1940s had been fully adult in Holmes's time, the physical and intellectual environments were not significantly different, and certainly attitudes and vocabularies had not changed much. It is those of us born and raised during and after the electronics revolution of the 1950s who need the thoroughly mechanistic, arrogantly optimistic nineteenth century explained to us.

It has been said that the Victorians were not so different from us after all, that today's institutions had most of their origins among the Victorians – but those who say so are the historians and sociologists who spent their own formative years before the computer and satellite communications changed the focus of everything. Perhaps thirty years ago we resembled the Victorians. We don't any more.

The truth is that the Victorians had almost nothing in common with us. They were the last of mankind – so far – to know real self-confidence, to thoroughly expect their world would endure. The brutal disillusionments of world war, depression, and nuclear uncertainty had not been divined. Their institutions, like their architecture, and their artefacts, were designed to be perpetuated as the pinnacle of human accomplishment – a feast of ethnocentric hubris we'll not soon match. It is only now, after appalling delay, that the combined technology and social conscience of the twentieth century are finally dismantling the ponderous oppressions of the nineteenth.

The passing of Victorianism is not a thing to be mourned. Objectively viewed, our Victorian heritage is a remarkably negative one. The era's merits have been swept away in a stream of history, and we are left to cope with the remnants of an artificial age.

The Victorian has been called the era of compromise, and not without a great deal of justice. Nearly every significant concept identifiable as uniquely Victorian was the result of compromise – compromise between progress and tradition, science and religion, wealth and poverty, privilege and freedom, enlightenment and intolerance, conscience and hysteria. It was an operable solution a century ago, when resolution could be put off and forgotten. Our own generation, however, clearly can no longer afford to take refuge in compromise – particularly the kind of anachronistic non-humanist compromise we have inherited from the Victorians.

Such fundamental attitudes make us infinitely different from them, despite the superficial physical similarities of our worlds. If they enjoyed a strong sense of security and belonging, they did so at the cost of a rigid code of social behaviour very much in conflict with our own concepts of personal liberty. If they had unparalleled cultural stability, it was at the expense of institutionalizing rather than solving the problems created by their own physical and economic expansion.

If they lived at the center of a world-wide economic empire, it was through an exploitive system that forced them to rationalize the cruellest racial and cultural theories at the expense of both scientific and theological integrity.

It is a tribute of sorts to the Victorians' thoroughness and sense of commitment to their own short sightedness that their institutions have stood so long, and that only in the face of self-destruction they made inevitable have we begun to recognise how inapplicable they are to a society responsive to man and nature together.

The need to dissolve the Victorians' social models makes it all the more essential that we genuinely understand them if we are to do the job right. This is not always easy, for if we blind ourselves to their more unfortunate circumstances (an outrageously easy thing to do), the final twenty or thirty years of Victoria's reign are perhaps among the most genuinely romantic in history.

Any man with a little money and a lust for adventure had no trouble finding it. Every continent still teemed with whatever combination of danger and potential riches the mind could imagine. The maps of Africa and South America were still largely blank if you craved utterly primitive conditions and none of the distractions of civilized life, and Central Asia and the polar regions were perhaps less exotic but equally challenging. Australia, South Africa, and the American West offered adventure without the hardship of exploration.

There were South Sea Islanders, East Indians, Red Indians, Africans, and Arabs ("niggers" all) to exploit the world over. Unless you were an officer the Army was for the lowest classes, but any battle-hungry Englishman could always find excitement fighting against (or with) filibusters in Central America, slave-traders in the Sudan, or nationalists in the Bahamas; or if you preferred, you could get a position as a war correspondent and join the jaunty campaigns against the crudely armed natives of Ashanti or the Indian frontier. It was the era of the "gentleman rankers" – the well-educated younger sons of the propertied classes who would never inherit at home and so went off abroad to fight, to settle, to plant, to administer, to explore, all for England and Empire.

It was the era too of the scientist and the civil engineer as hero. There was no popular anti-technology reaction to those days. There was disillusionment to be sure; the promised utopia of the machine had not materialized, and the Victorians understood that gears and levers only served to make folly more efficient – but they did not fear their machines. The most limited mind could comprehend the workings of a steam engine, take apart grandfather's watch, smell the gas seeping from the jet, puzzle out lifts and derricks and pumping stations, and instantly recognize the sound of the toilet valve failing again. (Today we have no such advantage; we can't see an electron, a circuit-card has no moving parts, and while intellectually we can grasp electronics theory, we just can't take the back off the pocket calculator and watch it for ourselves.) The Victorians believed creation to be orderly, uniform, and infinitely Newtonian. This concept of mechanistic simplicity they imposed upon everything, from cosmology to crime detection.

And for a brief flash of history, shorter than the span of a single human life, conditions were ideal for the emergence of a Sherlock Holmes.

Holmes's profession as a consulting detective depended on just the right combination of cultural elements – popular acceptance of scientific principles at a time when science was still in a stage which allowed a single individual a reasonable grasp of the whole; a stable society in which methods of observation, and deductive principles based on observation could be formulated and applied faster than the data upon which they were founded changed; and the existence of a moneyed middle class from which clients could be drawn. But that is only half the story.

If the science of deduction and analysis, as Holmes claimed, existed only as a course of lectures, there would be no Sherlock Holmes saga. Fortunately, Dr. Watson was a man of romantic and not of didactive bent.

For Holmes lived at the very center of the largest colonial empire the world will ever know. In and out of that sitting-room in Baker Street came a succession of gold millionaires, African explorers, Government officials, and foreign dignitaries – all the trappings of Empire – colorfully blended with representatives of the great British middle class, from tea-brokers to typewriter-girls to country doctors, for whom it was that the empire existed (and here we must include the men of Scotland Yard, the existence of civil police being one sure sign of a dominant middle class); it was only toward the end of his career, having attained a reputation for discretion, that Holmes was consistently sought out by his own country's nobility. His necessarily pedantic attitude towards his profession may even have made him insensitive to its inherent romanticism – but happily for us all Watson was there, to put flesh and blood on the stark bones of detection and in so doing produce one of the most immortal series of tales in literature.

Today colonialism is a tired anachronism, cities as great centers of culture and finance are gone (though the illusion lives on), media diffuse culture as well as knowledge to all, and the victory of the middle class is long conceded – yet the fascination with Sherlock Holmes is as strong as ever. After the silly perversions of the Holmes image by such as William Gillette and Basil Rathbone. (Holmes as tight-lipped derring-doer, Watson as comic sidekick, and performances all round by writers and actors who, if one didn't know better, you would swear never read a line of Holmes), there is a definite revival of interest in the great detective as a literary, and not a cinematic, figure.

The difficulty raised by this return to the original is the lack of familiarity with the Victorian milieu. Much of the vocabulary, institutions, and attitudes of the late nineteenth century have passed out of the modern American experience. For the reader who requires a fuller appreciation of Holmes through a reasonable understanding of the many allusions to Victorian lifestyle there is no longer easy access to definitions, explanations, and perspectives. So much has happened since Holmes's day that modern influences have crowded the nineteenth century right out of the dictionaries and encyclopaedias. The information that Watson's readers took for granted is no longer available without a knack for the historical approach. Hence *The Encyclopaedia Sherlockiana*.

Simply stated, then, this is a book about the historical background of the Holmes adventures. While it owes a great deal to the "Sherlockian" tradition, it is really not a part of it. It is based on the same prime assumption – that Sherlock Holmes and Dr. Watson were living historical personages, that the chronicles are based on actual incidents, and that Sir Arthur Conan Doyle acted as Watson's literary agent in placing them – and there the similarities end. The cult of "Sherlockiana" is a high-camp intellectual joke in which fact and fiction must be confused as thoroughly as possible. This work is established on precisely the opposite approach. It is not an "in" book, and it never speculates. In fact all references which are clearly imaginative are marked with an asterisk so that the reader immediately is made aware of the fact.

It is interesting (though not too surprising really) to observe that while Sherlock Holmes enjoys a world-wide popularity it is in the United States that his followers are most widespread, and that the bulk of Sherlockian scholarship has been done by Americans. Most of us are rather slavishly Anglophilic in the first place; we can idealize an England in which we don't live, yet when we choose to be we are far more objective observers of the British scene than the British themselves; and we don't have to read the stories in translation. So permit me to anticipate the criticism applied by so many English Sherlockians to America – written commentaries and point out that this is a book written by an American, and that it pretends to no other perspective.

Such an admission is perhaps more necessary than it would appear at first, for it has been my intention to produce a genuine companion-volume to the Holmes saga which a reader can consult comfortably as he reads. For this reason the language employed is a sort of Anglo-Victorian patois which to an Englishman may be stilted and even slightly comic, but to the American will blend with Watson's prose without distracting from the tone of the original. The style is carefully patterned on the reference works of the time, and the viewpoint assumed is a Victorian one.

Experimentation quickly shows that I cannot retain a period flavor to the language and at the same time provide a historical approach to the material. The solution is to present *The Encyclopaedia Sherlockiana* as if it had been written during the first decade of the twentieth century by a denizen of that era, a device which both provides a unified point of view and achieves a roundabout historical perspective which in the aggregate is even more successful than I had envisioned.

As a result this book takes almost no notice of events which occurred after 1914 (the only exceptions are death dates and biographical details of persons mentioned in the saga). Naturally the viewpoint is not a consistent one, and the outcome is a synthesis of English society in the years 1880-1910, with accent on the 1890s, which represents the general state of knowledge prevailing in Holmes's time. Understand that no information is given herein which not believed to be true by the Victorians themselves. (Where obligatory Sherlockian data occasionally is inserted such as in the dating of the chronicles, it has been designated clearly as such.)

The technique has posed the danger of my inadvertently expressing nineteenth-century ideas in terms which did not exist then. To take the most apparent example, Watson alludes repeatedly to Holmes's "dual nature" as perhaps the outstanding facet of the detective's personality. Holmes clearly was a mild manic-depressive – yet the term is not found in general use in works of the period and will not be found in this one either.

Contrarily, I am well aware that a cheetah is not a leopard – but the state of zoological classification was not all that refined in Holmes's day, and in the lay reference works of the time the cheetah was indeed defined as a variety of leopard, and so it is here. By a rigid adherence to such trivial standards can a reasonable atmosphere of authenticity be maintained.

While I have suppressed some Victorian attitudes, such as the blatantly racist allusions to non-Europeans, I have retained others, among them the practice of referring to wives and children under the names of their husbands and fathers, which not only saves space but also carries the right touch of nineteenth-century chauvinism. The use of population figures too is simple and, in these overpopulated times, a rather profound indication of the gulf between ourselves and the Victorians; all figures for the United States are based on the 1900 census, and all other population statistics are as of 1901, unless otherwise specified.

Each entry herein ideally consists of three parts – the *definition*, the *exposition*, and the *reference*. The *definition* is a single sentence describing the subject. If further information is required for clarity or for Sherlockian interest, the *exposition* is added; this can run from one sentence to several pages in length. Finally the *reference* provides a four-letter code to indicate in which story the item appears, often accompanied by a sentence putting it in context. Naturally this is not a universal practice; some subjects don't need definitions at all, and for others including an exposition or contextual sentence would be extraneous, clumsy, or distracting. In some articles, such as the one on Holmes himself, for example, or the one about SCOTLAND YARD, exposition and references are inextricably bound up with one another. A very few general terms too commonly used to specify contexts – POUND, for instance, or ENGLAND – carry no references at all; but these are kept to a minimum. Others consist of almost nothing but references, the entry entitled SERVANT being the most conspicuous example.

With some exceptions, items are entered just as they are worded in the stories to avoid confusion in looking them up, though in a few cases cross-references will direct the reader to a more serviceable heading. The work is liberally supplied with them whenever variant headings might suggest themselves, as well as among articles of related interest. This sort of thing reaches its logical extension in the article LONDON, which in two thousand words of exposition contains not one strong code and is effectively one long narrative cross-reference. To save space and to keep from interrupting the flow of information, cross-references are printed in SMALL CAPITALS without further designation.

Where Watson makes thinly disguised allusion to clearly identifiable places or things, either for literary purposes or through simple error, I have clarified the identification; but in adherence to the non-speculative nature of this book I have preferred to stay well on the conservative and avoid making an identification if the evidence is not all but conclusive. Thus Watson's GREAT ORME STREET is declared to be the very real *Great Ormond Street* in Bloomsbury; but even though the overwhelming Sherlockian consensus is that STOKE MORAN is actually the Surrey hamlet of *Stoke D'Aberon*, I have declined to assert this identification in the absence of more direct evidence and have labelled Stoke Moran as fictitious. I will be criticized more for what I have left out than for what I have included, and the reader who feels his interest in the Sherlockian cult being kindled by this volume should keep that fact firmly in mind. Fictitious entries are preceded by an asterisk (*), important exceptions to this rule being the story characters, who are not so designated, along with other obviously imaginary items such as elements of Holmes's many cases, published and unpublished.

One important assumption which is strictly followed is that in all cases, in the absence of clear evidence to the contrary, it is assumed that Watson's observations and memory are accurate and that his recital of events is presented with complete honesty. Obvious contradictions of fact are pointed out and occasionally explained, always with the presupposition that inconsistencies are the result of error rather than dissimulation.

I have acted also on the presumption that no one is going to resort to a book such as this without having first read Sherlock Holmes purely for enjoyment. I have not scrupled to give away a story's secrets if it seems necessary. At the same time I have presumed that the reader knows nothing about Victorian England other than what common knowledge has taught him and what he has been able to deduce from reading the tales. The more uninitiated reader may be dismayed to find that herein he will search in vain for any mention of a DEERSTALKER CAP, an INVERNESS CAPE, or a MEERSCHAUM PIPE, stereotypical symbols of Sherlock Holmes. All, alas, are apocryphal. They are a part of Sherlockian lore, but they are not part of Holmes as Watson depicted him. Sidney Paget, the famous illustrator of the stories for the *Strand* magazine, was fond of wearing the deerstalker (or "fore-and-aft"), and when he pictured Holmes in the provinces, he dressed him occasionally in one. But Holmes was always a man of propriety. The deerstalker is only worn in the country, and the Inverness is essentially a travelling-cloak to protect one from railway soot and road-mud. The image of Holmes prowling the gas-lit streets of London in this "traditional" garb is ludicrous.

The tales themselves will tell you that when the detective went abroad in the metropolis, he donned tweeds or the oppressively respectable Victorian frock-coat.

The curved meerschaum can be attributed to William Gillette, the American actor who originated Holmes on the stage in 1899. Gillette found he could not keep his hands free for other business and keep the ever-present pipe, essential to any characterization of Holmes, clenched in his teeth at the same time. He solved the problem by making use of the more balanced meerschaum which was far less of a strain on his jaw muscles. The American magazine illustrator Frederic Dorr Steele, who based his representations of Holmes on Gillette, perpetuated the image, and yet another cliché was born.

And you will never see the words, "Elementary, my dear Watson." Basil Rathbone may have been passionately fond of that expression, but Holmes never said it.

When we shed the mythology, however pleasant, and confine ourselves to the historical and cultural background of the Holmes saga, the first thing the researcher becomes aware of is the sheer mass of available material. The late Victorian and Edwardian eras may be the most minutely documented in history. Strikingly modern printing methods, cheap labor, a literate population, and a lack of competition from yet-to-be-invented media created a market for thousands of books on every conceivable subject. Economical photoengraving processes developed around 1890 made the popular illustrated magazine such as the *Strand* possible. And today's "unabridged" dictionaries and "universal" encyclopaedias are hardly worthy of the name compared to nineteenth-century standards. Reference works, of which there were many more then than there are today, could go into far greater detail for the simple reason that details did not change that radically from edition to edition – and when they did change they did so along what the lamenting scholars of the 1920s called "known lines of normalcy" and at generally predictable rates.

The material in this book is very largely derived then from what the Victorians had to say about themselves, and there is very little truly organised research herein. Most of the information is there for the gathering – if, as I did, you care to spend six weeks seeking it out. I have done a lot of simplifying, reorganizing, and rewording, for most nineteenth-century reference works subordinated clarity to completeness and scrupulous accuracy, but for the most part I have chosen to intrude myself as little as possible on a particularly eloquent age. There are a few really original discoveries, especially those of a Sherlockian nature, among these pages, and they will be found in their proper places, but to call attention to them would be self-defeating. The ego trip involved here is not based on any one subject's prominence, but on the unity, accuracy, and unprecedented completeness of the work. Energy is nothing without method, and I have striven consciously for what Holmes himself called "that supreme gift of the artist – the knowledge of when to stop."

There is something undeniably appealing about an age – epitomized by the life and talents of Sherlock Holmes – whose inhabitants genuinely believed themselves in control of their environment, who were yet untouched by the long-term consequences of their technology, who were contentedly unaware of such twentieth-century preoccupations as nuclear proliferation, ecology, and shrinking energy reserves. Still, we're better off if we temper the nostalgia with a few coarse realities. Victorian England is a very real and very immediate place for me – one I can enjoy and sympathize with, but seldom one I can admire, and never one to which I would like to see us return.

It is true that there were in Holmes's day none of the likes of computers, frozen dinners, and other nemesis of the simple life. There were also no antibiotics, no food and drug laws, no sanitation to speak of, no civil rights, often no right to criminal appeal, no child labor laws, no trade unions, no social security, no minimum wage. It has been pointed out that during the sixty-three years of Victoria's reign Great Britain engaged in more than two hundred overseas wars, most of them against primitive tribesmen in Asia and Africa; but admittedly none were nuclear. Environmentally we merely have exchanged the pollution that causes emphysema for the pollution that causes typhoid. And when you find yourself yearning for that uncomplicated era before our homes were invaded by all those energy-consuming, indifferently constructed appliances, just remember that in Sherlock Holmes's day all routine labor was done by the hands of an underprivileged, underpaid servant class who knew nothing of comfort and little of self-respect; and if that doesn't move you, please consider that, given the relative size of the upper and middle classes to the lower, you probably would have been one of them. The good old days have just begun.

Bloomington, Indiana
1 March 1977

Chapter 26

Miscellany IIII: 2008-2011

Daily Mail, Saturday, December 27, 2008

Question

Who is the most portrayed character in film?

Answer

Sherlock Holmes has been played by 72 different actors in 204 films. Basil Rathbone played him 14 times.

Antiques Roadshow Sunday 4 January 2009

At the above roadshow from Belfast, four photographs of the Cottingley Fairies (1917), plus the camera that took them were brought to the roadshow by Frances Griffith's daughter from Dublin. Also included was a photograph she took with the same camera (from Sir Arthur Conan Doyle) which showed a picture of 'real' fairies, according to Frances, as she took the photograph. The photographs and the camera were extremely rare said the expert, who suggested an amount of approximately £25,000-£30,000 as their value.

THE DAILY TELEGRAPH WEDNESDAY, JANUARY 21, 2009

British diplomat as Bollywood Holmes?...it's elementary

By Dean Nelson in New Delhi

A PIPE-SMOKING British diplomat is to star as Sherlock Holmes in a Bollywood production.
　　Simon Wilson, 50, Deputy High Commissioner in Calcutta, is using "Bollywood Diplomacy" to improve Anglo-Indian relations by appearing in a remake of *The Sign of Four* by acclaimed Indian director Ashoke Viswanathan.
　　Mr Wilson, a keen amateur thespian, initially agreed to help research Sir Arthur Conan Doyle's links to India and the role India played in the novel.
　　But after impressing the director, Mr Wilson was persuaded to follow in the footsteps of Peter O'Toole and Peter Cushing and star as Holmes.
　　In Mr Viswanathan's Indian version, a detective called Prashant Saigal is investigating a series of murders but hits a dead end. He seeks inspiration from the iconic British detective and – in true Bollywood fashion – Holmes emerges from a misty river, complete with cape and pipe.

The film, which also stars Victor Banerjee, the Indian actor who played Dr Aziz in *A Passage to India*, was shot on location in Shillong, the former Raj capital, which is known in India as the "Scotland of the East" for the green hills and colonial architecture.

Mr Viswanathan said "I wanted to do an Arthur Conan Doyle classic and we agreed on *The Sign of the Four*, in which Watson falls in love. My film is entirely set in India but we have a surreal vision of the original Sherlock Holmes who helps Saigal solve the case.

"We have Simon Wilson playing Sherlock, who I found to be a fine actor who could handle a pipe and speak at the same time. Most Indian actors can't do that."

Mr Wilson said his job as a diplomat meant he had little time for acting. Appearing in a cameo, however, gave him a rare chance to act as well as an opportunity to promote English literature and its ties to India.

"Many Indians are very well versed in English literature, there's a love for P.G. Wodehouse and Arthur Conan Doyle. They're very familiar with Sherlock Holmes. So I decided to do my bit," he said. "It would have been difficult for a non-pipe smoker."

The Sunday Telegraph SEVEN Magazine 25.01.09 Paperback/Books

TITLE DEED HOW THE BOOK GOT IT'S NAME

The Hound of the Baskervilles by Arthur Conan Doyle

The Hound of the Baskervilles (1901) was the story that reintroduced Holmes after his tumble into the Reichenbach Falls in 1893. Doyle redeployed his hero partly for the money – *The Strand* magazine coughed up double the usual fee – but also because he'd happened on an irresistible story. The spectral hound and the location in Dartmoor were suggested by his journalist friend, Fletcher Robinson; and it is at least possible that the Robinson family coachman, Harry Baskerville, whom Doyle met on his fact-finding tour of Dartmoor in May 1901, supplied the surname (although another strong candidate is the Baskerville family of Clyro Court, Hay-on-Wye). Support for the coachman theory comes also from the fact that Robinson, in his role as 'co-author', inscribed a copy of the novel to Harry Baskerville with apologies for using the name'. Harry went on to become a piece of walking Holmesiana, and died aged 91 in April 1962.

THE DAILY TELEGRAPH Friday, May 22, 2009

We still believe in Holmes, even in the age of DNA

150 years after his birth, Conan Doyle lives on in his greatest creation, says **Melanie McDonagh**

Sir Arthur Conan Doyle was born 150 years ago today, but it doesn't feel like that, does it? There are some authors you don't feel separated from by the mere passage of time; that's true of Conan Doyle, but still more of his most famous creation, Sherlock Holmes. He's the premier brand name in detective fiction, the archetype of the sleuth.

Of course, Conan Doyle didn't invent the concept of the analytical detective. This distinction belongs to Edgar Allan Poe and his C. Auguste Dupin, who came complete with the soon-to-be traditional detective brilliance and dim sidekick. But Conan Doyle achieved a feat that belongs as much to popular fiction as to great novels: he invented a character who was utterly memorable. Holmes's appeal shows no sign of diminishing, but in an odd way, he has become less relevant than ever. In my edition of the stories, the publisher assures readers that Scotland Yard had incorporated Holmes's scientific methods into its own investigations. But the science outran the deduction: practically every contemporary crime (and practically every contemporary crime drama) seems to revolve around the use of DNA or forensic evidence, which renders the Holmes method pretty well redundant. I can't, alas, think of a single modern murder that could have been cleared up by a man with a magnifying glass and a remarkable capacity for reasoning. It's the size of the DNA database that delivers modern criminals to justice.

The Sherlock Holmes novels, then, bring us back to a more human and edifying kind of crime, whose perpetrators aren't identified by scraps of genetic material at the crime scene, mobile phone logs or the simple assumption that it was the boyfriend/husband who dunnit. Today, the brilliant amateur could never edge out the professionals, because it's the police who have the technology. With Holmes, we're back in happier times, when ratiocination ruled.

Of course, an immortal character has some elements of caricature. Conan Doyle insisted that Holmes was, as a man, modelled on his old teacher, Dr Joseph Bell, with "his eagle face...his curious ways...his eerie trick of spotting details". It was that combination of instantly recognisable characteristics as much as the plots that the public fell for – though we don't now dwell on Holmes's cocaine habit. Poor Conan Doyle thought it was his historical novel, *The White Company*, that "would live and illumine our national traditions". Nope: it was the creation he "regarded as a lower stratum of literary achievement" who lived instead.

Conan Doyle stands out for other things than his writing. He was, for instance, a great champion of spiritualism, a creed he embraced after a series of bereavements. It's a reminder that even men of high intelligence can fall for hokum – as is his belief in the Cottingley Fairies, a hoax perpetrated by two girls who became famous for the photos they concocted at the bottom of their garden.

These days, we don't read his historical novels much, but the Brigadier Gerard stories, about the adventures of a Napoleonic officer, are funny and touching; *The White Company* certainly doesn't deserve oblivion; and his autobiography is very funny. I'm also a sucker for the Professor Challenger novels, or at least the first one, *The Lost World*, in which he gives Jules Verne a run for his money with a valley full of dinosaurs.

Ultimately, though, it is his famous sleuth for whom Conan Doyle will always be remembered – however for the fashions of detection drift from his flamboyant techniques.

Daily Mail, Monday, May 25, 2009

A wooden actor

QUESTION Was actor Basil Rathbone awarded the Military Cross in World War I for conspicuous bravery in the field while disguised as a tree?

ANSWER Second Lieutenant Basil St John Rathbone, of the 2/10th Liverpool Scottish Battalion, The King's Liverpool Regiment, reported for duty on May 23, 1917, at Erquinghem, a short distance west of Armentieres, where he was posted to B Company.

It was a sector of the front line known as Streaky Bacon and La Rolanderie Farms, where the men rested when not in the front line. My uncle William Frederick Bate, a member of the same regiment, was killed in action three days after Rathbone arrived at the front.

At the time that he won the Military Cross, Rathbone was Scouting Officer whose job it was to crawl out into No Man's Land, taking with him a sniper and one other, and to hide close to the enemy forward posts in an effort to collect useful information.

He persuaded his military superiors to allow him to use his gift to scout enemy positions during daylight, which was usually considered too dangerous. On one such expedition he shot dead a German, after coming face to face with him, crawling towards the British lines.

Rathbone had a considerable gift for disguise and camouflage – a gift he was later to attribute to his screen character Sherlock Holmes. It is the frequency with which Rathbone conducted these dangerous patrols that won him his Military Cross; both men who went with him on these raids were awarded the Military Medal.

In an interview in 1957 with Edward R. Murrow, the U.S. broadcast journalist, Rathbone related the story of how he disguised himself as a tree to get near the enemy camp to obtain information, although it might have been tongue in cheek.

'I went to my commanding officer, and I said that I thought we'd get a great deal more information from the enemy if we didn't fool around in the dark so much…and I asked him whether I could go out in daylight,' he said.

'I think he thought we were crazy. I said we'd go out camouflaged – made up as trees – with branches sticking out of our heads and arms. We brought back an awful lot of information and a few prisoners.'

Rathbone was only one of many brave young men who served with 'the Liverpool Scottish'. One other was their medical officer, Captain Noel Chavasse, V.C. and Bar, M.C., (R.A.M.C.). He was the only soldier serving in World War I to be awarded the Victoria Cross twice.

Stan Bate, St Helens, Merseyside

Daily Mail WEEKEND Magazine 30 May 2009

HOUSE AND HOLMES

House is back on Sky 1 this week. But did you realise the know-all doctor was inspired by the great Sherlock Holmes? Here are the tell-tale clues…

*Holmes and House both exhibit remarkable powers of observation and a tendency to come to rapid conclusions after the briefest examination of the circumstances.

*They both have only one close friend – Holmes had Dr Watson, House has Dr Wilson.

*House's name is obviously inspired by Holmes's. Gregory Shed wouldn't have worked nearly so well.

*Both the detective and the doctor share a fondness for recreational drugs. To relieve his boredom while not on a case, Sir Arthur Conan Doyle's fictional character indulged in cocaine and morphine. Some episodes suggest House also used hard drugs before he developed his current dependency on Vicodin, a prescription pain-reliever. In the episode *Distractions*, House used LSD to treat a migraine. And this man is a doctor?

*In the pilot episode of House, there is a patient called Rebecca Adler, while in the first Holmes short story, A Scandal in Bohemia, he is outwitted by Irene Adler.

*Neither man has the faintest idea what the word 'humility' means.

*In the episode *No Reason*, the man who shoots House has the surname Moriarty, echoing Holmes's nemesis, Professor Moriarty.

*In the episode *Failure To Communicate*, the physician asks his staff to solve a riddle about a room with an all-southern view and a polar bear. This is the same riddle given by the Victorian sleuth to Dr Watson in the 1985 film Young Sherlock Holmes.

*Both live in a residence numbered 221B. It must save on the rent and the bills, though there'd probably be terrible arguments over who had the last of the morphine.

*Conan Doyle based Sherlock Holmes on Joseph Bell, a doctor noted for deductive reasoning and skill in the new science of forensic medicine. The character of House has finally fulfilled the writer's original vision.

Daily Mail, Wednesday, July, 29, 2009

EPHRAIM HARDCASTLE

AN early Afghanistan casualty was Dr. John Watson, an assistant surgeon of the Army Medical Department invalided home after being shot 'at the Battle of Maiwand'. Watson, of course, was created by Arthur Conan Doyle as the companion of his fictional detective Sherlock Holmes. But there was a real Battle of Maiwand, in 1880, in which many British soldiers died.

BBC2 Friday 28.08.09 **Mastermind**

Roy Watson Davis – Teacher

Specialist Subject: **The Sherlock Holmes Films of Basil Rathbone**

Q Based on Sir Arthur Conan Doyle's *The Dancing Men* which of Roy William Neal's films opened with the word Switzerland emblazoned on the screen?

A *The Secret Weapon*

Q Which actress appeared in *The Spider Woman* as Andrea Spedding?

A Gale Sondergaard

Q "I won't forget that morning not if I live to be a hundred. I counted the men as they marched out of the yard, they'd hardly slept for weeks". Are the opening lines to which film?

A *Woman in Green*

Q Although the majority of the films were directed by Roy William Neal, who made the second film *The Adventures of Sherlock Holmes*?

A Alfred Werker

Q In which house on the west coast of Scotland did the seven men of the Good Companions live in the House of Fear?

A Drearcliffe

Q In *The Woman in Green* Dr Watson says that Professor Moriarty was hanged in which city only minutes before Professor Moriarty pays Holmes a visit?

A Montevideo

Q How is the body of Guy Davis identified even though it had been burnt beyond recognition?

A By his cuff-links

Q Which film starts with a bell tolling in a gloomy graveyard?

A *The Scarlet Claw*

Q In *The Secret Weapon* Dr Watson says that Sir Reginald Bailey played for which rugby club?

A Blackheath

Q What single word does the bird called Charlie utter several times in the Rat and Raven public house?

A Blood

Q Which art gallery auctioned the three musical boxes that are central to the plot of *Dressed To Kill*?

A Gaylord

Q What's the price of the grilled salmon in the Soho oyster house. It's clued in the number of the house that Holmes and Watson have to visit?

A 2/6

Q Which actor featured in *The Pearl of Death* as the Hoxton Creeper?
A Rondo Hatton

Q In *Sherlock Holmes in Washington* Holmes said that he will write a monograph some day on the noxious habit of accumulating useless what?

A Trivia

Q Better known for a later TV role, who plays Sir Henry Baskerville in the first of the Rathbone/Bruce films, *The Hound of the Baskervilles*?

A Richard Green

Q In *Pursuit to Algiers* Holmes comments to Watson that the late Professor Moriarty was a virtuoso on which instrument?

A The bassoon

Q What's the name of the firm of ornamental plasterers on whose premises Giles Conover finds the bust of Napoleon containing the Borgia Pearl?

A Gelder

Q In *Terror By Night* Inspector Lestrade pretends to be going on holiday to Scotland. Who does Sherlock Holmes say that he is giving an excellent imitation of?

A Izaak Walton

Daily Mail, Friday, November 13, 2009

Release the hound!

Question

A previous answer referred to squire Cabell, the ghostly hunter of Dartmoor, as the inspiration for Sir Arthur Conan Doyle's The Hound of the Baskervilles. Is this

correct? What about Lord and Lady Baskerville of Crowsley Park, Henley-on-Thames?

Baskerville was the name of the coachman employed by a family called Fletcher Robinson, who lived in the village of Ipplepen in Devon. The Baskerville family farmed in our village of Landscove and their original farmland abuts ours, which at one time, belonged to the vicarage.

Conan Doyle met journalist Bertram Fletcher Robinson during the Boer War and, both being interested in spiritualism, struck up a friendship. There has long been debate over the role played by Fletcher Robinson in the creation of The Hound of the Baskervilles. It was he who first entertained Conan Doyle with his ghostly folk stories from his home in Dartmoor.

Conan Doyle was impressed by the story of squire Cabell, a huntsman who sold his soul to the Devil and was dragged to the underworld by a pack of hellhounds. When he died in 1677, black hounds are said to have appeared around his burial chamber. This was the genesis of the Baskerville Hound.

Fletcher Robinson invited Conan Doyle to Ipplepen and the book may have been a joint venture. Fletcher Robinson's coachman, Harry Baskerville drove the pair around the moors, the arrangement being that his name would be incorporated into the book.

The book was a success and, as the royalties began to flow in, Conan Doyle paid £2,500, a quarter of the advance, to Fletcher Robinson.

Unfortunately, Fletcher Robinson died in 1907, age 36, of enteric fever,

prompting Doyle to write in the preface to The Complete Sherlock Holmes Long Stories (1929), that the story 'arose from a remark by that fine fellow whose premature death was a loss to the world.'

(**Compiler's note**: See the full preface at the conclusion of this chapter).

There is a Baskerville family grave at St. Matthew's Church, Landscove, and one day, when walking through the graveyard, I thought I'd entered a time warp.

Several men were walking about in tweeds, wearing deerstalker hats and smoking Meerschaums. They were members of a Conan Doyle society and were visiting scenes associated with The Hound of the Baskervilles, including the Baskerville grave adjacent to our nursery.

Raymond Hubbard,
Landscove, Devon.
PREFACE

The following stories paint Mr Sherlock Holmes and his activities upon a somewhat broader canvas where there is room for expansion. This expansion must express itself in action, for there is no room for character development in the conception of a detective. Whatever you add to the one central quality of astuteness must in my opinion detract from the general effect. Other writers may however succeed where I failed.

The *Study in Scarlet* was the first completed long story which I ever wrote, though I had served an apprenticeship of nearly ten years of short stories, most of which were anonymous. It represented a reaction against the too facile way in which the detective of the old school, so far as he was depicted in literature, gained his results. Having endured a severe course of training in medical diagnosis, I felt that if the same austere methods of observation and reasoning were applied to the problems of crime some more scientific system could be constructed. On the whole, taking the series of books, my view has been justified, as I understand that in several countries some change has been made in police procedure on account of these stories. It is all very well to sneer at the paper detective, but a principle is a principle, whether in fiction or in fact. Many of the great lessons in life are to be learned in the pages of the novelist.

There was no American copyright in 1887 when the *Study in Scarlet* was written, so that the book had a circulation in the United States, and attracted some attention. As a consequence Mr Lippincott sent an ambassador over to treat for a successor. He had commissions for several British authors, and invited Oscar Wilde and myself to dinner to discuss the matter. The result was *The Picture of Dorian Gray* and *The Sign of Four*.

Then came *The Hound of the Baskervilles*. It arose from a remark by that fine fellow, whose premature death was a loss to the world, Fletcher Robinson, that there was a spectral dog near his home on Dartmoor. That remark was the inception of the book, but I should add that the plot and every word of the actual narrative was my own.

Finally, there is *The Valley of Fear*, which had its origin through my reading a graphic account of the Molly McGuire outrages in the coalfields of Pennsylvania, when a young detective drawn from Pinkerton's Agency acted exactly as the hero is representative as doing. Holmes plays a subsidiary part in this story.

I trust that the younger public may find these romances of interest, and that here and there one of the older generation may recapture an ancient thrill.

ARTHUR CONAN DOYLE

June 1929

The Sunday Telegraph DECEMBER 13 2009

MANDRAKE BY RICHARD EDEN
Elementary role

JUDE LAW, who plays Dr Watson in Guy Ritchie's new film *Sherlock Holmes*, said last week that he used to watch a television series about the fictional detective.

The actor, 36, who portrays Watson as a rugged action hero, was, perhaps, too shy to mention that he did more than watch the series.

Mandrake recalls that he appeared in a 1991 episode in which he played a cross-dressing servant.

THE DAILY TELEGRAPH TUESDAY, DECEMBER 29, 2009

Elementary? Twist in the tale of Sherlock Holmes creator's house

By Gordon Rayner

WITH a film about one of the world's favourite detectives in cinemas this week, Sherlock Holmes is winning a new generation of fans.

But the fate of the country house where its creator, Sir Arthur Conan Doyle, wrote about his exploits remains a mystery. The writer built Undershaw at Hindhead in Surrey as a place where his wife Louisa could recover from tuberculosis.

It was in the study of Undershaw that the author penned Holmes's greatest adventure, *The Hound of the Baskervilles*, in 1901. He lived there until 1907 and entertained guests such as Bram Stoker, the author of *Dracula*. The house was run as a hotel for 80 years but over the past five years, it fell into a near-derelict state as it stood empty. The 36-room property is full of reminders of its celebrated former owner, including monogrammed door handles and stained glass windows bearing the family coat of arms.

Plans by a property developer who bought the site to divide it into flats were turned down but a new planning application to the council is expected within weeks.

But Conan Doyle enthusiasts want to see the house turned into a museum.

They have set up the Undershaw Preservation Trust aimed at either raising enough money to buy the property or finding a buyer who could restore it and keep it as a single private house. Lynn Gale, from the trust, said: "It will be a tragedy if Undershaw is not preserved and opened to the public.

"We believe it has a viable future as a visitor centre, museum and conference centre, but we are rapidly running out of time to make this a reality and this is the latest chance to save the building for the nation."

The plan is supported by the Victorian Society, which campaigns to save important 19th century buildings. A spokesman from the Society said plans to divide the house into apartments would "harm the historical interest of this house as Arthur Conan Doyle's family home".

MONDAY, MAY 10, 2010 **THE DAILY TELEGRAPH**

News Bulletin

Holmes clue leads to burglar

A burglary victim unmasked a thief using a clue described in a Sherlock Holmes story, a court heard. Scott Baldwin suspected he knew the burglar as his dog had not barked. He confronted his nephew Carl Nesbitt, 21, who confessed to stealing £700 and an Xbox console in January.

At Newcastle Crown Court, Judge Guy Whitburn said that, like the story *Silver Blaze*, it was a case of "the dog that didn't bark in the night". Nesbitt, of Chopwell, Gateshead was given a 51-week suspended jail term and ordered to carry out 100 hours community service.

Chapter 27

THE NEW ANNOTATED SHERLOCK HOLMES – VOLUMES I, II & III. Edited by Leslie S. Klinger. W.W.Norton & Company, Inc.

VOLUME I (2005)

Dust jacket

The twenty-four original Sherlock Holmes stories – with over 1,000 annotations that will fascinate the novice reader and delight even the most knowledgeable of fans.

If Sherlock Holmes is not the greatest detective in history of literature, there is little doubt that he is the most beloved. Tales of his brilliant use of observation and deduction to solve the most unusual and sensational crimes first appeared in the pages of the *Strand Magazine* in the late nineteenth century. The reading public quickly embraced the whodunits of Holmes and his colleague, Dr. John H. Watson, with a fervour that surpassed all other detective stories in history, electrifying Victorian readers everywhere, and Holmes soon became known as the quintessential detective.

A celebration of the 150th. Anniversary of Holmes's birth, the publication of *The New Annotated Sherlock Holmes* promises to delight faithful followers of the detective and inspire legions of new readers. In this first volume, renowned Sherlockian Leslie S. Klinger, one of the foremost Sherlock Holmes authorities in the world, collects the series of stories that were first published in the *Strand* from 1891 to 1893 and later gathered in book form as *The Adventures of Sherlock Holmes* (1892) and *The Memoirs of Sherlock Holmes* (1893). Largely presented as Watson's reports on various cases Holmes solved, this collection covers the early part of Holmes's career, from its beginnings to 1891. Among the most notable literary capers of the period are such legendary stories as "A Scandal in Bohemia," a tale of love and blackmail, the ingenious robbery hidden by "The Red-Headed League"; the poisonous villains of "The Speckled Band"; the suppressed "Cardboard Box"; Holmes's first case, "The 'Gloria Scott'"; the famous sports scandal "Silver Blaze," which made Holmes's reputation, and eighteen more.

The final story in the collection chronicles Holmes's famous battle with arch-villain Professor Moriarty at the Reichenbach Falls, where Holmes vanishes and is presumed dead. After the story appeared in December 1893, an anguished correspondent wrote to the author: "You brute!" and young City men put mourning crepe on their silk hats. Even the publisher of the *Strand* called the dispatch of Holmes "a dreadful event," yet it appeared that – barring divine intervention – Holmes's life had finally come to an end.

In this lavishly produced volume, readers will find hundreds of famous Sidney Paget and W.H. Hyde illustrations, along with the drawings of some long-forgotten illustrators. The 1,000-plus annotations examine some of the great issues of Sherlockians, among them the identity of an elusive snake ("The Adventure of the Speckled Band"), Watson's wandering wound, and alternative explanations of Holmes's "death" at the Reichenbach Falls. Other annotations evoke the history and rich Victorian milieu in which these stories occur, reflecting on such oddities as the "transportation" of convicts to Australia, the disposition of the Crown Jewels, and the state of the art of nineteenth-century hand-guns. Volume I also contains an insightful foreword by Klinger on "The World of Sherlock Holmes," which includes biographies of Holmes, Watson, and Arthur Conan Doyle, and provides an invaluable introduction to the fabled detectives.

Magically instructive, thoroughly engaging, and ultimately timeless, *The New Annotated Sherlock Holmes* will be an essential part of any home library.

About the author

LESLIE S. KLINGER, a lawyer and a member of the Baker Street Irregulars, is considered one of the foremost Holmes authorities in the world. He has published countless articles on Sherlockians and numerous books, including The Sherlock Holmes Reference Library, a multivolume work of Sherlockian scholarship. He lives in Los Angeles, California. Additional material can be found on Leslie S. Klinger's web site.

PREFACE

In 1968, when I was supposed to be engrossed in Law school studies, I received a gift of William S. Baring-Gould's *The Annotated Sherlock Holmes*, published the previous year. This magical pair of volumes entranced me and led me back to the stories that I had enjoyed when I was young(er) and had subsequently forgotten. More importantly, the books introduced me to the idea of Sherlockian scholarship, the "game" of treating the stories as biography, not fiction. In later years, as I avidly collected things Sherlockian, I dreamed that someday I, too, would produce an annotated version of the Canon.

Baring-Gould's *Annotated Sherlock Holmes* remained in print for more than twenty-five years and became the cornerstone of every Sherlock Holmes library. Yet it had its idiosyncrasies, with the stories arranged in the controversial chronological order created by Baring-Gould with footnotes that embraced, in many cases, Baring-Gould's personal theories regarding the life of Holmes. Sadly, Baring-Gould did not live to see publication of his greatest work, and as a result, occasional errors were not corrected. In contrast to the Baring-Gould edition, the *Oxford Sherlock Holmes*, published in 1993, presented the stories in nine volumes (as they were originally published in book form), but the scholarly notes largely ignored Sherlockian scholarship, concentrating more traditionally on an analysis of Conan Doyle's sources.

I set out to create for this edition an annotated text that reflects the spectrum of views on Sherlockian controversies rather than my own theories. In addition, this work brings current Baring-Gould's long outdated survey of the literature, including references to hundreds of works published subsequently. Recognizing that many of the events recorded in the stories took place in England over 100 to 150 years ago, it also includes much background information on the Victorian age, its history, culture and vocabulary. For the serious scholar of the Sherlockian Canon, there is an extensive bibliography at the end of Volume II. Chronological tables, summarizing the key dates in the lives of Holmes, Watson, and Conan Doyle and major world events, are set forth at the end of each volume. I have avoided "lawyerly" citations of the works consulted, but full citations may be found in the nine volumes of my *Sherlock Holmes Reference Library*, publisher by Gasogene Books.

Thirty-seven years have passed since publication of Baring-Gould's monumental work, and the world of Sherlock Holmes has grown much larger. This edition was created with the assistance of new resources that now exist for the serious student – Ronald L. DeWall's *The Universal Sherlock Holmes*, Jack Tracy's *Encyclopaedia Sherlockiana*, Steve Clarkson's *Canonical Compendium*, and scores of other handbooks, reference works, indexes, and collections, many in computerised format. It also reflects the aid of a new tool – the Internet, which makes accessible immense quantities of minute detail.

This is not a work for the serious student of Arthur Conan Doyle. While Doylean scholarship is vitally important, the reader of these volumes will not find reference to the literary sources of the stories or to biographical incidents in the life of Sir Arthur that may be reflected in the Canon. I perpetuate the gentle fiction that Holmes and Watson really lived and that (except as noted) Dr. John H. Watson wrote the stories about Sherlock Holmes, even though he graciously allowed them to be published under the by-line of his colleague and literary agent Sir Arthur Conan Doyle.

To keep this work from approaching the length of a telephone book, it is published in three volumes: The first two volumes consist of the fifty-six short stories that appeared from 1891 to 1927 (Volume I containing the stories collected in the volumes called *The Adventures of Sherlock Holmes*, *The Memoirs of Sherlock Holmes*, Volume II containing the stories collected under the titles *The Return of Sherlock Holmes*, *His Last Bow*; and *The Case-Book of Sherlock Holmes*; the third volume (to be published in 2005) presents the four novels, *A Study in Scarlet* (1887), *The Sign of Four* (1890), *The Hound of the Baskervilles* (1902), and *The Valley of Fear* (1915).

All in all, here is the complete record of the career of Mr. Sherlock Holmes. For the first-time reader of these tales, my best advice is to plunge immediately into the stories, skipping the introduction. Whether this is your first reading or your fifty-first reading of the Canon, I wish you joy in the experience, and I hope that you find that this edition enriches it.

LESLIE S. KLINGER

INTRODUCTION BY JOHN LE CARRE

DR WATSON DOESN'T write to you, he talks to you, with Edwardian courtesy, across a glowing fire. His voice has no barriers or affectations. It is clear, energetic, and decent, the voice of a tweedy, no-nonsense colonial Britisher at ease with himself. Its owner has travelled. He has knocked about, as they say, browned his knees. Yet he remains an innocent abroad. He is a *first class chap, loyal to a fault, brave as a lion*, and *the salt of the earth*. All the clichés fit him. But he is not a cliché.

Finer feelings confuse Dr. Watson. He is a stranger to art. Yet, like his creator, he is one of the greatest story-tellers the world has ever listened to. On the rare occasions he leaves the stage to Holmes, we long for him to return. Holmes – mercurial, brilliant, complex, turbulent Holmes – is not safe out there alone. Oh, he manages. He can dissemble, go underground, disguise himself to the point where his own mother wouldn't know him, he can act dead or dying, trawl opium dens, wrestle with Moriarty on a cliff's edge, or dupe the Kaiser's spy. But none of that changes the fact that when he is alone, he is only half the fellow he becomes the moment faithful Watson takes back the tale.

No amount of academic study, thank Heaven, no earnest dissertation from the literary bureaucracy, will ever explain why we love one writers voice above another's. Partly it has to do with trust, partly with the good or bad manners of the narrator, partly with his authority or lack of it. And a little also with beauty, though not as much as we might like to think. As a reader, I insist on being beguiled early or not at all, which is why a lot of books on my shelves remain mysteriously unread after page twenty. But once I submit to the author's thrall, he can do me no wrong. From my childhood onwards, Conan Doyle has had that power over me. I love his Brigadier Gerard, too, and his wicked pirate Sharkey, and his Professor Challenger, too, but I love Holmes and Watson best of all. He has the same power over my sons, and I look on with delight as one by one my grandchildren fall under his spell.

Peek up Conan Doyle's literary sleeve and you will at first be disappointed; no fine turns of phrase, no clever adjectives that leap off the page, no arresting psychological insights. Indeed, what you are looking at is a kind of narrative perfection: a perfect interplay between dialogue and description, perfect characterisation and perfect timing. No wonder that, unlike other great story-tellers of the nineteenth and early twentieth centuries, Conan Doyle translates without loss into practically any language.

Professional critics can't lay a glove on Conan Doyle, and never could. They could mock his spiritualism, his magpie obsessions, they could declare the later Holmes to be no longer the man he was. But nobody was listening then, and nobody is listening today. Now, as in his lifetime, cab-drivers, statesmen, academics, and raggedy-arsed children sit spellbound at his feet – proof, if proof were needed, that Doyle's modesty of language conceals a profound tolerance of the human complexity. Even in his own day, Conan Doyle had many imitators, all vastly inferior, though successful. If one of them, by some awful accident, had spawned the wicked Moriarty, it's a pound to a penny, Moriarty would have been a scheming Jew. If Joseph Conrad then an anguished Balkan radical hell-bent on the destruction of industrial society. But Conan Doyle carried no such baggage. He knew that evil can live for itself alone. He has no need of hate or prejudice, and he was wise enough to give the Devil no labels.

Reflect for a moment on the cunning with which Doyle places the reader mid-way between his two great protagonists. Holmes the towering genius is miles ahead of us, and we know we will never catch him up. We aren't meant to, and of course, we don't want to. But take heart: we are smarter by a mile than that plodding Dr. Watson! And what is the result? The reader is delightfully trapped between his two champions. Is there anywhere in popular literature a sweeter portrait of what Thomas Mann sonorously called the relationship between the artist and the citizen? In Holmes, we are never allowed to forget the artist's urge towards self-destruction. Through Watson, we are constantly reminded of our love of social stability.

No wonder, then, if the pairing of Holmes and Watson has triggered more imitators than any other duo in literature. Contemporary cop dramas draw on them repeatedly. They are almost single-handedly responsible for the buddy-buddy movie. The modern thriller would have been lost without them. With no Sherlock Holmes, would I ever have invented George Smiley? And with no Dr. Watson, would I ever have given Smiley his sidekick Peter Guillam? I would like to think so, but I doubt it very much.

I was nine years old at my second boarding school when the headmaster's brother, a saintly man with a golden voice, read us *The Adventures of Sherlock Holmes* once a week in the junior common room before bedtime. He followed the next term with *The Hound of the Baskervilles* and I hear him now, see his great bulk, with his bald head glinting before the coal fire.

"Footprints?"

It is Holmes, questioning Dr. Mortimer.

"Footprints?"

"A man's or a woman's?"

Dr. Mortimer looked strangely at us for an instant, and his voice sank almost to a whisper as he answered".

"Mr. Holmes, they were the footprints of a gigantic hound!"

Now read on. You have in your hand the Final Solution to the collected Sherlock Holmes stories, enriched by a lengthy and learned introduction. Do not be dismayed. Nobody writes of Holmes and Watson without love.

JOHN LE CARRE
October 24, 2003

VOLUME II (2005)

Dust jacket

The triumphant return of Sherlock Holmes – and the final thirty-two stories of the great detective's illustrious career.

After his famous grapple with his nemesis, Professor Moriarty at the Reichenbach Falls, Sherlock Holmes was presumed dead by almost everyone. From 1894 to 1901, no new stories appeared detailing his various exploits. The length of this hiatus did little to quell the increasing clamour among his legions of fans. Their desire was simple: the return of the greatest detective in history. They got their wish as the twentieth century began.

Volume II of Leslie S. Klinger's illuminating annotation of the Holmes canon includes all of the thirteen stories first published serially between 1903 and 1905, and later collected in book form as *The Return of Sherlock Holmes*, as well as those published sporadically between 1907 and 1927, which were later collected in book form as *His Last Bow* and *The Case-Book of Sherlock Holmes*. All of them appeared in the *Strand Magazine* along with hundreds of illustrations.

Two of the stories in Volume II ("The Adventure of the Second Stain" and "The Adventure of the Dying Detective"), even though they were not published until after 1900, relate to cases in Holmes's early career, which ended in 1891 with his disappearance. The remaining stories included here follow Holmes's return to the foggy streets of London until his retirement to the Sussex Downs in 1901. Also included are two post-retirement cases "The Adventure of the Lion's Mane" and "His Last Bow," the latter the only record of Holmes's secret war service in the years leading up to 1914.

Alongside the stories, over 1,000 annotations examine important Sherlockian problems, such as the identity of Watson's wives, where Holmes attended college, and what did, in fact, happen at the Reichenbach Falls. Still other notes yield fascinating culture and historical insights about the Victorian and Edwardian ages, examining an incredible range of topics, including annotations on Victorian bicycling, the development of fingerprinting, the history of the Boer War, the invention of the submarine, the growth of the railroads, the use of the vampire in literature, and the amazingly pervasive fear of premature burial.

Volume II also includes appendices that will prove indispensable to any Sherlockian, including an extensive bibliography and a listing of international societies dedicated to the study of Sherlock Holmes, as well as numerous Web sites for further study of the stories and the times.

VOLUME III (2006)

Dust jacket

The four brilliant novels of Sherlock Holmes, spanning the detective's illustrious career.

Arthur Conan Doyle is not only renowned for his fifty-six short stories featured in Volumes I and II of *The New Annotated Sherlock Holmes*, but also for his four classic novels that were published between 1887 and 1915, and which are celebrated here in Leslie S. Klinger's final volume of this historic literary publication.

In fact, four years before Sherlock Holmes made his mark in the *Strand Magazine* with the first appearance of the short stories, Conan Doyle had already written two novels. The first of these, *A Study in Scarlet*, was published in the long-forgotten 1887 edition of *Beeton's Christmas Annual* and provided readers with their first glimpse of the character who is now history's most famous detective. The sordid tale of murder and revenge recounts the initial meeting of Holmes and his lifelong friend and partner, Dr. John H. Watson, as they unravel their first mystery.

Conan Doyle's second book-length tale grew out of an eventful dinner with American publisher J.B. Lippincott and the young literary lion Oscar Wilde in 1889. Lippincott was seeking short novels for his new magazine; Wilde obliged with the controversial *Picture of Dorian Gray*, and Doyle produced *The Sign of the Four*; or *The*

Problem of the Sholtos (published in England under the shorter title *The Sign of Four*). Doyle's novel proved to be the thrilling precursor to the immortal short stories and features now-classic elements of the Victorian thriller, including a one-legged man, a pygmy, rogue Indian Army Officers, a river chase, and a stolen treasure.

By 1893, Conan Doyle had grown tired of the public's demands for more accounts of the brilliant, pipe-smoking detective and the good doctor, and the public was shocked when Doyle revealed that Holmes had perished at the Reichenbach Falls, at the hands of his malevolent enemy, Professor Moriarty. Then, in 1902, Conan Doyle created an international stir with the publication of *The Hound of the Baskervilles*. Although die-hard fans were disappointed to discover that the tale recounted a pre-Reichenbach case, the book rapidly became one of the first bestsellers of the twentieth century. In what has been hailed by critics as the greatest mystery novel of all time, Holmes deals with a diabolically clever murderer, a family curse, and a spectral hound on a fog-shrouded moors of England.

Rounding out this essential Holmes collection is *The Valley of Fear*, the last of the four novels, which appeared at the beginning of World War I. The book combines a compelling "locked-room" mystery, set in rural England, in which Holmes races to outwit Professor Moriarty, and a gripping tale of labor unrest and violence in the coal-mining country of Pennsylvania. Although the historical veracity of the American portion of the book has been challenged by modern historians, it has also been hailed as the first "hard-boiled detective" story.

The New Annotated Sherlock Holmes: The Novels gathers these four epic works into one volume, together with almost 1,000 annotations by Edgar-winning Holmes scholar Leslie S. Klinger. These annotations examine important Sherlockian problems, such as the identity of Watson's wives, the location of the real Baskerville Hall, Watson's war service (and the location of his mysterious war wound), and the date of the Sholto murder. Still other notes yield fascinating cultural insights about the Victorian age, examining an incredible range of topics, including phrenology, the treatment of typhoid, secret societies, the Pinkertons, the sport of singlestick, and the art of the violin.

Klinger has collected nearly 400 contemporary illustrations and period photographs, including the work of early American illustrators, the undeservedly forgotten German artist Richard Gutschmidt, and all of the legendary Sidney Paget's drawings for the *Strand Magazine*. This final volume also includes an extensive bibliography and a chronological table providing easy reference to dates in the lives of Holmes, Watson, and Conan Doyle.

Website: annotatedsherlockholmes.com

Chapter 28

The Case of Marion Gilchrist

Readers will have noted in Chapter 24, that mention was made of Peter Costello's book *The Real World of Sherlock Holmes* (1991). *The true crimes investigated by Arthur Conan Doyle.* Chapters 14 and 15 of his book were entitled **The Case of Oscar Slater** and **Why Miss Gilchrist Died**. (This is possibly the first mention of this [Gilchrist] case, confirmed by the author below).

The Case of Oscar Slater

IN THE SUMMER OF 1912 CONAN DOYLE was approached by the lawyer acting for a prisoner serving a life sentence for the brutal murder of an old lady of eighty-two in Glasgow in December 1908.

He was sent a copy of William Roughead's edition of *The Trial of Oscar Slater*, from which he learnt the disturbing facts of the affair, and felt compelled to take up the case. He did not find Oscar Slater himself, a German pimp and shady jewel merchant, an attractive figure – he could not sympathise with him as readily as he had with George Edalji, but the cause of proving him innocent was to involve Doyle for sixteen years.

Oscar Slater's trial constituted an even graver miscarriage of justice than the Edalji affair, one which to this day is not resolved. Here, for the first time, I will make explicit the full facts of the case as they were known to Conan Doyle, but which have never been related before.

On the rainy night of Monday, 21 December 1908, Helen Lambie, a maid employed by Miss Marion Gilchrist, left the second floor flat at 15 Queen's Terrace, West Princes Street, Glasgow to buy an evening paper. This was not an errand she did every night, but usually when her mistress was expecting visitors she did not want the maid to see.

(**Compiler's question**: Who and Why?)

It was then seven o'clock. Sometime in the next ten minutes Miss Gilchrist was murdered.

In the flat below lived Mr Arthur Adams and his mother and five sisters. He was not on intimate terms with Miss Gilchrist, but as she had long been anxious about burglars, he had arranged with her that she could knock on the floor if she needed help in an emergency.

At five minutes to seven Mrs Rowena Liddell, Mr Adam's sister, noticed a man leaning against the railings outside the house as she came in. He was very respectable, but had a distinctive long nose with a most peculiar dip. "You would not see that dip among thousands". (He could have been waiting for one of her sister's music students, though there was conclusive evidence later that someone had been watching the house for several weeks.)

Soon after seven Helen Lambie collected a penny for the paper, leaving on the table a half sovereign for the shopping to be collected on her return. She left Miss Gilchrist sitting at the table in the dining-room, her back to the fire, reading a magazine. On the way down the street Lambie paused to chat to a policeman on duty.

Suddenly the Adams family household were startled by three sharp bangs on the ceiling on the ceiling. Adams went out into the close and up the stairs. He gave at least three long, almost rude rings to the bell. The door to the close had been open. Her door was locked, but the gas was turned up in the hall. As he stood there he heard the sharp sound of wood breaking. He returned to his own flat, but his worried family urged him to go upstairs again as the noises were continuing – "the ceiling was like to crack."

Again he rang the bell. There was now no sound from within. While he stood there irresolute, Helen Lambie returned. One her way up from the street she too had been surprised to find the door open, wet footprints on the stair, and now Mr Adams at the door. He said he had heard a noise. She thought it might have been the clothes rack in the kitchen, which was held up by a series of pulleys, collapsing. She opened the door and entered the hall. Adams stood waiting on the threshold.

From the spare bedroom at the end of the hall, a man emerged. He came down the hall, passing Helen Lambie, who said nothing to him but went on into the kitchen. He passed Adams, and then once outside, sprinted down the stairs. Lambie had shown not the slightest surprise at seeing him: a crucial point in the case. She went into the kitchen, where the clothes rack was in order.

"Where is your mistress?" Adams asked. Lambie went into the dining room, and screamed out, "Oh, come here."

Miss Gilchrist was lying by the table, head towards the fireplace. A skin rug had been thrown over her. Lifting it, they found she had been brutally beaten. This is how William Park described it later: "The head had been severely battered, both eyes smashed in, and there were horrid gashes and cavities on the sides of the head, with other awful injuries to the face." Blood was everywhere. And yet the old lady was still alive, only dying as they knelt beside her.

Adams and Lambie ran downstairs. It was now ten minutes past seven. While the distraught girl wailed to the Adams family, Arthur Adams himself ran out into the street. Nobody like the fugitive was now in sight. The murderer had disappeared into the Black Glasgow night.

He returned with a policeman and his own doctor, Dr Adams. Dr Adams made an examination, and concluded that Miss Gilchrist had been beaten with the chair that stood nearby, and that the seat would have kept the blood to some extent off the clothes of the killer. But only to some extent. Arthur Adams and Lambie had not noticed blood on the clothes of the man in the hall.

Helen Lambie now ran off to the house of Miss Margaret Birrell, a cousin of the victim, to break the awful news to her. What passed at her house 19 Blythswood Drive, where Lambie arrived at 7.15, was later to be the subject of dispute. As it did not form part of the evidence at the trial we can pass over it for now.

On her return, Miss Lambie was questioned by the police, who had now arrived in force at the flat. Officially, she now said she was not certain she could identify the man in the hall.

The first policeman on the scene was Superintendent William Douglas, Western Division, and later Mr John Ord, Superintendent of the Glasgow CID. Whatever she told

Douglas at first, Helen Lambie later told Ord that the only thing that seemed to be missing from the apartment was a single diamond crescent brooch.

Aside from her claim, *there is no other evidence that any jewellery was stolen that evening*. There were pieces worth upwards of £3,000 in various parts of the flat. If robbery *was* the motive, it was curious these too were not looted.

All the man had left behind was a box of *Runaway* matches and a spent match used to light the gas in the spare bedroom. There the police found a small wooden box, in which papers were kept, which had been broken open (the sound of breaking wood heard by Arthur Adams?) and the papers it contained scattered on the floor. There was no blood on the box or the match.

Yet the police now took robbery to be the motive and issued an alert. They were looking for: "A man between 25 and 30 years of age, 5 feet 8 or 9 inches in height, slim build, dark hair, clean shaven, dressed in light grey overcoat and dark cloth cap. Cannot be further described."

It seemed odd to Conan Doyle, having reviewed the evidence thus far, that Miss Gilchrist should have admitted the man.

The doors were arranged that she could open the door close to the street mechanically and see who was coming up the stairs. If he were a stranger she could then lock her own door. There was no sign the flat had been broken into. Whoever he was, Miss Gilchrist herself had let her killer in.

But how, Conan Doyle considered next, had the police got on the trail of the man they now arrested. Apart from those given by Lambie and Adams, they obtained another, more detailed, description a few days later from a fourteen-year-old girl named Mary Barrowman of a man she claimed to have seen running from the house. (Her statements that she was in West Princes Street are hard to reconcile with Adam's claim that the street was empty, and her employer's later claim that she was mistaken about the day.) Another witness, an intelligent schoolteacher named Agnes Brown claimed that she had seen *two men* running away from the area on the night of the murder. One resembled the man seen by Adams and Lambie, the other was more heavily built. She was not called as a witness at the trial.

Then on Christmas Day the police received information that a German Jew named Oscar had been offering around for sale a pawn ticket for a diamond crescent brooch. The police visited his flat and learnt he and his mistress had gone to Liverpool with the intention of sailing to America.

Oscar Slater was pursued, eventually being arrested in New York. There at an extradition hearing, Adams, Lambie and Barrowman identified him as the man they had seen. There was no other evidence against him, beyond the fact that he was "identified" and that he had "fled". The brooch in the pawn office was proved to have been his own property, and not to have been stolen from Miss Gilchrist.

From the facts laid out before him, Conan Doyle concluded that the identification was tainted. Slater had been pointed out to the witnesses in a corridor before the hearing in New York, and Lambie and Barrowman had been coached in what to say.

But as so often in cases of miscarriages of justice, Oscar Slater's defence was badly handled. The police built "a case" against him. His way of life, as a pimp, gambler and jewel dealer was what convicted him, not the evidence. The jury, after being misdirected by Lord Guthrie, the judge, returned a verdict of guilty.

There was such a clear travesty of justice that 20,000 people signed a petition against his execution. Oscar Slater was reprieved and sent to Peterhead Prison for life.

There the case might have ended. The prison chaplain, John Lamond, a friend and biographer of Conan Doyle, heard Slater's claims to be innocent without a qualm. It never occurred to him that Slater might, in fact, have been falsely convicted. All too many people assumed that if Oscar Slater was in prison he was where he deserved to be.

Conan Doyle, basing himself on the evidence in Roughead's book, wrote a pamphlet about the case which was published in August 1912. It was not well received, and though he won a few solid supporters, the general reaction was to dismiss the matter.

He received a letter from one member of the jury, who said he had not been convinced by the evidence. It had not been shown at the trial how the murderer had got into the flat, and if the murder had been committed as the Crown claimed, there ought to have been blood on Slater's clothes: "I had a feeling all through the trial that there was a missing link somewhere."

The letter was printed by the *Daily Record* in Glasgow, which added that many people believed the murderer was still walking the streets of the city, albeit conscious-stricken. Such people could, so the paper said, point him out.

Time passed. Then at the end of March 1914 Conan Doyle received a letter from a Glasgow solicitor named David Cook. He was acting for a detective on the Glasgow police force named John Trench. Detective Lieutenant Trench alleged that when Lambie had called on Miss Birrell minutes after the murder, she had named to her the man she saw in the hall. Miss Burrell had warned Lambie not to say anything to the police. And though Trench had been to see Miss Birrell the evidence had been suppressed.

This added a whole new element to the case. Cook and Trench, supported by Conan Doyle, campaigned to have an enquiry. This was eventually held. It was unsworn and Miss Birrell and Helen Lambie denied Trench's allegations, especially about the identity of a person referred to as "A.B.", who was supposed to be the man in the hall that evening. Slater stayed in prison. Worse, Cook and Trench almost joined him. They were arrested on a charge of receiving stolen property, and though they were acquitted, their lives were ruined. This was in 1915, and the arrest came the day before Trench was to sail to the Dardanelles. John Trench died in 1919; David Cook two years later.

Time passed again. Conan Doyle spared little thought for Oscar Slater during the war years and after. In 1925 a fellow prisoner smuggled out of prison an appeal from Slater to Conan Doyle pleading with him to take up the case again. This he did, but once again the authorities turned down any hope of an enquiry.

A new figure now entered the case; William Park, a determined Glasgow journalist. Park found new evidence, that the brooch which had played a major part in the arrest of Slater was not stolen and that a new witness who saw a man running away from Miss Gilchrist's house on the night of the murder said it was not Slater. Encouraged by Conan Doyle, Park wrote a book about the case called *The Truth about Oscar Slater*. However, work on the subject had warped Park's judgement, and he was drinking heavily. Through his own firm the Psychic Press, Conan Doyle published the book in 1927, adding a preface of his own.

The book caused a sensation. Once again there were calls for an inquiry. The *Daily News* published an influential series of articles taking the case against Slater apart. In October 1927 Helen Lambie, interviewed in America where she now lived, withdrew her evidence, and a month later, Mary Barrowman also stated that she was now uncertain of *her* evidence. This was sufficient. On 14 November 1927, Oscar Slater was released from Peterhead Prison.

An appeal followed, and though in the usual way of lawyers, some of the evidence which was brought forward in support of Slater was not accepted, it was admitted that aspects of the trial had been unfair. Slater was pardoned, and a close-fisted government paid him £6,000 compensation. He returned to Ayr, where he lived quietly, dying in 1949. He and Conan Doyle later had a falling-out over the matter of who should pay for the appeal, but this was sorted out in the end to mutual satisfaction. Conan Doyle did not like Slater, but he was convinced that he had nothing to do with the murder of Miss Marion Gilchrist.

Conan Doyle and his friends likewise had no doubts about the identity of the "man in the hall", a man who could reveal the whole truth about the case.

His name was Francis James Charteris.

(**Compiler's note:** See the end of this chapter for further information in Peter Costello's new book).

Why Miss Gilchrist Died

ONE THING IS CERTAIN: MARION GILCHRIST was not killed for her jewellery by a common thief. She was killed by someone she knew, for reasons buried deep in the history of the Gilchrist family. For Conan Doyle the solution to the case lay in the events of that December evening and the strange behaviour of Helen Lambie, and in the text of Miss Gilchrist's will.

Miss Lambie, it will be recalled, did not challenge the man who came out of the spare bedroom and passed her as she was on her way into the kitchen. She did not challenge him for the simple reason that she knew well who it was. After she found Miss Gilchrist dying, she ran off to 19 Blythswood Drive where Margaret Birrell, a relative of Miss Gilchrist, lived. To her she poured out the horrible details of what had happened. What follows is their actual dialogue.

"Oh, Miss Birrell, Miss Birell, Miss Gilchrist has been murdered. She is lying dead in the dining room, and oh, Miss Birrell, I saw who did it."

"My God, Nellie, this is awful. Who was it, do you know him?"

"Oh, Miss Birrell, I think it was Dr Charteris. I am sure it was Francis Charteris."

"My God, Nellie, don't say that. Unless you are very sure of it Nellie, don't say that."

But Nellie Lambie was sure, and probably frightened. Later she repeated her claim to the police and that night Detectives John Pyper and James Dornan visited Miss Birrell. From them she heard that Helen Lambie had repeated the charge. Miss Birrell told her friends and also a member of Glasgow Corporation, who contacted Chief Superintendent Ord.

The next day another detective, none other than Lieutenant John Trench, called on her and took a statement. (This visit is confirmed in his police diary.) When he gave the statement into Ord, his superior seemed to be impressed."

"This is the first real clue we have got."

But later he told Trench: "I have been ringing up Douglas and he is convinced that Doctor Charteris had nothing to do with it." Superintendent William Douglas was in charge of the Western Division of the city, where the murder had taken place.

It now became the official line that Helen Lambie could not identify the man; though later she agreed to identify Oscar Slater as the man she had seen when police faced her with him in New York. She was a good girl, of a class that did what it was told. At least, what it was told by senior policemen in Glasgow in 1909.

Miss Birrell had told Trench that "Miss Gilchrist was not on good terms with her relations. Few, if any visited her." Dr Charteris was one of those few, as Helen Lambie was later prepared to admit at the secret inquiry, even as she denied the story of what happened on the night of the murder.

Marion Gilchrist was a curious woman, with a strange past. Rumour in Glasgow suggested that she had made a fortune as a dealer in stolen jewellery, though no concrete evidence had ever been uncovered.

Certainly she was rich, and afraid of something.

(**Compiler's question**: Where did jewellery worth £3,000 found in her flat come from?)

During the months before the murder there had occurred some strange events. In September, an Irish terrier, which had been a present, died. Miss Lambie thought it might have been something it ate, Miss Gilchrist was convinced it had been poisoned.

(**Compiler's question**: Why? Was this a symptom of her paranoia which included a fear of burglars?)

In November she changed her will.

As from 1 December neighbours had been aware of a man watching the flat. Some twelve people saw the man, at different times and in different clothes. From the confused details of their evidence – some said he was foreign-looking, others that he had a moustache – it may well be that two men were involved.

When Miss Gilchrist's death was officially registered on 23 December, the information was provided by another relative of hers, Mrs Mary McCall, who had come up from her home in Boscombe Court in Bournemouth in the south of England. None of her local relatives had, it seems, been prepared to come forward.

At probate Miss Gilchrist's estate was valued at £12,000. To her sister she left the life income on £2,000, which was to go to charities after her death. To other nieces and their children, £2,200 as legacies. After some other requests, including £20 to Helen Lambie, what remained of the estate, £6,280, went to an illegitimate daughter, Mrs Maggie Galbraith Ferguson, whose own daughter was named, significantly enough, Marion Gilchrist Ferguson.

Originally much of Miss Gilchrist's money had come from her father, and her peculiar way of life had only added to family tensions about the inheritance.

Her brother James had died some years before. His widow Mary had married Matthew Charteris, Professor of Materia Medica and Therapeutics at Glasgow University, who had died in 1897.

His father had been a plain schoolmaster, but his brother the Very Rev. Archibald Hamilton Charteris, Professor of Biblical Criticism at Edinburgh University, had been since 1870 one of the Royal Chaplains in Scotland.

Matthew Charteris had three sons. The eldest was Archibald Hamilton Charteris, then Professor of International Law at Glasgow University, and later at the University of Sydney. The youngest was a soldier, later Brigadier-General John Charteris. And the middle son was Francis James Charteris, like his father, a medical man. He eventually became a professor at the University of St Andrews.

The Charteris family was distinguished and well connected, indeed one of the most prominent families in Scotland.

Francis John Charteris was not related by blood to Miss Gilchrist, but was loosely viewed as being her nephew. He was born in 1875, making him about thirty-three at the time of the murder. All the witnesses agreed that the man they saw was a respectable young man in his middle thirties. He had studied medicine in Glasgow and Leipzig before opening a medical practice in Glasgow. How could such a person come to be suspected of involvement in a brutal murder?

The explanation which Charteris gave was a simple one. The following facts were his version of what happened that night, on the case. But they were not revealed during his life time.

At the time of the murder Francis Charteris was attending the birth of a baby boy. Later that evening he received a police message asking him to break the news of the murder to his mother. Going by the flat in West Princes Street he called in. There he found the police questioning Helen Lambie. Seeking to make clear to the police her impression of the man she had seen, she said "He was like Dr Charteris there."

It was this remark, according to his friends, that Detective Trench took up instantly, and from it grew his disgraceful action in 1914 which led to his dismissal. Charteris was the mysterious "A.B." whose identity had so puzzled everyone in the report of the inquiry.

It is said, unbelievably, for his own relatives gave evidence at the inquiry, that Dr Charteris was unaware of the rumours about him until 1951. These, as rumours will, became enlarged. He was said to be a drug addict, a drunkard, the owner of a brothel in Garnethill, and the organiser of shocking orgies at his lodgings as a student.

An addition was made to the legend to explain the initials used at the inquiry. It was said there were two men, one of whom was Austin Birrell, another relative of Miss Gilchrist's. He was said to have gone off his head and wandered about Glasgow in the 1930s mumbling about his remorse for the brutal crime.

Some of this information came out after Dr Charteris died on 4 July 1964. In 1969 another effort was made to clear the name of John Trench, but the application was dismissed by the Glasgow magistrates. The *Glasgow Herald* which had been no friend of Oscar Slater attacked Trench again in an editorial by Alistair Phillips. Trench's moral offence was still inexcusable. "What he did, by inflating his own sketchy and inaccurate second-hand knowledge of the early interrogations, was to impeach a respectable Glasgow physician who patently, and to the satisfaction of the procurator-fiscal and the very senior officers on the scene, had nothing to do with the crime."

It seems that even today in Glasgow there is one law for the shady pimp and another for the Royal Chaplain's nephew.

Trench's knowledge was not secondhand: he had taken part in the inquiry. He had interviewed Miss Birrell himself and had reported the matter to his superiors. That surely was the whole part of his claim. Nor does the account which Dr Charteris gave square with the events as recorded at the time and as recounted at the inquiry.

It was admitted at the inquiry that the alibi of "A.B." – Dr Charteris – had been investigated, which was odd indeed if his name had not been connected with the murder. He claimed that he was attending a birth at the time: we have no evidence that this was true. More crucially, Helen Lambie identified him, not to the police later in the evening, as he relates, but to Margaret Birrell within minutes of the murder.

Conan Doyle had few doubts about his guilt. And certainly, on the basis of what we now know, it would seem that a more searching investigation should have been made. One was certainly begun, as we can see both from the testimony of John Trench and the comments in the papers in December 1909 which had hinted that a "sensational arrest" was to be expected.

There are still those, as Conan Doyle knew in his time, who believe, contrary to all the evidence, that Oscar Slater had something to do with the crime. It is surely time that this rumour was scotched. I hope that by naming Dr Francis Charteris as one of those implicated in the murder of Miss Gilchrist, something will finally be done to clear the names of Oscar Slater and John Trench from the tragic consequences of the cover-up initiated by the police to protect the well-connected Charteris family.

I believe Francis Charteris and another relative went to the flat that night, perhaps by arrangement, perhaps not. Miss Gilchrist admitted them because she knew them. His companion knocked Miss Gilchrist out while Dr Charteris went to search for family papers in the spare room; Miss Gilchrist showed signs of reviving. His companion (clearly a disturbed personality) then beat her to death with the chair. While Charteris continued his search, his partner in crime left the flat and perhaps hid on the upper flight of stairs as William Roughead surmised, until the coast was clear. Surprised by the entrance of Helen Lambie and Mr Adams, Dr Charteris whom Helen recognised from a previous visit, walked coolly out of the flat, before running down the stairs and into the night, to be swallowed up in mystery.

That was what Conan Doyle believed. It may now be too late to prove him right, but some redress should be given to the tarnished reputation of Detective Lieutenant John Trench. It is never too late for justice.

The next book which mentions this case is Daniel Stashower's (1999) **Teller of Tales**.

The Edalji case had brought Conan Doyle a considerable reputation as a champion of the oppressed. Now, as he settled down to work in his new study (at Windlesham), a second, even more notorious criminal case claimed his attention. The story began on a grey December evening in Glasgow in 1908, when an elderly spinster named Marion Gilchrist sent her paid companion Helen Lambie, around the corner to buy a newspaper. When Miss Lambie returned ten minutes later, an unknown man rushed past her into the street. Entering the parlour, she found Miss Gilchrist dead on the floor. She had been bludgeoned to death. Her personal papers were scattered, and her jewels rifled, but only one item appeared to be missing – a diamond brooch.

Police were quick to implicate a German immigrant named Oscar Slater, who had recently pawned a diamond brooch. Slater appeared to confirm his own guilt by fleeing the country under an assumed name, aboard the *Lusitania*. When the liner reached New York, Slater was found in possession of a small upholsterer's hammer, thought to be the murder weapon. Extradition was threatened, but Slater returned to Britain voluntarily, convinced that he could easily prove his innocence.

Slater was guilty of many things – gambling, petty theft, and possibly even, prostitution – but he was not the murderer of Marion Gilchrist. As in the Edalji case, however, the police tailored the facts to fit the suspect, suppressing contrary evidence where necessary. Witnesses who had seen a mysterious man flee the victim's apartment were coached with Slater's photograph, and the suspect's alibi – he had been at home with his mistress and a servant – was overlooked. Worse yet, the only real piece of evidence linking Slater to the crime scene – the diamond brooch – did not match the description of the victim's jewelry and was indisputably shown to have been hocked before the murder took place. Astonishingly, Slater was found guilty and sentenced to death. No court of criminal appeal existed in Scotland at the time. Slater's only option, then, was to ask the government for mercy. Public opinion now turned in his favor, and a petition asking for clemency gathered a staggering twenty thousand signatures. Two days before the execution was scheduled to take place, Slater's sentence was commuted to life in prison.

In April 1910, a prominent Edinburgh lawyer named William Roughead published a booklet entitled "Trial of Oscar Slater," which set out the inconsistencies of the evidence and presented a transcript of the trial. Conan Doyle, who had already been approached by Slater's lawyers, was among those stirred by Roughead's accusations. Though he had little stomach for another investigation, he recognized that "this unhappy man had in all probability no more to do with the murder for which he had been condemned than I had." The Edalji case had discouraged him, however, and he knew that the officials in Slater's prosecution would close ranks in a similar manner. "What confronts you is a determination to admit nothing which inculpates another official," he wrote, "and as to the idea of punishing another official for offences which have caused misery to helpless victims, it never comes within their horizons."

For all of that, Conan Doyle felt obliged to do something. Once again he decided to publish a booklet, using his name and influence to attract a wider audience for Slater's grievance. With William Roughead's assistance, he assembled "The Case of Oscar Slater," published in the summer of 1912. It was an eighteen-thousand-word summary of the case that examined Roughead's information in greater detail. The booklet presented an effective rebuttal of many of the initially damning indictments of Slater's actions and motives. Slater had, for example, been travelling under a false name when he made his flight to America. Conan Doyle pointed out that Slater had made the trip in the company of his young mistress and wished to avoid being found out by his wife. This explanation, while not exactly laudable, did not make Slater guilty of murder. Slater had used his real name in a hotel in Liverpool before departure, Conan Doyle pointed out, something he would not have done had he been hiding from the police.

As for the hammer found among Slater's effects, Conan Doyle did not express much confidence in its value as a murder weapon. It was "an extremely light and fragile instrument," he insisted, and "any task beyond fixing a tin-tack, or cracking a small piece of coal, would be above its strength." A doctor who examined Miss Gilchrist's body at the crime scene offered some corroboration on this point; he concluded that the victim had been dispatched with a heavy mahogany chair, found to be "dripping" with blood.

"The Case of Oscar Slater," published cheaply to encourage a wide readership, revived the calls for a new trial. In the House of Commons, questions about the case were addressed to McKinnon Wood, the secretary of state for Scotland. The reply offered little cause for optimism: "No new considerations have, in my opinion, emerged such as would justify me in reopening the case."

Meanwhile, new disclosures came to light, along with further evidence of police negligence. Slater's alibi, it emerged, had been confirmed by a grocer named MacBrayne, who saw him standing on his own doorstep at the time of the murder. MacBrayne had not been called to testify at the trial. An even more disturbing revelation came from Lieutenant John Trench, a Glasgow police detective. After a long struggle with his conscience, Lieutenant Trench came forward with an electrifying piece of information: on the night of the murder, Helen Lambie, the victim's companion, had named the man fleeing from Miss Gilchrist's flat. That man was not Oscar Slater.

Incredibly, this allegation was not thought significant enough to warrant a new inquiry. For his trouble, Lieutenant Trench found himself dismissed from the force and denied a pension. Conan Doyle was mortified. "How the verdict could be that there was no fresh cause for reversing the conviction is incomprehensible," he wrote in *The Spectator*. "The whole case will, in my opinion, remain immortal in the classics of crime as the supreme example of official incompetence and obstinancy."

For the moment, all appeared lost. The next move – though Conan Doyle could not have known it at the time – would be Oscar Slater's.

In February 1925, even as he put the finishing touches on *The Land of Mist*, an urgent plea for help recalled Conan Doyle to the earthly plane. Sixteen years had passed since the imprisonment of Oscar Slater, the man Conan Doyle believed had been falsely convicted of the murder of Marion Gilchrist in Glasgow. In that time, Conan Doyle had made several attempts to reopen the case, but his efforts brought a stony silence from the Scottish authorities. "From time to time one has some word of poor Slater from behind his prison walls," he wrote, "like the wail of some wayfarer who has fallen into a pit and implores aid from the passers by."

In Peterhead Prison, on a remote stretch of Scottish coastline, Slater knew nothing of Conan Doyle's efforts on his behalf. Denied correspondence with the outside world, he engineered a desperate appeal. A fellow prisoner named William Gordon was due to be released. On a piece of waterproof paper from the prison bindery, Slater wrote an impassioned note. He then folded the coated paper into a tight bundle and persuaded Gordon to conceal it in his mouth. The ruse worked; Gordon submitted to a thorough search, but Slater's message was not discovered. On gaining his release, Gordon relayed the plea to Conan Doyle.

Conan Doyle could hardly ignore such a direct appeal. He sent a fresh barrage of letters to the secretary of state for Scotland, demanding that Slater's conviction be overturned. "Apart...from the original question of guilt or innocence," Conan Doyle wrote, "the man who has now served 15 years, which is, as I understand, the usual limit of a life sentence in Scotland when the prisoner behaves well."

As it happened, Slater had not been a model prisoner. Indignant now over his situation, he complained loudly about the deplorable conditions of the prison, and occasionally got into scuffles with other inmates. This had no bearing on the official reply to Conan Doyle's entreaties. He was notified that court officials found no justification for "advising any interference" in Slater's sentence.

Conan Doyle stepped up his effort, much as he had in the Roger Casement affair, with letters to influential friends and members of the press, along with public appearances where he aired Slater's grievances. Many others had taken up the case by this time, but no single supporter could rally public opinion as effectively as Conan Doyle, as Slater himself had recognized. With Conan Doyle putting his shoulder to the wheel, the campaign for Slater's release steadily gathered force over the next two years.

The turning point came in July 1927, with the appearance of a new book by William Park, a Glasgow journalist. Park, as Conan Doyle later described him, "had within him that slow-burning, but quenchless, fire of determination which marks the best type of Scotsman." He had spent years digging into the story, prompted by the disclosures of Lieutenant John Trench, the policeman whose forthright testimony had cost him his job. With Conan Doyle's help, Park gathered his findings under the title *The Truth About Oscar Slater*. Conan Doyle contributed a crisp foreword and published the volume through his own Psychic Press.

Drawing on Lieutenant Trench's impressions, Park presented a graphic reconstruction of the murder. In his view – an opinion shared by many – Miss Gilchrist had known her killer and opened the door to him willingly on the night of her murder. Then, in the case of a quarrel over a document in her possession, the old woman had been pushed to the floor, striking her head on a coal box near the fireplace. Seeing that the injury was serious, the visitor faced an urgent dilemma. If Miss Gilchrist recovered and identified him to the police, he would be charged with a violent assault. If she subsequently died, the charge would be murder. Summoning his resolve, the visitor picked up a heavy chair and bludgeoned the old woman to death. Snatching up the incriminating document, (**Complier's question**: What are the contents of this document and why should it be in the possession of Miss Gilchrist?), he fled the scene – passing Miss Gilchrist's paid companion, Helen Lambie in the corridor. According to Park, the murderer "slipped out unchallenged" because Miss Lambie knew him and had no reason to question his presence in the flat. Although libel laws prevented Park naming the suspect, Conan Doyle and many others had known of his involvement for some time. It was Francis Charteris, the victim's nephew, now a professor at St. Andrew's University.

(**Compiler's note**: Readers will have noted that this is the second time he has been mentioned).

Park's book touched off a press circulation war, with several newspapers vying to provide fresh revelations about the case. The *Empire News* registered a major coup when it published "Whey I Believe I Blundered over Slater," which purported to be a statement from Helen Lambie, who had since immigrated to the United States. According to Miss Lambie, the police had disregarded her statement that she recognized the man fleeing from the crime scene, and instead coached her to identify Slater. A rival newspaper, the *Daily News*, produced a second witness, who claimed that the police had offered her a £100 bribe to finger Slater.

(**Compiler's question:** Was this witness ever identified?)

On November 8, 1927, five days after the *Daily News* revelation, the secretary of state for Scotland issued a statement: "Oscar Slater has now completed more than eighteen and a half years of his life sentence, and I have felt justified in deciding to authorize his release as soon as suitable arrangements can be made." The timing of this decision, coming as it did amid a public clamor for a retrial, was not lost on the press. By releasing Slater, the government hoped to pre-empt any further disclosures.

Six days later, Oscar Slater walked through the gates of Peterhead Prison a free man. Under his arm, he carried a brown paper parcel containing all of his worldly possessions. A special railway car carried him to Glasgow, where a large crowd awaited him, but Slater could not bring himself to address his supporters or answer questions from reporters. He was offered refuge in a private home, and at the sight of a clean bed and a hot water bottle, he burst into tears.

Conan Doyle sent a message to Slater in Scotland: "This is to say in my wife's name and my own how grieved we have been at the infamous justice which you have suffered at the hands of our officials. Your only poor consolation can be that your fate, if we can get people to realise the effects, may have the effect of safeguarding others in the future."

Slater, though not entirely comfortable with the written word, sent a heartfelt response. "Sir Arthur Conan Doyle," he wrote, "you breaker of my shakels [*sic*], you lover of truth for justice sake, I thank you from the bottom of my heart and the goodness you have shown me. My heart is full and almost breaking with love and gratitude for you and your dear wife Lady Conan Doyle and all the upright men and women who for justice, (and that only) have helped me, me an outcast…."

Although Slater was a free man, he had not been pardoned. Conan Doyle now led the calls for a retrial, in the hope of clearing Slater's name and winning compensation for his false imprisonment. He updated his "Case of Oscar Slater" pamphlet and sent a copy to every member of Parliament, including the Honourable John Charteris, the Conservative member for Dumfriesshire, the younger brother of the man widely held to be the true murderer of Marion Gilchrist.

(**Compiler's question**: By whom and what was the motive?)

A special act of Parliament was passed to enable the Scottish Court of Criminal Appeal to reopen the case. As Slater had no money for legal costs, his supporters raised a defense fund, bolstered by a £1,000 guarantee from Conan Doyle. At the last moment, when Slater discovered that he would not be permitted to give evidence, he announced that he would withdraw his appeal. Conan Doyle responded with white hot fury, as Slater appeared to be scorning the efforts of the many people who had expended time and money on his behalf. Conan Doyle was so angry, it has been said, that he declared himself ready to sign a petition to have Slater's original death sentence carried out. In time, others persuaded Slater of his error and the appeal proceeded as scheduled.

Conan Doyle went to Scotland for the proceedings, meeting Slater for the first time. In contrast to his admiration for George Edalji, Conan Doyle never regarded Slater as anything more than a petty criminal. When Slater sent a silver cigar cutter as a token of his gratitude, Conan Doyle returned it immediately. It was the miscarriage of justice, rather than the man himself, that had aroused Conan Doyle's passions. Nevertheless, his account of the hearings, written for the *Sunday Pictorial*, demonstrated a keen sympathy for the plaintiff. "One terrible face stands out among all those others," he wrote of the courtroom. "It is not an ill-favoured face, nor is it a wicked one, but it is terrible nonetheless for the brooding sadness that is in it. It is firm and immobile and might be cut from that Peterhead granite which has helped to make it what it is. A sculptor would choose it as the very type of tragedy. You feel that this is no ordinary man but one who has been fashioned by some strange end. It is indeed the man whose misfortunes have echoed around the world. It is Slater."

After ten days of hearings, the original verdict was dismissed on a technicality. This was by no means the total vindication Slater's supporters had desired but a happy result nonetheless. Matters soon ran aground over the issue of compensation. The court awarded £6,000 to Slater, but left him responsible for the legal costs, which were settled with the funds contributed by Conan Doyle and others. Conan Doyle assumed that Slater would act quickly to reimburse his supporters. He did not. Slater argued that he should not have been held responsible for the court costs in the first place, and therefore could not be expected to pay them out of his settlement. At a stroke, Slater managed to alienate virtually every supporter he had. The money mattered little to Conan Doyle, but he bitterly resented Slater's intent to foist his debts on the people who had won his freedom. He also felt that William Park, whose book was so instrumental in winning the release, deserved some form of compensation for his long years of labor on Slater's behalf.

Slater would not yield. "You seem to have taken leave of you senses," Conan Doyle told him. "If you are indeed quite responsible for your actions, then you are the most ungrateful as well as the most foolish person whom I have ever known." The two men eventually reached a compromise that found Slater contributing £250 to the costs. In Conan Doyle's view, Slater had simply reverted to type, an opinion Slater quite naturally resented for the rest of his life.

Slater retired quietly to the town of Ayr, on the western coast of Scotland, where he devoted much of the time to wood carving. He made many friends in the community, and even remarried in 1936, at the age of sixty-six. His death twelve years later brought a curious notice in the local newspaper. It read: "Oscar Slater Dead at 78, Reprieved Murderer, Friend of A. Conan Doyle."

The third book on the case is Dr Andrew Norman's **Arthur Conan Doyle: Beyond Sherlock Holmes** (2007).

Further new information is found in the chapter entitled *Justice and Fair Play*, from which an excerpt is as follows:

…In the late 1980s the Slater case files were opened to the public. In them, former Special Branch Officer Thomas Toughill discovered an anonymous letter sent to the Secretary of State for Scotland the day before Slater was due to hang, accusing not Charteris but another man of the murder. This was Wingate Birrell (who, like Charteris, was also a nephew of Miss Gilchrist), who happened to be engaged to Lambie. Birrell had also visited Miss Gilchrist on the evening of her death and it appears that the two nephews were working in cahoots, with the connivance of Lambie who had admitted them to the house. While Charteris rummaged through the elderly lady's papers, Birrell's task was to distract her.

The reason for the visit of the two nephews was connected with the fact that shortly before her death Miss Gilchrist had changed her will, leaving the bulk of her estate to her, allegedly, illegitimate daughter. It is therefore believed, that Charteris may have been searching through the papers in order to find some evidence which would make his aunt's new will invalid.

(**Compilers note**: This answers my question from page 721).

However, the plan went dreadfully wrong when Birrell apparently lost his nerve and instead of simply distracting the elderly lady, battered her to death.

Doyle, who had procured the release of an innocent man from prison, did not live to see the real culprits identified. As for Birrell and his accomplice Charteris, they also died before the evidence of their guilt was forthcoming.

The penultimate book in this chapter is Russell Miller's **The Adventures of Arthur Conan Doyle** (2009). Chapter 16 of this book contains some new facts as follows in this excerpt:

…Following instructions, Helen Lambie *double-locked* the door behind her, knowing Miss Gilchrist feared being burgled.

…Both Lambie and Adams described a man they had seen as being about 5 feet 6 inches tall, dark-haired, clean-shaven, wearing a light-grey overcoat and a dark cap. Next day a 14-year-old girl, Mary Barrowman, who had been walking past Miss Gilchrist's flat at the time of the murder said she, too, had seen a man, but described him as tall and quite young with a crooked nose, wearing a fawn cloak or mackintosh, a round hat and brown boots. After further questioning, she changed her mind and produced a description much like that of Helen Lambie.

…Oscar Slater was a German Jew, named Joseph Leschziner, who was born in Silesia in about 1870, the son of a baker. At the age of 15 he left home, worked in a bank in Hamburg and then moved to Britain, where he changed his name to Slater and earned an erratic living on the fringes of the criminal fraternity, on racecourses and in gambling halls. He married in around 1902, but abandoned his wife and moved in with a French woman who called herself a 'nightclub singer' – a profession she probably combined with that of the world's oldest. Six weeks before the murder of Miss Gilchrist, the couple moved to Glasgow.

…Almost three years would pass before Conan Doyle became involved, somewhat reluctantly, at the instigation of Slater's lawyer, Alexander Shaughnessy. After the publication of Park's sensational 'The Truth about Oscar Slater', in July 1927, a number of newspapers revived the story.

…The breakthrough came when the *Empire News* tracked down Helen Lambie in the United States and, under the headline 'Why I believed I Blundered Over Slater', she confirmed that she had given the police the name and description of the man she had seen in the apartment on the night of the murder. He had visited Miss Gilchrist several times before and knew his way about the place, and she was normally sent out on an errand when he was due to arrive.

(**Compiler's note:** This answers my question on p. 743).

The police had ignored all this and persuaded her to identify Slater as the visitor.

PETER COSTELLO (2006) **Conan Doyle Detective. The TRUE CRIMES investigated by the creator of Sherlock Holmes.** Robinson.

The final book in this chapter is a revised and enlarged edition of Costello's (1991) book with a change of title. Other changes to this book compared to this earlier edition are noted as follows:

FOREWORD

They [the crimes] are told largely from his [Conan Doyle's] point of view, which means that they do not always coincide with other versions, but the documentation will allow interested readers to pursue them in greater detail.

Peter Costello

Dublin

(**Compiler's note**: The above sentence has been added to the paragraph towards the end which begins'…His biographers in the past' and ends '…either new or unfamiliar').

Chapters Fourteen and Fifteen have been combined in this new edition.

Chapter Fourteen

THE CASE OF OSCAR SLATER

'The whole case will, in my opinion, remain immortal in the classics of crime as the supreme example of official incompetence and obstinacy.'

Sir Arthur Conan Doyle,
The Spectator, 25 July 1914

(i) Murder in Queen's Terrace No new information

(ii) Why Miss Gilchrist Died

The case of Oscar Slater still arouses the fiercest controversy. Indeed, like other controversies, such as the assassination of President Kennedy, a flood of information is tending to rub out the simple outline which Conan Doyle accepted.

In 1993 Thomas Toughill, who had been for a time a policeman in Hong Kong, reinvestigated the affair in the light of all the documents, including released official files. He was a keen supporter of Trench's position and detailed much more evidence about the Charteris family than was available to Conan Doyle down to 1928 or to me when I was writing originally in the late 1980s.

But to show no case is ever closed, the distinguished writer and criminologist Richard Whittington-Egan published in 2001, a detailed rebuttal of the Trench *v.* Charteris position. His book was, again, based on a very careful appraisal of the evidence, and on what he had gleaned by further local investigation.

While all are agreed that Slater was innocent, of this crime at least, neither is agreed on other matters. Whittington-Egan concludes that the murder was committed in the course of a robbery, and that rumour in the city was later able to put a name to the crime. This, however, still seems unconvincing to me. Burglars always work quickly, ransacking the premises, throwing the contents of drawers around the rooms. There was none of that in the Gilchrist case. There was a very limited search of a bureau by one intruder, and a brutal attack on Miss Gilchrist by a second.

If the case comes down to the Charteris family as against common burglars I still think that Conan Doyle and Trench were right. The Scottish establishment covered up the case until 1928, protecting one of their own, and pinned the crime on Slater. Toughill thinks that they never wished for the return of Slater from New York. Perhaps it would have been better for him if he had not been so trusting of the Scottish authorities.

Those concerned with this ongoing debate, as opposed to Conan Doyle's view of the case, will be able to read Toughill and Whittington-Egan for themselves, and make up their own minds. Conan Doyle's own papers relating to the Oscar Slater affair, covering the years 1914-29, were bought (for £30,000) at Christie's in May 2004 by the Mitchell Library in Glasgow, to be added to their existing holdings on the case. Doubtless on the basis of this hoard of 145 items, other writers will in their time rebut Whittington-Egan and Toughill. However, I suspect the papers will serve only to reinforce the views of Trench and Conan Doyle, which I have summarized. Our hero's point of view will not, I think, be too easily discounted.

(Compiler's note: The conclusion of this chapter comprises the above information supplied to me by the Mitchell Library in Glasgow).

One final point: there can be little doubt that Conan Doyle's reputation and standing sank in the eyes of many influential people. His son Adrian told the critic and journalist Stuart P.B. Mais that in 1927 Conan Doyle was passed over for the offer of a peerage by Stanley Baldwin owing to the strong opposition from Queen Mary and the Archbishop of Canterbury, Dr. Randall Davidson. What reason could they have had? Conan Doyle had dismayed many Anglicans with his views over spiritualism and divorce. But was there more?

The Archbishop Randall Davidson was a Scotsman, born in Edinburgh of Presbyterian parents; and Anglican convert, he had been close to the Royal Household since 1882. It strikes me that their personal and public connections with Dr Charteris's uncle, the Very Rev. Archibald Hamilton Charteris, a Royal Chaplain for Scotland (1870-1908), might indeed have prejudiced these two and others in the Scottish Establishment against Doyle.

Was this rejection of Sir Arthur Conan Doyle by his country to be a legislator the final injustice of the Slater affair?

TD 1560 Oscar Slater Papers

Oscar Slater was convicted of the murder of Miss Marion Gilchrist at her home in West Princes Street, Glasgow in 1908. Suspicion fell on the German Jewish gambler initially on the basis of a pawned diamond brooch. He was extradited from New York, and stood trial in Edinburgh in 1909. His conviction, chiefly on the basis of his character and lifestyle, was accompanied by flawed identifications and suppressed evidence, but sufficient doubt remained for the death sentence to be commuted to imprisonment. Slater served 18 years of his sentence in Peterhead Prison before being given a free pardon by the Scottish Criminal Court of Appeal and awarded £6,000 compensation. Conan Doyle's 16-year campaign to free Slater began in 1912 with the publication of a booklet, *The Case of Oscar Slater* and even after Slater's release in 1927, the writer backed successful appeals for a pardon and for compensation together with the Glasgow journalist William Park.

This collection was purchased in May 2004 from The Conan Doyle Collection with funding assisted by the National Acquisition Fund.

TD 1560 Oscar Slater Papers

Contents

1 Letters from Oscar Slater
2 Letters from Sir Arthur Conan Doyle
3 Letters from William Park
4 Letters from David Cook
5 Miscellaneous letters
6 Press Cuttings

<u>1 Letters from Oscar Slater</u>

1 <u>Letter to [William] Gordon, n.d.</u> (smuggled out of prison under Gordon's dentures) "Gordon, my boy, I wish you in every way the best of luck and if you feel inclined, then please <u>do what you can for me</u>. Give to the English public you opinion regarding me, and also in other respects…Please don't forget to write or see Connan D."

2 <u>Letter from W[illia]m to Conan Doyle, n.d..</u>
Forwards the above letter from Slater, explaining how he got it out of prison. Asks to meet Conan Doyle to pass on a verbal message from Slater.

3 <u>Letter and typescript to Conan Doyle, 17 Nov (1927)</u>
"Sir Conan Doyle, you breaker of shackles, you lover of truth for justice sake", offering thanks to all who "have helped me, <u>me an outcast.</u>"

4 <u>Letter to Conan Doyle, 23 Nov 1927</u>
Thanks Conan Doyle for sending £3.0.0 to Peterhead Prison for him, though he mistakenly thought it had come from a Mr Boil. Asks if he knows who sent a money order for £6.6.0 in order to send his thanks.

5 <u>Letter to Conan Doyle, 25 Nov 1927</u>
Asks Conan Doyle's advice over whether to authorise agents Norman Macpherson & Dunlop, Edinburgh to act on his behalf.

6 <u>Letter to Conan Doyle, 7 Dec 1927</u>
Has seen Conan Doyle's appeal for funds in the Jewish Chronicle two days ago and "thought that half a dozen influential Jews…would have paid the bill like sportsmen. Dear Sir Arthur, it makes me <u>sick absolutely sick</u> to think on such actions." He offers to pay Conan Doyle half the expenses and if need be "<u>I pay it all</u>…All collected money must go back to the Jews and we will thank the few who have who have given for their kindness."

7 <u>Letter to Conan Doyle, 23 Dec 1927</u>
Asks Conan Doyle to accept a present which "although of no great value, it was dear to my heart, because I have handled it daily for more than 10 years."

TD 1560 Oscar Slater Papers

1 Letters from Oscar Slater

8 Letter to Conan Doyle, 2Jan 1928
Thanks Conan Doyle for the present of a smoking pipe. "Yesterday I went down to the shore to have a quiet smoke and except a little burning at the tip of my tongue, I have enjoyed it immensely." Includes a letter to Lady Conan Doyle, 2Jan 1928 thanking her for her kindness in sending him the nice Christmas gift.

9 Letter to Conan Doyle, 30, Mar 1928
Denies giving an interview which appeared in the daily express and states "I keep strictly to my contract…Your pipe, Sir, is dear to me, as a gift – to look upon it but to use it, it is a failure, then only by touching it my tongue starts to nip, and any attempt to fill the pipe makes my stomach heave up and down."

10 Letter to Conan Doyle, 2May, 1928
Thanks Conan Doyle for a recent letter but cannot deny that it has upset him greatly. "Sir Arthur I never have failed my friends yet!" Defends his character and explains where and who he is living with and who his friends are. Received £2000 from Allied Newspapers, after threatening to prosecute.

11 Letter to Conan Doyle, 5 May 1928
Glad that his last letter relieved Conan Doyle. Aware of the splendid work Mr Park has done for him and is very, very grateful for that, but "this great worker makes mistakes also". States that he offered to pay the expenses of the appeal alone and that was refused and at the time said "I am prepared to pay now, but nothing later."

12 Letter to Conan Doyle, 17 Jun 1928
"I think that I may have hurt you, my faithful friend, dear Lady Conan Doyle, and my other staunch supporters. But I am not sorry that I have acted as I did, because I only behaved, as any other animal would behave, who is free, yet lying bleeding and wounded on the ground, using his last strength, to lash furiously out again, when painfully treated."

13 Letter to Conan Doyle, 21 Jun 1928
Thanks Conan Doyle for his last letter which was "a very kind letter". Writes that after twenty years, his past is still thrown at him. "When in the witness box I would bother less, than the police about their past. My past was made public and was magnified, the Police-past must be suppressed-by hook or by crook."

TD 1560 Oscar Slater Papers

1 Letters from Oscar Slater

14 Letter to Conan Doyle, 21 Jul 1928

Thanks Conan Doyle for his congratulations but "they went to far in throwing muck at me in an open Court…This cruel 5 judges, this judges, <u>who knew the frame up of my case</u>, should have limited themselves a little and in not doing so, even the lay man in the street know now that my character was the staff for the Crown to lean on. I will fight and expose the All, - <u>All them who I know have taken my confidence and have betrayed me</u> – I shall fight regardless of consiquences."

15 <u>Letter to Conan Doyle and Lady Conan Doyle, 24 Jul 1928</u>
Sends heartfelt thanks for their congratulations on becoming a free man. Signed Oscar Slater (Leschziner).

16 <u>Copy letter to Conan Doyle, Nov 1929</u>
"I hereby undertake not to raise any action against you for damages on account of alleged slander prior to this date." Signed Oscar Leschziner (Slater).

2 <u>Letters from Sir Arthur Conan Doyle</u>

1 <u>Postcard to J Cuming Walters, editor of the Manchester City News, 2 Nov 1827</u>
Discusses Lambie's confession. "What a story! What a scandal! She says that the police <u>made</u> her say it was Slater. Third Degree! What a cess pool it all is!"

2 <u>Letter to Mr [Stanley] Baldwin, 13 Nov 1927</u>
The Oscar Slater business "will surely develop into a big political issue unless there is some inquiry into the scandal connected with the man's conviction. I regret that I cannot believe in the 'thorough investigation' by the Scots office alluded to in your former letter. There are limits to human stupidity and this is beyond them."

3 <u>Letter to Oscar Slater, 2 Aug 1928</u>
Urges that "you will get no compensation, not a penny, if you do not apply for it" and itemises payments due to lawyers and other contributors to the campaign for Slater's release.

4 <u>Copy of letter to Oscar Slater, 9 Aug [1928]</u>
Asks if Slater proposes "to relieve those who supported you of the costs of your defence…?" requesting a clear and direct reply.

5 <u>Letter to unknown recipient, 10 Oct 1929</u>
Accepts explanations for the delay in payment of £250 on the basis of Slater's ill health.

6 <u>Letter to unknown recipient, n.d.</u>
Expresses his sense of disgust at the circumstances of Slater's conviction which animated his campaign. "I was up against a ring of political lawyers who could not give away the police without also giving away themselves. There is no doubt that Mr Ure went too far in his speech for the prosecution…Oscar Slater never knew that Miss Gilchrist existed…The faked police persecution of their own honest Inspector [Detective Trench]…was a shocking business."

7 Letter to [Slater], n.d.
Insists "these bills have to be met now…I beg…you will send me a cheque by return for [£300]."

TD 1560 Oscar Slater Papers
3 Letters from William Park

1 Letter to Conan Doyle, 23 Sep 1914 (incomplete)
Pulls McKinnon Wood's speech to pieces and points out several distortions of evidence especially regarding the identification of Slater by Adams and Lambie.

2 Letter to Conan Doyle, 25 Sep 1914
Asks Conan Doyle to write to McKinnon Wood on the question of his Inquiry and White Paper. Thinks matters should be left to rest until after the war but is concerned that Slater may be dead by then as several ex-convicts have told him that Slater is "off his head."

3 Letter to Conan Doyle, 29 Sep 1914 (incomplete)
States that the Inquiry was not full and searching as McKinnon Wood stated in his White Paper. Mr Cook agrees that a letter from Conan Doyle to McKinnon Wood would be advantageous. Suggests questions for inclusion in his letter. Shows discrepancies in Mary Barrowman's sworn disposition and evidence at trial that discusses how this was not investigated properly in the Inquiry. Lists all the witnesses that were suppressed by the Crown and in some cases explains why.

4 Letter to Conan Doyle, 8 Oct 1914
Believes that McKinnon Wood is a "hopelessly stupid man…He is simply a promoted man in the street…It is our view…that the Trench business should only come in as episode to the main story of the sham inquiry and humbug report."

5 Letter to Conan Doyle, 7 Dec 1914
Has decided to proceed with a book on Slater's unfortunate position and has two new documents of a very damaging character. Plans to expose the police conduct, show how they prepared the case by selecting and rejecting witnesses and illustrate the discrepancies between statements at trial with those given secretly to police.

6 Letter to Conan Doyle, 14 May 1915
Brings attention to press reports over arrests of ex-Lieutenant Trench and Mr Cook and details the facts of the case. "There is an obvious reflection here on the character of the principals responsible for the agitation in favour of the liberation of Slater and it is proper that I should acquaint you with some of the facts, knowing as I do that they are both entirely innocent."

7 Letter to Conan Doyle, 20 May 1915
The Cook-Trench case is sub-judice so cannot comment on it, but can prepare. Crown seized the business books of Mr Cook this week this week but returned them quickly. "I shall be glad of any suggestions from you. You're keen acumen and experience of police methods may throw light on the mystery of the arrests." Encloses extracts from

the diary of ex-Lieutenant John J Trench, 14-23 Jan 1914 and a copy letter from Local Secretary of Guardian Ins[urance] Co., Glasgow to the Chief Constable, Glasgow, 19 Jan 1914 advising that the stolen property has been recovered apparently intact. Expresses his appreciation of the good offices of Detective Trench and is aware that without his assistance the matter couldn't have been carried through.

8 Letter to Conan Doyle, 7 Sep 1915
Informs Conan Doyle that Mr Cook has received c. 100 letters from law agents in Scotland congratulating him on the result of the trial. All condemn the prosecution and the majority express their conviction that the trial reveals nothing short of a legal tyranny in Scotland. "When we come, at the end of the war, to deal afresh with Slater's case, the ground of attack has thus been simplified into one of an assault against a system which encroaches upon the liberties of the subject…As you say we have had three scandals – the Slater Trial, the Inquiry and the Cook-Trench persecution. We have sufficient matter to bring some of the hidden busybodies to grief…On the whole I have a strong suspicion we shall be able to smack up the conspiracy which is at the back of the Crown."

9 Letter to Conan Doyle, n.d.
Regarding the Cook-Trench case of 1915 and encloses 'Verbatim Report of The Lord High Justice Clerk's Charge to the Jury in the trial before the High Court of Judiciary, 17 August 1915. His Majesty's Advocate against David Cook and John Thomson Trench'.

10 Letter to Conan Doyle, 9 Jun 1916
Brings Conan Doyle's attention to a new edition of the trial, edited by Mr Roughead which contains a resume of the proceedings in connection with the recent inquiry. Asks Conan Doyle to bring to the attention of the editor of the "Spectator" the legal contradiction of McKinnon Wood's opinion as to the result of the Inquiry. Has discovered that the police advertised the descriptions supplied by Barrowman, Lambie and Adams in the 'Glasgow Herald' on 29 Dec 1908. The advert described two men who were seen to leave the stair leading to the deceased's house. He believes the suppression of this advert and a secret police document produced at the Inquiry by Lieutenant Trench were deliberate fraud on the American Court who would have instantly dismissed the case against Oscar Slater if it had seen either document.

11 Letter to Conan Doyle, 13 Apr 1919
Hopes to secure the re-opening of the case once a series of articles on Slater have been completed. "It would be of uncalcuable service to receive from you a letter for publication on the subject, addressed Editor Sunday Mail, Glasgow."

12 Letter to Conan Doyle, 4 Feb 1925
Governor Walkinshaw, Glasgow Prison, exposed a "villainous attempt on the part of the police to secure the identification by a woman of a poor fellow who was on trial for a murder at Kirkintilloch." Compares this to the position Slater is currently in and highlights the fact that "the whole bungle was perpetrated by men who owed their positions to a Liberal Government."

13 Letter to Conan Doyle, 9 Feb 1925 (page 1 and 4 only)
Believes that there will be no move to liberate Slater and intends to publish a new book on the case at a later date. "It can be proved that the authorities put into a box at least one known perjurer…Every one who dares to disturb the dovecoat of Bureaucracy is a heretic and doomed to excommunication. The people of Britain do not realise how great a tyranny – a system of Leninism – exists in its midst."

14 Letter to Conan Doyle, 24 Mar 1926
Regarding new evidence of a witness and her description of "Dr. C". Thinks they should try and get Slater's appeal into the new Scottish Court, but fears they will be barred on some technicality of belatedness or inapplicability. Discusses Helen Lambie's testimony in the New York court and precognition. On Wednesday 23 Dec 1908 the 'Glasgow Evening News' published a 'sensational' story regarding a turn in events that the police were now hot on the track, not of the missing brooch, but of the will.

15 Letter to Conan Doyle, 13 Apr 1926
Park is writing a further article demanding an Inquiry or rehearing of the case under the new Scottish Criminal Appeal Court. "The police are not prosecutors, they are custodians of justice and the rights of a prisoner must me observed by them while sifting a case." Suggests Professor Glaister's evidence on the hammer was a fraud. Dr Adams, whose evidence was suppressed, declaring that Miss Gilchrist was murdered with a chair.

16 Letter to Conan Doyle, 16 Apr 1926
Has written to the editor of the 'Empire News' suggesting he should see his superior, Sir Thomas Berry, and get all his 'Allied Newspaper' group to form a crusade for a rehearing of Slater's case.

17 Letter to Conan Doyle, 25 Apr 1926
Informs Conan Doyle that the directors of the 'Allied Newspapers' are very seriously considering the start of a petition for rehearing Slater's case.

18 Letter to Conan Doyle, 18 Jun 1926
Mrs Trench still has the damning police document tracing the family history of the Charteris subject. He is trying to get photographs of Trench's official police diary which shows undoubtedly that he called on Miss Birrell on 27 Dec 1908 and made another call at the Birrell's early in January. Park had asked Trench, before his death, what the call was for and he answered "I was sent to tell her to shut her mouth about the Charteris business as we were after another man."

19 Letter to Conan Doyle, 30 Aug 1926
Informs Conan Doyle of the death of Mr JN Hart, the Procurator- Fiscal in the Slater case and the twelfth person of importance connected with the Slater tragedy to predecease the man who was condemned to death and escaped. On going through the late Lieutenant Trench's papers, he has across the original warrant, dated 2 Jan 1909. In

it Hart requests the power to search Slater's house for clothing etc. The document states that Hart has 'charged' Slater with the murder and he has 'absconded'.

20 Letter to Conan Doyle, 7 Sep 1926
Believes Hart is the blunderer and faker of the evidence against Slater regarding his supposed flight and thinks over twelve witnesses were suppressed altogether by Hart. He is assured the 'Empire News' means to go ahead with the petition for release after the coal strike.

21 Letter to Conan Doyle, 13 Oct 1926
Believes in truth, justice and morality and that all prison officials in Scotland subconsciously believe "let this man die out and save us all from a scandal that would shake the country's confidence in ourselves."

22 Letter to Conan Doyle, 26 Oct 1926
A lady has come forward who is possibly the person Lambie went to work for after the murder. A journalist is coming up from London and they hope to break down Barrowman to get a confession that she was not at the scene of the crime.

23 Letter to Conan Doyle, 22 Nov 1926
Writes about criminal jurisprudence and suggests ways to prevent suppression of witnesses. Should go for an investigation of the Scottish criminal system having the Slater case as the demonstration ground. Asks Conan Doyle if he should aim at a booklet or get a newspaper to take it up.

24 Letter to Conan Doyle, 31 Dec 1926
He is finishing the story of Oscar Slater case and will send a copy to Conan Doyle for his consideration. Is going to obtain Trench's official diary for 1908-9 from his wife and get photographs of the entries showing his call at Birrell's regarding 'AB'.

25 Letter to Conan Doyle, 3 Jan 1927
Sends Conan Doyle the completed manuscript of the proposed story for his consideration.

26 Letter to Conan Doyle, 12 Jan 1927
Believes the case will become a classic in respect of the exposure of police methods. Trench confided in Park all the secrets and much more than he told the Secretary for Scotland. "The man was in terror of dismissal: but yet forced by his conscience to speak."

27 Letter to Conan Doyle, 18 Jan 1927
After the Slater case, Ord was deposed and sent to a district office and the Chief Constable created a new Criminal Investigation Department. Discusses the evidence in the case – relatives blaming each other, matches, brooch, secret documents etc. Ord

bought a specific book for the case to insert statements of his officers which meant he could hold up statements. Statements were re-written by his clerk, at least one had post-dated information in it and by using this book, Ord was able to get rid of Trench's report on Lambie's confession.

28 Letter to Conan Doyle, 21 Jan 1927
Sends Conan Doyle the secret documents and points out that the word 'stronger' written in pencil on the document was written by Chief Constable Stevenson or so Trench claimed.

29 Letter to Conan Doyle, 25 Jan 1927
Sends some suggestions for Conan Doyle's preface. The institution of the new Criminal Appeal Court does not meet the position at all as an appeal is only connected with the things said and done at the trial.

30 Letter to Conan Doyle, 29 Jan 1927
Agrees that Conan Doyle should proceed with publication of the book. Park admires the preface Conan Doyle has written. Doesn't like to touch anything writes as it is a kind of sacrilege to do so, but gives a few suggestions anyway.

31 Letter to Conan Doyle, 31 Jan 1927
Writes about the preface Conan Doyle has written for his book. Trench died of decline and his widow and children were persecuted also. The petition for liberation campaign organised by the newspapers last May failed due to the coal strike, but editors hope to return to it. Only need to try and make it clear that social influences were at work regarding AB, whereas Slater was kicked about like an old shoe. Adam tried to please the police and Lambie and Barrowman were tools of the police.

32 Letter to Conan Doyle, 2 Feb 1927
Has received Conan Doyle's addition to the preface of the book and suggests some slight alterations. Attaches press cutting from 'Daily Mail' regarding Mr Justice Avory's comments on witnesses being shown photographs of prisoners before identification. Gives information on Trench's past career especially saving the life of an American, Warner, from the scaffold. He tried to save Slater and was <u>dismissed and ruined</u> for it."

33 Letter to Conan Doyle, 22 Feb 1927
Park and Mr Roughead have fixed up Cragie Aitcheson and a first class firm of law agents. Counsel have asked that the newspaper articles are stopped at once.

34 Letter to Conan Doyle, 18 Sep 1927
Park has mentioned to the Editor of the 'Express' to contact Conan Doyle regarding the secret document. A Jewish gentleman from Glasgow is keen to organise a public meeting in Glasgow to demand Slater's release and requests Conan Doyle to go to Glasgow and give an address on the case.

35 Letter to Conan Doyle, 21 Sep 1927

Discusses the preparation of Gilmore to release and that Ramsay Macdonald is on side. Suggests sending a copy of the secret police document to Macdonald and explains its implications. Suggests three sources of tampering and suppression – the police, the Fiscal and the Lord Advocate.

36 Letter to Conan Doyle, 23 Sep 1927
Very positive that Macdonald's letter finishes the business. The case has never been in such a healthy position and regards it as certain that Slater will be released soon. Trusts that Conan Doyle will send Ramsay Macdonald a copy of the secret document.

37 Letter to Conan Doyle, 4 Oct 1927
Approves of Conan Doyle's letter to Gilmour. Indicates how they will show at an Inquiry how the American Court of Extradition was fooled.

38 Letter to Conan Doyle, 5 Oct 1927 (torn in half)
Feels Gilmour cannot and dare not grant an Inquiry. The alternative for him is to face a faked inquiry and come through safely with the police and official life proved to be unsullied and put Slater in the wrong. Ramsay Macdonald will stand in the way of this. The only other way is compromise – get Slater out, soften the public apprehension by diplomatic utterance and palaver. Should inform Gilmour that a bundle of correspondence has come to light of great importance but do not show him the secret document.

39 Letter to Conan Doyle, 10 Oct 1927
Has information from an ex-convict that Slater had been transferred to Perth Asylum. Slater will go mad at Perth as it was the one thing he dreaded most while at Peterhead. Suggests Conan Doyle writes to Gilmour to ascertain if this is true. Disillusioned that the press are working the campaign as if it were theirs, not the book's.

40 Letter to Conan Doyle, 22 Oct 1927
Believes Gilmour will not release Slater. Suggests that Conan Doyle writes to Gilmour to find out what the position he has arrived at after the three month Inquiry. Also advises Conan Doyle to turn to Ramsay Macdonald and work up the forces of the opposition. "Get ready to prepare Parliament against [Gilmour's] statements. We must educate the members."

41 Letter to Conan Doyle, 25 Oct 1927
The Lambie confession has startled the country. Park has written to the 'Empire News' to explain fully what it means in relation to Slater and the secret document Park possesses. Lambie declared that the police pushed her off the AB identification by a systematic process of ridicule. Gilmour and his legal advisers are to consider the Lambie confession with the statements in the book.

42 Letter to Conan Doyle, 26 Oct 1927
Has read the Lambie confession and believes she must have been quite obstinate in refusals to say what the police wanted (though she was persuaded to drop the charge against AB). Encloses an analysis of the secret document.

43 Letter to Conan Doyle, 28 Oct 1927
Discusses the significance of the deposition to the New York court by Allan McLean regarding the pawn ticket which was taken five days after the police knew the brooch was Slater's. Suggests lodging a charge of fraud in sending the deposition to New York as it was intended to deceive the New York court and did deceive both the Foreign Office in London and the British Consul and legal adviser in New York. "This may explain why McLean hanged himself."

44 Letter to Conan Doyle, 28 Oct 1927
Regarding Conan Doyle's letter to Lord Strathclyde and his intention to write an article for the 'Empire News' entitled "Who Killed Miss G[ilchrist]." Quotes extracts from the Glasgow papers at the time when Lieutenant Trench called on Birrell and considers why Gilmour is delaying the inquiry.

45 Letter to Conan Doyle, 29 Oct 1927
Details why he thinks Lambie and Barrowman were corrupt and never should have been allowed in the box and explains that he had written to Ramsay Macdonald about the Lambie confession.

46 Letter to Conan Doyle, 31 Oct 1927
Regarding Conan Doyle's article on "Who did kill Miss G". Park is trying to locate Barrowman and has been briefing Macdonald in case he needs to confront Gilmour in the House of Commons.

47 Letter to Conan Doyle, Wednesday 9, n.d. (c. Nov/Dec 1927)
Slater has appointed his agents – Craigie Aitcheson and Mr Roughead. First consultation with Slater, Aitcheson and agents will take place on Friday. Discusses the scope of the inquiry and whether police can introduce new evidence. Need to consider a 'not proven' verdict which would carry no compensation.

48 Letter to Conan Doyle, 2 Nov 1927
Writes about a letter from a new witness who is convinced Lambie knows the murderer and is satisfied he was in the house when she left for the newspaper. Details information regarding the telegram to the Cunard Company in Liverpool and circumstances regarding the supposed flight of Slater.

49 Letter to Conan Doyle, 4 Nov 1927 (torn)
Writes that Lambie has been intimidated and that Barrowman was drilled into saying Slater was the man.

50 Letter to Conan Doyle, 5 Nov 1927
Barrowman made a statement to Park that Gordon Mellen had a statement already written down for her to sign when she went in his room at the 1914 inquiry. Believes Gilmour has not even started his inquiry and all his letters about a careful and exhaustive inquiry are more official falsehood.

51 Letter to Conan Doyle, 7 Nov 1927
Asks Conan Doyle to send a copy of the witness's evidence to Macdonald and Gilmour which says she is perfectly satisfied that the man was in the house at the time Lambie left. Also shows Miss Gilchrist had apprehensions of murder before Slater appeared in Glasgow and the safeguards she took point to her urgent fear of violence from quarter known to her.

52 Letter to Conan Doyle, 9 Nov 1927
Has forwarded Conan Doyle's article to 'Empire News' having made two little changes. He has written Gilmour charging Barrowman with perjury and if he refuses an investigation, Park will republish his book with new matter and make definite charges of fraud and perjury. Has also written to James Maxton and thinks the Clydeside 'Reds' are now hot on the job. Suggests how Ramsay Macdonald should respond to Gilmour in the House of Commons. Next line of attack is Mr Adams – Lambie told him the whole story about the man still being in the house and that the Adams' did not hear the bell ring.

53 Letter to Conan Doyle, 10 Nov 1927
Park is ready to resume the book and make definite charges of fraud and perjury if the inquiry is not granted. "If intelligence isn't there to essence the rottenness of the case, founded upon error, continued by fraud and finished with perjury, nothing will rouse [Sir John Gilmour] out of his official indolence." Discusses Barrowman's evidence.

54 Letter to Conan Doyle, 10 Nov 1927
Has re-read a letter from Sir J. Gilmour and believes he was trying to put Conan Doyle in the wrong as regards the production of documents. "Are we dealing here again with scoundrels, masquerading as gentlemen, who will cheat and lie and wriggle while the facts are striking any honest man dead?"

55 Letter to Conan Doyle, 11 Nov 1927
Believes that they have been betrayed and the Stewart's absence was pre-arranged. "The police and papists of Glasgow work hand in hand." The 'Glasgow Herald' published a disgraceful and lying statement that the book and the new evidence count for nothing. Park had given an article to the 'Evening Times' saying "Gilmour had granted release at the point of the bayonet."

56 Letter to Conan Doyle, 12 Nov 1927
Gilmour's decision was release "on License." Thinks he is worse than McKinnon Wood. Believes now is the time to disclose Ramsay Macdonald. Sends news of a new witness, Mrs Hamilton, who says Barrowman wasn't in the street at all.

57 Letter to Conan Doyle, 16 Nov 1927
Park has received a letter from James Maxton, M.P. stating that the whole Labour party was watching Gilmour. He is going to see Slater again to unlock the mystery of the police already watching the house and waiting to get a £200 reward by catching him as a fugitive instead of at his own house.

58 Letter to Conan Doyle, 19 Nov 1927

Details a list of questions that should be asked of the Lord Advocate of Scotland regarding the scope of the inquiry. Slater has signed an agreement with the 'Empire News' for £2000 but Slater's friends are dissatisfied with the whole arrangement. The man they sent to arrange it was insolent and aggressive and claimed to have a letter from Conan Doyle which did the trick. Park states they robbed him shamefully and refused to start a petition for Slater's release. Slater, Mr Phillips and others desired Park to write his story but that wasn't even considered. Believes Conan Doyle should not have interfered and recommended these people.

59 Letter to Conan Doyle, 23 Nov 1927
Craigie Aitcheson has been identified as Slater's barrister, but need to appoint a firm of solicitors who will then engage him. 'Empire News' articles were complicating issues and legal opinion was to stop them at once. Slater was paid £2000 for them and Park does not want him involved in possible litigation for breach of contract. Discusses funds and functions of the Court and the scope of the Inquiry. Suggests organising a small overlooking committee who would stand over and control the lawyers, which would include Park and Conan Doyle. Explains Slater has a secret about the case which is good, though doubts it could be proved. Sensational revelation regarding the address to the jury by Lord Guthrie – "the old rascal re-wrote the speech and introduced into the revision wholesale paragraphs and sentences which he never said to the jury at all." Explains he found the letter from Mr Jacobs, New York in the cuttings book of Mr Roughead, warning that the case in New York was a fabrication of the Glasgow police.

60 Letter to Conan Doyle, n.d. (c. Nov 1927)
Worried about the articles in the 'Empire News'. Legal opinion is to stop them immediately. "Empire News" have sold Scottish rights to the 'Sunday Mail' who previously published an article calling Slater a professional blackmailer. Disillusioned with other journalists gleaning information and publishing articles themselves and even suggesting they got Slater out of prison themselves. "I accordingly propose to drop the whole business. Slater has got his liberty: his innocence is proved in the book."

61 Letter to Conan Doyle, 25 Nov 1927
Thanks Conan Doyle for a cheque of £25. "You can not personally be bled in this awful fashion…I only accept this sum as a loan from you. The public, I hope, will come to the rescue and do its belated duty to you and Slater." Explains Slater's story of his arrest and flight. His house was being watched sometime before the murder to get him on a charge of immoral housekeeping. "This gives us a new theory altogether. Slater was being watched for another crime altogether and was rolled into the Gilchrist case as a handy sort of fellow to convict."

62 Letter to Conan Doyle, 27 Nov 1927
Explains that Ramsay Macdonald has written him a letter and was deeply interested. Discusses the grave danger of the police system and suggests improvement of the whole system of criminal procedure. Discusses the importance of a letter from Jacobs, New York to Judge Guthrie which stated that Slater was pointed out to Lambie and Barrowman before they identified him in court. "At the appeal the only point in which the prosecution can make any fight is identification."

63 Letter to Conan Doyle, 28 Nov 1927
Discusses whether it is worth re-setting and publishing. The 'Daily News' turned down the suggestion of an Oscar Slater Shilling fund, but the 'Jewish Chronicle' has intimated it is collecting. There is also a central fund in Manchester. Discusses possible costs of the case. Has received a copy of the Jacobs letter from Mr Roughead.

64 Letter to Conan Doyle, 1 Dec 1927
Four hundred circulars go out at the weekend asking for funds and there have been good notices in all the evening newspapers. Notes that another thousand copies the 2/6 edition are being printed. Palmer of the 'Daily News' tells Park that the official view is that the verdict will be maintained. Glasgow police have dug up some wonderful information but Park says to take no notice as "Human stupidity is entrenched in the Glasgow police system." Slater told Park this week that "he intended to endure Peterhead till the end of 20 years and then if no help came he intended to take his life."

65 Letter to Conan Doyle, 5 Dec 1927 (incomplete)
Details meeting with Counsel last Friday afternoon. Cragie Aitcheson believes Lambie "holds the secret."

66 Letter to Conan Doyle, 13 Dec 1927 (incomplete)
Discusses Lambie's statement to the 1914 Commissioner as a "bundle of falsehoods" and Barrowman's evidence and possible pay off with which he says "the police will need more than their available intelligence to catch us in any of their traps." Editors are on their guard against any temptation to destroy Barrowman's evidence with a payment of money.

67 Letter to Conan Doyle, 17 Dec 1927
Park has been told that Mary Barrowman expressed her gladness at Slater's release and declared her intention to go into the box and swear that the Fiscal had put her up to say that Slater was the man and that he was not the man who emerged from the West Prince St house. Suggests police are trying to trap them into paying Barrowman and has warned editors not to answer any letters. Their new witness, Mrs Brown, is being pestered by parties calling on her about her evidence.

68 Letter to Conan Doyle, 19 Dec 1927
Park received a letter from Lawson, 'Empire News' that suggests the supposed interview with Lambie was bogus. But Park says "there were material facts disclosed which he could not have invented, even if he were a Sherlock Holmes at filling up gaps of deductive logic." Discusses the fact that they will be able to break Lambie on cross-examination. Discusses the Jacob letter and suggests trying to find him.

69 Letter to Conan Doyle, 21 Dec 1927
Asks Conan Doyle if he can push the Jews in London as the fund is going too slowly. Also states Slater is a very independent soul. He wanted to stop the Glasgow fund declaring he would pay for everything out of his £2000 from the newspapers but Park refused to permit that.

70 Letter to Conan Doyle, 23 Dec 1927
Discusses Lambie's evidence in light of the Jacobs letter. "If the police produce Lambie as adhering to her evidence in Court, we have now such a plenitude of materials upon which to attack her credibility as to shake her to pieces."

71 Letter to Conan Doyle, 29 Dec 1927
Gives details of a man who has access to Lambie's mother's house and who is willing to help find where Lambie is. Also talks about the identification of Slater in the New York Court and the representations made by Detective Pyper to the jury in the Edinburgh trial regarding the identification.

72 Letter to Conan Doyle, 4 Jan 1928 (incomplete)
Craigie Aitcheson has been spending time looking over the case and sees daylight coming through the tangle. Believes the conviction will be quashed due to the Lord Advocate misleading the jury, but this would mean police conduct will not be touched at all. Need to get Slater's conviction quashed, compensation assigned and then ask for a new separate inquiry into police misconduct.

73 Letter to Conan Doyle, 17 Jan 1928
Discusses what Aitcheson will be able to do with Lambie and Detective Pyper in the box. Also discusses the half-sovereign found on the floor of the dining room, the fact that the murderer was probably already in the house and the fabrication of a man watching the house, seeing Lambie leave and entering to murder.

74 Letter to Conan Doyle, 21 Jan 1928
Very approving of Craigie Aitcheson and feels he is doing a good job. He is very methodical and desires several meetings to prepare a case that will be comprehensive, embracive and yet watertight. Worried about expenses and asks how the London fund is doing. Lists the documents regarding the case that he holds.

75 Letter to Conan Doyle, 8 Feb 1928
The 'Empire News' has made a shocking mess of the search for Lambie but Park feels they do not need her as the affidavits from America should kill identification. Points out that the 'Glasgow Herald' advert for two wanted men is significant. Keen for Miss Adams to be interrogated regarding her statement that Miss Gilchrist would not open her door to anyone when on her own.

76 Letter to Conan Doyle, 10 Feb 1928
Details further affidavits sent by Mr Goodheart in America relating to the extradition in 1909 consisting of the depositions of Lambie and Barrowman taken in Glasgow. Mr Goodheart is willing to come over and personally produce all affidavits and other documents from Washington.

77 Letter to Conan Doyle, 12 Feb 1928
Regarding the funds needed to fight the case again. In 1909 the prisoner and his defending counsel and agents had only £60 available for a trial which occupies four

days. This time, the defence needs to bring the witnesses and evidence which should have been forthcoming at the trial in 1909.

78 Letter to Conan Doyle, 14 Feb 1928
Discusses the whereabouts of Lambie as she has gone missing following her confession. Park thinks she has been spirited away because of the dread Birrell-Charteris group of her disclosures. Park is to write to Lawson, 'Empire News' to begin searching at Holytown to see if any postmarks can be gleaned from correspondence with her mother.

79 Letter to Conan Doyle, 28 Feb 1928
Discusses the two agents that will come across from America, which will be pointless if evidence regarding gross irregularities at the New York proceedings is disallowed.

80 Letter to Conan Doyle, 13 Mar 1928
Depositions sent to America in 1908 are nearly all a mass of police dictations. Asks Conan Doyle his opinion of Ord's admission on oath that Powell was to allow Slater to abscond. Discusses events on the night of the murder regarding Lambie leaving the house to get a constable and Adams finding the door open, also dispute between the colour of a coat.

81 Letter to Conan Doyle, 26 Mar 1928
Scottish Office and the Lord Advocate are confident the decision of the Court of 1908 will be upheld and intend to fight. Will not be surprised if Helen Lambie is brought forward by the police to reiterate that Slater is the man. Aitcheson will be prepared fully to cross-examine her regarding her trustworthiness. Mr Miller will go in the box and declare that the pawnticket was the only or paramount issue in the case when Slater was arrested in New York. Should highlight before the court the discrepancies in material statements by eye witnesses relative to identification.

82 Letter to Conan Doyle, 5 Apr 1928
Discusses new evidence from New York and that the fraud may be proved regarding the identification of the prisoner. "I think the case is now definitely won. At all costs, however, we must get the New York stuff in…the New York evidence can finish the case."

83 Letter to Conan Doyle, 24 Feb 1928
Thanks Conan Doyle for the £25 he sent, making a total of £50. When the appeal is imminent, suggests they put out notices to sell the book as the case will have much public interest (especially in America). Discusses Lambie's evidence, Adam's evidence and the police's secret document.

84 Letter to Conan Doyle, n.d. (page 2 only)
Park has had a letter from American author regarding another case who says at least in the British cases of miscarriages of justice, lives were not lost as the were in the Sacco-Vanzetti Case.

85 Letter to Conan Doyle, n.d.

"Who did murder Miss G!" Notes regarding why Trench was initially sent to Miss Gilchrist's house. Organisation of Glasgow police and the introduction of the Criminal Intelligence Department. Also notes from Trench's official diary.

86 Letter to Conan Doyle, n.d. (page 3 only)
Warns Conan Doyle to be careful with the original documents he holds regarding the case. Park is concerned that suspicious characters have been seen around his own house and worries that if stolen, they would lose an important weapon.

87 Letter to Conan Doyle, Monday, n.d.
Is in Glasgow to see Slater. Has written a statement for him to sign in order to stop press "stories". Has learned that Helen Lambie's husband went to America due to his wife's confession of the real murder. Thinks he might strike oil but must keep newspapers away.

88 Letter to Conan Doyle, n.d. (PS only)
Received copy of new book on Sacco-Vanzetti case from America which thanks Park "for his persistent effort towards justice for the lowly and the outcast."

89 Letter to Conan Doyle, n.d.
Conan Doyle appears to have written to Birrell asking the name of the accused man. Park believes she will die before she reveals the name now as it involves ruin and the possible hanging of her cousin. Thinks the family will send someone to America to buy off Lambie.

90 Letter to Conan Doyle, n.d. (PS only)
Park omitted answer of Conan Doyle's point regarding Dr. Charteris. Park can not help as he does not know his 'description'. At the Inquiry they said Dr. Charteris' name had never been mentioned rather than they found he had an alibi.

4 Letters from David Cook

1 Letter to Conan Doyle, 26 Mar 1914
Indicates the position of the Slater Case. David Trench is an officer of ability and integrity and has always been of the opinion that Slater is an innocent man. Mr MacKinnon Wood is in possession of a signed statement by Trench. Barrowman's original statement bears no relation to the evidence she gave at trial. Trench is prepared to swear at the enquiry that he received a statement from Lambie on 3 Jan 1909 that another man was the man whom she saw leave the house. Has copies of telegrams from head of police in Liverpool. Miss Birrell is prepared to swear that Nellie Lambie named the man who murdered Miss Gilchrist. Believes all original documents will be destroyed by the police, but Cook has copies of them.

2 Letter to Conan Doyle, 17 Apr 1914
The question of fact to be enquired into suggests to Cook that the enquiry will be more or less a farce. Suggests four points which require investigation. " I am bound to confess

that I am disgusted not only at the delay but at the failure wilful or otherwise to grasp the significance of the information furnished by Trench."

Encloses copy letter from James G. Millar, Sheriff of Lanarkshire, 17 Apr 1914. Questions the scope of the three questions and knows of no reason why the enquiry should be private. Depends greatly on the terms of Millar's reply as to whether Trench will associate himself with the investigation.

Encloses letter from David Cook to James G. Millar, Sheriff of Lanarkshire, 17 Apr 1914. Questions the scope of the three questions and knows of no reason why the enquiry should be private. Depends greatly on the terms of Millar's reply as to whether Trench will associate himself with the investigation.

3 Letter to Conan Doyle, 24 Apr 1914
The Inquiry opened yesterday. Trench was the last witness to be examined for the day and the Sheriff went for him like a pick-pocket. Somerville, excess clerk to the Central Railway Station and Duckworth of Liverpool will be examined today. Barrowman had to either have lied when she made her original statement or at the trial. There are too many reputations at stake to attain justice by means of a private Inquiry, so proposes publishing copies of the documents and emphasising the points hidden by the police. The police had evidence of a man, Duncan McBrayne, a licensed grocer in Lenzie, who saw Slater at 8.15pm at his own close mouth. When Slater was in the suburbs according to the Lord Advocate, he was actually in his own house and the police knew that.

4 Letter to Conan Doyle, 9 May 1914
Lord Strathclyde is bitterly opposed to any public enquiry, so thinks it will be prudent to have the whole case with the new facts published in a Scotch weekly with a circulation in England. Miss Birrell and Nellie Lambie have both denied what Trench has said so he intends to deal delicately with any allegations regarding Dr. Charteris. Believes no one has the right to say Dr. Charteris is the man, but do have the right to say if his name was mentioned by Lambie, there ought to be an end of the Slater case. Is seriously considering whether a book should be published with a criticism of the methods of the police, the action of the Lord Advocate and the conduct of the Judge.

5 Letter to Conan Doyle, 16 Jul 1914
The White Paper has been issued and it is ample as a warrant for at least a public enquiry. The contents show how much valuable information was suppressed at the trial. The theory of flight is destroyed and without it, the case is hopeless from the police's point of view. It is his intention to publish a book but feels it would be of little value compared to what Conan Doyle could do.

5 Miscellaneous Letters

1 Letter from W. Roughead to Conan Doyle, 18 July 1912
Thanks Conan Doyle for letter and kind reference to his book on the Slater trial. Will read Conan Doyle's pamphlet with great interest and if it re-awakens the public conscience in the matter, so much the better for Slater – and his publishers! General

disbelief that the Crown were able to secure a verdict and they made no effort to prove Slater had heard of Miss Gilchrist or the jewels.

2 Letter from Innes to Conan Doyle, 25 Aug 1912
Met with the new Secretary of State for War who "is keen to know about the Oscar Slater case and acknowledges that the police are not much bothered by scruples when they have a chance of scoring a conviction."

3 Letter from Arthur Cohen to Conan Doyle, 26 Aug 1912
Points out a wrong conclusion from page 10 of Conan Doyle's "Case of Oscar Slater." Clothes lines in the majority of kitchens are made of wood and therefore would make a noise if they fell to the floor. This could explain the noise heard by the Adams'. Hopes Conan Doyle's efforts to obtain the truth will meet with the success it deserves.

4 Letter from Denham to Conan Doyle, 26 Aug 1912
Has just read Conan Doyle's note on the Slater case and as a police officer and keen student of criminology, could not resist writing. Believes there was no case against Slater, that Lambie could have been an accomplice and details how things could have happened if she was.

5 Letter from Summerville to Conan Doyle, 27 Aug 1912
Have just read pamphlet on Oscar Slater. Points out that in Glasgow and other parts of Scotland, poles are suspended from the kitchen ceiling by cords fixed to pulleys. If these fell, they would make a noise.

6 Letter from Pat L Frorbes to Conan Doyle, 29 Aug 1912
Thanks Conan Doyle for "The Case of Oscar Slater". Seems marvelous to him that Scottish Police and a Scottish jury could ever have hounded and convicted a man on such rotten evidence or rather none at all. Spent the day with Robert Little, who knows the Lord Advocate. He says he is a man who does not care for the truth if it makes an effect. His mother was terribly upset and rendered ill by the Oscar Slater speech. Asks to be kept informed of any developments in the case.

7 Letter from W.E. Berridge to Conan Doyle, 29 Aug 1912
Has just read Conan Doyle's book on Oscar Slater but can not find mention of who succeeded to Miss Gilchrist's money and jewels and therefore had a motive in her death. Also thinks the bedroom contain no blood stains because the murderer must have riffled the box and then committed the murder.

8 Letter from J. Buyers Black, Insurance expert of the Scottish insurance Bureau to Conan Doyle, 4 Sep 1912
Following Conan Doyle's letter to the 'Daily Mail' of Sep 2 1912, writes to make him aware of what is an open secret in Scotland – that the Judiciary Office in Edinburgh have proof which points to Slater being the murderer in the case known as the Whiteinch murder. Also suggests an unsolved murder in Ashton Lane could be by Slater. Is perfectly obvious to him that Slater is guilty and it was apparently so to Lord Guthrie who was one of the most human Judges in Scotland.

9 <u>Letter from F.W. Smith to Conan Doyle, 21 Oct 1912</u>
Contacted the Detective Department of the Glasgow Police Office to inform them of a third party who may have been connected to the murder and was metaphorically told to mind his own business.

10 <u>Letter from William A. Goodhart to Conan Doyle, 28 May 1914</u>
Was Counsel for Slater at the time of the extradition proceedings and has been his personal counsel for some years in America. Never doubted his innocence. Had intended to assist in the trial in 1909, but the trial was advanced and he was unable to get there. Has always seemed to him that a grave doubt existed as to the identity of Slater. "I am personally of opinion that Slater is another Dreyfus and that he has not had justice done to him and I am reasonably convinced now as I always have been, that he is an innocent man." Pleased to do any service that those in charge of his case might require. Is unable to help financially but offers his time and services.

11 <u>Letter from John Munro to Conan Doyle, 2 Feb 1925</u>
Feels that Slater is innocent and encloses some particulars which he thinks will interest Conan Doyle. Includes letters from John Munro, husband of the servant of Miss Lawrie (Miss Gilchrist's sister) to Conan Doyle, n.d. Gives facts about the Slater case – one page of points he wishes to make and one page of particulars that may be of interest. States that Miss Lawrie was threatened and feared violence from her nephew.

12 <u>Letter from J. Stoddart, Falkirk Spiritualist Society to Conan Doyle, 3 Feb 1925</u>
A circle has been sitting for communications in Falkirk. "Stephanus" told the circle where a missing document could be found, named the real criminal, the street where he lived and where the murder weapon could be found. Also maintained that Slater would not suffer the death penalty.

13 <u>Letter from Geo[rge] Ritchie, Master Mariner to Conan Doyle, 9 Feb 1925</u>
May interest Conan Doyle to know that the late Lord Guthrie believed him innocent of the crime for which was sentenced. He stated so while on a visit to Iona in the presence of several people.

14 <u>Letter from Geo[rge] Ritchie to Conan Doyle, 15 Feb 1925</u>
Is in receipt of Conan Doyle's letter which he forwarded to his brother. Says he heard of Lord Guthrie's statement that Slater was innocent from Captain McLean and there is no doubt he made such a statement.

15 <u>Letter from A.M. Ritchie to George Ritchie, 17 Feb 1925</u>
Recalls Captain McLean's interest in Lord Guthrie's comments and how he prompted Lord Guthrie when he forgot the name of one witness. He has the impression that Lord Guthrie said in his private opinion that he thought Slater to be innocent.

16 <u>Letter from Ramsay Macdonald to Conan Doyle, 15 Sep 1927</u>
Has read Park's book and wrote to the late Lord Advocate, Macmillan, to look into the matter and advise him. Is expecting to hear back any day. Has written a private and

confidential letter to Sir John Gilmour stating the case cannot rest where it is and he cannot avoid a debate in the House of Commons.

17 <u>Letter from Ramsay Macdonald to Conan Doyle, 26 Sep 1927</u>
Glad that Conan Doyle has passed on the information regarding Slater and sees it is impossible to keep the matter out of the newspapers. Has been going further into the case and is quite convinced that Slater has received a horrible injustice and he must not only be released, but also cleared. His only regret is that someone did not bring it before him earlier.

18 <u>Letter from John Gilmour to Conan Doyle, 28 Sep 1927</u>
Received Conan Doyle's letter of 27 Sep 1927 regarding the Slater case and appreciates the points he makes. The whole position is receiving his careful consideration with his advisers.

19 <u>Letter from John Lamb, Scottish Office to Conan Doyle, 3 Nov 1927</u>
Directed by the Secretary of State to acknowledge Conan Doyle's letter regarding the case of Oscar Slater and to say the representations in it will receive consideration.

20 <u>Letter from R.A. Bennett to Conan Doyle, 21 Nov 1927</u>
Believes the Government ought to make adequate monetary provision for Slater's case being placed independently before the Scottish High Court. If it is necessary to raise a 'Slater Defence Fund' it would be desirable to have a committee to satisfy the public that the money is being properly expended and accounted for. Advises Conan Doyle to send an appeal or a personal letter to all the principal papers.

21 <u>Letter from Norman Macpherson & Dunlop to Conan Doyle, 28 Nov 1927</u>
Have had several meetings with William Park and Mr Roughead. Received a letter from Slater formally asking them to act for him and have accepted his instructions. Will write to Conan Doyle with an estimate of probable costs but they will not run to anything like Conan Doyle's estimates.

22 <u>Letter from William Roughead to Conan Doyle, 5 Dec 1927</u>
Had consultation with Oscar Slater and William Park which was most satisfactory. Describes Slater as very dignified, quiet and restrained. He sustained a long and searching examination by Aitcheson who agrees with Roughead that Slater kept nothing back and should make an excellent appearance as a witness. Had to take in Mr Marcus as he pledged himself to raise funds from his co-religionists, but he will not interfere with the conduct of the case. Counsel are of opinion that there is every hope the conviction will be quashed on the proceedings at the trial.

23 <u>Letter from E.P. Phillips to Conan Doyle, 14 Dec 1927</u>
Received a letter from Slater which was a copy of one sent to Conan Doyle. Slater hopes, if the decision of the Appeal Court is favourable, to distribute a sum of money equivalent of the amount collected on his behalf to Christian and Jewish Charitable Instutions. Slater is "living and quiet and retired life and enjoying his freedom with commendable reserve."

24 Letter from Norman Macpherson & Dunlop to Conan Doyle, 28 Apr 1928
Confirms Conan Doyle's liability is not to exceed £1000.

25 Letter from E.P. Phillips to Conan Doyle, 2 May 1928
There is no foundation in the reports which have reached Conan Doyle that Slater is meeting with ex-convicts and showing ingratitude to those who have done all for him. He is friendly with a young man, Carstairs, with whom he struck up an acquaintance in prison. Phillips sees no harm in the companionship as since his release, Carstairs has made an honourable effort to redeem and rehabilitate his character. As to Slater himself, his private and public conduct has been one of meticulous care and up to now has done nothing to prejudice his case and is sure he never will.

26 Letter from Norman Macpherson & Dunlop to Conan Doyle, 20 Jul 1928
Sends Conan Doyle the opinion of the court. Only one was given which was in the opinion of all the judges and delivered to the Lord Justice General. The conviction of Slater has been quashed due to the misdirection of the presiding Judge. Congratulates Conan Doyle on the success of the gallant efforts he has made over so many years. Two distinct injuries were done to Slater – his conviction and his detention in prison. It was wrong for the Judge to misdirect the jury, resulting in conviction. If Slater was guilty, he should have been given the death sentence. Someone must have advised that there was doubt about the proceedings resulting in the commutation of the sentence to one of penal servitude.

27 Letter from Norman Macpherson & Dunlop to Conan Doyle, 30 July 1928
If Slater does not claim compensation, he will not get it and if he delays, he will probably find public sympathy has gone. If he does not claim compensation, he should at least claim expenses. Mr Aitcheson, Macpherson & Dunlop, Mr Park, Mr Roughead, Conan Doyle and Mr Marcus all need payment.

28 Letter from P.E. Baker to Conan Doyle, 13 Sept 1929
Refers to clipping from a local newspaper and says "that in using the term, 'ungrateful dog', you really flatter Slater. As the owner of a well-bred dog, I cannot conceive how, even a mongrel dog, would be as undeserving as this. As I believe the common rat has yet to be proven of any real value to humanity, whereas, dogs have it, it might be more appropriate to use the term, 'Dirty Rat'."

29 Letter from Anthony Clyne to Conan Doyle, 14 Sep 1929
Advises Conan Doyle not to allow the costs dispute to blunt his enthusiasm for right and justice. "That I disagree so flatly with your views on various subjects should make my assurance more convincing."

30 Letter from Greenburg to Conan Doyle, 16 Sep 1929
Is very perturbed that Conan Doyle has taken action against Slater for money Conan Doyle guaranteed for Slater's appeal costs. Greenburg wrote and suggested that he would endeavour to collect the £300 through the Jewish Chronicle and thought Conan Doyle would do nothing further until he had given them the opportunity. The very bad

feeling between Conan Doyle and Slater is a sorry ending to what was something of a noble and successful endeavour.

31 Letter from Robertson, Chalmers, Auld & Hunter to Messrs. Oswald Hickson, Collier & Co., 20 Sep 1929
Sir Arthur Conan Doyle v Slater was not called yesterday and will now be called on 15 Oct 1929. Tells them to inform Conan Doyle that it is almost certain he will not go to Edinburgh to prove the case as in view of the evidence, it is impossible for Slater to put up a defence.

32 Letter from Lindsay C. Steele to Robertson Chalmers & Co., 11 Oct 1929
Regarding the disagreement between Conan Doyle and Slater over the payment of £250. Lindsay C. Steele had been in a position to pay the £250 as soon as he received it from Messrs J.W. & J. Mackenzie. Conan Doyle's comments on Slater's character and stating publicly that he was "an ungrateful dog and a liar" have wounded Slater's feelings and requests Conan Doyle to withdraw summons and arrestments and to tender an apology for the slanderous statement. If do not receive satisfactory reply, has instructions to proceed with an action with damages for the slanderous statements made by Conan Doyle and also against the newspapers who published them.

33 Letter from Robertson Chalmers & Co. to Messrs. Oswald Hickson, Collier & Co., 14 Oct 1929
Conan Doyle is abroad but presume that Messrs. Oswald Hickson, Collier & Co. agree to proceed with the action against Slater as Lindsay C. Steele made no personal assurance to pay the money. Publicity after the action was nothing to do with Conan Doyle or themselves. He seems only concerned with raising a fresh action against Conan Doyle for slander.

34 Letter from Norman M. Macpherson, of Norman Macpherson & Dunlop to Conan Doyle, 16 Oct 1929
Emphatically denies either he or Mr Dunlop did anything to prejudice Conan Doyle's claim against Slater. Asks Conan Doyle to refrain from using their name when communicating with the press.

35 Letter from L.I. Reade to Conan Doyle, 23 Oct 1929
Has just returned from France and sees some of the newspapers which discusses Conan Doyle's action against Slater. Was astonished at some of the statements Conan Doyle was purported to have made. Is sorry that he was given no help with his efforts last year to obtain adequate compensation for Slater as if he had, he may have succeeded and all this most unsavoury quarrel and litigation may have been prevented.

36 Receipt for £25 given by Conan Doyle to William Park for expenses incurred in connection with the defence of Oscar Slater, n.d.

37 Account for the Oscar Slater Appeal Fund for 1928 showing amount received by the Jewish Chronicle and paid to Messrs. Norman Macpherson & Dunlop (£673.10.3).

38 Copies of fifteen pieces of evidence from the Slater Case:
1 Report of the murder
2 Statement of Miss Margaret Birrell
3 Description of man leaving the close to Miss Gilchrist's, with note by Trench
4 Statement by Allan McLean, cycle dealer
5 Statement of William Powell, Detective Inspector
6 Wanted statement for Oscar Slater
7 Statement of Thomas Anderson, Detective Officer
8 Telegram from 'Devoir', Liverpool to Chief Constable, Glasgow
9 Telegram from 'Devoir', Liverpool to Chief Constable, Glasgow
10 Statements of Detective Chief Inspector Duckworth and Detective Sub Inspector Bell, Liverpool City Police
11 Statement of Mary Cooper and Catherine Fitzpatrick
12 Statement of Mary Barrowman
13 Statement of John Cameron
14 Statement of William Gordon
15 Statement of Colin McCallum

39 Photograph of entry in Trench's diary showing visit he made to interview Miss Birrell, Wed 23 (Dec 1908)

40 Essay by Gerald Newman, fellow inmate of Peterhead Prison, n.d. "The Soul-wracked case of Oscar Slater from Persecution and False Imprisonment Good Lord Deliver Me."

41 Essay by Gerald Newman, fellow inmate of Peterhead Prison, n.d. "Why is Oscar Slater kept in Prison by one who knew him."

42 List of contributions to the Oscar Slater Fund, n.d.

6 Press Cuttings

1 'Glasgow Evening News', 26 Aug 1912 (letter dated 17 Aug 1912)
Letters to the Editor
The Slater Case (regarding Slater's tickets to Liverpool/London)

2 'The Spectator', 25 Jul 1914
Letters to the Editor
The Oscar Slater Case

3 'Jewish Word', 29 July 1914
The Case of Oscar Slater
4 'Weekly News', 3 Oct 1914
"A disgraceful business"
Sir Conan Doyle says Trench Case
Reminds him of Dreyfus persecution
Scottish Secretary and his "personal honour"

5 'Sunday Mail and record', 13 Apr 1919
Was Oscar Slater guilty of murder?
Strong adverse comments by eminent men
Sir Arthur Conan Doyle's views

6 'Empire News', 27 Apr 1924
Oscar Slater's Own Story
Changed names and the fatality of a brooch

7 'Empire News', 4 May 1924
Oscar Slater's Story of a Night Journey to Liverpool

8 'World's Pictorial News', 10 May 1924
The Case of Lieutenant [Trench]
Detective broken by Oscar Slater Trial

9 'Empire News', 13 Apr 1924
In meshes of suspicion
Sir Arthur Conan Doyle and Oscar Slater Case
Oscar Slater's Own Story
Specially compiled from private documents
Oscar Slater and the Net of Suspicion

10 'Empire News' 8 Feb 1925
Why Slater is not released
Declaration after a thorough investigation of the mystery

11 'Sunday Express', 8 Feb 1925
Convict's Appeal to Conan Doyle
Why Slater is unlikely to be freed

12 'World's Pictorial News', 29 Mar 1925
Oscar Slater's hard life in Peterhead Prison
Crushed by the Refusal of Freedom

13 'Empire News', 28 Mar 1925
New document in Slater case
Revelation of another grave blunder in famous crime trial
Warrant granted under a false assumption

14 'Empire News', 28 Mar 1926
New witness for Slater
Prepared to give evidence on oath at inquiry
"Not same man"
Miscarriage of justice says Sir A Conan Doyle

15 'Empire News', 4 Apr 1926
Who killed Marion Gilchrist?
Blunder of a Brooch
How first theory against Slater was shattered. Visits of Lieutenant Trench

16 'Empire News', 11 Apr 1926
The New Witness in Slater Case
Call for release and full enquiry
Truth on the 'Empire News' Evidence
Weakness of Crown Case

17 'Empire News', 18 Apr 1926
Appeal demand in Slater case
Secret police document and the warning about two men
Girl who changed her view on Liner trip

18 'World's Pictorial News', 19 Apr 1926
Oscar Slater's Own Stories, and a message
Relatives eager to receive him in Germany if released

19 'Word's Pictorial News', 2 Jan 1927
Latest Prison interview with Oscar Slater
Hope abandoned by "thug" under life sentence
Two attempts at suicide
 Renewed petitions on ground of injustice
Already served his full term

20 'Empire News', 7 Aug 1927
[Disclo]sure of official d[ocuments]
Determination to fix the guilt on suspect: how the Lord Advocate and others were misled

21 'Daily Telegraph', 14 Sep 1927
Oscar Slater's Costs
Sir A Conan Doyle explains "I am terribly disappointed"

22 'Daily News', 24 Oct 1927
Oscar Slater
 Support for 'Daily News' Inquiry Demand
It was not Slater
Former Maid who identified him
Her alleged admission
Restitution
Sir A Conan Doyle on the next steps

23 'Empire News', 30 Oct 1927
Secret document in the Slater Case

Persons of 'Social Standing' involved: What inquiry would mean

24 'Empire News', 13 Nov 1927
Who did murder Miss Marion Gilchrist?
Name of a suspect given by a woman? – analysis of the motive

25 'The Daily News', 14 Nov 1927
There must be an inquiry

26 Unknown newspaper, n.d. (c. Nov 1927)
Oscar Slater
Release from prison this week
Inquiry demand
Conan Doyle's appeal to popular feeling
The farce of 1914
Public opinion roused
A campaign in Scotland

27 'Yorkshire Telegraph and Star', 6 May 1929
Slater Case
Reply to Sir A Conan Doyle
Paying of costs

28 'Evening News', 13 Sep 1929
Sir A Conan Doyle and Oscar Slater
"I worked 18 years for him – for abuse"
Cigars and Brighton

29 'The Daily Telegraph', 13 Sep 1929
Oscar Slater Costs Appeal
Sir A Conan Doyle's £1000 Guarantee
Legal step to recover large sum

30 'Daily Express', 13 sep 1929
Sir A Conan Doyle's claim on Slater
Legal action to recover £300 advance
Appeal costs
"The ungrateful man will not pay"

31 'The Yorkshire Herald', 13 Sep 1929
Echo of the Slater appeal case
Recovery of expenses
Sir A Conan Doyle's reported action

32 'The Star', 13 Sep 1929
Slater's Retort to Sir A Conan Doyle
No reply to "insults"

"Beneath the dignity of Oscar Slater"
Contesting Claim
Income tax worries at Brighton

33 'Evening Standard', 13 Sep 1929
Sir A Conan Doyle and Oscar Slater
Author says "I don't want presents from him"
Cigar-Cutter returned
"I would rather have my £300 paid"

34 'The Daily Mail', 14 Sep 1929
Sir A Conan Doyle's Challenge to Oscar Slater
"Publish our letters"
New statements in quarrel over £250
Lively exchanges

35 'Evening Standard', 14 Sep 1929
"When I fight him"
Oscar Slater on Sir A Conan Doyle's Claim
Two versions of £3
Author claims he kept the gift secret

36 'Liverpool Post and Mercury', 14 Sep 1929
A Strange Business – claims Government should have paid expenses and given more compensation

37 'City and East London Observer', 21 Sep 1929
(No headline) – latest development of the Oscar Slater case – dispute between Conan Doyle and Oscar Slater over costs

38 'Empire News', 22 Sep 1929
A New Slater Statement
Sir A Conan Doyle's Garbled Letter
"Absolutely False"

39 'Daily Telegraph', 18 Oct 1929
Oscar Slater
Sir Arthur Conan Doyle Enters Action

40 'Truth', n.d.
The Conviction of Oscar Slater

41 'Daily record', n.d.
Oscar Slater's Case
Mysterious Cable to New York Police
Probing of the false clue

42 Unknown newspaper, n.d.
Helen L[ambie]
Why I believe I blundered over Slater!
Sensational statements by Helen Lambie. What the police said
Truth about parade
"This marks end of the case"
Enormous importance of statement

43 Unknown newspaper (city edition), n.d.
"Mr M'Kinnon Wood has nothing to say!"
Glasgow Magistrates' views on the Trench case
Chief Constable and Scottish Secretary's letter

Chapter 29

The Latest Sherlock Holmes Films – Boxing Day 2009 & Christmas 2011

Daily Mail, Friday, October 3, 2008

Watch out for…by **Baz Bamigboye**

Elocutionary, Dr Watson

GUY RITCHIE has assembled a thoroughly British cast for his Sherlock Holmes movie.

But what, you might well ask, about Robert Downey Jr, the all-American star who plays Holmes?

'His accent is perfect!' Kelly Reilly insisted. Kelly plays Mary, the girlfriend of Dr Watson (Jude Law) in Sherlock Holmes, as the film is simply entitled.

'Remember Chaplin?' Kelly said, referring to Downey Jr's performance in the Richard Attenborough film. His impressive portrayal of the little tramp landed him a best actor Academy Award nomination.

'At the cast read-through, Robert's British accent was as good Sherlock I remember thinking: "He's got a Brit inside him, that man,"' Kelly laughed.

After being terrified in the stark thriller Eden Lake, Kelly's happy to be out of harm's way in Sherlock Holmes.

It's Downey Jr and Law who will face most of the danger when they confront the film's 'baddie' played by Mark Strong. Rachel McAdam has the main female part of Irene Adler, who enjoys a tempestuous relationship with the detective from Baker Street.

Eddie Marsan, James Fox and Hans Matheson are also in the film, which is now in production.

Gary Dexter

THE DAILY TELEGRAPH Saturday, February 14, 2009

Mandrake Tim Walker
A good Guy when the going is tough

While his marriage to **Madonna** was coming to an end as he directed his *Sherlock Holmes* film starring **Robert Downey Jr**, Guy Ritchie showed considerable grace under pressure.

"For one scene the stage hands had to mock up the massive hull of a ship at Chatham Docks," whispers my man with the clapperboard. "It was a tough, dirty job involving a lot of black paint. When they'd finished, Guy arranged for everyone involved to get a fleece jacket emblazoned with the words *Sherlock Holmes*. There was a flat cap too – just like Mr Ritchie wears. "They were lucky they didn't get deer stalkers."

THE DAILY TELEGRAPH THURSDAY, AUGUST 6, 2009

MANDRAKE BY TIM WALKER

Strange case of Sherlock Holmes, Dr Watson and a shared bed

While no one could have any doubts about where **Jude Law's** sexual interests lie in real life, the Watson that the actor plays to **Robert Downey Jnr's** Holmes in **Guy Ritchie's** film about the great sleuth has already set tongues wagging.

Reports from the set of *Sherlock Holmes* have suggested that the two residents of 221b Baker Street are portrayed very much as an item and even share a bed. This has alarmed the literary estate of **Sir Arthur Conan Doyle**, which guards the late author's most famous creation jealously. **Andrea Plunket**, the estate's manager, assures me she kept a close eye on things. "The suggestion that Holmes and Watson are portrayed as gay is a downright lie," she says.

I recall the late **Dame Jean Conan Doyle** telling me that her father made the two protagonists male to help "take his mind off sex". Sir Arthur had fallen in love with her mother, **Jean Leckie**, as his first wife, **Louise**, was dying of TB. Sir Arthur behaved impeccably, and it was only a year after his bereavement that he allowed himself to marry Miss Leckie. And think about sex again.

The Sunday Telegraph *Seven* **Magazine** 01.11.09

Christmas culture planner

From the Coen Brothers' latest to *The Snowman* on stage, we present an indispensable guide to the best of the rest of 2009. Compiled by Lucinda Everett.

FILM Will Guy Ritchie's take on Sherlock Holmes, starring Robert Downey Jr as Holmes and Jude Law as Watson, be a load of old cobblers?

The Sunday Telegraph/NOVEMBER 8 2009

To the Editor

A load of cobblers

SIR – "Will Guy Ritchie's take on Sherlock Holmes be a load of old cobblers?" asks *Seven's* Christmas culture planner (November 1). Of course it will: we need look no further than trailer stills showing Robert Downey Jr and Jude Law sporting designer stubble.

Late Victorian gentlemen were either bewhiskered or clean-shaven. Indeed, Holmes was able to deduce the position Watson stood in relation to the morning light coming through his window because of the "positively slovenly" state of one side of his imperfectly shaven chin.

Because film scriptwriters inevitably and wrongly think they can come up with stories and characters better than Conan Doyle's manifestations of Holmes on wide screen, in contrast to some fine renditions on radio and television, have ranged from garbled to nonsensical, Guy Ritchie's effort looks as though it will be at the far end of that spectrum.

Andy Connell
Appleby, Cumbria

THE DAILY TELEGRAPH Friday, December 11, 2009

Jude Law: the all-action Dr Watson
He wowed Broadway with his Hamlet – now Jude Law plays Sherlock Holmes's sidekick in a way never seen before. He talks to **John Hiscock**.

Jude Law is almost running on empty. When I speak to him he is nearing the end of a gruelling, but highly successful, three-month run in *Hamlet* on Broadway, following three months in the West End. He fears for his voice and is calling on deep energy reserves to keep him going. By the time he finishes his run he will have done 200 shows without a break of more than a day, spending six and a half hours on stage on Wednesday and Saturday matinee days.

Fortunately, he was at peak fitness when he took the role, having trained for four months, mainly in the boxing ring in preparation for playing Dr Watson to Robert Downey Jr's Sherlock Holmes in Guy Ritchie's all-action version of the adventures of

Sir Arthur Conan Doyle's detective. With a budget approaching £100 million, if it finds an audience, *Sherlock Holmes* is clearly destined by Warner Bros to be the first in a series of adventures featuring the reimagined 19th-century sleuth and his combative sidekick.

Fans' reaction on the internet has been sharply divided over Ritchie's vision of Holmes and Watson as brawling, two-fisted action heroes, dodging fireballs and inflicting brutal beatings on London's criminal classes, as they combat a sinister black magician. Law, however, sees his Watson as nearer the character created by Conan Doyle than the bumbling sidekick portrayed by Nigel Bruce to Basil Rathbone's Holmes in the Forties series of films.

"One of the dynamics missing from the earlier film interpretations was a more accurate representation of Watson," he says, although he admits he was a stranger to the books until he started work on the film. "I used to watch a television series in England with Jeremy Brett as Holmes and David Burke playing Dr Watson, but I never read the books. But once I'd read the script and started looking into the books, and then met Guy and Robert, I realised it was an opportunity to bring a new perspective to a character who has been so often portrayed slightly incorrectly."

Law, 36, is cheerful and upbeat as he settles into a chair in New York's Four Seasons hotel. One condition of his agreeing to an interview was that there were to be no personal questions, meaning he did not want to be asked about the break-up of his six-year marriage to actress Sadie Frost, his affair with the family nanny, his romance with his *Alfie* co-star Sienna Miller and the birth two months ago of a daughter to model Samantha Burke, whom the actor met on the set of *Sherlock Holmes* and with whom he had a brief fling.

Apart from his looks, image and reputation, Jude Law comes across as the most un-star like of film stars.

"I don't want to get to an age where I look back and say, 'Oh, I never did that,'" he says. "That was in my mind when I first met Robert Downey and I wanted to work with him, and so I said I'd do *Sherlock Holmes*. Two days later, I thought, "What am I doing? I'm going to play Dr Watson and this is insane because is it really what I want to do? Luckily, it evolved into a wonderful experience, but initially it was because of the reaction I had to Robert Downey and loving him as a man and the way he talked about how he was going to work. "The same thing applied when Ken Branagh asked me to play Hamlet (Branagh later pulled out.) He knows his Shakespeare and he knows his stuff. If he thinks I can do it, then I'll do it.' But after I'd said yes, I suddenly thought, 'Am I crazy? I'm going to be pulled to pieces for doing this and it's going to be two years of very, very hard work.' But it's fear. Fear and the challenge is what drives me." That Guy Ritchie's record as a director since *Lock, Stock and Two Smoking Barrels* is somewhat spotty did not deter him. "I thought it was a clever twist to take a man known for his modern, punchy, almost street films and apply him to the somewhat staid Holmes legacy," he says.

"Watson's just come back from the Afghan war, where he was awarded a medal of honour and there's no mention in the stories of him being bumbling or stupid. That came about in the Basil Rathbone movies because Rathbone wanted a comic actor to play opposite him so that he looked more important. I liked the opportunity of bringing back some of the more accurate and edgy qualities. I suppose we injected a slightly more energetic and visceral quality to their investigations."

Law is now in the enviable position for British actors of being able to choose his roles. Since he joined the National Youth Music Theatre at the age of 12, where he played the lead in *Joseph and the Amazing Technicolour Dreamcoat*, and from inauspicious beginnings as a car-stealing kid in the 1994 film *Shopping*, he weathered a string of bad films before his decadent playboy in Anthony Minghella's *The Talented Mr Ripley* brought Hollywood attention and an Oscar nomination. His second film with Minghella, *Cold Mountain*, won another Oscar nomination.

Prone in the past to periods of anxiety and self-doubt, he has satisfactorily answered his own questions about his acting abilities.

When his *Hamlet* run finishes he is looking forward to resting his voice and moving into the house he has bought in the country just outside London. He has a movie he has made before *Sherlock Holmes*, *Repo Men*, awaiting release and there is the possibility of a *Sherlock Holmes* sequel in the future but the obvious question is: what do you do after you've played Hamlet on Broadway?

"It's been on my mind quite a lot," he confesses, "because this is everything I could have wished for in a role and there is a part of me that thinks, "How will anything match this?' There are other Shakespearean roles that I really want to play and Ian McKellen said to me that the best thing to do is to look at the ones that you're getting to old to play, so there are roles like Henry V.

"A more optimistic way of looking at it is that with *Hamlet* behind me, once I've had a chance to recoup, having done something so great I might feel free to do slightly lighter and not so intense fare. I think it would be a mistake to want a bigger challenge. That would be when I would maybe make the wrong decision. But when you're in the middle of it it's really hard to know how you are going to feel once it's over. So I'll just have to wait and see."

'Sherlock Holmes' is released on Monday.

TELEGRAPH MAGAZINE 12 December 2009

PIPE DREAMS

The true nature of Guy Ritchie's new film, in which Sherlock Holmes is reinvented as a Victorian 007, remains something of a mystery. **Chloe Fox** goes behind the scenes to investigate. Photographs by **Alex Bailey**.

Judging by the number of hats worn by both cast and crew, on the set of *Sherlock Holmes*, this could only be a Guy Ritchie film. The setting is a disused ceramics factory in Shoreditch, London, transformed for the purposes of today's filming into a steamy, stinking 19th century pork slaughterhouse where Holmes and Dr Watson, played by Robert Downey Jr and Jude Law, are attempting to rescue a terrified woman from being flayed alive. Ritchie himself, in the midst of his divorce from Madonna and keeping a low profile behind the monitors, is in his trademark flat cap, while Downey Jr (and his stunt double) are sporting slightly puffier, more Victorian versions. Law is in some sort of trilby, while various members of the crew are wearing full-blown fedoras. Susan Downey, Robert's wife and the film's main producer, has opted for a modern fur-lined take on the deerstalker, the hat most commonly associated with Sherlock Holmes himself.

Since Holmes first appeared in print in 1887, Sir Arthur Conan Doyle's detective has imprinted himself on our cultural fabric – thanks in no small part to cinema. Holmes is listed in the *Guinness Book of World Records* as 'the most portrayed character', with more than 70 actors having played the part in at least 200 films. Over time, Conan Doyle's character has been eroded and the Holmes we think of is more likely to be the one portrayed by Basil Rathbone in the 14 films made by Universal Pictures between 1939 and 1946. It is this image that endures: an uptight, acerbic character ('Elementary, my dear Watson') with cloak, deerstalker and pipe.

Guy Ritchie has other plans.

'What you've got going on with our movie is a complete reinvention process of an iconic figure,' he says. 'We have gone back to the books themselves. In them, Holmes is a very compelling here: an inquisitive, tortured, complex genius, who is also an action man.' Ritchie's Holmes won't be seen wearing a deerstalker or Inverness tweed (neither of which he wore with any regularity in the books) – sometimes he won't be wearing a shirt at all. This Holmes will be a quick-witted, fleet-footed chaser, shooter and pummeller of criminals, a bare-knuckle boxer with an impish intelligence. 'Like James Bond in 1891,' according to Joel Silver, one of the film's nine producers.

That very little is known about Ritchie's film only adds to the hype. Even the plot is being kept largely under wraps. It is an original story – an amalgamation of elements from different books and something new – that sees Holmes and Watson trying to defeat Lord Blackwood (Mark Strong), an Aleister Crowley-esque character whose dealings with the occult see him hanged for murder – only to return from the dead. No Hollywood film would be complete without a smattering of beautiful women, thus the starlet-of-the-moment Rachel McAdams plays Irene Adler, the only woman ever to have got the better of Holmes, while Kelly Reilly plays Watson's love interest, Mary Morstan.

Sherlock Holmes potentially has the word 'franchise' written all over it: the A-list leading man (recently reinvented as an action hero with *Iron Man*) the Christmas release date, the toy action figures in production. There is talk already of a sequel. 'We hope there will be elements of Indiana Jones, *Pirates of the Caribbean*, Bond to a certain extent, 'Susan Downey says. 'We are not making a stuffy, period movie. We are making something really big and really fun.'

For the British-born writer and producer Lionel Wigram, Holmes has always had a modern relevance. 'As well as being heroic, he is very vulnerable, with all sorts of mental issues. His brain is his superpower, but it is also his curse; his mind can turn on him and lead him to be self-destructive. He is the kind of man who is happy to spend two weeks lying on a sofa playing the violin in between cases, and it felt to me like there was a way of expressing what he is in a modern way, in a way we hadn't seen before in other movies.

It took Wigram, an executive producer on the two most recent Harry Potter films, six months to work out the story and concept, along with the comicbook artist John Watkiss. Together they came up with a graphic novel which Wigram then took to Warner Brothers. In his original pitch, as an expression of how fresh he felt it could be, Wigram described his idea as a 'Guy Ritchie version of a Sherlock Holmes story'. From there, serendipity seemed to come into play. Susan Downey, who had just produced

Ritchie's *RocknRolla* for Warner, brought him in for meetings and Ritchie needed little persuasion.

'I was sent to boarding school between the ages of six and nine,' Ritchie says. 'Looking back, there was not a lot to recommend the experience, except for the bedtime stories we used to get if we were good.' Then, the children would be allowed to listen to audio tapes in their dormitory at bedtime. There were only two options: 20,000 *Leagues Under the Sea* or Sherlock Holmes. 'Holmes was by far the best,' Ritchie says. 'Plus, it was an audio story not a visual story so I got to develop my own ideas about who he would be.'

Originally, Ritchie wanted to make a film about Holmes as a young man, in the vein of *Batman Begins*, positioning somewhere between adulthood and the teenage Holmes of Barry Levinson's *The Young Sherlock Holmes*. But then, during a friendly discussion with Downey Jr about how best to reinvent an iconic figure, the two men engaged in a debate about where the character should go. 'Eventually, I just turned to Robert and said, "Why don't you play him?"' Ritchie says.

'I loved the idea of working with Guy, who brings on energy to the table that is very exciting,' Downey Jr drawls during a break from filming, spent eating a macrobiotic lunch with Law in the basement of a chair shop across the road from the location. 'I also couldn't resist the challenge of working on something that, even before we started, was somehow bigger than us. I found that prospect very humbling. I also found it very invigorating.'

With Downey Jr on board, the characterisation crystallised. Like the Holmes in the pages of Conan Doyle's books, Downey Jr has a mind that seems to run ahead of itself. He too has known what it is to battle internal daemons; his having taken him to prison and rehabilitation centres over the years. 'Holmes is the archetype of the tortured perfectionist,' Downey Jr says.

A honed and healthy 44, Downey Jr has also become something of an action man, deft at ashtanga yoga and the fast-paced aggressive Chinese martial art of wing chun. 'I seem to be returning to the warrior part of myself,' he smiles. 'On this set, the juices have been really flowing.'

For Downey Jr, who does as many of his own stunts as he can, there have been regular yoga sessions on set with various members of the cast and crew, including Ritchie himself. 'Oh yes, there were all the Hollywood trappings,' laughs the English production designer Sarah Greenwood. Fresh from working with Downey Jr on Joe Wright's *The Soloist*, Greenwood was unfazed. Less so, perhaps, than those of us who waited a good few hours for some interview time with Rachel McAdams, only to discover she had been delayed by a much-needed massage. 'Guy is the master of the chin-up,' she eventually confides, when asked what it was like working with Ritchie. 'There are chin-up bars all over the set.

For Greenwood, beneath the Hollywood trappings lay a lot of hard work. 'Initially, it felt like a very tricky brief,' she says. 'Well, how do you reinvent the wheel?' Above all else, her job was to make the film look and feel real. 'I was, as I always am, obsessed with detail.' Thus, during the 12 weeks of pre-production, Greenwood and her team saturated themselves with thousands of images from the period and trawled every corner of the country for locations. Their list was clear enough: a dockyard, a slaughterhouse, an office in the Houses of Parliament, Piccadilly Circus and Tower Bridge (under construction) *circa* 1891, a crypt underneath St. Paul's, 221b Baker Street. 'Overall, it wasn't quite girly enough for my liking,' Greenwood laughs. 'No pretty stately homes or anything. I only got one feminine fix and that Irene Adler's bedroom at Cliveden.

For the most part Greenwood was too 'manic' to notice where they were. 'I've never worked on a scale like this before. The budget seems neverending. We were never on a set – whether it was in London, Liverpool or Manchester – for more than three days. Our last location was in New York, where we filmed the interior shots of Baker Street and the Punchbowl Pub [a reference to the pub Ritchie owns in Mayfair] and built the top of Tower Bridge for the film's denouement. For those scenes, we had to ship over the props, because they didn't have anything English enough available in the States.'

'It was ridiculously hard work,' agrees the costume designer Jenny Beavan, who had to make so many costumes so quickly that she employed several buyers whose sole task was to scour the country for fabric. When she was first developing Holmes's look, Beavan went back to her *Byron* rail (left over from the 2003 BBC film starring Jonny Lee Miller). One particular item stood out: a black, ribbed velvet jacket, which had overtones of Vivienne Westwood-esque romanticism – 'the type you might have seen on a Rolling Stones album cover *circa* 1970.' Most importantly for her, the fitting-room relationship with Downey Jr was a collaborative one. 'He knew exactly what he wanted, down to the shape of his shirt.'

'Robert is one of the very few actors that I would take direction from,' says Greenwood, who has twice been nominated for an Oscar. Thus, when after two weeks' dressing the Baker Street set he walked in and declared it too tidy and in need of a sense of chaos and filth, she and the team obliged.

For Greenwood, as for so many, the casting of Jude Law was initially baffling. 'He came on board quite late on in the process and we all just said, "What?"', she says. Guy Ritchie, however, was in no doubt. 'I really, really wanted to get away from the idea of a stodgy, subservient Watson,' he explains. 'I wanted him to be a handsome, debonair and worthy sidekick to Holmes; a Sundance to his Butch, if you like.' He didn't have to look far for justification. 'In the books, Watson is a handsome, dashing military surgeon, stick-thin and nut-brown and just back from the Afghan War,' Wigram says.

For Law himself – whose first television job, aged 19, was a small role in the 1991 BBC Sherlock Holmes series starring Jeremy Brett – the role appealed on every level, not least in the opportunity it provided to immerse himself in the research process. 'Overnight, I became a big Conan Doyle fan,' he says. 'I went into the project thinking I was clear on who or what the character of Watson was and then I read the books and realised that there was a whole volume of stuff that I could put into this character and this partnership that had never really been explored before.'

'Jude and Robert have an incredible chemistry on set,' Rachel McAdams says. 'Their sense of fun and enthusiasm for the project is absolutely infectious.' They do look the perfect double act, laughing between takes, but they also huddle intensely with Ritchie, their third musketeer, to discuss a scene. 'For a while, we were working seven days a week,' Law says. 'On the days we weren't filming, we were buffing the script, watching stuff back, boning and perfecting the work.'

For Ritchie, who until the comparative success of *RocknRolla* last year had not had a hit on his hands since *Snatch* in 2000, *Sherlock Holmes* has been a high-pressure project. 'This is going to be very different from the movies I've made in the past,' he says cautiously. 'For a start, it has a linear narrative, whereas every film I've made before has had a multiple narrative.'

'Of course, we wanted Guy's dynamic energy but we didn't want it to be modern or anachronistic in any way,' Susan Downey adds. 'It won't be frenetic, except in the scenes that require it. In fact, Guy has shown a lot of restraint; a restraint appropriate to a period movie.'

'Sometimes I think about the pressure, and I can't even go there to be honest,' Ritchie says. 'In the end, whenever I'm making a movie, I think, what will people want to see? I hope I've achieved that. At the very least, I hope they come out of the cinema feeling like they've been taken on a good ride.'

'Sherlock Holmes' is released on Boxing Day

The Sunday Telegraph DECEMBER 13 2009

MANDRAKE BY RICHARD EDEN
Elementary role

JUDE LAW, who plays Dr Watson in Guy Ritchie's new film *Sherlock Holmes*, said last week that he used to watch a television series about the fictional detective.

The actor, 36, who portrays Watson as a rugged action hero, was, perhaps too shy to mention that he did more than watch the series. Mandrake recalls that he appeared in a 1991 episode in which he played a cross-dressing servant.

THE DAILY TELEGRAPH FRIDAY, DECEMBER 18, 2009

Film **Crash, bang, Watson** Guy Ritchie takes on Sherlock Holmes

Elemental, my dear Watson

Guy Ritchie spins a flashy, thunderous, all-action blockbuster around the Victorian super-sleuth and his sidekick.
Review by **Tim Robey SHERLOCK HOLMES**

There's an eccentric touch in the end credits for Guy Ritchie's *Sherlock Holmes*. They're beautifully done, freeze-framing all the proceeding mayhem into elegant graphic stills to recall Sidney Paget's original magazine illustrations. Then up pops the page for the movie's literary source – credited to "the late Sir Arthur Conan Doyle". How late can you get? Watching the pumped-up Victorian buddy movie, Doyle might have wondered what mad century he'd stepped into. You'll look in vain for a deerstalker on the head of Robert Downey Jr's Holmes. In the first scene he's busy cracking ribs. This Sherlock, we quickly discover, is a bare-knuckle boxer and man of action, whose phenomenal skills of amateur sleuthing are a virtual sideshow. Downey spends half the film stripped to the waist, diving away from explosions and repelling a 7ft French goon by bouncing hammers off his chest.

You can add a big dose of Captain Jack Sparrow raffishness: at one point Downey is tied naked to a pair of bedposts, which is not a pose we'd have often wanted from Peter Cushing.

Thanks to Downey, and thanks in surprising part to Ritchie, it's a totally enjoyable spin on the character – he's a slovenly headcase who can't look after himself, not an opium addict but neurotic, perma-bantering student of crime and combat. Jude Law's pally Watson – a definite plus – is essentially Danny Glover in *Lethal Weapon*, the stolidly reliable, long-suffering foil to his friend's quicksilver brilliance. Together, they confront the case of Aleister Crowley-ish serial killer called Lord Blackwood (Mark Strong, with a wonky front tooth), who is caught, sent to the gallows, pronounced dead, and then does a dastardly Lazarus routine.

With the help of a wicked bunch of Freemasons, his even more dastardly idea of Parliamentary reform is to introduce poison gas into the House – that'll teach them for the moats and duck houses.

The challenge here is finding any time for detection at all, in a movie so brusquely determined to power its way from one crash-bang-wallop set piece to the next. Three minor characters are killed off somewhere in the middle, less for any crucial plot purpose than to provide Holmes with some locked-room riddles to solve: Downey turns up, fondles a few clues, and then waits to the very end to tell us what they all mean. In each case, the puzzles are less ingenious than Sarah Greenwood's production design, which is just fantastic – a definite high point in the recent vogue for comic-book Victoriana.

As usual, Ritchie overdoes the flash; there's hardly a scene he doesn't want to edit back to front, and the opening sequence of Blackwood's capture, which he intends to feel like the overblown finale of a previous case, doesn't work at all. Still, it's fun flash, on the whole: powered by Hans Zimmer's antic score, the movie has a restless, try-it-on quality that keeps you on your toes.

Rachel McAdams, as American *femme fatale* Irene Adler, feels like very pretty window-dressing, because the script never decides what to do with her beyond setting up the shadowy sequel-hinting presence of an accomplice called Moriarty. Too often she and Law are competing for scenes. We want more Law! But that's a fairly sure sign this droll blockbuster has got you on its side.

Telegraph Rating *** out of five

Daily Mail, Friday, December 18, 2009

it's Friday!

Sherlock with a six-pack

Forget deerstalkers and pipes – Guy Ritchie's Holmes is a ruthless, brawling Victorian superhero who lives in squalor. And as for his friendship with Dr Watson…pass the smelling salts.

By **Michael Hellicar**

WE ALL have a mental picture of Sherlock Holmes in his deerstalker hat and heavy tweed cape, puffing on a Meerschaum pipe.

'Elementary, my dear Watson,' he loftily tells his confused sidekick as he uses his formidable powers of deduction to solve yet another case that has baffled Scotland Yard's finest.

But that's a caricature of the idiosyncratic Holmes – and a quotation – that never sprang from the pen of his creator, Sir Arthur Conan Doyle.

It is an image that has developed after more than 200 film and TV portrayals of the world's best-known fictional detective – with more than 70 actors having played him, from the suave Basil Rathbone to the thoughtful Jeremy Brett.

Anyone expecting to see the usual iconic image when Guy Ritchie brings his interpretation of Sherlock Holmes to the cinema screen on Boxing Day is in for a surprise.

For Holmes, played by Robert Downey Jr, has been rebooted and suited – when he's not stripped to the waist and showing off a six-pack. 'It's an adventure story,' says Downey. 'Holmes gets physical, down and dirty, and may the best man win.

'Inside that body, streaked with mud and sweat, is a ruthless fighting machine.'

'He's the superhero of the Victorian age. The James Bond of the 1890s. The first Bohemian martial arts fighter. He was solving dastardly crimes years before Miss Marple and Hercule Poirot were born.

'When I first read the script, I thought this is a fresh take on an old character, but then I read all the original stories and realised this is how Conan Doyle had envisaged Holmes all along.'

Says Ritchie: 'We show Holmes as a man with a brilliant mind, but a flawed personality. He's not the cool, languid figure of previous movies, but a tortured genius and a very complex man. He's lazy and can spend weeks just lounging around on his sofa.

'He's untidy, disorganised, scruffy and tends to depression. He's even got a personal hygiene problem, and is never comfortable in the company of women.'

According to Conan Doyle, Holmes staves off boredom with a seven per cent solution of cocaine in water, but this habit is only hinted at in the film.

Downey himself has had well-documented drug problems that have sent him to prison and rehab, but he told me this week that unlike Holmes, he didn't turn to narcotics through boredom.

'That was never really my relationship,' he said. But I can relate to Holmes through a shared restlessness and a hate of stagnation.'

ADDS Ritchie: 'When it comes to observation and deduction, there's no sharper eye or keener mind than Sherlock's. Add his skills as a bare-knuckle boxer, a single-stick fighter and exponent of the martial arts and you've got an incomparable crime-fighter.

'I know a lot of people will find our take on Holmes a bit of a travesty, but I am convinced this is the closest possible interpretation of what was in Conan Doyle's mind.

'I grew up loving the Holmes stories and could never quite reconcile how TV and movies saw Holmes with the way the author saw him.'

The same back-to-the-drawing board treatment has been given to Dr John Watson, played by Jude Law, almost unrecognisable with a moustache and sideburns. 'He's always been shown as playing very much second fiddle to Holmes' genius,' says Law.

'In countless films he just let Holmes take charge and doesn't really get involved in the action, apart from asking him at the end how he solved the crime.

'Watson is usually seen as small, portly and a bit pompous, and although he's a doctor, he's not particularly smart.

'But that's all gone out of the window in this film. I play him as a tall, slim, cultured, self-confident man, a gambler with an eye for the ladies and a veteran of the Afghan war.

'I'm the one who's the buttoned-up, polished professional, counter-balancing Holmes as the flaky, way-ward, eccentric dilettante.

'Intellectually, my Watson is Holmes's equal, and more socially accomplished. We share a flat at 221b Baker Street, but he has made it a tip, and in the film I'm moving out to get married, which Holmes doesn't like one bit.

'With his moodiness, he's not been the easiest person to live with, so I'm not sorry to go. Unlike other portrayals, my Watson is not subservient. We bicker like an old married couple and I'm not afraid to disagree with him, but he gets on my nerves.

'It's the kind of friendship you can have with only someone of the same sex; a person you adore, but who infuriates you.'

The story begins with London being terrorised by a series of ritualistic murders of young women. Scotland Yard's Inspector Lestrade hasn't a clue, but with Holmes and Watson on the case it's not long before they catch up with the culprit – the evil Lord Blackwood (Mark Strong). Blackwood who is based on the Satanist writer Aleister Crowley, is sentenced to death, but just before his execution he warns Holmes that he's not heard the last of him.

Later, when Blackwood's tomb is found open, but with another body in the coffin, fear grips the streets. Holmes is intrigued, but not scared. To him *the game is afoot*. Blackwood teams up with a group of establishment conspirators in a plot to destroy Parliament and give them absolute power over the country.

It won't spoil things to reveal that in the end, good, in the form of Holmes and Watson, triumphs (at the last minute) over evil. However, the denouement is reached only after a series of spectacular chases, explosions and action scenes in the House of Commons vaults, a slaughterhouse, a boatyard, churches, and on Tower Bridge. Holmes also takes part in a brutal bare-knuckle fight for a wager in an East End pub.

Location shooting took place in London, Manchester, Liverpool and Chatham, Kent. But Holmes and Watson's chaotic flat at 221b Baker Street was specially built at a film studio in New York.

In the books, Watson describes Holmes as 'the worst tenant in London'. He observes: 'He keeps his cigars in the coal scuttle, his tobacco in the toe of a Persian slipper and his unanswered correspondence is transfixed by a jack-knife in the very centre of his wooden mantelpiece.'

The set took two weeks to dress, with all Holmes's and Watson's personal belongings and furnishings specially flown in from England – 'nothing in the States looked authentic enough', says production designer Sarah Greenwood. But when Downey arrived, he declared it too tidy, and asked for more chaos and filth.

'But, as always he knew what he wanted and he was right,' says Greenwood. 'He'd even told me the shape of the shirt he thought Holmes should wear.'

Two other characters from the books find their way onto the screen: Irene Adler, a femme fatale (played by Rachel McAdams) and the only woman ever to outwit Holmes, earning his respect. And Holmes' arch enemy, Professor Moriarty, for whom she is working.

The revival of Holmes was initiated by British-born writer and producer Lionel Wigram, when he was working on the Harry Potter movies.

'I'd always been a fan, and I thought the character deserved a better and bigger portrayal on the screen that we'd ever seen. The problem was that although everyone in the world has heard of Holmes, he is perceived as stuffy and old-fashioned.

'I knew I'd have trouble persuading a studio to back me, so I had an illustrator draw up my story in a comic-strip and we turned it into a 25-page book.

'I wanted it to be seen as an adventure movie, like The Raiders Of The Lost Ark, a Bond film, or Pirates Of The Caribbean.

'A lot of the physical action in the original Holmes stories is mentioned only in passing. So I brought that element to life in the drawings, to show how exciting it would look on the screen.

'I also had Holmes drawn as scruffy and stubby, with a pistol in one hand and a sword in the other. Until they saw that drawing, the studio suits at Warner Brothers just didn't get it – but then they suddenly saw the possibilities, and threw themselves right behind the film.'

Ritchie was brought in to direct, and when Law was suggested to play Watson, 'it was instant bonding', says Downey. 'We bounced off each other, as if we'd been working in partnership for years.'

The only problem that remained was Downey's American accent. 'Holmes is too identifiably British ever to be played by a foreigner,' says Ritchie. 'Or so we thought. 'When I asked Robert to audition for the part with a British accent, he was flawless.'

Says Downey, 'I drew on my experience filming Chaplin, for which I'd had to perfect an English accent. Luckily, it came back to me.

His next step was to consult the original. 'I'd never read any Holmes before, and I found myself gripped.'

Law's only previous connection with Conan Doyle's fictional detective had been in 1991 at the age of 19, when he was cast as a stable boy in the BBC Sherlock Holmes series which starred Jeremy Brett.

'I went into this film knowing only what everyone else knows about Watson – the pudgy little chap immortalised in all those screen versions.

'Then I read the books and realised he wasn't like that at all, that he was good-looking, brave and slim with a strong character of his own. None of that had ever been explored in film before.'

For Sherlock Holmes fans, one mystery remains. In Ritchie's film, Holmes' arch enemy Professor Moriarty is seen only fleetingly. Is this because the producers are hoping to unveil Brad Pitt in the role in the next Holmes movie?

The producers are saying nothing, though the internet gossip is that it's a done deal.

As Holmes might say: 'Watson, there is a game afoot here.'

Daily Mail, Friday, December 18, 2009

Sherlock Holmes (12A)

Verdict: Great Visuals, rubbish script ** out of five

Review by **Chris Tookey**

When the sleuth is stranger than fiction

AFTER three flops in a row, diamond geezer Guy Ritchie tries his hand at Hollywood hackery with this big-budget attempt to create a new action-adventure franchise to rival Pirates Of The Caribbean.

The transformation of its creator's cerebral sleuth into a brawling, bare-knuckle fighter and action man with designer stubble will have most Arthur Conan Doyle fans howling like a whipped hound of the Baskervilles.

The plot is frequently incomprehensible, and Rachel McAdams's poorly photographed femme fatale could be edited out of the picture without making much difference. Most of the time, I hadn't a clue what she was doing, and she didn't seem to know either.

Robert Downey Jr suggests he must have misheard the title as Sherlock Hams. He can do Holmes's intellect and eccentricity, but isn't remotely Victorian.

As Watson, Jude Law is dull – which in the light of his recent screen performances, is a step up for him. But he's still oddly lightweight, like the X Factor's Joe McElderry attempting to give us his Disraeli.

The most enjoyable turn is by Mark Strong as principal baddie Lord Blackwood, a megalomaniac Mason with a keen interest in World domination and sacrificing virgins to Lucifer.

Strong manages to look in period, and approaches the role with the terrifyingly reptilian malice of Peter Mandelson. The other good news is that Victorian London is wonderfully photogenic, thanks to Jenny Beavan's costumes and Sarah Greenwood's production design.

Hans Zimmer's bombastic score was less to my taste, and Ritchie's direction is pacy and action-packed without showing the slightest flair for characterisation or story-telling.

The film gets off to a promising start and has its moments, but at 130 minutes it is half-an-hour too long, and the action fizzles out with a weak showdown on a half-built Tower Bridge and too many hints of a sequel.

I suspect Sherlock Holmes (released on Boxing Day) will do underwhelming business for a blockbuster, but unlike Ritchie's past three movies, it's not a disaster.

THE TELEGRAPH SATURDAY, DECEMBER 19, 2009

Film Review

Out on Boxing Day **Sherlock Holmes**

Slovenly, eccentric, bare-knuckle boxer, banterer *extraordinaire* – oh, and a pretty good amateur sleuth into the bargain – Robert Downey Jr's Holmes in this droll Victorian blockbuster is hardly one Conan Doyle would recognise. There's not a deer-stalker in sight, and Downey Jr spends half the film stripped to the waist – he's a man of action, not meticulous deduction, piecing together the entire the entire feeble-ish story about a resurrected arch-criminal (Mark Strong) and a plot against Parliament almost in passing. Jude Law's pally Watson, a definite plus, is essentially Danny Glover in *Lethal Weapon* – the stolidly reliable and long-suffering foil to his friend's quicksilver brilliance, while stuff explodes. Director Guy Ritchie overdoes the flash, as usual, but it's fun flash – the movie's almost needlessly elaborate editing keeps you on your toes – and this smashingly designed production is an enjoyable playground for his favourite sport: dandyish brawling.

Tim Robey

The Sunday Telegraph DECEMBER 20 2009

NEWS REVIEW

HOW I PUT THE FEAR FACTOR INTO SHERLOCK HOLMES

As a new film redraws the Victorian detective as a hard-bitten bohemian, Mark Strong, who plays the villain, tells **Olga Craig** about his part in the unlikely blockbuster.

The cockerel isn't exactly a conventional cast member of the traditional children's Nativity play. Not that that was bothering Mark Strong when he jumped on board a dawn flight from the Irish location of his latest film to London last week in time to see his eldest son Gabriel's acting debut as the raucous rooster in his school's Christmas performance.

"There he was, not five yet, with a yellow marigold glove on his head for a crest, opening the show with a song," Strong smiles with paternal pride. "I was just so proud that he had got up in front of 80 or so people and pulled it off. I'd been doing his lines with him and listening to him sing his song for ages. I would have moved heaven and earth to be there, though I have to admit I'm not entirely convinced there was a cockerel in the Nativity."

Now, purists would say there probably wasn't. But then purists have also been muttering darkly about the historical accuracy of Strong senior's own latest film, *Sherlock Holmes*, which is tipped to be one of the big blockbuster cinema releases this Christmas.

Directed by Guy Ritchie, whose reputation has taken a bit of a battering since producing a celluloid turkey or two, it controversially casts Robert Downey Jr as Sir Arthur Conan Doyle's Victorian sleuth and Jude Law as a rather dashing Dr Watson. Strong plays Dr Blackwood, the dastardly, occult-dabbling villain in a typical brainteasing Holmesian plot.

But, if you were expecting a Jeremy Brett-style cadaverous codger in a deerstalker hat, whose sidekick is a bit of a bumbling buffoon, then think again. Downey Jr's firecracker performance depicts Holmes as a gun-toting, bare-knuckle fighter who is an expert in the martial arts. He swaps his conservative headgear for a fedora but loses none of his incisive thinking or brilliantly observed deductions along the way. Watson, too, is the debonair doctor who is a war hero and just as happy as Holmes to have a gun in his hands, a thug by the neck or a fiancée in his thrall.

Though the film has been endorsed by no less an authority than the Baker Street Irregulars, a group of international Holmes experts, it has fallen foul of a few reviewers' pens simply because it redraws the fictional sleuth in a whole new way. That said, it is such an action-packed and intelligent romp that it is likely to spawn several sequels; there are rumours that Brad Pitt is lined up for the follow-up. And, while reviews have been mixed, it is bound to be a box-office biggie.

"I know, I know," says Strong, a little wearily. "People keep saying, 'It's Guy Ritchie. How can Guy Ritchie do Holmes? He does gangster movies. And to cast an American who isn't tall and aquiline as Holmes...' 'Believe me, this Holmes is much truer to the books than anything before. If you delve into them, you will see he was adept at martial arts, all that stuff. It's all a bit like people saying Dan[iel] Craig couldn't do James Bond just because he was blond.

"Honestly, Guy isn't at all bothered by those criticisms. He knew he could do Holmes in a way that served both his love of the Conan Doyle stories and his own style. He wasn't trying to shoehorn Sherlock into something he wasn't. And he knew he was getting a consummate professional in Downey Jr."

And Ritchie wasn't at all overawed by the legendary actor who, several years ago, fought back from a career spiral after a lengthy drugs battle to become an A-lister. "Robert fizzes at a higher level than the rest of us," says Strong. "He positively crackles with energy. At our first meeting to discuss the script, he went off into this sort of esoteric 10-minute monologue about his character. At the end of it, Guy sat back in his seat, looked straight at him and said, 'I didn't understand a f------ word of that.' I literally held my breath. Guy wasn't taking any bull----. Robert just said, 'Fine, OK.'"

The film hinges in part, Strong acknowledges, on the chemistry between Holmes and Watson. "We are aiming for a Butch Cassidy and Sundance relationship – what the glossy mags now call 'bromance.' It was perfect."

The successful relationships between Downey Jr, Law and Strong was the result, he says of Ritchie's able direction. "He creates an incredible environment on set; he is incredibly inclusive and doesn't have an ego. There is no shouting, no hierarchy. When there is down time, he likes to play chess or strum his guitar. He is as happy serving the coffee as the next guy."

This is the third time Strong has starred in a Ritchie film (after *RocknRolla* and *Revolver*), and he is a great admirer of the former Mr Madonna whose artistic merit, he believes, is much misunderstood. "*Lock, Stock and Two Smoking Barrels* was brilliant. So was *RocknRolla*, but people just said, 'Oh, it's only that old Guy Ritchie gangster stuff again.' It wasn't. It was what he knows and does well. *Revolver* was just too deep for some people. So what if he wanted to go off and do something different with his missus?" (*Swept Away*, the film he made with his former wife Madonna, was widely panned.)

While Strong describes a strong sense of camaraderie on location, Ritchie and Madonna's much publicised divorce was played out during the making of *Sherlock Holmes*. "We all respected his privacy," Strong says. "Work is the place you can escape from all that. The end of a 10-year relationship is heartbreaking for everyone involved. But Guy doesn't like newspapers around because he doesn't want anything to get in the way of the work."

His role as the irredeemable villain is a slight departure for Strong, a versatile actor whose parts have included the devious royal adviser Sir John Conroy in The Young Victoria, a psychologically unstable astronaut in Danny Boyle's Sunshine, and King John's vicious henchman Sir Godfrey in the forthcoming blockbuster Robin Hood – as well as several parts in the Prime Suspect series.

As to whether or not he triumphs or fails in *Sherlock Holmes*, that must wait for its release on Boxing Day. But, suffice to say, Strong's fight scenes are hugely exciting. "You should have seen my hands after filming," he says, holding out his hands. "Robert and I do a lot of punching. And believe me, he packs a mean punch."

Of Italian extraction, Strong, 40, was christened Marco Giuseppe Salussolia, but his mother changed his name by deed pole to enable him to integrate more easily with his peers. His first taste for the theatrical came as the lead singer of a punk band. "I had to be the singer because I couldn't play a musical instrument," he admits. "I couldn't sing very well either."

His initial ambition was to become a lawyer, but he dropped out of a German university to study acting at the Royal Holloway College in London to study acting at the Bristol Old Vic Theatre School. His big break was playing Tosker, the lovable rogue in the 1966 television political drama *Our Friends in the North*, which also lauched the careers of Gina McKee, Christopher Eccleston and Daniel Craig.

"I was a bit taken aback by our success," says Strong. "I remember walking down the road with Dan Craig and asking him, 'Do you think this is going to be any good?' We genuinely had no idea. We had been filming it for a year. But it served us well because it gave all of us our breaks. That is the randomness of acting. There are lots of seriously good actors out there but they never get that one break."

Strong has always said that Tinseltown wasn't for him. Now, he isn't so sure. "I've always said I wasn't the Hollywood type but now, here I am: I've just done Robin Hood and I'm about to film John Carter of Mars, a huge Disney/Pixar film. The good thing, though, is that I haven't had to leave the country."

And fatherhood is the reason that is so important. "It came along at the right time for me," says Strong, who has two sons. And, whilst his eldest, Gabriel, has now made his stage debut, Strong would prefer his boys did anything but acting. "There is so much insecurity," he says.

For all that, Strong, these days, has his choice of parts. "Stage or screen?" he muses, torn between them. "I have to say I absolutely love film. There is something utterly intoxicating about it. At first I thought it was cheating, doing retakes until you got it right. Now I see it as a way of refining a moment.

He is angered, though, about rumours that *Sherlock Holmes* was beset by production problems, requiring a wealth of re-shooting. "Categorically, that is utter bull----," he says. "The truth is that re-shoots happen on every film."

With so many parts being offered, Strong is seldom "resting", but when he does, family comes first. He is however, fond of poker. "My friends Dexter Fletcher [the actor] and Jamie Oliver and I like to play. My missus lets me go to that because Jamie always cooks for us before we play, and I always tell her, "Well, I can't turn down a meal from Jamie Oliver…"'

Sherlock Holmes is released on Boxing Day

Daily Mail, Wednesday, December 23, 2009

Ephraim Hardcastle

SOME cineasts sense a hint of 'homo-eroticism' in the performances of Jude Law and co-star Robert Downey Jr, pictured, in their new movie, Sherlock Holmes. The stars have encouraged this idea. Law says of Downey: 'I met him and I loved him. We trained together, we rehearsed together, we read together.' Downey on Law: 'Disappointingly, he is entirely heterosexual.' Might it be a ruse to attract the pink pound?

THE DAILY TELEGRAPH, THURSDAY, DECEMBER 24, 2009

My dear Watson Actor hints at gay Sherlock Holmes

The actor Robert Downey Jr is said to have unnerved studio bosses by hinting that the characters of Sherlock Holmes and Dr Watson in his new film are meant to be homosexual.

Downey Jr stars as the title character, Jude Law plays Dr Watson.

Appearing on **The Late Show with David Letterman** he was asked whether the two characters had a "different level of relationship" beyond solving crimes, he replied: "You mean that they were homos? That is what you're saying?"

The actor also suggested that Dr Watson's fiancée could be a cover for the relationship between the two main characters, and introduced a clip of Holmes wrestling by inviting the audience to decide if he was a "butch homosexual".

His jokes are said to have caused unease among studio executives who have been marketing the film as an action-packed adventure.

One Hollywood insider said that executives did not want the film to become "Brockeback Mountain 2", referring to the Oscar-winning movie about two homosexual cowboys.

Downey Jr has dropped a series of other hints about the subtext of the film, which was directed by Guy Ritchie and is released over Christmas.

He previously described the lead characters as "two men who happened to be room-mates, wrestle a lot and share a bed.

He added: "I had an idea of how he should be represented and from what I understand it's not quite how he's been previously represented."

Roger Johnson, the editor of *The Sherlock Holmes Journal*, said that in Arthur Conan Doyle's original stories the Victorian detective was "essentially asexual with no erotic interest in women or men."

He said Watson was "something of a ladies' man but a faithful husband to his wife".

Nick Allen
In Los Angeles

DEAL & SANDWICH EXPRESS December 24, 2009

Reviews

The game's afoot

THIS is Sherlock Holmes as we've never seen him before.

In Guy Ritchie's hands, the consulting detective is a man of action who's just as likely to be seen bare-knuckle fighting, deploying martial arts skills and crashing through dockside warehouses as using his considerable intellect to track down criminals.

Holmes fans may baulk at the thought of what Ritchie – director of geezers 'n' gangster thrillers like Snatch and Lock, Stock and Two Smoking Barrels – has done with "their man" but the film is an enjoyable enough conceit; it's a late Victorian romp that owes something to Alan Moore's League of Extraordinary Gentlemen graphic novels as well as Barry Levinson's 1985 Young Sherlock Holmes, a boy's own style adventure in which the fledgling sleuth battles a sinister cult.

Ritchie's film starts in confident fashion, as Holmes (Downey Jr) and his faithful sidekick (Law) gatecrash an occult ritual and save a young woman from being sacrificed. From the outset, it's clear Downey Jr's Holmes isn't afraid to use his fists alongside his mental faculties.

Holmes and Watson hand over the head of the cult, Lord Blackwood (Mark Strong) to Inspector Lestrade (Eddie Marsan) but it soon becomes evident that Blackwood is no ordinary criminal and actually seems to have supernatural powers.

He's sentenced to death but somehow survives the hangman's noose as Holmes finds himself up against an adversary who is as clever as he is well-connected and who is plotting to overthrow the Government and throw the country into turmoil.

Complicating matters for Holmes is the involvement of Irene Adler (Rachel McAdams) in this nefarious plot. A deceitful double agent who has bested Holmes in the past. Adler is in the employ of another mysterious villain. Despite his misgivings, Holmes is fascinated by and attracted to Adler and the feeling is mutual, leading to an enjoyable onscreen tension between the two. But the central relationship, of course, is between Holmes and Watson. Sir Arthur Conan Doyle's detective duo is one of the most enduring pairings in fiction and Ritchie rightly reinstates Watson not just as a foil for Holmes, but also as his equal.

Jud Law's Watson is a dynamic, have-a-go sort of chap, reliable and sensible, but not at all the bumbler that he's sometimes portrayed as. Indeed he's the stalwart and counterpoint that the erratic Holmes needs and the detective realises this – Holmes doesn't react well to the news that Watson is to marry his sweetheart Mary (Kelly Reilly) and move out of 221B Baker Street.

Downey Jr and Law make for a good team, bantering, bickering and even coming to blows at times. For purists, this Holmes may be too Bohemian, too action-orientated and maybe even a little smarmy. But I enjoyed Downey Jr's charismatic turn and his light-hearted approach to the role.

Ritchie's signature style of restless camera work. Stop-start fight scenes and action aplenty makes this a romp rather than a study in detection and reasoning.

This take on Holmes is more action adventure than unfolding mystery so it will not suit everyone's tastes. But as a fresh interpretation of well-known material and characters, it's a lot of fun.

Darryl Webber

THE DAILY TELEGRAPH, SAURDAY DECEMBER 26, 2002

NEWS REVIEW & COMMENT

Elusive case of the celluloid detective

Guy Ritchie has reinvented Sherlock Holmes as an action hero with homosexual leanings, but Conan Doyle's hero has always been a man of many faces, says **Philip Horne**

The new Sherlock Holmes film opens today, hoping to benefit from the season of goodwill. Will it be a Christmas turkey, or a cracker, full of delightful surprises? A little like the eternally bemused Dr Watson, we might feel amazed and baffled by Hollywood's latest eccentric-seeming-ploy turning the world's most famously cerebral detective, a literary icon of the late-Victorian period, into a big-budget-action-hero franchise (if it comes off, that is). Why do they think this is the moment, and why hire Brit-lad director Guy (*Lock, Stock*) Ritchie to do it, with Robert Downey Jr as Holmes and Jude Law as Watson?

The answer, perhaps, is simplicity itself – as Holmes would say. The enduring appeal of Conan Doyle's creation lies in the fact that Holmes means all things to all people. In addition, the stories are out of copyright, Holmes's name is universally recognised, even among 18-to-25-year-olds, and the films have an enviable commercial track record. The Holmes-Watson relationship is as classic as Jeeves and Wooster, Ritchie is a Londoner like Holmes and his last film (*RocknRolla*) was a hit. Downey just got big in *Iron Man*, Law has a devoted following and there hasn't been a major Holmes film for 20 years. Even those who love the books may go to the movie, if only to denounce it.

Filming Holmes is nothing new. Sir Arthur Conan Doyle's master detective was less than halfway through his literary career when he first hit the cinema screen, rather compromisingly in *Sherlock Holmes Baffled*(1903), a trick film in which a burglar breaks into 221B Baker Street and evades the master's grasp by repeatedly disappearing and rematerialising. Holmes had first appeared in print in 1887 (and on stage a mere six years later); the last story appeared in 1927, three years before Doyle's death.

By 1930 Holmes had been filmed in Britain, America, Scandinavia, Germany and France – and had been played by Mack Sennett (of *Keystone Cops* fame), John Ford's brother Francis, and John Barrymore (grandfather of Drew). He was also played, in 1916, by William Gillette, who was the original stage incarnation of the character, performing in the part more than 1,300 times, as well as being the author of the definitive 1899 theatrical version, revived successfully by the RSC in the 1970s.

Guy Ritchie's new version – full of jokey violence and explosions, and with a much-trumpeted gay subtext – has a lot to live up to. Downey is hugely talented, fortunately;

but devotees of the original stories and aficionados of the many film and television versions (223, according to IMDB.com) are notoriously hard to please.

Ritchie's first big studio film, for Warner Brothers, will at least be lively and much talked about, and, anyway, is just one more entry in a fertile history, over which Holmes has been played by actors ranging from Rupert Everett to Hans Albers (the great star of Nazi cinema), from Michael Caine to Stewart Granger, and Raymond Massey to Roger Moore.

Holmes is a gift for a great actor, with his swings between "the blackest depression" and obsessive activity. His pipe, cocaine habit and violin virtuosity make wonderfully distinctive and eccentric trademarks (the deerstalker does not appear in the stories).

The tales reliably produce their formulaic pleasures – of the dazzling deductions that amaze Watson, but are dismissed by Holmes as "elementary" (Doyle's Holmes never said "Elementary, my dear Watson"); of the reconstruction of the crime; of feats of disguise; of forensic knowledge (Holmes is a scientist-hero for the post-Darwinian age); of his thrilled, slightly paranoid sense of urban evil-doing: "He loved to lie in the very centre of five millions of people, with his filaments stretching out and running through them, responsive to every little rumour or suspicion of unsolved crime," Doyle writes. And there is his great rivalry with Professor Moriarty, with Irene Adler, played by Rachel McAdams in the new movie (as Watson says, "to Sherlock Holmes she is always the woman").

Among the vast range of film portrayals – not to mention well-loved television incarnations including Peter Cushing and Jeremy Brett – a few landmarks are worth singling out. Now almost forgotten, but still impressive, is Arthur Wontner, the English star of a series of films between 1931 and 1937, whose bony features gave him the necessary aquiline presence.

Wontner was eclipsed, however, by the glorious Basil Rathbone, a superbly intense and witty South African actor whose magnificent Sherlock Holmes is an iconic Hollywood figure – first in two Victorian-set films for 20th Century Fox, most famously *The Hound of the Baskervilles* (1939, director Sidney Lanfield). After a break as radio stars, Rathbone and his Watson, the rather shouty, buffoonish Nigel Bruce moved to Universal, where the franchise was reinvented in the wartime present-day, and with mostly new stories – starting with *The Voice of Terror* (1942), where the criminal enemy is the Third Reich. By common consent, the best of the twelve Universal pictures is *Sherlock Holmes and the Scarlet Claw* (1944), written and directed by the maestro Roy William Neill. Set in Quebec, it's enjoyably atmospheric and full of neat ideas ("For the first time, we've been retained by a corpse"). The sumptuous, earnest Hammer *Hound of the Baskervilles* (1959) gave us Holmes in colour for the first time with Peter Cushing putting his stamp on the part with great authority and Ritchie style, plenty of lurid action.

Things took off in the Seventies. In 1970 Billy Wilder, probably the only great director to have tackled Doyle's hero, gave us the quite delightfully witty, characterful and somewhat melancholy comedy-fantasia *The Private Life of Sherlock Holmes*, with the brilliant pairing of Robert Stephen as the troubled Holmes and Colin Blakemore, superb as a bristlingly priggish Watson. Wilder made brilliant with the gay reading of the Holmes-Watson friendship – Ritchie's not the first.

Liberties were in the air. In 1971 George C. Scott in the kooky *They Might Be Giants* played an insane former judge who believes he is Holmes. A lesser Wilder – Gene –

wrote and starred in the amiable, sub-Mel-Brooks farce, *Adventure of Sherlock Holmes' Smarter Brother* (1975).

In *The Seven Per Cent Solution* (1977), Nicholas Meyer had Nicol Williamson as the drug-addicted Holmes undergo psychoanalysis at the hands of Alan Arkin's Freud (Robert Duvall) was Watson, Laurence Olivier Moriarty). Peter Cook (Holmes) and Dudley Moore (Watson) spoofed *The Hound of the Baskervilles* (1978); and in 1979, *Murder by Decree* had Christopher Plummer's Holmes tracking down Jack the Ripper. In 1985 Chris Columbus wrote *Young Sherlock* Holmes (director Barry Levinson), a rather mechanical Spielberg production that echoes Indiana Jones and anticipates Harry Potter in its gothic-fantastic, effects-heavy extravaganza about Holmes's school days. And then in 1988 *Without a Clue* ingeniously made Ben Kingsley's Watson the real brilliant detective and Michael Caine's Holmes merely the drunken actor he hires as a front for his own activities.

If, then, Guy Ritchie's plays fast and loose with the sacred texts of the Sherlockian canon, it will be far from the first. It probably will win Doyle some new readers.

And even if it's awful and simply sends people back to the books, that in itself is a Christmas present worth having.

Philip Horne teaches literature and film at UCL

SEVEN **The Sunday Telegraph** MAGAZINE 27.12.09

FILM By Mike McCahill

THERE MUST BE Film-makers less qualified than Guy Ritchie to bring **Sherlock Holmes** back to the screen, but I'll be damned if I can think of anyone right now. With the exception of 2005's much-derided *Revolver* – an existential misfire that probed the deepest recesses of Jason Statham's mind – Ritchie has thus far limited himself to physical rather than intellectual pursuits. What use deduction when your protagonists are all tooled up and ready for a rumble?

So it is that Ritchie's Sherlock (a fidgety Robert Downey Jr) juggles case-solving with martial arts and bare-knuckle boxing. When he disagrees with Holmes, Jude Law's Watson retorts with a fist to the face: even the usually fragrant and demure Rachel McAdams, styled like a common harlot, is obliged to carry a billy club about her person.

It's a vulgarisation of not only its source but its director, whose usual energies dissipate having to turn every crime scene into a fight scene. We get the worst of Ritchie – the incoherent set-pieces, the ADD-ish ability to hold any shot longer than two seconds – without one hesitates to describe as his best, a committee-authored screenplay means there's none of the sometimes sparky banter with which this film-maker made his name. One deft touch right at the start, when the Warner Bros logo appears set in the London cobblestones, the rest, I'm afraid, is just cobblers.

Daily Mail, Monday, December 28, 2009

Janet Street-Porter

2009: A year that drove me crazy!

MY A-Z OF THE PEOPLE AND THINGS THAT MADE ME TRULY GRUMPY...

EROTIC. Guy Ritchie denigrates a British hero – by giving us an 'erotic' Sherlock Holmes. Robert Downey Jr, who plays Holmes to Jude Law's Watson, tells interviewers the two characters had a secret 'relationship' claiming they 'wrestled a lot and shared a bed'. News to literary experts, who reckon Holmes was completely asexual.

The Sunday Telegraph JANUARY 3 2010

NEWS

MANDRAKE BY TIM WALKER

Downey Jnr puts sequel to Sherlock Holmes in peril

TO THE EXECUTORS of the literary estate of Sir Arthur Conan Doyle, it is elementary. If Guy Ritchie wants to make a sequel to his blockbuster, *Sherlock Holmes*, he must never portray the sleuth and Dr Watson as anything more than just good friends.

Andrea Plunket, who controls the remaining US copyrights in the Holmes stories, was not amused when Robert Downey Jnr, who plays Holmes to Jude Lawson's Watson in Ritchie's film, said on a talk show that he felt the residents of 221B Baker Street were an item.

He introduced a clip showing him wrestling with Law, with an invitation to the audience to decide whether he was the more "butch" of the two. As for Watson's fiancée, Mary, played by Kelly Reilly, he said that she was merely a convenient "cover". Rachel McAdams, playing Irene Adler in Sherlock Holmes, would have had little allure for the sleuth, if Robert Downey Jnr is to be believed.

"I hope this is just an example of Mr Downey's black sense of humour," says Ms Plunket. "It would be drastic, but I would withdraw permission for any more films to be made if that is a theme they wish to bring out in the future. I am not hostile to homosexuals, but I am to anyone who is not true to the spirit of the books." Sir Arthur's daughter, the late Dame Jean Conan Doyle, told me he wrote the later books in the series to "take his mind off sex", which is why he resisted romantic themes. He had fallen in love with her mother, Jean Leckie, as his first wife, Louise was dying of TB. He behaved impeccably, and it was only a year after she died that he allowed himself to marry Miss Leckie.

Daily Mail, Thursday, January 7, 2010

THE IDEAL HOLMES SHOW

As the latest incarnation storms the box office, who IS the definitive Sherlock?

YOU need only three clues to his identity; a tweed cape, a deerstalker hat and a pipe. Elementary, my dear reader – Sherlock Holmes is back. Directed by Guy Ritchie, this latest incarnation sees the great detective – played by Robert Downey Jnr, reinvented as an arrogant, swashbuckling, womanising Victorian hero. But ever since Sir Arthur Conan Doyle penned the first Sherlock Holmes story – A Study in Scarlet – in 1887, his character has never been far from the limelight. There have been more than 260 Holmes films, two musicals, various radio plays – and even a ballet. All in all, more than 200 actors have played him.

Here, **CLAIRE COHEN** takes a look at the most distinguished…

1920 BRITISH actor Eille Norwood holds the record for playing Holmes – with 47 silent films.

1922 HOLMES was John Barrymore in this silent movie by William Gillette, who gave him the deerstalker and pipe.

1929 THE first Holmes to have sound starred Clive Brook. It also contains the first use of the phrase 'Elementary, my dear Watson'.

1939 BASIL RATHBONE is best-known for his articulate, acerbic portrayal of Holmes with a real ability to adopt a disguise.

1959 PETER CUSHING had a long association with the character – but would rather have swept floors than repeat the experience.

Daily Mail, Monday, January 11, 2010

LETTERS

Elementary casting

I'M NOT so sure that Peter Cushing would 'rather have swept floors than repeat the experience of playing Sherlock Holmes' (Mail). He first played Sherlock Holmes in 1959 and continued to play the character throughout his career.

Only ill health prevented him from reprising the role in the Eighties.

Further detective work might have uncovered that Patrick Macnee and Jeremy Brett are among the few actors to have played both Holmes and his loyal companion, Watson.

ROB Lane,
Derby.

1962 HAMMER film star Christopher Lee not only donned the deerstalker but also played Mycroft (Sherlock's brother).

1970 BILLY WILDER'S vision of Holmes as a man riddled with self-doubt drove classical actor Robert Stephens to despair.

1976 HOLMES popped up in New York looking rather like Roger Moore, at the height of his success as 007. Avengers star Patrick Macnee was Watson.

1978 THE spoof Hound of the Baskervilles has Peter Cook's Holmes wearing women's clothes and speaking in a Welsh accent. Dudley Moore plays Watson.

1979 ANGLO-Canadian film Murder By Decree saw Christopher Plummer's sensitive Holmes (with James Mason as Watson) on the trail of Jack the Ripper. It won five awards, including best actor for Plummer.

1982 TOM BAKER'S first role after leaving the Tardis – but he was accused of playing Holmes like Doctor Who.

1984 THE definitive Sherlock of his era, Jeremy Brett's study was a portrait of Holmes' obsessive mannerisms.

1985 NICHOLAS ROWE auditioned for Steven Spielberg's film Young Sherlock Holmes – solving his first case – while a pupil at Eton.

2002 TRUE to Conan Doyle's original character, Richard Roxburgh plays Holmes as a heavy smoker with a cocaine addiction.

2004 IN The Case of the Silk Stocking, Rupert Everett's Holmes shows the first sign of ruthlessness by shooting the main villain.

2009 FAR from the suave English gent of Holmes folklore, Robert Downey Jr, portrays him as a troubled man – 'a tortured genius'.

Daily Mail, Wednesday, January 13, 2010 LETTERS

Stately Holmes

CLAIRE COHEN'S entertaining spread (Mail) omitted to mention a Shakespearian actor often regarded as the finest Sherlock Holmes of his or any other generation.

Douglas Wilmer first played the role of Conan Doyle's sleuth in BBC TV's anthology series Detective, with Nigel Stock as Watson, and this adaptation of The Speckled Band became the first short story in a series of 13 episodes transmitted to great acclaim in 1965.

So memorable was the interpretation that when Gene Wilder needed a 'real' Sherlock Holmes for his 1975 spoof 'The Adventures of Sherlock Holmes' Smarter Brother (not Mycroft, but the even more fictional Sigerson), he selected Wilmer, with Thorley Walters as Dr Watson.

(Walters, incidentally, would play Watson again in a 1977 TV movie, Silver Blaze, which marked Christopher Plummer's debut as Holmes on film – two years before Murder By Decree).

Wilmer's definitive portrayal has been recognised with honorary membership of The Sherlock Holmes Society, and only last year this splendid actor published his autobiography, Stage Whispers.

CY YOUNG, London W10.

Daily Mail, Tuesday, January 19, 2010

From **Baz Bamigboye** at the Golden Globes Awards in Beverly Hills (Extract)

Robert Downey Jnr won Best Actor for Sherlock Holmes.

LETTERS

The whole Sleuth

AS REPORTED, Sherlock Holmes first appeared in 1887, but it wasn't until 1891 that he started a never-ending appeal when A Scandal in Bohemia was serialised in the Strand Magazine. His last appearance in those pages was in 1927 in Shoscombe Old Place, three years before Sir Arthur Conan Doyle's passing.

The original Strand Magazine artist for the Holmes series was Sidney Paget, who modelled the detective's figure on his brother. But it wasn't until 1899 – when the play Sherlock Holmes was procured by American impresario Charles Froham – that he was first played in the flesh by William Gillette.

I still have a framed version of his Vanity Fair supplement caricature as Holmes.

Charlie Chaplain played Billy The Page to Gillette's Holmes at the Duke of York's Theatre in 1905. In Dickson Carr's biography of Doyle, it's recorded that when the actor and author first met 'not even Sidney Paget had done so well in a drawing', so close was the comparison to the intended original.

Gillette played the sleuth on both sides of the Atlantic.

Another eminent actor who played Holmes was Arthur Wontner, born in 1875. His son, Sir Hugh, later became Lord Mayor of London.

ROGER JENKIN,
Penzance, Cornwall.

Daily Mail, Friday, March 12, 2010

Baz Bamingboye it's Friday!

Elementary, my dear Robert (Excerpt)

ROBERT DOWNEY JR told me that he had fun working with Jude Law on Sherlock Holmes. 'We all still like each other, which is a good thing,' said the actor. He added there will be a Sherlock Holmes 2, possibly ready to shoot late this year or next year, depending on the schedules of the two leads and director Guy Ritchie. 'Jude and I had good on-screen chemistry and you can't fake that,' Downey Jr told me.

THE DAILY TELEGRAPH, FRIDAY, MAY 14, 2010

Arts Culture Update

Mark Monahan on the role that launched Robert Downey Jr.

It was Robert Downey Jr's performance in the movie **Chaplin** – free inside tomorrow's paper – that first brought him global attention. Eighteen years on, it remains an astonishing piece of acting: smart, mercurial, and brilliantly capturing both the light and dark sides of the great man – small wonder it earned him an Oscar nomination.

And yet, by 1992, sharper-eyed cinemagoers had already noticed that this was an actor of unusual wit and energy, even if his projects had generally not yet been worthy of him. In particular, the glassy-eyed nihilism of his privileged West Coast junkie in the 1987's.

Less Than Zero stood out as a piece of character-acting, but also, with hindsight, as an unfortunate harbinger of the many real-life drugs-related brushes with the law that would follow.

Indeed, so self-destructive was Downey Jr that many wondered not merely about his acting future but about his future full-stop.

However, now that he is "clean", and with his supremely funny turn in 2008's *Tropic Thunder*, last year's buoyant Sherlock Holmes, and his wantonly brilliant playboy in the two Iron Man blockbusters under his belt, the promise he showed in *Chaplin* has finally been fulfilled.

Daily Mail Weekend 15 May 2010

PAY-PER-VIEW MOVIES

Simone Andrews reviews the pick of the premiers on your movie-on-demand service.

Sherlock Holmes (2009)

Guy Ritchie's reimagining of Conan Doyle's consummate sleuth isn't quite as 'cor blimey' as it could have been, but purists have still had something to say about its authenticity. In fact, Robert Downey Jr's Holmes is surprisingly faithful to Conan Doyle's darker vision as the man as a bohemian maverick; the plot is the main departure here, a fast and loose amalgam of many various stories, which pits Holmes and Jude Law's Watson against Mark Strong's sinister villain, Lord Blackwood.
Radio Times 15-21 May 2010

Films worth paying for by **Stella Papamichael**

Sherlock Holmes MYSTERY THRILLER

Stuffy period mystery this is not, as director Guy Ritchie approaches his take on Baker Street's finest in the manner of *Lethal Weapon*.

Radio Times 22-28 May 2010

Feedback

Stories with punch

In reviewing **Sherlock Holmes**, Stella Papamichael (RT, 15 May) likens it to an action movie, then notes that "this may rankle with fans of the original Conan Doyle stories", a common criticism of the film. But I suspect that, ironically, most critics who wrote this were not really thinking about the stories, but about the TV series.

I read the entire Holmes canon shortly before seeing the film, and in many ways – particularly the most apparently silly – it is surprisingly true to the stories. The scene where Holmes initials the wall of his rooms with pistol shots, is taken directly from Conan Doyle. The "slo-mo bareknuckle fight" is also in line with the stories, where Holmes is clearly described as an excellent amateur boxer.

The Sherlock Holmes stories are adventures as much as they are intellectual puzzles; there is a plentiful supply of direct physical conflict, and plots – particularly in the later stories – are just as implausible as that of the film.

Adam Williamson
Hale, Cheshire

Radio Times 22-28 May 2010

The National Movie Awards Wednesday 26 8.00p.m. ITV1

Best Adventure Movie – **Sherlock Holmes** Directed by Guy Ritchie.

EXPRESS, THURSDAY, JUNE 3, 2010

DVD REVIEW SHERLOCK HOLMES

THERE is probably no more enduring character in fiction than Sherlock Holmes – even his creator Sir Arthur Conan Doyle was unsuccessful in his attempt to kill him off. Still, anyone unlucky enough to have seen the wretched RocknRolla must have doubted the super-sleuth's ability to survive being the subject of a Guy Ritchie film.

Thankfully, they needn't have worried, as Sherlock Holmes turns out to be a hugely enjoyable romp.

Purist fans of the books may be offended (aren't they always?) but after ITV's perfect realisation of Conan Doyle's work with Jeremy Brett's definitive Holmes, there seems little point in complaining about a touch of reinvention.

The excellent opening sets the scene perfectly, with Robert Downey Jr's Holmes vaulting obstacles and vanquishing huge henchman en route to saving a damsel in distress, with Jude Law's Watson and Inspector Lestrade (Eddie Marsan) hot on his heels.

The episode is not only exciting, it is also integral to a witchcraft-and-freemasons plot which is quite in keeping with Conan Doyle and, gratifyingly, holds up to scrutiny. If the tone of the film is sometimes too jokey, and there is perhaps one fight too many, there are compensations aplenty – starting with the cast. Downey's performance is so physical he could almost be Indiana Holmes, but he is completely successful in conveying the character's remarkable intelligence. Law, meanwhile, is something of a revelation as Watson, and actually closer to the original stories than the genial old duffer seen in some supposedly more faithful adaptations. Throw in the ever dependable Marsan, doing a lot with not much as Lestrade, Mark Strong on top form as the dastardly Lord Blackwood and Rachel McAdams (femme fatale) as Kelly Reilly (understanding fiancée) very good as the woman in Holmes and Watson's lives, and you have a movie without a poor performance.

The big surprise here, though, is Ritchie, who shows that given a decent script, rather than his own abject efforts, he has genuine talent.

MIKE WHITEWAY

Daily Mail, Friday, July 23, 2010

it's friday!

BUT WHO'S GOING TO BE THE MOVIE MORIARTY?

FILMING for the follow-up to the Sherlock Holmes movie with Robert Downey Jr and Jude Law begins in October.

Daniel Day-Lewis is tipped to play Holmes's arch-nemesis Professor Moriarty. It has been said that director Guy Ritchie intended to cast Brad Pitt in the role, but his fee was too high.

The new film will be released in December next year.

Daily Mail, Saturday, July 24, 2010

GUY RITCHIE

GUY is on a professional high. His last film, Sherlock Holmes, was his most successful, and took a staggering £338 million at the box office.

He is putting the finishing touches to the script for a sequel and is in talks with Daniel Day-Lewis, who may play Moriarty. Jude Law and Robert Downey Jr will be reprising their roles as Holmes and Watson.

Filming starts this October and the movie is destined for release in 2011.

The Sunday Telegraph SEVEN MAGAZINE 02.01.11

FILM CHOICE by **Anne Billson**

Sherlock Holmes

Purists wanting to see Sir Arthur Conan Doyle's inimitable sleuth at work are advised to wait for the next TV episode with Benedict Cumberbatch. But if you're in the mood for a lively mismatched buddy action romp set in a quasi-Edwardian London where Nine Elms and Pentonville are curiously adjacent to Tower Bridge. Guy Ritchie's film fits the bill nicely, thanks mostly to the considerable charm of Robert Downey Jr as Sherlock and Jude Law as Dr Watson, with Rachel McAdams a bit of a third wheel as wily Irene Adler. It's a boisterous adventure for boys and girls, socked over with a full panoply of CGI-assisted visual gimmickry, in which our intrepid twosome pit their wits and fists against black magic cult leader Mark Strong. It may not be Conan Doyle, but it is entertaining.

LIVE THE MAIL ON SUNDAY DECEMBER 4 2011

ROBERT DOWNEY JR HOLMES AGAIN

The curious case of the Hollywood star, his secret séances and Britain's most eccentric sleuth

COVER INTERVIEW. ROBERT DOWNEY JR

INTERVIEW BY **JON WILDE**
PORTRAIT BY **SAM JONES**

MEGASTAR PAYDAYS, TWO MOVIE FRANCHISES AND A COMEBACK WORTHY OF SHERLOCK HOLMES. WHICH BEGS THE QUESTION…

WHAT'S THE DOWNSIDE?

Team Downey – yes, that really is the name – is based in an ultra-modern $6 million three-story building in the terminally hip bohemian district of Los Angeles. It exists purely to maintain Robert Downey Jr's thriving public image as the most irresistible brand on the block – actor, writer, producer, potential director. One entire wall on the ground floor is given over to pop-art portraits of every single employee, but by far the largest is that of Downey and his wife. The emphasis might be on team aesthetic, but there's no ambiguity about whose ultimately in charge. Ascend to the upper floors and you will find a large kitchen, three ridiculously plush bedrooms, a projection room and a terrace with barbeque and swimming pool.

On the expansive top floor, Downey greets me with a big movie-actor smile. With a regal curtsey and a self-mocking grin, he goes off in search of coffee for us both.

He's surprisingly slim and, at 46, the only hints of middle age and a few creases and flecks of grey in his goatee. His boyish enthusiasm remains undimmed. Having returned, he grabs a handful of vitamin bottles and a box of nicotine gum. 'I'm off the smokes again,' he explains.

I offer him my own brand, and his eyes light up with childlike delight. 'I can have these? Man, these are the British gums. The originals. These represent a solid day's worth of guarantee that I won't launch myself like a heat-seeking missile on an unsuspecting public. Now I'm ready to party!'

When I last met him in 2007, Downey was moaning he was the only actor in Hollywood earning the same as when he started out. Following his critically acclaimed performance in 1987's *Less Than Zero*, it soon became obvious that he was as troubled as he was gifted. Between 1996 and 2001, he became the poster boy for self-destruction, being repeatedly arrested on drug-related charges and finally spending a year in jail at the turn of the century. By the time he cleaned up for good in July 2003, he was only able to return to work – on the big-screen version of Dennis Potter's *The Singing Detective* – after close friend Mel Gibson paid the insurance bond. Subsequent movies had little box-office impact.

Then, in 2006, he landed the lead role in the comic-book adaptation *Iron Man*, which grossed over half a billion dollars on its release two years later. His next movie, *Tropic Thunder*, won him an Oscar nomination. The first Sherlock Holmes film made half a billion, as did 2010's *Iron Man 2*. What changed?

'Two words. Richard Attenborough. In '91, I came to London to film *Chaplin* with him. What he taught me was life-changing. I was 26 and knew a lot less than I thought I did. But I was willing to learn. Attenborough helped me to see that if I wanted to act on any meaningful level, I needed to immerse myself in what was happening with British acting in the Sixties. He made me aware that all those great actors – Burton, O'Toole, Finney, Courtenay – figured out the whole thing and mastered it. He taught me about economy of effort and efficiency, even when I was out partying all night and burning the candle at both ends. It's the raw emotion of the British model that's most informed my own approach to acting.

'On a more personal level, Attenborough told me that one day my ambition would supersede all my other impulses and set me straight. At that time I foolishly thought my ambition had been realised. The fact I was acting in movies, I couldn't see beyond that. Attenborough saw a bigger picture. How do you remain a fast bowler for more than one season and also retain the use of your arms when you retire? How do you sustain that? That's how Attenborough measured success. It took a long time for me to understand that properly.

'With *Iron Man*, I had to take on board all that Richard Attenborough taught me about ambition all those years ago. I realised I needed a plan. I looked at Keanu Reeves in *The Matrix*, Toby Maguire in *Spider-Man* and Johnny Depp in *Pirates* and thought, "I could do that kind of film." I then had to seize the day when it came. I fought harder for *Iron Man* than I've fought for any other movie. I prepared for the screen test so feverishly that I made it impossible for anybody to do a better job.'

It was a random phone conversation in 2008 with director Guy Ritchie that led to Downey being cast as a swashbuckling Sherlock Holmes for the 21st century, but Downey's fascination with the character's creator took root far earlier.

During filming in London in 1989, he regularly visited Conan Doyle Hall in Belgravia to observe séances. The hall was part of a large 175-year-old mansion that housed the Spiritualist Association of Great Britain, which for decades has invited members and non-members to witness the tilting of tables and levitation of wardrobes, aided by presences from beyond the grave. Its centrepiece was a large medium's cabinet containing the chair on which Conan Doyle wrote many of his Sherlock Holmes stories.

'I spent a lot of my spare time there,' says Downey. 'I'd go there mainly to sit in on the séances they conducted, where people would try to contact loved ones who'd passed away. It was fascinating. I went back recently to their new location near Victoria, because some of the plot of the new movie centres on fortune telling and mediums. If I've learnt anything, it's that it's possible to detect the presence of a deceased person in the room simply by the way the curtains move.'

Downey is completely serious; like Conan Doyle himself, he has a long-standing fascination with spiritualism and psychic phenomena – coexisting, in his case, with a dedication to yoga and wing chun kung fu.

'I'm not at all sceptical about clairvoyance,' he says. 'I've always been drawn to that stuff. Knowing that Conan Doyle shared my interests helped me make my mind up about taking the role of Sherlock.'

It's a decision he clearly doesn't regret, as 2009's *Sherlock Holmes* confirmed Downey's status as one of Hollywood's hottest stars. Last year alone he made an estimated $31.5 million, including a $15 million fee for starring in the second instalment of the franchise. But Downey makes a shocking confession to Holmes fans.

'Act three of Sherlock 1 was serviceable, but not really very good. With this new movie, we agreed it needed to be a big improvement. Sherlock 2 starts off good, gets better and has the best act three of any movie I have ever done. It's like the best sex of your life – if, that is, the sex of your life took two years from start to finish.'

He says he was daunted to be taking on the most frequently portrayed character in cinema history. 'I'm the 76th actor to do Sherlock, so there was a lot to live up to. Not since *Chaplin* had I done something where I felt the character was so iconic in the collective unconscious. To improve on the first Sherlock was one reason for doing a second film. Another reason was that I got the chance to film in England again.

'When I got the part, I voraciously made my way through the Conan Doyle books and was taken with his charming attention to detail. Watson remarks that Holmes keeps his tobacco in the toe of a Persian slipper. The interesting thing about that line is that it's a judgement, a source of wonder, and it also explains so much about the character of Sherlock. It's a wonderful eccentric observation. No nation on Earth can touch the English for eccentricity, though the Irish come close.

'I'm one eighth English. And it's an important eighth. My dad is half-Irish and I saw that eccentricity in him from an early age. For instance, he would stir his tea with an upside-down hammer. He would also claim to understand what the family terrier was saying when it barked. Now, there's two ways of looking at that behaviour. Maybe he preferred a hammer to a spoon. They're both made of wood, right? Maybe, just maybe, he could actually understand the language of dogs. Another way of looking at it is to say he was a wantonly eccentric kind of fellow.'

The influence of British culture on Downey isn't just restricted to his acting, it has affected his entire life. With an underground-fil-maker for a father and an actress mother, he travelled constantly in his early years, first visiting Britain at the age of six.

'My dad was working on a movie in London, so we sailed over from New York on the SS *France* ocean liner. I attended Perry House, a prep school in Chelsea. I was there to study classical ballet, but most of my time was spent being a complete moron, when I should have been working on my pirouettes. I also spent way too much time focused on Monica, the most beautiful English girl you could possibly imagine. Coming from Greenwich Village in New York, London was like another planet. The weather was grey, but everything else was in technicolour. I was completely charmed by it all. I found it all so civilised. Hell, even the sewer rats were polite.

'From then on, I was hooked on British culture. It started with the music. At six my dad introduced me to the Rolling Stones' *Let It Bleed* album. It meant much more to me than *Sesame Street*. I played it endlessly. Elvis Costello's *Imperial Bedroom* is my favourite album of all time. When it comes to music, the Brits beat the Americans hands down. There's no contest. But it's not just music. I'm fascinated by British history, from watching the changing of the guard at Buckingham Palace to the English countryside, the architecture, the street art. I've always adored British comedy, from Python to Billy Connolly to *Blackadder*, and I'm especially drawn to the cutting edge. It doesn't get any cooler than hanging out in The Punch Bowl with Jude Law and Stephen Fry and Guy Ritchie, trying to keep up with the quick-fire English banter. I love Frankie Boyle's work, but everything he says seems to be an instant controversy. Why should he compromise the simple truth that humour is about what's funny, not about what's morally right and wrong? I just hope that British comedy doesn't loose its nerve.'

It seems appropriate to elicit Downey's thoughts on Ricky Gervais, whose edgy presentation of this year's Golden Globes he appeared to denounce on a speech on the night. A genuine spat or good-natured jousting? 'For me, anything that's happening in public is going to have a level of gamesmanship to it. If someone really offended me, I wouldn't say anything about it publicly. I'd wait for a quiet moment and have it out to their face. Or, more likely, I'd shrug and ask myself why I should care.

'The media are always looking for a spat, and I have to say that I love it, even when it's about me. I love tabloid reality, for the reason that everything is true in the moment that you read it. It doesn't occur to me when I'm reading it that it must be made-up garbage. I'll take that kind of thing any day over sycophantic, over-respectful journalism where everyone is a member of the same club and all the uncomfortably sharp edges are smoothed over to save face. Which is just as bad as lying. The truth is I like Ricky Gervais and I've seen him around. I've just heard that he's been invited back to host the Golden Globes in 2012. So, he wins. End of story.

Downey is happily married to Susan, an influential Hollywood player who was a producer on several of his recent movies. Aside from Team Downey Building, they own a sumptuous home in LA, along with a $14 Million estate in the foothills of Malibu. He has an 18-year-old son, Indio, from his previous marriage to actress/singer Deborah Falconer, and he and Susan are expecting their first child together in February.

'It's funny,' he says. 'I used to say that I'd welcome a bullet to the forehead if I ever ended up as a 40-some-thing, remarried, marketable, big-action movie dad living in a cosy cul-de-sac in suburban LA. Now I am that guy. It just goes to show that I usually don't know what's good for me in life. But I'm getting better at knowing that stuff. I don't need to rub against the grain nearly as much as I used to. I'm 46 now, so the countdown to my half-century has begun. I'd have to be completely deranged not to stress about that.'

It seems turning 50 is the only downside that Downey can conjure. 'Life is good,' he says. 'With a new baby on the way, maybe I ought to think about slowing down a little. But I can't see that happening in the short term.'

And with that, the activity in the building becomes noticeably more hectic, as Guy Ritchie bounds up the stairs and announces his arrival to discuss Sherlock 3. Downey needs to get back to work. With laser-like sincerity he thanks me for coming so far to see him. Heading into his office to greet Ritchie, chewing rapaciously on his gum, he turns and says, 'Give my love to England. I do mean that.'

'Sherlock Holmes: A Game of Shadows' is released on December 16

FRIDAY, DECEMBER 16, 2011 **THE DAILY TELEGRAPH**

REVIEWS BY **ROBBIE COLLIN**

Sherlock does panto

The riotous return of Robert Downey Jr and Jude Law as Holmes and Watson is a cross-dressing romp'

There are two important questions worth asking about Guy Ritchie's second Sherlock Holmes film: it is a faithful rendering of Sir Arthur Conan Doyle's character; and, in the event that it isn't, does that actually matter? The answer to both is a foghorn-like no: Ritchie's brassy, vigorously silly romp has next to nothing in common with Conan Doyle's work save a handful of character names and the odd pipe, but what it lacks in authenticity it makes up for in sheer swashbuckling brio.

Robert Downey's Jr's portrayal of Holmes as a childlike, slightly dangerous mischief-maker perhaps owes something to Gene Wilder's Willy Wonka: let's just say if this man had anything to do with a criminal investigation, you wouldn't expect him to be the person solving it. At the film's opening, Holmes is distraught that his straight-arrow sidekick Dr Watson (Jude Law) is marrying his sweetheart Mary (Kelly Reilly) and leaving the detection business for good. However, on Watson's stag night, the pair uncover a plot to spark war in Europe that Holmes suspects may be the work of Professor Moriarty (played with husky malevolence by Jared Harris). Holmes and Watson embark on a madcap chase across the continent to thwart the detective's arch-nemesis, one that's rather heavier on action set-pieces and camp squabbling that it is on the actual detective work for which Conan Doyle's creation is best known.

A Game of Shadows is at once looser and more coherent than Ritchie's first Holmes film: while the 2009 original was an uneasy mish-mash of action and sleuthing, this is a *Boy's Own* adventure through and through. The elaborate scrapes that play out across various sumptuously detailed fantasy-historical settings recalls Disney's *Pirates of the Caribbean* series, but *A Game of Shadows* is frothier and funnier than those films; much less pompous and significantly more likeable.

Much of the appeal comes down to the Downey Jr – Law partnership. Cinema has seen its fair share of romance and bromance over the years; this, surely, is its first Holmance. The duo's knockabout schoolyard chemistry has improved immeasurably since the first film: Holmes and Watson are like a pair of naughty 11-year-olds, thick as thieves and bickering constantly. Stephen Fry adds to the fun as Holmes's dryly buffoonish brother Mycroft, a British diplomat who fondly calls his younger sibling "Shirley".

As tends to be the way when 11-year-old boys are in charge, all of the yucky girls are frozen out. Both Reilly and Rachel McAdams, who briefly returns in the role of Irene Adler, are swiftly sidelined by the plot, and Noomi Rapace's gipsy fortune-teller Simza – who joins Holmes and Watson on their adventure – is so underwritten she's virtually disposable.

Fortunately, there is someone on hand to redress the oestrogen imbalance: Holmes himself, who dons full drag in order to sneak on board a train crawling with Moriarty's minions. This leads to an uproariously daft punch-up, soundtracked by Hans Zimmer's thigh-slapping music-hall score.

The ensuing fight, along with most of the others in the film, is muddled, but it's carried by some witty ideas, many of which involve Holmes's borderline-superhuman ability to mentally spool back and forth through time. This is used most amusingly here than it was in the first film: Holmes beating a boxer by second-guessing his punches is a cop-out, but Holmes bested a soldier by sliding a booby-trapped lipstick into his ammo belt half an hour previously is priceless.

With the dead wood trimmed and the dud characters rewritten, *Sherlock Holmes: A Game of Shadows* could have been a sharper, more consistently enjoyable one hour-and-

45-minute romp. But, as it stands, it's such rollicking good fun – particularly the climax, set above a waterfall in the Swiss Alps – that it's easy to forgive the film its missteps with its cross-dressing lead, hissable villain and oodles of double entendre, Ritchie's film is the closest action cinema has ever come to pantomime – and that's meant as a sincere compliment.

Telegraph RATING 3 out of 5 stars.

REVIEW The Mail on Sunday December 18, 2011

THE CRITICS

Matthew Bond

It's all a bit...Rudimentary my dear Watson

Sherlock Holmes: A Game of Shadows

Two years ago Guy Ritchie's first stab at making a Sherlock Holmes picture was close to brilliant. His second, alas, is not in the same class. Yes, it has a barnstorming last half-hour and Jared Harris is outstanding as Holmes's nemesis, Professor Moriarty, but time and again there are signs that all the praise I and others deservedly heaped upon Ritchie has rather gone to his head.

Humour is the most obvious casualty. In the first film, it was driven by the dazzlingly quick repartee between Robert Downey Jr's hyper-manic Holmes and Jude Law's revelatory reinterpretation of Dr Watson. There are still echoes of that in *A Game of Shadows* but, with a fresh and noticeably inexperienced team of writer on board, the new approach seems to that when in pursuit of laughs, anything goes. So we have 21st Century vernacular being parachuted jarringly into the London of 1891. 'You're the one with no friends,' Watson accuses Holmes at one point, 'Shirley No Mates'.

We have Stephen Fry stripping inexplicably to the buff as Holmes's brother, Mycroft, and, worse of all, we have Holmes and Watson teaming up with a band of gipsies escaping on horseback...only for Holmes, apparently nervous equestrian, to be given a Shetland pony.

Now I know small boys will still be laughing at this but I was closer to weeping. And I haven't even mentioned the silly interior camouflage suits (for blending into rooms) or Holmes and Watson dancing together at a diplomatic ball.

The damage this sort of cavalier approach does to the underlying Holmes franchise is incalculable, particularly given the care Ritchie lavished on the first film. And, dare I say it, with the visual noticeably poorer than before this seems more of a money-making exercise.

But there are things still to admire and enjoy as Holmes forces Watson to give up his honeymoon and join him instead on a trans-European pursuit of the evil Moriarty, whom he believes is behind bombings that have brought the Continent to the brink of war.

Harris brings menace to nearly every scene he's in, and is almost single-handedly responsible for the film acquiring some edge and tension as we enter the final half-hour. Law is excellent too, cutting back on the military bearing, perhaps – Watson you may recall, is an Afghanistan veteran – but still getting the blend of loyalty, exasperation and engagingly gung-ho spirit pretty much spot-on. As for Downey Jr, an actor who does not need to be kept on a tight rein, he's still good but not as good as in the first film.

It's a disappointing outing for the female cast members. Rachel McAdams, who returns as jewel thief and occasional Holmes love interest Irene Adler doesn't last long, while Kelly Reilly, as the new Mrs Watson, never really recovers from being thrown from a train. As for poor Noomi Rapace, famous for her riveting performance as Lisbeth Salander in the original Swedish version of The Girl With The Dragon Tattoo, her first English language feature film leaves her with little more to do as a fortune-telling gipsy than looking mildly exotic.

The end result is undemanding, commercial holiday fun but nothing like as good as the original.

Kent on Sunday December 18, 2011
Hollywood makeover creates Holmes' Swiss castle in park

By Chris Britcher

KNOLE Park has a star role in the latest Hollywood blockbuster featuring super detective Sherlock Holmes.

The venue in Sevenoaks was transformed into a winter wonderland for director Guy Ritchie's Sherlock Holmes: A Game of Shadows which went on general release this weekend.

The film sees Robert Downey Jr reprise his role as the super sleuth, along with Jude Law as side-kick Dr Watson.

In the latest instalment the world-famous detective faces his arch-nemesis – Professor Moriarty, played by Jared Harris – and the action leads Holmes and Watson from England to France to Germany and finally to Switzerland.

When the location switches to Switzerland, Knole steps into the limelight.

Jane Maltby, marketing manager at Knole, explained: "Last autumn the cast and crew from A Game of Shadows came to Knole for five weeks, transforming Stone Court into the courtyard of a Swiss castle.

"Recreating the wintry conditions of Switzerland required a lot of fake snow and as you might imagine, fake snow does not do as it is told. Whereas real snow tends to sit where it falls, the artificial stuff wanders, particularly in a breeze. This meant that quite a lot of Knole experienced an early dusting of the white stuff.

"Once the drifts of fake snow were in place, Stone Court was used to mark the arrival of Holmes' arch enemy Professor Moriarty, by a wonderful Horse-drawn sledge. We're all delighted to see that this sequence has made it's way into the film's trailer – a mere 50 seconds in."

It is not the first time Guy Ritchie and his team have come to Kent. Scenes from the first Sherlock Holmes film were shot at Chatham's historic dockyard.

During filming, star Robert Downey Jnr was accidentally punched in the face by actor Robert Maillet, who played Dredger, drawing blood and leaving the Iron Man actor on the ground.

THURSDAY, DECEMBER 22, 2011 THE DAILY TELEGRAPH

Mandrake Tim Walker

Elementary error

Starring **Robert Downey Jr** and **Jude Law**, **Sherlock Holmes: A Game of Shadows** is the big Christmas film, but it has failed to impress **Baroness Bakewell** . She says it is so bad that she walked out of the cinema. "Saw truly awful Sherlock Holmes film last night. Left after 45 minutes…couldn't take any more. Conan Doyle must be spinning." One wonders what Joan Bakewell was doing, as a committed feminist, seeing a film about a man who admitted to not being a "whole-souled admirer of womankind".

Chapter 30

An Update On Undershaw

THE DAILY TELEGRAPH THURSDAY, JULY 6, 2006

Sherlock Holmes heritage threatened by homes By **Catriona Davies**

DEVELOPERS and conservationists are in dispute over plans to convert Sir Arthur Conan Doyle's Surrey house where he wrote *The Hound of the Baskervilles* and *The Return of Sherlock Holmes*, into four homes. Campaigners say that the unique history of Undershaw, built at Hindhead in 1897, is under threat if permission is granted to divide it.

They fear that internal fittings, such as the author's initials monogrammed on ground floor doors and stained glass windows bearing the family crest, will be lost, as will any public access. The Victorian Society, a heritage charity that is being backed by the Sherlock Holmes Society, has appealed to English Heritage for the house's listed building status to be upgraded from Grade II to Grade I to save the interior.

The 36-room house was a hotel from 1924 until 2004 but is now empty. Desmond Moore, a developer, originally applied to convert it into 13 flats but has now revised the plans to four homes. Three would be built in the main house and one in a garage in the grounds.

Kathryn Ferry, an architectural adviser to the Victorian Society, said: "Any scheme for subdivision could be hugely damaging and would mean that this vital part of our literary heritage is lost. Undershaw was the home of one of the best-known authors in the English language. It is time we recognised its importance."

However, Chris Atkins, of RDA Architects, working for Mr Moore's firm, Fossway, said the house was in a poor state of repair and that development would restore it as much as possible to its original state.

He said: "Many of the original features were destroyed when it was converted to a hotel and what is there at the moment is only a partial reflection of the house as it was.

"If nothing happens it will just fall to pieces because it is not viable as a house. It is too big and no one would buy it in its present condition. The features such as the monograms and the stained glass windows are not in pristine condition but they will be retained."

Conan Doyle paid £1,000 for the plot of land after his wife Louisa [*sic*] was diagnosed with leukaemia. He thought Hindhead would be a good place for her to convalesce because of its healthy microclimate.

Records suggest that the author drew up the first plans himself, before asking his friend Joseph Henry Ball, an architect, to complete the design. Conan Doyle and his wife lived there for 10 years until she died and he remarried. He wrote *The Hound of the Baskervilles* there in 1902 and resurrected *Sherlock Holmes* in 1904.

Bram Stoker, the author of *Dracula*, interviewed Conan Doyle at Undershaw. Afterwards he said: "It is so sheltered from cold winds that the architect felt justified by having lots of windows, so that the whole place is full of light.

"Nevertheless, it is cosy and snug to a remarkable degree and has everywhere that sense of 'home' which is so delightful to occupant and stranger alike'"

Julian Barnes set part of his 2005 novel *Arthur & George* at Undershaw. The Victorian Society argues that the home's literary associations put it on a par with Charles Darwin's home, Down House, in Kent, which is Grade I listed and an English Heritage property. Ideally, the society would like Undershaw to be kept as a single home but with some public open days. John Gibson, an author who has written books on Conan Doyle, expressed interest in buying the house for £1 million after the hotel closed, but missed out. He said: "I have been interested in this property for many years. This was the only house that Conan Doyle had built for himself. To gut it will destroy the integrity of the important building and all its connections." Nick Utechin, the editor of the *Sherlock Holmes Journal,* said: "no thought appears to have been given to the incredible importance Conan Doyle has in popular literary culture. We are not saying the house needs to be maintained exactly as it was, but it would be nice if something could be kept or if the public were able to look around it."

English Heritage said it would assess the Victorian Society's application to upgrade the listing then pass it's advice to the Department of Culture, Media and Sport for a decision.

TELEGRAPH PROPERTY **Saturday, October 20, 2007**

What's to become of it, Watson?

Undershaw, once Sir Arthur Conan Doyle's Surrey home, is on the market. **Sinclair McKay** takes a look at its past.

The game is afoot! And indeed, far from being elementary, this conundrum looks like a three-pipe-problem. The puzzle, my dear Watson, is this: what exactly is to become of the house that once belonged to Sir Arthur Conan Doyle, the creator of Sherlock Holmes?

Undershaw's the place. It is a striking, redbrick house just a little way back from the A3 at the Surrey village of Hindhead. Conan Doyle lived here from 1897 to 1907 with his wife Louise. It was here, also – as set out in the new biography by Andrew Lycett – that he began a relationship with Jean Leckie, who was later to become his second wife.

But the house is our concern, not the gossip of highbrow literary chroniclers. Conan Doyle had the place built by architect Joseph Henry Bell. After 1907, when he sold up, it fell into various hands; indeed from 1924 until 2004, the house became a hotel. Now, after years of standing sorrowfully empty, Undershaw has been boarded up against vandals, the council has ensured its roof is leak-proof and it has come on the market.

Sitting amid a prospect of tall trees and waving grass, commanding a view down a secluded valley to the South Downs, Undershaw is where the eerie *The Hound of the Baskervilles*, most famous of Conan Doyle's Sherlock Holmes stories, was written in 1902.

A familiar-looking, yet slightly odd construction – the asymmetry is striking – it was built in the Surrey-vernacular style. It is, says the local conservation office, a good example of the intellectual and art homes that sprung up during this period.

Close to the town of Haslemere, and about 40 miles from London, it is a world away from the deadly sucking embrace of Grimpen Mire or the deafening roar of the Reichenbach Falls, but it was clearly a tremendous home for Conan Doyle's fertile imagination and febrile energy. It was here that Conan Doyle made the decision to resurrect the detective, whom he had tried to kill off in a struggle with his arch-nemesis Professor Moriarty.

Also, it was from Undershaw that Conan Doyle thrust himself into politics and stood for Parliament as a Conservative candidate. He became a Deputy Lieutenant of Surrey, and joined the local Chiddingfield Hunt and the golf club. And it was here that he entered the Boer War as a volunteer army surgeon. It might be argued that after many peripatetic years, moving from Edinburgh, to Southsea, to London and then to Austria, Undershaw represented Conan Doyle's first really secure home as a successful author.

There's more, Watson: as anyone who has read Julian Barnes's recent bestseller *Arthur & George* will know, it was from Undershaw that Conan Doyle championed the case of George Edalji, falsely imprisoned for animal mutilation. According to Barnes, Conan Doyle also pursued his other passion as a ghost-hunting spiritualist. There is no evidence, sadly, that any furniture moved about of its own volition at Undershaw. But in other ways, the house itself is now taking dramatic centre stage.

In aesthetic terms, there is a reason why the place is so unusual: Conan Doyle commissioned his house specially to take into account the prognosis for his wife Louise, who was suffering from TB. The outlook in 1897 was not good, and she was expected to live a matter of months rather than years. This is the reason why the house has extra large windows, in order to make it a sunnier, airier place and one conducive to convalescence.

The aesthetics clearly did the trick, because Louise (known as "Touie") lived 10 years longer. In fact, in the late Victorian era, the Surrey air was very much sought after, the area in which Undershaw was built being known as "Little Switzerland". Undershaw became famous as a sort of literary hot spot, with visitors such as Bram Stoker, the author of *Dracula*, who came to interview Conan Doyle, and Virginia Woolf, who took photographs of everyone as they sat on the lawn. Another visitor was Jean Leckie; Conan Doyle always insisted that no impropriety took place during this period, but their marriage after Louise's death in 1906 was swift. Although it is being advertised as a hotel, there are many who hope that the new buyer will convert Undershaw back into the sort of quiet, single residence that Conan Doyle so relished.

There have already been genteel punch-ups over the subject. Especially pugilistic is the Victorian Society, which has long been pushing for the Grade II-listed house to be given greater protective status from English Heritage.

"We are pushing for Grade I-listing," says spokeswoman Heloise Brown. "English Heritage originally turned it down on the grounds that Conan Doyle wasn't on quite the same level as other authors such as Jane Austen or Elizabeth Gaskell. Our argument is that Sherlock Holmes has such an immense and universal appeal – there are 400 appreciation societies around the world – that the house really deserves extra protection."

And it is not just a question of big windows. Another feature was the inclusion of some specially commissioned stained glass, upon which were heraldic symbols purporting to be the Conan Doyle coat-of-arms. Sadly, not a huge amount of this has survived.

"There were some other extraordinary quirks, too," says Heloise Brown. "For instance, Conan Doyle asked the architect for internal doors that would open both ways. There was also a rumour that he had a secret door to the library."

Last year the local authority, Waverley Borough Council, stepped in to prevent the house being turned into 13 different "dwellings". At the time, it was owned by a company called Fossway. Christopher Atkins, from RDA Architects, speaking on their behalf, says: "It might have been his [Conan Doyle's] house once, but it has been through a number of different versions since. If it's left alone, it'll fall to pieces. The developer's intention is to provide a number of houses within the existing building and that will then provide the funding to enable it to be restored to its original position."

The Victorian Society was, and is, vehemently opposed to this. "We very much hope that it doesn't get split into flats," says Heloise Brown.

The Society's hopes for the house are ambitious.

"It's potential as a hotel is great. And so is its potential as a museum. We would like to see part of it open to the public.

* *Undershaw is up for sale through agents Lambert Smith Hampton in Guilford (01483 538181); Website:lsh.co.uk. Set in three acres, it is bordered lush woods, and has 14 bedrooms set over three rambling floors, comprising 10,000 sq ft. A spokesman says that no guide price is available as there are many options for interested parties to consider. As to renovation, the years of standing empty have taken their toll, not to mention the thieves who stole lead from the roof. Expect a big bill. To find out more about The Victorian Society, visit their website: victorian-society.org.uk.*

From The Victorian Society Friday 28 September 2007

News

Conan Doyle's former home up for grabs

News that Undershaw, the Grade II-listed Surrey home of Sir Arthur Conan Doyle, is up for sale has been welcomed by the Victorian Society, the national charity campaigning for the Victorian and Edwardian historic environment.

Joining forces with many of the 400 societies devoted to Conan Doyle and Sherlock Holmes around the world, the Victorian Society successfully fought plans to subdivide Undershaw into 13 dwellings last year. It is also pushing for its listing to be upgraded to bring the house where The Hound of the Baskervilles (1902) was written and guests such as Virginia Woolf and Bram Stoker entertained into line with historic buildings associated with other significant literary figures.

'The historical importance of Undershaw is indisputable,' said Heloise Brown, Conservation Adviser of the Victorian Society. 'It was the home of one of the best-known authors in the English language. Conan Doyle and Sherlock Holmes are world-famous figures and people around the world care deeply about the house that played such a part in their existence. We expect it will have wide appeal.'

Over the last eighteen months, the Victorian Society has been contacted by numerous people concerned about the future of the house and interested to know whether it might be available to buy. Run as a hotel until it closed in 2004, Undershaw, has been seriously neglected by its owner. Earlier this year, Waverley Council sent in workmen to carry out urgent repairs after the property was left inadequately boarded up, at the mercy of vandals and the elements.

'It's vital that the right buyer comes forward now,' continued Miss Brown. 'This is not just a charming and intriguing historic house, but a nationally and internationally significant building, too. In the hands of the right owner, it could be a wonderful asset again. We hope it gets that chance.'

To make enquiries about buying Undershaw, please contact Lambert Smith Hampton (01483 538 181).

THE DAILY TELEGRAPH TUESDAY, DECEMBER 29, 2009

Elementary? Twist in the tale of Sherlock Holmes creator's house

By Gordon Rayner

WITH a film about one of the world's favourite detectives in cinemas this week, Sherlock Holmes is winning a new generation of fans.

But the fate of the country house where its creator, Sir Arthur Conan Doyle, wrote about his exploits remains a mystery. The writer built Undershaw at Hindhead in Surrey as a place where his wife Louisa could recover from tuberculosis.

It was in the study of Undershaw that the author penned Holmes's greatest adventure, *The Hound of the Baskervilles*, in 1901. He lived there until 1907 and entertained guests such as Bram Stoker, the author of *Dracula*. The house was run as a hotel for 80 years but over the past five years, it fell into a near-derelict state as it stood empty. The 36-room property is full of reminders of its celebrated former owner, including monogrammed door handles and stained glass windows bearing the family coat of arms.

Plans by a property developer who bought the site to divide it into flats were turned down but a new planning application to the council is expected within weeks.

But Conan Doyle enthusiasts want to see the house turned into a museum. They have set up the Undershaw Preservation Trust aimed at either raising enough money to buy the property or finding a buyer who could restore it and keep it as a single private house. Lynn Gale, from the trust, said: "It will be a tragedy if Undershaw is not preserved and opened to the public.

"We believe it has a viable future as a visitor centre, museum and conference centre, but we are rapidly running out of time to make this a reality and this is the latest chance to save the building for the nation." The plan is supported by the Victorian Society, which campaigns to save important 19th century buildings. A spokesman from the Society said plans to divide the house into apartments would "harm the historical interest of this house as Arthur Conan Doyle's family home"'

Daily Mail, Saturday, March 13, 2010

It's a mystery that would even stump Sherlock Holmes. Why on earth are we letting Conan Doyle's home fall into ruin?

HOW I SEE IT by Robert Hardman

HE MANAGED to solve some of the most famous crimes in history using nothing more than a magnifying glass and a contemplative pipe or three of tobacco. So it's a pity he is not around to study this sorry little crime scene.

Who smashed these windows? Who sprayed this graffiti over these Victorian walls? Who pinched all the lead off the roof, allowing the rain to cascade through the house? And who vandalised these heraldic stained glass windows?

But there's actually a more troubling mystery here. How on earth could a nation which has produced the most famous character in modern fiction – inspiring a record 233 films and 400 fan clubs worldwide – simply stand by while his creator's legacy is erased? Even Sherlock Holmes would have been pushed to answer that one.

That, however, is the sad situation here at Undershaw, the enchanting spot on the Surrey-Hampshire-Sussex border where Sherlock's creator Sir Arthur Conan Doyle lived, loved and worked at the height of his powers. From the rubble-strewn bedrooms to the overgrown tennis court to the valley below, the whole place is in a dismal state.

The imposing late Victorian house – built in what experts like to call 'Surrey vernacular' – is boarded-up, dilapidated and awaiting next month's verdict by the local council's planning committee. If the current owner, a Virgin Islands-based property company, has its way, Undershaw will be gutted and redeveloped into eight executive homes.

Standing in its path, however, is an angry and energetic legion of Conan Doyle devotees who want Undershaw to remain a single house. 'I urge you to consider what future ages will adjudge a foolish, short-sighted and wanton act of vandalism,' writes Stephen Fry, once the youngest member of the Sherlock Holmes Society of London, in his submission to Waverley Borough Council.

Certainly, as far as the rest of the world is concerned, Britain has gone completely mad.

'I've been interviewed by a Russian television crew who simply could not believe what we are doing to our literary heritage,' says John Gibson, a retired chartered surveyor and co-founder of the Undershaw Preservation Trust, as he shows me round. 'Can you imagine any other country producing the most popular detective in history and not bothering to make something of it?'

Undershaw is our last proper link to an author who helped to define his age. Aside from the make-believe Sherlock Holmes Museum and gift shop in London's Baker Street, there really is nowhere else. Hence the importance of Undershaw.

It was beneath this patchwork ceiling of cracked plaster and bare beams that the Edinburgh-born GP composed some of his finest work.

It was here that he brought Sherlock Holmes back to life after his seemingly terminal encounter with the original arch-enemy Professor Moriarty. It was staring out across the uninterrupted 20-mile view of the South Downs that Conan Doyle produced arguably his most famous novel, The Hound of the Baskervilles.

That one Sherlock Holmes story alone has been turned into 24 films – more than the entire James Bond oeuvre put together.

Today, Conan Doyle would see nothing from his study because the shattered ground-floor windows are boarded up. But weave your way through the mess, tread gingerly up the stairs to the upper floors and the panoramic view across three counties has not changed one bit since a chum dropped in for lunch with the Conan Doyles in 1898.

He later described 'an endless sea of greenery, ranges of hills piling up, one behind the other, in undulations of varying blue. An expanse which, whether seen from near or far, in unity or detail, simply ravishes the eye with its myriad beauties'.

That visitor was a certain Bram Stoker, the creator of the second most-filmed character in fiction after Sherlock Holmes – Dracula (217 films and counting).

Conan Doyle's literary circle ranged from Oscar Wilde and HG Wells to the assistant at his local Post Office in Grayshott.

'Scarcely a day passed without his bursting like a breeze into the Post Office, almost filling it with his fine presence, and the deep tones of his jovial voice,' wrote Flora Thompson, author of Lark Rise To Candleford (she particularly enjoyed the social mayhem stirred up by the Conan Doyles' fancy dress ball in 1898).

By any standards, this house commands a substantial place in Britain's cultural history.

I may be in a leafy Surrey, but here is a monument to a genius of Irish lineage who conquered the world. And Undershaw is not just about Sherlock Holmes, Brigadier Gerard and all his other fictional creations.

Conan Doyle was a supremely eminent Victorian/Edwardian in so many ways. He was a man who abandoned his stellar literary career to go off to the Boer War as a medic, ending up writing the official history of the war.

He was also a gifted sportsman. As a cricketer, he bowled out WG Grace. As a footballer, he served as goalkeeper for the original Portsmouth Football Club (a position now enjoyed by England's David James).

There is a hell of a story hiding behind the rhododendron bushes next to the A3 at Hindhead. Conan Doyle chose this spot for his home because of the area's repute as 'Little Switzerland' so-named for its 800 ft altitude and clean air. Some of the great medical minds of the age, such as John Tyndall and Sir Johnathan Hutchinson, had championed the restorative qualities of life on the Surrey-Sussex border around Hindhead and Haslemere.

Conan Doyle was working as a doctor in Portsmouth when he met his wife Louise, known as 'Touie'.

By 1891, his success as an author allowed him to give up medicine and write full time in London. With two children and fame and fortune, the couple failed to spot Touie's deteriorating health until she was diagnosed with tuberculosis in 1893.

In 1896, Conan Doyle decided that urgent measures were required. Having tried clinics all over Europe, he paid £1,000 for a plot of land in Hindhead and spent another £7,000 building and equipping it with all the latest gizmos, including an electricity plant.

The house is still full of little touches with Touie in mind – including the shallow steps on the main staircase. 'Touie would be out of puff in no time, so he made the stairs as easily as possible,' explains Mr Gibson. The huge windows were built to provide optimum air and light for a housebound invalid.

Even amid today's wreckage, we still see a quirky monument to a great man's vanity.

In the main hall, once decorated with guns, prints and aspidistras, there remains a huge stained glass window incorporating the crests and names of all the grand families – 'Percy of Northumberland', 'Hawkins of Devonshire' – from whom Conan Doyle claimed he and his wife were descended. For all the neglect, this place still has strong echoes of the buzzing ideas factory it once was.

So why have things deteriorated this far? Four years ago, conservationists at the Victorian Society begged English Heritage and the Government to upgrade Undershaw from a Grade II – listed building (which means it is of special architectural or historical interest) to Grade II – starred (more than special) or Grade I (exceptional).

This is not just a matter of words. A Grade II listing means that only the local council needs to be consulted about alterations. A higher grading would make it a matter for national concern and invoke the attention of English Heritage.

Amazingly the Culture Secretary of the day, Tessa Jowell, refused the upgrade, arguing that the building was not of sufficient architectural or historic merit.

Now, I admit that Undershaw is no oil painting. But it is, surely, of enormous historic significance.

The Government has cheerfully given Grade I listings to other houses on the basis of literary links to, among others, Charles Dickens, Jane Austen, John Keats, Elizabeth Gaskell (Cranford) and Charles Kingsley (The Water Babies).

While I have no wish to poo-poo Cranford or The Water Babies, how could anyone claim that either is of more importance than Sherlock Holmes? Unless, that is, there is a spot of literary snobbery going on here.

In the end, the long-term security of this place may simply depend on the next General Election.

Undershaw falls within the seat of the Tory MP for Surrey South West, Jeremy Hunt, who is also Shadow Culture Secretary. If the Tories get in, Mr Hunt will be in charge of listing all buildings in England.

'While I could not be directly involved,' says the MP, 'I would very strongly support any change of listing.' For now, Mr Hunt wants to see the plan thrown out.

I was allowed inside by Michael Wilson, a respected architect hired by the owners, Fossway. Fossway bought Undershaw for £1.1 million in 2004, when it was a hotel and restaurant.

The place then sat empty while the new owners sought permission to redevelop. 'It was in a terrible state,' recalls Mr Gibson. 'I came here once and the front door was wide open with rain pouring through. I reported it to the council and came back two weeks later and it was still open to the world.'

Fossway's first planning application, in 2006 was kicked out. When the council looked ready to impose a compulsory purchase in 2008, the company brought in Mr Wilson to come up with a more respectable plan. It still involves chopping up the main house into three separate houses and adding another five.

Mr Gibson is particularly cross that Conan Doyle's original stables – still untouched, with the same cast iron stalls in place – are to be turned into a garage.

Mr Wilson argues that his plan is a sensitive solution which maintains the façade of the house and also provides a platform for the public to view the house from adjacent National Trust land. Mr Gibson is appalled. 'It will destroy the whole spirit of the place. You'll have Conan Doyle's drawing room in one house, his dining room in another and his study in another.'

Above all else, Conan Doyle's fans want a stay of execution which will maintain Undershaw as a single entity until a new buyer steps forward (Mr Wilson says Fossway would consider offers of £1.5 million).

Speaking from America, Stephen Fry says: 'There has never been a time when Conan Doyle has gone out of fashion.' He points out that yet another Sherlock Holmes Hollywood blockbuster has just hit the screen. 'Undershaw' is 'Underthreat', 'he declares. 'Surely we can all see that this is a disastrous mistake?'

Considering the Lottery has come up with £4.3 million for, say, a museum dedicated to the local artist George Frederick Watts, it would surely kindly on a bid to create the first and only museum dedicated to one of Britain's greatest author.

There is much ground to cover. Quite apart from Sherlock Holmes, Conan Doyle produced so many classic tales. The Lost World, for example. The original man-meets-dinosaur thriller, it inspired Michael Crichton of Jurassic Park Fame.

There was Conan Doyle's famous obsession with ghosts, spirits and fairies which led to much public ridicule. And then there was his love-life. During Touie's final years, he fell in love with the young Jean Leckie, whom he married as soon as was decent after his first wife's death in 1907.

He died in 1930, his global fame assured for eternity. Show a picture of a deerstalker to a passer-by in Tokyo or Timbuktu and they will say, simply, 'Sherlock Holmes'.

That is why a central piece of British literary history rests with a handful of Surrey councillors who must make up their minds next month.

Anyone can still object to Waverley Borough Council before next Friday (it's waverley.gov.uk and the planning reference is 0172).

(**Compiler's note**: From the above website: 05/02/2010 Pending Decision Undershaw Hotel, Hindhead Road, Hindhead GU26 6AH Conversion, extension and alterations to building to provide 8 dwellings, alterations to Lodge House and erection of a pavilion.

On Thursday night, the local town council in Haslemere voted to oppose the plans. This weekend, Mr Gibson is orchestrating a final push among fellow supporters.

The alternative? Elementary, my dear Watson: a cultural disaster which will puzzle the entire planet.

SATURDAY, MARCH 13, 2010 **THE DAILY TELEGRAPH**

In Brief

Conan Doyle Fight

Stephen Fry has joined the 1,500 people objecting to plans to convert the former country home of Sherlock Holmes author Sir Arthur Conan Doyle into flats. The actor said the destruction of Undershaw in Hindhead, Surrey, would be a "wanton act of vandalism".

Daily Mail, Wednesday, March 17, 2010

LETTERS

Man of Mystery

READING about Sir Arthur Conan Doyle's home, Undershaw (Mail), reminded me of something an elderly friend told me many years ago.

As a young woman, she was friendly with someone who'd worked as a handyman for Conan Doyle at Undershaw.

He told her that one of the upstairs rooms was permanently locked, staff were forbidden from entering and Conan Doyle had the only key.

After Conan Doyle's death, curiosity overcame him and he put up a ladder to the window and looked in. It was, he said, 'completely empty'.

Whatever the secret of the locked room, Conan Doyle took it to the grave. Or does anyone know differently?

ROGER VINCE,
Upper Brynamman, Carms.

Daily Mail, Wednesday, March 24, 2010

LETTERS

Frightful revelation…

FURTHER to the mysterious empty locked room at Sir Arthur Conan Doyle's mansion, Undershaw (Letters), in 1922 the great man wrote a short story entitled The Sealed Room. In it, on its being opened, the chamber revealed the horror of a body in a state of decomposition seated at a desk.

More significant perhaps are Conan Doyle's description of the house in the story and his musing that 'the cheap builder might rear a dozen £80-a-year villas upon the garden frontage' – a prescient speculation in view of the possibility that Undershaw could be developed into 'eight executive homes'.

J.D. PARR,
Romsey, Hants.

FRIDAY, DECEMBER 17, 2010 **THE DAILY TELEGRAPH**

Battle to save Conan Doyle home

A five-year battle to save the former home of Sir Arthur Conan Doyle has gone to the High Court after campaigners applied for a judicial review of a decision to allow development of the Grade II listed house.

Undershaw, in Hindhead, Surrey, is where the creator of Sherlock Holmes wrote many of his books, including *The Hound of the Baskervilles*, after he built it in 1897. It has remained largely unchanged since, and retains features including stained glass windows bearing the Conan Doyle family's coat of arms.

Plans to turn the house into a museum came to nothing, and with the building suffering from vandalism, Waverley borough council granted the owner permission to turn it into flats. The Undershaw Preservation Trust has lodged papers at the High Court requesting a judicial review of the planners' decision, which they say was unlawful.

THE DAILY TELEGRAPH SATURDAY, MARCH 19, 2011

Could Sherlock Holmes hold the key to Hindhead's future? (Excerpt)

Hindhead has also hit the headlines lately due to controversy surrounding a house built south of the crossroads by Sir Arthur Conan Doyle in 1897.

The author, whose wife suffered from tuberculosis, chose the village for its fresh air and wonderful views and helped to design a handsome family home on a three-acre site.

Undershaw – so named because it was downhill from George Bernard Shaw's place – became a hotel in 1924, then fell into disrepair after investors bought the property in 2004. Last June, Waverley Borough Council approved plans to divide the main building into three town houses, and building five further homes on the site.

Both locals and the literary world have raised objections, and in December the Undershaw Preservation Trust (web site: saveundershaw.com), founded by Conan Doyle scholar John Gibson, launched judicial review proceedings. The trust which is awaiting a date for the hearing, wants to see the house kept as a single dwelling – whether as a home, a hotel or an attraction that could put Hindhead on the map for a better reason other than traffic jams.

Chapter 31

The New TV Sherlock Holmes

The Sunday Telegraph SEVEN Magazine 04.01.09

2009 IN BAKER STREET

On the small screen, Benedict Cumberbatch will star in a modern spin on Holmes written by new *Doctor Who* supreme Stephen Moffat and *The League of Gentlemen*'s Mark Gatiss. Moffat updated a classic Victorian character in Jekyll last year, while Gatiss is a Sherlock Holmes buff, who has written his own series of novels about the era, featuring the dastardly spy Lucifer Box. It should be with us in the autumn. Place your bets on the truest likeness.

Daily Mail, Friday, October 17, 2008

21st-century Holmes in 221b Baker Street

BENEDICT CUMBERBATCH will play Sherlock Holmes in a modern-day setting.

Holmes will actually be a contemporary detective, not some sort of time traveller. Steve Moffat, who works on the Dr Who dramas, has written an hour-long pilot episode with Mark Gatiss. If senior executives at the BBC like what they see, a series will be commissioned.

Cumberbatch is one of the country's fastest-rising young actors and was seen last year in Joe Wright's film Atonement, Starter For Ten and plays at the Royal Court. He also starred in the splendid TV productions To The Ends Of The Earth and Stuart: A Life Backwards. It's not yet known whether any of Arthur Conan Doyle's stories will be updated, although some of them are very much set in time and place. Also, I wonder how many detectives inject themselves with cocaine and morphine as in the Victorian-era Holmes did? Another thing, if he resides on present-day Baker Street, how can he afford it?

Daily Mail, Friday, December 19, 2008

Watch out for...**Baz Bamigboy**

Martin Freeman who will play Dr Watson, opposite Benedict Cumberbatch's Sherlock Holmes, in a modern-day look at Arthur Conan Doyle's famous detective. Writer Stephen Moffat has penned a one-hour TV pilot drama with Mark Gatiss that places Holmes and Watson firmly in today's society. The Holmes-Watson friendship began in A Study in Scarlet with Holmes uttering the following: 'How are you? You have been to Afghanistan, I perceive.' The original Watson was in the second Afghan War and was wounded at the battle of Maiwand. In the new pilot, Freeman's Watson would have seen service in the present campaign in Afghanistan. Filming starts in the New Year, and if the show works, BBC TV will order a full series.

The Sunday Telegraph SEVEN Magazine 04.01.09

2009 IN BAKER STREET
On the small screen, Benedict Cumberbatch will star in a modern spin on Holmes written by new *Doctor Who* supremo Stephen Moffat and *The League of Gentleman*'s Mark Gatiss. Moffat updated a classic Victorian character in Jekyll last year, while Gatiss is a Sherlock Holmes buff, who has written his own series of novels about the era, featuring the dastardly spy Lucifer Box. It should be with us in the autumn. Place your bets on the truest likeness.

THE DAILY TELEGRAPH MONDAY, MARCH 22, 2010

In Brief

Holmes of 21st century

By Urmee Khan

SHERLOCK HOLMES is to police the mean streets of London in a new BBC series.
　The show **Sherlock** will star Benedict Cumberbatch as Holmes, while Martin Freeman will play his side-kick, Dr Watson. The writer Steven Moffat, said that although the period had changed, the characters had not.
　"Conan Doyle's stories were never about frock-coats and gas light: they were about brilliant deduction," he said.

Daily Mail, Friday, July 23, 2010

it's friday!

SHERLOCK'S GOT SEXY!

With nicotine patches instead of a pipe, taxis replacing hansom cabs and no deerstalker in sight (not to mention chiselled cheekbones) the new TV Holmes is a very 21st century hero.

By **Tim Oglethorpe**

HIS FAMILIAR tweed cape and deerstalker hat have been consigned to the wardrobe of history.

Now, Sherlock Holmes and his sidekick Dr Watson dress in 21st century smart-casual clothes.

The trademark Meerschaum pipe – on which Holmes would puff while pondering the intricacies of his latest case – has succumbed to the anti-smoking campaigners.

Instead, nicotine patches line his arm – an arm in the original stories would have had a tourniquet around it for the injection of illegal substances. 'This, Watson, is a three-patch problem', announces Holmes – an update to the 'three-pipe problem' that some of his knottiest cases rated.

He used to keep in contact with the world through cables and telegrams. Now, he texts on his mobile phone, carries a laptop and has a websight. Watson has replaced his regular dispatches to the Strand Magazine with a blog. So welcome to the 2010 Holmes and Watson, uprooted from the fog-shrouded streets of Victorian times and given a modern make-over by BBC1 in a new three-part drama.

It's the latest in a Sherlock Holmes renaissance which began last December with the release of the blockbuster movie starring Robert Downey Jr and Jude Law as Holmes and Watson – with a sequel in the pipeline.

Last month, Nintendo DS launched a new game, Sherlock Holmes And The Mystery Of Osborne House, and BBC radio has been reviving several previously broadcast Conan Doyle stories.

Meanwhile, Jeremy Paul's play, The Secret Of Sherlock Holmes has just opened in London's West End with Peter Egan and Robert Daws as the two principal characters.

But back to the BBC's three 90-minute updated dramas. Are they taking unacceptable liberties with a classic piece of crime fiction? And by dragging Holmes and Watson into the present day, have they brought a terrible curse down upon themselves?

Benedict Cumberbatch, the old Harrovian who plays Holmes, endured weeks of suffering before surviving a potentially fatal attack of pneumonia halfway through filming.

And Martin Freeman, best known for his role as Tim Canterbury in hit comedy The Office, experienced a fall which left him in agony – and in plaster.

Cumberbatch, 34, initially thought his pneumonia was nothing more serious than flu. 'Or a touch of man flu, as a few people on the production initially suggested,' he says, quietly-spoken, tall and gangly and now clearly restored to health.

'But it just wouldn't go away. It got nastier and nastier, my nasal passages became more and more bunged up, until, one weekend, I got really ill and felt ghastly. 'The doctor was called and the thermometer indicated I had a dangerously high temperature – pretty close to 104F – and pneumonia rather than flu. I was put on a course of powerful antibiotics and I slept and slept.

'The doctor who treated me had been concerned and it's probably just as well I had treatment when I did. I don't like to think what might have happened if I hadn't.'

Martin Freeman slipped while leaving his location caravan, on just the third day of filming in South Wales. 'The weight of my body was pressing down on my wrist and the pain, after impact with the metal steps leading from the caravan was indescribable,' says Freeman, 38.

'My wrist was put in plaster which I removed before I shot a scene and then put it back again when it was completed. I was in agony.'

THE production itself seems to have been blighted at every turn. The first pilot episode filmed at a reputed cost of £800,000, will never be shown.

BBC bosses decided it wasn't what they were looking for and told creators Steven Moffat – executive producer and head writer on Dr Who – and Mark Gatiss, who co-wrote and performed in The League Of Gentleman – to make the stories in the new three-part more intricate and detailed.

And when filming of the series did take place, it occurred during the coldest winter in Britain for 30 years. Says Freeman: 'On one day, we were standing in half an inch of ice cold water for ten hours, in a car park, and it was utterly miserable.

'It was so cold, my mind started to freeze – and this is a dialogue-heavy show with lots of lines to remember. I was struggling to say my words.

'The one consolation was that it made it easier for me to look miserable on screen, because Dr Watson has every reason to be depressed.

'He's a medical man, recently returned from the war in Afghanistan – the present one, not the Victorian one – where he worked as a surgeon and saw men dying.'

And that may just be the salvation, of this new, modern take on Sherlock Holmes: the link it makes, and the due respect it pays, to the original version.

In the first ever Sherlock Holmes story published in 1888, A Study in Scarlet, Watson had just returned from the second Angle-Afghan War after being wounded.

More than 120 years later, Freeman's Watson is doing the same, returning to England after military service in Kandahar.

'We pay homage to the original stories,' says Cumberbatch. 'Of course the world has changed, in terms of things such as transport and technology. But whereas Holmes and Watson would once have travelled around London by horse drawn cab, they now do it in a black taxi.

'And while Holmes would originally have used his powers of deduction to work out the provenance of a pocket watch, now he'll do the same to a mobile phone, and can tell a software designer by the tie he's wearing and an airline pilot by the condition of his thumb.

'The principles remain the same and I don't see why the Sherlock Holmes purists should be upset by our version, it's merely their hero using his skills in a different era.'

So no curse, then?

'I led a caffeine-free, chocolate-free, nicotine-free, fast food-free existence when I started filming and yet I still suffered a serious illness,' says Cumberbatch.

Adds Freeman, 'As for whether we are taking liberties by placing Sherlock Holmes and Dr Watson in the 21st Century, I admit I was wary to begin with.

'I had this dread of the scriptwriters moving the characters to 2010 London, giving them iPods, computers and modern clothes, and considering it job done. But I think that this version of Sherlock works; it captures the essence of the original.

'It's still about solving crimes, just using the tools available to the 21st century detective, rather than the 19th century sleuth. Sherlock Holmes wouldn't have used 18th century methods and tools in the 19th century, when the stories were set, so why should he use anything less than 21st century technology in the present day?

'And still at the heart of the drama is the relationship between Holmes and Watson. That's pivotal.'

The pair of them live in a flat at 221B Baker Street, just as they did in the original, and they still have a landlady called Mrs Hudson, played in this new version by Una Stubbs.

Holmes still has a clever brother, plays the violin and works with Scotland Yard's exasperated Inspector Lestrade (Rupert Graves).

In the first story, A Study In Pink, the pair of them barely get to know each other before Holmes is whisking Watson away to investigate the death of a young woman, found lying in a derelict house.

'Their friendship does develop, as it did in the original stories, but there's no suggestion they are more than just friends,' says Cumberbatch.

'I accept that two men looking for a flat share in the modern world is open to question but it's addressed wittily. I think Holmes was – and is in our modern interpretation – asexual, rather than gay or bisexual. I think he had an experience of a woman that left him badly burnt.'

A detective in 2010 – even one with his origins in the 1880s – will inevitably invite comparisons with other modern-day crime fighters.

Holmes can be brusque sometimes so is he the BBC's new version of Gene Hunt, now that the eighties retro cop from Ashes to Ashes has fired up his Audi Quattro and driven off into the sunset?

'I don't think he shares a lot in common with Hunt – Holmes isn't a red-necked, anti-feminist, he's just rude, direct and impatient,' says Cumberbatch.

'Mind you,' adds Freeman, 'I don't think there's a fictional detective since Sherlock Holmes that doesn't owe something to the man and they are everywhere now – Morse, Taggart, Poirot for instance – on TV.

'It's never been a problem updating James Bond to the 21st Century, even though his origins were the middle of the last century and his clothing of choice – right down to his Panama hat – was very different to what it is now that Daniel Craig is playing him.'

Cumberbatch says it is 'highly unlikely' that their modern Sherlock will go to a second series.

'It was only when we finished the first one that we saw a deerstalker and pipe for the only time.

'We were given souvenir versions of each. But they won't be making their way on to screen.

'Our Sherlock, and our Dr Watson, are 21st Century detectives, through and through, there's no place for Victoriana in their lives'.

JULY 24, 2010 TELEGRAPH **Review** MAGAZINE

21st-century Sherlock

Holmes has to get modern, says Mark Gatiss and Benedict Cumberbatch, the writer and star of the BBC's witty new version. By **Olly Grant**

"Come in, come in" says Mark Gatiss, stepping across a TV studio towards a shiny black door. Where could this lead? 221B says the number plaque. That's a clue. Through the door, then, and up some stairs. "Purists, note," says the writer, "17 steps. Just like the books. "And, all of a sudden, we're standing in the sitting room of the world's most famous detective.

This little domicile is the new home of Sherlock Holmes, who returns to our screens on Sunday for a three-part crime thriller, courtesy of BBC One. The series is called *Sherlock*, it stars *Small Island* actor Benedict Cumberbatch, and it was concocted by Gatiss and writer friend Steven Moffat, the man who now calls the shots on *Doctor Who* (for which Gatiss has also written episodes).

But while the accoutrements look familiar – there's the violin, a knife stabbed through a pile of post and the general untidiness – there's something different about this flat. A laptop on the dresser gives the game away. Good deduction: it's set in the present.

"Bringing it out of the fog," is how Gatiss describes the idea behind the series, which sees Holmes and his sidekick Watson (*The Office's* Martin Freeman) on the trail of serial killers and crime kingpins in 21st-century London. The opening episode is a loose reworking of the first Arthur Conan Doyle story, 1887's *A Study in Scarlet*, and hints that a modern-day Moriarty may be skulking in the shadows.

"I think it's worth saying that both [Moffat and I] are in love with Victoriana," says Gatiss, who is best known for his comic roles in *The League of Gentlemen* but has recently been ploughing a writing furrow, with a forthcoming *Poirot* and an adaptation of HG Well's *The First Men in the Moon* also to his name (he pops up in an acting role in *Sherlock* later, too). "We felt, however, that it was time to reclaim Holmes," he says. So don't expect to see any deerstalkers or velvet dressing gowns: this Holmes is a netbook and PDA kind of sleuth. Watson, meanwhile, is writing a blog and seeing a therapist.

So far, so 2010. But what will the traditionalists make of it? Cumberbatch – who is no stranger to playing geniuses, having previously incarnated Van Gogh, Stephen Hawking and Pitt the younger on screen – isn't fussed. "Why should we serve up what people have already had so sublimely already?" he says, referring to the countless TV shows and movies that have made Holmes, apparently, the most portrayed character in the history of film. "We're setting out to do something new," he says.

There are some good arguments why modernising Holmes might be an unexpectedly good idea. First, Conan Doyle's tales did once feel genuinely modern; snappy, action-orientated, always more concerned with plot than period details. Second, many of the Holmesian "trimmings" were invented by others; the curly pipe, for example, was introduced by playwright and actor William Gillette in the 1890s.

And third, Conan Doyle was possibly the least precious author in literary history. "May I marry Holmes?" Gillette asked him, while working on a stage adaptation (meaning marry him off). "You may marry him, or murder or do what you like with him," came the reply.

The new series has smoothly integrated modern details into its storylines. "There's a famous deduction in *The Sign of Four*," Cumberbatch says, "where Holmes examines Watson's watch and rather discourteously announces that his brother [who once owned it] is an alcoholic loner in need of money, but is too proud to come to Watson for it. We've got a version of that in this, but with a twist."

The twist is that the object is now a mobile phone – scuff marks around the power connection suggest it was regularly plugged in by shaking hands, hence probably by a drunk (Conan Doyle's version involved scratches around the keyhole used for winding up the watch).

Another neat reworking involves Watson's back story. Gatiss and Moffat have been able to follow Conan Doyle and make Sherlock's right-hand man an Army doctor injured in Afghanistan – from 1878 to 1880, Britain was engaged in the second Anglo-Afghan war, a costly, if temporarily successful, encounter with the country's tribal warlords.

Emphasising the new Watson's psychological scars – he is supposed to be blogging about his feelings – lends the character weight, and stops him becoming the buffoon so often played on screen, notably by Nigel Bruce in the 1940s Basil Rathbone films. "Because," says Gatiss, "Holmes wouldn't have an idiot as a friend; that's what weak people do."

This puts *Sherlock* firmly in the tradition of Jeremy Brett, the man often anointed as the screen's greatest Holmes. His Granada TV series, which ran from 1984 to 1994, grew out of a desire to rescue Watson from the ignominy of past portrayals.

It's too soon to say if the new Holmes will follow Brett into the pantheon of favourite Sherlocks. But he has a fighting chance. Cumberbatch's sleuth – Byronic, sociopath, often killingly funny – is just the right balance of psycho-nerd and winning eccentric, the sort of person you'd love to have as your flatmate. If you could stand the mess.

To judge by his conversation, Cumberbatch may even have fallen a little under the detective's spell himself.

"I have found myself casually [analysing] people on the train," he admits. "At the businessman, say, who has a pale line around his ring finger. I'd think, 'Hmm, I wonder what's going on there, then?' And I'd look at his shirt collar to see whether he had washed it, and the size of his luggage to see if he had been away overnight..."

He grins. "Well, you can't help but go there in your mind, can you?"

Radio Times 24-30 July 2010

New Drama of the Week: Sherlock Sunday 9.00pm **BBC1** 25 July 2010

Holmes and Watson transposed to modern London might sound like sacrilege but fear not, it's a clever, edgy thriller that breathes new life into the legend, and not to be missed.

The fabulous Baker Street boys

Lifelong Sherlock Holmes fan **Steven Moffat** has thrust his hero into the age of Twitter, but why?

W E'RE HERETICS, MARK Gatiss and I. Obviously, we are. Vandals in fact. Defilers of a sacred text. We've ripped Sherlock Holmes and Dr Watson from the thrilling gaslight of Victorian London and plonked them down among cash machines and Oyster cards and God help us, Twitter. Clearly we should be run out of town.

This is the case for the defence.

When I was a little *Beano*-reading *Doctor Who* fan – about nine or ten – I was desperate to know more about Sherlock Holmes. It was a name I'd heard. I knew he was some kind of policeman, I knew he had a funny hat, and I knew he was in a film called *The Hound of the Baskervilles*, which once came on the telly and got me sent to bed because it was "too frightening". I remember lying upstairs that night, too excited to sleep – because I could hear the baying of the terrible hound, and the rapid-fire voice of a policeman who fought monsters. I needed to find out more, because I knew already this was my kind of hero: if Doctor Who had been a detective, clearly he'd have been Sherlock Holmes.

Of course it wasn't easy back in the olden days of yore, before the internet, and DVDs – back then, Britain was entirely made of wood and lit by one enormous candle tended by the Queen – but we still had books. And one weekend, when my mum and dad dumped me at my grandparents, and I was a bit grumpy about it and stomped upstairs to my room, I found a book waiting for me on my bed. A present from my parents. An apology, even. On the cover was a deerstalker silhouette against yellow fog, and the utterly magical words "A Study in Scarlet – the first Sherlock Holmes adventure".

S OMETIMES YOU CAN'T read fast enough – but I'll tell you what, it wasn't the gaslight, it wasn't the hansom cabs or the fogs or any of the things I'd been told, years later, were SO important to Sherlock Holmes. It was the deductions. No, that's too dull a word. Let's call it what it was when I was ten. It was *the best superpower ever*! Sherlock Holmes glanced at Dr Watson and *deduced* he'd been to Afghanistan – and, talk about superpowers, Arthur Conan Doyle made me wait pages to find out how he'd done it.

And that was the thing, that was the best ever – Sherlock Holmes *explained*. Superman never told you *how* he flew, he just did. The Doctor never says a word about how the Tardis can be bigger on the inside (and I've gone to extraordinary lengths to find out), it just *was*. But Sherlock can't wait to tell you how the trick is done – and I couldn't turn the pages fast enough to find out. And no sooner had he explained, than he was at it again. My new hero walked into a room where a man lay dead – and announced that the murderer had a florid face.

How can he possibly know that, I thought, as I raced through the pages, now by torchlight under my bedclothes. How is that possible? And then, a terrible dark twist that no one could see coming! My gran walked in and confiscated my book and my torch. Oh, what a long, long night.

How? How could a crime scene tell Sherlock Holmes that a murderer had a red face? Do red faces have an effect on wallpaper? Were there tiny fragments of red face hanging in the air? Was the room a bit warm? The next morning, more pages at the breakfast table – and there it was, the answer. Perfect and logical and hidden in plain sight. And available from your local bookshop.

WHILE YOU'RE THERE, you might want to pick *The Sign of Four*. The second Sherlock Holmes adventure. At the very start, in the first couple of chapters, Sherlock takes Watson's pocket watch and only deduces his brother's entire life and death!!! Even at ten I was thinking, "Whoah, too far, no way can he land this one." But you're back from the bookshop now, now check it out. How clear, how brilliant. A genius writer making exposition (the curse of the plot) into a living hero on the page. As you read, though, you'll something else: the wealth of period data. Specifically, you'll notice there isn't much.

Well, of course not! Doyle was writing fast-paced, contemporary detective thrillers – he wasn't wasting time on what you could see from your own window. It was about story and surprise and jokes, and of course those mind-bending deductions. He wasn't – to state the obvious – writing a period piece.

Inevitably, though, a period piece is exactly what it became – partly thanks to the hundreds of TV and film adaptations featuring such great Sherlocks as Peter Cushing, Jeremy Brett and Robert Stephens, all of them firmly establishing the detective as an icon of a bygone age. A lovingly preserved relic; a suitable object for awe; a monolith from ancient times, looming out of the fog. And what I'm going on at great length (sorry) to say is that was never what Sherlock Holmes was to me.

A few years ago, I was on a train with the best and wisest man I have ever known – Who? Mark Gatiss, of course – and the subject of Sherlock Holmes came up. And, oh, a kindred spirit at last. We agreed we loved Victoriana and fogs and melodrama and a nice bit of posh shouting – but that was not what Sherlock Holmes was supposed to be! We agreed that of all the Holmes films, the ones we liked best were those guilty pleasures, the Basil Rathbone and Nigel Bruce adventures in modern dress, when they fought the Nazis. B-movies of course: cheap as chips, made in less time than it takes to type this sentence, and to any thinking person, quite clearly a heretical defilement of a sacred text – and if we're honest, a damn sight more fun than most Sherlock Holmes movies!

"Modern-dress Holmes," we said "Someone should do that again!"

"Someone probably will," we concluded – and then we both went into a bit of a sulk about how cross we'd feel when someone else did the idea we'd already had but accidentally forgotten to do anything about.

WE'D HAD THIS conversation maybe about 15 times – Mark and I only have three conversations, so we do this in strict rotation – when I mentioned it to the producer Sue Vertue. She gave me a funny look, and then – with seemingly no intervening moment of consciousness – I found myself at a meeting with Sue and Mark, where Mark and I were patiently explaining that we were both extremely busy, and probably unable to commit to a project of this size, and when would she like the scripts, please? Oh, she's a persuasive one Sue. Well, she must be, because all of a sudden we were making a pilot, and then we were making three 90-minute movies, and now we're about to show our mad dream of a modern Sherlock on actual, real television. Finally, I'd marry the girl if I wasn't (a) a bit busy at the moment (b) already married (c) to her.

So. Heresy be damned (well, it would be, wouldn't it?). Here it is, Sherlock Holmes and Dr Watson, reclaimed from the fog. An edgy, brilliant young man and his war-hero best friend, back where they belong – right now.

Elementary my dear… By David Brown

"Elementary, my dear Watson".

It's now thought that the first use of this phrase is actually in PG Wodehouse's *Psmith, Journalist* (1915) – it is certainly not attered by Holmes.

Holmes's deerstalker cap

This was never mentioned by creator Arthur Conan Doyle and only appeared in Sidney Paget's illustrations.

The curved meerschaum pipe

Again, this isn't in the stories and has since been attributed to a stage production starring William Gillette.

Watson – idiot or equal?

The image of the buffoonish sidekick was popularised by Nigel Bruce's film version. It isn't something that's recognisable in the doctor's narration on the page.

221b Baker Street

At the time of the original publication, the address didn't exist, though the street number was assigned to the Sherlock Holmes Museum in 1990.

The changing face of Sherlock

Basil Rathbone and Nigel Bruce **1939-46**

Bruce's bumbling, borderline annoying Watson was perhaps the perfect foil for Rathbone's angular, analytical and contained Holmes in 14 Hollywood films, most of which were set in contemporary times.

Peter Cushing and Nigel Stock **1968**

Cushing was the first Holmes in colour, both on film (in Hammer's *The Hound of the Baskervilles*, 1959) and on TV in the 1968 BBC1 series, in which he and Stock's Watson were true to Conan Doyle's originals.

Robert Stephens and Colin Blakely **1970**

In Billy Wilder's curious film *The Private Life of Sherlock Holmes*, Holmes was an affectionate parody of previous incarnations who indulged his habits for both the violin and drugs. Watson was, therefore, long – suffering.

Jeremy Brett and Edward Hardwicke **1984-94**

ITV's seminal adaptations of 41 (of 60) stories saw Holmes as a troubled genius. Hardwicke's Watson (David Burke played him in the first two series) was stoic and patrician.

Robert Downey Jr and Jude Law **2009**

In Guy Ritchie's film version of a brand-new story, Downey Jr's Holmes was a vain, hard-bitten martial-arts expert, while Law played Watson as redoubtable, in keeping with Conan Doyle's original.

Gareth McLean

Benedict Cumberbatch on Holmes

"He's brilliant at collating information. He uses science, he uses the internet, he uses technology. And he's as equally engaging on an intellectual level as he is on the understanding of human nature"

Martin Freeman on Watson

"He wants to be excited, because he's had a more exciting time than any of us would ever want to have, in a war. And he's come back home to nothing. The one thing we know about ex-service people is they can find civilian life really hard to adjust to"

Daily Mail 24 July 2010 **Weekend** Magazine

PICK OF THE WEEK

Sherlock

Remembering the BBC's most recent attempts at dramatising Sherlock Holmes – a risible Hound of the Baskervilles and the ludicrous Case of the Silk Stocking (starring Rupert Everett) – I approached Sherlock with a heavy heart. I was, however, won over in no time by an updating of Holmes and Watson that's been done with thought, zest, imagination and wit. The three-part series puts 21st-century technology – text messaging, email, the internet – at Holmes's disposal, thus transforming the possibilities of the plot, and at the same time makes full use of the grammar of 21st-century television to tell its stories. Think CSI with a brain and a sense of humour – and a vastly superior script. The first episode sets everything up smoothly, bringing Martin Freeman's Watson and Benedict Cumberbatch's fast-talking, dazzling, mercurial Holmes together – and creating what looks already like a great double act.

NIGEL ANDREWS

If you're a fan of Basil Rathbone and/or Jeremy Brett's portrayal of Sherlock Holmes, you're probably wary of any new Conan Doyle adaptations – but you miss this three-part series at your peril. Set in the present-day world, it begins with Army medic John Watson (Martin Freeman) returning to civilian life in London, where he soon finds himself sharing 221b Baker Street with the charismatic Holmes (Benedict Cumberbatch), a brilliant 'consultant detective' who helps Inspector Lestrade (Rupert Graves) with tricky cases, such as a spate of suspicious 'suicides'. Quirky, daring, darkly funny and superbly acted, this is the surprise of the year (so far).

SOPHIE HEATH

ROLE REPLAY: Dr John Watson

As the BBC's fresh, contemporary take on Conan Doyle's Sherlock Holmes stories begins, we take a look at at great detective's sidekick, Dr Watson. As Martin Freeman takes up the gauntlet tonight, he has his work cut out. Here are some of his predecessors…

Nigel Bruce (films/radio with Basil Rathbone, 1939-46):
Bruce frequently played blustering toffs, and his Watson (cruelly nicknamed Boobus Britannicus) was no exception – Holmes purists objected to his bumbling portrayal.

Ben Kingsley (Without A Clue, 1988):
A nice inversion of the usual formula had Kingsley's Watson as a supersleuth who employs a drunken, out-of-work actor (Michael Caine) as Holmes, and gets rather annoyed when he takes all the credit. Very clever.

Jude Law (Guy Ritchie's Sherlock Holmes, 2009):
Law's Watson is much truer to Conan Doyle's blueprint, while Ritchie's film follows the trend of his earlier works (Lock, Stock…et al). A match made in heaven? It certainly adds a new twist.

Radio Times Sunday 25 July **Sherlock** 9.00p.m. BBC HD

PICK OF THE DAY

DRAMA OF THE WEEK New Series

Some viewers will recoil from the very idea of BBC1 updating Conan Doyle's characters to modern London, with texting (*lots* of texting) and police tape and GPS and a doctor Watson who fought in Afghanistan. But the good news is, it works. What could have been a defiling of a sacred text comes off superbly.

Benedict Cumberbatch makes a disturbing, edgy Holmes, one who likes to whip corpses and keep human eyes in the microwave. The police he helps see him as a dangerous weirdo; when one calls him a psychopath, he snaps back, "I'm not a psychopath, I'm a high-functioning sociopath – do your research!"

While Cumberbatch provides the fireworks, it's the understated Martin Freeman as Dr Watson who is the glue that holds the story together, taking a flat-share with Holmes (at 221B Baker Street, of course) and providing a quietly brilliant foil as they tackle a series of linked suicides.

There are sharp lines (look out for the joke about nicotine patches), well-worked thriller twists and a neat device of having words (text messages, Holmes's thoughts) appear on screen now and then. But it's the central partnership that's key, and that looks as though it could run and run.

New series 1/3 A Study in Pink 25/7/10

It's London 2010 and war hero Dr Watson, fresh from military service in Afghanistan, meets the strange but charismatic genius Sherlock Holmes, who's looking for a flatmate. The pair form a strong alliance and set about solving a string of inexplicable suicides.

Inspector Lestrade is played by **Rupert Graves** in series one and three and Mrs Hudson by **Una Stubbs** in all three.

MONDAY, JULY 26, 2010 **THE DAILY TELEGRAPH**

Television & radio

THE WEEKEND ON TELEVISION

Meet the new Sherlock: an electrifying sociopath

By **Serena Davies**

BBC executives have a simple solution available to them to silence the constant carping about the quality of their drama output: cast Benedict Cumberbatch in every production going. He transfixed us in *Hawking*; he found poignancy playing a sexual inadequate in *Small Island*; he even made dramatic reconstructions interesting in a docu-drama about Van Gogh's letters – and now he's reinvented Sherlock Holmes.

However good the script, however zany the gimmicks, BBC One's **Sherlock** (Sunday) – which presents Arthur Conan Doyle's stories transposed to the present day – was always going to stand or fall on its Holmes. Last night we met him in *A Study in Pink* (a loose riff on *A Study in Scarlet*) and he was electrifying.

The character of Holmes as reworked by writers Mark Gatiss (the multi-talented *League of Gentlemen* comic) and Steven Moffat (*Doctor Who*'s new supreme) is a conceited, sociopathic ass whose genius ranges somewhere on the autistic spectrum, but who nevertheless possesses a sense of humour.

Cumberbatch conveyed all these facets within three seconds of our first encounter with him, when he happened to be flaying a dead body with a horsewhip (to research how quickly bruises came up). He was also filmed in such a way that, with a shock of blackened hair, his parchment-pale skin and liquid eyes took on a translucent quality that made him appear both sickly and mesmerisingly other-wordly.

Gatiss and Moffat have done very well in more than their casting. Their drama whipped along, was laugh-out-loud fumy and the 19th-to-21st century transpositions worked. Dr Watson (Martin Freeman, a dab hand at finding charisma in the average bloke) was now, for instance, an Army doctor injured in Afghanistan – as, funnily enough was the original Watson, who had fallen foul of the second Afghan war of 1878-1880.

We were introduced to Holmes, an eccentric layabout living in Baker Street, as a potential flatmate for the returning Watson when the murders of last night's mystery at hand were already taking place, so the plot came thick and fast. The murders looked like suicides, but were so similar in format that Holmes was convinced a serial killer was at work. Naturally, he was right.

Sherlock worked because it was having fun. It also let down the po-faced pretence that the suffocating abundance of TV detective shows often labour under: that the detective actually cares about the victims. This Holmes revelled in horror. "Four serial suicides and now a note. It's Christmas!" How have Barnaby, Taggart, Marple et al hidden their own jubilation for so long?

I have just one caveat regarding the hugely enjoyable programme. This is that its Sherlock Holmes was too legible. Basil Rathbone and Jeremy Brett, the greatest

Holmeses of the past, gave us characterisations so gentlemanly and clipped they couldn't work in a modern setting, but they also had their own delectable mystery, an opacity, that has been lost in *Sherlock*.

The new Sherlock is quite clearly a sociopath: we were told that he is incapable of friendship, has no interest in sex, and takes drugs. Quite gone are the hints, obfuscations and unsaids in Rathbone and Brett's films that meant we were never quite sure if Holmes was a total nut job or a jolly decent bloke. Here we have only a nut job – albeit a brilliantly portrayed one – and that, I think, is a bit of a shame.

THE DAILY TELEGRAPH TUESDAY, JULY 27, 2010

The riveting riddle of the enduring detective

The timeless appeal of Sherlock Holmes is due to Conan Doyle's powers of observation, says **Harry Mount**.

Sherlock, the BBC's new modern version of Sherlock Holmes, is a must-see for Sunday nights, and it's a long time since we've had one of those.

Benedict Cumberbatch's Holmes has an appropriately high opinion of his own brilliance, while not being arrogant – by his own admission, he is a high-functioning sociopath. His starved, etiolated features smack convincingly of the addict; his clothes – a broad-collared overcoat with scarf tightly knotted at the throat – nod back to Victorian England but also fit right into modern, fashionable Soho.

Martin Freeman's Watson – like Conan Doyle's original, a wounded Afghanistan veteran – is moving, as a man cut off from ordinary life by military service. He is also funny, with shades of his other sidekick character in *The Office*.

Written by Steven Moffat, Sherlock has the same knowing humour that Moffat brought to *Dr Who*; the wit that plays around with our knowledge of the original without ruining it by mockery.

But the real star of Sherlock remains Arthur Conan Doyle. Holmes is an extraordinary invention because he is more than a creature of his time. He is a man for all television seasons.

Lots of the joy of the original comes from the rich Victorian backdrop – the gloomy fog of London, the bleak moors of Baskerville country. But Holmes's allure spreads beyond period detail; his genius and mystery can be transferred to any age, but particularly to our own, obsessed as it is with television detectives.

So, there was instant comedy in Cumberbatch dismissing the expert opinions of forensic scientists and senior policemen. Where other detective shows would need a careful, drawn-out explanation of why our man is right and the others wrong, Holmes carries with him the assumed baggage that he is always right. He can afford to be dismissive and superior, yet we're still on his side.

In a convincing article on Holmes last Christmas – when Robert Downey Jr's Sherlock, a more traditional, less witty, Victorian version, came to the cinema – AN Wilson argued that Holmes was such a unique creation that he grew beyond Conan Doyle's control; that he developed characteristics beyond those planned by his creator. Wilson was – like Steven Moffat – convinced that Holmes is gay, even if Conan Doyle didn't intend it that way.

Whether this is or isn't true hardly matters. The thing is, it might be true. Conan Doyle created such a mysterious character – who also had such a range of distinctive characteristics – that he is recognisable in any age, and yet can also be easily moulded into the habits of that age.

There's great pleasure for Holmes, buffs too, in spotting how that modern moulding is done. When Cumberbatch is consumed by a case, it's not a "three-pipe problem" but a "three patch problem" (he's as keen on cigarettes as he is on cocaine). The Victorian Holmes spotted that Watson's brother was a drunk because there were scratches around the lock of his pocket watch, where he tried to open it under the influence, Cumberbatch works it out because there are scratches all around the charging socket in a mobile phone.

Any writer who observes the repeated details of the human condition as closely as this can jump the ages. And any character with universally desirable qualities – like Holmes's powers of deduction – remains eternally attractive.

Shakespeare – with the same gift for universal, ageless observation – can skip effortlessly from 16th-century Verona to modern gangland America, as he did in Baz Lurhmann's *Romeo & Juliet* [1996]. Jane Austen's *Emma* can be transformed seamlessly into Alicia Silverstone's Beverly Hills valley girl in *Clueless* [1995].

The acting and new writing must be good to survive the journey in the time machine; the original writing must be timeless.

Daily Mail, Friday, July 30, 2010

it's Friday! TV

The BBC's Holmes run

Paul Connolly's TV & Radio Week

Sherlock

THE phrase 'modern re-imagining' usually means 'cheap remake'. Just hearing that a show has been updated is often enough to have viewers running for the hills.

So, when **Sherlock** was announced by the BBC as a 'contemporary update' of Sir Arthur Conan Doyle's detective stories, my heart did not soar. I feared the worse. Would they have Holmes slouching about in low-slung jeans and referring to Dr Watson as 'bruv'?

Fortunately, it seems my imagination was a little florid. The first episode, A Study in Pink, was smart, funny and exciting. The writers, Mark Gatiss and Steven Moffat, who have both written for Doctor Who, did not jettison too much of Conan Doyle's genius.

Sherlock opened on Dr Watson's dreams of combat in Afghanistan. How contemporary, you might think, were it not for the fact that Conan Doyle's Watson was a veteran of an Afghan war, too. Watson was played by Martin Freeman, who captured the medic's loneliness and steel with precision. His chemistry with Benedict Cumberbatch's selfish Holmes, was glorious. Here was a team you could believe in as they investigated the deaths of four people.

There were nods to the original stories. In Conan Doyle's tales, nicotine-addict Holmes called an investigation a 'three-pipe problem'. Cumberbatche's Holmes had a 'three nicotine-patch problem.' Oddly enough, it was the plot that let down this otherwise first-rate episode. It doesn't bode well if a TV critic is yelling, 'It's the taxi driver!' at the screen a full five minutes before it dawns on the world's finest detective that a cabbie is responsible. And I rarely guess plot twists.

Daily Mail 31 July 2010 **Weekend** MAGAZINE

Seven Days NIGEL ANDREWS guide to the week's TV

Sherlock

Benedict Cumberbatch and Mark Freeman continue their great double act as the 21st-century Holmes and Watson in a fanciful episode involving an international secret society and a cipher that kills whoever sees it. In plot terms, a sad falling-off from last week's opener.

Sunday August 1

When you think about it, Sherlock Holmes's brilliant deductive powers are perfectly compatible with modern technology, so putting him slap-bang in present-day London was inspired – and anyway, deerstalkers are so last century. However, after last week's cracking opener, this second episode fails to live up to expectations. Benedict Cumberbatch and Martin Freeman are still terrific as Holmes and Watson, of course, but the far-fetched plot (involving the City and a Chinese circus) is stretched rather thinly over the 90 minutes – a surprise when you consider that this is the second of only three episodes. It's still entertaining enough – but it would have been even better with a chunk sliced out of the middle.

SOPHIE HEATH

Telegraph **Review** MAGAZINE 31 2010

What to watch

Sherlock

The qualities that make Sherlock Holmes such a compelling literary figure are the ones that rarely seem to make their way on to the screen: the almost inhuman coldness, the drug addiction, the hint of cruelty. This fantastic new drama series created by *Doctor Who* supreme Steven Moffat and *The League of Gentlemen*'s Mark Gatiss gives us a dark and glittering Holmes – "freak", the police call him – who is just so *right*, you want to go up and shake his hand.

Benedict Cumberbatch is brilliant in the role, adding sexual ambivalence to Holmes's lightspeed penetration. Mark Freeman is no less convincing as Dr Watson, sometimes attracted, sometimes appalled, but always astonished by his dangerous new flatmate at

221b Baker Street, while the decision to reset the story in contemporary London appears to be the work of an evil genius.

This week, the amateur detective and his disciple attempt to decipher the mysterious symbols that are appearing on walls all over the city. Anyone who sees them is dead within hours. There's also the little matter of paying the rent, which threatens to get in the way of their unpaid thrills.

Chris Harvey

The Sunday Telegraph **Seven** MAGAZINE 01.08.10

Television **Review**

Sherlock's elementary failings By JOHN PRESTON

Every so often when I'm watching TV, the tiny, invisible man who lives on my shoulder leans forward and whispers the single word 'Why?' in my ear. During the first episode of **Sherlock** (last Sunday, BBC One), he was practically apoplectic, jumping up and down and going 'Why? Why? Why did anyone think it was worth doing an updated Sherlock Holmes?'

Before proceeding, let us reflect on what gives the Holmes stories their appeal. Of course, there's the characterisation and the ingenuity of the plotting, but there's also the swirl of atmosphere, the elegance of the writing and its concision, the sense of nothing being wasted.

And now return to Sherlock. Soon after it started, a group of journalists were seen at a press conference when Detective Inspector Lestrade (Rupert Graves) was outlining his theories about the latest in a spate of apparent suicides. As he was doing so, the journalists' mobiles all started pinging simultaneously while captions flashed up on screen saying 'Wrong', 'Wrong', 'Wrong.'

This wasn't elegant, it was clumsy and crass. There was worse to come. While Steven Moffat's script was adroit and quite funny in it's depiction of Holmes and Watson's growing friendship, it was a lot less assured when it came to creating tension. Fatally, it seemed to have no idea on how seriously to take itself, opting for an uneasy blend of camp knowingness and cheap whizz-bang thrills.

The maddening thing about this was that Benedict Cumberbatch had the makings of a rather good Holmes, while Martin Freeman made a perfectly serviceable Watson. Inevitably, Watson had just returned from working in an Army hospital where – just as inevitably – he had contracted Post Traumatic Stress Disorder. Rupert Graves was fine as Lestrade, but then he always is. Has there ever been such an accomplished actor who's appeared in such an array of stinkers?

As well as being absurdly protracted, the denouement was plain absurd, involving Phil Davis appearing out of nowhere as a psychotic cabbie who makes people suicidal simply by talking to them. We've all been there, I suppose – except this was supposed to have some sort of plausibility about it. It didn't, not a whisper.

The Sunday Telegraph AUGUST 1 2010

THE WEEK THAT WAS

IT WAS A GOOD WEEK FOR...

Sherlock Holmes Britain's greatest detective – played by Benedict Cumberbatch in a new, modern-day adaptation – proved more than a match for the Hollywood A-list, with the first instalment of this new series attracting a million more viewers than Tom Cruise and Cameron Diaz's earlier appearance on *Top Gear*, as well as the adulation of the critics.

Daily Mail, Wednesday, August 4, 2010

Sandra Parsons

With just the right hint of mania and weirdly compelling face, Benedict Cumberbatch is brilliant as the new Sherlock Holmes, while Martin Freeman plays Dr Watson with perfect understated bewilderment. At last, a reason to look forward to Sunday evenings. Bliss.

Radio Times 31 July-6 August 2010

PICK OF THE WEEK

DRAMA OF THE WEEK

Sherlock

Our dashing duo have settled in together at 221b, but a bank security breach sucks them into a netherworld of codes and assassinations. Thrilling, feature-length fun.

PICK OF THE DAY

After last week's crackerjack opener things simmer down tonight. The script plays with elements of Conan Doyle plots (*The Dancing Men* and *The Sign of Four* and others for all I know) and after a low-key start, it turns into another sinuously satisfying mystery. Once again, there's a strong sense of sinister powers at work under the drab surfaces of London, where the everyday and the lethal rub shoulders. There's a nice scene where Watson struggles with a self-service checkout at the supermarket, while back at 221B, Holmes fights off a sword-wielding assassin – then never mentions it.

But the main case concerns a City bank where an intruder has sprayed mysterious symbols on the wall. What that has to do with a Chinese antiquities expert and a fearful journalist takes a while to emerge, via locked room mysteries, ciphers and a circus.

Through it all, Benedict Cumberbatch is magnetic as Holmes, his pale eyes always darting and sliding, taking everything in like the instinctive hunter he is, while Martin Freeman as Watson grounds things nicely. Even better, Watson has a potential love interest, played by the excellent Zoe Telford. She has no idea what she's letting herself in for.

David Butcher

FEEDBACK

Elementary error

Explaining the updating of Conan Doyle's stories in *Sherlock* (Sundays BBC1), RT's preview says it includes "a Dr Watson who fought in Afghanistan". So not like the Victorian original, then?

As described in *A Study in Scarlet* (1887), Holmes's friend served in the (real) Second Anglo-Afghan War, being invalided out following a wound received in the Battle of Maiwand. Poignantly, this is close to Helman, where British troops are engaged today.

Chris Rogers
Edgeware, north-west London

In our defence, Stephen Moffat did mention the Study in Scarlet link in his piece on the series.

MISSED IT? Catch up with the best of recent TV and radio

TOP NEW DRAMA

Sherlock

A scintillating reimagining, conceived by *Doctor Who* writers Steven Moffat and Mark Gatiss. Fresh, pacy, shamelessly clever and constantly stylish, it stars Benedict Cumberbatch as the master detective. He lets rip as perhaps the most dangerous and certainly the lippiest screen Holmes yet – but Martin Freeman is even better as Watson, moving elegantly from bewildered sidekick to feisty equal partner in this first episode. It's 90 minutes of non-stop vim. You can also see the Jeremy Brett version on ITV Player, but it'll look static compared to this.

New series 2/3 The Blind Banker 1/8/10

A mysterious cipher is being scrawled on walls around London. The first person to see the cipher is dead within hours of reading it. As Holmes and Watson investigate, they are plunged into a world of codes and symbols.

Daily Mail 7 August 2010 **Weekend** MAGAZINE

Seven Days **NIGEL ANDREW'S** guide to the week's TV

Sherlock

The third and final episode of the series is back to the entertaining form of the first, as Holmes and Watson become entangled in a fiendishly complicated mystery. Don't expect to keep up with the plot developments, just enjoy the ride.

Sherlock 8 August 2010

The third and final episode of the series finds Sherlock Holmes languishing in boredom – but not for long, as he and Watson are soon embarking on an adventure involving a sadistic bomber, a suspicious suicide, a blood-soaked car, a missile defence system, a pair of trainers belonging to someone 20 years dead, oh, and a fake Vermeer. It is, as it sounds, fiendishly complicated plot, so don't beat yourself up if you lose track. But who could be at the heart of it? Who indeed…(Sherlock Holmes fans don't need to think too hard.) This is the last of the series – already . If you're wondering whether there's more to come, well, it looks as if we haven't seen the last of Sherlock and Watson.

SOPHIE HEATH

SATURDAY, AUGUST 7, 2010 TELEGRAPH **Review**

Sherlock

The final episode of this updated detective drama may just be the best yet. Written by Mark Gatiss, who turns up again as Sherlock's elder brother Mycroft, it's dark and funny from the start. It begins with Sherlock (Benedict Cumberbatch) giving grammar lessons to a murderer in Belarus, before the scene shifts to London, where Martin Freeman's Dr Watson arrives back at 221b Baker Street to find his oracular flatmate "bored" and shooting at the walls. Freeman's immaculate comic delivery gets plenty of play as the plot thickens, starting with a surprise in the fridge, and moving on to a case of national importance brought to Sherlock by Mycroft. "A nice murder, that'll cheer you up," suggests Una Stubb's blithe landlady Mrs Hudson. He's about to get exactly that, and quite a lot more besides.
Chris Harvey

THE DAILY TELEGRAPH SATURDAY, AUGUST 7, 2010

Letters to the Editor

The BBC Sherlock Holmes is an elementary failure

SIR – Are there any other avid readers of Sherlock Holmes who deplore the current recreation of the great detective, as produced by the BBC?

I do not care how many enthusiastic reviews it may have had, but gad, Sir, give me top hats instead of bushy curls, frockcoats instead of open-necked shirts, hansom cabs instead of flash cars; give me Dartmoor and the alleys of Whitechapel.

Sir Arthur must be turning in his grave. May the gigantic hound savage those responsible.

Adrian Holloway
Minchinhampton, Gloucestershire

THE DAILY TELEGRAPH MONDAY, AUGUST 9, 2010

Letters to the Editor

Sherlock revisited

SIR – My reaction to the updated Sherlock Holmes series being screened on the BBC is very different from your correspondent, Adrian Holloway (Letters, August 7).

Like him I am an ardent Holmes fan; indeed, I was inspired from an early age to write detective novels through reading the stories. I admire the ingenious way Holmes and Watson have been updated and placed in a contemporary milieu.

The episodes I've seen have been well acted and directed, with the new Holmes and Watson exhibiting the nuances of the old team; uncannily so at times.

Rev John Waddington-Feather
Shrewsbury

SIR – I was relieved to find someone else had withstood the praise in the reviews for the update of Sherlock Holmes.

Although I cut my reading teeth on bound volumes of the *Strand Magazine*, it was not because of any sentimental loyalty to the detective hero that I found Sherlock so lamentable. The second episode failed in that *sine qua non* of all dramatic presentations: suspension of belief.

Leslie Rocker
Warminster, Wiltshire

Daily Mail, Monday, August, 9, 2010

Janet Street-Porter

HARSH HOLMES TRUTH

WHEN Stephen Fry accused the BBC of 'Infantilising' drama I thought it was a bit over the top. Having watched the much-hyped Sherlock I'm afraid I agree.

I'm a huge Holmes fan and even own a set of recordings of Basil Rathbone reading the original stories. My all-time favourite is Jeremy Brett (completely bonkers), closely followed by Rupert Everett (almost as tortured).

Mark Gatiss, who co-wrote this drama, created the wonderfully weird League of Gentlemen, so I had high expectations.

What a disappointment – this production was geared to the Doctor Who generation, where actions speak louder than words. Benedict Cumberbatch is never less than compulsive in the role, but Martin Freeman seemed oafish as Watson.

All they did was rush around delivering bite-sized morsels of dialogue – God forbid there should be anything as taxing as a fully formed sentence or a proper conversation.

The BBC seems scared of delivering drama with depth for an educated audience.

Daily Mail, WEDNESDAY, AUGUST 11, 2010

The case for Sherlock

HAVING read Janet Street-Porter's article about the excellent Sherlock BBC drama series I feel I must leap to its defence.

This rendition is very different from, and does not try to compete with, the inimitable Jeremy Brett. Well done to all concerned in this production. I look forward to a new series.

Mrs **Sian Roberts**,
Bedford

Radio Times 7-13 August 2010

PICK OF THE WEEK

Drama of the Week

Sherlock Sunday 8

There's a shiver of something special in tonight's closing episode. Our heroes face a series of evil challenges – but who is setting them?

MOMENT OF THE WEEK

Sherlock

In this week's episode there's a fabulous scene with a strong hint of Hitchcock, as Holmes and Watson tackle a formidable foe on the stage of a planetarium. As the three of them struggle, the projection system goes loopy, projecting images of the solar system and playing snatches of Holst. As punch-ups go, it's a cut above.

Television Edited by **Alison Graham**

Brilliant – but is that it?

Why must **Sherlock** disappear after just three episodes, asks **David Butcher**. We want more, but give it a twist.

THIS WOULD NEVER happen in America. After a grand total of three episodes (the last is on Sunday night), the brilliant **Sherlock** is over, for now. Finished. Seven million-odd fans will have to wait until next year for another series.

I mean to say – three episodes! In America, if you like episode one of something, you can be darn sure there will be 22 or more to follow, all cleaving like barnacles to the exact formula of the original. It's a ruthless, cookie-cutter approach, but at least it means you're not left in limbo just as you're getting hooked on something. Still, if **Sherlock** is taking an extended break, then let's take advantage of the fact, dry our tears, and set out a wish list for series two.

The main thing that's needed – and let's not beat about the bush here – is at least one half-decent female character who is not a) a clucking landlady (enjoyable as Una Stubbs Mrs Hudson is) or b) a tetchy policewoman given to addressing our hero as "Freak".

WHEN ZOE TELFORD arrived as Watson's love interest Sarah in episode two she looked like providing just what the, uh, Doctor ordered. She was likeable, laid-back and added a whiff of sexiness to the proceedings. Plus, she was Zoe Telford. In my book, Telford could read the Argos catalogue for an hour and it would be worth watching.

But it turned out that Sarah was only in the story to perform damsel-in-distress duties; the Chinese baddies tied her to a chair and pointed a crossbow at her as writhed and looked terrified. Once rescued, her services were no longer required.

So more of Sarah, please. And we also need more business for Mycroft, Sherlock's mysterious umbrella-twirling brother, as played with silky relish by Mark Gatiss. We like Mycroft, particularly as he's the only person who can talk to Sherlock on equal terms, rather then floundering in his slipstream.

And while we're on Gatiss, could he or fellow genius Steven Moffat please write *all* the episodes next time. Sorry, but episode two by Steve Thompson felt a teeny bit short on pizzazz. Look out for a couple of scenes in this week's finale – a fight in a planetarium and the chilling poolside climax – that show Gatiss at his outrageous best.

There are other niggles (more fights and chases wouldn't hurt; Watson needs to stop tutting at Holmes's insensitivity – it gets dull; and do we need 90-minute stories or would an hour be plenty?), but crucially: get out the cookie cutters if necessary and, please, give us lots more.

PICK OF THE DAY

DRAMA OF THE WEEK

Ooh, it's good this. Mark Gatiss is on script duty for the final episode and he writes this kind of thing better than anyone. Fizzing capers, puzzles within puzzles, mysteries interlocking in a larger picture that we don't grasp until a thrilling last-minute reveal…it's all here.

We start with a bored Sherlock lounging about at 221B, absent-mindedly firing a gun at the wall and berating the criminal classes for their inactivity. His brother, shadowy government mandarin Mycroft (Gatiss) wants him to take on a case of national importance, but Sherlock's not bovvered. Luckily, some explosive developments mark the start of a kind of deductive obstacle course devised by someone very evil for Sherlock to solve – against the clock.

It's all loopily enjoyable, with the thrill that comes with when bold writing, smart direction and dashing performances join hands. Sure, there's the odd blip, including a very silly Vermeer painting and Haydn Gwynne with a Czech accent. But whatever you do, don't quit before the dark final showdown. It'll send you to bed with a shiver.

David Butcher

WORLDPLAY OF THE WEEK

There are any number of sharp exchanges in tonight's finale, but perhaps the silliest comes when Sherlock performs one of his dazzling feats of deduction over a dead body washed up by the Thames. "Fantastic!" cries Watson. "Meretricious," shrugs Holmes, to which Inspector Lestrade can't help adding, "And a Happy New Year…"

DRAMA OF THE WEEK

9.00 Sherlock

3/3 The Great Game

A murder on a railway track, a clue in an empty room, a blood-soaked car and a priceless painting presage a terrifying game of cat and mouse as a crazed bomber pits his wits against the sociopathic detective and his sidekick.

Will Watson ever find anything elementary when Holmes tackles a ruthless bomber?

Feedback

Brilliant, Holmes!

The first episode of **Sherlock** (25 July BBC1) was an exceptionally well-made drama that honoured the original 19th-century stories, where Holmes relied on telegrams and newspaper advertisements, bringing them to a 21st-century milieu with mobile phones, PCs and so much that didn't exist in Conan Doyle's day.

I can imagine the glee in writer Steven Moffat's mind as he re-created the first meeting of Holmes and Watson, finding that Conan Doyle's line, "You have been in Afghanistan, I perceive," could be adapted so fittingly for a wounded soldier of 2010.

There were plenty of references to the original stories to entertain aficionados, but they didn't get in the way. **Sherlock** moved at a cracking pace, with clever ideas such as text messages and the clues Holmes notices as he examines the body flashing up on the screen.

The worst thing is that there are only three episodes. I wonder what Moffat and co-creator Mark Gatiss could do with a 21st-century version of *The Hound of the Baskervilles*?

Allan Palmer

Basingstoke, Hampshire.

David Butcher completely agrees with you about the brevity of this first series.

...As a lifelong Sherlockian, I have seen and read many pastiches, but few succeed. Writers fail to understand the friendship between Holmes and Watson and reduce the good doctor's role to that of a bumbling fool.

In **Sherlock**, this wasn't the case. We had two rounded characters, still within a world of cabs, poor lighting (courtesy of low-energy bulbs) and a cluttered Baker Street. The eccentricities of Holmes fitted perfectly into a world of texting and blogs. Even the relationship between Holmes and Scotland Yard were believable. Steven Moffat achieved the almost impossible task of reclaiming Holmes and Watson for our contemporary world.

Anna Jordan
Cullingworth, West Yorkshire

...The transposition to a contemporary setting has the magical effect of elevating Holmes above our almost religious fixation with the omnipotence of our technology, just as the original Holmes went beyond the technology of his own age. Benedict Cumberbatche's Holmes exploits technology as a tool for his brilliant deductive powers, restoring our belief in the fabulous lateral-thinking computer the human brain can be.

Couple this with the late-night chases, the frantic urgency and the explosive process of logic, and I'd go so far as to suggest this is how Conan Doyle might have written Holmes had he been writing now.

Guy de la Bedoyere
Welby, Lincolnshire.

Radio Times 14-21 August 2010

Television Edited by **Alison Graham**

Sherlock left me cold

Throw me a lifejacket, because I'm going to swim against the time: I thought **Sherlock** was cold and uninvolving. Yes, Benedict Cumberbatch and Martin Freeman were excellent as Holmes and Watson – I particularly admired the way Cumberbatch captured Holmes's "alone-ness".

But I didn't want to "admire" a drama, I want to love it; I want to be engaged and thrilled. I don't want to spend 90 minutes thinking "wow, this is technically perfect with a splendid sense of time and place and I don't mind the updating of Conan Doyle's original stories at all."

That's like applauding the scenery. I want joy, danger and excitement. **Sherlock** was beautifully crafted, but hollow.

Daily Mail, Wednesday, August 18, 2010

So where is the BBC's Baker Street?

By Chris Beanland

THE BBC adaptation of Sherlock Holmes has re-ignited the greatest mystery of all – where is 221B Baker Street? For it's modern version, the BBC stuck with the iconic address for Holmes, played by Benedict Cumberbatch with Martin Freeman as Watson. But they had a problem – Baker Street itself is now a major traffic artery, too loud for filming.

So the BBC recreated 221B half a mile away at 185 North Gower Street, above a café called Speedy's Sandwich Bar.

It is now reaping the rewards of the series' popularity, with fans flocking to take their pictures there.

The BBC's decision is entirely in keeping with the spirit of the books, because when Sir Arthur Conan Doyle first wrote about Holmes in 1887, the address didn't exist – the numbers on Baker Street reached only 100.

It was renumbered in the 1930's, with former building society Abbey landing the desirable 221.

For a period, Abbey even assigned staff to answer correspondence addressed to Holmes.

In 1990, a Holmes Museum opened on the street, and despite its address being 237, Westminster Council allowed it to adopt the number 221B. All Sherlock Holmes letters, however elementary, are now handled there.

Daily Mail, Thursday, August 19, 2010

Wimpy Holmes

IT DOES not take a great detective to deduce that, despite all the hype, the curly-haired, wimpish Benedict Cumberbatch was hopeless as Conan Doyle's famous sleuth. Basil Rathbone remains the one and only Sherlock Holmes.

Reg Knapp,
Ruislip, Middlesex.

Daily Mail, Tuesday, August 24, 2010

Holmes, I presume

AS AN aficionado of the Conan Doyle stories, I disagree with Reg Knapp's claim that Basil Rathbone was the one and only Sherlock Holmes (Letters).

That however must go to Jeremy Brett, whose more in-depth performance captured perfectly the complexity of Holmes. Rathbone's jolly hockey sticks approach is superficial by comparison.

Benedict Cumberbatch brought interesting new touches and eccentricities to the role.

I hope the BBC will treat us to more episodes of this excellent interpretation.

Barry Mccann
Blackpool, Lancs.
Radio Times 21-27 August 2010

Television Edited by **Alison Graham**

Elementary error

I'm not a fan, but I watched the final episode of **Sherlock** and loved the waspish, prancing Moriarty. Mmm, I wondered. I recognise that actor, now what's his name, and where have I seen him before. I shall check the credits.

Thwarted! I leapt forward, glasses on, all ready. But no, within seconds they'd shrunk to oblivion, unreadable, and I had to find, through a very circuitous route, the actor's name online (it was Andrew Scott, if you're interested). Come on everyone, this isn't funny and it isn't clever. Credits are there for a reason. So SHOW THEM!

THE SEARCH IS ON

Viewers had almost as much trouble pinning down Moriarty as Holmes and Watson.

FEEDBACK

A case of disappointment

The three episodes of **Sherlock** seen to date were uniformly farcical and obviously aimed at aficionados of *Doctor Who* and *Batman*. Episode one is the first instance in the canon where Holmes fails to solve the crime! The only bright spot was where he deduced that the victim had travelled from Cardiff and was expecting to stay one night in London. It showed something of his method but didn't lead to any denouement. Indeed, the crazed serial-killer taxi driver was at the door ready to confess all.

Episode two began with an attempt on Holmes's life and, in order to avoid attracting attention in mid-afternoon Baker Street, the assassin wore full Bedouin dress and carried a three-foot scimitar. Holmes defeated him using the sub-pantomime ruse of pointing over his attacker's shoulder, shouting, "Look out!" and downing his assailant with a single punch.

Forgive my apparent fixation with professional assassins. But they usually like to be unobtrusive. Not in episode three! Golum, the world's deadliest killer, can be looked up on the internet and he is literally, eight feet tall! But forget all that, does Holmes catch the criminal. No. Jim Moriarty pops up willingly to engineer a Mexican stand-off to hook the audience into the next series. Don't bother on my account.

Lawrie O'Connor
Ossett, West Yorkshire

FRIDAY, OCTOBER 15, 2010 **THE DAILY TELEGRAPH**

Television & radio

Holmes, Hollywood – and turning down the Hobbit

Why Martin Freeman is doing a bizarre new Radio 3 drama – but not the biggest movie ever. By **Olly Grant**

It must be tiring being Martin Freeman. As we speak, he's lining up a trip to Spain. "I'm backwards and forwards from Barcelona," he says, with a contented sort of sigh. It's for a feature film called *Animals*, he says, a half-English, half-Spanish fantasy with a mostly unknown cast, made by a young Catalan director whose best-known work is a BBC Three pilot that never became a series (*The Things I Haven't Told You*). Offbeat? A bit "It has a very beautiful script," he adds quickly.

These days, Freeman can afford to be picky. At 39, he's enjoying a career renaissance. He's just been in the most talked about TV drama: BBC One's *Sherlock*, playing Dr Watson. His name has even been linked to the star role in what could be the most expensive movie ever made (of which more later).

So perhaps we shouldn't begrudge him a few left field projects. The latest is a Radio 3 adaptation of BS Johnson's book, *The Unfortunates*, in which he plays a football reporter whose thoughts turn to the death of an old friend.

The Unfortunates is about as far from mainstream as you can get: a 1960s experimental novel; cult in its day but now rarely read; written in stream-of-consciousness by a man once described as "the most important young English novelist now writing" but who is, today, largely forgotten. Oh, and originally published as a book-in-a-box, with unbound chapters to be read at random.

"I just thought it was an interesting idea," says Freeman. "I hadn't heard of the book before. Or of BS Johnson. But I liked the idea of a book being published in no particular order, and of applying that to a radio version." The book's shapelessness has been played up in an intriguing way. "They did it like an FA Cup draw," he explains. "They put the chapters on little wooden balls and then drew them out [one by one] to get a random result."

The other thing that should be said about *The Unfortunates* is that its hero is typically Freeman; that is meat-and-two-veg ordinary; downbeat, humdrum. Playing the Englishman Everyman is Freeman's shtick. He rose to stardom doing it in *The Office* (2001-03) as Tim, and has flirted with it in subsequent roles, such as Arthur Dent in *The Hitchhiker's Guide to the Galaxy* (2005).

Hits have been thin on the ground since *The Office* – though Freeman has often insisted that his best roles have been the rarely seen ones, such a BBC Two's 2005 comedy *The Robinsons*. But then came *Sherlock*, where he was brilliant as a modern-day, war-scarred Watson, ironing the starch out of Benedict Cumberbatch's sociopathic Holmes. And even stealing the show, according to some.

Freeman says he was "taken aback" by the programme's success (it had more than 7million viewers and critics hollered its praises), but thinks it deserves the accolades. "It's the best British thing that's been on telly in ages," he says. "Quality will out, if that doesn't sound too arrogant. But why should I sound arrogant? I didn't write it. I just think it was undeniably good."

Ironically, though, *Sherlock* also presents him with a career-defining dilemma. His commitment to the filming dates for series two (due to be screened next year) meant that he had to decline the plummiest of movie roles: that of Bilbo Baggins in the much-delayed big screen version of *The Hobbit*, reportedly to be directed by *Lord of the Rings* supremo Peter Jackson, with a record-breaking £315m budget.

Freeman says he turned down Bilbo "with a heavy heart", but still hopes there might be a way of resurrecting the part, dates permitting. "If something could be worked out, that would be great," he says.

But, then again, he's also a famously unstarry actor who has spent most of his post-*Office* career eschewing the bright lights of L.A. He has admitted being "freaked out" by his first trip to Hollywood six years ago (to promote *The Office*) and recently described red carpet events as "four hours of my life lost". Could he really handle being the star of potentially the biggest film ever?

He mulls this over for a second. "Well," he says, "for a start, it wouldn't be in Hollywood [New Zealand is the likely location]. And I think Peter gives Hollywood a fairly wide birth himself. So it won't be all that Hollywoody."

"And anyway, I certainly wouldn't be stupid enough to say that I wouldn't do anything Hollywoody." He pauses. "It's just that I'm more of an Englishman, really, than a Hollywood man."

UPDATE

THE DAILY TELEGRAPH SATURDAY, OCTOBER 23, 2010

WORLD BULLETIN

Martin Freeman to play the Hobbit

Martin Freeman, the English actor best known for the role of Tim in comedy series *The Office*, will play Bilbo Baggins in *The Hobbit*, director Peter Jackson has announced.

"He is intelligent, funny, surprising and brave – exactly like Bilbo," he said.

The news comes amid speculation that a pay dispute between the studio Warner Bros and unions will drive the adaptation of the JRR Tolkien novel away from New Zealand, where the *Lord of the Rings* were shot.

Editorial Comment

Tim turned Hobbit

The choice of Martin Freeman as the actor to play Bilbo Baggins in the film of *The Hobbit* is of the greatest importance. No one is obliged to like the book or the film to be made from it, but it is bound to be popular. *The Return of the King*, the last in the *Lord of the Rings* trilogy, directed by Peter Jackson, drew the third biggest box office revenues of all time.

There is much behind the popularity. *The Lord of the Rings* is a fantasy, and audiences forget mundane realities while watching it. But it is also a myth, as JRR Tolkien intended above all, for English speakers. Thus it engages interest in the most real choices of all: heroism or compromise, mercy or revenge, vice or selflessness. This myth exercises a deep appeal in the war-torn 20th century, and the transition to terrorism in the 21st is unlikely to reduce the appeal. This is not to say the myth is outstandingly told – in the books or, certainly, in the films. But it is a tribute to the power of mythology that films which are incomprehensible without a thorough knowledge of the sources have captured a mass market.

Martin Freeman – nice Tim from *The Office* – hardly need change from his dressing-gown that saw him through *The Hitchhiker's Guide to the Galaxy*. But if *The Hobbit* is partly a domestic myth, Mr Freeman might even offer a person a too ordinary. Millions will be interested to see whether that is true.

Daily Mail, Saturday, October 23, 2010

Office star bags the Hobbit role

He is best known for his role in The Office. But all that is about to change for Martin Freeman.

The 39-year-old British actor has beaten some of Hollywood's biggest names to play Bilbo Baggins in the Lord of the Rings prequel, The Hobbit, chosen ahead of U.S. star Tobey Maguire.

Director Peter Jackson said there had 'only ever been one Bilbo Baggins for us' after meeting Freeman.

'There are a few times in your career when you come across an actor who you know was born to play a role, but this was the case as soon as I met Martin'.

Shooting will begin in the summer with the story being split into two separate films, set for release in December 2011 and 2012.

Freeman, who appears in Richard Curtis's Love Actually, and the BBC series, Sherlock, had previously revealed he turned down the role in The Hobbit to continue playing Dr Watson in Sherlock. But a delay in filming means that he can commit to both.

TUESDAY, NOVEMBER 30, 2010 **THE DAILY TELEGRAPH**

MANDRAKE TIM WALKER

Freeman's omission

Rather disappointingly, **Martin Freeman**, the 39-year-old actor who is to play Bilbo Baggins in **The Hobbit**, a Lord of the Rings "prequel," told me he had never read any of **JRR Tolkien**'s works before he got the part. He admitted at the **Evening Standard** theatre awards at the Savoy that he hadn't read any of **Sir Arthur Conan Doyle**'s books either before he played Watson to **Benedict Cumberbatche**'s Holmes in the BBC's **Sherlock**.

He said that he "knew" most of the stories from "television and the cinema." It's not quite the same thing, but the actor insists that he spent all of his youth reading the works of **George Orwell**.

Mandrake hadn't been aware that Orwell had written quite such a huge body of work.

UPDATE

THE DAILY TELEGRAPH MONDAY, MAY 23, 2011

Case closed: Sherlock wraps up Bafta victory

BBC One's reinvention wins best drama and supporting actor awards

By Anita Singh, Showbusiness Editor (Excerpt)

SHERLOCK, the television drama that reinvented Sir Arthur Conan Doyle's detective for a new audience, was the big winner at the television Baftas (British Academy of Film and Television Awards) last night.

The BBC One show won best drama series and Martin Freeman, who played Dr Watson, picked up the best supporting actor award. Appropriately enough, its success came on the 152nd anniversary of Conan Doyle's birth.

The programme starred Benedict Cumberbatch as Holmes and transposed the action to the present day. Freeman described it as the story "of a slightly dysfunctional relationship that really works".

Cumberbatch was nominated for the best actor award along with the *Doctor Who* star Matt Smith. However, both missed out when the prize went to Daniel Rigby for his performance as a young Eric Morecambe an BBC Two's *Eric and Ernie*.

THE DAILY TELEGRAPH TUESDAY, MAY 24, 2011

Mandrake Tim Walker

It's elementary, says Freeman. Holmes loved Watson

It is an issue that Sherlock Holmes's fans are as wary of plunging into as their hero was the Reichenbach Falls. **Martin Freeman** has, however, described the BBC series *Sherlock* as having "the gayest story in the history of television".

At the Baftas, where he picked up the best supporting actor award by playing Dr Watson to **Benedict Cumberbatche**'s Holmes, Freeman said he saw **Sir Arthur Conan Doyle**'s character as being profoundly in love.

"It's about the relationship between the two men and how it develops and how it changes," Freeman tells me. "It is about the things that wind each other up and the things that they genuinely love about one another as well. We all certainly saw it as a love story. These two people do love and kind of need each other in a slightly dysfunctional way, but it is a relationship that works. They get results."

It is just as well that Sir Arthur is no longer with us, or, indeed his daughter **Dame Jean Conan Doyle**. Shortly before her death in 1997, she told me that her father would have been aghast at such a notion.

"I think that he immersed himself in the story of these two men precisely because, at the time that he was writing these stories, he wanted to take his mind off sex," she explained. Her father had fallen in love with her mother, **Jean Leckie**, as his beloved first wife, **Louise**, died a long, lingering death from tuberculosis. Sir Arthur behaved impeccably, and it was only a year after he lost Louise that he allowed himself to marry Leckie.

Rupert Everett, when he played the detective in the BBC drama *Sherlock Holmes and the Case of the Silk Stocking*, said that he had seen it as "a love affair, albeit one that is not really expressible".

Still, as Holmes himself remarked to his live-in companion: "When you have eliminated the impossible, whatever remains, however improbable, must be the truth."

Daily Mail Weekend 24 December 2011

Sherlock, New Year's Day, BBC1

When the BBC's modern-day version of Sherlock Holmes finished in the summer of 2010 after just three episodes, it left more than nine million viewers begging for more. And the Beeb doesn't let us down, as a new three-episode run starts on New Year's Day. Not only are our dynamic duo – Benedict Cumberbatch's supersleuth and Martin Freeman's Dr Watson – tackling the Hound of the Baskervilles, but in A Scandal in Belgravia, the only woman ever to have turned Sherlock's head, Irene Adler (played by Spooks star Lara Pulver), appears.

Sherlock Holmes becomes obsessed with her and starts following her on Twitter. 'She's the one woman who ever caught his eye,' says writer Steven Moffat. 'Normally he avoids women because he knows they'll distract him, but he's met his match in her. We'd love to do 25 episodes a year, but getting everyone together even for three 90-minute episodes is tough. So that's why we've tackled some of Sherlock's biggest stories for this run.

Tim Oglethorpe

NIGEL ANDREW'S guide...

...If you want classy detective drama...**SHERLOCK**. The contemporary reimaging of Conan Doyle returns with three new episodes, and it's better than ever. The chemistry between Benedict Cumberbatch as Holmes and Martin Freeman as Watson is quite magical. In this opener, they encounter Irene Adler – the Woman.

Sophie Heath

Having narrowly escaped the clutches of a murderous psychopath, Sherlock Holmes and John Watson embark on a new round of adventures in the eagerly awaited second series of Conan Doyle's stories. With Watson's new blog an internet sensation, this first of three episodes finds countless potential clients traipsing through the door of 221B Baker Street in the vain hope of grabbing Sherlock's attention. The case that eventually does interest him brings him face to face with one of the very few people he finds himself unable to 'read' – a woman whose wiles could prove his undoing. Smart, witty, terrific.

THE DAILY TELEGRAPH TUESDAY, DECEMBER 27, 2011

I'm typecast because I'm posh, says Old Harrovian Sherlock

By Anita Singh

BENEDICT CUMBERBATCH, star of the BBC's *Sherlock* series, had admitted that "being a posh actor in England" limits the roles he is offered.

The Old Harrovian plays an Army major in Steven Spielberg's Forthcoming adaptation of *War Horse*, and has played screen characters as diverse as William Pitt the Younger and Prof Stephen Hawking. However, Cumberbatch said his background and accent had sent his career in a particular direction.

"I was brought up in a world of privilege. It can ostracise you from normal codes of society," says the 35-year-old. "Being a posh actor in England, you can't escape class-typing, from whatever side you look at it.

"I realised quite early on that, although I wasn't trying to make a career speciality out of it, I was playing slightly asexual, sociopathic intellectuals."

The son of two professional actors, Cumberbatch was educated at Brambltye preparatory school in West Sussex before attending Harrow. But he insists he is not an "archetypal product" of Harrow. After leaving school he studied drama at Manchester University before completing his training at the London Academy of Music and Dramatic Art.

The actor recently won a theatre award for his performance in *Frankenstein* at the National Theatre, and plays Sherlock Holmes in BBC One's modern take on the Arthur Conan Doyle stories.

Speaking to the *Radio Times*, Cumberbatch said he tried to avoid being typecast in "posh" roles. "The further away you can get from yourself, the more challenging it is. Not to be in your comfort zone is such great fun," he said.

Radio Times 31 DEC 2011 – 6 Jan 2012

The Sherlock and John show

Benedict Cumberbatch and Martin Freeman reveal how they turned literature's greatest crimefighting duo into cerebral sex symbols

Interview by Alan Franks

THE DEDUCTIVE GENIUS of the world's most famous sleuth is, of course, a joy to behold. It always has been, whether Arthur Conan Doyle's greatest creation is being portrayed by 1920s Hollywood star John Barrymore or by its most recent incumbent, the Old Harrovian heart-throb, Benedict Cumberbatch. But in the best adaptations, the unravelling of the mysteries plays second fiddle to the evolution of the relationship between Holmes and his right-hand man, Watson. Or Sherlock and John as we must call them, since that is what they call each other.

Away from the set of 221b Baker Street, Martin Freeman, who plays John, refers to his senior partner as Lord Cumberbatch. Or Cumberlord for short. He even calls him that to his face. A mighty clue, surely, that the professional association has bled into their private transactions. Cumberbatch gives a tolerant smile, taking it as the affectionate subordination it's probably meant to be. Hard to be forensically certain though, in an England where class digs can hurt as much as they did a century ago.

Just as the 35-year-old Cumberbatch seems fashioned by nature and nurture to play the young gentleman, as he memorably did last year in a Terence Rattigan revival at the National Theatre in London, so Freeman, five years older, married with two young children, looks free of any illusions about being officer material. Remember his amiable loser Tim Canterbury in *The Office*, or John, the modest stand-in actor in *Love Actually*.

The Cumberlord tag brings a thoroughly game response from the chap in question.

"I was brought up in a world of privilege," he concedes, in an accent that has taken the top edge off its expensive breeding, but is still a world away from the estuary. "It can ostracise you from normal codes of conduct in society. Being a posh actor in England, you can't escape class-typing, from whatever side you look at it. I realised quite early on that, although I wasn't trying to make a career specialty of it, I was playing asexual, sociopathic intellectuals."

You might well put Sherlock Holmes in that category. As Watson says of him in *The Sign of the Four*, he is "an automaton, a calculating machine". And as Holmes himself says of women: [They] are never to be entirely trusted – not the best of them."

Cumberbatch says he took to the challenge of the role "like a duck to water. It was about ferocious speed, casual disregard for other people's feelings, and the idea of treating life as an ever-expanding series of problems and potential adventures, right through from the smallest to the largest detail of behaviour or circumstance.2

Having said that, he adds that when it comes to mental aptitude, Freeman is by far the closer of the two to Holmes, and a superior actor into the bargain. Not to mention, all you could ever want from a colleague in the way of patience and support. If there were a list of patronage here, Freeman would surely have seen it coming and reacted accordingly. But there isn't, and he hangs his head modestly – apart from observing that there's nothing wrong with being a supporting actor (his Watson in the first Holmes series won him a Bafta award). "I mean, it's not as if the show is called *John* is it?"

They agree that their own relationship has been driven by the one they portray on screen; it could hardly have been otherwise, given the time they have devoted to inhabiting those fictive lives, and given that they had never met before landing the roles. Both are so familiar with their characters that, even though they have high praise for series co-creators Steven Moffat and Mark Gatiss, they would feel able to say if there was a line that struck a jarring note.

WHILE CUMBERBATCH, the son of professional actors, was going to Brambletye prep school in Rural Sussex, Freeman was growing up in what he describes as suburban Dickensian London. He had started playing squash at the club where his father ran the bar and his mother the kitchen. As a young teenager he thought about turning professional. Then he joined a youth theatre in Teddington, and the acting took over.

"There's more crossover in our backgrounds than we admit," says Cumberbatch.

"I didn't go to the oldest school in the world," replies Freeman.

"The fact that I did does not make me an archetypal product of that school."

"Some of my best friends went to posh schools, and they're very aware of not wanting to be that stereotype." "Well, we all want to escape our circumstances, don't we?" asks Cumberbatch. "Especially if you're an actor. It's the imaginative process that gets my juices going. The further away you can get from yourself, the more challenging it is. Not to be in your comfort zone is such great fun."

But then, when you become as successful as Cumberbatch has, something strange happens: being yourself in the eyes of others becomes harder. His godmother's grandson is obsessed with Sherlock Holmes and everything to do with him. "One day he said,' Gran what relative am I to him?' 'None', she said, 'I'm just his godmother.' 'No. He doesn't really exist.' 'But I've seen him. Do you think he wants to meet me?'"

Many do. He would love to satisfy all their inquiries with something suitably Holmesian in its ingenuity. He shakes his head ruefully at the thought that he simply hasn't the problem-solving capacity of the brilliant Scottish physician who invented the detective. Freeman suggests that just remaining enigmatic might be the answer. Benedict says, "Hmm," approvingly, but wishes he could do better than that.

He has been changed by the alchemy of public pretending, no doubt about it. The process will intensify with the second series – three more cracking episodes with Moffat, the man behind *Doctor Who*, League of Gentlemen member Gatiss and playwright/screenwriter Steve Thompson. Content is a closely guarded secret, but watch out for unexpected twists in *The Hounds of Baskerville* and *The Reichenbach Fall*. "Everyone wants to know how we're going to do the effing dog," says Moffat. Also expect a shift in the relationship between the two principals as Holmes's feared nemesis, Moriarty, played by Andrew Scott, makes his presence felt once more.

The new series coincides with the release of Steven Spielberg's movie of the stage hit *War Horse*, with Cumberbatch in one of the lead roles as Major Stewart. The exposure is making him value his privacy in a different way. He says he was alarmed to find himself being doorstepped by paparazzi last year when he and his long-standing partner Olivia Poulet, whom he had met at Manchester University were separating. "It was unnerving to think they knew where I lived…with fame you do get the most extraordinary perks and experience, whether it's chairing programmes or having a voice in the political field, because you happened to have a large audience who listened to you for three nights ago. It's both beneficial and odd. The usual yin-yang thing. But by and large good."

ONCE THEY HAD finished filming the new *Sherlock* series, the two actors were at work together almost immediately in the final part of Peter Jackson's *Hobbit* movie (due for release next December), in which Freeman plays Bilbo Baggins and Cumberbatch supplies the voice of the dragon, Smaug. Is this a good instance of escaping one's circumstances? They swap an after-you glance, waiting for the other to reply. Cumberbatch thinks hard, involuntarily making a Sherlock-at-work face. "As an actor, you can do weight loss, weight gain, put on silly noses, crazy accents, move like a dragon, inviting people to look at the fireworks and admire how different you're being. But with acting like that, it's all about look-at-me, when what you should be doing is helping the audience care about the person they're watching."

"I always think it's a bit of a red herring," says Freeman, "this business of whether you're pretending to be something different. I mean, Ben isn't like Sherlock [Cumberbatch nods], but you could only play that part really well if there is enough of a crossover. Same with any role, ever. Show me someone who's being nothing like they are in real life and I'll show you a rubbish performance. In every film De Niro's in, he's the best actor on God's earth, but he'll always pull the same De Niro face at some point. You're never going to go, 'Oh, I didn't know who that was.'"

What these two men have been through in the past two years is the acting equivalent of an intense flat share, with the BBC fulfilling the role of Mrs Hudson, John and Sherlock's landlady. Seeing them on the set of those timeless premises, with the flock fleur-de-lys on the wall and the Samsung flat screen on the table, they look like members of some highly idiosyncratic, time-warped sitcom. As Steven Moffat puts it, crime being solved by

Chapter 32

Sunday Times Magazine 14 March 2004
The Archive

CONAN THE LIBRARIAN

For 70 years, the location of Conan Doyle's archive has been a mystery worthy of his most famous creation, Sherlock Holmes. Now, as the case is solved, Philip Norman unwraps the literary treasures.

The great popular writers of the 18th and 19th century enjoyed a status that even today's most prize-garlanded novelist or biographer cannot imagine. The likes of Kipling, GK Chesterson and HG Wells were figures of huge social as well as literary influence; sages and oracles to whom their countless readers instinctively turned for a moral view of the world, a perspective on the past or prophecies of the future. Among these prime ministers of prose, none was more universally venerated than Sir Arthur Conan Doyle.

Conan Doyle has won immortality as creator of Sherlock Holmes, "the world's most famous man who never was", in Orson Welles's phrase. But the Holmes oeuvre represents only a fragment of an enormous output and a hugely varied, richly fulfilled life. He wrote numerous other novels and stories featuring serial heroes like the swaggering Napoleonic cavalryman Brigadier Gerard, the deceptively puny knight-at-arms Sir Nigel Loring, and the ferocious Professor Challenger, who discovers a lost world of dinosaurs and pterodactyls three generations ahead of Spielberg.

A qualified surgeon and eye specialist, he took a mobile hospital to the Boer war, wrote plays for Sir Henry Irving, stood twice, unsuccessfully, for parliament, was a historian, war lecturer and foreign correspondent, played cricket for the MCC, championed causes ranging from divorce-law reform to the Channel tunnel, became a consulting detective and righter of wrongs just like his greatest fictional creation. He devoted decades and a good part of his colossal earnings to the spiritualist movement, and was famously tricked by two mischievous young girls into believing in fairies.

The personal papers and memorabilia of Conan Doyle's great contemporaries have long since been laid out under glass at the British Museum or filed in the air-conditioned vaults of American universities. Yet, ironically, the writer who brings millions of pilgrims to London each year in search of Sherlock Holmes, Dr Watson and Professor Moriarty – and who has outsold JK Rowling and JRR Tolkien put together – can be studied in only the most fragmentary detail. Since Conan Doyle's death in 1930, aged 70, the whereabouts of his private archive has been a mystery as tantalising as any ever unfolded at 221B Baker Street.

The entire cache has now come to light and is to be auctioned on May 19 at Christie's for an estimated £2m. It is essentially the contents of Conan Doyle's study at his home near Crowborough, Sussex, on the day he wrote his last, immaculate pen-and-ink page. Its measures range from diaries, research notes and correspondence with world figures such as the US president Theodore Roosevelt, British leaders such as Lloyd George and Churchill, and the cricketer W.G. Grace, to intimate possessions such as his cash-book, wallet, and driving licence. Jane Flower, Christie's manuscript consultant, calls it the most exciting find she has seen in 25 years.

The story behind its final emergence into the saleroom is a highly involved one, saying much about the shadow that even the most benign great man can cast on their descendents. By his second wife, Jean Leckie, Conan Doyle had two sons, Adrian and Denis, and a daughter, Jean. Adrian, the only one to try literature, later produced some Sherlock Holmes stories in a passable imitation of his father. Denis married a spendthrift Georgian aristocrat named Princess Mdivani, who ended her days a resident in luxury hotels like the Savoy. Jean became an air commandant in the Women's Royal Air Force, and a dame. I met her once, and she told how, when she was small, her father would let her sit in his study while he wrote, so long as she never made a noise. She recalled the sound of his pen nib racing across the page with scarcely a pause for thought or correction.

Despite the royalties flooding in from Sherlock Holmes reprints, dramatisations and films, the family sold most of the story manuscripts to private collectors in the US. The archive stayed with Lady Conan Doyle, who devoted herself to the old-fashioned widowly task of putting her husband's papers "in order". After her death in the 1940s it passed to Adrian, who later moved to Switzerland. In 1949 he authorised a biography of his father by the mystery writer John Dickson Carr, the first outsider to gain access to the archive. Although bland and hagiographic, the book sparked a public row between Adrian and Mary, Conan Doyle's daughter by his first wife, who bitterly objected to its portrayal of her mother. More intriguing to Conan Doyle addicts was its appendix of archive papers that John Dickson Carr had access to but barely made use of.

After the death of Adrian's widow, Anna, in 1992, and of his sister Dame Jean Conan Doyle in 1997, a dispute within the surviving family maintained the veil of secrecy about the archive, by now stored in the strongroom of a London solicitors. Only with the settlement of this dispute could its existence be made public.

The papers were mostly kept in large manila envelopes annotated by Lady Conan Doyle, who invariably referred to her husband as "My Darling". In later years, Adrian added notes in a similar reverential vein. This is a palpable effort by mother and son to present Conan Doyle as a paragon of all virtues, though, as Flower agrees this hardly seems necessary. The big Scots medic with his walrus moustache, wherever one looks, seems to have been a lovely man. He was devoted to his first wife, Louise – "Touie" – who bore him two children and spent years stricken with tuberculosis. Though he fell for the beautiful Jean Leckie in Touie's declining years, he refused to go beyond friendship until he became a widower. The dominant female influence in his life was his mother, Mary Doyle, always referred to, half-heartedly, half-adoringly, half-warily, as "the Ma'am."

From one contemporary source at least, we learn that he spoke in much the same highly charged dialogue he wrote for Sherlock Holmes. PG Wodehouse recalled Conan Doyle talking about an American "writers' school" he found to be using his name without authorisation to recruit customers. "What most people at this point would have said would have been 'Hullo, this looks fishy,'" Wodehouse wrote. The way [Conan Doyle] put it when telling the story was, 'I said to myself, Ha! There is villainy afoot!'"

The archive contains mementoes from every era of his unstoppably vigorous three score years and ten. A leather folder preserves fragments of the first story Conan Doyle ever wrote, aged six – a characteristically all-action tale of hunters and tigers. Here are the illustrated logs he kept as a surgeon on the whaling ship Mayumba. (The nephew of the Punch artist "Dicky" Doyle, he was an accomplished draughtsman.) Here is the brass plate that hung outside his medical practice in Southsea, where he first began writing between consultations, and the Red Cross armband he wore as a volunteer in the Boer War. Here are his notes and drawings on heraldry for the medieval novels Sir Nigel and The White Company, which he himself thought – with good reason – were his greatest achievements as a storyteller. Here is his correspondence with his agent, AP Watt, in years when queues would form at bookstalls to devour the latest Holmes story in The Strand Magazine. As Flower has noted, sifting through the meticulously kept account books and royalty records, he could be "rather beady" about money. The autograph letters from fellow literary giants are enough to make any collector salivate. Here is one from Kipling, saying he read Rodney Stone "in one gulp" and still wants more. Here is one from HG Wells, commiserating over hostile reviews of A Duet, an atypical Conan Doyle novel about young married love that some denounced as "immoral". Here is an adulatory note from Oscar Wilde, who is almost wistful in praising the "simplicity and strength" of Conan Doyle's prose and regretting the "mist of words" in his own work that makes him always "throw probability out of the window for the sake of a phrase".

Here are the letters of his father, Charles, a figure as tragically mysterious as any at the heart of a Holmes investigation. Charles was an artist of erratic brilliance, whose alcoholism and mental instability cast a pall of insecurity on his son's early life. In 1889 he was committed to an institution, which the family did its utmost to cover up. He died in 1893, the same year his son tried to kill off Holmes by plunging him into thr Reichenbach Falls locked in combat with Professor Moriarty (though public demand and the huge fees offered by magazines brought him back a decade later).

It's perhaps too much to speculate what part filial guilt may have played in Conan Doyle's impulse to destroy his money-spinning creation. Certainly, he had first-hand knowledge of addiction when he gave Holmes a dependency on cocaine. And the theme of a prisoner with an anguished secret recurs in Holmes adventures like The Blanched Soldier and The Yellow Face.

Conan Doyle's reputation as a sage reached its height in the 1914-18 war, of which he later wrote a bestselling history. Years earlier he had predicted the crucial role of submarine warfare – unhappily, to deaf ears at the Admiralty. In an eerie echo of modern times, he also campaigned for troops at the front line to be supplied with proper body armour, as he did for sailors in the Royal Navy to have life jackets.

The archive includes letters from many serving officers, among them Sir Douglas Haig, the British commander-in-chief, to who Conan Doyle unsuccessfully gave his designs for a bulletproof vest. The device would have undoubtedly saved many lives, though, not alas, those of the two war casualties in his own family. One brown envelope is poignantly inscribed with a cross and the names of his eldest son, Kingsley (by his marriage to Touie), and his brigadier-general brother, Innes, both of whom died from influenza while debilitated by wounds sustained in action.

He mingled with the mightiest, but as the archive shows, a large part of his correspondence was with ordinary people writing to him for advice on almost any subject under the sun. His public expected him to be a real-life Holmes, and he did not disappoint them.

At times the problem would be exactly the kind of oddball mystery that Holmes relishes most. In 1909, for example, a woman named June Carver entreated his help in tracing a young Dane who had wooed and proposed to her, and then disappeared. It was almost an exact reprise of A Case of Identity, written in the 1890s. Conan Doyle spent months tracking down the Dane, establishing him to be almost a dodgy as Hosmer Angel, the missing man in the story. "A case of Sherlock Holmes work on My Darling's part," wrote Lady Conan Doyle.

Two cases found him pitted against the police and the Establishment as fearlessly as Holmes ever was. In 1907 he cleared the name of George Edalji, a young Parsee lawyer who had received a seven-year prison sentence after being convicted of mutilating farm animals. Disgusted by the undercurrent of racism in Edalji's treatment, Conan Doyle visited the scene, doubtless accompanied by his assistant Major Wood, the real-life Dr Watson. The clincher was his diagnosis of Edalji's astigmatic myopia, which made it impossible for the man to have attacked cattle and horses at dead of night as alleged. The gaps in the legal system exposed by Conan Doyle led directly to the institution of the Court of Criminal Appeal.

His longer crusade, stretching over 17 years, was on behalf of a man named Oscar Slater who was sentenced to death, later commuted to life imprisonment with hard labour, for the murder of a Glasgow woman on the flimsiest evidence in 1908. The archive includes a note from Slater to an about-to-be-released fellow convict urging him to "get in touch with Conan Doyle", which the recipient smuggled out under his dentures. Largely through Conan Doyle's persistent campaigning, Slater was exonerated of the murder and released in 1927. "Sir Conan Doyle" the freed man wrote to his champion as if at the conclusion of yet another Holmes story, "You breaker of my shackles, you lover of truth for justice sake, I thank you from the bottom of my heart for the goodness you have shown towards me."

Strangely, however, Conan Doyle received no further public recognition after his knighthood in 1902, conferred for his services in South Africa. Flower suspects part of the reason may have been his increasing involvement with spiritualism, which in the 19th century had been respectable, even chic, but by the time of the great war was looking embarrassingly suburban. Conan Doyle is believed to have spent some £250,000 – several million today – in advancing its cause. The archive contains certificates he received from spiritualist groups to whom he lectured in Australia and the US, as well as notes on séances, mediums and spirit manifestations. Tucked into his wallet is a description of a psychic message that impressed him, a picture of his lost son, Kingsley, and a jotted note about the "feeling of calm and restful happiness" with which he contemplates death.

The material has two notable absences. There is almost no Sherlock Holmes material, like the page on which Conan Doyle toyed with the notion of making Holmes's first name "Sherringford". And – possibly thanks to wifely tact – Flower has found no mention of the famous kerfuffle in 1917 when 10-year-old Frances Griffiths and 16-year-old Elsie Wright produced photographs they claimed to have taken of fairies dancing in a dell at Cottingley, Yorkshire. Today, they seem the most obvious hoax (as Frances would admit they were, 60 years later). Yet in The Strand Magazine for December 1920, Conan Doyle conceded "a prima-facie case" for their being genuine, and looked forward to further contacts with denizens of the fairy world. "The thought of them...will add a charm to every brook and valley and give romantic interest to every country walk," the big softie wrote. "We seem to be on the edge of a new continent, separated not by oceans but by subtle and surmountable psychic conditions."

Why sell off such an archive to individuals rather than in its entirety to an institution such as the British Library, where it might nurture the definitive biography of Conan Doyle, which has still not been written? While regretting the break-up of such a treasure, Flower says it couldn't have divided equitably between the remaining family members, nor sold outright as a piece of heritage. Libraries or museums might bid for the papers but would be less ready to acquire "trophy items" like the doctor's plate. The letters of his father, however, and other senior family members are not included in the sale, and may be offered to some national institution in the future.

Perhaps the most touching of the brown envelopes are those in which Lady Conan Doyle kept the early snowdrops her husband picked for her each spring on the anniversary of their first meeting. There is also the gold medallion he had specially made for her just before his death, inscribed "to the best of nurses", and the card that informed the public that ill health meant that he could no longer take up the cudgels on their behalf. The motto he kept on his study wall sums up his life and is good enough advice to any writer: "Don't tell me of luck, for it's judgement and pluck/And a course that will never shirk/To give your mind to it, and know how to do it/And put all your heart in your work."

MEN OF LETTERS

In 1989, JM Stoddart, the Philadelphia publisher, came to London seeking copy for his Lippincott's Monthly Magazine. The high point of his visit was a dinner party whose guests included two star potential contributors, the then plain Arthur Conan Doyle and Oscar Wilde. Despite their supreme dissimilarity as both writers and individuals, the two got on well, especially when Wilde proved a fan of Conan Doyle's novel Micah Clarke. It was on this occasion that Wilde made his famous observation, especially true of writers, that "anyone can sympathise with the suffering of a friend, but it requires a very fine nature – it requires in fact the nature of the true individualist – to sympathise with a friend's success". He also, atypically, made an HG Wells-ish prophesy that would prove uncannily accurate, saying that in future warfare "a chemist on each side would approach the frontier with a bottle". The dinner led Conan Doyle to offer Stoddart serialisation of The Sign of Four, a Sherlock Holmes novel with an Indian-mutiny back story, which opened with the great detective injecting cocaine (and also contains almost surreally nightmarish views of Victorian London). Conan Doyle's description of this corpse-ridden tale led Wilde in turn to recount the murder plot of his still-unwritten novella, The Picture of Dorian Gray, which Stoddart immediately snapped up. When the editor specified a length of 100,000 words, Wilde cabled back, "There are not 100,000 beautiful words in the English language." He tried to go about the story as Holmes's creator would do, even consulting a surgeon about the chemical disposal of Dorian's victim, Hallward. He also tried hard to emulate Conan Doyle's two-fisted prose style, while privately admitting: "I can't describe action; my people sit in chairs and chatter." Cordial as their first meeting was, the Wilde-Conan Doyle friendship did not ripen. When the two later ran across each other, Conan Doyle admitted he had not seen

Wilde's latest play, A Woman of No Importance. "Ah, but you must go," Wilde told him, "It is wonderful, it is genius." To Conan Doyle, the only explanation for such boastfulness, was insanity.

NUPTIAL AGREEMENT

Conan Doyle met his first wife, Louise Hawkins ("Touie"), when he was a struggling young GP. Her brother had incurable meningitis, and Conan Doyle took the boy into his house to care for him personally. The couple married in 1885, had two children, and enjoyed over 20 years of blissful happiness clouded only by Touie's health: just as Conan Doyle began to achieve fame as a writer, she was diagnosed with tuberculosis and given only a few months to live. Her husband refused to accept the verdict and took her to more beneficial climes in Switzerland and the Middle East, thereby prolonging her life by another decade. In 1897, Conan Doyle met a beautiful woman named Jean Leckie and, by his own later account, instantly fell in love with her. But with chivalry worthy of his fictional knights errant, he refused to begin a relationship with her until after Touie's death in 1906. They married a year later and remained as besotted as newlyweds until Conan Doyle's death in 1930. Yet, paradoxically, this paragon of marital fidelity became a champion of divorce-law reform. In 1909 he published a pamphlet attacking the inequality that allowed men to divorce solely on grounds of adultery but obliged women also to prove their husbands had deserted them for two years or been physically violent. The result was a royal commission echoing his call that "the cause for divorce shall be the same between the sexes" and that further grounds should be a three-year period of desertion by either partner. Conan Doyle's pamphlet, written with touches of true Holmesian scorn, can be seen as his parting from Catholicism and the start of his journey into spiritualism. "Every church has a right…to prescribe conduct for its own members," he wrote. "None has the right to enforce views upon the general public. If it pleases the ecclesiastical mind to consider that our present ethical customs should be regulated by its own particular interpretation of certain words uttered 2,000 years ago, then that is its own affair." In spiritualism he hoped to find a new morality to take the place of the old belief systems, which, for him, had lost all its relevance.

THE DAILY TELEGRAPH Thursday, May 20, 2004

£1m clues to life of Conan Doyle By Will Bennett Art Sales Correspondent

A LOST archive of letters and documents providing an insight into Sir Arthur Conan Doyle's life fetched £948,546 at auction yesterday.

The 3,000 letters, notes and hand-written manuscripts had been thought lost for 40 years until they were found a few months ago in the offices of a London solicitor.

The auction at Christie's in London, which led to the archive being split into almost 140 lots, was criticised by some enthusiasts of the Sherlock Holmes author. They said that it should have been kept together and preserved for the nation.

Christie's had hoped that the collection would fetch about £1.5 million but a quarter of the lots failed to sell.

Chapter 33

Sir Arthur Conan Doyle: An Obituary

THE DAILY TELEGRAPH, MONDAY, JULY 7, 1930

LETTERS TO THE EDITOR

CONSTANTINOPLE

ALLIES' "PRIZE" THAT WAS WELL LOST

RUSSIA IN POSSESSION

From SIR ARTHUR CONAN DOYLE

TO THE EDITOR OF "THE DAILY TELEGRAPH"

SIR – It makes one's heart bleed to read Mr. Churchill's account of our unnecessary failure to force the Dardanelles.

Mr. Churchill writes with such power – he is, in my opinion, the greatest living master of English prose – that he may produce a greater effect than the facts warrant. For consider the situation if we had then taken Constantinople and driven Turkey out of the war.

The possession of Constantinople had been promised to Russia, and we should now have been faced with a mighty Power which faced Europe upon a front extending from Archangel to the Mediterranean. If the Power were Bolshevik the situation would be terrible.

But even if we assume that a victorious Russia would have remained Imperial, would not that also have been a mighty danger when the counterpoise of Germany had been removed?

It may be that our failure was really more beneficial in the end than success would have been, and that this one more instance where the wisest plans of men have been set aside by that which is wiser still – Yours, & c.,

ARTHUR CONAN DOYLE.
Crowborough, July 4.

THE DAILY TELEGRAPH, TUESDAY, JULY 8, 1930

SHERLOCK HOLMES'S CREATOR

CONAN DOYLE'S VARIED CAREER

NOVELIST WHO BEGAN AS DOCTOR

CATHOLIC, AGNOSTIC AND SPIRITUALIST

By the late T.P. O'Connor

Sir Arthur Conan Doyle (whose death is reported on another page) was famous as the creator of Sherlock Holmes, one of the few living and permanent figures in the gallery of detective fiction.

Trained for the medical profession, Sir Arthur was in turn writer of fiction, war correspondent, playwright, historian of the South African campaign, and the sturdy champion of England in the Great War, and Roman Catholic who turned agnostic and afterwards became a strenuous advocate of spiritualism, and the man who did more than anyone to secure the release, after eighteen years, imprisonment, of Oscar Slater, who had been sentenced to death for the murder of a woman in Glasgow.

He came of Irish stock, his uncle being "Dicky" Doyle, the famous artist of *Punch*. His father was a public official in Edinburgh, where Conan Doyle was born on May 22, 1859. The family being strictly Roman Catholic, young Doyle was sent to Stonyhurst, and then came a year in Germany, and five years as a medical student in Edinburgh. During those student days his real education as a man of letters began, by studying the characters of some of the remarkable men who were professors in the medical school. One of them, Dr. Rutherford, stood for Professor Challenger; another, Dr. Joseph Bell, was the original Sherlock Holmes.

Bell had a wonderful power of diagnosis of ailments and character.

"Well, my man you've served in the Army?" he said to a civilian patient. "Aye, sir." "Not long discharged?" "No sir." "A Highland regiment?" "Aye, sir," A non-com, officer?" "Aye, sir." "Stationed at Barbados?" "Aye, sir."

"You see, gentlemen," he would explain, "the man was a respectful man, but did not remove his hat. They do not in the Army, but he would have learned civilian ways had he been long discharged. He has an air of authority, and he is obviously Scottish. As to Barbados, his complaint is elephantiasis, which is West Indian, and not British."

EARLY LITERARY EFFORTS

Conan Doyle had not long been in the medical school before the literary ferment was working on him; his allowance for his lunch was two pence, the price of a mutton pie; he often spent the two pence at a second-hand bookstall, and went fasting. A friend who had been impresses by the vividness of style in Doyle's letters to him, suggested that he had a talent for writing, and under this encouragement, Doyle wrote his first published tale, which was accepted by *Chamber's Journal*, and bought a fee of three guineas.

He got the post of medical man on a small vessel trading to West Africa, and had many wanderings and adventures. He fell a victim to a fever that nearly killed him. On his return he definitely started his career as a medical man at Southsea. He only had £10 as capital, he was a complete stranger. He had to pick up bits of furniture so as to make at least one room presentable for patients who might come; he cleaned up his own plate and did, in short, all the domestic work of a servant. He kept his small allowance of food in a trunk; and the trunk also had to serve as his dining table; and he did his own cooking on a gas stove.

Doyle seemed in danger of settling down to the sedate and uninteresting life as a family doctor when literature began at last to hold out some brighter prospects. James Payn accepted a story for the "Cornhill," and gave him a fee of £30. Doyle also stormed the impregnable fortress of "Blackwood." But he felt he was not getting "forrader," and that until he had produced a book he could not hope for large recognition. He was not quite satisfied with the marvellous M. Dupin, the greatest detective in Gaboriau. He thought the type of detective in fiction could be improved on, and then he bethought himself of Dr. Bell, who became Sherlock Holmes. And so began the now famous stories.

While Doyle was awaiting the publication of the first "Sherlock Holmes" book he spent much time and labour on a historical novel, which tried to reproduce the Puritans of the Cromwellian period. It was rejected by several publishers, but Arthur Lang finally got it taken by Longmans. Then he wrote his two historical novels, "The White Company" and "Sir Nigel" both dealing with English history of the period of Edward III. In after years Sir Arthur said that these two books, in his personal judgement, constituted his best literary work.

MEDICINE ABANDONED

In spite of these successes, and being as he insisted, a man of simple tastes and small wants, he might, in spite of growing success as a man of letters, have remained in Southsea but for a family incident – the threat of consumption to a little daughter. Koch had just been announced as the discoverer of a new and certain cure for consumption.

Acquaintance with Sir Malcolm Morris, the celebrated surgeon, helped to mature the germ already in Doyle's mind of trying his chances in London. Acting on the advice of Morris, he resolved to become an eye specialist, and went to Vienna to get intensive training. He took rooms in Montague street, and waited there for hours every day for patients who did not come, which in the end helped, for these idle hours gave him the opportunity of writing. It was thus he began the series of short stories in which Sherlock Holmes was the chief figure. While he was starting on this new departure, a fit of influenza threw him back on himself; and the, with a feeling of exultation, he made the big refusal, threw physic to the dogs, and started as a writer pure and simple. From this time forward he lived entirely by his pen.

BOXING ADEPT

A great misfortune fell upon him in the illness of his wife, which was diagnosed as consumption. He devoted years to her relief. Shut up with her in the solitude of Davos, he was enabled to devote himself entirely to literary work, and there began the "Brigadier Gerard" series. On his return from a lecture visit to America, he went to Egypt, where he became a war correspondent with the Expedition to the Sudan. He made the acquaintance of Kitchener, but turned back before the final advance to Khartoum. Returning to his literary work, Doyle found his next theme in a study of the big prize-fighters of the past; it was then he wrote "Rodney Stone" – one of his most popular works and one of his best written.

In most that he attempted Doyle succeeded, but one ambition eluded him – a seat in the House of Commons. He fought Central Edinburgh as a Liberal Unionist and then Hawick Burghs as a Tariff Reformer, but in neither case was he successful.

No sketch of Doyle would be complete which did not mention his great love of sport, including riding, shooting, skiing and boxing. At boxing he was something of an adept, always ready for a bout in gloves with a friend: once, indeed, he fought another man while they were both in evening dress after a party where they both had been guests. One of the offers which amused him was from an American newspaper which enabled him to come over and describe the fight between Jeffries and Johnson. His knowledge of prize-fighting and of boxing generally proved to be very useful; it accounts for the simplicity and the strength of the boxing scenes in "Rodney Stone"; the best descriptions of such feats since the days of George Borrow.

The last phase in the life and adventures of Doyle must be dealt with similarly. His religious creeds indeed showed throughout his life as a curious mutability; for beginning as a Roman Catholic, he went on to agnosticism, and ultimately turned to spiritualism.

EDALJI CASE

Mention has been made of the efforts of Sir Arthur to secure the release of Oscar Slater. Another convicted man he championed was G.R.T.Edalji, the Parsee, who in October, 1903, was sentenced to seven years' penal servitude for cattle maiming. Sir Arthur became convinced that there had been a miscarriage of justice, and he devoted the powerful advocacy of his pen to securing a reversal of the sentence. In January, 1907, THE DAILY TELEGRAPH published an article in which Sir Arthur gave the results of his investigation into the case, and it was largely as a consequence that at the end of three' years confinement, Edalji was released and pardoned.

Sir Arthur also took part in the agitation which resulted in the release of Adolph Beck.

Such, then, was Conan Doyle – a manly man, a tender man, a little rough-hewn in mind and body; the inventor of a being almost as popular as Robinson Crusoe; and the author of much innocent delight to his generation and perhaps generations to come.

Sir Arthur was twice married – first to Louise, daughter of Mr. J. Hawkins of Minsterworth, and secondly to Jean, daughter of Mr. J.B. Leckie.

THE DAILY TELEGRAPH, TUESDAY, JULY 8, 1930

SIR ARTHUR CONAN DOYLE

THE FAMOUS NOVELIST'S SUDDEN DEATH

LAST LETTER IN "THE DAILY TELEGRAPH"

THE DAILY TELEGRAPH regrets to announce the death of Sir Arthur Conan Doyle, which occurred yesterday at his Sussex home in Crowborough.

Sir Arthur had been ill since the autumn of last year, but recently the heart trouble from which he had suffered had become easier, and his death was unexpectedly sudden.

It was only yesterday, the day of his death, that a letter from his hand was published in THE DAILY TELEGRAPH dealing with the Dardanelles campaign, in connection with the articles which Mr. Churchill is contributing to our columns.

Mr. Dennis Conan Doyle considers that his father's death may have been accelerated by the fact he headed a deputation to the Home Secretary on Tuesday of last week.

"This deputation" he said, "was an attempt to get altered what my father considered the unfair laws relating to mediums. The speech he made on their behalf while in an unfit state hastened his end."

"A SPLENDID FATHER"

Lady Conan Doyle, two sons and one daughter were present at the bedside when Sir Arthur breathed his last. Mr. Adrian Conan Doyle paid the following tribute to his father:

"He was a good man and a splendid father, and he was loved – and was happy because he knew it – by all of us. My mother and father were lovers after the passing of the years as they were on the day they were married. Their devotion to each other at all times was one of the most wonderful things I have ever known. She nursed him right through his illness to the end – just as she, like all of us, had been about the world with him.

"His last words were to her, and they show just how much he thought of her. He simply smiled at her, and said: 'You are wonderful.' Never have I seen anyone take anything more gamely in all my life. Even when we all knew he was suffering great pain he always managed during the time he was conscious to keep a smile on his face for us."

SIR OLIVER LODGE'S TRIBUTE

Sir Arthur, the son stated, fully believed as a Spiritualist that when he "passed over" he would continue to keep in touch with his family. "And all his family believe so, too," he added. "There is no question that my father will often speak to us just as he did before."

Sir Oliver Lodge paid tribute to Sir Arthur's work for Spiritualism. "He never spared himself when the cause was a stake," Sir Oliver said. "Much more than most of us, he regarded himself as an apostle or missionary, and threw himself and all his belongings into the movement.

"Even among those impressed with the magnitude of the issue few are willing to sacrifice themselves to the same extent. His period of service is not ended."

A memoir by the late T.P. O'Connor appears on Page 811 with the facsimile of the last letter

This facsimile appears overleaf.

Chapter 34

New Books: October/November 2010/2011

THE SUNDAY TELEGRAPH/SEVEN MAGAZINE

Andrew Lycett enjoys three books that shed light on the life and genius of Holmes's creator.

ON CONAN DOYLE Or, The Whole Art of storytelling.

By **Michael Dirda.**

THE NARRATIVE OF JOHN SMITH.

By **ARTHUR CONAN DOYLE.**

THE HOUSE OF SILK.

By **ANTHONY HOROWITZ.**

By their enthusiasms you shall know them. Michael Dirda, a heavyweight of American literary criticism, might have chosen Philip Roth or some worthy classical author as the subject of this enchanting biographical study, which doubles as a paean to all aspects of the printed word. Instead he focuses on Sir Arthur Conan Doyle, whom he discovered as a boy (through the Sherlock Holmes story *The Hound of the Baskervilles*) and has been hooked on ever since.

As a result of that youthful encounter, Dirda developed a passion for the writings of this underrated craftsman – not just the Holmes stories and their mock scholastic cult, but also for the rest of his extensive output, from the exploits of the Napoleonic adventurer Brigadier Gerard and the scientific explorer Professor Challenger to dozens of little-read tales involving boxers, pirates, doctors and all sorts of spooky situations.

In light but authoritative fashion, Dirda expands on this lifelong bibliophilic affair, from the pleasures of seeking out the master's extra-Sherlockian adventure stories to his induction into the Baker Irregulars.

Along the way he came to admire the virtues of the author, with his gentlemanly qualities – expressed in his work as in his life – of honour, romance and good humour. Dirda finds these not just in Holmes but also in historical novels such as *The White Company*, the sort of thing Conan Doyle aspired to writing when he killed off his detective at the Reichenbach Falls. Dirda praises the "wonderful bounce and sweetness" of this book's narrative, seeing his hero's beloved Macaulay and Scott "behind the rhetorical sweep of even the simplest sentences".

Dirda is not alone in his devotion. As well as deft allusions to unexpected writers including Tolstoy and Dostoevsky, he works in references to authors, such as TS Eliot, who have paid literary homage to the Conan Doyle canon (witness his "grimpen" in

Four Quartets and his parody of the Musgrave Ritual in *Murder in the Cathedral*). They are in the same camp as PG Wodehouse who stated, "Conan Doyle was my hero. Others might revere Hardy and Meredith. I was a Doyle man, and I still am."

Looking at Conan Doyle's life, Dirda eschews strict chronology, preferring to interpret lesser known episodes to his hero's advantage. Thus Conan Doyle's warm recollection of meeting the black American abolitionist Henry Highland Garnet, in West Africa, is represented as evidence of his humanity – a quality apparent also in his support for the part-Parsee George Edalji, wrongly accused of animal mutilation (the stuff of Julian Barnes's novel *Arthur & George*) and in his opposition to slavery in the Congo.

Some might cavil at the space given to the Baker Street Irregulars and its canonical horseplay. But Dirda offers good value, arguing that French deconstructionists have nothing on the Irregulars when it comes to scouring Sherlockian texts and "finding latent, suppressed meanings hidden in 'endless minutiae'." Given the excellence of this introduction, it is interesting to see how two new publications match up to the master. *The Narrative of John Smith* is by the man himself, the partial text of an early "novel" which recently turned up in the British Library. It provides insights into Conan Doyle's perennial interest in topics such as medicine and religion, and shows flashes of his humour. However, as its editors acknowledge, this is a work in progress; a compendium of ideas, lacking narrative drive.

Still, as James Bond and Peter Pan, the demand for "continuation" material persists. Anthony Horowitz, the children's author, is the latest writer to turn his hand to Holmes.

The result is an exciting, well-crafted novel about the great detective's tussle with a murderous homosexual ring that somehow infiltrates Holmes's band of urchins, the original Baker Street Irregulars. Strong on period detail, it weaves in familiar elements of Holmes's character, methods and relationships with Dr Watson and other figures such as Inspector Lestrade. The only thing lacking is what Vladimir Nabokov (as noted by Dirda) called *shamanstvo;* the enchanter-quality of Conan Doyle himself.

That same, astonishing popularity has lasted to this day. Although Holmes appears in just 56 short stories and four novels, he is famously the one character most often portrayed on television and film. He has recently been modernised by the BBC and bowdlerised by Hollywood – the second film with Robert Downey Jr comes out at Christmas. There is currently a campaign (which I support) to give Jeremy Brett a posthumous Bafta for his brilliant depiction of the character throughout the Eighties.

My own addition to the Sherlock canon – the first to be given the imprimatur of the Doyle estate – received extraordinary attention when I announced it last January in the House of Commons at a dinner hosted by the 1,000 strong Sherlock Holmes society. I found myself on the *News at Ten*. *The Spectator* ran an editorial as did the *New York Times* – although neither seemed to think the book would be much good. So why Holmes has endured – and, more to the point, how did I dare to take on the mantle of the world's most successful detective?

In truth, when I was offered this assignment, just over a year ago, I did pause for at least half a second. Are publishers being overtly cynical, relaunching old characters in new adventures, adding prequels and sequels to cash in on bestselling names? The two new Bond novels – Sebastian Faulks's *Devil May Care* and Jeffrey Deaver's *Carte Blanche* – are perhaps to most obvious successes but an extraordinary range of novels, from *Madame Bovary* to *Just William*, have been given the same treatment. Why would any author want to tread in the shadow of such icons when surely the whole point of writing is to come up with something original.

I hesitated, as I say, very briefly and wouldn't have considered it but for one simple fact. I have always loved Sherlock Holmes – by which I mean the books, and not the character. I read them when I was about 17 and they stayed with me, driving me into a career writing detective fiction for both children (the Diamond Brothers) and adults (Midsomer Murders, Foyle's War. Holmes himself is not lovable. In fact it was Doyle's genius to make him cold, aloof, unfathomable, irritating, a drug addict even – and then to tie him in with the one person, whose warmth, decency and whole-hearted and unstinting admiration would humanise him. I have always thought of Holmes and Watson as having the greatest friendship in literature. For me it is this, and not the mysteries, or even the solutions, that makes us return to the stories with such pleasure.

The mysteries, though always elegant and intriguing, are often quite thin and, sometimes, there is no mystery. In *The Man With the Twisted Lip*, no crime is committed, while *The Adventure of the Crooked Man* is conspicuous by having little or no investigation. It's surprising how few of the stories in the first collection, *The Adventures of Sherlock Holmes*, contain murders. In later stories, Holmes reveals that deaths have been caused by a horse, by a jellyfish and by suicide.

This is not to criticise Doyle. It is simply to suggest that his mind was elsewhere and that, unlike Agatha Christie, he was less interested in the method and the mechanism of crime (I'm not sure there's a single Holmes story where we're blown away by the identity of the killer) than in the character of his two protagonists and the atmosphere in which they lived. And in this, of course, he triumphed. People assumed that Holmes was a real person while Doyle was alive, and some still believe it today.

Perhaps that is why writing *The House of Silk* was not exactly a challenge, which is to say I never felt intimidated. When you write an original novel, you're on your own. But I started well ahead of the game with a fantastic array of characters – not just Holmes and Watson, but Mycroft, Moriarty, Lestrade, the Baker Street Irregulars – a world so brilliantly defined by Doyle that I can conjure it up now with just a handful of words: fog, gas-lamps, hansom cabs, cobbled streets, the pipe, the Persian slipper, the various monograms. These were all gifts for a writer. And then there were the turns of phrase that I could more or less cherry-pick. "Elementary, my dear Watson" (although he never said it). "The game's afoot." How many authors are there who can arrange three or four words in the English Language and have themselves instantly identified?

This was my task as I saw it. I had to obey all Doyle's conventions. I decided very early on that, apart from one or two tiny details, I would add no new information – no speculation about Holmes's childhood or new romances. There would be no cameos from famous people – Queen Victoria or Jack the Ripper – because Doyle never did this and so it wouldn't seem appropriate. And I threw out any sense of chronology. *The House of Silk* is set in 1890, but I didn't worry too much about the historical time-line as Doyle certainly didn't. "Accuracy of detail matters little," he once wrote. "What matters if I hold my readers?"

My readers are, of course, modern and I knew I had to come up with an original story that would be fast-paced and twisty enough to hold their attention. I would use a 19th-century idiom, but carefully. Finally – and this was the biggest challenge – my publishers had commissioned 90,000 words, the length of an airport blockbuster (they hope).

But the Doyle novels are barely more than 40,000 words. Two of them have whole sections that take place abroad without Holmes or Watson being present. I did wonder how I could extend the length without damaging the delicate structures of the Doyle originals.

I think I've succeeded. I'm tempted to say that the book has turned out better than I could possibly hoped. And so much of that is down to Sir Arthur Conan Doyle. Unlike him, I am not a spiritualist. But as I wrote, I sometimes felt as if he were standing next to me, urging me on. I never had to search for words or descriptions. And although a book usually takes me seven months to a year, *The House of Silk* was finished in half that time. I am as proud of it as anything I have ever written and, no matter how it is received, how many copies it sells, I will never regret my time at 221b Baker Street in the company of two such remarkable men.

Writers FORUM

August 2011

Doyle's delayed debut

Sherlock Holmes creator Arthur Conan Doyle's debut novel is to be published for the first time in September, nearly 130 years after it was written. Conan Doyle was in his early 20s when he wrote *The Narrative of John Smith*, which apparently is not what modern readers might call a 'page turner'.

Jon Lellenberg, a Conan Doyle expert, said: 'What is interesting about it is not the story for its own sake but as a look inside the mind of this very young man – a struggling physician who is struggling even harder to become a published writer.'

To add even more difficulty to the fledgling literary career of the man who would shortly create one of literature's most famous characters in Sherlock Holmes, the original manuscript of *The Narrative* was lost in the post on the way to the publisher, and Conan Doyle had to rewrite it from memory.

Katalin Havasi

SATURDAY, NOVEMBER 5, 2011 THE DAILY TELEGRAPH
Comment

Damian Thompson ON SATURDAY

Sherlock back on the trail

So great is my devotion to Sherlock Holmes that, in addition to the "sacred canon" of the Conan Doyle stories, I own books in which scholars argue about whether an adventure can be dated to August 1887 or April 1888. Sad, I know, but its been an obsession since childhood. So I approached Anthony Horowitz's new Holmes novel, *The House of Silk* – the first to be approved by the Conan Doyle estate – in a spirit of scepticism. The verdict? I've read more accurate pastiches, but none that was so suspenseful. Besides, let's face it, the later Holmes yarns are feeble. (*The Mazarin Stone* is probably the worst short story ever written.) As someone once told Conan Doyle: "Holmes may not have been killed off at the Reichenbach Falls, but he was never quite the same afterwards."

OUTRAGE By Roger Oldfield

The true story of an extraordinary family obsessed till now by a dying pit-pony and Conan Doyle's world-famous campaign.

The Edalji Five and the Shadow of Sherlock Holmes.

Published by Vanguard Press, October 2010, price £11.99. Arthur Conan Doyle didn't just write mysteries, he actually solved a few. One of his most famous cases is the George Edalji case.

Roger Oldfield has written a book about the case, *Outrage: The Edalji Five and the Shadow of Sherlock Holmes*. Mr. Oldfield brings a unique perspective to the case as someone who has met descendents of individuals involved in the case.

Roger Oldfield recently told LitQuotes about the case and about his new book.

'SHERLOCK HOLMES AT WORK'. This was the headline in the *Daily Telegraph* on January 11 1907 when Sir Arthur Conan Doyle in the first of two articles announced to the world that he was taking up the case of George Edalji. The great novelist George Meredith, one of the many literary friends who wrote to congratulate him, put it this way: Sherlock Holmes, he said, had shown 'what can be done in the life of breath'.

There had already been a national outcry in 1903 when George Edalji of Great Wyrley in Staffordshire had been convicted of wounding a pony, the 8th of a series of barbarous outrages in his home village. The fact however that the very creator of Sherlock Holmes seemed in 1907 to be acting out the part of his own creation, the most famous character in British fiction, gave George Edalji's cause worldwide fame: newspapers from New York to Paris to Mumbai reported the developing events of 1907 with fascination. Conan Doyle not only acted as sleuth, scouring the scene of the crime and interviewing the major players; he also had his real-life Inspector Lestrade, in the shape of George Anson, Chief Constable of Staffordshire, whom he blamed for George Edalji's wrongful conviction.

The shadow of Sherlock Holmes has hung over the story ever since. 'It is a blot upon the record of English Justice,' Conan Doyle wrote in his *Memories and Adventures* in 1924, 'and even now it should be wiped out.' This was the verdict which echoed for decades through the pens of many of the dozens of his admirers and biographers – 'a very gentle, perfect knight' (Lamond, 1931), 'a brilliant vindication of Edalji' (Pemberton, 1936), 'the incarnation of the English conscience' (Nordon, 1968). Even Julian Barnes, who has revived worldwide interest in the story in his novel *Arthur & George* (2005), the bookies' favourite for the top literary prize in Britain in 2005, does not question Conan Doyle's view that Edalji was innocent.

There is evidence, however, which runs counter to the Conan Doyle view, as the local historian Michael Harley suggested in the 1980s. Roger Oldfield's, is the first to go behind the scenes and assess the evidence for and against George Edalji in full. A conclusion is reached on whether the man who believed in fairies had been taken in by the mild-mannered, middle class from Great Wyrley.

As for Julian Barnes's novel, that too is subjected to rigorous scrutiny and the general reader is given a glimpse into how far it remains true to the actual historical record.

Also new, and of special interest for Conan Doyle addicts, is an account of the extraordinary secret war which broke out between Conan Doyle and Chief Constable Anson. At one point their furious dispute led each of them to appeal to Winston Churchill for support. Anson was utterly contemptuous of the detective skills of the man many thought actually was Sherlock Holmes, and his seething hatred for the world-famous writer lasted until his death.

Roger Oldfield's book suggests that the shadow of Sherlock Holmes hanging over the story has obscured the fascinating history of the Edalji family as a whole. His research has uncovered a mass of new material about all five members of the family which has never been published before.

'unlikely to be surpassed as a comprehensive, intelligent, balanced and intensely readable account' – *The Newsletter of the Sherlock Holmes Society of London*

'certainly the best thing there is concerning the Edalji case on every count' – *D. Michael Risinger, Professor of Law, Newark, USA.*

© Roger Oldfield 2011

Conan Doyle's first novel, *The Narrative of John Smith*, will soon be published for the first time. This early, and uncompleted work of Conan Doyle will be published by the British Library.

Lost Conan Doyle novel to be published

The Narrative of John Smith, Sherlock Holmes author's previously unpublished debut novel, due out this autumn.

After languishing unpublished for almost 130 years, Sir Arthur Conan Doyle's first novel is set to be released for the first time this autumn.

The Narrative of John Smith was written when Conan Doyle was 23, and just a few years before the author published his first Sherlock Holmes story, A Study in Scarlet. It tells the story of a 50-year-old "opinionated Everyman" confined to his room by gout, laying out his thoughts and views on subjects from religion to war and literature through the conversations he has with his visitors, from a retired army major to a curate.

"As you may expect with the creator of Sherlock Holmes, there's a bit of a mystery around the manuscript," said Rachel Foss, lead curator of modern literary manuscripts at the British Library, which is publishing the 150-page book in November (2011).

"He wrote it in 1883 and 1884, when he was starting to try to establish himself in the medical profession and as a writer. He sent it to a publisher, but it got lost in the post, so he decided to try and redo it from memory. The manuscript we have is the novel as reconstructed from memory, and it stops around chapter six.

The book, said Foss, is "fairly loose in terms of plot and character", but it does provide "some hints towards the Sherlock Holmes stories to come". John Smith's housekeeper, Mrs Rundle, for example, "can be seen as a prototype for the garrulous Mrs Hudson, Sherlock Holmes's landlady".

"It gives a really fascinating insight into the early stages of [Conan Doyle's] development as a writer – his apprenticeship period…It represents his attempt to make the transition from short story writer to novelist," she said. "It demonstrates that there are things we can learn about him."

Stephen Fry said publication of the novel, which displays Conan Doyle's "boundless energy, enthusiasm and wide-ranging mind, not to mention [his] pitch-perfect, muscular and memorable prose", was "very very welcome indeed".

"The breadth, depth and scope of Conan Doyle's knowledge and curiosity is often overlooked. He was the first popular writer to tell the wider reading public about narcotics, the Ku Klux Klan, the mafia, the Mormons, American crime gangs, corrupt union bosses and much else besides," said Fry. "Someone, I think it was the noted Janeite Lord David Cecil, once said that Jane Austin was the kind of writer on whose laundry lists and notes to the milkman any keen reader would pounce. While Conan Doyle may not be considered to be in quite that category there can be no doubt that the heart of every lover of British writing will rejoice at this discovery of an early and as yet unpublished work by the creator of Holmes, Watson, Moriarty and Professor Challenger."

The Daily Telegraph Review November 12 2011

Book Review: Crime

The House of Silk By **Anthony Horowitz**

Sherlock Holmes is framed for murder by a dastardly secret society in Horowitz's inventive yarn, the first sequel ever to be endorsed by Conan Doyle's estate. I suspect the great Sir Arthur would have been dazzled by the frenetic pace, puzzled by the touchy-feely bits and outraged by some of the un-Victorian indelicacy, but would ultimately salute a brother writer who shares his aim of giving joy "to the boy who's half a man, or the man who's half a boy".

Jake Kerridge

THE DAILY TELEGRAPH MONDAY, DECEMBER 19, 2011

Charles Spencer

When Holmes netted Nessie

The first "grown-up" books I ever read were the Sherlock Holmes stories and their appeal has never faded. Conan Doyle grew notoriously tired of a character whose popularity the author felt eclipsed his more serious work, but posterity's verdict is with Holmes.

What's remarkable and hugely cheering is the game's still afoot and the great double act of Holmes and Watson is as vibrant in the 21st century as it was in the 19th. Indeed, we are currently living in the golden age of Sherlockiana. Anthony Horowitz's new Sherlock Holmes novel *The House of Silk* is superb – indeed, I would say it is better than any of Conan Doyle's own Holmes novels, which always feel padded out in comparison with the gripping short stories

The BBCTV series *Sherlock* starring Benedict Cumberbatch and Martin Freeman, set in the present day, just as the classic films starring Basil Rathbone and Nigel Bruce were in the 1940s, is a witty and inventive delight, and the good news is that there will be three more episodes early next year.

And though Guy Ritchie's new Sherlock Holmes movies starring Robert Downey Jnr and Jude Law are world's removed from Conan Doyle's originals, they are undoubtedly high class blockbuster hokum.

There is, however, one terrific Holmes film that is often overlooked and to which, I would particularly draw your attention. Billy Wilder's *The Private life of Sherlock Holmes* (1970) never achieved much commercial success and isn't in the same league as such Wilder masterpieces as *Sunset Boulevard* and *Some Like It Hot*.

It is nevertheless an enduring delight, often funny (there's a hilarious camp scene set at Covent Garden in which the corps de ballet wrongly suspect Dr Watson of being gay) but also gripping and imaginatively plotted with appearances by both Queen Victoria and the Loch Ness monster. Robert Stephens makes a louche, witty Holmes, Colin Blakely a delightful Watson while Genevieve Page adds a tingle of sex appeal as an Irene Adler-like *femme fatale* to whom the great consulting detective becomes dangerously attracted.

It's available for less than a fiver from Amazon and would make an admirable stocking-filler for any Holmes fan.

Chapter 35: Addendum

Daily Mail, Friday, February 12, 2010

FRIDAY BOOKS

BOOK OF THE WEEK **Sam Leith**

THE DEVIL & SHERLOCK HOLMES: TALES OF MURDER, MADNESS AND OBSESSION By **David Grann**. (Simon & Schuster £12.99) (Excerpt)

At first glance, Watson, what do we notice about the object under study? Yes, that's right: a paperback book. The game's afoot.

The title alludes to two notables, the front cover advertises 'murder, madness and obsession', and the obverse – yes, yes, 'back cover', if you will – says it describes an attempt to 'unravel the truth of 12 great real-life mysteries'.

The opening piece is the one on which the title hangs – telling the story of the 2004 death of the world's leading authority on the works of Sir Arthur Conan Doyle.

It's a cracker-what with a mysterious voice on the dead man's answerphone, skulduggery over a treasure trove of lost manuscripts, and what appears, at first, to be unsolvable murder but has a sadder and stranger outcome…

(**Compiler's note** – The reference above must be about the case of Richard Lancelyn Green which was detailed in Chapter 11 of this compilation.)

WEDNESDAY, FEBRUARY 24, 2010 **THE DAILY TELEGRAPH**

Mandrake Walker

Dismay that Bafta chooses not to commemorate Todd's life. (Excerpt)

…**Sir Christopher Lee** an old friend of **Richard (Todd)** who appeared with him in *House of Long Shadows* and a Sherlock Holmes film *Incident at Victoria Falls,* said: "It seems a remarkable omission as he obviously had a place in the history of British film-making. Many of his films are undoubtedly classics…"

[Richard Todd died just before Christmas aged 90].

Few, if any actors have figured as prominently in the history of British films as Richard Todd.

A Bafta spokesman said that "Every loss is equally important, but the time restriction of the obituaries section in the broadcast forces us to make small and necessary subjective selection."

Todd was on the list of 200 names "considered" for inclusion.

Daily Mail, Monday, March 8, 2010

Peter McKay

Cocaine nights of Sherlock

WE'RE told that 'Britain's love affair with cocaine is still growing'.

Some people in the TV, radio and newsprint media play up the use of cocaine because they're users themselves and enjoy thinking they're part of some wicked cult which has the likes of Kate Moss as a member.

But there's nothing new under the sun. There were probably as many users in the 19th century, including Arthur Conan Doyle's fictional detective Sherlock Holmes.

From The Sign of Four, 1890: 'Sherlock Holmes took his bottle from the mantelpiece, and his hypodermic syringe from its neat morocco case…Finally, he thrust the sharp point home, pressed down the tiny piston, and sank back into the velvet-lined armchair with a long sigh of satisfaction.'

Holmes justifies his coke habit to colleague Dr Watson by saying the damage it might be doing to himself is 'of small moment…I abhor the dull routine of existence. I crave for mental exaltation.'

So it is for many today.

Poor boobies, they're not happy 'in themselves', as my granny would put it. They have to stick chemicals up their noses to feel strong and clever. It's hardly a 'love affair', though, is it.

The Sunday Telegraph MAGAZINE **Seven** 14.03.10

TITLE DEED

HOW THE BOOK GOT IT'S NAME

The Adventures of Sherlock Holmes

By Arthur Conan Doyle

The Adventures of Sherlock Holmes (1892) was the first Sherlock Holmes collection – the first Holmes story had appeared five years before. Doyle dithered long and hard over the name of his hero and considered ' J. Sherrinford Holmes' and 'Sherrington Hope' before deciding on 'Sherlock Holmes'. It is not certain where Sherlock came from, but 'Holmes' has a concrete origin, in the name of Oliver Wendell Holmes, the American doctor and writer. Doyle was so star-struck by Dr Holmes that as a student he starved himself to buy Holmes's *The Autocrat of the Breakfast-Table*, and said 'Never have I so known and loved a man whom I never have seen'. He even made a literary pilgrimage to meet Holmes, though it was ill-fated. 'It was one of the ambitions of my lifetime to look into his face,' Doyle said, 'but by the irony of fate I arrived in his native city just in time to lay a wreath on his newly-turned grave.'

GARY DEXTER.

Daily Mail, Wednesday, March 31, 2010

ANSWERS TO CORRESPONDENTS Compiled by Charles Legge

An elementary error

QUESTION Did Sir Arthur Conan Doyle really play for Portsmouth FC?

AS A lifelong Portsmouth FC supporter, I wish that were the case, but alas it is not. It is a common misconception that Conan Doyle played for Pompey and an excellent book, popular in the city, Sherlock Holmes Was A Pompey Goalkeeper, perpetuates the myth.

After his writing became successful, Conan Doyle left a struggling doctor's practice in Southsea for pastures new in 1891. The professional football club Portsmouth FC wasn't founded until 1898.

My research for a forthcoming book about the city shows that while he was in Southsea, Conan Doyle played for an amateur club called Portsmouth Association Football Club.

This was not the forerunner of the professional club – that sprang from Portsmouth Royal Artillery, whose team played on the Services sports ground within the sound of the town hall chimes. Hence the famous Pompey Chimes – 'Play Up Pompey, Pompey Play Up' – sung by the supporters when the bells rang.

Conan Doyle was an ardent sporting man whose interests included bowls, boxing, ski-ing and baseball, which he tried to introduce to Britain after a visit to the U.S.

As a footballer he played in goal and 'at back', but he was no Gordon Banks or Bobby Moore. What skills he lacked he made up for by using his tall, robust, 15-stone frame and restless energy.

The story goes that, tired of kicking his heels in defence, he would often run the length of the pitch to support an attack – without ever receiving the ball – before running back.

However, he excelled at cricket. He was captain of Portsmouth Cricket Club and later played for Marylebone Cricket Club, once taking seven wickets for 51 runs against Cambridgeshire, making him one of the early Lord's legends.

Chris Horrocks, Southsea, Hants.

Email from Portsmouth Football Club (01/04/2010) in answer to my question on the above article, elicited the following reply:

'He (ACD) was a member of Portsmouth Football Association Club in the mid 1880s. More than ten years before Portsmouth Football Club as we know it today was formed'. **(Compiler).**

Daily Mail, Friday, April 2, 2010

It's Friday! Theatre

Elementary error, I fear, Sir Arthur

Arthur & George (Repertory Theatre, Birmingham)

Verdict: Sherlock-lite. Three Stars (out of five)
Review by Patrick Marmion

NOVELIST Julian Barnes and playwright David Edgar have gone to great lengths to create a cunningly un-Sherlock-like Conan Doyle drama. It's based on real-life events, when Sherlock Holmes's creator Sir Arthur Conan Doyle investigated a miscarriage of justice involving an Asian West Midlander called George Edaljii – a small-town Indian solicitor framed in a nasty case of horse slashing.

Like his fictional alter ego, Conan Doyle prides himself on being a man of sharp instinct, re-deploying Holmes's shrewd forensic intellect to his own personal ends.

It's a journey that leads him and his Watsonian assistant through a landscape of benighted country folk who, in time-honoured tradition, advise the upstart Londoner to 'leave it well alone'.

The ingredients of Barnes's 2005 novel about the episode and Edgar's staging bear all the hallmarks of a Conan Doyle classic.

Sadly, though, Sir Arthur is not allowed to get one over on Holmes with a real-life, last-minute rabbit-out-of-the-hat trick in which the dastardly villain is brilliantly exposed. Conan Doyle is instead more or less told off for the sin of pride in seeking to outwit his fictional creation.

Personally, I'd rather have had the brilliant hat trick, but there are elementary pleasures in Rachel Kavanaugh's production, which scales up a modest studio play for the Rep's chasm-like arena.

Chris Nayak as George, the hapless victim who becomes the cause celebre that gave us the Court of Criminal Appeal in 1907, is a loveable nerd whose innocence might have benefited from being more in doubt.

Kirsty Holles, Arthur's rather matronly love interest, exists, I fear, merely to satisfy political correctness, and tut-tut the menfolk for their clubbish misogyny.

Thankfully, Adrian Lukis saves the day as Conan Doyle. Although his Scottish accent only just makes it to Jedburgh, he gives the audience what they came for: an unmistakable Sherlock.

He is like a barrister addressing some invisible jury, halting mid-stride and stroking his chin at moments of insight. All that's missing is the cape and deerstalker.

TUESDAY, MAY 25, 2010 **THE DAILY TELEGRAPH**

News digest

Stately Holmes Sleuth's debut to fetch £400,000.

A rare inscribed copy of the book in which Sherlock Holmes made his first appearance is expected to fetch up to £400,000 when it goes under the hammer.

A copy of *A Study in Scarlet*, the debut novel by Sir Arthur Conan Doyle, is one of only two inscribed examples known to exist. Sotheby's will auction the work, which it described as "one of the rarest books of modern times", in London on July 15.

The work, published in *Beeton's Christmas Annual* in November 1887, had been rejected by a succession of publishers.

It sold out in 14 days and was republished, but Conan Doyle had given up all the rights for £25 and never received another penny for the work.

His inscription reads: "This is the first independent book of mine which was ever published, Arthur Conan Doyle."

Peter Selley, a senior specialist in Sotheby's books and manuscript department, said of the novel – the first inscribed copy to ever come up for auction: "It is highly unlikely that such a copy will ever become available again.

"The sale represents an opportunity to acquire the finest copy of the most important cornerstone of any collection of detective literature in the world."

(Compiler's note: See the close of this chapter for an update on this).

THE DAILY TELEGRAPH TUESDAY, JUNE 29, 2010

Bloomsbury Auctions
London, 8 July 2010
Strand Magazine
VOL. 1 – VOL 84, 1891-1897
A complete run that includes all the Arthur Conan Doyle issues
Est. £7,000-10,000

Saturday, July 3, 2010 TELEGRAPH WEEKEND

Book Club

Mystery of Sherlock's childhood revealed

A hew series uncovers the ace detective's youth. By **Christopher Middleton**

You don't have to be a detective to work out there's a murder mystery at the heart of our Family Book Club choice for July. However, the hero of *Young Sherlock Holmes: Death Cloud* is not quite the character we have all come to expect.

"I decided to make him just a younger version of his adult self," says Andrew Lane, the author commissioned by the Sir Arthur Conan Doyle estate to write a whole series of Young Sherlock books. "The thing is, Holmes is insufferable enough as an adult. Give him the same characteristics when he was a 14-year-old boy, and you'd just want to slap him around the face.

"Far more interesting, I thought, to develop him from scratch, to see him as an adolescent starting out in life and gradually acquiring the different aspects of his personality."

Not that it looks like he's going to reach adulthood, given the dangers he faces during the course of this first book in the series. Apart from the obvious hazard mentioned in the title, young Sherlock finds himself trapped inside a burning barn, attacked by savage dogs, surrounded by club-wielding thugs and at the wrong end of a riding whip wielded by sadistic megalomaniac Baron Maupertuis.

As with no Dr Watson to watch his back, the junior Holmes has to rely on the help of Matty, a wily young Victorian street urchin, and Virginia, the resourceful (and somewhat unnervingly attractive) daughter of his tutor, Amyus Crowe.

What, cry the purists? The famous misogynistic Holmes having anything to do with a woman who isn't either a client or Mrs Hudson, his landlady?

"He hasn't yet developed the massive distrust of women that he will have in later life," explains Lane. "But even at this early stage, we see the seeds being sown."

We certainly do. Apart from the sparky Virginia, most of the other females in young Sherlock's life are a poor advertisement for their sex: his mentally fragile (and absent) mother, the loopy aunt with whom he is sent to live and the malevolent housekeeper Mrs Eglantine, whose first words to him are: "Child, be aware you are not welcome here."

As well as not having acquired immunity to emotion, the teenage Holmes has also not perfected the powers of observation and analysis that will mark him out in later life. We only get one glimpse of his fledgling perspicacity when, by looking at the crumples in elder brother Mycroft's trousers, he can deduce by what mode of transport he has travelled (their father's carriage which has a clumsily repaired rip in the upholstery).

"A small bit of me regrets putting even that one scene into the book," admits Lane, a prolific crime and science-fiction writer in his own right (*Doctor Who*, *Torchwood*). "I really wanted to preserve the distinction between the young and old Sherlock."

An obsessive Holmes fan since childhood, Lane has gone to great lengths to capture the period detail, providing vivid descriptions of rail journeys, fair grounds and unhygienic public highways (the manure-rich streets of Farnham). And he has refused to allow anything into his books that might conflict with the original Conan Doyle stories.

The Sunday Telegraph MAGAZINE 15.08.10

theatre Extraordinary, Holmes

Jeremy Paul's homage to the great detective is thoroughly on the case. By TIM WALKER

Sir Arthur Conan Doyle sat down to write his Sherlock Holmes stories as some men would venture into cold showers. His, wife, Louise, was dying a long, lingering death from tuberculosis and he had found the love of another woman in Jean Leckie. Sir Arthur remained faithful to his first wife until the end, and, out of loyalty to her, only permitted himself to marry Jean a year after Louise's death.

Dame Jean Conan Doyle, Sir Arthur's daughter by his second marriage, was a jolly-hockey-sticks type of woman in the Joyce Grenfell mould, and she told me towards the end of her life that her father had made two men the central characters of his detective stories precisely because he wanted to put sex as far out of his mind as possible.

Predictably, she did not approve of Robert Stephen's dashingly romantic performance in the title role of *The Private Life of Sherlock Holmes*, and she was nothing less than aghast at the prospect of a pornographic film whose name she could not bring herself even to utter. Mercifully, *Sherlock Homo and Dr Wet Thong* did not, in the event, come out, in any sense of the phrase.

Had Dame Jean lived to see *Sherlock* – the BBC's attempt to set Sir Arthur's stories in a modern setting, starring Benedict Cumberbatch and Martin Freeman – she would not, I fear, have been a whole-hearted admirer. Still, adaptations that are true to the spirit of the original stories are still to be had.

The Secret of Sherlock Holmes would, I am certain, have pleased Dame Jean greatly. What Jeremy Paul has written amounts to *un hommage* to the books. There is a lot more of Peter Cushing's cold obsessiveness to Peter Egan's Holmes than Cumberbatche's lusty grandstander, and it is all the more faithful and welcome for that. Robert Daws is no bumbling slow-witted Nigel Bruce or Andre Morell as Watson, but a sensitive and intelligent man with whom one could readily imagine Holmes wishing to consort.

There is a splendidly atmospheric recreation of 221b Baker Street by the designer Simon Higlett, some bracing sound design and music by Matthew Bugg, and as for the director Robin Herford, he extracts every last ounce of atmosphere out of his limited budget in the tradition of all the great Hammer horror films. It all puts the grand into Holmes's guignol.

FRIDAY, AUGUST 20, 2010 **THE DAILY TELEGRAPH**

In Brief

Churchill 'inspired' by Conan Doyle

Winston Churchill's Battle of Britain speech, in which he said "never in the field of human conflict was so much owed by so many to so few", may have been inspired by Sir Arthur Conan Doyle.

John Michael Gibson, a scholar, has uncovered a passage in *The Refugees*, a historical novel admired by Churchill, that reads: "Never, perhaps, in the world's history has so small a body of men dominated so large a district and for so long a time." It refers to the American Indian tribe, the Iroquois, from which Churchill claimed descent.

THE DAILY TELEGRAPH WEDNESDAY, NOVEMBER 17, 2010

Obituaries (Excerpt)

Bernard Davies

Sherlock Holmes scholar who identified Baskerville Hall and the real 221B Baker Street

BERNARD DAVIES, who has died aged 86, devoted much of his life to the study of "the more neglected regions of Sherlock Holmes topography" and was also founder-president of the Dracula Society.

Davies joined the Sherlock Holmes Society of London in 1958 and made his mark the following year in the society's journal with a paper entitled *Was Holmes a Londoner?* quickly followed by *The Back Yards of Baker Street*. In both papers he drew on an unrivalled familiarity with the entire Conan Doyle canon and the results of years spent in the British Museum Reading Room poring over old maps, directions and, of course, back numbers of *Bradshaw's Monthly Railway* and *Steam Navigation Guide*.

In his first article, an exhaustive and comprehensively footnoted analysis of the most ephemeral of clues in the Sherlock Holmes stories led him to conclude that Holmes had in all probability been born and brought up "in the districts known loosely as Kennington and Stockwell, where his useful associations seem most concentrated".

In his second article he addressed the "abiding mystery" of the true location of No 221B Baker Street (which does not exist) and, by analysing fleeting references to the topography of the house and surrounding streets, made what Holmes aficionados regard as a "virtually unassailable" case for its being No 31 Baker Street.

In other papers (published by the Sherlock Holmes Society in 2008 in a two-volume collection entitled *Holmes and Watson: Travels in Search of a Solution*) Davies addressed such knotty problems as did *The Sign of Four* take place in September or July and was it in 1887 or 1888?"

A series of "radical rethinks on Baskervillean problems" yielded the conclusion that the most likely original for the village of Grimpen was the Devon village of Postbridge, and identified the nearby manor of Cator Court as the probable location of Baskerville Hall.

Davies admitted to playing the Holmesian game "with all the seriousness of a cricket match at Lords", and seemed to have picked up some of the Great Detective's methods and even his voice. Describing his apprenticeship he wrote: "My own ideas developed slowly during the years in which I was engaged in formulating principles for the topographical detection which, while they did not exclude the logical use of inference, placed it firmly on a basis of detailed map-work and research in the field."

A mere layman might have obtained the impression that Davies sometimes lacked a sense of proportion – as when he suggested that, "in terms of world influence," *A Study in Scarlet* "stands at least on a par with *Das Kapital*".

He was proud of the fact that one of his grandfathers had been a Metropolitan Police inspector who was drafted into Whitechapel at the time of the Jack the Ripper murders.

In his years as a professional actor, Davies took part in only one Sherlock Holmes production, playing two roles in a 1970 audio dramatisation of *Shoscombe Old Place*.

The same year (1958) he joined the Sherlock Holmes Society of London. By this time Davies had already devoted around a decade of his life to Holmes research. He went on to write some 30 meticulously researched papers which, in addition to topographical studies, included essays on the ancient Cornish language and a spirited defence of Dr Watson's war record. In addition he contributed to all but nine of the society's 25 expedition handbooks and gave numerous lectures and tours.

In 1984 he was made a member of the Baker Street Irregulars, the American Holmes society. He served as Chairman of the Sherlock Holmes Society of London from 1983 to 1986.

Daily Mail, Friday, November 26, 2010

Curious case of 221a

QUESTION Do we know who occupied 221a Baker Street, next door to Sherlock Holmes?

THERE was no actual Number 221a Baker Street. The 'b' in Sherlock Holmes's famous address represented the French designation *bis* (meaning twice), denoting the address is a subsidiary one, this case on an upper floor, Holmes's landlady Mrs Hudson being in residence on the ground floor.

In Sherlock Holmes's day, Baker Street was quite short, running north to south with numbered addressed from 1 to 85. There was no 221.

In 1930, some of the surrounding streets were renamed, buildings were renumbered and Baker Street became much longer. So 221 Baker Street became a real address.

In 1932, the original 221B Baker Street was demolished and the block of odd numbers from 215 to 229 was assigned to an Art Deco-style building known as Abbey House, home of the Abbey Road Building Society, which the society and its successor Abbey National occupied until 2002.

Subsequently, the inside of the building was demolished, though the distinctive façade and tower were retained, to be integrated into a new, mixed-use office, retail and residential development.

Abbey National sponsored the creation of the bronze statue of Sherlock Holmes that has stood at the entrance to Baker Street Tube station since 1999.

The firm received so much mail from Sherlock Holmes fans that it appointed a 'secretary to Sherlock Holmes' to deal with it.

Colin Jackson, London W6.
Daily Mail, Wednesday, January 19, 2011

80 years on, a novel new case for Sherlock (Excerpt)

By **Liz Thomas**

SHERLOCK Holmes is making a comeback in a new adventure more than 80 years after his creator died.

The book, which is expected to be released in September, will be written by Anthony Horowitz with the approval of Sir Arthur Conan Doyle's family and estate.

The title and plot of the story are still secret, but Mr Horowitz, best known for his Stormbreaker novels about teenage spy Alex Rider, said: 'My aim is to produce a first-rate mystery for a modern audience while remaining true to the spirit of the original.

'I fell in love with Sherlock Holmes stories when I was 16 and I have read them many times since.

'I simply could not resist the opportunity to write a brand new adventure for this iconic figure. 'The story will be set in the 19th century and Holmes will again live at 221b Baker Street.

It is the first time since Sir Arthur's death in 1930 that a new Holmes book has been authorised.

Sir Arthur wrote four novels and 56 short stories about the eccentric and brilliant detective.

His attempt to kill Holmes off in 1891 was so unpopular with readers that he was forced to bring him back just three years later and explain away his apparent death.

The novel comes amid renewed interest in the sleuth after Guy Ritchie's 2009 film adaptation starring Robert Downey Jr and Jude Law.

The BBC has also made a hugely popular series – set in modern times – starring Benedict Cumberbatch as the detective and Martin Freeman as sidekick Dr Watson.

Jon Wood, of the publisher Orion, said Mr Horowitz's 'passion for Holmes and his consummate narrative trickery will ensure this new story will not only blow away Conan Doyle aficionados but also bring the sleuth to a whole new audience'.

He added: 'We are incredibly excited by what an author of Anthony's quality can bring to the greatest of all British detectives.'

Daily Mail, Friday, January 21, 2011

BOOKS FICTION

THRILLERS BY GEOFFREY WANSELL

THE HOLMES AFFAIR BY GRAHAM MOORE Century

THE game's very much afoot in this charming evocation of the exotic world of fans of Sir Arthur Conan Doyle's legendary detective Sherlock Holmes.

The story concerns nerdy Holmes fanatic Harold White, who suddenly finds himself not only elected the youngest member of the elite Sherlockian Society of New York, but also forced to turn detective when one of the Society's luminaries is found dead in his hotel room. The great man was about to announce he'd discovered the whereabouts of one of Doyle's diaries, missing since his death a century before.

Shifting seamlessly between Victorian London and the friendship of Doyle and Dracula's creator Bram Stoker, a contemporary New York, it positively glows with its delight in everything Holmesian.

Every clue is cast exactly as the pipe-smoking master would have done it in Baker Street, and each is clear to the reader – if only they are clever enough to deduce it. A delight – and you don't need to be a Holmes buff to enjoy it.

Daily Mail, Wednesday, January 26, 2011

LETTERS

A curious case of the 'new' Sherlock adventure

WHY is such a fuss being made of the news that Anthony Horowitz is to write a new Sherlock Holmes adventure with the approval of the Conan Doyle estate, claiming it's 'the first time since Sir Arthur's death in 1930 that a new Holmes's book has been authorised' (Mail) and will 'imagine how Holmes would tackle the 21st century'?

There's no need to imagine: there are countless 'new' Holmes stories set in modern times, right into the 21st century. I'm reading Barry Grant's The Strange Return Of Sherlock Holmes, which came out last year along with his Sherlock Holmes And The Shakespeare Letter, both using the premise that Holmes is around today.

Parodies of Holmes began almost as soon as the first Holmes adventure, A Study in Scarlet, appeared in Beeton's Christmas Annual of 1887. One of the earliest was John Kendrick Bang's The Pursuit Of The Houseboat (1897), in which Sherlock is the leader of the Shades of Hades. There are thousands of parodies of Holmes, and it's true that the Conan Doyle estate tried to stop the publication of many of them.

One of the most famous in Sherlockian circles was the Ellery Queen-edited Misadventures Of Sherlock Holmes (1944) which, on publication, sent the Conan Doyle estate into apoplexy and ended with the book being withdrawn, ensuring it became a collector's item. The estates attitude, mainly due to Sir Arthur's son, Adrian, had already caused writers to dream up enterprising takes on the name Sherlock Holmes, including Robert L. Fish's Schlock Homes and Dr Watney and Bret Harte's Hemlock

Jones. Meanwhile, writers carried on using Sherlock Holmes, with or without the estate's permission.

From the very early days there was a constant flow of 'new' Holmes adventures, but with the publication in 1974 of Nicholas Meyer's The Seven Per Cent Solution, the floodgates opened and hundreds of authors tried their hand at writing one – and this has continued to the present day. So, there's nothing really new about a 'new' Sherlock Holmes story – a curious incident, indeed Dr Watson.

T. TURNER, London

Update: on the inscribed copy Conan Doyle's *A Study in Scarlet* – a phone call to Sotheby's today: 18.02.11, revealed that the book never sold and was returned to the seller.

Daily Mail Weekend Magazine 26 March 2001

Why am I killing off my hero? It's elementary, of course!

By Anthony Horowitz (Extract)

Sir Arthur Conan Doyle did it. Ian Fleming did it. JK Rowling did it. And now I've done it.

Authors have a strange and often unhappy relationship with their long-running creations. Doyle thought Sherlock Holmes – more of him later – got in the way of his more serious writing, particularly his historical novels, and pushed him off the Reichenbach Falls in the Swiss Alps without a second thought.

For me, there's the excitement of my adult book, a new Sherlock Holmes novel, coming out in the autumn. It came as a huge surprise when the Conan Doyle estate not only chose me to write the new novel but gave me complete editorial freedom.

I hesitated only briefly. On the one hand, I didn't want to be seen jumping on a bandwagon. We currently have the Robert Downey Jr films, and Steve Moffat and Mark Gatiss's brilliant modern update on BBC1. But I have always loved Holmes. The book I have written goes very much to the heart of the originals, with the language, the settings and the plot all scrupulously tailored to the 19th century. The violent crime in which Holmes finds himself involved also has a decidedly modern feel.

There is already film interest in the book (whose title I am not yet allowed to reveal). Apparently, Sherlock Holmes is the most filmed character in cinema history and it would be a thrill to add to the tally.

THE DAILY TELEGRAPH WEDNESDAY, APRIL 13, 2011

Jewel raid is straight from Sherlock Holmes

By Andrew Osborn in Moscow (Excerpt)

A GANG of Russian thieves bought a flat next to a jewellery shop and drilled through the wall over a period of weeks, in a robbery that has been likened to a plot from a Sherlock Holmes story.

The thieves appear to have drawn their inspiration from *The Red-Headed League*, a Sherlock Holmes story by Sir Arthur Conan Doyle that was first published in 1891. In the book, a pair of robbers dig up the basement of a pawnbroker's shop in London to break into a bank vault next door.

The thieves got the shop's red-headed owner out of their way by hiring him for an invented clerical job. The owner is improbably told that only people with red hair are eligible to do the job.

Holmes solves the case and catches the thieves in the bank vault.

THE DAILY TELEGRAPH WEDNESDAY, 18, MAY, 2011

Obituaries

Edward Hardwicke

Actor who played a Colditz escaper and Dr Watson to Jeremy Brett's Holmes (Excerpt)

EDWARD HARDWICKE, who died on Monday aged 78, was best known on television for playing Dr Watson in a Sherlock Holmes series in the 1980's, but had already come to public attention in the 1970's series **Colditz** as the character based on the real-life war hero Pat Reid.

Hardwicke had been suggested as the bumbling foil to Sir Arthur Conan Doyle's inscrutable sleuth by the actor David Burke, who had portrayed Watson in Granada Television's **The Adventures of Sherlock Holmes** (1984-85), alongside Jeremy Brett, the 117th actor to take the title role.

THE SUNDAY TELEGRAPH

AUGUST 14 2011

ANTI-MORMON, DEAR WATSON

Sherlock Holmes's first adventure, *A Study in Scarlet*, has been removed from reading lists for 11-12 year-olds in a Virginia school after a parent complained it was derogatory towards Mormons.

FEBRUARY 4, 2012 **THE DAILY TELEGRAPH review**

Bestsellers
FICTION Hardbacks

5 (-) Sherlock Holmes: The Complete Stories by Sir Arthur Conan Doyle

THE DAILY TELEGRAPH SATURDAY, FEBRUARY 4, 2012

Elementary **TV Sherlock leads to a case of expanding sales**

Book sellers have seen sales of Sherlock Holmes novels treble – thanks to the Benedict Cumberbatch effect.

Figures show Sir Arthur Conan Doyle's classic stories have been improved thanks to the latest television version of their hero.

Industry figures are thanking the actor Benedict Cumberbatch as Holmes with Martin Freeman as Watson who has been praised for his interpretation of the role.

Melanie Harris, of Waterstones the bookseller, said "It's been a real pleasure to see the impact *Sherlock* has had on book sales.

"The iconic character of Sherlock Holmes has enjoyed an enduring popularity ever since he first appeared on the page in 1887, and there have been several successful screen incarnations over the years.

"But Benedict Cumberbatch's powerful performance as the fictional detective has attracted a whole new army of fans."

Waterstones figures show that for most of 2011, fewer than 2,000 copies of Sherlock Holmes books sold each week. But during the new BBC series which puts original Conan Doyle stories in a modern setting, the figure has risen to more than 6,000.

Bibliography I

ADRIAN, J. (1991) **Detective Stories from The Strand**. Oxford University Press.

ASHLEY, M. (Ed) (2004) **New Sherlock Holmes Adventures**. Castle Books.

BREWER'S DICTIONARY OF PHRASE & FABLE (1997). Revised by Adrian Room (15th. edition). Cassell Publishers Limited.

BRITISH LIBRARY, THE (2003) © **Newspaper Articles**, 8 July 1930, 9 Oct 1953 & 22 July 1967. Newspaper Library, Colindale Avenue, London NW9 5HE. www. bl.uk.

BARNES, J. (2005) **Arthur & George**. Jonathan Cape.

BUTLER, I. (1973) **Cinema In Britain. An Illustrated Survey**. A.S. Barnes & Co. Inc.

CARR, C. (2005) **The Italian Secretary: a Further Adventure of Sherlock Holmes**. Little Brown.

CHABON, M. (2005) **The Final Solution**. Fourth Estate (h/b) Harper Perennial (p/b) (2006).

COSTELLO, P. (1991) **The Real World of Sherlock Holmes**. Carroll & Graf Publishers Inc.

DOYLE, ADRIAN CONAN. (1963) **The Exploits of Sherlock Holmes**. John Murray Paperbacks.

DOYLE, ADRIAN CONAN & JOHN DICKSON CARR. (1964) **More Exploits of Sherlock Holmes**. John Murray Paperbacks.

DOYLE, SIR ARTHUR CONAN. (1974) **The Adventures of Sherlock Holmes**. Book Club Associates.

DOYLE, SIR ARTHUR CONAN. (1974) **A Study in Scarlet.** John Murray & Jonathan Cape.

DOYLE, SIR ARTHUR CONAN. (1975) **The Return of Sherlock Holmes.** Book Club Associates.

DOYLE, SIR ARTHUR CONAN (1979) **The Sherlock Holmes Illustrated Omnibus**. Book Club Associates.

DOYLE, SIR ARTHUR CONAN (1979) **The 2nd Sherlock Holmes Illustrated Omnibus**. Nationwide Book Service.

DOYLE, SIR ARTHUR CONAN. (1981) **The Edinburgh Stories**. Polygon Books.

DOYLE, SIR ARTHUR CONAN. (1981) **The Penguin Complete Sherlock Holmes**. Penguin Books.

DOYLE, SIR ARTHUR CONAN. (1982) **The Celebrated Cases Of Sherlock Holmes. Treasury of World Masterpieces**. Book Club Associates.

DOYLE, SIR ARTHUR CONAN. (1987) **The Adventures of Sherlock Holmes**. Reader's Digest Association.

DOYLE, SIR ARTHUR CONAN. (1990) **A Study in Scarlet & The Hound of the Baskervilles**. Reader's Digest Association.

DOYLE, SIR ARTHUR CONAN. (1994) **Complete Sherlock Holmes & Other Detective Stories**. Harper Collins *Publishers*.

DOYLE, SIR ARTHUR CONAN. (1995) **The Return of Sherlock Holmes**. Reader's Digest Association.

>DOYLE, SIR ARTHUR CONAN. (2005) **The Very Best of Sherlock Holmes**. Axiom Publishing.

>DOYLE, SIR ARTHUR CONAN (2007) **Memories and Adventures.** Wordsworth Editions.

DRUXMAN, M.B. (1975) **Basil Rathbone: His Life and His Films**. South Brunswick & New York: A.S.Barnes.

EVERSON, W.K. (1972) **The Detective In Film**. The Citadel Press, Secaucus, New Jersey.

GARDNER, J. (1974) **The Return of Moriarty**. Berkley Fiction.

GORDON, R. (1985) **Great Medical Mysteries**. Arrow Books Limited.

GREEN, RICHARD LANCELYN (1985) **The Further Adventures of Sherlock Holmes. Collected & Introduced by Richard Lancelyn Green. After Sir Arthur Conan Doyle**. Penguin Books.

GREEN, RICHARD LANCELYN & GIBSON, JOHN MICHAEL. (1999) **A Bibliography of A. Conan Doyle**. Hudson House.

GREENBERG, M.H., LELLENBERG, J.L. & STASHOWER, D. (Eds). (2001) **Murder in Baker Street**. Robinson London.

HALL, R.L. (1977) **Exit Sherlock Holmes**. Sphere Books Ltd.

HALLIWELL, L. (1989) **Halliwell's Filmgoer's Companion**. (9th.edition). Grafton Books.

HALLIWELL, L. (1999) **Halliwell's Who's Who In The Movies**. (13th. edition Edited by John Walker). Harper Collins *Entertainment*.

HARDWICK, M & M. (1962) **The Sherlock Holmes Companion**. John Murray, London. (1999) Senate.

HARDWICK, M. (1983) **The Private Life Of Dr. Watson. Being the Personal Reminiscences of John H. Watson, M.D.** Weidenfeld & Nicolson, London.

HIGHAM, C. (1976) **The Adventures of Conan Doyle.** Hamish Hamilton, London.

HORSLEY, E.M. (Ed) (1986) **Hutchinson 20th Century Encyclopedia**. Century Hutchinson Limited.

KLINGER, LESLIE S. (Ed). (2005) **The New Annotated Sherlock Holmes: Volume 3: The Novels**. Norton.

KURLAND, M. (Ed). (2003) **My Sherlock Holmes – Untold Stories of the Great Detective**. St. Martin's Press.

MACINTYRE, B. (2000) **The Napoleon of Crime: The Life And Times of Adam Worth.** Flamingo.

MALTIN, L. (1987) (Ed) TV Movies and Video Guide. **Penguin Books.**

MILLER, R. (2008) **The Adventures of Arthur Conan Doyle**. Harville *Secker*.

NORBU, JAMYANG (2000) (Ed) **The Mandala of Sherlock Holmes**. John Murray.

PETRIE, G. (1995) **The Hampstead Poisonings. A Mycroft Holmes Adventure**. Ian Henry Publications. Players Press.

POUND, R. (1966) **The Strand Magazine 1891-1950**. Oxford University Press.

RATHBONE, B. (1956, 1962) **In and Out of Character: An Autobiography**. New York: Doubleday.

REDMOND, C. (1993) **A Sherlock Holmes Handbook**. Simon & Pierre.

RENNISON, N. (2005) **Sherlock Holmes: The Unauthorised Biography**. Atlantic Books.

ROBERTS, B. (2001) **Sherlock Holmes and the Crosby Murder**. Constable Crime.

SHERLOCK HOLMES GAZETTE (1995) **A Case of Identity.** Spring 1995 (No.11). Peter Harkness.

SHERLOCK Magazine, Issue 57 Dec. 2003. **The Lady of the House** (Part One) by John Hall. Atlas Publishing.

SHERLOCK Magazine, Issue 58 Feb.2004. **The Lady of the House** (Part Two) by John Hall. Atlas Publishing.

SHERLOCK Magazine, Issue 59 April 2004. **The Case of The Conk-Singleton Forgery** by THOMSON, J. Atlas Publishing.

SHERLOCK Magazine, Issue 59 April 2004. **Mrs Hudson of the Movies** by David Stuart Davies. Atlas Publishing.

SHERLOCK Magazine, Issue 60 June 2004. **Newsdesk**. Atlas Publishing.

SHERLOCK Magazine, Issue 60 June 2004 **On the Scent of the Hound of the Baskervilles** by RICKMAN, P. Atlas Publishing.

SHERLOCK Magazine, Issue 63 December 2004 SHERLOCK **STATESIDE** By **Pat Ward**. Atlas Publishing.

SHERLOCK Magazine, Issue 66 June 2005. **Baker Street Bulletin**. Atlas Publishing.

SHERLOCK Magazine, Issue 68 September 2006. **Keeping the memory Green**. Atlas Publishing.

STASHOWER, D. (1999) **Teller of Tales: The Life of Sir Arthur Conan Doyle**. Allen Lane.

STOCKWELL, A. (2003) **The Singular Adventures of Mr. Sherlock Holmes**. UPSO Limited.

SUTHERLAND, J. (1988) **Companion to Victorian Fiction**. Oxford University Press.

THOMAS, D. (1999) **The Secret Cases of Sherlock Holmes**. Carroll & Graf.

THOMSON, J. (1990) **The Secret Files of Sherlock Holmes**. Constable. London.

THOMSON, J. (1992) **The Secret Chronicles of Sherlock Holmes**. Constable. London.

THOMSON, J. (1993) **The Secret Journals of Sherlock Holmes**. Constable. London.

THOMSON, J. (2004) **The Secret Notebooks of Sherlock Holmes**. Allison & Busby.

WALLER, P. (2002) **The Hound of the Baskervilles: Hunting the Dartmoor Legend**. Devon Books.

WELLER, P. with RODEN, C. (1992) **The Life and Times of Sherlock Holmes**. Bracken Books.

www.Edinburgh.room@edinburgh.gov.uk

www.siracd.com

www.ingramcontent.com/pod-product-compliance
Lightning Source LLC
Chambersburg PA
CBHW081821230426
43668CB00017B/2340